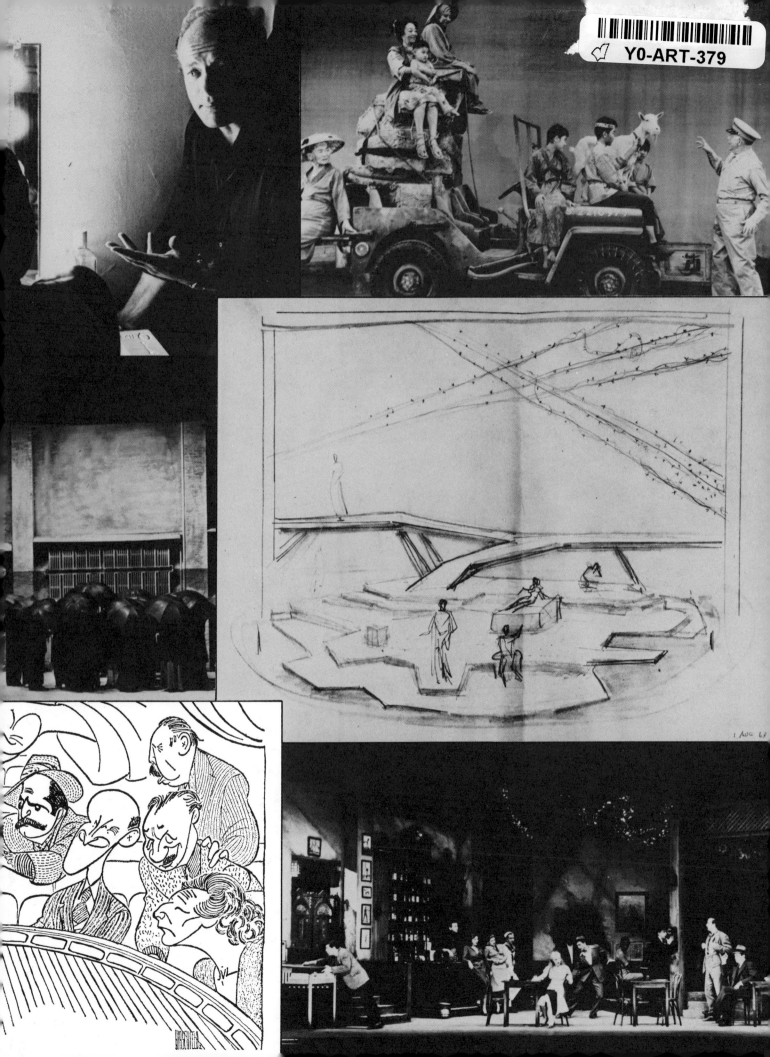

Dictionary of Literary Biography

Twentieth-Century American Dramatists

Part 2: K-Z

Dictionary of Literary Biography

1: *The American Renaissance in New England,*
   ed. Joel Myerson (1978)

2: *American Novelists Since World War II,*
   ed. Jeffrey Helterman and Richard Layman (1978)

3: *Antebellum Writers in New York and the South,*
   ed. Joel Myerson (1979)

4: *American Writers in Paris, 1920-1939,*
   ed. Karen Lane Rood (1980)

5: *American Poets Since World War II*, 2 volumes,
   ed. Donald J. Greiner (1980)

6: *American Novelists Since World War II*, Second Series,
   ed. James E. Kibler, Jr. (1980)

7: *Twentieth-Century American Dramatists*, 2 volumes,
   ed. John MacNicholas (1981)

Dictionary of Literary Biography • Volume Seven

Twentieth-Century American Dramatists

Part 2: K-Z

Edited by John MacNicholas
University of South Carolina

A Bruccoli Clark Book
Gale Research Company • Book Tower • Detroit, Michigan 48226
1981

Planning Board for
DICTIONARY OF LITERARY BIOGRAPHY

John Baker
Richard L. Darling
William Emerson
A. Walton Litz
Orville Prescott
William Targ
Alden Whitman

Matthew J. Bruccoli, *Editorial Director*
C. E. Frazer Clark, Jr., *Managing Editor*
Richard Layman, *Project Editor*

Copyright © 1981
GALE RESEARCH COMPANY

Contents

*Indicates master entries

Contents

Permissions

The following persons and institutions generously permitted the reproduction of photographs, manuscripts, or archival materials: Billy Rose Theatre Collection, The New York Public Library at Lincoln Center, Astor and Tilden Foundations, pp. 6, 15, 29, 36, 43, 51, 59, 64, 71, 72, 92, 114, 117, 124, 128, 135, 142, 145, 154, 159, 170, 181, 187, 194, 202, 210, 215, 229, 234, 241, 254, 265, 268, 273, 274, 302, 309, 313, 325, 343, 352, 369, 404; Hoblitzelle Theatre Arts Collection, The Humanities Research Center, The University of Texas at Austin, pp. 91, 97, 102, 157, 158, 376, 404; The Granger Collection, pp. 56, 155; Gene Bagnato, p. 77; Clemens Kalischer, p. 149; Frederic Ohringer, p. 172; Cynthia Mac Adams, p. 279; Megan Terry, p. 286; Mark Morrow, pp. 344, 347; Dennis E. Anderson, p. 412; Tess Sleinkolk, p. 419; Linda Blase, p. 422; Robert Ashley Wilson, p. 438; *Chicago Tribune*, p. 448; A. Vincent Scarano, p. 452.

Acknowledgments

This book was produced by BC Research.

Margaret A. Van Antwerp and Inge Kutt were the in-house editors.

The production staff included Janet E. Black, Joyce Fowler, Sharon K. Kirkland, Cynthia D. Lybrand, Nadia Rasheed, Cynthia H. Rogers, Karen L. Rood, Shirley Ross, Walter W. Ross, Robin Sumner, Cheryl A. Swartzentruber, Theodora J. Thompson, Carol J. Wilson, and Lynne C. Zeigler.

The editor would like to acknowledge also the indispensable assistance he has received from the following people and organizations: the staff of the Billy Rose Theatre Collection of the New York Public Library at Lincoln Center, Astor and Tilden Foundations, especially Richard Buck, Dorothy Swerdlove, Paul Myers, and Simon Rosenblatt; The Humanities Research Center at The University of Texas at Austin, especially Ellen Dunlap, Timothy Spragen, and Daniel Jones; Mary Sue Birkhead Jones of The Dallas Theater Center; Charlotte Ball of The Goodman Theatre; Bella Itkin and Randy Larsen of The Goodman School of Drama; Ron Litke of The Newberry Library; Nancy Hereford of The Mark Taper Forum; Howard Stein, Chairman of the Department of Drama, The University of Texas at Austin; Patti Gillespie, Chairman of the Department of Theatre and Speech, University of South Carolina; and George Geckle, Chairman of the Department of English, University of South Carolina. Anne Dixon and Jacquelyn Price did the necessary library research with the valuable assistance of the following librarians at the Thomas Cooper Library: Michael Havener, Donna Nance, Harriet Oglesbee, Jean Rhyne, Paula Swope, Jane Thesing, Ellen Tillett, Gary Treadway, and Beth Woodard. Photographic copy work for this volume was done by Pat Crawford of Imagery, Columbia, South Carolina, and William Pessoni of Lexington Labs, New York.

Finally, grateful acknowledgment is due the subjects of entries in this book who were kind enough to read their entries for accuracy. Without the assistance of all these people, this book would not have been possible.

Dictionary of Literary Biography

Twentieth-Century American Dramatists

Part 2: K-Z

Dictionary of Literary Biography

GARSON KANIN
(24 November 1912-)

PRODUCTIONS: *Born Yesterday*, 4 February 1946, Lyceum Theatre, New York, 1642 [performances];

The Smile of the World, 12 January 1949, Lyceum Theatre, New York, 5;

The Rat Race, 22 December 1949, Ethel Barrymore Theatre, New York, 84;

The Live Wire, 17 August 1950, Playhouse Theatre, New York, 28;

Die Fledermaus, new English libretto by Kanin for Johann Strauss's opera, 20 December 1950, Metropolitan Opera Company, New York;

Do Re Mi, music by Jule Styne, lyrics by Betty Comden and Adolphe Green, 26 December 1960, St. James Theatre, New York, 400;

A Gift of Time, adapted from Lael Tucker Wertenbaker's *Death of a Man*, 22 February 1962, Ethel Barrymore Theatre, New York, 92;

Come On Strong, 4 October 1962, Morosco Theatre, New York, 35.

SELECTED BOOKS: *Born Yesterday* (New York: Viking, 1946);

The Smile of the World (New York: Dramatists Play Service, 1949);

The Rat Race (New York: Dramatists Play Service, 1950);

Fledermaus, new libretto by Kanin for Johann Strauss's opera (New York: Boosey & Hawkes, 1950);

The Live Wire (New York: Dramatists Play Service, 1951);

Do Re Mi [novel] (Boston: Little, Brown, 1955);

Blow Up a Storm (New York: Random House, 1959; London: Hamilton, 1961);

A Gift of Time, adapted from Lael Tucker Wertenbaker's *Death of a Man* (New York: Random House, 1962);

Come On Strong (New York: Dramatists Play Service, 1964);

Remembering Mr. Maugham (New York: Atheneum, 1966; London: Hamilton, 1966);

Cast of Characters: Stories of Broadway and Hollywood (New York: Atheneum, 1969);

Tracy and Hepburn (New York: Viking, 1971; London: Angus & Robertson, 1972);

Hollywood (New York: Viking, 1974; London: Hart-Davis, MacGibbon, 1975);

One Hell of an Actor (New York: Harper & Row, 1977; London: Barrie & Jenkins, 1979);

It Takes a Long Time to Become Young (Garden City: Doubleday, 1978; London: Prior, 1979);

Together Again! The Great Movie Teams (New York: Grosset & Dunlap, 1979);

Movieola (New York: Simon & Schuster, 1979; London: Macmillan, 1980);

Smash (New York: Viking, 1980).

Actor, director, dramatist, and screenwriter, as well as author of several novels and memoirs, Garson Kanin is remembered today primarily for a single play, *Born Yesterday* (1946), the first and most successful of his works for the stage. *Born Yesterday* found a place in the hearts of several generations of enthusiastic Kanin followers, and it is a popular play even today, nearly thirty-five years after its first performance. It has made the lists of best American plays and appears in several anthologies. *Born Yesterday*, deservedly the highlight of Kanin's career as a dramatist, is scarcely the only play Kanin wrote, nor is it the only one of his plays worthy of attention. Considering the range of his activities in other fields, however, it is remarkable that he wrote and directed a play which holds such a permanent place in American drama.

Kanin was born in Rochester, New York, the son of David M. and Sadie Levine Kanin. He attended James Madison High School and, in 1932, entered the American Academy of Dramatic Arts, where he studied for two years. Having prepared for the theatre, in 1933 Kanin began what was to become a lifelong education in the theatre, performing for the first time at age twenty-one in *Little Ol' Boy* (1933) and subsequently in *Spring Song* and *Ladies' Money* (both 1934), *Three Men on a Horse*, *The Body Beautiful*, and *Boy Meets Girl* (all 1935), *Star Spangled* (1936), and several other productions. During these early years, when Kanin was not performing in Broadway plays (and in two instances when he was), he assisted his friend George Abbott in directing *Three Men on a Horse*, *Boy Meets Girl*, *Brother Rat* (1936), and *Room Service* (1937).

Kanin himself directed *Hitch Your Wagon* (1937) and *Too Many Heroes* (1937), and after the war a whole string of plays, some of which are among Broadway's all-time favorites: *The Diary of Anne Frank* (1955), *A Hole in the Head* (1957), and *Funny Girl* (1964). In 1950 he directed *Die Fledermaus* for the Metropolitan Opera, having himself written a new English libretto, and in 1962 he adapted for the stage Lael Tucker Wertenbaker's book *Death of a Man*, the author's story of her husband's fatal bout with cancer. Kanin's adaptation, *A Gift of Time*, with Henry Fonda and Olivia de Havilland in the leading roles, received good reviews and was moderately successful. It is an important play, one of the few tragic dramas on which Kanin has worked, a play, in the words of critic Howard Taubman, which "affirms the values of life even as it looks steadily at death."

Though death has seldom been one of Kanin's theatrical preoccupations, it is certainly not a subject of which he has been entirely unaware. During the war Kanin took an active part in the war effort ultimately responsible for the victory in Europe. An enlisted man assigned initially to the Signal Corps Training Film Section at Fort Monmouth, New Jersey, Kanin quickly rose to the rank of sergeant, was commissioned an officer, and sent to the Office of Strategic Services, where he was promoted to captain while serving in the European theatre of operations. In the service Kanin contributed to the Allied cause film and screenwriting experience going back to 1937, directing *Ring of Steel* and *Fellow Americans* (both 1942) and *Salute to France* (1946) for the offices of War Information and Emergency Manpower. In 1945, with Carol Reed, Kanin di-

rected *The True Glory*, the War Department's official film report of the war in Europe, for which he and Reed received an Academy Award and citations from the New York Film Critics Circle and National Board of Review. Immediately after the war, Kanin wrote his first play, *Born Yesterday*, which he directed at the Lyceum Theatre in 1946.

Set in Washington, D.C., in September 1945, *Born Yesterday*, "a funny play with unfunny implications," is concerned with the seamier side of politics and the American dream: congressional skulduggery and influence peddling, the industrial bullying of government by self-serving men of wealth and power. Harry Brock, a millionaire junk dealer from Cleveland, arrives at the foot of Capitol Hill bellowing demands and holding a fistful of dollars and a briefcase full of legislation. The dollars he spends lavishly on a $265-a-day hotel apartment; the legislation he intends to squeeze out of Congress with the help of Sen. Norval Hedges, whom Brock's attorney, Ed Devery, has managed without too much trouble to get on the payroll.

When Hedges and his wife come to call on the Brock entourage, they are introduced to the roughneck junk man's mistress, Billie Dawn, an ex-chorus girl with little or no education but dynamite looks and the proverbial "heart of gold." Billie's monosyllabic self-consciousness and obvious lack of interest in either the Washington scene or its social elite suggest to Ed Devery that what "the dumb blond" needs is a tutor. Devery recommends Paul Verrall, a young writer for the *New Republic* who lives down the hall. Momentarily uncertain, Verrall agrees to take the job—for two hundred dollars a week and the opportunity to sit in on the Brock-Hedges machinations.

There are opportunities for more than eavesdropping. Physically attracted to Verrall, Billie is impressed as well with his good manners, quiet way, and educated sensitivity and anger toward a situation in which she, as well as Brock, is involved: Billie holds controlling interest in more than half of Brock's properties and signs her name daily to contracts and other documents she knows nothing about, implicating herself in everything the tycoon and his lawyer put their minds to. Staring near-sightedly through new spectacles at the newspapers, books, and articles Verrall assigns her to read, Billie dredges up memories of a decent childhood and an honest, loving father she has not met for over a decade, and she begins to change. "I like to like what's better to like," she says. She refuses to sign the papers. "The whole damned history of the world," Verrall has said, "is the story of a struggle between the selfish and the unselfish." She demands to know which side she is on. She demands her right to become more and better than she has been in the past, with Brock and even before. She learns what Verrall and the audience already know about education: "The idea of learning is to be bigger, not smaller."

The scheme recommended by Devery to Brock blows up in their faces. Newly enlightened, "born yesterday" into a life of freshened self-awareness and the promise of personal integrity, Billie threatens everything. Called on the carpet, Verrall pleads facetiously yet sincerely on Billie's behalf: "Education is a difficult thing to control or to channel, Harry. One thing leads to another. It's a matter of awakening curiosity—stimulating imagination—developing a sense of independence." Having both been slapped around by Brock and his henchman, their lives threatened, Verrall and Billie call Brock's bluff, holding as they do all the evidence, and prance off victorious with the papers they need to write an expose. Brock, Devery, and Hedges are left wondering why the "dumb chump" and the "crazy broad" did not accept their one hundred thousand dollar bribe.

Kanin's primarily social theme has to do with the individual's responsibility to uphold the rights of all, rich and poor alike, in America and abroad. Brock's plan, which is to corner the postwar scrap iron market in Europe and the world, disregards the immediate needs of already devastated populations. In this sense, *Born Yesterday*, as it unfolds on a plush set amid the trappings of opulence and ostentatious illiteracy, is a microcosm of wealth and power misused in the interests of a handful of selfish people. Billie's metamorphosis from within this setting is symbolic perhaps of "the good in all of us," the good resident in the seamiest of situations. Her father's love for her despite disappointment, Verrall's care and burgeoning love for her and his persistent involvement in both her intellectual and physical life give her the strength to protect the rights of others as well as her own. Kanin is heavy-handed in his treatment of this theme, and his plot is as weak and transparent as his characters are brilliant; but his ideas make for good theatre, now as then.

Born Yesterday is an entertaining play. It is a good play. The jokes are hilarious, even today. In 1946, the critics and playgoers loved the play, especially the characters Brock and Billie: "a marvelous combination of wit and indignation," wrote Howard Barnes; "great good fun," wrote Burton Rascoe, "ribald, adult, witty, and clever . . . it draws home an ancient message with an air of timeliness and melodramatic force." Today, the play's perennially relevant subject compensates for the melodrama (however persistent the taste for melodrama on the Broadway stage), and the play is revived frequently in little theatres and university playhouses. In the late 1940s, *Born Yesterday* played to hundreds of thousands of New York patrons—Kanin himself a great hit as director and entrepreneur as well as playwright—closing finally in 1950 after 1642 performances.

In 1949, a year or so before *Born Yesterday* had completed its initial Broadway run, Kanin wrote and directed two new plays: *The Smile of the World*, which opened in January 1949, and *The Rat Race*, which opened the following December. Both plays are fast-paced tragicomedies in which continuity and overall structure receive less attention than do ideas and dialogue.

The Smile of the World, in certain respects the least successful of Kanin's plays, is a continuation of or variation on the general theme introduced in *Born Yesterday*: the corruption of American institutions and the destruction of the moral and social fabric by individuals responsible to the governed and to loved ones and friends, who relinquish out of personal malice or weakness the trust placed in them by others. Set in 1923 in the Washington home of Chief Justice Reuben Boulting and his wife Sara, the play offers a striking resemblance in theme to Shaw's *Candida* and Ibsen's *A Doll House*, though for substance Kanin draws on the life and times of the American jurist, Oliver Wendell Holmes, Jr. (1841-1935), "the play's off-stage hero." In contrast to Chief Justice Holmes, with whom Reuben Boulting works on the Supreme Court, Boulting himself is stuffy, narrow, and complacent, the shadow of a public man and a travesty of the idealistic young attorney his wife first met and fell in love with many years before. Sara Boulting has lost all but the most careless and mundane interest in her husband, the years of compromise and increasing apathy having left Boulting less the object of her respect than of her pity, and finally, of her disgust and scorn. Even Boulting's own mother (a light-hearted soul to whom Kanin assigns his funniest lines) is less than pleased with what her son has become. To make matters worse for Boulting, Sara finds herself attracted to her husband's clerk, Sam Fenn, the epitome it would seem of the compassionate liberalism she once admired so very much in her husband. She deserts Boulting, despite his last-minute appeal that in other hands (or perhaps in another play structured more carefully) might have

Garson Kanin and Ruth Gordon

redeemed Boulting's conceit and apathy and made Sara's actions more dramatic. Finally, Sara rejects also the young clerk, many years her junior, the difference in their ages an all too present reminder of the effects of time and of disappointments revisited.

Like Billie Dawn in *Born Yesterday*, Sara Boulting is sustained by memories of Boulting when he stood for something she too could believe in. Like Billie, Sara is Kanin's central character, a foil to Reuben Boulting as Billie is to Harry Brock. Unlike Billie, however, whose memories are dredged up for an immediate, dynamic, and compelling purpose, Sara is faced not with a renaissance but with resorting to dreams that become in time a travesty of intellectual sustenance and finally collapse under their own weight. Dreams and ideas are rarely self-sustaining, but they must be brought to life—and then kept alive—by people who are informed by them and for whom, in turn, the ideas stand symbolically as a kind of monument. Good theatre generally requires flesh-and-blood characterization, however monumentalized the characters may become in ideas. In this respect, Sara Boulting and indeed all of the characters except Boulting's mother fail to live up to standards set by Kanin himself in *Born Yesterday*; none of Kanin's central

characters in *The Smile of the World* is sufficiently real and substantial to carry the weight of ideas Kanin assigns.

The Smile of the World received mixed reviews. Kanin's first play was still a hit, and critics and playgoers alike had anticipated dramatic comedy like *Born Yesterday*, if not comedy more farcical and exaggerated than that, but they were disappointed. Though praised by John Lardner as "a writer of marked talent" and for ignoring safer paths to examine life's "deeper meanings," Kanin had managed to hit the discordant note once too often. Brooks Atkinson summed up much of the critical reaction: "all message and no drama . . . a dull play." Robert Coleman, put out with Kanin for writing *The Smile of the World* "with more intelligence than heart," complained that though Kanin's matter is sufficient, even abundant, his characters are not: "There are the materials here for a moving play, but they seldom move you. It is hard to feel sympathy for the three corners of a triangle representing ideas rather than people." Apart from general criticism of Kanin's listless structuring of the play—his characteristic plotlessness—the most pointed remarks seem, in retrospect at least, to have been aimed at the inappropriateness of Kanin's tragicomic handling of important social issues. The play closed on Broadway almost immediately, having had the shortest run of any play Kanin had or would ever set his mind to.

Set surrealistically in what Kanin refers to as "a piece of Manhattan," his second play of 1949 concerns the relationship of a young man and woman who share a furnished room in the theatre district. Gus Hammer, the protagonist of *The Rat Race* and a saxophone player who has just arrived in New York from the Midwest, is eager for success, enthusiastic, optimistic about the future. His roommate, Helen Brown, a taxi dancer (if not quite the "dance hall trollop" one critic suggests), is far less certain than Gus of what the theatre may still have to offer; she is in fact hopelessly pessimistic, bitter, disillusioned, having abandoned all hope and aspiration of ever becoming a Broadway star. Helen lives continuously in the past, sustained from one day to the next by the fading memory of a dance contest she won years before. Though Helen's bitterness is cheapening and pathetic, she is more sympathetic than Gus, whose naive assumptions and unwarranted confidence are almost certainly doomed from the outset.

Kanin's message in *The Rat Race* would seem to be that the theatre and theatrical life in general are a kind of maze in which the youthful, the vigorous, and the aspiring are deceived, as often as not, by their own false hopes and naive ambitions. Gus is and will continue to be deceived often, and Helen's great burden and conflict is past deception and disappointment. But the two characters are rather nicely balanced in Kanin's melodrama, Gus's optimism providing Helen intermittent relief from her own nagging disillusionment, Helen's pessimism anticipating and averting the constant and inevitable trouble Gus gets them into. In the end, though there is little doubt that their problems will continue to mount, frustrating Gus's plans and aggravating Helen's hopelessness and tendency to despair, the two are resolved to stay together, to stick it out, providing mutually the human contact and reinforcement both so desperately require. It is not Gus and Helen, the human elements in Kanin's play, that we are meant to criticize, but rather the scene, the environment generally in which these two characters find themselves, the New York theatre world of the late 1940s: "the cold and merciless reality of a city callous to failure," as critic Richard Watts put it.

Though it had a longer run than *The Smile of the World*, if anything *The Rat Race* was received with greater disapproval, even ridicule by critics, who in some cases were becoming more and more annoyed with Kanin for not coming up with another boisterous crowd-pleaser like *Born Yesterday*. Kanin's disgust with social conditions in New York and sympathy with the plight of aspiring young performers were interpreted by some as pessimism pure and simple, a "negative philosophy." Robert Coleman found Kanin's play "remote and unbelievable." Robert Garland demeaned it as an "aimless rooming-house idyll." Although these criticisms were in a sense unfair and naive, the critics did have an important point that needed making: the play lacks a sense of purpose that might permit it to rise above the tragic melodrama of the opening scenes. Despite his obvious sympathy for Gus and Helen, Kanin abandons them, putting them at a distance from himself, from the audience, from any salvation one might wish for them. Kanin "has not managed enough suspense and continuity in his story to make [it] absorbing," wrote John Chapman. "There are many incidents and many little gems in the play, but the story is so fragmentary that it failed to arouse my concern." Once again, it is the story, the plot and structure of the dramatization, that the critics feel has eluded Kanin. Whether out of respect for the author of *Born Yesterday*, or disillu-

sionment with the happier plays esteemed by the critics, a select audience of Kanin admirers kept *The Rat Race* at the Ethel Barrymore Theatre for several months.

The Rat Race had been at least a limited success by anyone's standards, and in August 1950 Kanin opened at the Playhouse Theatre with *The Live Wire*, set in New York in the late summer of 1949. The play had done well on the summer circuit, and the theatregoers were still anxious for another Kanin success. They were still unprepared, however, for any negativism or, as one critic put it, "bitterness of spirit."

Kanin was unconcerned with the critical attitudes and public euphoria of the late 1940s. Pinning his hopes once again on repartee and racy dialogue—and to a lesser extent on characterization—Kanin contented himself in *The Live Wire* with another theme from the theatre's rag and boneyard of unemployed actors. *The Live Wire*, like *The Rat Race*, is a play about youth and vigor and naivete, a play in which indigent theatrical hopefuls, eight young actors out of work but undaunted, pool their meagre resources and limited talents and rebelliously set up house in a Quonset hut on a vacant lot. All is well until "a liar, a crook, and a chiseler" named Leo Mack moves in, provokes dissension by messing up the place, borrowing money no one has to spare, and stealing his friend's girl, managing shrewdly to get for himself most of the publicity a pair of *Life* reporters give the commune: his photograph appears on the cover. It is Leo, of course, who ends up with a Hollywood agent and a bid to do pictures.

Again, Kanin's theme is the ill effect of desultory theatrical existence on vibrant and energetic young men and women whose chances for success are extremely limited, as much by their own lack of ill will, inhumanity, and selfishness as by external circumstances. While Gus and Helen in *The Rat Race* are entrapped in the maze of false hopes and broken dreams, relieved only by the glimmer of humanity in one and fully recognized if naive humanity in the other, in *The Live Wire* Kanin reveals a way out. It is not exactly injustice that Kanin depicts in *The Live Wire*, though injustice and incivility abound at each level of reality (commune, district, city, and nation), but the evolution of human types that succeed because they must. It is a social theme that deals with the breaking of faith and abuse of friendship but extends beyond the concerns of individual characters. Leo is "the live wire," with the same capacity for good as well as evil. He could be like Ursula Poe, "the larcenous rockette who gets her come-uppance from a bigger heel than she is," or like Brian Freer, "a smooth-talking high-powered Hollywood agent" and "power-house talent salesman" who steals the play from the other characters in the third act. As the critics' labels suggest, these are stock characters, pretty much to be expected in plays *about* the theatre. Though the dialogue was still some of the best in town, even Kanin's characterizations were beginning to fall apart, and there was little in this play, as in the others, to keep character, thought, and action on the same track.

The Live Wire was poorly reviewed by critics and audiences alike. Though fast-paced and "flawlessly" cast and directed by Kanin himself (Brooks Atkinson found the acting "excellent throughout"), *The Live Wire* suffers from the same malady encountered in the two previous plays: instability of plot, indecisiveness, the sacrifice of meaningful and meaningfully structured action to pace and "sharply bantering dialogue," topical jokes that in retrospect have lost their full power to amuse and, even in 1950, were not fully appreciated (or particularly well taken by the critics), all creating a kind of shapelessness that ultimately makes the play inconsequential. The theatre crowd was uneasy, having been disappointed by two Kanin plays in a row. The critics too were disappointed. Having written a not unfavorable review, Atkinson concluded that Kanin's "playwriting is less decisive than his direction." Several of the other critics were less charitable: *The Live Wire* "lacks the humorous inventiveness and imagination we expect of Mr. Kanin," wrote Richard Watts; "Mr. Kanin hasn't yet recaptured his prior form." *Born Yesterday* remained the play to surpass, but Kanin had not been able to equal it. Not quite a funny play, as one critic put it, *The Live Wire* ran for twenty-eight performances, closing long before the end of the season.

However discouraging (or not) the events of 1949-1950 might have been for Kanin, it is important to keep in mind that for this versatile man the Broadway playhouse is scarcely his only refuge. As noted earlier, Kanin's career as a director of plays and motion pictures spans all of the years from the mid-1930s to the present, and his many successes are legend. A great believer in television's dramatic potential and potential for intimacy and depth of characterization, Kanin directed *Born Yesterday* for television in 1956, and he has since done several special media adaptations for family viewing in the home. His articles and short stories have appeared in countless periodicals, from *Esquire*, *Ladies' Home Journal*, and *Paris-Match* to the *Atlantic Monthly* and *Virginia Law Review*. His novels and reminiscences are impressive, given the constant demands made on his time and energy, his mental and physical resources, by both the Broadway and Hollywood establishments, the Screen Directors' Guild, Writers' Guild, Academy of Motion Picture Arts and Sciences, Jewish Theatrical Guild, and many other organzations. But Kanin has always had a knack for making things work in several different ways, as can be seen in both his book and musical *Do Re Mi*.

In 1955 Kanin wrote and published a slight but thoroughly entertaining novelette entitled *Do Re Mi*, the story of a gang of four very small-time hoods who decide to elbow their way into the juke box racket. Their story is told from the most unbecoming of city jails in the first person by their leader, a Runyonesque tough guy named Hubie Cram: "I am sitting here," says Hubie, "in the sneezer. Taking the fall for Fatso. Again. They got a television now, only the food was better last time." The story Hubie tells is a funny one of the gang's untimely and irreverent expansion into not only the recording business, but unfortunately also into the well-established terrain of a bigger and wiser corporation of much tougher hoods. When Hubie's chanteuse, Nan Needles, runs off to Atlantic City with the opposition's good-looking front man (reminiscent of Billie and Paul's liaison in *Born Yesterday*), Hubie decides that enough is enough. But when the gang breaks in on the lovers, the cops bust the whole lot, and Hubie is off to jail—again.

In 1960, with Hubie, played by Phil Silvers, out of jail and singing, dancing, and playing everything from the piano to the drums on the Broadway stage in Kanin's own musical adaptation, the slight, eighty-nine page novelette really came into its own. Seldom have book and musical achieved such a happy continuity. Seldom has the director of a successful musical built good entertainment out of his own material. Kanin made some changes, of course, in the original story, giving his characters broader gestures, more openness and sympathy, more naievete and comic humility. In a legitimate business deal Hubie is offered two hundred juke boxes, all polished chrome and flashing lights, the kind we imagine now in old-fashioned ice cream parlors. "It's Legitimate," Hubie sings in one of the show's opening numbers, a nightclub scene shared with Hubie's long-suffering and less than enthusiastic wife, Kay. The trouble, of course, is that Hubie cannot be satisfied with a measly juke box concession, however appealing the take. Always coming up with new ideas, he decides that the recording

I have been working with Gene &
whatever else happens on his job,
or has happened or will happen —
the experience with him makes it all not
only worthwhile, but eternally valuable.

He is the very definition of a
professional. The work comes first —
ahead of any other consideration or
responsibility to person place or thing.
Before himself, even. I honestly
believe that if I were not around
to arrange for some food once in a
while — he ~~would~~ ^we not^ eat at all.

He attends every single performance,
including matinees \ I sit in his seat
and take his notes in the dark \ They
are voluminous, often cryptic, always
smart.

Afterward, I type them up and
bring them to him \ He is usually
already at work, typing steadily \
He is a better typist than I am \ I
put the notes down beside him, he
says, many months, without
looking up. I leave and wait
for him to call me, which he does

business is where the real money is, and in a later scene holds an audition for singers. Tilda Mullen, the singer who finally catches his eye, has what it takes: with beauty and a voice to match, she is a sure fire juke box starlet and the key to Hubie's success—or so he thinks. But Tilda falls in love with John Henry Wheeler, Hubie's rival in the recording business, and the flap that occurs when Hubie tries to even the score lands everyone in a senate subcommittee investigation.

There are some wild moments in Kanin's musical adaptation of *Do Re Mi*, for instance when Hubie gives Tilda a singing lesson and has to teach each of the band members to play his instrument, and there are some funny, low-keyed lines: Hubie and Kay, curled up in bed reading newspapers—he the *New York Mirror*, she the *Daily News*—oblivious to each other, until Kay turns to Hubie and asks, innocently, "Did a fish bite a woman in Asbury Park in yours?" Even the critics laughed, and the theatregoers who sat beside them laughed also—through 400 performances. *Do Re Mi* was one of the greatest of Kanin's successes on Broadway, second in popularity only to *Born Yesterday*, and in critical esteem it was quite respectable. "The first-nighters taxed their ribs laughing and blistered their palms applauding," wrote Robert Coleman. "It's a smasheroo. A red-hot ticket." Richard Watts found Kanin's musical "fast, professional, tuneful, funny, and delightful . . . rare fun." And even Walter Kerr succumbed to the magic of Kanin's unpretentious efforts: "It's fun. Silly fun, loud fun, fast fun, old-fashioned fun, inconsequential fun, grand fun. . . . As entertainment . . . it's delectable."

Kanin's last play for the New York stage, *Come On Strong*, produced in 1962, had a slightly longer run than *The Live Wire*, but it was not a success, certainly nothing to compare with *Do Re Mi* or *Born Yesterday*. Critically speaking, from the standpoint of theme as well as plot and characterization, *Come On Strong* is scarcely better than *The Smile of the World*, which dealt at least with a theme of some general importance. Set in New York and Hollywood, *Come On Strong* concerns two young people, Virginia Karger and Herbert Lundquist, who live together, fight and make up, then separate. Virginia marries an older man, who dies on their wedding night. Herbert consoles Virginia, but the couple fight again, and Herbert walks out, this time presumably for good. Virginia goes to Hollywood and becomes a star. Several years later, Herbert, a photographer on assignment for *Life*, is asked to photograph Virginia for the magazine. The love affair is resumed, all of their differences get patched up, and Herbert and Virginia live happily ever after.

It is difficult to say precisely what Kanin's theme in *Come On Strong* is supposed to be. The boy-meets-girl, boy-loses-girl, boy-finds-girl plot is so hackneyed that one is compelled to pry beneath the surface action of the play to find meaningful substance. It is evident once again, as in *The Rat Race* and *The Live Wire*, though less obviously so, that ambition thwarting the personal happiness of otherwise innocent people and the devastating theatrical ambiance of New York and Hollywood have a lot to do with Herbert and Virginia's troubles. Yet Virginia is not of the same caliber even of Helen Brown; she certainly has not the dynamic inner strength and fortitude of either Billie Dawn or Sara Boulting. Virginia is vain and selfish. She is unsure of herself, despite her beauty, talent, and Hollywood success. When the chips are down she grasps at straws, twirling a baton in a pathetic attempt to bring back small memories of her earliest years in the limelight. Virginia really has very little in common with Kanin's strongest heroines except this tendency to live briefly, from time to time, in the past. But the strength of character and characterization Virginia derives from this is insignificant in comparison with the marvelous effects memory has on some of the earlier heroines. Though Virginia is more intelligent than, say, Billie Dawn, she is nevertheless not drawn by Kanin to the same grand proportions nor made out of the same strong stuff of integrity, self-respect, and determination.

Come On Strong was received with contempt. "A hoax? Possibly. A nightmare? Beyond question. But a play?" asked Howard Taubman. "Say it isn't so, Mr. Kanin." There was still criticism of Kanin's gossipy dialogue and uncertain plotting, and for the first time even Kanin's characterizations were challenged. Not only that, but the critics were still calling *Born Yesterday* the "everlasting standard," as Taubman put it: "how could the writer of *Born Yesterday* let *Come On Strong* see the light of a stage? Its trite plot is the kind of thing that films have abandoned, and its characters are so shopworn that television would look askance at them."

Hollywood had no doubt made its mark on Kanin, but it is more likely that the themes and characters that had grown out of World War II's self-righteousness and the postwar era's self-conscious fervor had simply faded in the late 1940s and early 1950s, and had become completely out-dated by 1962. Kanin seemed beset almost from the beginning by audiences looking for something else, for "emotional depth" in *The Smile of the World*, for structured action and greater continuity in all of the plays, for less "negative philosophy" and "bitter-ness" in 1949 and 1950, for more perhaps in 1962. Kanin's plays, though they faced the facts head on, seldom met precisely the emphasis and interests of the moment. With the exception of *Born Yesterday*, they seldom coincided with the temper and inclina-tions of the times. If Kanin never topped his first performance, however, it is partially the result of his own genius: *Born Yesterday*, the play, along with Harry Brock and Billie Dawn, the characters, are

deservedly classics of the modern American theatre.

–John Bruce Cantrell

Screenplays:
A Double Life, by Kanin and Ruth Gordon, Universal, 1947;
Adam's Rib, by Kanin and Gordon, MGM, 1950;
Pat and Mike, by Kanin and Gordon, MGM, 1952;
The Marrying Kind, by Kanin and Gordon, Columbia, 1952;
It Should Happen to You, Columbia, 1954;
The Rat Race, Paramount, 1960;
Some Kind of a Nut, United Artists, 1969;
Where It's At, United Artists, 1969.

George S. Kaufman

Ina Rae Hark
University of South Carolina

BIRTH: Pittsburgh, Pennsylvania, 16 November 1889, to Joseph and Henrietta Myers Kaufman.

MARRIAGE: 15 March 1917 to Beatrice Bakrow; children: John, Anne; 26 May 1949 to Leueen McGrath, divorced.

AWARDS: Pulitzer Prize for *Of Thee I Sing*, 1932; Pulitzer Prize for *You Can't Take It With You*, 1937; Antoinette Perry Award (Best Director) for *Guys and Dolls*, 1951.

DEATH: New York, New York, 2 June 1961.

PRODUCTIONS: *Someone in the House*, by Kaufman, Larry Evans, and Walter C. Percival, 9 September 1918, Knickerbocker Theatre, New York, 32 [performances];
Jacques Duval, adapted from Hans Muller's play, 10 November 1919, Blackstone Theatre, Chicago;
Dulcy, by Kaufman and Marc Connelly, 13 August 1921, Frazee Theatre, New York, 246;
To the Ladies!, by Kaufman and Connelly, 20 February 1922, Liberty Theatre, New York, 128;

No, Siree!, by Kaufman and Connelly, 30 April 1922, Forty-ninth Street Theatre, New York, 1;
The 49ers, by Kaufman and Connelly, 7 November 1922, Punch and Judy Theatre, New York, 15;
Merton of the Movies, by Kaufman and Connelly, 13 November 1922, Cort Theatre, New York, 398;
Helen of Troy, New York, by Kaufman and Connelly, score by Harry Ruby and Bert Kalmar, 19 June 1923, Selwyn Theatre, New York, 193;
The Deep Tangled Wildwood, by Kaufman and Connelly, 5 November 1923, Frazee Theatre, New York, 16;
Beggar on Horseback, by Kaufman and Connelly, adapted from Paul Apel's play, 12 February 1924, Broadhurst Theatre, New York, 224;
Be Yourself, by Kaufman and Connelly, score by Lewis Gensler and Milton Schwarzwald, 3 September 1924, Sam H. Harris Theatre, New York, 93;
Minick, by Kaufman and Edna Ferber, 24 September 1924, Booth Theatre, New York, 154;
The Butter and Egg Man, 23 September 1925, Long-acre Theatre, New York, 241;

The Cocoanuts, score by Irving Berlin, 8 December 1925, Lyric Theatre, New York, 375;

The Good Fellow, by Kaufman and Herman J. Mankiewicz, 5 October 1926, Playhouse Theatre, New York, 8;

The Royal Family, by Kaufman and Ferber, 28 December 1927, Selwyn Theatre, New York, 343;

Animal Crackers, by Kaufman and Morrie Ryskind, score by Kalmar and Ruby, 23 October 1928, 44th Street Theatre, New York, 213;

The Still Alarm in *The Little Show*, 30 April 1929, Music Box Theatre, New York, 321;

June Moon, by Kaufman and Ring Lardner, 9 October 1929, Broadhurst Theatre, New York, 272;

The Channel Road, by Kaufman and Alexander Woollcott, 17 October 1929, Plymouth Theatre, New York, 60;

Strike Up the Band, by Kaufman and Ryskind, score by George and Ira Gershwin, 14 January 1930, Times Square Theatre, New York, 191;

Once in a Lifetime, by Kaufman and Moss Hart, 24 September 1930, Music Box Theatre, New York, 401;

The Band Wagon, by Kaufman and Howard Dietz, 3 June 1931, New Amsterdam Theatre, New York, 262;

Eldorado, by Kaufman and Laurence Stallings, 26 October 1931, Shubert Theatre, New Haven;

Of Thee I Sing, book by Kaufman and Ryskind, score by George and Ira Gershwin, 26 December 1931, Music Box Theatre, New York, 446;

Dinner at Eight, by Kaufman and Ferber, 22 October 1932, Music Box Theatre, New York, 243;

Let 'Em Eat Cake, by Kaufman and Ryskind, score by George and Ira Gershwin, 21 October 1933, Imperial Theatre, New York, 89;

The Dark Tower, by Kaufman and Woollcott, 25 November 1933, Morosco Theatre, New York, 57;

Merrily We Roll Along, by Kaufman and Hart, 29 September 1934, Music Box Theatre, New York, 155;

Bring On the Girls, by Kaufman and Ryskind, 22 October 1934, National Theatre, Washington, D.C.;

First Lady, by Kaufman and Katherine Dayton, 26 November 1935, Music Box Theatre, New York, 244;

Stage Door, by Kaufman and Ferber, 22 October 1936, Music Box Theatre, New York, 169;

You Can't Take It With You, by Kaufman and Hart, 14 December 1936, Booth Theatre, New York, 837;

I'd Rather Be Right, by Kaufman and Hart, score by Richard Rodgers and Lorenz Hart, 2 November 1937, Alvin Theatre, New York, 289;

The Fabulous Invalid, by Kaufman and Hart, 8 October 1938, Broadhurst Theatre, New York, 65;

The American Way, by Kaufman and Hart, 21 January 1939, Center Theatre, New York, 164;

The Man Who Came to Dinner, by Kaufman and Hart, 16 October 1939, Music Box Theatre, New York, 739;

George Washington Slept Here, by Kaufman and Hart, 18 October 1940, Lyceum Theatre, New York, 173;

The Land Is Bright, by Kaufman and Ferber, 28 October 1941, Music Box Theatre, New York, 79;

The Late George Apley, by Kaufman and John P. Marquand, 21 November 1944, Lyceum Theatre, New York, 384;

Local Boy Makes Good in *The Seven Lively Arts*, 7 December 1944, Ziegfield Theatre, New York, 182;

Hollywood Pinafore, 31 May 1945, Alvin Theatre, New York, 52;

Park Avenue, by Kaufman and Nunnally Johnson, score by Arthur Schwartz and Ira Gershwin, 4 November 1946, Shubert Theatre, New York, 72;

Bravo!, by Kaufman and Ferber, 11 November 1948, Lyceum Theatre, New York, 44;

The Small Hours, by Kaufman and Leueen McGrath, 15 February 1951, National Theatre, New York, 20;

Fancy Meeting You Again, by Kaufman and McGrath, 14 January 1952, Royale Theatre, New York, 8;

The Solid Gold Cadillac, by Kaufman and Howard Teichmann, 5 November 1953, Belasco Theatre, New York, 526;

Silk Stockings, by Kaufman, McGrath, and Abe Burrows, score by Cole Porter, 24 February 1955, Imperial Theatre, 478;

Amicable Parting, by Kaufman and McGrath, 3 June 1968, Off Broadway Playhouse, Camden, N.J., 5.

BOOKS: *Dulcy*, by Kaufman and Marc Connelly (New York & London: Putnam's, 1921);

To the Ladies!, by Kaufman and Connelly (New York & London: French, 1923);

Merton of the Movies, by Kaufman and Connelly (New York & London: French, 1925);

Beggar on Horseback, by Kaufman and Connelly, adapted from Paul Apel's play (New York: Boni & Liveright, 1925; London: Benn, 1925);

Minick, by Kaufman and Edna Ferber (New York: French, 1925; London: French, 1930);

If Men Played Cards as Women Do (New York & London: French, 1926);

The Butter and Egg Man (New York: Boni & Liveright, 1926; London: French, 1926);

The Royal Family, by Kaufman and Ferber (Garden City: Doubleday, 1928);

June Moon, by Kaufman and Ring Lardner (New York & London: Scribners, 1930);

Once in a Lifetime, by Kaufman and Moss Hart (New York: Farrar & Rinehart, 1930; London: Gollancz, 1932);

The Good Fellow, by Kaufman and Herman J. Mankiewicz (New York: French, 1931);

Of Thee I Sing, by Kaufman and Morrie Ryskind (New York: Knopf, 1932; London: Gollancz, 1933);

Dinner at Eight, by Kaufman and Ferber (Garden City: Doubleday, 1932; London: Heinemann, 1933);

Let 'Em Eat Cake, by Kaufman and Ryskind (New York: Knopf, 1933);

Merrily We Roll Along, by Kaufman and Hart (New York: Random House, 1934);

First Lady, by Kaufman and Katherine Dayton (New York: Random House, 1935);

Stage Door, by Kaufman and Ferber (Garden City: Doubleday, Doran, 1936; London: Heinemann, 1937);

The Dark Tower, by Kaufman and Woollcott (New York & London: French, 1937);

You Can't Take It With You, by Kaufman and Hart (New York: Farrar & Rinehart, 1937; London: Barker, 1938);

I'd Rather Be Right, by Kaufman and Hart (New York: Random House, 1937);

The Fabulous Invalid, by Kaufman and Hart (New York: Random House, 1938);

The American Way, by Kaufman and Hart (New York: Random House, 1939);

The Man Who Came to Dinner, by Kaufman and Hart (New York: Random House, 1939; London: English Theatre Guild, 1945);

George Washington Slept Here, by Kaufman and Hart (New York: Random House, 1940);

The Land Is Bright, by Kaufman and Ferber (Garden City: Doubleday, Doran, 1941);

Six Plays by Kaufman and Hart, introduction by Kaufman (New York: Modern Library, 1942);

The Late George Apley, by Kaufman and John P. Marquand (New York: Dramatists Play Service, 1946);

Bravo!, by Kaufman and Ferber (New York: Dramatists Play Service, 1949);

The Small Hours, by Kaufman and Leueen McGrath (New York: Dramatists Play Service, 1951);

Fancy Meeting You Again, by Kaufman and McGrath (New York: Dramatists Play Service, 1952);

The Solid Gold Cadillac (New York: Random House, 1954).

The theatre world affectionately dubbed George S. Kaufman "The Great Collaborator," and that epithet pinpoints his particular genius. Only one of his full-length plays was not a collaboration or adaptation. His other famous activities in addition to his writing—as a director and as one of the wittiest members of the Algonquin Round Table group—also involved collaboration of a sort. He excelled at producing humorous dialogue and at shaping material so that it played well, but he had little interest in (and perhaps little talent for) creating original dramatic plots or complex characters. But despite differences among the works he produced with a Moss Hart or a Marc Connelly or an Edna Ferber, recognizably Kaufmanesque elements run throughout his best plays: the naive, not-too-bright young man out to make his fortune; the wise-cracking independent young woman who comes to his aid; the traumas involved in preparing to entertain company; and a satirical eye cast in the direction of big business, politics, American bourgeois mores, and, especially, show business. A sizable majority of his twenty-five hits contain at least one character connected with the theatre, films, or the music business.

Kaufman was born in Pittsburgh in 1889, a descendant of early German/Jewish immigrants to the region. A year before his birth his only brother, Richard, died at the age of two, and his emotionally unstable mother Nettie therefore neurotically overprotected George. As a result Kaufman grew up with ineradicable phobias about food, failure, physical contact, illness, and death. Nevertheless, his childhood was not on the whole unhappy. He enjoyed playing baseball and card games, reading—Mark Twain and W. S. Gilbert were early favorites—and attending plays and vaudeville shows. At fourteen he wrote his first play, "The Failure," in collaboration with a friend, Irving Pichel, who later became a successful Hollywood actor and director. Kaufman also acted in plays performed by the dramatic society at Rodeph Shalom Temple, his family's synagogue.

After graduating from high school in 1907,

Kaufman entered law school at the Western University of Pennsylvania (later the University of Pittsburgh). But he contracted pleurisy during his first semester and withdrew. When recovered, he did not return to school but undertook a series of short-lived jobs, as a member of a surveying team, as a clerk in the Allegheny County Tax Office, and then as stenographer to the controller of the Pittsburgh Coal Company. In 1909 his father found him a post as salesman for the Columbia Ribbon Company, which the elder Kaufman managed. Kaufman remained in this job for three years.

At the same time, however, he had begun his writing career by contributing comic items to the "Always in Good Humor" column in the *New York Evening Mail* edited by the celebrated FPA—Franklin Pierce Adams. Adams recognized Kaufman's talent for crafting witticisms and printed his submissions frequently. To emulate his mentor, Kaufman signed his pieces with his initials only, and since he had been given no middle name, he arbitrarily added the letter *S* to become GSK. In later years he said that the initial honored his grandfather Simon Kaufman, and librarians have zealously, but erroneously, added the middle name Simon to all the author cards for Kaufman.

In 1912 Frank Munsey, publisher of the *Washington Times*, asked Adams to recommend someone to write and edit a humor column for his paper. Adams mentioned Kaufman, and Munsey hired him sight unseen. Kaufman moved to Washington, D.C., and his column "This and That with Sometimes a Little of the Other," debuted on 9 December. Things went well until late November 1913, when Munsey, a virulent anti-Semite, visited the newsroom and saw the very Semitic-looking Kaufman for the first time. "What is that Jew doing in my city room?" Munsey exclaimed; Kaufman was soon notified that his 1 December column would be his last.

The elder Kaufmans had in the meantime moved to Manhattan, and upon his dismissal Kaufman went to New York and moved in with them. Within two months Adams had gotten him another job, as a reporter for the *New York Tribune*. Kaufman would remain a newspaperman for seventeen years, primarily with the *New York Times*, where he started on the drama desk in 1917 and soon became drama editor, a position he would retain until 1930, even after he had become established as a successful playwright.

On a visit to his sister Ruth and her husband in Rochester in 1916, Kaufman met and quickly became engaged to the assertive and intelligent Be-

atrice Bakrow. They were married on 15 March 1917 and moved into an apartment on Central Park West. Beatrice soon became pregnant, but in November 1918 the baby, a boy, was stillborn and Beatrice was rendered incapable of bearing any more children. (The Kaufmans subsequently adopted a daughter, Anne.) The impact of the tragedy on the neurotic Kaufman was to make him impotent with his wife. Although the two remained devoted in all other respects, by mutual consent they both turned to others for sexual gratification. Kaufman later developed a reputation as an accomplished ladies' man—sex was the only kind of touching he could tolerate, but he tolerated it marvelously—particularly after his name was the most prominent of those publicized through the Mary Astor "diary" scandal.

Through his newspaper work Kaufman met and became intimate with such sophisticated Manhattanites as Dorothy Parker, Robert Benchley, Alexander Woollcott, and Heywood Broun, whom he would join for legendary battles of wit over the lunch table at the Algonquin. Working on the *Times* drama desk also reawakened Kaufman's interest in playwriting and provided him with contacts in the theatrical business that would eventually enable him to write for the stage. In 1917 Burns Mantle brought Kaufman's name to the attention of Henry Stern, who wished to begin an agency to develop plays by unproduced playwrights. Kaufman wrote for Stern a farce called "Going Up" about an impoverished young man who gets involved with altering the dollar amounts on checks to his own advantage. Although Stern and Mantle liked the play, they could interest no producer in putting it on. However, one, George C. Tyler, upon reading the play, made note of Kaufman as a writer with a future.

Therefore, when Tyler was trying to get a play about a gentleman crook into shape after a failed road tryout in the autumn of 1917, he called in Kaufman to serve as a rewrite man. Others had preceded and would succeed Kaufman at this task, but his contribution was the only one deemed significant enough to earn him author credit with the original writers, Larry Evans and Walter C. Percival. The finished product, *Someone in the House*, opened 9 September 1918 and closed after only thirty-two performances and mediocre reviews.

Kaufman's involvement with *Someone in the House* proved far more significant than its undistinguished run might indicate, however. Tyler had cast in the supporting role of Helene Glendenning a gifted British actress with little American exposure:

Lynn Fontanne. He wanted Kaufman to rewrite the part to showcase Fontanne's talents; Kaufman responded by modelling Helene on Dulcinea, a character of FPA's invention who exuded naive optimism and spoke predominantly in cliches. Fontanne handled this role expertly and received glowing notices, in contrast to those of the play as a whole. When Tyler three years later decided to produce a play starring Fontanne as this same character, he naturally offered the project to Kaufman. (Kaufman had in the meantime ill-advisedly adapted for Tyler *Jacques Duval*, Hans Muller's gloomy Danish melodrama about a French medical researcher, his wife, and the wife's lover who becomes the doctor's patient. The material was totally unsuited to Kaufman's talents and the play closed out of town.) He agreed on the condition that he could collaborate with Marcus Cooke Connelly, a fellow newspaperman with whom he had unsuccessfully been trying for a year to come up with a viable script for a three-act comedy.

In the new play Connelly and Kaufman openly acknowledged the source for their heroine by calling her Dulcinea Smith and giving Adams "a bow" beneath the title, *Dulcy*, in the playbill and on the title page of the published version. The play finds Dulcy attempting to promote the merger between her husband Gordon's small costume jewelry firm and the larger Forbes corporation by inviting the Forbes family to her Westchester home for a weekend. She also schemes to arrange an elopement between Forbes's daughter Angela and Vincent Leach, an effete Hollywood scenarist. In the course of the overplotted proceedings, which also involve a missing pearl necklace, an ex-convict butler, and a lunatic impersonating a millionaire, everything Dulcy does has results disastrously opposite to those she intends, yet in the end Gordon has the merger on most favorable terms and Angela has married not Leach, but Bill Parker, Dulcy's acerbic brother, one of the few sensible characters in the play. Opening on 13 August 1921, *Dulcy*, despite Kaufman's conviction that it would be a failure, ran for 246 performances and established Kaufman as a preeminent Broadway dramatist. It was a position he would not lose until illness debilitated him at the end of his life forty years later.

The play contains many elements that would reappear in other Kaufman/Connelly collaborations and in Kaufman's work with others. First there is the basis of the comedy in confrontations between the wisecracking knowledgeable *eiron*, here Bill Parker, and to a lesser extent, Mr. Forbes, and complacent often self-deluded *alazons* like Tom Sterrett,

George S. Kaufman

the gung-ho advertising executive, and Leach, the pretentious screenwriter. (It is fitting that while both these braggarts seek the hand of the ingenue, Angela, Bill wins her in the end.) One of the play's finest comic scenes involves the reactions of Bill and Forbes to Leach's lengthy recitation of the scenario for his upcoming epic film, *Sin*. The overall discomfiture and exasperation that Forbes must suffer from Dulcy's misguided efforts to entertain him produce much more humor today than do the heroine's addlepated effusions divorced from the magic of Fontanne's performance. Besides being bored by Leach and by the piano recitals of "Schuyler Van Dyck" (the disguised lunatic), Forbes must sit in the soft armchairs his hostess insists on rather than in the straight-backed chair his sore back requires; the eloping couple borrow his car, leaving him stranded; as entertainments Dulcy suggests bridge and golf, which he abhors; and when he discovers a billiard table, promising an amusement he enjoys, she has misplaced the billiard balls.

Kaufman, a workaholic, who played as energetically as he worked, reacted neurotically to the prospect of poor service, uncertain food prepared by strangers, and directionless leisure. Perhaps for that reason, anxious preparations to entertain ill-assorted combinations of visitors and the disastrous social events that ensue occur frequently in his drama. The incompatibility of the bourgeois business world to which Forbes and Gordon Smith belong and the eccentric artistic milieu of Leach would also provide dramatic conflict in many Kaufman plays, as would the situation of a young woman helping her man to success. In later plays, however, the man possesses Dulcy's bumbling earnestness and the woman hardheaded common sense.

This is certainly the case in the next Kaufman/Connelly collaboration, *To the Ladies!* (1922). Its protagonist is Leonard Beebe, another husband seeking career advancement, this time in the piano manufacturing firm of John Kincaid, who believes that "there is a great romance in pianos. Some day, perhaps, it will be written." Leonard shares Kincaid's enthusiasm, but his ardor far exceeds his intelligence. He believes the claims made for various self-improvement aids in the classifieds and has invested heavily in a bogus Florida land scheme. Like many Kaufman heroes to follow, he is also complacently overconfident as to the success his abilities should lead to. Leonard does succeed, but only through the agency of his wife Elsie, whose demure, acquiescent manner masks her shrewd maneuverings on her husband's behalf. When, after typical anxieties about the impending visit, the Kincaids drop in on the Beebes in act 1, Elsie is recognized as a kindred soul by Mrs. Kincaid, who for years has unobtrusively made all her husband's business decisions for him. She approves of Elsie and procures a promotion for Leonard.

Leonard's second advancement occurs during the comic highlight of the play, the Kincaid company banquet. The authors satirize the excesses of such gatherings with deadly accuracy, parodying each style of boring presentation. Leonard and two other aspirants for promotion are to give speeches also; he has memorized one from a "Be-a-Popular-Speaker" manual. Unfortunately the first speaker has chosen the same selection. When her husband is made speechless by this calamity, Elsie, saying he has laryngitis, extemporaneously gives as Leonard's a sincere, low-key address that wins him the job. Kincaid later discovers this deception and wants to replace Leonard. Elsie and Kincaid's wife, Myrtle, dissuade him by pointing out that most men succeed only through their wives. The play ends with Elsie and Myrtle congratulating themselves on the recruitment of another "able woman," Mrs. Fernandez and arranging to lunch together on "Tuesday—as usual."

Following *To the Ladies!* Kaufman and Connelly wrote sketches for two revues and a satire on the supposed simplicity of small-town life, which after several title changes and a rocky road trip in 1922, opened and soon closed on Broadway in 1923 as *The Deep Tangled Wildwood*. Also during 1922, however, they produced a successful comedy, *Merton of the Movies*, which from a half century's distance appears as the freshest of their collaborations. It also established the pattern—a naive young man from the sticks comes to the big city, gets involved in show business, and bumbles his way into unlikely success—that would recur in Kaufman plays written without Connelly such as *The Butter and Egg Man* (1925), *June Moon* (1929), and *Once in a Lifetime* (1930).

Based on a serial by Harry Leon Wilson, *Merton of the Movies* traces the fortunes of a general-store clerk from Illinois, who, stirred by his resemblance to screen hero Harold Parmalee and by the fan magazine descriptions of his idol Beulah Baxter, vows to go to Hollywood to make "serious pictures" and "enrich the American public." Upon his arrival Merton spends days without food or money, hanging around the Parmalee-Baxter sets and hoping for a part. He is taken in tow by a wise and cynical stunt girl, "Flips" Montague, whose friend Jeff Baird, a slapstick comedy director, finds in Merton's attempts to emulate Parmalee a wonderful source of parody. They persuade Merton that they are filming a serious Western in which he should give his best dramatic performance; with him thus deceived they produce a hilarious spoof that establishes Merton as a comedy star. Although the truth initially crushes Merton, he finally realizes that comedy can be as valuable as drama and reconciles himself to a career with Baird and a marriage with Flips.

Much of the humor of the play is incidental to this plot and derives from the shrewd observations of Hollywood idiocies that pass before the audience as Merton awaits his opportunity to act as an extra. Particularly amusing are the bits of bizarre scenarios discussed by director Sigmond Rosenblatt and his scenarist Weller. The contrast between Merton's idealized images of Parmalee and Baxter and their actual characters also generates considerable comedy. Parmalee is a pompous idiot, and Miss Baxter is a petty, vain woman who has slept her way to the top. Although Kaufman in 1923 had never visited Hollywood, he considered it a sham, business masquerading as art, where success came through sheer chance. His opinion would not change over the years, even though he would later go to California to rewrite scripts for various studios.

Next the collaborators provided a book for the

already titled and scored musical *Helen of Troy, New York* (1923). They turned to their favorite theme, the foibles of the business world, and wrote a farce about life in a collar company. The musical ran for six months on Broadway but died quickly in the public memory. Then in early 1924 the pair embarked upon what would be their last successful collaboration, *Beggar on Horseback*. It was also their most theatrically ambitious in that it was based on an experimental German play by Paul Apel, *Hans Sonnenstössers Höllenfahrt*, and contained expressionist and surrealist elements.

Most of the play comprises the dream of impoverished composer Neil McRae after he has, on the advice of a childhood friend, proposed to the daughter of a wealthy bourgeois family from his midwestern hometown. Through the marriage he hopes to acquire enough money to complete the symphony he is struggling to write amidst the jobs as an arranger he takes on to support himself. In so doing he must break off with the girl he really loves, his New York neighbor Cynthia Mason. In the dream the Philistine banality and materialism of the Cady family, only slightly exaggerated from their actual conversation, interferes with Neil's art far more than his poverty ever did; at last, exasperated beyond endurance, he murders the entire family. After a trial staged like a play—during which the Cadys spring back to life and prevent Neil from playing his symphony as a defense for his actions—he is incarcerated in the Cady Consolidated Art Factory where composers, writers, and painters are forced to turn out prodigious quantities of hack work for the delight of the masses. Awakening from this awful warning, Neil breaks his engagement to Gladys Cady and proposes to Cynthia.

The Cadys embody the foibles of the provincial, business-minded middle class that are the primary target of satire in all the Kaufman/Connelly plays. Mr. Cady abandoned an ambition to become a judge when he discovered how little money judges make; his chief interests are golf and the affairs of his widget factory. Mrs. Cady sits in a rocking chair, knitting and gossiping; her favorite recreation is off-key hymn singing. Their son Homer is a peevish, lazy hypochondriac who says unkind things to Neil at every opportunity. Despite the avant-garde trappings, the world of the play is that of *Dulcy* and *To the Ladies!* And although *Beggar on Horseback* received high critical praise as a daring intellectual drama when it opened, even Kaufman, viewing a revival years later, noted that it had dated badly.

Kaufman and Connelly wrote one more play, an indifferent and short-lived musical, *Be Yourself*, but by the time of its opening in 1924 Kaufman the compulsive writer had clashed with the less driven Connelly, and the two decided to end their partnership. Kaufman would work subsequently with many collaborators, most importantly Edna Ferber, Morrie Ryskind, and, of course, Moss Hart. But the one full length play he wrote that was not a collaboration or adaptation, *The Butter and Egg Man*, is very much on the Kaufman/Connelly model. It concerns the efforts of unscrupulous Broadway producers Jack McClure and Joe Lehman (an Irish-Jewish partnership to be repeated with Gilhooley and Lippman in *Of Thee I Sing*, 1931) to obtain financing for a dreadful musical melodrama, *Her Lesson*, that they have acquired without paying royalties. They find their "butter and egg man"—an out-of-towner with a bankroll—in Peter Jones from Chillicothe, Ohio, who wants to parlay $20,000 quickly into $50,000 in order to buy the hotel at which he works. Enchanted by Lehmac Productions' charming secretary Jane Weston, he lets himself be talked into investing in the play.

Her Lesson has a terrible road tryout in Syracuse; after a vain attempt by all concerned to fix the play—a situation Kaufman knew well—the producers decide to close it. Frantic at the loss of his bankroll, Peter offers to buy them out. He raises the necessary cash from the stagestruck assistant manager of the Syracuse hotel, Oscar Fritchie, who is even dumber than he. Peter has meanwhile picked up just enough of Lehman's fast-talking ways to succeed in the theatre business. *Her Lesson* miraculously arrives on Broadway a hit.

Many reversals occur in the third act of *The Butter and Egg Man*, with the upshot that Lehman buys back the play just in time to be slapped with a plagiarism suit, Peter talks Oscar into investing his share of the profits in the Chillicothe hotel, and Jane and Peter, after an estrangement brought about by his brush with theatrical success, reconcile and leave for Chillicothe where they will marry and and manage the hotel. This ending represents the only time in Kaufman's many treatments of the naive Midwesterner versus the big city sophisticate that he advocates a retreat to the provinces. But in all other respects the play differs little from those that preceded it, particularly in Jane's role as guide to the inexperienced Peter.

What *The Butter and Egg Man* lacks in originality it makes up for in Kaufman's insider's knowledge of the theatrical world he is mocking and in the pointed jibes of Fanny Lehman, Joe's ex-wife who has no real function in the play except to deliver wisecracks. While Kaufman definitely wrote better with collaborators, this play demonstrates that he could turn out competent comic entertainment on his own. However, he never attempted a solo outing again and was always on the alert for new collaborators.

The first he found after breaking with Connelly was the already prominent fiction writer Edna Ferber. Kaufman approached her in 1923 about dramatizing her story "Old Man Minick." She consented, beginning a partnership that would last off and on for the next twenty-five years. It was, however, often a strained partnership, partly because Ferber fell in love with Kaufman and he did not reciprocate. Of all his collaborators Ferber nevertheless seems to have had the most noticeable influence on the finished product. With their melodrama, sudden death, and moralizing the plays are more Ferber/Kaufman than Kaufman/Ferber.

Minick, which opened in September 1924, a year before the premiere of *The Butter and Egg Man*, gave little indication of the success they would eventually achieve together. Ferber's tale about an elderly widower who comes to stay with his son and daughter-in-law, disrupts their lives, and then must overcome their guilt (in order to enter the retirement home where he has friends and really would prefer to live) had few themes to bring out the best in Kaufman. The one effective sequence concerns the frantic preparations for the meeting of Nettie Minick's civic club at her apartment, the banality of the club's business, and the total collapse of the gathering due to Minick's interference. Here Kaufman is on home ground, exposing trivial bourgeois values.

In 1927 Kaufman and Ferber got together again on a play with a subject comfortable for both. For Kaufman it was the well-known territory of the Broadway theatre, for Ferber the fortunes of a family dynasty, three generations of actors in the Cavendish clan, patterned after the Barrymores. *The Royal Family* (1927) unfolds in a series of hectic, dialogue-filled scenes with many characters running about the stage talking at cross purposes. Rather than having a well-defined plot, it presents several conflicts. The central one involves the opposition of two ways of life—secure, dull materialism and domesticity versus the erratic, egocentric, but fulfilling life in the theatre.

Julie Cavendish ponders giving up her stage career to marry ex-suitor, now millionaire industrialist, Gil Martin, and move to South America. Her daughter Gwen struggles to accommodate her developing acting career to her love for society scion Perry Stewart. The differences between philistine and artist are, as always in Kaufman, irreconcilable. As Martin describes the joys of life among his "very fine" friends the Zamacos, "He's a Spaniard of the highest type—very big cattle man. She was a Kansas City girl—Krantz—you know—daughter of Julius Krantz—packer," Julie's resolve to get away from the madness of the acting profession weakens. Although Gwen does marry Perry and bear his son, she is soon planning to go back on the stage and start the baby, named Aubrey for his great-grandfather the Shakespearean actor, on the same path. It is clear that Gil and Perry will always be outsiders in their women's lives.

While they become one set of fools to be defeated by the wisecracks of Julie and her mother Fanny, those theatre people who are not true artists serve as another set. Paramount among them are the conceited hams Herbert Dean and his wife Kitty, who, lacking talent and having lost youth, must descend from the legitimate theatre to vaudeville melodrama. They contrast with grande dame Fanny who, despite her age, is prevented from making a triumphant comeback tour only by the illness that leads to her death at the final curtain. Fanny's black sheep son Tony also comes in for some of the same type of satire, while providing much of the play's humor as well, as he exaggerates the events of his own life into a never-ending melodrama. Tony has the true Cavendish talent, but he has sold out to Hollywood (as much a sin to Ferber as to Kaufman); he spends most of his time, not acting, but either evading women he has seduced and abandoned or hiding out from the reporters his scandals attract.

At the end of the play, however, Tony is returning to the stage, playing Christ in an updated version of the Passion play; all the other members of the family are returning to the stage as well. Although Fanny's death mutes the happiness of the conclusion, just prior to her demise she has asserted of baby Aubrey's imminent debut: "He's a Cavendish, and he's going to carry on. We always have and we always will. When one drops out there's always another one to take his place." *The Royal Family* celebrates this continuity of the family acting tradition, which becomes a metaphor for the persistence of the theatre itself.

In 1929 Ferber began trying to interest Kaufman in a play about a fashionable society dinner party and the various people—with their various self-serving motives—who attend. But Kaufman felt the vignette structure required by Ferber's concept would be technically impossible to stage. By 1932 the success of the similarly structured *Grand Hotel* and Ferber's persistent entreaties persuaded him to change his mind. Once the two began work on *Dinner at Eight* (1932) he warmed to the theme, and the anticipated difficulties with unity disappeared.

Although the audience meets them in separate scenes, the destinies of each of the dinner guests are complexly intertwined. The hostess, Millicent Jordan, is so busy trying to score a social coup by entertaining visiting British nobility that she doesn't notice her husband Oliver's failing health and failing business. The latter is threatened by a stock takeover, behind dummy agents, by Ferberesque self-made Montana millionaire Dan Packard. Unaware of his scheme, Oliver has had Millie invite the rough-hewn Packard and his vulgar wife Kitty to the dinner. Packard agrees to come because he needs to meet Lord Ferncliffe in order to further his empire-building ambitions. Also on the guest list is Dr. Talbot, the physician who alone knows that Jordan is dying and who has had an affair with Kitty Packard. Two former stars, Carlotta Vance and Larry Renault, now broke and past their acting prime, are also to grace the table; both have done things that have adversely affected their hosts. Carlotta has sold the Jordan stock her old admirer Oliver advised her to buy in the past, thus making the Packard takeover possible. And Renault has seduced the Jordans' daughter Paula away from her wealthy fiance.

By the actual time of the dinner, one of the least propitious of the many nervously planned at-home entertainments in the Kaufman canon, most of the characters have received a comeuppance. The guests of honor, the Ferncliffes, cancel out at the last moment, disappointing Packard and nullifying the raison d'etre for the whole affair. What's worse, Millicent must fill in with her decidedly non-fashionable cousins Hattie, the Kaufman wise-cracker of the play, and Ed. She has suffered a further blow when a quarrel among the servants results in the destruction of the lobster dish that was to crown the meal. The doctor decides to return to his wife and to break off with Kitty. Evicted from his hotel for nonpayment of his bill, with no acting jobs on the horizon and no money for whiskey, Renault commits suicide; but Paula has gone to break off her engagement before the news reaches her. Carlotta learns that she has inadvertently ruined her old friend. *Dinner at Eight*, unlike most of Kaufman's plays, balances its criticism of pretension and double-dealing with little affirmation of the eventual triumph of common sense and decency.

The next Kaufman/Ferber collaboration restored such a balance. *Stage Door* (1936) contrasts several sets of show-business people, playing off those who prostitute their talent to Hollywood fame against those who remain true to the higher ideals of the legitimate theatre. The play is set in a New York boardinghouse for aspiring female performers, the Footlights Club, modeled on the real-life Rehearsal Club. With Margaret Sullavan playing the lead role of Terry Randall, the play was a substantial hit and would have run even longer if pregnancy had not forced Sullavan to leave the show.

Kaufman and Ferber wrote two more plays together, but neither repeated the success of the preceding trio of hits. *The Land Is Bright* (1941) is pure Ferber, a multigeneration saga of a western robber baron and his descendants, who get and spend money irresponsibly, pursue decadent life-styles, make loveless marriages, and often end violently. The last generation, however, profiting from the marriage of one of the sons to a competent, nonmaterialistic wife and shaken by events in Hitler's Europe, vows to enter public service to make up for all the family has gouged from the country. Such a concept provided little scope for Kaufman's comic gifts except in the opening scene when the head of the clan's former Montana sidekicks reacts in disbelief to the gaudy, nouveau riche appointments of his New York City mansion.

The team's last collaboration, *Bravo!* (1948), is more Kaufmanesque, although its focus on a group of European refugees trying to start over in America derives from a preoccupation of Ferber's that also figures in *The Land Is Bright*. The central character Zoltan Lazko, a formerly eminent East European playwright, supposedly based on Ferenc Molnar, lives with a diverse collection of fellow countrymen in a New York brownstone. (One feels as though one has gone home with Boris Kolenkhov, the emigre Russian ballet master of the earlier, Kaufman/Hart collaboration *You Can't Take It With You*, 1936.) Their struggles provide many effective comic moments and sharp dialogue exchanges, but the contrived plot, which alternates between pathos and satire, fails to find a place for all the characters. As a whole, the play does not jell. So as it began, the Kaufman/Ferber collaboration ended on an insignificant note.

Kaufman first sought the help of Morrie Ryskind, another frequent collaborator during the late 1920s and early 1930s, when he was working on the book of *The Cocoanuts* (1925), an Irving Berlin musical starring his new friends the Marx Brothers. The play concerns Florida land speculation at a run-down hotel owned by Groucho, with Zeppo as the desk clerk, Harpo and Chico as two wacky guests, and Margaret Dumont, in her first appearance with the brothers, as a bewildered sane one. Of course, plot never mattered much to the Marxes; Kaufman and Ryskind's primary task involved coming up with copious wisecracks for Groucho to "ad lib" at will. Groucho was one of the few performers Kaufman grudgingly allowed to tamper with a script, and Kaufman was one of the few dramatists Groucho trusted to write for him.

Therefore Kaufman was summoned for the book of the next Marx Brothers musical *Animal Crackers* (1928), and Ryskind, who had worked uncredited on *The Cocoanuts*, this time received full coauthor billing. Like the later *Dinner at Eight, Animal Crackers* deals with the going awry of a party as social coup, this time a weekend at the estate of Mrs. Rittenhouse (Dumont). She has arranged to show off to her guests both the noted African explorer, Captain Spalding (a role which gave Groucho his theme song "Hooray for Captain Spalding!"), and a valuable painting. But her envious, scheming neighbors exchange the painting for a forgery; a second copy then turns up; and general anarchy, abetted by Harpo and Chico, ensues before the confusion is cleared up and all the romantic subplots happily resolved. Both these stage successes helped to launch the Marx Brothers' movie careers. Although Kaufman did not join Ryskind in adapting them for the screen, at the request of MGM's Irving Thalberg, whom he admired, he did later contribute to the original screenplay of *A Night at the Opera* (1935).

The Marxes having gone to Hollywood, Kaufman and Ryskind for their next Broadway venture turned to a more focused musical satire, originating in Ryskind's interest in politics. *Strike Up the Band* (1930) is a Gilbert-and-Sullivan-style extravaganza about a businessman who stages a war as a profit-making venture. After the authors experienced some difficulty in completing a producible script, the play ran a respectable 191 performances. But their political satire that followed it soon eclipsed *Strike Up the Band* in the history of the theatre. *Of Thee I Sing* opened 26 December 1931, ran over one hundred performances longer than any previous Kaufman play, and became the first musical comedy to win the Pulitzer Prize for drama.

Of Thee I Sing does not satirize any particular politician or party but ridicules the American system of presidential politics. Two assumptions underlie most of the play's humor: first, that competency to run government concerns neither candidates nor electorate during a presidential race; second, that the office of vice-president reduces its holder to a nonentity. Neither point is very original, but the Kaufman / Ryskind plot, aided by the George and Ira Gershwin score, turned it into delightful theatre.

Worried about his party's declining popularity, the advisers of incumbent John P. Wintergreen seek a campaign gimmick to insure his reelection. After polling a chambermaid, who informs them that, after money, people care most about love, the party hacks arrange for Wintergreen to run on a love platform. The winner of a Miss America-like beauty contest will be his bride. But at the last minute he cannot go through with the stunt, having fallen in love with the corn muffins baked by the unglamorous but practical pageant coordinator Mary Turner.

Wintergreen easily wins the election, but the contest winner, Southern belle Diana Devereaux, stirs up public opinion against him for jilting her. Then the French government joins in the protest when it discovers that Miss Devereaux comes from a long line of illegitimate descendants of Napoleon. However, Mary's pregnancy placates the populace, and the French are satisfied when vice-president Throttlebottom, whom no one ever recognizes, finally gets to perform a duty—to act in place of the president and marry Diana.

Individual scenes and the whole musical mode point up the fantasy elements of the play. At a rally the candidates' speeches are upstaged by a wrestling match going on at the same time in the same hall; Throttlebottom can only enter the White House as an awestruck tourist; the Supreme Court, by tossing dice, rules on whether the presidential infant will be a boy or a girl (in the end Mary has twins, one of each sex); Mary worries over the number of lamb chops required by the officials who cannot be prevented from coming to state dinners. Yet the exaggerations have just enough basis in truth to make the satire wickedly effective. While the vice-presidential jokes seem somewhat stale today, the depiction of the presidency as 99% public relations hype is more relevant than ever.

Kaufman and Ryskind would never duplicate the success of *Of Thee I Sing*. A sequel, *Let 'Em Eat Cake* (1933), again featuring Wintergreen and Throttlebottom as played by the now popular comedy team of William Gaxton and Victor Moore and dealing with international rather than domestic politics, veered too far into fantasy to work as satire.

Bring On the Girls (1934), another political satire and their first nonmusical collaboration, closed in tryouts. These failures, coupled with a swing to the right in Ryskind's political views, ended their playwriting partnership.

During the late 1920s and early 1930s Kaufman was involved with three other hits written with people other than his usual collaborators. In 1929 he offered to help Ring Lardner dramatize his short story "Some Like Them Cold." It concerned the romance between one of Lardner's grammar-fracturing, dumb but overconfident provincials who goes to the big city and the hometown girl he meets in a railway station. She shares his simple tastes and naive aspirations and longs to fill all his domestic needs. In the story he drops her for a "cool" sophisticated New Yorker, but Kaufman persuaded Lardner that the play would be more commercially viable if the young man, Fred, became intimidated by the demands of this gold-digging creature, Eileen, and eventually allowed himself to be led back into the arms of his faithful Edna by the acerbic but kindhearted Tin Pan Alley pianist Maxie Schwartz.

Happy ending aside, the combination of the antisentimental, witty Kaufman and cynical, witty Lardner results in the most tough-minded and consistently funny version of the much-used Kaufman plot involving the simple-minded and untalented young man who inexplicably succeeds in show business, this time as a songwriter. *June Moon*, the title of one of his hits as well as of the play itself, has two wisecracking characters, Maxie and Lucille Sears, the neglected and straying wife of Fred's composer Paul Sears; when their sarcasm collides with Fred's banal, earnest effusions, the play has few rivals in the Kaufman canon:

FRED: I like Bronxes best. They're nothing but gin and
    orange juice. I don't know why they call it a Bronx.
MAXIE: It's great orange country, up there.

....

FRED: I seen the Goddest [*sic*] of Liberty, too—I mean the
    statue. It cost a million dollars and weighs 225 ton.
MAXIE (*gently*): She ought to cut out sweets.

Kaufman also worked with Howard Dietz on the comedy sketches for the highly successful musical revue *The Band Wagon* in 1931, and in the mid-1930s he collaborated with Washington columnist and society insider Katherine Dayton to produce *First Lady* (1935), an entertaining amalgam of the Kaufman / Ryskind political extravaganzas and the Kaufman / Connelly plays about women arranging their husbands' careers. The plot, which does not warrant close scrutiny, has two rival Washington hostesses, Lucy Chase Wayne, granddaughter of a former president, and well-worn beauty Irene Hibbard competing to become First Lady. When Lucy suspects that Irene will divorce her aging Supreme Court justice husband in order to marry an up-and-coming young Western senator, Gordon Keane, she starts a "Carter Hibbard for President" boom in order to divert Irene's attention. But her scheme backfires when Hibbard, backed by a powerful newspaper chain and a satirically presented national women's organization, becomes the leading contender for the party's nomination. Only a scandal from Irene's past saves the day by forcing Hibbard to withdraw from the race and leaving the nomination available for Lucy's husband Stephen, the secretary of state. As a final twist, Keane, now safely steered romantically toward Lucy's Southern belle niece, reveals that he was born in Canada and thus disqualified from ever running for president.

Most of the action occurs before or during one of Lucy's parties, and the number of acidulous comments made by the various Washington wives in attendance makes it clear that the plot only serves as an excuse for a witty survey of social life in the nation's capital, where a hostess arranging a dinner partner for a friend can remark, "I can give you a Cuba attache, unless they have a revolution before dinner."

Far more significant than any of Kaufman's other collaborations during the 1930s, however, were the plays he wrote with Moss Hart; Kaufman and Hart are now linked in the public consciousness as firmly as Gilbert and Sullivan. The circumstances of their first collaboration, when Hart sought help from Kaufman in 1929 for rendering his script of *Once in a Lifetime* stageworthy, and the agonies of multiple rewrites and dismal tryouts before the play's triumph on Broadway, as detailed by Hart in his autobiography *Act One* (1959), have become a theatrical legend of sorts. Although Kaufman, who also directed and acted the part of Lawrence Vail, claimed in his opening night speech that the play was eighty percent Moss Hart, *Once in a Lifetime* is ironically the most Kaufmanesque of all their collaborations. As Hart admitted, it had been inspired by *Merton of the Movies* and *June Moon*. Succeeding Kaufman / Hart plays would more strongly reveal Hart's preference for comedy over satire, for the creation of more psychologically complex characters, for the theatrically innovative, and for significant rather than perfunctory romantic plots. Even *Once in a Lifetime* has the profusion of characters, episodic plotting, and onstage chaos that typifies the Kaufman / Hart comedies.

The play takes place during the crisis that swept Hollywood with the advent of sound. Three out-of-work vaudevillians, fast-talking Jerry Hyland, his cynical girl May Daniels, and their dumber-than-dumb partner George Lewis head west with a scheme to pass themselves off as elocution experts. Silent stars are so desperate to learn how to deliver lines that May and Jerry soon find themselves with many opportunities at the Glogauer Studios. Given the capricious nature of Hollywood success, they lose them just as quickly, and almost lose each other when Jerry's absorption in getting ahead at all costs alienates May. In the meantime, however, Indian nut-cracking George has become a hit director of films starring his equally dim-witted actress girl friend Susan Walker. Although he shoots the wrong script and makes numerous technical errors, the critics hail his latest film as cinematically daring and innovative. With the studio at his feet, he demands that May and Jerry be rehired, and they resolve their romantic differences.

As in *Merton of the Movies*, it is the absurd nature of life in Hollywood rather than the mechanics of the plot that generates the comedy. Kaufman and Hart look at the plight of New York playwrights brought out to write dialogue and then forgotten; at the accidents that pass for art; at the vulgarity of the big studio bosses Glogauer, whose precise whereabouts and phone extension are constantly announced by a page, and the aptly named Schlepkin brothers, one of whom is always "schlepping" home to the Bronx to care for their elderly mother; at the lack of any values save monetary ones. All these faults are pointed up through the running commentary of May, who serves double duty as romantic lead and wisecracking female.

Fearful of losing his individuality in his admiration for Kaufman, Hart did not immediately seek another collaboration. Three and a half years later, his confidence bolstered by psychoanalysis and some success on his own, he approached Kaufman, who had remained a close friend, with an idea for a play spanning several decades in the career of a successful but shallow Broadway playwright. Richard Niles has betrayed friends, lovers, and his own talent for quick material gain. The plot was about as hackneyed as it sounds, but *Merrily We Roll Along* (1934) depended for its success on a gimmick Hart had come up with: the action unfolded in reverse order, as in Harold Pinter's recent *Betrayal*. A character based on Kaufman's friend Dorothy

Parker also enlivened the proceedings with her biting, drunken comments. Nevertheless, although their previous hit guaranteed decent ticket sales, the second Kaufman / Hart effort did not really deserve the recognition it received from the public. For collaborators to lead Kaufman into "serious" drama was always a mistake.

The next Kaufman / Hart collaboration was definitely not a mistake. *You Can't Take It With You*, the story of an eccentric family and its efforts to resist the agents of social conformity, would run longer than any other Kaufman play, would win him his second Pulitzer Prize, and would achieve classic status in the American theatrical repertory along with such other celebrations of daffy individualism as *Arsenic and Old Lace* and *Harvey*.

Head of the household is "Grandpa" Martin Vanderhof, a successful businessman who had many years ago realized that he hated his work. So he simply retired to collect snakes and stamps and drop in annually on the Columbia University commencement exercises. His daughter Penny Sycamore is a hobbyist who abandoned painting for playwriting when a typewriter was mistakenly delivered to the house. Penny's husband Paul manufactures fireworks in the basement with the help of permanent houseguest Mr. DePinna, the iceman who came to make a delivery one day and never left. Their elder daughter Essie is an untalented but dedicated ballerina who also makes "Love Dreams" candy for her husband Ed to peddle around town. Ed includes in each box one of the selections from various books that he enjoys printing on his printing press. He also accompanies Essie on the xylophone. Her ballet teacher, Russian emigre Boris Kolenkhov, also visits frequently, particularly at mealtimes, casually presided over by black servants Rheba and Donald.

Two problems threaten the happiness of this blissful household. The one "normal" member of the family, Penny and Paul's younger daughter Alice, has fallen in love with her boss's son and fears that his conservative, materialistic family will never accept her unconventional one. And the Internal Revenue Service is inquiring into Grandpa's nonpayment of income taxes while the FBI is concerned about some of the candy box inserts that Ed has copied from Communist tracts.

Everything comes to a head during the most calamitous of all Kaufman's calamitous parties when Alice's fiance Tony purposely brings his parents to dinner on the evening *before* Alice has scheduled a formal entertainment with everyone on his best behavior. Tony admires the nonconformity of the family and wants his parents to see them as they really are. They certainly get the opportunity. The Kirbys arrive at a moment when all members of the household are simultaneously pursuing their eccentric interests in the living room—a wonderful comic moment. None of the odd varieties of food in the house will suit Mr. Kirby's nervous stomach, a drunken actress is sleeping it off upstairs, Mrs. Kirby reveals during a word-association game that her husband substitutes business for sex, G-men invade the house and haul everyone off to jail as all the fireworks in the basement explode.

Of course the last act solves all difficulties. Tony and Grandpa convince Mr. Kirby that making money is not the sole aim of life. With the elimination of the familial incompatibility that had made Alice vow never to see Tony again, the young lovers can happily marry. And because the family had buried a former lodger under the name Martin Vanderhof, Grandpa can persuade the government that he is dead and therefore owes no taxes. The play ends as all sit once more around the family table—with a former Russian Grand Duchess dishing up blintzes—and Grandpa thanks God for making everything work out all right.

An expert blend of humor, whimsy, and sentiment, *You Can't Take It With You* is Kaufman's best and most popular play, but it is also not very typical of the mainstream of his work. Except for the famous interview with the IRS in which Grandpa quizzes the agent about what would be done with his money should he decide to pay taxes, the play contains little social satire. And one has difficulty, despite Kaufman's long history of distaste for the business world, imagining him, as compulsive worker, endorsing the philosophy Grandpa states to Mr. Kirby: "Don't see anybody I don't want to, don't have six hours of things I *have* to do every day before I get *one* hour to do what I like in—and I haven't taken bicarbonate of soda in thirty-five years. What's the matter with that?" Although Grandpa is generally interpreted as a wise man whose apparent craziness is far saner than that of the world at large, it is no wonder that Kaufman described the whole household as "a slightly mad family" who do "some swell mad things."

Kaufman and Hart would return to the idea of a house overrun with slightly mad people in *The Man Who Came to Dinner* (1939) four plays later, but in that interval they turned to a series of episodic theatrical spectacles that depended more on staging or stars than on their own comic gifts. *I'd Rather Be Right* (1937) was a political satire with a musical score by Richard Rodgers and Lorenz Hart. The

revue was not about a fantasy politician as in the Kaufman/Ryskind musicals, but satirized, by name, Franklin D. Roosevelt, his cabinet members, and his quarrels with the Supreme Court justices (who pop out from behind bushes if the president even mentions making a new law), as well as such other topical institutions as the Federal Theatre Project. The framework for the satire is a dream—but the audience learns this only at the end of the play—in which a young couple meets FDR during a July Fourth celebration in Central Park and asks him to balance the federal budget so that the boy can get a raise that will enable them to marry. All the comically conceived schemes to do so fail, but the president inspires them with enough faith in the country to get married despite the prevailing economic uncertainty. The play owed most of its success not to this scenario, but to the spirited performance in the FDR role of George M. Cohan.

In 1938 Kaufman and Hart offered their most elaborate production, *The Fabulous Invalid*, a history of the American theatre. It begins with the opening of the Alexandria, a fictional theatre, and, after the premiere performance, the death of one and the suicide of the other of the husband and wife stars of the show. But they are permitted to stay on earth as ghosts as long as the theatre continues. This conceit allows Kaufman and Hart to stage a series of tableaux of scenes from famous plays of the century, utilizing elaborate sets and multimedia effects.

However, as the Alexandria deteriorates from showcase stage to movie theatre to seedy burlesque house, it appears that the ghosts may be doomed to leave earth. Then a young group of actors, modeled on Orson Welles's Mercury Players, buys the building and vows to restore its status as a legitimate theatre. As in *The Royal Family*, the dramatic tradition continues. Despite the ambitiousness of the production and its expression of both authors' deep love of the stage, it had the shortest run (65 performances) of any Kaufman/Hart play.

This failure did not deter them from trying another historical pageant in January 1939. *The American Way* is a cavalcade chronicling the rise to prominence and concomitant personal setbacks of immigrant German cabinetmaker Martin Gunther from the turn of the century through World War I to his death at the hands of Bundist thugs as he tries to convince his grandson to stick by American democratic ideals and not be seduced by Fascist propaganda from the homeland. A sentimental flag waver, this play had a cast of 250, striking sets and costumes, but a weak script. It fared better than the previous pageant only because the troubles in

Europe had made patriotism fashionable.

In October 1939, Kaufman and Hart finally returned to the type of drama they did best with *The Man Who Came to Dinner*. It is the story of the stuffy middle-class Mesalia, Ohio, household of the Stanleys, which is totally disrupted by the celebrated journalist and personality Sheridan Whiteside when he injures his leg on their front stoop after having accepted their dinner invitation during a lecture tour. Taking over the house and servants, terrorizing his nurse, dropping famous names with every breath, Whiteside is a caricature of Kaufman's good friend Alexander Woollcott. Two other friends, Noel Coward and Harpo Marx, appear under the names Beverly Carlton and Banjo. But the play is hilarious even to an audience that knows nothing of the characters' real life prototypes.

Since most of the comedy derives from Whiteside's egotistical manipulations and outrageous put-downs, like his famous entrance line "I may vomit," the plot is slight. It concerns the decision of his indispensable secretary Maggie Cutler to marry local newspaperman and aspiring dramatist Bert Jefferson and remain in Mesalia. Partly for selfish reasons and partly because he believes Maggie would regret such a marriage, Whiteside schemes to break up the lovers by bringing in nymphomaniac actress Lorraine Sheldon to vamp Jefferson. But when he realizes how deep Maggie's love for Bert is, he conspires with Banjo to remove Lorraine—in a

mummy case—just as quickly as he summoned her. His injury healed, he finally departs the Stanley residence, only to fall once again down the porch steps. He is carried in, threatening to sue them for $350,000, as Mr. Stanley throws up his hands in despair, Mrs. Stanley faints, and the curtain falls.

The Stanleys suffer a sort of reverse of Neil McRae's nightmare in *Beggar on Horseback*, as they are conventional people driven mad by artistic eccentrics. One cannot help but pity them, but they and their small-town friends are so rigid and dull that Whiteside retains audience sympathies despite his monstrous behavior, particularly when he helps the Stanley children June and Richard to achieve their ambitions over parental objections. *The Man Who Came to Dinner* presents the familiar Kaufman conflict between provincial bourgeois and New York-based artist, and there is little doubt as to his preference.

Kaufman and Hart's last play together, *George Washington Slept Here* (1940) is also a comedy, but more farcically slapstick than those that preceded it. It deals with the efforts of Newton and Annabelle Fuller to restore a ramshackle country house in Bucks County, Pennsylvania (where both Kaufman and Hart had country houses), in which the father of our country had supposedly spent the night. After many complications the house is left a shambles, and the poor Fullers learn that Benedict Arnold, not Washington, was the famous occupant. Although not as tedious as *Merrily We Roll Along* or *The American Way*, the play was decidedly inferior in conception and comic imagination to *Once in a Lifetime*, *You Can't Take It With You*, and *The Man Who Came to Dinner*.

During the 1940s the continuous success Kaufman had known since the opening of *Dulcy* began to lessen. He was no longer working with Hart, and his last two collaborations with Ferber in 1941 and 1948 were, as noted previously, not successful. While his adaptation of *The Late George Apley* with J. P. Marquand in 1944 was a hit, *Hollywood Pinafore* (1945), his updating of Gilbert's libretto for *HMS Pinafore* (retaining Sullivan's original score) to a movie studio setting flopped. The only other full-length play he wrote during the decade, *Park Avenue* (1946), a musical written with Nunnally Johnson and scored by Arthur Schwartz and Ira Gershwin, also had a brief run.

The decline in Kaufman's output during these years resulted partially from the personal upheaval of Beatrice Kaufman's sudden death in 1945. By 1949, however, he was married again, to thirty-five-year-old British actress Leueen McGrath. To-

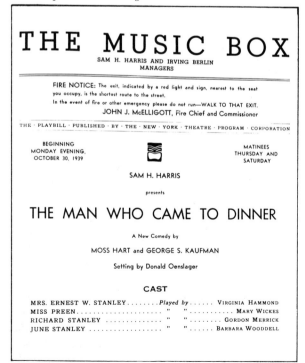

Playbill

gether they wrote several plays to feature her, but only two, *The Small Hours* (1951) and *Fancy Meeting You Again* (1952), were ever produced. They ran only twenty and eight performances respectively. Kaufman's marriage to McGrath ended in divorce in 1957, but the two remained close friends until his death.

Eventually success returned. From 1948 to 1952 Kaufman gained national prominence dispensing his pointed wit on the radio and television panel show *This is Show Business*. In 1950 he directed the long-running hit musical *Guys and Dolls* for which he received his only Tony Award, as best director. Then in 1953, with new collaborator Howard Teichmann, he wrote *The Solid Gold Cadillac*, a Cinderella-style fable about an elderly actress who thwarts the plans of four conniving executives to swindle the stockholders of a large corporation. Given a sinecure as stockholder relations officer, Laura Partridge charms all the small stockholders with her letters so that they send her enough proxies to fire the four wicked officers and take over the company, with the help of its former president who had ill-advisedly accepted a government post in Washington. The effect is rather that of Carlotta Vance in *Dinner at Eight* deciding to save Oliver Jordan's company from Dan Packard rather than selling him her shares. The satire of the business world goes back to *To the Ladies!* and *Dulcy*, although the businessmen here are truly vicious characters rather than mere pompous fools. *The Solid Gold Cadillac* ran for 526 performances, making it the third longest-running of Kaufman's plays. He followed this success in 1955 with his last script to be produced, the hit *Silk Stockings*, the musical version of the movie *Ninotchka*, which he adapted with McGrath and Abe Burrows. His career as a director, which began auspiciously with his staging of the Hecht / MacArthur smash, *The Front Page*, in 1928 and included, in addition to twenty-four of his own plays, such notable productions as *Of Mice and Men*, *My Sister Eileen*, as well as *Guys and Dolls*, also ended on a successful note with Peter Ustinov's *Romanoff and Juliet* in 1957.

Kaufman never gave up developing new projects—he was working with Connelly again just before he died—but his health, weakened by prostate trouble and a series of small strokes during the 1950s, permitted none of his projects to come to fruition in the four years before his quiet death on 2 June 1961 at the age of seventy-two.

Although Kaufman originated the aphorism "Satire is what closes on Saturday night," his primary strength as a dramatist was as a satirist of those follies most basic to American society, whether in the domestic, business, political, or entertainment spheres. Because he abhorred displays of emotion, and always let his collaborators write the love scenes, one can be fairly safe in crediting them also with providing the occasional feelings of tenderness or pathos the plays generate. To Kaufman goes praise for the laughs, for the crackling flow of wit. And very few of his more than forty plays to reach Broadway closed on their first Saturday night.

His satire had no profound reforming purpose. His targets were fools, not knaves. He wrote for the popular theatre, with an eye for the commercially viable, and few playwrights have had a better eye. He crafted his first hit in 1922 and his last in 1955, and although some have dated, it is still an even bet that if a classic comedy of the 1920s or 1930s is being revived, Kaufman's name will be on the playbill. The continuing revivals of his best plays in community and regional theatres and the appearance of three biographies in the 1970s indicates that interest in the man and his works is still strong. Although one cannot claim Kaufman as a great literary artist, he was one of the great men of the American theatre, and that theatre does not seem likely to forget him soon.

Screenplays:

Business Is Business [short] by Kaufman and Dorothy Parker, Paramount, 1925;

If Men Played Cards as Women Do [short], Paramount / Famous-Lasky, 1929; included in *Star-Spangled Rhythm*, Paramount, 1942;

Roman Scandals, by Kaufman, Robert E. Sherwood, George Oppenheimer, Arthur Sheekman, Nat Perrin, and W. A. McGuire, Goldwyn / United Artists, 1933;

A Night at the Opera, by Kaufman, Morrie Ryskind, and James Kevin McGuinness, Metro-Goldwyn-Mayer, 1935.

Other:

The Still Alarm, in *The Little Show* (New York: French, 1930);

Charles Goren, *Better Bridge for Better Players*, introduction by Kaufman (Garden City: Doubleday, 1942).

Periodical Publications:

"Notes on an Infamous Collaboration," *Theatre Magazine*, 50 (December 1929): 24;

"Jimmy the Well-Dressed Man: A Vaudeville Act with Music," *Nation*, 134 (15 June 1932): 676-677;

"All We Need is Horse Sense," *New Yorker*, 11 (25 May 1935): 36;

"Einstein in Hollywood," *Nation*, 147 (6 August 1938): 128-129;

"Seeing Things," *Saturday Review*, 28 (11 August 1945): 22-23;

"School for Waiters," *New Yorker*, 23 (2 August 1947): 48-51;

"The Great Kibitzer's Strike of 1926," *New Yorker*, 25 (12 November 1949): 37-38;

"Does Newark Have to Be Where It Is?" *New Yorker*, 29 (19 September 1953): 33;

"Musical Comedy—or Musical Serious?," *New York Times Magazine*, 3 November 1957, p. 24;

"Memoir," *New Yorker*, 36 (11 June 1960): 39.

References:

George Freedley, "George S. Kaufman, 1889-1961," *Modern Drama*, 6 (December 1963): 241-243;

Malcolm Goldstein, *George S. Kaufman: His Life, His Theater* (New York: Oxford University Press, 1979);

Moss Hart, *Act One* (New York: Random House, 1959);

Russell W. Lembke, "The Esthetic Values of Dissonance in the Plays of George S. Kaufman," Ph.D. Dissertation, Iowa State University, 1946;

Lembke, "The George S. Kaufman Plays as Social History," *Quarterly Journal of Speech*, 33 (October 1947): 341-347;

Scott Meredith, *George S. Kaufman and his Friends* (Garden City: Doubleday, 1974);

Howard Teichmann, *George S. Kaufman, an Intimate Portrait* (New York: Atheneum, 1972).

Papers:

George S. Kaufman's papers, including copies of unpublished and unproduced plays, are at the Wisconsin Center for Theatre Research, University of Wisconsin, Madison.

GEORGE KELLY
(16 January 1887-18 June 1974)

PRODUCTIONS: *One of Those Things*, 1913;

Finders-Keepers, 1916;

Mrs. Ritter Appears, 1917;

The Flattering Word, 1919;

Poor Aubrey, 1922;

The Weak Spot, 1922;

Mrs. Wellington's Surprise, 1922;

The Torchbearers, 29 August 1922, Forty-eighth Street Theatre, New York, 128 [performances];

Smarty's Party, 1923;

The Show-Off, 5 February 1924, Playhouse, New York, 571;

Craig's Wife, 12 October 1925, Morosco Theatre, New York, 360;

Daisy Mayme, 25 October 1926, Playhouse, New York, 113;

A La Carte, 1927;

Behold, the Bridegroom, 26 December 1927, Cort Theatre, New York, 88;

Maggie, the Magnificent, 21 October 1929, Cort Theatre, New York, 32;

Philip Goes Forth, 12 January 1931, Biltmore Theatre, New York, 98;

Reflected Glory, 21 September 1936, Morosco Theatre, New York, 127;

The Deep Mrs. Sykes, 19 March 1945, Booth Theatre, New York, 72;

The Fatal Weakness, 19 November 1946, Royale Theatre, New York, 119.

BOOKS: *Finders-Keepers* (Cincinnati: Kidd, 1923);

The Torchbearers (New York: American Library Service, 1923; London: French, 1924);

The Show-Off (Boston: Little, Brown, 1924; London: French, 1924);

The Flattering Word and Other One-Act Plays (Boston: Little, Brown, 1925; London: French, 1925);

Poor Aubrey (New York: French, 1925);

Craig's Wife (Boston: Little, Brown, 1926; London: French, 1926);

Daisy Mayme (Boston: Little, Brown, 1927; London: French, 1927);

Behold, the Bridegroom (Boston: Little, Brown, 1928; London: French, 1928);

Philip Goes Forth (New York, Los Angeles & London: French, 1931);

Reflected Glory (New York, Los Angeles & London: French, 1937);

The Deep Mrs. Sykes (New York & Los Angeles: French, 1946);

The Fatal Weakness (New York: French, 1947).

George Edward Kelly was born to John Henry and Mary Costello Kelly on 16 January 1887 in

Schuylkill Falls, Pennsylvania. He was the next to youngest of ten children in a prominent Philadelphia family. His brother John was an Olympic rowing champion, chairman of the Democratic City Commission of Philadelphia, state secretary of revenue, and father of Grace Kelly, later Princess Grace of Monaco. Another brother was Walter B. Kelly, renowned as vaudeville's "Virginia Judge." George was educated privately by his parents, though he was awarded an honorary A.F.D. by LaSalle College in 1962. At age twenty-five Kelly entered the world of the theatre as an actor in a national touring production of *The Virginian*. Subsequently, he toured with *Live Wires* (1913) and *The Common Law* (1914). The road to his career as a playwright was paved by his entrance into vaudeville as an actor in Paul Armstrong's *Woman Proposes* (1915), for he soon turned to writing his own material. After a year in the army, he created for himself the roles of Eugene Tesh in *The Flattering Word* (1919) and Eugene Aldrid in *Finders-Keepers* (1916), among others, and toured the country between 1918 and 1922 with his own sketches. Kelly's first full-length play, *The Torchbearers*, opened on Broadway in 1922. In all, ten Kelly plays were produced, and the first three of them—*The Torchbearers*, *The Show-Off* (1924), and *Craig's Wife* (1925)—gained widespread popularity. His next three plays—*Daisy Mayme* (1926), *Behold, the Bridegroom* (1927), and *Maggie, the Magnificent* (1929)—suffered decreasing public success. After one more play, the slightly better-received *Philip Goes Forth* (1931), Kelly left for Hollywood, claiming that the New York stage had "practically no appeal right now for the writer interested in a serious, analytical study of characters and situations." While enjoying the warmer weather, Kelly worked as a script consultant for MGM; the only film he contributed to in a substantial way, however, was *Old Hutch* (1935), starring Wallace Beery. Kelly had only three more plays produced after this, *Reflected Glory* (1936), *The Deep Mrs. Sykes* (1945), and *The Fatal Weakness* (1946), each of which had increased difficulty in meeting the tastes of Broadway. He stopped staging plays, but he did not stop writing them. There remain four plays which have never been published or staged: "Where the Heart Is," "When All Else Fails," "Can Two Walk Together," and "Rude Awakening." He wrote a television play about Perle Mesta for Shirley Booth in 1956. In 1957 he moved to a retirement community in Sun City, California, where he lived until shortly before his death on 18 June 1974 in Bryn Mawr, Pennsylvania.

George Kelly was a versatile man of the theatre. He knew the craft of acting and stagework thoroughly and always insisted on staging his own plays, paying particular attention to matters of pace and precision. His work has been highly acclaimed in many quarters. *Craig's Wife* won a Pulitzer Prize (1926); five of his works are included in Burns Mantle's *Best Plays* (*The Show-Off*; *Craig's Wife*; *Daisy Mayme*; *Behold, the Bridegroom*; and *The Fatal Weakness*); and he received numerous awards and prizes, including an Achievement and Creative Arts Award from Brandeis University (1959), the Philadelphia Creative Arts Theatre Award (1962), the Gold Medal from the Women's Theatre Club of New York City (1968), and the Drama Award of Distinction from the California Alpha chapter of Theta Alpha Phi (1968).

Various critics have undertaken to define the nature of the Kelly play because it is a distinctive type. Generally, it is circumscribed in structure and circumspect in theme. Kelly's plays are well made. The panoply of inconsequential stage actions exercises the eye, and the natural rhythm of the dialogue engages the ear. His stage is conventional; scene changes are few; the actions of the characters are unspectacular. Kelly relies upon the situations he creates to entertain the audience. However, Kelly had in mind serious entertainment. "I believe in the theatre of ideas," he said, and his ideas usually take the form of social satire centered around two subjects: career and family.

His first play, *The Torchbearers*, deals with a sweet but unthinking wife, Paula Ritter, who becomes stagestruck. Under the energetic and inept guidance of the small-town impresario Mrs. Pampinelli, Paula is awarded the lead in a catastrophic benefit performance; she receives the role partly for her superior "dramatic instinct" and partly because the original lead withdrew in mourning over her husband's sudden death. When Mr. Ritter sees his wife make a fool of herself on stage, he forbids her to make any more public performances. She agrees, and the play ends as a comedy. The satire in the play is based on the depiction of the little theatre movement (represented by Mrs. Pampinelli and her maladroit crew of thespians) as misguidedly idealistic and "enthusiastic" in the eighteenth-century sense of the word. The human frailty which Kelly represents is one's tendency to try to be something he is not. Paula is not a talented actress, but her vanity allows Mrs. Pampinelli to convince her that her ignorance of acting is much less a liability than her natural dramatic instinct is an asset. Although *The Torchbearers* has been criticized for its lack of plot, the characterization of Mrs. Pampinelli presents such a redeemingly lively portrait of the crusading little theatre enthusiast, carrying the torch of culture to the masses, that the play is, on the whole, a success.

The Torchbearers left followers of the legitimate theatre wondering who this new and entertaining playwright was; Kelly did not wait long to provide an answer. His comedy *The Show-Off*, which opened two years later, was a clear success. Heywood Broun called it "the best comedy which has yet been written by an American." It was recommended by the Pulitzer committee for the prize, but Hatcher Hughes's *Hell-Bent for Heaven* won it instead. So appealing was this play that at three separate times it was made into movies, the best of which starred Red Skelton. William Almon Wolff adapted it into novel form, too, though Kelly was not pleased with the results. *The Show-Off* succeeds in the same way *The Torchbearers* does, by its colorful and vital characterization. Kelly developed this "transcript of life in three acts" from his one-act *Poor Aubrey* (1922), which concerns the efforts of Aubrey Piper to impress Mrs. Cole, a friend of his wife, Amy. Aubrey is the core of both these plays and is more of a caricature than a character. He is the stereotypical windbag and braggart, so intent upon impressing others with his imaginary importance that he constantly distorts reality to suit the image of himself he wishes to create. He lies to increase his stature and then believes his own lies. In *Poor Aubrey*, Piper is married to Amy but living with her widowed mother, Mrs. Fisher, because he cannot support his extravagances. *The Show-Off* takes place some time before, when Aubrey is only courting Amy and Mr. Fisher is still alive. In *The Show-Off* Amy marries Aubrey; Mr. Fisher dies; Aubrey wrecks a car he borrows, running into a policeman in the process; and young Joe Fisher makes a scientific discovery which earns him a fortune. There is perhaps more to the plot in this than in any of Kelly's other plays, but still the plot is not the important part. Each bit of action is only an excuse for Aubrey to display his vain posturing, which is the source of the play's amusement. Yet the epigraph indicates that Kelly intended perhaps a more thoughtful response to the play: "That's where all the trouble starts—gettin' married." Kelly himself never married, although he had a long romance with Tallulah Bankhead, but the subject of marriage recurs frequently in his plays. It is ironic that Amy deserves even less sympathy than Aubrey. By accepting Aubrey as her husband, she inflicts a sizeable monetary loss upon her brother-in-law Frank Hyland, and

causes her mother much exasperation and irritation.

The Pulitzer-Prize-winning *Craig's Wife* is Kelly's most Strindbergian drama. Its portrait of Harriet Craig as a heartless, grasping materialist supplies the primary evidence for the misogyny charges against him; to be fair, though, Kelly did not consistently create unestimable female characters. In this same play, for example, both Irene Austen and Ethel Landreth are solid and good people.

Craig's Wife is as much a character drama as *The Torchbearers* or *The Show-Off*. Walter Craig discovers that his wife is obsessed with gaining complete control over the beautiful house and its elaborate furnishings. His aunt, Irene Austen, warns him, but he is not convinced until he becomes a suspect in a murder case and learns that Mrs. Craig has more regard for her reputation in the community than she does for him. When he learns his wife's true nature, he leaves her, and the play ends with Mrs. Craig alone in the empty house she has now succeeded in gaining control of. She is sobbing in realization of her life's failures. This is Kelly's most tragic play because Mrs. Craig is his most potentially destructive character. Other Kelly characters are self-delusive in ways which cause them pain and trouble, but Mrs. Craig sets out consciously to manipulate others. She has the excuse that she was mistreated in her childhood, but that is not sufficient absolution for the extent of her moral crimes. Once again, marriage is a key issue. Walter Craig gives his niece Ethel some advice about her prospective marriage to Smith College professor Eugene Fredericks, which could be the moral norm for this play and other Kelly plays as well: "The only thing I think you need to consider really seriously—is whether or not you are both absolutely honest with each other."

Kelly took the issue of control of a house, which had played such an important part in *Craig's Wife*, and fashioned another play around it, *Daisy Mayme*. The major creation here is Daisy Mayme Plunkett, a brassy, expansive, and winning personality who has taken up with seventeen-year-old May Phillips at Atlantic City, where Cliff Mettinger, May's uncle, has taken her to help ease the pain of her mother's death just one month ago. Daisy returns with May and Cliff to their large old home to find Laura Fenner, Cliff's sister, engaged in some very possessive housework there. Mrs. Fenner plans to persuade Cliff to take her and her husband to live with him there after May goes off to school. And she

George Kelly

has a plan for her daughter Ruth, too: perhaps Cliff can be persuaded to give Ruth one of those new houses he is building as a wedding present. Daisy opens Cliff's eyes to the way he is being manipulated, and at the end she and Cliff agree to enter into a very sensible marriage. Daisy is neither so maniacal as Harriet Craig nor so lighthearted as Aubrey Piper, but she is an entertaining figure and the center of the play. Although Kelly called it a comedy, he pursued in a systematic way the theme that people willing to sacrifice themselves for others are often coldly taken advantage of. The only real spot of high comedy comes with Mr. Chauncey Filoon, Cliff's ninety-year-old neighbor who, because of partial deafness and the advancing eccentricities of old age, is able to insult the determined and serious Mrs. Fenner with gleeful impunity.

The problem of marriage had been a consideration in each of Kelly's first four plays, and in *Behold, the Bridegroom* he finally approaches it directly. Tony Lyle, a very wealthy and very spoiled young woman, has wandered in and out of numerous love affairs, feeling no sense of responsibility or obligation in any of them. When she meets Spencer Train, who puts no value on her hollow charms of sophistication, she recognizes the irreversible direction her life has taken. In despair Miss Lyle

lapses into declining health, and the play ends on that note. *Behold, the Bridegroom* does not succeed as well as Kelly's other plays. One critic feels that it lacks the intensity of expression which blank verse could have given it and which its subject requires. More central to the problem, however, is the lack of variety in the plot. We get a close view of the tragic figure of Tony Lyle sustained through three complete acts. There is little relief for the audience, and the result is melodrama rather than tragedy.

The more serious Kelly tried to be, it seems, the less success he had, for his next play, *Maggie, the Magnificent*, lasted through only thirty-two performances. Margaret Reed's artistic sensitivity, which she seems to have inherited from her dead father, puts her in conflict with her coarse and aggressive mother. This incompatibility climaxes when mother slaps daughter in the face during an argument and is resolved when Margaret leaves home and goes to live with a wealthy family more suited to her temperament where, with the objectivity provided by some distance, she is finally able to accept her mother. One measure of this play's relative lack of success is the fact that it is the only one of Kelly's produced plays which has never been published.

Kelly's next two plays return to the subject of his first: the theatre. Philip Eldridge, the title character of *Philip Goes Forth*, goes forth from his hometown to New York City to make his way as a playwright over the objections of his father, who wants him to enter the family business. Philip takes a part-time job at the Ramona Novelty Company to support himself while he writes plays and eventually comes to realize that he is more interested in business than in the theatre. At the beginning of the play, Philip is self-deluded; he adopts an exaggerated pose of the sensitive artist who sees potential dramatic value all around him. The difference between him and Aubrey Piper is the level of self-awareness each takes into his pose. Philip pretends to be more sure of his artistic destiny than he really is, in reaction to his father's violent insistence that he enter business. Aubrey, on the other hand, is completely, complacently, and swaggeringly self-delusive, and that is the source of his comic stature.

Although *Reflected Glory* was Kelly's next play to appear on stage, it was written in 1929. It presents a situation that is so much the reverse of *Philip Goes Forth* that it might well have been titled "Muriel Stays Put." Muriel Flood is a famous and talented actress tempted to leave the stage for the more stable and secure life of husband and home. She rejects one suitor, Tom Howard, in a period of vacillation, but eventually accepts another, Leonard Wall. Her discovery that he is already married and has a history of affairs with actresses makes her realize that her real home is in the theatre. The subject of *The Torchbearers*, *Philip Goes Forth*, and *Reflected Glory* is not the theatre but personal honesty and self-knowledge. Housewifery, business, the theatre—all are appropriate occupations to those who are suited for them. Throughout Kelly's plays, he seems to have put a high value on the ability to see the role that one is meant to play and on the steadiness to play that role without being attracted and distracted by other parts.

Both of Kelly's last two plays explore the theme of a wife suspicious that her husband is having an affair. In *The Deep Mrs. Sykes*, Caroline Sykes will not be convinced of the truth of the fact that her son, not her husband, is infatuated with Irene Taylor, a concert pianist who has recently married a neighbor of the Sykeses. Mrs. Sykes's two main flaws—her jealous egotism and her self-delusion—are ruthlessly examined. She resents Mrs. Taylor because her piano playing commands people's attention, and she reinforces her ill feeling by convincing herself that her intuition is so strong as to be irrefutable when it tells her that Mrs. Taylor is receiving the affections of Mr. Sykes. In *The Fatal Weakness* Mrs. Espenshade receives an anonymous letter informing her that her husband is having an affair with Claudia Hilton, his osteopath. Like Mrs. Sykes, Mrs. Espenshade has a weakness, and hers is a delusive romanticism which interferes with the conduct of her real life. Even after Mrs. Espenshade has definite proof of her husband's behavior, she avoids discussing it with him because she is captivated by the romance of his love for Miss Hilton. As her delusion brings on the destruction of her marriage, her daughter's meretricious conception of a liberated marriage fades into a more sensible view, and she and her husband resolve their differences. Both *The Deep Mrs. Sykes* and *The Fatal Weakness* underscore Kelly's campaign against self-deception, and, as always, he is careful to point out the consequences: domestic chaos and destruction.

Throughout his career, George Kelly was a practical moralist. He was interested in some of man's basic weaknesses: vanity, egotism, excessive romanticism, greed. It is perhaps a shortcoming in his work that his objections to these qualities were too didactic. If he had investigated the source and nature of these human flaws, rather than the immediate problems that they cause domestic life, and if his sense of original sin had been mixed with a greater amount of wonder, then his plays might have more to offer that is universal and undying. Still, he is an able playwright, an insightful craftsman; and it may be unfair to quibble over the value of his message, which a later age may regard in a different light. When he stopped offering his plays for production, he did so because the theatre had changed. And he left this advice for future playwrights: "Avoid vulgarity. Do not say the thing they expect or want you to say. Don't go too far."

–*Jack Wright Rhodes*

Screenplay:
Old Hutch, MGM, 1935.

Other:
One of Those Things, in *One-Act Plays for Stage and Study*, Third Series, ed. Percival Wilde (New York: French, 1927).

References:
Carl Carmer, "George Kelly," *Theatre Arts Monthly*, 15 (April 1931): 322-330;

Barrett Clark, "George Kelly," in his *An Hour of American Drama* (Philadelphia: Lippincott, 1930), pp. 50-61;

Florence Crowder, "Up from Vaudeville to the Front Rank of American Dramatists," *Letters*, 5 (February 1932): 29-33;

Paul A. Doyle, "George Kelly: An Eclectic Bibliography," *Bulletin of Bibliography*, 24 (September-December 1963): 173-174, 177;

Irving Drutman, "Anybody Here Seen Kelly?," *New York Times*, 3 December 1967, II: 1, 5;

Lodwick Hartley and Arthur Ladu, "George Kelly," in *Patterns in Modern Drama* (New York: Prentice-Hall, 1948), pp. 248-251;

Foster Hirsch, *George Kelly* (Boston: Twayne, 1975);

Joseph Wood Krutch, "The Austerity of George Kelly," *Nation*, 137 (30 August 1933): 240-242;

Edward Maisel, "The Theatre of George Kelly," *Theatre Arts*, 31 (February 1947): 39-43;

Montrose J. Moses, "George Kelly," *Theatre Guild Magazine*, 7 (July 1930): 15-17;

John Van Druten, "Small Souls and Great Plays," *Theatre Arts Monthly*, 11 (July 1927): 493-498;

"Where Are They Now?," *Newsweek*, 75 (2 February 1970): 12;

Kenneth White, "George Kelly and Dramatic Device," *Hound and Horn*, 4 (April-June 1931): 384-400;

Arthur Wills, "The Kelly Play," *Modern Drama*, 6 (December 1963): 245-255.

Sidney Kingsley

Paul M. Bailey
University of Texas at Austin

BIRTH: New York, New York, 22 October 1906, to Robert and Sonia Smoleroff Kirshner.

EDUCATION: B.A., Cornell University, 1928.

MARRIAGE: 25 July 1939 to Madge Evans.

AWARDS: Pulitzer Prize and Theatre Club Award for *Men in White*, 1934; Theatre Club Award for *Dead End*, 1936; New York Drama Critics Circle Award, Federated Women's Club Award, Catholic Dial Award, Newspaper Guild Front Page Award, and Theatre Club Award for *The Patriots*, 1943; Edgar Allen Poe Award for *Detective Story*, 1949; Newspaper Guild Page One Citation, 1949; New York Drama Critics Circle Award and Donaldson Award for *Darkness at Noon*, 1951; Medal of Merit from the American Academy of Arts and Letters, 1951; Yeshiva University Award for Achievement in Theatre, 1965; D.Litt., Monmouth College, West Long Branch, New Jersey, and Ramapo College of New Jersey, 1978.

PRODUCTIONS: *Men in White*, 26 September 1933, Broadhurst Theatre, New York, 357 [performances];
Dead End, 28 October 1935, Belasco Theatre, New York, 684;
Ten Million Ghosts, 23 October 1936, St. James Theatre, New York, 11;
The World We Make, adapted from Millen Brand's *The Outward Room*, 20 November 1939, Guild Theatre, New York, 80;
The Patriots, 29 January 1943, National Theatre, New York, 172;
Detective Story, 23 March 1949, Hudson Theatre, New York, 581;
Darkness at Noon, adapted from Arthur Koestler's novel, 13 January 1951, Alvin Theatre, New York, 186;
Lunatics and Lovers, 13 December 1954, Broadhurst Theatre, New York, 336;

Night Life, 23 October 1962, Brooks Atkinson Theatre, New York, 63.

BOOKS: *Men in White* (New York: Covici Friede, 1933; London: Gollancz, 1934);
Dead End (New York: Random House, 1936);
The World We Make, adapted from Millen Brand's *The Outward Room* (New York: Dramatists Play Service, 1939);
The Patriots (New York: Random House, 1943);
Detective Story (New York: Random House, 1949);
Darkness at Noon, adapted from Arthur Koestler's novel (New York: Random House, 1951);
Lunatics and Lovers (New York: Random House, 1955);
Night Life (New York: Dramatists Play Service, 1964).

Many contemporary critics of the drama and theatre, if they consider Sidney Kingsley at all, tend to dismiss him with a brief mention of his work and an acknowledgment that his plays are either dated or insignificant. And indeed, his plays would seem behind the times to a modern audience. However, such a summary dismissal of Kingsley's dramatic contributions is perhaps unwise, for while he is certainly not a playwright of the caliber of Eugene O'Neill or Arthur Miller, he has nonetheless been an important asset to the social conscience of twentieth-century American theatre. Kingsley has devoted his playwriting career to the forceful illumination of serious, difficult social issues in American society.

Every age of the theatre has had its social critics, from Euripides in ancient Greece to socially aware playwrights of the present day. Kingsley belongs in that dramatic tradition. He made his first appearance as a professional playwright in the turbulent 1930s, when American theatre was struggling with new techniques and increasing social awareness. The thread of social activism runs through every one of Kingsley's plays, and some of his works propose positive solutions to difficult social issues. He is not afraid, for example, to address topics such as street crime in one instance and the nature of democracy in another. If Kingsley is prevented from consideration as a major dramatist, it is because his plays lack any transcendent quality which will make them appealing to audiences or readers of a later time. Though his plays were exciting when first performed, they have not aged well. His dramatic techniques seem frozen in the 1930s, and nowhere is this more pronounced than in his writing style. His characters are drawn in heavy, dark strokes until they become types rather than subtle living creations. Plots are consistently predictable. His plays, instead of being rich in dramatic texture, tend to be single-leveled melodramas written in the sharp, unpoetic style of realism which emerged in the 1930s.

Nevertheless, despite the apparent transience of his work, Kingsley shows himself to be a skilled, if sometimes obvious, dramatic craftsman. Precisely because his characters are types, they are readily identifiable, and a reader or audience member, quickly discerning where sympathies should lie, can achieve an immediate and somewhat uncritical involvement in the play. The plots themselves, regardless of superimposed romantic subplots or obvious turns in the action, remain strangely compelling. Kingsley's ability to tell a story sometimes overcomes the deficiencies of subject or style.

Kingsley's dramatic reputation rests on a total of only nine professionally produced plays spanning a period of twenty-nine years, from 1933 to 1962. He surprised Broadway in 1933 with his first play, *Men in White*, and followed it two years later with another success, *Dead End*. His next two plays, *Ten Million Ghosts* (1936) and *The World We Make* (1939), suffered from serious conceptual and stylistic flaws and were considered regressions in Kingsley's art as playwright. With the 1940s and the early 1950s, he was once again successful with *The Patriots* (1943), *Detective Story* (1949), and *Darkness at Noon* (1951), only to be very disappointing in his last two works, *Lunatics and Lovers* (1954) and *Night Life* (1962), which were generally regarded as poorly written or simply insignificant.

Kingsley was born Sidney Kirshner, in New York City on 22 October 1906. After public school on the Lower West Side, he attended Townsend Harris Hall high school, graduating in 1924. While at high school, he began writing one-act plays, directing, and acting. He won a scholarship to Cornell University and went on to earn his B.A. in 1928. Studying under A.M. Drummond at Cornell, he

continued to write short plays and direct them. In 1928 he won an award for the best one-act play written by a student for a work entitled "Wonder-Dark Epilogue." After his graduation from Cornell, Kingsley worked for a time as an actor with the Tremont Stock Company in the Bronx. He played a small role in a play called *Subway Express* by Eva Kay Flint and Martha Madison (produced in 1929). It was then, according to an essay in *Current Biography*, that Kingsley "apparently decided that he would never be a Barrymore." From there, his life takes on a story-book quality. He moved to California in 1929 and worked as a play reader. Then he became a scenario reader for Columbia Pictures. But he was also struggling with a play of his own. This play, which took three months to write and some three years to polish, was about doctors and their work, and he called it "Crisis." It was repeatedly optioned but a production failed to materialize until Sidney Harmon, James Ullman, and the now legendary Group Theatre joined forces to present it. The play, directed by Lee Strasberg, opened at the Broadhurst Theatre in New York on 26 September 1933 bearing the new title, *Men in White*.

Men in White is a tribute to the medical profession and the doctors who sacrifice personal happiness in order to devote themselves to the betterment of medical care. Kingsley in fact dedicated his work to "the men in medicine who dedicate themselves, with quiet heroism, to man." The play centers on the fortunes of a young intern named George Ferguson. He is bright, talented, dedicated to his work, and he plans to study with Dr. Hochberg, the respected chief of surgical staff at a large hospital. George is also engaged to marry Laura Hudson, whose wealthy father is a sometime patient of Hochberg's. In a succession of scenes, George saves a patient by justifiably alienating an older (but incompetent) doctor; loses another patient; and has a serious argument with Laura, who becomes upset because his work is taking so much time and suggests that their engagement is perhaps not a very good idea. A lonely young nurse named Barbara Dennin, who harbors an admiration for George, discovers him in his room at the hospital, tired, discouraged, and depressed about Laura. He is called away momentarily, but she takes off her nurse's cap with the clear implication that she plans to stay. Months pass, and Dr. Hochberg, noting that Laura's wedding plans distract George from his work, becomes determined to impress upon Laura the importance of George's career. He invites her to observe an operation that George is about to perform. The patient is the former nurse Barbara

Dennin, who is suffering from an infection caused by a sloppy back-room abortion. Before being wheeled into surgery, Barbara tells George that she always loved him. Laura, standing nearby, hears and realizes that it was George's baby that was aborted. George resolves to marry Barbara despite Hochberg's insistence that such a step would ruin his promising career, but Barbara unexpectedly dies. George is distraught that, even with all his knowledge, he was unable to save her. Hochberg assures him that medical progress can be made in preventing such deaths, but that it takes the dedication of young men like George. As Hochberg says, "It's not easy for any of us. But in the end, our reward is something richer than simply living. Maybe it's a kind of success that world out there can't measure . . . maybe it's a kind of glory, George. . . . Yes, question as much as we will—when the test comes we know—don't we, George?" Laura, who has been understandably upset by George's infidelity, affirms her love for him by deciding to stay with him, but George ends the engagement and dedicates himself completely to medicine.

The thematic implication in this play is clear: to be a fruitful member of the medical profession requires absolute dedication, regardless of the personal cost. The characters of the play, drawn in bold and clear strokes, illuminate this theme. George and Hochberg are essentially sympathetic characters. Hochberg is portrayed as the paternal figure in the hospital, full of wisdom and patience, the stabilizing guide for the young doctors. George is more complex. He is a potentially valuable member of the medical community, but when he becomes involved in other allegiances chaos sets in as shown through the plight and death of Barbara Dennin. However, when George devotes himself entirely to medicine at the end of the play, it seems that all the death and destruction he has initiated are redeemed by this one affirmative decision. The full consequences of his indecision are not explored. He nevertheless remains a sympathetic character by virtue of his eventual dedication to medicine.

Kingsley also portrays characters antithetical to Hochberg and George. Dr. Cunningham is Hochberg's opposite; where Hochberg is patient, wise, and dedicated, Cunningham is rich, abrasive, and ultimately a quack who cares more for the impression he leaves on a patient than for actual medical care. He has influence, a lavish office, and wealthy patients, but it is he that George contradicts in a case involving the medication to be given to a little girl. George overrules Cunningham and saves the patient's life. It is doctors like Cunningham, Kingsley implies, that give medicine a bad name. George's counterpart is Levine, who was once a young doctor with the same opportunities for advancement as George. But Levine abandons his opportunities for the love of a woman. He marries her, and when she falls seriously ill he returns to the hospital for help. He appears as a poor, unhappy, beaten man; indeed, he is scarcely recognized by his former mentor Hochberg. Levine is intended to be a portrait of George in the future should he abandon his dedication to medicine.

Men in White betrays some of the stylistic pecularities which surface repeatedly in later works. The characters are one-dimensional and starkly drawn. The play is written in short, choppy, unpoetic lines which deprive characters of subtle feeling or reflection. But, although the work is dated, it is imbued with a sense of optimism in the future and in progress, and as a reflection of attitudes in the 1930s it remains historically significant.

The critical response to the production of *Men in White* was generally favorable. John Mason Brown was virtually alone in his conclusion that the script was "piffling" and "mildewed in its hokum," although many modern critics might agree. The majority of critics in 1933 sided with Joseph Wood Krutch in his review in the *Nation*: "Where other plays of this sort were shrill or hysterical, 'Men in White' is eloquent with the eloquence of calm understatement." The play was popular, running 357 performances on Broadway and sustaining a substantial run in London as well. It garnered a host of awards, including the Theatre Club Award and a Pulitzer Prize, and in 1934 was adapted into a film by Metro-Goldwyn-Mayer starring Clark Gable as George Ferguson.

In 1935, after a trip to Europe, Kingsley brought his second play, *Dead End*, to Broadway. It retains perhaps the greatest historical significance for its substance and style of production. It also proved to be Kingsley's longest-running play. *Dead End* was cast and staged by Kingsley and produced and designed by the visionary designer Norman Bel Geddes. The play opened (appropriately enough) at the Belasco Theatre on 28 October 1935, and the curtain rose to gasps from the audience, for Bel Geddes had designed a setting as stunning as any created by Belasco himself. On one side of the stage was a slum tenement; on the other, a new apartment building for the wealthy; in the middle, a street which dead-ends at New York's East River. For the river, Bel Geddes flooded the orchestra pit, and throughout the play the slum children dived, swam, and splashed. This was one of the most realistic settings ever to grace a stage in America, and it was in this spectacular environment that the story of how crime is bred in a poor society unfolded.

The play traces essentially two distinct plots which occasionally overlap and finally converge into one. The first plot concerns Tommy, a boy from the slums, and several of his young friends. They begin the play by shouting, cursing, stripping down and swimming in the river, and assaulting another boy. In the nearby new apartment building live a man named Griswald and his young son Philip. Tommy steals Philip's watch and Griswald tries to retrieve it by locking Tommy in a stranglehold. Tommy produces a knife and slashes Griswald, who is not seriously hurt but very angry. Tommy flees and hides.

The second plot concerns a young architect named Gimpty. Slightly crippled in one leg and presently out of work, he spends his time down at the wharf looking after the boys, whose problems he understands, having grown up there himself. He loves a girl named Kay, and though she loves him, the need for security makes her leave him for a rich man. Gimpty also strikes up a friendship with Tommy's older sister Drina, which later evolves into a romance. One day a childhood friend of Gimpty's returns to the waterfront—only now he is Baby Face Martin, a notorious, callous killer. Gimpty informs the FBI of Martin's whereabouts, and in an explosive scene they gun him down. Gimpty receives a substantial reward for his efforts. The two plots converge at this juncture when Tommy returns and, at Drina's insistence, gives himself up to the police. Griswald is anxious to press charges and have Tommy sent to reform school, but Gimpty pleads Tommy's case stating that the reform school will only make him a hardened criminal like Martin. Griswald does not relent. As Tommy is taken away, Gimpty vows to Drina that he will spend his reward money on the best lawyer available to help Tommy, and they leave together.

With *Dead End* Kingsley is attempting to illustrate how a society which allows extreme wealth and extreme poverty to coexist will breed crime. The implied solution is for society to understand and eliminate poverty. Kingsley articulates this theme by creating antithetical characters such as Gimpty and Martin, Tommy and Philip. Like Dr. Hochberg, Gimpty is a paternal figure, rather inconspicuously supervising the boys of the slum. He has a good heart but becomes bitter when, due to his slum background and present poverty, he is deprived of a good job and his girl. Martin, on the other hand, is cynical and cruel, and serves as a warning to other slum dwellers as well as society. In

one of the more telling scenes of the play, even Martin's mother refuses to have anything to do with him. Martin is what Gimpty would have become had he gone into a life of crime, and it is flatly stated that Tommy will become like Martin if he is sent to reform school. Tommy, as contrasted to the rich and pampered Philip, is the victim of social and economic inequities. Although he is a thief and injures Griswald, he remains sympathetic because he is only a boy struggling against powerful forces. As Kingsley points out, with proper guidance Tommy could become a useful citizen.

Dead End suffers from the same strengths and weaknesses as *Men in White*. It is immediately clear which characters are intended to be sympathetic and which are not. The plot is predictable. The story is weakened substantially by romantic subplots which seem imposed on the central action. The depiction of Gimpty's broken romance with Kay is perhaps justifiable, for it illustrates the extent to which Gimpty is deprived of all his hopes by economic circumstances. However, his awkward relationship with Drina seems to serve little dramatic purpose. If there are signs that Kingsley matured as a dramatist in *Dead End*, they can be found in the dialogue. The way society has shaped the young boys is shown by their tough, crude language and habits, although the stereotyped characters and the use of slang may make the play seem dated to today's audiences. Nevertheless, Kingsley's social concerns give the play significance. The effectiveness of *Dead End* led to one of the few examples in theatre history of a play moving its audiences to effective action outside the theatre. In New York, some sixty clergymen requested copies of the script for use in sermons, and the Boys' Club recorded an increase in donations, mostly from people who had seen the play. One senator declared that the play had been instrumental in pushing forward slum clearance legislation.

The opening press for the play was generally favorable. Percy Hammond of the *New York Herald-Tribune* praised the play as "a substantial thriller, full of violence and romance, and with an aim to give you food for thought." Burns Mantle likened it to a newsreel of the cradle of public enemies. Some critics, however, wondered whether the impact of the play came not from the play itself but from the acting and the staging. John Anderson of the *New York Evening Journal* commented, apropos of the setting, "You can lead a play to water, but you can't make it think." And Joseph Wood Krutch decided that the play made for exciting theatre but was not necessarily good drama: "The real reason is that, without being false, it lacks either that originality of incident or that freshness of feeling at least one or the other of which is necessary to make a play great." He concluded, therefore, that *Dead End* was "very high-grade hokum." If the work was indeed hokum, audiences were very fond of it. It ran on Broadway for 684 performances. Lillian Hellman adapted the play for the 1937 United Artists movie *Dead End*, in which Humphrey Bogart starred as Baby Face Martin, and the "Dead End Kids" became a part of film history and the American language.

A year after the premiere of *Dead End*, Kingsley wrote, directed, and produced *Ten Million Ghosts* on Broadway, and it qualifies as his greatest critical and popular disaster. It is the story of how greedy munitions manufacturers were able to extend World War I for profit. The central character, a young Frenchman named Andre, loves Madeleine, who is the daughter of one of the largest munitions manufacturers in France. Also seeking Madeleine's hand is Zacharey, a munitions salesman. When the war erupts Andre becomes an aviator and discovers that, in a seeming conspiracy to prolong the war, Germany and France are ignoring each other's iron mines, allowing the continued mining of the material necessary for the manufacture of war goods. Determined to expose the conspiracy, Andre sets off on his own private bombing mission; he fails to destroy the mines and is killed. Zacharey weds Madeleine under the shadow of an implication that another war looms on the horizon.

This portrait of greed and profiteering was given a lavish and expensive production in 1936 which most critics felt the script could not justify. Edward Reed bluntly stated that he felt the play presented "banality of situation, wooden dialogue, preachment rather than persuasion. . . ." Burns Mantle felt that the failure of the play was due not so much to the script or the production as it was the politics of the work. The play, he suggested, "veered so sharply to the left in argument as to limit its appeal." Whether it was bad drama or merely bad protest, the play closed quickly with a run of only eleven performances.

Kingsley's next Broadway offering, *The World We Make* (1939), fared a little better than *Ten Million Ghosts*, but it was nonetheless regarded as a failure. Based on the novel *The Outward Room* by Millen Brand, the play tells the story of a young girl who escapes from a mental asylum to the slums, wanders into a laundry, falls in love with a man, and ultimately finds relief from her severe emotional problems in the daily routine of the laundry. After

she realizes that others need her as much as she needs them, she makes her own world of sanity.

The production received a mixed critical response. Most reviewers felt the spectacular laundry-room set was an appropriate environment for the play and the unusually fine performances were highly praised. Brooks Atkinson liked the play because Kingsley had "not lost the compassion of a fine study of character fulfillment." Joseph Wood Krutch objected to the slum dwellers in the play: he felt they were just too nice. And Stark Young felt that the script's mixture of fairy tale, psychiatry, reality, and fantasy lacked unity: "There are many agreeable moments . . . but taken seriously, the play struggles with too many planes to be successful." *The World We Make* was not popular; it closed after eighty performances.

The 1930s saw the production of four of Kingsley's plays; half were considered successes, half failures, and critics were seriously questioning Kingsley's abilities. But the decade also gave Kingsley one of his greatest personal successes: his marriage to actress Madge Evans. She was appearing at the Ogunquit Playhouse in Maine when, on 25 July 1939, Kingsley whisked her away to a justice of the peace after a performance . She had reportedly not even changed out of the dress that was her last-act costume. It is appropriate that, with such a theatrical marriage, both would continue to work in the theatre and enhance one another's talents.

Kingsley spent forty-six weeks writing his next play, his first offering of the 1940s, *The Patriots*, which focuses on Thomas Jefferson, Alexander Hamilton, and the nature of democracy. The first draft was finished in March 1941, reputedly the day before Kingsley was inducted into the army. (He was discharged in 1943.) Stationed near New York and encouraged to refine the play, he found odd times among his army duties to polish and rewrite the script. Once he thought he had found a place above a barracks where he could work in quiet, only to discover to his dismay that it was actually a firing range. Nevertheless, he was able to complete the play and even attend some rehearsals. *The Patriots* opened at the National Theatre on 29 January 1943, with Madge Evans in the role of Jefferson's daughter Patsy.

The play is a defense of a democracy "of the people" and a warning against those who would vest excessive governing power in a privileged few. At the time of its production, it was also an appeal for unity in the face of World War II. By setting the play in the late eighteenth century and examining the conflict between Thomas Jefferson and Alexander

Hamilton, who disagreed over the way America should be governed, Kingsley was able to present political views pertinent to the 1940s. Having just returned from his position as American ambassador to France, Jefferson presents himself to President Washington, who offers him the post of secretary of state. Jefferson, wishing to return to the quiet of his Virginia home, refuses, but Washington is able to convince him that the country needs his leadership. Jefferson's belief in a democracy of the people puts him into conflict with Hamilton, who is trying to create a moneyed aristocracy through his policies as secretary of the treasury. As their differences increase, the French Revolution imposes itself upon American politics. The people accuse Hamilton of being a monarchist; Hamilton and his followers accuse Jefferson of trying to bring the French Revolution to America through his democratic principles. Jefferson is soon longing once again for the quiet of his estate saying to his daughter Patsy: "Do you know, dear, my only pleasure? For an hour or so every evening I sit and dream of Monticello." He decides to resign, but Washington, sensing the unrest among the people, refuses the resignation and calls upon Jefferson and Hamilton to work together. The final act shifts to the presidential election of 1801. Washington is dead; the electoral system is in shambles; and Congress has been trying to decide for hours who will be president. Once again, Hamilton and Jefferson face each other, Hamilton calling the people a "great beast" and Jefferson rejoining: "You have never properly estimated the character of the American people." Neither will compromise his political beliefs. However, when Jefferson offers to break the deadlock by supporting Aaron Burr for president, Hamilton proves himself to be a patriot. Realizing that Burr is unfit for office, he swings his support to Jefferson, setting aside his personal ambitions for the benefit of the country. The play ends with Jefferson making his inaugural address as president of the United States.

The form of historical drama accentuates the weaknesses in Kingsley's method of characterization. He is clearly sympathetic to Jefferson's idea of what a democracy should be and wishes to portray the statesman as the protagonist of the play, but nowhere is the one-dimensional quality of Kingsley's characters more apparent than in his rendition of a heroic Jefferson and a morally bankrupt Hamilton. Jefferson is a man who only wants to live in peace at Monticello, mourn his deceased wife, and enjoy his grandchildren, but he sacrifices his personal happiness for the betterment of man. He

excoriates political parties. By contrast Hamilton is painted in lurid colors. He is not above personal vendettas for political ends; he is blackmailed for an extramarital affair; and he accuses Jefferson of all manner of political underhandedness. Kingsley is able to support his theme, but at the cost of rich character portrayal and historical accuracy. Indeed, some critics charged that he had virtually rewritten history, or at best distorted it, with uneven and biased portraits of Jefferson and Hamilton. However, despite its shallow characterizations, the play illuminates its emotional theme with some objectivity. *The Patriots* appeared during World War II while America was embroiled in a political crisis not unlike that in the play. The historical format gave Kingsley license to support his democratic ideals and call for unity with reasoned (if not calm) detachment. All the decisions within the play seem more crucial because of the historical perspective, and Kingsley is thereby able to intensify the atmosphere of a crisis. Perhaps the greatest advantage of Kingsley's historical subject matter is its timelessness. In *The Patriots* Kingsley dramatizes the universal theme of how best to govern using characters removed from his own time. As a result the play, while not Kingsley's most significant work, may well be his most enduring. It comes nearer to trans-

Sidney Kingsley

cending the stylistic influence of the 1930s than any of Kingsley's other dramatic offerings.

The Patriots received a warm popular and critical response. Some observers complained that Kingsley had tampered with history and others felt the parallels of historical crises were overstated, but most critics found the work successful drama, if inaccurate history. A few noted the stylistic ripples created by Kingsley's lifting speeches directly from history. Stark Young's assessment best reflects the wide critical consensus toward the play: "It puts us, for a change, in good company, on a fine plane. It is thoughtful, full of warm feeling, and its general content is rich, honest, and noble as regards its application to our day." Audiences agreed; the play ran 172 performances. Kingsley's peers awarded it a host of honors, including the Drama Critics Circle Award, the Theatre Club Award, and the Newspaper Guild Front Page Award.

Kingsley's only other dramatic contribution of the 1940s was *Detective Story*, which opened at the Hudson Theatre on 23 March 1949, its author once again in the director's chair. The play, which is a plea for justice tempered with mercy, concerns the consequences of intolerance, and it was particularly lauded at the time of production for its strikingly authentic recreation of a New York police precinct station.

The plot centers on a tough cop named McLeod and his treatment of two criminals who have been brought into the detective squad room. The first offender is a young man named Arthur. A former war hero with no previous criminal record, he is brought in for stealing a small sum of money from his boss. Driven to the crime by what he thought was a desperate love for a beautiful woman named Joy, he soon discovers it is her sister Susan for whom he feels genuine affection. Susan stays with him at the police station and offers to pay back the stolen money if only Arthur's boss will drop the charges against him. The boss agrees, but McLeod will not hear of it and insists on throwing the full force of the law against the young man. Refusing to consider either Arthur's proven good character or the circumstances of his crime, McLeod continues to view him as a criminal like all the others he has arrested. The second case involves a sleazy abortionist named Schneider who practices his illegal trade with the full knowledge that some of his young patients have died as a result of his carelessness. Angered by yet another death, McLeod loses his temper and strikes Schneider several times, sending him to the hospital. But it is learned that McLeod's wife, Mary, had also required Schneider's

services years before she met her husband. Mary attempts to explain the circumstances of her transgression by saying that she was young, new to the city and made a mistake, but McLeod will not listen: "Everything I hate . . . even murder. . . . What the hell's left to understand?" He pronounces their marriage finished and ignores all advice to change his decision. Finally, following an intense confrontation between McLeod and Mary, a thief who had been arrested earlier seizes a gun from one of the policemen. McLeod is shot trying to retrieve it. Dying, he realizes that his inability to allow for human failure has cost him the thing he valued most: his marriage. Acting upon a newfound sense of compassion he relents in the matter of Arthur, allows the charges to be dropped, and dies a more understanding, if broken, man.

Kingsley stated in an interview that his purpose in *Detective Story* was to demonstrate the inherent dangers to a society which does not carefully control its police force. McLeod, the character Kingsley created to illustrate his point, is the epitome of intolerance and refuses to moderate his behavior. He is not controlled by either the public or his superiors. Though the police lieutenant cautions McLeod not to lay hands on Schneider because of the criminal's threats of legal retaliation, he beats him nonetheless. Susan, representative of the citizenry, is unable to persuade McLeod to drop the case. Indeed, McLeod's own happiness is ultimately destroyed by his compulsion to prosecute all crimes fully, regardless of the circumstances in which the crime was committed. Kingsley cautions that a police state would lack mercy and human understanding, the qualities which prevent justice from becoming tyranny.

It may be that *Detective Story* is an allegory of a police state, but it is dramatically compelling on an emotional level due to the intricate evolution of McLeod's character. Clearly McLeod's harsh attitude toward Schneider is justified, but he seems unable to comprehend that not all offenders are vicious. Only when his wife has left him and he is lying on the floor dying from a gunshot wound does he realize that he is a human being without human feeling. In his last moments he comes to understand the value of forgiveness and he is able to perform one act of charity by setting Arthur free. The structural pattern is familiar: the central character is undone by a mistake or flaw but recognizes the causes of his undoing before the final catastrophe. It is this pattern which moved John Gassner to write: "With this play, Kingsley came close to turning adult melodrama into naturalistic tragedy."

The play remains a melodrama primarily because of Kingsley's familiar single-dimension characterizations, which are inconsistent with tragedy. McLeod retains the form of a tragic hero but lacks the depth. The other characters embody types rather than appearing as real people: Arthur is pathetic; Mary is a victim; Susan is innocent and understanding; the newspaperman Joe is softhearted; and Schneider is slimy and cowardly. The developing romance between Arthur and Susan provides a contrast to the troubles between McLeod and his wife, but it does little to propel the overall action of the play. Nevertheless *Detective Story*'s comment on the nature of a police state and its plea for humanitarian ideals endow it with significance it might otherwise lack.

Most reviewers were pleased with the production, noting particularly the fine performances and the effective atmosphere of the detective squad room. But, as Brooks Atkinson rightly observed, "It takes thirty-four characters and a hopper full of colorful minor incidents to prove the main point. The machinery of 'Detective Story' is unwieldy in comparison with the size of the product." Nevertheless, even those who found weakness in the script affirmed Kingsley's ability as a dramatic craftsman to create exciting theatre. Joseph Wood Krutch felt that *Detective Story* was "to my mind quite the best melodrama of the year and none the worse for having a moral." The production ran for 581 performances, and in 1951 Paramount adapted the play into a film.

Kingsley's next play, *Darkness at Noon*, has generally been considered his last significant effort. Based on a novel by Arthur Koestler, the play examines the fate of an aging revolutionary in Stalinist Russia and is thematically an echo of *Detective Story*.

Set in March of 1937, the story involves a former revolutionary, Rubashov, who has been arrested during a purge and placed in a prison for political offenders. The commandant of the camp, an old revolutionary comrade named Ivanoff, informs him that he has been charged with involvement in a conspiracy to kill the leader of the revolution. False evidence is presented, and Rubashov is asked to confess to a crime he did not commit. Ivanoff and his young assistant Gletkin differ over the best way to expedite the confession. Gletkin wants to force it out of Rubashov with physical torture, but Ivanoff wants Rubashov kept comfortable and given time to reflect, for he realizes that his prisoner will confess as an act of party loyalty. Weeks pass, and Rubashov, reflecting through flashbacks on his years of service to the party, does indeed decide to confess to his old friend Ivanoff. But on being brought to the commandant's office, Rubashov discovers that Ivanoff has himself been purged and Gletkin is now in command. Perceiving Gletkin to be a callous brute, Rubashov resists confessing, and Gletkin employs harsher methods, beating the old man and keeping him awake under a bright light enduring lengthy interrogation. After days of questioning Gletkin discovers Rubashov's weakness: a woman he once loved named Luba. On Gletkin's order, she is killed. When informed of the deed, Rubashov once again relents and agrees to a confession, his spirit broken. In his cell awaiting execution, Rubashov begins to realize that creatures such as Gletkin are the natural result of the early revolutionary ruthlessness he and his comrades had practiced. Human feeling and human understanding have been sacrificed to the success of the revolution. He says to himself, "My hundred and eighty million fellow prisoners, what have I done to you? What have I created? If History is all calculation, Rubashov, give me the sum of a hundred and eighty million nightmares. Quickly calculate me the pressure of a hundred and eighty million cravings. Where in your mathematics, Rubashov, is the human soul? At the very beginning you forgot what you were searching for?" His confession completed, Rubashov is led to his execution.

Like *Detective Story*, *Darkness at Noon* is the story of a human being who has lost all human feeling or compassion. Both Rubashov and McLeod are undone by their mistake, and both recognize their error before death. Like McLeod, Rubashov helped create a police state through inflexibility and cruelty. However, the consequences of inhumanity are greater in *Darkness at Noon*, for the play involves not a detective squad room but an entire people under the yoke of tyranny created by a revolution gone sour.

Kingsley's thematic vehicle is, of course, Rubashov. From his tender romance with Luba it becomes clear that he is not a cruel individual. However, the success of the revolution dictated costly decisions and gradually Rubashov hardened his heart to human suffering. In one scene Rubashov says to Luba as they listen to Beethoven: "This music is dangerous. When you listen to this and realize that human beings can create such beauty, you want to pat them on the head. That's bad. They'll only bite your hand off." Rubashov is seen through flashbacks making extraordinary decisions for the benefit of the party at the expense of human happiness: in one instance he prevents a justified strike among Italian workers; in another he betrays a fellow comrade to the Nazis. Yet it is not until his impending death that Rubashov perceives the truth; his cruelty has begotten cruelty. He tries to convey this truth to Gletkin as he is being led away to execution. You cannot, he says, build a paradise out of concrete, and he calls Gletkin "my son." Gletkin replies perfunctorily that he is not Rubashov's son, to which the old man replies: "Yes, you are. That's the horror."

In *Darkness at Noon*, Rubashov is the only character developed with any depth; the others are one-dimensional: Gletkin is violent, crude, vicious; Luba is sweet and long-suffering; and Ivanoff seems to lack character altogether. Rubashov's catharsis at the end of the play is considerably weakened because Kingsley fails to show the emotional and psychological forces acting upon him. Technically, the play contains a stylistic difficulty which complicates the achievement of crisp pacing: in the prison scenes the various inmates communicate with one another by tapping on the walls of their cells, repeating their lines out loud as they tap them. This interesting technique has the tendency to slow the progress of the play but, despite its stylistic weaknesses, the play is important because of Kingsley's social concerns.

Critical responses to *Darkness at Noon* varied widely, the greatest controversy centering on whether Kingsley did justice to Koestler's book. The novel is a psychological portrait of all three principal characters: Rubashov, Ivanoff, and Gletkin; the play develops only Rubashov. Brooks Atkinson felt the play was a disappointment compared with the novel: "somewhere between the novel and the theatre the intellectual distinction has gone out of the work. For Mr. Kingsley is less a writer than a showman in this theatre piece, and his melodrama comes with elements of the glib propaganda play that we find so distasteful when it is on the other side." John Gassner reflected that even Rubashov was not sufficiently developed as a character: "Kingsley's character was too greatly worn down by gnawing reminiscences to be anything but an essentially passive victim. He flickered out instead of undergoing a tragic explosion and illumination." But by contrast, Wolcott Gibbs wrote: "I think Mr. Kingsley has done an admirable job of conveying the spirit of Koestler's book." Most critics praised *Darkness at Noon* for the atmosphere but found it a flawed melodrama. Harold Clurman had the harshest criticism for the play. Noting Kingsley's talent for atmosphere, color, and preachment, he went on: "He has, however, no psychological in-

sight, no poetic eloquence, no capacity to convey the quality of any inner state." The play therefore became for Clurman "a *Reader's Digest* melodrama, intricate without suspense, psychological without characters, philosophical without mind, violent without effect." Winner of the New York Drama Critics Circle Award, *Darkness at Noon* sustained a run of 186 performances.

Kingsley's final two Broadway offerings, *Lunatics and Lovers* and *Night Life*, have usually been regarded as negligible contributions to the theatre, not representative of Kingsley's ability, although many of his familiar dramatic techniques appear in both works. *Lunatics and Lovers*, which opened at the Broadhurst Theatre on 13 December 1954, was a critical failure but a commercial success, running 336 performances. Kingsley's first venture into the realm of farce, the play involves two con artists who are trying to influence the judge who is hearing their tax case. Their weapon is the judge's great weakness: women. Their antics also involve a dentist, his wife, and a prostitute who holds court in a bathtub. Mechanically, the play is skillfully crafted, but it lacks any of Kingsley's customary social awareness—a redeeming quality it badly needs.

Most theatre critics felt the play was well written but lacked substance. The consensus was that Kingsley was simply out of his element. Harold Clurman wrote: "The play has no theme or even a trace of social comment and, what is much more damaging in a farce, very little situation or complication of situation." Maurice Zolotow rightly reflected this majority opinion: "Kingsley has tried to intoxicate himself with the wine of Bacchus, but his sobriety has conquered all."

Perhaps Kingsley himself felt uncomfortable in the farce genre, for in his next play (and his last appearance on Broadway to date), he returned to socially oriented realistic drama. The play, *Night Life*, was a critical and popular failure, opening at the Brooks Atkinson Theatre on 23 October 1962 and closing after only sixty-three performances. In an interview shortly before opening, Kingsley stated the theme of his play: "It is not enough to give lip service to an ideal. The great need in our time is to refashion—revitalize—the myths by which men live." To illuminate his theme, Kingsley creates the painfully realistic atmosphere of a New York key club and introduces a number of stock characters: a crooked labor boss, a movie starlet, a furniture dealer (who is the hero of the piece), and many others. He develops the play through a stream-of-consciousness technique, resulting in a number of lengthy but significant speeches. Unfortunately some critics found the speeches only served to interrupt the flow of the play. Richard Watts, Jr., best described its central flaw: "Its serious weakness, I think, is that the elements of melodrama and the aspects of intellectual parable, though striking in themselves, rarely combine in a successfully integrated pattern, the one adding strength to the other, but rather tend to get in each other's way, with the result that the play ends by seeming inferior to the sum of its parts." Critics praised the performances by the large cast but often found little to admire in the play itself. If there was one comment which reflected the widespread critical frustration with *Night Life*, it was John McCarten's statement in the *New Yorker*: "But why go on? The performances are excellent, but the play is another matter." In *Night Life* Kingsley failed where he had so often previously succeeded by not sufficiently supporting his social theme with an adequately structured melodrama.

Kingsley has not presented a new work on the Broadway stage since *Night Life* in 1962, but he remains an active participant in the theatrical community. He is a member of the influential Dramatists Guild and has served as president and vice-president of that organization; for a time he was on the board of directors of the Cafe La Mama Experimental Theatre Club. Early in the 1970s, Kingsley began work on a trilogy of plays with the collective title of "The Art Scene." The first of the plays, "Man With a Corpse on His Back" was completed in 1973.

Joseph Wood Krutch once wrote: "Mr. Kingsley's plays have always been completely devoid of what we call 'literary quality,' and for that reason there is a kind of seriousness with which they cannot possibly be taken." He continued, however: "But I know of no other contemporary American who can take a topic . . . and turn out a more stageworthy piece, full of shrewd if not too profound observation crisply and humorously embodied in recognizable types." This is perhaps the most apt description of Kingsley's dramatic works. As American dramatic writing has increased in sophistication, the stylistic weaknesses of Kingsley's plays have become more pronounced. In his orientation toward his subject matter, a definite shift may be noted: in the earlier plays, his heroes received dramatic sympathy as a result of their dedication to their work and ideals; in his later plays—particularly in *Detective Story* and *Darkness at Noon*—the protagonists suffer painful defeat because of their excessive dedication to work and ideals. His skill as a dramatic craftsman has indeed created works which are genuinely stageworthy by virtue of the excitement and sympathy they invoke, but he can never be considered among the foremost rank of dramatists because he had been unable to transcend his early formative playwriting practices.

Yet Kingsley has been among the few dramatists who have been the social conscience of the American theatre. All of his major works are infused with optimism, with the hope that unjust personal or social conditions can and should be changed. His career has been devoted to banishing complacency and to voicing the certainty that the often flawed American society can be substantially improved. The hope and social dedication he has skillfully embodied in his plays have assured him a place in American theatrical history.

References:

John Anderson, "Kingsley and Bel Geddes Picture Slum Play Covering Waterfront," *New York Evening Journal*, 29 October 1935, p. 14;

Brooks Atkinson, Review of *Darkness at Noon*, *New York Times*, 15 January 1951, p. 13;

Atkinson, Review of *Dead End*, *New York Times*, 29 October 1935, p. 17;

Atkinson, Review of *Detective Story*, *New York Times*, 24 March 1949, p. 34;

Atkinson, Review of *Lunatics and Lovers*, *New York Times*, 14 December 1954, p. 44;

Atkinson, Review of *Men in White*, *New York Times*, 27 September 1933, p. 24;

Atkinson, Review of *Ten Million Ghosts*, *New York Times*, 24 October 1936, p. 23;

Atkinson, Review of *The World We Make*, *New York Times*, 21 November 1939, p. 19;

Howard Barnes, Review of *The Patriots*, *New York Herald-Tribune*, 30 January 1943;

Harold Clurman, "From Lorca Down," *New Republic*, 124 (5 February 1951): 22-23;

Clurman, "Theatre," *Nation*, 180 (1955): 18;

Clurman, "Theatre: Good Show," *New Republic*, 120 (11 April 1949): 25-26;

John Gassner, *Theatre at the Crossroads* (New York: Holt, Rinehart & Winston, 1960), pp. 142-143;

Wolcott Gibbs, "Cops and Causes," *New Yorker*, 25 (2 April 1949): 50;

Gibbs, "Moscow and Madrid," *New Yorker*, 26 (20 January 1951): 54;

Gibbs, "Standard Brands," *New Yorker*, 30 (25 December 1954): 38-40;

Percy Hammond, "The Theatre," review of *Dead End*, *New York Herald-Tribune*, 29 October 1935;

Joseph Wood Krutch, "Drama: An Event," *Nation*, 137 (1933): 419-420;

Krutch, "Drama: Sure Fire," *Nation*, 141 (1935): 575-576;

Krutch, Review of *The World We Make*, *Nation*, 149 (1939): 627-629;

Krutch, Review of *The Patriots*, *Nation*, 156 (1943): 248-249;

Krutch, Review of *Detective Story*, *Nation*, 168 (1949): 424-425;

Thomas Lask, "Kingsley's Return," *New York Times*, 21 October 1962, II: 3;

Burns Mantle, *Best Plays of 1936-37* (New York: Dodd, Mead, 1937), pp. 422-423;

Mantle, *Contemporary American Playwrights* (New York: Dodd, Mead, 1938);

Mantle, " 'Dead End' as Alive as Steam," *New York Daily News*, 29 October 1935;

Margaret Marshall, Review of *Darkness at Noon*, *Nation*, 172 (1951): 92-93;

John McCarten, Review of *Night Life*, *New Yorker*, 38 (3 November 1962): 111-112;

Lewis Nichols, Review of *The Patriots*, *New York Times*, 30 January 1943, p. 11;

Edward Reed, "Other New Plays," *Theatre Arts Monthly*, 20 (1936): 932;

Howard Taubman, Review of *Night Life*, *New York Times*, 24 October 1962, p. 44;

Richard Watts, Jr., "Two on the Aisle," *New York Post*, 18 November 1962, p. 15;

Stark Young, "Full of the Moon," *New Republic*, 101 (13 December 1939): 230;

Young, "American Patriots," *New Republic*, 108 (15 February 1943): 211-212;

Maurice Zolotow, "The Season On and Off Broadway," *Theatre Arts*, 39 (February 1955): 90.

ARTHUR KOPIT
(10 May 1937-)

PRODUCTIONS: *The Questioning of Nick*, October 1957, Harvard University, Cambridge, Mass.; 28 December 1973, Stage 13, New York;

Gemini, November 1957, Harvard University, Cambridge, Mass.;

Don Juan in Texas, by Kopit and Wally Lawrence, December 1957, Harvard University, Cambridge, Mass.;

On the Runway of Life, You Never Know What's Coming Off Next, April 1958, Harvard University, Cambridge, Mass.;

Across the River and Into the Jungle, December 1958, Harvard University, Cambridge, Mass.;

Sing to Me Through Open Windows, April 1959, Harvard University, Cambridge, Mass.; revised version, 15 March 1965, Players Theatre, New York, 24 [performances];

Aubade, 1959, Harvard University, Cambridge, Mass.;

Oh Dad, Poor Dad, Mama's Hung You in the Closet and I'm Feelin' So Sad: A Pseudoclassical Tragifarce in a Bastard French Tradition, 7 January 1960, Harvard University, Cambridge, Mass.; 5 July 1961, Lyric Opera House, London; 26 February 1962, Phoenix Theatre, New York, 454;

Asylum, or, What the Gentlemen Are Up To, Not to Mention the Ladies, March 1963, Theatre de Lys, New York; closed in previews; *And As for the Ladies*, 1964; produced again as *Chamber Music*, 1965, Society Hill Playhouse, Philadelphia;

The Conquest of Everest, 1964, New York; 20 November 1970, Assembly Theatre, New York;

The Hero, 1964, New York; 3 October 1970, Playbox, New York;

The Day the Whores Came Out to Play Tennis, 15 March 1965, Players Theatre, New York, 24;

Indians, 4 July 1968, Aldwych Theatre, London, 34; 6 May 1969, Arena Stage, Washington, D.C., 40; 13 October 1969, Brooks Atkinson Theatre, New York, 96;

What Happened to the Thorne's Place, 1972, Peru and Landover, Vt.;

Louisiana Territory; or, Lewis and Clark–Lost and Found, 1975, Middletown, Conn.;

Wings, 3 March 1978, Yale Repertory Theatre, New Haven, Conn., 28; 21 June 1978, Newman Theatre, New York;

Secrets of the Rich, 1978, O'Neill National Playwrights Conference, Waterford, Conn.

BOOKS: *Oh Dad, Poor Dad, Mama's Hung You in the Closet and I'm Feelin' So Sad: A Pseudoclassical Tragifarce in a Bastard French Tradition* (New York: Hill & Wang, 1960; London: Methuen, 1962);

The Day the Whores Came Out to Play Tennis and Other Plays (New York: Hill & Wang, 1965; London: Methuen, 1969)—includes *The Questioning of Nick*, *Sing to Me Through Open Windows*,

Chamber Music, *The Conquest of Everest*, and *The Hero*;

Indians (New York: Hill & Wang, 1969; London: Methuen, 1970);

Wings (New York: Hill & Wang, 1978).

Born in New York City, Arthur Kopit grew up in Lawrence, Long Island, where his father worked as a jeweler. Upon his graduation from high school in 1955, Kopit entered Harvard University on scholarship. Despite a major in engineering, the youthful undergraduate proved his versatility in the arts. During his last three years at the university, he won two playwriting contests, saw seven of his plays produced at Harvard, and directed six of them himself. His first one-act drama, *The Questioning of Nick*, written during the spring of 1957 for the Dunster House Drama Workshop, took Kopit only three or four days to write. Drawing from his personal experience as a high-school basketball player, Kopit wrote of a teenage athlete's rebellious attitudes, an arrogant pose splintered by interrogation experts at police headquarters. *The Questioning of Nick* focuses on Nick, the product of a tough, immigrant environment, who has never had much of a chance for a decent life. His mother cleans tables at a restaurant to eke out a living. Rejected even by the local street gang, the Black Angels, because he is merely a punk, Nick desperately tries to impress the police by bragging about his position on the basketball team. The officers, however, expose and humiliate him as a nonentity. In a pathetic moment, he sinks in utter defeat.

Although *The Questioning of Nick* is a serious play, Kopit's natural inclination turned early to humorous satire. In collaboration with Wally Lawrence, he composed *Don Juan in Texas* (1957), a farcical takeoff on the American Western. The bumbling hero, wandering soap salesman Alvin Smithers, comes to a town that is excitedly awaiting the arrival of Billy the Kid. Word has it that the Kid is going to stop the railroad from laying tracks through his mother's cabbage patch. Since none of the local citizens knows what the notorious outlaw looks like, they mistake the newcomer Smithers for the legendary Kid, and his soap business is an overnight success. Several of the figures in the cast foreshadow the playwright's technique of personifying the animal world and anthropomorphizing objects, in this case livestock and cactus plants.

Again drawing on first-hand observation, Kopit placed his next hero, a fifteen-year-old boy bent on adventure, in the hands of two carnival strippers with hearts of gold. Kopit's Nefertiti with a Southern drawl steals the show by her outrageous antics as a striptease dancer in *On the Runway of Life, You Never Know What's Coming Off Next* (1958). Kopit's next play, *Across the River and Into the Jungle* (1958), is a parody of Ernest Hemingway's 1950 novel *Across the River and into the Trees*. Kid Congo heads an expedition in search of a movie star whose plane has crashed en route to Johannesburg. Her agent wants her back, not because he is concerned over her welfare but because she has not yet fulfilled her contract. The natives are polka dotted rather than black, and the cast's writer figure finally completes his first sentence for a work to be published in *Esquire*. Kopit uses the writer's speeches to satirize the stylized grammar of Ernest Hemingway's *A Farewell to Arms*.

In his senior year, Kopit returned to a sober vein. *Aubade* (1959) is a dancer's hour-long monologue on the disappointing nature of love. *Sing to Me Through Open Windows* (1959) is an eerie mood play in which the circus motif of *On the Runway* becomes grotesque rather than funny. Another venture, *To Dwell in a Palace of Strangers*, concerns the mysterious intrusion of a former friend who unsettles the life of the hero. During this developmental period, the blend of humor and earnestness in Kopit's writing established his dominant tendency toward the tragicomic mode.

In the first play to bring him international attention, Kopit combined wild exuberance with pathos. *Oh Dad, Poor Dad, Mama's Hung You in the Closet and I'm Feelin' So Sad* (1960) has been presented in London, Paris, and West Germany as well as in New York and at Harvard. This satire mimics the conventions of avant-garde drama, specifically the theatre of the absurd. Kopit's fantastic characters are placed in a capricious situation, and the dialogue is composed of non sequiturs. The setting is a beach hotel suite in Havana, Cuba, in which both props and characters romp madly through a burlesque that resembles a perverse nightmare. Reminiscent of Tennessee Williams's cast in *The Rose Tattoo* (1950), the characters' names are appropriate to the rose motif. Dad (who is deceased but whose corpse is nonetheless conspicuously active), his widow, and his son are the Rosepettles. The widow's suitor is Commodore Roseabove; her son's temptress, Rosalie. A piranha fish, distinguished by its dietary preference for Siamese cats, answers to Rosalinda. An added note of Williams parody is Mrs. Rosepettle's windy monologue in scene 3, in which she effusively describes how she became in-

Arthur Kopit

volved with her former husband. The style of this speech caricatures Williams's penchant for the confessional monologue.

The play is a grotesquerie focusing on women who devour men, noticeably the weaker sex. These females' counterparts in the natural world are carnivorous plants and fish. Details are playful and varied, yet the idea is somewhat monotonously repeated from scene to scene. Mrs. Rosepettle is a moneyed traveler who is accompanied on the international circuit by her son, addressed as Albert or Edward or Robinson after his father. (His true name is Jonathan.) Even in death, the ill-fated husband remains in his voracious spouse's clutches. His stuffed, preserved body forms part of Mrs. Rosepettle's luggage, and his festooned coffin is precariously balanced in the closet of her hotel room. Jonathan is also kept captive. Mrs. Rosepettle regularly locks him in the suite so that the world will not contaminate him before she can decide how to ensure his future international eminence. His development stunted by a possessive mother, Jonathan is seventeen but looks and acts like a stammering ten year old. He spends his days playing with collections of stamps or coins and reading.

Mrs. Rosepettle likewise shuts out reality from her existence. She requires that thick, black velvet curtains be hung in her rooms, and her excursions take the form of raids on the beach, where she searches out lovers and kicks sand into their faces. Kopit suggests a reasonable basis for Mrs. Rosepettle's cynical attitude toward sex. Her own initiation into conjugal lovemaking on her wedding night had been traumatic: she was carelessly used and dismissed. Capitalizing on her sole sexual encounter as a justification for her spiteful revenge, she thereafter tortured her spouse in his sleep. Eventually her domination over him caused his fatal heart attack. The widow is a man hater, crusading against sex and love, luring eligible bachelors into flirtations fearsome in their consequences. Her virulent campaign almost smothers the Commodore, who succumbs to an asthmatic attack under stress.

Perverted mothering is also a result of a life without love. Because Mrs. Rosepettle views the outside world as a threatening environment in which rejection is supreme, she assures herself that preventing her son from achieving normal maturation has saved him from a hypocritical society. She has kept Jonathan pure: "His skin is the color of fresh snow, his voice is like the music of angels, and his mind is pure." If Jonathan is kept chaste, his spirit will stay innocent; he will never have to face the loathsome state of manhood. According to her scheme of effective child rearing, both radio and telephone are censored. The television set contains no picture tube. Jonathan is allowed to write letters to strangers whose names and addresses he culls from the telephone directory, but his letters do not reach the mailbox. At night he is pinned down with blankets tucked so tightly that he is immobilized. All this repression results in Jonathan's turning to voyeurism. With his telescope, he espies Rosalie, a disarmingly sweet baby doll of nineteen, who turns out to be as ironfisted as Mrs. Rosepettle. Her ambition is to maneuver Jonathan out of his mother's tentacles and into her own. In the bizarre seduction scene, Rosalie gets her victim to Mrs. Rosepettle's sacred bed and almost divests him of his last garment. Coitus is interrupted when Dad tumbles out of the closet, landing on top of the temptress. The terrified Jonathan asphyxiates Rosalie, and destroys his mother's predatory vegetables and animals as well. Mrs. Rosepettle herself, however, remains invincible and triumphant. Jonathan learns that life is much safer behind his spectacles or the lens of his telescope.

Using macabre humor to distance the viewer from the stage action, Kopit exposes the psychological danger in a society which blindly adheres to a belief in stereotyped roles, such as those of husband, child, or mother, and to platitudes about the blessings of home and family life. In *Oh Dad*, the perception of females as devourers is masked by visual extravaganza and elaborate paradox. Yet, within this atmosphere of fantasy and abandon, designed to provoke both horror and laughter, Mrs. Rosepettle emerges finally as a monstrous panzer machine of hate. *Oh Dad* won the Vernon Rice Award and the Outer Circle Award in 1962.

The terror that tortures a deranged mind suffuses the emotional atmosphere of *Asylum* (1963), later retitled *Chamber Music* (1965). This piece is written in an impressionistic style which underscores the suggestibility of eight paranoiac women confined to a ward in an institution for the insane. The inmates assume the identities of celebrated individuals: they believe themselves to be the wife of Mozart, the explorer Osa Johnson, Gertrude Stein, movie actress Pearl White, Amelia Earhart, Joan of Arc, and Susan B. Anthony. Unaccountably, they decide that the men's ward is a threat and unanimously agree to send a dead body there in the middle of the night as a show of strength and a warning. Amelia Earhart is arbitrarily chosen to be the sacrifice; she is clubbed and strangled to death by the other seven. The play ends on an ironic note as the attendant enters the meeting room and thinks that the dead woman is napping. *Chamber Music* is sometimes perceived as a reflection of anxiety in the nuclear age.

Sing to Me Through Open Windows and *The Day the Whores Came Out to Play Tennis* were presented as a double bill on the New York stage in the spring of 1965. In these plays, the mother image of *Oh Dad* recedes, replaced by a focus on a father-son relationship. The fable *Sing to Me Through Open Windows*, written during Kopit's undergraduate days, is an experiment in expressionism which projects a boy's memory of a lost father figure. Andrew Linden, just out of the seventh grade, visits Ottoman Jud, a magician, and his butler, Loveless the Clown, in their obscure circus, where they entertain him with a series of tricks and illusions. He learns from their theatrical magic that a guiding fatherhead does not have to be a person. The magician is a paternal presence revealing that innocence must fade, that imagination must be free, and that poetry is a fragile art. When the magician warns, "I have vanished," the boy watches him disappear, aided by Loveless, into a trunk. At the final curtain, snow falls, suggesting that nothing lasts, neither belief nor disbelief, neither hope for a father nor despair over the loss of one.

In *The Day the Whores Came Out to Play Tennis*, the prestigious father Franklin Delano Kuvl feels contempt for his son, Herbert, who is more of a sissy and less effectual than Jonathan Rosepettle. The elder Kuvl belongs to Cherry Valley Country Club, where the two older generations of men, long-term members of the executive committee which runs the club, are empty-headed vulgarians. The younger members are outright nincompoops or self-inflated boors who show no regard for their elders. Kopit's play is a light parody of Anton Chekhov's *The Cherry Orchard* (1904) in which the Russian aristocrats' estate is about to be sold to pay their debts, the final crisis intensified by the thud of axes chopping down the cherry trees at the drama's close. At the end of Kopit's play, the audience listens to tennis balls striking against the shutters of the clubhouse amid tumbling plaster. The settings of the two plays match: the rooms are both nurseries, the time is dawn, the month is May, the air cold and frosty. Even the remark that the room's windows are closed has been adopted from Chekhov's stage directions. Although the Cherry Valley scions are not Russians but upper-class Jewish-Americans, their names retain a Russian flavor—Ratscin, the treasurer, for example, and the still more conspicuously parallel name Gayve. Gaev or Gayeff was the fifty-one-year-old bachelor in Chekhov's play who must bid farewell to a familiar life of ease. In Kopit's play, he is the secretary of the Cherry Valley Country Club and wears misbuttoned pajamas—almost like a child. Kopit's sophisticated mockery connects, besides, the Chekhovian theme of the decline of the landed aristocracy with the vanity motif in the Hemingway novel *The Sun Also Rises* (1926). In all three works—Chekhov's, Hemingway's, and Kopit's—stubborn refusal to adjust to change results in ruin. Herbert Kuvl's excitement over the "great lines" in *The Sun Also Rises* undercuts the seriousness of the action. This technique of alluding to a work not integrally related to the dramatic action is Kopit's way of satirizing contemporary writers who adapt previously developed themes from already successful literature. Nevertheless, corresponding to the emergence of a new social order in Chekhov's play and the sense of loss after World War I in *The Sun Also Rises*, an overthrow of the old order occurs in *The Day the Whores Came Out to Play Tennis*. And in Kopit fashion, the transition is accomplished by strong women who prevail over weak men.

The Cherry Valley Country Club is a male enclave operated according to terms of rigid convention. The eighteen or twenty whores who brazenly show up on the tennis courts represent the outside world. Without ever actually appearing onstage, this external force easily effects a triumphant coup against the club's hierarchy. President Kuvl calls the pilot committee to meet in the nursery room of the club, where the members talk but take no positive action. All they can do is bemoan their loss. The whores, representative of a lower, exploited social stratum, have no use for the established country club, so they demolish it with their tennis balls.

The play's farcical tone is supported by costume. Since the men are summoned to a dawn parley, they arrive wearing a motley assortment of last night's tails and tuxedos, long underwear, and pajamas. The whores have driven up in Rolls-Royces equipped with one-way mirrors for windows. Herbert Kuvl sits astride a hobbyhorse. Vaudevillian stunts erupt intermittently: cigars explode; the wrapper on a bar of chocolate conceals a jack-in-the-box butterfly; a door panel opens, and a bottle of tequila zips into the room; tennis balls fly through the windows. Behind all the nonsense, however, Kopit has built a case against America's urban middle class. The country club is a familiar symbol for social-climbers' aspirations. Because of the successful members' complacency, however, their self-contained world collapses, and their sequestered way of life ends. *The Day the Whores Came Out to Play Tennis* is an imaginative fantasy with a perceptive warning about what lies beneath society's surface frivolity.

The Hero and *The Conquest of Everest*, both produced in New York in 1964 and in 1970, are two additional examples of expressionism written about the time that *Sing to Me Through Open Windows* was launched at Harvard in 1959. Both are plays of situation rather than plot. To emphasize a world in which words cannot be trusted, no dialogue occurs in *The Hero*. The short scenario describes a pantomime in which the two characters, A Man and A Woman, represent all human beings who persist in carrying on the business of life when existence seems meaningless. In the tradition of Samuel Beckett, the setting is a desert, void, whose one significant figure is A Man, tattered and exhausted, stumbling across the stage. The map that he pulls from his pocket is a symbolic pattern of his lifetime, and the scene's sunrise, followed by sunset, represents the limited cycle of A Man's life. Much of the map has been torn away, suggesting the Man's depleted sources and energy. The equipment he carries with him is grossly inadequate for surviving the desert: an attache case, a salt shaker, opera glasses,

and a paint box. But he laughs. And he makes an admirable, though comic, attempt to pull himself together in order to mount another feeble attack on adversity. With his paintbox, he sketches his own oasis, trying to make art out of the unpromising material at hand. Art brings him a measure of order and security. And his ability to laugh about the realities of the human condition represents a heroic, positive force in a hopeless situation.

A Woman enters and preens. The two individuals conduct a mating ritual. A Man gives her a sandwich of rocklike hardness, the only gift he has to offer. They share the sandwich and then join in creating mutual body warmth against the cold and darkness around them. Kopit's experiment demonstrates that wordless communication is of critical importance.

Chaos is the important element in *The Conquest of Everest*, again a short skit, reinforcing the point that people have little of consequence to say to one another. As in *The Hero*, a man and a woman figure are the main characters, joined by an obtrusive Chinese soldier. Mount Everest is diminished to a mere slope, conquered with ease by two naive schoolteachers on an American Express tour. Details of character and setting are as basic as those in the preceding play. The names are generic—Mr. Almanstar is exploring the world, accompanied by Miss Almenside, who is his female counterpart. In the biting cold of the Himalayas, the two Americans walk barefooted, dressed in summer clothes. They beat the Chinese machine gunner to the mountain's crest, accidentally break a Coca-Cola bottle over his head, and remain oblivious to his anger because he speaks in Chinese, which they do not understand. In a soliloquy that serves as the adventure's epilogue, the Chinese soldier, shifting into lyrical, if broken, English iambic pentameter, maintains that in order to rise to any challenge, "One only needs not know what one is doing."

One of the most important American dramas of the 1960s is *Indians*, the foremost of Kopit's plays with editorial points of view. The playwright undertook an intensive study of American history before transfiguring the legendary West into a dreamscape of the nineteenth century. With a Rockefeller Foundation grant in 1968, Kopit and his wife were able to attend the Royal Shakespeare Company production in London, and then to start major revisions at Villa Serbelloni at Lake Como in Italy. The revised version, first produced at the Arena Stage in 1969, contains thirteen scenes. *Indians* is an eloquent satire which rivets attention on America's greed and racism during the nineteenth century. Although the set for the opening scene suggests an objective approach, Kopit did not intend his play to be labeled documentary. When members of the audience enter the auditorium, they see three glass cases onstage. No curtain intervenes. No backdrop or sets depict realistic locales. The glass museum cases housing effigies of Buffalo Bill, Sitting Bull, and a buffalo skull with rifle and bloodstained Indian shirt suggest a stark theatre of fact, reminding viewers that Indian culture in the United States has been brutally reduced to pathetic artifacts.

The central argument of *Indians* is that the United States has consistently used romantic myths and legends to glorify sordid political policies. The idea for the play received impetus from the Vietnam conflict, particularly from incidents of American soldiers' gunning down Vietnamese citizens. In scene 13, Colonel Forsyth echoes a speech by General Westmoreland: "Of course innocent people have been killed. In war they always are. And of course our hearts go out to the innocent victims of this." *Indians* acutely shows the cost of believing that oppressing the weak is an unavoidable, though lamentable, consequence in the fight to protect or enlarge national goals. A prevailing white majority have continually worked to suppress minorities believed to be their inferiors. *Indians* is concerned with guilt over the American Indians' treatment; this theme has obvious parallels to America's abuse of Asians and blacks as well. But calling attention to the plight of the downtrodden was not Kopit's main intent. Principally, he wanted to show that Hollywood movies and Western tall tales have manipulated facts in order to suit the white audience. Much of the play's conflict is generated through William Cody (Buffalo Bill), who *knows* what the Indians are suffering, yet who has become a celebrity by perpetuating the legends which justify genocide. He is therefore an appropriate representation of the white majority's dilemma. The schism between the actual hunter and scout and his Wild West persona is at once comic and tragic. Hired by railroad builders to provide buffalo meat for the laborers, Buffalo Bill probably killed single-handedly more buffaloes than any other sharpshooter. Yet he was sympathetic toward the Indians, realizing too late that he had annihilated their major food supply. He had never considered the consequence of his actions. In his career as mediator, he made personal attempts to persuade Washington officials that the government had a moral obligation to redress wrongs committed at the Indians' expense. On the other hand, however, Cody ventured into the entertain-

ment world as a flamboyant pioneer showman. In this role, he hired Indians to play parts which undermined their pride by reducing them to incompetent villains and humiliated flunkies. Cody's Wild West Show converted battlefield slaughter into widely appealing, rollicking and profitable entertainment. Kopit noted and took exception to the mockery of history in that gaudy circus, which he felt was a telling spectacle of American hypocrisy. In the end, Cody becomes the playwright's symbol for the exploiter whose self-aggrandizement was at the expense of the defeated.

Indians explores a period in Western history when heroes were being created by such dime novelists as Ned Buntline, who has a substantial role in the play. Buntline realizes that he can invent a persona around Cody which will make a lot of money. To counterpoint Buntline's phony eulogizing, Kopit, by contrast, characterizes Buffalo Bill in authentic perspective. He is an aging performer, reduced to hawking two shows a day in a ghost town. The modern audience sees Bill's spectaculars for the degrading grotesqueries they were, in which Indians were maligned and their slaughter by white troops celebrated. The core of the drama is William Cody's tortured attempt to justify his behavior and rationalize his position as an American hero. He is a self-deluded liberal who has helped to destroy with false promises those he has intended to save.

Without sentimentalizing, the play highlights the contrasting dignity and innocence of Spotted Tail, Sitting Bull, and his tribesman John Grass. Vignettes from the cheap tableaus of Buffalo Bill's Wild West Show are interspersed with flashbacks that reveal the blunt reality of historical incident. Cody's personal doubts surface in his opening monologue when he tries to convince the audience that he is a man with a blameless past. Even so, his self-condemnation is apparent when he proclaims himself "A GODDAM HERO!" His compulsion to self-aggrandize escalates. In scene 3, with Ned Buntline standing by, taking notes for a biographical article, Cody brags exaggeratedly of his exploits. The Russian visitor, Grand Duke Alexis, becomes overexcited by stories of Cody's prowess against the Comanche and, in his attempt to demonstrate his own bravery, he grabs a rifle and fires blindly into the dark, killing Spotted Tail. Cody is stunned by his friend's death, but, in order to protect the mythic self-image he has been building, he compromises his integrity by lying to the Duke and Buntline, assuring them that the fallen man is an enemy Comanche rather than an Indian of mixed Sioux, Cherokee, and Crow blood. His Buffalo Bill persona not only conceals the less heroic side of his true personality but also goads him into corrupting those qualities in himself that are decent.

That decency is expressed in the brief scene 4 which recreates the 1886 government commission's hearing of Indian grievances at Standing Rock reservation. Cody's defense of Sitting Bull's tribe to the senators is fervent. But in scene 5, he enters the cage where Geronimo is held prisoner and turns his back. The gesture of turning his back demeans and insults a proud but now powerless captive who was once regarded with dread and awe.

The pivotal event in scene 7 is Ned Buntline's "Scouts of the Plains," a play within the play, which Kopit pushes to hilarious farce. A poker-playing president and his first lady, both formally dressed, attend the White House performance. They watch an outlandish presentation of Western life in which Cody and Wild Bill Hickok play themselves and the Indian roles are performed by an Italian, a German, and a troupe of Brooklyn extras. Once the melodrama is under way, Hickok balks at having to act out a pretense of himself and decides to behave naturally rather than according to Buntline's stilted script. Following his own inclinations, he knifes Buntline and rapes the Italian actress. The scene dramatically points out the discrepancy between fact and the whitewashed version of it in adventure stories of the Old West. The essence of Kopit's style is that he infuses the humorous tradition of the tall tale with the tragic nonheroic temper of black humor.

Kopit's Indian figures heighten the discrepancy between the white man's promises and the facts of history. In scene 9 Chief Joseph movingly confesses to the spectators that he agreed to join Buffalo Bill's Wild West Show in exchange for broken pledges that his people would be fed. A second incident calling attention to the Indians' humiliation occurs during the ritual sun dance, which is re-enacted in the show to demonstrate Indian bravery under torture. In an imitation of the actual dance, participants use conspicuous chest harnesses to prevent real muscle pain. Watching from the sidelines, John Grass is finally overcome with shame over this debasement of a time-honored test for measuring a man's courage and endurance. He thrusts himself among the dancers, takes the barbed ends of the thongs hanging from the top of the sun dance pole, rips open his shirt, hooks the barbs into his bare chest, and dances. The centrifugal force generated by the dance shreds his muscles, and he collapses, blood streaming. Cody's cradling Grass as the scene fades reinforces the contrast between the Indian's pride and the showman's debasement.

In a third illustration of oppression, Sitting Bull in scene 11 protests to the senators that his people are being treated like beasts. The Great Spirits have chosen him to be the proud leader of an entire nation. As a worthy chief who has devoted his life to his people, he has a right to his pride. On behalf of his people, he asks for the benefits that human beings deserve. In a subsequent meeting between Cody and Hickok, surrealistically represented, the audience learns that the army has answered Chief Sitting Bull's ardent plea by massacring his tribe.

As an ironic defense of the government's Indian policy, Buffalo Bill recites in scene 13 a long series of indictments against an administration that has repeatedly broken faith with the people native to this country. The play itself has been a series of impasses between two alien systems. The white culture has greedily demanded full ownership of the land, while the Indian believes man's access to all land is free. Like air, it can be possessed by neither individual nor company. The two sides do not understand each other despite Buffalo Bill's tries. He is a well-intentioned though inept man caught between his sense of honor and the demands of a white culture believing in manifest destiny and the power of gold. Kopit's social drama shows Cody trying to resolve the grievances of the dispossessed tribes and attempting to adjust the legalistic attitudes of the senate investigating committee. But the confrontation between spokesmen from both sides leads nowhere. And the play ends on a note of pathos. *Indians* reveals the tragic consequences of incomprehensible exchanges between peoples speaking different languages. And the complexity of communicating through language has continued to obsess the American dramatist.

During the decade following *Indians*, Kopit was a Fellow at the Center for the Humanities at Wesleyan University in Middletown, Connecticut, in 1974-1975; playwright-in-residence at Wesleyan in 1975-1976; then CBS Fellow at Yale in 1976-1977. In 1978 appeared Kopit's innovative drama *Wings*, an inventive work that underscores the frustration of linguistic noncommunication. Dedicated to his father, who suffered a critical stroke in 1976, Kopit's *Wings* dramatizes the mind of a stroke victim deprived of the ability to create coherent language. As he did for *Indians*, again the playwright undertook exhaustive research, this time in the fields of aeronautics and speech abnormalities resulting from traumatized brains. He also worked directly with recuperating patients at Burke Rehabilitation Center in White Plains, New York, where his father received therapy after release from the hospital.

In its original form, *Wings* was a radio play commissioned for National Public Radio. After its success, Kopit expanded and adapted it for the stage. The actual performance takes only ninety minutes; the struggle by the protagonist to reassemble her fragmented world covers a two-year period. The patient is Emily Stilson, an elderly lady who suffers a left cerebral infarction while she is sitting quietly at home, reading. No theatre intermission interrupts the progress and setbacks of Mrs. Stilson's recovery. Her experience is condensed into a single act, broken into four scenes. The stroke itself occurs in a short prelude, followed by the stages of her fight, referred to as "Catastrophe," "Awakening," and "Explorations." The few props making up the set include several chairs, one bench, a hospital bedside table, and a couple of black screens that convey an impression of corridors through which the audience sees activities outside Mrs. Stilson's consciousness. These revolving screens also function as mirrors for a mind's chaotic landscape. Though the play calls for a cast of nine, the work is mostly a dramatic monologue by the main character.

In the opening prelude, the stroke is indicated visually by Mrs. Stilson's staring into the room bewilderedly as the lights go out one by one. When the clock finally stops ticking, a din of noise crashes in on her. Emily Stilson loses consciousness; thereafter, she loses touch with the world. Her speech is gravely impaired. When she can form verbal sounds, her words are largely gibberish. When others speak intelligibly to her, she often hears what they say as meaningless mumbo-jumbo. One of the doctors, for instance, asks her to repeat the sentence "We live across the street from the school." She replies with "Malacats on the forturay are the kesterfats of the romancers." And when she listens to two physicians conferring about her, she hears their exchange as "Pollycadjis" and "Sewyladda."

Demonstrating the idea of confusion on all sides, Kopit has constructed the play so that the audience observes the action mainly through Mrs. Stilson's own chaotic state of awareness. While her outward behavior remains halting and, for the most part, inarticulate, the spectators hear her thoughts as soliloquies. She is unable to make connections between the world of objects and the proper names for them. She works through the painful beginnings of communication with the medical staff. A tremendous strain behind applying the right iden-

tifying word to the utensil for cleaning her teeth indicates the continual frustration in her struggle to relearn basics. Once she makes some headway, the determination to succeed turns that exhausting effort into an adventure. She begins to extend herself, to mix with other patients. From a state of removal in which she does not recognize her children when they come to support her, she advances to form a companionable and affecting bond with Amy, her therapist.

As is the case with all human beings, Mrs. Stilson has much more depth and substance than her own or an observer's words can express. Playgoers suffer with her effort and rejoice when she finds and releases the right word or phrase. Her battle represents man's continual struggle to articulate. Mrs. Stilson further demonstrates that the resolve to continue wrestling with the difficulties of self-expression can make verbal communication adventurous.

As a young woman, before she became wife and mother, Emily Stilson worked as a stunt pilot, sometimes flying her Curtiss Jenny, sometimes daringly walking on the wings, soaring above the world. As a stroke victim, she is similarly detached from ordinary reality. In her mind, she comes to associate her alternating setbacks and triumphs with her experiences while flying. Loss of verbal control is like flying upside down or through a snowstorm. The exhilaration of success is like facing the wind atop an airplane wing. Because her new situation is unexplored territory to her, venturing ahead seems like a night flight in which she is lost and terrified. She makes up her mind to keep going in the dark. Mrs. Stilson is suspended between life and death, and the life that she is exploring is as foreign to her as death. When she suffers a second attack, she goes out on "wings." The metaphor used to describe her youthful defiance of death represents her awareness of death. The conclusion of *Wings* thus pays homage to the invincibility of the human spirit.

Kopit has proved himself versatile in both comedy and serious drama. He is among the foremost American playwrights in the theatre of the absurd, yet his work testifies to his compassion and deep concern for the human race. He expresses his views of tragedy in a tough, unsentimental attitude, and the comic framework in which most of his work is composed provides a crucial perspective for sobering insights into human pain and disaster. His techniques establish a sense of distance which reminds viewers that art is not intended to be literally true. Through his experimental efforts, he has extended the use of language, bearing testimony to the value of the theatre as the domain of imaginative power. Kopit's wit, mastery of verbal manipulation, and surety of instinct identify him as a major virtuoso in contemporary theatre.

–Carol Harley

Screenplay:
Oh Dad, Poor Dad, Mama's Hung You in the Closet and I'm Feelin' So Sad, Paramount, 1967.

Television Scripts:
The Questioning of Nick, WNHC, 1 June 1959;
The Conquest of Television, NETV, 1966.

Other:
An Incident in the Park, in *Pardon Me, Sir, But Is My Eye Hurting Your Elbow?*, ed. Bob Booker and George Foster (New York: Geis, 1967).

Periodical Publication:
To Dwell in a Palace of Strangers, act 1, *Harvard Advocate* (May 1959).

References:
Robert Brustein, "Bagatelles and Jacks," *New Republic*, 152 (10 April 1965): 24;
Harold Clurman, "The Kopit Plays," *Nation*, 200 (5 April 1965): 373-374;
John Gassner, "Broadway in Review," *Educational Theatre Journal*, 14 (May 1962): 169-171;
Henry Hewes, "The Square Fellow," *Saturday Review*, 45 (17 March 1962): 35;
Vera M. Jiji, "*Indians*: A Mosaic of Memories and Methodologies," *Players*, 47 (June-July 1972): 230-236;
John Bush Jones, "Impersonation and Authenticity: The Theatre as Metaphor in Kopit's *Indians*," *Quarterly Journal of Speech*, 59 (December 1973): 443-451;
Anthea Lahr, ed., "A Dialogue Between Arthur Kopit and John Lahr," in *Indians* (New York, Toronto & London: Bantam, 1971);
Edith Oliver, "Off Broadway: And Lies and Lies and Lies," *New Yorker*, 41 (27 March 1965): 146-147;
David L. Rinear, " 'The Day the Whores Came Out to Play Tennis': Kopit's Debt to Chekhov," *Today's Speech*, 22 (Spring 1974): 19-23.

CHARLES MACARTHUR
(5 November 1895-21 April 1956)

PRODUCTIONS: *Lulu Belle*, by MacArthur and Edward Sheldon, 9 February 1926, Belasco Theatre, New York, 461 [performances];
Salvation, by MacArthur and Sidney Howard, 31 January 1928, Empire Theatre, New York, 31;
The Front Page, by MacArthur and Ben Hecht, 14 August 1928, Times Square Theatre, New York, 281;
Twentieth Century, by MacArthur and Hecht, 29 December 1932, Broadhurst Theatre, New York, 154;
Jumbo, by MacArthur and Hecht, 16 November 1935, Hippodrome, New York, 221;
Ladies and Gentlemen, by MacArthur and Hecht, adapted from Ladislaus Bus-Fekete's play, 17 October 1939, Martin Beck Theatre, New York, 105;
Fun to Be Free, Patriotic Pageant, by MacArthur and Hecht, 1941, Madison Square Garden, New York;
Johnny on a Spot, 8 January 1942, Plymouth Theatre, New York, 4;
Swan Song, by MacArthur and Hecht, adapted from Ramon Romero and Harriett Hinsdale's *Crescendo*, 15 May 1946, Booth Theatre, New York, 158;
Stag at Bay, by MacArthur and Nunnally Johnson, 6 February 1974, School of Theatre, Florida State University, Tallahassee.

BOOKS: *A Bug's-Eye View of the War* (Oak Park, Ill.: Pioneer Publishing, 1919);
The Front Page, by MacArthur and Ben Hecht (New York: Covici Friede, 1928; London: Richards & Toulmin, 1929);
War Bugs (Garden City: Doubleday, Doran, 1929);
Ladies and Gentlemen, by MacArthur and Hecht (New York, Los Angeles & London: French, 1941);
Fun to Be Free, Patriotic Pageant, by MacArthur and Hecht (New York: Dramatists Play Service, 1941);
The Stage Works of Charles MacArthur, ed. Arthur Dorlag and John Irvine (Tallahassee: Florida State University Foundation, 1974)—includes *Lulu Belle, Salvation, The Front Page, Twentieth Century, Ladies and Gentlemen, Johnny on a Spot, Swan Song*, and *Stag at Bay*.

Charles MacArthur's significance as a playwright lies in his contribution to the development of American comedy in the 1920s and 1930s. The slick, unrestrained, confidently wisecracking slices of life which appeared on the New York stage in that era delighted and entertained a generation of theatregoers. MacArthur, with his collaborator Ben Hecht, was at the forefront in the development of American comedy with the plays *The Front Page* (1928) and *Twentieth Century* (1932). Tennessee Williams later credited them with taking "the corsets off the American theatre."

Charles MacArthur was one of nine children born to fundamentalist evangelist William Telfer MacArthur and his wife Georgianna. He left his Scranton, Pennsylvania, home at age seventeen and worked that summer for a newspaper in Oak Park, Illinois. He then worked for a local Chicago news service, the *City Press*, but soon advanced to a better job as a reporter for the *Chicago Herald-Examiner*. Except for a hitch in World War I which he later humorously recalled in *War Bugs* (1929), MacArthur remained a reporter in Chicago both for the *Examiner* and the *Chicago Tribune* until the early 1920s. He married reporter Carol Frink in 1920; they were divorced in 1926. A move to New York to work for the *American* was a springboard for MacArthur. In New York he became a member of the Algonquin Round Table, a group of literary and performing artists, and playwriting became a fulltime occupation. In 1948-1949 he was editor of the *Theatre Arts Magazine*. MacArthur had an attractive personality. All who write about him mention his personal charisma and charm, and he was a favorite of many of the leading creative figures of his day. On 17 August 1928 MacArthur married actress Helen Hayes. They had one child, Mary, and adopted another, James. MacArthur suffered increasing ill health in his later years and died of chronic nephritis in 1956.

MacArthur's first New York play was a collaboration with a distant relative, Edward Sheldon, a well-established playwright whose career was handicapped by an illness which left him blind and bedridden by 1920. Their play *Lulu Belle* (1926) chronicles the adventures of a black courtesan, Lulu Belle, who lures the innocent George Randall to abandon his wife and children for her, but later abandons him for a wealthy French viscount. The scorned lover gets revenge in a climactic murder. The cast of the play included one hundred blacks and fifteen whites, the whites taking the leading roles in blackface, as was still the custom at that time.

The play was melodrama on a grand scale. It was produced and directed by the noted impresario David Belasco, and the finished product shows strong evidence of his influence. Belasco's trademark was the orchestration of spectacle, with meticulously detailed sets and exact attention to lighting effects. Though popular response to the play was positive, critical response was negative. Critics complained that the plot and story were lost in a jumble of scenic detail. The heavy melodrama, unrelieved by humor, was ponderous and overdone.

MacArthur's second collaborator was Sidney Howard, also a journalist-turned-playwright, whose *They Knew What They Wanted* (1924) had won the Pulitzer Prize. Their joint effort, *Salvation* (1928), is about a woman evangelist, Bethany, whose spiritual purity and honest goodness are contrasted with the scheming avarice of her mother, her manager, and her publicity agent. They oppose her romance with Victor, the tenor who appears with her, for crass financial reasons. The pair marry anyway, but after Bethany discovers that Victor, too, has less than pure motives, she leaves them all to search for her own salvation.

Salvation suffers from a lack of cohesiveness in intent and form. The play's plot is predictable and the attitude it takes toward the characters and situations is shallow and unconvincing. There is a tentative humor which wars with an earnest seriousness. The characters of Whittaker and Brady (foreshadowing Webb and O'Malley in *Twentieth Century*) are MacArthur's first portrayals of the reporters who often appear in his plays, and they provide the first evidence that MacArthur was most successful as a playwright when he drew his characters from life. Though the critics praised Pauline Lord's portrayal of Bethany, the play was roundly attacked by the critics and closed after thirty-one performances.

MacArthur's most successful collaborations were with Ben Hecht. The prolific Hecht was a published novelist and produced playwright before he teamed up with MacArthur in the 1920s. In the mid-1920s they wrote a play called "The Moonshooter," the manuscript of which was misplaced; Hecht later asserted that the play was "the best work MacArthur and I ever did together." MacArthur and Hecht worked together on five Broadway productions as well as many Hollywood screenplays. According to Hecht, they followed the same procedures in writing together for twenty years. Hecht would sit with pencil and paper on his lapboard while "Charlie walked, lay on a couch, looked out of a window, drew mustaches on magazine cover girls, and prowled around in some fourth dimension." Hecht credited their success with the fact that they had complete faith in each other's judgment.

The first and most luminous collaboration of this team was *The Front Page*. MacArthur and Hecht had first known each other when they were both newspaper reporters in Chicago, and it was to these days that they turned for inspiration for *The Front Page*, which takes place in the press room of the Chicago Criminal Court Building on the eve of a murderer's scheduled execution. The main characters are newspapermen drawn from reporters the authors knew in Chicago. Ace reporter Hildy Johnson, on the verge of quitting his job to marry and move to New York, comes upon a scoop he cannot refuse as the escaped murderer literally drops into his hands. The wildly farcical plot revolves around Hildy's efforts to conceal the escapee from the other reporters and the authorities; the efforts of his tyrannical boss, Walter Burns, to secure the story and keep his ace reporter; and the efforts of Hildy's fiancee and future mother-in-law to wrest him from the newspaper world. *The Front Page* challenged the traditions of American comedy, since the actions of the lively characters became the core of the play. As one critic wrote, the play is a "heavily underlined, savagely good-humored caricature of newspaper life." The affectionately humorous characterizations and the skillfully honed honest newspaperman's dialogue combine with elements of melodramatic surprise to keep the audience in laughter.

The critics applauded *The Front Page*, enjoying its fast-paced, rowdy brand of entertainment. The authors, producer Jed Harris, director George S. Kaufman, and the cast received enthusiastic praise. Some critics did complain about the coarseness of the play's language; Burns Mantle, while naming it one of the ten best plays of 1928-1929, reproved it for being brazenly profane. Others, such as George Jean Nathan, praised the dialogue as the play's strength and defended the profanity which "always oozes out of the characters' mouths as naturally as their tobacco juice." The play has remained one of the durable pieces of American comedy; successful revivals occurred on Broadway in 1946 and 1969.

MacArthur and Hecht continued their irreverent madcap satire in their next collaboration, *Twentieth Century*. Here the thrust of the satire is "artistic temperament," a prime character trait of many of their associates in Hollywood and on Broadway. The action of the play occurs as the express train Twentieth Century Limited makes its run from Chicago to New York. The flamboyant producer, Oscar Jaffe, near bankruptcy after several flops, tries to persuade his former star Lily Garland, who has "gone Hollywood," to return to him and assure his renewed success. The train (whose movement was simulated by complicated techniques which revealed selected compartments of the train at different times and produced visual and sound effects of passing scenery) is peopled by such characters as a pair masquerading as honeymooners, two bewildered Nuremburg passion players, a religious maniac, and a classic masculine-looking lesbian.

MacArthur and Hecht repeated their success in satirizing characters drawn from real life. The play was based on a play, "The Napoleon of Broadway" by Charles Bruce Milholland, which treated the personality of Morris Gest, a producer for whom he had worked. The MacArthur-Hecht version added elements from the personalities of David Belasco and Jed Harris to create Oscar Jaffe, their grandiloquent impresario, and the characters of Oliver Webb and Owen O'Malley were based on Harris's general manager and press agent. The authors' real skill again lay in raising specific comedic elements in real personalities to a level of universal humor. If they were somewhat less successful in *Twentieth Century* than in *The Front Page*, it may be because their focus on the world of the theatre was

Charles MacArthur, 1936

somewhat diluted by the diverse minor characters and the train setting, while in *The Front Page* setting, characters, and plot joined in unified focus on the zany newspaper world.

Critical reaction to *Twentieth Century* was generally favorable; critics praised the gusto of the satire and enjoyed this slapdash cartoon of the theatre world. Some thought the story ran a little thin and noted that the third act, which was completed more than a year after the first two, was not quite up to standard. The first run of the play would probably have been longer if it were not for the collapse of the United States banking system in the depressed economic climate of 1932. *Twentieth Century* has stood the test of time. It was made into a successful movie starring John Barrymore and Carole Lombard (1934) and was revived successfully on Broadway by ANTA in 1950. Most recently, in 1978 a musical adaptation by Betty Comden and Adolph Green entertained Broadway theatregoers.

MacArthur and Hecht next ventured into the world of circus extravaganza, writing a story for *Jumbo* (1935), a Billy Rose production, which was primarily circus spectacle and only secondarily a play. Their script, which treated a Romeo-and-Juliet theme about lovers whose parents were rival circus owners, was largely discarded when it became apparent that dialogue was lost in the caverns of New York's Hippodrome. Critics were favorable to the production, but mentioned the awkwardness inherent in trying to combine circus and musical comedy.

MacArthur was never able to repeat the success of *The Front Page* and *Twentieth Century*. His attention turned increasingly to writing screenplays in the 1930s, and his later Broadway efforts were not successful. *Ladies and Gentlemen* (1939), another collaboration with Hecht, was the only play MacArthur ever wrote as a vehicle for his wife, Helen Hayes. The play is a behind-the-scenes picture of a murder trial which shows the leavening effect of a woman's intuition upon her eleven jury colleagues. The situation is complicated when the woman, who alone believes in the defendant's innocence, falls in love with the married jury foreman, thus setting up a love triangle which parallels that in which the defendant was a participant.

The play is slow-paced, unimaginative, and sentimental. Though some of the authors' flair for satire is displayed with some jabs at the jury system and Hollywood personality types, the basic structure of the play has grave faults. This play, about a trial which is never seen, about jurors who are too numerous to be well-developed characters, lacks

any sustaining interest and at best is a pleasant romance. The critics praised Miss Hayes's performance but wondered why she did not choose a play more worthy of her talent.

MacArthur's one solo venture on the Broadway stage was the ill-fated *Johnny on a Spot* (1942), a wildly farcical caper set in the world of politics. On the eve of his election to the United States Senate a Southern governor dies at a local brothel. The play centers on the efforts of the governor's administrative assistant, Nicky Allen, to keep the truth from the public until after the election, while keeping his own position and love life intact.

The play is energetic and lively, but not very funny. The main character, Nicky, is a scamp in the MacArthur tradition, but instead of the positive affection which an audience feels for reporter Hildy Johnson or impresario Oscar Jaffe, Nicky evokes a negative reaction; he is a conniving, low-down politico whose cause does not seem very noble or attractive. Although the play has some good dialogue and flashes of the MacArthur humor, it lacks animation. When the play opened in January 1942, only a month after the Japanese attack on Pearl Harbor, neither the country nor the critics were ready for a frenzied farce. Unanimously rejected by the critics, it swiftly closed.

The final MacArthur-Hecht Broadway collaboration involved an attempt to revitalize a dead article. The suspense melodrama *Crescendo* by Ramon Romero and Harriett Hinsdale, which had failed in Philadelphia a few months earlier, was revised by MacArthur and Hecht and opened in New York as their *Swan Song* (1946). The play revolves around a child prodigy pianist whose relationship with her maestro and whose life are threatened by the jealous brother of the maestro's previous prodigy, who had supposedly committed suicide but was actually murdered by her brother. The melodrama was hardly tight enough to sustain suspense. MacArthur and Hecht added sprightly dialogue, including some acerbic jabs at the critics, but the structure of the play severely limited the expression of their gifts. The mild interest the play does engender arises from the attractive personalities of the maestro and his daughter as well as the charm and pianistic skills of the young prodigy. The critics were unanimously cold, asserting that MacArthur and Hecht should not have bothered to rewrite *Crescendo*.

MacArthur left several unfinished and unproduced playscripts. Three of these, "The Good Time" (with Edward Sheldon), "My War With the U.S.," and "The One I Love the Best" (with Ludwig

Bemelmans), have not been released by the MacArthur family because the author did not consider them ready for production. One other play, thought lost until it was discovered among the MacArthur papers at the Wisconsin Center for Theatre Research, was a collaborative effort with Nunnally Johnson entitled *Stag at Bay*. They began work on this play in 1939, but apparently it was not completed until 1954. Efforts to have the play produced at that time were unsuccessful; it received its premier performance in 1974 at Florida State University, the home of the Charles MacArthur Center for Development of American Theatre.

The plot of *Stag at Bay* was based on one of MacArthur's favorite anecdotes about his friend John Barrymore. It seems that Barrymore had forgotten that he had a daughter, and when reminded of this fact he went immediately to her boarding school to visit. There he charmed staff and students, but his daughter would have nothing to do with him. Bart Starling, the Barrymore character in *Stag at Bay*, has a similar experience. The play displays most of MacArthur's successful techniques. The hero is a loveable scamp, the world of Hollywood is lampooned, and the laughs abound as the errant father encounters the sedate girls school. If the play is an insubstantial piece of fluff, the satire less sharp, and the characters less colorful than in *The Front Page* and *Twentieth Century*, *Stag at Bay* does share the same qualities to a lesser extent and is genuinely entertaining.

Comedy, excitement, salty dialogue, and rapidly paced melodrama were the dominant goals of Charles MacArthur's theatre. At his best he accomplished them skillfully, as he transformed humorous elements in actual personalities into universals which everyone recognized. He subjected the world of newspapers and New York-Hollywood artistic pretensions to a sharp but always benevolent satire which has delighted generations of audiences. His heroes, like himself, were scamps, but something of his own genial spirit was infused into his characters and is appreciated by his audiences. When MacArthur departed from his own experience or tried to delve beneath the surface of his zaniness, he was less successful as a playwright. At his best, though, he was very good, and with *The Front Page* and *Twentieth Century* he made a memorable contribution to the development of American comedy.

—Jane Isley Thesing

Screenplays:

The Sin of Madelon Claudet, MGM, 1931;
Rasputin and the Empress, MGM, 1933;
Crime Without Passion, by MacArthur and Ben Hecht, Paramount, 1934;
Barbary Coast, by MacArthur and Hecht, Goldwyn, 1935;
The Scoundrel, by MacArthur and Hecht, Paramount, 1935;
Once in a Blue Moon, by MacArthur and Hecht, Paramount, 1935;
Wuthering Heights, by MacArthur and Hecht, United Artists, 1939;
Gunga Din, by MacArthur and Hecht, RKO, 1939;
The Senator Was Indiscreet, United Artists, 1948.

References:

Ben Hecht, *Charlie: The Improbable Life and Times of Charles MacArthur* (New York: Harper, 1957);
John Crawford Irvine, "An Analysis of Character Delineation in Selected Playscripts of Charles MacArthur and His Collaborators," Ph.D. dissertation, Florida State University, 1976.

Papers:

MacArthur's papers are at the Wisconsin Center for Theatre Research at the University of Wisconsin, Madison.

ARCHIBALD MACLEISH
(7 May 1892-)

PRODUCTIONS: *Union Pacific: A Ballet*, libretto by MacLeish, music by Nicholas Nabokoff, and choreography by Leonide Massine, 25 April 1934, St. James Theatre, New York, 4 [performances];
Panic: A Play in Verse, 14 March 1935, Imperial Theatre, New York, 3;
The Trojan Horse: A Play, 1952, BBC Radio, London; 23 October 1953, Poets' Theatre, Cambridge, Mass., 1;
This Music Crept by Me Upon the Waters, 1953, BBC Radio, London; 23 October 1953, Poets' Theatre, Cambridge, Mass., 1;
J. B.: A Play in Verse, 22 April 1958, Yale University Theatre, New Haven, 6; 11 December 1958, ANTA Theatre, New York, 364;
The American Bell, music by David Amram, 1962, Independence Hall, Philadelphia;
Herakles: A Play in Verse, 27 October 1965, Lydia Mendelssohn Theatre, University of Michigan, Ann Arbor, 14;

The Play of Herod, prose narration by MacLeish, 27 December 1968, Church of St. Mary the Virgin, New York, 3;

Scratch, 6 May 1971, St. James Theatre, New York, 4.

SELECTED BOOKS: *Songs for a Summer's Day* (New Haven: Yale University Press, 1915);

Tower of Ivory (New Haven: Yale University Press, 1917; London: Milford, 1917);

The Happy Marriage and Other Poems (Boston & New York: Houghton Mifflin, 1924);

The Pot of Earth (Boston & New York: Houghton Mifflin, 1925);

Nobodaddy (Cambridge, Mass.: Dunster House, 1926);

Streets in the Moon (Boston & New York: Houghton Mifflin, 1926);

The Hamlet of A. MacLeish (Boston: Houghton Mifflin, 1928);

Einstein (Paris: Black Sun Press, 1929);

New Found Land: Fourteen Poems (Paris: Black Sun Press, 1930; Boston & New York: Houghton Mifflin, 1930);

Conquistador (Boston & New York: Houghton Mifflin, 1932; London: Gollancz, 1933);

Poems 1924-1933 (Boston & New York: Houghton Mifflin, 1933; London: Boriswood, 1935);

Panic: A Play in Verse (Boston & New York: Houghton Mifflin, 1935; London: Boriswood, 1936);

Public Speech: Poems by Archibald MacLeish (New York: Farrar & Rinehart, 1936; London: Boriswood, 1936);

The Fall of the City (New York: Farrar & Rinehart, 1937; London: Boriswood, 1937);

Air Raid (New York: Harcourt, Brace, 1938; London: Lane / Bodley Head, 1939);

Land of the Free: U.S.A. (New York: Harcourt, Brace, 1938; London: Boriswood, 1938);

America Was Promises (New York: Duell, Sloan & Pearce, 1939; London: Lane / Bodley Head, 1940);

The Irresponsibles: A Declaration (New York: Duell, Sloan & Pearce, 1940);

A Time to Speak: The Selected Prose of Archibald MacLeish (Boston: Houghton Mifflin, 1941; London: Allen & Unwin, 1941);

The American Cause (New York: Duell, Sloan & Pearce, 1941);

American Opinion and the War: The Rede Lecture (New York: Macmillan, 1942; Cambridge, England: Cambridge University Press, 1942);

A Time to Act: Selected Addresses (Boston: Houghton Mifflin, 1943; London: Allen & Unwin, 1945);

The American Story: Ten Broadcasts by Archibald Mac-Leish / The Admiral / The Names for the Rivers / The American Name / The Discovered / The American Gods / The Many Dead / Ripe Strawberries and Gooseberries and Sweet Single Roses / Between the Silence and the Surf / Nat Bacon's Bones / Socorro, When Your Sons Forget (New York: Duell, Sloan & Pearce, 1944);

Actfive and Other Poems (New York: Random House, 1948; London: Lane / Bodley Head, 1948);

Poetry and Opinion: the Pisan Cantos of Ezra Pound (Urbana: University of Illinois Press, 1950);

Freedom Is the Right to Choose: An Inquiry into the Battle for the American Future (Boston: Beacon Press, 1951; London: Lane / Bodley Head, 1952);

Collected Poems 1917-1952 (Boston: Houghton Mifflin, 1952);

The Trojan Horse: A Play (Boston: Houghton Mifflin, 1952);

This Music Crept by Me Upon the Waters (Cambridge, Mass.: Harvard University Press, 1953);

Songs for Eve (Boston: Houghton Mifflin, 1954);

J. B.: A Play in Verse (Boston: Houghton Mifflin, 1958; London: Secker & Warburg, 1959; revised edition, New York: French, 1958);

Poetry and Experience (Boston: Houghton Mifflin, 1961; London: Lane / Bodley Head, 1961);

Three Short Plays / The Secret of Freedom / Air Raid / The Fall of the City (New York: Dramatists Play Service, 1961);

The Collected Poems of Archibald MacLeish (Boston: Houghton Mifflin, 1963);

The Dialogues of Archibald MacLeish and Mark Van Doren, ed. Warren V. Bush (New York: Dutton, 1964);

The Eleanor Roosevelt Story (Boston: Houghton Mifflin, 1965);

An Evening's Journey to Conway, Massachusetts (Northampton, Mass.: Gehenna Press, 1967);

Herakles: A Play in Verse (Boston: Houghton Mifflin, 1967);

A Continuing Journey (Boston: Houghton Mifflin, 1968);

The Wild Old Wicked Man and Other Poems (Boston: Houghton Mifflin, 1968; London: Allen, 1969);

Scratch (Boston: Houghton Mifflin, 1971);

The Human Season: Selected Poems 1926-1972 (Boston: Houghton Mifflin, 1972);

The Great American Fourth of July Parade: A Verse Play for Radio (Pittsburgh: University of Pittsburgh Press, 1975);

New and Collected Poems 1917-1976 (Boston: Houghton Mifflin, 1976);
Riders on the Earth: Essays and Recollections (Boston: Houghton Mifflin, 1978);
Six Plays (Boston: Houghton Mifflin, 1980).

In a distinguished and kaleidoscopic career spanning more than six decades Archibald MacLeish, chiefly renowned as a major American poet, has also served as soldier, educator, lawyer, journalist, librarian, political essayist, literary critic, social commentator, statesman, philanthropist, and playwright. This vast diversity of endeavor reflects his fundamental philosophy of art, including poetry and drama, that casts aside ivory-tower isolationism in favor of a spirited activism that leaves no corner of life unexplored. MacLeish himself best summarized the matter in 1958 when he wrote for *Atlantic Monthly*: "To declare, as the American aesthetic seems to do, that the effort to act upon the external world in the making of a work of art is a betrayal of the work of art is a misconception of the nature of art. The nature of art is action, and there is no part of human experience, public or private, on which it cannot act or should not." By resolutely adhering to this philosophy in print and on the stage, MacLeish has repeatedly "brought himself into sharp conflict with those who are partisan in politics, orthodox in religion, and dogmatic in art."

MacLeish wrote only seven stage plays and one libretto between 1924 and 1971. But it is difficult and unwise to segregate MacLeish the poet from MacLeish the playwright. His plays, with the sole exception of *Scratch* (1971), are composed in the same distinctive blank verse that marks his poetry. Furthermore, his plays flow from the same sources as his poetry—current events, American folklore, classical mythology, and biblical parable. Most important of all, his plays focus on the same ultimate goal. Never content simply to mirror his age, MacLeish has always striven to fulfill his own stringent demand: "Poets, deserted by the world before, / Turn 'round into the actual air: / Invent the age! Invent the metaphor!" Thus, as poet and playwright, MacLeish has toiled to unearth the metaphors that would provide a sense of direction to American life through some of the most turbulent decades of the twentieth century. As some testimony to his success, *Time* magazine, in August 1979, named him a national leader "who has steadily, over a long and distinguished career, held up to our people a spectacle of greatness."

MacLeish was born in Glencoe, Illinois, the son of prosperous Chicago merchant Andrew Mac-

Leish and his wife Martha Hillard MacLeish. Private study at the Hotchkiss School in Lakeville, Connecticut, prepared him for Yale University. There, during his freshman year, the *Yale Literary Magazine*, for which MacLeish would later serve as editor, published his first poem. Four years later, in 1915, his *Songs for a Summer's Day* won the Yale University Prize for Poetry. By his own admission, MacLeish was more interested in football and swimming than academics. Nonetheless, he was elected to Phi Beta Kappa in his junior year and graduated with the A.B. degree in 1915.

"To avoid going to work," MacLeish next entered Harvard Law School. Marriage to singer Ada Hitchcock came the following year on 21 June 1916. They eventually had four children. World War I interrupted, and MacLeish spent most of 1917 and 1918 with the U.S. Army in France. He began service as a private with a hospital unit but soon transferred to the field artillery, saw action at the front, and rose to the rank of captain. His first volume of poetry, *Tower of Ivory*, appeared in 1917 as he fought in France. After the war he returned to Harvard, where he received his LL.B. in 1919. Graduating at the head of his class, MacLeish still confessed that he "could never believe in the law." For a year he remained at Harvard to teach classes in constitutional and international law. Then, in 1920, he went to work for the prestigious Boston law firm of Choate, Hall, and Stewart.

By the winter of 1923, however, MacLeish was no longer content to be a weekday lawyer and weekend poet. On the very day he was elected to partnership he resigned the practice of law and made plans to take his wife and two children to Paris. There he lived, studied, and perfected his craft among the greatest literary figures of the era—including Ernest Hemingway, James Joyce, F. Scott Fitzgerald, and Ezra Pound. At the same time he also came into contact with T. S. Eliot, E. E. Cummings, and William Butler Yeats. Particularly influential were Eliot and Pound, who introduced MacLeish to the innovative work of nineteenth-century French poets and great Oriental poets such as Tu Fu and Li Po. Eliot also alerted MacLeish to the potential of drama as a means of poetic expression, especially when making use of legend, folklore, and mythology. But in marked contrast to Eliot and Pound, whose disillusionment led them into permanent exile from American shores, MacLeish had no intention of remaining abroad. He returned to the United States and took up what would become a lifelong residence on a farm in Conway, Massachusetts.

Archibald MacLeish, 1933

These crucial years between 1923 and 1928 have been called his "expatriate period," but Mac-Leish disdains the labels "expatriate" and "Lost Generation," whether applied to himself or other writers of 1920s Paris. "It was not the Lost Generation which was lost," he argued, "it was the world out of which that generation came." It may be claimed, in fact, that MacLeish discovered himself in Paris both as a poet and as an American. He dates the beginning of his life from 1923 and notes that his years in a foreign country gave him a new perspective on the value and potential of American democracy. Since Paris, biographer Signi Falk observed, MacLeish "has persisted in expressing in both verse and polemical essay the need of Americans to revitalize the principles of individual liberty." Paris, ironically, helped mold MacLeish into a distinctively American poet.

During his sojourn in France, MacLeish not only passed from obscurity to eminence as a poet; he also took his first step as a fledgling playwright with *Nobodaddy*. A closet drama, producible but unproduced, the play was written before 1925 and published in America in 1926. The title comes from William Blake, who joined "nobody" and "daddy" to create a derisory name for the grim God of prohibitions often associated with the Old Testament.

Ironically, God exists in the play only as the invisible Gardener, who brings the life-giving rain but is perceptible to Adam and Eve only as an ominous wind moving through the trees. In MacLeish's own words, *Nobodaddy* is an appropriation of the biblical parable of Eden meant to dramatize "the condition of self-consciousness in an indifferent universe."

Not long after the play opens, the innocence of Eden is invaded by the serpent, a voice inside the head of Adam urging him to eat the forbidden apple or, in other terms, to overthrow blind obedience, assert his own rational will, and rise to the station of God. Adam succumbs to the temptation and, along with Eve, eats the fruit. To their amazement God is silent and does not strike them dead. What follows, however, is a torrent of shame and superstitious terrors. Wrenched with guilt over their deed, Adam and Eve cast themselves into exile by fleeing into a desert wasteland beyond Eden.

In act 3 the focus shifts to Cain and Abel, but the action remains glued to the same philosophical conflict pursued in act 1 and act 2. Abel represents the fanatical mystic who hopes through blind obedience and sacrifice to appease God and win a return to the paradise of Eden. Cain represents the equally fanatical proponent of reason and free will who, like Milton's creation, would rather rule in hell than serve in heaven. Naturally, the two brothers are constantly at odds, and their struggle comes to a climax when Abel attempts to sacrifice a ram to God. Shocked by the idea of such a senseless slaughter, Cain strikes out and kills Abel. The irony of the situation is unmistakable as Cain, in his effort to prove the superiority of reason over superstition, takes the life of his brother.

As might be expected of a first play, *Nobodaddy* is awkward and ambiguous. More dramatic poem than drama, static argument dominates the play until Abel enters in act 3. MacLeish himself called *Nobodaddy* a poem. Furthermore, the work raises many questions while providing few answers. As R. P. Blackmur noted: "Man is the ruin as well as the triumph of God." Through Cain and Abel, God is both worshiped and scorned, leaving man's final relationship to God quite nebulous. Perhaps this is due to the fact that MacLeish's second son died shortly before the play was written. Whatever the reason, *Nobodaddy* is unfulfilling drama, yet of particular note because many of its ideas and many of its conflicts would surface three decades later in *J. B.*

MacLeish spent part of 1929 in Mexico, retracing by mule pack the paths of explorer Hernando Cortés. Out of the adventure came *Conquistador*, a long narrative poem that chronicles the conquest of Mexico by Cortés. *Conquistador* carried MacLeish to a wider popular audience and his first Pulitzer Prize for poetry in 1932. Still, it was necessary for him to supplement his income from poetry by signing on as an editor for Henry Luce's *Fortune* magazine. MacLeish remained at that lucrative position until 1938, writing well-documented articles on contemporary social and political problems.

First contact with the professional stage came for MacLeish in 1934 when he wrote the libretto for *Union Pacific*, a ballet based on the construction of the first transcontinental railroad and the golden spike ceremony, marking its completion, on 10 May 1869, at Promontory Point, Utah. Scored by Nicholas Nabokoff, choreographed by Leonide Massine, and produced by the Monte Carlo Ballet Russe, *Union Pacific* opened at the Saint James Theatre on 25 April 1934 with assistance from the Federal Theatre Project. Audience response was tumultuous and Siegfried Wagener, special correspondent for the *Neue Freie Presse*, called the ballet "as refreshing as a glacial wind on a midsummer day" in a nation "obsessed with economic worries." Wagener went on to say: "This production is an artistic event of the first importance to America because here, for the first time, a purely American theme has been thought out and presented in choreographic form and set to music." For MacLeish, *Union Pacific* was the first of several dramatic works, including plays, radio dramas, and television shows built upon American history, folklore, or legend. In addition to its four-performance run at the Saint James Theatre, *Union Pacific* toured widely in the United States and Europe.

As evidenced by his third play, *Panic* (1935), MacLeish's work during the 1930s exhibited a steadily ascending social consciousness in response to the Great Depression. Set in New York City, 1933, at the apex of the banking crisis during which many banks failed for lack of capital, *Panic* spotlights a financial titan known only as McGafferty. In blind fear of the unseen enemy threatening them with hunger and death, the other New York bankers and the unemployed mob all look to McGafferty to deliver them from the impending doom of economic collapse. McGafferty, however, is impotent both as a banker and as a leader. He lacks everything necessary to fulfill his role as popularly elected financial savior. The last half of the play shows his precipitous decline into a stupor of incapacitating indecision, hastened by the suicide of a colleague and the news of a banking moratorium. In the end, facing his own economic ruin, the humiliation of failure, and the anger of the mob, McGafferty himself escapes through suicide.

Though far less enigmatic than *Nobodaddy* before it, *Panic* may still perplex the reader because the dominant theme of the play does not emerge from the actions of the central character, McGafferty; it emerges from the actions of the wealthy bankers and the poor unemployed. Both groups, pampered before the crisis by varying degrees of material wealth and comfort, display a shocking willingness to peddle their individual freedom to McGafferty in exchange for continued prosperity. Here is the warning MacLeish would repeat again and again in prose and verse—crisis, economic or otherwise, endangers individual liberty and begets the tyranny of demagogues.

Because of its unique verse form, *Panic* is of particular note in MacLeish's evolution as a playwright. Dissatisfied with archaic verse forms dating back as far as Elizabethan England, MacLeish sought a new form more in tune with the rhythms of contemporary American speech. The result, seen in *Panic*, is an accentual meter, which counts the number of stresses in a line rather than the number of syllables. This is the verse form MacLeish would remain with in all of his subsequent dramas except *Scratch*.

Panic was scheduled for and ran for only three performances at the Imperial Theatre in New York beginning 14 March 1935. Critical response was in keeping with the economic and political nature of the play. Spokesmen for the right viewed it as an attack on capitalism and suspected MacLeish of leaning toward communism. Ironically, spokesmen for the left, including V. J. Jerome of *New Masses* magazine, viewed *Panic* as soft on capitalism and marred by "doctrinal ambiguities." Jerome was particularly upset by the portrayal of the unemployed masses as a faceless chorus and by the final suicide of McGafferty. Jerome wanted the end to come via "the stormy assault of the proletariat" and lamented: "It is the self-destruction of the bourgeoisie in the play that robs the proletariat of its historic revolutionary role."

In the late 1930s MacLeish stood with Franklin Roosevelt in his efforts to alert Americans to the dangers of the ever-growing totalitarian regimes in Europe. Evidence of this can be seen in MacLeish's first two radio plays, *The Fall of the City* and *Air Raid*, broadcast by CBS radio in 1937 and 1938, respectively, as part of the pioneering Columbia Workshop. In *The Fall of the City* the metropolis falls because its inhabitants will not defend themselves against invasion. In *Air Raid* a village is destroyed and its inhabitants killed because they will not take shelter from enemy planes. In both plays death is the price paid for ignoring the lethal realities of war, a clear warning for isolationists in America.

With the coming of World War II, MacLeish devoted himself to public service to the virtual exclusion of his art. Following his controversial appointment as Librarian of Congress in 1939, a post he held with distinction until 1944, MacLeish was also appointed director of the U.S. Office of Facts and Figures, 1941-1942; assistant director of the Office of War Information, 1942-1943; and Assistant Secretary of State, 1944-1945. In the latter post he worked toward the founding of a world organization of nations as the best hope for a lasting peace. At the close of the war he was instrumental in creating the United Nations Educational, Scientific and Cultural Organization (UNESCO).

Between 1939 and 1947 MacLeish published numerous volumes of political prose but only one volume of poetry, *America Was Promises* (1939). His only other artistic output came in the form of radio broadcasts such as *The States Talking*, 1941, and *The American Story*, 1944. Patriotic and highly successful, *The American Story* was actually ten separate broadcasts dramatizing the birth and rise of America from the time of Christopher Columbus to the time of George Washington. MacLeish's only religious radio play, *The Son of Man*, was broadcast by CBS in 1947.

MacLeish returned to Harvard University in 1949 as Boylston Professor of Rhetoric and Oratory, teaching creative writing and English literature. Finding teaching challenging and rewarding, MacLeish remained at Harvard until 1962, enjoying the long vacations that afforded him time to write poetry and drama. His *Collected Poems 1917-1952*, published in 1952, won him a second Pulitzer Prize for poetry along with the Bollingen Prize and a National Book Award.

Following an interval of more than eighteen years, two short plays by MacLeish reached the stage for one night in 1953. *The Trojan Horse* and *This Music Crept by Me Upon the Waters*, originally broadcast over BBC radio in 1952 and 1953 respectively, were both performed by the Poets' Theatre in Cambridge, Massachusetts on 23 October 1953. Like *The Crucible* by Arthur Miller, which premiered in January of the same year, *The Trojan Horse* employs historical parallel to warn against the re-

pugnant, self-destructive fear and suspicion generated by the followers of Joseph McCarthy. In the play, dialogue between the Blind Man and the Girl serves as choral commentary for the action, a device foreshadowing *J. B. This Music Crept by Me Upon the Waters*, frequently compared to T. S. Eliot's *The Cocktail Party*, is a melodious mood play of ambiguous meaning. With its ten characters and contemporary, Caribbean island setting, the play delves into different attitudes toward happiness and paradise. In the end every chance for happiness is either missed or squandered. Though there is little consensus on the matter, a plurality of critics saw the play as a slap on the wrists of Americans who have paradise within their grasps but, for whatever reason, let it slip away.

The Trojan Horse and *This Music Crept by Me Upon the Waters* were written for radio or for reading without scenery in the manner of Dylan Thomas's *Under Milk Wood*. Despite the advent of television, MacLeish remained loyal to radio because it offered "the promise of a true theatre for poets; a theatre in which the imaginative ear, not the pedantic eye, would provide the audience . . . a theatre also in which poetry could regain what it cannot long exist without—a public."

Commercially and critically, MacLeish earned the great bulk of his reputation as playwright with *J. B.* Originally staged by the Yale School of Drama in April 1958, *J.B.* played at the Brussels World's Fair in September and opened at the ANTA Theatre in New York on 11 December 1958. After a run of 364 performances, the play closed on 24 October 1959. In published form, *J.B.* was a best-seller and translated into many foreign languages. Later productions were mounted in many nations including England, France, Egypt, Israel, and Mexico.

Essentially the Book of Job transplanted into the twentieth century, *J.B.* asks how man, with dignity and hope, can love and serve a god who allows so much evil to exist in the world. The action unfolds under a giant circus tent, recreating the universe-as-big-top analogy earlier seen in MacLeish's own poem "The End of the World." As a play-within-a-play, *J.B.* begins with the entrance of two ragtag gentlemen named Mr. Zuss and Nickles. The pair discover and don masks of God and Satan, thus setting the inner play into motion. For the rest of the play Zuss and Nickles each fulfill a dual role, one deified and one human. Together they act as a Greek chorus, both taking part in and commenting upon the action of the play, Zuss as orthodox believer and Nickles as rebellious cynic.

When we first see Job's modern counterpart,

Orson Welles, Archibald MacLeish, and William Robson

J. B., he is celebrating Thanksgiving with his wife and children. Prosperous and happy, J. B. is overflowing with love of God. Then, the senseless misfortunes begin. One son is killed overseas in an absurd accident following the Armistice. One daughter is brutally raped and murdered by a sexual psychopath. Two other children die in a gruesome automobile accident. The last child perishes when J. B.'s bank is bombed. In each case, the news is borne to J. B. by callous messengers—drunken soldiers, photographers with glaring flashbulbs, raincoated policemen, and steel-helmeted civil defense officers. J. B. himself is stricken with boils and, with his wife Sarah, left the pitiful survivor of an atomic blast. Sarah, however, soon leaves, urging J. B. to denounce God and surrender life. As the first half of the play comes to a close, J. B., wounded and bewildered, cries out: "Show me my guilt, O God!" God responds with agonizing silence.

In the second half comes the parade of comforters, giving no comfort at all. Bildad expounds Marxist jargon about collective humanity. Eliphaz, a Freudian psychiatrist, talks about guilt as an illusion. Finally, Zophar, a theologian, argues that guilt is an inevitable part of being human. J. B. rejects the panaceas of all the comforters but finds the words of Zophar most cruel because they imply a gamester-God who creates sin to punish sin. With nothing left to do, J. B. simply restates his faith and trust in God. This time God answers, in the form of a distant, disembodied voice over the public address system. But to J. B.'s surprise, God speaks only to question him and rebuke him for his presumptuousness in trying to instruct the Lord. In MacLeish's words, J. B. "has not been answered at all—he has merely been silenced." Humbled by God's chiding, J. B. repents. Not long after, Sarah returns to him out of love and together they resolve to begin a new world.

This was the version of *J. B.* staged at Yale University. Before the play reached New York, however, it underwent a significant metamorphosis, mostly at the behest of director Elia Kazan. The multiscene structure of the original gave way to a more conventional two-act form. Zuss and Nickles, segregated from the J. B. scenes in the Yale version, were more fully incorporated into the total action of the play. Most significant, especially in terms of later critical opinion, was the addition of what Kazan called a recognition scene, in which J. B. rejects both complacent ignorance and cyni-

-2-

113

trees and pastures as they had from the beginning when
they were brought there first as slaves. But you you
belonged to nothing on that island but the happiness
you were afraid to find.

Oh, some of us who went there then were happy. Women
mostly, wearing the warm wind like a scarf, delighting
in it. Others, most often men, were lost. They drank
too much. Pretended love. Played games. Still others,
one or two, became themselves a moment and then lost the
moment.

And then, a generation after the first planes came down
the curve of the Antilles, that whole world was gone.
There were two hotels in every sandy cove of every island
and the icy contrails of enormous jets webbed the sky,
and there was no Far left to go to anywhere ...

End of that Introduction

Silence
the sound of the sea on a reef far out,
the sound of a soft wind in palm trees,
the sea on the reef,
the wind in the palms,

then suddenly a raucous record — rock and roll
a door opens,
the record drowns the sea sound and the wind,

A woman's voice:

Chuck!

     Turn that thing off!

Revised typescript

cism in facing the ills of the world. Instead, he finds hope and salvation inside himself, inside the human heart, saying to his wife: "The candles in the church are out. / The lights have gone out in the sky! / Blow on the coal of the heart / And we'll see by and by...." From a solid majority of the critics, *J. B.* harvested high praise. John Gassner called it "an exalted work of the dramatic and poetic imagination in a generally commonplace theatre." John Ciardi of the *Saturday Review* called it "great poetry, great drama, and ... great stagecraft" and added, "the poetry and the drama are organically one." Dudley Fitts, mixing prophecy with praise, wrote: "A passionate work, composed with great art ... a signal contribution to the small body of modern poetic drama, and it may very well turn out to be an enduring one." Citing the emotional power of the play, Samuel Terrien of *Christian Century* observed that even "the most blase audience submits to the spell in an almost unbearable experience of empathy." Finally, Brooks Atkinson, writing for the *New York Times*, said: "It portrays in vibrant verse the spiritual dilemma of the twentieth century."

Transforming a familiar story, however, invites comparison with the original, and here the critics butted heads. In the view of Henry Hewes, *J. B.* "adds precious little to what has already been said more beautifully in the Bible." In a more orthodox vein, another spokesman for *Christian Century* concluded: "While Mr. MacLeish's drama is a brilliant recreation of the story of Job, the character of J. B. is completely foreign to that of the hero who speaks in the biblical poem." Joseph Wood Krutch disagreed with both of these critics, saying: "MacLeish's interpretation is strong and interesting, neither merely repeating what the biblical drama says nor perverting it into something else."

Without doubt, the religious implications of the recognition scene in *J. B.* stirred the greatest controversy and inspired the most biting detractions. Scores of critics, religious and secular, agreed with Martin D'Arcy of *Catholic World* that "evil cannot be solved within us; help and grace must come from outside, from a God." As Brooks Atkinson added, "a declaration of individual independence from God differs from cursing God only in degree, and it weakens the force of the purity of J. B.'s character." Henry Van Dusen alone came to MacLeish's defense in the matter of religious doctrine, arguing in *Christian Century* after the detractors had spoken: "If MacLeish has recourse to human integrity and human love for the answer to J. B.'s need, it is, again, because the biblical Job offers him nothing beyond obeisance before an arbitrary and heartless

Cosmic Power." All critics concurred on one final point: *J. B.* was a genuine rarity—a commercially successful religious verse play.

Moving into the 1960s, MacLeish wrote two plays for television and a highly successful screenplay. *The Secret of Freedom* appeared on NBC in 1960. *An Evening's Journey to Conway, Massachusetts*, written to celebrate the bicentennial of MacLeish's adopted hometown, was shown by WNET in 1967. In 1965 MacLeish wrote the screenplay for *The Eleanor Roosevelt Story*, an effort which won him the Academy Award for Best Feature Documentary in 1966.

Mad Herakles by Euripides served as some inspiration for MacLeish's seventh play, *Herakles*. Staged by the University of Michigan at Ann Arbor in 1965, *Herakles* follows Professor Hoadley, an egomaniacal American scientist who visits Athens after receiving the Nobel Prize. Herakles of the classical myth performs magnificent feats for the good of his people but goes mad and kills his own wife and sons. Hoadley of the MacLeish parody harnesses power for the welfare of mankind but loses touch with his own humanity and alienates his own wife and son. Mrs. Hoadley, like Megara of the Greek tragedy, pleads for love to no avail. Professor Hoadley brushes her aside in his mad pursuit of godhead. Like Cain in *Nobodaddy*, his will is rebellious, and he is not content simply to serve man and God. Overall, the action of the play implies that Hoadley's error is the error of many other scientists in contemporary America.

When they saw *Herakles*, many critics felt it was a better effort than *J. B.* John Wain of the *New Republic* found *J. B.* "so disastrously inferior to the original as to be positively agonizing" but said of *Herakles*, "there isn't that crippling sense of second-handedness." On a different point, Ernest Sandeen wrote for *Poetry* magazine: "*Herakles* surpasses MacLeish's *J. B.* of a decade ago because it entrusts more to the audience.... There is no lack of thought or feeling in *Herakles* but these are invested in the main characters who are held to one simple, clean line of dramatic development. The dilemma they pose is left to the audience to ponder." Karl Shapiro gave MacLeish credit for harvesting "from the tangle of myths and cults of Hercules the parable of the antihumanist modern."

During the upheaval of the late 1960s, MacLeish witnessed a battle between law and order on the one hand and individual liberty on the other that threatened to destroy the Union. In response he wrote *Scratch*, his only prose play. Suggested by "The Devil and Daniel Webster," a short story by

Stephen Vincent Benet, *Scratch* employs the legend of the famed Yankee orator as a plea for liberty *and* union. MacLeish also felt the play was an appropriate fable for an age of affluence when men sold their souls and individual freedom in return for creature comforts on the installment plan.

Scratch premiered at the Saint James Theatre on 6 May 1971, but closed after a run of only four performances. The critics did not find much to like in this MacLeish play. Henry Hewes called it "too arbitrary for a drama, too ambiguous for a history, and too shallow for a biography." Jack Kroll of *Newsweek* censured MacLeish for turning "a charming and beautifully scaled story into an inflated and disastrously abstract play." The most vocal detractor was Martin Gottfried, who called the dialogue "incomprehensible in both content and in plain words," the theme "unoriginal and empty," and the whole an example of the "obsolete values of literary theatre."

For his latest dramatic effort, MacLeish returned to a beloved medium and wrote *The Great American Fourth of July Parade: A Verse Play for Radio*. Read at the Carnegie Music Hall in Pittsburgh on 18 April 1975, the play dramatizes the philosophical and personal battles between John Adams and Thomas Jefferson.

In retrospect, most observers agree with Allan Lewis, who concluded that MacLeish would have earned no enduring reputation as a dramatist at all were it not for *J. B.* The judgment is severe but just, considering the fact that all other MacLeish plays combined held the stage for less than thirty performances. MacLeish, however, was never primarily concerned with commercial success. In the face of realism and naturalism, he simply wanted to sustain an endangered species—poetic drama—of which he wrote: "Its essence is precision, but precision of the emotions, not the mind. Its quality is to illuminate from within, not to describe from without. Its language is not communication, but experience." Certainly *J. B.* will be remembered for its rarity as a religious verse drama in an age of secular prose. Certainly MacLeish will be celebrated as a playwright who insisted upon poetry and humanism in an age of global disaster and national cynicism.

–*James L. McWilliams III*

Screenplays:
The Spanish Earth, by Ernest Hemingway with additional material by MacLeish and Lillian Hellman, Contemporary Historians, 1937;
Grandma Moses, Falcon Films, 1950;
The Eleanor Roosevelt Story, Allied Artists / American International, 1965.

Television Scripts:
The Secret of Freedom, NBC, 1960;
An Evening's Journey to Conway, Massachusetts, WNET, 3 November 1967.

Radio Scripts:
The Fall of the City: A Verse Play for Radio, CBS, 11 April 1937;
Air Raid: A Verse Play for Radio, CBS, 27 October 1938;
America Was Promises, music by Nicholas Nabokoff, CBS, 5 April 1940;
The States Talking, CBS, 1941;
The American Story: Ten Broadcasts by Archibald MacLeish, NBC, February-April 1944;
The Son of Man, music by Johann Sebastian Bach, CBS, 1947;
The Great American Fourth of July Parade: A Verse Play for Radio, Carnegie Music Hall, Pittsburgh, 18 April 1975.

Other:
Union Pacific, in *The Book of Ballets*, ed. Gerald Goode (New York: Crown, 1939), pp. 235-237;
The States Talking, in *The Free Company Presents . . . A Collection of Plays About the Meaning of America*, ed. James Boyd (New York: Dodd, Mead, 1941), pp. 219-237;
The American Bell, in *Let Freedom Ring: The Story of Independence Hall and Its Role in the Founding of the United States* (New York: American Heritage, 1962).

Periodical Publications:
"A Stage for Poetry," *Stage*, 13 (November 1935): 38-39;
"Poetry and the Public World," *Atlantic*, 163 (June 1939): 823-830;
"The Poet as Playwright," *Atlantic Monthly*, 195 (February 1955): 49-52;
"The Isolation of the American Artist," *Atlantic Monthly*, 201 (January 1958): 55-59;
"The Men Behind *J.B.*," by MacLeish, Elia Kazan, and Alfred de Liagre, Jr., *Theatre Arts*, 43 (April 1959): 60-63.

Bibliographies:
Arthur Mizener, *A Catalogue of the First Editions of Archibald MacLeish* (New Haven: Yale University Library, 1938);
Edward J. Mullaly, *Archibald MacLeish: A Checklist* (Kent, Ohio: Kent State University Press, 1973).

References:
Brooks Atkinson, "From 'Job' to 'J. B.,' " *New York Times*, 4 May 1958, II: 1;
Atkinson, "MacLeish's 'Panic,' " *New York Times*, 16 March 1935, p. 18;
Atkinson, "Poet's Epic of Mankind Staged at Yale," *New York Times*, 24 April 1958, p. 37;
Atkinson, "When 'J. B.' Worried," *New York Times*, 10 May 1959, II: 1;
R. P. Blackmur, "A Modern Poet in Eden," *Poetry*, 28 (September 1926): 339-342;
John Ciardi, "The Birth of a Classic," *Saturday Review*, 41 (8 March 1958): 11-12, 48;
Signi Lenea Falk, *Archibald MacLeish* (New York: Twayne, 1965);
Dudley Fitts, "Afflictions of a New Job," *New York Times Book Review*, 23 March 1958, p. 3;
Henry Hewes, "Hope Springs External," *Saturday Review*, 54 (29 May 1971): 55;

Hewes, "A Minority Report on 'J.B.,' " *Saturday Review*, 42 (3 January 1959): 22-23;
Hewes, "Play by Meters," *Saturday Review*, 37 (6 March 1954): 26;
Joseph Wood Krutch, "The Universe at Stage Center," *Theatre Arts*, 42 (August 1959): 9-11;
Charles Morgan, "The Poet in the Theatre," *The Yale Review*, 24 (Summer 1935): 834-841;
Ernest Sandeen, "This Mortal Story," *Poetry*, 112 (June 1968): 199-201;
Grover Smith, *Archibald MacLeish* (Minneapolis: University of Minnesota Press, 1971);
John Wain, "Mr. MacLeish's New Play," *New Republic*, 157 (22 July 1967): 25-30.
Papers:
Archibald MacLeish's papers are on deposit with the Library of Congress, Washington, D.C.; Yale University, New Haven, Connecticut; and Harvard University, Cambridge, Massachusetts.

DAVID MAMET
(30 November 1947-)

SELECTED PRODUCTIONS: *Lakeboat*, 1970, Marlboro Theatre Workshop, Marlboro, Vt.;
Duck Variations, 1972, St. Nicholas Theater Company, Goddard College, Plainfield, Vt.; 16 June 1976, Cherry Lane Theatre, New York, 273 [performances];
Sexual Perversity in Chicago, Summer 1974, Organic Theater Company, Chicago; 16 June 1976, Cherry Lane Theatre, New York, 273;
Squirrels, 1974, St. Nicholas Theater Company, Chicago;
American Buffalo, 23 November 1975; Goodman Theatre Stage Two, Chicago, 12; 16 February 1977, Ethel Barrymore Theatre, 135;
Reunion, 6 January 1976, St. Nicholas Theater Company, Chicago; 18 October 1979, Circle Repertory Theatre, New York;
The Water Engine, 11 May 1977, St. Nicholas Theater Company, Chicago; 6 March 1978, Plymouth Theatre, New York, 16;
Dark Pony, 14 October 1977, Yale Repertory Theatre, New Haven; 18 October 1979, Circle Repertory Theatre, New York;
A Life in the Theatre, 20 October 1977, Theatre de Lys, New York, 244;
The Woods, 11 November 1977, St. Nicholas Theater Company, Chicago; May 1979, Shakespeare Festival Public Theatre, New York;

The Revenge of the Space Pandas, or Binky Rudich and the Two-Speed Clock, November 1977, St. Nicholas Theater Company, Chicago;
Mr. Happiness, 6 March 1978, Plymouth Theatre, New York, 16;
Lone Canoe, May 1979, Goodman Theatre, Chicago;
The Sanctity of Marriage, 18 October 1979, Circle Repertory Theatre, New York;
Shoeshine, 14 December 1979, Ensemble Studio Theatre, New York.

BOOKS: *American Buffalo* (New York: Grove, 1977);
Sexual Perversity in Chicago and The Duck Variations (New York: Grove, 1978);
The Water Engine and Mr. Happiness (New York: Grove, 1978);
A Life in the Theatre (New York: Grove, 1978);
The Revenge of the Space Pandas or Binky Rudich and the Two-Speed Clock (Chicago: Dramatic Publishing, 1978);
The Woods (New York: Grove, 1979);
Reunion and Dark Pony (New York: Grove, 1979).

"In this country of incessant obbligatos accompanying all activity—music in offices, and elevators, tapes in cars, radios in restaurants—Mamet has heard the ultimate Muzak, the dissonant din of people yammering at one another and not connecting. He is a cosmic eavesdropper who's caught the American aphasia," wrote Jack Kroll in

Newsweek (28 February 1977). The recipient of this plaudit is David Mamet, who has had nearly twenty plays produced since 1972 and has been heralded as the most important new playwright to come out of the 1970s. His reputation has been built on a large body of work, his first national recognition coming with the Broadway opening of *American Buffalo* in February 1977. Although the play received mixed critical notices, nearly everyone conceded that Mamet possessed a unique ear for American idiom. Christopher Porterfield of *Time* said that Mamet recreated a "forlornly eloquent" language with "cadences of loneliness and fear."

Mamet attributes his gift for and obsession with language to various influences dating from his childhood. Born 30 November 1947, Mamet grew up in a Jewish enclave on Chicago's South Side. His mother, the former Leonore June Silver, was a teacher and his father, Bernard Morris Mamet, a lawyer with a penchant for semantics. He remembers his father stopping dinner-time conversation until Mamet or his sister found more precise words for what they were trying to say. After his parents' divorce in the late 1950s, Mamet lived in the Chicago suburb of Olympia Fields with his mother and attended a private school in Chicago. While still in high school, he worked as a busboy at Chicago's Second City, an improvisational comedy cabaret, which spawned such talents as Mike Nichols and Elaine May. To this experience and to his years of piano lessons, Mamet attributes his understanding of the rhythms of action and speech. During his high-school years, Mamet also worked backstage at the Hull House Theatre in Chicago. His love of writing was further encouraged by his father in whose office Mamet spent hours composing dialogue at a typewriter.

Mamet studied literature and drama at the open, experimental Goddard College in Plainfield, Vermont, where he received a B.A. degree in 1969. His first play, a revue called "Camel," was written to fulfill his thesis requirement in English literature.

In the midst of his Goddard education, Mamet took some time off (1968-1969) to study acting at the Neighborhood Playhouse School of the Theatre in New York City, under the direction of Sanford Meisner, an original member of the Group Theatre and a staunch advocate of the Stanislavsky method as interpreted by Meisner and his cofounders of the Group Theatre: Lee Strasberg, Harold Clurman, Cheryl Crawford, and Morris Carnovsky. In an interview with Dick Cavett, Mamet said that his study of the Stanislavsky method, especially the exercises in concentration, taught him about writing. It was there that he learned to understand the principles of continuous action and "moment-to-moment." In another interview, with Ross Wetzsteon, Mamet further explained his debt to the Stanislavsky method for teaching him "the way the language we use, its rhythm, actually determines the way we behave, more than the other way around." Although Mamet spent some time as a supporting actor on the New England straw-hat circuit, he quickly abandoned acting for writing and directing because, he says, "My perceptions of what acting could be were very far off in the distance from my ability to implement them."

After completing his studies at Goddard, Mamet was hired as a teacher at Marlboro College in Marlboro, Vermont, partially on the strength of his idea for an unwritten play, since one of the requirements for this postion was a play that could be put into production. Mamet's *Lakeboat*, a one-act play dealing with the merchant marine, was subsequently staged by his students in 1970. Finding himself back in Chicago after one academic year, Mamet worked as a cabdriver, short-order cook, factory worker, and telephone salesman. Many critics attribute his astute ear for idiom and cadence to this apprenticeship among the working class. Richard Eder wrote, in a lengthy profile on him in the *New York Times*, that Mamet concentrates on the "apparent wasteland of middle American speech . . . the language of the secretary, the salesman, the file clerk, the telephone lineman, the small-time clerk, the semi-literate college kid." Mamet himself, however, dismisses the influence of these experiences on his style by saying he took these jobs to eat, not eavesdrop: "The only materials I gathered were groceries."

In 1971 he returned to Goddard College as a drama instructor and artist-in-residence. In the process of teaching his acting classes Mamet found it easier to write scenes for his students to perform than to involve himself in the sometimes frustrating search for appropriate material by others. With some of his best students, Mamet formed an ensemble acting group, which he called the Saint Nicholas Company. They performed modern classics as well as Mamet's plays. Mamet moved back to Chicago in 1972. Soon several of his plays, among them *Duck Variations* (1972) and *Sexual Perversity in Chicago* (1974), were being given productions at a number of the smaller experimental theatres there, and *Sexual Perversity in Chicago* won the Joseph Jefferson Award, given annually to the best new Chicago play. In August 1974 Mamet, Steven Schachter, William H. Macy, and Patricia Cox founded the Saint Nicholas Players, a reincarnation of the earlier Goddard group with a similar repertoire. He resigned from the group in May 1976 because of "irreconcilable artistic differences."

After a few years of submitting his scripts to New York producers, a double bill consisting of *Duck Variations* and *Sexual Perversity in Chicago* was produced in December 1975 by the Saint Clement's Theatre, an Off-Off-Broadway New York theatre. That twelve-performance showcase led to an Off-Broadway production at the Cherry Lane Theatre which opened on 16 June 1976 and toted up a highly respectable run of 273 performances. *Time* also included them in its list of the "ten best" plays of 1976.

Duck Variations is a series of vignettes about two old men sitting on a park bench. Their musings, which cover the gamut of subjects from the weather to death, are loosely connected by their observations of the habits of ducks. It is a gentle, charming play which Mamet said grew out of "listening to a lot of old Jewish men all my life, particularly my grandfather."

Sexual Perversity in Chicago, also a series of brief scenes, shows the progression of a relationship between a young man and woman and the influence of two of their friends on the development of that relationship. The characters are young, urban, presumably "swinging" 1970s singles. Jack Kroll of *Newsweek* called it a "sleazy sonata of seduction involving two couples." For one of the first times Mamet tackles a theme which recurs in much of his later work: the destructiveness of myths. *Sexual Perversity in Chicago* examines the myth of male sexuality and what must be done to prove and maintain it. Richard Eder said that *Sexual Perversity in Chicago* was a "dazzling set of variations on how the sex hunt destroys communication between men and women." And, indeed, the men and women in this play talk and behave according to the proscriptions of a formalized mating ritual which has nothing to do with their individuality or their capacity to communicate. One critic called the language (which is highly obscene in parts) "too clever," but most agreed that Mamet had made a deadly hit in an outrageously satirical manner on the sometimes unfortunate courting habits of the 1970s.

While *Duck Variations* and *Sexual Perversity in Chicago* played out their run Off Broadway, a revised version of *American Buffalo* opened on Broadway at the Ethel Barrymore Theatre on 16 February 1977. *American Buffalo* had had its premiere at the Goodman Theatre Stage Two in Chicago on 23 November 1975; after twelve performances it moved to the Saint Nicholas Theater Company in Chicago and subsequently, in February 1976, to St. Clement's in New York—the same theatre that had first produced *Duck Variations* and *Sexual Perversity in Chicago*.

Set in a dilapidated junk shop owned by one of the characters, *American Buffalo* has a loosely constructed plot which centers on the efforts of three low-life city toughs to steal a coin collection and more specifically, a particularly valuable American buffalo nickel, which may or may not exist. As in most of Mamet's plays, the plot is so minimal as to provoke criticism of "static" situations and "passive" characters. Mel Gussow of the *New York Times*, however, calls these works plays of "indirect action." This lack of movement seems quite intentional on Mamet's part because, as he told Wetzsteon, "words create behavior . . . our rhythms prescribe our actions." In that same interview Mamet observed, "One critic in Chicago says I write the kind of plays where a character wakes up in Act I and finally gets around to putting on his bathrobe in Act III." In a more specific defense of *American Buffalo* he said in the promotional issue of *Decade* in 1978: "even after Beckett and Pinter, there are people . . . who think that three men's talking for two acts about a break-in which they do not commit does not constitute a plot." About the language of *American Buffalo* Mamet says: "Of course, it's not really spoken speech at all; it's dramatic writing that happens to have rhythms similar to those of spoken speech." In this play and in others, Mamet makes a stylized use of certain portions of dialogue. He explains in the script notation: "Some portions of the dialogue appear in parentheses, which serve to mark a slight change of outlook on the part of the speaker—perhaps a momentary change to a more introspective regard." These parentheses tend to become obtrusive for the reader. They set apart the lines they enclose and make the reader wonder whether he is missing some hidden meaning. Mamet's scripts make large demands upon actors. He borrows

Harold Pinter's use of pauses, though they seem to have a different function in Mamet's plays. In Pinter's plays, the pauses reflect reality while the dialogue verbalizes the characters' subconscious thought patterns. In Mamet's plays the pauses serve to heighten the naturalistic nature of the language because they always appear to be immediately motivated by character and situation.

American Buffalo, like other Mamet plays, does not rely on external plot or movement. What the play provides instead is a subtle development of character created out of inner movement and conflict. This is a risky method which depends upon nuance of mood—a method with which Mamet is successful in varying degrees. The character portraits in *American Buffalo* are, however, skillfully constructed archetypes of modern man involved in the struggle for survival against the crumbling facade of American myth. Mamet himself contends that the play is about the dishonest ethics of the American corporate structure, and "an essential part of American consciousness, which is the ability to suspend an ethical sense and adapt in its stead a popular, accepted mythology and use that to assuage your conscience like everyone else is doing." Most of the critics agreed that though this was an interesting speculation, in reality, the play's import was something less than that—or at least different. Although highly naturalistic in style and tone (the junk-shop set was so lush and detailed as to be distracting), *American Buffalo* works well on a symbolic level. The constant specter of the proud, noble buffalo, a common symbol of the American heritage, but made nearly extinct by the advent of civilization, is juxtaposed with the background of the junk shop, making an arresting battleground for the three principal characters. The shop itself is a place full of old memories and values that have been discarded, a microcosm of a society that can no longer sustain its weak members with the mythical promise of success. Mamet compares the three principals to cavemen since they are forced to use atavistic talents and ultimately each other in order to survive.

Using character as the major plot device greatly increases the importance of how each character speaks and what he says. Christopher Porterfield of *Time* described the speech of these three men as an "incrustation of street slang, nonsequiturs, malapropisms and compulsive obscenity." The effectiveness of the scatological language is diminished by overuse. At best this language is the song of the alienated, the dispossessed—a litany of expletives which stems from a real despair over the

JEAN(C)   I think he made the story up. (PAUSE)
            THIS CHURCH ... THE CRAYONS
            "Wind and fire makes it round..." (PAUSE)

            "Friends and physicians"...And that one:

            "Friends and physicians could not save

            This mortal body fromthe Grave

            Norxskpikxpkpxßrpxpxpapfpapxpapkppp.

            Wkpxp£ppipp

            Do you remember?

EDWARD   Yes.

JEAN   "Til Christ shall cause me to appear ."

            "Nor can the grave confine me here

            When Christ shall call me to appear."

            That was my favorite by far.

            Saint...what? That's funny...(PAUSE) Saint...what?

GAEY ——   Some Gaellic name. It was so old .

            The man said it was built when?|

EDWARD   The tenth century.   (PAUSE)

JEAN   I felt such peace. He said come back the next day.(PAUSE)

    and   It would be open then. You sat on the gravestone and

            you smoked a cigarette. Do youremember?
                            I knew it(PAUSE)
            Something moved us then. To be toghether. I waS moved.

            It made us, what, I thought. More open. To ourselves.

            A certain...what? Shared sensitivity. That our life was

    not endless.

John Hopkins
243-7006
Shirley

loss of civilization, warmth, and humanity. The three characters in *American Buffalo* feed off each other in a parasitic manner, alternately destroying and rebuilding each other's egos. They cannot live harmoniously together, but they would be lost without the constant interaction that forms the basis of their microscopic society.

American Buffalo solidified Mamet's place in contemporary drama. It ran 135 performances and was voted the best American play of 1976-1977 by the New York Drama Critics Circle. In 1976 Mamet was awarded an Obie for distinguished playwriting on the basis of *Sexual Perversity in Chicago* and *American Buffalo*. More importantly, however, Mamet's first Broadway production implied that he was capable of creating a unique American language for the theatre.

In February 1977, *A Life in the Theatre* opened at the Goodman Theatre in Chicago, and on 20 October 1977 a production starring Ellis Rabb and Peter Evans opened at the Off-Broadway Theatre de Lys in New York. *A Life in the Theatre* is a series of vignettes featuring a young actor and an old actor who have vastly different approaches to their craft. It encapsulates in a witty and charming manner the history of twentieth-century acting and the conflict between old and new methods. Mamet describes it as "an old-fashioned play with the connections taken out." The two men interact, both backstage in their dressing room and on stage, in very clever parodies of almost every theatrical style. This play was cited as "a love letter to the theatre" by one critic and as a "tedious, offensively banal caricature of . . . the theatre" by another. But Mel Gussow's reaction in the *New York Times* to the Chicago production is an example of the general opinion: "The play is Mr. Mamet in a light-hearted mood. It is slight but it does not lack consequence. It has bite and it also has a heart."

Also in 1977, Mamet married the actress Lindsay Crouse. His growing reputation was reflected in the invitation from Yale University to give a playwriting course in 1977. The following year he was named associate director and playwright-in-residence of the Goodman Theatre in Chicago. Moreover, his second Broadway production, *The Water Engine*, opened at the Plymouth Theatre on 6 March 1978. This piece was first written for radio and broadcast on "Earplay" on National Public Radio. The stage version was first produced by the Saint Nicholas Theater Company in Chicago in May 1977, and was subsequently produced by Joseph Papp at the New York Shakespeare Festival Public Theatre in December 1977. Papp moved the play to

Broadway in 1978, along with a companion piece, *Mr. Happiness*, hitherto unperformed.

The plot of *The Water Engine* is probably Mamet's most complex to date. Gussow called it so intricate as to be able to "serve as a subject for a Hollywood epic." It functions on two levels of reality as a representation of a Chicago radio studio in 1934 and as an actual radio play. Again Mamet's theme is the pervasiveness and the destructiveness of the American dream, showing how greedy corporations strangle the impulse of private enterprise. The theme, though similar, is handled in a more straightforward manner in *The Water Engine* than in *American Buffalo*. In *The Water Engine*, Charles Lang has invented an engine which runs on water, and after refusing to surrender the plans to an unscrupulous "big business" man, Lang and his sister are murdered—but not before he can mail the plans to a young friend, a radio announcer. The complexities of the play give it a richness and density missing in much of Mamet's other work. The size of the cast, too, is unusual for a Mamet play: there are eight characters in *Water Engine* instead of the usual two or three. The language here verges intentionally on the melodramatic as does the plot, for, as Richard Eder explained in the *New York Times*, for Mamet "Melodrama has become myth."

Mr. Happiness, the short piece accompanying *The Water Engine*, reinforces the style and theme of the longer play. The only character is Mr. Happiness—an unctuous, self-righteous man who answers letters from the lovelorn over the radio. He deals with an old maid afraid to get married because she must care for her aging mother, a policeman in love with a woman not his wife, and an adolescent boy with a limp who cannot find the courage to ask a girl to the prom. Mr. Happiness, in his self-aggrandizing role, pontificates on traditional "American" virtues. To these people with real problems, he offers empty cliches, reflecting the American myth of the "quick answer." Again the themes touched upon are alienation and the inability to communicate on any but the most shallow level.

The Woods, Mamet's next play, received its first production in Chicago at the Saint Nicholas Theater in November 1977 and then was performed at the Shakespeare Festival Public Theatre in May 1979. Mamet describes this play variously as about "a man and a woman on vacation in a family cottage in the north woods coming to grips with the fact of love"; a "two-character play about a crisis of intimacy"; and "a celebration of heterosexual love." Although Richard Eder in his review of the Chicago production thought that this was Mamet's best play to date, Eder was resoundingly outvoted by critics of the New York production. They found Mamet's language "self-conscious" and "affected," and one critic even dismissed it as a "doodle" of an otherwise talented playwright. This criticism is aimed at the stilted quality of the language (he has eliminated the use of contractions), the seemingly meaningless repetitions, and Mamet's focus on the language's rhythm and form rather than on its function and content. The male character was cited as being undeveloped and passive, and again the lack of plot and dramatic conflict was lamented. But Mamet insisted, "What I write about is what I think is missing from our society. And that's communication on a basic level." That could certainly be the theme of *The Woods*, and in the play Mamet seems to accept this condition as immutable. The two characters make little attempt to communicate. They seem to have made up their minds about who they are and what their relationship is and should be. Essential conflict is missing in the play. Ultimately the audience does not care about their plight.

In *Lone Canoe*, Mamet has again pared his language, trying to fulfill his ultimate aim of condensing a speech into a single line or even a single word. *Lone Canoe* played at the Goodman Theatre in May and June 1979. This play seems to be Mamet's attempt to deal with yet another American myth: the noble red man. Julius Novick of the *Village Voice* called attention to its "stiffness" and "hollowness," and even Eder, usually a staunch supporter of Mamet's work, said that here the "sparseness is empty and forced. In *Lone Canoe* Mr. Mamet's tightrope has broken. He has plunged right into the middle of the awkwardness and banality he was hovering above."

In October 1979, Mamet directed three of his one-act plays at Circle Repertory Theatre. (*Reunion* and *Dark Pony* had been previously performed by the Yale Repertory Theatre in 1977.) The first two are very short pieces, barely ten minutes each. *The Sanctity of Marriage* is about a husband and wife on the verge of separation. In the second, *Dark Pony*, a small daughter and her father are driving home late at night, and the father is telling her the story of a young Indian brave and his beloved pony. This play was described as "a lovely, tiny moment of a play" by one critic, but the piece de resistance was a somewhat longer playlet called *Reunion* about a father and his adult daughter. The unhappily married woman has sought out her ex-alcoholic father, now a restaurant employee, whom she has not seen in years. C. Lee Jenner, a critic for *Other Stages*, com-

mented, "Mamet seems to be trying to see how much of the usual dramatic paraphernalia he can pare away from his language and still have something recognizable as theatre. Plot is gone; the situations are static; character development is sketchy. Even setting has been kept to a minimum . . . what Mamet keeps to hold his words to the stage are relationships, needs and mood." Indeed, the relationship in this vignette is probably the strongest manifestation of character interaction and interdependency yet evidenced in his writing. The characters in *Reunion* at least attempt to reach beyond the confines of the sparse language to a new dimension of humanity and warmth. Despite one critic's reaction that Mamet's "words spin out as a somewhat monotonous, if often lifelike, chant celebrating a cliche," *Reunion* suggests the real and deep characters Mamet is capable of creating.

Mamet's most recent production was *Shoeshine*, a short contribution to an Off-Off-Broadway one-act festival at Ensemble Studio Theatre. As two advertising men exchange office banalities while sitting in a shoeshine parlor, a third customer accuses the shoeshine man of stealing his wallet. The play represents another brief moment whittled away to a singular isolated dramatic pause. The content is slight, but Mamet's realistic language is again very effective.

Mamet has written a number of other plays, most of which were produced in his early days in Chicago, primarily at the Saint Nicholas Theater. Among them were *Squirrels*, a piece about writers, and *Marranos*, about the Inquisition in Lisbon. His works also include several children's plays: *Mackinac*, *The Poet and the Rent*, and *The Revenge of the Space Pandas or Binky Rudich and the Two-Speed Clock*. He has recently completed the screenplay for a remake of James M. Cain's novel *The Postman Always Rings Twice* for United Artists and has also written the screenplay for a movie version of *Sexual Perversity in Chicago*.

Mamet's work is so fragile that, more than most other dramatic work, it depends strongly on the understanding and delicacy of his directors and actors. He is a playwright of nuance and mood. His work is uneven, and some parts are outright failures. But Mamet introduces most of his plays in Chicago's Off-Loop or New York's Off-Off-Broadway theatres, where his experiments are tested. Mamet is a playwright who takes the risk of failure.   *–Patricia Lewis and Terry Browne*

References:

Richard Eder, "David Mamet's New Realism," *New*

York Times, 12 March 1978, VI: 40, 42, 45, 47; Ross Wetzsteon, Interview with David Mamet, *Village Voice*, 5 July 1976, pp. 101, 103-104.

CARSON MCCULLERS
(19 February 1917-29 September 1967)

PRODUCTIONS: *The Member of the Wedding*, 5 January 1950, Empire Theatre, New York, 501 [performances];
The Square Root of Wonderful, 30 October 1957, National Theatre, New York, 45.

SELECTED BOOKS: *The Heart Is a Lonely Hunter* (Boston: Houghton Mifflin, 1940; London: Cresset, 1943);
Reflections in a Golden Eye (Boston: Houghton Mifflin, 1941; London: Cresset, 1942);
The Member of the Wedding (Boston: Houghton Mifflin, 1946; London: Cresset, 1947);
The Member of the Wedding: A Play (New York: New Directions, 1951);
The Ballad of the Sad Café: The Novels and Stories of Carson McCullers (Boston: Houghton Mifflin, 1951; London: Cresset, 1952);
Collected Short Stories and The Novel The Ballad of the Sad Café (Boston: Houghton Mifflin, 1955);
The Square Root of Wonderful (Boston: Houghton Mifflin, 1958; London: Cresset, 1958);
Clock Without Hands (Boston: Houghton Mifflin, 1961; London: Cresset, 1961);
Sweet As a Pickle and Clean As a Pig (Boston: Houghton Mifflin, 1964; London: Cape, 1965);
The Mortgaged Heart, ed. Margarita G. Smith (Boston: Houghton Mifflin, 1971; London: Barrie & Jenkins, 1972).

Carson McCullers is best known as a novelist, for it is her early novels, written when she was in her twenties, that assure her position among the preeminent writers of her generation. But McCullers's published work also includes two plays, and the first of these, a dramatization of her novel *The Member of the Wedding* (1946), established her reputation as a playwright as well. The play is of interest for several reasons. It is, as Gerald Weales has noted, one of the few examples in American drama of a novelist's successfully adapting her own work for the stage. Furthermore, its dramatic structure was innovative, rejecting conventional plotting devices in favor of an emphasis on character, theme, and mood. A commercial and critical triumph, the play ran 501 performances, won the New York Drama Critics Circle Award in 1950 for best play of the season, took two Donaldson awards in 1949-1950 as best play and best first play by an author, and was included in Burns Mantle's *Best Plays of 1949-1950*. Its enthusiastic reception led the National Institute of Arts and Letters, in selecting McCullers for membership in 1952, to cite "her rare talent as a dramatist." This glowing judgment proved premature. Her second play, *The Square Root of Wonderful* (1957), was a dismal failure, and she never wrote another.

There is little in McCullers's background to suggest that she would become a Broadway playwright. At the time she wrote the dramatic version of *The Member of the Wedding* she had seen, she said, "only about ten plays in [her] life, including high school *Hamlets*." Only two of these plays had been Broadway productions. Nevertheless, she had long exhibited a flair for the dramatic. One of the recollections she often shared with interviewers was of her first venture into playwriting. Born Lula Carson Smith, she grew up in Columbus, Georgia, where as a teenager she discovered Eugene O'Neill. Her admiration for his work inspired her first play, which she described as "a three-acter about revenge and incest." Her next effort was a two-character play entitled "The Fire of Life," in which Jesus Christ and Nietzsche confronted each other speaking rhymed verse.

The young writer soon abandoned drama in favor of short stories and novels, however. At the age of seventeen she traveled alone to New York, where she studied writing at Columbia University and New York University. Her first published story, "Wunderkind," appeared in *Story* magazine in 1936, when she was nineteen. Three novels followed: *The Heart Is a Lonely Hunter* in 1940, *Reflections in a Golden Eye* in 1941, and *The Member of the Wedding* in 1946. Like all McCullers's best work, these early novels are Southern in setting and material and share as a primary theme the essential, painful solitude of the human heart. The critical attention they attracted established McCullers as a major literary figure.

In 1937 she married Reeves McCullers, whom she later divorced and remarried. It was not a traditional marriage; though they were close friends for many years, the couple lived together only sporadically. Carson McCullers often preferred the company and attentions of other creative people. During the early years of her career she was, in Gore Vidal's words, "*the* young writer," highly publicized

Tennessee Williams and Carson McCullers

and admired by members of the literary establishment.

It was in this period that McCullers met Tennessee Williams, who was to be her lifelong friend and who first suggested that she adapt *The Member of the Wedding* for the stage. She spent the summer of 1946 on Nantucket Island with Williams, he working on *Summer and Smoke*, she on the dramatic version of *The Member of the Wedding*. Though they worked, Williams says, at the same table, reading their work to each other in the evenings, he discounts any direct influence on McCullers's play. To her biographer, Virginia Spencer Carr, he wrote, "In no sense of the word was I Carson's mentor. . . . Carson accepted almost no advice about how to adapt *The Member of the Wedding*. I did not suggest lines to her more than once or twice, and then she would usually have her own ideas and say, 'Tenn, honey, thank you, but I know all I need to know.' "

Between Nantucket and Broadway the play went through a number of revisions, including an ill-fated attempt at collaboration with another playwright, Greer Johnson. The play as finally produced was not the collaboration but McCullers's

own version, revised by her with further suggestions from Tennessee Williams.

It is probably true, however, that in writing her play McCullers was guided more by her novel than by Williams's advice. The novel's lyrical mood, its three sensitive characterizations, and even much of its idiosyncratic dialogue are transferred to the stage almost intact. Like the earlier work, the dramatic version of *The Member of the Wedding* is a poignant study of adolescent pain and growth. Its central character, Frankie Addams, is an awkward, motherless twelve-year-old living in a small Southern town. Excluded by her peers, she spends the long summer afternoons in the kitchen with John Henry West, her seven-year-old cousin, and Berenice Sadie Brown, the earthy, eloquent Negro housekeeper.

In the play as in the novel, the theme is loneliness. Frankie, trapped in the terrible void between childhood and adolescence, laments, "The trouble with me is that for a long time I have been just an 'I' person. . . . All people belong to a 'we' except me. . . . Not to belong to a 'we' makes you too lonesome." The other characters counterpoint Frankie's loneliness. The child, John Henry, has yet to face the complexities of Frankie's world; he needs only to be accepted by Frankie and Berenice. The adult, Berenice, knows loneliness as fundamental and inescapable. She has had four marriages, three of them loveless, and she is a black woman in a white world. A secondary theme of racial injustice is suggested through the bitter violence of Berenice's foster brother, Honey Camden Brown.

An often-voiced criticism of the play, first expressed by New York reviewers and echoed by subsequent critics, is that it is structurally weak. A typical comment was that of Brooks Atkinson in his *New York Times* review: "The play has no beginning, middle or end." Certainly it is not the well-made play audiences expected in 1950. The first two acts are virtually plotless, consisting of a series of vignettes in which the three characters share their memories and fantasies. Yet while the structure is unconventional, it is theatrically sound, for the sketches are unified by a clear, urgent dramatic action, Frankie's intense need to find her "we of me." Harold Clurman, who directed the 1950 production, identifies the play's central action as a "struggle for connection." Frankie pursues that struggle relentlessly. Seizing upon her brother's wedding as a symbol of the connection she longs for, she makes elaborate plans for becoming a member of the wedding and going away with her brother and his bride.

The third act erupts into activity. Frankie is ejected from the car in which the bride and groom are leaving and runs away; John Henry dies; Honey hangs himself in jail. Yet the delicate play is not transformed into melodrama, as some critics have charged, for its focus remains constant. The decision to limit the action to the kitchen (a barroom scene was cut in the out-of-town tryouts) reinforces the theme of loneliness by centering attention not on the tragic events but rather on their effects on Frankie and Berenice. As the play ends, Frankie has found her "we" in friends her own age. Essentially untouched by tragedy, she has yet to experience the irrevocable loneliness that, in McCullers's works, accompanies maturity. In the final scene Berenice is left alone in the empty kitchen, her solitude intensified and inconsolable.

In performance, *The Member of the Wedding* is an emotionally powerful play, artfully merging character, theme, and action. New York theatre critics, recognizing the play's appeal but perplexed by its unusual structure, attributed much of the success of the 1950 production to its stars, Julie Harris, Ethel Waters, and Brandon de Wilde, and to

its director, Clurman. More recent criticism has correctly recognized the play's fluid structure as one of its strengths. John Gassner and Clive Barnes are among several critics who have noted that the play's "plotless" structure is in the tradition of Chekhov. Reviewing a 1975 New York revival, Barnes found McCullers's play reminiscent of *The Cherry Orchard*, citing her foreshadowing of social revolution in the South and her use of a "Chekhovian ending."

McCullers was exhilarated by the recognition and the financial rewards her play brought. She sold the film rights to Hollywood producer Stanley Kramer for $75,000, using part of the money to buy her mother's home in Nyack, New York, where she lived much of the rest of her life. With characteristic intensity, she had, she said, fallen in love with the theatre, and she soon drafted a second play. But the years before its 1957 production as *The Square Root of Wonderful* were difficult ones for McCullers. In 1953 her husband committed suicide in France, where they had been living. Frightened by his despondency, she had returned to America some weeks before his death, and she refused to mourn him. Then in 1955 the death of her mother, on whom she was particularly dependent, affected her profoundly.

These personal tragedies, McCullers later

Jo Mielziner, Carson McCullers, and José Quintero

said, inspired the final version of *The Square Root of Wonderful*. Its central character, Mollie Lovejoy, is a naive and charming woman whose "sense of joy in life" was modeled after the playwright's mother. Mollie's ex-husband, Phillip, is, like Reeves McCullers, a would-be writer who takes his own life. Mollie's relationship to Phillip is much like that of Carson and Reeves McCullers; finally, the play is clear only when it is viewed as McCullers's attempt to exorcise her guilt over her husband's death. She intended a life-death theme: Phillip, incapable of love, chooses death, while Mollie, who loves life, learns that her love cannot save him. The theme is only tenuously developed, however, and it must compete for focus with a jumble of other characteristic McCullers themes. The pain and loneliness of love and the passage of time are suggested, but neither theme is clearly developed.

Nor are the blurred themes the play's only weakness. It is flawed by lifeless characters, two of whom, Phillip's mother and sister, are maladroit caricatures of Amanda and Laura Wingfield in Tennessee Williams's *The Glass Menagerie*. The plot, though more conventionally structured than that of *The Member of the Wedding*, lacks the focus of a strong dramatic action; Mollie's search for love is much more tentative than Frankie's.

The play's problems were apparent long before its New York opening. Since its first draft years earlier, *The Square Root of Wonderful* had undergone a number of revisions, several of them guided by McCullers's close friend, Arnold Saint Subber, who produced it. By the time it opened on Broadway in 1957, it had been subjected to a series of directors and to so many rewrites that the disastrous reviews came as no surprise. Advance ticket sales kept it running for forty-five performances.

McCullers was devastated by this failure. She had been in poor health for years, having suffered her first stroke when she was only twenty-four. In the decade following the production of *The Square Root of Wonderful*, she endured a series of painful illnesses, and her work suffered. She never completed another play. Edward Albee dramatized her novella *The Ballad of the Sad Café* in 1963, an adaptation which McCullers encouraged but which she found disappointing. At the time of her death in 1967, she had been collaborating with Mary Rodgers on a musical version of *The Member of the Wedding*. The project was abandoned, however, and *F. Jasmine Addams*, the musical which was produced in 1971 at New York's Circle in the Square, does not use McCullers's script but that of Theodore Mann.

In her preface to the published version of *The*

Square Root of Wonderful, McCullers wrote, "It is rare that a writer is equally skilled as a novelist and a playwright." Certainly, though McCullers's reputation as a novelist is secure, her talent for playwriting is more difficult to assess. In recent years, few have tried; serious criticism of her plays has been rare. An attempt to evaluate her contribution to the theatre must take into account her admittedly scant knowledge of the theatre as well as the uneven quality of her two plays. The inevitable conclusion is that McCullers was not a skilled playwright; rather, she was an intuitive one. She acknowledged the improvisational design of *The Member of the Wedding*: "I must say I did not realize the proper dimensions of this play, the values of the unseen qualities involved, until the work had taken on its own life." In this first play, written in her early creative years and based on her own soundly constructed novel, her intuition served her well. But in writing *The Square Root of Wonderful*, she had no previous design to build upon, and her dramatic instincts, decimated by illness and time, were unreliable. She left the American theatre a small and strange legacy: one sensitive, theatrically effective play, and another that is of interest only because its author is Carson McCullers.

–Sara Nalley

Periodical Publications:
"How I Began to Write," *Mademoiselle*, 27 (September 1948): 191, 256-257;
"The Vision Shared," *Theatre Arts*, 34 (April 1950): 28-30.

Bibliography:
Robert F. Kiernan, *Katherine Anne Porter and Carson McCullers: A Reference Guide* (Boston: G.K. Hall, 1976).

References:
Brooks Atkinson, "At the Theatre," *New York Times*, 6 January 1950, p. 26;
Clive Barnes, " 'Member of the Wedding' Wears Well," *New York Times*, 3 January 1975, p. 14;
Virginia Spencer Carr, *The Lonely Hunter: A Biography of Carson McCullers* (Garden City: Doubleday, 1975);
Harold Clurman, *Lies Like Truth* (New York: Macmillan, 1958), pp. 62-64;
Clurman, "Some Preliminary Notes for *The Member of the Wedding*," in *Directors on Directing: A Source Book of the Modern Theater*, ed. Toby Cole and Helen Krich Chinoy, revised edition (Indianapolis: Bobbs-Merrill, 1963), pp. 380-389;

Oliver Evans, *The Ballad of Carson McCullers* (New York: Coward-McCann, 1966);

John Gassner, *The Theatre in Our Times* (New York: Crown, 1954), pp. 78-79;

Alfred Kazin, *The Inmost Leaf* (New York: Harcourt, Brace, 1955), pp. 127-135;

Margaret B. McDowell, *Carson McCullers* (Boston: Twayne, 1980);

Jordan Y. Miller, *American Dramatic Literature: Ten Modern Plays in Historical Perspective* (New York: McGraw-Hill, 1961), pp. 426-428;

John van Druten, *Playwright At Work* (New York: Harper, 1953), pp. 189-190;

Gerald Weales, *American Drama Since World War II* (New York: Harcourt, Brace & World, 1962), pp. 174-179, 198.

Papers:

Carson McCullers's papers are in the Humanities Research Center at the University of Texas, Austin.

TERRENCE MCNALLY
(3 November 1939-)

SELECTED PRODUCTIONS: *The Lady of the Camellias*, adapted from Giles Cooper's play based on Alexandre Dumas's novel, 20 March 1963, Winter Garden Theatre, New York, 13 [performances];

And Things That Go Bump in the Night, 4 February 1964, Guthric Theater, Minneapolis; 26 April 1965, Royale Theatre, New York, 16;

Tour, in *The Scene*, November 1967, Mark Taper Forum, Los Angeles; in *Collision Course*, 8 May 1968, Cafe Au Go Go, New York, 80; 7 August 1968, Berkshire Theatre Festival, Stockbridge, Mass.;

Next, 7 August 1968, Berkshire Theatre Festival, Stockbridge, Mass.; 10 February 1969, Greenwich Mews Theatre, New York, 707;

Botticelli, 7 August 1968, Berkshire Theatre Festival, Stockbridge, Mass.; 7 October 1969, Mark Taper Forum, Los Angeles;

Sweet Eros and *Witness*, 21 November 1968, Gramercy Arts Theatre, New York, 78;

Noon, in *Morning, Noon and Night*, by McNally, Israel Horovitz, and Leonard Melfi, 28 November 1968, Henry Miller's Theatre, New York, 52;

Cuba Si!, 9 December 1968, Theatre de Lys, New York, 2;

Bringing It All Back Home, 1969, La Mama Experimental Theatre Club, New York;

Bad Habits: Ravenswood and Dunelawn, 1971, John Drew Theatre, East Hampton, New York; 4 February 1974, Astor Place Theatre (transferred 5 May 1974 to Booth Theatre), New York, 126;

Where Has Tommy Flowers Gone?, 7 October 1971, Eastside Playhouse, New York, 78;

Let It Bleed, in *City Stops*, 8 May 1972, Bronx Community College, New York;

Whiskey, 29 April 1973, Theatre at St. Clement's Church, New York, 7;

The Tubs, January 1974, Yale Repertory Theatre, New Haven; revised as *The Ritz*, 20 January 1975, Longacre Theatre, New York, 400.

BOOKS: *And Things That Go Bump in the Night* (New York: Dramatists Play Service, 1966);

Apple Pie: Three One-Act Plays (New York: Dramatists Play Service, 1968)—includes *Tour*, *Next*, and *Botticelli*;

Sweet Eros, Next, and Other Plays (New York: Random House, 1969)—includes *Botticelli*, *Next*, *¡Cuba Si!*, *Sweet Eros*, and *Witness*;

Noon, in *Morning, Noon and Night*, by Israel Horovitz, McNally, and Leonard Melfi (New York: Random House, 1969);

¡Cuba Si!, Bringing It All Back Home, Last Gasps (New York: Dramatists Play Service, 1970);

Where Has Tommy Flowers Gone? (New York: Dramatists Play Service, 1972);

Whiskey (New York: Dramatists Play Service, 1973);

Bad Habits (New York: Dramatists Play Service, 1974);

The Ritz and Other Plays (New York: Dodd, Mead, 1976)—includes *The Ritz*, *Bad Habits*, *Where Has Tommy Flowers Gone?*, *And Things That Go Bump in the Night*, *Whiskey*, and *Bringing It All Back Home*.

Terrence McNally, known primarily for *Next*, *Where Has Tommy Flowers Gone?*, *Bad Habits*, and *The Ritz*, achieved prominence as a bitingly comic writer in 1968, when six of his plays were produced. His subjects are the major upheavals of the 1960s and 1970s: the Vietnam War, fascism, the draft, middle-class morality, political revolution, presidential assassination, youth and rebellion, popular culture, and changes in sexual codes. His more recent work is exuberant, lyrical, and farcical, sharply contrasting with the tone of outrage and anger noted in the beginning of his career.

Born in Saint Petersburg, Florida, McNally grew up in Corpus Christi, Texas. His parents, Hubert Arthur and Dorothy Rapp McNally, both native New Yorkers, introduced him to the theatre by taking him at the age of seven to see *Annie Get Your Gun* (1946), starring Ethel Merman. After his graduation from high school, McNally left Corpus Christi in 1956 to attend Columbia University in New York. In his senior year he collaborated on a college variety show. After graduating Phi Beta Kappa in 1960 with a bachelor's degree in English, he went to Mexico on a Henry Evans Traveling Fellowship which he had won for his work in a creative writing class. In Mexico he wrote a long one-act play which he sent to the Actors Studio in New York. Molly Kazan, wife of director Elia Kazan, saw promise in the script but also realized that the playwright had no theatrical experience. She offered McNally a job as stage manager at the Actors Studio, and as a result he became acquainted with the Kazans, Lee Strasberg, and Kim Hunter while learning how plays are produced. Also through the studio's connections, McNally was offered a job as a private tutor in Europe. Never having been to Europe, he decided to take the offer. When he arrived in Europe in 1961, he discovered, much to his surprise, that he had been hired to teach the children of John Steinbeck. For the next year McNally toured the world with the Steinbeck family, forming a close relationship with them.

The following year McNally received the Stanley Award for the best original play at the New York City Writer's Convention, held at Wayne College on Staten Island; his entry was "This Side of the Door" (after revisions it became *And Things That Go Bump in the Night*). Also in 1962 Susan Strasberg introduced him to director Franco Zeffirelli, who was interested in staging the younger Alexander Dumas's *The Lady of the the Camellias*. Zeffirelli asked McNally to rework the adaptation written by English dramatist Giles Cooper. Although Zeffirelli's production, which opened on Broadway in March 1963, closed after thirteen performances, McNally had received his first Broadway credit. During this period McNally shared an apartment with Edward Albee. The two exchanged ideas and commented on each other's work, but McNally did not rely upon the already well-known Albee to have his plays produced. McNally's first recognition for independent production came in 1964, when he received a grant from the Rockefeller Foundation to produce *And Things That Go Bump in the Night*.

The play was scheduled to be produced along with two of Arthur Kopit's one-act plays, *The Day the Whores Came Out to Play Tennis* and *Mhil'daiim*, at the Tyrone Guthrie Theatre in Minneapolis. McNally and Kopit became the center of a sensational scandal when the University of Minnesota removed the production from the list of plays to be seen by their season-ticket subscribers on grounds that it was offensive to public taste. Both playwrights were indignant at this censorship: Kopit withdrew his plays, but McNally went ahead with production. The fight over censorship had brought to the unknown playwright a great deal of publicity, and reviewers from New York were present at the premiere on 4 February 1964 to evaluate the play that had caused so much scandal. *And Things That Go Bump in the Night* came to the attention of producer Theodore Mann, who decided to produce it in New York.

The play presents a family of unrepresentative types who inhabit a combination basement apartment and atom-bomb shelter. The father, Fa, sits almost silently in a corner, occasionally uttering prophetic cries of doom while Grandfa, an old, old man, a moral center of the action, eagerly looks forward to the coming morning when he is to be removed to a home for the insane. At the head of this clan is the mother, Ruby, a former diva given to oracular pronouncements via tape-recorded messages, who appears to be nothing less than the devil incarnate. The son, Sigfrid, twenty-one years old, and the daughter, thirteen-year-old pig-tailed Lakme, are a demented duo who entice innocent strangers to the basement for evenings of macabre game-playing and torture. Tonight's victim is Clarence, who was a friend of Sigfrid's in elementary school. Clarence has been picked up by the marauding youngsters while he was at a protest rally carrying a placard which says on one side "There Is Something Out There" and on the other "We Shall Prevail." As the play begins Ruby's strident voice is uttering commands, endearments, conciliations, Italian-language interjections, and non sequiturs. Ruby is desperately afraid of whatever evil lurks out there in the world; her paranoia sets the tone for the play. This paranoia is emphasized by the fact that the family's living quarters are sealed off from the world by a heavy iron door, and the grounds are encircled by a lethal, electrically charged fence.

The characters spend most of the play alternately bickering and making up, with much sibling rivalry and a hint of oedipal fixation. None of them has even a touch of human sympathy. McNally's message is transmitted through Ruby's recorded, nihilistic communiques which deny man's worth and the wisdom of institutions: man "shall *not* inherit the earth . . . it has already disinherited *us*." With a sort of insane logic Ruby reasons that as people are now without faith they must find their way in the darkness, which is light enough. As people are without hope, they must turn to despair, which has its own consolations. And if people are without charity, they must "suckle the bitter root of its absence." This vision is delivered in sadness, for Ruby knows that the cruelty she and her family inflict on others, and the pain that is their only reminder they are alive, are but temporary antidotes. Ruby fears the monstrous thing that lies out there in the darkness, which by implication is worse than the hell she creates.

Sigfrid has invited Clarence to the house to make homosexual advances to him. Clarence is not a completely unwilling victim, and Sigfrid succeeds in seducing him while Lakme takes photographs without Clarence's knowledge. Ruby, Lakme, and Sigfrid then sadistically play a game with Clarence, berating and humiliating him with slides and a taped soundtrack presentation of the seduction. Clarence flees outside into the night and is electrocuted by the fence. Clarence's death causes Sigfrid to question the virtue of their actions, but Ruby replies that in order to survive in this horrible world they need guests like Clarence to comfort them. At the end of the play, however, Ruby and the family are threatened by a loud and menacing thumping outside their door.

Reviews of McNally's first play were mainly unfavorable; critics condemned it for its violence, dismal vision of mankind, and its bizarre action. Many compared it unfavorably to Charles Addams's cartoons and to Edward Albee's *Tiny Alice*. The play had its admirers, however. The profusion of letters attacking the *New York Times*'s negative review caused Howard Taubman to write a second article defending his first, and the *Village Voice* published a favorable review of the play.

From 1963 to 1965 McNally was the film critic for the *Seventh Art* magazine; in 1966 he received a Guggenheim Fellowship for playwriting, which allowed him to concentrate on writing one-acts. In November 1967 *Tour* opened at the Mark Taper Forum in Los Angeles. During the 1968-1969 season he had seven one-act plays produced: *Next, Botticelli, Sweet Eros, Witness, Noon, ¡Cuba Si!,* and *Bringing It All Back Home*. It is notable that four of these plays focus upon the Vietnam War, either directly by representing soldiers in the war, or indirectly by dramatizing the schism between those who remained at home and those subjected to being drafted and killed. *Tour*, presented at New York's Cafe Au Go-Go in *Collision Course*, "an omnibus of eleven plays" by various authors, depicts the surrealistic journey of an American couple. While touring the Italian countryside, they write a postcard to their son in Vietnam and suddenly have hallucinations that transform the ordinary vistas of rural Italy into the horrifying landscape of Southeast Asia.

Despite the play's brevity, McNally deftly draws a picture of complacent Americans who even in their desire to appear liberal and unprejudiced betray their xenophobia and provincialism. The man, Mr. Wilson, proclaims that they are not the "run-of-the-mill American Express oriented, enterobioform, boiled-water, bourbon-daiquiris-in-the-Dolomites-type tourist," and then proceeds to hurl racial slurs at their inept driver. Superficially the couple are Babbitts showing disdain for the unfamiliar, yet they become almost sympathetic figures as their world begins crumbling before their startled eyes. Their spiritual expedition through a hostile world reveals a collapse of external security, a moral framework eroded by the pressures of a society in which they are as much victims as victimizers. At the heart of the play is their pathetic concern for their soldier son who is fighting and, in their fantasy, napalming helpless civilians and leperous mendicants. The couple are frightened at their shared responsibility for such horrors but have no way to redeem themselves.

McNally's ability as a writer of comedy was confirmed with his extremely popular and successful farce *Next*, produced on 7 August 1968 at the Berkshire Theatre Festival in Massachusetts. Opening on a double bill with Elaine May's *Adaptation* (1969) at the Greenwich Mews Theatre in New York, it ran for 707 performances. The central character of *Next*, Marion Cheever, is caught in an implausible situation. Forty-eight years old and overweight, Cheever has been ordered to take a physical examination before being drafted into the army. The examination is conducted by a female, Sergeant Tech, whose first words to him are "you have ten seconds to strip." The stolid implacability and asexuality of his female examiner only increases Cheever's nervousness; Cheever, having no desire to enter the army, wants to fail the examination. At one point the modest man drapes the American flag about his rotund figure, but his dignity is finally stripped away as he fails the psychological test, an inane display of one-upmanship. While Cheever does not want to be

drafted, he feels disgraced when found unacceptable. After the sergeant has exited, Cheever adopts her pompous mannerisms and authoritarian attitude and delivers a monologue that parodies the whole examination. As he continues, his voice becomes more strident, and he releases his frustrations in a virtuoso monologue which questions how society determines who is and is not acceptable.

Harold Clurman concluded that *Next* launched "an exacerbated attack on the mechanics of a civilization which is taken as an acceptable, because inescapable, norm. The flaw—though it should be emphasized that this sketch is one of McNally's better efforts—is that the farcical opening fails to anticipate the final onslaught." The reviews in general were extremely favorable, praising both McNally and the lead actor, James Coco.

Botticelli opened with *Next* at the Berkshire Theatre Festival. Set in the jungle of Vietnam, its situation is presented with chilling simplicity: two soldiers, Wayne and Stu, are seen crouching ready to ambush the enemy. To pass the time, they play an intellectual guessing game called Botticelli. Wayne has selected a famous cultural hero of history. Stu tries to guess the identity, guided only by the infor-

mation that the name begins with *P*. Names such as Proust, Paderewski, Pushkin, Pasternak, Pepys, and Pope, all incorrect, suggest a world that is in sharp contrast to the one in which they are operating. Stu never guesses the right name, but together they shoot the enemy. *Botticelli* demonstrates how soldiers of necessity construct methods to keep from going crazy in the midst of senseless violence; also it suggests that there is no reason for the violence—it, too, has become a game without an answer.

Sweet Eros and *Witness* opened as a double bill in November 1968. The protagonist of *Sweet Eros* is one of McNally's recurring types—a personable, engaging, talkative young man of Byronic sensibilities, colossal ego, and sadistic yearnings who is fulfilling a fantasy. He has found that he cannot love or be loved. Because he requires a passive receptacle for the outpourings of his ego, without engaging any emotional responsibilities, he kidnaps a girl, takes her to his place in the country, ties her to a chair, and strips her naked. Meanwhile, he tells her his life story. The girl struggles initially, but seems quite reconciled in the end. The implication is that all people want is to be taken care of—to quit struggling against the forces of evil, darkness, chaos—and to retreat into dependency. The engaging and quick humor of the young man in part compensates for his cruelty. The play suggests that "people don't like to be loved" because "what they want is simpler."

Witness is a humorous treatment of another personable young man who attempts to assassinate the president of the United States. Because he does not want his actions to be interpreted as the product of a deranged mind, he captures an encyclopedia salesman and ties him to a chair so that the salesman can witness the attempted slaying and testify subsequently in court that the young man understood the nature of his actions. In the first scene the young man engages in an obscene phone conversation with the girl upstairs who is conducting a survey on happiness for the president's Commission on Our National Purpose. As the conversation ends, a window washer, who has periodically appeared through a backstage window, enters the room. A representative of the vulgar American proletariat, a "Native New Yorker," mad at the world and raging at the excess of freedom his class has been granted, he plans to write a book about all the queer things he has witnessed on the job, calling it "Things I Seen Washing Windows." He thinks shooting the president is a good idea. The protagonist also invites the girl upstairs in to witness the assassination. Neither the window washer nor the upstairs neighbor finds it unusual that a man sits bound and gagged in the chair next to them. McNally, in a rather humorous manner, shows how the American public has become desensitized to brutal occurrences. Moreover, the American public does not want to know what takes place around them; they only want to be left alone. The window washer, who refers to himself as a man of the street, even though he is forty stories up, reveals how people are afraid of responsibility: "I've got so much fucken freedom I don't know what to think anymore. . . . give me some rules that you can make stick for a change, draw some line, and watch me tow it." *Sweet Eros* and *Witness* both emphasize the need for greater attention to one's responsibilities, be they personal or social. The unifying image of *Witness* and *Sweet Eros* is the individual bound to a chair: in each play a desperate act seems to be the result of an abdication of personal and social responsibility. The young man in *Witness* feels compelled to act, not because he believes in killing people, but because he wants to prove that killing people changes nothing.

In *Noon*, produced in 1968 on a bill with *Morning* by Israel Horovitz and *Night* by Leonard Melfi, is McNally's most compassionate play to date. It still retains the characteristic type of humor apparent in the earlier plays, but it also suggests McNally's new concern with characterization as he studies the problems of interpersonal communication. Unlike many of his other plays, it has a positive ending.

The plot of *Noon* is McNally's most bizarre. An ambiguous, unseen character named Dale has placed personal advertisements, and answered others, for various kinds of sexual partners. The first to arrive at the noon rendezvous point, a deserted loft in New York City, are Kerry, a homosexual in his early thirties, and Asher, a virginal heterosexual in his twenties, each of whom mistakes the other for Dale. While they talk past each other, revealing their sexual preferences but generally not communicating, Kerry's glib talk and quick hands have Asher stripped to his underwear. But after Asher sniffs the amyl nitrate capsule Kerry has brought, he falls asleep while Kerry undresses. The next person to arrive is Allegra, a bored suburban housewife who was content until her "creep-liberal-intellectual-lawyer husband" introduced her to pornographic books and then could not keep up with her sexually. Allegra tells her sorry story to the sleeping Asher while Kerry hides in the closet. Just as she finishes undressing, Asher awakens, is confronted with his fantasy come alive and alarmingly close, and runs screaming from the room. As Allegra curses at Dale (whom she believes Asher to be), Beryl and Cecil, a middle-aged, sadomasochistic couple from Westchester County, arrive.

Eventually all five gather to figure out who Dale is. With such a group of people one might expect an orgy, but ironically their tastes are incompatible. In the midst of a general depression Dale telephones from a bowling alley in Paramus, New Jersey, and invites everybody but the homosexual for a party. A general exodus ensues. Kerry is left despondent but putting up a defiant front. Alone in the room he begins to gather his things and make ready to leave. And then he hears a distant voice on the stairs. Kerry, believing it to be Dale, spruces himself up and begins to smile. Curtain.

In this tightly controlled play, McNally demonstrates the human desire to communicate and the unhappiness that results from improperly received signals. While the Young Man in *Sweet Eros* has already given up on communication, the characters in *Noon* are so eager to relate that they advertise for companionship. That Dale tricks them is disillusioning, but they continue to hope. Their need for some sort of communion is so great, and the alternatives so nonexistent, that they are willing to risk further humiliation in a wild goose chase to Paramus. Despite his rejection by Dale, Kerry, the character most sympathetically portrayed, is eager to hope again, unwilling to entertain the possibility that the unknown final caller might not be Dale at all, but only a sixth misguided seeker, come newly upon the scene to start the tragic cycle spinning again. Again McNally keeps his ending tentative. In *And Things That Go Bump in the Night* the curtain falls upon a horrified family awaiting the coming of an ever louder thumping menace, but the menace remains outside in the dark. Kerry's promised assignation is still on the stairs, and the play ends with neither affirmation nor denial.

¡Cuba Si! also demonstrates McNally's developing talent for characterization. A whimsical look at revolution, the play presents a girl called Cuba, a supporter of Fidel Castro, who has for two years been permitted to establish a "beachhead" in Central Park, while she spouts revolutionary rhetoric and awaits the arrival of fellow Castro supporters. Though most bystanders regard her as merely a curious tourist attraction, a crusty old *New York Times* reporter reluctantly allows her to engage him in a virtually nonstop talkathon. The play exploits many polarities—the Left versus the Right, young versus old, for example—and there is much ranting and raving. But *¡Cuba Si!* is sustained by its personable young female protagonist, whose at-

titude toward her revolutionary purpose can be read as a statement of McNally's serious commitment to his art and in part an explanation of his method. After Cuba has "dispatched" a would-be infiltrator of her camp, she turns to the shaken reporter and exclaims, "That's revolutionary politics, sweetheart. You think because I laugh I play games?" In the same way, McNally creates a surface of hilarious, hysterical comedy to cover his messages.

Bringing It All Back Home (1969), McNally's fourth treatment of the Vietnam conflict, captures the American nuclear family at all its white middle-class worst. The son is on drugs and seems concerned only with having sex with his girl friend. The daughter has already had one abortion and is afraid that others will gossip, even though it is common knowledge that most of the girls in her high school are also sexually active. The father wears a flashy bowling shirt and windbreaker, kisses the daughter with a little too much eagerness, and shouts commands in military fashion, while the mother walks about with her head in a portable hair dryer, effectively shutting out the world. They are all very excited because the body of the older son Jimmy, a soldier, is being brought home today, and a television news team is coming to interview the family. The black newscaster, Miss Horne, is an extremely effective satiric weapon. She bosses the family as they try to please her by displaying their very meager talents for the national television audience. Once in a while, when the other characters are offstage, Jimmy sits up in his coffin and addresses the audience. While the others have made up events to suit themselves, Jimmy tells the truth about his death: he stepped on a land mine, and "after a minute or two it hurt like hell. You have your guts hanging out and see how it feels!" When Miss Horne informs the family that Jimmy died in slow agony ("forty-five minutes of pain and terror [while] he sat under a tree holding his large intestine in the palm of his hand"), the family reacts in disbelief and orders the "black troublemaker" out of the house. The son wants to know what channel the program will be on; the daughter whether they will be in color.

In 1969 McNally won his second Guggenheim Fellowship and worked on several plays. His next major production was *Where Has Tommy Flowers Gone?*, produced in October 1971. Many regard it as McNally's best play. In subject it looks back to the latent fascism and macabre cruelties of *And Things That Go Bump in the Night*, and in structure it looks forward to the free-for-all gymnastics of *The Ritz*.

The action is episodic, and realism is ignored as the play condemns and celebrates all the forces affecting a boy born in the 1940s, raised in the 1950s, and confused and traumatized in the 1960s. The central character, Tommy Flowers, is another of McNally's sensitive, slightly diabolical young anti-heroes. His identity seems to be a composite of popular culture of the 1950s. In a series of flashbacks and loosely connected episodes, Tommy revolts against the emptiness of official attitudes. In a flashback set in 1952, Tommy is asked in his civics class: "Who are the ten most admired men today in America and why?" He writes down "Holden Caulfield" (The hero of J. D. Salinger's novel *The Catcher in the Rye*, 1951) ten times, because Caulfield is not a "phony." Tommy receives an F for his answer and takes the test again and writes the preferred answers—Harry Truman, Dwight Eisenhower, etc.—but considers himself a phony for yielding to authority. (It is noteworthy that the protagonist of *Witness* signs his letter explaining the reason for the attempted assassination "Holden Caulfield.")

Tommy engages in one-man guerilla warfare by blowing up with homemade bombs the Vivian Beaumont Theatre, the Philharmonic Hall, the New York State Theatre, and the Metropolitan Opera House—all parts of New York's Lincoln Center for the Performing Arts—but not before disguising himself and auditioning in off-key falsetto and contrived Italian accents for various roles. He is laughed off the stage but succeeds in making the acquaintance of a dim-witted tour guide, Greta Rapp, who is enamored by his forwardness and excited by the destruction. She goes home with him.

Tommy is a con artist for whom morality does not count. Only the act, and getting away with the act, is important. Tommy does gain some audience sympathy, however, not only for his good spirits and boisterousness but also because of an underlying sensitivity which compels him to gather about himself the rudiments of a family—a girl friend named Nedda Lemon who plays the cello, an old man who serves as surrogate father and regales all with made-up tales of his great days as an actor, and a dog named Arnold. The prankish tone of the play forcefully conveys the notion that random violence and sabotage are inevitable weapons to a society that does not tolerate individualism or deviation from established norms. Tommy Flowers has necessarily gone underground because authority—whether it is academic, parental, economic, or political—abhors the nonconformist. Yet Tommy's refusal to make any conciliatory gesture when confronted by

1.

The setting is the dining hall at Rosewood Manor. Formerly a boys'
camp, Rosewood Manor's dining hall is a plan, long, many-windowed
room. There are no wall decorations. There are two long tables with
benches. The room is spotless. The overall impression is one of austerity
except for the green tress that may be glimpsed through the open
windows.

At rise, it is a beautiful summer morning in late July. Sunlight floods
into the room. Birds are singing in the trees. The state is bare.
Ten seconds of this.

HAMILTON (HAM, for short) and RUDI enter. HAM is 74 years old and delicate.
RUDI is 68 years old and less delicate.

                                HAM
The piano isn't here. I knew it.

                                RUDI
Typical.

                                HAM
It's outrageous.

                                RUDI
They don't care.

                                HAM
What are we going to do?

                                RUDI
There's a piano in the lounge.

                                HAM
They'll all be watching some game show.

                                RUDI
Who did you ask to get it?

                                HAM
Lucky.

                                RUDI
That one! Frenchie had to ask him five times before he got a desk
for his room. I wouldn't be surprised if he were on drugs.

                                HAM
It's a different generation. They don't remember anything.

                                RUDI
They don't care.

                                HAM
Well, this is getting us nowhere. Shall we go back?

                                RUDI
I wanted to rehearse.

                                HAM
I know.

authority deprives him of his family, and in the end he is a pathetic, lonely figure, however successfully picaresque his characterization has been.

Bad Habits (1971) consists of two thematically related one-act plays entitled *Ravenswood* and *Dunelawn*. Both plays are set in sanatoriums and depict the actions and habits of those within. In the first play, *Ravenswood*, a powerful and highly honored Dr. Jason Pepper treats couples with marital problems. One couple, the Pitts, are newlyweds who have conflicting careers in show business; they hope that Dr. Pepper will be able to prevent them from becoming another Hollywood marital casualty. Harry Scupp became a patient following his wife's latest attempt on his life. The Scupps, instead of fighting, take their frustrations out on one another by trying to kill each other. The third couple, a homosexual pair, Hiram Spane (of the Newport Spanes) and Frances Tear (of the Baltimore Tears) have been living at Ravenswood so long they plan never to leave. Dr. Pepper's unique form of therapy consists of allowing everyone to have exactly what he wants, ranging from unlimited liquor to a high cholesterol diet. The treatment seems to work; the patients appear healthy, happy, and well adjusted.

The second asylum, Dunelawn, seeks the solution to the patients' problems from another angle, by attempting to remove all vices. Dunelawn wants to make its patients perfect. At Dunelawn the patients, kept in straitjackets and confined to wheelchairs, are docile. They have various inclinations, being alcoholics, or transvestites, or sadists. Two nurses have immediate control. The first, Ruth, is a woman disappointed in love, having been rejected years before because of her slovenly appearance. She has since straightened out and is a model of decorum and priggishness for Nurse Becky Hedges to emulate. They both worship Dr. Toynbee who is insane himself and mutters nonsense words of advice to the straitjacketed patients and signals the proper time for massive injections of passivity serum. The bizarre comedy of *Bad Habits* was well received, winning the Elizabeth Hull-Kate Warriner Award for 1973-1974 and an Obie in 1974, and running for 126 performances.

Whiskey (1973), McNally's greatest commercial failure (seven performances), is also a bizarre comedy. The characters are a horse named Whiskey and a group of television actors, the Lush Thrushes, who star with Whiskey in the longest-running show in the history of television. They also want to perform in a musical variety show. Though most often offstage, Whiskey makes his presence known, cantankerously causing havoc through his outbursts. In

their first live appearance as an act, the Lush Thrushes— I. W. Harper, his wife Tia Maria, Jack Daniels, Johnny Walker, and the lovely if loose Southern Comfort—get booed off the stage of the Houston Astrodome. As they perform their music, Whiskey becomes hostile and refuses to come onstage. The horse knows he is the only one in the act that can carry a tune.

The balance of the action takes place in a squalid hotel room where one by one the characters give drunken, tearful renditions of their own sorrowful life stories, colored by both sexual clowning and self-pity, much like the final statements of characters in earlier McNally plays, but here unforgivably inconsequential. Clever as the portraits are, they lack human depth, and the audience is ultimately unconcerned.

Undaunted, McNally produced another madcap farce after the failure of *Whiskey*. First entitled *The Tubs* (1974), the revised version premiered in New York as *The Ritz* in January 1975 and had a run of 400 performances on Broadway. The extremely fast-paced farce does not even attempt plausibility of plot. The scene is a New York City gay bathhouse named the Ritz. An overweight heterosexual, Gaetano Proclo, is attempting to avoid his brother-in-law, Carmine Vespucci, who is out to kill Proclo. Arriving in New York, Proclo asks a taxi driver to take him to a place where he would never be discovered. The taxi driver brings Proclo to the Ritz bath house, and when Proclo enters he is unaware that it is a homosexual hangout. Vespucci has been ordered by Proclo's father-in-law to kill Proclo so that Vespucci can assume full control of the family business, a Mafia-sponsored sanitation route. At the Ritz Proclo must simultaneously avoid being discovered by another heterosexual, Carmine's detective, Michael Brick; fight off the advances of gay "chubby chasers" who cannot understand why Proclo will not cooperate; and decline the attentions of a third-rate female cabaret singer, Googie Gomez, who mistakenly believes that Proclo is a big-time producer and will put her in a big show. There is much moving about in chase sequences, slamming of doors, and contrived occurrences. It turns out that Vespucci owns the Ritz. When Proclo threatens to expose Vespucci as a homosexual, Vespucci is beaten at his own game, and Proclo retains his interest in the family business. Reviews of the play were mixed, but the spirited comedy maintained its large audience.

The direction that McNally's career will take in the future is still uncertain. He is capable of producing a wide variety of dramatic effects from grisly horror to exuberant farce. He is extremely skillful with anti-heroic protagonists. The range of his satire extends from intensely personal matters to broad social themes. Nearly all of his plays attack complacency, smugness, and mindless acquiescence to authority. His weaknesses stem from occasional uncertainty of tone or intent and from dramatic structures which threaten to fall apart because of their fragmented, episodic nature. His ear for dialogue, however, is sharp; McNally is capable of making his heroes very appealing to a wide audience. Unquestionably he is one of the best satiric playwrights to write during and after the Vietnam War.

–William Mattathias Robins and Craig L. Downing

Other:
Tour, in *Collision Course*, ed. Edward Parone (New York: Random House, 1968), pp. 85-97.

Periodical Publication:
Terrence McNally, "Theatre Isn't All on Broadway," *New York Times*, 28 April 1974, II: 1.

Interview:
Richard Shepard, "Three Young Playwrights Talk Shop," *New York Times*, 10 December 1968, p. 54.

MARK MEDOFF
(18 March 1940-)

PRODUCTIONS: *Doing a Good One for the Red Man*, June 1969, Dallas Theater Center, Dallas;
The Froegle Dictum, 1971, Albuquerque;
The Kramer, March 1972, American Conservatory Theatre, San Francisco; 9 October 1973, Mark Taper Forum, Los Angeles, 6 [performances];
The Wager, January 1973, HB Playwrights Foundation Theatre, New York, 21; 21 October 1974, Eastside Playhouse, New York, 104;
When You Comin Back, Red Ryder?, 25 June 1973, Circle Repertory Theatre, New York, 19; 6 December 1973, Eastside Playhouse, New York, 228;
The War on Tatem, 1973, New Mexico State University, Las Cruces;
The Odyssey of Jeremy Jack, by Medoff and Carleene Johnson, December 1974, New Mexico State University, Las Cruces;
The Halloween Bandit, 1976, Huntington, New York;

The Conversion of Aaron Weiss, 13 October 1977, Guthrie 2, Minneapolis, 22;
Firekeeper, 2 May 1978, Kalita Humphreys Theatre, Dallas, 39;
Children of a Lesser God, 25 October 1979, Mark Taper Forum, Los Angeles, 55; March 1980, Longacre Theatre, New York.

BOOKS: *Four Short Plays* (New York: Dramatists Play Service, 1974)—includes *The Froegle Dictum, Doing a Good One for the Red Man, The War on Tatem*, and *The Ultimate Grammar of Life*;
When You Comin Back, Red Ryder? (New York: Dramatists Play Service, 1974);
The Odyssey of Jeremy Jack, by Medoff and Carleene Johnson (New York: Dramatists Play Service, 1974);
The Wager (New York: Dramatists Play Service, 1975).

Mark Medoff's plays have been gaining attention at a steady rate since his first commercial success, the 1974 Off-Broadway production of *The Wager*. A faculty member at the New Mexico State University, he has, in the past few years, gained much critical and public respect as a playwright. *The Wager* and *When You Comin Back, Red Ryder?* (1973) had impressive runs, and *Children of a Lesser God* (1979), which premiered in Los Angeles, has been successfully transferred to Broadway.

Mark Howard Medoff was born in Mount Carmel, Illinois, to Lawrence R. Medoff, a physician and Thelma Butt Medoff, a psychologist. He attended the University of Miami, where he received his B.A. in 1962. Then, after a two-year pause in his formal education, during which he was supervisor of publications and assistant director of admissions for the Capitol Radio Engineering Institute in Washington, D.C., he worked toward his master's degree in English at Stanford University, graduating in 1966. Since then Medoff has been associated with the New Mexico State University, Las Cruces, as instructor from 1966 to 1971; as assistant professor from 1971 to 1974; as associate professor of English since 1974; as writer-in-residence since 1966; and as dramatist-in-residence since 1975. He and his second wife, Stephanie Thorne, whom he married in 1972, have three daughters.

In 1974 Medoff won a Guggenheim Fellowship; his play *When You Comin Back, Red Ryder?* earned an Obie for distinguished playwriting, an Outer Circle Critics Award for best playwriting of the 1973-1974 season, the New Mexico State University Westhofer Award for excellence in creativity, the Outer Circle John Gassner Award; and for his acting in this play he won the Jefferson Award. Five of his works have been included in Burns Mantle's *Best Plays: The Kramer, When You Comin Back, Red Ryder?, The Wager, Firekeeper,* and *The Conversion of Aaron Weiss.* Medoff has also been active in the production aspect of the theatre. A member of the Actors' Equity Association and the Writers Guild of America, he has served as a director for his own *Red Ryder,* as well as for Samuel Beckett's *Waiting for Godot,* Paul Zindel's *The Effect of Gamma Rays on Man-in-the-Moon Marigolds,* Harold Pinter's *Jacques Brel Is Alive and Well and Living in Paris* and *The Birthday Party,* and Dale Wasserman's version of *One Flew Over the Cuckoo's Nest.* He has played the roles of Andrei Bolkonski in *War and Peace,* Marat in Peter Weiss's *Marat/Sade,* Pozzo in *Waiting for Godot,* Teddy in *Red Ryder,* Harrold Gorringe in Peter Shaffer's *Black Comedy,* and Bro Paradock in N. F. Simpson's *A Resounding Tinkle.*

Thematically, Medoff is concerned with the various conflicts involved in a person's attaining an accurate view of himself, and the plays generally center on one or more characters' struggles to communicate and reveal some sort of harsh truth to one another, as in *Red Ryder,* or else, as in the case of *The Wager*'s main character, John Leeds, to avoid communication altogether. Medoff explores how people use sex, violence, and language to control others; his major plays—*The Kramer, The Wager, When You Comin Back, Red Ryder?*—have atmospheres of emotional strain which he intensifies through preoccupations with guns, crude language and, in particular, verbal threats. Typically, Medoff's protagonist is a male who uses sex to exhibit power and thus to gratify himself physically and psychologically. He threatens to become violent when the subtler techniques of control lose their effectiveness, and his struggle for superiority makes him a harsh but truth-bearing savior. However, his act of emancipation does not automatically free those he confronts. He savagely forces upon them a revelation about themselves, then disappears— leaving them to decide how to act in the future. Whether Medoff's bossy, loudmouthed, zealous men actually accomplish anything worthwhile is doubtful. They are too boorish to earn true respect. Obviously, the playwright does not intend them to be merely boorish, but also forceful in their knowledge and perceptions since they take upon themselves the difficult job of dislocating people from ruts of blind behavior. Four early one-act, experimental plays—*Doing a Good One For the Red Man* (1969), *The Froegle Dictum* (1971), *The Ultimate Grammar of Life* (published in 1974 but never produced), and *The War on Tatem* (1973)—indicate the beginnings of his concern with the dramatic use of sex and violence in defining problems of personal communication. In each of these plays he seems to be isolating a particular problem in order to refine his handling of it. Although these plays are not noteworthy, they were valuable apprentice work for Medoff.

In *The Wager,* first produced in 1973, Leeds and Ward, two graduate students at an unspecified university, share an apartment. When the first act opens they have been living together a year, and, immediately, in a brief lecture presented by Leeds and illustrated on a portable blackboard, the conflicting interests of the roommates are evident. Leeds is cold and intellectual; he tells the audience, with frosty composure, of Ward's latest sexual interests. Ward has been making advances toward Honor Stevens at the swimming pool. When her husband, Ron, arrives, he demonstrates his athletic prowess by swimming forty laps. Leeds explains that Ward is not discreet because he wants Ron to have no doubts about the encroaching threat to his marriage. Leeds is an intellectualizer; Ward is a man of action unconcerned about consequences; Ron is a scientist whose main desire is to live contentedly with Honor; and Honor is a young, attractive woman capable of a certain ruthlessness, much like Leeds. Ward offers Leeds a wager: that he, Ward, can seduce Honor in some agreed-upon amount of time. Leeds alters the bet, suggesting they bet not on whether Ward succeeds with Honor, but whether her husband will kill Ward or make an attempt on his life within forty-eight hours of the seduction. Because Ward seduces her in merely an hour, the bet is changed again, so that Honor must be seduced twice in the forty-eight hour period. When Ron finds out from Leeds, who reluctantly answers Ron's questions about Honor's downfall, he unexpectedly reappears in Leeds and Ward's apartment with a submachine gun to murder Leeds, rather than Ward. Incapable of such violence, however, he abandons his intent at the last moment and leaves the stage, trying to reconcile himself with dignity to the divorce Honor insists she has long wanted. Meanwhile, Ward rushes off to spend a weekend with an old girlfriend. Honor remains onstage with Leeds, and the play ends with a suggestion that through such disruption they will begin to understand and appreciate each other.

Even if *The Wager* had not had its successful run Off Broadway when produced there in 1974, it would still have to be regarded as one of the major achievements of Medoff's career because it incorporates all the elements found in his work. Violence, both physical and emotional, is the very foundation of the play. For example, Leeds wears a revolver in a shoulder holster from beginning to end, once shooting a picture on the wall to intimidate Ward, who stands beside it. The wager itself is an invitation to murder, and when Ron threatens Leeds with the machine gun, Leeds's life momentarily hangs in the balance. Emotionally, all four characters suffer waves of violence, and all but Ron are deliberate inflicters of pain. Besides the tension Leeds so relentlessly cultivates with his obnoxious, at times unbearable, cleverness, sex is also a problem which cannot be separated from those of violence and communication. Medoff shows the various ways human beings use sex: to validate conquest, to mark personal boundaries, to incite violence, and to quell it. Finally, Leeds is the fully developed type of character who surfaces in Medoff's other plays. He is the ruthless catalyst whose activities gradually give each character (or couple) a clearer view of himself (themselves). He has no respect for intimacy. Both critical and public response to *The Wager* were generally favorable, though critics found precedents for this work in that of other playwrights. For example, John Simon, in *New York* magazine, claims *The Wager* is similar to the plays of Tom Stoppard.

The Kramer, which premiered in San Francisco in 1972, is a strange, brief play with an ethereal, dreamlike quality. Medoff's stage directions describe the locale as "Mind space." The set consists of platforms at various levels, and spotlights illuminate the platform on which a particular scene is enacted. The play presents Art Malin's rise from assistant to the admissions officer of a secretarial school to a possible future in the State Department, by riding the coattails of Bart Kramer. Kramer is aggressive, ruthless, adept at rapid corporate advancement, and interested (for some unknown reason) in aiding Malin. He gradually changes Malin's manner of dress and speech, and advises Malin to find a new wife. Malin ultimately rebels against Kramer's help, although at first he appreciates and desires it. In the end, he remains with his wife even though she is unattractive and unintelligent. He sabotages Kramer's further advancement by contacting Kramer's future employers at the State Department and revealing to them Kramer's questionable ethics. In retaliation, Kramer, like an infuriated fairy godmother, destroys Malin's personal possessions and casts him back out on his own. The other characters are secondary to Malin and Kramer. Kramer is an

Mark Medoff

image of a sleazy perfection; Malin exudes slovenliness and lack of ambition. But the school's director who is intimidated by Kramer, the switchboard operator who desires an affair with Malin, Malin's useless wife, and a student who abandons her crippled husband in order to marry Kramer, are not developed in significant detail.

Medoff's thematic preoccupations are present in this play but are not strongly developed. Power, ambition, the effect of role models, and the desire to aggrandize oneself are presented with less clarity than in Medoff's next major production, *When You Comin Back, Red Ryder?* Both plays examine the effect of an almost supernaturally perceptive and powerful figure who appears from nowhere to take control of directionless lives.

The Wager and *When You Comin Back, Red Ryder?* together established Medoff's reputation. *Red Ryder* takes place on an early Sunday morning in a run-down diner in rural New Mexico at the close of the 1960s. Just as the characters of *The Wager* are a cross-section of types brought together by a common interest, so are those in *When You Comin Back, Red Ryder?*. Stephen Ryder works a night shift at the diner, and when Angel, a chubby waitress, arrives for work at six each morning, he lingers in order to chat with her. He talks often of leaving town, but it is only talk. He is afraid to leave. He dresses like a tough young man of the 1950s with his cigarette package rolled up in his shirt sleeve, but his toughness is a weak facade. He likes to be called "Red," which was the name of his cowboy idol and which he claims was his nickname as a child. Angel is pathetically desperate for Stephen's affection and laughably simpleminded. But Stephen and Angel never establish a genuine rapport because they lack confidence in themselves. Richard and Clarisse, the travelers, are a well-to-do married couple from New York. She is a concert violinist, and they are en route to a performance.

The central character of the play, Teddy, appears late in the first act. His manner is alert, uneasy, and distinctly alters the slow pace and depressed mood established in the long colloquy between Angel and Stephen in the opening scene. Teddy was a hippie and also a soldier in Vietnam. Now he is returning with his compliant but edgy girl friend from Mexico—they have presumably smuggled some drugs—and he demands to have his van repaired. But he does not seem primarily interested in having his van fixed, although he pulls out a gun and threatens harm if it is not fixed immediately. He holds the people in the diner captive and amuses himself by forcing them to acknowledge their actual feelings toward each other. Richard is revealed as a weakling living vicariously through his wife's accomplishment, contributing merely financial security to the relationship, but still behaving as if he were Clarisse's lord. Clarisse clutches her violin case and, as the morning progresses, aggressively confesses her growing contempt for Richard. Teddy humiliates Stephen repeatedly, forcing him to run around in a circle, slapping his hip as if he, Stephen, were the cowboy hero Red on a horse. He exposes Stephen's sexual inexperience and the inept way in which Stephen has shown an interest in Angel. Stephen, of course, constantly threatens retribution, but he is all talk and his public unmasking forces him to recognize that he is barely more than a self-pitying adolescent who constantly complains, procrastinates, and pretends to be a tough guy. At the play's end Stephen leaves town, looking for a new life. It is clear that he would never have left his position at the diner had he not met up with the ferocious intruder.

In *When You Comin Back, Red Ryder?*, once again Medoff explores the various ways in which honesty is deliberately suppressed and violence becomes necessary in order to release frustration, force communication, and disrupt established patterns of behavior. The title of the play implies that

personal fantasy can become destructive when it defines one's outlook on life. Red Ryder, Stephen's cowboy hero, will never come back to deliver Stephen in the manner Stephen likes to imagine. Instead, Stephen's deliverance is effected by a vicious and terrifyingly lucid ex-hippie who forces Stephen to relinquish his image of himself as a tough guy. Stephen's pose was paralytic. Teddy's role is reminiscent of Hickey's in Eugene O'Neill's *The Iceman Cometh*. In each play the catalyst is an unwanted psychopathic prophet whose truth is painfully and bitterly perceived. How convincingly Medoff dramatizes the necessity of violence is debatable. Teddy claims to be on a hurried trip to Mexico, yet later events show he has already smuggled his contraband into the country, undetected by border guards. Why is he behaving in a way that increases the probability that he will be caught? He does not appear to wish subconsciously to be caught and punished. This, however, is a minor difficulty in a play of undeniable power and skill. The play was well received by most critics and enjoyed a long run in New York.

Following *When You Comin Back, Red Ryder?*, Medoff wrote four more plays of secondary importance: *The Odyssey of Jeremy Jack* (1974), a children's play on which he collaborated with Carleene Johnson, *The Halloween Bandit* (1976), a short play produced in Huntington, Long Island, *The Conversion of Aaron Weiss* (1977), another play depicting the travails of a distressed graduate student, and *Firekeeper* (1978), which was included in *Best Plays* of the year; none of these efforts achieved popular success.

On the other hand, Medoff's most recent work, *Children of a Lesser God*, may insure his standing as one of America's promising playwrights. The play chiefly concerns a deaf woman, Sarah, and the man she marries, James Leeds, an excellent instructor at a school for the deaf. Sarah is an ex-student who refuses to learn to speak or read lips. She prefers remaining in her janitorial job and living in solitude to adapting herself to society in order to attain a better position in it. Both characters are exceptionally intelligent, and both are determined to remain independent. Leeds diligently tries to make Sarah value speech, secretly convinced he will someday overcome her resolve. She refuses to give in. This conflict causes the audience to perceive the advantages of her silent world. Is it so inferior, after all, to the world of the "normal"? Their marriage suffers, in time, and Medoff again presents a situation in which he can investigate people's urges to control each other. Leeds is unable to accept Sarah's desire to remain in the isolated world which is of value to her, and tries to manipulate her. *Children of a Lesser God* exploits a stark, absolute communication problem. Unlike his previous plays, this one does so without the threat of physical violence. There are no guns. *Children of a Lesser God* has almost unanimously captured the praise of critics and at this writing appears to be headed for a long run on Broadway. At this point in his career, Medoff's

reputation rests upon three plays, which are concerned with psychological stress and emotional violence: *The Wager*, *When You Comin Back, Red Ryder?*, and *Children of a Lesser God*. These plays confirm his place in contemporary drama and suggest, in their form and outlook, that Medoff's voice will continue to address the problem of self-isolated personalities making themselves felt without disintegrating.

–*Paul Sagona*

Arthur Miller

Jeffrey Helterman
University of South Carolina

BIRTH: New York, New York, 17 October 1915, to Isidore and Augusta Barnett Miller.

EDUCATION: A.B., University of Michigan, 1938.

MARRIAGE: 1940 to Mary Grace Slattery, divorced; children: Jane and Robert, 1956 to Marilyn Monroe, divorced, 1962 to Ingeborg Morath; children: Rebecca.

AWARDS: Hopwood Award (University of Michigan) for *Honors at Dawn*, 1936; Hopwood Award for *No Villain*, 1937; Theatre Guild Award for *They Too Arise*, 1938; New York Drama Critics Circle Awards for *All My Sons*, 1947, and for *Death of a Salesman*, 1949; Pulitzer Prize for *Death of a Salesman*, 1949; Antoinette Perry (Tony) Award for *The Crucible*, 1953; Drama Critics Circle Award for *A View from the Bridge*, 1955; Honorary Doctor of Letters, University of Michigan, 1956; National Institute of Arts and Letters Gold Medal for Drama, 1959; President of P.E.N., 1965-1969; Brandeis University Creative Arts Medal, 1969-1970.

SELECTED PRODUCTIONS: *The Man Who Had All the Luck*, 23 November 1944, Forrest Theatre, New York, 4 [performances];
All My Sons, 29 January 1947, Coronet Theatre, New York, 328;
Death of a Salesman, 10 February 1949, Morosco Theatre, New York, 742;
An Enemy of the People, adapted from Ibsen's play, 28 December 1950, Broadhurst Theatre, New York, 36;
The Crucible, 22 January 1953, Martin Beck Theatre, New York, 197;

A View from the Bridge (one-act version) and *A Memory of Two Mondays*, 29 September 1955, Coronet Theatre, New York, 149;
A View from the Bridge (two-act version), 11 October 1956, Comedy Theatre, London;
After the Fall, 23 January 1964, ANTA Washington Square Theatre, New York, 208;
Incident at Vichy, 3 December 1964, ANTA Washington Square Theatre, New York, 99;
The Price, 7 February 1968, Morosco Theatre, New York, 425;
The Creation of the World and Other Business, 30 November 1972, Shubert Theatre, New York, 20; revised as *Up From Paradise*, 23 April 1974, Power Center for the Performing Arts, Ann Arbor, Mich.;
The Archbishop's Ceiling, 30 April 1977, Eisenhower Theatre, Kennedy Center for the Performing Arts, Washington, D.C.;
The American Clock, adapted from Studs Terkel's *Hard Times*, Spring 1980, Spoleto Festival, Charleston, S.C.

BOOKS: *Situation Normal* (New York: Reynal & Hitchcock, 1944);
Focus (New York: Reynal & Hitchcock, 1945; London: Gollancz, 1949);
All My Sons (New York: Reynal & Hitchcock, 1947; Harmondsworth, U.K.: Penguin, 1961);
Death of a Salesman (New York: Viking, 1949; London: Cresset, 1949);
An Enemy of the People, adapted from Ibsen's play (New York: Viking, 1951);
The Crucible (New York: Viking, 1953; London: Cresset, 1956);
A View from the Bridge: Two One-Act Plays (New York:

Viking, 1955)—includes *A Memory of Two Mondays*; (New York: Dramatists Play Service, 1956);

A View from the Bridge: A Play in Two Acts, revised editon (New York: Dramatists Play Service, 1957; London: Cresset, 1957);

Collected Plays (New York: Viking, 1957; London: Cresset, 1958);

The Misfits (New York: Viking, 1961; London: Secker & Warburg, 1961);

Jane's Blanket (New York: Crowell-Collier, 1963; London: Collier-Macmillan, 1963);

After the Fall (New York: Viking, 1964; London: Secker & Warburg, 1965);

Incident at Vichy (New York: Viking, 1965; London: Secker & Warburg, 1966);

I Don't Need You Any More: Stories (New York: Viking, 1967; London: Secker & Warburg, 1967);

The Price (New York: Viking, 1968; London: Secker & Warburg, 1968);

Psychology and Arthur Miller, by Miller and Richard I. Evans (New York: Dutton, 1969);

In Russia, by Miller and Inge Morath (New York: Viking, 1969; London: Secker & Warburg, 1969);

The Portable Arthur Miller, ed. Harold Clurman (New York: Viking, 1971);

The Creation of the World and Other Business (New York: Viking, 1973);

In the Country, by Miller and Morath (New York: Viking, 1977);

The Theater Essays of Arthur Miller (New York: Viking, 1978);

Chinese Encounters, by Miller and Morath (New York: Farrar, Straus & Giroux, 1979);

The American Clock, adapted from Studs Terkel's *Hard Times* (New York: Viking, 1980).

Arthur Miller was born in Manhattan, the son of a middle-class ladies' coat manufacturer and a schoolteacher mother. He has a brother who became a businessman and a sister who was an actress. Although he went to grammar school in then fashionable Harlem, Miller was forced to move to Brooklyn when his father suffered major losses right before the Depression. Today, fifty years after his move to Brooklyn, Miller lives the life of a country squire on 400 acres of Connecticut countryside, where he gardens, mows, plants evergreens, works as a carpenter, and writes four to six hours every morning in an isolated studio. There is both a real and metaphoric sense of planting new roots, but he remains haunted by the old. The Depression still troubles him: "It seems easy to tell how it was to live

in those years, but I have made several attempts to tell it and when I do try I know I cannot quite touch that mysterious underwater thing."

In the Depression years, Miller lived on Gravesend Avenue in the Midwood section of Brooklyn and says that his house was constantly visited by salesmen uncles who filled the air with their boastful talk. He attended James Madison and Abraham Lincoln high schools in Brooklyn where he was an average student. Of his reading, Miller says that "until the age of seventeen I can safely say that I never read a book weightier than Tom Swift and the Rover Boys, and only verged on literature with some Dickens." When he graduated from Abraham Lincoln in 1932 in the depth of the Depression, his parents could not afford to send him to college, nor were his grades good enough to get him in. The University of Michigan turned him down because of his academic record, and years later, none of his high-school teachers could remember having taught the Pulitzer Prize winner.

During those days Miller was much more of an athlete like Biff Loman in *Death of a Salesman* (1949) than the man who would become America's "intellectual" playwright. He would, in fact, never become quite comfortable with that mantle. Miller has never been an intellectual playwright in the sense of Jean Genet in *The Balcony* (1960) or Edward Albee in *Tiny Alice* (1964): he is rarely concerned with the nature of being or reality, but rather with social issues. In the 1940s and 1950s, however, to be involved with social issues was to be an intellectual.

After his high-school graduation, Miller worked for two and a half years at various jobs including a long stint at an auto supply warehouse, which becomes the setting for his one-act play, *A Memory of Two Mondays* (1955). Miller claims that, like Bert in that play, he saved thirteen dollars of his fifteen-dollar-a-week salary to pay for his college education. During this time, Miller was also a crooner for a small Brooklyn radio station, but his growing love for Dostoevski led to a new and successful application to the University of Michigan.

At Michigan, Miller supplemented his income with various jobs: first as a mouse tender in a university laboratory and then as a night editor on the *Michigan Daily*. Miller began to write plays while he was at college and won two of the university's five-hundred-dollar Hopwood playwriting awards for "Honors at Dawn" (1936) and "No Villain" (1937). "No Villain," revised as "They Too Arise" (and revised again later as "The Grass Still Grows"), won the Theatre Guild Award for 1938, and the cash prize of $1250 encouraged Miller to become engaged to Mary Grace Slattery, whom he married in

1940. Miller was briefly associated with the Federal Theatre Project, which paid promising young playwrights a wage for working on plays. He expected to have a play of his produced by the project, but the program was curtailed before production could begin. At this time, he also wrote half-hour radio scripts for such shows as the "Cavalcade of America" and the "Columbia Workshop." Miller found the radio plays useful for learning dialogue, but he also felt severely limited by the special demands of the shows. He complained that because of the producers' notion of what the audience could understand, there could be no subtlety of characterization, "every emotion in a radio script has to have a tag."

In 1944, Miller toured army camps as a researcher, gathering background material for the filming of Ernie Pyle's *Story of GI Joe* (1945). Miller turned his research into a wartime journal called *Situation Normal*, which was published that year. He worked hard to keep his journal free of the flag-waving patriotism that was the stuff of most Hollywood treatments of the war effort. As he toured such places as Fort Dix, Camp Croft, and Fort Benning, he became increasingly concerned with the soldiers' thinking about the aims of the war. His description of a GI back from New Georgia in the southwest Pacific is a striking revelation of the new perceptions brought to the average American soldier by life in combat.

Miller's first Broadway play, *The Man Who Had All the Luck*, opened in 1944 but ran for only four performances. The play was almost universally panned by the critics, who punned unmercifully on the title, though most saw promise in the young playwright if he could keep his characters from so much speech making. The play tells the story of a young garage mechanic, David Beeves (David Frieber in the published version), for whom everything always turns out right. Instead of rejoicing in his luck, however, David becomes more and more frightened because he cannot believe he deserves the gifts fate has handed him. He keeps hoping for small doses of trouble because he firmly believes in the notion of compensation—an idea put forth in Emerson's essay of the same name—according to which the good and the bad in life are ultimately doled out equally.

David's luck is not only incredible, but everything seems connected as if the fates could undo the string with one tug. His garage becomes a success when the state decides to put a highway next to it. His real test as a mechanic comes when he is brought a rare car, a Marmon, for repair. Although he does not know how to fix the Marmon, a Viennese refugee mechanic (and philosopher) happens along to give him instructions. The Marmon, in turn, helps David win the girl he loves when it accidentally runs over the girl's father as he is on his way to shoot David because the father opposes the couple's marriage. For a time David fears that his unborn child will be the gods' chance for revenge, but despite a nasty fall she has taken, his wife gives birth to the healthy boy he wished for. David then lets his luck ride on a decision to develop a mink ranch, seeing this as an operation that can be governed by no other force than luck. At this point, he is no longer trying to earn a living, but rather, deliberately tempting the gods.

In *The Man Who Had All the Luck* a basic Miller plot is established: the rivalry of two brothers for the affection of the father. The father has given all his love to David's brother in the hope of making the brother a baseball star and has kept the boy in the basement from age ten learning how to pitch. When the brother ascends from his cellar to the real world of baseball, he cannot cope with men on base and fails in his attempt to become a major leaguer. David cannot understand why he has succeeded while his brother, for all his effort, has failed.

In addition to his brother, David is confronted by a cynic in a wheelchair who argues that man is no more than a jellyfish unable to control his fate. This philosophy is countered by the Viennese mechanic who argues that man is free when he works. David seems to prove this point when for the first time he succeeds by dint of his own efforts and not by luck: he saves the minks by picking all the silk worms, poisonous to minks, off the fish the minks eat. The only problem with this treatment of the hard-work philosophy is that the baseball-playing brother works just as hard as David and yet he fails. With the hindsight gained from Miller's later plays, one would have to believe that the secret reason David succeeds is not because of hard work, but because his father has favored his brother. This rivalry for the affection of a parent remains in force throughout Miller's work, down to *The Creation of the World and Other Business* (1972) where the ultimate fraternal rivals, Cain and Abel, struggle because Eve loved Abel best.

In 1945, Miller turned out *Focus*, a rather successful (90,000 copies) novel about anti-Semitism. The title refers to the metamorphosis the hero undergoes when he gets a new pair of glasses. Not only does he begin to see things more clearly, but everyone else sees him differently as well: Newman, a gentile, looks like a Jew with his glasses on, and people begin to suspect that his real name is Neumann. He is a basically timid man who is afraid of his colleagues at work, afraid of women, afraid of his neighbors. The novel opens when Newman ignores the cries of a rape victim because she has a foreign accent, and he rationalizes that a foreign woman out so late could only be a prostitute. He takes the same attitude to the office where he works in the personnel department identifying Jewish job applicants.

When his glasses make him look too Jewish, Newman is relegated to a clerical desk in a corner. He quits in outrage, but finds that he cannot find another job until he goes to a Jewish firm. While Newman is facing the pressures of anti-Semitism at work, his neighbors are forming a vigilante committee against the presence of Finklestein, a Jewish grocer in their community. Although he is involved in the passive phase of this anti-Semitism, Newman, spurred on by his own experiences with Jew-haters, acts to save Finklestein from night raiders. At the end of the novel, Newman redeems himself by taking up a baseball bat and coming to Finklestein's aid.

The novel is melodramatic with Newman's shifts in character overstated throughout, but two major themes of Miller's later plays surface here. The first, man's responsibility for all of his fellowmen, is clearly delineated in Miller's next play, *All My Sons* (1947), and a more specific aspect of that theme—all men are responsible for and have a share in the suffering of the Jews—becomes the central concern of *Incident at Vichy* and an important side issue in *After the Fall*, both produced in 1964.

Miller's first successful play, *All My Sons*, bears the stamp of Ibsen's influence in its style, its theme, and even its plot. Miller aimed the play's realism at a broad-based audience and deliberately excised all the bookishness of his early drafts. He changed, for example, the play's original title, "The Sign of the Archer" (a reference to Kate's interest in astrology), because it was too literary. He made the dialogue of *All My Sons* as plain as possible to fit both the blue-collar Keller household and nineteenth-century theories of realism. The play is "well-made" in the nineteenth-century sense of the term as well, with neatly-articulated crises leading to an overwhelming crisis.

Miller notes that his treatment of chronology is modeled on Ibsen's method of having characters spend much of the present discussing the past. The closest parallel is Ibsen's *The Wild Duck* (1884) where every action in the present works toward revelation of the past. Because Miller found this talky exposition of past events one of the most artificial devices of dramatic realism, he experimented in his next play, *Death of a Salesman*, to work out problems of exposition more fluidly.

The thematic concerns of *All My Sons* are also Ibsen's. Like Gregers Werle in *The Wild Duck*, Chris Keller is an idealist who insists on dredging up the past so that the truth may set everyone free. As in Ibsen's play, the revelation of the truth destroys everyone it is supposed to cleanse. The secret hidden in the past is basically the same as that which plagues Gregers's father in *The Wild Duck*. Chris's father, Joe Keller, has sent the air force the defective engine parts which caused the deaths of twenty-one flyers; then he left his partner to take the blame. The father's guilt is magnified because his eldest son, Larry, is a pilot who is missing and presumed dead. Although Larry did not fly one of the defective P-40s, his death becomes central to the moral crisis of the story.

Although Ibsen is considered a dramatic realist, he continually imposed symbols on the realistic surface of his plays, particularly by using commonplace details to make thematic statements about his characters. So, for example, when Hjalmar Ekdal in *The Wild Duck* is first seen at his occupation of retouching photographs, Ibsen suggests that this is a man who does not like the truth as it is. Miller accomplishes the same task with the casual prop of a newspaper. Joe Keller resolutely refuses to read the news because he fears finding the truth. Instead, he reads the want ads because his lie is based on his belief that he is pursuing the life that every American wants. Chris, on the other hand, reads the book section, which hints that he is an intellectual until it is revealed that he reads the reviews but never the books themselves: he is someone who wants to appear knowledgeable about the finer things in life, though he has no acquaintance with their substance.

The most important symbol in *All My Sons* is the apple tree planted as a memorial to Larry. A storm has blown the tree down the night before the action of the play begins, and everyone's ideal memory of Larry will also be destroyed in the play. When Chris, dressed in his best pants, is seen sawing off the remains of the tree, it is clear that he is trying to remove the dominant presence Larry still has on his family. Chris's mother, Kate, warns him that he will soil his good pants, and his attempt to expunge Larry's memory does cast mud on Chris's self-image.

At first, the play's theme seems to pit the relentless honesty of Chris Keller, who also is a World War II veteran, against the crass pragmatism of his father and the maudlin sentimentality of his mother. This theme is echoed in the life of a neighbor, a doctor who dreams of doing selfless research like Don Ameche in a Warner Brothers movie, but yields instead to his wife's demands that he make more money. The doctor's discomfort in Chris's presence seems to reflect his own failure to live up to his beliefs the way Chris has to his. As the action progresses, however, the neatly opposed values within the Keller household turn out to be more complex than expected.

The first crack in Chris's idealistic armor appears when he refuses to let his father change the company's name to Keller and Son. Although he wants to believe his father is innocent, Chris knows Joe is guilty. He also knows that his conscience will force him to leave the company if he admits his father's guilt to himself. Keeping his name off the plant is Chris's halfhearted way of disassociating himself from his father's act.

Kate, the mother, appears to use astrology unrealistically to prove that her son Larry is not dead. She reads the stars to prevent Chris from marrying Larry's former girl friend. Her argument is that allowing the marriage would be an admission of Larry's death. As it turns out, Kate is protecting the fiction of Larry's survival not for her own sentimental reasons, but because she knows her husband would blame himself for Larry's death, even though the defective airplane part is not directly responsible. Kate realizes that the hope of Larry's survival is all that allows Joe to live with his guilt.

Chris's investigation of the past unearths more truth than anyone can bear. A letter from Larry to Ann, his former girl friend and now Chris's fiancee, proves to be the key to the mystery, conveying more than anyone expects it to. Ann introduces it at first to prove to Kate that Larry is dead so that she will give the young people her blessing to marry. Chris doesn't know the contents of the letter except that, according to Ann, it establishes once and for all that Larry is dead. He reads it aloud to his father without having read it himself and then realizes that he has gone too far: in the letter Larry announces that he will commit suicide because he knows his father was responsible for the defective parts and therefore for the deaths of his brothers-in-arms. This direct blame for his son's death is too much for Joe Keller. While Chris, idealistic to the last, is insisting to Kate, "once and for all you can know there's a universe of people and you're responsible to it, and unless you know that you threw away your son because that's why he died," Joe goes into the house and shoots himself. Chris's last words recognize the enormity

of his error in demanding the whole truth: "Mother, I didn't mean to—"

Earlier in the play, Chris, a war hero, speaks effusively about dying for one's fellowman in Europe when honor made a difference. Miller questions whether it is as easy to live for one's fellowman as it is to die for him. Also haunting Chris is the fact that he is alive while others, including his brother, who fought in the war are dead. This theme of the guilt of those who escape is central in *The Man Who Had All the Luck*, and it reappears in *After the Fall* as well.

Although the men in the play seem tough-minded at first and the women merely dreamers, it turns out that Kate and Ann are the only ones willing to face reality in all its ugliness. They may try to shield their men from the truth, but they never hide it from themselves. Their great virtue lies not only in knowing the truth, but also, like Regina Ekdal in *The Wild Duck*, in knowing how much of it ought to be suppressed. Linda in *Death of a Salesman* and Beatrice in *A View from the Bridge* (1955) have much the same quality.

When *All My Sons* won the New York Drama Critics Circle Award in 1947, Miller was established as an important young playwright, particularly since the competition included Eugene O'Neill's *The Iceman Cometh*. In retrospect, the critics' choice seems somewhat off the mark; Miller's work is a solid piece and an important milestone in his career, but it is not a match for O'Neill's masterpiece.

The critics may just have been foresighted. Miller's next play, which won their award in 1949, was comparable to O'Neill at his best. *Death of a Salesman* was that wonder of wonders, a masterpiece that came easily. The play tells how its protagonist, Willy Loman, a middle-class salesman whose youth is but a memory, decides to end his life. He is loved by his wife, Linda, and he has two sons, Biff and Happy, whom he has tried to raise to become men of influence and power. Biff, the older son, now in his thirties, has not lived up to Willy's expectations, goals which were set when Biff was a high-school football hero. When Biff's plans to borrow money to go into a sporting goods business fail, he confronts Willy with his version of the truth and then breaks down and weeps. Willy feels at last that his son loves him and commits suicide in the automobile so that Biff can have the life insurance money.

The basic script was turned out in six weeks when Miller went off to a small house that he had built with his own hands on some property in Connecticut. Miller's skill with tools is an ability he shares with his hero, but Willy Loman can never turn his mechanical ability into part of a positive self-concept. Almost everything he owns breaks down in the course of the play, but Willy is too busy being a salesman to fix anything. Though the writing of *Death of a Salesman* came easily, the same was not true of the backing. Angels shied away from the pessimistic title, the radical plans for staging, and the revolutionary set design of Jo Mielziner. Mielziner's set played a major part in making the journeys into Willy's memory believable. After *The Man Who Had All the Luck*, Miller became convinced that shifting scenery was one of the quickest ways to turn the audience's attention from the dramatic focus of the play. He wanted a set where characters could move through time and space without moving props. As he conceived of the play, exposition would become part of the action on stage and not a story told by one of the characters. Mielziner, who had just come from designing the set for *A Streetcar Named Desire*, where lighting had played an important part in distinguishing the brutal Stanley Kowalski from the fragile Blanche Dubois, constructed a set in which the skeleton of Willy's house became all the places called for in the play—not only the house itself, but also a business office, a hotel room, a restaurant, and finally the cemetery. An arbitrary convention neatly separated the present from the past: characters from the present observed the wall lines and used the doors to enter the rooms, while characters from the past walked through the "walls."

The lighting of the play, particularly the use of various kinds of magic lantern shows, allowed instant changes in time and place that would have

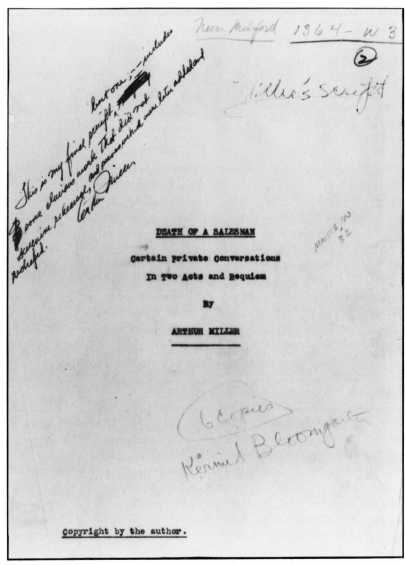

Title page of penultimate typescript for Death of a Salesman

Death of a Salesman

taken minutes in a conventional set. The return to the glory days of Biff's youth, for example, was signaled by projecting a springlike, leafy green pattern on walls and furniture. The apartment houses that hem in Willy's home in his old age were produced by back lighting so they could be removed to suggest the earlier, more hopeful days.

The set helped establish the dual quality of the play, which is both a realistic study of the decline of one man, and at the same time, a symbolic presentation of the pursuit of the American dream. Miller set out to be nothing less than a modern Sophocles of everyday man in this play. His essay "Tragedy and Modern Man" suggests that Willy, the "low man" on life's totem pole, is the Oedipus for this generation: "I think the tragic feeling is evoked in us when we are in the presence of a character who is ready to lay down his life, if need be, to secure one thing—his sense of personal dignity." Critics have denied that Miller established Willy's dignity on the grounds presented in the essay and suggest that Willy's fate is perhaps pathetic. Miller, distinguishing a lesser form from tragedy, argues that "pathos rules where . . . a character fought a battle he could not possibly have won." Many critics do not believe that Willy could have fulfilled his dream.

The American dream and its delusions are everywhere. Though the present time of the play takes place in Brooklyn, all parts of the United States are continually invoked. Willy is the New England man for his company, an explorer who has opened up the territory for them, and his son Biff has followed Horace Greeley's classic advice to "go west, young man!" though with less sanguine results than Greeley foresaw. Biff loves the outdoors and hates offices, and so his father's plans for Biff's becoming a big shot are foiled when Biff works on a ranch. Biff's trip west is a sure sign he will never become a Southern gentleman and scholar / athlete at Thomas Jefferson's University of Virginia, a school he cannot enter because he failed his senior math class. Willy's father, like Willy's brother Ben more myth than man, is the archetypal Yankee peddler peddling the products of his imagination across the land: "he'd drive the team right across the country; through Ohio, and Indiana, Michigan, Illinois . . . stop in the towns and sell the flutes that he'd made on the way." This is the dream; the reality is less inspiring: whipped American cheese—an adulteration of an already processed "food product," cars and appliances that break down before they are paid for, and the tape-recorded voice of Willy's boss's son naming the capitals of all the states. Pathetically, the boy's mechanical voice becomes the prelude to Willy's being fired.

There are two incarnations of the successful American dream in the play: Willy's brother Ben and a salesman named Dave Singleman. Ben is the man who succeeds without working; he has all the luck. There is no sense that Ben is a real character, but only a representation of the dream of instant wealth and success: he heads for Alaska, but gets his directions mixed up and accidentally ends up in Africa where he stumbles on diamond mines. A dream figure of Ben offers to take Willy on his next venture to Alaska, but Willy refuses; he has his own version of this ideal: "The whole wealth of Alaska passes over the lunch table at the Commodore Hotel, and that's the wonder, the wonder of this country, that a man can end up with diamonds here on the basis of being liked!"

Willy's dream of success then is to end up like Ben, but not by any fanciful journeys to Darkest Africa or frozen Alaska, but by selling himself. It is significant that the audience is never told what Willy sells because, as he makes clear, his real product is himself. This makes the need to sell far more important and personal than would otherwise be imagined. The inability to sell means there is something wrong, not with the product, but with the salesman. Willy ties up both his self-image and his manhood in his career. His standard of being well liked is not a casual thing, but the basis of his identity. His memory of Dave Singleman is a description of a life well lived: "What could be more satisfying than to be able to go, at the age of eighty-four, into twenty or thirty different cities, and pick up a phone, and be remembered and loved and helped by so many different people? . . . when he died—and by the way he died the death of a salesman, in his green velvet slippers in the smoker of the New York, New Haven and Hartford, going into Boston—when he died, hundreds of salesmen and buyers were at his funeral." This funeral serves as a contrast to Willy's own at the end of the play, attended by no one except his immediate family and Willy's friend Charley. Instead of making the contrast merely ironical, Miller reminds us of the love Willy has inspired despite his faults. Charley insists: "He's a man way out there in the blue, riding on a smile and a shoeshine. . . . A salesman is got to dream, boy. It comes with the territory."

Most of Willy's frustrating encounters with the American dream occur before the present time of the play. In the present he is occupied with finding some legacy to pass on to his sons, Biff and Hap. This becomes nearly impossible when, at age sixty-two, Willy is fired. After years of wandering,

Biff has returned and Willy dreams of his two boys going into business for themselves. In Mielziner's expressive set, which turned the boys' beds into secret elevators, the two boys are apparently sleeping in full view of the audience when they make an entrance dressed as teenagers. From this early point on, the audience accepts the rapid transitions in time as the play moves in and out of Willy's memories of his relationships with his sons, particularly with Biff.

Willy never stops selling himself, and selling means improving the product—making it sound better than it is. His reports of his selling trips, even on his best days, are always exaggerations. The step to outright lies is only a small one, and Hap inherits this trait from his father. Biff goes along with Willy's petty cheating until he discovers that Willy has cheated even his own wife. From this point on, Biff uses petty thievery, not to get ahead, but to guarantee his own failure.

The more Willy's salesmanship falters, the more it becomes not merely a proof of his identity but a test of his masculinity as well. Willy continually asserts his manhood, both through Biff's athletic prowess and through his own ability to use tools. He continually denigrates his friend Charley, and Charley's son Bernard, for being unmanly. Charley cannot work with his hands, and Bernard is in short pants too long. The major crisis of the past time of the play turns on Willy's confusion of salesmanship and masculinity.

When Biff is unable to graduate from high school because he has failed a math test given by a teacher he had previously antagonized by mimicking him, he turns to Willy for help. Biff has been following in his father's path, looking for the easy way, so instead of preparing to go to summer school he goes to Boston hoping his father can talk the teacher out of flunking him. Meanwhile, Willy, already losing his touch as a salesman, has seduced a buyer not so much for the seduction itself, but to prove he is still a man. When Biff finds the two of them together, suddenly all of the cheating that Willy has condoned—taking materials from construction sites, copying a classmate's math homework, permanently borrowing basketballs from school—becomes reprehensible. For Biff the worst thing about Willy's affair in Boston is that he has given nylon stockings to the woman while Biff's long-suffering mother has had to repair her old stockings.

Since Biff now equates success with dishonesty, he refuses to succeed and wanders from job to job, always leaving when he has a chance to get ahead. As a way of insuring failure, he steals something from his employers. In the present time of the play, Biff steals a pen from a man who might back him and his brother, which dooms Willy's dream of the two boys becoming salesmen of athletic equipment.

Just as entrapped in his father's twisted ideals is Hap, the son who has remained at home. He has become a salesman like his father, but he has debased the notion of selling himself so that the dream behind it is gone—only the technique is left. Hap is almost a parody of his father, but like his brother Biff, he ruins everything he has a chance of completing. Instead of stealing things, Hap steals the

Willy's horror is multiplied when—through Miller's use of surrealistic techniques—Willy's memory of events with the buyer in the Boston hotel room impinges upon his present distress.

The boys' desertion leads to a tremendous argument about the lies that have been told in the house, but finally the barriers that have been built up for so long between Willy and Biff are broken down, and father and son are reunited. This brings Willy back to his original problem of providing a legacy for his boys. He decides that only by suicide can he leave his boys anything. The suicide also appeals to him because he expects a grand funeral

---

Week beginning Monday, February 28, 1949 • Matinees Wednesday and Saturday

KERMIT BLOOMGARDEN and WALTER FRIED
present
ELIA KAZAN'S Production of

DEATH OF A SALESMAN

A New Play by ARTHUR MILLER
Directed by ELIA KAZAN
with

LEE J. COBB   ARTHUR KENNEDY

MILDRED DUNNOCK   HOWARD SMITH   THOMAS CHALMERS

CAMERON MITCHELL   ALAN HEWITT

Setting and Lighting by JO MIELZINER
Incidental Music Composed by ALEX NORTH
Costumes by JULIA SZE

CAST
(In Order of Appearance)

WILLY LOMAN .... LEE J. COBB
LINDA .... MILDRED DUNNOCK
HAPPY .... CAMERON MITCHELL

Playbill

---

women of the men he works for. Hap as "salesman" is seen at work when he picks up a girl in the restaurant. The pickup is an exchange of facades. Hap passes himself off as a champagne salesman and his has-been brother as a football star, while the obvious bar girl passes herself off as a model. The scene is a prelude to one of the cruelest pieces of business in modern stage history. The restaurant was to be the setting for the triumphant announcement that Biff had gotten backing for the boys' new career. Instead, when Willy arrives, Biff not only announces that he has failed, but then he and Hap go off with the girls when Willy goes off sick to the bathroom.

like Dave Singleman's. Such a funeral will prove to his boys that he was well liked: "All the old-timers with the strange license plates—that boy will be thunderstruck, Ben, because he never realized—I am known!"

The failure of the funeral to turn out like this suggests that Willy may also be wrong about the insurance paying off. The audience is never told whether or not it does, but the company would not pay the family if it could establish that Willy's death was a suicide. Furthermore, it is not certain whether or not Willy paid the overdue premium on the insurance, though Miller makes his borrowing the money for it into an important scene. Despite the likelihood that Willy's plan to leave a cash legacy for his boys has failed, it seems proper to see his death as tragic rather than pathetic. Acting destructively because of misconceived ideals is the stuff of tragedy, particularly in Shakespeare and Ibsen. Brutus, Othello, and Hedda Gabler are no more able to right things through their tragic deaths than is Willy Loman.

The critical and financial triumph of *Death of a Salesman* catapulted Miller into the front rank of American dramatists. The play won Miller's second Drama Critics Circle Award and a Pulitzer Prize in 1949. The royalties for *All My Sons* had paid for Miller's house in Brooklyn, but with Miller's characteristic disdain for props, it had remained half-furnished. The more than two-year run of *Death of a Salesman* furnished the house handsomely. In addition to the royalties for the Broadway production, there were two road companies that performed the play, soon to become a movie, and, perhaps most lucrative of all, a part of the repertory of almost every local theatre in the country.

In 1950, Miller's adaptation of Ibsen's *An Enemy of the People* was produced on Broadway. The work strengthened Miller's already strong ties to Ibsen, but it also signaled his interest in a new type of hero. Up to this point Miller's heroes dissipated their energies in the pursuit of misguided ideals. For the most part, Ibsen's heroes are of this mold as well, but Peter Stockmann's courage in the face of his town's moral cowardice needs no defensive explanation like that which Charley gives for Willy Loman at Willy's funeral. Stockmann is a doctor who refuses to permit the town to build a spa after he finds disease in the water supply. He becomes the town's enemy because his rectitude threatens its profits. The chief action of the play is the gradual turning of the entire town against a man who was once one of its most respected citizens.

A hero of this kind emerges in Miller's next play, *The Crucible* (1953). Although John Proctor has his weaknesses, they seem more like classical tragic flaws than the skewed idealism of Willy Loman or Chris Keller. At the end of the play, the audience has no sense at all that the hero's death has been an empty gesture.

The Crucible is set during the Salem witchcraft trials and the analogies with Senator Joseph McCarthy's "witch-hunts" for communists were immediately perceived by the critics. Miller's comments on the play at this time encouraged such comparisons and the play's relevance becomes even more striking a few years later because Miller himself was called (in 1956) before the House Committee on Un-American Activities. In a classic case of life imitating art, Miller took the precise position Proctor took before his Puritan judges. Just as Proctor is willing to implicate himself but refuses to name other dabblers with witchcraft, so Miller named himself, but refused to identify any others involved in communist-front activities.

Despite the contemporary relevance, the historic setting of the play brought about a change in the style of Miller's language. His first three plays are filled with the naturalistic dialogue of the American middle class, but the setting in Puritan New England allows Miller to use a much more formal pattern of speech. Miller sees his style in this play as more poetic than anything else he has done. Although at times the dialogue seems leaden, Miller for the most part makes exemplary use of this new style, its biblical echoes, its metaphorical richness, and its ethical basis. One could hardly imagine Proctor's speech denouncing his own lechery couched in modern English.

Like *An Enemy of the People*, *The Crucible* is about making moral choices in the face of community pressure and about the irrational basis of that pressure. In fact, for most of the play, the audience's emotion is more involved in the growing witch-hunt hysteria than in Proctor's taking a moral position against it. Miller promoted the emphasis on the mass hysteria when he excised Proctor's confrontation with Abigail from the printed version of the play. In this scene, Abigail sees herself purified from sin by the purgatorial fire of their passion. Her unshakable faith in passionate love makes Proctor uncertain that she is acting out of hypocrisy. Since Proctor's sense of guilt and consequent moral uncertainty stem from his adulterous relations with Abigail, removal of the scene changes the play from Proctor's tragedy to the community's crime. Most productions since the 1958 Off-Broadway run, most significantly Olivier's London production in 1965, have omitted the scene.

Since his concern is with the sources of the madness which was plaguing his own time as well as that of the Puritans, Miller explores the multifaceted causes for the growth of the witch-hunt. The first sources, social or economic, are rational. Rev. Parris, the village minister, finds it useful to explain his daughter's indecent behavior by attributing it to witchcraft rather than to his own inability to raise her properly, and Mr. Putnam, the town's richest man, finds great advantage in having his rival landowners charged with witchcraft. Because of her testimony, Abigail Williams, a serving girl and something of a slut, raises herself to a position of power in the town. As the fever grows, however, its sources lie more and more in the irrationality of the human psyche as both individual and mass hysteria take over the town. Paranoia surfaces: Mrs. Putnam's unfocused despair over the loss of her infants in childbirth turns to a more comforting hatred of Rebecca Nurse. Both Mrs. Putnam and Rev. Parris see a kind of inverse election in being tormented by the devil. Miller very convincingly describes the "positive" effects of paranoia. The "victims" of the witches begin to value themselves more highly than those who have been left alone, since it comforts them to know that someone, even Satan, is constantly watching out for them. The culmination of the mass hysteria occurs when the girls of Salem, egged on by the calculated deceptions of Abigail, truly believe that they see the devil in the form of a gigantic bird.

Miller also observes the tremendous force that mere accusation had at this time, something that was evident as well in the McCarthy witch-hunts. A man's career could be ruined if he were merely asked, "Are you now or have you ever been a member of the Communist party?" The power of accusation is seen in the town's reaction to the charges made by two servants, Abigail, who deliberately uses accusation for her own purposes, and Mary Warren, a timid girl who is overwhelmed by the great prominence she gains simply by accusing people of greater stature in the community. Mary's transformation is more interesting than Abigail's because she is a basically good, honest person who struggles against the power that the trials suddenly give her. In his revision of the play, Miller pays much more attention to Mary than Abigail, precisely because he wants to show how good men, even when wanting to do right, yield to the pressure of the group.

The growing corruption of much of the community is balanced by a number of characters who grow in self-understanding and courage as the excesses of the tribunal continue. The most radical change is in Rev. Hale, who comes to Salem as a certifier of witchcraft and finally realizes the horror he is helping to perpetrate. He loses his convictions when he confronts the twisted logic of the chief judge, Deputy Governor Danforth. Hale, once a cold man of principle, ends up by asserting: "Life is God's most precious gift; no principle however glorious, may justify the taking of it." A similar change occurs in Proctor's wife, Elizabeth, who comes to recognize how her denial of life has

contributed to the disasters in the town and in her household. She has blamed her husband for his sexual misconduct and ultimately realizes that her own coldness is to a large extent responsible for his behavior. Both learn the strength they possess in the love they share, but in an ironic conclusion, Elizabeth, who has never lied in her life, lies for her husband when he needs her to tell the truth: Proctor can escape from the tribunal by proving Abigail is a harlot; Elizabeth, now reconciled with her husband, lies about his affair with Abigail because she believes that he is being charged with lechery.

In the topsy-turvy world created by the witch-hunts, lies and the truth cease to have their accustomed values. Giles Corey, whose farm Putnam covets, finds himself in an untenable position once accused of witchcraft. If he denies the charge he will be hanged, but if he accepts the charge he will lose all legal rights and therefore his property. Instead of answering the tribunal's indictment, Corey submits to the torture of pressing. He is crushed to death, but his silence protects his farm for his sons.

In a complex decision, Proctor decides to lie to save his life. His choice is not made out of cowardice but for two other reasons. First of all, because of his adultery and his failure to live an exemplary life, he finds himself unworthy of sharing the martyrdom of the others whose ideal behavior makes their refusal to confess saintly. Second, he feels that he owes his wife the life of love they have not shared up to this point. She was willing to lie for him; now he will give up his honor for her. Proctor signs his confession, but refuses to confess that he knows of anyone else who has dealings with the devil. His judges grudgingly accept this limited confession, but when Proctor realizes the document will be used as propaganda to make other men confess, he tears the pardon and marks himself for the gallows.

Miller felt that both the audience and the critics were very uncomfortable with the theme of witch-hunting in the McCarthy era. *The Crucible* opened to polite, lukewarm reviews; "it got respectful notices, the kind that bury you decently," and after a run of a few months it closed. The play was very popular in Europe, however, and Miller was planning to attend the Brussels opening in 1954 when he was denied a passport by the State Department. The denial of the passport was just the beginning of Miller's troubles with the government over his alleged leftist sympathies. *The Crucible* was revived Off Broadway in 1958 to glowing praise from the same critics who yawned over it five years earlier. This production ran for more than six

21

John (He is weeping)
What say I?! Why, what may I say when goodness calls me good?
I say ~~I~~ I never thought to hear it while I live. It is
a wonder, a wonder, Mister Hathorne.... ~~xxxxxxxxxxxxxxx~~
~~xxxxxxxxxxxxxxx~~ this bride never spoke praise lightly.
~~I~~

                    Hathorne
Will you open with us or will you not?

                    John
They will die to keep their good names white, ~~xxxx~~---I
~~think~~ I cannot spoil them.

                    Hathorne
Then you are one with them.(?)

                    John
(With fury now) Why do you live?, Hathorne, why do you
live!

                    Hathorne
Are you one with them? Say your mind.

                    John
If it must be that I am one with them or one with you--
and there be no footing in between--~~xxxxxxxxxxxxxxx~~ then if I
mistake not the balance of my soul~~xxxxxxxxxxxxxxx~~ it is
one with them.
                    Hathorne   (Parris and Cheever go out at once)
Willard, take ~~i~~them.

                    Elizabeth
~~xxxx~~ (Cries out) John!

                    John
(With a cry) Weep no farewells! I tell you goodness dies
today, and if goodness dies then sure it ~~there~~ lived
and God is clear, God lives, and we will meet, surely!
~~Give them no tears!--and~~ I, I need them not~~xxxxxxxx~~--
you have given me better. (Softly, with great wonder)
I have my soul now. ~~xxxxxxxxxxxxxxxxxxxxxxxxxx~~

for

                              (Rebecca walks with difficulty to
                               Elizabeth, and kisses her; then
                               starts out, but stumbles. John
                               catches her)
                    Rebecca
(With a restrained little laugh of apology that calls out
all her trembling fear)
...I've not had my breakfast.

                              (John supports her out, Martha with
                               them; followed by Hathorne and Willard.
                                        (Cont'd)

The Crucible, revised typescript

hundred performances and established *The Crucible* as the second most popular play in the Miller canon.

In 1955, Miller brought two one-act plays, *A Memory of Two Mondays* and *A View from the Bridge*, to Broadway on the same bill. The plays were completely different in tone and theme. *A Memory of Two Mondays* is a nostalgic glance at Miller's teenage years about which he says that nothing "was written with greater love," while *A View from the Bridge* is a taut tragedy, like "some re-enactment of a Greek myth which was ringing a long-buried bell in my own subconscious mind." In 1956, Miller expanded *A View from the Bridge* into a two-act play that opened in London.

A Memory of Two Mondays is an impressionistic view of Miller's days as a stock clerk in an auto supply house after he graduated from high school. The Miller figure, an eighteen-year-old boy named Bert, is different from the rest of the workers because he will get out of the petty microcosm that is the life of the others. "It is a little world, a home to which, unbelievably perhaps, these people like to come every Monday morning, despite what they say." The play is made up of two scenes six months apart, one in summer, the other in winter. The events of the two days are similar, but the impression each day gives is very different. In the first scene, the small triumphs and tragedies of life seem rich. In the central business of the scene all of the workers combine to protect one of their number, a drunk, from being fired. In their charade, Bert courageously and cleverly outwits the boss. The characters seem imbued with a strength and dignity that goes beyond their petty stations in life: the slightly lecherous advances of an old man seem to be the energy of life; a man with the ability to find a part for an antique auto seems almost the keeper of the racial memory; and Bert's determination to read Tolstoy's *War and Peace* on the subway appears to be the triumph of intellect over circumstance. All of the characters seem filled with hope about new cars, getting married, or next weekend's date.

An important device for changing mood is the lighting, which shifts in the middle of the play from warm summery tones to cold wintry ones. All of the hopes of the first half of the play are quashed. The new car has proven too expensive to run; the old lecher has lost his wife and his energy; the weekend date has turned into a tawdry affair between a woman who is losing her youth and a married man. Although the drunk of the first scene is reformed, he has become joyless in his triumph over alcohol, while a poetry-spouting Irishman of the first scene has become the new alcoholic, with liquor-scrambled brains incapable of retaining the fourth line of a verse. Bert, whose departure for college should be the hope of the play, still has not finished reading his epic novel and there seems little sense that he ever will. More upsetting is the fact that no one seems to care about his departure and that in six months his existence will be forgotten altogether.

One of the notions Miller stresses is how the survival of this community even at a very minimal level depends upon its insularity. Bert and the poetic Irishman take it upon themselves to clean the filthy windows of the warehouse with the hope of brightening things up. Instead, the view of the world outside, including a run-down whorehouse, makes the workers less content with their lot. Like Gregers Werle in Ibsen's *The Wild Duck*, Bert's attempt to bring light only calls attention to the dirt.

In "Tragedy and the Common Man" Miller argues that it is possible to write tragedy in the classic Greek mode about the plight of modern man. Though the essay was written almost immediately after *Death of a Salesman*, it is in *A View from the Bridge* that Miller creates his contemporary classical tragedy. The tense conflict of loyalties in the play's protagonist, Eddie Carbone, reveals the same undiscovered passion and misconception of events in an essentially good man that is at the heart of *Oedipus Rex*. Eddie fits Miller's definition of the tragic hero in "his inherent unwillingness to remain passive in the face of what he conceives to be a challenge to his dignity, his image of his rightful status."

A View from the Bridge, set in the Italian-American community in Brooklyn, New York, presents Eddie's downfall coming about as the result of his incestuous longing for his young niece Catherine, who lives with him and his wife Beatrice. Because he is so jealous of her, he cannot abide her growing interest in other men. When Catherine is attracted to an illegal alien, Rodolpho, Eddie, who is also Italian, betrays Rodolpho to the immigration authorities, precipitating his own fatal confrontation with Rodolpho's brother Marco.

The play is narrated by Eddie's lawyer Alfieri, a calm and reasonable man who perceives basic passions accurately. Alfieri functions like the chorus of a Greek play: he provides commentary on the action but is unable to stop its inevitable flow. Similarly, the immigration officers are just as implacable as the Furies that hound Orestes. Furthermore, the Italian-American community provides the necessarily rigid system of values which allows classical tragedy to take so precisely the measure of man: violating the laws of the community is just as dangerous to Eddie as Oedipus's trying to spurn the oracle at Delphi. The existence of the community and its code makes Eddie's betrayal of Marco and Rodolpho not merely a personal vendetta, but a rupture in the order of things.

When *A View from the Bridge* was first produced on Broadway as a one-act play, it nearly foundered on Miller's insistence that Eddie's conflict with his world be presented as the spare collision of two forces. The telegraphic diction and nonnaturalistic style of acting left the audiences cold. Miller was trying to counter what he perceived to be the prevailing romanticism on Broadway, but he could not find a way to make Eddie's Brooklyn accent formal. The right style for the play was found, somewhat accidentally, when Peter Brook put it on in London with actors accustomed to playing Shakespeare. Their inability to capture the Brooklyn dialect combined with their training in playing larger-than-life roles to give the commonplace world of the community of Red Hook the stature of ancient Thebes. For the two-act London production, Miller expanded the role of Eddie's wife, Beatrice, adding a dimension of sympathy lacking in the one-act version.

Miller makes it clear that the Sicilian-American community in the shadow of the Brooklyn Bridge has grown up clinging to ancient codes of justice and revenge that are fully as exacting as those of Sophocles' Thebes. In the play the rules of the community are established early with the report of a disturbing incident: when a young boy betrays illegal immigrants ("submarines") staying in his father's house, he is beaten by his father and made an outcast by the community.

In Red Hook, there is no crime greater than treachery. As the play opens, the surface harmony of the Carbone household is about to be shattered by the arrival of Marco and Rodolpho, two other "submarines." The tension already in the house is seen in Eddie's relationship to his seventeen-year-old niece, Catherine. He has kept her from growing up—by keeping her in school, by not letting her go out with boys, by monitoring what she wears—ostensibly because he wants to do his best for his sister's child. Eddie is unwilling to face the real reason for his protectiveness: he has fallen in love with her. He refuses even to consider the possibility, though it is clear to Beatrice that Catherine's sexual maturity has destroyed their marriage. Since Eddie cannot admit to himself that he has betrayed his sister, he begins to project his guilt upon others, especially upon Rodolpho.

Marco, an ox of a man, has come to America to earn money for his family in Italy and plans to return, but Rodolpho has come to stay. Catherine falls in love with Rodolpho and Eddie begins to find fault with him. Like Othello, whose refusal to admit his own jealousy leads to incredible accusations, Eddie begins to see foulness everywhere because he will not see it in himself.

At first Eddie accuses Rodolpho of using Catherine as a "passport," marrying her so that he can stay in America because he is the husband of a citizen. When Catherine refuses to believe this allegation, Eddie raises a new specter: he suggests that Rodolpho, who likes to sing, sew, and cook, is a homosexual. With the issue of homosexuality, Miller shows how tragic events snowball from the protagonist's first mistake. The accusation is at first a logical maneuver on Eddie's part, much like Putnam and Parris's using accusations of witchcraft for their own advantage in *The Crucible*. Its purpose is to substantiate Eddie's claim that Rodolpho could be after Catherine only because he wants to stay in America. Little by little, Eddie's own manhood becomes tied up in the charge: the more he proves Rodolpho is not a man, the more Eddie can convince himself of his own manhood. Eddie is no longer a young man, and his sexual relations with his wife have deteriorated. For this reason, Rodolpho's youth threatens Eddie's virility and much of the last half of the play is a test of Eddie's manhood disguised as a test of Rodolpho's.

Miller begins to convert the verbal anger to physical conflict when Eddie teaches Rodolpho to box so that he can beat him up "fairly." Eddie stages the boxing lesson to parade his masculinity before Catherine, but it ends up differently from the way he expects. Marco picks up a heavy chair by one leg to demonstrate that he is strong enough to kill a man with his bare hands. The scene ends with Marco silently challenging Eddie to mock his brother a second time. Tension between the two fills the stage as the scene ends. In the inevitable flow of this tragedy, it is only a matter of time before Eddie will shame Rodolpho more brazenly and Marco will use his deadly hands.

In great tragedy, the smallest gestures can be earth shattering to the audience when they have been set up to make the tragic denouement unavoidable. For example, Othello's slapping Desdemona in front of her peers is perhaps more shocking than his murdering her in the privacy of their bedchamber. Miller sets up such a moment when, in rapid succession, Eddie kisses Catherine and then Rodolpho. The audience is astounded each time. When Eddie finds the two lovers coming from her bedroom, he kisses Catherine passionately. He cannot cope with this evidence of the lovers' intimacy, so he impugns Rodolpho's masculinity by offering Catherine a kiss meant to show her what a man's kiss is really like. Even at this point, Eddie will not admit that the kiss is an acknowledgment of his own passion rather than an object lesson for his niece. Eddie's self-deception is so great that he is genuinely shocked at the end of the play when Beatrice confronts him with the truth about his feelings for Catherine.

The implications of Eddie's second kiss are even more far-reaching. Knowing how embarrassing such a kiss would be in the ultramasculine Sicilian community, Eddie kisses Rodolpho to shame him, perhaps hoping that Rodolpho will strike back and give Eddie an excuse to kill him. Eddie later tries to use the fact that Rodolpho cannot break out of his embrace as further proof of his homosexuality, arguing that he could have gotten free but that he did not want to. The kiss seems also to be the Sicilian kiss of death, Eddie's warning to Rodolpho that he means to destroy him, and finally, it is a Judas kiss, warning the audience that Eddie will betray Rodolpho.

Eddie's betrayal of Marco and Rodolpho must be bought at a terrible price. Like Creon in Sophocles' *Antigone*, Eddie calls on the law of the land to subvert a higher law. The difference is that Eddie's loyalties are with the law he rejects. The situation dictates that the tragic hero's crime extends far beyond the needs of his vengeance. Not merely does the betrayal ruin Rodolpho, but it also must destroy Marco, and therefore take the bread out of the mouths of Marco's children. Miller extends the crime against the community even further by planting two additional "submarines" in Eddie's building for the immigration authorities to find. Like Hamlet, who kills a half-dozen innocent people to carry out his revenge on Claudius, Eddie finds that fate can be pushed in a certain direction, but once started, its avalanche cannot be controlled. The price paid is, of course, not merely the unwitting destruction of others; Eddie is shamed before the community and inevitably killed by Marco. When Alfieri, Miller's narrator in the play, describes Eddie, he is also describing the quintessential Millerian hero—the man who may do things wrong but who does them with every ounce of his being: "Most of the time now we settle for half and I like it better. But the truth is holy, and even as I know how wrong he was, and his death useless, I tremble, for I confess that something perversely pure calls to me from his memory—not purely

good, but himself, purely, for he allowed himself to be wholly known and for that I think I will love him more than all my sensible clients."

A View from the Bridge won Miller his third Drama Critics Circle Award, and the production of the two one-act plays in 1955 marked the end of a fruitful eight-year period of playwriting. He was now to enter a nine-year period of personal and political problems that would keep him from finishing a new play until 1964.

In 1955, Miller was divorced from Mary Grace Slattery, and in the same year his troubles because of his leftist interests began in earnest. He had been working with the New York Youth Board on a film about juvenile delinquents when the American Legion and the Catholic War Veterans applied pressure to have the project dropped because of Miller's "Communist ties." He had, after all, been refused a passport the previous year as a "person believed to be supporting the Communist movement." The pressure by the two groups was successful and work on the film ceased.

Two years later, Miller was called before Representative Francis Walter's Committee on Un-

American Activities. Miller chatted amiably with the committee members about his opinions on Ezra Pound, Elia Kazan, Howard Fast, Red China, and the repeal of the Smith Act, the 1940 law that made it a federal offense to advocate violent overthrow of the government or to be a member of any group devoted to such advocacy. The committee was most cordial in discussing these matters with Miller, but then asked Miller about his attendance at a meeting of Communist writers in 1947. Miller refused to take the Fifth Amendment and freely admitted that he had been at the meeting, though he denied ever being a member of the Communist party. The committee then asked him to name other writers who were there. At this point, Miller, like Proctor in *The Crucible*, said that his conscience would not permit him to name any others. Since the committee already knew from other sources who had attended the meeting, it is clear that the questions were asked to see if Miller would implicate his colleagues. Proctor's judges too were not so much interested in knowing the names, but in having Proctor betray his fellows.

Because of his refusal to answer the committee's questions, Miller was put on trial for contempt of Congress. The judge decided that Miller's motives were commendable, but that his position was legally indefensible, and he found Miller guilty on two counts of contempt. Miller's sentencing was deferred pending an appeal. In the following year, 1958, Miller's conviction was overturned on a technicality by the U.S. Court of Appeals.

In 1956, Miller married Marilyn Monroe, sparking headlines of the "Pinko Playwright Weds Sex Goddess" variety. The marriage at first was more successful than the cynics predicted with Monroe almost reverent in the presence of her intellectual husband. She was tired of her "dumb blonde" roles and thought her marriage to Miller might end the typecasting: "If I was nothing but a dumb blonde, he wouldn't have married me." Despite her deference to his work habits, Miller soon fell into Monroe's orbit rather than vice versa. He became involved in her financial arrangements and her script choices, pushing her to make *Some Like It Hot*, her most successful movie. She was not particularly pleased, however, that Miller thought her perfect for the quintessential "dumb blonde" part of Sugar Kane. Miller also persuaded Yves Montand to star with her in *Let's Make Love*. Montand and his wife, Simone Signoret, had starred in a French production of *The Crucible*, and both were close friends of Miller's. The marriage began to founder as Monroe found herself unable to bear

Miller's child. Though he seemed to be working constantly, Miller produced no new plays during their marriage. Eventually, he created a screenplay, *The Misfits*, as a vehicle for his wife. The screenplay is a revision of a short story he wrote soon after his divorce from Mary Grace Slattery. While in Nevada waiting for his divorce, Miller joined a group of cowboys who were rounding up mustangs to sell them for dog food. The mustangs, because they were too small to ride, were called "misfits." Miller was particularly impressed by the mechanization of the West as he watched the cowboys using trucks and light planes in their roundup. In his story, Miller tells of three such cowboys whose lives become as mechanized as the tools of their trade. Clearly they are as much misfits as the horses they pursue.

Marilyn Monroe's part of Roslyn, the dance hall girl, was grafted onto the original story. Roslyn identifies with the mustangs as fellow victims of life and ultimately convinces the cowboys to give up their work. Monroe was not happy with the part Miller wrote for her. She saw it as another "dumb blonde" role, with Roslyn using feminine rage instead of articulate logic to change the men's minds. "He was supposed to be writing this for me. He could have written me anything and he comes up with this. If that's what he thinks of me, well, then I'm not for him and he's not for me," she complained. In addition to her quarreling with Miller over the role he had created for her, she began to argue with him about whose picture it was. It had been written as a present for her after her last miscarriage, but Miller began to get angry with her for being late to the set of *his* picture. They left Hollywood separately and within the year (1961), they were divorced. The filming of *The Misfits* became even more traumatic for both of them when Clark Gable, who starred as Gay Langland, suffered a fatal heart attack on the last day of shooting. Miller attended the funeral, but Monroe did not.

When Miller rewrote his short story, he put some of his personal life into the part of Gay who trades his freedom for married life with Roslyn. In the film the marriage marks the beginning of a new kind of responsible manhood. Miller says of Gay that he "has lived across the frontier all his life, but because he finally gets related to this woman, now he can choose something else—the gratification offered by their relationship." Perhaps Miller perceived this ideal in his relationship with Monroe, but the reality was something else. As she slid further and further into dependence on alcohol and drugs, he found himself unable to help her and frustrated

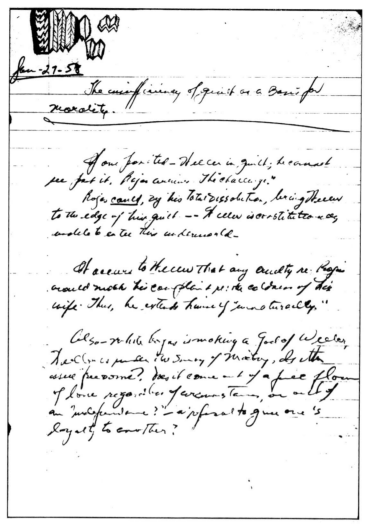

Notes for After the Fall

by his inability to do so. Nonetheless, Miller had never worked harder on a project than on *The Misfits* continually staying up after midnight, revising the script, trying to get Monroe's part right for the next day's shooting. Two months after the death of Gable, Monroe was in Mexico filing for divorce.

The Misfits would be Monroe's last film; after her divorce from Miller, she began work on *Something's Got to Give*, a film for director George Cukor. The problems on the set escalated even beyond those on *The Misfits*, and Monroe left the set with her future in Hollywood up in the air. Two months later, on 4 August 1962, she was found dead from an overdose of sleeping pills. Joe Dimaggio arranged the funeral, barring all of Hollywood from the simple ceremony at Westwood Cemetery. Miller, who had recently married Ingeborg Morath, one of the photographers for *The Misfits*, did not attend the funeral.

In 1964 Miller finished *After the Fall*, his first play in nine years, for the Lincoln Center Repertory Company. The central theme of the play is how its protagonist, Quentin, can come to terms with his past. Dominated by Quentin's memory, the action of the play is expressionistic throughout, using an open space in which various people and events come and go, always confronting Quentin's judging mind. In this episodic structure the recurrent matter to be resolved is the nature of guilt, the limits of personal responsibility for the lives of others, and the means of expiation for crimes real or imagined. Three crises in Quentin's life are vividly presented: Nazi death camps, the suicide of Quentin's beautiful but neurotic wife, Maggie; and Quentin's confrontation with the anti-Communist House Committee on Un-American Activities.

When *After the Fall* opened most of the interest was in how closely the character of Maggie resembled Marilyn Monroe. Many of the critics saw Miller engaged in a tawdry game of marry-and-tell in which he used the central character, Quentin, as a mouthpiece to excuse his inability to keep Monroe from killing herself. Miller's denial of the autobiographical element only pitched the critical furor higher, and critics paraded the parallels between Miller's life and Quentin's. Like Quentin, Miller was the son of a wealthy man who went broke during the Depression; like Quentin, Miller had his share of troubles with the House Committee on Un-American Activities; like Quentin, Miller was greatly troubled by guilt for not having suffered in German concentration camps; but most importantly, like Quentin, Miller married a sensuous woman for whom love was the only salvation, and he was not able to save her.

Despite the initial interest in the autobiographical elements, the play's greatest weakness is not that the characters are too lifelike, but that they are too abstract: whomever they may be modeled upon, all the characters come to represent principles which Quentin is trying to sort out in his life. Since the play purports to take place in "the mind, thought and memory of Quentin," one might say that Miller has succeeded in reducing human beings to attitudes, but this theoretical success does not produce satisfactory character interaction. Characters from various points in Quentin's life emerge from the shadows of the nonrepresentational set to enact their lives. The voices overlap, and often characters from different plot lines will speak out of context on an incident to which they are not related. The effect of this multilevel chorus is not the deepening of understanding, but rather the flattening of human experience as one event too neatly parallels another. It is ironic that Miller has Quentin voice the play's theme with the observation, "We are killing one another with abstraction."

Although the play is mostly about Quentin's relationship with women, Quentin's emotional problem originates in the quintessential Miller plot: a failing father has two sons—one who goes off to seek ideals, the other who remains behind to help the father cope with the collapse. In *After the Fall* Miller focuses on the son who leaves home and never gets over his guilt for deserting his father. The father and the brother, Dan, are little more

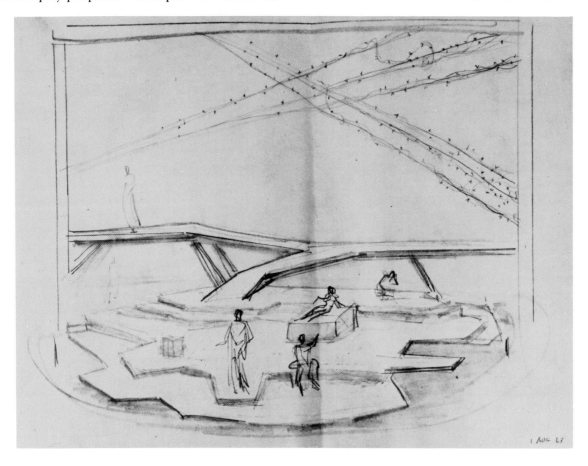

Stage design by Jo Mielziner for After the Fall

than shadows, but their voices are trumpets of guilt. Whenever Quentin does something he considers shameful, they remind him that despite his desertion his family is always behind him.

Quentin's mother provides one of the female role models in the play, and in many ways his life is a reaction against her manipulation of the family. Quentin's earliest memory is his mother's deserting him for a week while she goes to the beach with his older brother and then tries to buy back his love with a toy. His mother treats his father in the same way. She spends most of her time destroying his ego until the collapse of his business reduces him to misery and dependence. Then she takes great pleasure in being the comforter. Parallel to Quentin's mother is Elsie, the wife of Quentin's former law professor who treats her husband like a little boy by continually reminding him of his dependence on her. Elsie is completely contemptuous of her husband until he is crushed by antileftist investigations, at which point she becomes his protector.

In addition to the women who treat men like little boys so they can smother them with salvation, there are the martyrs who need to be saved. The martyrs include Felice, whom Quentin gives the courage to get a nose job; Holga, who needs reassurance that she is not guilty for escaping the ovens at Auschwitz; and finally Maggie, who wants to believe she has some value beyond her flesh. Basically, Quentin's life is a flight from the first kind of woman to the second, but he never fully realizes that the second kind of woman creates a greater dependency in the man than the first. Like most of the women in Ibsen's *Hedda Gabler*, Quentin is so bent on saving people that he seems at a loss when there is no one to save. Significantly, he first takes Maggie to bed after he has straightened out a legal problem of hers. "I can't even go to bed without a principle," he says. Once he has begun to save her, he can sleep with her. The play is set up as a *demande d'amour*, a request for the audience to decide an unresolved question about love. Quentin has had unsuccessful marriages with two women (Louise and Maggie) and asks if he should marry a third, Holga. The women certainly parallel Miller's three wives; however, it seems likely that the self-centered Quentin will fail in his third marriage as well.

The play's title refers to the Fall from Eden and the loss of innocence. In the foreword to the play, Miller says, "through Quentin's agony in this play there runs the everlasting temptation of Innocence, that deep desire to return to when, it seems, he was in fact without blame. . . . But the closer he examines those seemingly unified years the clearer

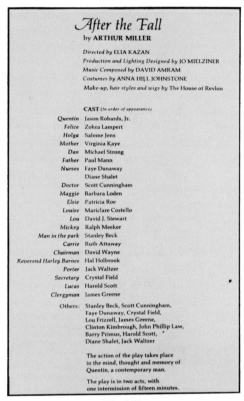

Playbill

it becomes that his Paradise keeps slipping back and back." Like David Beeves in *The Man Who Had All the Luck*, Quentin feels he has never quite paid for his sins, and so he is wracked by guilt. Furthermore, Quentin cannot possibly pay for his crimes because they are sins of omission. He has not stayed with his father; he has not communicated with Louise; he has not died at Auschwitz; he has not been forced to choose between his friend and his career as he expected. This last "crime" illustrates Miller's point and the absurdity of Quentin's obsession with guilt. Quentin has committed himself to defending Lou, his law professor, against the Committee on Un-American Activities, knowing that his law firm will fire him if he takes the case. Understandably, Quentin has some qualms about his commitment. He is relieved when Lou releases him from his commitment by taking his own life, but then he feels guilty because he is relieved rather than upset. Miller's comment on the murder of Abel in reference to this play pinpoints Quentin's (and Miller's) own obsession with guilt: "The first real 'story' in the Bible is the murder of Abel. Before this drama there is only a featureless Paradise. But in that Eden there was peace because man had no consciousness of himself. . . . Presumably we are being told that the human being becomes 'himself' in the act of becoming aware of his sinfulness. He 'is' what he is ashamed of." Miller's parallel between the Old Testament's story of Cain and Abel and the events in *After the Fall* is, however, quite misleading. Murdering one's brother is one thing, but Quentin's sins of omission are something else. It is easy to discern one's own character from his sins; but one's concept of himself is necessarily more amorphous when it is determined by what one has not done. Shame over things which, in retrospect, one ought to have done but did not is radically different from shame over a positive transgression. Furthermore, the list of one's responsibilities grows the more one is an idealist. For someone like Quentin with a salvation complex, everyone's misfortunes become his responsibility so his fund of guilt is endless.

The title's reference to Eden is also a reminder that Eve is the only woman who was literally an extension of her husband's self and not a separate personality. After the Fall, all lovers are separate individuals, but Quentin's relations with women founder on the question of how separate they should be. He leaves Louise because she has become a separate person, not dependent upon him for emotional support nor existing to provide him with praise and comfort. On the contrary, he leaves Maggie because she is never a separate person. Maggie begins their relationship with adoration for Quentin and ends with blame, but her self-image is always based on him, not on herself. Quentin has an Adam's rib complex: he can deal with women only insofar as they are extensions of himself.

At the end of 1964, Miller wrote a second play for the Lincoln Center Repertory, *Incident at Vichy*. As the play opens, seven actors are seen frozen in "attitudes expressive of their personalities and functions." Even though the characters begin to move once the play starts, almost all of them remain locked in their own personalities for the rest of the play. *Incident at Vichy* tests those personalities to see whether anything, even the specter of the concentration camps, can stir them out of their rigidity. The seven men, all living in Vichy France, have been rounded up by the Nazis and it becomes increasingly clear that they have been caught in a racial purity dragnet. One by one, they are marched to the interrogation room, and as their circle grows smaller, those remaining argue about their fate and about the nature of humanity. What must be decided ultimately is whether or not the Nazis can strip them of every shred of human dignity.

Miller brilliantly shows the deepening of the moral crisis. At first, all try to believe that the interrogation is routine—that they have been brought in for a simple check of credentials. As the situation worsens, each tries to separate himself from the rest of the group by finding a reason for the Nazis' wanting to destroy the others while leaving him alone: the other is a gypsy, a Communist, a Catholic, a Jew. Each wants to convince himself that he is better off not being one of *those*: "Each man has his Jew; it is the other . . . the man whose death leaves you relieved that you are not him, despite your decency." It becomes clear that for most men, real decency fails when the alternative is self-destruction.

As the Nazis continue to take away the survivors, those who deem themselves moral individuals find their morality tested. Bayard, a Communist, finds a measure of courage in playing the role of spokesman of the people, even though he is alone. Miller suggests that role-playing is too fragile a response to stand up to such assaults on human dignity as the measuring of penises. As Bayard is taken he assumes "an artificial and almost absurd posture of confidence." No matter how great his bravery, he has not gotten out of his self, producing the irony of a Communist who has nothing in common with anyone else.

The final survivors, Leduc, a Jewish psychiatrist, and Von Berg, an Austrian Catholic aristocrat, debate the subject of personal responsibility in such matters. Leduc makes claims for responsibility while Von Berg notes the tendency of his own class to shirk its duty. Leduc's concern with responsibility finds a sensitive nerve in the Nazi major who is in charge of the investigation. The major, a regular army officer, is horrified by the business of racial policies, so Leduc pushes him to act, to stop the horror in some small way. The major undercuts Leduc's idealism when he tempts him with freedom: "If you were released and the others were kept . . . would you refuse?" When Leduc cannot deny he would take the pass to freedom, he loses his hold on the major's sympathies; the major returns to the work he loathes.

After his failure with the major, Leduc cross-examines Von Berg, whose beliefs make him an unlikely hero. Von Berg is able to make sense of the Nazis on aesthetic terms because they are, in a way, like him and his class in being beyond rationality. Like an aristocrat's maintaining the trappings of his rank even while destitute, the Nazis' destruction of the Jews is awesome because it does not make economic sense: "The fact that it costs money and uses up trains and personnel—this only guarantees the integrity, the purity, the existence of their feelings. . . . They are poets, they are striving for a new nobility, the nobility of the totally vulgar."

Although he vows that he hates the Nazis, Von Berg's logic would seem to leave him open to change his loyalty. Leduc argues that Von Berg had a chance to act on his loathing of the Nazis, but failed to take it. Furthermore, it is not enough that Von Berg feels guilty about this failure; it is his duty to act and take responsibility for his fellow human beings. It is here that Miller takes his characters a step beyond *After the Fall*. Quentin was overwhelmed by complicity of his fellow human beings—in fact, even in the deaths of concentration camp victims he had never seen—but his guilt never led him to being crushed so that another could survive. In *Incident at Vichy*, Von Berg takes this next step. When he comes out of the interrogation room, he holds a pass for freedom. He has been declared not guilty of brotherhood with his fellow prisoners: he is free. Von Berg understands, however, that no man can deny his bond with humanity and still remain a human being. He has learned that not only does rank have obligations, but so does humanity. He hands the pass to Leduc and accepts fully his complicity in the human race. Quentin's problem seems to be that he has never had so neat a chance to pay the price of admission to the human race.

After Miller had two plays produced with the Lincoln Center Repertory (both performed at the company's temporary headquarters at the ANTA Washington Square Theatre), he broke with the theatre's governing board over its repertory policy. Miller felt that the company was not trying to develop a true repertory theatre like those in Europe. For this reason, he returned to Broadway with his next play, *The Price* (1968).

The Price is a most traditional piece of theatre, harking back to *All My Sons*, not only in its theme of defining the price one pays for the choices in life, but also in its technique of the characters uncovering the past by retelling events to reveal one incompletely understood motive after another in their present lives. The play has almost no present time; it is almost all recognition, as its setting soon makes clear. A policeman, at the brink of retirement, decides to sell his deceased father's furniture from the attic of a condemned brownstone. The play's title refers, first of all, to the price he can get for the furniture from a secondhand-furniture dealer. The play is set entirely in the attic and the claustrophobic set, which puts a whole houseful of furniture in one room, reinforces what Miller has been saying in all his plays: at some point in one's life everything important from the past will be set out and a price will have to be put on it.

The hero, Victor Frank, like Biff in *Death of a Salesman* or Chris in *All My Sons*, is an idealist whose refusal to compromise has cost him dearly. Like those other idealists of Miller's, however, there is something hollow at the core of his virtue. Victor sets out to bargain with the furniture appraiser, but he does not know how to bargain about either furniture or life.

The ninety-year-old furniture dealer, a marvelous comic creation named Gregory Solomon, is a shape-shifting con man, whose varied life contrasts brilliantly with Victor's dull lifetime on the force. In the course of their dealings, Solomon claims he was a vaudeville acrobat, a sailor in the British navy, the husband of three or four wives (he loses count), and the president of the New York furniture dealers' association. The audience is meant never to be certain how much of Solomon's stories are true: he exists as a foil for Victor. Victor, at fifty, is past the earliest retirement age for a policeman, and he feels that it is too late in his life to make a new start. Solomon, the former acrobat, is far more flexible than Victor, a man forty years his junior. Victor is afraid to face the future, but Solomon comes out of retirement to face the challenge of selling Victor's once expensive, but now nearly worthless, furniture. Victor has dreams of doing "something in science," but he fears making a commitment because starting in science now will mean he has wasted his life to this point. The uncovering of the past will reveal he could have started thirty years earlier.

Victor's father, like Quentin's in *After the Fall* and Miller's own father, went bankrupt in the Depression, and Victor made the choice to stay with him rather than pursue his own dreams. He sees himself as the noble son who sacrificed his own future—he was always good in science—for his broken father, while his brother went off and became a success as a doctor. As a policeman, he can point to his life as one of public-spirited self-sacrifice. The lynch pin of his sacrifice is his resentment of his brother Walter, whom he has not seen in half a lifetime. The sale of the father's furniture brings them together for a bruising confrontation.

The audience has been prepared to dislike Walter as a selfish, money-hungry physician who not only deserted his father, but also later refused to lend Victor the money he needed to go to college. The two men have not spoken since Walter turned down Victor's request. When Walter appears, the audience's suspicions seem to be confirmed. Walter is appalled at the low price that Victor has accepted for the furniture and offers a devious scheme for making a great deal of money out of it. Instead of selling the furniture, Walter will have Solomon overapprais it outrageously and then give it to charity, thereby reaping a huge profit in the form of a tax refund. When Walter offers to give the whole amount to Victor, it seems like blood money to pay off his guilt at having refused the loan years before. As the story unfolds, however, Victor's nobility loses much of its luster.

Both brothers' lives have been reactions to the father's failure. Walter has pursued money and success voraciously, hoping to insulate himself from his father's fate. The result has been a nervous breakdown and divorce. He sees his life as a continual striving that has left no time for living, and he envies the full life he thinks Victor has lived.

Victor, on the other hand, has confused cause and effect in his sacrifice for his father. Victor's version of his life is as follows: his father was broke and broken in spirit so he had to sacrifice his future by taking a job he did not like to support his father; the job drifted into an unwanted career, and his life was wasted because he was caring for his father; his brother helped ruin his life by refusing him a loan to pay for his education.

The long-hidden secret revealed at this time is that the father was not broke—though his millions were gone, he still had $4,000, a huge sum during the Depression and certainly enough to tide him over while his son finished school. Even more shocking is the revelation that Victor knew about the money, not to the penny, but he knew that his father was not destitute. This knowledge changes the meaning of his self-sacrifice: his father's poverty becomes his excuse for not succeeding rather than his reason. Like his brother, Victor does not want to repeat his father's fall, but he takes the opposite path to safety. Walter tries to get so high up nothing can reach him; Victor avoids a dangerous fall by not trying to scale the heights at all. It is also likely that Victor uses the excuse of his father's poverty to avoid direct competition with his brother. Victor had always been the smarter one in school, but at the time he was ready to go to college, Walter was already established as a doctor. As Walter points out, the loan was not necessary: if Victor did not want to take his father's money, he could have sold the family's harp, which even in the Depression was worth enough to pay for his tuition. Victor has kept the harp all these years, ironically symbolizing his desire to be an "angel" above the common wants of men.

As in all Miller plays, motivations remain complex even when they are explained, and here Walter's explanation is a little too facile: his father's weakness of character and refusal to admit he had any money do not really excuse Walter's neglect, and Walter's judgment that he should not have supported Victor's education because the money was there may be legally correct, but it is a judgment as harsh as Cain's about Abel—Walter has refused to be his brother's keeper.

As the revelations continue, Victor's staying with his father is seen to be more than cowardice: he had given his father, who trusted no one in the world, someone to believe in. It was not an act of love—for there was no love in the family's wealthy household—but an illusion of love to keep his father from falling apart. Victor's wife, Esther, sees that maintaining the illusion has generated its own love, and so the play ends on a note of muted optimism. Esther has just learned that she has reason to be bitter about her husband's wasted life, but in watching the brothers fight she realizes what is missing from their relationship: "It always seems to me that one little step more and some crazy kind of forgiveness will come and lift up everyone." She takes the step and walks out with her life and her marriage intact.

With all Miller's concern with the loss of innocence and the conflict between two brothers, it was inevitable that he would return to the archetype in the book of Genesis. He had already written *After the Fall*; he moved to before the Fall in *The Creation of the World and Other Business*. The play is a comic retelling of the Adam and Eve and Cain and Abel stories, but the "other business" in the title refers not only to these stories, but also to the comic stage business or "shtick." The play is a light comedy that is also supposed to make a philosophic statement. In the program, each act is given a philosophic question to answer—"When Every Man Wants Justice, Why Does He Go On Creating Injustice?"—but it is unclear whether the questions are ironic counterpoints to the action or mere pretension.

Most of the humor of the play comes from anachronisms—God talking about Notre Dame, an angel playing Beethoven on a bassoon, Adam thinking about volleyball when he sees Eve's behind—and from mixing biblical language with modern slang. The comic aspect of Adam and Eve's attempt to learn about sex is embarrassingly heavy-handed. When Lucifer says "he's sticking it in her ear now," groans are the only possible response.

The play is a debate between God and Lucifer about the nature of good and evil with the Genesis stories used to illustrate their positions. For the most part, Lucifer is the more attractive of the pair, but his character seems confused, rather than paradoxical as in Milton or Shaw. At times, he seems to be a Promethean liberator of mankind, at other times an earthly dictator looking for subjects to rule. The tree is the tree of sexual knowledge, and Lucifer urges Eve to eat its fruit so that God can have the grandchild he wants. Lucifer, for all his wit, does not seem to recognize the absurdity in God's behavior. God wants Adam and Eve to be fruitful and multiply, but they cannot because the tree holds the secret of how it is done; then, when they do eat from the tree, God is furious that they have disobeyed his prohibition.

In the Cain and Abel story, Miller seems to lose his sense of humor entirely. Lucifer, who is for the coexistence of good and evil because it equates him with God, tries to keep Cain from killing his brother, but even he cannot untangle the ultimate sibling rivalry. Like Quentin, Cain hates his brother because Abel was his mother's favorite. Miller has told his story one time too many.

The play was a bomb. It closed after twenty performances, with the critics attacking it unmercifully. Though some of the reviews were downright abusive, the worst were by the critics who condescended to Miller as the great man fallen on hard times. Miller angrily blasted the critics and stomped off to his home in Connecticut.

Miller was not yet finished with Eden, and the following year he turned *Creation of the World* into a musical for which he wrote the lyrics. He directed the performance of *Up from Paradise* at his alma mater, the University of Michigan.

Perhaps because he was so badly stung by the New York critics, Miller took his next play, *The Archbishop's Ceiling* (1977) to the Kennedy Center for the Performing Arts in Washington, D.C. The play is a response to Soviet treatment of dissident writers. It is set in some European Communist state where the hero, a renowned novelist named Sigmund, is pondering his fate. He has written an outspoken letter to the United Nations condemning conditions in his country and now he must choose between exile and trial for treason. Three other people are involved in his decision: Marcus, a rival novelist who was once a rebel like Sigmund, but now has come to terms with the regime; Adrian, a bestselling American author who feels his success has come too easily; and Maya, an actress who was the lover of both European writers and the subject of novels by all three.

Sigmund's choice is the result of a four-cornered debate marked by shifting loyalties and the emergence of personal and professional jealousy and admiration. The play takes place in a room in what was once the archbishop's palace, and all of the characters believe that the ceiling is bugged, though none is certain that is the case. The fact that it is the archbishop's ceiling suggests that speaking in the room is like speaking under a heaven which may or may not be filled with a God, who may or may not be listening. Miller makes wonderful use of the uncertainty: everything said in the room is spoken for the benefit of both the ceiling and the other characters in the room. Only by catching every nuance can a character pick up the others' real meanings, and even then there is uncertainty—the other characters may be untrustworthy, or all the others may be acting out an elaborate game set up by the government to manipulate Sigmund.

Though there are reminiscences of Jean Genet's *The Balcony* in the multiple possibilities of illusion (Maya's name can mean "the illusions that sustain man"), Miller allows himself his most optimistic conclusion since *The Man Who Had All the Luck*. Sigmund chooses to stay, gets Marcus to support his radical position, and convinces Adrian and Maya to smuggle out parts of his novel. Though it is likely they will be caught, their heroism is unlike anything in Miller's work except John Proctor's death in *The Crucible*.

The play's credo then reaffirms what Miller had said about human possibility twenty years earlier in the introduction to the *Collected Plays* (1957): "The past half century has created an almost overwhelming documentation of man as a nearly passive creation of environment and family-created psychological drives. If only from the dramatic point of view, this dictum cannot be accepted as final and 'realistic' any more than man's ultimate position can be accepted as his efficient use by state and corporate apparatus." Miller's commitment to this ideal both in his personal life and in his drama has made him one of the two or three most significant playwrights of his generation, both in this country and in Europe.

Since his 1962 marriage to Ingeborg Morath, Miller's life has become considerably less frenetic than it was throughout the 1950s and early 1960s. His Connecticut home is no longer a retreat from the attacks of the House Committee on Un-American Activities and the breakneck pace of Hollywood, but a place of calm where he can discuss literature with neighbors like William and Rose Styron. During this period he has successfully collaborated with his wife, writing the text for three books of photographs she has put together: two illustrate their travels in Russia and China respectively and the third portrays the pleasures of the Connecticut countryside.

He has continued to work at his craft. His latest plays, though not yet on Broadway, have been produced and mark further investigation into the two subjects that trouble him most: the Depression and the Nazi terror. *The American Clock*, produced at the 1980 American Spoleto festival in Charleston, South Carolina, is a series of vignettes of life during the Depression and its effect on the American family. The play, based on Studs Terkel's *Hard Times*, reasserts Miller's belief in the moral strength of the family unit. Miller has also written the screenplay for the 1980 television production of *Playing for Time*, Fania Fenelon's story of how she survived in Auschwitz by being part of the prison camp's female orchestra. The portrayal of individual courage in the face of brutal dehumanization is even more searing than in *Incident at Vichy*.

Although his work of the last decade has not matched the great creative surge of the late 1940s and early 1950s, Miller in his later plays continues to investigate complex moral decisions, where each man must weigh his individual conscience against the laws of the society in which he lives. That society may be made up of a nation, a community, or a family, and the hero may concur with its laws generally, yet his beliefs will be tested to a point where external verities no longer provide a useful absolute. At this point the hero must rely on his conscience. This is no easy decision and the choice made by conscience may be wrong, but Miller applauds the man who has the courage to make that choice. In his personal life as well as in his writings, Miller has never wavered from this belief.

Screenplays:
The Witches of Salem, Kingsley-International, 1958;
The Misfits, United Artists, 1961.

Television Script:
Playing for Time, CBS, September 1980.

Other:
"The Man Who Had All the Luck," in *Cross-section: A Collection of New American Writing*, ed. Edwin Seaver (New York: Fischer, 1944), pp. 486-552.

Periodical Publications:
"The Plaster Masks," *Encore*, 9 (April 1946): 424-432;
"Tragedy and the Common Man," *New York Times*, 27 February 1949, II: 1, 3;

"Arthur Miller on 'The Nature of Tragedy,' " *New York Herald-Tribune*, 27 March 1949, V: 1, 2;
"The 'Salesman' Has a Birthday," *New York Times*, 5 February 1950, II: 1, 3;
"A Modest Proposal for the Pacification of the Public Temper," *Nation*, 179 (3 July 1954): 5-8;
"The American Theatre," *Holiday*, 17 (January 1955): 90-98, 101-102, 104;
"A Boy Grew in Brooklyn," *Holiday*, 17 (March 1955): 54-55, 117, 119-120, 122-124;
"The Family in Modern Drama," *Atlantic Monthly*, 197 (April 1956): 35-41;
"The Playwright and the Atomic World," *Colorado Quarterly*, 5 (Autumn 1956): 117-137;
"The Writer in America," *Mainstream*, 10 (July 1957): 43-46;
"The Shadows of the Gods," *Harper's*, 217 (August 1958): 35-43;
"Bridge to a Savage World," *Esquire*, 50 (October 1958): 185-190;
"My Wife Marilyn," *Life*, 45 (22 December 1958): 146-147;
"The Bored and the Violent," *Harper's*, 225 (November 1962): 50-52, 55-56;
"On Recognition," *Michigan Quarterly Review*, 2 (Autumn 1963): 213-220;
"Our Guilt for the World's Evil," *New York Times Magazine*, 3 January 1965, pp. 10-11, 48;
"The Role of P.E.N.," *Saturday Review*, 49 (4 June 1966): 16-17;
"Literature and Mass Communication," *World Theatre*, 15 (1966): 164-167;
"The Contemporary Theater," *Michigan Quarterly Review*, 6 (Summer 1967): 153-163;
"Arthur Miller on *The Crucible*," *Audience*, 2 (July-August 1972): 46-47;
"The Limited Hang-Out: The dialogues of Richard Nixon as a drama of the antihero," *Harper's*, 249 (September 1974): 13-14, 16, 18-20.

Interviews:
Virginia Stevens, "Seven Young Broadway Artists," *Theatre Arts*, 31 (June 1947): 53-56;
Henry Hewes, "Broadway Postscript: Arthur Miller and How He Went to the Devil," *Saturday Review*, 36 (31 January 1953): 24-26;
John Griffen and Alice Griffen, "Arthur Miller Discusses *The Crucible*," *Theatre Arts*, 37 (October 1953): 33-34;
"*Death of a Salesman*: A Symposium," *Tulane Drama Review*, 2 (May 1958): 63-69;
Philip Gelb, "Morality and Modern Drama," *Educational Theatre Journal*, 10 (October 1958): 190-202;

Kenneth Allsop, "A Conversation with Arthur Miller," *Encounter*, 13 (July 1959): 58-60;

Allan Seager, "The Creative Agony of Arthur Miller," *Esquire*, 52 (October 1959): 123-126;

Henry Brandon, "The State of the Theatre," *Harper's*, 201 (November 1960): 63-69;

Alice T. McIntyre, "Making *The Misfits* or Waiting For Monroe or Notes from Olympus," *Esquire*, 55 (March 1961): 74-81;

Barry Hyams, "A Theatre: Heart and Mind," *Theatre: Annual of the Repertory Theatre of Lincoln Center*, 1 (1964): 56-61;

"Freedom in the Mass Media," *Michigan Quarterly Review*, 6 (Summer 1967): 163-178;

"Arthur Miller Talks Again: A Chat with a Class in Stage Direction," *Michigan Quarterly Review*, 6 (Summer 1967): 179-184;

Olga Carlisle and Rose Styron, "The Art of the Theatre II," *Paris Review*, 38 (Summer 1968): 61-98;

Robert A. Martin, "The Creative Experience of Arthur Miller," *Educational Theatre Journal*, 21 (October 1969): 310-317;

Josh Greenfield, "Writing Plays is Absolutely Senseless, Arthur Miller Says, 'But I Love It. I Just Love It,'" *New York Times Magazine*, 13 February 1972, pp. 16-17, 34-39;

Robert Corrigan, "Interview: Arthur Miller," *Michigan Quarterly Review*, 13 (Fall 1974): 401-405;

Robert A. Martin and Richard D. Meyer, "Arthur Miller on Plays and Playwriting," *Modern Drama*, 19 (December 1976): 375-384;

Christian-Albrecht Gollub, "Interview With Arthur Miller," *Michigan Quarterly Review*, 16 (Spring 1977): 121-141.

Bibliographies:

Martha Eisenstadt, "Arthur Miller: A Bibliography," *Modern Drama*, 5 (May 1962): 93-106;

Harriet Ungar, "The Writings of and about Arthur Miller: A Checklist 1936-1967," *Bulletin of the New York Public Library*, 74 (February 1970): 107-134;

Tetsumaro Hayashi, *An Index to Arthur Miller Criticism*, second edition (Metuchen, N.J.: Scarecrow Press, 1976);

George Jensen, *Arthur Miller: A Bibliographical Checklist* (Columbia, S.C.: J. Faust, 1976).

References:

Henry Adler, "To Hell With Society," *Tulane Drama Review*, 4 (May 1960): 53-76;

Richard Barksdale, "Social Background in the Plays of Miller and Williams," *College Language Association Journal*, 6 (March 1963): 161-169;

Barclay Bates, "The Lost Past in *Death of a Salesman*," *Modern Drama*, 11 (1968): 164-172;

C. W. Bigsby, "The Fall and After: Arthur Miller's Confession," *Modern Drama*, 10 (1967): 124-136;

Bigsby, "What Price Arthur Miller? An Analysis of *The Price*," *Twentieth Century Literature*, 16 (1970): 16-25;

Guerin Bliquez, "Linda's Role in *Death of a Salesman*," *Modern Drama*, 10 (1968): 383-386;

Paul Blumberg, "Sociology and Social Literature: Work Alienation in the Plays of Arthur Miller," *American Quarterly*, 21 (1969): 291-310;

Harold Clurman, "Director's Notes: *Incident at Vichy*," *Tulane Drama Review*, 9 (Summer 1965): 77-90;

Larry Cook, "The Function of Ben and Dave Singleman in *Death of a Salesman*," *Notes on Contemporary Literature*, 5 (1975): 7-9;

Robert Corrigan, "The Achievement of Arthur Miller," *Comparative Drama*, 2 (1968): 141-160;

William Dillingham, "Arthur Miller and the Loss of Conscience," *Emory University Quarterly*, 16 (1960): 40-50;

John Ditsky, "Stone Fire and Light: Approaches to *The Crucible*," *North Dakota Quarterly*, 46 (1978): 65-72;

James Douglass, "Miller's *The Crucible*: Which Witch is Which?," *Renascence*, 15 (1963): 145-151;

Alan Downer, "Mr Williams and Mr. Miller," *Furioso*, 4 (Summer 1949): 66-70;

Tom Driver, "Strength and Weakness in Arthur Miller," *Tulane Drama Review*, 4 (May 1960): 45-52;

Arthur Epstein, "A Look at *A View from the Bridge*," *Texas Studies in Literature and Language*, 7 (1965): 109-122;

Stephen Fender, "Precision and Pseudo-Precision in *The Crucible*," *Journal of American Studies*, 1 (1967): 87-98;

Alfred Ferguson, "The Tragedy of the American Dream in *Death of a Salesman*," *Thought*, 53 (1978): 89-98;

B. S. Field, Jr., "Hamartia in *Death of a Salesman*," *Twentieth Century Literature*, 18 (1972): 19-24;

Norm Fruchter, "On the Frontier," *Encore*, 9 (January 1962): 17-27;

Arthur Ganz, "The Silence of Arthur Miller," *Drama Survey*, 3 (1963): 224-237;

Ganz, "Arthur Miller: After the Silence," *Drama Survey*, 3 (1964): 520-530;

James Goode, *The Story of "The Misfits"* (Indianapolis: Bobbs-Merrill, 1963);

Barry Gross, "Peddlar and Pioneer in *Death of a Salesman*," *Modern Drama*, 7 (1965): 405-410;

Gross, "*All My Sons* and the Larger Context," *Modern Drama*, 18 (1976): 15-27;

Ronald Hayman, "Arthur Miller: Between Satire and Society," *Encounter*, 37 (November 1971): 73-79;

Philip Hill, "*The Crucible*: A Structural View," *Modern Drama*, 10 (1967): 312-317;

Robert Hogan, *Arthur Miller* (Minneapolis: University of Minnesota Press, 1964);

Sheila Huftel, *Arthur Miller: The Burning Glass* (New York: Citadel, 1965);

Albert Hunt, "Realism and Intelligence," *Encore*, 7 (May 1960): 12-17;

Joseph Hynes, "Arthur Miller and the Impasse of Naturalism," *South Atlantic Quarterly*, 62 (1963): 327-334;

Esther Jackson, "*Death of a Salesman*: Tragic Myth in the Modern Theatre," *College Language Association Journal*, 7 (September 1963): 63-76;

Irving Jacobson, "Family Dreams in *Death of a Salesman*," *American Literature*, 47 (1975): 247-258;

Stuart James, "Pastoral Dreamer in an Urban World," *University of Denver Quarterly*, 1 (1966): 45-57;

George Kernodle, "The Death of the Little Man," *Tulane Drama Review*, 1 (January 1956): 47-60;

Allen Koppenhaver, "*The Fall* and After: Albert Camus and Arthur Miller," *Modern Drama*, 9 (1966): 206-209;

Lawrence Lowenthal, "Arthur Miller's *Incident at Vichy*: a Sartrean Interpretation," *Modern Drama*, 18 (1975): 29-41;

Robert Martin, "Arthur Miller's *The Crucible*: Background and Sources," *Modern Drama*, 20 (1977): 279-292;

Emile McAnany, "The Tragic Commitment: Some Notes on Arthur Miller," *Modern Drama*, 5 (1962): 11-20;

Leonard Moss, *Arthur Miller* (New York: Twayne, 1967);

Edward Murray, *Arthur Miller: Dramatist* (New York: Frederick Ungar, 1967);

Benjamin Nelson, *Arthur Miller: Portrait of a Playwright* (New York: McKay, 1970);

Arthur Oberg, "*Death of a Salesman* and Arthur Miller's Search for Style," *Criticism*, 9 (1967): 303-311;

Orm Överland, "The Action and Its Significance: Arthur Miller's Struggle with Dramatic Form," *Modern Drama*, 18 (1975): 1-14;

Brian Parker, "Point of View in Arthur Miller's *Death of a Salesman*," *University of Toronto Quarterly*, 35 (January 1966): 144-157;

Henry Popkin, "Arthur Miller out West," *Commentary*, 31 (1961): 433-436;

Popkin, "Arthur Miller's *The Crucible*," *College English*, 26 (1964): 139-146;

John Prudhoe, "Arthur Miller and the Tradition of Tragedy," *English Studies*, 43 (1962): 430-439;

Raymond Reno, "Arthur Miller and the Death of God," *Texas Studies in Literature and Language*, 11 (1969): 1069-1087;

Paul Siegel, "Willy Loman and King Lear," *College English*, 17 (1956): 341-345;

John Stinson, "Structure in *After the Fall*: The Relation of the Maggie Episodes to the Main Themes and Christian Symbolism," *Modern Drama*, 10 (1967): 233-240;

Clinton Trowbridge, "Arthur Miller: Between Pathos and Tragedy," *Modern Drama*, 10 (1967): 221-232;

Gerald Weales, "Arthur Miller: Man and His Image," *Tulane Drama Review*, 7 (September 1962): 165-180;

Weales, "All About Talk: Arthur Miller's *The Price*," *Ohio Review*, 13, no. 2 (1972): 74-84;

Dennis Welland, *Arthur Miller* (Edinburgh: Oliver & Boyd, 1961);

Sidney White, *Guide to Arthur Miller* (Columbus, Ohio: Merrill, 1970);

William Wiegand, "Arthur Miller and the Man Who Knows," *Western Review*, 21 (1956): 85-103;

Ralph Willet, "A Note on Arthur Miller's *The Price*," *Journal of American Studies*, 5 (1971): 307-310;

Samuel Yorks, "Joe Keller and His Sons," *Western Humanities Review*, 13 (1959): 401-407.

Papers:

The University of Michigan at Ann Arbor, the University of Texas at Austin, and the New York Public Library have collections of Miller's papers.

JASON MILLER
(22 April 1939-)

PRODUCTIONS: *The Circus Theater (Perfect Son, Circus Lady,* and *Lou Gehrig Did Not Die of Cancer),* 23 February 1967, Triangle Theatre, New York, 10 [performances];

Lou Gehrig Did Not Die of Cancer, 2 March 1970, Equity Theatre, New York, 3;

Nobody Hears a Broken Drum, 19 March 1970, Fortune Theatre, New York, 6;

That Championship Season, 2 May 1972, Estelle Newman Theatre (transferred 14 September 1972 to Booth Theatre), New York, 988.

BOOKS: *Stone Step* (Brooklyn, N.Y.: Jadis / Yumi Editions, 1968);

Its a Sin to Tell a Lie, Circus Lady, and *Lou Gehrig Did Not Die of Cancer* (New York: Dramatists Play Service, 1970);

Nobody Hears a Broken Drum (New York: French, 1970);

That Championship Season (New York: Atheneum, 1972; London: Davis Poynter, 1974).

Jason Miller attained his reputation as an important American playwright solely on the attention and acclaim given *That Championship Season* (1972), his second full-length play. In addition to writing plays, Miller has published some poetry, but much of his energy since the success of *That Championship Season* has gone to acting.

Miller, born John Miller in Long Island City, New York, is the only child of John Miller, an electrician, and Mary Miller, a special education teacher. His background is solidly Irish Catholic, a significant factor in considering his work; Miller credits the Catholic ritual as the source of his theatre sense. His family moved shortly after his birth and Miller grew up in Scranton, Pennsylvania, living there, he says, "until I was twenty-one, twenty-two."

Miller attended Scranton's St. Patrick's High School, specializing in athletics and delinquency until one of his teachers pointed him in the direction of a theatrical career. The nuns there made a measurable difference in his priorities, "especially Sister Celine." According to Miller, "She gave me encouragement at a time when I might have stolen cars."

Sister Celine, who taught rhetoric, public speaking, and debating, recognized the potential in Miller's deep, strong voice and convinced him to study elocution. Under her tutelage, he became something of a local celebrity as an elocution contest

champion. Acting was a short step away, and Miller participated in St. Patrick's production of Laurence Housman's *Victoria Regina* during his senior year.

Miller studied theatre and playwriting at Scranton University (B.A., 1961), though his athletic prowess was what had originally attracted the school. This education was extended to include drama study at the Catholic University of America in Washington, D.C. (1962-1963). While in college, Miller garnered a first-place prize in the Eastern Jesuit Play Contest for a one-act entitled "The Winners," his first playwriting attempt.

In 1963 Miller married Linda Gleason, another Catholic University drama student and daughter of television and motion picture actor Jackie Gleason. (They have three children and were divorced in 1973.) They made a meager living in Washington performing a short program of Shakespeare for high schools before moving to New York City. Miller received some minor Off-Off-Broadway roles and bit parts in soap operas for television in New York, but got more notable employment as an actor in regional companies, including Baltimore Center Stage, the Champlain Shakespeare Festival, and the Cincinnati Shakespeare Festival. In intervening periods Miller earned money to pay bills through a variety of jobs: truck driver, messenger, waiter, welfare investigator.

Miller also struggled for recognition as a writer during this period. In 1967, three of his one-act plays, *Perfect Son, Circus Lady,* and *Lou Gehrig Did Not Die of Cancer,* were given ten performances at the Off-Off-Broadway Triangle Theatre under the title *The Circus Theater.* The production received little attention, although *Circus Lady* was later included in Stanley Richards's *Best Short Plays of 1973,* and *Lou Gehrig Did Not Die of Cancer* was presented as an Equity Theatre Informal for three performances in 1970 and included in Richards's *Best Short Plays of the World Theater 1968-1973.* In 1968 a small volume of Miller's poetry, *Stone Step,* also appeared in print.

Nobody Hears a Broken Drum, Miller's first full-length play, was produced Off Broadway, opening at the Fortune Theatre on 19 March 1970. Though there are few thematic similarities between *Nobody Hears a Broken Drum* and Miller's second play, *That Championship Season,* both reflect vividly the author's religious background (virtually all Miller's characters are Catholic), as well as his preference for the conventionally structured well-made play. Some critics found the lack of innovation irritating, but Miller defends his motives. "I want to tell a story," he said in a 1972 *New Yorker* interview. "I'm not ashamed of entertainment." In *Nobody Hears a Broken Drum* Jamie O'Hanlin leads a group of striking Irish miners in a Pennsylvania coal town in 1862. The men become a part of the vigilante group the Molly Maguires and begin a somewhat clumsy fight for justice. Jamie is dedicated but self-destructive, and is finally abandoned by the group and martyred.

Critics were fairly unanimous in their condemnation of the production as over-long and predictable. Miller received some positive reaction, though in limited and qualified amounts. Marilyn Stasio of *Cue* magazine pointed out Miller's gift for language and potential for the future, while Edith Oliver, after enumerating several major and fatal flaws, wrote in the *New Yorker* that the play was on the whole "an impressive accomplishment for a relatively inexperienced dramatist." Most reviews echoed Clive Barnes's sentiments in the *New York Times* that the play had "no dramatic excitement" and the plot was "contrived and pasteboard." *Nobody Hears a Broken Drum* closed after a six-performance run. Though immensely disappointed, Miller learned a great deal from the experience and rewrote the play in 1973. The revised version, however, has yet to be produced.

In 1970, after the failure of *Nobody Hears a Broken Drum*, Miller began work on *That Championship Season*. Most of the play was written in Fort Worth, Texas, where Miller was acting in a minor role at the Windmill Dinner Theatre in a production of Neil Simon's *The Odd Couple*. Although guiding his new play to production proved to be a difficult task, Miller had met producer Joseph Papp while working on the manuscript of *That Championship Season* and was commissioned by Papp as an actor. Miller played the role of Rogozhin in Robert Montgomery's *Subject to Fits*. The play opened at Papp's Public Theatre in New York City on 14 February 1971, and Miller received favorable reviews for his performance. Moreover, *Subject to Fits* was an important project for Miller because it allowed him to work with its director, A. J. Antoon, who later directed *That Championship Season*.

Papp was given first opportunity to produce *That Championship Season*, but was hesitant, worried that Miller might have overdrawn the central character of the coach and that some speeches were overwritten. Miller offered the play to other Broadway producers, and some were interested, though they planned to use the play as a vehicle for a well-known actor to assure success. Miller was dissatisfied with that possibility and with the help of

Antoon organized a reading of the play in an attempt to convince Papp to produce it. The plan worked, and Papp agreed after making some editorial suggestions which Miller acknowledged as beneficial. Finally the play was cast with an ensemble of experienced but relatively unknown actors and opened at the Estelle Newman Theatre on 2 May 1972.

That Championship Season is set in Pennsylvania's Lackawanna Valley, Miller's home territory, at the twentieth annual reunion of a high school championship basketball team. Four team members meet, as they do each year, at the home of their coach. Because the middle-aged men still hold the same phony, petty values that had led them twenty years earlier to use unscrupulous tactics to win the championship game, their lives are void of quality and honor. The group includes George, who has become mayor of the town; Phil, who has become a wealthy businessman; Tom, now an unemployed alcoholic; and Tom's brother, James, principal of a junior high school. The central character, however, is the coach (they all still refer to him as "the coach"), who, though retired, maintains close contact with his "boys." Prominently displayed in his living room is the large silver trophy with the team members' names inscribed upon it—a sacred memento of "that championship season" of Fillmore High School's 1952 basketball team.

The chief irony of the play is that little has changed since these people left high school. They betray each other while claiming to be friends. George, up for reelection as mayor, is frightened that he may lose to his Jewish opponent. He needs Phil's money to run a campaign. Phil is involved in a strip-mining operation which environmentalists oppose, but George as mayor permits Phil to have access to certain lucrative tracts of land. Moreover, Phil has been having an affair with George's wife. When George discovers this, he threatens to kill Phil; but after some discussion with the coach, George decides that he must "pay the price" in order to keep Phil's backing and win the campaign. He decides to overlook Phil's behavior and rationalizes that his wife's motive was probably to help his career anyway.

James has chafed at his relatively humble position in the high school and is counting on George's endorsement of him for the post of superintendent of schools in return for being George's campaign manager. Phil and the coach, however, realizing that George's opponent is a formidable threat, decide to employ a Philadelphia advertising agency to run the campaign. James, hurt and angry, gets into

Jason Miller

a fight with Phil and threatens to spread the news about George's wife as well as other damaging gossip. Phil reveals also that James, in George's absence, had proposed his own candidacy for mayor. George, overwhelmed with this betrayal, becomes physically ill. Suddenly realizing he cannot make it to the bathroom, he vomits into the handiest nearby container—the team trophy—thus ending the second act.

In the third act the coach expresses concern that his boys are not working together smoothly as a team. Tom, who has fallen down the stairs in his drunkenness, keeps reminding them of things they would like to forget. Conspicuously absent from these reunions is the fifth team member, Martin, who was the best player and who scored the winning basket as time ran out. In the third quarter, however, when they were losing the game, the coach had instructed Martin to debilitate the tall black center on the opposing team. Martin put him out of the game by breaking his ribs. Afterwards, Tom says, Martin wanted the coach publicly to refuse the trophy. The coach, whose goal is to win at all costs, refused, and afterwards Martin would not associate with the coach, who claims that his boys are his real

trophies. George, Phil, and James support the coach and consider that Martin had strange ideas. The coach thinks the country has lost its real leaders—men like Joseph McCarthy, John F. Kennedy, George Patton. These men understood the need to be winners. In his nostalgic mood, he replays the recorded radio narration of the last moments of their championship game. Overcome with emotion, the coach's boys profess loyalty and brotherly love. They take a photo of the coach holding the trophy as the play ends. Miller's character study of men who refuse to examine the moral bankruptcy of their lives and their perverted values of competition was extremely successful.

Miller understudied two of the actors in the Off-Broadway production, which ran for 144 performances at the Estelle Newman Theatre before it moved to the Booth Theatre on Broadway on 14 September 1972 for an additional 844 performances. The play closed 21 April 1974. *That Championship Season* won the New York Drama Critics Circle Award in 1972 and the Tony Award for the best play of 1972-1973. Miller won also the Drama Desk Award for Most Promising Playwright of 1972 and the Pulitzer Prize in 1973.

There was little critical disagreement over the qualities of *That Championship Season*, particularly its energy and the fine detail with which Miller developed his characters. T. E. Kalem in *Time* magazine called the play "a drama of searing intensity, agonized compassion and consummate craftsmanship," and Marilyn Stasio noted in *Cue*, "It is Miller's achievement that these men emerge not as grotesques, but as flesh-and-blood human beings." Several critics found it difficult to praise a modern play that made no experimental strides. In *New York* magazine, John Simon wrote, "*That Championship Season* is not a work of innovative art; but as a well-made, commercial, traditional yet freshly felt and thought-out play, it is perfect." Producer Joseph Papp pointed out, "Its simplicity is deceptive—but it is this simplicity translated into recognizable human form that gives the work its extra-ordinary power."

Miller has concentrated on acting since *That Championship Season* and is recognized as a formidable talent. His most memorable role is that of Father Karras in Warner Brothers's 1973 film *The Exorcist*. Miller was nominated in 1974 for an Academy Award for Best Supporting Actor for that portrayal. He also starred as a gangster in *The Nickel Ride* for Twentieth Century-Fox, released in 1975 to negative critical reaction. Miller has appeared in numerous television films, including *A Home of Our*

Own, *Fitzgerald in Hollywood*, and *The Dain Curse*, and is currently working on television projects. Though his acting career has dominated his energy since 1973, Miller has completed a screenplay for the motion picture version of *That Championship Season*. Its production is still pending.

That Championship Season has carved Miller a niche as a notable contemporary dramatist. *Time* called the play one of the ten best of the 1970s, a gesture suggesting the play's well-deserved place among America's stage literature. Most importantly, *That Championship Season* has demonstrated Miller's ability and potential as a dramatist.

—Jonathan Hershey

Other:

"Veil," "The Call," "Tenement Sky," "Web," "Gate," *Poetry*, 117 (January 1971): 235-239.

Interviews:

"On the Set," *New Yorker*, 48 (20 May 1972): 32-33;
Jerry Tallmer, Interview with Jason Miller, *New*

York Post, 23 September 1972, p. 15.
Glenn Loney, Interview with Jason Miller, *After Dark*, 5 (January 1973): 49;

References:

Clive Barnes, "Nobody Hears," review of *Nobody Hears a Broken Drum*, *New York Times*, 20 March 1975, p. 55;
T. E. Kalem, "The Dust of Glory," review of *That Championship Season*, *Time*, 99 (15 May 1972): 59;
Charles Michener, "Double Champ," review of *That Championship Season*, *Newsweek*, 80 (25 September 1972): 124;
Edith Oliver, "Off Broadway," review of *Nobody Hears a Broken Drum*, *New Yorker*, 46 (28 March 1970): 84-85;
John Simon, Review of *That Championship Season*, *Hudson Review*, 25 (Winter 1972-1973): 616-625;
Simon, "Winners as Losers," review of *That Championship Season*, *New York*, 5 (22 May 1972): 78.

LANGDON MITCHELL
(17 February 1862-21 October 1935)

SELECTED PRODUCTIONS: *Deborah*, 22 February 1892, Avenue Theatre, London, 5 [performances];
Don Pedro, 26 May 1892, Strand Theatre, London, 1;
In the Season, 26 May 1892, Strand Theatre, London, 1;
Ruth Underwood, 26 May 1892, Strand Theatre, London, 1;
Becky Sharp, adapted from William Thackeray's *Vanity Fair*, 12 September 1899, Fifth Avenue Theatre, New York, 116;
The Kreutzer Sonata, adapted from Jacob Gordin's Yiddish adaptation of Tolstoy's novel, 10 September 1906, Lyric Theatre, New York, 19;
The New York Idea, 19 November 1906, Lyric Theatre, New York, 66;
The New Marriage, 19 October 1911, Empire Theatre, Syracuse, 3;
Major Pendennis, adapted from Thackeray's *Pendennis*, 26 October 1916, Criterion Theatre, New York, 76.

BOOKS: *Sylvian and Other Poems*, as John Philip Varley (New York: Brentano, 1885);

Poems (Boston & New York: Houghton, Mifflin, 1894);
Love in the Backwoods (New York: Harper, 1897);
In the Season (New York & London: French, 1898);
The Picture Book of Becky Sharp (Chicago & New York: Stone, 1899);
The New York Idea (Boston: Baker, 1908);
Understanding America (New York: Doran, 1927).

Langdon Mitchell is known primarily for his comedy *The New York Idea*, which premiered in New York in 1906. An extraordinary comedy of manners which satirizes the American way of marriage and divorce, the play boasts witty dialogue, vital characters, and strokes of theatrical genius. Acted superbly by an ensemble that included Minnie Maddern Fiske and Marion Lea (Mitchell's wife), the play has survived the test of time, having been produced in several successful revivals and included in no less than twelve anthologies of American plays. Although most readers and playgoers probably associate Mitchell's name with only *The New York Idea*, his literary works, though few in number, included dramatizations of novels, original plays, essays, and poems.

Early in his career, Mitchell's plays were regarded as harbingers of a new, tough, taut dramaturgy for the American theatre. The critical reception of his work was generally favorable, with praise heaped upon the two plays he wrote for Minnie Fiske, *Becky Sharp* (1899) and *The New York Idea*. William Winter described the former as "four artfully planned, neatly constructed, and tersely written acts," and the British critic William Archer praised the latter as "from the intellectual point of view, the most remarkable piece of work I have encountered in America." Other critics compared Mitchell to Arthur Wing Pinero, Henry Arthur Jones, and George Bernard Shaw.

Evaluated retrospectively by Arthur Hobson Quinn, Montrose J. Moses, and Allan Halline, Mitchell's work is praised for its universality, "a quality which makes his work enduring." Mitchell would have been pleased with that judgment since he admired work which addressed itself beyond an immediate locale or social class. Unfortunately, since the 1930s there has been no critical evaluation of Mitchell's work. The inclusion of *The New York Idea* in anthologies and in summer stock seasons is the only testament to his play's endurance.

Mitchell's career seems to be a particularly charming blend of preparation and happenstance. As the well-educated son of the physician and novelist Silas Weir Mitchell, Langdon Mitchell was born into the highest social circle of Philadelphia in 1862. A love of literature was obviously instilled in Mitchell at an early age; he was educated at St. Paul's School in New Hampshire and studied law at Harvard and Columbia. Before being admitted to the New York bar in 1886, Mitchell studied abroad in Dresden and Paris for three years. His enchantment with the theatre may have begun during those years, for his first play, *Sylvian*, was published one year before he was admitted to the bar. In the scant biographical information available on Mitchell, it appears that after being admitted to the bar he went to London where in 1892 he married the British actress Marion Lea and premiered four of his plays.

The talent that flowered in *The New York Idea* was nowhere in evidence in *Sylvian*, which was never produced. A seventeenth-century romantic tragedy set in Cordova, Spain, this closet drama is a student's imitation of Shakespeare, Webster, and Dryden. Written in blank verse and prose, the play presents a two-faced young man (Sylvian) who declares his love simultaneously for the actress Perdita and the Lady Olivia. When Olivia taunts Sylvian by falsely demonstrating Perdita's unfaithfulness, Sylvian conspires to kill Perdita by assuming a role in the play in which Perdita is performing. True to heroic tragic form, several murders are committed, ending in the stabbing death of Sylvian.

Contrary to his own dictum that drama "must entertain, divert, interest, exhilarate, excite, please and carry away," Mitchell's play is negligible except for the attitudes and preoccupations of the young author which surface in the text. Mitchell's fascination with the theatre had begun by this time: both Sylvian and Perdita are performers in the play, and a play-within-a-play construction is used for the climactic scene. But the playwright's fascination with the theatre is far from positive. For both Sylvian and Olivia the word "actor" is pejorative. Olivia says to Sylvian: "Sweet-swearing liar / Honey-tongued hypocrite; sir, thou hast been / A very complete actor." The liveliest denouncement, however, is Sylvian's about Perdita: "Actress, actress, the word sticks in my mind like some cursed hornet's sting; sticks, festers, sticks, will not out. Player's a better word; which your dictionary will tell you is one that doth expose her general person to the public view; in what antic postures, with what unseemly gestures this or that mannikin may categorically direct." Mitchell's ambivalence about the theatre, or perhaps his desire not to exploit his father's name, may have been his justification for publishing this play under his pseudonym, John Philip Varley.

Having abandoned his desire to write plays plotted with revenge, unfaithful loves, and violence, Mitchell turned again to the theatre in 1892 with his bride Marion Lea appearing in three of his four plays that premiered in London. Of the four plays, only *In the Season* is available for study in a Samuel French acting edition. A gentle comedy of manners about the prideful misunderstanding between a couple in the middle of London society, *In the Season* offers the first glimpse of Mitchell's talent for comedy, characterization, and dramatic action. The play celebrates youth and poses the problem of trust between the sexes, a theme on which Mitchell elaborates in his two novellas which comprise *Love in the Backwoods* (1897).

The plot of *In the Season* is simple: a lovely young woman, Sybil March, doubts the sincerity of her favorite beau, Fairburne, because he chastized her for her association with the jaunty Mr. Chester. Sybil writes a letter to Fairburne ending their relationship. Sir Harry Collingwood, a friend to both lovers and an ardent admirer of Sybil, asks for her hand in marriage. When she gracefully refuses his offer, Sir Harry arranges a private tete-a-tete between Fairburne and Sybil. After many false starts, the two delicately declare their love for each other.

The strength of this play is in the restraint of the emotions, the intelligence of Sybil, and the wit of the dialogue, as in the following exchange, which suggests Mitchell's capacity for comic deflation of language:

SIR HARRY: . . . You care so much for your own home, I can scarcely imagine you ever being willing to leave it.

SYBIL: I never shall be.

SIR HARRY: How about the Fairy Prince—when he blows his horn at your castle gate?

SYBIL: (*settling cushions comfortably*) It's a cracked horn, it won't blow; or if the horn is sound, then it's the Prince that's cracked.

Following the successful year in London, Mitchell returned to New York. *Poems* (1894) and *Love in the Backwoods* were published. In 1898, Mitchell's career took an exciting turn. The American actress Minnie Maddern Fiske and her husband-manager were looking for a playwright to adapt Thackeray's novel *Vanity Fair* (1848) with Becky Sharp as the main character. Finally Minnie Fiske chose Mitchell on the basis of his critically successful one-act plays in London.

Becky Sharp, which premiered in New York in 1899, was controversial in its fidelity (or lack of it) to the novel but earned plaudits for both the playwright and the actress. Starring, in addition to Minnie Fiske, Tyrone Power and Maurice Barrymore, the play spawned several rivals in London and a plagiarized version in Upstate New York against which Mitchell filed a restraining order. Playing continuously for nearly two years, the play was revived successfully through the 1930s. Mitchell's version was by far the most successful of the theatrical adaptations of *Vanity Fair*.

Mitchell's task in *Becky Sharp* was to condense the span of the "novel without a hero," focus on Becky, and devise dramatic action for the narrative. Critics have pointed out that *Vanity Fair* is "devoid of what may be called a theatrical situation." Mitchell filled that void by concentrating all the action into four acts. The first act, set at Miss Crawley's residence in May 1815, establishes Becky's manipulation and guile as she talks her way into and out of people's lives. In the second act, at the Duchess of Richmond's ball in June 1815, Becky ingratiates herself with the men, insults the women, and outrageously flirts with her friend Amelia's husband against the backdrop of the Napoleonic invasion. The climactic scenes take place in act 3, in which Becky's high living and her husband Rawdon's gambling debts push her to the brink of arranging a private supper in her room with the lascivious, but wealthy, Lord Steyne. Some critics feel that Mitchell wisely capitalized on the only dramatic scene in the novel—the discovery by Rawdon of Becky and Lord Steyne—and wrote his play forward and backward from that point. The denouement in act 4 shows a piously penitent Becky alone in the Pumpernickel lodgings in 1828 eagerly resuming a life of opportunism and deceit.

Mitchell's attraction to the story is obvious. His entire career is marked by a strong sensibility which lucidly renders the elements of his characters' decisions and which recognizes the social values of honesty, work, and friendship. Becky's line of "living comfortably on absolutely nothing a year" becomes an ironic refrain throughout the play as she wheedles and plots her way up and down the social and financial ladders. Caught up in nineteenth-century English society, Becky is both victim and victimizer. A victimizer of the weak, Becky is a survivor of the fittest in intelligence and bravado. A victim of economic circumstance wherein she is dependent on someone else's money and position, Becky is a moral loser without a spiritual identity. Called a "play of eternal petty tragedy," *Becky Sharp* is Mitchell's only successful serious drama.

Nevertheless, ardent admirers of *Vanity Fair* quibbled with some of Mitchell's choices of characterization, setting, and sequence of scenes as they later did with his adaptation of another Thackeray novel, *Pendennis* (1850). These quibblings were

Langdon Mitchell

dismissed by some as little trivialities, but William Winter enumerated them in his grudging assessment of the play. Winter sees Becky as "scarcely anything more than the unrelieved incarnation of vicious, repulsive, aggressive selfishness"—qualities which he felt were not so absolute in the novel. Winter's comment may hold up for the reader of the play, but hardly for the audience in a performance. Becky's sudden shifts from hypocrisy to despair due to her disillusionment make a statement about a character in moral chaos by whom an audience could not help but be intrigued. Rather than write a didactic drama wherein the heroine's sins make an audience feel superior and untouched, Mitchell chose to portray the ambivalence of Becky, whose schemes are reprehensible but whose will to survive generates an enduring energy.

Continuing to use Mitchell's talents, in 1906 Minnie Fiske commissioned Mitchell to adapt *The Kreutzer Sonata* for Bertha Kalich and to revive *Becky Sharp* in order "to keep Mitchell's name fresh in the public mind"; she also encouraged him to write a new comedy (*The New York Idea*) as the main offering for her 1906-1907 season.

When examined together, *Becky Sharp* and *The New York Idea* share a strength: the vibrant characterization of the female lead. Shifting his focus from the faithful but passive and uninteresting type represented by Perdita in *Sylvian*, Mitchell worked steadily at creating central female characters who dazzle with their intelligence and vitality. It may be argued that the tendency to write such roles was Mitchell's own since he already showed such proclivity in *In the Season*. However, that he was writing expressly for Minnie Fiske cannot be underestimated as an influence on his method of characterization. In his later essay "Substance and Art in Drama" (1928), Mitchell stresses that the playwright must know the practice of the theatre, especially the rehearsal process. In a letter written about *The New York Idea*, Mitchell hints again at the playwright's need to be adaptable to the demands of dramatic action and the playing of a scene onstage: "The play was written for Mrs. Fiske. The choice of subject was mine. I demanded complete freedom in the treatment, and my most wise manager, Mr. Harrison Grey Fiske, accorded this. The play was produced and played as written, with the exception of one or two short scenes, which were not acceptable to Mrs. Fiske; that is, she felt, or would have felt, somewhat strained or unnatural in these scenes. Accordingly, I cut them out, or rather rewrote them." The parts of both Becky Sharp and Cynthia Karslake (in *The*

New York Idea) are written with grand strokes of color wherein the actress must change strategies and play with eloquence, irony, humor, and pathos. A formidable task for any actress in the role, these qualities precisely matched Minnie Fiske's theatrical talents.

The New York Idea represents the full flowering of Mitchell's dramatic talents. His fierce intelligence and clear attack on frivolity are coupled with witty dialogue and carefully orchestrated scenes. The play focuses on two divorced couples, the Phillimores and the Karslakes. Cynthia Karslake is preparing for her marriage to the boring, but ever correct, Judge Philip Phillimore. The Phillimore family, steeped in social convention, is outraged by Cynthia's lack of decorum shown in part by her interest in horse racing. Having divorced her previous husband on a whim when he could not take her to the races, Cynthia realizes the even more restraining trap she is setting for herself as the future Mrs. Phillimore. Pondering her dilemma, in act 1 Cynthia is unprepared for the visit of her former husband, John Karslake, to the Phillimore house on a business matter. Complicating the touchiness of divorced couples' meeting, Mitchell contrives to introduce into the scene Vida Phillimore, who immediately sizes up Cynthia's predicament.

Act 2 takes place the day after, on Cynthia's wedding day, at Vida's boudoir, where Vida manages to arrange for Cynthia and John to meet on the pretext of John's selling one of Cynthia's favorite horses. Cynthia asserts that her involvement with John is over, and in a burst of fevered confusion, she asks John to be her best man. Exhilarated by this decision, she takes up the offer of a sporting Englishman, Sir Wilfrid Cates-Darby, to run off to the races. Karslake is left to explain the probable delay in the wedding ceremony.

Act 3 pushes the play to its crisis with the jubilant Cynthia returning hours late for her wedding and finding the upstanding Phillimores angry and uncomprehending. Philip Phillimore stoically dismisses the guests. Cynthia nearly breaks her match with Philip, but his logical persuasion gets the better of her until Vida returns. Wanting Cates-Darby for herself, Vida contrives to make Cynthia jealous about Vida's relationship with John. So adroitly does she accomplish this that Cynthia, halfway up the altar, stops the wedding and runs off to keep John from marrying Vida.

The riotous shenanigans of act 3 resolve into gentle comedy in act 4 as Cynthia learns that Vida and Cates-Darby are married. While she and John assess their marriage and divorce, he receives a call from his lawyer stating that their divorce was not legal. John and Cynthia reconcile.

Critics praised *The New York Idea* for its satirical view of New York society's lackadaisical attitude toward marriage and divorce. As John Karslake says in the play: "Uncle Sam has established consecutive polyandry,—but there's got to be an interval between husbands! The fact is, Judge, the modern American marriage is like a wire fence. The woman's the wife—the posts are the husbands." Cynthia, the spoiled girl-wife who married and divorced on whim acknowledges the acute social embarrassment divorce brings: "I repeat then, if there's to be nothing but marriage and divorce, and remarriage, and redivorce, at least, those who *are* divorced can avoid the vulgarity of meeting each other here, there, and everywhere!"

A legal issue, as well as satire of society, is at stake in the play. As a lawyer, Mitchell was probably aware of the nationwide campaign for a uniform divorce law in 1905. Mitchell denies that his legalistic concerns influenced the play: "When I was writing the play, I had really no idea of satirizing divorce or a law or anything specially temperamental or local. What I wanted to satirize was a certain extreme frivolity in the American spirit and in our American life—frivolity in a deep sense—not just a girl's frivolity, but that profound, sterile, amazing frivolity which one observes and meets in our churches, in political life, in literature, in music; in short, in every department of American thought, feeling, and action." Frivolous thinking, lack of commitment, and the engulfing nature of social conventions are the targets for the play. If it were simply about American divorce laws in 1906, the play would have lost its large audience over the years.

Several critics have commented on the celebratory nature of *The New York Idea* where real love triumphs, the courage to flout social expectations is abetted, and the passionate side of nature is valued as much as the intellectual. Margaret Mayorga says the play is an isolated comedy of manners which broke its own ground in 1906 and was not rivaled "until Jesse Lynch Williams wrote *Why Marry?* in 1917." On the other hand, John Corbin of the *New York Times* (30 December 1917) chastizes Mitchell for never assessing the cause or the remedy for bad marriages. In this case, Corbin refuses to acknowledge the satire of the play and regards the play as a social drama. Despite Corbin, critics consistently acknowledge the vivacity of the play, which

achieved widespread recognition. Max Reinhardt produced it in 1916 under the title *Jonathan's Daughter*.

Although the play pushes perilously close to farce at times in the scenes between Vida and Cates-Darby, Mitchell manages to restrain the humor. In fact, an unauthorized British production failed when played strictly as farce. An Oscar Wilde aura pervades a few of the scenes, especially the tea scene when Cynthia and Vida first meet. Similar to Wilde's Gwendolyn and Cecily scene in *The Importance of Being Earnest* (1895), the women assume gentility and breeding on the surface while the cups, saucers, and tea things bounce around in repressed rage. Verbally the play enlarges on the wit shown earlier in *In the Season*, extending to all the main characters as they channel their energies into repartee, retort, and occasional conceits.

Unfortunately, the flowering of talent in *The New York Idea* was not to be repeated. Minnie Fiske commissioned *The New Marriage* in 1911, but Mitchell was in Paris and worked slowly when abroad. Fiske closed the play after three performances, refusing to pay Mitchell any more money for rewriting "his foggy play." Seemingly inactive in the theatre after the failure of *The New Marriage* and the lukewarm success of *Major Pendennis* (1916), Mitchell left several plays in manuscript, two of which ("Before Dawn" and "The Second Generation") pursue the problem of divorce in legalistic rather than satiric terms.

Details of Mitchell's life remain obscure. A shy man who barely tolerated the spotlight, he turned to the writing of essays for the *Atlantic Monthly*, *Century*, *American Mercury*, and the *Virginia Quarterly Review*. Many of these essays were compiled and published in *Understanding America* (1927). Although Mitchell's reputation as a playwright rests upon a small body of work—the most important of which was closely tied to his artistic collaboration with Minnie Fiske—his plays were regarded highly enough to earn him the first chair of playwriting at the University of Pennsylvania (1928-1930). Mitchell died in October 1935.

–Kathleen Conlin

Other:

"Substance and Art in Drama," in *The Art of Playwriting*, by Mitchell and others (Philadelphia: University of Pennsylvania Press, 1928), pp. 32-46;

Becky Sharp, in *Monte Cristo and Other Plays*, ed. J. B. Russak (Princeton: Princeton University Press, 1941), pp. 197-283.

References:

Archie Binns, *Mrs. Fiske and the American Theatre* (New York: Crown, 1955);

Donald Nelson Koster, "The Theme of Divorce in American Drama, 1871-1939," Ph.D. dissertation, University of Pennsylvania, 1942, pp. 56-60, 91-94;

Margaret G. Mayorga, *A Short History of the American Drama: Commentaries on Plays Prior to 1920* (New York: Dodd, Mead, 1932), pp. 257-259, 271;

Montrose J. Moses, ed., *Representative Plays by American Dramatists*, vol. 3 (New York: Blom, 1921), pp. 598-604;

Arthur Hobson Quinn, *A History of American Drama from the Civil War to the Present Day*, vol. 2 (New York: Harper, 1927), pp. 62-68;

William Winter, *The Wallet of Time*, vol. 2 (New York: Moffat, Yard, 1913), pp. 273-278.

Papers:

Langdon Mitchell's papers are available in the Manuscript Collection at the University of Pennsylvania.

WILLIAM VAUGHN MOODY
(8 July 1869-17 October 1910)

PRODUCTIONS: *A Sabine Woman*, 12 April 1906, Garrick Theatre, Chicago; revised as *The Great Divide*, 3 October 1906, Princess Theatre, New York, 238 [performances];

The Faith Healer, 19 January 1910, Savoy Theatre, New York, 6.

BOOKS: *The Masque of Judgment* (Boston: Small, Maynard, 1900);

Poems (Boston & New York: Houghton Mifflin, 1901);

A History of English Literature, by Moody and Robert Morss Lovett (New York: Scribners, 1902);

The Fire-Bringer (Boston & New York: Houghton Mifflin, 1904);

A First View of English Literature, by Moody and Lovett (New York: Scribners, 1905);

The Faith Healer (Boston & New York: Houghton Mifflin, 1909; revised edition, New York: Macmillan, 1910);

The Great Divide (New York: Macmillan, 1909);

The Poems and Plays of William Vaughn Moody, 2 vols., ed. John M. Manly (Boston & New York: Houghton Mifflin, 1912);

Selected Poems of William Vaughn Moody, ed. Lovett (Boston & New York: Houghton Mifflin, 1931).

William Vaughn Moody's five plays skillfully blend the romanticism and the realism of two eras. Chiefly remembered as a transitional playwright and poet, Moody bridges the gap between traditional forms of the nineteenth century and experimental designs of the twentieth century. Although his ambitious trilogy of philosophical verse plays (*The Masque of Judgment*, *The Fire-Bringer*, and *The Death of Eve*) was never staged, his prose dramas (*The Great Divide* and *The Faith Healer*) establish his dramatic reputation as a pioneer of modern theatre. Moody's importance lies in the way he used his abilities as a poet to expand the limits of realistic melodrama.

Born in Spencer, Indiana, Moody grew up in New Albany, Indiana, on the Ohio River, directly across from Louisville, a center of commerce for the area. Before Moody was born, his father, Burdette Moody, had been a riverboat captain, traveling to and from New Orleans; however, when the Civil War erupted, Moody's boat was confiscated in Memphis and his piloting on the river was ended. Eventually he served as the employee of his brother-in-law's iron works business in New Albany, unhappy at the loss of his former freedom on the river. William Moody's aspirations were deeply influenced by his mother's love of art, music, and literature. As Moody grew up, she guided him, even though she became a near-invalid.

At the New Albany High School Moody edited a school newspaper, the *Minute-Man*, which was dedicated to attacking "evil institutions and abuses" in society. Graduating first in his class in 1885, Moody delivered for the valedictory speech his essay entitled "The Evolution of History." He was encouraged in his writing by the school's principal, R. A. Ogg, who suggested that Moody pursue a college education in the East.

Moody's mother died in 1884, his father in 1886. More on his own now, he taught high school at Corydon Pike, Indiana, near New Albany, for a year and began to read extensively and write poetry. In 1887 he went to Poughkeepsie, New York, to tutor a student for the Yale entrance exams, and he attended Riverview Academy to prepare for college himself. He graduated from Riverview in 1889 with the highest average in the school's history and entered Harvard on a scholarship of $400, supplementing his income with a loan of $1,000 from an uncle and by tutoring, proctoring, typing, and editing.

In his first year at Harvard, Moody published poems and a short story in the college's literary magazines, the *Advocate* and the *Monthly*. As a result of these publications, Moody became closely associated with others interested in literature: Robert Morss Lovett, Hutchins and Norman Hapgood, and Robert Herrick—all on the *Monthly*'s editorial board which Moody himself was invited to join even though he was a first-year student. Many recent Harvard graduates kept in touch with the *Monthly*'s activities, and consequently Moody met several prominent writers and intellectuals, including George Pierce Baker and George Santayana, who were members of the Harvard faculty by then.

After completing his bachelor's degree in three years, he toured Europe the following year as tutor for a young man. Returning to Harvard, he received a master's degree in 1894, then worked as an instructor in the English department of Harvard and Harvard Annex (Radcliffe), assisting in Lewis E. Gates's writing courses. One of his associates was Josephine Preston Peabody, whom Moody met in 1895 at Harvard's English Club. She was a special student at the Annex and had enrolled in classes taught by Gates and George Pierce Baker. Peabody was already publishing poetry in the *Atlantic Monthly* and *Scribner's*, and she went on to establish herself as a playwright. In later years she and Moody remained friends, and he frequently offered constructive criticism of her work.

From 1895 through 1898 Moody taught English at the University of Chicago. Anxious to pursue his writing career, however, he arranged to teach half the year and remain on leave the other half. At the end of the fall term of 1899, he left Chicago for Boston and then New York, spending all of 1900 to complete his *Poems* (1901). His student record of academic brilliance was matched by his reputation as a fine teacher and scholar; nevertheless, Moody did not like the duties of teaching, especially the monotonous task of correcting themes. His letters during this period refer with disgust to the "spiritual beggary" of "hack teaching." Moody's academic aloofness is suggested by his students' calling him "The Man in the Iron Mask"; perhaps because he was shy and taciturn, a colleague commented that, "It took Moody a pipeful to make a remark."

In 1901 Moody received an attractive offer from the University of California to teach for one semester at full salary—an offer which the University of Chicago matched, additionally permitting Moody to request another year's absence. The financial success of his textbooks on English literature, which he co-authored with his friend Robert Morss Lovett, enabled Moody to remain free from teaching. Except for a three-month stint in 1903, he did not teach again, although he stayed on the university register through 1908 as an assistant professor on leave.

With his teaching days over, Moody devoted himself completely to writing a prose drama, *A Sabine Woman* (later revised as *The Great Divide*), produced in Chicago in April 1906. In addition to *A History of English Literature* (1902) and *A First View of English Literature* (1905), he had already published book reviews, poems, two verse dramas, and editions of writers such as Bunyan, Coleridge, Milton, Scott, and Homer. Moody's talent was recognized by his election to the National Institute of Arts and Letters in 1905. *The Great Divide* was received as a play of exceptional merit when it opened in New York in October 1906 for a successful run of 238 performances. While his second stage production, *The Faith Healer* (1910), did not enjoy this same popular success, Moody won critical acclaim for his plays' high merits. Moreover, in 1908 Moody received an honorary Doctor of Letters degree from Yale.

Critics have speculated that Moody's work as a playwright might have been second only to that of Eugene O'Neill had he lived longer than forty-one years. Having suffered a severe typhoid fever attack in March 1908, he was nursed by his longtime friend, Harriet Brainard, whom he married on 7 May 1909. Faced with the beginnings of blindness while honeymooning in England, he returned with her to southern California as his health deteriorated. He wrote one act of *The Death of Eve* but became too seriously ill to complete it. They moved to Colorado Springs in October 1910 in a last attempt for his recovery, but Moody died of a brain tumor on 17 October 1910.

A man of fine critical and creative intellect, Moody reflects his profound sensitivity and intelligence in his poetic and prose dramas. His chief merit as a dramatist lies in his highly lyrical poetic dramas rather than in the prose dramas that were praised by his contemporaries. Moody himself said that he regretted having given so much of his precious time to prose, for his true genre was poetry.

He strongly believed that modern life could be presented best on stage in the poetic medium. However, he was concerned as well about the limitations inherent in theatre. In 1909 he wrote a friend, describing his concern with the physical nature of the stage: "I am torn between the ideal aspect of the theme and the stage necessities—the old, old problem. Perhaps in the end I will let the stage go to ballyhoo, and write the thing as I see it, for that justly lighted and managed stage of the mind, where there are no bad actors and where the peanut-eating of the public is reduced to a discreet minimum. But this—after all—is an uncourageous compromise." Nevertheless, his reputation as a playwright lies foremost with his prose plays, in which he managed to address the moral and metaphysical concerns of his day. His use of mythic symbolism, realistic detail, fine craftsmanship, and direct confrontation of contemporary problems makes his plays fine examples of American drama during the first decade in the twentieth century.

Moody's trilogy of verse dramas reflects his conservative attitude toward prosody. He adhered strictly to traditional forms and techniques in meter, diction, syntax, and rhetoric. At their best, these plays reflect intensely emotional and serious themes; at their worst, they deteriorate into bathos and exalted moral idealism marked by rhetorical extravagance.

The Masque of Judgment (1900), written first but placed second in the trilogy, celebrates the dignity of man's rebellion against God. Set in Miltonian landscape, from the time of the Incarnation to the Judgment Day, it focuses on protagonist/archangel Raphael's conversations with Uriel and Michael. Other dramatis personae include an assortment of celestial "Spirits" and emblematic figures from the Book of Revelation: Spirits of the Seventh Lamp of the Throne, the Angel of the Pale Horse, the Lion and the Eagle of the Throne, Spirits of the Sacred and the Lost, and the Spirit of the Morning-star. These personifications of religious abstractions are used to define man's conflict with God. Ending with the destruction of heaven, the masque shows Moody's disapproval of the Puritans' God of wrath and of their concept of man's original depravity. The prelude and five acts (blank verse alternating with rhymed lyrics) dramatize the sanctity of the

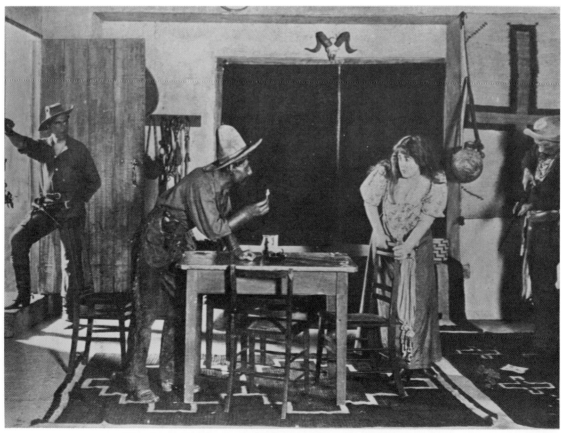

The Great Divide, *Henry Miller and Margaret Anglin center stage*

human spirit, even when it defies God's authority.

The Fire-Bringer (1904), written second but the first play in the trilogy, stresses one's supreme duty to rebel in order to assert his dignity, his free will: one's physical and intellectual desires are more important than submission to his Creator. The play celebrates Prometheus, who, because he has struggled with the gods and been punished by Zeus for bringing back fire from Olympus to Deukalion and Pyrrha and for warning men of the deluge, is a symbol of man's necessary rebellion against God. The poem's purely lyric quality (especially in Pandora's songs), more sympathetic portrayal of human qualities, more compact structure, more direct motives, and more concrete action have all been cited as reasons for *The Fire-Bringer*'s being even better than *The Masque of Judgment*.

The incomplete play, *The Death of Eve*, would have finished the trilogy by showing the triumph of love over hatred and sin. Moody planned to reconcile God and man through Eve, who had separated them when she committed the original sin in the Garden of Eden. In the one-act fragment, Eve attempts to lead the Serpent, now ruling heaven with declining strength, back to the place of her sinning. In the following acts of the play, Eve and her descendants were to have been relieved of the burden of sin, making impossible any separation of God and mankind. Thus, Eve's atonement for her defiance of God is logically the basis for reuniting God and man. Eve is venerated as the eternal mother and wife; as symbol of Woman, she is the spirit of life itself which assures the renewal of the world, restoring happiness, truth, and beauty on earth. This projected conclusion of the trilogy has been praised as the best suited of the verse dramas for stage production because of its dramatic unity, concreteness, and human characters. Solving the cosmic problem of man's separation from God, *The Death of Eve* represents an appropriate culmination of Moody's dramatic career in 1910, for it epitomizes the best of his poetic art and his evolving philosophy of life. These three verse plays are unified by the thesis that God and mankind are intertwined. They embody the enduring themes that faith and love are essential for meaning in life; that revolt against the restraints to freedom (found in each main character: Prometheus, Raphael, and Eve) is necessary for the human spirit; and that the individual must believe in the joy of both body and spirit.

The Great Divide (1906), Moody's most popular play, reflects many of the themes of the verse plays, especially the idea that love is the redeeming force that can merge divisive opposites. This three-act prose play depicts a refined Eastern girl, Ruth Jordan, being won over eventually by a rough Western man. The title of the play refers to two opposing codes—those of the East (Calvinistic, socially stratified, cultured) and the West (unrepentant, democratic, rude). In act 1 Ruth chafes at her Eastern strictures. She is engaged to be married to Winthrop Newbury, a young doctor who has come out to Arizona with Ruth and her brother Philip, but she finds Newbury dull and uninteresting. She responds warmly to the rough and magnificent country, so different from the East, and left alone for a while by her family, she sings a song which expresses unfulfilled aspirations. As she goes to bed, three drunken men (two of them Mexicans) break into the cabin. They start to throw dice for Ruth. Attracted to one of them, Stephen Ghent, she promises to give herself to him in return for his protection from the Mexicans. Ghent buys one of the Mexicans off with some gold nuggets and, outside the cabin, chases the other Mexican away in a gunfight. Then Ghent and Ruth consider their situation (she threatens to kill herself; he requests she shoot him), but she goes to live with him at the site of his gold mine. She is powerfully attracted to his strength and manliness even though she feels humiliated at having been bought by Ghent's actions. In the second act it is revealed that Ruth's brother's business has failed and that he is returning to New England; that Ghent's gold claim has been successful; and that Ruth, now pregnant with Ghent's child, has worked to buy herself back. Using only her own money, she has purchased the string of gold nuggets back from the Mexican, and she gives it to Ghent. The opposing philosophies are starkly presented in their conflict: Ghent claims her by nature's law of passion; Ruth reclaims herself by financial accounting and insisting upon penance. She leaves Ghent and returns to New England.

In act 3 it appears that Ruth has lost interest in her life. Her motherhood is joyless. Ghent, however, has rescued her brother's business from debacle and comes to New England to renew his relationship with Ruth. After a stormy confrontation with Ruth's mother, in which Ruth reveals how she had met Ghent, Ruth finally sees him. Ghent proclaims that "whiskey, and rum, and the devil" brought them together: "I tell you now I'm thankful on my knees for all three!" He gives her the string of gold nuggets again, which she places around her neck, asking him to teach her to live according to his code of the West.

The conflict of *The Great Divide* no doubt arose

in part from Moody's having lived both in the East and Middle West. Moreover, Moody's father had instilled in him a love of travel, romance, and adventure, no doubt relating many of his experiences as a riverboat captain. Here, as in his poetic dramas, Moody denounces Puritan dogmas of sin, suffering, and sacrifice, and he advocates the freedom, joy, and selfishness of love. Ghent is the modern prototype of the ideal Promethean hero found in *The Fire-Bringer*. By using prose and a contemporary American setting, Moody succeeds in expressing his philosophy through a realistic drama that audiences could accept.

The Great Divide is notable in American drama because it introduced a different emphasis of realistic technique. It broke from the Belasco tradition of minutely representational sets and language, and employed instead a greater complexity of characterization and conflict. Although not wholly free from broad strokes of melodrama, the characters of Ruth and Ghent are not simplistic, and the resolution of their love is not achieved by a conventional tying of loose ends. Moreover, the tone of the play is governed by lyricism and symbolic gesture not imported from Europe but achieved largely through Moody's own experience as a poet. In these respects, *The Great Divide* marks a distinct turning point in the American tradition.

The Faith Healer (1910) has a message about the power of love similar to that which pervades *The Great Divide*, yet it was not as successful on stage. The protagonist of this prose drama is a faith healer, Ulrich Michaelis, whose wanderings take him to the midwestern farmhouse of Matthew Beeler, whose wife Mary has not walked in five years. Michaelis, however, cures her. He also falls in love with Mary's niece, Rhoda, who appears to prevent his ministering to the sick. In this struggle between human love and spiritual devotion, Michaelis renews his mission to heal the sick and learns to accept Rhoda's love to strengthen his spiritual powers. His antagonists are Dr. Littlefield, Rhoda's former lover, who represents the dogmatism of science, and the Rev. Culpepper, who epitomizes established religion's opposition to the occult. It has been suggested that *The Faith Healer* failed to be successful on stage because Michaelis's faith-healing miracles were too implausible; moreover, the actor in the title role was not at all credible. However, Moody's success lies in his imaginative treatment of one of his favorite themes—the conflict between man's spiritual and sexual needs.

Moody's development as a playwright, from *The Masque of Judgment* to *The Faith Healer*, demon-

William Vaughn Moody

strates the creative genius he brought to American drama. Although his prose dramas were more acceptable to modern taste than his verse plays, his work as a whole is marked by high literary ideals applied to universal themes. Moody is perhaps better known as a poet. While his plays are rarely anthologized, his poems (such as "Gloucester Moors," "The Menagerie," "On a Soldier Fallen in the Philippines," "Thammuz," and "An Ode in Time of Hesitation") can frequently be found in modern literary anthologies. Early in his career his poetry had received widespread recognition. Two years after his untimely death, Harriet Monroe, editor of the influential *Poetry*, included a Moody poem in the magazine's first issue (October 1912); and in the second issue she reviewed Manly's *Poems and Plays of William Vaughn Moody* by praising the "spontaneity" of his masque and the "simple austerity" of *The Death of Eve*. Moody's achievement, according to Monroe, lies in "the beginning of great things" to come.

Even if Moody never fully achieved his vision of drama as a poetic form of liberating the human spirit, he succeeded in protesting against restrictive social and moral codes and in reaffirming a vision of emotional, spiritual, and sexual fulfillment. The work of William Vaughn Moody contains nearly all the chief ideas and creative motifs of modern drama. In their book-length studies on Moody, David Dodds Henry, Martin Halpern, and Maurice F. Brown agree that Moody deserves a higher reputation in modern drama than he has been accorded. While his celebrated play, *The Great Divide*, won such critical acclaim as being called "the present high water mark in American drama" by a *New York Sun* reporter (23 February 1908), Moody's reputation suffered a decline after 1925 due to changes in literary sensibility. Nevertheless, his serious ideals and far-reaching intellect contributed a great deal to twentieth-century drama. His brief life and relatively small dramatic output relegate him to the stature of a minor playwright, yet his achievement in *The Great Divide* alone is significant enough to be considered a pivotal moment in the evolution of American drama.

–*Laura M. Zaidman*

Other:

John Bunyan, *The Pilgrim's Progress*, edited by Moody (Boston: Houghton Mifflin, 1896);

Samuel Taylor Coleridge, *The Rime of the Ancient Mariner*, and James Russell Lowell, *The Vision of Sir Launfal*, edited by Moody (Chicago: Scott, Foresman, 1898);

John Milton, *The Complete Poetical Works of John Milton*, edited by Moody (Boston: Houghton Mifflin, 1899);

Sir Walter Scott, *The Lay of the Last Minstrel*, edited by Moody (Chicago: Scott, Foresman, 1899);

Scott, *Marmion*, edited by Moody (Chicago: Scott, Foresman, 1899);

Scott, *The Lady of the Lake*, edited by Moody (Chicago: Scott, Foresman, 1900);

The Iliad of Homer, books 1, 6, 22, 24, trans. Alexander Pope, edited by Moody and W. W. Cressy (Chicago: Scott, Foresman, 1900);

The Poems of Trumbull Stickney, edited by Moody, George Cabot Lodge, and John Ellerton Lodge (Boston & New York: Houghton Mifflin, 1905);

Selections from De Quincey, edited by Moody (Chicago: Scott, Foresman, 1909).

Letters:

Some Letters of William Vaughn Moody, ed. Daniel Gregory Mason (Boston & New York: Houghton Mifflin, 1913);

Letters to Harriet, ed. Percy MacKaye (Boston: Houghton Mifflin, 1935).

Biography:

Maurice F. Brown, *Estranging Dawn: The Life and Works of William Vaughn Moody* (Carbondale & Edwardsville: Southern Illinois University Press, 1973).

References:

Nash O. Barr, "The Lyrist and Lyric Dramatist," *The Drama: A Quarterly Review*, no. 2 (May 1911): 177-206;

Sculley Bradley, "The Emergence of the Modern Drama," in *Literary History the United States*, vol. 2, ed. Robert E. Spiller and others (New York: Macmillan, 1948), pp. 1013-1015;

Charles H. Caffin, "The Playwright," *The Drama: A Quarterly Review*, no. 2 (May 1911): 206-211;

Martin Halpern, *William Vaughn Moody* (New York: Twayne, 1964);

David Dodds Henry, *William Vaughn Moody: A Study* (Boston: Humphries, 1934; republished, Darby, Pa.: Folcroft Library Editions, 1973);

Arthur Hobson Quinn, "William Vaughn Moody and the Drama of Revolt," in his *A History of the American Drama from the Civil War to the Present Day*, revised edition, vol. 2 (New York: Appleton-Century-Crofts, 1936), pp. 1-26;

Martha Hale Shackford, "Moody's *The Fire-Bringer* for To-day," *Sewanee Review*, 26 (1918): 407-416.

Papers:

The Archives and the Houghton Library at Harvard University, the Princeton University Library, and the University of Chicago Library have collections of Moody's papers.

Clifford Odets

Beth Fleischman
University of South Carolina

BIRTH: Philadelphia, Pennsylvania, 18 July 1906, to Louis J. and Pearl Geisinger Odets.

MARRIAGE: 8 January 1937 to Luise Rainer, divorced. 14 May 1943 to Bette Grayson, divorced; children: Nora and Walt Whitman.

AWARDS: George Pierce Baker Drama Cup for *Waiting for Lefty*, 1935; New Theatre-New Masses Theatre Contest winner for *Waiting for Lefty*, 1935; Award of Merit Medal for Drama, American Academy of Arts and Letters for *The Flowering Peach*, 1961.

DEATH: Los Angeles, California, 14 August 1963.

PRODUCTIONS: *Waiting for Lefty*, 5 January 1935, Civic Repertory Theatre, New York; 26 March 1935, Longacre Theatre (transferred 9 September 1935 to Belasco Theatre), New York, 159 [performances];
Awake and Sing!, 19 February 1935, Belasco Theatre, New York, 184;
Till the Day I Die, 26 March 1935, Longacre Theatre, New York, 135;
Paradise Lost, 9 December 1935, Longacre Theatre, New York, 72;
Golden Boy, 4 November 1937, Belasco Theatre, New York, 248;
Rocket to the Moon, 24 November 1938, Belasco Theatre, New York, 131;
Night Music, music by Hanns Eisler, 22 February 1940, Broadhurst Theatre, New York, 20;
Clash by Night, 27 December 1941, Belasco Theatre, New York, 49;
The Russian People, adapted from Konstantin Simonov's *The Russians*, 29 December 1942, Guild Theatre, New York, 39;
The Big Knife, 24 February 1949, National Theatre, New York, 109;
The Country Girl, 10 November 1950, Lyceum Theatre, New York, 235; revised as *Winter Journey*, 12 March 1968, Greenwich Mews Theatre, New York, 15;
The Flowering Peach, 28 December 1954, Belasco Theatre, New York, 135; adapted as *Two by Two*, by Peter Stone, Richard Rodgers, and Martin Charnin, 10 November 1970, Imperial Theatre, New York, 352;
The Silent Partner, 11 May 1972, Actors Studio, New York, 12.

SELECTED BOOKS: *Three Plays by Clifford Odets* (New York: Covici-Friede, 1935)—includes *Awake and Sing!*, *Waiting for Lefty*, *Till the Day I Die*;
Rifle Rule in Cuba, by Odets and Carleton Beals (New York: Provisional Committee for Cuba, 1935);
Paradise Lost (New York: Random House, 1936);
Waiting for Lefty (London: Gollancz, 1937);
Golden Boy (New York: Random House, 1937; London: Gollancz, 1938);
Rocket to the Moon (New York: Random House, 1939);
Six Plays of Clifford Odets (New York: Random House, 1939)—includes *Waiting for Lefty*, *Awake and Sing!*, *Till the Day I Die*, *Paradise Lost*, *Golden Boy*, *Rocket to the Moon*;
Night Music (New York: Random House, 1940);
Clash by Night (New York: Random House, 1942);
The Big Knife (New York: Random House, 1949);
The Country Girl (New York: Viking, 1951); republished as *Winter Journey* (London: French, 1955);
The Flowering Peach (New York: Dramatists Play Service, 1954).

Clifford Odets is known primarily as a proletarian playwright of the 1930s, although this label is misleading. Odets's first few plays, which catapulted him virtually overnight to fame and affluence, reflect the experience of the Great Depression and have an explicit socialist message. Beginning with *Golden Boy* (1937), however, Odets broadened the scope of his plays, thus drawing severe criticism for allegedly abandoning his ideological direction. Actually, this charge has little validity; an examination of Odets's plays reveals that his basic theme, the struggle of the individual to maintain his integrity, remains constant, and that it is Odets's tone which undergoes change—from militancy to moderation.

Odets's own family was decidedly middle-class. He was born in Philadelphia; during his early childhood, his father Louis, a Jewish Russian immigrant, held various jobs selling newspapers and peddling salt, and his mother worked in a factory. When he was six, the family (Odets has two younger sisters) settled in the Bronx, where his father rose from a position as feeder in a printing plant to become the owner. Although Odets has said he was "a worker's son until the age of twelve," the family lived in one of the first apartment buildings in the Bronx that had an elevator, and they owned a Maxwell automobile, two sure indicators of financial success. They later returned to Philadelphia, where Louis Odets became vice-president of a boiler company and owned an advertising agency, which he sold upon his retirement for two hundred thousand dollars. Despite a financially secure childhood, Odets claimed to have been "a melancholy kid," probably resulting from his stormy relationship with his father, who had plans for his son to enter his advertising business; but from an early age, Odets wanted to become an actor. Because he considered it "a waste of time," he dropped out of Morris High School in 1923 after two years and tried to write poetry. Odets recalled in an interview that on one occasion his father, furious with his son's rebelliousness, smashed his typewriter. Later, of course, his father replaced it, and eventually gave his permission for Odets to attempt a career on the stage.

Odets had, during the next seven years, a series of minor jobs in the theatrical world. He acted with the Drawing-Room Players, a neighborhood company which presented one-act plays in the Heckscher Theatre, and with Harry Kemp's Poet's Theatre. He also worked as an announcer for a small radio station in the Bronx, wrote radio plays, gave performances as a roving reciter specializing in the poems of Rudyard Kipling, and played in vaudeville for a dollar a night. At the age of twenty, he was hired as a juvenile in Mae Desmond's Stock Company, which performed primarily melodrama, but he apparently was not particularly talented as an actor. His first association with the Broadway stage

came in 1929 when he was hired as understudy to Spencer Tracy in Warren F. Lawrence's *Conflict*. A member of the cast introduced Odets to the Theatre Guild, which led him to join the Group Theatre in 1930. This event marked the actual beginning of Odets's career.

The ten-year history of the Group Theatre has been chronicled in Harold Clurman's *The Fervent Years* (1975). It was an organization of actors and directors founded by Clurman, Lee Strasberg, and Cheryl Crawford as a collective theatre, a group of individuals whose plays would reflect their values and attempt to change the society of which they were a part. Ideally, the Group Theatre would be a training ground for actors, in which a unified method (closely modeled on the theories of the Russian theatrical director, teacher, and actor, Konstantin Stanislavsky) would be used by the directors to mold the actors into a single organism; because the production itself was most important, there would be no "stars." Although the Group Theatre occasionally failed to live up to its ideals and was periodically plagued by internal disputes, it was vigorously applauded by critics and has had a lasting impact on the American theatre. There is no question that it had an overwhelming influence on Odets; in 1936 he remarked, "I don't think I would ever have written a play if it hadn't been for the Group." He joined the Group Theatre as an actor and played a few minor roles in plays such as Paul Green's *The House of Connelly* (1931) and Sidney Kingsley's *Men in White* (1933). Scarcely noticed by reviewers and increasingly frustrated over his floundering career, Odets began to write a play about Beethoven. The following year he wrote in his diary: "Here I am writing the Beethoven play, which when it is finished may not even be about Beethoven. Why not write something about the Greenberg family, something I know better, something that is closer to me?" Apparently this idea inspired Odets to work on the play which later became *Awake and Sing!* (1935).

Meanwhile, as the Depression continued and Odets found it increasingly difficult to survive (he lived with several other members of the Group Theatre in a large, poorly heated apartment), he sought the solution to the problems of the suffering masses in the Communist Party, which he joined in 1934 and left after eight months. In 1952, testifying before the House Un-American Activities Committee, Odets explained his feelings during the 1930s: "Literature was passed around, and in a time of great social unrest many people found themselves reaching out for new ideas, new ways of solving depressions or making a better living, fighting for one's rights. . . . The rights to be steadily employed, for instance. I believe at that time there were perhaps fifteen or sixteen million unemployed people in the United States, and I myself was living on ten cents a day. . . . They were horrendous days that none of us would like to go through again. . . . [I] finally joined the Communist Party, in the belief, in the honest and real belief, that this was some way out of the dilemma in which we found ourselves."

Written during his association with the Communist Party, *Waiting for Lefty* (1935), Odets's first produced play, has been called "the definitive specimen of the whole proletarian drama in America." It was inspired by the New York taxi strike of February 1934, although Odets claimed that when the play was written, he had "never been near a strike." He wrote the play for the New Theatre League, which was seeking plays for workers that might be presented in any meeting place or hall. Clurman reports that the first performance of *Waiting for Lefty*, a Sunday benefit performance for the *New Theater Magazine* on 5 January 1935 at the Civic Repertory Theatre in New York, was a significant moment in the history of the American theatre: "When the audience at the end of the play responded to the militant question from the stage: 'Well, what's the answer?' with a spontaneous roar of 'Strike! Strike!' it was something more than a tribute to the play's effectiveness, more even than a testimony of the audience's hunger for constructive social action. It was the birth cry of the thirties. Our youth had found its voice." Today's readers may be somewhat mystified as to what all the excitement was about; *Waiting for Lefty* seems simplistic—its message is heavy-handed, and its characters are shallow stereotypes. Yet the play does have its merits and is frequently touching. Malcolm Cowley says in *The Dream of the Golden Mountain* (1980), "*Lefty*, for all its faults, comes as close to being classic as anything that directly emerged from the proletarian school."

Odets structured the play as a series of brief vignettes, each of which spotlights certain individuals and shows how their problems reflect the larger conflict which forms the framework of the play. (Odets rearranged and substituted scenes after the original production; the version included in *Six Plays of Clifford Odets*, 1939, will be discussed here.) The play opens with the "Union Assembly Hall Scene," in which Harry Fatt, a union organizer, is attempting to dissuade the members of the taxi drivers' union from striking. The play is staged so that the theatre becomes the union assembly hall,

with the union officials sitting facing the audience and actors playing union members planted in the audience. It quickly becomes obvious that the taxi drivers are eager to strike and are awaiting the arrival of Lefty Costello, a leader who will support them. One man, Joe, speaks out, shouting that the country is "on the blink," and he comes onstage to argue in favor of a strike. As he does so, the lighting changes as the second scene, "Joe and Edna," begins, showing Joe at home having a confrontation with his wife. Because Joe brings home only six or seven dollars a week, scarcely enough to support the

Clifford Odets

family, Edna demands that he do something to improve their life and threatens to leave him. Edna knows nothing about politics, but she recognizes the inequities of the economic system which permits the capitalist to become wealthy while the worker's children go hungry, and she bitterly attacks Joe for allowing the situation to become critical. Joe is finally stung into action, and the scene shifts back to the union hall, where he says, "We gotta walk out!" Next to be spotlighted is Miller in "Laboratory Assistant," who now drives a taxi because he was fired from his previous job as research assistant when he refused to compromise his ideals. The scene shows him being offered a promotion by Fayette, a capitalist manufacturer of poison gas; his new position will require him to spy on his co-worker, a respected chemist. Finally Miller realizes that what Fayette is offering is harmful to mankind as well as degrading, and, in a rage, he strikes him. The next scene, "The Young Hack and His Girl," depicts two young people, Sid and Florrie, who want to get married but are forced to separate because Florrie's brother will not allow her to marry a poor taxi driver. In "The Labor Spy Episode," the focus shifts back to the union meeting, where a labor spy, Clayton, is exposed by one of the taxi drivers in the audience, who turns out to be his own brother. In "The Interne" scene which follows, Dr. Benjamin, a Jew, has been asked to resign from the hospital staff. His friend, Dr. Barnes, hints that anti-Semitism might be the motive. Furthermore, an incompetent physician, who is the nephew of a senator, will be replacing him. Dr. Benjamin muses that perhaps he will go to Russia to live but decides that his work is here in America, and he takes a job driving a cab. The final scene in the play is "The Agate Episode," in which Agate Keller takes the floor to urge the members not to wait for Lefty but to strike now. His speech is impassioned, and when a man comes in to announce that Lefty has been found shot to death, the men rise to their feet in a unified call to "Strike!"

Harold Clurman remembers that when the Group Theatre members first read *Waiting for Lefty*, they were "struck by its originality and fire," and Joseph Wood Krutch in the *Literary History of the United States* (1963) calls the play "ingenious and forthright." It was an immediate success when it opened on Broadway, and by July of 1935 it had been produced in thirty cities across the country. Although the play was acclaimed primarily as a political statement, one can argue that beyond the issue of the taxi strike, *Waiting for Lefty* asserts the right of every individual to have his share of human dignity. The villain in the play is not just capitalism, but any system or set of values which strips a man of his self-worth and destroys personal relationships. Michael J. Mendelsohn further suggests that *Waiting for Lefty* shows a skill in technique and imagination that is unusual in a first play and has an artistry not found in the other proletarian plays of the 1930s. Unfortunately, Odets's name has been irrevocably linked with *Waiting for Lefty*, while many of his better plays are often overlooked. Certainly *Awake and Sing!*, which was actually written prior to *Waiting for Lefty* but not produced by the Group Theatre until the latter was already a hit, is a more lasting contribution to the American theatre.

Awake and Sing! takes its title from Isaiah 26: 19—"Awake and sing, ye that dwell in dust." According to the list of characters, "all of the characters in *Awake and Sing!* share a fundamental activity: a struggle for life amidst petty conditions." Like *Waiting for Lefty*, the play condemns the economic system which traps individuals into a treadmill of hopelessness. It is not, however, an angry diatribe. Instead, it is a full-length, three-act play which examines the relationships, ambitions, and frustrations of the members of a struggling Jewish working-class family, the Bergers. The plot centers on the efforts of the youngest members of the family to escape their environment. Ralph, the son, a romantic and naive dreamer, works as a clerk and complains that all he wants is "a chance to get to first base." Hennie, the beautiful, self-reliant daughter, has several admirers, including Schlosser, the janitor, whose wife ran off and left him with a young child, and Moe Axelrod, a boarder in the Berger household, who lost a leg in the war and is now a petty racketeer. Their father, Myron, is a "born follower" who has known nothing but failure yet never admits defeat and continues to live in the past. Their mother, Bessie, is a strong-willed, domineering woman whose motivation is to preserve the respectability of her family; she forces the pregnant Hennie to marry Sam Feinschreiber, a lonely, sensitive man who is deluded into thinking that the baby is his. Ralph is appalled when he discovers what his mother has done and is shocked to learn that his grandfather, Jacob, a Marxist idealist, did nothing to prevent it. The family circle is completed by Uncle Morty, a shrewd, cynical businessman and sensualist who personifies economic success. By the end of the play, Ralph and Hennie achieve some sort of escape. Hennie leaves her husband and child and runs off to Cuba with Moe Axelrod. Ralph becomes spiritually reborn when Jacob, who is not a man of action, names Ralph as beneficiary of his insurance policy and commits suicide, after giving him the advice which he himself was never able to follow: "This . . . I tell you—Do! Do what is in your heart and carry in yourself a revolution. But you should act. Not like me. A man who had golden opportunities but drank instead a glass tea." The play ends on a positive note with Ralph's affirmative speech: "I'm twenty-two and kickin! I'll get along. Did Jake die for us to fight about nickles? NO! 'Awake and sing,' he said. Right here he stood and said it. The night he died, I saw it like a thunderbolt! I saw he was dead and I was born! I swear to God, I'm one week old! I want the whole city to hear it—fresh blood, arms. We got 'em. We're glad we're

THE · PLAYBILL · PUBLISHED · BY · THE · NEW · YORK · THEATRE · PROGRAM · CORPORATION

BEGINNING
TUESDAY EVENING,
FEBRUARY 19, 1935

NRA
WE DO OUR PART

MATINEES
THURSDAY AND
SATURDAY

THE GROUP THEATRE, INC.

presents

THE GROUP THEATRE ACTING COMPANY

in

"AWAKE AND SING!"

By CLIFFORD ODETS

"Awake and sing, ye that dwell in dust."—Isaiah 26:19

Production directed by HAROLD CLURMAN

Setting by BORIS ARONSON

CAST

(In the order of appearance)

MYRON BERGER . . . . *Played by* . . . . ART SMITH
BESSIE BERGER . . . . " " . . . . STELLA ADLER
JACOB . . . . " " . . . . MORRIS CARNOVSKY

Playbill

living." Clearly, the theory of economic determinism underlies *Awake and Sing!* There is no villain in the play except the economic system; the characters have all been gravely affected by their financial circumstances. Moe and Morty, who have achieved success as capitalists, are crippled, one physically, the other spiritually. The remaining characters are victimized by capitalism. Bessie and Myron are, in the words of Michael Mendelsohn, "chained to their own bourgeois attitudes and slogans, leading a hopelessly false life." Presumably Hennie and Ralph will ultimately be like their parents unless they make the individual effort to escape, and Odets believes that they have indeed broken the cycle.

However, the ending of the play has drawn considerable criticism. Hennie's flight is undeniably irresponsible, and her destination, Havana, is highly suspicious. In 1935, Cuba was ruled by the Mendieta dictatorship, and Gerald Weales has pointed out that the Cuban Tourist Commission resorted to advertisements in American newspapers to assure potential tourists that they would be safe in Cuba. Moe, with his false values, is an unlikely hero; to him, "it's all a racket—from horse racing on down. Marriage, politics, big business—everybody plays cops and robbers." Additionally, Ralph's al-

leged transformation does not truly indicate that his life will be any different in the future. The audience is merely *told* Ralph has changed. His final speech is impassioned and seems full of conviction, but there is no proof that Ralph is now capable of action, nor is there any concrete suggestion of what he will do to improve his situation. Indeed, in the third act he is still incapable of dealing decisively with his girl friend, Blanche. Odets, however, did not intend the ending of *Awake and Sing!* to be ambiguous; he repeatedly emphasized in interviews the optimistic nature of the play. Despite this flaw, the play is remarkable for its power, realism, and brilliant dialogue. Edward Murray believes that "few works in American drama reveal so well what happens to a family when natural relations are perverted."

Odets's third play is more explicitly political than *Awake and Sing!* When the hour-long *Waiting for Lefty* was brought to Broadway by the Group Theatre, a companion play was needed. For this purpose, Odets wrote *Till the Day I Die* (1935), a play in seven scenes inspired by a letter Odets had read in *New Masses*, which described the torture and breakdown of a German underground worker by the Nazis. Although it was the first successful anti-Nazi play to appear in New York, *Till the Day I Die* is considered the slightest of Odets's plays; its relatively long run was due to the popularity of *Waiting for Lefty*. It tells the story of Ernst Tausig, a Communist worker who is arrested by the Nazis and tortured. Even though they smash his hands (he is a violinist), he refuses to divulge any information, so the Nazis release him, intending to use him as a decoy to capture other members of the underground. He is reunited briefly with Carl, his brother, and Tilly, his common-law wife who is pregnant with his child, and he tries to tell them how the Nazis plan to use him. At a meeting, Ernst's fellow workers decide to blacklist him after hearing the charges against him: he had accompanied the Nazis on raids, he was seen standing at the door as prisoners were taken in for interrogation, he was wearing new clothes—all ploys by the Nazis to make him appear to be a traitor. In the final scene, Ernst returns to Carl and Tilly, a broken and sick man, in an effort to clear his name. He begs Carl to kill him: "Take the gun. Carl, you loved me once. Kill me. One day more and I'll stand there like an idiot identifying prisoners for them." When Carl refuses, Ernst walks offstage, saying, "Do your work, comrades." The play ends with Ernst's suicide:

TILLY (*for a moment stands still, then starts for room. Carl stops her*): Carl, stop him, stop him. (*Carl holds her back.*)

CARL: Let him die. . . .

TILLY: Carl. . . . (*Shot heard within.*)

CARL: Let him live. . . .

Till the Day I Die is clearly a propaganda play intended to alert audiences to the horrors of Nazism and the need to combat it. Unfortunately, it is not particularly convincing, due to its lack of verisimilitude, the sentimentalization of its characters, and some political misconceptions. The central character, Ernst, is never developed beyond the stereotype of the noble resister; as Gerald Weales suggests, the play focuses less on what he does (until the final suicide) than on what is done to him. In addition, the play proposes that the proper weapon against Nazism is Communism, a notion which was shown to be false, particularly after the signing of the Berlin-Moscow pact in 1939. *Till the Day I Die* was the last of Odets's plays to deal explicitly with a particular political problem.

Paradise Lost, Odets's fourth play produced during 1935, takes a more indirect approach. Although Odets wrote in the preface to *Six Plays* that it was his favorite of the early plays, it was not well received; it was probably not understood by the critics who were expecting a realistic play similar to *Waiting for Lefty, Till the Day I Die*, and *Awake and Sing!* The play has often been called Chekhovian,

because Odets himself mentioned Chekhov in a publicity release. However, he later denied that the play was influenced by a reading of Chekhov, and R. Baird Shuman suggests that it may be more readily compared with the plays of Sean O'Casey. *Paradise Lost* has also been likened unfavorably to *Awake and Sing!*; Joseph Wood Krutch, for example, wrote that the play "seems like nothing so much as an improbable burlesque of *Awake and Sing!*" However, Odets intended for the audience to consider the symbolic meaning of what is on the surface a realistic play. As he explained, the hero of the play is "the entire American middle class of liberal tendency." Each of the members of the Gordon household represents a middle-class value, and the steady decline within the play symbolizes the decay of these false values during the 1930s. Shuman explains that "Odets is not for a moment trying to imply that only *a* family is destroyed; indeed, a huge segment of society is being swallowed up—morally, economically, spiritually—in one of the most pervasive social upheavals to occur in the United States during its history. The author is concerned in *Paradise Lost* with this all-encompassing social situation which he portrays microcosmically through one very limited group of characters."

The head of the household, Leo Gordon, a small businessman who designs handbags, represents the best middle-class characteristics; he is artistic, intellectual, and compassionate. Clara, his wife, has found fulfillment in her three children. The children each embody a virtue: Ben is a former Olympic hero, Julie is a bank clerk with great prospects for financial success, and Pearl is a classical pianist. Other characters in the play include Leo's friend Gus Michaels, whose small business has failed, leaving him little to do but collect stamps; Gus's daughter, Libby, who marries Ben; Sam Katz, Leo's unscrupulous business partner; Sam's wife, Bertha, disappointed by her inability to have children; Kewpie, a petty gangster and friend of Ben's; and Mr. Pike, a former itinerant worker, now a furnace man, who represents America's pioneer stock but utters Marxist ideals. In the course of the play, the Gordons experience one catastrophe after another. A shop delegation from Leo Gordon's business complains that the workers are being denied a decent living wage, a condition which Leo had not been aware of because he left the running of the factory to Sam, who is revealed to be an embezzler. Despite Sam's protestations that raising wages would result in financial ruin, Leo agrees to the delegation's demands, and the business eventually goes bankrupt. The older son, Ben, has a weak heart and, notwithstanding vague promises from his friends and acquaintances, is unable to find employment and earn a living for his family until Kewpie invites him to participate in a robbery, where he is killed by the police. The second son, Julie, has made a fortune on paper, but he is incurably ill with encephalitis. The daughter, Pearl, loses her lover, Felix, because he is unable to find employment as a violinist and must go to another city to get a job; as a result, Pearl completely withdraws from the world and spends her lonely days playing her piano. Act 3 finds the Gordons about to be evicted, having lost their business and their house. The play ends, however, in typical Odetsian fashion with a final impassioned speech. Leo, undefeated by all of his losses, bursts forth with a vision of optimism for the future: "That was the past, but there is a future. Now we know. We dare to understand. Truly, truly, the past was a dream. But this is real! To know from this that something must be done. That is real. We searched; we were confused! But we searched, and now the search is ended. For the truth has found us. . . . Oh, yes, I tell you the whole world is for men to possess. Heartbreak and terror are not the heritage of mankind! The world is beautiful. No fruit tree wears a lock and key. Men will sing at their work, men will love. Ohhh, darling, the world is in its morning . . . and *no man fights alone!*" Critics were particularly harsh in their comments about this speech. It is the same problem of Ralph's final speech in *Awake and Sing!* all over again, only this time there is even less internal evidence to support Leo's conversion. Clara Bagley, in her review in *Worker*, remarked that the only apparent reason for Leo's speech is that "it is eleven o'clock and the curtain must come down." *Paradise Lost* was a commercial failure, and it marked the end of the first phase of Odets's career as a playwright.

During 1935 Odets remained concerned with the sufferings of the downtrodden and oppressed, despite the success which transformed him into a celebrity. In fact, that summer he led a commission to Cuba to verify reports that the Mendieta regime had suspended civil liberties in that country. On their arrival in Havana, the members of the commission were arrested and forced to return to the United States. After lodging a protest with the Cuban Consul General, the commission published a pamphlet, *Rifle Rule in Cuba*, and Odets began a play (which he never finished) which was intended to bring the incident to the attention of the public. At the same time, however, as a successful writer, Odets began to receive offers from Hollywood, starting with $500 a week after the opening of

Waiting for Lefty and apparently going as high as $4000 a week when *Awake and Sing!* was established as a hit. To Odets, Hollywood represented "sin" and a desertion of the values held by the Group Theatre. However, with the failure of *Paradise Lost*, Odets accepted an offer of $2500 a week from Paramount, rationalizing his decision on the grounds that he could help the Group Theatre by sending it money, which he did. His first Hollywood effort was the screenplay *The General Died at Dawn* (1936), a melodrama with some minor political overtones. When the movie was released, reviewer Frank S. Nugent titled his review, "Odets, Where Is Thy Sting?"; the New York critics generally agreed that Odets's career as a playwright was over and that he had sold out to Hollywood. They were proven wrong; after an interlude in Hollywood, during which he wrote two other screenplays ("Gettysburg," which was never filmed, and "Castles in Spain," which was rewritten and produced as *Blockade* in 1938) and married Luise Rainer, Odets returned to New York, where he worked with the Group Theatre until 1941.

Odets wrote *Golden Boy* for the Group Theatre and subsidized the cost of the production, and the play rescued the Group Theatre from a severe financial crisis. It was the greatest commercial success of Odets's career, and the movie rights were eventually sold for $75,000. *Golden Boy* also ushered in a new period in Odets's career. As Shuman suggests, "It is much broader in scope than the earlier plays, and shows clearly that the author is unwilling to remain ideologically static and produce political propaganda for the remainder of his life. His concern is for man and the forces which dictate human destiny." According to Harold Clurman, *Golden Boy* is the most subjective of Odets's plays, reflecting the compromise Odets made by going to Hollywood. To a certain extent, this is true. The hero of the play is Joe Bonaparte, the son of an Italian fruit vendor, who decides to forsake a potential career as a concert violinist in order to become a successful prizefighter. In the course of his rise to the top, Joe unintentionally kills the former champion during a bout. When this happens, he realizes what he has sacrificed for success, and the play ends with his death in an automobile accident. Gerald Weales suggests that *Golden Boy* is a variation on the Faust theme, "the story of a young man who sells his soul (goes against his nature) and discovers, too late, that he has made a bad bargain."

The other characters and the symbolic elements in the play serve to reinforce this thesis. Joe's family represents genuine values. His father, who has saved for a lifetime to buy Joe an expensive violin, believes in self-fulfillment; he is Odets's spokesman when he says, "Whatever you got ina your nature to do isa not foolish!" Joe's sister Anna and her husband Siggie have a marriage based on love and mutual respect. His brother Frank is a representative of the Congress of Industrial Organizations, a conscientious man whose life is dedicated to the betterment of society. Yet Joe rejects his family when he gives up the violin for boxing gloves and enters the world of commercial success. There he is treated like a commodity by individuals like Tom Moody, his manager, who exploits him in order to obtain financial security so he can divorce his wife and marry Lorna, his girl friend and secretary; and by Eddie Fuseli, a racketeer who "buys a piece" of him. Joe himself is a sensitive introvert who becomes a boxer in order to achieve financial success and to revenge past insults resulting from his odd name and his optical deformity (he is "cock-eyed," symbolizing his inability to focus clearly on what is important to him). After he breaks his hands during a fight at the end of the second act, which means he can no longer play the violin and which symbolizes his complete break with his former values, he exults, "Hallalujah! It's the beginning of the world!" He buys a Deusenberg automobile, a symbol of materialism and speed, and thinks he has found love in Lorna. But the death of his opponent, the Chocolate Drop, brings him to the realization that he has actually destroyed himself. Odets does not specify whether or not the fatal accident at the end of the play is a suicide. It does not matter. As Weales suggests, "even if it is an accident, it is no accident."

Even before *Golden Boy* was produced, Odets had been working on a play entitled *The Silent Partner*, which focussed on the shift of power from bosses to workers in a factory town during the Depression and which he claimed would be the best labor play ever produced. However, the play is very similar to *Waiting for Lefty*, and it was not performed during his lifetime. (On 11 May 1972, *The Silent Partner* was produced by Actors Studio in a limited engagement as a special showcase production that included both readings and staged portions of the play.) Over the next four years, Odets wrote three plays dealing with relationships between men and women. It is likely that this preoccupation stemmed from his own marital problems (he was divorced from Luise Rainer in 1941). When the first of these, *Rocket to the Moon*, opened in 1938, Odets defended himself against charges that the play lacked substance by saying that "the roots of love and the meaning of it in the present world need surely to be comprehended as much as the effect of a strike on its activists."

According to Clurman, the theme of *Rocket to the Moon* is the "difficult quest for love in the modern world." The three pivotal characters form a conventional triangle, but the underlying assumption of the play is that society is responsible for the predicament they are in. Ben Stark is a rather timid, middle-aged dentist who is frustrated with his marriage and his dental practice. His wife, Belle, a domineering shrew whose only pregnancy ended with a stillborn child, will not permit him to risk his secure business by moving to a new location and disapproves of his pretty young secretary, Cleo, a naive and romantic girl who is seeking love and excitement. The inevitable affair between Stark and Cleo develops and is complicated by two other men who also vie for Cleo's attentions—Mr. Prince, Belle's suave widower father, whose marriage was unhappy, and Willy Wax, a Broadway director and a ladies' man. To Cleo, the three men represent respectively passion, security, and glamour; at the end of the play, she rejects all three and leaves to seek "a whole full world, with all the trimmings." As for Stark, he seems to have reached a higher level of self-awareness, as his closing lines indicate: "For years I sat here, taking things for granted, my wife, everything. Then just for an hour my life was in a spotlight. . . . I saw everything clearly, realized who and what I was. Isn't that a beginning? Isn't it?" The element of economic determinism is underscored in the play by two minor characters. Phil Cooper, a dentist who shares offices with Stark, represents the professional man whose career and personal happiness are ruined by the Depression; he complains, "Who's got time to think about women! I'm trying to make a living!" Frenchy, a chiropodist, philosophizes on the conflict of the work ethic and the love ethic:

FRENCHY: . . . Love is no solution of life! Au contraire, as the Frenchman says—the opposite. You have to bring a whole balanced normal life to love if you want it to go!

STARK: Yes, I see your point.

FRENCHY: In this day of stress I don't see much normal life. . . .

This viewpoint has been apparent, to a greater or lesser degree, in all of Odets's plays—from Joe and Edna in *Waiting for Lefty* to Joe and Lorna in *Golden Boy*; in this sense, *Rocket to the Moon* is not really the departure from social criticism that reviewers complained it is. It does, however, have its weaknesses, primarily in the characterizations of Stark and Cleo.

Stark is simply too insignificant to be seen as heroic, and Cleo is regarded by many as silly and childish. Furthermore, the failure of the Starks' marriage seems to be due as much to their emotional weaknesses as to the Depression, thus undermining the ideological foundation of the play. However, the play does successfully depict what Weales terms a spiritual dislocation in which no one dares risk anything. The title itself refers to taking chances; Mr. Prince says to Stark, "Why don't you suddenly ride away, an airplane, a boat! Take a rocket to the moon! Explode!" Stark and Cleo are able to do this, and presumably their lives are better for it.

Odets's next play, *Night Music*, which was produced in 1940, also has a conventional "boy meets girl plot." Clurman, in his introduction, writes "The play stems from the basic sentiment that people nowadays are affected by a sense of insecurity; they are haunted by the fear of permanence in all their relationships; they are fundamentally *homeless*, and, whether or not they know it, they are in search of a home, of something real, secure, dependable in a slippery, shadowy, noisy and nervous world." The play's action begins on a Saturday evening in Manhattan when the brash, wisecracking hero, Steve Takis, who is transporting two monkeys to California as part of his job with a movie studio, accidentally meets Fay Tucker, a struggling young actress. The monkeys frighten Fay, and Steve is arrested. The two young people spend the weekend together, Steve provoking quarrels most of the time because of a series of accidents (Steve has lost his wallet; the play in which Fay was acting has closed). When Fay's father and her fiance, both of whom represent middle-class complacency and narrow-mindedness, arrive to take Fay home with them, she rejects their kind of life, and by Monday, the end of the play, Steve and Fay have fallen in love. Acting as a sort of guardian angel for the young couple is Abraham Lincoln Rosenberger, a detective who is dying of cancer, but who symbolizes life lived to the fullest ("I am in love with the possibilities, the human possibilities," he says). Several minor characters Steve encounters are also homeless: a sailor, a beggar, a sleeping man, a drunk, and a whore.

In *Night Music*, Odets deliberately experimented with structure, music, and setting. Joseph Wood Krutch in his review calls the structure of the play "centripetal"; Edward Murray believes it is more accurately "centrifugal." Steve is the center of the structure, and the action proceeds outward from this center. Murray suggests that Steve may be viewed as the hub of a wheel with all of the other characters revolving around him, the re-

sulting movement conveying the theme of homelessness. In addition, the play includes incidental music composed by Hanns Eisler. Weales notes that *Night Music* is "unusual in its attempt to present a total theater experience in which text, performance, music and sets worked together to convey a prevailing mood." Apparently music and slide projections were employed primarily to sustain the mood during the scene changes. Setting is more significant in this play than in previous Odets plays. Each of the eight settings (a police station, a stage-door exit, the lobby of the Hotel Algiers, adjoining hotel rooms, Central Park, a restaurant, the World's Fair, and the airport) is a public place, reemphasizing the theme of homelessness.

Despite Odets's attempts to provide the play with unity, the reviewers were unanimous in their criticism of its structure. Shuman notes that the concentrated action does not result in a "heightened intensity" but instead suggests that Fay and Steve's relationship is merely superficial. In addition, Steve's basic problem is private, not public. Edward Murray notes that Steve's homelessness stems from a search for a lost mother, not from poverty. Fay's search, likewise, has a psychological foundation; she is suffering from an existential malaise. *Night Music* closed after a brief run, probably because, as Shuman suggests, it bewildered rather than enlightened audiences. Odets, according to Clurman, assumed wrongly that we all "recognize our homelessness, that we all believe the rootlessness and disorientation of his hero to be typical, that we all know that most of the slogans of our society are without substance in terms of our true emotions." The play was revived briefly in 1951; critics discussing the play then and in more recent years have had increasingly positive things to say about it. Michael J. Mendelsohn believes it is Odets's most underrated play, and Weales says it is one of Odets's plays for which he has the greatest affection. Yet it has never been successful as a theatre piece.

The third of Odets's plays to deal with love relationships is *Clash by Night*, which premiered in 1941; it also suffers from a blurring of psychological and sociological motive. Like *Rocket to the Moon*, the play presents a triangle, but its characters are less sympathetic, and the violent ending makes the play pessimistic. Although Odets attempted to build an ideological base into his play, the banality of the plot reduces it to a depressing melodrama. Using Matthew Arnold's poem "Dover Beach" (1867) as a point of reference, Odets attempts to show that modern life is indeed a confused struggle on "a darkling plain," "Where ignorant armies clash by night," and that the prevailing concept of love is false and artificial and will not provide any real alternative to the loss of meaning in life. The subplot in *Clash by Night* shows a pair of young lovers, Joe and Peggy, prevented from marrying by financial hardships, who finally decide to marry in the last act; Joe makes a concluding affirmative speech, ending with "it's time to love and face the future!" However, the subplot is not well integrated into the play (Clurman says it "represented a kind of ideological afterthought") and is negated by the hopelessness of the ending.

The characters in *Clash by Night* are members of the lower-middle class living on Staten Island. Mae Wilenski, thirty, is a bored, lonely housewife with a seven-week-old baby. Her husband, Jerry, is a somewhat stupid but good-natured carpenter. His father, a Polish immigrant who lives with the couple, is afraid that he will be deported back to Poland because he has never learned to read, so he is constantly pretending to read the newspaper; he is a pathetic figure of loneliness and social disorientation. In act 1, Jerry invites his friend Earl to board with them, and Earl eventually becomes Mae's lover; at the end of the play, Jerry murders Earl. Beyond this, there is very little action in *Clash by Night*, but Odets has built symbolic elements into the play which are intended to clarify the thesis that American society is on the brink of disaster, that the working class, lulled into a false sense of well-being by the trappings of popular culture, is actually baffled, discontented, and full of repressed violence—ripe for fascism. For example, Mae hums songs like "The Sheik of Araby" and "Avalon" (popular escapist songs) and says she enjoys going to the movies, Earl works as a projectionist in a movie theatre, and the murder takes place in a projection booth while a typically frivolous movie is playing. Also, the character of Vince, Jerry's uncle, is intended to represent fascism. He is a despicable villain who goads Jerry into violence. In Joe's affirmative final speech, he predicts that the next step after disillusionment is fascism: "I see what happens when we wait for Paradise. Tricky Otto comes along, with a forelock and a mustache. Then he tells them why they're blue. 'You've been wronged,' he says. 'They done you dirt. Now come along with me. Take orders, park your brains, don't think, don't worry; poppa tucks you in at night!' . . . And where does that end? In violence, destruction, cripples by the carload!"

The difficulty with the play is that although these symbolic elements are present, they are not obvious; what is obvious is that Mae and Jerry are crippled by their emotional problems. Mae's discontent seems to stem largely from her comparing Jerry with her former lover, a "big, comfortable" politician who gave her "confidence." Murray suggests that Mae might be searching for a father surrogate, in which case it is doubtful that she would be content with any man. As far as Jerry is concerned, he is infantile in his behavior and has a clear mother fixation; when he learns what has developed between his wife and Earl, he says, "I can go sleep in poppa's room, if you don't wanna talk to me, momma—I mean, Mae," and the scene ends with his picking up a teddy bear which cries out, "Momma, momma." Any connection between these psychological factors and the larger social environment is unexplained by Odets. Weales suggests that Odets is wrong to consider popular culture to be the cause of a widespread social problem; if anything, it is a symptom. That audiences did not accept Odets's premise and that they assumed the tragedy had private rather than public causes is obvious from the fact that when the play opened—twenty days after the attack on Pearl Harbor and sixteen days after Nazi Germany declared war on the United States—the reviewers scarcely mentioned the politi-

Form letter for New Theatre *Magazine*

cal implications and dismissed the play as a sordid triangle.

The failure of *Clash by Night* marked the end of the second phase of Odets's career. Although he was well established as an important playwright by the end of 1941 (Random House had published *Six Plays of Clifford Odets* in 1939), he was at a crossroads: his marriage ended in divorce, and the Group Theatre, plagued by internal dissension, disbanded. (*Clash by Night* had begun as a Group Theatre production, but finally was produced by Billy Rose.) After contributing to the war effort by writing an adaptation of Konstantin Simonov's *The Russians* (a patriotic melodrama, extolling the heroism of the Russian people, immensely popular in Moscow, but not well received in New York) which was produced in December 1942 by the Theatre Guild as *The Russian People*, Odets returned to Hollywood. During the next few years, he wrote three screenplays: *None But the Lonely Heart* (1944), which he also directed; *Humoresque* (1946); and *Deadline at Dawn* (1946); plus a number of scripts which were never produced. He married Bette Grayson in 1943. Although Odets was well paid (on 2 March 1949, *Variety* reported that his income during his last year in Hollywood ran into six figures), he apparently had a great distaste for the work he was doing, saying, "I took my filthy salary every week and rolled an inner eye around an inner landscape." His attitude toward Hollywood remained ambivalent; he tried to convince himself that he could work for the betterment of humanity through the medium of cinema, but his scripts never reached a high level of achievement. Stefan Kanfer, in *A Journal of the Plague Years* (1973), suggests that Odets was always uncomfortable in Hollywood and never forgave himself for submitting to the lure of the high salary. Nevertheless he adopted the Hollywood life-style. Kanfer relates that on one occasion, when Odets was still married to Luise Rainer, he became angry when she gave her staff a night off and served the guests herself. "In Hollywood, one has servants," he told her. "Otherwise why come here?" He returned to New York for the production of *The Big Knife*, written in 1948 and produced in 1949, which was interpreted by critics as a direct attack on Hollywood.

The Big Knife is the story of Charlie Castles, a highly successful movie actor, who has been offered a four-million-dollar, fourteen-year contract by Marcus Hoff, a motion-picture tycoon. Charlie does not want to sign the contract. Feeling that he has lost his integrity by acting in cheap films, he wishes to return to the New York stage; his wife, Marion, who

is now living apart from him, threatens to divorce him if he does sign. The situation is complicated by the fact that, several years earlier, Charlie had killed a child in a hit-and-run accident for which his friend Buddy Bliss had taken the blame and served a prison term. Now Marcus Hoff is threatening to make the truth known if Charlie refuses to sign the contract. Out of fear, Charlie agrees to sign, but once he does so, he realizes that he has sold his self-respect. When he learns of the studio plot to murder Dixie Evans, the starlet who was in the car with him the night of the accident, to prevent her from talking, Charlie comes to a full awareness of what his "success" means and commits suicide.

Odets claimed that the play was more than an indictment of Hollywood: "This is an objective play about thousands of people, I don't care what industry they're in. . . . I have nothing against Hollywood per se. The big knife is that force which seeks to cut people off in their best flower." Yet most reviews, like that in the *Daily Mirror*, complained that, "after spending seven years in Hollywood turning out movie scripts at fancy wages, Clifford Odets has returned to Broadway to belabor the source of his handsome income." Apparently Hollywood held a different opinion, and a successful film version of *The Big Knife* was produced in 1955.

There are obvious similarities between *The Big Knife* and *Golden Boy*: both heroes choose materialism over idealism and end in suicide. However, the character of Charlie Castles is more complex than that of Joe Bonaparte. Joe soon realizes that material success will not make him happy, but Charlie is a man who "at once both loves and hates his success," according to Weales. Joe's accidental killing of the former champion is the critical moment of his life, but Charlie is able to live with the death of the little girl on his conscience; he can even sleep with Buddy's wife while Buddy is in jail for him. He only stops short of deliberate murder. At one point in the play, Charlie says, "Macbeth is an allegory, too: one by one, he kills his better selves." Apparently Odets had *Macbeth* in mind when he was writing *The Big Knife*, and in an interview he referred to Dixie Evans as "Banquo's ghost." It is possible to view Charlie Castles's depraved environment as an equivalent of the moral squalor of *Macbeth*'s witches, which pressures Charlie to yield to his darkest yearnings. To Murray, Charlie Castles is "the most tormented character Odets ever created. . . , sickened by compromise and driven to self-destruction in an effort to expiate his sins." Therefore, to view *The Big Knife* as simply an attack on the values of Hollywood is to disregard the fact that Charlie Castles's problems result from flaws in his character as well as the corrupting influences of society.

Two other attributes of *The Big Knife* should also be mentioned. First, the language in an Odets play is usually a strong point, and this play is no exception. The critics praised the verbal power of the dialogue; Kappo Phelan, for example, admired the play's "astonishing rhetoric." Secondly, the minor characters in the play are remarkable; Weales believes that "theatrically, they are the best thing in the play." Marcus Hoff is the stereotype of the oily villain, but his habit of uttering convoluted speech makes him especially memorable. Smiley Coy, Hoff's factotum, personifies cruelty camouflaged by friendliness. Nat Danziger, Charlie's agent, is paradoxical; although he seems to be a good man, of the same mold as Joe Bonaparte's father, he advises Charlie to sign the contract—and he stands to gain a considerable amount of money if Charlie does so. Odets's incisive portrait of Patty Benedict, the gossip columnist, may have been modeled on Hedda Hopper.

Odets's next play, *The Country Girl* (1950), also has an actor as its hero, but it is entirely a psychological study—it is the one Odets play which clearly does not have a "message" in the political sense. After *Golden Boy*, it is Odets's most commercially successful play, with its 235 performances, although he claims that he wrote it for money and never cared for it. In the play, Bernie Dodd, an enthusiastic young director, offers Frank Elgin, an aging alcoholic actor, a leading role in a Broadway play. Lacking confidence in himself, Frank is reluctant to accept. His wife, Georgie, is about to leave him, but decides to stay when he assumes responsibility for himself and takes the part. At first, primarily because of the lies that Frank has told him, Bernie thinks that Georgie's severe emotional problems would be a hindrance to Frank's comeback. Then, when Frank crumbles under the pressure of his role and gets drunk, Bernie realizes that actually Frank is dependent on Georgie, and not the other way around. Bernie and Georgie have a brief romance and work together to help Frank, who, at the end of the play, gives a triumphant performance.

If there is a theme in the play, it is what Weales calls "willful blindness." The theatrical world, with its deliberate falsity, is an especially apt setting. Each of the three characters begins with a self-created set of illusions which he is forced to shed in the course of the play, thereby gaining new insights. Frank believes his own lies, plays the role of a happy man, unable to admit that his lack of confidence has made

him an alcoholic and, though dependent on Georgie, he pretends that his wife is neurotic. Bernie, according to Weales, tries to "fit Frank and Georgie into preconceived roles," and refuses to see the reality of the Elgin marriage, which becomes more and more obvious to the audience. Georgie, who is, as the title suggests, the central character, also lives a self-created lie. She has convinced herself that Frank is dependent on her and that she must protect him; she refers to herself as an "old lady" and acts more like Frank's mother than his wife. However, as Shuman has suggested, "were Frank to take command of the situation, Georgie would be thoroughly miserable." The ending of the play is ambiguous; although Frank has recognized the truth about himself and has been able to make a comeback and Georgie has decided to stay with him, her speech points to future conflicts due to their new awareness and roles: "Neither of us has really changed. And yet I'm sure that both our lives are at some sort of turning point. There's some real new element of hope here—I don't know what. But I'm uncertain . . . and you, Frank, have to be strong enough to bear that uncertainty." Ambiguity in the ending of a political play like *Awake and Sing!* is a weakness, but in a psychological play like *The Country Girl*, it is a virtue. More than other Odets plays, *The Country Girl* has been successfully revived; in 1968 it was updated and produced as *Winter Journey*, Odets's second title for the play. Odets was correct when he termed the play a "theater piece"; free from topicality, the play has a universal appeal.

In the spring of 1952, Odets was called to testify before a Subcommittee of the House Un-American Activities Committee. In the course of his testimony, he mentioned the names of individuals he believed to have been members of the Communist Party during the 1930s. Kanfer points out that Odets actually "named" no one, because the people he mentioned were either dead or had already been named to the HUAC. Nevertheless, the act of testifying gave him a "sense of incalculable revulsion." Kanfer reports Odets wept at the funeral of John Garfield (who had acted in several of Odets's plays and whose sudden death was precipitated by his being blacklisted), and Clurman in *All People Are Famous* (1974) says that Odets went weeping to Garfield's widow to confess that he had not testified as he should have. He had not testified against Garfield at all; he stated to the Committee that he did not know Garfield to be a Communist. However, he did name, among others, Tony Kraber, a producer whom Odets knew from his Group Theatre days, as a former member of the

Party. Kanfer writes that when Kraber answered his doorbell in the middle of the night a few weeks later, he found Odets there, who said "I named you" and ran off. Apparently his guilt continued to torment him for years, and after 1952 he wrote relatively little.

Odets's last play was *The Flowering Peach* (1954), an adaptation of the biblical story of Noah. In writing it, Odets drew on a long tradition of plays based on the deluge (particularly André Obey's *Noah*, 1931) and borrowed elements found in them: domestic comedy, dialect humor, anachronisms, and modern philosophical argument. When the play was produced in 1954, there was the suggestion that Odets had a contemporary interpretation in mind, that the ark was a symbol of the bomb shelter. This view has some validity but is not essential for an appreciation of the play. The play was well received and was nominated for the Pulitzer Prize, but that award was given instead to Tennessee Williams's *Cat on a Hot Tin Roof*. In 1970 a musical adaptation of *The Flowering Peach*, *Two by Two* by Peter Stone, Richard Rodgers, and Martin Charnin, had a successful run on Broadway.

In Odets's play, Noah, according to Weales, is a "somewhat seedy patriarch, rather too given to drink." The play begins as Noah awakens from a dream in which he has been told by God of the coming events. His family, of course, doubts him, until the animals begin to arrive. The first scenes consist of gentle Jewish-family comedy, and the serious nature of the play does not begin to emerge until the philosophical confrontation between Noah and his youngest son, Japheth. Noah is a staunch advocate of acceptance of God's will; Japheth, a rationalist, challenges a God who would destroy so many people and refuses to board the ark. After Japheth is knocked out and physically carried aboard, their differences continue. Japheth wants to use a rudder to steer, and Noah believes that God will steer the ark for them. Noah is proved wrong when the ark strikes a submerged object and springs a leak, and he is forced to admit that perhaps God would accept some human assistance. Noah's gentle and patient wife, Esther, tries to keep the peace between father and son. Her motivation is to keep the family together; she dies of old age at the end of the voyage as the sons and their wives go off in different directions to start new families. Noah's two other sons, Shem and Ham, are less important characters. Shem is a businessman and opportunist who nearly causes the ark to sink by hoarding manure from which he intends to manufacture dried manure briquettes that he can sell later. Ham is a playboy who no longer loves his wife, Rachel, and lusts after Goldie, a woman Noah brought along as a wife for Japheth. However, Japheth doesn't love Goldie, but Rachel. A wife-swapping arrangement would please everyone involved except Noah, who believes that it is against God's commandments. Goldie and Rachel are pregnant, and before Esther dies, she asks that Noah agree to the alternate marriages, which he eventually does. True to the biblical version, the ark lands on a mountaintop in April, the month of rebirth. Japheth and Noah have both changed—the son is no longer rebellious, and the father has learned that it is better to maintain order through love than through blind adherence to God's commandments. Noah's closing speech is, in typical Odetsian fashion, affirmative and optimistic: "Thank you, Lord above, thank you. . . . But what I learned on this trip, dear God, you can't take away from me. To walk in humility, I learned. And listen, even to *myself* . . . and to speak softly, with the voices of consolation. Yes, I hear you, God—Now it's in man's hands to make or destroy the world . . . I'll tell you a mystery."

Mendelsohn suggests that these last words of Odets's to be spoken on Broadway are a fitting valedictory. His last play, although permeated with the same optimism that inspired his plays of the early 1930s, is considerably gentler in tone. Odets himself had learned to "speak softly, with the voices of consolation." After *The Flowering Peach* closed in 1955, Odets returned to California, where he lived for the rest of his life. He said he intended to write more plays, but he did not. He wrote three screenplays, *The Sweet Smell of Success* (1957), *The Story on Page One* (1960), which he also directed, and *Wild in the Country* (1961); in 1963 he was working on scripts for "The Richard Boone Show", a television drama series, when he was hospitalized for an operation for ulcers. He died of cancer three weeks later. His eulogy, written by Harold Clurman and delivered by Danny Kaye, stressed his humanitarian message and his gift of love. Odets said of his own work, "All of my plays . . . deal with one subject: the struggle not to have life nullified by circumstances, false values, anything."

Although his techniques changed considerably during the course of his career, from the strident call for action of *Waiting for Lefty* to the quiet allegory of *The Flowering Peach*, Odets always wrote about the individual trying to maintain his sense of identity in the midst of an often hostile world. His plays are filled with brilliant dialogue, an emphasis on the importance of the family, and a profound belief in the dignity of the human race. Although

Odets as a playwright is clearly not of the stature of Eugene O'Neill, Tennessee Williams, or Edward Albee, he rightfully has a respected position in the history of American drama.

Screenplays:
The General Died at Dawn, adapted from Charles G. Booth's story, Paramount, 1936;
Blockade, United Artists, 1938;
None But the Lonely Heart, adapted from Richard Llewellyn's novel, RKO, 1944;
Deadline at Dawn, adapted from William Irish's novel, RKO, 1946;
Humoresque, adapted by Odets and Zachary Gold from Fanny Hurst's novel, Warner Brothers, 1946;
The Sweet Smell of Success, adapted by Odets and Ernest Lehman from Lehman's story, United Artists, 1957;
The Story on Page One, Twentieth Century-Fox, 1960;
Wild in the Country, adapted from J. R. Salamanca's *The Lost Country*, Twentieth Century-Fox, 1961.

Interviews:
"Odets at Center Stage," *Theater Arts*, 47 (May 1963): 16-19, 74-75; (June 1963): 28-30, 78-80;

"How a Playwright Triumphs," *Harper's*, 233 (September 1966): 64-70, 73-74.

References:
Harold Cantor, *Clifford Odets, Playwright-Poet* (Metuchen, N.J.: Scarecrow Press, 1978);
Harold Clurman, *The Fervent Years* (New York: Harcourt Brace Jovanovich, 1975);
Michael J. Mendelsohn, *Clifford Odets, Humane Dramatist* (Deland, Fla.: Everett / Edwards, 1969);
Edward Murray, *Clifford Odets: The Thirties and After* (New York: Ungar, 1968);
Robert Baird Shuman, *Clifford Odets* (New York: Twayne, 1962);
Gerald Weales, *Clifford Odets, Playwright* (New York: Pegasus, 1971).

Papers:
Typescripts of "I Got the Blues" (original title of *Awake and Sing!*), *The Silent Partner*, and "The Cuban Play," and continuity scripts of three screenplays are at the Library of Congress. Typescripts of variant versions of a number of the published plays and one screenplay are in the Performing Arts Research Center of the New York Public Library at Lincoln Center.

Eugene O'Neill

George H. Jensen
Chicago, Illinois

BIRTH: New York, New York, 16 October 1888, to James and Ellen Quinlan O'Neill.

EDUCATION: Princeton University, 1906-1907; Harvard University, 1914-1915.

MARRIAGE: 2 October 1909 to Kathleen Jenkins, divorced; children: Eugene Gladstone, Jr.; 12 April 1918 to Agnes Boulton, divorced; children: Shane, Oona; 22 July 1929 to Carlotta Monterey.

AWARDS: Pulitzer Prize for *Beyond the Horizon*, 1920; Pulitzer Prize for *Anna Christie*, 1922; National Institute of Arts and Letters Gold Medal Award for Drama, 1923; election to the National

Institute of Arts and Letters, 1923; Litt.D., Yale University, 1926; Pulitzer Prize for *Strange Interlude*, 1928; Nobel Prize for Literature, 1936; Pulitzer Prize and New York Drama Critics Circle Award for *Long Day's Journey into Night*, 1957.

DEATH: Boston, Massachusetts, 27 November 1953.

PRODUCTIONS: *Bound East for Cardiff*, 28 July 1916, Wharf Theatre, Provincetown, Mass.; 3 November 1916, Provincetown Playhouse, New York;
Thirst, Summer 1916, Wharf Theatre, Provincetown, Mass.;

Before Breakfast, 1 December 1916, Provincetown
    Playhouse, New York;
Fog, January 1917, Provincetown Playhouse, New
    York;
The Sniper, 16 February 1917, Provincetown
    Playhouse, New York;
In the Zone, 31 October 1917, Comedy Theatre, New
    York;
The Long Voyage Home, 2 November 1917,
    Provincetown Playhouse, New York;
Ile, 30 November 1917, Provincetown Playhouse,
    New York;
The Rope, 26 April 1918, Provincetown Playhouse,
    New York;
Where the Cross Is Made, 22 November 1918,
    Provincetown Playhouse, New York;
The Moon of the Caribbees, 20 December 1918, Prov-
    incetown Playhouse, New York;
The Dreamy Kid, 31 October 1919, Provincetown
    Playhouse, New York;
Beyond the Horizon, 2 February 1920, Morosco
    Theatre, New York, 111 [performances];
Chris, 8 March 1920, Atlantic City, N.J.; revised as
    Anna Christie, 2 November 1921, Vanderbilt
    Theatre, New York, 177;
Exorcism, 26 March 1920, Provincetown Playhouse,
    New York;
The Emperor Jones, 1 November 1920, Provincetown
    Playhouse (transferred to Selwyn Theatre),
    New York, 204;
Diff'rent, 27 December 1920, Provincetown
    Playhouse, New York, 100;
Gold, 1 June 1921, Frazee Theatre, New York, 13;
The Straw, 10 November 1921, Greenwich Village
    Theatre, New York, 20;
The First Man, 4 March 1922, Neighborhood
    Playhouse, New York, 27;
The Hairy Ape, 9 March 1922, Provincetown
    Playhouse, New York, 127;
Welded, 17 March 1924, Thirty-ninth Street
    Theatre, New York, 24;
*The Ancient Mariner: A Dramatic Arrangement of
    Coleridge's Poem*, 6 April 1924, Provincetown
    Playhouse, New York, 29;
All God's Chillun Got Wings, 15 May 1924, Province-
    town Playhouse (transferred to Greenwich
    Village Theatre), New York, 100;
S.S. Glencairn, 14 August 1924, Barnstormer's
    Barn, Provincetown, Mass.; 3 November
    1924, Provincetown Playhouse, New York, 99;
Desire Under the Elms, 11 November 1924, Green-
    wich Village Theatre, New York, 208;
The Fountain, 10 December 1925, Greenwich Vil-
    lage Theatre, New York, 24;

The Great God Brown, 23 January 1926, Greenwich
    Village Theatre, New York, 283;
Marco Millions, 9 January 1928, Guild Theatre, New
    York, 92;
Strange Interlude, 30 January 1928, John Golden
    Theatre, 426;
Lazarus Laughed, 9 April 1928, Community
    Playhouse, Pasadena, Cal., 28;
Dynamo, 11 February 1929, Martin Beck Theatre,
    New York, 50;
Mourning Becomes Electra (*Homecoming*, *The Hunted*,
    and *The Haunted*), 26 October 1931, Guild
    Theatre, New York, 150;
Ah, Wilderness!, 25 September 1933, Nixon Theatre,
    Pittsburgh; 2 October 1933, Guild Theatre,
    New York, 289;
Days Without End, 8 January 1934, Henry Miller's
    Theatre, New York, 57;
The Iceman Cometh, 9 October 1946, Martin Beck
    Theatre, New York, 136;
A Moon for the Misbegotten, 20 February 1947,
    Hartman Theatre, Columbus, Ohio; 2 May
    1957, Bijou Theatre, New York, 68;
Long Day's Journey Into Night, 10 February 1956,
    Kungl. Dramastika Teatern, Stockholm; 7
    November 1956, Helen Hayes Theatre, New
    York, 390;
A Touch of the Poet, 29 March 1957, Kungl. Dramas-
    tika Teatern, Stockholm; 2 October 1958,
    Helen Hayes Theatre, New York, 284;
Hughie, 18 September 1958, Kungl. Dramastika
    Teatern, Stockholm; 22 December 1964,
    Royale Theatre, New York, 51;
More Stately Mansions, 11 September 1962, Kungl.
    Dramastika Teatern, Stockholm; 31 October
    1967, Broadhurst Theatre, New York, 142.

BOOKS: *Thirst and Other One Act Plays* (Boston:
    Gorham Press, 1914);
Before Breakfast (New York: Shay, 1916);
The Moon of the Caribbees and Six Other Plays of the Sea
    (New York: Boni & Liveright, 1919; London:
    Cape, 1923);
Beyond the Horizon (New York: Boni & Liveright,
    1920);
The Emperor Jones, Diff'rent, The Straw (New York:
    Boni & Liveright, 1921); republished as *Plays:
    First Series, The Straw, The Emperor Jones, and
    Diff'rent* (London: Cape, 1922);
Gold (New York: Boni & Liveright, 1921);
The Hairy Ape, Anna Christie, The First Man (New
    York: Boni & Liveright, 1922);
The Hairy Ape and Other Plays (London: Cape, 1923);
Beyond the Horizon and Gold (London: Cape, 1924);

All God's Chillun Got Wings and Welded (New York: Boni & Liveright, 1924);

The Complete Works of Eugene O'Neill, 2 vols. (New York: Boni & Liveright, 1924);

Desire Under the Elms (New York: Boni & Liveright, 1925);

All God's Chillun Got Wings, Desire Under the Elms, and Welded (London: Cape, 1925);

The Great God Brown, The Fountain, The Moon of the Caribbees and Other Plays (New York: Boni & Liveright, 1926); republished as *The Great God Brown Including The Fountain, The Dreamy Kid, and Before Breakfast* (London: Cape, 1926);

Marco Millions (New York: Boni & Liveright, 1927; London: Cape, 1927);

Lazarus Laughed (New York: Boni & Liveright, 1927);

Strange Interlude (New York: Boni & Liveright, 1928; London: Cape, 1928);

Dynamo (New York: Liveright, 1929);

Lazarus Laughed and Dynamo (London: Cape, 1929);

Mourning Becomes Electra (New York: Liveright, 1931; London: Cape, 1932);

Ah, Wilderness! (New York: Random House, 1933);

Days Without End (New York: Random House, 1934);

Ah, Wilderness! and Days Without End (London: Cape, 1934);

The Iceman Cometh (New York: Random House, 1946; London: Cape, 1947);

Lost Plays of Eugene O'Neill (New York: New Fathoms, 1950)— includes *Abortion*, *The Movie Man*, *The Sniper*, *Servitude*, and *A Wife for a Life*;

A Moon for the Misbegotten (New York: Random House, 1952; London: Cape, 1953);

Long Day's Journey Into Night (New Haven: Yale University Press, 1956; London: Cape, 1956);

A Touch of the Poet (New Haven: Yale University Press, 1957; London: Cape, 1957);

Hughie (New Haven: Yale University Press, 1959; London: Cape, 1962);

More Stately Mansions (New Haven & London: Yale University Press, 1964; London: Cape, 1965);

Ten "Lost" Plays (New York: Random House, 1964; London: Cape, 1965)—includes *Thirst*, *The Web*, *Warnings*, *Fog*, *Recklessness*, and *Abortion*;

"Children of the Sea" and Three Other Unpublished Plays (Washington, D.C.: Microcard Editions, 1972)—includes *Bread and Butter*, *Now I Ask You*, and *Shell Shock*;

Poems 1912-1944, ed. Donald C. Gallup (Boston: Ticknor & Fields, 1980).

In the 1910s the American theatre, long dominated by melodramas, dictatorial producers (most of whom were artless magnates), and an audience more drawn by stars—preferably British—than good scripts, was finally ready to establish its own identity. The change had begun in the late nineteenth century with a generation of earnest though ultimately ineffective playwrights: James A. Herne, Bronson Howard, David Belasco, Augustus Thomas, Clyde Fitch, and William Vaughn Moody. Belasco's experiments with lighting, set construction, and special effects made the American theatre equal and, in some ways, superior to the European theatre. The American innovations of the nineteenth century and the dramas of Henrik Ibsen, August Strindberg, and George Bernard Shaw brought more of the next generation's talent to the theatre. George Jean Nathan, Barrett H. Clark, Joseph Wood Krutch, Alexander Woollcott, Kenneth Macgowan, Heywood Broun, and Burns Mantle formed a critical battery willing to demand and capable of appreciating good drama. Robert Edmond Jones, Lee Simonson, and Cleon Throckmorton added to Belasco's developments in scenic design. Young energetic intellectuals began forming experimental theatre groups to encourage good productions and good playwrights. Lawrence Langner, Helen Westley, Philip Moeller, and Edward Goodman formed the Washington Square Players in 1914 in New York; George "Jig" Cook, Susan Glaspell, and friends formed the Province-town Players in 1915. The catalyst and symbol of this collection of talent, the rejection of melodrama, and the establishment of American drama became Eugene Gladstone O'Neill, America's first great playwright. His career, so tied to this generation of theatrical personnel, should be judged within its historical context, as a reaction against melodrama and a search for a theatrical aesthetic to replace it.

O'Neill was born into the very theatrical world he would help to displace. He was born in a New York hotel on Forty-third and Broadway on 16 October 1888. His father, James O'Neill, Sr., who had worked with James A. Herne and David Belasco in the early 1880s, was then on tour. O'Neill, Sr., spent most of his career playing the title role in *The Count of Monte Cristo* (1846), a melodrama adapted from Alexandre Dumas's novel. Eugene, since he grew up with melodrama, knew its dangers and limitations. Also crucial to his development as a playwright was the nature of his family life. Structured on guilt, betrayal, and accusations, it is, implicitly or explicitly, in most of his plays. Ellen Quinlan O'Neill, his mother, felt betrayed when, three months after her marriage, her husband was sued by Nettie Walsh, who claimed James O'Neill, Sr., was married to her and was the father of her child. Jamie, Ellen's firstborn, passed measles on to Edmund, her secondborn, who died soon afterward. Ellen became a drug addict after a doctor administered morphine while she was recovering from Eugene's birth. She later blamed her addiction on her husband, claiming that he was too miserly to pay for a competent doctor.

For the first seven years of his life O'Neill traveled with his parents. He was educated first in authoritarian Catholic schools—St. Aloysius Academy for Boys in Riverdale, New York, from 1895 to 1900, and De La Salle Institute in New York City, from 1900 to 1902—and later at Betts Academy, a nonsectarian preparatory school in Stamford, Connecticut. In 1906-1907 he spent less than a year at Princeton. He was suspended in April for breaking a window in a railroad stationmaster's house and did not return.

After leaving Princeton O'Neill perfunctorily worked at a few jobs, but his life was for the most part aimless and dissipated. In 1907-1908 he worked at the New York-Chicago Supply Company. In the following year he met and married Kathleen Jenkins. His father, who disapproved of the marriage, arranged for him to prospect for gold in Honduras. After contracting malaria, O'Neill returned to New York but did not live with his wife. On 5 May 1910 Kathleen gave birth to O'Neill's first son, Eugene Gladstone, Jr. O'Neill and Kathleen were divorced in 1912.

One month after the birth of his son, O'Neill sailed as a seaman on the *Charles Racine*, a Norwegian square-rigger. He jumped ship in Buenos Aires, where he worked a few jobs but generally lived hand-to-mouth, begging for food along the waterfront. In spring 1911 he returned to New York on the *Ikala*, a freighter which would, with his other sea voyages, inspire the *S.S. Glencairn* series of one-act plays. After living at Jimmy-the-Priest's, a waterfront dive, for a few months, he shipped out on the *New Yorker* and returned on the *Philadelphia*, both luxury liners. The voyages provided material for *The Hairy Ape* (1922). He returned to Jimmy-the-Priest's, where he attempted suicide by taking an overdose of Veronal. He was then reunited with his family and toured with his father's *Monte Cristo* company.

At the end of 1912, after a short career as a journalist with the *New London Telegraph*, O'Neill entered Gaylord Farm Sanitorium to be treated for tuberculosis. During his six months in the sanitorium, probably feeling, at times, close to death

Eugene O'Neill

(his maternal grandfather died from tuberculosis), O'Neill reassessed his life. He entered the sanitorium a dabbler in poetry; he left resolved to become a serious writer.

In the fall and winter of 1913-1914, while living with the Rippin family in New London, O'Neill began his apprenticeship. Having grown up with *The Count of Monte Cristo*, O'Neill had little choice but to begin by writing melodramas. Though he had read Ibsen, Strindberg, and Shaw (authors who had evolved from but transcended nineteenth-century melodramas), these models were less accessible, except in printed form, than American melodramas. In the early twentieth century, theatrical experiments in Europe were not easily transplanted to America. The unavoidable model, then, was the melodrama, in which plot was more important than characterization. O'Neill eventually broke from the tradition of melodrama by making characterization more important than plot.

A Wife for a Life (1950), O'Neill's first play, written in the spring of 1913 and not produced in his lifetime, is characteristic of his early works. It is a melodrama in which a great deal of stage time is devoted to exposition and action, little to the development of character. In the one-act play, two miners share the same claim. They had become partners after Jack, in his thirties, saved the Older Man, in his fifties, from drowning. The Older Man was searching for a man he suspected of being his wife's lover. Through Jack's reminiscences, the Older Man learns that it was Jack who was in love with his wife and that his wife, despite her love for Jack, had remained true to her wedding vows. The Older Man is tempted first to kill Jack, half-drawing his gun, and later to destroy a telegram from his wife to Jack. In an inexplicable reversal, he decides instead to accept all responsibility: "In this affair I alone am to blame." He sends Jack off to his wife and ends the play with a modified version of John 15:13: "Greater love hath no man than this, that he giveth his wife for his friend."

The two-dimensional characters, the movement of the plot toward disaster, with a quick reversal toward a happy ending, and the simple moral are characteristic of melodramas. Yet within this short play, which O'Neill later referred to as a "vaudeville skit," are some embryonic themes of the mature playwright. Even in this early play, O'Neill used the set for more than decoration: "On the horizon a lonely butte is outlined, black and sinister against the lighter darkness of a sky with stars." The butte, like the elms in *Desire Under the Elms* (1924), is the play's inanimate character influencing the actions of the animate characters. It is a scenic image of O'Neill's determinism. The Older Man, a cynic, self-isolated from civilization, is the prototype of characters in *The Iceman Cometh* (1946). He also makes reference to the ghosts that will haunt the characters of *Mourning Becomes Electra* (1931): "I cannot be a ghost at their feasts." These undeveloped themes, all of which are incompatible with the aesthetic of melodrama, reveal that the germinating impulse of the play is tragic; it strains against the seams of its melodramatic framework.

After *A Wife for a Life*, O'Neill began to write steadily, completing some twenty-four plays in the next four years. His next play, written in fall 1913, but not produced in his lifetime, was *The Web*. Rose, who recently became a mother, is a prostitute who, pathetically, has tuberculosis, a communicable disease. Steve, her pimp, still forces her to walk the streets to support his drug and drinking habits. When Steve gives Rose one week to abandon her child, they argue. Tim, a neighbor, bursts in with a gun drawn and orders Steve out. As Tim and Rose talk, they discover a common history. Rose is trapped in prostitution, and Tim is trapped in a life of crime, his most recent felonies being a jailbreak and a bank robbery. They begin to feel that there is hope for a better life with each other. Rose agrees to

help Tim elude the police, and Tim gives Rose money. Steve, who has listened from the fire escape, shoots Tim, throws the gun into the room, closes the window, and flees. The police, who have been closing in on Tim, enter and accuse Rose of murder. The turn of events is as sensational and improbable as any in melodrama, but the play, as *A Wife for a Life*, has characteristics antithetical to melodrama. It does not end happily, and O'Neill adds a third dimension to the characters. Rose is a prostitute, but her concern for her child, her despair, her pathetic grasping for a new life with Tim, and O'Neill's already acute ear for dialect make her more than a prostitute.

In *The Web* O'Neill explored realism; in *Thirst*, written in fall 1913 and produced in summer 1916, he explored, as he would in *The Hairy Ape*, what he would later refer to as supernaturalism, which to O'Neill meant going beyond realism by using symbolism in a basically realistic play. In *The Hairy Ape*, where his supernaturalism is more developed, O'Neill felt that Yank was a particular character and yet a representation of mankind. The three characters of *Thirst*—a gentleman, a dancer, and a West Indian mulatto sailor—are nameless, as much representations of a class or type of character as individuals, and the dialogue is stylized rather than dialectal. They are on a life raft on "fantastic heat waves," surrounded by sharks. The dancer, consumed by the "mad fixed idea" that the sailor has water, offers a necklace, then herself, for a drink. When the sailor rejects her, she dances: "She is like some ghastly marionette jerked by invisible wires." She dies after the exhausting dance, and the sailor, telling the gentleman that they will now eat and drink, begins to sharpen his knife. Attempting to preserve his values, the gentleman tries to stop the sailor. They both fall overboard, leaving only the necklace on the raft. The theme of what should be regarded as O'Neill's first experimental play is confused. The dancer abandons her moral values, the gentleman tries desperately to maintain his, and the sailor, like Melville's Queequeg, seems to be a pragmatic savage. Yet, they all die.

Recklessness (1950), a parlor melodrama written in fall 1913 but not produced in his lifetime, is uncharacteristic of O'Neill's later work. Mildred Baldwin, whose parents forced her into a loveless but lucrative marriage, is having an affair with Fred, her chauffeur. After learning of the affair, Baldwin tells Fred that Mildred is ill and sends him for a doctor in an unsafe racing car. The second scene focuses on Baldwin's maliciousness. Knowing that Fred has died in an auto accident, Baldwin questions his wife about the affair and promises to grant her a divorce. As Mildred is thanking him, some men carry in Fred's body. Mildred shoots herself, and Baldwin calmly lights a cigar. Because of the play's provocative story line, it was sold to Hollywood and provided the plot for two B-movies.

Warnings, written in fall 1913 but never produced, was an advancement for the young playwright in one important sense: it was his first attempt to move beyond the limited scope of one-act plays. Though *Warnings* is in one act, it has ten characters, two scenes, and a change of sets. The first scene presents Knapp, a wireless operator for the S.S. *Empress*, and his family in their Bronx flat. O'Neill is able to create sympathy for Knapp as one who has been beaten by fate through his inability to raise himself and his family from their minimal subsistence. The set adroitly reveals the family's life-style: "Several gaudy Sunday-supplement pictures in cheap gilt frames are hung at spaced intervals around the walls. . . . On the wall above the table is a mantelpiece on the middle of which a black marble clock ticks mournfully." In the scene Knapp, who has just learned that he is going deaf, is convinced by his wife, made "prematurely old by the thousand worries of a pennypinching existence," to work for one more voyage. The second scene shows the repercussions of Knapp's decision. Because Knapp was unable to hear a warning, the S.S. *Empress* struck a derelict and is sinking. When Knapp learns that he is responsible, he shoots himself. The first scene is a vivid and rich portrait of the Knapp family, similar to that of Robert Mayo's family in *Beyond the Horizon* (1920), and it presents the dramatic conflict of Knapp's having to choose between providing for his family and endangering the S.S. *Empress*. The second scene, however, is barren and reaches a premature climax.

The action of *Fog*, written in winter 1914 and produced in 1917 by the Provincetown Players, occurs after a shipwreck. A man of business, a poet, a Polish peasant woman, and her dead child are drifting in a lifeboat without oars. The lifeboat, shrouded by a slowly dissipating fog, is the forum for a debate between the man of business, who is materialistic, optimistic, and self-serving, and the poet, who is spiritualistic, melancholic, and altruistic. The man of business, who had to swim to reach the lifeboat, thinks that the child's death is a tragedy. The poet, who is weary of life and planned to go down with the ship, feels that the child is much better off dead. After the lifeboat drifts next to an iceberg, a steamer's whistle is heard. The poet insists that they not call out, for that would draw the ship

into the iceberg. A lifeboat from the ship, however, returns for them, someone claiming to have heard a child crying. The play is, ultimately, an odd mixture. The first part is a philosophical debate between the man of business and the poet. The dichotomy, similar to that of Apollo and Dionysus in Nietzsche's *The Birth of Tragedy* (1872), is developed in later O'Neill plays, especially in *The Great God Brown* (1926). The end of the play, a rescue precipitated by the cries of a child, is pure sensationalism.

In 1914, after finishing *Fog*, O'Neill collected his plays in *Thirst and Other One Act Plays*, the printing costs of which were deferred to his father. Critic Clayton Hamilton, who suggested the publication, reviewed it for *Bookman*, but O'Neill remained a struggling, developing playwright, unproduced and relatively unread.

In spring 1914, O'Neill wrote his first full-length play, *Bread and Butter* (1972). The play, not produced in his lifetime, expanded the major conflict of *Fog*, that between the man of business and the poet. Edward Brown, Sr., a self-made hardware merchant in Bridgetown, Connecticut, and his effacing wife are, as their home indicates, hopelessly middle-class and artless. Edward Brown, Jr., the eldest son, an alderman as well as manager of the family business, is equally philistine. Harry, the second son, is working in the family business, but his drinking, cynicism, and wit (he is drawn from Jamie, O'Neill's older brother) set him apart from his family. John, the youngest son, is the artist. The conflict of the play is between John and his family. John wants to study art in New York, but his father wants him to study law. With the support of Maud Steele, his fiancee, and her father, both of whom want John to become a commercial artist, he is able to convince his father to subsidize his art education. After studying in New York for a few years, John reluctantly returns to Bridgetown, marries Maud, works in her father's business, and begins to drink heavily. Maud, who abandons even her superficial appreciation of art, grows closer to Edward. The marriage becomes like "two corpses chained together." Maud feels that John has no sense of propriety and is a failure in her father's business. John, who overhears Edward offering to take care of Maud, resents having given up art for his marriage. Each accuses the other of infidelity, and John escapes the marriage through suicide. The theme, the tragedy that evolves from subverting temperament, is repeated in *Beyond the Horizon*.

Bound East for Cardiff, written in spring 1914 and produced in 1916, is the first play in a series involving the crew of the S.S. *Glencairn*. The plays all deal with the friendships that bind the crew and bring meaning to their lives, and with the emotions that drive them apart. The major literary influence on the play is Joseph Conrad's *The Nigger of The 'Narcissus'* (1897). The title of the first American edition of Conrad's novel was *Children of the Sea*, which was also the original title for *Bound East for Cardiff*. Both works portray a crew's reactions to a dying shipmate. In *Bound East for Cardiff*, Yank is dying; Driscoll, his best friend, and the rest of the crew are nursing him. Yank goes through stages as he prepares to die. At first he cannot accept his own death: "I'm goin' to—" He regrets having spent his life as a seaman and wishes that he had settled down on a farm. As he and Driscoll reminisce about their voyages, Yank seems to find some validation of his life in his adventures with his friend. Finally, Yank begins to prepare for death by setting his life in order. He asks Driscoll if he was wrong to stab a man in Cape Town, and Driscoll reassures him that it was self-defense. He also asks Driscoll to divide his pay among the crew and to buy some candy for a barmaid who was kind to him. Before he dies, Yank sees a pretty woman dressed in black. Shortly after he dies, a fog surrounding the ship lifts. *Bound East for Cardiff*, with relatively little plot but strong characters, is one of the best plays of O'Neill's early career. It was the first of his plays to be produced and one of the first to be performed by the Provincetown Players.

In *Abortion*, written in spring 1914 but not produced until 1959, O'Neill returned to the theme of determinism. As the one-act play opens, Jack Townsend has just won the championship for his college baseball team by pitching a three-hitter. In the study of his dorm room, his family, roommate, and fiancee praise his character and athleticism. The irony of the praise becomes apparent when, left alone with his father, Jack confesses that during the past year, he seduced a town girl and paid for her to have an abortion. Jack explains his actions by saying that he was like "the male beast who ran gibbering through the forest after its female thousands of years ago." He was doomed by his own biological urges. Joe Murray, the tubercular brother of the seduced girl, enters and is left alone with Jack. He tells Jack that his sister died after the shoddy abortion and he attempts to shoot Jack, but Jack takes the gun from him. As students cheer Jack outside his window, he puts the revolver to his head and pulls the trigger.

The Movie Man, written in spring 1914 but not produced until 1959, is one of O'Neill's few com-

edies. It is both a satire on filmmakers and Latin-American revolutions and a parable of the selfish motives behind apparent altruism. Henry Rogers and Al Devlin, filming a real Mexican revolution for Earth Motion Picture Company, are awaiting the next two events in their filming schedule: the storming of a nearby town, brought nearer as the generals become drunker, and the execution of Ernesto Fernandez, who must be killed because he is the enemy of one of the revolutionary generals. Anita Fernandez, daughter of the condemned man, solicits the aid of Rogers. When Gomez, the commander in chief, decides to storm the town at midnight, Rogers reminds Gomez that they have a contract which forbids night attacks—because the crew needs light to film—and that, if the contract is broken, the film company will cease to finance the revolution. Rogers eventually agrees to allow the night attack providing Gomez releases Fernandez. Anita, thanking Rogers, tells him that she and her father will regard him as a brother. Rogers questions, "Only—a brother?" Retreating in confusion, Anita tells him, "Who knows?"

David Roylston, the protagonist of *Servitude*, written in summer 1914 and published in 1950, is a novelist and playwright whose major theme is the influence of "the narrowing environment of the

Kenneth Macgowan, O'Neill,
Robert Edmond Jones at O'Neill's house in Bermuda

conventional home" on the individual and the need for the individual to become a Nietzschean superman and overcome his environment (that is, to break from the constrictions of marriage). In act 1 Ethel Frazer visits Roylston late in the evening and tells him that, after being exposed to his works, she became disillusioned with her stockbroker husband and set out to begin a life of her own. She claims to be Roylston's creation because she changed after reading his fiction. Roylston, once he realizes that she has missed her train, asks her to stay the night. In act 2, the next morning, Mrs. Roylston returns home to discover Mrs. Frazer. Because Roylston has received many love letters from readers, Mrs. Roylston assumes that Mrs. Frazer is her husband's mistress. She then begins a confession—one of O'Neill's favorite techniques for exposition. She reveals that her husband married her because he felt duty-bound. She was his father's stenographer. When Roylston's father found out that they were in love, he fired her. Roylston, feeling responsible, proposed. Mrs. Roylston, who believes that love is servitude, says that during the first years of their marriage, she supported the family, shielding and protecting her husband so that he could write. In act 3 Mrs. Frazer, who is now disillusioned with the egotistical Roylston, dispels his sense of self-importance with criticism. Roylston admits that he is not a "brilliant genius" tied to a "poor ignorant creature" of a wife: "Whatever I am she has made me." He resolves to be a man worthy of his wife's love. The relationship between Roylston and his wife is similar to the relationship between Cornelius Melody and his wife, Nora, in *A Touch of the Poet* (1958). Melody is an egotist whose self-concept is destroyed by humiliation; Nora is the wife whose happiness is in serving her husband. The major difference between the two plays is that Melody, unlike Roylston, is unable to accept the disintegration of his self-image.

In September 1914 O'Neill took George Pierce Baker's English 47 course on playwriting at Harvard. Baker, considered the father of American drama, taught some of the most important writers and theatrical artists of the early twentieth century, including Sidney Howard, George Abbott, Thomas Wolfe, Lee Simonson, and Theresa Helburn. While at Harvard O'Neill collaborated with Colin Ford on "Belshazzar," a biblical adaptation (later destroyed); "Dear Doctor," an adaptation from a magazine story (also destroyed); *The Sniper*, a one-act; and "The Personal Equation," an unpublished full-length play.

The Sniper, produced in 1917 by the Provincetown Players, is a simple story of revenge. Rougon is a Belgian peasant whose farm has been demolished and son killed by the invading Prussians. He enters carrying his son's body. A priest is able to calm him temporarily, but when Rougon learns that his wife has also been killed, he begins shooting at Prussian soldiers. Rougon is captured and shot.

In "The Personal Equation," Tom Perkins, a merchant marine, joins the International Workers Union to rebel against his father, a loyal worker for Ocean Steamship Company, and because he loves Olga Tarnoff, a second-generation socialist. The play touches on several social issues, including free love and the labor movement, but the climax is reached when Tom and a few crew members try to sabotage the engines of the S.S. *San Francisco*. Tom's father, who works on the engines and feels that they are his friends, "accidently" shoots his son to prevent the sabotage. The final scene is set in Tom's hospital room. Perkins and Olga meet in the room and agree to nurse Tom, now deranged as a result of the wound. They have found the personal equation that transcends political differences.

Baker, who found promise in the works that O'Neill wrote at Harvard, invited him to return for a second year of study. O'Neill, though he later said the experience was valuable, declined the offer. After living for almost a year in Greenwich Village, spending much of his time in a bar known as The Hell Hole, O'Neill moved to Provincetown, Massachusetts. He became involved with the Provincetown Players, who on 28 July 1916 produced his *Bound East for Cardiff*. Stimulated, he began to write again. During the summer he wrote "Atrocity," "The G.A.M." (both destroyed), and *Before Breakfast* (1916). *Before Breakfast*, like Strindberg's *The Stronger*, is a short dialogue dominated by one character. Mrs. Rowland's only solace in her disappointing life is in taunting Alfred, her husband. As she prepares breakfast, she criticizes her husband, who remains offstage, for his laziness, lack of character, inability to find a job, and even his inability to hold his liquor: "You'd better give up drinking. You can't stand it. It's just your kind that get the D.T.'s. *That would be* the last straw!" Finally, Mrs. Rowland, who married her husband after becoming pregnant, criticizes him for impregnating a girl named Helen. The play ends as Mrs. Rowland discovers that Alfred has slit his wrists.

Although he was still primarily a writer of one-act plays, O'Neill was beginning to develop a reputation in the theatre. In November 1916 the Provincetown Players moved their theatre to New

York and in their first season produced *Bound East for Cardiff* (O'Neill had one line as the mate), *Before Breakfast* (O'Neill played the role of Alfred), *Fog*, and *The Sniper*. A year later the Washington Square Players produced *In the Zone*.

During the winter of 1917 O'Neill and Agnes Boulton lived together in Provincetown. It was a productive period during which O'Neill completed five plays, one of which was *Now I Ask You*. This play satirizes the Greenwich Village bohemians of the 1910s and the melodramatic elements of the Ibsen dramas that influenced O'Neill's early plays. In the prologue, a flash-forward to the play's end, Lucy Ashleigh puts a revolver to her head. As the curtain drops a shot is heard. In act 1, the day before Lucy's wedding, Mrs. Ashleigh advises her future son-in-law Tom to agree with Lucy's avant-garde ideas. When Lucy enters, she tells Tom that she does not want to marry and would prefer a "free love" relationship. Far more conventional than she pretends to be, Lucy is surprised and frightened when Tom agrees with her. Mrs. Ashleigh achieves a compromise by suggesting that they go through with the ceremony but draw up their own wedding contract, which could include clauses on free love. In act 2 Lucy, who has recently seen Ibsen's *Hedda Gabbler*, is suffering from the ennui of married life. Her only relief is flirtation with Gabriel, who is living with her artist friend Leonora Barnes. In act 3 Tom unhappily flirts with Leonora to make Lucy jealous. The bohemians' underlying conventionality becomes more evident as Gabriel and Lucy are shocked by the possibility that Tom and Leonora are having an affair. Gabriel even confesses that he and Leonora have been secretly married for two years. As Tom and Leonora are preparing to leave for the evening, Lucy repeats the action of the prologue. She puts a revolver to her temple, and a shot is heard. In the epilogue the others discover Lucy sprawled on the floor and think that she is dead. Then Tom remembers that the gun was not loaded; the shot sound came from a tire blowout.

In the Zone, produced in 1917, is the second of the S.S. *Glencairn* series. In *Bound East for Cardiff* the death of Yank brings harmony to the crew; in *In the Zone* suspicion divides them. The play is set in 1915 in the forecastle of the S.S. *Glencairn*, which is transporting dynamite through the war zone. The crew's fear of submarines and saboteurs makes them suspicious of Smitty, who is more refined and aloof than the others. Several of the crew members, who have seen Smitty hiding a black box, convince themselves that he is a spy. They first submerge the box in water, thinking that it is a bomb, and then, after

Smitty enters and is restrained, open it—breaking the unwritten seaman's code of respecting each other's privacy. They find a package of love letters. By reading the letters, they learn that Smitty's real name is Sidney Davidson and that his girl friend, unable to tolerate his drinking, ended their relationship. The crew, satisfied that Smitty is not a spy, crawl into their bunks and roll over to face the wall.

The Long Voyage Home, which premiered in November 1917, is the third of the S.S. *Glencairn* series. In it, alcohol disrupts the crew's unity. While on shore leave, Driscoll, Cocky, and Ivan are escorting Olson to a ship that will take him home to Sweden. On the way, they stop at a disreputable waterfront bar. Olson, who does not want to miss his ship or lose his money, drinks ginger beer, but the others drink heavily. When Ivan passes out, Driscoll and Cocky carry him to a boardinghouse. The bartender drugs Olson's ginger beer, steals his money, and then delivers him to the *Amindra*, a tramp steamer in need of an extra hand. Olson, whose drinking prevented him from returning home earlier, is let down by the drinking of his crewmates.

Ile, also produced in November 1917, is a one-act sea play set in Captain and Mrs. Keeney's cabin on board the *Atlantic Queen*, a whaling ship. The ship is locked in ice. Though the ice has broken to the south and the crew is considering mutiny, Keeney refuses to turn toward home. He is obsessed with the idea of always returning with a full hull of whale oil (or *ile*). Mrs. Keeney is the victim of her own fixed idea. Her storybook idea of sailing life as free, adventurous, and romantic enticed her to sail with her husband. Because of the severity and boredom of the voyage, she begs her husband to return home immediately. He agrees, but when the ice breaks to the north, he changes his mind and continues. Mrs. Keeney, losing her sanity, begins to play an organ wildly. The relationship presented is found in many of O'Neill's plays, including *Long Day's Journey Into Night* (1956). The husband, obsessed with his career or some other fixed idea, neglects his wife; the wife, unable to reconcile her romantic notions with the reality of her marriage, is driven insane.

The Moon of the Caribbees, which was produced in 1918, the final play of the S.S. *Glencairn* series, continues the theme of harmony and chaos. The *Glencairn* is anchored off a West Indies island. The crew, waiting for native women to bring them fruit and—without the Captain's knowledge—rum, listen to a "melancholy Negro chant." Since the chant depresses some of the crew and makes Smitty remember things that he became a sailor to forget, Driscoll sings "Blow the Man Down." Though the chantey brings unity to the crew, dissension arises almost as soon as the native women climb on board. After drinking the rum, the crew fight each other and Paddy is knifed. The play ends with the brooding native music which is "faint and far-off, like the mood of the moonlight made audible."

In *The Rope*, written in winter 1918 and produced in April 1918, Abraham Bentley, the prototype for Cabot in *Desire Under the Elms*, is a stingy, senile, Bible-quoting monomaniac. When his son Luke stole one hundred dollars from him, Bentley hung a noose in the barn. Before Luke ran off to sea, Bentley told him to hang himself with the noose if he ever returned. All of the characters, except for Bentley's granddaughter, are motivated by money. Bentley's daughter, Annie, and son-in-law, Sweeney, are trying to take the farm from him. Bentley's stinginess, according to his daughter, killed his first wife, and he mortgaged the farm for his second wife. When Luke returns, he and Sweeney agree to hunt for and divide the mortgage money they feel that Bentley must have hidden. The play ends ironically. As the idiotic granddaughter plays by swinging on the noose, a bag of gold coins falls. The child uses the coins to play "skip-rock."

Beyond the Horizon's theme is simple: be true to your nature. The play, written in winter 1918, contrasts the two Mayo brothers: Robert, sickly and poetic, and Andrew, practical and a born farmer. In act 1 Robert is about to ship out with his uncle to seek freedom, mystery, and beauty. After he discovers that Ruth, with whom he and his brother grew up, loves him, he decides to stay and become a farmer. Andrew, who also loves Ruth, decides to sail in Robert's place. Both brothers go against their nature, and both suffer. In act 2 Robert, though he works hard, is unable to manage the farm effectively. His marriage and his health deteriorate. Andrew, who returns for a short visit, finds sea life dissatisfying. In act 3 the farm, Robert's health, and his marriage have further deteriorated. Andrew, who has lost his money speculating, returns with a doctor but is too late. Robert dies of consumption. The play was an important watershed in O'Neill's career. With it he moved from little theatres in Greenwich Village to prominent producers on Broadway. It was first produced experimentally by John Williams as a matinee feature. Because of critical praise, it was brought to the Morosco Theatre in 1920.

Written in the summer of 1918, shortly after O'Neill married Agnes Boulton (on 12 April), and produced a year later, *The Dreamy Kid* is, perhaps, more important for what follows it than for itself. The simple one-act is about a young black gangster called Dreamy who visits his dying grandmother even though he is wanted for murder. As the play ends, Dreamy is holding his grandmother's hand in one hand, his gun in the other, and is waiting for the police to charge through the door. In the play O'Neill was experimenting with black characters and dialect; what he learned from writing *The Dreamy Kid* enabled him to write *The Emperor Jones* (1920) and *All God's Chillun Got Wings* (1924).

In *Where the Cross Is Made*, a one-act written and produced in fall 1918, O'Neill experimented with the relationship between the stage action and the audience. The play is set in Captain Bartlett's room which is decorated as a cabin and built onto a seaside house where he lives with his son and daughter. Seven years ago while shipwrecked on an island, Bartlett and three of his crew found what they believed to be lost treasure. They buried it, made a map, and after they returned to San Francisco, the three crew members went back for the treasure in the *Mary Allen*. Even though he received word that the *Mary Allen* had sunk, Bartlett has been waiting for the ship's return. His insane vigil places a strain on his son, Nat, who knows that the treasure is only paste, but nonetheless wants to believe in the treasure. On the night that Nat has asked a doctor to take his father to a sanatorium, more to preserve his own sanity than to restore his father's, Captain Bartlett shouts, "Sail-ho." Nat also sees the *Mary Allen*, but Sue, his sister, sees nothing. The ghosts of the crew, seen only by Nat and his father and the audience, enter and give a map to Bartlett. By having the ghosts onstage, O'Neill was attempting to make the audience believe in the treasure also.

In the fall of 1918 O'Neill also wrote *Shell Shock*. This one-act play, published in 1972 but not produced in his lifetime, is set in a New York bar during World War I. In it, he begins to develop his theme of pipe dreams: men cannot function if they face reality unbuffered. As the play opens, Herbert Roylston, just back from the front, tells Robert Wayne, who was sent to New York to treat shell-shock victims, how a mutual friend saved his life. After Roylston was wounded and left for dead in no-man's-land for three days, he screamed and briefly stood up. Then Jack Arnold, his major, rushed to him and carried him to safety. As Roylston is exiting to write some letters, Arnold, sent home to be treated for shell shock, enters. He tells Wayne about the horrors of war and how

Painting by Charles Ellis of the Provincetown group at Christine's Restaurant: (clockwise from top)
Christine Ell, George Cram Cook, O'Neill, James Light, and Charles Collins

cigarettes, which he began to smoke to clear the stench of rotting bodies, became an obsession. He then confesses that—thinking Roylston was dead—he went out into no-man's-land and carried him back because he needed a cigarette and hoped that he could find one on the body. Wayne is able to convince Arnold that he saw Roylston stand up and that he did not carry the body back for cigarettes. Once Arnold believes in his pipe dream, or what Ibsen called a life-lie, Wayne pronounces him cured.

The Straw was written in 1918 and 1919 and produced in 1921. In act 1 Eileen, suffering from tuberculosis, learns that she will have to leave her family and go to Hill Farm Sanatorium. Since her mother died, Eileen has found meaning in serving her family. Now that she is ill, however, she finds little support. Her father is more worried about the expense than her health, and her boyfriend fears that he may contract the disease. At the sanatorium Eileen meets Steven Murray, a journalist with aspirations of becoming a fiction writer. Eileen encourages him to write and offers to type his stories. By act 2 Murray has sold a story, and Eileen has fallen

in love with him. When the patients are weighed (a weight gain indicates an improvement) Eileen has lost three pounds and Murray has gained three. The sacrificing Eileen has symbolically given Murray, who is now healthy enough to leave, three pounds. At Eileen's request, the two meet at a crossroads, and she confesses that she loves him. In act 3 Murray returns to the sanatorium for a checkup. A nurse tells Murray that Eileen is dying and that she would be happier in her last days if she believed that he loved her. Murray agrees, and while asking Eileen to marry him, he discovers that he actually does love her. The ending supports O'Neill's belief that love is best expressed through sacrifice. Only when Murray is acting in Eileen's behalf can he discover love. Critics were held by the play's interesting characters, but, largely because of poor direction and management, it closed after twenty performances.

In the summer of 1919, O'Neill and Agnes moved to an old Coast Guard station in Peaked Hill Bars, Massachusetts. They both drank heavily and argued frequently. On 30 October 1919, O'Neill's second son, Shane, was born. O'Neill, who was never close to any of his children, suggested to Agnes that they move Shane's crib into the basement, where the child would be less distracting. But, despite the changes in his family life, O'Neill continued to write steadily.

Gold, written in the winter of 1920 and produced in 1921, is a full-length version of *Where the Cross Is Made*. In act 1 Captain Bartlett and a few of his crew, shipwrecked on an island in the Malay Archipelago, find what they believe to be gold. Before they are rescued, Jimmy Kanaka, with Bartlett's passive permission kills the cook and cabin boy, whom the other crew members do not trust. In act 2 Bartlett and the remainder of his crew are stocking a new ship to return for the gold. Mrs. Bartlett, who heard her husband talking of the murders in his sleep, refuses to christen the ship as she has always done. She finally agrees to christen it, but only after Bartlett threatens to take Nat, his son, on the voyage. Act 3 begins shortly after Mrs. Bartlett, despite being weak from an illness, has christened the ship. Bartlett, who is obsessed with the gold, is neglectful of her. Sue, Bartlett's daughter, who wants her father to remain with her mother, convinces her fiance to sail in her father's place. In act 4 Bartlett is waiting for the ship to return even though word has arrived that it has sunk. While a doctor is making arrangements to have Bartlett committed, Bartlett is able to infect Nat with his madness, but only temporarily. Nat is able to realize that the trinkets Bartlett brought back with him are just brass. Though *Gold* is technically a better play than *Where the Cross Is Made*, it takes four acts rather than one to develop the same themes: the effects of guilt on the individual and the effects of one person's insanity on his family. *Gold* closed after thirteen performances.

Anna Christie (1921), which went through several painful revisions between 1919 and 1920, was originally entitled "Chris Christopherson." During the revisions, the emphasis shifted from Chris to Anna. In act 1 Chris, who is the captain of a coal barge, and Maggie, who lives with him, learn that his daughter, Anna, is to meet him at Johnny-the-Priest's saloon. After Maggie agrees to move out and Chris leaves to sober up, Anna enters. Maggie, a tough woman who has lived a hard life, realizes immediately that Anna has been a prostitute. Anna tells Maggie her life story. Her father left her to be raised by relatives on a farm in Minnesota; one of her cousins seduced her; she then worked as a nurse but soon turned to prostitution. In act 2, set on the fog-enshrouded barge, Anna feels clean because the fog hides her past. Mat Burke, a shipwrecked sailor, comes alongside and quickly attempts to seduce Anna, who reacts by hitting him. Mat respects her for her reaction and proposes. In act 3 Anna tells Mat that she will not marry him and relates her past. Both Chris and Mat leave to get drunk. In act 4 Mat returns to ask Anna's forgiveness. He has decided to ship out after they are married and will send Anna his money. When Chris enters, also to ask Anna's forgiveness, he announces that he has signed for a voyage on the same ship as Mat. The play was wrongly criticized for having a happy ending. Anna, who was once abandoned by her father, is about to be abandoned by her future husband and again by her father. Further, Chris's final words refer to the "ole davil sea," which has ruled and destroyed the men in his family for generations. Despite the mixed reviews, the play won a Pulitzer Prize and ran for 177 performances.

The Emperor Jones, written in fall 1920 and produced in November, is perhaps the most remarkable of O'Neill's early plays. Scene 1 is set in the emperor's palace on an island in the West Indies. All but a native woman stealing a few artifacts have deserted the court because the overtaxed islanders are about to rebel. They would have rebelled long before but Brutus Jones, a black American who became emperor, convinced them that he could only be killed by a silver bullet. In the scene Smithers, a white trader who helped instate Jones and now vacillates between hatred and genuine admiration for him, tells Jones that he had better resign as emperor. Jones is not worried because he feels that the myth about the silver bullet, his religion (though he has "put it on the shelf"), and his escape plan will save him. During Jones's flight through the forest, the natives in pursuit beat a drum. The rate of the drumbeat is seventy-two beats per minute at first—corresponding to a normal heartbeat—but, as Jones's flight becomes more frantic, the beat accelerates. In a series of scenes depicting his flight, Jones experiences events from his past and racial heritage. In scene 2 he encounters "formless creatures" that represent his fears; when he fires his revolver at them, they disappear. In scene 3 he encounters Jeff, a Pullman porter whom Jones killed during a dice game. Another bullet is used to dispel this ghost. In scene 4 Jones finds himself a member of a chain gang of blacks. He attempts to kill the white guard with his imaginary shovel, but, realizing that he does not have a shovel, he has to shoot the ghost again. In scene 5 Jones is placed on an auction block. He is about to be sold when he fires two shots, one at an auctioneer and one at a planter. In scene 6 Jones faces a Congo witch doctor who demands that he sacrifice himself to a god, represented by a crocodile head. Jones uses his last bullet, the silver one he was saving to kill himself if worse came to worst, to dispel the crocodile. In scene 8 Jones's body, stripped of its clothes as Jones is stripped of his pretentions, is brought before Smithers and Lem, the leader of the revolt. He is then killed by silver bullets made from melted money.

The play marks a turning point in O'Neill's career. In fact, Travis Bogard wrote of it, "Not only the literate American drama, but the American theatre came of age with this play." *The Emperor Jones* was the first American play to adapt expressionistic techniques. The play, however, is more than an imitation of European plays. O'Neill effectively uses the scenic design of the play (sets, lights, and sound) to bring the audience into Jones's psyche. The combination of techniques and their effects was revolutionary, but O'Neill, even though the play was successful and ran for 204 performances, did not write only in the mode of *The Emperor Jones*. In the 1920s he continued to experiment: with expressionistic techniques in *The Hairy Ape*; with masks in *The Great God Brown* and other plays; with spoken thoughts in *Strange Interlude* (1928) and *Dynamo* (1929); with a chorus in *Lazarus Laughed* (1928); with sets in *Desire Under the Elms*; and with lighting in *Welded* (1924). During this period he also wrote histories and traditional plays. It was a period during which O'Neill was certain of the kind of play he did not want to write but was not certain of the kind of play he did want to write. He was thoroughly divorcing himself from melodrama as he experimented with a variety of dramatic forms that might replace it.

Diff'rent, a more traditional play that was also written in fall 1920 and produced in December, illustrates the destruction that comes from trying to meet an impossible ideal. In act 1 Emma and Caleb are to be married in two days. Emma loves Caleb because she thinks he is different—better than other men, like the heroes in the romantic novels she has been reading. When Emma learns that the town is laughing about a South Sea island woman who, during Caleb's last voyage, seduced him, she breaks off the engagement. Her mother and Caleb's sister try to convince her that Caleb's actions were natural, but Emma vows never to marry. Caleb, equally idealistic, vows to wait until she changes her mind. In act 2 Emma, who has not matured emotionally, is an eighteen-year-old in the body of a forty-eight-year-old. She has redecorated her home and dressed as a 1920s flapper to attract the atten-

tion of Benny Rogers, Caleb's nephew. With Benny, Emma relives her aborted relationship with Caleb. The relationship with Caleb was different because Emma wanted it to fulfill her idea of love; the relationship with Benny is different because it is pathetically unnatural. The act reaches a melodramatic denouement as Benny, to revenge himself on Caleb, whom he resents for his stinginess, asks Emma to marry him. When Caleb learns of it, he hangs himself. As the play ends, Emma goes insane and begins marching to the barn to join Caleb. Even though the critical reception was tepid, the play ran for 100 performances.

In *The First Man*, written in winter 1921 and produced in 1922, O'Neill depicts the two destructive forces to the family: the quest of a romantic ideal and the narrow-mindedness of a puritanical society. In act 1, set in Bridgetown, Connecticut (the same setting as *Bread and Butter*), Curtis Jayson, who was influenced by the stories of Bret Harte, is about to begin a five-year expedition in search of the first man, the missing link. Since their two daughters died, Curtis and his wife, Martha, have been nomadic, he working as an anthropologist and she as his assistant. While Curtis was writing a book in Bridgetown, Martha spent a great deal of time with Edward Bigelow, Curtis's college friend who has been marked by the town as an infidel. In act 2, the next day, Curtis tells Martha that he has arranged for her to accompany him on the expedition; Martha tells him that she cannot go because she is pregnant. The news destroys Curtis's romantic ideal of the two working together; he tells her, "You have blown my world to bits." The Jayson family, who disapprove of Martha's familiarity with Bigelow, assume that the child is not Curtis's. In act 3, while Martha is having a difficult childbirth, Curtis tells Bigelow that he hopes the child will be stillborn and thus not separate him from Martha. The child, the first son in that generation of Jaysons, is born healthy, but Martha dies in childbirth. In act 4, after Martha's funeral, Curtis has refused to see the child, whom he considers a murderer, and still plans to join his expedition. His family, concerned about forestalling a scandal, is finally so blunt in expressing their suspicions that Curtis learns what the rumors in Bridgetown have been. In an act of defiance, he claims his child, leaves him in the care of a kindly aunt, and then departs, vowing to take the child with him on later expeditions. O'Neill seems to imply that the child will somehow trigger a new step in the evolution of man, perhaps the evolution of a Nietzschean superman, but the point is not made clear. The play is also flawed by an overabundance of characters, allowing little stage time for any of them to develop, and obscure motives for the few character changes that do occur. *The First Man* closed after twenty-seven performances.

The Hairy Ape, written in fall 1921, is O'Neill's clearest treatment of one of his most important themes: modern man has lost his place in the universe; he is isolated from his history, his fellow men, and his purpose. Yank, different from the Yank in *Bound East for Cardiff*, is a stoker on a transatlantic liner and feels that he is part of the engines. When Mildred Douglas, the daughter of a millionaire, descends into the forecastle, she is shocked at the sight of Yank and calls him a beast. The encounter destroys Yank's unity with the engines, and he then begins an odyssey to reestablish his self-esteem and regain his sense of belonging. On Fifth Avenue in New York, where the rich parade like marionettes, Yank fights a gentleman and is thrown into jail. After spending time in jail, where the cells "disappear in the dark background as if they ran on, numberless, into infinity," Yank attempts to revenge himself on Mildred by joining the Industrial Workers of the World. The socialists, who think that Yank must be a secret-service spy, refer to him as a "brainless ape." In the final scene Yank climbs into the ape cage at the zoo and is killed by the gorilla. The final stage direction reads: "And, perhaps, the Hairy Ape at last belongs." The short, compact play, which made use of expressionistic techniques, was so successful that it had to be moved from the small Provincetown Players' theatre to a large one.

In *The Fountain*, written in 1921 and 1922 and produced in 1925, O'Neill used the story of Juan Ponce de Leon and his search for the fountain of youth to present, as he would with his other historical plays, his view of salvation. Juan, whose affair with Maria de Cordova and whose duel with her husband resulted in exile from the Spanish court, travels to Puerto Rico on Columbus's second voyage. Twenty years later, after Juan has become governor, Beatriz, Maria's daughter, the "personification of youthful vitality," travels to Puerto Rico to bring Juan a patent to find the western route to Cathay. Juan falls in love with Beatriz and becomes obsessed with finding the fountain of youth. Through torture and promises, Juan eventually convinces Nano, an Indian, to lead him to the fountain. Nano leads Juan to a spring where other Indians ambush him. While wounded, Juan sees figures arise from the stream, Beatriz wearing the mask of an old hag, then a Chinese poet, a Moorish minstrel, and others. Through the figures' expres-

sionistic dances, during which Beatriz unmasks, Juan realizes, "All things dissolve, flow on eternally!" In the final scene, months later in a Cuban monastery, Beatriz and Juan's nephew arrive as Juan is dying. Juan discovers that his love for Maria has been reborn in his nephew's love for Beatriz. *The Fountain*'s theme, that immortality is found in the continuity of generations and nature, has filled out many great sonnets, but it makes for a simplistic, drawn-out play. It closed after twenty-four performances.

Welded, written in 1922 and 1923 and produced in 1924, is an experimental combination of a Strindbergian love-hate relationship and the expressionistic evolution of the superman. Through the play, Michael Cape, a playwright, and Eleanor, his wife, who acts in his plays, are both encircled by spotlights, which are like "auras of egoism." They have an idealistic view of marriage that is disrupted by the strength of their egos. Michael says of the marriage, "Our marriage must be a consummation demanding and combining the best in each of us! Hard, difficult, guarded from the commonplace, kept sacred as the outward form of our inner harmony!" As the play opens, Michael has just arrived home and the two are about to spend an evening alone when John, a friend and the producer of Michael's plays, visits briefly. Michael is jealous of John and angry because Eleanor flees the apartment. They both—as a means of revenge—attempt to have an affair. Eleanor runs to John but is unable to consummate the affair because she thinks that she sees Michael standing before her. Michael visits a "bovine stolid type" prostitute, whom he sees as a symbol of "the tortures man inflicts on woman," but is also unable to consummate the affair. In the final act they are able to overcome the "vanity of personality" and are united in the desire to find a greater love. Michael says, "Our life is to bear together our burden which is our goal—on and up! Above the world, beyond its vision—our meaning!" There are many faults with the play. The experimental lighting, the stylized dialogue, and the symbolic acting seem contrived. The play, however, is important because in it O'Neill first began to experiment with the technique of spoken thoughts; in act 1 Michael and Eleanor sit side by side and, while remaining motionless, speak their thoughts. The technique is further developed in *Strange Interlude*.

All God's Chillun Got Wings, unlike *Welded*, concentrates on the destructiveness of love. Jim Harris, a black, and Ella Downey, a white, are children when the play begins. Despite their racial differences, a childhood romance develops. Ella outgrows her affection for Jim, becomes the girl friend of a white boxer, and has a child by him, but Jim remains in love with her. After Ella is deserted by the boxer and her child dies, Jim becomes her protector. Even though Jim, studying to become a lawyer, has been unable to pass the bar exam because of the tension he feels while being examined by "white faces," he tells Ella that he wants to be her "black slave." They are married and spend two years in France, where, despite the lack of prejudice, Ella leads an isolated life. Because the isolation also makes Jim feel that he is not a real man, the two return to New York so that Jim can retake the bar examination. In New York Ella, who is unable to isolate herself from the outside world even in her own home, begins to lose her sanity. She feels threatened by Jim's attempt to pass his exam, and begins to vacillate from love for Jim to fear of his success. At one moment she tells Jim not to take the examination, the next she tells him that she wants him to pass. After failing the examination for the second time, Jim also loses mental balance. They both regress into childhood: Jim kneels before Ella and becomes her "black slave." The ending, showing O'Neill's maturation from the suicide finales of his early career, is fitting for a marriage based on unhealthy motives: Ella wanted someone to feel superior to and Jim wanted someone to make him feel less inferior.

All God's Chillun Got Wings, because of its miscegenation theme, brought the play censorship and O'Neill a letter from the Ku Klux Klan. New York City government did not allow children to act in the opening scene, so it was read to the audience. Despite, or perhaps because of, the censorship, the play ran for 100 performances.

Desire Under the Elms, written in the first half of 1924, is set in 1850 in and around the Cabot farm in New England. Over the farm hover the elms which seem to control the actions of the characters: "They appear to protect and at the same time subdue. There is a sinister maternity in their aspect, a crushing, jealous absorption. They have developed from their intimate contact with the life of man in the house an appalling humaneness. They brood oppressively over the house. They are like exhausted women resting their sagging breasts and hands and hair on its roof, and when it rains their tears trickle down monotonously and rot on the shingles." The characters in the play, like the crushing, jealous, oppressive elms, vie for possession of the farm; their possessiveness generates isolation and loneliness.

The play opens as Cabot is about to return with a new wife. Before he returns, Eben, Cabot's

son by his second marriage, buys rights to the farm from Simeon and Peter, Cabot's sons by his first marriage, with money that the stingy Cabot had hidden. Eben feels that the farm is rightfully his because his mother's family sued Cabot for the deed to the farm. Cabot, to end the suit, married Eben's mother. Once Cabot arrives with his new wife, Abbie, a three-way struggle develops for possession of the farm. Abbie and Eben eventually have an affair and a child. The lovers' motives are similar to those in *All God's Chillun Got Wings*; Eben wants to revenge himself on his father, and Abbie wants a child to secure her rights to the farm. The relationship, unlike that in *All God's Chillun Got Wings*, develops. When Cabot tells Eben that Abbie had a child in order to prevent him from inheriting the farm, Eben accuses her of betraying him and threatens to leave. To prove that she loves Eben, Abbie kills the child. Though initially shocked (he reports her to the sheriff), Eben later sees the significance of the murder and shares the blame. He says to Abbie, "If I'm sharin' with ye, I won't feel lonesome, leastways." Because of the explicit treatment of adultery and the rather bizarre means of expressing love, the play was banned in several cities, including London and Boston. But, as with *All God's Chillun Got Wings*, the play was successful, running for 208 performances.

Like O'Neill's other historical plays, *Marco Millions*, written between 1923 and 1925 and produced in 1928, is concerned with the salvation and destruction of the soul. In the prologue, as businessmen debate the religious significance of a sacred tree, each claiming it as a symbol of his own religion, the coffin of Kukachin, granddaughter to Kublai Kaan, is pulled onto the stage by slaves. Kukachin, who represents the triumph of the soul and love over death, rises and speaks to the Christian businessman: "Say this, I loved and died. Now I am love, and live. And living, have forgotten. And loving, can forgive." In the first act, set twenty-three years earlier, Marco Polo is a young man wooing Donata. The young Polo has a soul, but the materialism of his father and uncle soon destroy it. In the second scene, set in the papal palace, the Polos are waiting for a new pope to be chosen. Before returning to Cathay, they want to fulfill a request from Kublai Kaan, that the pope send him 100 wise men from the West. Once the pope is chosen, he tells the Polo brothers to take Marco in place of the wise men. In the next scenes Marco begins to learn how to be a salesman and a trader and, in the process, loses his desire to write poetry. In the final scene of the act, the Polos present them-

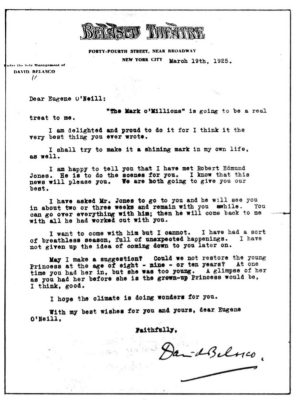

Letter from David Belasco to O'Neill

selves to Kublai, who, because he is amused with Marco's foolishness, appoints him to a government position. In act 2, fifteen years later, Kukachin, who has since fallen in love with Marco, is about to be married to the Khan of Persia. Kublai Kaan, who is beginning to weary of Marco, says that the Venetian "has memorized everything and learned nothing." Since Marco is returning to Venice, Kukachin asks that he escort her to Persia. During the voyage, Marco saves Kukachin's life several times, but remains soulless. He returns to Venice and Donata, now overweight and the symbol of material greed. The epilogue occurs in and outside the theatre as the audience exits. Marco Polo, discovered sitting in the first row, rises and walks out with the audience, obviously perplexed by the play's meaning. He enters a limousine and "resumes his life."

It was a few years before the play, an unusual blending of pageant, satire, and history, found a producer. The Provincetown Players had failed to grow with O'Neill and did not have the resources to produce it. David Belasco and other Broadway producers considered the play but were eventually frightened by the high production costs and the uncertainty of an audience. In 1928, the Theatre Guild, which had the resources of a large subscription audience and a desire to promote developing

playwrights, finally agreed to produce it. The play ran for ninety-two performances in New York and was later even more popular on the road, but, more importantly, a relationship was established with the Theatre Guild that would last for the rest of O'Neill's career.

Though O'Neill used masks occasionally in earlier plays, *The Great God Brown* is the first play devoted to restoring masks to the theatre. O'Neill felt that, with masks, the modern theatre could "express those profound hidden conflicts of the mind which the probings of psychology continue to disclose to us." The mask is a defense, a pose, a lie that a character presents to the world to protect the vulnerable self beneath it. Only rarely can a character feel secure enough to unmask and reveal his true self. The mask, O'Neill felt, was an unfortunate necessity. It protects the self, but maintaining a mask (the strain of living a lie) dissipates, haunts, and isolates the self. In O'Neill's words, "One's outer life passes in a solitude haunted by the masks of oneself."

In *The Great God Brown* O'Neill combines his theory of masks with a theme developed in preceding plays: the conflict between a soulless, materialistic businessman and a poet-artist. William Brown is the materialist, an architect who designs buildings that look like tombs. Dion Anthony (whose name combines Dionysus and St. Anthony) is the artist and a boyhood friend of Brown's. Margaret shares the love of both men. At the beginning of the play Dion wears a mask of Pan; he is the artist who wants to immerse himself in life. As the play develops, his mask becomes a mocking, Mephistophelian shield to protect his "supersensitive" self. Dion can only unmask before Cybel, outwardly a prostitute, inwardly an earth goddess. She understands and accepts Dion's true self. He says of Cybel, "You're strong. You always give. You've given my weakness strength to live." At first, Margaret, who understands and accepts Dion's mask, wears a mask of her own features; after years of dealing with Dion's alcoholism, her mask becomes a pleasant pretense to hide her tortured self.

The plot of the technically complex play, similar to Ibsen's *The Master Builder* (1892), is simple. Brown, who needs Dion's creativity to enhance his staid designs and "to reassure him he's alive," hires Dion to work in his architectural firm. When Dion dies of a heart attack, a complication of his alcoholism, Brown assumes Dion's identity and creativity by wearing his mask, visiting Cybel and being a husband to Margaret. Ironically, Brown—while wearing Dion's mask—is shot by the police for murdering Brown. When this simple plot is encased in poetic dialogue and the mask schema, it seems more complicated. Surprisingly, however, the play was accepted by critics and the public; it ran in New York in 1926 for 283 performances.

In *Lazarus Laughed*, written in 1925 and 1926 and produced in 1928, masks are used in a different way. O'Neill later wrote of the play, "I advocate masks for stage crowds, mobs—wherever a sense of impersonal, collective mob psychology is wanted." The play opens shortly after Lazarus has been revived by Jesus. Lazarus, who has already died and thus does not fear death, is the only character who does not wear a mask. The other characters, Lazarus's family, the Romans, and a chorus of forty-nine Greeks, legionnaires, and Roman senators, representing different periods of life, wear masks. The large chorus is an important element in the play. It reacts to and chants Lazarus's message from beyond death, that "death is dead," that men kill because they are afraid to die, and that man can revèl in life through laughter. With Lazarus chanting his message and the chorus echoing it, the play almost becomes an opera. As with *The Great God Brown*, the techniques are complex, the plot and theme simple. Lazarus offers salvation, but the chorus, representing mankind, is ultimately unable to accept it. Lazarus is burnt alive by the Roman Caligula because he wants to prove that there is death. The play, produced in California by the Pasadena Community Playhouse, ran for twenty-eight performances.

In *Strange Interlude*, written in 1926 and 1927, O'Neill achieved a scope and depth not often found in modern realistic drama. The Theatre Guild production began at 5:15 and ended at 11:00; the audience was allowed an hour break after act 5. Spoken thoughts—O'Neill's version of the aside—created a sensational effect. By presenting the characters' thoughts as well as what they actually say, O'Neill added depth to the characters and complexity to the dynamics between characters. In the production the spoken thoughts were differentiated from dialogue by a contrast between motion and stillness. While one character was speaking his thoughts, the other characters remained motionless. During the traditional dialogue, the characters moved about freely. Though the technique and the way it was staged seem awkward, the audience adjusted to it.

The action of the play evolves from Nina Leeds's relationships with the male characters. The play opens after her fiance, Gordon, has been killed in World War I. Though her father convinced Gordon to delay the marriage, Nina feels guilty about never having slept with him. To punish herself, she leaves her father, works as a nurse, and sleeps with several maimed soldiers. After her father dies, she returns home only to have others control her life. Ned Darrell, the doctor for whom she worked at the clinic, and Charlie Marsden, a family friend and a writer of sexless novels who is emotionally crippled by ties to his mother, convince Nina to marry Sam Evans, one of Gordon's college friends, and have children. Her mother-in-law, after revealing that the Evans family suffers from genetic insanity, advises Nina to have an abortion and then have a child by a healthy man. Nina follows her advice and has a child by Ned Darrell. For the first time, her life is complete. She is a wife, mother, and mistress. But the vitality she experiences from a fulfilled life, the strange interlude, is short-lived. Her husband dies, her lover returns to his work, and her son marries. Her life has come full circle as she is left with Charlie Marsden, a lifeless father figure. In the play Nina attempts to escape from the influence of what she calls "God the Father" (guilt, distance, and death) and seek out "God the Mother" (compassion, union, and life). She succeeds—but only briefly.

The play established O'Neill as a popular playwright and writer. The Theatre Guild expected to lose $500,000 on it, but, instead, it ran for 426

Eugene and Agnes with children Oona and Shane, 1926

performances. It sold over 100,000 copies in hardback and earned O'Neill over $250,000. The play's popularity, however, also brought problems. It was banned in Boston, and in 1929 Georges Lewys, claiming similarities to her novel *The Temple of Pallas Athene*, sued for plagiarism. The suit, which Lewys lost, received nationwide press coverage.

Though the preliminary notes for *Dynamo* were made in 1924, the play was not finished until 1928. It was the first play of what O'Neill hoped would be a trilogy on religion in the modern world. The second play in the trilogy was *Days Without End*, not completed until 1933. The third play was never written. O'Neill wrote in the playbill of the trilogy's theme: "The playwright today must dig at the roots of the sickness of today as he feels it—the death of the Old God and the failure of science and materialism to give any satisfying new One for the surviving primitive religious instinct to find meaning for life in, and to comfort its fears of death with." The statement is more true of *Dynamo* than of *Days Without End*.

Reuben Light, the protagonist of *Dynamo*, is the son of a preacher. Their next-door neighbor, Ramsay Fife, an atheist who worships electricity, uses Reuben, who is in love with Fife's daughter, Ada, to bait Reverend Light. Fife invents the story that he is wanted for murder and tells Reuben to keep it secret. To avoid a beating, Reuben tells the secret to his father. When Reverend Light tells the police and the joke is revealed, Reuben and his father argue. Reuben rejects his father's god, a paternal god of guilt, and runs away from home. When Reuben returns fifteen months later, his father blames him for his mother's death. Like Nina Leeds in *Strange Interlude*, Reuben tries to escape the masculine god of guilt by seeking a feminine god of compassion. For Reuben the feminine god is the dynamo, to which he prays and from which he receives forgiveness. The guilt, however, returns. After Reuben and Ada make love in the dynamo room, he feels guilty. He then kills Ada and is electrocuted as he attempts to achieve spiritual union with the god of the dynamo. He is unable to find comfort in traditional religion or the new religion of science.

Dynamo closed after fifty performances and would have closed sooner if it were not one of the Theatre Guild's subscription plays. O'Neill blamed the failure on his inability to attend rehearsals—he was living with Carlotta Monterey in France—and his marital problems—he was undergoing a divorce from Agnes Boulton during the play's composition.

Almost as an act of atonement, O'Neill extensively revised the play before publication.

On 22 July 1929, after a protracted and bitter divorce from Agnes, O'Neill married Carlotta Monterey in Paris. Though they traveled, O'Neill and Carlotta lived mostly in France, where he wrote *Mourning Becomes Electra*. Carlotta valued her role as the writer's wife, guarding to an extreme O'Neill's privacy. She limited visits and isolated O'Neill from some of his friends. In May 1931, the O'Neills returned to New York for the production of *Mourning Becomes Electra*.

This trilogy is pivotal in O'Neill's career, for it was both a new experiment and an end to experiments. In the fall of 1928 he conceived a play that would be a "modern psychological approximation of Greek sense of fate." Written between 1929 and 1931, *Mourning Becomes Electra* was ostensibly structured on Aeschylus's *Oresteia* and went through a series of aborted experiments. O'Neill incorporated but later abandoned spoken thoughts (like those in *Strange Interlude*), half-masks, and stylized soliloquies (probably an attempt to develop a language for tragedy). The six drafts of false starts and abandoned experiments indicate that O'Neill was moving away from the avant-garde toward a simpler, more traditional theatre. In the transition, however, his experiments were not lost; they were, instead, subtly incorporated into his later plays.

Homecoming, the first play in the trilogy, is set in the tomblike Mannon mansion shortly after the Civil War and centers on the competition between Christine Mannon and her daughter Lavinia. Lavinia is an Electra figure; she hates her mother and competes with her for the affection of her father, brother, and Adam Brant. Brant, whose father was the disgraced David Mannon (Lavinia's great uncle) and whose mother was a Mannon servant, blames his parents' harsh life on the Mannon family and seeks revenge by courting Lavinia and having an affair with Christine. The romance between Brant and Christine is, like the romance in *Desire Under the Elms*, founded on unnatural motives, but it evolves into love. The play reaches a climax when Christine poisons her husband. In *The Hunted*, the second play, Lavinia, who knows that her father was murdered, convinces Orin, her brother, to help her kill Brant. Brant's murder precipitates Christine's suicide. In the final play, *The Haunted*, Orin and Lavinia are unable to escape their past. They travel to a South Sea island, which is Orin's ideal of a sinless paradise. Orin is unable to shed his puritan morality, but Lavinia, more like her

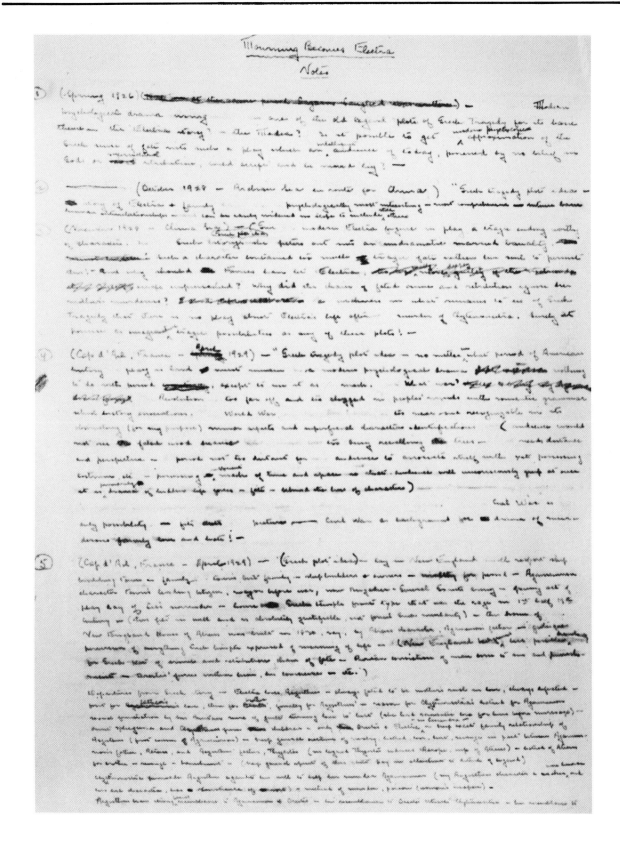

Notes for Mourning Becomes Electra

Carlotta O'Neill's copy of the final manuscript for Mourning Becomes
Electra *with inscription by O'Neill*

Carlotta and Eugene O'Neill

mother than she realizes, has an affair with a native. After returning to the Mannon house, Orin commits suicide and Lavinia, whose guilt returns, resolves to entomb herself in the Mannon mansion.

Philip Moeller, who directed this play as well as *Strange Interlude*, criticized it for being "too big for its size." Even though it is as long as *Strange Interlude*, *Mourning Becomes Electra* does not have the earlier play's depth and complexity. Critics, however, welcomed the trilogy as one of O'Neill's best plays; some called it his masterpiece. It ran for 150 performances in 1931.

Days Without End, the second play of an unfinished trilogy, was begun in 1927; the difficult composition ended in 1933. In the last of his avant-garde plays, O'Neill uses a mask to present John Loving, who becomes disillusioned with Catholicism after losing his parents. He wants to find a substitute for religion in his love for Elsa, his wife, but he is afraid of placing faith in his love and becomes cynical to protect himself from the possibility of his wife's death. The ambivalence is represented onstage by two actors: the first actor plays John, the seeker of faith; the second actor plays the other side of his personality, Loving, the cynic, and

wears a tortured, mocking mask of John the seeker. John speaks most of the dialogue; Loving occasionally interrupts with cynical lines. The other characters react to John and Loving as one, but are aware of the dissonance of Loving's cynical interruptions.

The complication of the plot evolves from an affair that John Loving has with his wife's best friend and his attempt to atone for his guilt. After telling Elsa the plot of a novel he is writing, which is a thinly disguised version of his own search for faith, his love for Elsa, and his adultery, John Loving asks her if she would forgive the character in the novel. Elsa says she could not, and she eventually realizes that the novel is her husband's story, that he has defiled their ideal marriage, their faith in each other. She then rushes out into the cold and contracts pneumonia. The play closes as John Loving leaves Elsa's bedside—just as she forgives him—to pray at the foot of a cross. As John prays to a god of love, Loving, his cynical self, dies at the foot of the cross "like a cured cripple's testimonial offering in a shrine," and word comes that Elsa's fever has broken. Critics, somewhat confused by the play, felt that O'Neill was now a reformed Catholic. In the final scene, however, John Loving accepts the love—not the dogma—of Christianity: "Life laughs with God's love again! Life laughs with love!" Audiences were as confused as the critics, and the play, which premiered in 1934, closed after fifty-seven performances.

In fall 1932, while living at Sea Island, Georgia, during the difficult composition of *Days Without End*, O'Neill dreamed the plot of *Ah, Wilderness!* (1933), which he called a "Nostalgic Comedy." He quickly wrote what he intended to be a light comedy of a childhood that he wished he had lived, yet, unintentionally, he wrote about Richard Miller's initiation into his family's use of guilt as a subtle means of dominance. Only in recent years have critics acknowledged the darker side of the Miller family.

As the play begins on 4 July 1912, Richard is naive, idealistic, and poetic. He is in love with Muriel McComber, but the romance is virtually ended in act 1. Muriel's father, after reading Richard's love poetry to her, orders her to cease seeing him. To console himself, and as an act of rebellion against his father, Nat, and his mother, Essie, Richard goes to a bar with one of his brother's classmates at Yale and two disreputable girls and becomes drunk for the first time. Richard's drunkenness is parallel to his Uncle Sid's drunkenness earlier in the day. Sid, Essie Miller's brother, has for years been in love with Lily, Nat Miller's sister. Lily refuses to marry Sid because of his drinking but still retains control over him by making him feel guilty for becoming drunk, then by graciously forgiving him. Sid is so relieved to be forgiven that he becomes totally servile. After Richard comes home drunk, his parents treat him as Lily treated Sid. After receiving a message from Muriel, Richard meets her at midnight on the following evening. During their talk Richard manages to make Muriel feel partially responsible for his drunkenness. He is beginning to learn the value of guilt. In the final scene Richard's father decides to punish him for his drinking by not letting him go to Yale. Richard is pleasantly surprised at his father's punishment. He had been planning to forego college and to get a job on his father's newspaper in order to marry Muriel much sooner. But Nat Miller's threat not to send his son to college was only a threat; "only half concealing an answering grin," he tells Richard that he must go to Yale and stay until he graduates, whether he likes it or not. The play concludes with a heartfelt reconciliation between Richard and his parents. As Richard leaves the room, he and his father hug each other and, much to his father's surprise, Richard kisses him. When the play opened in 1933 with George M. Cohan

playing the role of Nat Miller, critics and audiences found it a pleasant comedy. It ran for 289 performances and would have run longer if Cohan had not decided to leave the cast.

After the production of *Ah, Wilderness!*, O'Neill became an exile from Broadway for twelve years. He and Carlotta moved to the West Coast. From afar, O'Neill was able to criticize the commercialism of the New York theatre industry and begin work on what he hoped would be his magnum opus, a cycle of nine plays entitled "A Tale of Possessors Self-Dispossessed." Although O'Neill worked on the cycle into the 1940s, most of the plays were written or planned in late 1934 and 1935. The origins of the cycle can be traced back to "On to Betelgeuse," a play that he worked on in 1928 and 1929. It was revised into "The Life of Bessie Bowen" in 1932 and later into "Hair of the Dog." Though "On to Betelgeuse" was written much earlier, the cycle actually evolved from the "Calms of Capricorn" trilogy, which traced the history of Sara Harford and her sons. The action of "The Calms of Capricorn," which occurs in 1857, begins on a clipper ship docked in Boston harbor and follows a trip through the South Atlantic to San Francisco. In the play Sara Harford is fifty years old, and her sons are in their twenties. "The Earth's the Limit" is set in 1858 in a San Francisco hotel and on top of a pass in the Sierras. Sara and her sons apparently become involved in trade and, perhaps, privateering. The third play, "Nothing Is Lost Save Honor," covers the years 1862-1870. In it, the Harford brothers make a fortune from unethical railroad deals. The play is the moral culmination of the trilogy. Within the three plays, which move from the poetic clipper ship to steam-driven trains, is the theme that would be embodied in the cycle: the members of the Harford family gain the world but lose their souls. O'Neill expanded the cycle to nine plays: "The Greed of the Meek," "Or Give Us Death," "A Touch of the Poet," "More Stately Mansions," "The Calms of Capricorn," "The Earth's the Limit," "Nothing Is Lost Save Honor," "The Man on Iron Horseback," and "Hair of the Dog." The first two plays were so long, as long as *Strange Interlude*, that O'Neill considered splitting each into two plays, which would have expanded the cycle to eleven plays. The ambitious project eventually became unmanageable; it was too large and interconnections between plays made it too complicated. In June 1939 O'Neill shelved the cycle, after which he returned to it only periodically. In winter 1952-1953 he and Carlotta attempted to destroy all of the cycle except *A Touch of the Poet*, the only one he completed. The unfinished *More Stately Mansions* (1962) survived by accident.

In *A Touch of the Poet*, which was produced in 1958, Sara Melody meets Simon Harford, her future husband. Although Sara's father, Cornelius Melody, maintains the pretensions of an Irish gentleman and an officer in the British army by keeping an expensive horse and his old uniform (more subtle forms of a mask), he is a poor innkeeper in New England. Sara's mother, Nora, is a self-sacrificing wife who understands Cornelius's need to assume a Byronic superiority. Sara met Simon Harford, who remains offstage for the entire play, while he was living in a cottage near her father's inn. When he became ill, Sara brought the idealistic youth to the inn to nurse him and calculatingly seduce him into marriage. The Harfords reject the proposed marriage and attempt to bribe Sara into leaving New England. Cornelius, who feels that his family has been insulted, leaves in his uniform to duel Simon's father. After brawling with the Harford servants and police, Cornelius returns in a tattered uniform, his pretensions dissolved, and shoots his horse, the symbol of his superiority. Sara, who had previously despised Cornelius's posing, tries to restore her father's self-esteem. The play had a successful run of 284 performances on Broadway.

More Stately Mansions, produced on Broadway in 1967, is set four years after the end of *A Touch of the Poet* and continues the story of Sara's relationship with Simon. Simon, now less idealistic, is a successful businessman living with his mother, Deborah, and his wife, Sara. Each character struggles to possess the others through love. As Horst Frenz says, love "is transformed into desire to possess . . . which never brings victory but only inner impoverishment and ultimately loss of identity." Deborah loses her sanity and any connection with reality, and Simon becomes his wife's child. Sara is left in control of the Harford business and her three sons. The two surviving plays are a strong indication of the cycle's direction; Sara and her sons will grow more materialistically successful but any idealism in the two branches of the family—in Sara's mother and the young Simon—will be destroyed in the process.

In June of 1939, when O'Neill decided to put the cycle aside, he began one of the most productive phases of his career. In the next few years, despite his failing health (he was suffering from a hereditary nervous disease that brought a loss of motor control), he would write *The Iceman Cometh*, *Long Day's Journey Into Night*, *Hughie* (1958), and *A Moon for the Misbegotten* (1947), four of his best plays.

The Iceman Cometh, written in the latter half of 1939, is set in Harry Hope's saloon and boardinghouse. In act 1 the characters, all of whom live on pipe dreams and lies that buffer the harshness of reality, are sleepily waiting for the arrival of Hickey, a traveling salesman. He visits once a year to drink, buy drinks for others, celebrate Harry's birthday, and tell jokes about his wife's affair with the iceman. Before Hickey arrives, Don Parritt rents a room. He knew Larry Slade, who lives at Harry's, when Don's mother and Larry were radicals in "the movement." Don tells Larry that he is trying to hide from the police, who have recently arrested his mother. When Hickey arrives, he is, to the suprise of all, sober. He claims to have overcome his reliance on whiskey and pipe dreams and wants to show the denizens of Harry Hope's how to do the same. In act 2, where the setting of Harry's birthday party evokes the Last Supper, Hickey disrupts the festivities by dispelling everyone's pipe dreams. Larry's dream is that he is in the grandstand, no longer interested in life; Hickey shows him that he is still a vulnerable idealist. In act 3, where the set almost becomes a circus with Hickey as a ringleader, the characters, stripped of their pipe dreams, attempt to leave the bar and do what they have been putting off until tomorrow for years. They all return, devastated failures. In the final act Hickey and Parritt

Playbill

confess in counterpoint: Hickey that he murdered his wife to end the suffering he had been causing her, and Parritt that he turned in his mother for money. Both men have a common motive; they were unable to live up to the ideals of the women in their lives. After the confessions, Harry Hope and his friends return to their pipe dreams and drink. Hickey and Parritt react to their sense of inadequacy by destroying the women who set unrealistically high standards for them; Harry Hope and his friends react to their sense of inadequacy by fabricating pipe dreams.

Because O'Neill felt that *The Iceman Cometh* would be ill received during the war, it was not produced until 1946. The press coverage of the first new O'Neill production in thirteen years briefly brought him back to the public. It was, however, also the last new play to be produced on Broadway in his lifetime, and, after the 136 performances, critical interest in O'Neill began to decline. A revival of *The Iceman Cometh* in 1956, which ran for 565 performances, initiated an O'Neill revival.

O'Neill made notes for *Long Day's Journey Into Night*, his masterpiece, in June 1939. He wrote it in 1940 and revised it in spring 1941. In many ways, *Long Day's Journey Into Night* is the play O'Neill had been trying to write all of his career. After twenty-seven years of playwriting, he had finally broken from melodrama and perfected his own theatrical aesthetic.

The play, set in New London, Connecticut, in 1912, depicts the Tyrone family during a crisis. Mary, the convent-bred mother, is in the process of trying to overcome her drug addiction. The youngest son, Edmund (O'Neill gave the name of his brother who died as a child to his self-portrait), is a journalist and has what the family refer to as a "bad cold," later to be diagnosed as tuberculosis. James, the father, a successful actor, is land poor; he buys large tracts of real estate to alleviate his fears of dying in the poorhouse. Jamie, the older brother, an actor in his father's company, is a cynical alcoholic. As Timo Tiusanen states, there are a large number of unfinished statements in the play. With unfinished statements and other devices, O'Neill achieves subtly what he attempted to achieve in earlier plays with masks or spoken thoughts. He is able to hint at the characters' inner lives and show that the family, though dependent on each other, is afraid to face reality (that Edmund has tuberculosis), be honest with each other (Jamie adds water to the whiskey bottle after he drinks from it), and trust each other (Mary realizes, from suspicious stares, that the others fear her return to drugs).

Their need for mutual support is in conflict with obsessive lying, betrayal, and destructiveness. Mary blames her addiction on her husband, who, she feels, was too miserly to pay for a good doctor when Edmund was born; Jamie, conscious of his own inadequacies, attempts to convince Edmund that he will never become a writer. Even though the men make some attempt to be more honest with each other in a long confessional scene, the honesty comes with the aid of alcohol and will probably pass. The play ends as Mary descends the stairs wearing her wedding dress, lost in drugs and the past. The structure of the Tyrone family will not allow one character to change until they all change, and that is unlikely.

Because of the autobiographical elements of the play, O'Neill did not want *Long Day's Journey Into Night* published or produced until twenty-five years after his death. O'Neill's widow, however, allowed it to be produced by the Royal Dramatic Theatre in Stockholm in February 1956, two and a half years after he died. A New York production followed in November and had a very successful run of 390 performances.

In November 1940 O'Neill decided to begin a series of one-act plays entitled "By Way of Obit." Originally, he planned five plays. Each play would have one character who would deliver a monologue to a life-sized marionette, representing "The Good Listener." He later expanded the series to eight plays and added a second character to be the listener. Some of the plays that were planned were about a railroad man, a man in Jimmy-the-Priest's saloon who recited Homer, a character named Thompson who was connected to a "rat idea," and a minstrel. Only *Hughie*, written in the spring of 1941, was completed, and it was not published or produced during O'Neill's lifetime.

Hughie is set in a run-down New York hotel lobby in the summer of 1928. After the funeral of Hughie, to whom he felt close, Erie Smith, a gambler with pretensions of being a Broadway sport, went on a binge. The friendship, though both men valued it, was limited. Erie told Hughie embellished stories and outright lies about gambling and relationships with chorus girls. Hughie, trapped in a boring job and a static marriage, created his own fantasies from Erie's stories. When Erie returns to the hotel after his binge and asks for his key, he tries to recreate the friendship between him and Hughie with the new clerk. The clerk, who at first is too consumed in his own boredom and fantasies to listen, eventually responds to Erie, and a new bond seems to be forming at the play's end. The friendship, however, will be, as was Erie and Hughie's, limited; it is really a relationship between Erie's stories and the clerk's fantasies. It does not improve the quality of their lives significantly; it only makes them a little less lonely and pathetic.

In fall 1941 O'Neill made the notes for *A Moon for the Misbegotten*, which would be his last play. Written in 1942 and 1943, it evolved from an episode in act 1 of *Long Day's Journey Into Night*, a story that Jamie tells about an Irishman who outwits a New England aristocrat. The play begins with an enactment of Phil Hogan's triumph over a New England oil tycoon. The oil tycoon rides to Hogan's house to complain about the Irishman's pigs wallowing in his ice pond. Before the tycoon leaves, Hogan drags him through the pigpen. The episode brings Jamie Tyrone, whose father leases the farm to Hogan, to the scene. Jamie, who faces the world with the "mask" of a hardened cynic, and Josie Hogan, a large woman who faces the world with the "mask" of the village slut, are brought together. They both understand the other's hidden self. Jamie knows that Josie is actually virginal, and Josie is aware of Jamie's sensitivity. Through long confessions, the characters achieve a closeness missing in their lives. In 1947 the Theatre Guild produced the play, but casting and censorship problems caused it to close after playing in three cities. It was O'Neill's last contact with the theatre.

After the failed production of *A Moon for the Misbegotten*, he wrote no new plays. Though his nervous disorder, his loss of motor control, made it difficult to hold a pencil without trembling, he still could have written. He owned a crude dictating machine, a gift from the Theatre Guild, but was unwilling to use the machine for composing. He claimed that he could not write without pencil and paper. Some of his friends felt that he was passively waiting for death. He died in 1953 apart from the theatre that he had helped to reshape.

Before O'Neill began to write, most American plays were poor imitations or outright thefts of European works. By the 1920s he was hailed in America as the most promising of the young playwrights and was also gaining an international reputation. A few decades later he was the model for the American playwrights who followed. Tennessee Williams, Arthur Miller, Edward Albee, and others could begin their careers in a tradition which O'Neill, more than any other playwright, had established. This legacy to his successors is of incalculable value.

An epigrammatic evaluation of O'Neill's career might be that he wrote some of the very best and some of the worst plays of the twentieth century. *The Emperor Jones*, *The Hairy Ape*, *Desire Under the Elms*, *Strange Interlude*, *Mourning Becomes Electra*, *A Touch of the Poet*, *The Iceman Cometh*, *Hughie*, and *A Moon for the Misbegotten* are all great plays, and *Long Day's Journey Into Night* is one of the greatest plays of Western literature. *The Great God Brown*, *Lazarus Laughed*, and other failed experiments, though the products of a dramatic genius, are, in one way or another, embarrassingly bad. A fairer evaluation would incorporate an understanding of O'Neill's need for experimentation. The variety of modes in which he wrote, especially during the middle period of his career, was his way of discovering how the theatre might be transformed into a medium for his thoughts. A still fairer evaluation of his career would include an appreciation for the magnitude of his accomplishments given the significant obstacles he encountered. He had to create American drama as an art form before he could begin to write great American plays.

Other:

Bound East for Cardiff, in *The Provincetown Plays*, *First Series* (New York: Shay, 1916);

Before Breakfast, in *The Provincetown Plays*, *Third Series* (New York: Shay, 1916);

The Dreamy Kid, in *Contemporary One-Act Plays*, ed. Frank Shay (Cincinnati: Kidd, 1922);

Benjamine DeCasseres, *Anathema!*, foreword by O'Neill (New York: Gotham Book Mart, 1928).

Periodical Publications:

"Tomorrow," *Seven Arts* (June 1917): 147-170;

"Strindberg and Our Theatre," *Provincetown Playbill*, 1 (1923-1924): 1, 3;

"The Playwright Explains," *New York Times*, 14 February 1926, VIII: 2;

"Memoranda on Masks," *American Spectator* (November 1932): 3;

"Second Thoughts," *American Spectator* (December 1932): 2;

"A Dramatist's Notebook," *American Spectator* (January 1933): 2;

"Prof. G. P. Baker," *New York Times*, 13 January 1935, IX: 1;

The Ancient Mariner, *Yale University Library Gazette*, 35 (October 1960): 61-86.

Bibliography:

Jennifer McCabe Atkinson, *Eugene O'Neill: A Descriptive Bibliography* (Pittsburgh: University of Pittsburgh Press, 1974).

Biographies:

Arthur Gelb and Barbara Gelb, *O'Neill* (New York: Harper, 1962);

Louis Sheaffer, *O'Neill: Son and Playwright* (Boston: Little, Brown, 1968);

Sheaffer, *O'Neill: Son and Artist* (Boston: Little, Brown, 1973).

References:

Jacob H. Adler, "The Worth of *Ah, Wilderness!*," *Modern Drama*, 3 (December 1960): 280-288;

Doris M. Alexander, "Captain Brant and Captain Brasshound: The Origin of an O'Neill Character," *Modern Language Notes*, 74 (April 1959): 306-310;

Alexander, "Eugene O'Neill and Charles Lever," *Modern Drama*, 5 (February 1963): 415-420;

Alexander, "Eugene O'Neill and *Light on the Path*," *Modern Drama*, 3 (December 1960): 260-267;

Alexander, "Eugene O'Neill as Social Critic," *American Quarterly*, 6 (Winter 1954): 349-363;

Alexander, "Eugene O'Neill, 'The Hound of Heaven' and the 'Hell Hole,'" *Modern Language Quarterly*, 20 (December 1959): 307-314;

Alexander, "*Lazarus Laughed* and Buddha," *Modern Language Quarterly*, 17 (December 1956): 357-365;

Alexander, "The Missing Half of *Hughie*," *Tulane Drama Review*, 6 (Summer 1967): 125-126;

Alexander, "*Strange Interlude* and Schopenhauer," *American Literature*, 25 (May 1953): 213-228;

Robert J. Andreach, "O'Neill's Use of Dante in *The Fountain* and *The Hairy Ape*," *Modern Drama*, 10 (May 1967): 48-56;

Andreach, "O'Neill's Women in *The Iceman Cometh*," *Renascence*, 18 (Winter 1966): 89-98;

Sverre Arested, "*The Iceman Cometh* and *The Wild Duck*," *Scandinavian Studies*, 20 (February 1948): 1-11;

Judith E. Barlow, "*Long Day's Journey Into Night*: From Early Notes to Finished Play," *Modern Drama*, 22 (March 1979): 19-28;

Lennart A. Björk, "The Swedish Critical Reception of O'Neill's Posthumous Plays," *Scandinavian Studies*, 38 (August 1966): 331-350;

Clara Blackburn, "Continental Influences on Eugene O'Neill's Expressionistic Dramas," *American Literature*, 13 (May 1941): 109-133;

Travis Bogard, *Contour in Time* (New York: Oxford University Press, 1972);

William R. Brashear, "O'Neill and Shaw: The Play as Will and Idea," *Criticism*, 8 (Spring 1966): 155-169;

Oscar Cargill, N. Bryllion Fagin, and William J. Fisher, eds., *O'Neill and His Plays: Four Decades of Criticism* (New York: New York University Press, 1961);

Frederic I. Carpenter, "The Romantic Tragedy of Eugene O'Neill," *College English*, 6 (February 1945): 250-258;

Leonard Chabrowe, "Dionysus in *The Iceman Cometh*," *Modern Drama*, 4 (February 1962): 377-388;

Norman Chaitin, "O'Neill: The Power of Daring," *Modern Drama*, 3 (December 1960): 231-241;

Barrett H. Clark, "Aeschylus and O'Neill," *English Journal*, 21 (November 1932): 699-710;

Clark, "Eugene O'Neill and the Guild," *Drama*, 18 (March 1928): 169-171;

Clark, *Eugene O'Neill: The Man and His Plays* (New York: McBride, 1929);

Marden J. Clark, "Tragic Effect in *The Hairy Ape*," *Modern Drama*, 10 (February 1968): 372-378;

Dorothy Commins, *What Is an Editor? Saxe Commins at Work* (Chicago: University of Chicago Press, 1978);

Matthew T. Conlin, "The Tragic Effect in *Autumn Fire* and *Desire Under the Elms*," *Modern Drama*, 1 (February 1959): 228-235;

Carl Dahlstrom, "*Dynamo* and *Lazarus Laughed*: Some Limitations," *Modern Drama*, 3 (December 1960): 224-230;

Cyrus Day, "*Amor Fati*: O'Neill's Lazarus as Superman and Savior," *Modern Drama*, 3 (December 1960): 297-305;

Day, "The Iceman and the Bridegroom," *Modern Drama*, 1 (May 1958): 3-9;

Helen Deutsch and Stella Hanau, *The Provincetown: A Story of the Theatre* (New York: Farrar & Rinehart, 1931);

Walter P. Eaton, "The Eugene O'Neill Collection," *Yale University Library Gazette*, 18 (July 1943): 5-8;

Edwin A. Engel, *The Haunted Heroes of Eugene O'Neill* (Cambridge: Harvard University Press, 1953);

Doris V. Falk, *Eugene O'Neill and the Tragic Tension* (New Brunswick: Rutgers University Press, 1958);

John J. Fitzgerald, "The Bitter Harvest of O'Neill's Projected Cycle," *New England Quarterly*, 40 (September 1967): 364-374;

Fitzgerald, "Guilt and Redemption in O'Neill's Last Play: A Study of *A Moon for the Misbegotten*," *Texas Quarterly*, 9 (Spring 1966): 146-158;

Winifred L. Frazer, *Love as Death in 'The Iceman*

Cometh' (Gainesville: University of Florida Press, 1967);

Frazer, " 'Revolution' in *The Iceman Cometh*," *Modern Drama*, 22 (March 1979): 1-8;

Horst Frenz, *Eugene O'Neill* (New York: Ungar, 1971);

Frenz and Frederic Fleisher, "Eugene O'Neill and the Royal Dramatic Theatre of Stockholm," *Modern Drama*, 10 (December 1967): 300-311;

Frenz and Martin Mueller, "More Shakespeare and Less Aeschylus in Eugene O'Neill's *Mourning Becomes Electra*," *American Literature*, 38 (March 1966): 85-100;

John Gassner, *Eugene O'Neill* (Minneapolis: University of Minnesota Press, 1965);

Virgil Geddes, *The Melodramamadness of Eugene O'Neill* (Brookfield, Conn.: Brookfield Players, 1934);

Karl-Ragnar Gierow, "Eugene O'Neill's Posthumous Plays," *World Theatre*, 7 (Spring 1958): 46-52;

Isaac Goldberg, *The Theatre of George Jean Nathan* (New York: Simon & Schuster, 1926);

William Goldhurst, "A Literary Source for O'Neill's 'In the Zone,' " *American Literature*, 35 (January 1964): 530-534;

Peter L. Hays, "Biblical Perversions in *Desire Under the Elms*," *Modern Drama*, 11 (February 1969): 423-428;

Theresa Helburn, *A Wayward Quest* (Boston: Little, Brown, 1960);

James Milton Highsmith, "The Cornell Letters," *Modern Drama*, 15 (May 1972): 68-88;

Highsmith, " 'The Personal Equation': Eugene O'Neill's Abandoned Play," *Southern Humanities Review*, 8 (Spring 1974): 195-212;

Vivian C. Hopkins, "*The Iceman Cometh* Seen Through *The Lower Depths*," *College English*, 11 (November 1949): 81-87;

H. G. Kemelman, "Eugene O'Neill and the Highbrow Melodrama," *Bookman*, 75 (September 1932): 482-491;

Janis Klavsons, "O'Neill's Dreamer: Success and Failure," *Modern Drama*, 3 (December 1960): 268-272;

Lawrence Langer, *The Magic Curtain* (New York: Dutton, 1951);

Kenneth Lawrence, "Dionysus and O'Neill," *University Review*, 33 (Autumn 1966): 67-70;

Marguerite Loud McAnerny, "Eleven Manuscripts of Eugene O'Neill," *Princeton University Library Chronicle*, 4 (February-April 1943): 86-89;

Jordan Y. Miller, *Eugene O'Neill and the American Critic* (Hamden, Conn.: Archon Books, 1973);

Miller, "Eugene O'Neill's Long Journey," *Kansas Magazine*, 26 (1958): 77-81;

Miller, "The Georgia Plays of Eugene O'Neill," *Georgia Review*, 12 (Fall 1958): 278-290;

Arthur H. Nethercot, "The Psychoanalyzing of Eugene O'Neill," *Modern Drama*, 3 (December 1960): 243-256; 3 (February 1961): 357-372;

Henry F. Pommer, "The Mysticism of Eugene O'Neill," *Modern Drama*, 9 (May 1966): 26-39;

Edgar F. Racey, Jr., "Myth as Tragic Structure in *Desire Under the Elms*," *Modern Drama*, 5 (May 1962): 42-46;

John Henry Raleigh, "Eugene O'Neill," in *Fifteen Modern American Authors: A Survey of Research and Criticism*, ed. Jackson R. Bryer (Durham: Duke University Press, 1969), pp. 301-322;

Raleigh, "O'Neill's *Long Day's Journey Into Night* and New England Irish-Catholicism," *Partisan Review*, 26 (Fall 1959): 573-592;

Raleigh, *The Plays of Eugene O'Neill* (Carbondale: Southern Illinois University Press, 1965);

R. Dilworth Rust, "The Unity of O'Neill's *S. S. Glencairn*," *American Literature*, 37 (November 1965): 280-290;

John T. Shawcross, "The Road to Ruin: The Beginning of O'Neill's Long Day's Journey," *Modern Drama*, 3 (December 1960): 289-296;

Richard Dana Skinner, *Eugene O'Neill: A Poet's Quest* (New York: Longmans, Green, 1935);

Timo Tiusanen, *O'Neill's Scenic Image* (Princeton: Princeton University Press, 1968);

Egil Törnqvist, *A Drama of Souls* (New Haven: Yale University Press, 1969);

Törnqvist, "Ibsen and O'Neill: A Study in Influence," *Scandinavian Studies*, 37 (August 1965): 211-235;

Törnqvist, "Nietzsche and O'Neill: A Study of Affinity," *Orbis Litterarum*, 23 (1968): 97-126;

Thomas F. Van Laan, "Singing in the Wilderness: The Dark Vision of O'Neill's Only Mature Comedy," *Modern Drama*, 22 (March 1979): 9-18;

Paul D. Voelker, "Eugene O'Neill and George Pierce Baker: A Reconsideration," *American Literature*, 49 (May 1977): 206-220.

Papers:

Most of O'Neill's manuscripts are housed in the Beinecke Library at Yale University and at the Library of Congress. Additional manuscripts are housed at the University of Texas at Austin, Princeton University, Harvard University, and Cornell University.

JOHN PATRICK
(17 May 1906-)

SELECTED PRODUCTIONS: *Hell Freezes Over*, 28 December 1935, Ritz Theatre, New York, 25 [performances];

The Willow and I, 10 December 1942, Windsor Theatre, New York, 28;

The Hasty Heart, 3 January 1945, Hudson Theatre, New York, 204;

The Story of Mary Surratt, 8 February 1947, Henry Miller's Theatre, New York, 11;

The Curious Savage, 24 October 1950, Martin Beck Theatre, New York, 31;

Lo and Behold!, 12 December 1951, Booth Theatre, New York, 38;

The Teahouse of the August Moon, adapted from Vern Sneider's novel, 15 October 1953, Martin Beck Theatre, New York, 1027;

Good as Gold, 7 March 1957, Belasco Theatre, New York, 4;

Juniper and the Pagans, 10 December 1959, Colonial Theatre, Boston;

Everybody Loves Opal, 11 October 1961, Longacre Theatre, New York, 21;

It's Been Wonderful, September 1966, Albuquerque Little Theatre, Albuquerque;

Scandal Point, September 1967, Albuquerque Little Theatre, Albuquerque;

Everybody's Girl, September 1968, Albuquerque Little Theatre, Albuquerque;

Love Is a Time of Day, 22 December 1969, Music Box Theatre, New York, 8;

A Barrel Full of Pennies, 12 May 1970, Playhouse on the Mall, Paramus, N.J.;

Lovely Ladies, Kind Gentlemen, 28 December 1970, Majestic Theatre, New York, 16;

Opal Is a Diamond, 27 July 1971, Flat Rock Playhouse, Flat Rock, N.C.;

The Savage Dilemma, 19 May 1972, Long Beach Community Theatre, Long Beach, Cal.;

The Dancing Mice, June 1972, Berea Summer Theatre, Berea, Ohio;

Macbeth Did It, July 1972, Flat Rock Playhouse, Flat Rock, N.C.;

The Enigma, 12 June 1973, Berea Summer Theatre, Berea, Ohio;

Opal's Baby, 26 June 1973, Flat Rock Playhouse, Flat Rock, N.C.;

Roman Conquest, 25 July 1973, Berea Summer Theatre, Berea, Ohio;

A Bad Year for Tomatoes, 1974, John Patrick Dinner Theatre at the You Are Cabaret Dinner Theatre, North Royalston, Ohio;

Divorce, Anyone?, 1975, John Patrick Dinner Theatre at the You Are Cabaret Dinner Theatre, North Royalston, Ohio;

Opal's Husband, 1975, Flat Rock Playhouse, Flat Rock, N.C.;

Noah's Animals, 1975, Berea Summer Theatre, Berea, Ohio;

Suicide, Anyone?, 1976, Fortuna Theatre Club, St. Thomas, Virgin Islands;

People!, October 1976, John Patrick Dinner Theatre at the You Are Cabaret Dinner Theatre, North Royalston, Ohio;

Opal's Million Dollar Duck, 1979, School of Performing Arts, St. Thomas, Virgin Islands;

Girls of the Garden Club, July 1979, Berea Summer Theatre, Berea, Ohio;

That's Not My Father, 1979, Fortuna Theatre Club, St. Thomas, Virgin Islands.

SELECTED BOOKS: *The Willow and I* (New York: Dramatists Play Service, 1943);

The Hasty Heart (New York: Dramatists Play Service, 1945);

The Story of Mary Surratt (New York: Dramatists Play Service, 1947);

The Curious Savage (New York: Dramatists Play Service, 1951);

The Teahouse of the August Moon (New York: Dramatists Play Service, 1957);

Everybody Loves Opal (New York: Dramatists Play Service, 1962);

It's Been Wonderful (New York: Dramatists Play Service, 1966);

Anybody Out There (New York: Dramatists Play Service, 1972);

A Bad Year For Tomatoes (New York: Dramatists Play Service, 1975).

John Patrick has achieved immense popularity and financial success as a playwright and screen writer. Having written over thirty plays, coauthored nineteen films, and having adapted several works into major motion pictures, he is highly regarded as a craftsman who has made a fortune entirely from his writing. Of his plays, the best known are *The Willow and I* (1942), *The Hasty Heart* (1945), *The Curious Savage* (1950), *The Teahouse of the August Moon* (1953), and *Everybody Loves Opal* (1961). *The Teahouse of the August Moon*, adapted from Vern Sneider's novel, has proved to be his most durable work. It earned him a Pulitzer Prize (1954), an Antoinette Perry (Tony) Award for best play (1954), the Drama Critics Circle Award for Best Play (1954), the Theatre Club Award, *Billboard* magazine's eleventh annual Donaldson Award (1954), and the Aegis Award (1954). Tonies were also given to two of the play's actors, David Wayne (Best Actor) and Paul Ford (Best Supporting Actor) as well as to its set designer, Peter Larkin. The director, Robert Lewis, received the Critic's Award for best director.

Born in Louisville, Kentucky, to John Francis and Myrtle Osborn Goggan, John Patrick Goggan was abandoned by both parents and shuffled in and out of foster homes and boarding schools. Of the numerous prisonlike boarding schools, he remembers only two: St. Edwards School in Austin, Texas, and Holy Cross School in New Orleans. He drifted through hobo camps as a teenager and at nineteen found his way to San Francisco where he became an announcer for KPO Radio. When he received his first writer's by-line, he legally dropped his last name. From 1929 to 1933, Patrick wrote more than eleven hundred scripts for "Cecil and Sally," a series later picked up by NBC. He continued to write for NBC Radio from 1933 to 1936. In 1940 Patrick's adaptations of classics were performed on NBC Radio by Helen Hayes. From 1941 to 1944, Patrick was an ambulance driver in the American Field Service. He served with Montgomery's Eighth Army in Egypt, with the British Ninth Army in Syria, and for a time with the South-East Asia Command under Lord Mountbatten. While in the service, he contracted malaria twice. Patrick took courses at Harvard University and Columbia University, although he never received an academic degree.

In 1935 Patrick's first play was produced on Broadway. *Hell Freezes Over* received uniformly bad reviews and closed after twenty-five performances. There is no surviving script for this melodrama about a dirigible crash in Antarctica. Despite the failure of the play, Patrick was offered a three year contract as scriptwriter for Twentieth Century-Fox in Hollywood. From 1936 to 1939, he coauthored nineteen films scripts with Lou Breslow and other team writers and developed his craft as well as his eye for commercial success. His later major film adaptations—*The President's Lady* (1953), *Three Coins in the Fountain* (1954), *Love is a Many-Splendored Thing* (1955), *Teahouse of the August Moon* (1956), *High Society* (1956), and *The World of Susie Wong* (1960)—were popular and financially successful. *Les Girls*, for which in 1957 he won the Screenwriters Guild Award and the Foreign Correspondents Award, was presented to Queen Elizabeth at a command performance. Adapted from James Jones's novel, the Academy Award-winning *Some*

Came Running was the top grossing film of 1959 and followed *Les Girls* in *Film Daily*'s listing of the ten best films of the year. *Gigot*, however, proved unsuccessful; *The Shoes of the Fisherman* (1968) is Patrick's most recent filmscript.

As a playwright, Patrick has always considered himself a craftsman first, an artist second, and an entertainer always. His scripts are sentimental and relentless in their affirmation of man's better qualities. Unpretentious, often brilliantly and outrageously theatrical, they have had enormous appeal for audiences all over the world. Despite the often caustic criticism by New York reviewers that at times has been justified, Patrick's plays have successfully entertained popular audiences. His ability to hold an audience was formed over a period of time. After the disastrous *Hell Freezes Over*, he attempted a gothic psychological drama set in the Deep South in 1900. The 1942 production of *The Willow and I* established the careers of Martha Scott and Gregory Peck, but the show folded after twenty-eight performances—in spite of many positive reviews. *The Willow and I* presents the relationships of two sisters, one gentle and introverted and the other outgoing and assertive, with a young man. As the gentle Mara is about to marry young Robin Todd, her sister Bessie threatens suicide, and in the strug-

John Patrick

gle for the gun, it fires, jolting Mara into a trance that lasts for forty years. Robin and Bessie marry and have a son, Kirkland, and Robin dies. After his death, Mara is eventually shocked back into reality by a thunderstorm. At first mistaking Kirkland for her former lover, she eventually accepts the truth, and he, fascinated by his aunt, decides to use her as the subject for a special painting. As he works, he tells his mother not to interfere because he has found fulfillment. The play ends with the implication that what ought to have been has come to pass and that mother and child are united. The strange, haunting story is unique among Patrick's plays, and reveals depth not usually found in his work. Certainly it reflects his mastery of mood and atmosphere and provides challenging roles. Royalties paid steadily by amateur groups since the play's release in 1942 have confirmed the play's popularity.

Patrick's third drama, *The Hasty Heart*, was quite successful in winning over audiences and critics in London as well as New York. Set in a British field hospital similar to the one in Assam, Burma, in which Patrick was treated for malaria, its characters are based on patients he had known there. The principal character, a dour Scot named Lachlen McLachlen, was drawn from two Scots whom Patrick had known while serving with the British.

At the center of *A Hasty Heart* is a simple theme, one found throughout Patrick's plays—that man is not made to live alone and that he needs to give and to receive love. When the ward nurse informs the other patients that the fiercely private Scot is dying, they make an effort to offer friendship. When "Lachie" discovers the reason for their friendliness, he is humiliated and embittered by their pity. The men, however, react harshly to his arrogance. Their honest, quick anger jolts him out of self-pity and Lachie learns to accept and to give friendship.

Patrick's first major success, *The Hasty Heart*, was written while Patrick was returning on a transport ship from North Africa to Newport News, Virginia. Having no typewriter and little paper, he jotted in cramped longhand on copy paper, wastebasket scraps, letterheads, wrapping paper, and finally on toilet tissue. Since wartime censorship policies demanded that all material composed aboard ship be confiscated and checked, he persuaded one of his fellow passengers, a flier, to hide the jumbled manuscript in a concertina. After having passed safely through customs, the pilot mailed the play to Patrick's New York address.

The New York production of *The Hasty Heart*

established Richard Basehart (Lachie) as a stage actor, secured Earl Jones (father of James Earl Jones) his first Broadway role, and provided Patrick with a substantial financial profit. For every performance during its six months on Broadway and two years in London, he received between five and ten percent of the gross and a percentage on scripts that were sold. He was thus able to buy sixty-five acres of farmland in Rockland County, New York, on which he later established his estate, Hasty Hill. For years it served as the place where he wrote and practiced organic farming and raised prize-winning Aberdeen-Angus cattle, Saanen goats, and Suffolk sheep.

Patrick's last early drama, *The Story of Mary Surratt* (1947), is his only passionate, almost didactic work. By his own admission quick to invent facts as his plays need them, he nonetheless spent considerable time researching the trial of the simple woman who was hanged by a military court for her alleged role in the Lincoln assassination. Although all of his plays treat human dignity, this emotional drama is not only a plea for human justice but also a statement of outrage over its miscarriage.

The first-nighters shouted bravos and encores, and several critics praised the new historical drama. In remaining true to history, however, Patrick painted Mary as a basically simple and undramatic heroine. For this the major critics faulted the script. Closing after only eleven performances, the play failed even to excite the amateur theatres. Such reluctance on the part of the popular audiences suggests that they were not ready at the end of the war to view any play, regardless of its merit, which depicted their country's military injustice.

With such limited success in somber subjects, Patrick turned to comedy. His next play, *The Curious Savage*, established his international reputation. It is one of his best comedies and remains a box-office success in regional and community theatres. Though it ran for only thirty-one performances on Broadway, it earned Patrick some $83,000 in royalties the first year that it was released to amateur groups and eventually became the third most often produced contemporary play in America, second only to *Life With Father* and *Arsenic and Old Lace*. In twenty years, the play earned over $400,000 for Patrick and in 1971 it was included in the repertory of the Vinohrady Theatre in Prague, along with works by Shakespeare and Gorki. It has also been produced in Poland, Hungary, and the U.S.S.R. The "Curious Savage" is eccentric multimillionaire Mrs. Ethel P. Savage, who has been committed to an asylum by her greedy children who wish to gain control of her estate. The play contrasts the gently mad inmates with the rapacious children to demonstrate the insanity of greed. Though the play's critical reception was not entirely negative, some critics felt the subject matter, insanity, to be in bad taste.

Not bothered by the critical opinion, Patrick continued to write in his characteristically light vein. The following year, *Lo and Behold!* (1951), a farce about ghosts, drew mixed reviews, the majority being unfavorable. Though Leo G. Carroll, Lee Grant, Doro Merande, and Cloris Leachman won praise, the script itself was condemned by critics. Though unsuccessful on Broadway, *Lo and Behold!* also became popular in regional and community theatres. Walter Kerr, whose review summarized critical opinion of the play, made a generally accurate assessment of Patrick's comedies. First praising the playwright as a "genuine humorist with an off-beat slant on the process of making people laugh," Kerr then censured him for "still fooling around with the more obvious, gauche, and all but amateur plot twists which intrigue the theatrical novice." The critic predicted that when Patrick "gets past his absorption with the merely eccentric and begins to lavish his talents on something reasonably down to earth, he is going to write a nice, fat hit."

It was Vern Sneider's novel about American occupation in Okinawa that provided Patrick a solid source for stage scripting, and when Patrick adapted it, the "nice, fat hit" was even greater than he, his backers, or Walter Kerr had ever dreamed. Eventually proclaimed by critic John Mason Brown as the best goodwill ambassador this country could have, *Teahouse of the August Moon* delighted audiences in England, West Germany, France, Mexico, Scandinavia, Holland, Belgium, Israel, Yugoslavia, Russia, Austria, Spain, Uruguay, Argentina, South Africa, and Japan. Although marred briefly by a controversy over Patrick's being awarded a Pulitzer Prize (some critics felt that Sneider should have received more credit), his fame was firmly established by the play.

The gentle satire on the American military's attempt to bring democracy to Okinawa was popular particularly in countries familiar with American occupational forces; such audiences were delighted that Americans could so gleefully poke fun at themselves.

Teahouse of the August Moon begins with an introductory monologue by Sakini, an Okinawan translator, who has become one of the most endearing characters in modern American theatre. At times wise and long-suffering and at others intuitive and childlike, he speaks with gentle conviction a

credo formulated by Patrick when he studied briefly with Harvard sociologist Pitirim Aleksandrovich Sorokin, author of *Social and Cultural Dynamics* (1937-1941). Condensing the Russian's thesis, Patrick has Sakini introduce his story by stating, "Pain makes man think. Thought makes man wise. Wisdom makes life endurable."

To begin the official democratization process, the blustering Colonel Purdy sends Captain Fisby, a former literature teacher, and Sakini to the village of Tobiki, where they are to supervise the construction of a pentagon-shaped schoolhouse and develop the island's economy. Sakini, wearing a floppy shirt, baggy shorts, oversized GI boots, and falling-down socks, convinces the captain that the people need a teahouse rather than a school. The captain agrees, and the colonel, vexed by Fisby's muddled report, suspects that he has "gone native" and sends a psychiatrist to observe him. The doctor also falls under the spell of Sakini and his people, however, and immediately begins applying his expertise as an organic farmer (Patrick himself is an authority on organic gardening).

Sakini and Fisby, soon discovering that the potato brandy made by the islanders will sell faster than their souvenirs, develop the industry. Eventually, Tobiki becomes a textbook example of American democracy at work, but the colonel threatens Fisby with court martial when the alteration of the original orders is discovered. A U.S. senator intervenes, however; Fisby is released, the teahouse is rebuilt after Purdy has it destroyed, and the colonel himself is converted. Sakini closes the play with his initial paraphrase of Sorokin.

Teahouse of the August Moon remains Patrick's most financially successful stage play. While running simultaneously in New York and London, the play earned Patrick $5000 per week and paid back the backers' initial investment of $100,000 after only six and a half weeks on Broadway. Weekly profits from the play averaged $6,200, and the ticket lines were so long that the area between Forty-fifth Street and Ninth Avenue became known as "Hong Kong Alley."

Such a reception did not assure success on Broadway for later Patrick plays. *Good as Gold* (1957), a political satire about an idealistic scientist who discovers how to transform gold into a miraculous dirt which will produce fabulous crops, closed after four performances, and *Juniper and the Pagans* (1959), previewed in Boston and Philadelphia, never reached New York.

In 1961, however, Patrick produced his first of a successful series of plays about Opal Kronkie, a

Teahouse of the August Moon

crusty but lovable junk collector. Although *Everybody Loves Opal* closed after twenty-one performances in New York, it became and remains a hit in summer theatres, the leading role attracting such comediennes as Jean Stapleton, Martha Raye, Imogene Coca, and Peggy Cass. Typical of all Patrick plays, it contains no profanity or sexual overtones, and love is triumphant over greed when the three petty crooks who try to kill Opal for her insurance are captured by her affection. Although the Opal scripts have yet to appear on television, Patrick has received $10,000 in advances from networks.

His growing popularity with community theatres prompted Patrick to write scripts exclusively for them. Albuquerque Little Theatre, in Albuquerque, New Mexico, presented *It's Been Wonderful* (1966), *Scandal Point* (1967), his only thriller, and *Everybody's Girl* (1968). *A Barrel Full of Pennies* premiered in 1970 at Playhouse on the Mall in Paramus, New Jersey.

His two most recent Broadway productions proved unsuccessful but pivotal: *Love is a Time of Day* (1969) closed after eight nights and *Lovely Ladies, Kind Gentlemen* (1970), a musical version of *Teahouse*

of the August Moon, after sixteen. Receiving a particularly harsh review from Clive Barnes, *Lovely Ladies, Kind Gentlemen* also failed because of the script's outdatedness. Tensions during the Vietnam era made a comedy about Asians seem inappropriate.

Stung by the Broadway failures, Patrick began to write exclusively for community theatres. The Berea Summer Theatre, sponsored by Baldwin-Wallace College in Berea, Ohio, enjoyed successful premieres of *The Dancing Mice* (1972), *The Enigma* (1973), *Roman Conquest* (1973), *Noah's Animals* (1975), and *Girls of the Garden Club* (1979). The college presented Patrick with an honorary doctorate, and the You Are Cabaret Dinner Theatre complex in adjacent Royalston named one of its theatres after him, premiering *A Bad Year for Tomatoes* (1974) and *Divorce, Anyone?* (1975). North Carolina's state theatre, the Flat Rock Playhouse, in Flat Rock, N.C., opened *Opal is a Diamond* (1971), *Macbeth Did It* (1972), *Opal's Baby* (1973), and *Opal's Husband* (1975).

Patrick now resides on Saint Thomas in the Virgin Islands on an estate which overlooks the

Atlantic and the Caribbean. In 1979 *Opal's Million Dollar Duck* opened at the School of Performing Arts in Saint Thomas, and the island's Fortuna Theatre Club presented *Suicide, Anyone?* (1976) and *That's Not My Father* (1979). A lifelong admirer of Socrates, Patrick has written "The Indictment," a play in which the philosopher is the main character. It is scheduled for production in Santa Barbara in 1980.

The success of John Patrick is not only a classic rags-to-riches story, but also a chart of the major trends in the American entertainment industry. Writing successfully for radio in its heyday, for Broadway, for big-budget movies of the 1950s, and finally for the emerging regional and community theatres throughout the country, Patrick will be remembered as a superb craftsman of popular comedies.

–John Marion

Screenplays:
Charlie Chan at the Race Track, by Patrick and others, Twentieth Century-Fox, 1936;
Educating Father, by Patrick and others, Twentieth Century-Fox, 1936;
36 Hours to Kill, by Patrick and others, Twentieth Century-Fox, 1936;
High Tension, by Patrick and others, Twentieth Century-Fox, 1936;
Midnight Taxi, by Patrick and others, Twentieth Century-Fox, 1937;
Dangerously Yours, by Patrick and others, Twentieth Century-Fox, 1937;
The Holy Terror, by Patrick and others, Twentieth Century-Fox, 1937;
Time Out For Romance, by Patrick and others, Twentieth Century-Fox, l937;
Sing and Be Happy, by Patrick and others, Twentieth Century-Fox, 1937;
Born Reckless, by Patrick and others, Twentieth Century-Fox, 1937;
One Mile From Heaven, by Patrick and others, Twentieth Century-Fox, 1937;
Big Town Girl, by Patrick and others, Twentieth Century-Fox, 1937;
Look Out, Mr. Moto, by Patrick and others, Twentieth Century-Fox, 1938;
Five of a Kind, by Patrick and others, Twentieth Century-Fox, 1938;

International Settlement, by Patrick and others, Twentieth Century-Fox, 1938;
Battle of Broadway, by Patrick and others, Twentieth Century-Fox, 1938;
Mr. Moto Takes A Chance, by Patrick and others, Twentieth Century-Fox, 1938;
Up the River Heaven, by Patrick and others, Twentieth Century-Fox, 1937;
Big Town Girl, by Patrick and others, Twentieth Century-Fox, 1937;
Look Out, Mr. Moto, by Patrick and others, Twentieth Century-Fox, 1938;
Five of a Kind, by Patrick and others, Twentieth Century-Fox, 1938;
International Settlement, by Patrick and others, Twentieth Century-Fox, 1938;
High Society, adapted from Philip Barry's play, *The Philadelphia Story*, MGM, 1956;
Teahouse of the August Moon, MGM, 1956;
Les Girls, adapted from Vera Caspary's novel, MGM, 1957;
Some Came Running, adapted from James Jones's novel, MGM, 1958;
The World of Susie Wong, adapted from Paul Osborn's play and Richard Mason's novel, Paramount, 1960;
Parrish, adapted from Mildred Savage's novel, for Warner Brothers, 1961;
Gigot, adapted from Jackie Gleason's story, Twentieth Century-Fox, 1962;
The Main Attraction, Seven Arts, 1963;
The Shoes of the Fisherman, adapted from Morris West's novel, MGM, 1968.

Television Scripts:
Teahouse of the August Moon, "Hallmark Hall of Fame," NBC, 1962;
The Small Miracle, adapted from Paul Gallico's short story, "Hallmark Hall of Fame," NBC, 1973.

Reference:
Michael Hall, "John Patrick: Playwright of the August Moon," master's thesis, University of Florida, 1972.

Papers:
The John Patrick Collection is deposited at the Rare Book Department of Boston University.

DAVID RABE
(10 March 1940-)

PRODUCTIONS: *Sticks and Bones*, 10 February 1969, Varsey Theatre, Villanova University, Villanova, Pa.; 7 November 1971, Florence Sutro Anspacher Theatre (transferred 1 August 1972, John Golden Theatre) New York, 366 [performances];

The Basic Training of Pavlo Hummel, 20 May 1971, Estelle R. Newman Theatre, New York, 363;

The Orphan, 30 March 1973, Florence Sutro Anspacher Theatre, New York, 53;

Boom Boom Room, 8 November 1973, Vivian Beaumont Theatre, New York, 37; revised as *In the Boom Boom Room*, 20 November 1974, Florence Sutro Anspacher Theatre, New York, 31;

Burning (reading), 13 April 1974, Martinson Hall, New York;

Streamers, 30 January 1976, Long Wharf Theatre, New Haven; 6 April 1976, Mitzi Newhouse Theatre, New York, 478.

BOOKS: *The Basic Training of Pavlo Hummel* (New York: French, 1969; London: French, 1972; New York: Viking, 1973);

Sticks and Bones (New York: French, 1972; London: French, 1973);

The Orphan (New York: French, 1975);

In the Boom Boom Room (New York: Knopf, 1975; London: French, 1975);

Streamers (New York: Knopf, 1977).

David Rabe achieved national recognition in 1971 when two of his plays, *The Basic Training of Pavlo Hummel* and *Sticks and Bones*, opened in New York within six months of each other. Productions of *The Orphan* (1973), *Boom Boom Room* (1973), and *Streamers* (1976), presented during the next five years, marked him as a playwright of exceptional quality and promise. The five plays depict contemporary American life as a senselessly violent battlefield. Whether placed in the context of the Vietnam War, recycled Greek mythology, or seedy urban life, the plays present an America in which inexplicable rage bursts into physical and verbal violence.

Rabe's plays have commanded serious public and critical attention for a variety of reasons: each is compellingly topical and sensational; each is a full-length drama written in an era when other serious dramatists had turned to the one-act form; and each

was produced by Joseph Papp's New York Shakespeare Festival—one of America's most prestigious production organizations. Further, the plays move to bloody resolutions; central characters are stabbed with switchblades, blown apart with hand grenades, brutally beaten. Gross and idiosyncratic language matches the intensity of the physical violence; long diatribes often center on racial or sexual conflicts. But the language, however seamy and aggressive in tone, is also mordantly humorous and strangely lyrical. The mixture of these qualities in the theatre results in a singular and distinctive dramatic voice.

David William Rabe was born in Dubuque, Iowa. His father, William Rabe, was a high school teacher and later a meat packer; his mother, Ruth McCormick Rabe, was a department store worker. Rabe was educated at Loras Academy, where he played football, and at Loras College, both Catholic institutions in Dubuque. After receiving his B.A. in

David Rabe

1962, Rabe went to Villanova University in Pennsylvania for a master's degree in theatre. Before he completed his graduate work, Rabe was drafted and served in the U.S. Army from January 1965 to January 1967 as a specialist fourth class. The final eleven months of Rabe's tour of duty were spent in Vietnam.

This period, which provided the experience from which Rabe fashioned his three Vietnam plays, was a turning point in his life. He was assigned to a support group for hospitals, and though never engaged in combat, he witnessed fighting at close range. Rabe was impressed by the youth and inexperience of most of the American front-line troops and viewed much of the war as havoc wrought by "kids, just kids. You don't realize how young most of our army is over there until you see them, troops fresh off the line, standing around some bar like teenagers at a soda fountain, talking coolly about how many of their guys got killed in the last battle."

Rabe has repeatedly emphasized how returning to the United States was profoundly disorienting: "Strange things began to happen to me . . . everybody seemed totally removed from the war." People were interested only in stories about massacres and corruption. In fact, Rabe said, "people were interested in debating the war but . . . didn't want to hear about the war itself." "I'll tell you what it was like," Rabe said in an interview. "It was a carnival—exciting, vulgar, obscene."

When he returned from Vietnam, Rabe went back to school at Villanova, where he received his M.A. degree in 1968. He married Elizabeth Pan in 1969, and they had one son before the marriage ended in divorce. In 1979 Rabe married actress Jill Clayburgh.

The Basic Training of Pavlo Hummel opened its 363-performance run at the Estelle R. Newman Theatre with William Atherton as Pavlo. Rabe was acclaimed a "new and authentic voice of our theatre" by Clive Barnes of the *New York Times*. In 1971 Rabe received the *Village Voice*'s Obie Award for distinguished playwriting and a Drama Desk Award for most promising playwright; the play won the Elizabeth Kate Warriner Award of the Dramatists Guild Council for the 1970-1971 season's best play on a controversial subject. The title character is a complex creation: a teenager, he is lost, emotionally separated from his indifferent mother, despised by his older and extremely callous half brother, ignored by his girl friend, and abandoned by his father. He desperately wants to belong, to have a family of his own. This need cements his ties to the U.S. Army. He is something of an anti-hero whose misguided pluck one cannot help but admire at times.

Yet he is also a compulsive liar, as well as a nearly psychotic misfit who steals from his fellow soldiers, and who attempts suicide to get attention.

Pavlo's perception of reality is depicted by the use of a character that only Pavlo sees or talks to, a dead black soldier named Ardell. Ardell, whose characterization serves to reveal the confused state of Pavlo's mind, moves in and out of the action and helps to establish its expressionistic tone. The scenes in both acts move backward and forward in time: now in the training camp, now in the hospital, then in the jungle; now back to the training camp, then in a brothel, and so on.

Pavlo wants to become a model soldier. He is fascinated by his drill sergeant, a near archetypal figure named Sergeant Tower. Pavlo seeks the confident masculine power over others and the sense of belonging that he imagines soldiers as having. As he dons his dress uniform, his alter ego Ardell says, "You so pretty, baby, you gonna make 'em cry." But despite the authority his uniform implies, Pavlo remains as hopelessly inept and friendless at the end of basic training as he was at its beginning. During leave, his brother has no time for him, and even in uniform, Pavlo cannot attract a girl. When he was young, his mother would point out to him rugged movie heroes, frequently soldiers in war movies, and say each was his father. When Pavlo now demands to know his real father's name, his mother refuses.

Once Pavlo gets to Vietnam, however, things are different. In the surreal carnival of death, even a complete misfit can function. Pavlo has his first sexual experience with a Vietnamese whore and feels he is becoming a man. He finds his niche as a medic, picking up from the battlefields the wounded and, mostly, the dead. It is a job only Pavlo could love. "When they been out here a couple days, man, that's when it's interesting," Pavlo tells Ardell. "You go to pick 'em up they fall apart in you hands, man. They're mud. Pink mud." Rabe's point is that the horror of war often lies in the soldiers' disassociation from the suffering they both inflict and experience. Pavlo is in fact wounded three times and receives the Purple Heart. Though he finally realizes the obvious—he might get killed out there—he continues hauling the dead. Strangely, there is a sort of foolhardy valor in the work he does.

Pavlo frequently recalls an experience from his youth, of swimming in the Hudson River: "They'd said there was no current, but I was twisted in all that water, fighting to get up . . . all my air burning out, couldn't get no more. . . . an I was going down, fighting to get down. I was all confused, you see, fighting to get down, thinking it was up. I hit sand. . . . I pounded the bottom. I thought the bottom was the top." The motif of hitting bottom is reiterated in an anecdote about the explorer Magellan. A maimed soldier says: "So one day [Magellan] wants to know how far under him to the bottom of the ocean. So he drops all the rope he's got. 200 feet. It hangs down into a sea that must go down and down beyond its end for miles and tons of water.... He thinks because all the rope he's got can't touch bottom, he's over the deepest part of the ocean. He doesn't know the real question. How far beyond all the rope you got is the bottom?"

It is a senseless death, not a valiant one, that awaits Pavlo. He argues with another soldier in a brothel over the whore he has been with before. Although he has no illusions about the girl, Pavlo insults the other GI and kicks him in the groin. Later, that soldier lobs a grenade through a window, and Pavlo is killed. Pavlo's death has little to do with Vietnam. Ardell prompts Pavlo, now dead, to give his opinion of the army, the civilians back home, all of life. "It all shit," Pavlo says. Ardell urges from Pavlo a stronger statement. Pavlo responds, "SHHHHHHHHHHIIIIIIIITTTTTTTTTT! . . ." The play is much like Pavlo's scatological scream, a coarse outcry against the senselessness of the war. The play also suggests that one never knows how far down the bottom is until one gets there.

One shortcoming of *The Basic Training of Pavlo Hummel* is a confusion of styles. Ardell and Sergeant Tower are schematic characters, serving a satiric purpose, while Pavlo and his fellow soldiers are deftly individualized and real. More importantly, however, the conception of Pavlo's character is unrelievedly bleak, in accordance with Rabe's theme, and the result is a grueling theatre experience.

Though the dead soldiers have left the war and all worldly worries behind them, and though some survivors might eventually forget Vietnam, the handicapped soldiers came home with permanent reminders of the war. *Sticks and Bones* considers the burden of such reminders. While *The Basic Training of Pavlo Hummel* was still playing, this second play opened to newspaper and broadcast reviews that were often supportive. Martin Gottfried, for example, called Rabe "an extraordinary playwright" and the play "striking and original." After a run of over a hundred performances, *Sticks and Bones* was transferred to Broadway where it ran for 245 performances. In 1972 Rabe won the Antoinette Perry (Tony) Award for best American play, a New York Drama Critics Circle Special Citation, an Outer Circle Award, and the *Variety* poll of New York drama critics as the most promising playwright. However, despite such acclaim, *Sticks*

and Bones did not find an audience in sufficient numbers to justify its Broadway engagement; profits from other projects of the New York Shakespeare Festival were used to support its run.

Sticks and Bones begins as a Vietnam veteran named David, who was blinded in the war, is dropped off at his home by a barking sergeant major and receives a wary welcome from his family: father, Ozzie; mother, Harriet; and brother, Ricky. The opening and character names suggest the kind of black comedy that follows in *Sticks and Bones*. The family's cartoonlike resemblance to the characters in the popular television show, "The Adventures of Ozzie and Harriet," is quite deliberate. Rabe uses the maimed soldier's return to trigger the characters' reappraisal of themselves. Rabe's satirical sword cuts at least two ways: to indict the sanitized public image of the American family which the media promulgates and to scathe those who are content to think that such a bland, complacent self-image can accommodate the truth of American activity in the war. The humorous and grim vignettes that make up the play vary greatly in tone. Harriet wanders empty-headed through many scenes, blithely serving fudge, milk, and cookies. She appears to believe that a nice snack will disarm any threat. David attacks his mother with his white cane. When David seems troubled his family priest talks to him, offering nothing but platitudes.

The most vital sections of *Sticks and Bones* concern the introspection his son's return triggers in Ozzie. Those moments have a caustic vitality. Ozzie reconsiders the promise of his youth, realizing, "I grew too old too quick." His youth is recollected as a dream, a memory of winning footraces, a revery of innocent and natural sexual desire. But the beauty of those images does not satisfy him: "Listen. I mean, I look for explanations. I look inside myself. . . . as I would look into water or the sky . . . the ocean. They're silver. Answers . . . silver and elusive . . . like fish. But if you can catch them in the sea . . . hook them as they flash by. . . . when you're adrift and starving . . . they . . . can help you live." Finally, Ozzie makes a list of everything he owns, has it printed, and says that when asked who he is, he will proudly hand out this list—the answer to what you are is what you have bought. It is an insanely logical conclusion in a materialistic, technologically bloated society.

David, however, has seen and felt too much to ignore the past. He reveals that he loved a Vietnamese girl, Zung, who is quite pretty. His parents are scandalized by the thought that their son has committed miscegenation. Like Ardell in *The Basic*

151

intrigues of the old man and the moon sharing the information

that each hand gained on me, their evaluation of my nature, my

strenghts and frailites, the betterto devise a plan to give them

what they desired from the course of my life, an insidious stratagey

that would include all my attemtps to dianose or detect it's existence so

it would seem a destiny, or fate, whose intricicies and influences woould

forever fool me, so that I would never be on my own, and whereI

might most experei ce myself an individual be, according to their

design and projotion, most spellbound by the mo n's enchantment,

the old man's narratives and need.

    This is a conception that has snuck up on me, the old

man huddled in collusion with the moon, and I want to

unleash myself from it, if I can. It's too hedious to

contemplate, delivering all the horror of a glacial abyss, the

cold, the dark, the shimmering, It makes the universe a scheemer

beyond my ingenuity or appeal. If they are in cahoots,

than they are *agents* of a universe that is clandestine, mean

and duplicite and I have no hope.

"Pogs," revised typescript

Training of Pavlo Hummel, Zung reappears throughout the play, but only David can see her. David does not, in short, seem to be reentering American society or sharing his family's notions of what is normal. Since he will not adapt himself to his family's views and since they are not capable of sharing his understanding or experience, they decide to excommunicate him—permanently. Ozzie, Harriet, and Ricky persuade David to slit his wrists. The family provides the razor, along with silver pans and some kitchen towels to catch the blood. David bleeds to death on stage.

Sticks and Bones examines the sometimes destructive reappraisal of American institutions and beliefs which the war triggered. However, the problem of style that mars *The Basic Training of Pavlo Hummel* is a major defect here: the contrasting bursts of poetry, parody, and pathos do not cohere; the writing is compelling but the mixture of the obvious and the obscure is, finally, unsatisfying.

Rabe's next play, *The Orphan*, is loosely based on the Oresteia trilogy by Aeschylus, and retells several interlocking Greek myths related to the Trojan War, which like Vietnam was a long, debilitating struggle fought on foreign soil. The critical response was unanimously negative and *The Orphan* closed after only fifty-three performances. A year later, in 1974, after considerable rewriting, *The Orphan* opened for a short Off-Broadway run that, again, baffled audiences and critics alike.

In the first act of *The Orphan*, Agamemnon sacrifices his daughter, Iphigenia, and Agamemnon subsequently is murdered by his wife, Clytemnestra, and her consort, Aegisthus. The second act portrays Agamemnon's son, Orestes, taking revenge on both of his father's slayers.

Rabe employs techniques which may be called experimental, though they are hardly new. There are jumps in space and time, repetitions of action, a narrator who interrupts with pseudoscientific monologues, and portentous anachronisms: an unseen phone rings, a priest carries in a briefcase certain bones used to foretell the future, a girl on LSD talks of seeing God. Orestes' revenge is likened to the Vietnam War protests; its conflicting and overlapping psychological motivations are debated. The god Apollo offers Orestes insight through the use of hashish and hallucenogenic mushrooms. In the final minutes, the girl who told of seeing God relates a story that at first seems to describe the revenge Orestes is taking as she speaks. In the end, however, it is unmistakably a retelling of the Charles Manson Family killings. These heterogeneous elements may evoke the Vietnam War years, but the implied thematic equation (that senseless violence in America somehow had its origins in the Vietnam experience just as Orestes' matricide had its fated beginnings on the battlefields of Troy) is unconvincing and undramatic. But, to an extent, Rabe's natural talent for dialogue and confrontation breaks through. Several of the brief scenes are built with clarity and economy, and the language of the Greek characters, though simple in construction, conveys some grandeur and a measure of poetry. Still, the play does not have the narrative energy to overcome the speciousness of its central idea.

Rabe abandoned his obsession with the Vietnam War for his fourth play, *Boom Boom Room* (1973), a savage character study of a woman, played by Madeline Kahn, who fights personal disintegration. The reviews were decidedly mixed. While acknowledging Rabe's "unmistakable talent for dialogue and characters," Edwin Wilson of the *Wall Street Journal* concluded that the three-hour-long play "does not pull together." Nevertheless, *Boom Boom Room* was nominated for a Tony award as best American play of the season. After considerable revision, and with an altered title, *In the Boom Boom Room* played thirty-one additional performances beginning 20 November 1974, with a new cast at the Anspacher Theatre. Critical response was again tepid.

The protagonist of the play is a young go-go dancer, Chrissy, who works in a tawdry bar in Philadelphia but yearns to be a dancer in New York.

The central problem of the play is that Chrissy seems to have very little sense of her own identity and personal worth. She attempts to form a set of values by talking with others, but she selects poor sources of information or intelligence. She compares her own sexuality with that of other dancers. She resorts to astrology for advice about her personal life. Without quite understanding the cause, she permits herself to be exploited by men. She marries Al, a petty crook who uses her for sexual gratification, then leaves her. Her father was also a felon and treated Chrissy's mother in much the same manner as Al treats Chrissy. In a touchingly pathetic scene, Chrissy attempts to understand her father, as he reveals that he has been emasculated by disease and corrective surgery.

In the Boom Boom Room is essentially a static play, for Chrissy suffers but never learns or adapts. She is repeatedly humiliated. Her attitude toward her job is emblematic of her approach to her friends and family: "when you are trying to be with a person who has dances in her head all the time, and who is a special kind of person—I mean, I have dreamed of ballet all my life and other kinds of dancing-so-you-tell-a-story. Of which go-go is a poor facsimile—and that kind of person must be treated very specially, or they will get upset with you as I just did." Chrissy is searching for a way to fulfill her need to love and to believe in her own personal self worth, but she can neither ask for nor take what would fulfill her. The people in her life, however, have no such weakness or humility. A male homosexual who lives below her either wants to dress like her in a pink go-go bunny outfit or to dress her to look like a man and call her "Christopher." One of her fellow dancers, a lesbian, tries to seduce her. Her mother, so Chrissy asserts, had not wanted a child and had tried to abort her; her father may have used her incestuously. Al enters and leaves her bed without so much as asking. In one grueling scene, presented as a frequent occurrence, Al and Chrissy get into an argument. It begins with verbal violence, profanity, and accusations, and ends with physical violence. In the dark, Chrissy yells, "Don't hit my face, don't hit my stomach, don't hit my face. . . ." In the play's coda, Chrissy is shown dancing in New York City. Topless and wearing a mask over her head, Chrissy is stripped of all vestiges of identity. She is left a body that may arouse desire but has not experienced love.

The chief virtue of *In the Boom Boom Room* is the poignant way in which Rabe has used street language to represent Chrissy's naive mind. The slang, vulgarisms, and obscenity are woven—at times almost poetically—into a fabric which shows that Chrissy, like Pavlo Hummel, is somehow immune to real insight. The naturalistic dialogue anticipates Rabe's next play, *Streamers*.

Produced in 1976 and directed by Mike Nichols, *Streamers* is the most powerful of Rabe's five produced plays. Originally staged at the Long Wharf Theatre in New Haven, *Streamers* moved to the Newhouse Theatre at Lincoln Center with the same director and designers and four of the original actors. With isolated exceptions the play and its production were highly praised. Clive Barnes cited the "dramatic power" of the play and commended its "dramatic idea." *Streamers* won the New York Drama Critics Circle Award as the best American play of 1976.

In an army barracks in Virginia in the mid-1960s, three soldiers from different backgrounds have established a sort of surrogate family while they await assignment in Vietnam. The main character, Billy, is a midwesterner, and, like many Americans, alternately liberal and conservative, forgiving and judgmental, self-aware and naive. Billy is one of the few whites to strike up a friendship with Roger, a black man who views the army as a refuge from the handicaps of his race. Their friendship has its varying rhythms, being at times warm and open and at other times formal. Also sharing the quarters is Richie, a moneyed New Yorker who taunts Billy by professing, in a farcical manner, a homosexual desire for him. Billy and Roger react uncertainly to Richie's taunts, responding with laughter and occasionally with anger. Sometimes it seems this sexual teasing is Richie's idea of a joke, but Richie becomes so insistent that one wonders whether Richie's yearning for Billy might be in earnest.

In spite of their differences, the three, by sharing quarters and their fear of service in the war, have become a unit. They are united, too, in their respect for their older sergeant, Rooney. Rooney appears with his buddy since World War II, Sergeant Cokes, who has been returned from Vietnam with leukemia. The two old friends stumble into the cadre room, drunkenly celebrating their reunion. In the ensuing set piece, touching and grimly humorous, the two sergeants tell the boys how a man dies. A man, they say, dies singing, and before they stumble off again, they sing a dying man's song about parachutes that fail to open, a song that gives the play its title. Ironically these lyrics are sung to the melody of "Beautiful Dreamer":

Beautiful streamer
Open for me,
The sky is above me,
But no canopy.

The sense of family these men share, created out of compromise and courtesy, is disrupted by the appearance of Carlyle, a black draftee from another company who is just out of basic training. With an animal drive that is pathological in its intensity, Carlyle will accept no compromise. The only courtesy he knows is ghetto street-jive. Carlyle frightens Billy and Richie but he reminds Roger of his roots. The two blacks form a quick, if shallow, friendship, and the breakup of the familial trio begins. When Roger convinces Billy to join him and Carlyle for a night of city low life, the breakup is completed. At Carlyle's first appearance, he was a disturbing outsider, but having won over first Roger and then Billy, he has left Richie as the odd man out. However, Richie tries to get back in and to make a point with Billy by offering Carlyle sex. Feeling he has made their room his home, too, Carlyle asks the others to leave. Roger grudgingly agrees, but Billy will not budge because he feels homosexuality is wrong not only for himself but for anyone else as well. Carlyle asks Roger and Billy, "What I'm gonna do? Don't you got no feelin' for how a man feel? I don't understand you two boys. Unless you a pair of motherfuckers. That what you are, a pair of motherfuckers? You slits, man. DON'T YOU HEAR ME! I DON'T UNDERSTAND THIS SITUATION HERE. I THOUGHT WE MADE A DEAL!" Carlyle then tells Richie, "YOU GET ON YOUR KNEES, YOU PUNK, I MEAN NOW, AND YOU GONNA BE ON MY JOINT FAST OR YOU GONNA BE ONE BUSTED PUNK. AM I UNDERSTOOD?" An argument builds. In the midst of a murderous rage, Billy has a realization: "THAT IS RIDICULOUS," he shouts. "YOU UNDERSTAND ME? I DON'T HAVE A GODDAMN THING ON THE LINE HERE!"

But Billy's rage will not be checked. He lashes out at Richie with a string of vile epithets. When he turns and calls Carlyle a "sambo," there is the flash of a switchblade and Billy is mortally wounded. In contrast to the plunging parachutist singing as he plummets, Billy's death is agonizingly slow and pathetic. Suddenly a laughing Sergeant Rooney stumbles onto the bloody scene. With drunken bravado (and a broken whiskey bottle for a weapon) he tries to prevent Carlyle's escape, and Carlyle stabs him to death also.

A long and precisely controlled denouement

begins with the entry of the military police who arrest Carlyle. After they have cleared the barracks of the bodies, leaving Roger and Richie alone with their horror and guilt, Sergeant Cokes drunkenly lurches in. He and Rooney were playing a game of hide and seek, and now he wonders where he might find his friend. The boys do not have the heart to tell him that Rooney is dead, so when he asks why Richie is crying, they say it is because he is queer. Cokes reacts to that revelation with surprising gentleness: "There's a lotta worse things in this world than bein' a queer. I seen a lot of 'em, too. I mean, you could have leukemia. That's worse. That can kill you. I mean, it's okay. . . . I mean, maybe I was queer I wouldn't have leukemia. Who's to say? Lived a whole different life." In a lengthy monologue, carefully balanced between comedy and pathos, Cokes tells about the slapstick day he and Rooney have just shared. His tipsy recollections bring him back around again to the parachute that would not open, so he gently sings "Beautiful Streamer," this time in mock-Korean. The rounded nonsense syllables serve as lullaby and lament and form a delicate and effective closure to the play.

Streamers is Rabe's most complex play because in it he gives the most intense, yet objective, treatment to basic human needs—particularly the need to form coherent social and personal bonds. It is a pessimistic play because one must face the bleak reminder that *any* group achieves identity as a result of excluding others—whether intentionally or not. Carlyle's deepest rage proceeds from his clear apprehension that he has no home. He belongs nowhere. Richie, Billy, and Roger have a place and a mutual understanding. Rabe uses army life to represent how personal territory can be formed, protected, or destroyed. The action of *Streamers* has little connection with the Vietnam War. The tiny unit depicted in the barracks is clearly emblematic of a larger world, yet this realization never intrudes upon the realistic treatment of the barracks life.

In short, like Rabe's other plays, *Streamers* has a variety of topics to explore: masculinity, territoriality, failures of communication, fear of dying, and race relations. It is, however, impossible to resolve these thematic elements into one simple and satisfying statement of what *Streamers* is about. But in performance, this play gives the impression of artistic wholeness due, in part, to its style. Like *In the Boom Boom Room* and *The Basic Training of Pavlo*

Hummel, Streamers is unschematic, violent, and often strangely lyrical. But unlike those earlier plays, *Streamers* is wholly realistic. It employs a single setting and each of its three scenes is continuous in time. Most importantly, the characters are individualized and real. Being so touchingly human, their respective fates are as moving as the fortunes of relatives or close friends.

As David Rabe enters his fifth decade, a final assessment of his career is premature. For now, it is clear that while *The Orphan* is a totally failed experiment, *Streamers* has the promise of becoming a new American classic. To varying degrees, the remaining three plays are flawed, but unique expressions of contemporary life. Rabe is still searching for new forms to express his understanding of life. His best work is marked by intensity of confrontation and a penchant for lyrical, if obscene and often scatological language. He appears willing to use varied theatrical formats. He blends humor and fear expertly and shows no tendency toward sentimentality. One expects his to be a marked and powerful voice as he writes plays of greater maturity.

—*James A. Patterson*

References:

Clive Barnes, "David Rabe Presents 'Sticks and Bones,' " *New York Times*, 8 November 1971, p. 53;

Robert Berkvist, " 'If You Kill Somebody,' " *New York Times*, 12 December 1971, II: 3;

Robert Brustein, "Drama in the Age of Einstein," *New York Times*, 7 August 1977, II: 1;

Mel Gussow, "A Rich Crop of Writing Talent Brings New Life to the American Theatre," *New York Times*, 21 August 1977, II: 1;

Walter Kerr, "He Wonders Who He Is—So Do We," *New York Times*, 30 May 1971, II: 3;

Kerr, " 'House' Is Not A Home," *New York Times*, 2 May 1976, II: 5;

Kerr, "When Does Gore Get Gratuitous?," *New York Times*, 22 February 1976, II: 1;

Bob Prochaska, "David Rabe," *Dramatics* (May/June 1977): 18;

"Rabe," *New Yorker*, 47 (20 November 1971): 48-49.

Papers:
David Rabe's papers are in the Mugar Memorial Library, Boston University.

Elmer Rice

Fred Behringer
University of Tennessee at Chattanooga

BIRTH: New York, New York, 28 September 1892, to Jacob and Fanny Lion Reisenstein.

EDUCATION: LL.B., New York Law School, 1912.

MARRIAGE: 16 June 1915 to Hazel Levy, divorced; children: Robert, Margaret. 12 January 1942 to Betty Field, divorced; children: John, Judith, Paul. 1966 to Barbara A. Marshall.

AWARDS: Pulitzer Prize for *Street Scene*, 1929; Canada Lee Foundation Award for *The Winner*, 1954; Litt.D., University of Michigan, 1961.

DEATH: Southampton, England, 8 May 1967.

SELECTED PRODUCTIONS: *On Trial*, 19 August 1914, Candler Theatre, New York, 365 [performances];

The Iron Cross, by Rice and Frank Harris, 13 February 1917, Comedy Theatre, New York;

The Home of the Free, 22 April 1918, Comedy Theatre, New York;

For the Defense, 19 December 1919, Playhouse Theatre, New York, 77;

Wake Up, Jonathan, by Rice and Hatcher Hughes, 17 January 1921, Henry Miller's Theatre, New York, 105;

It Is the Law, 29 November 1922, Ritz Theatre, New York, 121;

The Adding Machine, 19 March 1923, Garrick Theatre, New York, 72;

Close Harmony, by Rice and Dorothy Parker, 1 December 1924, Gaiety Theatre, New York, 24;

The Mongrel, adapted from Hermann Bahr's play, 15 December 1924, Longacre Theatre, New York, 34;

Is He Guilty?, adapted from Rudolph Lothar's play, *The Blue Hawaii*, September 1927, Boston;

Cock Robin, by Rice and Philip Barry, 12 January 1928, Forty-eighth Street Theatre, New York, 100;

Street Scene, 10 January 1929, Playhouse Theatre, New York, 601; musical version, music by Kurt Weill, lyrics by Langston Hughes, 9 January 1947, Adelphi Theatre, New York, 148;

The Subway, 25 January 1929, Cherry Lane Theatre, New York, 35;

See Naples and Die, 26 September 1929, Vanderbilt Theatre, New York, 62;

The Left Bank, 5 October 1931, Little Theatre, New York, 241;

Counsellor-at-Law, 6 November 1931, Plymouth Theatre, New York, 293;

Black Sheep, 13 October 1932, Morosco Theatre, New York, 4;

We, the People, 20 January 1933, Empire Theatre, New York, 50;

Judgment Day, 12 September 1934, Belasco Theatre, New York, 94;

Between Two Worlds, 25 October 1934, Belasco Theatre, New York, 32;

Not for Children, 24 November 1935, Fortune Theatre, London; 25 February 1936, Community Playhouse, Pasadena, Cal.; 13 February 1951, Coronet Theatre, New York, 7;

American Landscape, 3 December 1938, Cort Theatre, New York, 43;

Two on an Island, 22 January 1940, Broadhurst Theatre, New York, 96;

Journey to Jerusalem, 5 October 1940, National Theatre, New York, 17;

Flight to the West, 30 December 1940, Guild Theatre, New York, 136;

A New Life, 15 September 1943, Royale Theatre, New York, 69;

Dream Girl, 14 December 1945, Coronet Theatre, New York, 348;

The Grand Tour, 10 December 1951, Martin Beck Theatre, New York, 8;

The Winner, 17 February 1954, The Playhouse, New York, 30;

Cue for Passion, 25 November 1958, Henry Miller's Theatre, New York, 39;

Love Among the Ruins, 1963, University of Rochester, Rochester, N.Y.

BOOKS: *On Trial* (New York: French, 1919);

The Adding Machine (Garden City: Doubleday, Page, 1923; London: French, 1929);

The Passing of Chow-Chow (New York: French, 1925);

Wake Up, Jonathan (New York & London: French, 1928);

Close Harmony, by Rice and Dorothy Parker (New York: French, 1929);

Cock Robin, by Rice and Philip Barry (New York & Los Angeles: French, 1929);

Street Scene (New York & Los Angeles: French, 1929; London: French, 1929); *Street Scene*, [musical] (New York: Chappell, 1948);

The Subway (New York & Los Angeles: French, 1929);

See Naples and Die (New York & London: French, 1930);

A Voyage to Purilia (New York: Cosmopolitan Books, 1930; London: Gollancz, 1930);

The Left Bank (New York & Los Angeles: French, 1931; London: French, 1931);

Counsellor-at-Law (New York: French, 1931);

The House in Blind Alley (New York: French, 1932);

We, the People (New York: Coward-McCann, 1933);

The Home of the Free (New York & London: French, 1934);

Three Plays without Words (New York & London: French, 1934)—includes *Landscape with Figures*, *Rus in Urbe*, and *Exterior*;

Judgment Day (New York: Coward-McCann, 1934; London: French, 1938);

Two Plays (New York: Coward-McCann, 1935)—includes *Not for Children* and *Between Two Worlds*;

Imperial City (New York: Coward-McCann, 1937);

Black Sheep (New York: Dramatists Play Service, 1938);

American Landscape (New York: Coward-McCann, 1939);

Two on an Island (New York: Coward-McCann, 1940);

Flight to West (New York: Coward-McCann, 1941);

A New Life (New York: Coward-McCann, 1944; London: Gollancz, 1945);

Dream Girl (New York: Coward-McCann, 1946);

The Show Must Go On (New York: Viking, 1949; London: Gollancz, 1950);

The Supreme Freedom (Whitestone, N.Y.: Graphics Group Books, 1949);

Seven Plays (New York: Viking Press, 1950)—includes *On Trial*, *The Adding Machine*, *Street Scene*, *Counsellor-at-Law*, *Judgment Day*, *Two on an Island* and *Dream Girl*;

Not for Children (New York: French, 1951);

The Grand Tour (New York: Dramatists Play Service, 1952);

The Winner (New York: Dramatists Play Service, 1954);

Minority Report (New York: Dover Publications, 1954; London: Heinemann, 1963);

Cue for Passion (New York: Dramatists Play Service, 1959);

The Living Theatre (New York: Harper, 1959; London: Heinemann, 1960);

Love Among the Ruins (New York: Dramatists Play Service, 1963);

Three Plays (New York: Hill & Wang, 1965)—includes *The Adding Machine*, *Street Scene*, and *Dream Girl*;

The Iron Cross (Dixon, Cal.: Proscenium Press, 1965).

As a major American playwright, producer, and director, Elmer Rice contributed significantly to the development of a mature American drama in a career which spanned over fifty years. Although he is perhaps best remembered for his dramas of social significance, he also wrote mystery melodramas, romantic comedies, fantasies, and satirical comedies. Of the nearly thirty Rice plays produced in New York, two are considered great American plays, several were major commercial successes, and several were crashing failures.

Rice was born Elmer Leopold Reisenstein and raised in upper Manhattan. At age fourteen, after only two years of high school, his family's financial difficulties forced him to go to work. In 1907 he worked as a claims clerk, and from 1908 to 1914 he worked in his cousin's law firm. During this time he earned a New York State Board of Regents certificate, the equivalent of a high-school diploma, and attended the New York Law School. Rice's early work experience helped to shape his particular view of reality. As a young file clerk, he read depositions which gave detailed accounts of immoral or illegal behavior. Rice saw the law as a "majestic instrument" of justice but found that in practice "trickery and coercion" were the rule. Rice later wrote that because he had been "profoundly influenced" by his mother's "goodness, forbearance, honesty, decency, [and] loving-kindness," he was "then shocked to find in the conduct of most adults a lack of dignity and of integrity, and a disregard for the sensibilities and well-being of others." This confrontation between his own values and the behavior he observed in others led him to believe that a major portion of the world's activity was dominated by dishonesty, viciousness, and corruption. In 1930 he wrote in the introduction to his unpublished autobiography that with respect to "the social, religious and moral codes" of his generation: "I have found almost every article to be at variance with what seems to me to be the facts of the external world . . . almost everything that the vast majority of my fellow-countrymen today believe, is false."

In his teens Rice's reading ran toward "books that exposed the social structure's weaknesses and evils" and he began to evolve a radical outlook. A number of the nineteenth-century social dramatists dominated his attention, but George Bernard Shaw's writings finally provided the catalyst for something of a conversion experience. When he read *Plays, Pleasant and Unpleasant*, "the effect was cataclysmic." Rice described it as "the most revolutionary event to happen in my life, in an intellectual sense." From a complete reading of Shaw, Rice emerged a socialist, and it is significant that what convinced him "of the evils of the capitalist system and its concomitant institutions was literature rather than economics." His was an idealistic rather than practical socialism, what he described as being of the "utopian variety." He never joined a party, claimed that he had never been able to read Marx, and refused to engage in the "factional squabbles" of the Left.

This independence of mind and activity permeated all areas of his life. He felt that something must be wrong with the institutional approach to education when, after a year of studying a few hours at night without supervision, he was able to pass the exams for four years of high-school work. Later, he discovered in law school that he could absorb the work in a few hours of independent reading, spend his time in lectures reading plays, and still graduate cum laude. Although Rice belonged to organizations throughout his life, he favored those, such as the American Civil Liberties Union, which existed to promote the independence he so prized. He characterized himself in the 1930s as a revolutionary and vigorously denounced injustice. As a result, for many years he appeared on lists of radicals in

Elmer Rice

spite of his patriotic, solidly American position. Perhaps his need for independence functioned even in his strictly commerical writing. After suffering in his childhood the frustration of a family constantly worried about money, he was determined that he would always remain financially independent. He unashamedly wrote a number of plays from what he called "no nobler impulse than a realistic desire to make a comfortable living."

In a highly characteristic act Rice, an intelligent, self-styled radical, who for all his sense of humor was pugnacious and precipitant in the extreme, suddenly quit his job at the law firm only a few weeks after being admitted to the New York bar. He was twenty-one years old and had nothing in mind but a vague wish to write plays. Less than eight months later *On Trial* (1914) opened in New York. According to the description of reviewer Burns Mantle, the "pale young dramatist stood up in a stage box" to receive an ovation unlike any Mantle had ever witnessed.

Called by *Billboard* "the greatest dramatic and artistic triumph" in New York for years, *On Trial* is based on a simple and effective technical device, the flashback. First used in the American theatre in this melodrama, the flashback was facilitated by a jackknife stage (an arrangement of platforms which pivoted like the blades of a knife). Louis Sherwin of the *New York Globe* called the dramatic effect of the flashback "overpowering" and noted that it enabled "the author to tell an old, threadbare story in such a striking, original manner that the whole thing seems absolutely new."

The "threadbare story" is of the innocent girl, May, seduced by the promises of an unscrupulous married man. The man, Trask, turns up years later and forces May to submit to him again, threatening to reveal her secret to Robert, the man she has married. Robert learns what has happened; Trask is murdered under mysterious circumstances; and May disappears. At this point the trial and the play begin. The search for the real murderer moves forward in the trial plot as the story of May's rape is told through the use of flashbacks. The play develops in a standard, albeit skillfully managed way, through a series of sensational events including the cross-examination of May's young daughter and the sudden reappearance of May herself, each plot gaining in effect and momentum from the other. The murderer is discovered through a clever trap, and the husband and wife are reunited.

Insignificant now, except as Rice's first success and as an example of his early stagecraft, *On Trial* was such a sensation on its opening night in 1914 that at the second intermission George M. Cohan offered Rice thirty thousand dollars for the rights to the play. Unable to believe that such an offer could be genuine, Rice turned it down thinking that Cohan was priming him for a practical joke. Rice eventually made one hundred thousand dollars from the run of his play.

His success, of course, brought new opportunities. Eagerly seizing his advantage, Rice developed some skill at public speaking through an engagement at the Socialist Press Club and frequent participation in the Sunday-night forum at the Church of the Ascension. An idealistic, young activist, Rice edited a weekly bulletin for the Church of the Ascension, and during 1915-1916 directed the dramatic activities at the University Settlement. In an effort to help "young people to break through the enforced clannishness of the ghetto," he initiated an exchange of dramatic activities to "break down insularity" between the city's various settlement houses. In 1915 he married Hazel Levy and they had two children. Rice also made a trip to North Carolina in 1916 to investigate child labor, marched up Fifth Avenue in a parade supporting women's suffrage, and went to Washington in 1917 with a New York group to participate in a national protest against World War I.

These political activities gave rise to Rice's serious writing during this period. He had not been impressed with the critics' response to his first play. His models were Shaw and Henrik Ibsen, and he felt that *On Trial* was nothing more than skillful stagecraft. He wished to contribute to a serious American theatre and struck out in new directions. With Frank Harris he wrote *The Iron Cross* (1917), a play with a "feminist theme: war seen from a woman's point of view." In 1916 the horrors of child labor which he had witnessed in North Carolina inspired *The House in Blind Alley*. In 1918 *A Diadem of Snow*, a short play about the Russian Revolution, was published in Max Eastman's radical journal, the *Liberator*.

Rice failed to get professional production for any of these plays, but with his eye on a career as well as on artistic success, he pursued concurrently a commercial line of work. In 1919 *For the Defense*, a mystery melodrama with a quasi-legal theme, was produced in New York and had a short run. In 1921 *Wake Up, Jonathan*, a drama written with Hatcher Hughes, was somewhat more popular, and in 1922 *It is the Law*, another mystery melodrama adapted from a story by Hayden Talbot, was a moderate success. Perhaps inevitably, prompted by both financial need and curiosity, Rice also accepted an offer in Hollywood, where he spent two unhappy years under contract to the Goldwyn studio.

Rice reported that he was weighted down with a "feeling of futility and frustration" by the postwar political situation in America and concerned about his work as a creative writer when he was seized with a vision of a new play one night in 1922. "Suddenly, as though a switch had been turned or a curtain raised" he saw a play, "wholly unrelated to anything I had ever consciously thought about." He completed the play in seventeen days. He stated later that *The Adding Machine* (1923) emerged whole, that he never rewrote it.

Rice's most metaphysical play, this expressionistic drama is also his most negative view of the possibility of human life and society. *The Adding Machine*, "a little removed from the road of all Elmer Rice plays," as Meyer Levin noted in 1931, is Rice's 1920s "art-for-art's sake" play, his outcry against the philistinism of American technological culture. In this play the universe is depicted as a mechanistic system, a business, in fact, operated on the principles of efficiency and economy. The Cosmic Fixer explains to the bookkeeper-protagonist, Mr. Zero, that having presided over the demise of the dinosaurs on a cost-efficiency basis, he is now doing away with Zero in like fashion. Zero kills his boss when told that he has been replaced by superior technology, the adding machine. Tried, convicted, executed, and transported to "a pleasant place," Zero finds heaven intolerable because of all the disreputable sorts of people there. A thoroughly degraded being, Zero cannot accept happiness when finally, after a life of frustration, it is available to him.

Perhaps always most successful when he is treating mundane detail, Rice in *The Adding Machine* transforms the trivia of American popular culture in the 1920s into the universe as Zero perceives it. After being sentenced to die for murder, Zero is put in a large cage, and a barker presents him to a crowd as if he were an example of a remarkable species. In a scene based upon the most familiar and commonplace of events, a day with the family at the zoo, Rice captures society's two-pronged impulse: to disassociate itself from a murderer while simultaneously edging closer to the source of the violence. This juxtaposition of the grotesque and the utterly familiar characterizes Rice's approach throughout the play.

Rice's penchant for explicit theoretical exposition, not much noted by critics of this play but so often deplored in his political plays, obtrudes in the final scene. In hell, the obsessive Zero operates an adding machine, but learns that he must return to earth, that his soul is still good for further use. One of the managers of hell, Lieutenant Charles, tediously traces Zero's development from a monkey, to a builder of the pyramids, a rower in the Roman galleys, a potato-digging serf in an iron collar, to his present state as a "bunch of mush." The ponderous effect of this explanation is offset somewhat by the character of Lieutenant Charles, who hates the system he is forced to perpetuate. He symbolizes the corrupt, brutal man who insists on the truth and still has compassion for other losers.

Much of the popularity of *The Adding Machine* is attributable to the range of its satirical tone. Parts of the play, such as the family scenes, have a light, even delicate tone; others, including the trial scene, create what Joseph Wood Krutch described as "the spell of the nightmare." For such a play to contain a wide range of humor is unusual. The graveyard scene, in which souls wander about awaiting their fate, includes such moments of whimsy as mosquitoes troubling the dead (a problem helped some by smoking a Camel cigarette). There are frequent moments of grotesquery, such as the appearance out of a grave of The Head who, disturbed by the noisy corpses in conversation, tosses a skull to chase them away like alley cats. The play also contains broad and bawdy humor. For weeks Zero watched the whore, Judy, undress in the next building at night. He finally reported her to the police under pressure from his jealous wife. When Judy finds Zero's fresh grave, she wishes to entertain her present customer on the newly packed mound as a joke on her betrayer.

Although the original Theatre Guild production in 1923 saw a rather short run and drew some negative critical response, it was referred to as "deeply interesting," "a genuine contribution to American drama," and "the best and fairest example of the newer expressionism." Since the 1920s the popularity of *The Adding Machine* has been immense. Revived in New York, produced successfully in London and Paris, translated into many languages, it has also received innumerable college and university performances. The play has been assessed by critics as "one of the most original plays of the American stage . . . nothing short of brilliant" (John Gassner) and "one of the most penetrating and most critical of the many portraits of the 'little man' so popular in the drama of the twenties" (Alan Downer). It continues to be one of Rice's best-known and most popular plays.

The Adding Machine established Rice's reputation as a serious artist but did not solve his financial problems. Realizing that it would be less expensive to live in Europe than in New York, and wishing no longer to delay that experience, Rice took his family to Paris in the mid-1920s and remained there for several years. Many of his observations in Paris would later form the basis of his play, *The Left Bank*, produced in 1931. The same pattern of work continued. He wrote experimental plays which were turned aside by New York producers, and commercial plays which brought him no satisfaction but provided an income and continuing activity.

Toward the end of the decade, Rice was increasingly unhappy about his career. Feeling that he "lacked the qualifications of a good writer" and finding no other occupation appealing, he decided to settle for regarding writing as a trade, to forego "dreams of excellence and eminence," and "to be content with breadwinning competence." He began work upon *Street Scene*. The play, which was rejected by practically every producer in New York as having no potential, was finally produced in 1929 only because William Brady was desperate for a play with which to make a comeback. The play not only became Rice's greatest hit, but is thought by some to be his greatest artistic achievement. *Street Scene* won for him the Pulitzer Prize in 1929.

Rice stated that the "intended total effect [of *Street Scene*] was a panoramic impression of New York." The entire action takes place in front of an old brownstone apartment building. The tenement serves as a unifying device for a multifaceted plot and as a metaphor for the teeming life of the city. Rice commented on the range of characters, pointing out that his cross section of the lower middle class represented "various national origins, religious faiths, political opinions and degrees of education" and "included shopkeepers, clerks, artisans, students, a schoolteacher, a taxi driver, a musician, janitors, policemen." As in many of Rice's plays, his intention was to capture the whole sweep of life: "birth, death, love in its many aspects, economic problems, ideological conflicts, selfishness, self-sacrifice, kindness, malice, fears, hopes, aspirations." The slice-of-life approach accounts to a large degree for this play's strong appeal. Again Rice's mastery of the commonplace enhances the scenes: neighbors on the front steps engage in gossip; mothers attempt to control their children; young people make love; neighbors scurry frantically to aid the preparations for a birth; a family is evicted, the furniture piled on the sidewalk; or a music lesson is attempted. As Joseph Wood Krutch pointed out, "we have never previously realized just how characteristic these familiar things were."

Although Rice has reported that *Street Scene* was "influenced by the work of the seventeenth century French painter Claude Lorrain," the power of the play lies not in the surface reality, but rather in the intense struggles beneath. Anna Maurrant desperately struggles to find some happiness in life and resorts finally to a sexual affair. The stagehand, Maurrant, sensing his world dissolving, resists by attempting to force his notion of duty and honor upon his disintegrating family. Shirley, the daughter of the old Jewish radical, Kaplan, clings tenaciously to the only security she has, her relationship with her brother Sam. Mrs. Jones appears to have given up finding any happiness, but her resentment and anger force her to exercise gossip as a weapon of great viciousness. In like fashion, the color and accuracy of Rice's dialogue should not obscure the fact that its prime virtue is its activeness. One of the major forces driving the play is its emotional intensity—the snap and the dramatic vitality of the language.

Rice called *Street Scene* the most experimental play he ever wrote. Part of his method was the interweaving of a number of plots involving a large number of characters, a method he was to employ frequently in later plays. The great majority of incidents are short; interest and excitement are created with sharp changes in mood and tempo; gradually a mosaic takes shape as the patterns emerge. But for all the variety, one central melodramatic plot unifies and moves the play. The story—of Anna's love affair, Maurrant's discovery, the double murder, his gunpoint confrontation with his neighbors as he escapes, the arrival of Rose in time to see her mother carried away, Maurrant's capture and his parting from his daughter—develops with broad, theatrical strokes. Joseph Wood Krutch felt that the climax achieved "unusual intensity" in "a scene of violence which made even the hardened playgoer grip his seat and stifle [an] involuntary and agonized" shriek.

In spite of the violence, oppressiveness, and loss in the play, the central idea is one of affirmation. The daughter, Rose, struggles to choose between two men. Her boss promises her a stage career if she becomes his mistress. Sam is willing to forego law school and a career in order to marry her. In the end, Rose realizes that it is wrong for people "to belong to anybody but themselves," and that she must find in herself the strength to live. The idea of the influence of environment upon character plays a role here, and Krutch could even discover an implied "criticism of a society which generates slums and compels human beings to live in them." But Rice emphasizes the notion that not only is happiness possible, but that it is, in large part, a matter of personal choice.

Made into a successful film after its long run, *Street Scene* has remained one of the most popular of American realistic plays. Alan Downer called it "selective realism at its best," and Krutch felt that Rice "never again wrote so good a play." After *Street Scene* Rice himself felt that he could finally begin a serious and satisfying career in the theatre: "*Street Scene* not only solved my economic problems but resolved my doubts as to my place in the theatre. I knew now that I wanted to go on and in which direction."

Street Scene was also important to Rice as his first professional directing experience. Thereafter, he directed all of his own plays, except *The Subway* (1929, which premiered two weeks after *Street Scene*), plus a number of plays by other playwrights including Robert Sherwood, S. N. Behrman, and Maxwell Anderson. In addition, after 1930 he also produced all of his own plays.

Street Scene was followed by the failure of two rather unimportant plays. *The Subway* is of interest now only to specialists, while *See Naples and Die* (1929) has little interest of any kind. His next two plays are of more enduring value, and may, along with *Street Scene* be seen as a step in the development of Rice's social drama. The plays, *The Left Bank* (1931) and *Counsellor-at-Law* (1931), exhibit an increasing awareness of the deepening social crisis at the beginning of the 1930s, but they remain a step removed from the plays of the next stage in Rice's development, the plays of overt political commitment.

Produced two years after the great stock market crash, *The Left Bank* clearly suggested that the country had reached a time for reevaluation, for turning from the childishness of much of the 1920s to face the difficult problems of the 1930s. Claire, the wife of John, an expatriate American writer in Paris, comes to the realization that rebellion was part of her youth, and that now she must "face the realities of . . . life, instead of running away from them." She realizes that John's pose as a rebel is merely an excuse for failure.

It is interesting, however, that the play does not refer specifically to social or political conditions in America. Rather than criticizing America's problems, the play affirms traditional American values. The discredited writer, John, protests that America is unfit for a civilized man to live in, that as a sensitive individual, he cannot tolerate the "buffooneries of a plutocracy." The conservative American, Waldo, conventional and relatively unsophisticated, appears to Claire to be an attractive and mature alternative to John. Waldo demonstrates that although he is simple and unworldly, his virtues of honesty, strength, a capacity to love, responsibility, and common sense are important in building a mature life.

Although the exposure of the expatriate fallacy and the rediscovery and affirmation of traditional American strengths are ideas central to the play, much of the appeal of *The Left Bank*, as in *Street Scene*, lay in the creation of a particular milieu. The depiction of the famous American artist community at play, immersed in free sexual activity and general dissipation, provided the twin pleasures of titillation and morally superior condemnation. In much the way Elizabethan audiences loved images of a distant and exotic orient, American audiences of the 1920s and early 1930s thrilled to images of Paris. Thus, *The Left Bank* operated to a large degree by satisfying an interest in Parisian plumbing and interior decoration, poor telephone service, and excellent wine. In this respect *The Left Bank* marks an advance in Rice's appreciation of—and willingness to use—more sophisticated devices of commercial playwriting.

Counsellor-at-Law opened in November 1931, one month after *The Left Bank*, and it too created with vividness a particular milieu, the hard-driving, cynical world of a successful New York lawyer. This romance of corruption and ambition in a realistic mode abounds with contemporary references such as sudden financial ruin, leaps from high windows, illicit sexual intrigues in high society, conflicts between Communist agitators and police, the difficulties of the poor, and transatlantic cruises by the rich. Specific in its references to the social difficulties of the early 1930s, *Counsellor-at-Law* does not, however, offer a satisfactory critique. Rather the play simply exploits these images for their contemporaneity.

As social drama, *Counsellor-at-Law* is equivocal in the extreme. In one respect George Simon, the counsellor, appears as a kind of anti-business hero. A quasi-Robin Hood, he preys on the rich, who, when caught in foolishness or depravity, require someone smart and tough to rescue them. On the other hand, George (who has fought his way up from poverty) offers free legal aid to the poor. Also the play has certain elements of a class drama as George becomes a victim of class bias and snobbery. Married to a society woman whom he worships, he suffers her rejection, the snubbing of his own children, and finally her sexual betrayal. Furthermore, the technique of using George's office and its switchboard to present American society in microcosm implies that the exposure of George's world amounts to a criticism of the entire society.

Counsellor-at-Law is compromised by its melodramatic exploitation of the sordid characters George traffics with. Deep in his rounds of aiding a "blond bedroom artist" in extortion for breach of promise and obtaining the release of women who murder their husbands, George is distracted by the threat of ruin by a political enemy. George rejects his partner's suggestion that they resort to traditional Sicilian techniques for the solution, but then uses spying, theft, and blackmail to ensure his safety.

As character study or as expose, the play is at least vivid. As a step in Rice's deepening inclination toward social criticism, it is significant. But as social drama intended to change the world, *Counsellor-at-Law* fails. George himself is so deeply implicated in the workings of this world—his struggles are developed so exclusively for their excitement—that in the end the play finally glorifies the cynical, hard-bitten realist who knows that the world is corrupt and plays by its rules. Both *The Left Bank* and *Counsellor-at-Law* were successful in their New York productions, although they received somewhat mixed reviews. Krutch later estimated that *The Left Bank* amounted to only a "rather amusing comedy." *Counsellor-at-Law* was evaluated by John Gassner as a "vivid character study," and Krutch remarked on the "gallery of characters so justly drawn that one recognizes them as exquisitely lifelike."

The success of *Street Scene* and the Pulitzer Prize brought Rice greater prestige as a public figure. Increasingly during the first half of the decade Rice used this influence for political purposes. Both as a member of the American Civil Liberties Union, on whose national board he sat for many years, and as a private citizen, he involved himself in fights against censorship, resistance to Fascism, aid to European refugees fleeing Nazi persecution, and in criticism of militarism and capitalism. Although his position was always independent and always in support of American ideals and democratic traditions, he was sometimes mistaken for a communist. As ardent as he became in his revolutionary stance, however, Rice always carefully avoided doctrinaire approaches to which so many American intellectuals during the period fell prey. Perhaps political plays so unexpectedly strong for Broadway simply shocked some people, for whatever the difficulties with the plays, they were never unclear in their political positions.

Rice's political plays were not intended primarily as commercial entertainment but as social instruments to change the society. Rice, the experimenter, used his plays not for indoctrination but agitation. He stated that he wished to advance no "definite political program," nor could he pretend "that there is any specific remedy which will cure our ills." He did feel, however, that if he could stir people through an appeal to their idealism and humanitarian impulses they could be made to "see in vivid and interesting human terms what may appear dull and uninteresting in the columns of a newspaper." He theorized that a strong emotional release would bring an audience "to a deeper and more vital understanding," that the audience would leave the theatre not only with "a sense of exhilaration" but with "an ordered and coherent picture of what to the spectator outside the theatre seems mere confusion and chaos." This new view, he hoped, would produce political action.

We, the People (1933) attempts to agitate through dramatizing a great number of instances of injustice. In twenty scenes the economic and social breakdown of American society is shown to cause great suffering among the middle and lower classes. The rich, however, go on living luxuriously, seeking to deal with economic collapse by resorting to war, and with social unrest through evasion, propaganda, police violence, and judicial suppression. In spite of the play's focus on a great number of characters involved in several plots, one idea persists: injustice is real and widespread, and the rich will use any means necessary to protect their power while letting the poor suffer. In *We, the People* the intensity of injustice and suffering mounts until it becomes impossible for even those characters most well-disposed toward the establishment to deny the truth any longer. In the last scene, a number of characters from the different plots, radicalized to different degrees but all awakened to the injustice, join to plead for the reestablishment of traditional American democratic principles in order to save the country.

The play's strength lies in the forceful dramatization of intense suffering. In 1933 with the economic crisis deepening, *We, the People* was devastatingly immediate in its depiction of the conflict and frustration within families, the humiliation of working men unable to support their families, the shock at the loss of opportunities for marriage, education, even menial work, and the brutal response to dissidence: careers ruined for voicing dissent, men shot down while demonstrating against labor cutbacks. The play's weakness lies in its diffusion. The number of injustices cited in the dialogue becomes distracting; the minor plots fragment and weaken the action.

The critics cited both these problems, but they were most disturbed that they had encountered a piece of strong political propaganda. Although it is shown in the play that the business community has difficulties, no sympathy is created for these figures because the wealthy pass on the burden of economic difficulties to the poor. In contrast to *Counsellor-at-Law* no powerful figures jump from the windows in this play. However, some of the critics felt that the problems cited in *We, the People* were not worth serious attention. Robert Garland of the *World Telegram* was moved even to insult, referring to "Mr. Rice's sociological jitters." Brooks Atkinson felt that "a good deal of clarity and elemental emotion" had been sacrificed. Paradoxically, he also felt that the play had "much cumulative power." An Associated Press story indicated that in spite of Rice's failure to

Maxwell Anderson, Robert Sherwood, George M. Cohan, and Elmer Rice

produce "an ordered and coherent picture" in the minds of the critics, he was successful in stirring his audience. It was reported that the dialogue twice drew applause "which was replied to with a storm of hisses, and for about half a minute the action of the play was halted until the commotion had subsided." The final curtain, the wire story noted, was met with "such applause as has greeted few Broadway plays this season."

Rice's next play, a courtroom melodrama, *Judgment Day* (1934), unleashed a high-spirited attack upon fascism, and, in contrast to the structure of *We, the People*, was focused on one place and one action. The play exposes the brutality and illegality of a fascist government in its efforts to destroy the People's Party leadership by accusing the party of an attempt upon the Leader's life. The agitational values of external excitements are fully exploited through repeated disturbances of courtroom decorum by George, the heroic young dissenter who repeatedly protests the illegality of the proceedings and denounces the court (once he is dragged off yelling); through an explosion in an adjoining room which, of course, the People's Party is accused of; a

report of several instances of torture and death in the prison; and finally through two shooting deaths at the end of the play. The psychological violence is even more disturbing. Lydia, the young wife of the Party Leader, is falsely accused of bribing an official with offers of sex and of an illicit relationship with George. Her daughter is mentally tortured on the stand and finally viciously told that her father is dead. Rakovski, the Minister of Culture and Enlightenment, violates the sanctity of the judges' room and demands that the judges capitulate to the government's wishes to destroy the dissenters. The government breaches all principles of justice with false charges and repeated lies by bribed witnesses.

The play unapologetically propagandizes by identifying and attacking an enemy. The fascists embody unrelieved malignancy and the dissenters unblemished heroism. The production was pitched at a high emotional key and succeeded as intended. In Krutch's opinion, *Judgment Day* administered a "good sound beating . . . to the nerves of the spectator." It met with a mixed critical reception. Atkinson called it "a pretty clumsy play" and felt, somewhat remarkably, since the play is anything but unclear, that it was "difficult to decide what Elmer Rice is up to in *Judgment Day*." Gilbert Seldes wrote that "out of sheer excitement" he had had his "faith in the theatre restored." Seldes, who was familiar with Douglas Reed's *The Burning of the Reichstag* upon which the play was based, also thought, contrary to a number of complaints about the excesses of the play, that "the play actually stays way behind the mad extravagances of the actual trial." The play enjoyed a successful run in London several years later.

As *We, the People* and *Judgment Day* respond to capitalism and fascism, respectively, the next play Rice produced, *Between Two Worlds* (1934), responds to communism. The action takes place on a ship between New York and Europe and centers upon the confrontation between American and Russian points of view. The young socialite, Margaret, aimless and pampered, encounters the brutal but vital and realistic Russian revolutionary, Kovolev. Their brief sexual involvement constitutes the central dramatic event, but it is too weak to support the play's ideological conflict. The many minor plots intermingle in a delicate rhythm to contrast both the weakness of the misled but essentially sound American culture and the brutality of the vital Russian culture. The conclusion suggests a more viable future, if America can learn from the realistic outlook and strength of purpose of the revolution. The play contains a number of excellent, if not profound, characterizations, but the failure to fully dramatize the central conflict weakens the play. *Between Two Worlds* received almost unanimously negative reviews and closed after a four-week run.

Rice's political plays become more understandable in their proper context of the larger political action which occupied Rice throughout the 1930s. In the course of his efforts as a political activist, he articulated a social vision, including the relationship which he saw the theatre might have to a new society. He maintained that the source of the world's social and political difficulties was capitalism. He stated explicitly that he believed that peace in the world would be impossible "until economic nationalism and imperialist aggression have been rooted out." He called for nothing short of the "overthrow of the capitalist system and the substitution of some form of collectivism." Such ideas from a Broadway playwright, understandably, were met with alarm. But Rice was equally clear about the means which he felt were appropriate and acceptable for the accomplishment of the

new order. He believed that once aroused, the large body of people who desired a better world would find American democratic structures suitable to effect an evolution from capitalism to advanced socialism. He did not rule out the need for violence in nondemocratic countries, but he rejected its use in democratic states.

Rice was equally explicit in his statements about the theatre. He wrote that the American theatre was characterized by "crass and shallow worldly wisdom," "naive and banal sentimentality," and "snobbishness and callous flippancy." The theatre, he said, was "in the hands of businessmen, of real estate operators and entrepreneurs" whose only interest was to make money. He envisioned healthier possibilities, and in 1933 he wrote a major article for the *New York Times*, "Project for a New Theatre," in which he set out the relationship which he felt could be established between the society and art, between the artist and society, and between the audience and the theatre. He rejected the elitist status of art, "the art of the cloistered few, the art of a handful of specialists that smells of the lamp and bears the thumbprints of the academy," stating that art should instead function in society as a replacement for a broken church, an art which has "rediscovered its essentially religious origins." As for the artist's relationship to society, Rice believed that the artist should be dragged "into the forum, face to face with his time." He diagnosed the artist's present detachment from society as a result of the loss of the function of art. The artist, he claimed, "finds himself cut off from the main stream of society and to his bewilderment and chagrin is forced to exercise his creative gifts in a secluded and stagnant backwater." If his art had to face radical exposure to "the vulgar and skeptical gaze of the illiterate," the artist might again "learn to listen to the rhythm of the arena." The relationship of the audience to the theatre must also change, Rice believed. He deplored the fact that the theatres in New York reached less than ten percent of the potential audience, and insisted upon the need for the theatre to be accessible to the whole society, with the highest priced tickets fixed at one dollar. Although aware of the need to avoid a doctrinaire philosophy, Rice maintained that a serious audience could be attracted to a theatre whose general policy favored "the establishment of a new social order in which existing economic and social injustice is eliminated." Furthermore, a broader involvement of the audience in the life and activities of the theatre would be sought by serving as "the cultural centre of the community," providing a site for a wide range of nontheatrical, social, and political activities. Thus Rice proposed that the playwright should function not as an entertainer but as a political activist with a broad social vision. He viewed his plays as social instruments intended to affect national political policy.

An unfortunate controversy with the New York critics followed the failure of *Between Two Worlds*. In a speech at Columbia University, Rice, in some offhand indiscreet remarks, attacked the critics as incompetent on both professional and personal grounds. Although many of Rice's objections were valid, he expressed himself so vehemently that the notion that he was simply picqued at the reception of his plays has persisted. He announced that he was retiring from Broadway and possibly from writing plays altogether. He did withdraw from Broadway and did not produce another play until 1938, but his theatrical activities continued unabated. In 1935 Rice promoted among a number of prominent theatre artists an idea for a new organization. The Theatre Alliance was formed, and plans were developed for a company which could put into practice the ideas which Rice had outlined two years before. The organization did not receive the necessary federal support, and Rice shifted his energies to the Federal Theatre Project. Rice was involved in very early conversations with Hallie Flanagan, National Director of the Federal Theatre Project, about its goals and organization. Although he was wary about the possibility of bureaucratic interference in the work, he accepted the directorship of the New York project late in 1935. After repeated frustrations, Rice resigned in protest over the censorship of the first production of the living newspaper (a dramatization of a news story), *Ethiopia*, in January 1936. In 1938 he organized a continuing production group, the Playwrights' Company, with Maxwell Anderson, Sidney Kingsley, S. N. Behrman, and Robert Sherwood. Although the company did not realize many of Rice's idealistic goals, it provided another means to continue his efforts, and it became a major theatrical force in New York.

As the threat of fascism grew in Europe Rice's political goals shifted. In the early 1930s his goal was the establishment of a new world order, one which he felt was imminent and which would be brought about by the united efforts of concerned people. The tactic during this period was primarily one of criticism and attack in order to educate and to rally the forces for change. *We, the People*, *Judgment Day*,

and to a degree, *Between Two Worlds*, are part of this effort. But in the late 1930s, it became clear to Rice that the most important goal was the protection of democracy. To this end he employed symbols which would make understandable to Americans the traditions and institutions of American democracy which were being threatened both from abroad and from within.

As part of his new political effort Rice wrote *American Landscape* (1938). The slight plot involves the gathering of a New England family, including the ghosts of the ancestors, to meet a family crisis. Frank Dale, the grandfather, is ready to sell the family factory to a large concern which will close it to remove the competition. Frank is inclined to sell the ancestral house to a German-American organization which will use it for a Nazi youth camp. Before he can decide, he suffers a heart attack and dies. In his will he leaves the business to his children who now propose to fight for the family's American traditions.

Capitalism and fascism are described as twin threats to the American tradition, with the greater emphasis upon fascism. The solution is to rally round traditional ideals, throw off distraction and sloth, and give the most vital elements in the society, represented by the young people, a chance to reestablish a healthy situation. The play suggests no program, but hints that vigor and unionization will play a large part.

The ancestral ghosts play a large role in the family's deliberations throughout the play. Their presence emphasizes that a family's tradition and accumulated experience both provide aid and make claims in the present. The device operates to amplify family bonds and embodies traditional values which conflict with present trends and ideas. But as John Gassner commented, "the imaginative device of bringing ancestral apparitions on the stage was not sufficiently primed for successful operation." The general conclusion of the critics was that the play was static.

In *American Landscape* Rice addressed the danger of fascism, but he viewed it as a local danger, one that comes from within. By 1939 the situation was looking more grave. Malcolm Goldstein has noted in *The Political Stage* (1974) that Rice's next play, *Two on an Island* (1940), "curiously . . . contains no mention of the war." His explanation is that Rice "was too appalled by the prospect of a second global holocaust to take immediate notice of it in his writing." In the summer of 1940, with the air attack on Britain underway, Rice still could not overcome his pacifist convictions to sign a plea for American military intervention which Robert Sherwood published as a full-page advertisement in the *New York Times* under the title "Stop Hitler Now." But by the end of the year Rice had changed his mind.

Flight to the West, which opened in December 1940, is a pro-war play. The struggle of two pacifists, one a young Jew, the other an older liberal writer, comprises the central action. They confront the true nature of the enemy and decide that they must oppose fascism with force if democracy is to survive. In his usual fashion, Rice combines a number of plots which in this play fuse to make the central confrontation of the play that of fascism and democracy. A mystery plot hinges on the discovery and entrapment of two agents: the German diplomat, Walther, is passing instructions to a disguised German agent, Vronoff, who intends to conduct subversive activities in California. A revenge plot revolves around the realization by Marie, the Belgian exile, that Walther commanded the German artillery battery which destroyed the city of Louvain, killing her family. A love story develops the conflict between Charles, a young Jew, and his wife, Hope, when she learns that he is considering becoming a military pilot just as she is struggling with the fear of bringing a child into a torn world. The decisive moment arrives when Marie attempts to shoot Walther, and Charles saves him by stopping the bullet with his own body. The debate which follows elucidates the meaning of Charles's act as an irrational sanity which affirms the value of life in contrast to the rational madness of the Nazis.

Rice's skill as a commercial playwright is evident in the manipulation of the play's dramatic techniques, such as Marie's seizures of hatred, the attempted murder, the secret conversations involving codes and subversive plots, and in the cluster of theatrical events inherent in developing the central metaphor of the play: the airplane flight from Europe to America, including the sighting of points along the Atlantic route, and radio messages. All of the dramatic and theatrical elements, however, support the strong propagandistic emphasis in the play upon the fraternal connections between the British and the Americans, the Jew as a fighter for American values, the activities of the American businessman to appease Hitler while collecting a fortune, the savagery of the Nazis as an attack upon civilization itself, the revelation of German subversion in the United States, and, of course, the conversion of the liberals to a pro-war position.

Rice attempted to present the political con-

flicts in a comprehensible, immediate way and to find symbols which would affirm the traditions of America from which he felt the nation must draw its strength. Like *The Adding Machine*, *Between Two Worlds*, and *Two on an Island*, *Flight to the West* is a pilgrimage play. The airplane journey leads to a new political position. Also, as in a number of his plays, such as *Street Scene*, *Counsellor-at-Law*, and *Between Two Worlds*, Rice develops a world in microcosm through the use of the airplane as a unifying device. Toward the end of the flight various plots fuse as all the sympathetic characters unite against the Nazis. The journey becomes a contemporary reenactment of the voyage to the New World and a call for a militant reaffirmation of New World democratic values and strengths.

Rice's support of the war which included service on the advisory council of the Writer's War Board, and articles and speeches in support of Roosevelt and the war effort in general, as well as this pro-interventionist play, was a source of some difficulty to Rice, who had been a pacifist for thirty years. His private papers contain manuscripts of short pieces on the war which are strained in their efforts to both support the war effort and yet resist its attendant racial hatred, violence, and the curtailment of civil liberties.

Rice wrote one other play with political implications during the war, *A New Life* (1943), which strongly asserted that while freedom and independence were worth fighting for, capitalism and a government controlled by minority interests were not. But during World War II reservation of this sort was likely to be ignored, and the attempts to find devices to make the play more popular such as a love story, highly colloquial language, a variety of types of characters, and even an exceptional scene of an onstage birth did little to make for success. It is possible that Rice's own ambivalence contributed to the difficulties. Whatever the case, the result was a minor play.

Rice also had more personal matters on his mind. He had finally divorced his first wife long after their marriage had become simply a formality and had wed the beautiful and talented actress Betty Field in 1942. He later confessed that his "new-found happiness" took much of his attention from the political questions which had previously absorbed him. He wrote: "I was not indifferent to world events, nor had my loathing of war abated; but I was not as wrought up as I had been twenty-five years earlier." Although he claimed that he did not write the play specifically for Betty Field, *Dream*

Girl (1945) is certainly an expression of his new happiness, and it provided Field with a virtuoso role.

In *Dream Girl* Rice returned to expressionist techniques with which the main character acts out her fantasies. The play is strictly an entertainment piece, but it is executed with such exuberance and developed with dialogue so sharp, bright, idiomatic, and alive that *Dream Girl* has become one of Rice's best known plays. The comedy takes place during one day in Georgina's life. Her brother-in-law, with whom she believes herself to be in love, learns that his wife is leaving him and asks Georgina to marry him. A businessman invites her to spend a week with him in Mexico. A brash newspaperman woos and wins her from her fantasies and marries her. This event-packed day is intensified by Georgina's fantasies, into which the immature girl escapes at every available moment. She sees herself on a radio show trying to solve the problem of her "incestuous" love; in a hospital to be recognized as the true, spiritual mother of her brother-in-law's twins; in court where she is acquitted by an admiring jury for murdering the newspaperman who had criticized her writing; in Mexico for an illicit affair with a moral ending; and in the streets as a whore scornful of the world. The fantasies and reality converge when the newspaperman shows her how to live with him in a tougher but more rewarding world.

The New York critics were ecstatic over the play, commenting on its "charm," "wit," "gaiety," and "gusto," and announcing that Georgina was a "penetrating portrait." Krutch thought it a "very agreeable divertissement" and commented that "Mr. Rice's farce-comedies . . . [are] cheery, fundamentally wholesome, and rather more thoroughly American than a good deal of what passes for American Comedy."

Rice never again had much success with a new play and after the early 1940s he kept his political activity and his playwriting separate. Of the plays produced in New York in the 1950s, *Not For Children* (1951), which had been written in the 1930s, was badly received. *The Grand Tour* (1951), *The Winner* (1954), and *Cue For Passion* (1958) demonstrate some of the technical proficiency for which Rice is noted but failed to please the critics, find an audience, or prove to be of an enduring interest. Rice continued to work in the American Civil Liberties Union, to fight against censorship, to appear on lists of dangerous radicals, and to produce and direct with the Playwrights' Company. Although he was remarkably active through the last years of his life,

the period between the early 1920s and the middle 1940s remains the most productive and important part of his life during which he made a significant contribution to the American theatre's efforts to forge a vital relationship to the society.

Screenplays:
Help Yourself, adapted from Wallace Irwin's "Trimmed in Red," Goldwyn, 1920;
Doubling for Romeo, Goldwyn, 1921;
Street Scene, United Artists, 1931;
Counsellor-at-Law, Universal, 1933.

Other:
A Diadem of Snow in *One-Act Plays for Stage and Study*, 5th series, edited with an introduction by Rice (New York: French, 1929);
The Gay White Way in *One-Act Plays for Stage and Study*, 8th series (New York: French, 1934).

Periodical Publications:
"The Playwright as Director," *Theatre Arts Monthly*, 13 (May 1929): 355-360;
"Toward an Adult Theatre," *Drama Magazine*, 25 (February 1931):5;
"Project for a New Theatre," *New York Times*, 8 October 1933, X: 1;
"Elmer Rice Says Farewell to Broadway," *New York Times*, 11 November 1934, IX: 1, 3;
"Theatre Alliance," *Theatre Arts Monthly*, 19 (June 1935): 427-430;
"Apologia Pro Vita Sua, Per Elmer Rice," *New York Times*, 25 December 1938, IX: 3.

References:
Alan S. Downer, *Fifty Years of American Drama* (Chicago: Regnery, 1951);
Frank Durham, *Elmer Rice* (New York: Twayne, 1970);
John Gassner, *Masters of Drama* (New York: Dove, 1954);
Malcolm Goldstein, *The Political Stage* (New York: Oxford University Press, 1974);
Robert Hogan, *The Independence of Elmer Rice* (Carbondale & Edwardsville: Southern Illinois University Press, 1965);
Joseph Wood Krutch, *The American Drama Since 1918* (New York: Random House, 1939);
Meyer Levin, "Elmer Rice," *Theatre Arts*, 16 (January 1932): 54-62;
Gerald Rabkin, *Drama Commitment: Politics in the American Theatre of the Thirties* (Bloomington: Indiana University Press, 1964).

Papers:
Rice's manuscripts and personal papers, including correspondence, financial records, and theatrical scrapbooks, form the Elmer Rice Collection in the Humanities Research Center, the University of Texas at Austin.

JACK RICHARDSON
(18 February 1935-)

PRODUCTIONS: *The Prodigal*, 11 February 1960, Downtown Theatre, New York, 167 [performances];

Gallows Humor, 18 April 1961, Gramercy Arts Theatre, New York, 40;

Lorenzo, 14 February 1963, Plymouth Theatre, New York, 4;

Xmas in Las Vegas, 4 November 1965, Ethel Barrymore Theatre, New York, 4;

As Happy As Kings, 16 March 1968, New Theatre Workshop, New York, 3.

BOOKS: *The Prodigal* (New York: Dutton, 1960);

Gallows Humor (New York: Dutton, 1961);

The Prison Life of Harris Filmore (London: Eyre & Spottiswoode, 1961; Greenwich, Conn.: New York Graphic Society, 1963);

Xmas in Las Vegas (New York: Dramatists Play Service, 1966);

Memoir of a Gambler (New York: Simon & Schuster, 1979).

Jack Richardson's most significant contribution to American drama has been his iconoclastic experimentation with paradox and such various elements of the theatre as existential situations, myth, historical settings, realistic staging techniques, the conventions of the morality play, and bizarre characters. Richardson is one of the few talented individuals who utilized the exhortation for rebellion and experimentation from the 1960s to produce a brand of theatre that is both good and unique.

Jack Carter Richardson was born to Arthur and Marjorie Richardson in New York City. Immediately after graduation in 1951 from Collegiate School, a high school in New York City, he acted in summer stock at the Grist Mill Playhouse in Andover, New Jersey, and in the fall studied acting for three months at the American Theatre Wing in New York. He found, though, that his talent was limited. He enlisted in the army, where he served from 1951 to 1954 and was stationed in Korea, Frankfurt, and Paris (where he took courses at the University of Paris). He completed a B.A., cum laude, in philosophy at Columbia University in two and one half years (1954-1957) and was elected to Phi Beta Kappa. An Adenauer Fellowship for Germanic studies allowed him to do graduate work in Munich on the German existential philosophers. While in Munich, he lectured in German on William James and Dewey. In 1957 Richardson married Anne Grail Roth; they have one child, Emily. Before returning to the United States in 1958, he completed his first play, *The Prodigal*.

Between 1958 and 1965, he devoted himself to the theatre. The Off-Broadway production of *The Prodigal* in 1960 won him immediate praise and international recognition and evoked enthusiastic statements about his promise as one of America's leading playwrights. He received the Vernon Rice Award and an Obie for *The Prodigal* and was later awarded a Guggenheim Fellowship (1963) and a Brandeis University Creative Writing Award (1963). Walter Kerr called *The Prodigal* "a permanent contribution to the contemporary theatre," while George Wellwarth said, without qualification, that it was "undoubtedly the most brilliantly written new American play to come out since the end of World War II." Richardson's second play, *Gallows Humor* (1961), did well also, although the praise was occasionally qualified. Such positive response augured a long career in the theatre.

However, when Richardson wrote two plays, *Lorenzo* (1963) and *Xmas in Las Vegas* (1965), that were not on a par with *The Prodigal* and *Gallows Humor*, critical reaction was extremely harsh, so that by 1966 he had decided not to continue writing plays. Robert Coleman said, for example, that "'Lorenzo' isn't a lengthy play, it just seems that way," and *Time*'s critic accused Richardson of having "glutted the Broadway commodity exchange with pretentious bosh delivered in bloated rhetoric." One other play, written in the early 1960s, was produced nonprofessionally in 1968.

Since 1965, Richardson has written no new plays and has concentrated instead on other genres. An autobiographical novel, *Memoir of a Gambler*, appeared in 1979, but he has written mostly dramatic and literary criticism. In 1966, he became the regular theatre critic and sometime essayist for *Commentary* (contributing from two to six articles each year). He has also contributed to *New World Writing*, *Theatre Arts*, *Botteghe Oscure*, *Transatlantic Review*, *Show*, *Second Coming*, *Esquire*, *Harper's*, *New*

York Review of Books, the *New York Times Book Review*, and *Playboy*. He acknowledges having been influenced by Shaw, Mann, and Chekhov. His name has been mentioned in conjunction with those of Sartre, Beckett, Anouilh, Genet, Dürrenmatt, and Frisch. But he is, he says, "anti-Sartre" (despite the fact that Richardson's *The Prodigal*, like Sartre's *Les Mouches*, recasts the myth of Orestes) and he disagrees with the other writers on substantial issues. It is evident, though, that he has read these playwrights and has absorbed many of their existential concerns.

In *The Prodigal*, Richardson deals with the classical myth of Orestes' reaction when his father, Agamemnon, returns home to Greece—by posing an existential "situation" in which an individual must choose between two difficult options. Orestes is torn between antithetical forces: history (which dictates that he avenge his father's murder by Clytemnestra, Orestes' mother) and his personal desire to remain uncommitted. Much like modern man he has begun to perceive the weaknesses in the old, heroic conception of man (represented by Agamemnon, the individualistic warrior-hero who willingly sacrifices his daughter and Orestes' sister, Iphigenia, in order to inspire his men). On the other hand, Orestes dislikes with equal intensity the alternatives of acquiescence (represented by Aegisthus, the weak bureaucrat who has no individual will) and indifference. Consequently, Orestes seeks to withdraw into personal concerns. He struggles to exert his own will but eventually capitulates to his historical destiny when he and his sister Electra kill their mother.

Richardson's accomplishment in *The Prodigal* is substantial. He has said that he was trying "somehow to bring ideas and characters together in a manner which gave both more importance than could be hoped for from the naturalistic stage." He succeeded in his goal because, in addition to introducing lucid discussion of ideas, he uses myth to create vital characters who enact the theoretical issues under debate. Gerald Weales has commented that Richardson created nothing more than "perambulating points of view," but Weales can make this statement only by overlooking significant elements of the play. For example, Orestes highlights the impersonal, more-than-human aspect of the old conception of man when he violently rejects Agamemnon—as a father, not as a hero—for having sacrificed Iphigenia in the name of the heroic code. Agamemnon, in turn, brings the theoretical controversy to life in dramatic terms when he responds to his family's rejection with bewilderment—a stageable human emotion (he expected to

return with glory for having fulfilled the code, only to find that his son hates him and that his wife has taken a lover).

Despite the brilliance of the play, a number of features—the existential dilemma, the sharp distinctions between old and new conceptions of man, the frequent statements by Orestes that he wishes to remain uninvolved—led a number of critics, including Martin Esslin and Alan Downer, to associate Richardson with existentialist or absurdist values. This reaction is understandable but incorrect. Some existentialists create characters who are guilty of "bad faith" as negative models in order to provoke readers into a realization that the character's life is unacceptable by existential standards. However, an author may have a different intent when he depicts an existential failure: he may believe that man, regardless of how much he desires choice, is not capable of exercising freedom effectively. Such seems to be the case in *The Prodigal*. Richardson rejects the notion that his work is existentialist or absurdist, indicating in a self-interview that he belongs to no "school" and that he is more concerned with posing paradoxes which reveal the complexity of human experience.

Richardson also differs from the existentialists in the measure of his active concern with a large historical and social context. While Sartre, Beckett, and Camus allude to the individual's responsibility in a larger framework, their chief priority is unquestionably the individual's struggle with himself; history provides a background or vehicle for exposition of the individual's plight. In *The Prodigal*, Richardson's concern for historical issues and events is as important as his concern for the individual's dilemma. He is interested in Orestes' choice among Agamemnon, Aegisthus, and studied indifference, but he is equally concerned with man's changing conception of his limitations and with the role history plays in this situation.

Richardson disagrees with his contemporaries on one final point. Even though he believes that paradox is a condition of life, he disagrees with thinkers who contend that meaning is inaccessible, and he will not, as the absurdist playwrights do, condemn all conventional forms (plot, character depth, and language). He notes: "Now as much as a man dislikes being called an anachronism in his own lifetime, I must admit the new forms . . . hold little interest for me." He admires the plays of Beckett and Genet but says: "Their worlds, however, are not mine." Thus, Richardson uses normal structure, logical language, and straightforward argumentation, and he strives for clarity.

Though the critics (especially George Wellwarth) generally liked the play, virtually none of them understood Richardson's philosophical position thoroughly. The one exception was a French reader, Gilbert Debusscher, who advanced a cogent argument that Richardson should be considered one of America's leading playwrights. However, since Debusscher's article, published in *Revue des Langues Vivantes* (1971), has not been translated, it has had little effect on American critics

Jack Richardson

or the American reading public. When Richardson ceased to write plays, *The Prodigal* slipped into obscurity, even though literary biographers continue to express admiration for it.

Gallows Humor, like its predecessor, presents a thought-provoking "situation." The play opens with a prologue by the character Death (reminiscent of the medieval morality play) about the present-day difficulties in distinguishing the dead from the "living dead." Richardson presents practical examples of the difficulty when Walter, a murderer awaiting execution, and Phillip, his executioner, experience existential crises and nausea—the result of a realization that the law and habitual activity are

deadening. Prior to the action of the play, Walter's rebellion against the order in his life and the illogicality of the law has prompted him to murder his wife. In part 1, he is on death row preparing himself for execution. While in prison he has returned to the law with a vengeance, by establishing an obsessive routine that will render choice unnecessary and spontaneity impossible. In the figurative sense, he has died before the execution and so anticipates no difficulty in coping with the event. Only hours before the execution, though, in order to counter complaints about the cruelty of capital punishment, the warden provides Walter with a prostitute, Lucy. This intrusion, much to Walter's horror, threatens to make him live again, as he did during the murder. He resists Lucy's concerted attempt to make him enjoy her services, but eventually he chooses the play's life force—Lucy. This segment of the play seems to present a standard existential argument: most persons become so mired in "the law" and social propriety that they lose sight of their individual identities, but here one individual chooses to "live." Taken alone, the conclusion suggests that man is capable of living well in an existential sense, even if only momentarily.

Part 2 of the play upsets neat assumptions that this work is to provide an airtight argument for existential values. The second segment shocks the audience immediately because Phillip (the executioner) and Martha (his wife) are played by the actors who had assumed the roles of Walter and Lucy in part 1. Death's introductory comment about having difficulty distinguishing the hangman from the hanged becomes deliciously ironic: the hangman and the victim are, in fact, indistinguishable visually. The executioner's crisis arises after he has lived most of his life in a deadening routine. His initial attempt at "living" occurs when he asks the warden if he might wear a black mask (i.e., establish his identity) at Walter's execution. Wearing the mask is a shocking violation of contemporary standards (the executioner should not—in the 1960s—look like one). Phillip establishes an identity as a rebel by attempting to wear the mask. The crisis is complicated shortly after Phillip's request when he discovers his wife and the warden in a passionate embrace (they, too, are living for the first time). Martha's infidelity prompts him to make an attempt to leave her. She reacts to his threatened revolt with such disdain that he tries to murder her, but he is unable to do so. As the play closes, he has capitulated to the old life and has become an existential failure.

There are a number of deliberate parallels

between Walter's and Phillip's situations (lives dominated by mind-numbing habit, dissolution of orderly existence, and a murder attempt), but the results are essentially different: Walter succeeds in living while Phillip does not. The significance of Walter's success is diminished, of course, by the fact that it occurs only moments before the execution, so that he gains no opportunity to "live" outside the confines of the death-conferring prison. Thus, despite existential elements, Richardson refuses to confirm the existential code in this play. On the other hand, it is not antiexistential either, because Walter does "live" temporarily. The play poses questions and provokes thought, but Richardson refuses to offer solutions, suggesting only that success and failure, living and dying, are inextricably bound together, a point that is reflected in the mixed form of the play (a tragicomedy).

Although the juxtaposition of the two perspectives—condemned man and his executioner—is striking, *Gallows Humor* is, in one regard, not as powerful as *The Prodigal*. The first existential crisis, which led to Walter's murderous act, is presented through exposition (a flashback) instead of dramatic action. Nevertheless, two visual aspects of the play significantly bolster the dramatic potential. Most important is the shock that derives from the role doubling, a constant reminder to the audience that each man simultaneously harbors both life and death principles within himself (the potential to live a significant life or to live an ordered but meaningless routine). The second noteworthy visual element is the dramatic potential that Lucy provides in part 1 as she begins undressing to entice Walter into bed with her. The spoken lines of enticement are minimal, but, given a sensitive performance, this element of the play effectively engages the audience in Walter's crisis over whether or not to live well in his final moments.

While the topic of this play is similar to that of *The Prodigal*, in *Gallows Humor* Richardson presents significant variations. He alters the form from myth to an updated version of the morality play and shifts from concern with historical issues to the problems of an unheroic, private individual who feels trapped by the trivia of daily life. He also complicates the philosophical dilemma by juxtaposing a character who seems to be an existential success with one who fails.

The critical response to *Gallows Humor* was generally favorable, but the somewhat misguided, negative perceptions were sounded. Harold Taubman praised the work, noting that Richardson's "inventions are spirited and his observations pene-

trating," but Harold Clurman complained, as did others, that he detected a "certain forcing, a willful deliberation of the mind rather than a spontaneous expression of the spirit." Gerald Weales also bemoaned the fact that the play's simple point "is smothered in repetition that would be bearable only if the lines were much funnier than they are." Weales seems to miss the point of the play with this objection—these lives *are* nauseatingly repetitious and while there are comic elements in the situation, the play is not primarily comedy because Richardson intends that the repetition, indeed, become unbearable. In spite of these few negative reactions, the play succeeded, and Richardson was able to rally support for a Broadway debut of his next effort.

Lorenzo reached Broadway and won Richardson an award from *Saturday Review* (runner-up, Most Promising Playwright—Broadway Debut, 1962-1963), but Richardson knew that the play was unlikely to succeed either critically or financially. The commercial failure of this effort was to have a devastating effect on Richardson's dramatic career. An intellectual history play set in central Italy during the Renaissance, Richardson's third dramatic offering does not provide diversions such as the powerful, immediate conflict in *The Prodigal* or the comic elements in *Gallows Humor*. Lorenzo, the leader of an itinerant dramatic troupe, contends that art can exist apart from political issues (specifically, military conflict). Philippo, a naive idealist, also believes that he can prompt social change without his being tainted by the military/political force necessary to bring it about. Both men learn through painful lessons administered by the powerful General Van Miessen that such is not the case. Just as it seems that the play will end on a pessimistic note, with art and idealism thoroughly discredited as potent social forces, Lorenzo's son, Giorgio, returns to assert that while art may not exist aloof from all of history's negative, violent manifestations, it serves an important function by helping man make sense of his own actions and by providing continuity. Richardson's point is that man must discard sentimental, unduly optimistic appraisals of his abilities without capitulating to cynicism and degradation. The playwright's solution is tempered, mature art.

Richardson raises a set of serious, interesting questions in *Lorenzo*, and before the play ends, he creates several powerful characters (Van Miessen, Lorenzo, and Giorgio) and an engaging conflict. There are two major problems, though: several characters remain shadowy (Ricardo and Philippo) and the intellectual conflict emerges long before the dramatic, visual conflict. The emotional conflict does not develop, even in nascent form, until the third scene, and it only becomes compelling at the end of act 1 (more than halfway through the play). The long, abstract discussions of the relation between art and life, occurring early in the play before the audience fully understands their purpose, fail to engage the listener, while the arresting emotional conflict develops too late to salvage the play. The play's material is worthwhile; perhaps had Richardson rearranged the sequence in which he presented dramatic and intellectual issues, the drama might have fared better with the public. John McClain and George Wellwarth liked *Lorenzo*, while Frederick Lumley, Henry Hewes, and the *Newsweek* critic credited Richardson with a valiant, if flawed, attempt to create serious, intellectual drama for Broadway. Most of the critics, though, especially powerful voices such as Walter Kerr's, were negative, with several asking when Richardson would develop from a playwright with enormous potential into one who was accomplished.

Broadway backers retained sufficient confidence in Richardson's commercial appeal to support a production of *Xmas in Las Vegas*, but the play failed miserably. *Xmas in Las Vegas* is about a hapless gambler, Edward Wellspot, who drags his family to Las Vegas each year (seventeen times now) to be with him while he challenges fate and seeks to become fabulously wealthy. The annual trip functions as an ironic, almost cruel, inversion of the American dream (symptomatic of contemporary disillusionment with the dream), because instead of trusting in hard work and self-reliance, father Wellspot (passively waiting for success) trusts that a once-a-year bout with fate will suffice. Of course it never does.

The play includes a curious mixture of traditional and experimental devices. Richardson employs a standard plot, normal language, and conventional staging, but he incorporates implausible events and characters who are bizarre, one-dimensional caricatures. For example, the father is a schlemiel who never loses hope; his wife, Eleanor, mindlessly follows him but is humorously afflicted with visions of pornographic angels whenever Edward loses at gambling (a rebuke from the Episcopal Church); and their daughter, Emily, who has failed in four marriages, sleeps almost all of the time (loss of hope). If the audience accepts these characters as humorous caricatures, they can be effective, but if the viewer requires plausible characters who display complex emotions and evoke empathy from the audience, this group fails ignobly. Richardson,

ahead of his time, did not find many critics who were taken by the Wellspot menagerie.

In spite of the unusual characterization, the play might have survived had the dramatic conflict been handled more effectively. Unfortunately, Richardson develops the decisive confrontation between Edward Wellspot and fate very late in the play, without building sufficient interest or suspense prior to this scene. As a result, the early portion of the play seems to consist of little more than the aimless utterances and shenanigans of some very strange individuals (only later does the reader learn their significance). When the confrontation culminates in Edward's ignominious defeat, an experience that breaks his spirit just as he thought that he was graced with a magnificent winning streak, the event ironically precipitates two promising developments: the casino owner, Olympus, offers to marry Emily, and Lionel, the son who had until this point accomplished little beyond periodic suicide attempts, assumes his father's optimism, symbolizing that hope will persist even if fate crushes a hardy, albeit hapless, individual such as Edward Wellspot.

The play's ending generated controversy (some critics dubbing it implausible and some inappropriate), but given Richardson's belief that life is a gamble and that gambling, a chaotic act, allows man to live as he seldom does when meandering through his oppressive daily routine, the ending makes sense. The question, then, is not whether the ending is appropriate but whether the audience agrees with Richardson's philosophy that gambling can constitute a state of grace.

Critical reaction to *Xmas in Las Vegas* was vitriolic. Kerr, Watts, Taubman, the *New Yorker* critic, and a few others panned the play so thoroughly that it did not receive many other reviews. John McClain, a former supporter, said bluntly: "There is almost no excuse for *Xmas in Las Vegas*." Wilfred Sheed suggested, astutely, that perhaps the material would be more effective in novel form. (*Memoir of a Gambler* illustrates Sheed's point.) Shortly after the failure of *Xmas in Las Vegas*, Richardson stopped writing plays. He had written another play in the early 1960s, *As Happy As Kings*, about a Mrs. Dartonian, who tries to persuade her son that life is worth living (he wants to commit suicide as his father had). Although the play was produced nonprofessionally in 1968, it never received serious attention (Off-Broadway production, publication, or reviews).

Richardson has also written a screenplay and two novels. The screenplay *Juan Feldman*, is a light satire on liberal attitudes from the 1960s about cultural deprivation. The novels, *The Prison Life of Harris Filmore* (1961) and *Memoir of a Gambler*, on the other hand, are substantial. The plot and theme of *The Prison Life of Harris Filmore* are similar to those of *Gallows Humor*: a man who has lived with rules and customs as though they were "necessary conditions, without which living would be disastrous," commits a crime—embezzlement, his one act of rebellion— and discovers, once convicted, that he likes the determined existence of prison life better than life in the chaotic, freedom-burdened, outside world. The tone in this novel, though, is different from that in *Gallows Humor* because it is primarily satirical and humorous. Occasionally, intrusive narrative comments mar the satirical tone of *The Prison Life of Harris Filmore*; for the most part, though, it is an interesting variation on Richardson's main theme. The novel did not attract a great deal of attention, but the *Times Literary Supplement* offered a positive review, noting that, unlike many satires, this is an "extremely funny book, in which the background is sufficiently well described to be convincing and the characters of the satire express their views with fluency and freedom."

If Richardson lost the fine edge on his writing after *Gallows Humor* (the result, perhaps, of experimentation with new forms), he restored it with *Memoir of a Gambler*, which projects a serious, if more seasoned, perspective. *Memoir of a Gambler*, an autobiograhical chronicle of Richardson's obsession with gambling, has the intensity and the sharpness of focus that distinguish his first two plays. The reader follows him up and down his emotional roller coaster through intense excitement; degrading loss of his sense of self-worth; a sense of terrifying powerlessness; sterile, pleasureless obsession; and a voyeuristic fascination with the gambler's plight. Early in the book, which is narrated without self-pity, it becomes clear that Richardson's obsession with gambling is a visible manifestation of an inner struggle over meaning in life. The symbolism in *Memoir of a Gambler* is more effective than that in *Xmas in Las Vegas* because in the earlier work, the symbolism is not supported by rounded characters who make the problem come alive, whereas in this text the intense characterization and autobiographical experience emerge first and the symbolism second, as an integral corollary.

Another asset of the latest effort derives from the ending. The earlier works close with the characters failing to exercise choice, but Richardson does not discuss resignation or how the characters feel about having capitulated (perhaps he had not yet accepted resignation as the solution). In *Memoir of a Gambler* he uses a discussion with the devil to indicate that he has mastered his obsession with gambling because he has learned that it, too, is incapable of bestowing meaning on life. The tone at the close is not triumphant because Richardson, weary of struggling, has decided to "acquire a taste for paradox and resignation," but there is a sense of satisfaction in the realization that he has survived a painful encounter with the problem of meaning, during which he went very far down before he rose to offer, not a sentimental platitude, but a sobering, persuasive account of his real and metaphysical tribulations.

The unevenness of Richardson's career is, unfortunately, common among serious American dramatists. In exploring the forces that trap men, Richardson sought to experiment with various means of presenting his understanding of man's dilemma (during a seven-year span he utilized a classical myth, a tragicomic morality play involving role doubling, a history play, a gallery of grotesques, and a satire). While addressing these ambitious goals, he sought to satisfy Broadway backers. The diversity in form, though, was most likely the key to his problem. Any writer working with a new form is apt to experience initial difficulties until he masters its idiosyncratic demands. But the financial pressures of a Broadway production do not allow the playwright the time to adjust at his leisure. Had Richardson given himself more time, he might have worked his way through some of the natural difficulties, but he left the theatre before such an opportunity arose.

Difficulties with Broadway and the critics aside, Richardson's dramatic accomplishments are still noteworthy: *The Prodigal* and *Gallows Humor* are good plays that challenge the audience to confront the problems of choice and paradox. Moreover, recognition is in order for Richardson's courage (perhaps audacity) in experimenting and working against the grain of current intellectual fashion even though the experimentation might jeopardize his career.

–Richard Ziegfeld

Other:

Juan Feldman, in *Pardon Me, Sir, But Is My Eye Hurting Your Elbow?*, comp. Bob Booker and George Foster (New York: Geis, 1967), pp. 60-73.

Periodical Publications:

"Classical Method in Playwrighting," *New York*

Herald-Tribune, 14 August 1960, IV: 1;
"Jack's First Tape: A Self Interview," *Theatre Arts*, 46 (March 1962): 64-65, 73-77;
"On Reviewing Plays," *Commentary*, 42 (September 1966): 77-82;
"O'Neill Reconsidered," *Commentary*, 57 (January 1974): 52-54;
"Reviewing Plays," *Commentary*, 57 (April 1974): 71-73.

References:
Robert Brustein, "New American Playwrights," in *Modern Occasions*, ed. Philip Rahv (London: Kennikat, 1966), pp. 130-131;
Gilbert Debusscher, "Jack Richardson, dramaturge americain," *Revue des Langues Vivantes* (Brussels), 37 (1971): 44-63, 128-151;
Debusscher, "Modern Masks of the Orestes: *The Flies* and *The Prodigal*," *Modern Drama*, 12 (December 1969): 308-318;
Alan S. Downer, "Total Theatre and Partial Drama: Notes on the New York Theatre, 1965-1966," *Quarterly Journal of Speech*, 52 (October 1966): 231-232;
Martin Esslin, "Der Common Sense des Nonsense," *Sinn oder Unsinn: Das Groteske im Modernen Drama*, Theater unserer Zeit, vol. 3 (Basel: Basilus, 1962), p. 144;
Rosette Lamont, "Death and Tragi-comedy: Three Plays of the New Theatre," *Massachusetts Review*, 6 (1965): 381-402;
Alan Lewis, "New-Play Madness and Some New Voices," *American Playwrights and Playwrights of the Contemporary Theatre* (New York: Crown, 1965), pp. 190-211;
Frederick Lumley, *New Trends in 20th Century Drama* (London: Oxford University Press, 1967), pp. 319, 332-333;
Eric Mottram, "The New American Wave," *Encore*, 11 (January-February 1964): 35-41;
Don Ross, " 'The Critics' Taste is Quite Good' Says Off-Broadway Hit Playwright," *New York Herald-Tribune*, 28 February 1960, V: 1, 5;
Gerald Weales, *American Drama Since World War II* (New York: Harcourt, Brace & World, 1962), pp. 215, 220-221;
Philip Weissman, "*Mourning Becomes Electra* and *The Prodigal*: Electra and Orestes," *Modern Drama*, 3, no. 3(1960): 257-259;
George E. Wellwarth, "Hope Deferred—The New American Drama," *Literary Review*, 7 (Autumn 1963): 16-21;
Wellwarth, *Theater of Protest and Paradox: Developments in the Avant-Garde Drama* (New York: New York University Press, 1971), pp. 337-344.

HOWARD SACKLER
(19 December 1929-)

PRODUCTIONS: *Uriel Acosta*, 1954, University of California, Berkeley;
Mr. Welk and Jersey Jim, 1960, Actors Studio, New York;
The Yellow Loves, 1 February 1962, Poet's Theatre, Boston, 6 [performances];
A Few Enquiries (Sarah, The Nine O'Clock Mail, Mr. Welk and Jersey Jim, and Skippy), 1965, Theatre Company, Boston;
The Pastime of Monsieur Robert, 1966, Hampstead Theatre, London; 1969, American Conservatory Theatre, San Francisco;
The Great White Hope, 12 December 1967, Arena Stage, Washington, D.C.; 3 October 1968, Alvin Theatre, New York, 557;
Semmelweiss, 4 November 1977, Studio Arena Theatre, Buffalo, 29.

BOOKS: *Want My Shepherd: Poems* (New York: Caedmon, 1954);
The Great White Hope (New York: Dial, 1968; London: Faber & Faber, 1971);
A Few Enquiries (New York: Dial, 1970)—includes *Sarah, The Nine O'Clock Mail, Mr. Welk and Jersey Jim*, and *Skippy*.

The Pulitzer Prize, the New York Drama Critics Circle Award, and a Tony—any play which sweeps the three most coveted awards for a given Broadway season secures for its creator a place in twentieth-century theatre history. Such a coup was achieved by Howard Sackler's *The Great White Hope* for the 1968-1969 season. The phenomenal recognition accorded Sackler at the end of the 1960s may have made him internationally famous, but he had been successfully earning his living in the theatre prior to 1968. Even though none of his plays has received the stellar prominence of *The Great White Hope*, Sackler has had, and continues to have, an active and productive life in the theatre.

Born in New York City to Martin and Evelyn Rapaport Sackler, Howard Sackler spent a large portion of his early life in Florida. He later returned to New York to attend Brooklyn College, from which he received a B.A. in 1950. In 1963 Sackler married Greta Lynn Lungren, and they are the parents of two children. He maintains a residence in London, where he does most of his work for Caedmon Records, and also has a home off the Mediterranean coast of Spain on the island of Ibiza, where he does much of his writing. The recipient of numerous awards and grants, Sackler is a poet, a playwright, a screenwriter, a recording industry executive, and a director.

It was always Sackler's intention to be a writer, but not necessarily a playwright. In an interview with Lewis Funke, Sackler says, "I didn't begin writing seriously for the theatre until I was about 24. I began writing poetry and continue to write poetry." Not long after college, he published a volume of verse entitled *Want My Shepherd: Poems* (1954). His poetry has also been published in the *Hudson Review*, *Poetry* magazine, *Commentary*, and *New Directions* annuals. Sackler admits the influence of Eliot and Auden on his poetry and, more specifically, the influence of Eliot's verse drama on his own ventures into that genre.

Relying on the craft which he had practiced the most, Sackler wrote his first play, a long one-act called *Uriel Acosta* (1954), in verse. In the interview with Funke, he says that for this initial effort at playwriting, he "needed the security of writing in verse." Based on an actual event, *Uriel Acosta* describes the plight of a Portuguese Jew who lived in the generation before Spinoza (1632-1677). When he was an undergraduate at Brooklyn College, Sackler received the idea for the play from a Spanish teacher, Professor Bernadette, who expressed interest in the character of Acosta. In Sackler's play, because of the Inquisition, Acosta is forced to flee to Amsterdam. Arriving with a preconceived idea of the life of Jews there, Acosta is disenchanted when he discovers that his fellow Jews are actively and profitably engaged in mercantilism. Committed to the prophetic spirit of his religion, he publicly chastizes the Jewish community, and, as a result, meets with adversity and unhappiness. The play was produced at the University of California at Berkeley and received, in 1954, the Maxwell Anderson Award for verse drama.

The second play that Sackler wrote, *The Yellow Loves* (1962), concerns the nineteenth-century French poet Tristan Corbière (1845-1875). Corbière's personality was affected by poor health and by his belief that he was an extremely unattractive man. In the play, his affair with the mistress of a French colonel temporarily improves his self-esteem. Mistakenly believing that he has successfully competed with someone more manly than he, Corbière is horrified to discover that the colonel neither cares nor treats him with any new respect. *The Yellow Loves* was Sackler's first prose play, and it won the University of Chicago's Charles H. Sergel Award for playwriting in 1959. Despite the recognition Sackler received for his first two plays, they merely represent the work of a promising young playwright and are not memorable additions to the canon of twentieth-century drama.

Additionally, during Sackler's first few years out of college he entered the field of screenwriting. He was author of the screenplays for *Desert Padre* (1950), *Fear and Desire* (1953), and *Killer's Kiss* (1955)—all done for a young director named Stanley Kubrick. By the time his first play was produced in 1954, and with the publication of a book of his poetry, and the production of three of his screenplays, Sackler's writing career was off to a commendable beginning for a man who was barely twenty-five.

In the early 1950s he was the recipient of a Rockefeller Foundation grant (1953) and a Littauer Foundation grant (1954). At the New School for Social Research in New York City, Sackler directed readings of Shakespeare's *King John* in March 1953, Sophocles' *Women of Trachis* in February 1954, and T. S. Eliot's *The Family Reunion* in November 1954. In 1953, Sackler founded and became production director for Caedmon Records. Under the auspices of Caedmon, he has directed well over two hundred productions, including the medieval morality play *Everyman*; Shakespearean plays such as *Pericles* and *Titus Andronicus*; Goldsmith's *She Stoops to Conquer*; Rostand's *Cyrano de Bergerac*; and Eliot's *Murder in the Cathedral*. At Caedmon, Sackler has worked with and directed such highly skilled and respected actors as Paul Scofield, Sir Ralph Richardson, Rex Harrison, Margaret Leighton, Dame Edith Evans, Claire Bloom, Albert Finney, Julie Harris, and Jessica Tandy. His association with Caedmon marks a contribution of considerable significance to twentieth-century drama.

Sackler's enterprises at Caedmon occupied much of his time during the middle years of the 1950s and caused a brief hiatus in his career as a dramatist. Toward the end of the decade and on into the 1960s, however, Sackler once again turned his attention to playwriting. He also wrote the screenplay for and directed the English adaptation of the Czechoslovakian film version of *A Midsummer Night's Dream* in 1961. Although Sackler's *A Few Enquiries*, a collection of four one-acts produced in 1965 and published in 1970, represented a departure from strict reliance on poetry or historical subjects, poetic elements and historical settings are employed. Even though Sackler tells us in his author's note, they "were conceived as a program, to be played together as an evening in the theatre," each can be viewed separately.

The first, *Sarah*, a mysterious play with ten characters, is set on a bare stage at a Victorian ballet theatre and involves the investigation into the tragic and accidental death by fire of a young ballerina named Sarah Webster. From the opening cross-examination of the coroner through the understudy's reenactment of Sarah's final dance, which is accompanied by the mother's sobs, the play is concise and cohesive. It is a funereal mood piece, shrouded in mystery. Sackler handles the mid-Victorian theatre setting well and creates the mood of a Degas painting. The language of the play, even when specialized (as represented by the use of archaic dance terms), rings true.

The Nine O'Clock Mail was written for Canadian television in 1965, and, after its production as part of *A Few Enquiries*, it appeared on the same bill in 1967 at the Charles Theatre in Boston with two considerably better plays: Lanford Wilson's *The Madness of Lady Bright* and Leroi Jones's *Dutchman*. Sackler's play, set in the suburban living room of Ted and Cynthia, examines Ted's obsessive ritual of waiting, on edge, for the morning mail. Ted is obviously past the point of listening to reason, but his wife tries futilely. The play is not a very compelling attempt to depict modern man gone off the deep end. Providing the dramatic conflict is the disintegrating, neurotic relationship between husband and wife, largely caused by the effect of Ted's ritual on their sex life. By playing on the words *mail* and *male*, Sackler makes it clear that the regeneration of Ted's masculinity depends on the arrival of the postman. At the very end of the play, while reading his mail, Ted summons Cynthia by unplugging the vacuum cleaner. As the curtain comes down, she enters, with lipstick and eye makeup on, long hair flowing, and kneels seductively beside Ted. Martin Gottfried calls the play "coy and pop-psych" and says that it has a mechanical climax that is just barely supported by characters and dialogue.

Like *The Nine O'Clock Mail*, Sackler's *Mr. Welk and Jersey Jim* (first produced by the Actors Studio in 1960) eventually wound up on the same bill with two very reputable modernist plays, in this case with Ionesco's *Rhinoceros* and Pinter's *The Collection*, at Washington's Arena Stage in 1966. However, unlike *The Nine O'Clock Mail*, *Mr. Welk and Jersey Jim* is a strong and interesting play. It is a two-character play set in the seedy, turn-of-the-century office of Mr. Welk, a lawyer. Into this scene comes the client-victim, a flashy two-bit crook named Jersey Jim. The encounter between the irritable lawyer and the simple, devil-may-care client turns into a battle of words and wit. As the two characters rehearse a cross-examination, sadism and masochism color the lawyer-client relationship. The surprise ending, in which Jersey Jim chokes to death on a statute that he has ripped from a law book and stuffed into his mounth, is heavily symbolic, but it works because it evolves out of the dialogue and the well-drawn characters and is not simply tacked on for effort.

Mr. Welk and Jersey Jim is a play about words and how they may literally choke us. The language is sparse and poetic, Sackler's use of idiomatic expressions from the period helping to place the play firmly in a specific time. The play conjures up visions of vaudeville and, according to Gottfried, can be viewed as "a song and dance about words." The playwright's indictment of the law, and, by extension, the convoluted language the law employs, is severe. Not only is the law inhuman, he seems to be saying, but it is also cruel, torturous, and murderous.

Skippy, the last play in *A Few Enquiries*, is contemporary, urban, and mysterious. The play is set in a liquor store owned by Harry Weiman, about sixty years old, and Muriel, his wife, who is in her fifties, and the action occurs on a day when the store is robbed by a nervous Puerto Rican youth. Although the robbery is a central event, the play is primarily concerned with Harry's quest to alleviate his secret guilt from childhood over the accidental death of Skippy, his brother. This old pain has surfaced because of the recent death of his mother. Harry's bravery and kindness are supported throughout by his understanding and loving wife. The tension and violence surrounding the robbery serve to strengthen the couple's relationship so that they can face Harry's pain when, in a well-written monologue at the end of the play, Harry finally tells Muriel about Skippy's death and the guilt he has carried for fifty years. *Skippy* has an atmosphere of modern realism and dialogue that is both sincere and an outgrowth of character. *Skippy* is a fine character play that demonstrates how powerfully the past can threaten to dominate the present, a situation that makes Harry Weiman's survival skill, evidenced both in his confession of past guilt and his refusal to be defeated by urban violence, all the more admirable.

The next of Sackler's plays to be produced was a highly stylized, full-length play in prose called *The Pastime of Monsieur Robert*. Written in the early 1960s and first produced in London in 1966, the play is set in a chalet in eighteenth-century France. Observing the classical unities, the action takes place in twenty-four hours. The character of Monsieur Robert is based in part on the aristocratic French writer the Marquis de Sade (1740-1814). Monsieur Robert has survived imprisonment and the disillusionment of the Revolution. Retiring to his chateau, he, with the help of an old actor and his servants, puts on endless charades. For example, the entire household participates in a reenactment of the fall of the Bastille. However, a fantasy of a more personal nature most intensely engages Monsieur Robert's imagination. With his wife playing the part of his mother-in-law, whom he blames for his years of incarceration, Monsieur Robert acts out the revenge he desires. At the end of the first act, the mother-in-law actually arrives at the chateau, and the real and the imaginary worlds begin to merge. The second act, then, is concerned with his preparation to kill her. Discovering that his mother-in-law will not conform to his notion of her, Monsieur Robert must force her to become the monster he has imagined. *The Pastime of Monsieur Robert* is a tightly written drama that explores the effects of isolation on the imagination, and it deserves to be performed more often.

In 1964 Sackler had returned to an outline for a play that had been germinating in his mind for many years. The original stimulus for *The Great White Hope* was an old photograph of Jack Johnson, (the first black heavyweight boxing champion), lying on the canvas in Havana and taking the count from the referee, as he lost his title to Jess Willard in 1915. Further, Sackler had spent some time in Cuba, and a friend's mother there told him that she had seen Jack Johnson training for that fight. Sackler told Funke that his initial plan "was to make a musical play of it—of a more narrative and less tragic style. Something which took Johnson, Jefferson, as I call him, from the pre-Reno days to the end of his life when he wound up in the 40's in Hubert's Flea Circus. I was going to use music of each period and wind up with music of Artie Shaw and Benny Goodman in the 40's." This first version, only a detailed outline, was called "Jack and the White Hope."

As the play evolved, however, Sackler aban-doned the idea of a musical. Influenced by his many years of working with Elizabethan drama, the structure for *The Great White Hope* began to fall into place, and the first draft was finished in February 1967. Revisions were done between March and the play's December opening at the Arena Stage in Washington, D.C. Here was yet another attempt by Sackler to write a verse play based upon a historical event, but this time popular and critical success awaited the playwright.

Conceived on an epic scale, *The Great White Hope* chronicles the rise and fall of a black heavyweight champion, Jack Jefferson. The play's title refers to the white world's hope that a white man can defeat Jefferson and give the title back to the whites. Covering the years 1908-1915, the play is set in the United States, Europe, Mexico, and, finally, Cuba. There are three acts, with nineteen scenes, several of them with large crowds. Besides Jefferson, who is depicted as a proud and noble man of great depth and humanity, other major characters include Ellie Bachman, his white girl friend; Clara, his former black girl friend; Goldie, his manager; Tick, his trainer; and Mrs. Jefferson, his mother. All of these characters, as well as many minor characters, are drawn with great detail and skill, adding constant support in a play that clearly and unabashedly focuses on its central character.

Despite criticisms that it resembles a three-ring circus with too many side shows, the play moves steadily and in a unified manner toward its denouement. By the end of the third scene of act 1, Jefferson has defeated Brady, the white champion, and ascended to the throne as heavyweight champion. He returns victorious to his hometown of Chicago, opens his own bar, flaunts his white mistress, and incurs the wrath of the white establishment. The victim of a plot to dethrone him, Jefferson is arrested for violating the Mann Act and charged with transporting his white girl friend across state lines for immoral purposes. With the help of a black baseball team, he jumps bail and goes into exile in Europe. Act 2 takes place mostly on the European continent in the years just before World War I. Although he has escaped going to jail in America, Jefferson and Ellie are trapped and imprisoned by his exile. Forced to perform undignified jobs in order to survive, his humiliation reaches its pinnacle in a cabaret in Budapest when he impersonates Uncle Tom to Ellie's Little Eva. By the end of the act, he has decided to go to Mexico to train for what is to be his final fight. In Act 3 Jefferson turns down an offer of a pardon in exchange for throwing the championship bout, loses Ellie, who

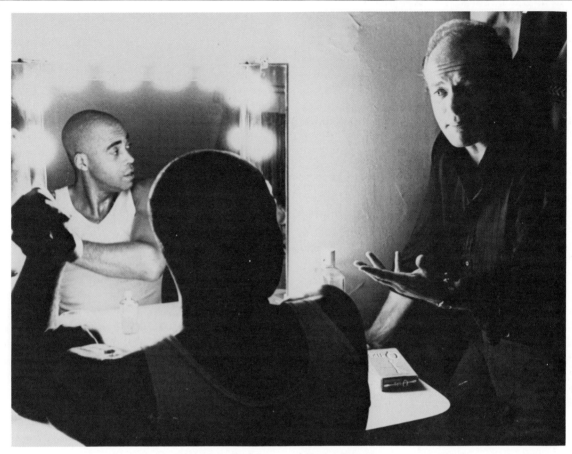

James Earl Jones and Howard Sackler

loves him, when she commits suicide, and relinquishes his title to the new white hope in a particularly bloody battle. The tragic cycle has been completed.

Many people are surprised to discover that *The Great White Hope* is written in verse. The language is not high-flown, but is, instead, the poetry of the vernacular. As Sackler told Funke: "I was guided by two short playlets that T. S. Eliot wrote in the 20's called *Sweeney Agonistes* and *Fragment of an Agon*, where he used jazz rhythms and syncopated American speech. . . . I was following Eliot's lead in using a loose four-beat line throughout and using a kind of unrhymed, non-iambic verse which would catch American speech patterns." The resulting dialogue is not stilted. Moreover, the play employs an effective pattern of symbolism. The obvious symbol of the boxing ring, as well as the backdrop of World War I as an outward representation of the great struggle within the central character, does not seem contrived. Before moving to a proscenium theatre in New York for its long run, the play had its world premiere in the round at Washington's Arena Stage, where the symbol of the ring was quite effective. According to Marion Trousdale in "Ritual

Theatre: *The Great White Hope*," the Arena production gave the play "a kind of ticker tape immediacy" and did "what Aristotle said a play should do, and what few playwrights know how to do—it imitated an action by means of an action." With its many scenes and locales, the play is structurally not unlike those of Brecht or Shakespeare. Sackler's experience with directing Shakespeare influenced the materials he assembled into *The Great White Hope*. In spite of numerous characters and sprawling geographical settings, the play is tightly focused upon its strong central character. Even the scenes without Jefferson cannot be viewed as digressions since they all relate to him.

In the classical sense, the central theme of *The Great White Hope* is how hubris can destroy a man. The scene, close to the end of the play, with Jefferson distraught over the body of his dead mistress, brings up the image of Othello and Desdemona. Sackler's play is not the equal of Shakespeare's tragedies, but he has written a work of great scope and placed a man of enormous stature at its center. On a sociological level, the strained race relations depicted were topical and important when the play appeared in the late 1960s. Although some may choose to view the play, as Richard Gilman did in the *New Republic*, "as a splendid liberal occasion" for whites, the merit of the play does not rest on its topicality.

In 1970, the film version of *The Great White Hope*, for which Sackler had written the screenplay, was released, and later in the decade he added more movie credits to his name with the release of *Bugsy* (1973) and *Jaws II* (1976). Also, with the appearance of his play *Semmelweiss*, he continued to demonstrate his interest in historical drama. Directed by Edwin Sherin, who had directed *Mr. Welk and Jersey Jim* and *The Great White Hope*, it was staged at the Studio Arena Theatre in Buffalo, New York, in the late fall of 1977. A play about Ignaz Philipp Semmelweiss (1818-1865), a Hungarian physician who was one of the discoverers of the principle of antisepsis, *Semmelweiss* delineates the obstacles encountered by the doctor, whose work preceded Lister's. Dr. Semmelweiss, whose enemies ridiculed him and saw to it that his work was not accepted, was broken financially and mentally by his struggles. In scope, the play, with its three acts, twenty scenes, and sixteen characters, has more in common with *The Great White Hope* than with the plays Sackler wrote prior to 1967.

In addition to his directorial work for Caedmon Records, throughout his career Sackler has directed for stage, film, and television. Among his stage credits are productions of *Hamlet* in Dublin in 1957, Samuel Beckett's *Krapp's Last Tape* for an Irish and European tour in 1960, and John Webster's *The Duchess of Malfi* in Los Angeles in 1976. For television, Sackler directed the much-praised *Shakespeare: Soul of an Age* for NBC in 1964. Importantly, he has admitted, in his interview with Funke, that this aspect of his career in the theatre has had an "inestimable" influence on his writing: "It's an education, directing great plays. And as a writer, living with these plays, one is compelled always to refer to the standard they set; it acts almost as a conscience." In fact, directing has occupied a large portion of Sackler's time during his thirty years in the theatre. It is quite possible that Sackler's achievements as a director for stage, film, television, and Caedmon Records could vie for prominence with his work as a playwright.

Sackler's strength as a playwright lies in his ability to handle diverse speech patterns, time periods, settings, moods, and characters. Strains of ritualism, violence—both overt and hidden—death, and fantasy make their way into his plays. As Martin Gottfried has noted in his introduction to *A Few Enquiries*, it is difficult to call Sackler's work either realistic or abstract, concluding that Sackler's plays are "classical and poetic while being modern in their treatment of the stage."

Even though more than half of Sackler's plays to date employ historical bases, and several are in verse, his work, as a whole, cannot be strictly labeled by its themes, techniques, or concerns. Except for T. S. Eliot and Maxwell Anderson, no other twentieth-century American dramatist has been as concerned with the fusion of history and poetry as Sackler has. And yet his stature as a playwright has not been sufficient to invite comparison with the author of *Elizabeth the Queen* and *Winterset*. Of his penchant for historical people and periods, Sackler told Funke that "the subjects that seem to involve me are real subjects. I use them in a sort of fictional way. . . . My goal in dealing with any subject for a play is to take it from the level of history or anecdote to the level of universal experience."

Sackler's reputation seems to rest on *The Great White Hope*. He had been writing plays, however, for at least fifteen years before he was catapulted to fame and praised as a playwright. Since the *Great White Hope*, he has not had another play that even approximates that work's critical and popular success. Unfortunately, because of the scope and demands of *The Great White Hope*, it does not receive many revival productions. The one-acts, on the other hand, especially *Sarah*, *Mr. Welk and Jersey Jim*, and *Skippy*, are certainly manageable and deserve to be performed more often. Sackler's varied and prolific career demonstrates that he is not, as many people believe, a "one-play" man.

–*Robert W. Hungerford*

Screenplays:
Desert Padre, RKO, 1950;
Fear and Desire, Stanley Kubrick Productions, 1953;
Killer's Kiss, United Artists, 1955;
A Midsummer Night's Dream, adapted from the Czechoslovakian film version, Showcorporation, 1961;
The Great White Hope, Twentieth Century Fox, 1970;
Bugsy, United Artists, 1973;
Jaws II, Universal, 1976.

Television Script:
The Nine O'Clock Mail, Canadian television, 1965.

References:
Clive Barnes, Review of *The Great White Hope*, *New York Times*, 4 October 1968, p. 40;

Lewis Funke, *Playwrights Talk About Writing: 12 Interviews with Lewis Funke* (Chicago: Dramatic Publishing, 1975), pp. 39-67;

Richard Gilman, Review of *The Great White Hope*, *New Republic*, 159 (26 October 1968): 36-39;

Martin Gottfried, Introduction to *A Few Enquiries* (New York: Dial, 1970);

Walter Kerr, Review of *The Great White Hope*, *New York Times*, 13 October 1968, D1;

Marion Trousdale, "Ritual Theatre: *The Great White Hope*," *Western Humanities Review*, 23 (Autumn 1969): 295-303;

Ross Wetzsteon, Review of *The Great White Hope*, *Village Voice*, 10 October 1968, pp. 45-46.

Papers:

Sackler's papers are at the Humanities Research Center, University of Texas, Austin.

William Saroyan

H. W. Matalene
University of South Carolina

BIRTH: Fresno, California, 31 August 1908, to Armenak and Takoohi Saroyan.

MARRIAGE: 24 February 1943 to Carol Marcus, divorced 1949; remarried 1951, divorced 1952; children: Aram, Lucy.

AWARDS: New York Drama Critics Circle Award and Pulitzer Prize for *The Time of Your Life*, 1940; Academy Award for *The Human Comedy*, 1943; California Literature Gold Medal for *Tracy's Tiger*, 1952.

SELECTED PRODUCTIONS: *My Heart's in the Highlands*, 13 April 1939, Guild Theatre, New York, 44 [performances];

The Time of Your Life, 25 October 1939, Booth Theatre, New York, 185;

A Theme in the Life of the Great American Goof, 11 January 1940, Center Theatre, New York;

Love's Old Sweet Song, 2 May 1940, Plymouth Theatre, New York, 44;

Across the Board on Tomorrow Morning, February 1941, Pasadena Community Playhouse, Pasadena; March 1942, Theatre Showcase, New York; 17 August 1942, Belasco Theatre, New York, 8;

The Beautiful People, 21 April 1941, Lyceum Theatre, New York, 120;

Hello Out There, 10 September 1941, Lobero Theatre, Santa Barbara; 29 September 1942, Belasco Theatre, New York, 47;

Jim Dandy, 1941, Pasadena Community Playhouse, Pasadena;

Talking to You, 17 August 1942, Belasco Theatre, New York, 8;

Get Away Old Man, 24 November 1943, Cort Theatre, New York, 13;

The Hungerers, *The Ping Pong Game*, and *Hello Out There*, 23 August 1945, Provincetown Playhouse, New York;

Sam Ego's House, 30 October 1947, Circle Theatre, Hollywood;

Don't Go Away Mad, 9 May 1949, Master Institute Theatre, New York, 2;

The Son, 31 March 1950, Circle Theatre, Hollywood;

Once Around the Block, 24 May 1950, Master Institute Theatre, New York;

A Lost Child's Fireflies, 15 July 1954, Round-up Theatre, Dallas;

Opera, Opera, 21 December 1955, Amato Theatre, New York;

The Slaughter of the Innocents, 1957, The Hague;

Ever Been in Love with a Midget, 20 September 1957, Congress Hall, Berlin;

The Cave Dwellers, 19 October 1957, Bijou Theatre, New York, 97;

Sam, The Highest Jumper of Them All: or, the London Comedy, 6 April 1960, Stratford East Theatre Royal, London;

Settled Out of Court, by Saroyan and Henry Cecil, 19 October 1960, Strand Theatre, London;

The Dogs: or, the Paris Comedy, 1960, Vienna;

High Time along the Wabash, 1 December 1961, Purdue University Playhouse, Lafayette;

Ah Man, music by Peter Fricker, 21 June 1962, Aldeburgh Festival, Suffolk, England;

Bad Men in the West, 19 May 1971, Stanford University, Stanford;

People's Lives, by Saroyan and others, August 1974, Manhattan Theatre Club, New York;

The Rebirth Celebration of the Human Race at Artie Zabala's Off-Broadway Theatre, 10 July 1975, Shirtsleeve Theatre, New York.

SELECTED BOOKS: *The Daring Young Man on the Flying Trapeze and Other Stories* (New York: Random House, 1934; London: Faber & Faber, 1935);

Inhale & Exhale (New York: Random House, 1936; London: Faber & Faber, 1936);

Three Times Three (Los Angeles: Conference Press, 1936);

Little Children (New York: Harcourt, Brace, 1937; London: Faber & Faber, 1937);

Love, Here Is My Hat (New York: Modern Age Books, 1938; London: Faber & Faber, 1938);

The Trouble with Tigers (New York: Harcourt, Brace, 1938; London: Faber & Faber, 1939);

The Hungerers, A Short Play (New York, Los Angeles, London & Toronto: French, 1939);

Peace, It's Wonderful (New York: Modern Age Books, 1939; London: Faber & Faber, 1940);

My Heart's in the Highlands (New York: Harcourt, Brace, 1939);

The Time of Your Life (New York: Harcourt, Brace, 1939);

Subway Circus (New York, Los Angeles, London & Toronto: French, 1940);

The Ping-Pong Game (New York, Los Angeles, London & Toronto: French, 1940);

Three Plays: My Heart's in the Highlands, The Time of Your Life, Love's Old Sweet Song (New York: Harcourt, Brace, 1940);

A Special Announcement (New York: House of Books, 1940);

My Name Is Aram (New York: Harcourt, Brace, 1940; London: Faber & Faber, 1941);

Jim Dandy (Cincinnati: Little Man Press, 1941); republished as *Jim Dandy, Fat Man in a Famine* (New York: Harcourt, Brace, 1947; London: Faber & Faber, 1948);

The People with Light Coming Out of Them (New York: Free Company, 1941);

Three Plays by William Saroyan: The Beautiful People, Sweeny in the Trees, Across the Board on Tomorrow Morning (New York: Harcourt, Brace, 1941); republished as *The Beautiful People and Other Plays* (London: Faber & Faber, 1943);

Saroyan's Fables (New York: Harcourt, Brace, 1941);

Razzle-Dazzle (New York: Harcourt, Brace, 1942; revised edition, London: Faber & Faber, 1945);

The Time of Your Life and Two Other Plays (London: Faber & Faber, 1942);

The Human Comedy (New York: Harcourt, Brace, 1943; London: Faber & Faber, 1943; revised edition, New York: Harcourt, Brace & World, 1971);

Dear Baby (New York: Harcourt, Brace, 1944; London: Faber & Faber, 1945);

Get Away Old Man (New York: Harcourt, Brace, 1944; London: Faber & Faber, 1946);

The Adventures of Wesley Jackson (New York: Harcourt, Brace, 1946; London: Faber & Faber, 1947);

Hello Out There (New York, Hollywood, London & Toronto: French, 1949);

Don't Go Away Mad (New York, Hollywood, London & Toronto: French, 1949);

Sam Ego's House (New York, Hollywood, London & Toronto: French, 1949);

Don't Go Away Mad and Two Other Plays: Sam Ego's House; A Decent Birth, A Happy Funeral (New York: Harcourt, Brace, 1949; London: Faber & Faber, 1951);

The Assyrian and Other Stories (New York: Harcourt, Brace, 1950; London: Faber & Faber, 1951);

Rock Wagram (Garden City: Doubleday, 1951; London: Faber & Faber, 1952);

Tracy's Tiger (Garden City: Doubleday, 1951; London: Faber & Faber, 1952);

The Bicycle Rider in Beverly Hills (New York: Scribners, 1952; London: Faber & Faber, 1953);

The Laughing Matter (Garden City: Doubleday, 1953; London: Faber & Faber, 1954);

Mama, I Love You (Boston & Toronto: Little, Brown / Atlantic Monthly, 1956; London: Faber & Faber, 1957);

The Whole Voyald and Other Stories (Boston & Toronto: Little, Brown / Atlantic Monthly, 1956; London: Faber & Faber, 1957);

Papa You're Crazy (Boston & Toronto: Little, Brown / Atlantic Monthly, 1957; London: Faber & Faber, 1958);

The Slaughter of the Innocents (New York, Hollywood, London & Toronto: French, 1958);

The Cave Dwellers (New York: Putnam's, 1958; London: Faber & Faber, 1958);

The William Saroyan Reader (New York: Braziller, 1958);

Sam the Highest Jumper of Them All, or the London Comedy (London: Faber & Faber, 1961);

Here Comes, There Goes, You Know Who (New York: Simon & Schuster / Trident, 1961; London: Davies, 1962);

Settled Out of Court, by Saroyan and Henry Cecil (London: French, 1962);

Me (New York: Crowell-Collier / London: Collier-Macmillan, 1963);

Not Dying: An Autobiographical Interlude (New York: Harcourt, Brace & World, 1963; London: Cassell, 1966);

Boys and Girls Together (New York: Harcourt, Brace & World, 1963);

One Day in the Afternoon of the World (New York: Harcourt, Brace & World, 1964; London: Cassell, 1965);

After Thirty Years (New York: Harcourt, Brace & World, 1964);

Short Drive, Sweet Chariot (New York: Phaedra, 1966);

Look At Us (New York: Cowles, 1967);

I Used to Believe I Had Forever Now I'm Not So Sure (New York: Cowles, 1968; London: Cassell, 1969);

Letters from 74 Rue Taitbout, or Don't Go, But If You Must, Say Hello to Everybody (New York & Cleveland: World, 1969); republished as *Don't Go, But If You Must, Say Hello to Everybody* (London: Cassell, 1970);

The Dogs, or the Paris Comedy and Two Other Plays: Chris Sick, or Happy New Year Anyway, Making Money, and Nineteen Other Very Short Plays (New York: Phaedra, 1969);

Short Plays (New York: Phaedra, 1969);

Days of Life and Death and Escape to the Moon (New York: Dial, 1970; London: Joseph, 1971);

Places Where I've Done Time (New York: Praeger, 1972; London: Davis-Poynter, 1973);

The Tooth and My Father (Garden City: Doubleday, 1974);

Sons Come and Go, Daughters Hang in Forever (New York, St. Louis & San Francisco: McGraw-Hill, 1976);

Chance Meetings (New York: Norton, 1978);

Obituaries (Berkeley: Creative Arts Book Co., 1980).

In the spring of 1939, when the work of William Saroyan first reached the New York stage in the form of a one-act play entitled *My Heart's in the Highlands*, Sidney B. Whipple of the *New York World-Telegram* accused Saroyan and his producers of conducting a "painful experiment . . . for one purpose—to test the I.Q. of the public and the crit-

ics." There is considerable justice in this philistine response, for when the play was published, Saroyan included in the volume its perplexed and conflicting reviews, and he added a preface, in which he pilloried "A number of drama critics [who] sincerely regretted they couldn't understand this simple play, and a number [who] were bored by it." Children, he wrote, were better prepared to cope with him than were the Eastern *cognoscenti*. And as Saroyan's subsequent plays were produced and published, he continued to surround them with autobiography and self-explanation, contemptuous of the social and cultural attitudes of his new Broadway public and of the critics shaping those attitudes.

For this contempt Saroyan cannot really be blamed, and, perhaps, should be praised. Born in 1908, far from the northeastern cultural metropole, to Armenian immigrants in Fresno, California, Saroyan lost his father, Armenak (whose English was good) in 1911 and spent the next four years in an Oakland orphanage, while his mother, Takoohi (whose English was poor), worked in San Francisco, visiting her children on weekends. When Saroyan was seven, the family was reunited in Fresno, where Armenians, he says, "were considered . . . unattractive foreigners," and where he "despised those Armenian boys who toadied to 'the American.'" In Fresno, he began combining work at odd jobs—frequently as a newsboy or as a telegraph messenger—with public school.

Looking back on this childhood, Saroyan has found in it his beginnings as a playwright: "By the time I was eight," he has written, "I was beginning to understand that there was something to the art [of inventing roles to play and playing them], and that I had the privilege of controlling it." In the role of a newsboy he says he learned "nonchalance, ease, poise, repartee, and the art of entrance and exit, particularly into and out of saloons and gambling joints." In fact, "It was all drama . . . all for my own amusement in a region where amusement was rare and difficult." Even school "was full of drama," though Saroyan's teachers, "the dullest, most ignorant and least imaginative people in the world," were not entertained.

As for the theatre of high culture, Saroyan first approached it as something alien, obscure, possibly "great," but probably fraudulent. His uncle took him to an Armenian-language version of *Othello*, which he has recalled as a "great experience," but more for its rant than for its sense, because he "understood less than ten per cent of the words." At fourteen, he read, and "the same day wrote a very good play in imitation of [the] worldly and brilliant style" of Oscar Wilde's *Lady Winder-mere's Fan* (1892). This feat, Saroyan records, "was very easy," but he knew even then that "the environment was wrong" for him. Wilde's parody of Mayfair was not Saroyan's own poor, dilapidated, casual, healthy, and funny Fresno. Nor was Ibsen, in whose *Ghosts* (1881) Saroyan's uncle had acted in school, to be the playwright's model. Ibsen was "great" for Saroyan because he was "dull," obscure, "cagey, crafty, calculating," and not as "real" as was vaudeville.

It was not the canonized theatre, then, as hallowed and publicized by critics in distant cultural capitals, but an early and constant exposure to folk and popular theatre that Saroyan has acknowledged as having governed his development into a recognized playwright. The day before one Christmas, at a Punch and Judy show, he was given his first taste of actual theatrical performance. Then, at the movies, he saw a silent Western; and he claims that after the age of ten, by bartering newspapers or simply by sneaking in, he made his way "into every

theatre in . . . Fresno . . . ; into every circus that came to town; into the County Fairs; [and] into the summer stock company shows." From this experience, in collecting for publication his initial Broadway successes, Saroyan has concluded that "the education [of a playwright] must include many things, the least of which is . . . a course in a school or university on the art."

The playwright left school at the age of fifteen and never graduated, but he coped proudly with work and with his decision to become a writer. He worked in his uncle's law office, in the vineyards around Fresno, in grocery stores, and in the post office. He made good use of the public library. He boasts that at nineteen he had become the San Francisco Postal Telegraph Company's youngest branch manager. Within a year, he had published his first short story in a San Francisco literary magazine. At thirty, he had a national reputation as a writer of short fiction.

Meanwhile, his work had caught the eye of an important director and producer in the liberal,

Caricature by Al Hirschfeld of S. J. Perelman, S. N. Behrman, Sidney Kingsley, William Saroyan, Garson Kanin, Howard Lindsay, Russel Crouse, and Lillian Hellman which appeared in the New York Times *(9 September 1962).*

Eastern theatrical world. In the winter of 1937, Harold Clurman, the founder, in 1931 (with Lee Strasberg and Cheryl Crawford), of the Group Theatre, wrote to Saroyan "asking him if he would be interested to write for the theatre." Clurman, the son of a New York doctor, had been an organizer of theatrical ventures from the age of six. He was the author of a Sorbonne thesis on French drama from 1890 to 1914. While in Paris just after World War I, before it had made its mark on New York, Clurman had seen the Moscow Art Theatre; and he had attended Jacques Copeau's antirealist Théâtre du Vieux Colombier, which had been in New York during the war, propagandizing French civilization's resistance to the Hun. With the Group Theatre, Clurman tried for ten years to establish a consistent force for Modernism and social commitment on the Broadway stage. Despite his success in short fiction, then, Saroyan might be expected to have been excited by Harold Clurman's interest in him; but in response to Clurman's query about writing for the stage, Saroyan's "reply, pencil-scribbled on a penny postcard, admitted he had entertained the thought, but when he did write a play he would insist on directing it himself."

At about the same time, William Kozlenko, the editor of the *One-Act Play Magazine*, suggested to Saroyan that he turn "The Man with the Heart in the Highlands," one of his short stories, into a dramatic script. The result was a little play with the same title, which Kozlenko published in the December 1937 issue of his magazine, and which he reprinted in a collection of one-act plays he edited for Scribners in 1938. Saroyan then added to *The Man with the Heart in the Highlands*, changing its title to *My Heart's in the Highlands*, and explaining, when he eventually published the longer play after its 1939 Broadway run, that he "could not resist the impulse to carry out the theme to its present completion."

In *The Fervent Years* (1945), his memoir of the Group Theatre, Harold Clurman recalls that it was a play with this latter title—not the original *The Man with the Heart in the Highlands*—which Molly Day Thatcher, the wife of Elia Kazan, gave him to read during his voyage home from the Group's London success in the summer of 1938, and he decided, despite Kazan's reservations, that the Group would act Saroyan's play during the coming New York season. Somehow, therefore, Saroyan had overcome his reticence about allowing strangers to direct his work, and *My Heart's in the Highlands* went into production with the Group even though Clurman recalls that "we hardly dared show it to anyone;

it would have been like an admission of lunacy." He did, however, show it, in rehearsal, to the board of the Theatre Guild, in hopes that the Guild would assure *My Heart's in the Highlands* of a run by offering it to subscribers. This, however, the board hesitated to do, and the Group therefore pressed on with the play as an "experiment," investing $9,000 in what Clurman calls a "most modest" production, which was originally scheduled to close after five performances.

Clurman saw Saroyan's script as "fable," and accordingly appointed Robert Lewis, with his aptitude "for the non-realistic forms," to direct it. Some of the actors found *My Heart's in the Highlands* both artistically and ideologically objectionable, and one or two, Clurman recalls, "balked at . . . Lewis as director." The Group's business manager, with an eye on the books, advised that the production be dropped; but Clurman was steadfast: "The Group is not a bank," he wired back, "proceed with Saroyan play."

Saroyan himself seems to have had nothing to do with the Group's production. Writing in 1957, he recalls having been en route from Mexico City to New York on opening night, unaware that his play was being performed. He says that on reaching New York and hearing that his play had opened, "I thought I would go and see it and find out for myself what it was that was happening on the stage." He reports having found its casting and direction not as he would have done them, and remarks that he has never (as of 1957) seen a production of *My Heart's in the Highlands* that he really liked. Still, he found the Group's work generally "pretty good," considering that it was the work of theatre people, most of whom (Saroyan complains) "have no sense of the theatre [but] are just there, as the fulfillment . . . of a bitter determination to *be* there."

When *My Heart's in the Highlands* was published in 1939, Saroyan went through the motions of gratitude to the Group for having made his writing into an actual play. But Clurman recalls that "Most of the criticism" of the Group's production "issued from Saroyan himself . . . , [who] thought of his play as virile realism, not at all as fable . . . , [and who] did not approve of Bobby Lewis's delicate stylization [even though] much of the play's success was due to it." Lewis had chosen Herbert Andrews to design the set, and Clurman notes that "if the set . . . was obviously not 'true to life' it was because the director believed . . . a different type of stage picture [was necessary] to achieve [Saroyan's] vision."

The specifications governing set design in the text of *My Heart's in the Highlands*, as well as those in the original *The Man with the Heart in the Highlands*, do not, despite Saroyan's polite acknowledgement of everything the Group contributed to his play, reflect what was done in bringing the play to Broadway. The first of Saroyan's published stage directions specifies "An old white, broken-down frame house with a front porch, on San Benito Avenue in Fresno, California [with] no other houses near by, only a desolation of bleak land and . . .sky." During scenes when this set is in place, actions in the house are heard but not seen. Other scenes take place in "The living room of [the same] house," where a meager table, a couch, stools, chairs, a vase, and some books are to be found. While the living room is in place, most actions in the street are specified as heard but not seen. Still, at the end of the play, Johnny's family can leave the living room and (presumably) be seen as "They walk up the street." Two other scenes are set in "The Inside of Mr. Kosak's Grocery Store," which can be made to look "more poverty stricken than before."

Saroyan calls for no curtains or blackouts. Hence, contrary to the practice of conventional realism, all set changes take place in view of the audience, in front of the desolate backdrop of land and sky, which is constantly in view whether the scene is Mr. Kosak's, the living room, or the exterior of San Benito Avenue. The color and brightness of the backdrop are to be changed by the lighting as dictated by stage directions specifying the weather and the time of day. These changes—from sunset to dawn, to the dark of a thunderstorm, to rain, to sunshine, and back again to sunset—generally follow shifts in the mood of the action rather than changes of setting. It is the backdrop, then, which Saroyan seems to have envisioned as "symbolic." The sets, on the other hand, no matter how they are changed, Saroyan wanted "realistic" enough to be identifiable with one of the locales of his childhood.

It would appear, however, that both to save money and to implement Harold Clurman's feeling that *My Heart's in the Highlands* was "fable," Herbert Andrews made the decor much sweeter and more abstract than Saroyan wanted it. Photographs reproduced in Clurman's memoir and in *Theatre Arts Monthly* (June 1939) show how Andrews's set broke with the requirements of Saroyan's stage directions. Rather than providing two different sets, one for the living room and one for the exterior of the house, Andrews combined these locales. At stage right, on a diagonal receding slightly from the audience as it approaches the center of the stage, Andrews placed a platform perhaps four feet high, which is reached by a stairway with a banister rising from stage right to a landing in the middle of the stage. The landing, much of which is visible, could suggest Saroyan's front porch. The stairway, however, looks more like interior stairs than porch steps, and nothing really suggests the exterior of a broken-down white house. On Andrews's platform, visible because it has no walls downstage or stage right, is the living room, which is reached either through a door from the landing, or (presumably) from the kitchen, offstage right. The living room is backed by a wall with a curtained window and with a shelf for a few household effects. There are some stools around a table made from a barrel.

At stage left, along a diagonal parallel to that of his platform, Andrews placed a rigidly rectilinear ramp, which narrows slightly to suggest perspective as it recedes from the audience, and which rises from downstage center until it vanishes upstage left at a level slightly higher than that of the living room. Andrews's ramp is far more suggestive of an open road to infinite horizons than of San Benito Avenue in Fresno, California. Moreover, dominating the middle of the stage, Andrews put an enormous, stylized, cutout evergreen tree, which rises absolutely straight at the upstage center corner of the living room landing from behind the downstage center foot of the ramp. All of the evergreen's branches form absolute rectangles either with its trunk or with each other. Andrews's evergreen negates Saroyan's call for a metaphorically desolate backdrop "of bleak land and sky."

One cannot help feeling, therefore, that the Group's realization of *My Heart's in the Highlands*, while it was striking and somewhat novel, merited Saroyan's criticisms, misled his first reviewers as to the tone of his play, and helped to establish the tradition that Saroyan was an uninterpretable sentimentalist; for as Clurman notes, it was the visual aspects of the Group's production—for which he, Lewis, and Andrews were responsible—which dominated the responses of the Broadway critics. Whipple of the *New York World-Telegram* announced, "The Group Theatre has gone in for surrealist drama." John Anderson of the *New York Journal American* called Saroyan "the Salvador Dali of the drama, a surrealist playwright whose [work] could be compared favorably with a fur-lined teacup." And John Mason Brown of the *New York Post* proclaimed that "Mr. Saroyan has managed to widen the theatre's horizons by escaping from facts and reason . . . abundantly aided by the Group, [and] by Herbert Andrews's admirable *surrealist* settings." *Time* magazine, summarizing the reaction of the New York press, passed along the idea that

My Heart's in the Highlands was a "surrealist" play—"a rather helpless identification," as Clurman, showing an insider's familiarity with modern art, has pointed out. Curiously, the setting Saroyan seems to have wanted looks far closer to the mainline surrealism of Salvador Dali's scenographic style, or of petrified, arid backgrounds in Paul Delvaux and Yves Tanguy, than does the setting Andrews gave him, with its gratuitous tree, which (as Mordecai Gorelik points out in *New Theatres for Old*) is deliberately "childlike," like a "picture book."

Saroyan's play is a coherent and detailed statement of the most pervasive belief in his writing. This is the belief that human life takes on value and meaning through direct, hedonic excitation of the five senses by two classes of stimuli—those produced by people and those produced by nonhuman nature. In the former case, Saroyan sees people, ideally, as constantly engaged in various kinds of direct exchanges which excite the love of life in the partners to these exchanges. For Saroyan, a properly functioning economy includes exchanges not only of goods and specialized services, but also of kindnesses and civilities. In the ideal exchange, Saroyan feels, the partners know what they need and like, and feel in their bones that they are getting what they need from each other. Workers in the Saroyan economy perceive themselves as doing favors for one another, and are constantly grateful not only for the gratifications others produce for them, but also for the chances others give them to experience the sensuous joy of using the special, productive skills which they have learned and refined. In Saroyan, the social, the economic, the hedonistic, and the aesthetic, ideally, are one. This ideal unity is approached by the mutual regard which Saroyan finds in humble people like the Armenians of Fresno, and he thinks it would be attained if established Western culture had not lost track of real, material value and invented the unattainable value of "greatness."

As the hero of Saroyan's prize-winning novel *Tracy's Tiger* (1951) knows, real value is simply, directly, and immediately sensed: "Good coffee," he says, tastes like "coffee"; "the *best* coffee" tastes like "good coffee," and "the difference between *good* and the *best* coffee" is "Advertising." That is, it is a socially imposed value, artificially superadded to the pleasurable taste of coffee itself. The obvious misery of most social life, for Saroyan, results from the actions of people who are struggling to experience great, "advertised" values, which are not really and sensuously there. Cravings for "greatness" cannot be satisfied because one can never know, of

William Saroyan

one's own, sensory knowledge, whether one has actually felt the great experience which someone else reports, or "advertises" having had. Moreover, for Saroyan, the exchange of work for the "advertised" value of other work, merely increases life's quotient of real misery, while it conjures up the illusion that "greatness" can be experienced. In Saroyan's writing, people are never really great; they are only good or bad. Like the coffee of *Tracy's Tiger*, people either make life immediately pleasant for one another, or they do not. Either by their courtesies or by their labors, good people produce unambiguous gratifications for each other. Beyond this, all is publicity and illusion. There is no "best" coffee, and there are no "best" people.

In a story entitled "Seventy Thousand Assyrians," Saroyan brings home the cost to humanity of trying to be "great" when it could be happy being good. He reports a conversation with Theodore Badal, an Assyrian who is cutting hair for fifteen cents in a San Francisco barber college. They exchange commiserations over the plights of Assyrians and Armenians in the West-dominated modern world. Indeed, Badal points out that there are only seventy thousand Assyrians left alive, anywhere. "We went in for the wrong things," he says.

"We went in for the simple things, peace and quiet and families. We didn't go in for machinery and conquest and militarism. We didn't go in for diplomacy and deceit and the invention of machine guns and poison gasses. Well, there is no use being disappointed," Badal concludes, "We had our day, I suppose."

In short, Saroyan believes that misery is the result of learned insatiability—that the rich and powerful make themselves as wretched as those they oppress because they must struggle constantly to learn, to teach, and to maintain respect for unreal value distinctions which are not immanent in the body's direct contacts with its objects of sensation, whether those objects are animal, vegetable, mineral, human, or humanly produced. The powerful must "advertise" false needs, and part of their "advertising" is accomplished through their power to decide what is or is not great art. In the modern West, "serious" art is self-expressive, but the critics who produce and maintain the list of great works and artists mistakenly equate an artist's self-expression with his Romantic tendency simply to replicate in art the misery of his social and economic life without trying to negate that misery by making his public's physical and social environment more unambiguously sensuous and empathic, as Saroyan thinks an artist should. *My Heart's in the Highlands* offers a sort of populist version of aestheticism. It reveals that for Saroyan, as for Oscar Wilde, "Art is our spirited protest, or gallant attempt to teach Nature [both human and nonhuman] her proper place."

As Saroyan brings up the curtain on *My Heart's in the Highlands*, the effects of the modern-art system's "advertising" for artificial value distinctions are instantly seen and heard. Johnny, a nine year old not yet contaminated by aspirations to culture as defined by established critics, is seen on the porch of the broken-down white house. He is "eagerly . . . trying to understand the meaning of . . . everything"—of a mournful train whistle, of "a small overjoyed but angry bird," and of "A fourteen-year-old boy on a bicycle, eating an ice-cream cone and carrying newspaper bags, [who] goes by . . . oblivious of the weight on his shoulders and of the contraption on which he is seated, because of the delight and glory of ice cream in the world." Meanwhile, inside the house, self-insulated from all the valuable sounds, sights, sensations, and tastes being soaked up outside by Johnny and the newsboy, Johnny's father, a poet, is heard struggling after the right alliteration in which to complain of "the long silent day" as it seems to his "sore

solemn . . . lone lorn heart." Somehow, he has lost track of sources of value obvious to the hedonistic young outside. And rather than listen to him suffer, Johnny tries standing on his head. For him, the mastery of his body feels good for its own sake. For the newsboy, the mastery of the body feels good even when it is not done entirely for its own sake, but is exchanged as work in the economy for the product (like ice cream) of other people's competences, the consumption of which increases the sensuous value of one's own time. But for the grown-up poet, time is not to be filled with the pleasurable sensations of bodily competence, of production, of consumption, and of empathic admiration for the different competences of others. He has matured in the individualistic, self-expressive, post-Romantic West; and time, for him, must be killed with poetic laments over the disappearance of value, for him, from a world on whose real pleasures he has learned, since childhood, simply to turn his back.

Just as Johnny achieves a headstand, an old man named Jasper MacGregor enters, playing on a bugle "the loveliest and most amazing music in the world . . . 'My Heart's in the Highlands.' " Like Johnny's father, MacGregor wants to be a serious artist. He introduces himself as an actor who has done Shakespeare on the London stage, but Johnny's father alone honors MacGregor's impulse to pass for a serious artist. To Johnny and the neighbors, MacGregor is a folk musician whose bugle can increase the sensuous quality of life on San Benito Avenue, and it is not in exchange for Shakespearean gloom and bombast, but for bugling to make them "weep, kneel, [and] sing the chorus" that Johnny and the neighbors are willing to honor MacGregor and bring him food.

For eighteen days, MacGregor is happy to remain on San Benito Avenue as a working artist who makes survival enjoyable for other workers who make survival possible. But then he falls victim to his old ambition to succeed in the grimmer arts canonized not by hedonistic children and workers, but by owners of money and power: the arts which replicate the miseries of real life and treat them as inevitable. The offer of a chance to play Lear—even in the annual show at the old people's home from which he has escaped—lures MacGregor back to its confines, and with him goes the musical competence he has been able to barter for enough of the neighbors' food to keep him, and to keep the poet's family, in exchange for shelter in the poet's house.

Johnny begins to resent the fact that he has again been reduced to begging food from the neighborhood grocer by a grown-up's addiction to serious art, expressive of personal pain; but his father remains hopeful. Concluding from Mac-Gregor's success as a bugler that "The people love poetry but don't know it, that's all," Johnny's father writes new poems. But it is not to the people he goes with his new poems. Like MacGregor, Johnny's father still craves recognition from the cultural establishment, not from the friendly and supportive workers he knows on San Benito Avenue, but from the distant editors of the *Atlantic Monthly* who "don't buy *poetry*, [but] *scare* you to death."

Only after the *Atlantic Monthly* rejects his new poems does the poet come to understand whom he is writing for and what his poems are really worth. He sees no difference between Eastern editors who would spurn his poems and European leaders who have embroiled the innocent masses in World War I. "Go ahead," he addresses critical and political powers who would promulgate values not obvious to children, "kill everybody. Declare War on one another. Take the people by the thousands and mangle them. Their poor hearts and their poor spirits and their poor bodies. Give them ugliness. Pollute their dreams. Horrify them. Distort them with hatred for one another. Befoul the legend of the living, you maniacs whose greatness is measured by the number you destroy. . . . You frauds of the world. You wretched and ungodly. . . . You won't kill *anything*. . . . There will always be poets in the world." He knows at last that the value of his poetry does not depend on its usefulness to an establishment of critics in the business of teaching people to yearn for experiences of value which the senses cannot feel. Good poetry, he now knows, is not self-pity made famous, but is art in which the reader recognizes the poet's hope of making the life of his audience more beautiful, more meaningful, less forgotten. Accordingly, the poet takes his new poems to Mr. Kosak, the grocer from whom Johnny has been begging. He offers Mr. Kosak the poems not to cancel his debt for the groceries, but to recognize the grocer's kindness. "Don't you see," he tells Mr. Kosak, "poetry must be *read* to be poetry." And he goes on: "It may be that one reader is all that I deserve. If this is so, I want that reader to be you." Whereupon Mr. Kosak humbly accepts the poems. When he reads them, he and his little daughter are profoundly moved by a passage in which the poet specifically acknowledges that his new writing is offered as his part in an exchange of kind remembrances by which people must sustain themselves amid the pain of living by artificial, socially imposed values, and in the face of death.

Thus does Saroyan's poet learn the real value of art, which (like all real values in Saroyan) is simply and immediately obvious to the uninstructed senses of a child and does not need to be "advertised" by an establishment of critics. With this, and all establishments, the poet makes no further attempt at accommodation. Behind with his rent, he agrees to move on, leaving the meager things with which he has furnished the broken-down house so that the next tenants, a poor young couple with a new baby, may use them. There is no work for anyone, and Mr. Kosak, after feeding the unemployed of San Benito Avenue on credit, is reduced to feeding his own family out of the dwindling stock of his grocery store. Johnny is now supporting the poet's household by bringing home fruit from the farms around Fresno. It is not stealing, the poet assures him, because "stealing is where there's unnecessary damage or cruelty to an innocent one, so that there may be undeserved profit or power to one who is not innocent." The implication is that most existing property arrangements, though legally sanctioned, are in reality no more than theft.

It is Johnny, as the family's provider, however, who (as always) is not permitted the self-indulgence of absolute high-mindedness. His father's notion of what is and is not stealing does not keep Johnny from fleeing home in guilt and terror and barricading his family in when he imagines that a fruit farmer and his dog are after him. And his troubles are not over when the man outside turns out not to be an angry farmer, but MacGregor, escaped again. The old man has been betrayed. At the old people's home, they tried to take away his bugle, and he has escaped to play a last, faltering solo and to die among his friends on San Benito Avenue.

While MacGregor plays, little Esther Kosak further involves Johnny in the problem of whether or not unbending, vulnerable innocence is, in fact, decent. In recognition of the poems her father has read to her, Esther gives Johnny money—her entire savings for Christmas, but nevertheless, money—the cruel world's loathsome medium of exchange which inhibits the circulation of real empathy and real competence among people who know they need one another. Torn between the purity of Esther's purpose and the foulness of her coins, Johnny throws them against the wall, sobbing "Who the hell wants that stuff?"

In the end, however, Johnny himself wants Esther's money. Saroyan never makes the boy explain why he changes his mind about the coins he has flung away, but after a certain point in Mac-Gregor's strange dying speech, Johnny begins moving about the stage, picking Esther's coins up and looking at them closely, as if seeing them in a different, more favorable light. It is a gesture of accommodation with things as they are, and Saroyan leaves it to his audience to see that Johnny makes this gesture as a result of something Mac-Gregor communicates to the boy.

A number of motives may plausibly be assigned to MacGregor's final speech, which is a ranting improvisation on Lear's disillusionment and death: MacGregor, perhaps, decides to do a theatrical improvisation in order to spare his friends the pain of realizing that he is, in fact, dying; or, MacGregor decides to dramatize his death in order at last to realize his life's ambition, regardless of the tastes of his public; or (finally) MacGregor chooses to act *King Lear* in order to comment, by indirection, on the meaning of his own life. All three motives are possible. But it is certain that, at first, Johnny is moved by MacGregor's performance, for when the old man complains that his "wits" are turning, "Johnny goes to him, and kneels," presumably deeply concerned. At first, MacGregor reacts to him, including him in his improvisation, but almost immediately, he puts Johnny off: "Come on, my boy, how dost my boy? Art cold?" he asks. But then he says, "Let me alone! Wilt break my heart?" And while MacGregor "Holds the bugle before him" as Lear holds the dead Cordelia, Johnny begins picking up Esther Kosak's coins.

It is as if Johnny, at first moved to empathy with MacGregor's failed aspirations, is suddenly warned off by the old man himself. There is great bitterness in the old man's dying comparison of his bugle to Cordelia's corpse. Like Lear, MacGregor has been insatiable. Just as Lear has rejected the genuine love of Cordelia for the more formal, conventional protestations of Goneril and Regan, so the insatiable MacGregor has turned down the genuine esteem his bugle has procured him on San Benito Avenue for the more canonical regard to be won, at the center of culture and power, by the Shakespearean actor. And it appears that when the old man's act threatens to inculcate the same insatiability in Johnny, he pushes the boy off—warning him not to follow the path he has himself taken. Johnny takes the old man's warning, and, in picking up the coins, he appears to have learned the lessons of Mac-Gregor's life: that one must be satisfied to produce what people know, immediately and sensuously, that they want; that money exchanged for desired work is not dirty; and that one can still feel good about accepting money, so long as it is earned satisfying the sensuous, rather than pandering to the insatiable. In short, to be happy at all, one must be

happy in spite of the fact that society will not tolerate one's romantic attempts at passing personal misery off in the name of Art.

The play therefore ends with Johnny's recognition that the poet's principled refusal to enter the economy and work for money, though validated as artistic integrity by the post-Romantic art system, is, in its way, an act of aggression in which the artist (though on a smaller scale) is as much of a parasite upon the worker as is the capitalist whom the self-expressive artist claims to oppose. "I'm not mentioning any names, Pa," the boy says, accusingly, as the final curtain comes down, "but something's wrong somewhere."

Harold Clurman recalls that the "excellent press" that greeted *My Heart's in the Highlands* "hastened a change of the [Theatre] Guild's schedule [which] gave [Guild] subscribers a chance to see" Saroyan's play. Enough of them did to give the play a modest run of forty-four performances, rather than the originally projected five; and when the Drama Critics Circle voted on the best New York play of the season of 1938-1939, John Mason Brown and George Jean Nathan voted for *My Heart's in the Highlands*.

According to Saroyan, these votes secured him an invitation to the annual dinner of the Drama Critics Circle, at the Algonquin, where he found himself across the table from the actor / impresario Eddie Dowling, who offered to buy, "sight unseen," any new Saroyan play. Within a week, Saroyan says, he had finished the draft of something he called "The Light Fantastic." Its title changed, it was to become the best known and most acted of Saroyan's plays, *The Time of Your Life* (1939). The playwright recalls its having been read and mentioned in *Newsweek* by George Jean Nathan, who suggested the title "Sunset Sonata"; and he gratefully acknowledges that, true to his word, "Dowling drew up a contract with me and advanced me an enormous sum of money" for the new script at a time when he was "simply broke." But despite Dowling's eagerness to become Saroyan's next producer, Clurman indicates that "Saroyan brought *The Time of Your Life* to me on completion." He regrets having rejected it for its "self-indulgence, [its] flagrant braggadocio of undiscipline, [its] thoughtless and almost cheap bathos . . . as if after the directness and simplicity of *My Heart's in the Highlands* Saroyan was seeking to popularize not only his message but his reputation. . . ." Apparently, then, *The Time of Your Life* went into production with Dowling and the Theatre Guild only after Clurman turned it down.

Again, as with *My Heart's in the Highlands*, there

were profound differences between the playwright and his company over the mounting of Saroyan's new play. In his note to this play in *Three Plays* (1940), Saroyan is as mannerly in acknowledging the contributions of the theatre people to *The Time of Your Life* as he had been in the first publication of *My Heart's in the Highlands*; but again, while recalling (in 1957) "Opening Nights I Have Known," Saroyan takes a harsher tone. He acknowledges that the play went through four or five revisions after the speedy first draft. Moreover, there were other changes. A line and some stage business were suggested by actor William Bendix, who played Krupp. Roles were written in or taken out of the play to accommodate local ordinances governing the use of child performers while the play toured before its Broadway opening. And when Saroyan's cousin Ross Bagdasarian came up from Fresno to San Francisco asking him to write a part into *The Time of Your Life* for him, the playwright obliged, sending young Bagdasarian along "to New York with the part and a letter." It was Bagdasarian who wired Saroyan "at the last minute that [he] had

Playbill

better have a look at the play right away because . . . it didn't look right." Saroyan reports that in New Haven, after one or two performances, he "took over the directing of the play," having learned, absolutely, that "a play is achieved or miscarried on the boards by its director." Less than three weeks later, on 25 October 1939, the play opened at the Booth Theatre in New York.

The published text of *The Time of Your Life* begins with an explicit statement of the play's "moral," as if (this time) Saroyan were specifically guarding against the misinterpretation and mystification under which Broadway's thespians and critics had hidden *My Heart's in the Highlands* in interpreting it. Saroyan planned for this moral to be read over a loudspeaker before the curtain, but the plan was abandoned and the moral survives only in print. It remains a touchstone for Saroyan's interpreters. It begins, "In the time of your life, live, so that in that good time there shall be no ugliness or death for yourself or for any life your life touches." To do this, Saroyan goes on to explain, one must "Be the inferior of no man, nor of any man . . . the superior." Moreover, one must put aside the conventional forms of materialism and fleshliness, from which "the obvious" in social life (its cruelty and inequality) results, and one must bring out the kindliness and gentleness of which man is also, obviously, capable, but which "have been driven into secrecy and sorrow by the shame and terror of the world." But even though one must encourage virtue during the only time in which one's moribund body has life, one may well be forced to kill, without regret, to resist the spread of "the obvious" against people too spontaneously kind to defend themselves against it. As recently as 1976, in an interview (published in 1977 in the journal *Soviet Literature*), Saroyan was still essentially paraphrasing sentences from this statement when asked if he had "any kind of motto."

The plotting of *The Time of Your Life* is in keeping with the didactic impulse of this moral. At crucial junctures in *My Heart's in the Highlands*, such as MacGregor's death, Saroyan had trusted his audience to piece together the characters' motives and his judgments of their motives from actions which the characters themselves never explain. But in *The Time of Your Life*, the playwright makes his characters state their motives or discuss the motives of others, thus providing *The Time of Your Life* with more verbal guides to interpretation than Saroyan had included in his first play.

The Time of Your Life is set in "Nick's . . . an American place: a San Francisco waterfront honky-tonk." Among the various characters who staff or patronize Nick's bar sits the expensively dressed, thoughtful, but "bored" figure of Joe, "At a table." Like his presence in such a place, Joe's conduct is anomalous enough to demand explanation. He buys out a newsboy's remaining papers, but hardly reads them. He dictatorially sends the innocent, boyish Tom on "crazy" errands, but is acknowledged as a benefactor whose charity once saved Tom's life. He seems not to work, yet he is

to find out if it's possible to live . . . a civilized life . . . a life that can't hurt any other life." Later, in act 5, Joe makes it clear that his strange charities are by way of atonement. He has been maimed by conventional success: "I *earned* the money I throw away," he says. "I stole it like everybody else does. I hurt people to get it . . . I've got a Christian conscience in a world that's got no conscience at all. . . . I'll always have money, as long as this world stays the way it is. I don't work. I don't make anything. . . . I drink. . . .

The Time of Your Life

visibly well-off. He has even had Nick lay in a supply of champagne—not the usual drink of his clientele—for him. When Kitty Duval, a prostitute with whom Tom is in love, enters, Joe alone treats her with respect. Still, when Kitty puts aside her initial defensiveness and asks Joe to dance, he refuses, almost in a panic. And when Tom returns, Joe gives him five dollars and tells him to dance with Kitty.

But at the beginning of the second act, Joe's contradictory toughness, tenderness, and fear of potential intimacies receives an explanation. To Mary L., Joe's female counterpart in alienation, Joe explains that for three years, he has "been trying . . .

Well, you can't enjoy living unless you work. . . . There isn't anything I can do that won't make me feel embarrassed. Because I can't do simple, good things. I haven't the patience. And I'm too smart." Though he has money and does not write, Joe's predicament is, once again, that of the poor poet in *My Heart's in the Highlands*. He has been spiritually ruined—left stranded, without a means of valuing himself—after "maturing" normally in a stratified society which proliferates false values, and which does not value real satisfactions: the body's competences for work, for love, and for guiltless aggression to protect work and love from the incursion of the false.

As it was in *My Heart's in the Highlands* the post-Romantic Western art system is again portrayed as deeply involved in the failures of the stratified society because of its confusion of self-expression with aggression based on acceptance of alienation as man's necessary condition. McCarthy, a longshoreman-intellectual, makes this clear. Treating the body as the basis of his philosophy, McCarthy explains himself as follows: "I'm a man with too much brawn to be an intellectual, exclusively. I married a small, sensitive, cultured woman so that my kids would be sissies instead of suckers. A strong man with any sensibility has no choice in this world but to be a heel, or a *worker*. I haven't the heart to be a heel, so I'm a worker. I've got a son in high school who's already thinking of being a writer. . . . Every maniac in the world that ever brought about the murder of people through war started out in an attic or a basement writing poetry. It stank. So they got even by becoming important heels. . . . Right now on Telegraph Hill is some punk who is trying to be Shakespeare. Ten years from now he'll be a senator. Or a communist." Canonized culture as promulgated by the schools, then, is for "sissies," and it is but a short step from the cultivated sissy to the maniacal "heel," bent, in the name of greatness and high standards, upon imposing his own misery upon others who can still feel, spontaneously, when they are well-off.

Such a spontaneous person is Krupp, the policeman, who has been taught to be ashamed of his want of social and cultural sophistication, but who nevertheless decides to quit the police force rather than go on keeping "law and order" for people possessed of what passes for political and cultural legitimacy, who, he knows, are "all crazy." In *The Time of Your Life*, Krupp's words spell out the message which Saroyan had dramatized in the children's acrobatics, ball games, and whistling demonstrations of *My Heart's in the Highlands*. "We've got everything," Krupp notes, "but we always feel lousy and dissatisfied just the same." And he goes on to enumerate the kinds of direct, sensuous experience which no one needs special cultivation to feel are really valuable: "It's wonderful to get up in the morning and go out for a little walk and smell the trees and see the streets and the kids going to school and the clouds in the sky. It's wonderful just to be able to move around and whistle a song if you feel like it, or maybe try to sing one. This is a nice world. So why do they make all the trouble?" This is Saroyan's constant question, and in *The Time of Your Life*, Blick, the "head of the lousy Vice Squad," is the character in whom his answer to it lies.

During act 1 Nick's proves itself "a good, low-down, honky-tonk American place that lets people alone." Despite his gruffness, Nick has a heart and an eye for artistic talent. He has hired Harry (first played by Gene Kelly), a dancing comic, and Wesley (played by Reginald Beane), a black piano player who has staggered in, fainting from hunger, in hopes only of food and a job cleaning up. Together, they play and dance, while Nick's various customers pursue their various interests. Saroyan's stage direction specifies that "There is deep American naiveté and faith in the behavior of each person. No one is competing with anyone else. . . . there is unmistakable smiling and humor in the scene; a sense of the human body and spirit emerging from the world-imposed state of stress and fretfulness, fear and awkwardness, to the more natural state of casualness and grace. . . . Into this scene and atmosphere comes Blick . . . the sort of human being you dislike at sight. . . . the strong man without strength . . . the weakling who uses force on the weaker." The mere presence of Blick "begins slowing down" the dancing, the music, and even the mechanical toy with which Joe is playing at his table. Blick refuses the drink Nick offers him and warns Nick against permitting streetwalkers to frequent his bar. Everything stops. "There is absolute silence and a strange fearfulness and disharmony in the atmosphere now." Nick accuses Blick of sexual hypocrisy and of trying "to change the world from something bad to something worse. Something like yourself." In a fury, Blick leaves, promising to return in the evening.

When he does, he proves the truth of Nick's accusations and brings on the climax of the play. Blick begins interrogating Kitty, who claims that she is a burlesque dancer out of work. An old fraud named Kit Carson, who, throughout the play, has been exchanging tall tales about himself for drinks, comes chivalrously to Kitty's defense. Blick takes Kit out and beats him. Then, putting Kitty to the test, Blick forces Wesley to play the piano while she proves to him she can do a striptease. Joe, well dressed as usual, comes to her rescue, but it is Wesley, the black man, on whom Blick's cowardly fury descends when Wesley joins in Joe's protest against Blick's treatment of Kitty. Tom enters, sees Kitty crying, and hears Blick beating Wesley offstage. He threatens to kill Blick, but Joe, having made possible Tom's entry into the world of work and love from which he feels himself cut off, restrains Tom and sends Kitty off to marry him.

Then, taking from his pocket the revolver after which he has sent Tom on one of his whimsical purchasing errands, Joe himself assumes the responsibility of eliminating Blick. He walks to the door through which are heard the sounds of Wesley's beating, cocks the pistol, "aims very carefully, and pulls [the] trigger. . . ." But "There is no shot." Old Kit Carson has left the gun unloaded. Nick quiets Joe as Blick reappears, "panting for breath" after beating Wesley. Threatening Blick's life, Nick warns him never to return and throws him into the street. Outside, two shots are heard, and Nick, who has run out to investigate the shots, returns with the joyful news of Blick's death and of the fact that "none of the cops are trying to find out who [Blick's killer is]." Joe is in a daze, apparently unable to settle how he feels about himself after his first really responsible act. His charities have merely been attempts to use the fruits of established socio-economic life to mitigate its ill effects upon those who cannot accept the grim disciplines that produce those fruits, such as they are. But intending to kill an enforcer of the insane, established order is a different matter. In acting on that intent, however unsuccessfully, Joe has risked everything, from his unearned access to the labor of others, to life itself.

But as Joe is leaving, still dazed, he meets old Kit Carson, who is just entering. The two "look at one another knowingly." "Somebody just shot a man. How are you feeling?" Joe asks Kit; and the old fraud, able to take himself seriously for the first time in his life, proudly takes credit for Blick's death. His only regret is that he "had to throw the beautiful revolver into the Bay." Kit's new dignity apparently reassures Joe about the worthiness of his own intent to kill Blick; "with great admiration and affection," Joe gives Kit the revolver that did not fire and leaves Nick's with a hearty wave for all. Evidently, his alienating acceptance of established social craziness is at an end.

The play had an initial run of 185 performances, but it lost $25,000. Still, *The Time of Your Life* was chosen best play of the 1939-1940 season by the New York Drama Critics Circle, and, more important, in May of 1940, it also won a Pulitzer Prize, which resulted in an immediate fall revival and an eventual road tour.

The Pulitzer Prize carried not only great prestige, but also an award of $1,000. Unlike the poet of *My Heart's in the Highlands,* therefore, Saroyan, in winning the Pulitzer, had been received at last in the sanctum where canonizers scare poets to death and admit plays to the status of "culture." In his two Broadway successes, however, Saroyan had proclaimed his opposition to institutions which tell people what to value beyond what they feel in life

and in art. Now, therefore, the sincerity of this opposition was to be tested.

In a telegram to the Pulitzer judges at Columbia University (which the *New York Times,* unaccountably, found "prolix"), Saroyan rejected the prize. The playwright's wire reminds the board of his anticipatory announcement that he would reject the prize if it were offered him, and it explains that "I do not believe in prizes or awards in the realm of art, and have always been particularly opposed to material or official patronage of the arts by government, organization, or individual, a naive and innocent style of behavior which, nevertheless, I believe, vitiates and embarrasses art at its source." *My Heart's in the Highlands* had been concerned with the problem of eliminating canonizing middlemen from the "source" of art in direct dealings between artists and hedonistic perceivers who are not taught by prize committees what to feel and say about the work of artists. *The Time of Your Life* had, likewise, been specifically committed to encouraging people not to be ashamed of their impulses to value what immediately feels good and humane. Hence, Saroyan's rejection of the Pulitzer Prize for his play was quite consistent with his notions about the political economy of art. For him, art was not to be one of the means of legitimizing "the obvious," but was rather to be one of the chief nonviolent antidotes to power and restorers of the damage done by critics and policers who do not respect what even children know in their bones that they need.

As late as 1968, in a note to a "very short play" called *Making Money,* Saroyan bluntly reiterated the contempt of Official Culture which made him refuse his Pulitzer Prize. "I find [*Making Money*] funny," he says, "but I must remark that a number of very good editors don't agree. Well, that's what makes great literature, as we say. Six or seven friends telling one another in print that each of them is the greatest going—and *voilà,* eminence, or should one say mincemeat? Let the reader decide—I say this is a very funny play. If you find it funny, too, please tell somebody, because I never knew anybody yet who didn't want to know about a piece of funny writing."

For a time, it appeared as if Saroyan might hold his own in his rebellion against the official art system and have his way on the New York stage. But things eventually went against him, and in *Places Where I've Done Time,* a memoir published in 1972, he reports that "I used to like the theatre . . . , but [it] also has become something neither enjoyed nor needed." Nevertheless, five consecutive Broadway seasons, from 1939 until 1943, included productions of Saroyan; and during these years, until he was inducted into the army in October of 1942, New York's productions *of* Saroyan became productions *by* Saroyan, as he had wished from the start.

In January of 1940, his ballet, *A Theme in the Life of the Great American Goof*, opened, and in May of that year, *Love's Old Sweet Song* began a run of forty-four performances at the Plymouth Theatre, produced, like *The Time of Your Life*, by Eddie Dowling and the Theatre Guild, and (also like *The Time of Your Life*) much revised and largely directed by Saroyan himself while it was being prepared for Broadway. *Love's Old Sweet Song* carries on the themes and character types with which *My Heart's in the Highlands* and *The Time of Your Life* had been concerned. In revenge for a prank, a telegraph messenger and his brother forge a telegram to be delivered by their colleague, the unwitting prankster, to an attractive, middle-aged spinster named Ann Hamilton. The forged wire announces the return of one Barnaby Gaul, who claims to have briefly met Miss Hamilton twenty-seven years before, while whistling "Love's Old Sweet Song" in front of her house. In the wire, this Barnaby Gaul also claims to have been nurturing his love for Miss Hamilton ever since. No such brief encounter had ever really occurred, but no sooner has Miss Hamilton's imagination been quickened by the forged telegram than a stranger arrives whose appearance roughly matches the wire's description of the fictitious Barnaby Gaul. The stranger is confused when the telegraph messenger and Miss Hamilton keep prompting him to remember her, but when the boy lets him read the wire he is supposed to have sent, the stranger instantly decides to take on Barnaby Gaul's identity and become the long-lost, unknown admirer Miss Hamilton obviously hopes he is.

In actuality, Gaul (originally played by Walter Huston) is a traveling swindler—a medicine salesman, somewhat reminiscent of MacGregor in *My Heart's in the Highlands* or of Joe or Kit Carson, in *The Time of Your Life*. He, too, has given himself over to living out hopeful lies, since the truth—"the obvious," as Saroyan had called it in the moral to *The Time of Your Life*—is such an insane, inhumane, body-violating guide to living. As Gaul tells Windmore, a subscription salesman for *Time* magazine and (hence) a purveyor of "the obvious," "I have studied the reasons for things: for disgrace, for wretchedness, for disease, for stupor. No man in the world knows better than I why these tragic things occur in that most miraculous and magnificent creation of the hand of God: the noble body

which is man. *You* bring news of world-wide madness and horror to the living every Friday. You make of universal crime a topic for idle reading. You tell the people of foolishness everywhere, every week. That's fine. *I* bring *hope* to the people. I have here in these bottles a medicine. . . ." The problem faced by the messenger boy, Georgie Americanos, and his Greek immigrant family, is to keep the mountebank from backing out of his first really responsible act and abandoning the kindly impulse that had led him to bring real hope to Ann Hamilton by assuming the fictitious identity of Barnaby Gaul. It is again the problem of encouraging virtue not to be ashamed of itself, which is spelled out in the moral of *The Time of Your Life*. Some of the encouragement is supplied by Georgie's father, Stylianos Americanos, a wrestler and "World's Heavyweight Champion [of] Kern County," but, in the end, Gaul himself recognizes that his love for Ann Hamilton has been real—not just another swindle. He stops being afraid of his impulse to love her and he proposes that Miss Hamilton join him in his travels.

As before, Saroyan is concerned in *Love's Old Sweet Song* with the complicity of the media, including the art system, in perpetuating "the obvious." While Gaul flees and Miss Hamilton and the Americanos family pursue him, Miss Hamilton's house is occupied by a family of Okies, Cabot and Leona Yearling and their eleven children. They are being shadowed by Elsa Wax, a cynical former Vassar girl, now a *Life* magazine photographer, and by Richard Oliver, an idealistic unpublished writer who plans to write a novel about the Yearlings so that "The pitiable plight of these unfortunate people [may become] not the concern of one man alone, but of the whole nation." "Something's got to be done for them," Oliver insists. "All right, *do* something. What can you do?" Elsa demands, and Oliver is only able to respond by calling her "a Fascist." "Talk! Talk! Talk! That's all I hear, ever since you intellectuals started following us around," Cabot Yearling concludes on behalf of the *lumpenproletariat*, the poor without hope or initiative: "When do you folks aim to let us rest?"

Recalling (in 1957) the opening night of *Love's Old Sweet Song*, Saroyan attributed the play's failure to the refusal of "New York intellectuals, as they are inaccurately called," to tolerate this attack on the emptiness of their announced commitment to the poor. He was perfectly satisfied that "all of our hard work in Philadelphia and in Baltimore had not been in vain" and that the Broadway premiere was "flawless." In *Places Where I've Done Time* he reports the details of this hard work. It had involved transforming *Love's Old Sweet Song* from "a farce-tragedy, if there is such a thing," into "a farce from beginning to end," after three performances in Philadelphia. In Baltimore, Saroyan writes, "my work was mainly to watch rehearsals and to remove flaws and to enlarge or heighten values"—no mean task since the cast included "eleven kids ranging from sixteen down to three," and "a rather eccentric Greek I had hired in New York outside the Guild Theatre offices on 52nd Street [who] could never be made to pick up his cues. . . ." When Saroyan threatened him with replacement by a professional actor, however, the Greek performed so well that "even Walter Huston was confused. 'This man has *got* to be a professional,' he said. 'He couldn't have improved so quickly if he weren't. . . .' "

Obviously, Saroyan remains proud of his work in staging his plays. His insistence on doing so cannot, however, have been easy for Broadway's producers, directors, actors, and critics to deal with. In 1972, for instance, he remembers the specifics of what, in 1957, he had quietly called "taking over the directing" of *The Time of Your Life*: "my cousin told me in unmistakable language that the play was being murdered by a lot of arty-farty people. . . . My career as an American playwright was at stake. I told the producers I would direct the play. I told them to get rid of the director, the scene designer, and various other people. The producers were scheduled to open in Boston in three days. I told them to meet the schedule. They thought I was mad of course, but then what could they lose? The play was quite plainly a total loss. . . . A new set was installed on the stage. Bogus Stanislavsky-style actors were fired and replaced by working actors—who looked right and moved right. The critics in Boston saw a performance after only three days of rehearsals and previews, and the producers were amazed that the critics thought so well of the play. Perhaps I *did* know what I was doing, after all. . . . My cousin reported the backstage news every night: 'Everybody thinks you're crazy, except the girl who plays Mary L.'

"Next night, 'The guy who plays Kit Carson thinks you're working a miracle.'

"Finally, he reported that everybody got the idea, even the producers." In any event, the Broadway ventures with which the playwright followed *Love's Old Sweet Song* were all his own.

The biographer Howard R. Floan reports that "For his next play, *The Beautiful People*, [Saroyan] took over the casting and directing himself and financed the play with money coming in from a

successful road tour of *The Time of Your Life* and from wide sales of [his novel] *My Name is Aram* in the stores and through the Book-of-the-Month Club." Saroyan himself reports that he put $11,000 into *The Beautiful People*, which opened at the Lyceum Theatre on 21 April 1941.

In *The Beautiful People*, Saroyan again expresses his concerns for encouraging people to negate "the obvious" and to create a working economy in which people exchange real values—not only currency, advertised goods, and grimly contracted services, but also civility, recognition of decent impulses, and love. Jonah Webster and his two youngest children, Agnes (seventeen years old) and Owen (fifteen years old), are living in an old house in San Francisco on a twenty-four-dollar pension check that keeps arriving in the mail every month for one Wilbur M. Stonehedge, now deceased. Jonah's oldest child, Harold, has gone to New York to become a musician. The old house in San Francisco is full of mice, for which Owen keeps setting traps; but Agnes, pitying the mice, keeps finding and burning the traps. She is "Saint Agnes of the Mice," Owen explains to a lady who has come looking for Jonah, and the mice keep praying for her and bringing her offerings—sometimes even spelling out her name, in flowers, across the floor. This "fairy-tale," as the lady calls it, turns out, however, to have a plausible, material explanation, as one might expect in Saroyan. Owen himself has been murmuring the mice's prayers and bringing the floral offerings, as Jonah explains to Father Hogan after Owen has fallen into the pipe organ at church while seeking to recognize and substantiate his sister's saintly fantasy by bringing home a mouse which she says has taken sanctuary there. "Father Hogan, if I do not encourage the imaginations of my children, I also do not hinder them. . . . It's not enough to make a record of the world—it's necessary to change it! And you cannot begin to change it from the *outside*. The image of the good must first be real to the *mind* before it can inhabit substance and occupy space. My world is myself and my kinship with all other things. And my delight is my children. We are exactly the same as all other people, but I know we live better than the rich and better than the poor, because the values which make rich and poor are without image or reality, and the real values are the only values we recognize and cherish. . . .Even in the eyes of the world, we *would* be better, . . . if the world itself would be, but since it isn't, we refuse to exchange our values for its values." Secretly, however, Jonah has been worrying that New York may have destroyed the goodness of his older son,

Harold, whose cornet music the family often fancies can be heard across the continent. "I've lost faith," Jonah confesses to Father Hogan, "because I believed goodness was a coin for exchange more powerful than any coin minted by any government—the *only* coin. . . . My children must not know that what I have taught them may be useless in this world." But the end of *The Beautiful People* suggests that Jonah's teachings are holding their own. Prim, the vice-president who has been sent to inform the Websters that the Stonehedge pension check will no longer be coming, has found a welcome with them anyway, and is moved to continue the checks with an additional ten dollars a month. And Harold returns, playing his cornet, and bringing with him a young man in need of a home. With this "miracle," the curtain falls.

With full control of the production, the playwright was able to confound Broadway by acting upon notions of the proper relationship between artist and spectator already suggested by his plays. First, with opening night less than one week away, Saroyan offered the public free tickets to dress rehearsals of *The Beautiful People*. On 15 April 1941, a large crowd consisting mostly of students, housewives, and aspiring thespians, and stretching for 300 feet down West Forty-fourth Street to Broadway, quickly grabbed up the 850 tickets Saroyan had to offer. The *New York Times* reported that a thousand people were turned away and that many of the free tickets distributed were swapped, scalped, and gambled for, in an appropriately Saroyanesque manner, on the sidewalk outside the Lyceum Theatre. "Perfecting a play without an audience is like trying to improve an orchestra without musicians," Saroyan explained. *The Beautiful People* "in its present state is still an unfinished product and therefore not for sale."

Then, after the play had run for a little more than two months, on 2 July, Saroyan and his press agent, Leo Freedman, advertised that anyone who disliked *The Beautiful People* could have his money back, "just present the stub of your ticket to the boys in the box office and go home with every cent of your money—and no hard feelings." According to the *Times*, the offer remained in effect for two weeks, during which the Lyceum staff made bets on which spectators would ask for refunds and satisfied theatregoers sometimes rebuked those in line waiting to get back their money. In withdrawing the offer, Saroyan claimed that it had been unnecessary. He thanked the public for the overwhelming confidence in his work, which it had revealed by the fact that 1½ percent of the receipts during the

fortnight of the offer were refunded. Saroyan closed the play on 2 August, after a run of 120 performances, which Floan, relying on the remarks the playwright published with *The Beautiful People*, says "took it out of the red and encouraged Saroyan to consider further productions." In 1957, however, Saroyan reported that "I could have closed with my own money doubled, but I kept it going until the $11,000 had been used up." Though the latter proceeding is quite within character and according to principle for Saroyan, it nevertheless is described in a paragraph in which he recalls *The Beautiful People* as having "opened at the Belasco," not at the Lyceum, as it actually did.

Next, on Broadway, as the first of what he hoped would be a series of his productions of his plays, under the rubric of "The Saroyan Theatre," Saroyan produced and directed his two one-act plays, *Across the Board on Tomorrow Morning*, and *Talking to You* (both in 1942). *Across the Board on Tomorrow Morning* had had two prior productions, the first (in February 1941) at the Pasadena Playhouse in California, and the second in New York (in March 1942) at the Theatre Showcase, ending an evening begun with Nicolas Evrienov's *Theatre of the Soul*. The Pasadena production, according to Floan, though not directed by Saroyan, still showed the playwright's interest in changing the norms under which audiences see plays. Saroyan specified that *Across the Board on Tomorrow Morning* was to be given twice in succession each evening so that spectators who wished to see it again might do so. For the Saroyan Theatre's production of *Across the Board on Tomorrow Morning*, the playwright again felt free, as he had done in casting *The Time of Your Life* and *The Beautiful People*, not to rely exclusively on professional actors. The cast included, as George Jean Nathan reported, "a hatcheck girl [from] the Stork Club, . . . a broke poet [from] Greenwich Village, and a couple of Filipinos [from] the Automat" who, by all accounts, stole the show. As Pablo and Pancho, two dishwashers in Callaghan's restaurant and bar, they emerge (like irate sociologists) from the kitchen to lecture Pinkerton, a Wall Street type who will not deign to speak with some of his fellow patrons, about his total ignorance of the plight of Filipino boys in America.

The playwright has recalled the fate of the Saroyan Theatre with some bitterness. In *Places Where I've Done Time*, he writes of closing his deal with Lee Schubert for the use of the Belasco Theatre. The memoir contrasts Schubert's sententious piety about the place as a shrine of the American theatre with Saroyan's sense of it as "dusty, haunted by [the spirit of Belasco,] a fraud who never suspected so much, and by his banal ideas and his . . . insatiable capacity for enjoying the favors of . . . women [desperate to go on the stage]." Schubert is quoted as telling Saroyan, "Any way that I can help, I am at your service. Go in [to the Belasco] with a free heart. Don't worry about business matters." Thus assured, Saroyan opened *Across the Board on Tomorrow Morning* and *Talking to You* on 17 August 1942.

As it had been over his direction of *The Beautiful People*, drama criticism remained divided over the playwright's work in mounting the two one-acts of the Saroyan Theatre. Stark Young, in the *New Republic*, had sensed a validity in Saroyan's refusal to allow Broadway to deck *The Beautiful People* in "wheezy old loads of stagecraft," snapping it up, stereotyping it, clipping and narrowing it. And Young saw "a certain elusive but fine [lyric] weaving and pressure of rhythms" which he did not think the established likes of Eddie Dowling could have brought "from the heart of" *Talking to You*. But the usually patronizing tone in which Brooks Atkinson wrote about Saroyan took on bluntness in treating his direction of the Saroyan Theatre. "Although Mr. Saroyan is an affable chap with an attractive slant on people, his [static and literal-minded] stage directions is like the compounding of a felony," Atkinson wrote. "He needs a professional director." According to Floan, Atkinson "echoed the judgment of many."

In 1972, Saroyan recalled that despite Lee Schubert's initial assurances, Schubert gave notice that the Saroyan Theatre was to vacate the Belasco "by the end of the week [after eight performances], when the terms of the written agreement were technically faulted because the box office intake fell below a certain [weekly minimum]." The failure of *Across the Board on Tomorrow Morning* and *Talking to You* marked the beginning of the end for Saroyan on Broadway.

Nevertheless, before 1942 was over, yet another Saroyan one-act play which had premiered a year earlier in California came to the New York stage. It was *Hello Out There*, a script for two performers, in which the roles were taken, on Broadway, by Eddie Dowling (who also directed) and Julie Haydon—the Joe and Kitty Duval of the first *Time of Your Life*. *Hello Out There* opened on 29 September 1942 at the Belasco, as the curtain raiser for a revival of G. K. Chesterton's *Magic*, but the critics felt that Saroyan's piece was clearly the highlight of the evening. As Atkinson saw it, "Some professionals have taken hold of a short play by

Saroyan and the results are stunning." It is possible, however, that New York was stunned by *Hello Out There* because it was the most conventional Saroyan script yet acted there.

The play is plainly realistic, set in the jailhouse of a small town called Matador, Texas, where a young drifter, brought there, unconscious, for his own protection after having been accused of rape and beaten up in a nearby town, is tapping on the floor, as if in Morse code, with a spoon. "Hello—out there!" he begins calling; and after a while, he is answered by "A girl's voice, very sweet and soft." For fifty cents a day, it develops, she cleans the Matador jail and cooks for whatever inmates it may happen to have. Her father has always eked out a living by stealing from her and by feigning a disability so as to collect "a little relief from the government." The townspeople have always laughed at her, but in his restless sleep while she was caring for him in the jail house, the prisoner said he liked her, and she has returned in the hope that this first evidence that someone might have feeling for her will continue after he begins recovering from his beating. From the moment he hears her voice, even before the sad facts of the girl's life are known, the prisoner recognizes a soul mate in the girl—someone "as lonesome as a coyote," as he is, himself. And through the bars of his cell, to which she cannot find the key, they exchange love and recognition, just as the poet of *My Heart's in the Highlands* had done in bringing his poems to Mr. Kosak in recognition of the grocer's kindness. Again, Saroyan is concerned with dramatizing people's basic capacity to exchange moral support, even in the face of "the obvious."

But "the obvious" has its way with the lovers of *Hello Out There*. The girl goes out for cigarettes, and while she is gone, the husband of the woman the prisoner is accused of having raped arrives at the head of a lynch mob, which waits outside while he enters the jail to confront his wife's alleged rapist alone. The desperate prisoner tells the husband that he "met [the man's wife] at a lunch counter." "She came in and sat next to me," he says, "There was plenty of room, but she sat next to me." The prisoner tells the husband that his wife seemed lonesome—that she began talking about a tune on the jukebox to no one in particular, and that he answered her in simple recognition of her apparent loneliness. He admits that he walked the woman home and that he would have taken her to bed had she not then asked him for money and revealed to him that he had picked up not a kindred sufferer in need of comfort, but a prostitute out to profit from his own apparent suffering. The prisoner challenges the husband to call his wife in and confront her with these facts; but the husband "is [too] frightened," and drawing a gun, he shoots the caged prisoner three times and flees from the jail as his victim "falls to his knees," calling again, "Hello—out there!"

The girl comes running back, and hears the prisoner tell her "I'll be with you always—God damn it. Always!" as he expires. The husband reappears with two friends, one of whom unlocks the cell as a woman, the alleged victim of the prisoner's rape, enters. She satisfies herself that the prisoner is, in fact, dead as "Her husband looks at her with contempt." When the husband and one of the other men begin to carry the body off, the girl, "suddenly, fiercely" tries to interfere, but the alleged rape victim "slaps the girl and pushes her to the floor," hissing "Listen to the little slut, will you?" The mob leaves with the body, and the curtain falls as the girl "looks straight out [at the audience], and whispers . . . Hello—out—there! Hello—out there!"—challenging the audience to support her resistance to "the obvious."

Floan follows the critical majority who look upon *Hello Out There* as Saroyan's "finest one-act play," remarking that it was written "with more unswerving singleness of purpose than Saroyan gave to any other play." But Saroyan has been his own best critic, and in 1955, in an essay entitled "Art for Man's Sake: A Minority View," published in the *Nation*, he repudiated *Hello Out There* as his own capitulation, in spite of himself, to the tradition which requires great art to replicate "the obvious." "If [like Shakespeare] you're going to have murder and madness in art, then you're going to have them in life, too," Saroyan wrote. And he goes on to repent having "permitted [himself, in *Hello Out There*,] to write out of violent material." "It was the easiest play I ever wrote," he confessed; "I therefore consider the play worthless, if not in fact a mistake, the high opinion of others notwithstanding." "To report chaos and hate is not to put order into chaos or to banish hate," Saroyan said, and he reaffirmed his constant position that "The potentials for order and love are inherent in human life and just as easy to achieve as their opposites—and certainly a lot more practical, if nothing else."

Within a month of Dowling's version of *Hello Out There*, Saroyan was embroiled in one of history's greatest outbreaks of "the obvious"—the one he had anticipated in *My Heart's in the Highlands*. In October of 1942, he was sworn into the U.S. Army, where he remained for the duration of World War II. His military service ended what Floan has called "The Time of His Life"—the period of tremendous productivity in which Saroyan tried to mount a frontal assault on the content, forms, and institutions of the American stage. His parting shot was fired in New York at the Cort Theatre on 24 November 1943, when *Get Away Old Man* opened under the direction of George Abbott, featuring Edward Begley and Richard Widmark in the chief roles. In publishing it, Saroyan tersely remarked that "The play was poorly received by the drama critics of the New York papers, and closed Saturday, December 4, after thirteen performances." Not all of the poor reviews, however, were very well informed about Saroyan's work in the theatre; the *New York Times* critic Lewis Nichols, for instance, quipped that " 'Get Away Old Man' still has a long road to travel before it is another 'Once in a Lifetime.' " So, presumably, would *The Time of Your Life*.

Get Away Old Man continues the analysis of the political economy of art begun in *My Heart's in the Highlands*. But rather than presenting that analysis from the viewpoint of an obscure, unpublished poet, Saroyan now presents it as a dramatic exposé of a recently concluded chapter in his own literary and theatrical success—his involvement with Hollywood in writing *The Human Comedy*, the screenplay for which he received an Academy Award, and which, transformed into a novel, became his most widely read work. As Floan reports, "In December, 1941, Saroyan moved into an office at Metro-Goldwyn-Mayer in Hollywood with the understanding that he would write 'a thoroughly American movie.' To the surprise of those who did not know him well, he declined to discuss contracts or salary until his scenario was ready.

"In February [of 1942] he finished *The Human Comedy* and the studio, well pleased, paid him sixty thousand dollars. But at this point difficulties arose, for Saroyan had set his heart on directing the picture and the studio objected. . . . he tried to buy back the script for eighty thousand dollars; but MGM refused. He gave vent to his anger and disappointment in an explosive article which appeared in *The Daily Variety*, a Hollywood trade paper: 'Why I am No Longer at Metro-Goldwyn-Mayer, or the California Shore-Bird in Its Native Habitat, or Brahms Double Concerto in A Minor.' " Apparently, he also retreated to San Francisco and, in no more than the six days in which he had completed the first draft of *The Time of Your Life*, he wrote *Get Away Old Man*.

The play dramatizes the conflict between a Hollywood producer named Patrick Hammer (played by Begley) and a writer named Harry Bird (played by Widmark). Hammer has made his way in the world by capitulating to "the obvious." He admits he is "a crook . . . But who isn't?," missing the constant Saroyan point that most people are not. For Hammer, "You can't survive in this world and live like a decent human being" without being "a crook." As a poor Dublin child, Hammer loved from afar a little rich girl, who spat at him when they finally met in the street. "I was murdered," Hammer complains, sentimentally, "as if they had put a knife in my heart." And he gloats of having had his revenge on the rich and powerful. "Their loveliest came to me . . . humiliated, seeking my favor. . . , their women hating me and pretending in their nakedness to love me." His mind a steady driveling of platitudes about the filmmaker's power and responsibility in the modern world, Hammer needs Harry Bird, who he says is like his son, to write the great film that will finally redeem the life Hammer has spent serving "the obvious." But Harry finds love and tells Hammer, "Get away, old man." The writer leaves with his girl, and the final curtain comes down as Hammer frantically telephones an aide to bring "the son of a bitch" back, and arranges an assignation with the undiscovered actress he plans to introduce in Harry's unwritten film.

In 1957, Saroyan recalled the premiere of *Get Away Old Man* as "the only opening night of any of my plays I have ever gone to." By the end of the second act, audience reactions had told him that the play was "a flop," and the experience convinced him that Broadway should see no more Saroyan unless it saw Saroyan as staged by its author. Explaining fourteen years of withdrawal from the Broadway stage, Saroyan writes that "From that year to this I have kept my plays away from Broadway, waiting for the time when I might produce them with my own money again. In May of this year [1957] I decided that I might never again be able to do that, and so I allowed another of my plays to appear on Broadway: 'The Cave Dwellers.' " *The Cave Dwellers* (1957), as of 1980, is the last of Saroyan's plays to be produced on a Broadway stage.

Meanwhile, on 9 January 1943, Saroyan had been elected to the department of art and literature at the National Institute of Arts and Letters. He had reached the peak of his recognition as an American writer. Then, on 24 February 1943, from Dayton, Ohio, where Saroyan was on duty with Signal Corps, came the news that Carol Marcus, the eighteen-year-old daughter of a vice-president of the Bendix Aviation Corporation, the former bridesmaid of Gloria Vanderbilt, the actress who

had made her Broadway debut in *Across the Board on Tomorrow Morning*, had been married to the thirty-four-year-old Saroyan by John Edwards, a justice of the peace. It was big news, for the war and his marriage clearly began the decline of the writer's reputation.

Not every play Saroyan published during "The Time of His Life" was produced on Broadway, and he mentions two—"The Hero of the World" and "Something About a Soldier" (respectively written just before and just after *Love's Old Sweet Song*)—which seem to have remained unpublished as well as unproduced in New York. David Kherdian's *A Bibliography of William Saroyan 1934-1964* lists a total of twenty-four published plays, mostly one-acts, mostly unproduced on Broadway, from *The Man with the Heart in the Highlands*, in 1938, until *Get Away Old Man*, published in 1944. Three of these were broadcast as radio plays in 1940 and 1941.

But Saroyan's Broadway years had not only been a period of serious literary and theatrical productivity. "The Time of His Life" had also been a time for the good life—for world travel, for drinking, for wenching, and for gambling. He was a celebrity—"the fabulous Saroyan," Brooks Atkinson patronizingly called him—and he faced the temptations of celebrity. Rather than sheltering him from these temptations, his marriage (as he has several times written about it) drastically compounded them. *Little* has been his constant adjective for his wife. The realization that he was in trouble seems to have begun setting in with a vengeance in 1947, the year in which he next published a play, *Jim Dandy, Fat Man in a Famine*, which had been acted at the Pasadena Community Playhouse in 1941. In the winter of 1947, the Saroyans, now including a son, Aram (born 25 September 1943), and a daughter, Lucy (born 17 January 1946), moved into a very fashionable rented house in Mill Neck, Long Island. "The arrangements of renting had been made," Saroyan writes in *Places Where I've Done Time*, "by the little woman's little mother . . . because [though exorbitantly expensive] it was perfect for the giving of parties." He adds, "Everybody knew that after three years in the Army and two years back in society, so to put it, I was broke and in debt, but . . . [Carol] and her little mother always believed—why, for that boy money is the easiest thing in the world to make, by the hundreds of thousands of dollars. . . . They were good at throwing around the titles of some of my novels and plays in relation to various motion picture companies, producers, directors, actors and actresses, but they spoke from ignorance. They had not read any of the plays or novels. . . ." Meanwhile, Saroyan records in a *Saturday Evening Post* article on "The Funny Business of Marriage," he became a roaring social lion, drinking too much, "going along at a good clip, writing 30 or 40 words a day like clockwork," and permitting himself to be endlessly talked at about "new books, new plays, new ideas, new liberalism, new ways to care about the poor people, the several minorities, the rejected, the despised [until] instead of writing 30 or 40 words a day I wrote only 15 or 20."

When the lease on the house in Mill Neck expired, the couple returned to San Francisco, where "the little bride" was miserable until, in 1948, they moved back again to New York. In April of 1949, the marriage broke up. Saroyan reports that he "wandered around [Europe] in a daze for three months," eventually going, via New York and San Francisco, "to Las Vegas, to establish residence in Nevada [for] the necessary six weeks in order to obtain a divorce." In Las Vegas, "drinking and gambling every day and all night," Saroyan lost $50,000—including a $36,000 advance from "a big publishing house [on] three books." During this troubled time, Saroyan had three more full-length plays published, all in 1949: *Don't Go Away Mad*, *Sam Ego's House*, and *A Decent Birth, A Happy Funeral*. Of these plays, Floan remarks that "they tend to repeat the weak points of his produced plays without adding any new dimensions." *Sam Ego's House*, produced in 1947, had opened in the round in Hollywood; and in 1949 an invited audience saw the Abbe Practical Workshop present *Don't Go Away Mad* Off Broadway at the Master Institute Theatre in New York.

Divorced in 1949, the Saroyans married a second time in 1951, and the union quickly ended once again in disaster. The playwright recalls having considered suicide. "I was bankrupt," he writes, "in debt to the Tax Collector for about fifty thousand dollars, about half that much to others, most of them merchants who had sold [the same little bride] stuff." Since his second divorce in 1952, Saroyan has never remarried. Still, *Places Where I've Done Time* indicates that throughout the 1950s his penchant for gambling and his financial troubles persisted.

The Cave Dwellers, the last Saroyan play to appear on Broadway, like *The Time of Your Life*, was written at the Great Northern Hotel in New York during a very brief span of time (the first eight days of 1955), while Saroyan was in town for the City Center Theatre's revival of *The Time of Your Life*. But as Saroyan indicated in his introduction to the published version of *The Cave Dwellers* in 1958, literary

history was not repeating itself: "the Tax Collector in 1939 hadn't yet decided that the reason the U.S. Government was always so sorely pressed for money was that I was spending too much for fun instead of turning it all over to him.

"Still furthermore, while I was writing *The Time of Your Life* in 1939 I knew that if the producer of my first play, Harold Clurman, didn't want it (he didn't), Eddie Dowling did, sight unseen, and that it would go into immediate production; whereas, while I was writing *The Cave Dwellers* in 1955 I believed that the play would not be produced for many years." On 19 October 1957, under the direction of Carmen Capalbo, *The Cave Dwellers* began a run of ninety-seven performances at the Bijou Theater, New York, with Wayne Morris, Susan Harrison, Eugenie Leontovich, and Barry Jones in the principal roles as the Duke, the Girl, the Queen, and the King.

In dedicating the play to the New York critics, whose reviews he published with *The Cave Dwellers*, Saroyan calls attention to the fact that the published play reflects "a number of changes . . . impelled [by Saroyan's] dislike of what [he] saw" at the Bijou. It was "an unbiased bystander," according to Saroyan, "a man out to paint [the] back porch" of the house on the beach at Malibu, where the playwright had lived since his second divorce, who "told [Saroyan] to let a play-producer have one of [his] plays" instead of "sticking to [his] long-range plan." "The people love poetry but don't know it, that's all," the poet of *My Heart's in the Highlands* had sensed; and apparently, the "miracle" of one of them telling Saroyan to let go of *The Cave Dwellers* seemed to confirm the poet's hunch.

A number of the play's critics have noted in *The Cave Dwellers* a new debt to the postwar theatre of France, notably to Samuel Beckett's *Waiting for Godot* (1952). For Harold Clurman, in the *Nation*, "Its 'philosophy' might be called sugared existentialism": "We do not know why we are here, we cannot comprehend the universe we are in, we shall never understand the great pattern, if pattern there be, of life. No matter: there is goodness, there is love—even hate is love. We get up in the morning, go to bed at night, in between we play wondrously—and that is enough. We require no more, for the spectacle is bright and even the dark is light enough." Briefly, *The Cave Dwellers* tells the story of various refugees from "the obvious" who take shelter in an abandoned theatre, scheduled for demolition, and allegorically called "The World." The King is an old clown; the Queen is an old actress; the Duke is an ex-prizefighter; and they are joined at the beginning of the play by the Girl, and later, by Gorky, a performing bear, and by the bear's trainer, his wife, and their newborn baby. Won at first by the Duke's kindness (much as the kindness of the prisoner had won the girl of *Hello Out There*), the Girl of *The Cave Dwellers* nevertheless falls in love at first sight with a mute boy who has chased the Duke back to the theatre with a crate of milk the Duke has stolen for the baby (much as Johnny had apparently been chased for stealing fruit in *My Heart's in the Highlands*). The Duke offers to go with him to the police, but the boy "shakes his head, turns and goes."

Meanwhile, outside, throughout the play, are heard the noises of demolition work going on in adjacent buildings. Each day, the King goes forth to try to earn some sustenance for the cave dwellers by clowning in the street. One day, the King returns, furious at having lost a shoe. He tells the Queen that he has tried to entertain the wrecking crew outside "after a whole day of failure." They have claimed that demolition gives them laughs enough, and when the King has offered to make them cry instead, they have bet him a coin from each of them against one of his shoes that he cannot bring one tear to even a single eye. And as things have soon appeared, he cannot. "What the devil's happened to the world? to the workers," the King asks. "Not one tear in one eye. . . . they even *offered* me coins, but I refused them," he says. "You had no right to refuse coins," the Queen protests. "Did I have a right to fail?" he asks in response; and the scene ends with this important question unanswered. Clearly, the issues concerning the morality of art with which Saroyan had concerned himself at the close of *My Heart's in the Highlands*, when Johnny silently picks up the coins he has earlier flung against the wall, were once again very much on Saroyan's mind in his last Broadway play.

In the end, however, the King has not failed. The Boss of the wrecking crew and his black helper appear to plan the destruction of the theatre. They are immediately sympathetic to the plight of those living in it, and the Boss directs his helper to have the crew call in sick for two days so that the cave dwellers can have time to find other accommodations. When the Queen asks the Boss why he is being so easy on them, he tells her that it is not for the sake of the baby, but in recognition of the greatness of the performance in which the King lost his shoe that he is letting them stay in the doomed theatre over the weekend. The Boss confesses that "he worked, and worked well, and all we did was laugh—all except one, Queen, that I know of—myself! . . . My-

self, and more than likely Jamie [his helper], too. . . . And more than likely each of the others, too, each of us unwilling, Queen, *unwilling* to let the other know of his pity and love for his Father. *That* is why." And when the grace period is over and the play is about to end, the Boss returns, "Goes to the King, looks at him intently," and says, "Good luck, Father. Good luck, all." Thus does Saroyan's last Broadway venture end as another dramatization, like *The Time of Your Life*, of the possibility of refusing to capitulate to "the obvious" by refusing to be ashamed of one's equally obvious impulses to "pity and love."

Throughout his career, Saroyan has been patronized and underinterpreted. One senses that critics have been less interested in discovering and teaching Saroyan's message than they have been in congratulating themselves for having been so democratic as to have admitted to the canon of recognized literature the work of an uneducated, penniless Armenian from Fresno—at least for as long as he seemed amusing. Brooks Atkinson's review of the Theatre Showcase production of *Across the Board on Tomorrow Morning*, in March of 1942, offers the best case in point. The play, he writes, "wastes a lot of words over metaphysical matters that Mr. Saroyan does not understand but cannot seem to get out of his head." What those "metaphysical matters" really are Atkinson does not explain.

Saroyan's gift as a playwright is not the gift for sentimental fantasy for which he has generally been tolerated. It is actually a gift for humane and rational analysis. Essentially, he is a pragmatist. His career-long habit of writing one-act plays (some of them are only minutes long) is evidence of Saroyan's analytic bent. *The Ping-Pong Game* (first published in 1940 and produced in 1945) analytically reduces to an actual, rule-structured game the way in which Western culture organizes exchanges of aggression between males and females. Similarly, *Making Money* ("written in 1956, [Saroyan thinks]," collected in 1968 in *I Used to Believe I Had Forever Now I'm Not So Sure*, and produced on educational television in November of 1970) analytically reduces his beliefs about money to the catechistic dialogue of an elementary school class. Or, again, in the sketch called *Dentist and Patient* (one of thirty-one sketches in Saroyan's *Anybody and Anybody Else*), collected in *The Best Short Plays, 1968*, Saroyan analytically reveals the irony he has always seen in exchanging for money competences that really make life feel better. The patient in the play, "a millionaire, retired," has made far more money than the dentist. But he has

225

made his money without doing anything but "cheating"—merely manipulating his investments among "gold, silver, paper, stocks, bonds, and . . . all the other forms [money] takes." Meanwhile, the dentist has been going through life making people's teeth better, unaware that others get away with charging a lot more money for dentistry.

Equally aware, in a way that most left-leaning intellectuals in America are not, of the absurdity of existing political, economic, and social arrangements and of the grave moral risks of changing them, Saroyan at his best has remained a prophet without honor in his country. From the beginning, however, he has understood his situation clearly. "In fairness to my critics," he wrote in publishing *Love's Old Sweet Song*, "I acknowledge the *partial* truth and validity of every charge brought against my work, against myself personally, and against my methods of making my work public." He goes on, "What is lacking in their criticism is the fullness and humanity of understanding which operates in myself, in my work, and in my regard for others. The essence of my work is honor, honesty, intelligence, grace, good humor, naturalness, and spontaneity, and these things do not appear to be nicely balanced in my critics. Consequently, it is difficult for them to make sense in themselves of that which is complicated and unusual for them. What should enlarge them because of its understanding, drives them more completely behind the fort of their own limitations." And he goes on to deny, one by one, the most persistent charges made against him—those of "exhibitionism," "mindlessness," and "formlessness." On each count, his best writing for the stage supports these denials.

Since 1958, Saroyan has maintained an apartment in the Montmartre section of Paris. Then, in 1964, he bought two adjacent "brandnew and cheap" houses "across from a vineyard" in Fresno. In 1979, the San Francisco author Herbert Gold wrote of two decades of acquaintance with Saroyan in the *New York Times Book Review*: "He was dividing his time between Fresno—because the company of the Armenians there and the local melons were good—and Paris, with a few short visits a year to camp out with relatives in San Francisco." Gold also reported, "He was well into the process of disengagement from the literary scene." "I'm growing old! I'm falling apart! and it's VERY INTERESTING!" Gold quoted Saroyan as saying.

Though he continues to have plays published, Saroyan seems largely to have disengaged himself from American theatrical production itself since the early 1960s. In 1960, the *Times* of London reported that "Mr. William Saroyan . . . moved into the Theatre Royal, [took] some two dozen of the regular company and proceeded to make up from scratch a play for, with and (spiritually speaking) about them." This was *Sam The Highest Jumper of Them All: or, the London Comedy*. In the same year, he collaborated with Henry Cecil on an adaptation for the stage of a mystery story by Cecil. This was produced in London as *Settled Out of Court*, and the *Times* could distinguish none of Saroyan's characteristic traits in it at all. Also in 1960, a production of *The Dogs: or, the Paris Comedy* opened in Vienna. A year later, Saroyan was writer-in-residence at Purdue University, and his *High Time Along the Wabash*, a group of one-acts on the subject of racism in Indiana was acted at the University Playhouse. In 1975, Saroyan was in New York for *The Rebirth Celebration of the Human Race at Artie Zabala's Off-Broadway Theatre*. He then told the *New York Times* that he lived in Paris for tax purposes, that he was always busy on five different writing projects at once, and that over the years he had lost $2,000,000 gambling.

Nevertheless, hardly a year goes by in which professional actors somewhere in America do not revive *The Time of Your Life*. *My Heart's in the Highlands* has been made into an opera and televised, and other Saroyan plays are occasionally featured on television. *My Heart's in the Highlands* and *The Time of Your Life* are collected in popular and school anthologies of American drama, and on the basis of those plays, the place of William Saroyan in the history of the American theatre still seems as secure as he always told us it would be. Indeed, on 18 November of 1979 Saroyan became one of the initial inductees to the Theatre Hall of Fame at the Uris Theatre in New York City.

Screenplays:
The Good Job, Loew, 1942;
The Human Comedy, MGM, 1943.

Television Scripts:
The Oyster and the Pearl, 1953;
Ah Sweet Mystery of Mrs. Murphy, "Omnibus," NBC, 1 March 1959;
The Unstoppable Gray Fox, "GE Theatre," CBS, 1962;
Making Money and Thirteen Other Very Short Plays, ETV, 12 November 1970.

Radio Scripts:
Radio Play, "Columbia Workship," CBS, 1940;

The People with Light Coming Out of Them, "Free
    Company," CBS, 1941;
There's Something I Got to Tell You, 1941.

Other:

Dentist and Patient and *Husband and Wife*, in *The Best
    Short Plays, 1968*, ed. Stanley Richards (Rad-
    nor, Pa.: Chilton Press, 1968);
The New Play, in *The Best Short Plays, 1970*, ed.
    Richards (Radnor, Pa.: Chilton Press, 1970).

Periodical Publications:

Once Around the Block, *American Mercury*, 69 (De-
    cember 1949): 663-675;
The Oyster and the Pearl, *Perspectives USA*, no. 4
    (Summer 1953): 86-104;
"The Time of My Life," *Theatre Arts*, 39 (January
    1955): 22-24, 95;
"Art for Man's Sake: A Minority View," *Nation*, 180
    (23 April 1955): 364-366;
*Cat, Mouse, Man, Woman,*and *The Accident*, *Contact 1:
    The San Francisco Journal of New Writing, Art
    and Ideas* (1958);
*Four Plays: The Playwright and the Public, The Hand-
    shakers, The Doctor and the Patient, This I Believe*,
    Atlantic Monthly, 211 (April 1963): 50-52;
"The Funny Business of Marriage," *Saturday Even-
    ing Post*, 236 (5 October 1963): 44-45;
"Something Else on My Mind," *New York Times*, 31
    July 1974, p. 33;
"Poetry for Profit," *New Republic*, 178 (4 March
    1978): 29.

Interviews:

Annie Brierre, "William Saroyan à Paris," *Nouvelles
    Littéraires*, 1665 (30 July 1959): 5;
Budd Schulberg, "Saroyan: Ease and Unease on the
    Flying Trapeze," *Esquire*, 54 (October 1960):
    85-91;
Zori Balayan, "Arguments for Soviet Power. . . ,"
    Soviet Literature, no. 12 (1977): 159-166;
Herbert Gold, "A 20-Year Talk with Saroyan," *New
    York Times Book Review*, 20 May 1979, pp. 7,
    49-51.

Bibliography:

David Kherdian, *A Bibliography of William Saroyan
    1934-1964* (San Francisco: Beacham, 1965).

References:

Frederic I. Carpenter, "The Time of William
    Saroyan's Life," *Pacific Spectator*, 1 (Winter
    1947): 88-96;
Harold Clurman, *The Fervent Years* (1945; re-
    printed, New York: Harcourt Brace
    Jovanovich, 1975), pp. 228ff;
William J. Fisher, "What Ever Happened to
    Saroyan?," *College English*, 16 (March 1955):
    336-340, 385;
Howard R. Floan, *William Saroyan* (New York:
    Twayne, 1966);
Mordecai Gorelik, *New Theatres for Old* (1940; re-
    printed, New York: Octagon Books, 1975),
    pp. 201-202, 228-229, 260-261;
James H. Justus, "William Saroyan and the Theatre
    of Transformation," *The Thirties: Fiction,
    Poetry, Drama*, ed. Warren French (Deland,
    Fla.: Everett/Edwards, 1967), 211-219;
Harry Keyishian, "Michael Arlen and William
    Saroyan: Armenian Ethnicity and the Writer,"
    in *The Old Century and the New: Essays in Honor
    of Charles Angoff*, ed. Alfred Rosa (Rutherford,
    N.J.: Fairleigh Dickinson University Press,
    1978), pp. 192-206;
Edward Krickel, "Cozzens and Saroyan: A Look at
    Two Reputations," *Georgia Review*, 24 (Fall
    1970): 281-296;
Lawrence Langner, *The Magic Curtain* (New York:
    Dutton, 1951), pp. 320-326;
Ran Sapoznik, "The One-Act Plays of Thornton
    Wilder, William Saroyan and Edward Albee,"
    Ph.D. dissertation, University of Kansas,
    1975;
Thelma J. Shinn, "William Saroyan: Romantic
    Existentialist," *Modern Drama*, 15 (September
    1972): 185-194;
Stark Young, "Saroyan Directing, Note," *New Re-
    public*, 104 (12 May 1941): 664;
Young, "Hello Out There," *New Republic*, 107 (12
    October 1942): 466.

EDWARD SHELDON
(4 February 1886-1 April 1946)

PRODUCTIONS: *Salvation Nell*, 17 November 1908, Hackett Theatre, New York, 71 [performances];

The Nigger, 4 December 1909, New Theatre, New York;

The Boss, 30 January 1911, Astor Theatre, New York, 88;

Princess Zim-Zam, 4 December 1911, Harmanus Bleeker Hall, Albany, N.Y.;

Egypt, 18 September 1912, The Playhouse, Hudson, N.Y.;

The High Road, 19 November 1912, Hudson Theatre, New York, 71;

Romance, 10 February 1913, Maxine Elliott's Theatre, New York, 160; revised as *My Romance*, lyrics by Rowland Leigh, music by Sigmund Romberg, 19 October 1948, Shubert Theatre, New York, 95;

The Garden of Paradise, 28 November 1914, Park Theatre, New York, 17;

The Song of Songs, 22 December 1914, Eltinge Theatre, New York, 191;

The Jest, 9 April 1919, Plymouth Theatre, New York, 77;

The Lonely Heart, 24 October 1921, Baltimore;

The Czarina, adapted from Melchior Lengyel's play, 31 January 1922, Empire Theatre, New York, 136;

Bewitched, by Sheldon and Sidney Howard, 1 October 1924, National Theatre, New York, 29;

Lulu Belle, by Sheldon and Charles MacArthur, 9 February 1926, Belasco Theatre, New York, 461;

Jenny, by Sheldon and Margaret Ayer Barnes, 8 October 1929, Booth Theatre, New York, 111;

Dishonored Lady, by Sheldon and Barnes, 4 February 1930, Empire Theatre, New York, 127.

SELECTED BOOKS: *Salvation Nell* (New York: Hauser, 1908);

The Nigger (New York: Macmillan, 1910);

Egypt (New York: Tower, 1912; London: Chiswick Press, 1912);

Romance (New York: Macmillan, 1914);

The Garden of Paradise (New York: Macmillan, 1915).

Edward Sheldon's unobtrusive influence on the American theatre was assessed in the *New York Times* in 1941: "If America has a theatrical center, it is a little known one, the New York apartment of Ned Sheldon, a man who has been an invalid for many years." Despite the significance of his dramas, Sheldon's actual contributions to the theatre will never be fully catalogued because he declined to advertise his services to playwrights, actors, producers, and directors. Sheldon's biographer, Eric Wollencott Barnes, concludes that between 1930 and 1946 "there was no season . . . which did not see at least one play in which he had some part, and frequently two or three."

Edward Brewster Sheldon, the son of Theodore and Mary Strong Sheldon, was born in Chicago in 1886. His father's wealth and his mother's cultural vitality colored young Ned's boyhood. By the time he entered boarding school, Sheldon was an inveterate playgoer. His theatrical apprenticeship did not begin, however, until his entry into Harvard University in 1904. There he joined Prof. George Pierce Baker's course in playwriting. He received his A.B. in 1907 and his A.M. the following year.

As an assignment in Baker's class, Sheldon wrote his first drama, "A Family Affair," which he sent—at his instructor's instigation—to a dramatists' agent in New York, Alice Hauser. A reader with keen intuition, Hauser recognized Sheldon's promise and encouraged him to submit another script. The product was *Salvation Nell*, which was presented in New York in 1908 by Minnie Maddern Fiske; its success assured Sheldon's career as a professional playwright. His subsequent dramatic successes outnumbered his failures, and his future seemed bright indeed.

At the height of his achievement, however, Sheldon was stricken with virulent arthritis, which at first restricted his movement, then finally confined him to bed. Yet he continued to write, although his joints stiffened and blindness followed. A period of collaboration succeeded *The Lonely Heart* (1921), his last original drama, and after 1930 Sheldon wrote no more plays.

For the remainder of his life, Sheldon's theatrical activities were confined to doctoring the plays of others, suggesting actors for particular roles, and dispensing counsel to scores of callers who sat at his bedside and marveled at his unabated intellectual force and matchless selflessness. With little pain and no warning, Sheldon died in his bed on 1 April 1946.

Critics have suggested that the value of Sheldon's plays is proportionate to their degree of realism, which has been particularly noted in *Salvation Nell*, *The Nigger* (1909), and *The Boss* (1911). When Sheldon began to write romantic plays, such as *Romance* (1913), he was accused of escapism, of abandoning the principles on which his earlier and better plays were based. This interpretation, however, ignores the fact that all of Sheldon's dramas contain romantic elements, even those that stress environmental determinism. *Salvation Nell*, *The Nigger*, and *The Boss* are principally love stories played against a backdrop of carefully calculated, realistic detail. The subsequent romantic dramas are only slightly less rich in realistic minutiae. Sheldon composed his earliest works at a time when Ibsen's social-problem plays were receiving their first American hearings. While still in boarding school, Sheldon had read the Norwegian's plays. Alice Hauser, moreover, was Ibsen's representative in America, and Minnie Maddern Fiske was presenting Ibsenian dramas when she accepted *Salvation Nell*. The young playwright could hardly have escaped Ibsen's influence, and Sheldon followed Ibsen's example of abandoning realistic social-problem plays in favor of more idealistic conceptions.

Celebrity came to twenty-two-year-old Ned Sheldon with the production of *Salvation Nell*. Although Sheldon arranged the incidents of the plot in a causal but sometimes confusing sequence, Nell Sanders's story is simple. While a charwoman in a disreputable saloon, Nell becomes pregnant by drunken ne'er-do-well Jim Platt, who, out of jealousy, nearly kills a man who makes advances toward Nell. By the time their baby is born and Platt is paroled from prison, Nell has turned from her former life and become a member of the Salvation Army. Love and respectability seem within her grasp when an unrepentant Platt returns to complicate her life. Nell finally transmits her religious convictions to Platt, who gives up his criminal associations for the purity of her love. Though the plot is certainly melodramatic and romantic, the element that made the play credible was its realistic diction, setting, and costumes. Its subject matter, moreover, had been presented in a new and powerful light—sufficiently powerful to prompt a revealing comment made to Sheldon by Eugene O'Neill: "Your *Salvation Nell*," O'Neill said, "was what first opened my eyes to the existence of a real theatre as opposed to the unreal. . . ." When Nell says to Platt, "You an' me didn't have no chance did we, Jim? An' it ain't our fault if we don't come quite up ter the mark," the issue of environmental deter-

Edward Sheldon

minism is raised. Squalor, poverty, drunkenness, crime—all contribute to Nell and Jim's problems. In Ashton Stevens's words, Sheldon "serves up Hell's Kitchen piping hot."

The characters indigenous to working-class New York are differentiated largely by dialect. Nell's world is primarily Irish, but Sheldon also depicts Greeks and Italians, whose polyglot dialects create the melting-pot environment of the play. The dramatist, however, seldom sacrifices clarity for exactitude of dialect. Copious stage directions describe details of the setting and costuming of the play. By manipulating these elements within large ensemble scenes, Sheldon uses realistic techniques to depict the mood and environment that partially dictate the actions of the characters. In his subsequent dramas Sheldon continued to combine romantic plots and characters with realistic diction and spectacle.

From the problems of urbanization, Sheldon turned to racism. "For perhaps the first time since before the Civil War a playwright boldly presented the problem of color free from contempt, on the one hand, or from maudlin sympathy, on the other," Randolph Edmonds wrote about *The Nigger*. As in *Salvation Nell*, Sheldon wraps his social consciousness in the garb of romantic melodrama with realistic elements of spectacle and speech. Philip Morrow, scion of an aristocratic Southern family, wins the governorship as a white supremacist, only to discover through the machinations of the villain that Morrow's grandmother was a black woman. Governor Morrow faces the loss of political influence but fears even more that his fiancee, Georgiana, will desert him. Given time to consider the problem and to realize that she truly loves Morrow, Georgiana urges him to deny his black heritage, but Morrow refuses to do so, saying: "You see, what my gran'fathah did t' my gran'mothah isn't all—it's what ev'ry white man has done t' ev'ry niggah fo' the las' three hundred yeahs! An' it's time for some one to pay up, even if he wasn't extra keen on bein' the pa'ticulah chosen man." So Morrow pledges to devote his life, education, and wealth to the betterment of the black race, his race.

The Nigger is rife with comments about "lynching, discrimination and miscegenation that created a sensation on the American stage." Sheldon realistically depicts some aspects of Southern village life: "political lobbying, partisan journalism, . . . crass commercialism. . . , the use of troops to quell a race riot, the political rise of the 'White Negro' [a black man who abandons his own race], coupled with open hostility toward the Negrophile." As in *Salvation Nell*, his stage descriptions fully describe costumes and scenery. *The Nigger* provoked an avalanche of critical reaction, much of it scornful of the title. *Cosmopolitan* magazine dubbed it one of "The Ten Dramatic Shocks of the Century."

Somewhat less melodramatic than *The Nigger* was Sheldon's next play, *The Boss*, "a study of the political boss who is also a contractor and who has made a success by building up a modern feudal system, whose bases are the mutual loyalty of chieftain and follower." Despite his numerous villainies, Michael Regan is sympathetically portrayed. His wife Emily married him to prevent her father's financial ruin, but she has grown to respect him for acting according to his code of behavior. Sheldon implies that the love of a good woman will redeem even Mike Regan. Suspicious financial dealings, union organizing, strikes, labor riots, and their concomitant effects on the people involved are basic issues of the play. Once again Sheldon constructed a drama of love and clashing emotions but imbued it with contemporary significance by introducing social consciousness and realistic sights and sounds.

Romance pervades *Princess Zim-Zam* (1911), Sheldon's first failure in the theatre. Set in a tent show at Coney Island, the action involves snake

charmer Tessie Casey and millionaire Peter Milholland, who announces, "I'm twenty-four years old, I'm on the loose, and I'm looking for romance." His liaison with Tessie, however, is ill-fated, as were *Princess Zim-Zam* and Sheldon's subsequent drama, *Egypt* (1912). The heroine, Egypt, is the daughter of a white man and a Gypsy woman. Reared by Gypsies, Egypt is forced to live with her father and to marry a white man, but before the union is consummated, Egypt elopes with her Gypsy lover. Six years and five children later, Egypt meets her white husband and asserts, "I don't think it matters how much God gave or the devil took—nothing matters if we do our best, as we were born to do, and live hard every minute of the long, long day—and love the road we travel—till we die." *Egypt* was not a commercial success.

The High Road (1912) is a play of love and politics. The protagonist, Mary Page, who years before the opening of the play was sexually indiscreet, has spent her life working in a factory and trying to improve the lot of working girls. After Mary meets and falls in love with the governor of the state, who seems assured of winning the presidency, a villain threatens to expose her disreputable past, but Mary thwarts him by volunteering to admit her error and to expose his ruthless tactics. Audiences hotly debated the moral implications of "a fallen woman" in the White House. Sheldon had created another cause celebre and precipitated another war of words both in the press and in pamphlets. With Mrs. Fiske and Carl Sandburg as champions, Sheldon's play drew capacity audiences.

The colorful life of operatic singer Lina Cavalieri provided the inspiration for *Romance*, the drama for which Sheldon is primarily remembered by two generations of playgoers. Included in Burns Mantle's *Best Plays of 1909-1919*, *Romance* describes the fondly remembered affair of a prominent bishop, then an upcoming rector, and a stormy, amoral singer named Margherita Cavallini. At the height of his infatuation with her, Cavallini rejects his love because she knows her reputation would impede his advancement in the church. The drama is rich in emotional conflict, interesting characters, and a roseate stereoptical view of New York society of a bygone age. Audiences responded warmly to Sheldon's depiction of elemental human feelings; the play was seen in England, Scotland, France, Norway, Sweden, Spain, Egypt, India, the Orient, Australia, New Zealand, and Africa. "In *Romance*, Sheldon reached the peak of his success as a playwright," according to Barnes, and there is no reason to doubt his conclusion.

Sheldon's career was one of contrasts. His triumph with *Romance* was succeeded by a colossal failure, his adaptation of Hans Christian Andersen's "The Little Mermaid." In the dramatization, called *The Garden of Paradise* (1914), the producers discovered that a doomed romance between a mermaid and a mortal could not compete for an audience anxiously watching the confrontation of powers in war-torn Europe. The producers lost $50,000 on the production and went into bankruptcy.

Sheldon continued to write adaptations. Hermann Sudermann's naturalistic *Das hohe Lied* (1908) was the source of *The Song of Songs* (1914), and Sem Benelli's *La Cena della Beffe* (1909) was the original of *The Jest* (1919). Both were moderately successful at the box office, but structurally *The Jest*, which was named by Burns Mantle as one of the best plays of 1919-1920, is the superior drama, and as acted by John and Lionel Barrymore, it proved to be quite an excellent theatre piece.

The Lonely Heart (1921) was never seen in New York, but the drama is interesting as an indication of the direction of Sheldon's artistry. External forces shaped the destinies of Sheldon's previous characters, but in *The Lonely Heart*, the playwright explores the inner reaches of his characters. Sheldon depicts his protagonist at four crises of his life in each of which he confronts a vision of the mother who died in giving him birth. He was, thus, deprived of the maternal love from which he might have drawn the wisdom and fortitude to sustain him at the crossroads of his adult life.

Only collaborative efforts followed *The Lonely Heart*; of these plays, only one was particularly successful. In *Lulu Belle* (1926), written with Charles MacArthur, Sheldon returned again to the problem of race. Lulu Belle, a mulatto cafe chanteuse, is the riotous embodiment of Harlem in the Roaring Twenties whose hedonism leads her into many indiscriminate love affairs. When the singer finds herself in Paris as the mistress of a French nobleman, a jilted lover from her past appears and kills her. As Loften Mitchell says, "The play was colorfully produced, but it was sheer melodrama that did no more than capitalize on the popularity of Harlem during that era."

In addition to his produced dramas, Sheldon copyrighted several others: *The Man Who Was Dead* (1916); *Alice in Wonderland* (1917); and *St. Ursula* (1921), written with Zoë Akins. *The Boss* was novelized by J. W. MacConaughy in 1913 and *Romance* by Acton Davies in 1915.

As a playwright, Edward Sheldon had a productive and fulfilling career. His plays achieved notable success in production, and it is likely that their theatricality rather than their literary qualities will be remembered. He had the ability to present strong emotions in carefully constructed melodrama. In this sense he was a child of his age. Sheldon was an irrepressible romantic, and, as Lionel Barrymore said, "the theatre's acolyte and its people's priest."

–*George B. Bryan*

References:

Eric Wollencott Barnes, *The Man Who Lived Twice: The Biography of Edward Sheldon* (New York: Scribners, 1956);

Ima Honaker Herron, *The Small Town in American Drama* (Dallas: Southern Methodist University Press, 1969), pp. 208, 210-212;

Walter J. Meserve, *An Outline History of American Drama* (Totawa, N.J.: Littlefield, Adams, 1965), pp. 199-201;

Loften Mitchell, *Black Drama: The Story of the American Negro in the Theatre* (New York: Hawthorn Books, 1967), pp. 39, 86;

Garff B. Wilson, *300 Years of American Drama and Theatre* (Englewood Cliffs, N.J.: Prentice-Hall, 1973), pp. 330-331, 335.

SAM SHEPARD

(5 November 1943-)

SELECTED PRODUCTIONS: *Cowboys* and *The Rock Garden*, 16 October 1964, St. Mark Church in-the-Bowery, New York;

Up to Thursday, 10 February 1965, Cherry Lane Theatre, New York, 23 [performances];

Dog and *Rocking Chair*, 10 February 1965, La Mama Experimental Theatre Club, New York;

Chicago, 16 April 1965, St. Mark Church in-the-Bowery, New York;

Icarus's Mother, 16 November 1965, Caffe Cino, New York;

4-H Club, 1965, Cherry Lane Theatre, New York;

Fourteen Hundred Thousand, 1966, Firehouse Theater, Minneapolis;

Red Cross, 20 January 1966, Judson Poets' Theatre, New York;

Melodrama Play, in *Six from La Mama*, 12 April 1966, Martinique Theatre, New York;

La Turista, 4 March 1967, American Place Theatre, New York, 29;

Cowboys # 2, 12 August 1967, Old Reliable, New York;
Forensic and the Navigators, 29 December 1967, St. Mark Church in-the-Bowery, New York;
The Unseen Hand, 26 December 1969, La Mama Experimental Theatre Club, New York;
Operation Sidewinder, 12 March 1970, Vivian Beaumont Theatre, New York, 52;
Shaved Splits, 29 July 1970, La Mama Experimental Theatre Club, New York;
Mad Dog Blues, 4 March 1971, St. Mark Church in-the-Bowery, New York;
Cowboy Mouth, 2 April 1971, Transverse Theatre, Edinburgh; 29 April 1971, American Place Theatre, New York;
Back Dog Beast Bait, 29 April 1971, American Place Theatre, New York;
The Tooth of Crime, 17 July 1972, Open Space, London; 7 March 1973, Performing Garage, New York, 123;
Nightwalk, by Shepard, Megan Terry, and Jean-Claude van Itallie, 8 September 1973, St. Clement's Church, New York, 15;
Geography of a Horse Dreamer, 2 February 1974, Theatre Upstairs, London;
Little Ocean, 25 March 1974, Hampstead Theatre Club, London;
Action and *Killer's Head*, 4 April 1975, American Place Theatre, New York;
Buried Child, 1978, Theatre de Lys, New York, 157.

BOOKS: *Five Plays by Sam Shepard* (Indianapolis: Bobbs-Merrill, 1967)—includes *Icarus's Mother*, *Chicago*, *Melodrama Play*, *Red Cross*, and *Fourteen Hundred Thousand*;
La Turista (Indianapolis: Bobbs-Merrill, 1968);
Operation Sidewinder (Indianapolis: Bobbs-Merrill, 1970);
The Unseen Hand and Other Plays (Indianapolis: Bobbs-Merrill, 1971)—includes *The Unseen Hand*, *4-H Club*, *Shaved Splits*, *Forensic and the Navigators*, *The Holy Ghostly*, and *Back Dog Beast Bait*;
Mad Dog Blues and Other Plays (New York: Winter House, 1972)—includes *The Rock Garden*, *Cowboys # 2*, *Cowboy Mouth*, *Blue Bitch*, and *Nightwalk*;
Hawk Moon (Los Angeles: Black Sparrow Press, 1972);
The Tooth of Crime and Geography of a Horse Dreamer (New York: Grove, 1974);
Angel City, Curse of the Starving Class and Other Plays (New York: Urizen Books, 1976)—includes

Angel City, Curse of the Starving Class, Killer's Head, Action;
Buried Child, Seduced, Suicide in B♭ (New York: Urizen Books, 1979).

Sam Shepard is considered by many critics to be the most important playwright in the Off-Broadway theatre movement. His unique blend of styles—using mythical American heroes, rock and roll music, poetically unconventional language—and his ability to create vivid dreamlike images set Shepard apart from more traditional American playwrights. No other American playwright has won more than two Obie awards, while Shepard has collected ten—for *Chicago* (1966); *Icarus's Mother* (1966), *Red Cross* (1966), *La Turista* (1967), *Forensic and the Navigators* (1968), *Melodrama Play* (1968), *The Tooth of Crime* (1973), *Action* (1975), *Curse of the Starving Class* (1977), and *Buried Child* (1979), which also won the Pulitzer Prize for Drama.

Sam Shepard was born Samuel Shepard Rogers in Fort Sheridan, Illinois, on 5 November 1943 to Samuel Shepard and Elaine Schook Rogers. The son of a career army officer, Shepard spent his childhood years moving from base to base. Among his early childhood memories are experiences of his family stationed on Guam: "I remember the tin roofed huts that we lived in, . . . and the rain would make this incredible sound on the tin roof. Also there were a lot of Japanese on the island, who had been forced back into living in the caves, . . . All the women were issued with army Lugers, and I remember my mother shooting at them."

After his father left the service, the family moved to South Pasadena, California, to live with an aunt. Shepard's father went to night school to complete his college degree, and his mother worked as a teacher. His father was fond of Dixieland music and played drums for a band to supplement his income. Later, the family moved to Duarte, California, and settled down on an avocado ranch. Shepard liked the atmosphere of the ranch and enjoyed working with horses and other animals. He also began playing his father's set of drums, starting his lifelong involvement with rock and roll music and its subculture.

He recalls when his first interest in theatre began: "I hardly knew anything about the theatre—I remember once in California I went to this guy's house who was called a beatnik by everybody in the school because he had a beard and he wore sandals. . . . and he sort of shuffled over to me and threw this book on my lap and said, 'Why don't you dig this,' you know . . . it was *Waiting for Godot*." In 1960 Shepard wrote a play in California, which he describes as "a sort of Tennessee Williams imitation, about some girl who got raped in a barn and her father getting mad at her or something . . . I forget. But the first play I wrote in New York was *Cowboys*."

Family life, however, did not provide Shepard with many fond memories. His father was strict and the ranch only moderately successful. Although he did graduate from Duarte High School in 1960, he did not enjoy studying. He enrolled in Mount Antonio Junior College in 1960, but stayed only one year. When an opportunity to leave home presented itself, he took it. Shepard joined a touring repertory group called the Bishop's Company, which played in churches across the country. "Everything just got so hysterical in my family," he remembers, "that, ah, I fled the scene."

Shepard arrived in New York in 1963, nineteen years old, with only a few months of professional acting experience. Charles Mingus, Jr., a high-school friend who was working in New York as a painter, became Shepard's roommate. Mingus helped Shepard find a job as a busboy at the popular jazz club, The Village Gate. While working at the club, Shepard met Ralph Cook, founder of Off-Off-Broadway's Theatre Genesis. Shepard had few close friends in New York, but Cook remembers how Mingus and Shepard lived: "in the wierdest apartment I ever saw . . . a genuine cold-water flat over on Avenue C. Charlie had painted the walls, and there was garbage all over the place. They'd go out and play cowboys and Indians right in the street, and Sam did crazy things, like if he saw a cab coming and it wouldn't stop, he'd jump on top of it and ride it down the street." *Cowboys* (and its revised version *Cowboys # 2*) grew out of this street playing of Mingus and Shepard.

Cook encouraged Shepard to write plays instead of the poetry he had been writing. Apparently, Shepard took this advice seriously because on 16 October 1964 his first production (two one-acts called *Cowboys* and *The Rock Garden*) was staged by Theatre Genesis at Saint Mark Church in-the-Bowery. This was also the first production by Theatre Genesis. The company was made up largely of actors who were also working at the Village Gate jazz club along with Shepard and Cook.

The Rock Garden is a short one-act in three scenes with three characters: a man, a woman, and a boy. Shepard has acknowledged that the origin of the play concerns his decision to leave home. In the first scene the man reads a magazine while the woman and boy sip milk, exchanging silent glances. The scene ends with the woman dropping her glass, spilling the milk. In the next scene, the woman is in bed with several blankets over her. The boy is seated next to the bed in a rocker, dressed only in underwear. The woman tells the boy stories about her father, occasionally asking the boy for a glass of water or another blanket. Each time the boy returns with the requested item he has on another article of clothing, until he is fully clothed. Then, the man enters as the boy leaves. The man sits in the rocker and finishes the conversation. The final scene is between the man and boy, although the boy never looks at the man. The man begins elaborating on mowing the lawn, painting the fence, and working on the rock garden, possibly even starting more rock gardens. Every now and then the boy falls off his chair. As the man becomes excited telling the boy how nice it will be fixing up the garden and the orchard surrounding it, the boy asks short questions about the work. After the man finishes, the boy begins his only monologue in the play. It is an extremely explicit speech about the boy's favorite sexual pleasures. It is spoken very conversationally, almost like the man's speech. When the boy is finished, the man falls over, and the lights black out.

The Rock Garden employs several techniques which occur throughout Shepard's work: a stage nearly devoid of furniture presenting a simple and open acting space (he almost never uses a box set) and a story line which does not proceed by cause and effect sequences. Bits and pieces of characterization are presented in no apparent order. Shepard's fragmented character development achieves poignancy through vivid, nearly poetic dialogue and an exploration of his characters' memories through lengthy monologues. In his later works, however, Shepard almost abandons the use of long monologues in favor of more conversational dialogue. *The Rock Garden* also shows Shepard's use of explicit sexual terms for shock value, comic relief, and the formation of vivid mental pictures. In fact, the orgasm scene was later used in the Broadway show *Oh! Calcutta!* and earned Shepard the modest sum of sixty-eight dollars a week in royalties. Most of the critics regarded Shepard's first works as "bad imitations of Beckett." Shepard was almost ready to give up and return to California, when the *Village Voice* gave the plays a rave review.

Encouraged by this praise he began to write plays so quickly that even he has lost count of the number. Between 1964 and 1974 he wrote over two dozen plays, many of which have been produced both in the U.S. and abroad. Shepard refers to some of his early work with something less than enthusiasm, saying, "*Up to Thursday* was a bad exercise in absurdity, I guess. This kid is sleeping in an American flag, he's only wearing a jockstrap . . . It was a terrible play, really. . . . *Dog* was about a black guy—which later I found out it was uncool for a white to write about in America. It was about a black guy on a park bench, a sort of *Zoo Story* type play. I don't even remember *Rocking Chair*, except it was about somebody in a rocking chair."

Between 1964 and 1970 Shepard wrote successfully and prolifically; during that period he received six Obie awards for playwriting. His method of writing is a form of improvisation, according to his own description: "I used to write very fast, I mean I wrote *Chicago* in one day. The stuff would just come out, and I wasn't really trying to shape it or make it into any big thing." The experimental methods Shepard followed had ready outlets in several of New York's Off-Off-Broadway theatres, which were flourishing because of grant support, young and perceptive audiences, and low costs of production. During the 1960s Shepard's living was meager, but enjoyable. Although he had plays being produced throughout the city and one premiere production at the Firehouse Theatre in Minneapolis, Minnesota, Shepard recalls feeling "at home for the first time" at Theatre Genesis: "Whenever I was feeling lost on the streets, I never went back to my apartment. I always ended up going back to the theater [Genesis], and, I mean, it was literally home—I slept there, ate there, not continuously, but I spent a lot of time there."

Shepard's second Obie winner, *Icarus's Mother* (1965), concerns five people on a picnic who have finished their meal. As the lights come up, they are all lying on their backs. They begin to belch and look at the sky while waiting for a fireworks display. Their conversation soon focuses on a jet flying across the sky and an argument erupts over whether it is leaving a vapor trail or skywriting. At this point, Bill becomes overly agitated, wondering at the pilot's intention, and yells at the plane to go away. The plane seems to offer some kind of a threat. Instead of the action continuing along this line, building to a climax and resolution, the characters begin discussing other obsessions. The plane is mentioned not much later as a giggling Jill tells everyone that the pilot swooped very low while she and Pat were having a pee in the middle of the beach, crouched "like a couple of desert nomads."

Sam Shepard

At the end of the play, Frank claims that the plane crashes during the fireworks display, and the girls corroborate his story. The action is simple, and the flow of imagery sometimes overpowers both character and structure. The conversation shifts suddenly and unexpectedly and changes shape like the windblown clouds the picnickers mention, needing only a key word or phrase to alter its course. *Icarus's Mother* explores the nature of fantasy and daydream. The climax of the play occurs in a highly rhetorical passage referring to the plane's crashing. The sound and color of the long-awaited fireworks display punctuates this speech, yet these final effects reveal nothing about the five observers.

Icarus's Mother reflects several of Shepard's attitudes toward the nature of theatre. He places paramount emphasis upon intensity of image, whether verbal or physical: "An image can be seen without looking at anything—you can see something in your head, or you can see something on stage, or you can see things that don't appear on stage, you know. The fantastic thing about theatre is that . . . you can be watching this thing happening with actors and costumes and lights and set and language, and even plot, and something emerges from beyond that. . . ."

Melodrama Play, written and first performed in 1966 but winning an Obie in 1968, is a strange story in which Peter, a huge bodyguard, holds his rock star client and friends captive, physically threatening them and telling them odd stories. He shoots the star's girl friend, which does not cause much stir in the other characters, and clubs the star unconscious. Peter then sits the others on the couch and says to them, "I'd like to ask you both what you think of me as a person. Just frankly. Don't be afraid of hurting my feelings or anything like that. Just tell me what you think." Further head beatings and verbal attacks within two lengthy monologues belie Peter's concern about the way other people think of him. At the end of the play, Peter's club is poised over the head of another character as the girl and one of the men suddenly come back to life and exit, giving the play its melodramatic twist. Shepard's preoccupation with self-identification and resurrection is central to this play and to much of Shepard's career. Says Shepard of this theme: "The idea of dying and being reborn is really an interesting one, you know. It's always there at the back of my head." Perhaps his Episcopalian upbringing planted this concern deeply in his mind. When talking of his early religious and environmental influences, he says, "You can't escape, that's the whole thing, you can't."

An actress named O-Lan Johnson was cast in the 1967 premiere of Shepard's *Forensic and the Navigators*. In 1969 she and Shepard were married at Saint Mark Church in-the-Bowery. They have one son, Jessie Mojo, born a year later. In *Forensic and the Navigators*, Shepard focuses on two co-conspirators, Emmet and Forensic, in their argument over how to go about capturing a fortress. The play suggests that the fortress is a prison or mental institution, but one is never certain. Suddenly, a girl, Oolan, enters flipping a pancake, and the fight ceases abruptly. Shortly, a knock is heard on the door, creating a fear in the room. Two "huge men . . . dressed like California highway patrolmen" enter. Called the Exterminators, they are well armed. Although they appear quite ominous, they speak with innocuous politeness, becoming bewildered in their roles and susceptible to Oolan's charms. By the time they leave, they are as frightened of their home office as Forensic and Emmet were at the knock on the door. At the end of the play another knock is heard, suggesting a repetitious cycle of menace. *Forensic and the Navigators* anticipates Shepard's *The Tooth of Crime* (1972) by insinuating early in the play a violent threat, only to have the threat recede into a nonviolent anti-climax.

Shepard's next four plays—*The Unseen Hand* (1969), *Operation Sidewinder*, *Shaved Splits* (1970),

and *Mad Dog Blues* (1971)—are marked by a bizarre blend of verbal and visual images using mythic heros, science fiction characters, cowboys, Indians, rock and roll stars, and musical passages. His purpose is to capture the energetic diversity of American culture in an off-beat and poetic form. His use of myth is highly stylized: "Myth speaks to everything at once, especially the emotions. By myth I mean a sense of mystery and not a traditional formula." Shepard often depicts several characters in varying—and extreme—states of consciousness. His plays are sometimes described as "trips," and many scenes have a hallucinatory quality. The characters themselves are often drugged and intoxicated on music or on their own language as it sweeps them into euphoric visions or utter despair. The everyday world does not usually have a place in Shepard's earlier works. Instead, the fantasy of his plays tears down and ridicules the middle-class world. Paradoxically, however, his plays often mourn the loss of traditional moral values.

Shepard's background as both poet and musician has undoubtedly left a lasting mark on his playwriting. *Operation Sidewinder*, first produced on 12 March 1970 at the repertory theatre of Lincoln Center in New York, is an excellent example of how he combines the roles of poet, musician, and playwright. The farcical action revolves around the attempts of many different factions of American society to find and use an experimental Sidewinder computer for their own purposes. The computer, invented by Dr. Vector (a mad scientist working for the air force) and created in the form of a large rattlesnake, has escaped and crawled into the desert. Although the computer was originally designed to trace unidentified flying objects, Dr. Vector's ultimate dream is realized when the computer chooses ". . . to go off on its own accord. It has chosen to be free and exist on its own." The action moves quite rapidly, as first one group of characters, then another, become involved in the intricate plot line: the air force wishes to use the Sidewinder computer to track U.F.O.s; the Indians see it as their mythological Snake-god come to save them from the final destruction; the blacks want to use it to gain power and overthrow the government; Honey, a beautiful but foolish blonde, and a young man (both products of a plastic society) merely try to give the computer back and rid themselves of responsibility. In the final scene, the Sidewinder transforms into the Indian god as the government troops surround the Indians worshiping the Sidewinder and attempt to recapture it. Such playful and satiric action is amplified by Shepard's production techniques. He assaults the senses of the audience by the use of intense sound and lights, and by various chants and songs. Political and religious symbols are jumbled together, creating a dreamlike effect. The psychological resonance of stylized production, and not its sociological satire, is Shepard's aim. However, the play was severely attacked by critics and proved financially disastrous.

Following the production of *Operation Sidewinder*, Shepard and his wife and son moved to London, England, where they lived for over three years. In England Shepard's output did not diminish. Among other plays, he wrote *The Tooth of Crime*, *Geography of a Horse Dreamer* (1974), and *Little Ocean* (1974). Reflecting on his experience in New York, Shepard concluded: "the difference between living in New York and working in New York became wider and wider. . . . And also I was into a lot of drugs then . . . I didn't feel like going back to California, so I thought I'd come here—really to get into music, you know . . . I had this fantasy that I'd come over here and somehow fall into a rock 'n' roll band. It didn't work. . . ." While in London, however, Shepard did write and produce some of his finest works.

The Tooth of Crime (first produced in London in July 1972) deals with a rock and roll hero, Hoss, and his struggle to be free to choose his own destiny in the restrictive game of the "Great Killer Race." The character of Hoss seems to be an outgrowth of earlier characters from Shepard's plays. The imagery of this play creates a world in which rock and roll stars kill one another to gain status, "turf," and the gold record, the symbol of success in the recording industry. The play depicts a society which worships raw power. In *The Tooth of Crime*, however, the rules of power are under the rigid control of the "Game Keepers," who, like gods, are unseen and omnipotent. The protagonist, Hoss, begins the show by singing "The Way Things Are." Its lyrics include the following lines: "You may think every picture you see is a true history of the way things used to be or the way things are. . . . So here's another fantasy about the way things seem to be to me." The first song, then, informs the audience that the play operates as a fantasy and its action is presented from Hoss's perspective.

In *The Tooth of Crime* Shepard uses Hoss as a hero with a forgotten cause. He no longer knows why he is fighting to stay at the top of his profession. Happiness and satisfaction, he realizes, do not automatically come with success. A vague uneasiness about a revolutionary force outside the Game

Keepers' dominion turns into a real threat when Hoss learns that Mojo Root Force (a rival rock group) has taken over Vegas, Hoss's next conquest, and that a mysterious Gypsy Killer is on his way for a final showdown. Hoss cannot understand how things could have changed so much and reflects, "without a code, it's just crime."

The play's constant references to killing and Hoss's love of knives and guns create in the audience an expectation of physical violence. In the first act, for example, Hoss slashes and stabs a blood-filled dummy in his preparation for confronting the Gypsy Killer. When Crow, the Gypsy Killer, arrives, he speaks an entirely new language. His self-created image is wholly his own, and totally different from that of Hoss. Crow is filled with contempt, arrogance, and violence when he takes the stage. His nonchalant attitude toward the fight and his vicious, biting tongue and alien style taunt Hoss to challenge Crow to a fight of verbal and singing styles instead of one of knives, "Just to prove I ain't outside." A referee (dressed in traditional black and white stripes) officiates the match, complete with microphones and flashing lights.

The duel between Crow and Hoss, then, is a conflict of identities rather than physical weapons; hence the physical imagery of the play presents a deliberate anti-climax. But personal identity in *The Tooth of Crime* seems utterly removed from any basis other than the popularity of a trend recognized and sanctioned by the mass media. Hoss—amid his knives, guns, black leather clothes, alcohol, and psychedelic drugs—even wonders whether there is such a thing as a farmer any more. The "crime" in *The Tooth of Crime* is apparently a surrender of personal identity to an outside and completely amoral system of power defined by ephemeral popular trends. An individualist in such a system cannot long endure. Consequently, Crow's attack of vicious insults and imagery overwhelms Hoss and leaves him defeated by a technical knockout called by the referee. In extreme anger Hoss shoots the referee, an act which puts Hoss outside the game forever. After Hoss realizes the consequences of his actions, he asks Crow to teach him to become a Gypsy. Crow complies, but only after Hoss agrees to give him all of his possessions. As Crow tries to reshape Hoss into a different pattern, Hoss realizes that he cannot change and forget his past. Hoss is a broken man, with a broken code, but he regains his honor by choosing his own destiny. He commits suicide and leaves Crow to carry on with the insanity of the game. Death, then, symbolizes the ultimate freedom, which Hoss has sought all along.

Geography of a Horse Dreamer does not have the same intensity of language that marks *The Tooth of Crime*. Shepard is aware of this issue: "It's not a play that's investigating a whole complicated language scheme." This play uses language from the 1930s in a Raymond Chandler and Dashiell Hammett style, "very idiomatic of a period in America which was really strong." Shepard's enjoyment of the dog racing in England helped in formulating the idea for *Geography of a Horse Dreamer*. Fingers, a member of an eastern gambling syndicate, keeps a Wyoming cowboy named Cody prisoner so that he, Cody, can successfully dream horserace winners. The syndicate is displeased by Cody's slump and a doctor prepares to remove surgically the dreaming bone from Cody's skull. The show ends violently when Cody's two huge cowboy brothers burst in with shotguns and brutally blast the doctor and two syndicate henchmen, but decide to spare Fingers. Shepard himself directed the premiere production in London and commented that directing had helped him to imagine various possibilities of producing plays: "I used to be dead set against rewriting on any level. My attitude was that if the play had faults, those faults were part and parcel of the original process, and that any attempt to correct them was cheating. . . . I began to see that [the production] always demanded a different kind of attention than the written form that it sprang from." *Geography of a Horse Dreamer* was the first play that Shepard directed.

Also written and performed in England was *Little Ocean*, a short series of sketches with three women concentrating on attitudes toward pregnancy and childbirth and ending with the idea of the mother turning into a "little ocean" at the moment of bearing the child. The title implies that the mother for a brief moment is at one with the world. Shepard's wife played the lead. Peter Ansorge, reviewing the premiere at Hampstead, remarked that the play "suffers a little from Shepard's recent attempts to create a kind of geographical limbo—a theatrical halfway house between America and England."

Following Shepard's return to the States in 1974, *Action* (1975) premiered at the American Place Theatre. The play begins in silence as two hairless men and two slovenly women sip coffee, while the lights of a Christmas tree blink in the background. The characters take turns trying to find their places in a book they have been reading, but they are unsuccessful. One of the men becomes agitated and smashes two chairs to bits. Soon, the turkey is served without any of the usual trimmings.

Shepard has set up an image of bleakness and poverty in an unpredictable world. Another of the men tells a story about a family of moths infatuated with the flame of a candle. One moth eventually flies directly into the fire and bursts into flames. The leader of the moths turns to the others and says, "He learned what he wanted to know but he was the only one who understands it." The play ends as one of the men describes how his life changed when he was arrested once. It was then that he found out that he "was in the world. I was up for grabs. I was being taken away by something bigger. . . . I had no idea what the world was. I had no idea how I got there or why or who did it. I had no references for this."

Action is exemplary of many of Shepard's plays in that the search for meaning in life depends also upon the search for a reference point from which to start. Harold Clurman's review of the play in the *Nation* commented on the difficult relationship between abstraction and meaning: "All is 'symbol.' In most traditional art, symbolic significance emerges from a context of action (or imagery) 'imitating' or suggesting a continuity of recognizable behavior and phenomena in a real world. In these Shepard plays the symbols are only notations or abstractions. The context which they are presumed to note are [sic] taken for granted."

Shepard's next major play, *Curse of the Starving Class* (1977), deals with a family on the verge of falling to pieces. Weston, the father, is continually drunk and the mother is trying to sell the house and escape to Mexico with two nearly grown kids. The old refrigerator and stove figure prominently in the action as everyone peeps into the ice-box hoping to find something edible. As the play opens, Wesley, the son, is cleaning up the debris of a smashed door. When his mother, Ella, tells him to leave it for his father to clean up, Wesley berates her for calling the police on his father. As Ella starts cooking the last of the bacon for breakfast, Wesley begins a long monologue about the images that flashed through his mind the evening before when the door was broken down by his father. Wesley takes the broken door away, and Emma, the daughter, enters to look for the chicken that she raised for her 4-H project. She has prepared a speech and illustrative charts about how to cut up a chicken for frying. But her mother starts telling her about menstruation, since Emma is having her first period. When Emma learns that her mother has boiled the chicken, she screams and leaves the kitchen. Wesley becomes angry over the screaming and urinates all over his sister's charts. From off-stage Emma continues the screaming match with her mother: "SO NO ONE'S

STARVING! WE DON'T BELONG TO THE STARVING CLASS!" The remainder of the action concerns the argument over selling the house and Ella's attempt to leave home. Weston has ceased drinking and cleaned up the house; he no longer wants to sell it. However, Ella has decided to become a criminal. Wesley is apparently following in his father's footsteps and beginning to be a violent drunk. *Curse of the Starving Class* utilizes a setting which seems drawn from Shepard's upbringing on the avocado ranch. The uproar of the family may well be based on autobiographical material.

Shepard's latest Obie winner and winner of the 1979 Pulitzer Prize for Drama, *Buried Child*, has been called a departure from his previous work. In many ways this is true. The setting and characterizations are more detailed and realistic. The set is stark but recognizable as a living room with an outside porch, door, and stairway. A television is used throughout much of the play. The character development follows more or less a direct cause and effect pattern seldom used in Shepard's previous plays. Many critics and audiences have found *Buried Child* easier to understand than Shepard's earlier work because of its more conventional structure. "If I was gonna write a play that would win the Pulitzer Prize, I think it would have been that play, you know. It's sort of a typical Pulitzer Prize-winning play," says Shepard. "It wasn't written for that purpose; it was kind of a test. I wanted to write a play about a family."

The play depicts the history of a midwestern farm family. Dodge, a whiskey-drinking grandfather, spends most of his time on the sofa watching television. Tilden, Dodge's oldest son, is mentally deranged and living in the past. Bradley, Tilden's brother, has a wooden leg and is an ominous figure until his leg is taken away and he is rendered helpless. Vince, Tilden's son, with his girl friend, Shelley, has come to visit after a six-year absence, only to find that his family does not recognize or want him. Only Halie, Dodge's wife, recognizes him. As the action unfolds, a secret begins to leak out concerning a dead child, born long ago of an incestuous relationship between Tilden and Halie. Dodge drowned the child and buried it in the back yard. Shelley learns this as Vince leaves to buy a bottle of whiskey for Dodge. Vince, however, does not return until the next day. When he does return, roaring drunk, he smashes bottles all over the house, and intimidates everyone to the point that

Dodge names him the heir to the farm. Vince throws Bradley's leg outside and makes him crawl after it. Shelley leaves the family to carry on alone. Halie's concluding offstage monologue refers to the corn growing in the back yard, even though it has not been planted for years. Tilden, covered with mud, enters the house and carries the decomposed corpse of the disinterred child up the stairs to her.

Buried Child, like *Curse of the Starving Class*, presents a bleak picture of family life. It is uncompromising, if more melodramatic, in its portrayal of how generations wound and alienate each other. The awarding of the Pulitzer Prize to Shepard for *Buried Child* raises the question as to whether Shepard's work may be reaching a larger audience. Shepard's ability to write lyrically yet brutally about the fantasies and myths which shape American consciousness is unique in current theatre. His prolific output and his restless energy are present in even his lesser efforts. He continually searches for new methods of expression. These qualities place him in the forefront of contemporary American playwrights.

–David W. Engel

Television Scripts:
Fourteen Hundred Thousand, "NET Playhouse," 1969;
Blue Bitch, BBC, 1973.

References:
Charles R. Bachman, "Defusion of Menace in Plays of Sam Shepard," *Modern Drama*, 19 (December 1976): 405-415;
Kenneth Chubb, "Fruitful Difficulties of Directing Sam Shepard," *Theatre Quarterly*, 4 (August 1974): 17-25;
Chubb, "Interview: Metaphors, Mad Dogs and Old Time Cowboys," *Theatre Quarterly*, 4 (August 1974): 3-16;
Harold Clurman, "Theatre," *Nation* (24 February 1979): 221;
Randall Craig, "Experimental," *Drama*, 121 (Summer 1976): 75-76;
Craig, "Plays in Performance," *Drama* (Autumn 1973): 30-37;
Walter Donohue, "American Graffitti," *Plays and Players*, 21, no.7 (April 1974): 14-18;
Michael Vermeulen, "Sam Shepard—Yes, Yes, Yes," *Esquire*, 93 (February 1980): 79-86.

Robert Sherwood

Carol Johnston
Clemson University
and
Richard W. Johnston
Barnwell, South Carolina

BIRTH: New Rochelle, New York, 4 April 1896, to Arthur Murray and Rosina Emmet Sherwood.

EDUCATION: B.A., Harvard University, 1918.

MARRIAGE: 29 October 1922 to Mary Brandon, divorced; 15 June 1935 to Madeline Hurlock Connelly.

AWARDS: Pulitzer Prize for *Idiot's Delight*, 1936; Pulitzer Prize for *Abe Lincoln in Illinois*, 1939; Litt.D., Dartmouth College, 1940; National Institute of Arts and Letters Gold Medal for Drama, 1941; Litt.D., Yale University, 1941; Pulitzer Prize for *There Shall Be No Night*, 1941; Academy Award for Best Screenplay for *The Best Years of Our Lives*, 1946; Litt.D., Harvard University, 1949; Gutenberg Award, 1949; Pulitzer Prize for *Roosevelt and Hopkins*, 1949; Bancroft Prize for Distinguished Writings in American History, 1949; honorary doctorate, Bishop's University, 1950.

DEATH: New York, 14 November 1955.

PRODUCTIONS: *The Road to Rome*, 31 January 1927, Playhouse, New York, 392 [performances];
The Love Nest, adapted from Ring Lardner's short story, 22 December 1927, Comedy Theatre, New York, 25;
The Queen's Husband, 25 January 1928, Playhouse, New York, 125;
Waterloo Bridge, 6 January 1930, Fulton Theatre, New York, 64;
This Is New York, 28 November 1930, Plymouth Theatre, New York, 59;
Reunion in Vienna, 16 November 1931, Martin Beck Theatre, New York, 280;
Acropolis, 23 November 1933, Lyric Theatre, London, 12;

The Petrified Forest, 7 January 1935, Broadhurst Theatre, New York, 194;
Idiot's Delight, 24 March 1936, Shubert Theatre, New York, 120;
Tovarich, adapted from Jacques Deval's play, 15 October 1936, Plymouth Theatre, New York, 356;
Abe Lincoln in Illinois, 15 October 1938, Plymouth Theatre, New York, 472;
There Shall Be No Night, 29 April 1940, Alvin Theatre, New York, 115;
The Rugged Path, 10 November 1945, Plymouth Theatre, New York, 81;
Miss Liberty, music by Irving Berlin, 15 July 1949, Imperial Theatre, New York, 308;
Small War on Murray Hill, 3 January 1957, Ethel Barrymore Theatre, New York, 12.

BOOKS: *The Road to Rome* (New York: Scribners, 1927);
The Queen's Husband (New York & London: Scribners, 1928);
Waterloo Bridge (New York & London: Scribners, 1930);
This Is New York (New York & London: Scribners, 1931);
The Virtuous Knight (New York: Scribners, 1931);
Reunion in Vienna (New York: Scribners, 1932);
The Petrified Forest (New York & London: Scribners, 1935);
Idiot's Delight (New York & London: Scribners, 1936; London: Heinemann, 1938);
Tovarich, adapted from Jacques Deval's play (New York: Random House, 1937; London: French, 1938);
Abe Lincoln in Illinois (New York & London: Scribners, 1939);
There Shall Be No Night (New York: Scribners, 1940);
Roosevelt and Hopkins (New York: Harper, 1948); republished as *The White House Papers of Harry*

    L. Hopkins, 2 vols. (London: Eyre & Spottis-
woode, 1949);

Small War on Murray Hill (New York: Dramatists
Play Service, 1957).

In the 1930s few living American playwrights
were better known than Robert Emmet Sherwood.
Offstage, when he served as an adviser to the president of the United States, and onstage, through
productions such as *The Road to Rome* (1927), *Reunion in Vienna* (1931), *The Petrified Forest* (1935),
Idiot's Delight (1936), *Abe Lincoln in Illinois* (1938),
and *There Shall Be No Night* (1940), his humanitarian
ideals vitalized the American conscience during the
period between the two world wars. Sherwood is
best remembered for undergoing a philosophical
conversion that turned the pacifist liberalism of his
early works into the strident militarism of his later
works. But, Sherwood's protagonists are seldom
liberals or militants; they are, like the playwright
himself, romantics—individualists in conflict with
the rigidity of Coolidge "prosperity." His plays are
concerned with the themes of war and romance.
Sherwood believed that the American writer "is
afraid that if he leaps upward on a flight of fancy, he
may bump his head against a star and tumble to
earth, landing in a laughable and undignified position." Those writers who espoused the "low-down,"
who honored fact at the expense of fantasy, proposed to "destroy illusions, by exposing the hokum
from which 'illusions' arise." But "hokum" and illusion were, as Sherwood knew, not only the lifeblood
of the theatre, but also an essential part of the
human response to reality. "To be able to write a
play for performance in a theatre," he noted, "a
man must be sensitive, imaginative, naive, gullible,
passionate; he must be something of an imbecile,
something of a poet, something of a liar, something
of a damn fool. . . . He must not shrink from the old
hokum; he must actually love it."

"Something of a poet" and "something of a
damned fool," Robert Sherwood was descended
from a line of artists and patriots. The Sherwood
family was artistic; the Emmet family was animated
by the cause of Irish freedom. The Sherwoods were
conservatives; the Emmets liberals. Sherwood's
mother, Rosina Emmet Sherwood, merited an entry
in *Who's Who* on the basis of her artwork; Sherwood's paternal grandmother, Mary Elizabeth Wilson Sherwood, a social gadfly, was the author of
hundreds of articles and over twenty books; Sherwood's father, Arthur Murray Sherwood, a successful investment broker, was also a theatre buff who
had, in his youth, been active in Harvard's Hasty

Pudding Club, as well as the founder and first editor
of the *Harvard Lampoon*. Robert Emmet, the
younger brother of Sherwood's great-great-
grandfather, Thomas Addis Emmet, had been the
leader of the ill-planned assault on Dublin Castle on
23 July 1803. His eloquent speech at the dock and
his subsequent hanging made him a martyr to the
Irish cause. More levelheaded than his fiery
younger brother, Thomas Addis Emmet was exiled
to America that same year and later developed a
reputation as an important lawyer. It is reported
that on his death the city flags of New York were
lowered to half-mast.

Sherwood's childhood was spent at the idyllic
Skene Wood a stately three-hundred-acre estate in
Westport, New York, which had as a backdrop the
Adirondacks and Lake Champlain. At Skene Wood,
he outgrew his short pants, lost the chubbiness of
childhood, and grew to a prodigious height (at
maturity he stood well over six and a half feet). In
addition, it was amid the natural beauty of Skene
Wood that Sherwood began his literary career. At
age seven, prefiguring his role as the editor of the
old humor magazine called *Life*, Sherwood edited a
small handwritten family newspaper, the *Children's
Life*. A year later, some thirty years before he
wrought Alan Squier's destiny in *The Petrified Forest*,
he attempted a revision of Dickens's *A Tale of Two
Cities*, purportedly to save Sydney Carton from his
"shabby end." By his tenth birthday, Sherwood was
regularly entertaining his family and friends with
amateur productions of which, today, only the
names remain: "Tom Ruggles' Surprise," "How the
King Was Saved," and "The Curse of the Bacchus."

The records of Sherwood's childhood transgressions seem uneventful: dangling a beetle before
the face of an invalid grandmother, wandering off
from the family estate without warning or permission; still, Sherwood was considered a difficult
child. At age nine he was sent off to the Fay School at
Southborough, Massachusetts. Several years later,
in 1909, he entered the prestigious Milton Academy
and began his preparation for Harvard.

An unconventional student, Sherwood
seemed blissfully unconcerned with academics. He
was fun-loving and active and, at Milton at least, his
violations of the rules were legendary. It is reported
that he once set an entire schoolroom on fire in the
process of attempting to destroy the record of his
offenses, and, when lauded for saving the entire
school from destruction (he succeeded in putting
the fire out), he insisted on setting the record
straight by identifying himself as the culprit who
had started it. He was a constant contributor to the

Robert Sherwood

school's monthly magazine, the *Milton Orange and Blue* (which he edited in his senior year), president of the Civics-Literature Club, a member of the Dramatic Club and Dance Committee, and a letterman in football. His grades, however, were so poor that he was denied a graduating diploma and presented, instead, with a certificate of attendance. In the midst of his complete disciplinary and academic disgrace, his fellow students voted him class valedictorian.

After a summer of being tutored, Sherwood entered Harvard in the fall of 1914. There he became editor of the *Redbook*, a magazine produced by the freshman class, though he was failing freshman English, and by the end of his first year was again on academic probation. He missed class regularly, seemed totally uninterested in scholarship, and instead, centered his attention on clubs and extracurricular literary activities. He was an active member of the Hasty Pudding Club, for which he wrote two plays: *A White Elephant* and *Barnum Was Right*. The first was staged by the Hasty Pudding Club in the spring of 1916 (Sherwood's name was deleted from the program because of his academic difficulties); the second was produced after Sherwood was awarded his degree in 1918. In addition, Sherwood was a prolific contributor to the *Harvard Lampoon*

and served as its editor in his senior year. Despite these notable achievements, Sherwood was thrice expelled from Harvard before the United States entered World War I.

The trauma of war, its threat or its effects, was the thematic background against which Sherwood staged all of his dramas. Rejected by the army and navy because of his height, Sherwood enlisted in the Canadian Expeditionary Force and was assigned to the 42nd Battalion of the 5th Royal Highlanders, known as the Canadian Black Watch. He spent nearly six months on active duty with his brigade in France. Gassed at Vimy Ridge in July 1918, he walked back to his battalion after being treated at the front. A month later his battalion was among the first to go over the ridge at Amiens, where Sherwood was again gassed, and then wounded in both legs. He was hospitalized initially in Amiens and was returned to London on a stretcher. In his preface to *There Shall Be No Night*, Sherwood wrote briefly of his experience as a common soldier in the Canadian army. He focused not on his experiences at the front, but instead (as he would in his plays) on the casualities of war, wounded soldiers such as an Australian who had been terribly burned by liquid fire and a South African Jew who would never walk again. His observations strengthened his abhorrence for war.

Although warned that his experiences at the front had damaged his heart and exhorted to accept the limitations of invalidism, Sherwood accepted a demanding position as motion-picture critic at *Vanity Fair* magazine after his graduation from Harvard. The post was largely the result of a successful *Lampoon* burlesque of *Vanity Fair*, which had impressed the magazine's editor, Frank Crowninshield. At *Vanity Fair* Sherwood shared an office with two fellow employees whose wit and liberal philosophy reinforced his own: Robert Benchley and Dorothy Parker. The three rebelled against the dictates of the editorial staff on more than one occasion and were dismissed from the magazine in January 1920; all three were hired by *Life* magazine that same year. Sherwood worked at *Life*, first as a motion-picture critic and, additionally, after 1924 as its editor. He served the magazine in both these positions until 1928. With Benchley and Parker, Sherwood became the often unobtrusive member of a circle of sharp-tongued theatre enthusiasts, known as the Round Table, who gathered regularly at the Algonquin Hotel. In the company of people such as George S. Kaufman, Marc Connelly, and Laurence Stallings, Sherwood's natural inclination toward the theatre was stimulated and nourished.

There, also, he met his first wife, Mary Brandon, whom he married on 29 October 1922. Sherwood's success as *Life*'s editor brought him a salary of $10,000 a year; however, his life-style was extravagant. By 1926 he was sufficiently in debt to require extraordinary efforts to lighten his financial burden; he turned to playwriting.

Sherwood wrote his first professional play, *The Road to Rome*, in 1926, reportedly over a three-week period at the Harvard Club. Although mixed reviews greeted its opening at the Playhouse in New York on 31 January 1927, it was an immediate popular success and ran for 392 performances. With the notable exception of *Abe Lincoln in Illinois*, Sherwood's maiden attempt at the New York theatre provided him with his longest-running production. It was a strong showing for a new playwright, and it gave Sherwood a measure of financial stability.

The Road to Rome was inspired by what Sherwood termed his "unashamedly juvenile hero-worship for Hannibal." The story is a tongue-in-cheek history lesson with parallels to the concerns of post-World War I America, a reminder to the population that even their most honored historical and political leaders were both human and fallible. Its irreverent handling of history and its use of modern attitudes and colloquialisms in dealing with antiquity drew comparisons to Shaw, a difficult comparison for an inexperienced playwright to survive. *The Road to Rome* was a good indication of the kinds of plays that Sherwood would write in the future. If it could be criticized for a lack of Shavian incisiveness, it could also be praised for its superb characterization, its sprightly and spirited dialogue, and the appealing sophistication of its comedy.

The play is built around a single question that had seemingly bothered Sherwood since his youth: why had Hannibal crossed the Alps to destroy Rome and yet purposely turned away from the gates of Rome on the eve of apparent victory? In his preface to the play, Sherwood retraced Hannibal's military career, as well as the history of the conflict between Rome and Carthage. Admitting that he had taken poetic license with history (*The Road to Rome* pictures Hannibal at the gates of Rome, fresh from a victory at Cannae which had taken place five years earlier), Sherwood suggests that after the battle of Cannae, the Carthaginian general had turned introspective—"that he paused to ask of himself the devastating question, 'What of it?' and that he was unable to find an answer." Sherwood's Hannibal is motivated equally by reason and the irrational urge to wage an imperialistic war. On his way to Rome

Hannibal encounters Amytis, the beautiful, strong-willed, and articulate wife of a Roman senator, Maximus Fabius. Amytis generates the central conflict of the play: should Hannibal yield to the impulse to sack Rome merely for plunder and glory, or should he yield to reason and renounce a pointless barbaric war?

Sherwood depicts Rome as a narrow-minded and sterile society, dominated by a sense of duty and totally unaware of the arts. Imaginative, art-loving, and totally individualistic, Amytis is an alien presence who is unappreciated in a society devoted to the mediocre, a woman who prizes beauty and passion above blind devotion and duty. Irrepressible, sexual, and alive, she stands in brilliant contrast to the sterility of Rome and the death caused by war. At the end of the first act, she leaves Rome, ostensibly to find safety in Ostia with her mother but in reality to find Hannibal. During the entire second act, set in Hannibal's camp, Amytis questions Hannibal's motives, planting doubts in the general's mind about his planned assault on Rome with her discussion of the human cost of war. Finally, as he plans to kill her because of the infectious sanity of her words, she seduces him. Amytis's sexuality overpowers Hannibal's rational defense of his war. In the morning, a rejuvenated and youthful Hannibal turns from Rome leaving a possibly impregnated Amytis in safety with her husband Fabius.

The Road to Rome is, in the Shavian sense, a comic drama of ideas, although its thesis gives a greater emphasis to the emotions than Shaw's plays normally do. To those men who had fought in World War I only to return to an indifferent America, Amytis's pacifism seemed an eloquent expression of their own beliefs; they tended to see the play in terms of a clear-cut confrontation between martial and pacifist views. Reviewers, however, were troubled by the inconsistency of her character. As *New York Times* critic Brooks Atkinson commented, Amytis appears to go to Hannibal's tent not to save Rome, but to fulfill her unfulfilled sexual longings. She argues with Hannibal, not for the purpose of saving lives, but for the purpose of reducing him to sexual submission. Sherwood's theme, however (one that he would outline more fully in the preface to *Reunion in Vienna*), is represented also by Hannibal's own incipient romanticism, a romantic's belief in the beauty of life, an ideal that Amytis finally succeeds in appealing to and that is instrumental in saving Rome. Sherwood pictures this, seductively, in terms of a sexual liaison that impels Hannibal to turn his back on Rome.

As Life's motion-picture critic and editor,

equally at home at the Algonquin and Thanatopsis clubs as he was on Broadway, Hollywood, or London, Sherwood stood at the center of the theatre boom of the 1920s. But his success with *The Road to Rome* prefaced four lean years, and it was not until 1931, after writing four unsuccessful plays, that Sherwood managed to produce another hit. In December 1927, not quite a year after the opening of *The Road to Rome*, Sherwood's second play, a dramatization of Ring Lardner's short story "The Love Nest," opened at the Comedy Theatre in New York. Where Lardner's brilliant story stripped the mask of domestic tranquillity from a marriage to reveal a wife driven to madness by the part she had been cast to play in her own marriage, Sherwood's melodrama reduced the woman to running off with the butler. *The Love Nest* closed, much to the playwright's relief, after 25 performances. Sherwood's next theatrical venture, *The Queen's Husband* (which opened only a month later), met with better success, but was still disappointing. It ran 125 performances. This thin, predictable comedy was Sherwood's speculative response to a visit made to the United States by Queen Marie of Romania the preceding year. The play centers on a bored and henpecked ruler who prefers checkers to politics and on the traditionally ill-betrothed princess in love with a commoner. After a revolution the king consolidates his power as monarch and the princess is allowed to elope with her lover, the son of a wholesale plumber. The play lacks the strength of characterization and the power of theatrical illusion that marked *The Road to Rome* and is, at best, a pedestrian tale.

In 1930 the playwright's fourth production, *Waterloo Bridge*, a wartime tale of love and fidelity, opened at the Fulton Theatre where it ran for sixty-four performances. The story of a young American soldier and a chorus girl who has turned to the world's oldest profession, *Waterloo Bridge* elicits a certain wistful sympathy, but lacks vitality. It translated more effectively to the screen where it has since assumed the reputation of a perennial remake, with adaptations produced by Universal in 1931 and Metro-Goldwyn-Mayer in 1940 and 1956. *This Is New York* (1930), a banal comedy inspired by Sherwood's desire to defend his favorite city from the anti-New York sentiments which had plagued Al Smith's presidential campaign, opened at the Plymouth Theatre later that year. In this play a North Dakota senator's daughter becomes part of the scandalous New York scene only to prove that narrow-minded provincialism can cause greater harm than the corruption of bootlegging and drug addiction. The play closed after fifty-nine performances.

Consistently, these plays lacked the comic touch and sparkling characterization that had led to the success of *The Road to Rome*. They are important, however, for the light they shed on the development and continuity of Sherwood's thought between 1927 and 1931. In at least one respect both *The Queen's Husband* (1928) and *This Is New York* recall Sherwood's *The Road to Rome* while looking forward to his second major achievement, *Reunion in Vienna*. In *The Road to Rome* Sherwood pictured the demigods of Roman history as contemporary in their vernacular and, at best, half-hearted and uncertain about their grand military enterprises. The parallels between Sherwood's Rome and the intolerant conformity of Coolidge "prosperity" were clarified by Sherwood in his preface, where he wrote, "the spirit of Fabius Maximus and his brother boosters has become the spirit of America today. History is full of deadly and disturbing parallels and this, it seems to me, is one of the most obvious parallels of all." Amytis's individualism was pitted not only against the conformity of Sherwood's Rome, but also against the intolerance of postwar America. Similarly, Sherwood's audiences were accustomed to seeing royalty, statesmen, and psychiatrists as revered figures. In *The Queen's Husband* a monarch is as roundly abused as a farmhand, while in *This Is New York* a racketeer seems the only man of decent impulses as he confronts a U.S. Senator who is full of cant. The development of this theme culminates in *Reunion in Vienna* in which the passion of a febrile, epileptic taxi driver seems ultimately more significant than the logical inquiry of a practicing psychiatrist.

Sherwood's sixth professional play, *Reunion in Vienna*, has been likened by most of Sherwood's critics to a lilting and lovely Viennese waltz. It opened at the Martin Beck Theatre on 16 November 1931, starring Lynn Fontanne and Alfred Lunt in the roles of Elena Krug and Prince Rudolf Maximillian von Habsburg, a Viennese aristocrat-turned-cab-driver in post-World War I Europe. It marked the first of Sherwood's associations with the Theatre Guild, yielded the playwright a substantial financial success, and redeemed his reputation. *Reunion in Vienna* ran for 280 performances and within two months of its premiere brought the playwright over $80,000 in film rights. Although preproduction controversy centered on the validity of Sherwood's treatment of psychoanalysis (one of the Theatre Guild's members considered himself an expert on it and was disturbed by the play's cavalier attitudes toward it), postproduction controversy revolved around whether the success of the play was the result of Sherwood's craft or the dazzling brilliance of the Lunts. Most critics could scarcely get beyond their praise of the Lunts to note the name of the playwright. However, for Sherwood, *Reunion in Vienna* was an occasion; after four seasons of lackluster productions he had finally produced a play that equalled the success of his first attempt.

Sherwood conceived of the play in 1929 while traveling in Europe with his wife, Mary Brandon. It was his first return to Europe after the war and he went to Vienna to see an Austrian production of *The Road to Rome*, retitled *Hannibal Ante Portes*. While there he was taken to the Hotel Sacher, a remnant of the Hapsburg era. Amid the opulence of a pre-World War I setting he was introduced to Frau Sacher (the original for Frau Lucher of *Reunion in Vienna*), a despotic, cigar-smoking hostess rumored to throw parties for those once-aristocratic patrons who hunger for the past. Two years later, Sherwood set to work writing a play that was to use Frau Sacher's hotel as its setting.

Sherwood, in his typically intense style, dashed the comedy off in two weeks and sent copies to the Theatre Guild and to the Lunts. The Theatre Guild agreed to produce the play, and the Lunts, anxious to do the kind of drawing-room comedy that best suited their talents, chose to do *Reunion in Vienna* rather than O'Neill's *Mourning Becomes Electra*.

Reunion in Vienna is the hybrid product of Sherwood's trip to Vienna and *The Road to Rome*. As a play it is far more successful than its predecessor; the dialogue is more graceful and less propagandistic and the characters more vital. Yet, the parallels are obvious. The first act of the play takes place in the home of Anton Krug, a successful Viennese psychiatrist whose stoic veneration of science mirrors Fabius Maximus's stoic veneration of Rome. His wife, Elena, the ex-mistress of the Archduke Rudolf Maximillian von Habsburg, is an alluring woman whose sexuality, like that of Amytis, is stifled by her surroundings. Whereas the parlor talk in Sherwood's first play revolved around the advisability of rendering oneself up to die for the good of Rome, the parlor talk in the home of Anton Krug revolves around offering oneself up to the great god, Science, "the gospel of the better life." The crisis turns not on Hannibal's encampment at the gates of Rome, but on the clandestine return of Elena's lover, the Archduke Rudolf Maximillian, to Vienna.

Rudolf, like Hannibal, is a man of tremendous vitality. Unlike Hannibal, however, he is past the time of his official power. Exiled, he has been driving a taxicab in Nice. He cannot bang on the doors of Vienna as Hannibal could at the gates of Rome; he can only slyly and secretly return to attend a party of faded aristocrats at Frau Lucher's. Still, he is the third party to a triangle which pits the debilitating forces of rigid conformity and proper social action against the luxury of individualism.

Krug's confidence in his control of all situations leads to his insistence that his wife join in a reunion at Frau Lucher's with her old lover on the logical assumption that ten years of penury would have resulted in the archduke bearing more resemblance to an aging taxicab driver than to a dashing young Habsburg. Rudolf, however, turns out to be as irrepressibly engaging as ever. In an action totally of Sherwood's invention and audacious in its theatricality, Rudolf greets his ex-mistress at Frau Lucher's by slapping her face before kissing her passionately. It is a gesture that she returns later in the act—the preface to a relationship which lacks conventionality, but is inspired by an enduring passion. In the course of the second act, the quintessentially emotional Rudolf confronts the quintessentially intellectual Anton. The two are on the verge of a brawl when the arrival of the police makes it necessary for Anton to intercede on Rudolf's behalf. This requires Anton to leave Elena alone with Rudolf who is, necessarily, somewhat reluctant to take advantage of his intercessor's wife. Alone with Elena in her home, Rudolf responds: "As effective a bit of foul play as I have ever witnessed! He's tricked me into his debt—put me on my honor. He knows that I have that. It runs in the Habsburg blood—honor and epilepsy." In the face of the psychiatrist's intervention Rudolf feels devitalized and emasculated; he is no longer the nephew of an emperor, but a taxi driver, dressed up. Nostalgic memory is a dispiriting force for Rudolf until Elena finally decides to make love to him. Revitalized, Rudolf awakes to a fine Vienna morning, devours the kidneys meant only for Anton, and exits—not with Hannibal's response to Fabius's comment that he has no sons ("You may have. . . .")—but with the satisfaction of knowing that he has "contributed something" to Anton and Elena's union.

The gaiety and frivolity of *Reunion in Vienna* stands in remarkable contrast to the nihilism of Sherwood's preface, a preface, it is well to remember, which was written upon the occasion of the presentation of the play to Scribners for publication in 1932. Sherwood would write in 1941 that in this preface he had come closer than he ever had before to a statement of what he was trying to write. "This play," Sherwood wrote, "is another demonstration of the escape mechanism in operation." He pessimistically pictured man as "a soldier who spreads a sheet of wrapping paper over his bivouac to keep out the airplane bombs." The Age of Reason, he suggested, had given birth to a "monster" in light of which man "submerges himself in the mass" and falls "meekly into line." In response to this sterile use of reason, Sherwood's comedies had offered the illusion of the theatre itself, as a means of countering nihilism. These plays gain remarkable strength when read as stories of people who, even in the face of lamentably inappropriate circumstances, face life with an undefeated spirit and a sense of gaiety. But Sherwood was beginning to question such optimism.

Sherwood wrote *Reunion in Vienna* in a state of melancholy. Privately, his marriage to Mary Brandon was floundering; publicly, the Depression, spreading unemployment, and the rise of figures like Mussolini, Stalin, and Hitler seemed to have invalidated the hopes that had arisen in the course of making peace a decade before. As Sherwood looked around him, it seemed clear that, having lost his religion, man had become the victim of politics and science. He addressed his *Reunion in Vienna* to a despairing age, but his social comment, sugarcoated as sophisticated comedy, was received merely as delightful or at best superficial amusement. The pessimism of Sherwood's preface is therefore pertinent to an understanding of the direction his career would take. The actions of Elena Krug and the Archduke Rudolf suggest that the age, one in which the human heart had been disarmed by the "sour distillations of a maturing intellectualism," required emotional rather than intellectual solutions. The spirit of the *Reunion in Vienna* preface was to become central to Sherwood's best works and would drive him into a decade of productivity which would earn him three Pulitzer prizes.

Sherwood wrote his seventh play, *Acropolis*, in 1932. It is unpublished but, after being politely turned down by the Theatre Guild, was produced in 1933 in London where it closed at the Lyric Theatre after only twelve performances. The play's central theme revolves around the conflict of Athenian aestheticism and Spartan militarism in ancient Greece. This type of opposition was, of course, central to all of Sherwood's work, and, as the militarism of European politics increased, the substance of his plays seemed more and more a reflection of changing world conditions.

The year 1934 proved to be a turning point in Sherwood's life. His marriage to Mary Brandon had proved unsuccessful and he found himself falling in love with Madeline Hurlock Connelly, the wife of his close friend, Marc Connelly. Sherwood went to Reno, filed for a divorce, and later married Madeline Connelly on 15 June 1935. While in Nevada he explored the Old West, the echoes of pioneers, and the relics of American folklore and legend. Looking at a road map he came across a spot intriguingly named "The Petrified Forest." He immediately set to work on a new play.

The Petrified Forest, the most starkly allegorical and improbable of Sherwood's works, marked his coming to maturity as a playwright. It has been criticized for its overt sentimentality and its melodrama, its static point of view, and the pessimistic philosophy of its protagonist. One critic referred to it as one of "the most amoral hodgepodges of philosophy that ever rejoiced the hearts of our dramatic critics and fashionable audiences." Yet, in its projection of that pattern of ideas present in Sherwood's earlier works, it is his most remarkable play. Setting its theatricality aside, the play Sherwood fashioned as he sat in his twenty-five-dollar-a-week office in Reno was a dramatic structure worthy of the Old West: a battle of ideas represented by the standoff of the old gunfight in which disillusioned intellectualism, personified in Alan Squier, meets and is outdrawn by the personification of violent reality, a gangster named Duke Mantee. The play is set, however, in the 1930s rather than in the 1870s: the two cowboys are transformed into their modern-day equivalents, and the old saloon has been transformed into the Black Mesa filling station. Duke Mantee, a murderer and bankrobber, carries a submachine gun rather than a pistol, and the disillusioned intellectual, Alan Squier, divested of belief in God and man, stands unarmed.

Alan Squier arrives at the filling station, run by an old pioneer, Gramp Maple, his dull son, Jason, and Jason's daughter, Gabby. Gabby is a vital young girl who dreams of romance and of being reunited with her mother in France. The Black Mesa stands on the edge of The Petrified Forest, a living world turned to stone, which Alan Squier describes as "the graveyard of the civilization that's been shot from under us ... the world of outmoded ideas. ... Platonism—Patriotism—Christianity—Romance—the economics of Adam Smith. ..." The location is suitable because, except for the youthful Gabby whose future balances tenuously on her ability to realize her dreams, all of the characters of the play have outlived their usefulness. The old man, Gabby's grandfather, is a relic of the past; his son, an American Legionnaire, belongs to an organization which promotes memories rather than realities; Boze Hertzlinger, the young halfback who meets Gabby, is incapable of looking beyond his college days; the stuffy banker is a victim of his own success; the banker's wife is a victim of her own sexual frustration; and the young intellectual is, in his own words, the member of a "vanishing race. . . . Brains without purpose. Noise without sound." When Duke Mantee, a latter-day Billy the Kid, arrives, he makes hostages of everyone present. In order to insure Gabby's future, Squier makes Gabby the beneficiary of his insurance policy and persuades Mantee to kill him. Mantee agrees and after shooting Squier flees into the night to an almost certain death. Squier dies in Gabby's arms.

The plot structure, despite its emphasis on the love interest between Gabby and Alan Squier, centers on the relationship between Squier and Duke Mantee. The gangster and the intellectual have an intuitive bond between them which seems to have no rational base, a bond which is somehow strengthened by their impending destruction. Squier's passive intellect is ineffectual and Mantee's violence is amoral. In a world of chaos, the men who are able to act with decisiveness are desperate and evil; the idealistic intellectuals are doomed by their own natures to be ineffectual. If the world is to be saved at all it must be saved by humanitarian values translated into action, and both Mantee and Squier lack this ability.

The Petrified Forest is the pivotal point upon which Sherwood's philosophy turned. It is the first of his plays in which romantic idealism fails and—despite Squier's insistence on dying in the romantic tradition—it fails miserably. Gabby, the sole hope of the drama is, at the end, left pitifully exposed in a world of Boze Hertzlingers and Jason Maples. The position of modern man, unable to integrate his conscious will and his moral philosophy, is one of only unrelieved tragedy.

The concerns of the American people, a nation torn between self-imposed isolationism and the emergence of European fascism, consumed Sherwood's interest in the years between *The Petrified Forest* and World War II. So presciently did Sherwood's dramas of this period describe current world tensions and so sensitively did they reflect the agonized shifting of the American conscience, that his plays seem more journalistic than dramatic. *Idiot's Delight*, a stirring play on what Sherwood then called "the next world war," was written in a time of

such instability that although the play was begun in November 1935, one month after Mussolini's invasion of Ethiopia, by its opening in March 1936 Hitler had already invaded the Rhineland. It was the last play that Sherwood would write in the spirit of pacifism fostered by his disillusioned response to World War I, the last of his plays in which his protagonists would choose to die without rising to defend their beliefs. With the onset of the war, Sherwood's pacifism came full circle. *Abe Lincoln in Illinois*, his best-known drama, found in this beloved American figure a symbol of the times in which "a democratic people of humble origins and inward struggles slowly awakened to the dreadful problems of reality"; and in *There Shall Be No Night* he expressed his philosophy regarding the war against the Axis Powers as he idealized one family's fight to preserve the liberty of their nation. Each of these three dramas was awarded the Pulitzer Prize. With the exception of Eugene O'Neill, no other American playwright has been so consistently honored.

Like *The Petrified Forest*, *Idiot's Delight* is structured on the simple device of gathering a group of people of various backgrounds and opinions together and isolating them in a pressure-filled situation for the purpose of exploring a central theme. In *The Petrified Forest* the theme centered on the monstrous anxiety produced by an age paralyzed by unreasoning brutality and sterile intellectualism; in *Idiot's Delight* the topic is war—not the war that Sherwood had lived through—but the one that loomed ahead. The play takes place in the Hotel Monte Gabriele in the Italian Alps near the frontiers of Switzerland and Austria where a group of civilians representing various points of view—a scientist; a labor leader; a bourgeois-couple; a munitions manufacturer and his mistress, an American showgirl in the guise of a Russian adventuress; and a small-time American vaudevillian—are being temporarily detained by the Italian government. Although each of them hates war, none can prevent it, and when war finally comes, each takes refuge in his own nationalism: the scientist, a distinguished German bacteriologist on the verge of discovering a cure for cancer, gives up his mission to return to his fatherland to work on nerve gas; the labor leader, a supposedly internationally minded pacifist, gives up his life in front of a firing squad yelling, "Vive la France!"; a member of the bourgeoisie, a young English artist, forgets his painting and his honeymoon in his impatience to get home and join up; and a munitions manufacturer, Achille Weber, threatened by his mistress's antiwar comments, escapes to safety leaving her behind. At the end only

Harry Van, the American showman, and Irene, the American showgirl, elect to remain. As the bombs fall around them, he launches into a jazz version of "Onward, Christian Soldiers."

This heavy-handed ending to the play, a tacked-on symbol of militant Christianity, at first seems inappropriate—an audacious piece of schmaltz conceived to lighten the audience's despair as the curtain drops on a scene of impending death and destruction. There are, however, two conflicts at work in the play: a conflict between pacifism and militancy, in which liberalism proves ultimately to be the weakest of forces in a world dominated by fear and suspicion, and a conflict between disillusionment and faith, represented in the characters of Irene and Harry Van. Where the first conflict results in World War II, the second presents the only true alternative to this doom. The problem posed in the drama is implicit in the title: is God, as Irene views him, a poor, lonely old soul, sitting up in heaven, with nothing to do but play solitaire? Is life nothing more than "Idiot's Delight," "a game that never means anything and never ends?" This question as it is posed in the play is frequently overlooked simply because Harry's muddled answer is far less dramatic and articulate than Irene's devastating response to her munitions-manufacturer lover on the mutilations that result from war. (Irene's often-quoted description of the future which lay before a young English couple, a future in which he confidently fights at the front to protect hearth and home, while she, shattered, lies in a cellar wrecked by an air raid, was improvised by Lynn Fontanne and is not contained in Sherwood's first draft of the play.) Still, in the preface to *There Shall Be No Night*, Sherwood referred to Harry Van's speech as being most representative of his ideas: "I've remained," Harry comments, "an optimist because I'm essentially a student of human nature. . . . it has been my job to dissect suckers! I've probed into the souls of some of the God-damnedest specimens. And what have I found? . . . Faith in peace on earth, and good will to men—and faith that 'Muma,' the three-legged girl, really has got three legs." Harry, like Sherwood, eventually believed that, however the meek might be bulldozed or gypped, they would eventually inherit the earth.

Like many dramatists, Sherwood tends to repetition; the structural similarity between *The Road to Rome* and *Reunion in Vienna* is significant in that it reveals Sherwood's ability to rework the material of one play, introducing new ideas and developing old themes, to produce a new and, frequently, superior work. *Idiot's Delight*, Sherwood's

first Pulitzer Prize-winning drama, is similarly a reworking of the themes and structures of the works that preceded it. The pacifist doctrines espoused by Irene sound remarkably similar to the arguments of Sherwood's prototypal heroine, Amytis; the technique of presenting profound social comment against a backdrop of frivolity and wit is reminiscent of *Reunion in Vienna*; and the passive acceptance of death implicit in Irene and Harry Van's decision to remain at the Hotel Monte Gabriele in many ways parallels Alan Squier's acceptance of death at the hands of Duke Mantee. In all four plays—*The Road to Rome*, *Reunion in Vienna*, *The Petrified Forest*, and *Idiot's Delight*—a woman, romantic and vital, becomes the answer to a man's quest for the meaning of life. In the first two plays she revitalizes him and becomes his reason for living; in the latter two plays she becomes his reason for dying. Another item common to all of these plays is a background of war and violence threatening one or more of the characters, a background of tension to which the characters respond and for which they are not personally responsible.

In *The Petrified Forest* Alan Squier lumped patriotism, Christianity, and romanticism with the economics of Adam Smith and identified them with the stone stumps of prehistory. Modern man, confronted by the labyrinthian thoughts of Freud and Marx, could no more depend on these old verities than he could return to his mother's womb. Still, the resolution of each of Sherwood's major works in some way turns on some combination of these verities. Both *Abe Lincoln in Illinois* and *There Shall Be No Night* stress a need for the support of democratic values in the form of a renewed patriotism.

If Robert Sherwood had functioned only as a dramatist, his ideas would have found a receptive audience; however, the same spirit that animated his ancestor, Robert Emmet, inspired Sherwood to a more active participation in the social and political movements of his time. By the end of World War II, Sherwood had become the most politically conspicuous of the active American dramatists: in 1937 he served as president of the Dramatists Guild and became a founding member of the Playwrights' Company; in 1940 he was appointed special assistant to the secretary of war and was named president of the American National Theatre and Academy (ANTA), an organization chartered by Congress for the purpose of bringing the American theatre to all the American people; in 1942 he was appointed director of the Overseas Branch of the Office of War Information; in 1945 he was appointed special assistant to the secretary of the navy;

and in 1949 he was awarded his fourth Pulitzer Prize, not for drama, but for his biographical-historical study of the wartime relationship between Franklin Delano Roosevelt and his controversial aide, Harry Hopkins—a relationship that Sherwood had observed at first hand. In addition to promoting the entry of the United States into World War II, Sherwood openly opposed racism, fought for the screenwriters' union, and worked as part of a ghostwriting team that provided Roosevelt with most of his post-1940 speeches. When he died, in 1955, he was a revered public figure, a literary figure whose humanitarian ideals had led him into the political arena.

Sherwood became involved in the movement for active unionism that infected New York dramatists and screenwriters throughout the 1920s and 1930s. In New York the playwrights banded together under the banner of the Dramatists Guild, an organization which energized the active resentment that playwrights had felt against the dictatorial actions of managers and producers and which represented playwrights as a bargaining agent. In 1935 Sherwood became secretary of that organization and, in 1937, its president. The most notable result of Sherwood's presidency and the most formidable expression of his resentment of those managers who had irked him in matters of casting and artistic judgement was the formation of the Playwrights' Company.

Riding together in an elevator following an especially tedious Dramatists Guild meeting, Sherwood, Maxwell Anderson, and Elmer Rice adjourned to a neighboring bar where all three entered into a vehement discussion on the heavy-handed prerogatives that the Theatre Guild had taken with their productions. The Guild, while producing some of the best works of American dramatists, often subjected these same playwrights to unwarranted harrassment concerning casting, revisions, and subsidiary rights. In a spirit of fraternal revolt, Sherwood, Anderson, and Rice, later assisted by Sidney Howard and S. N. Behrman, revived an often projected but seemingly impossible dream, the foundation of the Playwrights' Company (1938) in which playwrights would produce and reap the profits of their own plays. The agreement among the playwrights was that the company would produce any script written by a member so long as the budget did not exceed $25,000 and, in turn, each playwright was to be in complete charge of his own production, free to call upon the others at any time for assistance. Sherwood, who had just

completed *Abe Lincoln in Illinois*, offered it up to the company as their first production.

The least theatrical of Sherwood's dramas, *Abe Lincoln in Illinois* is the most historically astute. His "The Substance of 'Abe Lincoln in Illinois,'" a sixty-one page supplement to the drama appended to the Scribners edition (1939), describes his research in depth. In dealing with an individual portrait of an oft-eulogized American leader such as Lincoln, Sherwood walked a narrow line between poetic license and fact. Few audiences would expect the same diligent respect for detail in the depiction of a character such as Hannibal, for instance, that they would for a man whose integrity, humility, and loyalty had become universally recognized. Still, Sherwood needed to present the facts of the man's life in a way sufficiently dramatic to interest an audience already familiar with those facts. In a departure from the structure of his earlier plays, Sherwood's *Abe Lincoln in Illinois* is loose and episodic. The primary divisions of the play are twelve chronologically ordered scenes focusing on dramatic moments in Lincoln's life. Through all this Lincoln is portrayed as a charming young man—rent by bitterly conflicting emotions. The Lincoln of the drama is a destined creature resisting his destiny, a man whose undirected romanticism ultimately turns to a brooding recognition of his own duty.

Abe Lincoln in Illinois was an allegory of the times, clearly establishing a parallel between the development of the attitudes of the American people prior to 1940—the movement from appeaser to fighter—and the development of Lincoln's attitudes prior to the Civil War. The drama spans thirty years of Lincoln's life from his early twenties to his election, focusing on the metamorphosis of a melancholy, indecisive youth into a man of moral conviction and decisive action. The play begins with Lincoln as postmaster in Salem, Illinois, touches on his affection for Ann Rutledge, and follows his election to the state assembly and his years as a Springfield lawyer. In Springfield he meets and proposes to an ambitious Mary Todd, only to jilt her on their wedding day; however, he returns to her out of a sense of duty and marries her. After debates with Douglas, Lincoln is elected president and departs for Washington—a man duty-bound to both wife and country.

Had Sherwood written *Abe Lincoln in Illinois* earlier in his career, he would have undoubtedly focused on Lincoln's love for Ann Rutledge. Instead, while Sherwood chooses to identify this love as the inspiration for Lincoln's entering politics, he dispenses with the story of these star-crossed lovers with Ann's death at the end of the first act. "Sweet and pretty as Ann undoubtedly is—," Judge Bowling Green comments, "she'd only be a hindrance to him." To Abe, Ann represents a romantic belief in the possibility of life, a belief which Abe describes as a "beauty and purity in people—like the purity you sometimes see in the sky at night." This beauty might inspire a man to higher things, but, taken as a guide for living, could only blind him to the realities of his course. In Abe's movement from Ann Rutledge to Mary Todd, the play shifts from the solutions of emotionalism to those of moral commitment. As nagging and unattractive as Mary Todd Lincoln looms against her husband's gentle inoffensiveness, she ultimately represents duty and destiny. Although Lincoln cannot love her, he is by necessity bound to her. Following Ann Rutledge's death, Lincoln is always moved by a sense of obligation rather than by a spontaneous yielding to his emotions. Lincoln's decision to spurn Mary Todd in the play's sixth scene is equated with his decision to turn his back on politics, to mind "his own business," and to let the Union stand or fall on the Constitution. His return to her in the eighth scene of the play, following his encounter with a pioneer family and his recognition of their birthright, is ultimately a decision not to resist his own destiny. Where *Idiot's Delight* closed with a rousing rendition of "Onward, Christian Soldiers," *Abe Lincoln in Illinois* closes with "John Brown's Body"—the curtain falling on the words "His soul goes marching on." The unwritten conclusion of the play, the horrors of the Civil War and Lincoln's death by assassination, was already present in the audience's mind.

Abe Lincoln in Illinois altered Sherwood's life—at no other point in his dramatic career had Sherwood so clearly restated the American dream—and at few other points in the history of the nation did it seem so desperately to need restatement as on the eve of World War II. In a moment of widespread doubt, Sherwood urged the nation on to a conscious sense of its destiny; in a moment of national despair he gave it purpose.

On Christmas Day 1939, Sherwood listened to a radio broadcast from Finland by Bill White, the son of William Allen White, editor of the *Emporia* (Kansas) *Gazette*. The younger White, an American correspondent caught in the midst of Russia's invasion of Finland, described the Christmas he had just spent with exhausted Finnish troops at the front. The butchering of Finland had been going on for

nearly four weeks, and the heroic resistance of the vastly outnumbered Finns mobilized Sherwood's moral imagination. In telling the story of Abe Lincoln, a man of peace forced to face the hard issue of war, Sherwood had retraced the development of his own thought. As Russia invaded Finland, Sherwood found himself faced with an equivalent moment in history, one in which passive resistance seemed more an abdication than an instrument of moral will. In the coming year he wrote *There Shall Be No Night*, a firm denouncement of American isolationism, which he believed to be more the result of misinformed self-interest than of a true pacifism. The ends of true pacifism, he began to reason, lay beyond the rugged path of militarism. By the end of 1940 he had publicly identified himself with the interventionist causes in America and become their most outspoken advocate.

There Shall Be No Night opens with a radio broadcast from Finland. The eminent Finnish neurologist, Dr. Kaarlo Valkonen, recipient of the Nobel Prize for his work with and understanding of mental diseases, is being interviewed by an American newsman. The scene is the peaceful home of Dr. Valkonen. Despite the enlightened pacifism of Valkonen (as his son Erik comments, his parents live together in the future—"the future as my father has imagined it—not the one that may be made by unimaginative men"), his description of the mental diseases attacking individuals serves as a metaphor for the larger world, which Sherwood sees to be equally insane. In his own words, Valkonen decries the tendency of men to "find the easy way out— when man to *be* man, needs the experience of the hard way." This concept of "the rugged path," which originates in Lincoln's recitation of Keats's "On Death" in the first act of *Abe Lincoln in Illinois*, reaches its fullest philosophical development in *There Shall Be No Night*. Valkonen must admit, along with Sherwood, that men who fight barbarism, not for glory but in an agonized effort to preserve the traditions of freedom, partake in the fulfillment of human destiny. With the invasion of Finland by the Russians, Valkonen's ideals of pacifism are steadily beaten back by the course of events. The doctor's son goes to battle and is killed, and the doctor himself is forced to lay down the ideals of his profession and take up the gun in defense of his homeland. He remains, however, a liberal who, although recognizing the need to fight for the liberty of his country, refuses to give up those humanistic convictions central to his pacifism. For men like Valkonen, it is indeed a grim resignation that enables them to say of their own militancy, "This is an evil job—but I have to do it." Ultimately, it is this decision to fight for peace rather than for self-glorification that makes them men capable of conquering rather than submitting to inhumanity.

Finland had succumbed to the Russian invasion by the time that *There Shall Be No Night* opened at the Alvin Theatre on 29 April 1940. Sherwood was immediately condemned as a warmonger by some, hailed as a great patriot by others. He quickly achieved a conspicuous position as the most outspoken and persuasive of the American interventionists. In his valedictory address to the Dramatists Guild a year earlier, Sherwood had expressed what had become with him a sense of the growing power of the word. "There is," he commented, "a new and decisive force in the human race, more powerful than all the tyrants. It is the force of massed thought—thought which has been provoked by words, strongly spoken." It was this force that Sherwood sought to unleash in *There Shall Be No Night*.

In May 1940, Sherwood joined a group of interventionists, the Committee to Defend America by Aiding the Allies, and immediately became its leading spokesman. Taking $24,000 from his own pocket, he wrote and paid for a full-page advertisement of historic significance. His "Stop Hitler Now!" advertisement appeared on 10 June 1940 in more than a hundred newspapers throughout the country. The advertisement, a powerfully worded discussion of the long-range goals of Hitler's aggression, appeared on President Roosevelt's desk the following day as reporters filed into his office for the usual Tuesday afternoon conference. In an unusual move, Roosevelt praised the advertisement and its author for providing the American people with a piece of work of extreme educational value. It was not Sherwood's first contact with Roosevelt, a man with whom he would become more closely associated in the future, but it did mark the beginning of the administration's interest in the playwright's politics. On the radio, at mass rallies, at small meetings, in newspaper interviews, Sherwood argued his cause. By the end of the summer Sherwood had been formally approached by the White House and had become a close if unofficial associate of the president. Along with Harry Hopkins and Samuel Rosenman, Sherwood became a member of a notable team responsible for drafting most of Roosevelt's speeches.

The next four and a half years found Sherwood at the center of the most dramatic situations of the time, clearly apart from that world of theatri-

cality and illusion that most delighted him. By the close of 1940, he had been appointed special assistant to the secretary of war (a largely honorary post that occupied little of his time), and shortly after the entry of the United States into World War II, he was named director of the Overseas Branch of the Office of War Information. By 1942 he found himself in charge of a department of eighteen hundred employees with an annual budget of between twenty and thirty million dollars. The Office of War Information was responsible for establishing shortwave radio stations, dropping leaflets on Germany, and supplying information to the people of France. As its director, Sherwood was enmeshed in the administrative duties for which the vocational experience of a playwright had left him unprepared. In September 1944 he resigned in order to take a more active part in Roosevelt's reelection campaign.

As Sherwood became increasingly involved in government, he became less and less the playwright. Never again would he have the success of *There Shall Be No Night*. Following the war he wrote two original dramas, *The Rugged Path* (1945) and *Small War on Murray Hill*, produced posthumously in 1957, both on war themes and both unsuccessful. The needs of postwar America had changed, and Sherwood's thoughtful responses to the needs of a nation facing war were no longer applicable. The postwar years were not totally uneventful, though, for in 1948 he published his mammoth treatise on the relationship between Roosevelt and Harry Hopkins, *Roosevelt and Hopkins*. Sherwood died on 14 November 1955.

Despite the eminence that Sherwood gained in the 1930s, few critics today would identify him as a great figure in the American theatre. His plays are seldom revived, and his name is overshadowed by those of playwrights such as Eugene O'Neill and Tennessee Williams. The current lack of interest in Sherwood's dramas raises certain questions: Why should the same plays that so passionately sparked the imagination of the American people in the 1930s have proven so temporal? Do Sherwood's plays merit literary attention or are they the artifacts of a bygone era, best remembered as documents of one generation's muddled search for meaning? Can the principles of one generation serve as more than footnotes to the generations that follow? The questions are more easily posed than answered; still, some conclusions are possible.

It would not be fair to suggest that Sherwood's dramas achieve literary greatness; they do not. Several are more of interest to the student of theatre history than they are to the student of literature.

But this is not to say that his plays lack universality or literary value. All authors are, to some extent, prisoners of their times; still, it seems the best literature manages to appeal on some level to other ages as well. There is a tendency on the part of Sherwood's critics to reduce the playwright's work to its simplest elements and to discuss the internal dialogue of ideas on which the plays are structured. Almost all that has been written on Sherwood centers on the development of his pacifism while ignoring his romanticism, the quality of his characterization, and the general effectiveness of the drama as played on the stage. Sherwood's dramas are consistently articulate, at their best brilliantly witty and often eloquent probings of an enlightened mind into a civilization undergoing the throes of recognizing its own possible destruction. As long as men question the validity of their response or lack of response to entrenched and militant nationalism, Sherwood's dramas will have something of value to offer them.

To some extent, Sherwood's dramas are structured on an appeal to the political consciousness of the 1930s. They gain intensity when performed before audiences aware of the conflict between internationalist and isolationist views; they gain tension from the audience's awareness of the immediate possibility of totalitarian aggression. These political underpinnings may very well account for the unpopularity of Sherwood's dramas in the 1960s and 1970s when the national conscience turned against its own aggressive tendencies, rather than questioning its right to intercede in the aggressions of others. The pacifism that followed the Vietnam War, for instance, bears a greater semblance to the pacifism that followed World War I than it does to the determination that preceded World War II. To this extent, much of Sherwood's work is clearly temporal, but temporal in the sense that it addresses itself to a specific world situation rather than to a specific decade.

The dramatization of an age of anxiety is no little feat. It is well to remember that while Sherwood's plays turned headlines into dialogue, they did so with a sensitivity to the needs of the stage and to the virtues of dramatic form. Their success lay in the fact that they played well and immediately communicated to the audience the intelligent compassion and genuine concern for mankind that marked Sherwood both as a man and as a dramatist.

Screenplays:
Cock of the Air, by Sherwood and Charles Lederer, United Artists, 1932;

The Scarlet Pimpernel, by Sherwood and Arthur Wimperis, London Films, 1935;
The Ghost Goes West, London Films, 1936;
Thunder in the City, by Sherwood and Aben Kandel, Atlantic Films, 1937;
The Adventures of Marco Polo, United Artists, 1938;
The Divorce of Lady X, by Sherwood and Lajos Biro, London Films, 1938;
Idiot's Delight, MGM, 1939;
Abe Lincoln in Illinois, RKO, 1939;
Rebecca, United Artists, 1940;
The Best Years of Our Lives, RKO, 1946;
The Bishop's Wife, by Sherwood and Leonardo Bercovici, RKO, 1947;
Man On a Tightrope, Twentieth Century-Fox, 1953.

Other:
The Best Moving Pictures of 1922-23, edited by Sherwood (Boston: Small, Maynard, 1923).

Periodical Publications:
"The Dramatic Life of Abraham Lincoln," *Life* (14 February 1924): 24;
"Renaissance in Hollywood," *American Mercury*, 16 (April 1929): 431-437;
"Beyond the Talkies, Television," *Scribner's*, 86 (July 1929): 1-8;
"Extra! Extra!," *Golden Book*, 11 (January 1930): 19-23;
"Do You Like the Talkies? Yes," *Golden Book*, 11 (April 1930): 52-53;
"Inaugural Parade," *Saturday Review of Literature*, 9 (4 March 1933): 461-462;
Letter to the editor, *New York Times*, 15 April 1934, X: 2;
"To Summer—and Return," *New York Times*, 19 March 1939, XI: 2;
"The Vanishing American Playwright," *Saturday Review of Literature*, 23 (1 February 1941): 12;
"Harry Hopkins," *New Republic*, 114 (11 February 1946): 180-181;
"He Was a Political Genius," *New Republic*, 114 (15 April 1946): 537-538;
"Jim Crow in Washington," *New Republic*, 115 (11 November 1946): 623;
"Please Don't Frighten Us," *Atlantic Monthly*, 183 (February 1949): 77-79;
"Footnote to a Preface," *Saturday Review of Literature*, 32 (6 August 1949): 130, 132, 134, 135;
"Most Terrible Drama of All Time," *Saturday Review of Literature*, 33 (21 October 1950): 22-23;
"Of Durability," *Saturday Review of Literature*, 34 (17 March 1951): 22;

"The Third World War," *Collier's*, 128 (27 October 1951): 19-31ff;

"The Big Stone Book," *American Heritage*, 5 (Winter 1953-1954): 3-5;

"Elmer Davis in a Former 'Life,' " *New Republic*, 130 (18 January 1954): 12;

"There Is No Alternative to Peace," *Fortune*, 52 (July 1955); 84ff.

References:

S. N. Behrman, "Old Monotonous," *New Yorker*, 16 (1 June 1940): 33-40; (8 June 1940): 23-33;

Harvey Breit, "An Interview With Robert E. Sherwood," *New York Times Book Review*, 13 February 1949, p.23;

John Mason Brown, *The Ordeal of a Playwright: Robert E. Sherwood and the Challenge of War* (New York, Evanston, & London: Harper & Row, 1970);

Brown, *The Worlds of Robert E. Sherwood: Mirror to His Times 1896-1939* (New York: Harper & Row, 1962);

Eleanor Flexner, "Robert E. Sherwood," in *American Playwrights; 1918-1938* (New York: Simon & Schuster, 1938), pp. 272-282;

John Gassner, "Robert Emmet Sherwood," *Atlantic Monthly*, 169 (1942): 26-33;

Edith J. R. Isaacs, "Robert Sherwood: Man of the Hour," *Theatre Arts Monthly*, 23 (1939): 31-40;

John Howard Lawson, "The Technique of the Modern Play," in *The Theory and Technique of Playwriting* (New York: Putnam's, 1936), pp. 142-146;

Walter J. Meserve, *Robert E. Sherwood: Reluctant Moralist* (New York: Pegasus, 1970);

Casper H. Nannes, "Evolution of a Liberal," in *Politics in the American Drama* (Washington, D.C.: Catholic University Press, 1960), pp. 151-159;

"U. S. Propaganda," *Time*, 40 (12 October 1945): 44, 46;

S. J. Woolf, "A Playwright Enlists In The War Of Ideas," *New York Times*, 7 July 1940, VII: 8, 16.

Neil Simon

Sheila Ennis Geitner
Asheville, North Carolina

BIRTH: Bronx, New York, 4 July 1927, to Irving and Mamie Simon.

EDUCATION: New York University, 1944-1945; University of Denver, 1945-1946.

MARRIAGE: 30 September 1953 to Joan Baim; children: Ellen, Nancy. 25 October 1973 to Marsha Mason.

AWARDS: Emmy Award for "The Sid Caesar Show," 1956-1957; Antoinette Perry (Tony) Awards for *Little Me* and for *Barefoot in the Park*, 1963; Tony Award for Best Playwright, 1965;Sam S. Shubert Award, 1967-1968; Writers Guild awards for best screenplay for *The Odd Couple*, 1969, *Last of the Red Hot Lovers*, 1970, *The Out-of-Towners*, 1971, *and The Prisoner of Second Avenue*, 1972; *Cue* magazine's Entertainer of the Year award, 1972.

PRODUCTIONS: *Catch a Star!*, by Neil Simon, Danny Simon, and others, 6 November 1955, Plymouth Theatre, New York, 23 [performances];

New Faces of 1956, by Neil Simon, Danny Simon, and others, 14 June 1956, Ethel Barrymore Theatre, New York, 220;

Come Blow Your Horn, August 1960, Bucks County Playhouse, New Hope, Pa.; 22 February 1961, Brooks Atkinson Theatre, New York, 677;

Little Me, adapted from Patrick Dennis's novel, music by Cy Coleman, 17 November 1962, Lunt-Fontanne Theatre, New York, 257;

Nobody Loves Me, 1962, Bucks County Playhouse, New Hope, Pa.; produced again as *Barefoot in the Park*, 23 October 1963, Biltmore Theatre, New York, 1532;

The Odd Couple, 10 March 1965, Plymouth Theatre, New York, 965;

Sweet Charity, adapted from Federico Fellini's screenplay *Nights of Cabiria*, music and lyrics by Cy Coleman and Dorothy Fields, 29 January 1966, Palace Theatre, New York, 608;

The Star-Spangled Girl, 21 December 1966, Plymouth Theatre, New York, 262;

Plaza Suite, 14 February 1968, Plymouth Theatre, New York, 1097;

Broadway Revue, by Simon and others, November 1968, Bloomgarden Theatre, New York;

Promises, Promises, adapted from Billy Wilder and I. A. L. Diamond's screenplay *The Apartment*, music by Burt Bacharach, lyrics by Hal David, 1 December 1968, Shubert Theatre, New York, 1281;

Last of the Red Hot Lovers, 28 December 1969, Eugene O'Neill Theatre, New York, 706;

The Gingerbread Lady, 13 December 1970, Plymouth Theatre, New York, 193;

The Prisoner of Second Avenue, 11 November 1971, Eugene O'Neill Theatre, New York, 788;

The Sunshine Boys, 20 December 1972, Broadhurst Theatre, New York, 538;

The Good Doctor, adapted from Anton Chekhov's short stories, music by Peter Link, lyrics by Simon, 27 November 1973, Eugene O'Neill Theatre, New York, 208;

God's Favorite, 11 December 1974, Eugene O'Neill Theatre, New York, 119;

California Suite, 30 June 1976, Eugene O'Neill Theatre, New York, 445;

Chapter Two, 4 December 1977, Imperial Theatre, New York;

They're Playing Our Song, music by Marvin Hamlisch, lyrics by Carole Bayer Sager, February 1979, Imperial Theatre, New York;

I Ought to Be in Pictures, 3 April 1980, Eugene O'Neill Theatre, New York.

BOOKS: *Adventures of Marco Polo: A Musical Fantasy*, by Simon and William Friedberg (New York: French, 1959);

Heidi, adapted by Simon and Friedberg from Johanna Spyri's novel (New York: French, 1959);

Come Blow Your Horn (London & New York: French, 1961; Garden City: Doubleday, 1963);

Barefoot in the Park (New York: Random House, 1964; London & New York: French, 1967);

The Odd Couple (New York: Random House, 1966; London: French, 1966);

Sweet Charity (New York: Random House, 1966);

The Star-Spangled Girl (New York: Random House, 1967);

Plaza Suite (New York: Random House, 1969);

Promises, Promises (New York: Random House, 1969);

Last of the Red Hot Lovers (New York: Random House, 1970);

The Gingerbread Lady (New York: Random House, 1971);

The Prisoner of Second Avenue (New York: Random House, 1972);

The Sunshine Boys (New York: Random House, 1973);

The Good Doctor (New York: Random House, 1974);

God's Favorite (New York: Random House, 1975);

California Suite (New York: Random House, 1977);

Chapter Two (New York: Random House, 1979);

They're Playing Our Song (New York: Random House, 1980);

I Ought to Be in Pictures (New York: Random House, forthcoming 1981).

One of America's most popular and prolific playwrights is Neil Simon. Having seventeen Broadway productions to his credit, as well as screenplays and television scripts, Simon has entertained audiences for over twenty years. He has been hailed as the most formidable comedy writer in American theatre, and it is this reputation, based on his early plays, that has dogged Simon relentlessly and prevented his being considered a serious dramatist by many critics. They have at times refused to look beyond the writer's "detonatingly funny"quips and punchlines to the subject matter in his plays. Though Simon has often been accused of sacrificing meaning and depth to a good joke, this charge is only occasionally true. Even in Simon's lightest comedies there are undertones of seriousness. Much like Philip Barry of a generation ago, Simon feels that his comedy approaches serious themes, and he rejects the notion that tragedy and comedy do not mix. Simon views life as a mixture of the sad and funny, and drama as a reflection of life.

Marvin Neil Simon was born in the Bronx, New York City, to Mamie and Irving Simon (a garment salesman). Nicknamed "Doc" because of his examining the family with a toy stethoscope as a child, Simon grew up in New York City, the setting for nearly all of his plays. One of his early childhood memories defines the outlook of his playwriting career. Once he climbed up on a stone ledge to sneak a look at an outdoor movie—a Charlie Chaplin film. "I laughed so hard I fell off, cut my head open and was taken to the doctor, bleeding and laughing. . . . My idea of the ultimate achievement in a comedy is to make a whole audience fall onto the floor, writhing and laughing so hard that some of them pass out." As an accomplished playwright, Simon understands the connection between pain and laughter. He apparently approves of his nickname Doc, for the implied comparison between the work of a playwright and the function of a doctor—to relieve suffering. That the central character in one of his later plays, *The Good Doctor* (1973), is both a physician and a playwright seems in retrospect inevitable.

At the age of sixteen Simon graduated from DeWitt Clinton High School, and shortly thereafter entered New York University under the U.S. Army Air Force Reserve training program. In 1945 he was sent to Colorado on active duty where he attended the University of Denver. Discharged from the service as a corporal in 1946, Simon went to work at the New York offices of Warner Brothers where his older brother, Daniel (Danny), also worked. Danny and Doc heard that Goodman Ace of CBS was scouting for new comedy material, so the pair submitted some of their work. They were hired immediately—a coup that launched Simon's career.

For the next fifteen years Simon wrote for the "Robert Q. Lewis" show (CBS radio); the "Phil Silvers Arrow Show" (NBC, 1948); the "Tallulah Bankhead Show" (NBC, 1951); the "Jackie Gleason Show" (CBS); and the "Red Buttons Show" (CBS). In 1952-1953 the two Simons wrote sketches for camp shows in Tamiment, Pennsylvania, which were later adapted for the commercial stage as *Catch a Star!* (1955). The Simons also contributed material to *New Faces of 1956*, a stage musical produced in that year. Danny Simon eventually left writing to become a television director, but Neil Simon continued to write for television until the Broadway premiere of his first play, *Come Blow Your Horn* (1961).

Simon's philosophy is contained in his comedies, and the only incongruity in his play would be a situation without humor. Even illness and death have their funny sides, and, as an intelligent observer of people, Simon understands how they use laughter. Whether serious or frivolous, Simon's plays employ humor as a defense, as an escape, as a weapon, or as low comedy—farce, burlesque, and slapstick. Often he approaches comedy philosophically, combining all these types of humor with intelligent and sensitive commentary on modern life. This analysis comes with a warning, and it is impossible to categorize unequivocably everything funny in a Simon play. Situations and characters cross-pollinate. Humor as a defense can become humor as

a weapon, for instance, and in Simon's work, as in life, most of what is funny is funny for a combination of reasons.

In commenting about his work Simon claims that he does not write simply to get the one-liner joke: "Trying to show people how absurdly they live their lives. That's what I'm trying to do. I do it through the medium of comedy, but I don't do it just to get a laugh from the audience." Simon has the ability to perceive how comic life is. In his plays he takes a sad situation or conflict and exposes its humor; the laughter he evokes is cathartic and sometimes reassuring.

Come Blow Your Horn demonstrated that Simon could construct a complicated plot. It is the story of two sons, Alan and Buddy, who work for their father, a wax-fruit manufacturer. Alan, the older, is a swinging bachelor replete with apartment and an entourage of willing bedmates. The plot of *Come Blow Your Horn* revolves around Buddy's leaving the nest and adopting Alan's life-style. In act 1 Buddy is a quiet, obedient son who takes his job seriously. Alan is his opposite. Among the plot complications are Buddy's confrontation with his father over Buddy's leaving home, Buddy's first seduction attempt, Alan's losing a major account, the boys' mother leaving their father, and Alan's difficulties

Neil Simon

with Connie, his only "different" girlfriend.

By act 3 Alan and Buddy have changed places. In only three weeks, Buddy has become the smooth-talking bachelor and Alan is lovesick for Connie and concerned about wax fruit. In the last scene Dad shows up to confront his wife and sons. He finally accepts Buddy's growing up, apologizes to Mom, and is reconciled with Alan who has landed two large accounts and announced his engagement to Connie.

An autobiographical account of Danny and Doc's leaving home, *Come Blow Your Horn* has many of Simon's trademarks—witty dialogue, successful character types, and happy endings. It lacks the polish of his subsequent works, and the constant ringing of the doorbell and telephone to keep the plot moving gets annoying. But critics hailed its author as a promising and talented writer.

Simon's next effort was to write the book for *Little Me* (1962), a musical adapted from a novel by Patrick Dennis. In 1963 *Barefoot in the Park* opened and was a tremendous success, running for 1532 performances. *Barefoot in the Park* has four major characters. Corie Bratter is a newlywed who is "lovely, young, and full of hope for the future." Her husband, Paul, is a sedate, stuffy young man just beginning his career as a lawyer. Ethel Banks, Corie's mother, first outlines the conflict in the play when she says to Corie, "You're so impulsive. You jump into life. Paul is like me. He looks first." Corie's mother has pointed out that although opposites attract, they also irritate, exasperate, and injure one another. Victor Velasco is the weird upstairs neighbor who has to climb through the Bratter's bedroom window to his apartment because the landlord has locked him out for being behind with his rent. Corie decides that Velasco is the perfect match for her widowed mother, so she arranges a dinner date between them.

The evening is a fiasco, and it constitutes most of the dramatic action. Paul, Corie, Victor, and Ethel, after spending the evening together, experience some harsh realities: Paul and Corie's differences become all too apparent. Corie calls Paul a stuffed shirt, and Paul thinks Corie is too impulsive. They decide to divorce. Corie's mother, who after spending the night in Velasco's apartment has realized the folly of her own stuffiness, encourages Corie to "give up a little of you for him." Her advice is barely spoken when Paul returns to the apartment drunk and boasting of having walked barefoot in the park in February. He climbs to the roof as Corie, horrified, decides she wants the old, "safe" Paul back.

Barefoot in the Park is a more mature effort than *Come Blow Your Horn*. The comedy stems from Simon's unique and humorous characterization. The characters suffer from too much polarity; each is planted too firmly in his own opinions, and it is this rigidity that Simon pokes fun at. Although there is a running gag—the walk up six flights to the Bratter's apartment—the play is less dependent upon such contrivance than was *Come Blow Your Horn*. Beneath Simon's delightful craftsmanship is the writer's statement: successful relationships are built upon compromise and tolerance. *Barefoot in the Park* is a perennial favorite of Simon audiences. It was adapted as a television series, which appeared on ABC during the 1970-1971 season.

In *The Odd Couple* (1965) Simon took the same premise of *Barefoot in the Park*—the problems involved when opposites live together—and explored what happens when neither will compromise. *The Odd Couple* opens with Oscar Madison's weekly poker game. Oscar-the-slob appears in his natural habitat—amid cigar smoke, moldy green sandwiches, and warm beer. The other poker players are Speed, a sarcastic, quick-witted cynic; Roy, Oscar's typically dull accountant; Vinnie, a simpering neurotic who drags his family to Florida in July because the rates are lower then; and Murray, the bungling cop. Felix, Oscar's opposite, is missing from the game, and the men are worried about him. When Felix finally shows up, he announces that his wife has thrown him out of the house. In a weak moment the divorced Oscar offers Felix a sanctuary. After Felix accepts and moves in, he and Oscar find the same problems in divorce that they had encountered in marriage.

The idea for *The Odd Couple* was Danny Simon's. Neil Simon took his brother's idea, "What's funny about divorce?," and worked it into what he thought would be black humor. But what started out as anger and bitterness becomes a more benevolent acceptance of the inevitable in life: sometimes behavioral patterns cannot be broken, and to fight them is to beg frustration.

Much of the humor in *The Odd Couple* is achieved through exaggeration: Felix and Oscar are stylized characters; Felix's grief is overblown; the poker players are caricatures. In *The Odd Couple* Simon makes the absurd believable, and the audience can see parts of themselves in Felix and Oscar. Tom Prideaux accurately observed a basic element in Simon's success: "Neil Simon is not only selling entertainment. By making a modern audience feel that its foibles and vices are not too serious because he makes them seem so funny, Simon is also selling a sort of forgiveness: absolution by laughter." *The Odd Couple* was enthusiastically received on Broadway and also developed as a television series.

By Simon's own admission, *The Star-Spangled Girl* (1966) was a flop. It is the story of two struggling radicals, Andy and Norman, who live in San Francisco and publish *Fallout*, a protest magazine. Set in the late 1960s the play tries to play upon the popularity of radicalism but ends up being a second-rate love story.

Sophie Rauchmeyer moves in next door to Andy and Norman. Norman falls hopelessly in love with Sophie and spends the full three acts pursuing her. He follows her to work, follows her home, dogs her at the grocer's, waxes her floors, and makes such a nuisance of himself that Sophie loses her job. Sophie must find another job to pay her rent, so she becomes *Fallout*'s secretary. All the while quiet Andy is trying to calm Norman and keep *Fallout* from bankruptcy. Andy even dates the landlady, a woman who wears silver lame jumpsuits and rides a motorcycle (a character the audience never meets), so they will not be evicted for back rent. He lies to their creditors and hounds Norman to leave Sophie alone. In a predictable but not too successful ending Andy and Sophie fall in love. Norman is devastated at first, but realizes that his attraction to Sophie has only been physical. All are reconciled; the magazine gets back on its feet; and Norman is now the one dating the landlady. *The Star-Spangled Girl* is fatally weakened by contrivance: why did Sophie not just wallop Norman to get rid of him? Sophie is better drawn than the other characters; she has a charm that almost redeems her . . . that is, until the end when she succumbs to Andy and presumably to his radical politics.

Most critics agreed that *Plaza Suite* (1968) was Simon's philosophical prelude to *Last of the Red Hot Lovers* (1969). As critic Jack Kroll noted, in *Plaza Suite* Simon "fiddled around unsuccessfully with 'serious' overtones in his palimpsest of gags." However, *Plaza Suite* as serious drama is more successful upon reflection. This is the first of Simon's "sketch" plays; it contains three one-act segments which take place in the same suite of the Plaza Hotel in New York. Its variety and sensitivity are remarkable as it deals with delicate problems: a couple in a moribund marriage; a middle-aged pair tempted into adultery; and two parents who cannot communicate with their grown daughter.

"Visitor from Mamaroneck" involves forty-eight-year-old Karen Nash, "a pleasant, affable woman who has let weight and age take their natural course," and her husband Sam, a "mea-sured, efficient, economic" man who looks much younger than his fifty years. The two had spent their wedding night in Suite 719. It is now their twenty-fourth anniversary, and Karen is making an effort to rekindle their marriage. Sam is not interested in saving the marriage; he is content with the pleasures of his own good looks, his work, and his secretary, Jean. When Karen discovers that he is having an affair with Jean, Sam offers this explanation:

SAM: It's me Karen, not you.

KAREN: I'll buy that. What's wrong with you, Sam?

SAM: I don't know . . . I don't know if you can understand this . . . but when I came home after the war . . . I had my whole life in front of me. And all I dreamed about, all I wanted, was to get married, and to have children . . . and to make a success of my life . . . Well, I was lucky . . . I got it all.

KAREN: Then what is it you want?

SAM: I just want to do it all over again.

Sam is an honest if not endearing character, and Simon carefully portrays his sense of middle-age panic. The same panic surrounds Karen, but her pain masks itself in jokes about Sam's affair, about growing old, and about her fears for the future. Her humor is a defense against the overwhelming hurt that threatens to control her. There are witty lines in "Visitor for Mamaroneck," but the tone is miserably sad; the audience is left with the feeling that Karen and Sam will not solve their problems.

Jesse Kiplinger in "Visitor from Hollywood" is "Mr. Famous Hollywood Producer" who has been cuckolded by three wives and who has come to New York in search of his high-school sweetheart, Muriel Tate, who he feels, is the one decent woman who can convince him that life is not all delusion and deceit. Muriel, legitimately impressed by Jesse's stature in the movie industry, agrees to meet him for drinks in Suite 719. What Jesse thought would be a tender meeting between two old friends becomes an awkward seduction scene between two strangers. Both Jesse and Muriel need solace—Jesse from his confusing rat race and Muriel from her boring suburbia. They both have a need for affection; they both settle for sex. The seduction scene is riotously funny but contains real pathos. Although it seems that Jesse and Muriel never reach each other beyond a superficial level, they at least assuage each other's pain. The humor in "Visitor from Hollywood" relieves the tension in this awkward situation and demonstrates how Simon uses comedy to underplay a serious scene.

The "Visitors from Forest Hills" are Norma and Roy Hubley. They have rented Suite 719 and the Plaza Ballroom for their daughter Mimsey's wedding, but Mimsey has locked herself in the bathroom and refuses to get married. "Visitors from Forest Hills" is farce; its hilarious, albeit improbable, situations stem from the Hubleys' efforts to communicate with Mimsey. Norma is somewhat concerned with her daughter's happiness, but more involved with her own misery. Roy is indebted to every rental agency in New York City, and he is $8,000 worth of angry. The couple screams, rants, pleads, whispers, and even tries to climb through the bathroom window to talk to Mimsey. Mimsey finally emerges, not at her parents' pleading, but because her fiance, Borden, storms to the door and shouts, "Mimsey? This is Borden . . . Cool it!" The ending is perhaps too contrived, but it is effective in stating how little the Hubleys communicate in relation to how much they talk. There is much physical activity in this sketch which contrasts nicely to the lack of constructive emotional activity between the parents and Mimsey. Simon makes excellent use of the sketch format in *Plaza Suite*. The structure enables him to explore the theme of communication in various ways, thus suggesting the complexity of this theme.

Barney Cashman, who is the "last of the red hot lovers," is an appealing new version of Sam Nash from *Plaza Suite*, and most critics agree with Marilyn Stasio that with this effort Simon "steps distinctly out of polite-comedy circles and into the arena of the black humorists." In *Last of the Red Hot Lovers* Cashman faces middle age with no more eagerness than Sam Nash does, so he decides to introduce excitement into his life via adultery. The play is divided into three acts, corresponding to Barney's three seduction attempts. Barney's would-be lovers are Elaine Navazio, a depressed, cynical chain smoker who asks only for quick sex and no complications; Bobbi Michele, an amateur nightclub singer with a staggering list of mental problems including paranoia and delusions of grandeur; and Jeanette Fisher, "the singularly most depressed woman on the face of the Western Hemisphere. . . . She wakes up to gloom and goes to bed with gloom . . . and fills in the in-between hours with despair." Like many of Simon's characters, Elaine, Bobbi, and Jeanette are exaggerations, but whereas Simon generally uses exaggeration for comic effect, in *Last of the Red Hot Lovers* he employs it for thematic enrichment. Simon has concentrated an enormous malaise in these three women, and Barney Cashman is an innocent who would try to understand, if not cure it.

Last of the Red Hot Lovers contains several zany moments which elicit guffaws. But Simon is not laughing at the expense of these miserably unhappy characters; he is constructing a satire on a society that produces such aberrations as Elaine, Bobbi, and Jeanette. *Last of the Red Hot Lovers* is not merely a comedy, but a commentary in the manner of Joseph Heller's *Catch-22* (1961). It is a thoughtful, intelligent, funny treatment of suffering and anxiety. Finally, just as Barney realizes that adultery will not cure his discontent, the audience realizes that Simon's intent is to attack despair through comedy. *Last of the Red Hot Lovers* ridicules society's foibles and reassures the audience that there are "decent, loving, gentle" people like Barney Cashman.

Simon's next play, *The Gingerbread Lady* (1970), is, according to Edythe McGovern, "essentially a drama rather than a comedy . . . humorous only to the extent that there is some funny dialogue stemming very naturally from characters who live in a world where wisecracks serve to mask almost constant cries for help." *The Gingerbread Lady* is a consciously serious effort by Simon, and predictably his audiences resented this nearly total departure from comedy, which received mixed reviews from critics.

The protagonist in the play is Evy Meara, an unsuccessful singer who has just returned from a sanatorium for alcoholics. Her hospitalization seems to have been apocalyptic, marking a fresh start for Evy and the beginning of a productive life. However, *The Gingerbread Lady* depicts Evy's downfall: she succumbs to the pressures of loneliness, discontent, and demanding friends and returns to the bottle for consolation. In a tacked-on ending Simon constructs hope for Evy by having her keep a date with her former husband who, because of his interest in their daughter, Polly, wants to keep tabs on Evy's recovery. But even the upbeat ending, written chiefly to please the play's producers, cannot undercut the morbid tone and the sad perplexity of *The Gingerbread Lady*.

Adding to the play's disturbing tone are Evy's friends, Toby and Jimmy. Jimmy is a forty-one-year-old homosexual actor who clings to the futile hope of becoming a star. Probably a thoughtful, kind person at one time, Jimmy is now a demanding man too consumed by his own unhappiness to offer Evy constructive counsel. Toby Landau is a former beauty queen whose preoccupation with her own beauty is maniacal. Her life is spent trying to preserve a face and body that betray her age in spite of her efforts. Evy's daughter, Polly, is the only nontragic character in *The Gingerbread Lady*. Intelligent, caring, and hopeful, she is not blind to Evy's faults, nor does she expect an instant and lasting recovery from her mother; but she is not a defeatist, and it appears that Polly's love can somehow sustain Evy. By act 2, however, Evy is on another binge. Toby and Jimmy have unwittingly chipped away Evy's defenses, and Polly's expectations, though not demands, are too heavy a burden for Evy to shoulder.

Alcoholism is a complex problem, and in *The Gingerbread Lady* Simon has dramatized some very somber aspects of the disease. He offers no solutions, but poses some troubling questions: is Evy's drinking a defense or a weapon? It is possible that Toby and Jimmy contribute to Evy's problems out of malice (misery loves company) rather than ignorance? Does Evy drink because she cannot cope with her life, or does her inability to cope contribute to a disease over which she has no control? Evy, like all alcoholics, is caught in a cycle, and unless she and Polly can break that cycle, Evy will destroy herself and quite possibly her daughter. The tone of *The Gingerbread Lady* is not fundamentally humorous. Evy is a tragic character, and her attempts to hide behind quips and sarcasms only contribute to her stature as such. At this writing *The Gingerbread Lady* is being adapted for screen under the tentative title "Only When I Laugh."

In 1971 Simon "made another stab at unorthodoxy," according to reviewer Tom Prideaux, "and hit the jackpot with *The Prisoner of Second Avenue*." It is the story of Edna and Mel Edison versus urban blight. In the course of the play Mel's apartment is robbed, he loses his job, his air conditioner will not turn off, his water will not turn on, and his upstairs neighbor drenches him with a bucket of water every time he steps out on the balcony to register his complaints. Mel has a breakdown—it is his way of coping—so Edna goes to work. But by act 3 Edna has lost her job, and as the play closes it is Edna who is having a breakdown and Mel who offers consolation.

The Prisoner of Second Avenue shows Simon's deep concern for the growing indifference in modern society. The play is reminiscent of *Last of the Red Hot Lovers*, although its tone is not quite so disturbing. Determined to find humor in Mel and Edna's situation, Simon has artfully distributed witty comments, comic gestures, and little incongruities in character that inspire laughter. Simon also introduces Mel's relatives as an added comic touch. The sisters are quite funny, but *The Prisoner of Second Avenue* could have worked just as well without them. This play has none of the black comedy of *Last of the Red Hot Lovers*, but there is a strong undercurrent of sadness and seriousness throughout the play. Its anger and bitterness are contained, never allowed to undercut Simon's faith in Edna and Mel's ability to keep up their end of the fight.

"Spend a few afternoons around the Friars Club, a hangout for aging comedians, and a pencil, a pad, and a discriminating ear will record for you some of the funniest and saddest dialogue you ever heard," suggests Simon in his preface to Edythe McGovern's *Not-So-Simple Neil Simon* (1978). While everyone cannot spend an afternoon at the Friars Club, one has only to see *The Sunshine Boys* (1972) for a poignant, comic look at those aging comedians. It is the story of a retired and estranged vaudevillian comedy team, Willie Clark and Al Lewis, and the efforts of Ben Silverman, Clark's nephew, to reunite the pair for a special television appearance. *The Sunshine Boys* is one of Simon's favorites; in a *Playboy* interview he referred to it as his best work so far. Critics were enthusiastic about the play, giving Simon credit for his profound comic vision. William Empson, in writing about John Gay's *The Beggar's Opera* (1728), said a comedy could be "stupidly enjoyed" by those who are ignorant of its social or satirical intents. By this token *The Sunshine Boys*, with its vaudevillian dialogue and sketches, can entertain and amuse those who are unaware that Willie Clark and Al Lewis are faced with very real and painful problems. But for the more sensitive viewer, Simon offers an accurate and sympathetic account of the tolls of old age: failing health, forced retirement, absentmindedness, and relatives with good intentions who do not know what to do with old people. Willie Clark represents the struggle against encroaching age: he stubbornly refuses to move from a depressing apartment, though it is clear he is being victimized by his landlord. Al Lewis represents resignation to old age: he has meekly moved in with his daughter in New Jersey (a fate worse than death for a die-hard New Yorker). Ben Silverman must somehow reconcile these two "mighty opposites." He fails as far as the television show goes, but at the end of the play it is determined that Clark will move into the actors' retirement home. Quite by coincidence Lewis is making the same move.

The final moments of *The Sunshine Boys* contain genuine pathos. Although Lewis and Clark continue to spar with each other, it is apparent that the two share great affection and tenderness. Also, there is a tone of quiet acceptance in their voices, as if the two have embraced their old humor as a steadying influence in a time of bewildering changes.

The Good Doctor is a collection of vignettes suggested by Anton Chekhov's short stories. It satisfies Simon's desire to show people how absurdly they live their lives. There is a sense of surrealism present in the clever dialogue that is Simon's forte. But the dialogue is not stichomythic; it is clever in its economy and tone. The twenty-six characters in *The Good Doctor* are played by only three men and two women—a stroke which lends continuity to the sketches. The strongest unifying factor in *The Good Doctor* is the Writer who offers his wry comments on the action (and who could only be Neil Simon): "I have no choice. I am a writer. While I'm writing, I enjoy it. And I like reading the proofs; but as soon as it appears in print, I can't bear it. I see that it's all wrong, a mistake, that it ought never to have been written, and I am miserable. . . . Then the public reads it: 'Yes, charming, clever . . . charming but a far cry from Tolstoy' . . . and so it will be to my dying day. . . . Charming and clever, charming and clever. Nothing more. And when I die my friends will walk by my grave and say, 'Here lies so and so, a good writer, but Turgenev was better.' "

There are those who enjoyed this Simon effort because it has the Chekhovian flavor of sustained irony and profound insight. Perhaps Simon has unwittingly overshadowed his considerable talents by volunteering to ride in tandem with one of last century's greatest. Jack Kroll's concern may be justified: "What concerns me is what Chekhov, who can take care of himself, has done to Simon."

God's Favorite, which premiered in 1974, was Simon's effort to "justify the ways of God to men." If anyone can extract humor from the story of Job, it is Neil Simon, and he does create a play with some knee-slappers. But *God's Favorite* resorts to caricature and topical jokes that are ultimately unsatisfying. Joe Benjamin, the Job character, is a wealthy businessman plagued with an obnoxious family, which includes his wife, a jewelry fanatic; his smart-aleck son, David; the twins, Sarah and Benjamin, whose combined I.Q. is only 160; and two servants, Mady and Morris. All characters are patently absurd, and they betray Simon's promise to make all his characters likable "even when . . . exposing their worst faults." The audience cannot identify with these people because the characters beg disbelief.

The only redeeming character in *God's Favorite* is Sidney Lipton, invented by Simon as God's messenger. A middle-class drudge, Lipton is more believable than any of the Benjamins and often elevates the humor to a more respectable level. His role is good farce. Clive Barnes states that *God's Favorite* is "not one of Simon's best" plays. And Simon admits that the play "was simply not done skillfully enough."

In *California Suite* (1976), the playwright returns to the one-act structure of *Plaza Suite*, this time

with two farces and two serious pieces. "Visitor from New York" pits an avid New Yorker, Hannah, against a transplanted New Yorker in California, William (now called Billy). Hannah and Billy are divorced, and Hannah has journeyed to Los Angeles to retrieve their daughter who has run away from New York to live with her father. The meeting between this couple allows Simon to launch a scathing satire on Southern Californians, as Billy looks like a forty-seven-year-old Troy Donahue. Simon also satirizes New Yorkers, showing that Hannah, in all her superiority, is terribly unhappy. Their dialogue is really insult-swapping; their language is incisive and often abusive. It is not difficult to understand why the couple divorced. The humor resides in the intelligence of the dialogue and the rapid-fire retorts that the couple exchange. Hannah's sarcasms and snide remarks are an example of how Simon's characters use humor as a defense. Billy is not as malevolent, but Hannah's attack forces him to construct a defense, in this case humor. The lines, though often funny, are revealing. Hannah's lack of confidence and her threatened authority as a mother are apparent in her banter as well as in her mannerisms. Also, even though Billy is the object of much abuse, it is clear that he too is a sensitive, concerned parent. Hannah leaves her daughter with Billy, and "Visitor from New York" ends on a sad and desperate note.

In "Visitor from Philadelphia" background information is unimportant. It is a comedy of situation, a farce which relies for most of its humor on the presence of a prostitute in Marvin Michaels's bed. Arriving in California for his nephew's bar mitzvah, Marvin finds waiting for him in his hotel room a hooker hired by his brother. The hooker is in bed unconscious from consuming too much alcohol when Millie, Marvin's wife, arrives in the suite. Simon's comedy here is relentless; the laughter that begins in the first moments does not subside until the end. In this sketch Simon provides a much-needed relief from the bitterness of the first sketch. Because Marvin is such a likable character (we know, for instance, that he has never been unfaithful), this sketch is elevated slightly above pure farce. His good nature and Millie's willingness to forgive his transgressions make the play end on a positive note.

"Visitors from London" is in the same style as "Visitor from New York," but with fewer light moments and much more pain. Diana Nichols and her husband, Sidney, are in California because Diana, an actress, has been nominated for an Academy Award. Like Hannah and Billy, Diana and Sidney are experts at "wit and parry," and like Hannah,

Diana's verbal acrobatics mask a deep-seated unhappiness. Diana is an insecure woman with complex and contradictory feelings about her husband. Sidney is a homosexual, or more accurately, a bisexual, for whom marriage represents conformity and financial security. At first the relationship seems tolerable, although we sense that the couple is nearing dangerous territory.

After the award ceremony, Diana is drunk and bitterly disappointed, presumably at not having won the Oscar. Diana's "wit and parry" descends to an abusive attack upon Sidney for having made a date with a young actor whom he met at the ceremonies. Sidney calmly tolerates Diana's abuse; in fact, his control suggests that Diana's outbursts are not infrequent. Diana's agony is powerfully portrayed by Simon. She is fighting a futile battle. Sidney is also portrayed with understanding. He has his own guilt to wrestle, and he gently reminds Diana that their marriage is mutually satisfying in some ways. Each finds sanctuary in the other, and so the marriage survives. The serious moments in "Visitors from London" are never sacrificed for laughs; the pain that is portrayed initially is sustained to the end.

California Suite ends on a light note: "Visitors from Chicago" is pure, delightful farce. Mort and Beth Hollender are vacationing with their best friends, Stu and Gert Franklyn, but after four weeks "four people taking a vacation together can get very testy." The proverbial last straw has fallen. Beth has broken her foot on the tennis court and Mort blames it on the Franklyns' having played dirty tennis. He accuses Stu of deliberately lobbing the ball over Beth's head when Stu knew her shoe was untied. An argument ensues, and tempers get hotter and hotter until a verbal battle becomes a free-for-all. The fight scene is almost cartoonlike with its cursing, groin-kicking, and teeth-smashing while the two wives sit on the bed and exclaim "shit." As the scene ends Mort is sitting on Stu:

MORT: And tell me you had a good time on our vacation . . . Tell Me!!!

STU: I had a good time.

MORT: Especially the Japanese restaurants.

STU: Especially the goddamned restaurants. Let Me UP!

MORT: And you want to take another vacation with us next year!

STU: Crack my ribs!! Crush me!! I won't say that! (*The curtain starts to fall*)

MORT, BETH AND GERT: Say it! Say it! Say it!

Stu acquiesces, but he secretly holds fast to his opinion, "I had a better vacation when I had my hernia operation."

There is no unity of place in *California Suite* as there was in *Plaza Suite*. There are unities, however. Each playlet examines a relationship at a painful and explosive moment. In "Visitor from Philadelphia" and "Visitors from Chicago" Simon treats these moments comically by exaggerating the problems and the characters' responses. In "Visitor from New York" and "Visitors from London" Simon almost underplays the explosive moments. Diana, Sidney, Hannah, and Billy have insulated themselves against reality, and Simon slowly chips away each one's facade to reveal the truth. It is a subtle revelation, one understood more fully upon reflection.

Chapter Two (1977) is autobiographical. It is based on Simon's recovery period after the death of his wife, Joan, in 1973 and his subsequent marriage to actress Marsha Mason. In many ways it is Simon's best play, offering a fine balance of sadness and delight, of despair and hope. George Schneider is three months a widower. His marriage to Barbara had been idyllic, and he has convinced himself that with her he had reaped all the happiness he was entitled to. Despite the efforts of his younger brother, Leo, to get George back into circulation, he is content with his memories. Then accidentally George encounters Jennie Malone. She is also reeling from a loss: she has just finalized her divorce. Neither George nor Jennie is ready for another relationship, but when they meet, they like each other instantly. What ensues is a whirlwind romance. They fall in love, and after a three-week courtship, they marry. The first act of *Chapter Two*, which ends with the wedding, is high comedy. Although George's situation is not laughable, Simon insists there are humorous aspects to being alone. George pokes fun at his own misery. He is in a laugh-to-keep-from-crying situation, and he finds it is as easy to do one as the other. The humor in act 1 is never derisive; in fact it has a cathartic effect on the audience, as it must have on George.

In act 2 the tone shifts drastically. George, in his exhilaration at being able to love again, has inadvertently cheated himself out of the necessary mourning period for Barbara. He feels guilty and believes he is compromising his memories of Barbara by being in love with Jennie. He leaves Jennie, presumably to sort out his feelings. The emotion in act 2 is overwhelming. Jennie is devastated when George leaves, and the audience is angered because people they care about have been hurt. George is being bombarded by new feelings and haunted by old ones. The only relief from this agony comes in a comical scene between Faye, Jennie's friend, and

Leo, who have arranged to have an affair at Jennie's old apartment. And even this comic scene has undertones of unhappiness since both Faye and Leo are stuck in unhappy marriages. But the bungled meeting between the two provides the only good laugh in act 2.

Chapter Two ends on an optimistic note. After several days away from Jennie, George realizes that he cannot compartmentalize his emotions, as if some of his feelings belong to Jennie and his other feelings to Barbara. He knows he has problems, but he realizes that in Jennie he has a caring and capable guide. The audience is relieved and happy when George returns to Jennie, but it would be incorrect to call this a happy ending. Simon's final statement seems to be, "They will try to live happily ever after, and they may very well succeed."

Simon's most recent production, *I Ought to Be in Pictures* (1980), also blends pathos and humor. It is an intimate portrayal of the efforts of nineteen-year-old girl, Libby, to establish a relationship with her father, who deserted her mother many years ago. Herb, the father, moved from New York after the divorce, and his formerly successful career as a screenwriter has been halted by writer's block. Herb's outfit of dirty clothes and baseball hat do not conform to Libby's image of her cherished father. After much biting discussion and anguished confession, Libby and Herb reach out to each other. She even physically pins her father to the floor and demands to know why he divorced her mother. Herb thinks that his wife has no sense of humor. Critical response to *I Ought to Be in Pictures* has been mixed, but in the drama two important points have been reiterated. First, in a Simon-created world, even one that is bleak and depressing, a sense of humor is essential for survival. Second, in the world according to Simon, a man best remembered for quips and punches, there are many things that are unfunny.

At this point in his career it is impossible to discern how long Simon's productivity will continue or whether he will alter the dominant style of his writing. His unquestionable and nearly unprecedented popularity may have become a straitjacket: when an audience sees a Simon play it automatically expects a certain kind of play. If Simon writes a play which defies popular expectations, how can it receive a fair hearing? However, whatever success Neil Simon continues to enjoy will not be taken for granted; he is still trying to create the perfect play where "for 119 minutes the audience is hysterical with laughter, but for the last minutes they are so moved that they leave the theater in a daze."

Screenplays:

After the Fox, United Artists, 1966;

Barefoot in the Park, Paramount, 1967;

The Odd Couple, Paramount, 1968;

The Out-of-Towners, Paramount, 1970;

Plaza Suite, Paramount, 1971;

Last of the Red Hot Lovers, Paramount, 1972;

The Heartbreak Kid, adapted from Bruce Jay Friedman's short story, Twentieth-Century Fox, 1972;

The Prisoner of Second Avenue, Warner Brothers, 1975;

The Sunshine Boys, MGM, 1975;

Murder by Death, Columbia, 1976;

The Goodbye Girl, Warner Brothers, 1977;

The Cheap Detective, Columbia, 1978;

California Suite, Columbia, 1978;

Chapter Two, Columbia, 1979;

Seems Like Old Times, Columbia, 1980.

Television Script:

The Trouble with People, NBC, 12 November 1972.

Other:

Seesaw, adapted from William Gibson's *Two for the Seesaw*, text edited by Simon, 18 March 1973, Uris Theatre, New York, 296 [performances].

References:

Goodman Ace, "Take a Letter," *Saturday Review*, 50 (28 January 1967): 12;

James Alan Bernardi, "The Plays of Neil Simon: The First Decade of Dramatic Development," Ph.D. dissertation, University of Denver, 1976;

Harold Clurman, "California Suite," *Nation*, 223 (3 July 1976): 30;

Brendan Gill, "The Last of the Red Hot Theories," *New Yorker*, 45 (10 January 1970): 64;

Stanley Kaufmann, "Last of the Red Hot Writers," *New Republic*, 164 (16 January 1971): 22;

A. Levy, "Doc Simon's Rx for Comedy," *New York Times Magazine*, 42 (7 March 1965): 43;

Lawrence Linderman, "Playboy Interview with Neil Simon," *Playboy*, 26 (February 1979): 57-78;

Edythe M. McGovern, *Not-So-Simple Neil Simon: A Critical Study* (Van Nuys, Cal.: Perivale Press, 1978);

Helen McMahon, "A Rhetoric of American Popular Drama: The Comedies of Neil Simon," *Players*, 24 (September 1977): 12-15;

T. Meehan, "Unreal Hilarious World of Neil Simon," *Horizon*, 21 (January 1978): 70-74;

Tom Prideaux, "He Loves to Kill Them," *Life*, 58 (9 April 1965): 39;

Ellen V. Simon, "My Life with a Very Funny Father," *Seventeen*, 38 (November 1979): 154-157;

John Simon, *Uneasy Stages: A Chronicle of the New York Theater* (New York: Random House, 1975).

LAURENCE STALLINGS
(25 November 1894-28 February 1968)

SELECTED PRODUCTIONS: *What Price Glory?*, by Stallings and Maxwell Anderson, 5 September 1924, Plymouth Theatre, New York, 435 [performances];

First Flight, by Stallings and Anderson, 17 September 1925, Plymouth Theatre, New York, 11;

The Buccaneer, by Stallings and Anderson, 2 October 1925, Plymouth Theatre, New York, 20;

Rainbow, by Stallings and Oscar Hammerstein II, 21 November 1928, Gallo Theatre, New York, 30;

A Farewell to Arms, adapted from Ernest Hemingway's novel, 22 September 1930, National Theatre, New York, 24;

Virginia, by Stallings and Owen Davis, 2 September 1937, Center Theatre, New York, 60;

The Streets Are Guarded, 20 November 1944, Henry Miller's Theatre, New York, 24.

BOOKS: *Plumes* (New York: Harcourt, Brace, 1924; London: Cape, 1925);

Three American Plays, by Stallings and Maxwell Anderson (New York: Harcourt, Brace, 1926)—includes *What Price Glory?*, *First Flight*, and *The Buccaneer*;

The First World War–A Pictorial History (New York: Simon & Schuster, 1933; London: Daily Express, 1933);

The Doughboys (New York: Harper & Row, 1963).

What Price Glory? by Laurence Stallings and Maxwell Anderson was produced by Anthony Hopkins at the Plymouth Theatre in New York City in 1924 and was immediately hailed by critics as "the most sensationally successful of the important plays of 1924-25." Stallings is also the author of *Plumes* (a novel published in the same year), numerous short stories, articles, reviews, and two other plays, but

What Price Glory? remains his most important contribution to American drama. More than just another antiwar drama, this realistic play which focuses on ordinary soldiers in World War I was lauded for its objectivity, simplicity, and power. Critics praised it as "a milestone in the development of the modern theatre toward pure naturalism in dialogue," and Harlan Hatcher concluded in 1935: "Taking his work in all forms as a single whole, Laurence Stallings has done more than any one American author to cut away the romantic glamour of war and to expose its wretchedness."

When *What Price Glory?* was produced, a new trend in American theatre was developing. Playwrights such as Eugene O'Neill, Elmer Rice, Maxwell Anderson, and Stallings were striving to reach an American audience which had lived through World War I, a conflict which stripped away much of the glamour of war. This audience had not yet emotionally assimilated the war and needed plays which would, as Joseph Wood Krutch points out, "clarify their responses and give them an emotional release." *What Price Glory?* fulfilled these needs.

Born in Macon, Georgia, on 25 November 1894 to Larkin Tucker and Aurora Brooks Stallings, Laurence Stallings was from his youth fascinated by war, partially because of the stories of revered Civil War heroes still circulating in the South. His father was a shy man who was employed as a bank clerk; his mother, who had a strong interest in music and literature, was the dominant influence on Stallings's upbringing. After high school, he entered Wake Forest University in North Carolina in 1912, where he majored in classical studies and biology, played football, and was editor of *Old Gold And Black*, the campus literary magazine. He also began dating Helen Purefoy Poteat, whom he was later to marry. She was the daughter of his biology professor, William Louis Poteat, the president of the college. The teacher which most impressed him, however, was Helen's brother Hubert, a demanding classics professor who "struck terror in [me] early in the game." After Poteat caught Stallings using a pony in a Latin class, Stallings worked very hard and scored high grades thereafter. Although he indulged in drinking forbidden beer and was punished for painting on a statue of a nude, Stallings was designated by a campus magazine as "the widest read man in college." He completed the course work for his bachelor of arts degree in 1915, however it was not actually conferred until the next year. Stallings's undergraduate life at Wake Forest formed much of the background for his autobiographical novel *Plumes*

(1924), which he dedicated "To An Unknown Soldier, Helen Purefoy Poteat."

In 1915 Stallings went to Atlanta (his parents had moved there in 1911) to accept his first job as a reporter for the *Atlanta Journal*. He enlisted in 1917, accepting an appointment as a second lieutenant in the Marine Corps, and was assigned to active duty in October. In 1918 he went to France with the Second Division, Forty-seventh Company, Third Battalion, of the Fifth Marines. The young soldier was involved in heavy action at Chateau-Thierry and was seriously wounded on the last day of battle at Belleau Wood. As Stallings led his men in a grenade attack on a machine gun nest, a bullet struck his right leg, ripping his kneecap off. As he fell he threw the grenade and destroyed the nest. He recovered consciousness in the hospital and successfully pleaded with the physicians not to amputate his leg. He remained in France for eight months nursing his stiff leg, which had been put back together. He received the Croix de Guerre and the Silver Star for his action and returned to the United States. After his marriage to Helen Poteat on 6 March 1919 the couple moved to Washington, D.C. so that he could be near the Walter Reed Hospital for medical attention. He started reporting for the *Washington Times*. Unfortunately, in 1922, Stallings suffered a bad fall, reinjuring his leg; this time amputation was necessary.

When Stallings was released from the hospital, he and Helen Stallings made a short trip to Europe, then returned to New York where he joined the staff of the *New York World*. At the *World* he soon became a book reviewer and wrote more than four hundred articles during his first year. He also associated with such well-known writers as Edna Ferber, George S. Kaufman, Marc Connelly, Robert Sherwood, and Dorothy Parker in the now legendary Algonquin Round Table.

With Maxwell Anderson, another *World* reporter, Stallings wrote his most significant work, *What Price Glory?*. It was an effective collaboration, with Stallings supplying his firsthand experience of war while Anderson organized and rewrote Stallings's drafts. Acclaimed by both audiences and critics, *What Price Glory?* nearly won the Pulitzer Prize, losing to Sidney Howard's comedy *They Knew What They Wanted* (1924). *What Price Glory?* deals with the reactions of American soldiers in France to World War I. The play opens in "A room in a French farmhouse—now a U.S. Marine company headquarters," where three soldiers, Gowdy, Kiper, and Lipinsky are discussing women, the arrival of the new top soldier, Quirt, and their reasons for

joining the marines. Immediately evident is their lack of traditional patriotism. One soldier joined "to see the girls," another because he "had a brainstorm that day and signed on the dotted line." This unglamorous view of war is continued throughout the play.

The two main characters, Captain Flagg and Sergeant Quirt, are seasoned soldiers who respect each other on the battlefield. Flagg explains to his company that Quirt "is one of the best god damn soldiers that ever destroyed a memorandum receipt." They are, however, adversaries in romance. Flagg has been enjoying the favors of the pretty young French camp follower Charmaine (she is described as "a drab" in the stage instructions). When he takes a short leave, she jumps into the waiting arms of Quirt, who is newly assigned to Flagg's company. Eight days later Charmaine's father, Pete, claims that a man in Flagg's company has "trampled the one flower of his life." Pete wants 500 francs and a quick marriage. Flagg, not aware that Quirt has also become Charmaine's lover, counters with an offer of 300 francs and "any son-in-law he wants out of the whole damn army." When Pete points to Quirt, Flagg is stung, and decides to force Quirt to marry Charmaine and shackle him with a two-thirds allotment of Quirt's salary to her. A general appears in the middle of their negotiations to plan a new attack. He is not impressed by Quirt's protestations that it was a courtship with "honorable intentions on both sides." The general orders Quirt to sign the allotment for Charmaine or stand trial, then he leaves. However, Quirt extricates himself by saying that if Flagg insists upon having him marry Charmaine, he (Quirt) will not go on the attack: "if this sergeant goes in, he goes in single." Flagg, having no other sergeant, admits defeat, and as they go to battle he consoles Charmaine, "This war's lousy with sergeants. There'll be thirty along in thirty days."

The farcical tone of the first act implies how cheap life at the front is; however, the second act has only grim humor and demonstrates the brutal reality of this implication. Act 2 takes place in a cellar near the front lines. The soldiers rest here or are brought in when they are injured. Flagg comforts those who are wounded or hysterical; Quirt arrives with a wounded leg, which Flagg is certain he received intentionally so that he might leave the fighting in order to get back to Charmaine sooner than Flagg. Quirt leaves, and just as Flagg is about to dash out after him, a badly wounded soldier comes in, requiring Flagg's attention.

Act 3 is set at Charmaine's father's tavern and

the romantic farce continues. When Flagg arrives, he and Quirt get drunk and decide to fight. In an overly complicated and unconvincing sequence, the men decide to gamble and fight for Charmaine. Just as it seems clear that Flagg has won her and that Quirt has run away, a runner comes to call the company back to battle. Quirt, who because of his wounded leg could stay behind with Charmaine, does not, and appears at the last moment with the final words of the play: "What a lot of God damn fools it takes to make a war! Hey, Flagg, wait for baby!"

The two main characters are similar in many ways. Both drink hard, brawl readily, chase women, and fight bravely. Flagg is "a fine, magnificently endowed man," admired by his soldiers, Quirt included. Though both men return to the fighting, they are not naive about the war; both accept war and duty pragmatically. They do their best at their jobs with no respect wasted on their superiors. Flagg thinks that those who are running the war have no idea of the reality of it: "Damn headquarters! It's some more of that world-safe-for-democracy slush!" Even the romantic episodes involving Charmaine are not love scenes; they are actions typical of men only temporarily in a country, taking advantage of one of the numerous "soldiers' sluts," as they are called in the play.

The view that "war is hell" is made graphically clear in act 2 (the act for which Stallings is reputed to be almost solely responsible) by the soldier Gowdy: "Harry was unconscious—halfway—holding half his guts in his bare hands and hollering for somebody to turn him loose so he could shoot himself." Reactions to this horrifying episode range from callousness to insanity. Gowdy says of his captain: "Flagg's gone crazy now. Raving crazy. Hasn't slept for five nights. We'll be sitting on him in another night like he's had tonight." Kiper replies: "The whole damned universe is crazy now." The young marine who becomes hysterical at the sight of his friend's wound adequately sums up the feelings of most of the soldiers: "What price glory now? Why in God's name can't we all go home?"

What Price Glory? depicts men's individual responses to war rather than any broad philosophy regarding war. The characters are trapped in a situation which they cannot idealize nor justify. To resolve this dilemma, Joseph Wood Krutch suggests that their "justification had to be made in terms of that witty animality which alone had been left to them." The characters "learned to compensate for the loss of all usual human independence and security with ribald indulgence in certain licenses re-

specting language and conduct which the conditions of a soldier's life enormously enlarge."

Also in 1924 Stallings published *Plumes*, a novel whose main theme is the young hero's disillusionment with war. It traces, largely through flashbacks from 1922, the responses of Richard Plume to World War I. The flashback structure presents Richard before the war as a handsome young man, in stark contrast to the wounded and bitter man he has become. Chapter 2 of book 1 chronicles his family history, beginning in 1685 with the first Plume to come to America. The subsequent Plumes fought in every American war: the Indian wars, the Mexican War, the Revolution, the Spanish-American War. So, like Stallings, Richard had grown up on war stories. After being wounded in World War I, Richard begins his search for the meaning of suffering, leading finally to the realization that there is no meaning. His steady move toward this nihilistic view of the world is one of the causes for the growing estrangement between him and his wife, Esme, who, unlike her husband, is becoming more romantic. At the end of the novel, Richard is learning to cope in a world where all is absurdity; he sees that the "plumes" of life (representative of military honor) are meaningless. His main hope is that his son will not follow in his footsteps.

Plume's war experiences cause an estrangement from his own past since his forbears were proud soldiers. Harlan Hatcher said that *Plumes* represented accurately "the pitiful after-effects of the War upon one of its heroes mutilated in body and soul by the carnage. With blazing resentment it attacked the system that produced such irresponsible wastage and human suffering to no end."

In the wake of the success of *What Price Glory?*, Stallings and Maxwell Anderson continued their collaboration. *First Flight* and *The Buccaneer*, both historical romances, were produced in rapid succession in September and October, respectively, of 1925. Both were failures. Both have protagonists who place adventure and career above personal relationships with women (as do Flagg and Quirt). *First Flight*, set in 1788, depicts Andrew Jackson as a cunning but likable, fiery but practical twenty-year-old. He has just become an attorney for the state of North Carolina. While he is on his way to Nashville to keep the men there from transforming the territory into a new state, he stays at a roadside inn and becomes involved in a romance with Charity, a nubile fifteen-year-old. This romance, combined with a political argument, leads to a conflict with the other men at the tavern, who are also compcting for the charms of Charity. Jackson outwits his competitors, kills one who drunkenly assaults him, then leaves Charity behind, sacrificed to his political aspirations. The title refers to the first flight from romance taken by the hero—presumably there will be many more—as he pursues his adventurous career.

In theme and technique *First Flight* resembles its companion piece. *The Buccaneer*, set in the 1600s in Panama City, concerns the career of the English adventurer, Sir Henry Morgan. He has many loves, the chief one being Lady Neville, a strong-willed woman who cannot resist him. Morgan is apprehended and must stand trial in England for crimes against the crown. Charles II, however, pardons him, and the play concludes with a stirring speech in which Morgan spurns the dull, heartless existence of petty thieves and obsequious courtiers in "the rotten center of an empire." He asks for volunteers to join him in his trip to Jamaica—if "there's a man among you." The only one to step forth, however, is Lady Neville; her gesture ends the play.

Audience and critical response to these two plays were negative, perhaps because of Stallings's inability to write imaginatively of something he had not experienced, and perhaps, as Krutch suggests, because the plays did not "touch any contemporary emotions," as *What Price Glory?* had done so successfully.

With the success of *What Price Glory?* and the publication of *Plumes*, Stallings became a celebrity and attracted the attention of Hollywood. Irving Thalberg, a young production executive of MGM, introduced Stallings to director King Vidor, who wanted to make a film of Stallings's short story "The Big Parade" (1924). Stallings, quite restless, did not wish to remain in Hollywood to produce a film script, and Vidor literally followed Stallings back to New York and finally coaxed a scenario out of him.

The short story is similar to *What Price Glory?* in its portrayal of the emptiness of the pomp and glory of war. An unnamed American lieutenant is ordered to bring eight men from the front to Paris to march in a Fourth of July parade. From the original company of ninety men only nine remain. They must therefore draw straws to determine who stays behind. During the parade, the lieutenant realizes that the man who had to stay behind (a sympathetically portrayed undertaker's assistant from Brooklyn) will not survive. The story's effectiveness arises from its skillfully wrought mood conveying the lieutenant's weary appreciation of the brutal irony of how some people in war are chosen

Laurence Stallings

to live, some to die. The 1925 film based on "The Big Parade" established Vidor's career as a director and made its lead, John Gilbert, a star. However, Stallings never enjoyed writing for the screen, although he did write more in later years.

In 1926 Stallings and his wife left New York for a farmhouse, Forest Home, in Blanche, North Carolina, where he continued his writing, concentrating mainly on short stories. In 1928 he returned to New York and collaborated on a musical, *Rainbow*, with Oscar Hammerstein II. It was produced that year, then later made into a film, *Song of the West*. Also in that year Sylvia, the Stallingses' first child, was born. In 1931 Stallings began working for the *New York Sun* as a literary reviewer. During this period he met Ernest Hemingway and adapted *A Farewell to Arms* (1929) for the stage and screen.

Meanwhile, he continued writing and publishing short stories and began working on *The First World War: A Pictorial History* (1933), which is noteworthy not only for its vivid photographs of World War I, but also because of its ambiguous nature—it seems as much a prediction of the war to come as an objective look at World War I. Stallings wrote the introduction and also laconic captions for most of the 500 photographs. The irony and horror of a war that is justified by cultural aspirations seem to be the target of Stallings's introduction: "Man made this world in four years, and saw that it was good, if we are to believe in Versailles." The photographs were sufficient evidence to show how Stallings's generation had suffered at the hands of the military expert: "one who carefully avoids all the small errors as he sweeps on to the grand fallacy." At the time of its publication, the book provoked controversy, especially between two well-known literary figures, Archibald MacLeish and Malcolm Cowley. MacLeish contended that the book was antiwar propaganda, Cowley that it was time for veterans to admit that they had fought in vain. The philosopher Kenneth Burke in *The Philosophy of Literary Form* (1941) analyzed this debate and Stallings's pictorial history in considering the nature of "the poet's contradictory response, one best represented in war literature."

In 1934 Stallings became editor of the popular Fox newsreel series *Movietonews*. The following year he was also appointed literary editor of the *American Mercury* and in 1936 was promoted to associate editor. In 1935 and 1936 he toured Ethiopia filming the Italian incursion there for *Movietonews*. When he returned to the United States he separated from his wife and they were divorced on 1 December 1936. The following March he married his secretary at Fox, Louise St. Leger Vance. The couple moved to California where he signed a contract with MGM as a screenwriter. Even though he had previously expressed a distaste for movie work, he needed the money. *Northwest Passage* (1940) is probably his best known screenplay. Nineteen thirty-nine marked the birth of Stallings's first son, Laurence, Jr.; his last child, Sally, was born in 1941.

During World War II Stallings returned to the marines for active duty; he was stationed at the Pentagon for most of the war, but in his self-described capacity as an adviser or interviewer, he traveled in Africa, Europe, and England. Arthur Krock, Stallings's friend and a reporter for the *New York Times*, was convinced that he was involved in army and marine intelligence work. In 1943 Stallings retired as a lieutenant-colonel and returned to California. There he continued screenwriting and also wrote another play, *The Streets Are Guarded* (1944), set during World War II. It had a disappointing run, however, closing after twenty-four performances. Burns Mantle countered general opinion by asserting that the play deserved a better hearing.

Stallings did little writing for many years until Max Wyeth of Harper and Row publishers urged him to expand his essay, "The War to End War," which had been published in 1959. Stallings did so,

researching the military tactics and compaigns of the American Expeditionary Force in World War I, and producing a book entitled *The Doughboys* (1963). Again, his focus is on the individual and his response to war. Near the beginning of the book Stallings describes his purpose: "I sing not so much of arms . . . as of the man himself, conscious of being unable to summon him back in entirety, and heartsick of enduring the melancholy of trying to recover long buried remembrances of things past." *The Doughboys* succeeds in celebrating those unsung heroes of the Great War. It was to be his last work. Stallings's remaining leg, also injured in World War I, had to be amputated in 1963. The next year he was honored by his home state of Georgia "for his contributions and his service to his country." Laurence Stallings died of a heart attack 28 February 1968. He is buried in Rosecrans Veterans' Cemetery at Point Loma, California.

Stallings will always be associated with the trauma and alienation which occurred as a result of World War I. In addition to the achievement of *What Price Glory?*, which he shares with Maxwell Anderson, Stallings wrote sharp contemporary accounts of battle and published numerous short stories, which were admired by no less a judge than Ernest Hemingway. Stallings's "Vale of Tears" was included in the collection of stories, *Men at War: The Best War Stories of All Time*, edited by Hemingway in 1942. Stallings, like Hemingway's Nick Adams, had seen the insanity of war at close range yet did not retreat into platitudes about the meaning of sacrifice. His achievement as a dramatist will endure for its accurate portrayal of brave men fighting simply because they were brave in a world whose political confusion had made carnage commonplace.

–Lisa Hodgens

Screenplays:
The Big Parade, MGM, 1925;
What Price Glory?, MGM, 1926;
Northwest Passage, by Stallings and Talbot Jennings, MGM, 1940;
Jungle Book, United Artists, 1942.

Periodical Publication:
"How A Great Play is Written," by Stallings and Maxwell Anderson, *Current Opinion*, 77 (November 1924): 617.

References:
Joan Brittain, *Laurence Stallings* (Boston: Twayne, 1975);

Eleanor Flexner, *American Playwrights: 1918-1938* (New York: Simon & Schuster, 1938), pp. 80-81;

Jean Gould, *Modern American Playwrights* (New York: Dodd, Mead, 1966), pp. 121-123;

Harlan Hatcher, *Creating the Modern American Novel* (New York: Farrar, 1935), p. 227;

Joseph Wood Krutch, *The American Drama Since 1918* (New York: Random House, 1939), pp. 29-41, 53-54;

Archibald MacLeish and Malcolm Cowley, "Lines for an Interment," *New Republic*, 76 (20 September 1933): 159-161;

MacLeish, "The Dead of the Next War," *New Republic*, 76 (4 October 1933): 214-216.

DAVID STARKWEATHER
(11 September 1935-)

SELECTED PRODUCTIONS: *Maggie of the Bargain Basement* (ballad opera), music by Starkweather, 1956, Madison, Wis.;

Excuse Me, Pardon Me, 1957, Wisconsin Union Play Circle, Madison, Wis.;

The Family Joke, 1962, La Mama Experimental Theatre Club, New York;

You May Go Home Again, 1963, Caffe Cino, New York;

A Practical Ritual to Exorcise Frustration after Five Days of Rain, music by Allan Landon, 27 March 1970, Circle Theatre, New York;

The Poet's Papers, 17 March 1971, Tufts University, Medford, Mass.;

The Straights of Messina, 28 November 1973, Circle Theatre, New York.

Starting in the early 1960s, a new theatre movement began gathering momentum in New York City. Writers, actors, and directors began producing plays on makeshift stages, first in coffeehouses and bars, and then in churches and lofts. This movement was soon dubbed "Off-Off-Broadway." Many of the writers whose plays were first performed here have gone on to substantial commercial and critical successes in the more established arenas. Others of the original Off-Off-Broadway playwrights continue to write for small audiences and to employ highly experimental techniques and unusual themes. Their plays have not received much attention in recent years, especially as the number of Off-Off-Broadway theatres

has grown so rapidly. David Starkweather is a writer who seems to fall into the latter category.

Emerging in 1962 with a play entitled *The Family Joke*, Starkweather proceeded to write at least seven additional plays between that date and 1969. The plays' actual production histories are sketchy, but he does seem to have been successful in having a number of them produced during that time in theatres that later became famous as landmarks of the movement. *The Family Joke* was produced at La Mama Experimental Theatre Club in 1962, while a play which Starkweather completed the following year, *You May Go Home Again* (1963) was performed at the Caffe Cino.

La Mama and the Cino, both located in lower Manhattan, were unknown operations at that time. They have subsequently become synonymous with Off-Off-Broadway and, in the years since, have taken on a kind of mythic stature. The Cino was actually a cafe where espresso and pastries were the sole bill of fare until owner Joe Cino came into contact with various theatre people and decided to open his establishment to the production of plays as well. Ellen Stewart, the "Mama" of La Mama, was a dress designer who decided her true vocation lay in producing plays. She then went about finding spaces suitable for such endeavors.

A native of Madison, Wisconsin, Starkweather migrated to New York sometime after graduating from the University of Wisconsin in 1957 with a B.A. in speech. His father, Walter, was a wholesale television and radio salesman; his mother, Norma Shroyer Starkweather, a librarian. In a biographical statement published at the time of a 1965 production of *You May Go Home Again*, Starkweather mentions having written and acted in plays when he was a boy growing up in Madison. With the help of two friends, these productions were put on each summer in the boys' backyards. This early interest in theatrical expression remained with him. In college, he was still writing plays, albeit of a more formal nature. A "ballad opera" he composed during his student days, entitled *Maggie of the Bargain Basement*, was produced while he was at the university in 1956, and a one-act play he wrote the year he graduated won first prize in a playwriting competition sponsored by a local group called the Wisconsin Union Play Circle. The one-act, *Excuse Me, Pardon Me*, was produced by the group during that same year (1957). In fact, this script was given a further life when it was subsequently produced on an educational television network in Louisiana.

It is almost impossible for a young playwright to support himself from his plays initially, especially when the work is conceived along nontraditional, even avant-garde lines, and Starkweather was no exception to the rule. During the period when he first lived in New York, Starkweather supported himself as an actor, manager, or as a driver for a touring theatre company. He later worked for some time as an editor of a New York City visitors' guide, the *New York Visitors Reporter*.

The world Starkweather began to create in his plays was a decidedly stylized one. Like most recent experimental work, Starkweather's plays question the assumptions upon which the prevailing theatre was based. There is no linear narrative progression where events proceed in an orderly fashion. Rather, the sense of time is very subjective and changeable. Language too is used in a nontraditional way—not to further the story, but rather as an entity unto itself. The words often seem to be used to create an emotional climate—tense, poetic, satirical. Words as supplication. Words as weapons. In addition, the words often seem scored as if in a musical composition, this being just one of the parallels in Starkweather's work to musical forms.

The characters of Starkweather's plays are not recognizable flesh-and-blood men and women, dis-tinguished by individual quirks and perspectives. Rather, they are types (in the best sense of the word) who, at times, carry definite symbolic overtones. Perhaps best defined as "Everyman" figures or essences, they are often not even distinguished by individual names, but just by their labels or functions. The "Executioner" of *You May Go Home Again* (1963) and the "Secretary of the Ulterior" in *The Poet's Papers* (1971) are examples. This sort of characterization takes the plays further from the realm of the specific, adding to the sense of a heightened, almost mythic reality where basic, even primeval, conflicts are often being worked out.

You May Go Home Again was the first of Starkweather's plays to be published. Its two-week run at the Caffe Cino was directed by the author, with the assistance of Stanley Rosenberg and Paula Mason. The music was composed by Lucas Mason and the costumes created by Ya Yoi. Starkweather has called the play "a domestic Noh in one-act." Its central character and the consciousness through which the action of the play is perceived is the Executioner. From the first description of this character it is apparent that a reality larger than life is being attempted. The character's costume has a

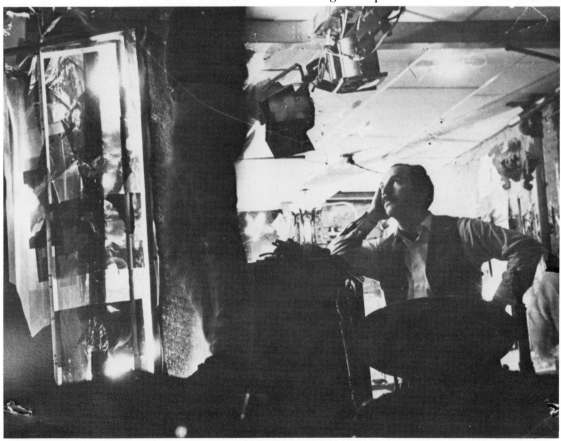

David Starkweather

"fantastic" quality, complete with tiny mirrors which reflect the light. The setting is a "bridge," not a bridge which connects any two specific geographical points, but rather a metaphoric bridge, one joining two states of mind, the poles of past and present, love and hate, guilt and acceptance.

The use of music is central to the play's conception. The text calls for a musician to be "prominently located between the Executioner and the stage." Music is used to counterpoint the Executioner's actions. When he mimes severing two heads, the musician simultaneously whacks a block of wood with a hatchet. Moans, blubbering, and giggles are just a few of the sounds called for. At various points, the text reads like a sound score for a musical composition with words as just one element in the score. Here then is one of the links to the Japanese Noh drama, where music is an integral part of the work.

The use of mime is another link. Very often, an almost choreographic effect is called for, with the characters enacting everyday events as if those events constituted a "methodical, somnolent ritual." To obtain the effect he is after, Starkweather stipulates in the stage directions that the mime be "not simply pantomimic." Instead, the physical movements of the actors create a contrast or counterpoint to the rhythms of their speeches.

The story of *You May Go Home Again* revolves around a homecoming—the Executioner returning for his sister's wedding. The play traces an emotional, as well as a physical, journey undertaken by the solitary, Beckett-like figure of the Executioner back to his roots. The family group is comprised of Mother, Father, the sister, Linda, and a brother, Peter. All are recognizable types—the controlling Mother overtly dominates the ineffectual Father, while Linda and Peter bicker between themselves. At times, the passages spoken by the family members rely on the familiar absurdist use of cliches; at other times, Starkweather employs other nontraditional stylistic devices. For example, each character comes to be associated with a particular sound. Father, for one, becomes associated with the sound of a bucket being filled with water. Another device has two conversations being carried on simultaneously. The dialogue courses back and forth between different perspectives. At one point, it appears the Executioner will not be attending the wedding. The family then proceeds to travel over water by boat to fetch him. By this time, the Executioner is referred to as David, not coincidentally the name of the playwright. "I told you not to come but you came anyway," the Executioner tells the family. "I warned you but you did not turn back. Don't you know there are reasons I have always run from you, trying to escape you?" Themes of punishment and retribution become evident as the Executioner seeks to come to terms with his past. "Don't you see I must kill you to ever live?" he finally asks.

All ends brightly, however, as the Executioner is "transformed" in the course of one last ritual movement. By removing his elaborate costume an "unassuming, almost boyish" young man is revealed. The Executioner identity of the character has now been replaced fully by the David identity. The unforgiving, destructive elements in his soul have been reconciled with the innocent and loving elements. Therefore, the play ends joyfully with the sound of "prolonged bells and celebrations," the Executioner's ax continually "turning into flowers."

The Poet's Papers is the second Starkweather play to be published. While it is much different from *You May Go Home Again* in tone and substance, it shares with the earlier play innovative stylistic devices and a unique nonrealistic structure. Time is again a very fluid dimension with the action ricocheting back and forth between various bases. Characters are changeable, assuming different sexes as well as personae at the drop of a hat. And, lastly, music—or, more accurately, sound—is again central to the playwright's conception.

Where *The Poet's Papers* differs markedly from the first play is in its attitudes. The dark, brooding quality of *You May Go Home Again* has been replaced with a light, highly satiric point of view. The absurdist flavor suggested at moments in *You May Go Home Again* is felt much more strongly here. Certain scenes are overtly comic and much of the actors' "business" quite farcical. This is not to say that Starkweather does not address serious issues. Aside from the often biting political satire, the role of the artist in society, and the dichotomy between reason and emotion are two of the issues Starkweather is raising.

Written in 1967 (four years after *You May Go Home Again*), *The Poet's Papers* ends the first period of Starkweather's work. A number of plays were written in the intervening years, but scripts are unavailable. Among these are "Owey Wishy, Are You There?" (1964), "The Assent" (1967), and "The Wish House" (1966). *The Poet's Papers* was produced in 1971 at Tufts University.

Early in this play, an announcement is made that the Poet has died. The President and his advisers (aptly named the Secretaries of Logic, Reality, and the Ulterior) then begin a search for a proper memorial to this dead artist. Scorned in his lifetime, the artist is, of course, celebrated in death. Starkweather here introduces a novel touch—inserting simple line drawings of possible plans for such a memorial into the text. While the President and his advisers are conferring, Starkweather indicates that "construction workers" are to be on stage, actually building a monument before the audience's eyes. This idea of "building" works quite nicely when contrasted with such themes in the play as a "falling apart" or "tearing down" of known social institutions, an only partially comic vision of the end of the world. In a time reversal, Starkweather introduces the Poet. Though he is said to have died, the Poet and his Wife wander through the scenes, adding to the play a touching human dimension as well as a large part of its philosophical underpinning.

The text's first words are an evocation of sound: "An ubiquitous, primeval sound arises, filling the darkness." Next a primitive procession of strange animals parades by, carrying placards. Soon, "an orchestra begins tuning." When the President appears, he is carrying a violin and preparing to play in the orchestra along with the other musician politicians. The scene takes place in the House of Representatives where a joint session of Congress is convening. The world then is seen as one large orchestra, an organism comprised of many intricate parts which can only fulfill its function (the creation of beautiful sound) with the cooperation of all.

In a reenactment of the Poet's marriage, the Poet's Wife is envisioned as a she-wolf. In their subsequent wanderings, these two define one of the play's key polarities. The Poet's Wife seems to represent the physical forces of nature—sexuality, appetite, passion. She is concerned with nurturing and bodily functions. She is always putting her hands on her "female parts and howling." The Poet, on the other hand, seems to represent reason: "Ideas are the only weapons men possess . . . And all ideas are merely relationships. Established in our minds by contrast and similarity . . . And, if all ideas are relationships, all thoughts can be expressed in structures." From this, he is able to deduce that "science is the search for meaning . . . implicit in the structures around us." Yet he is able to see a place for art: "Man's Art specializes in extravagant hypotheses. For there is nothing we can know of the world beyond the mind save by metaphors in the language of the senses." Starkweather here could well be describing his own creative process as a playwright. His play is nothing as much as a "structure," through which "all thoughts can be expressed."

Form and content become one. And it is this very "language of the senses" which he relies on to convey meaning.

The actors who had been playing the President and his three advisers are transformed into a pair of uncommon Kings and Queens. It is here that the absurdist quality in Starkweather's writing reaches its apex. The King and Queen of the Anals and the King and Queen of the Orals now proceed to enact a series of fantastic masquerades that are startling at times, uproarious at others, but which are always bizarre almost to the point of being surreal. This is a vision of the world where the natural order is reversed—men find themselves married to men, the only logic is illogic, and chaos and confusion reign supreme. The Poet, at one point, ends up performing for the Kings in the guise of a woman dressed as an exotic dancer, and then for the Queens as a man in the uniform of a military guard. As the chaos accelerates—one scene tumbling into another, almost free-form in its structure—Starkweather again looks to sound to provide an emotional foundation for what is happening. The sound in this case is a heartbeat. It is used repeatedly throughout the last section of the play, "throbbing as it grows louder and louder."

Starkweather's work is difficult and complex. While some parts of it are more accessible than others, none of it is easy. To a middle-class theatre audience, schooled on routine bedroom farce and workmanlike domestic drama, it must seem baffling. To a daring, intellectually curious audience, on the other hand, it is a challenge. Starkweather received a CAPS grant (New York's Creative Arts Public Service Grant) in 1976 and a Rockefeller Foundation grant in 1978. These indicate that he intends to continue writing avant-garde works for the same kind of audience that gave him his first hearing.

–*Bruce Serlen*

Other:

The Poet's Papers, in *New American Plays, Volume III*, ed. William M. Hoffman (New York: Hill & Wang, 1970), pp. 27-76;

You May Go Home Again, in *The Off-Off Broadway Book*, ed. Albert Poland and Bruce Mailman (Indianapolis: Bobbs-Merrill, 1972), pp. 17-24.

Reference:

Arthur Sainer, *The Sleepwalker and the Assassin, A View of the Contemporary Theatre* (New York: Bridgehead Books, 1964), pp. 108-109.

Papers:
The theatre collection of the New York Public Library at Lincoln Center has some of Starkweather's papers.

JOHN STEINBECK
(27 February 1902-20 December 1968)

PRODUCTIONS: *Of Mice and Men*, 23 November 1937, Music Box Theatre, New York, 207 [performances]; musical version, 4 December 1958, Provincetown Playhouse, New York, 37;

The Moon Is Down, 7 April 1942, Martin Beck Theatre, New York, 71;

Burning Bright, 18 October 1950, Broadhurst Theatre, New York, 13.

SELECTED BOOKS: *Cup of Gold* (New York: McBride, 1929; London & Toronto: Heinemann, 1937);

The Pastures of Heaven (New York: Brewer, Warren & Putnam, 1932; London: Allan, 1933);

To a God Unknown (New York: Ballou, 1933; London & Toronto: Heinemann, 1935);

Tortilla Flats (New York: Covici Friede, 1935; London: Heinemann, 1935);

In Dubious Battle (New York: Covici Friede, 1936; London & Toronto: Heinemann, 1936);

Of Mice and Men [novel] (New York: Covici Friede, 1937; London & Toronto: Heinemann, 1937);

Of Mice and Men: A Play in Three Acts (New York: Covici Friede, 1937);

The Red Pony (New York: Covici Friede, 1937);

The Long Valley (New York: Viking, 1938; London & Toronto: Heinemann, 1939);

The Grapes of Wrath (New York: Viking, 1939; London & Toronto: Heinemann, 1939);

The Forgotten Village (New York: Viking, 1941);

Sea of Cortez (New York: Viking, 1941); republished as *The Log from the Sea of Cortez* (London, Melbourne & Toronto: Heinemann, 1958);

The Moon Is Down [novel] (New York: Viking, 1942; London & Toronto: Heinemann, 1942);

The Moon Is Down: Play in Two Parts (New York: Dramatists Play Service, 1942; London: English Theatre Guild, 1943);

Bombs Away (New York: Viking, 1942);

Cannery Row (New York: Viking, 1945; London & Toronto: Heinemann, 1945);

The Wayward Bus (New York: Viking, 1947; London & Toronto: Heinemann, 1947);

The Pearl (New York: Viking, 1947; Melbourne, London & Toronto: Heinemann, 1948);

A Russian Journal (New York: Viking, 1948; London, Melbourne & Toronto: Heinemann, 1949);

Burning Bright: A Play in Story Form [novel] (New York: Viking, 1950; Melbourne, London & Toronto: Heinemann, 1951);

Burning Bright: Play in Three Acts (New York: Dramatists Play Service, 1951);

East of Eden (New York: Viking, 1952; Melbourne, London & Toronto: Heinemann, 1952);

Sweet Thursday (New York: Viking, 1954; Melbourne, London & Toronto: Heinemann, 1954);

The Short Reign of Pippin IV (New York: Viking, 1957; Melbourne, London & Toronto: Heinemann, 1957);

Once There Was A War (New York: Viking, 1958; London, Melbourne & Toronto: Heinemann, 1959);

The Winter of Our Discontent (New York: Viking, 1961; London, Melbourne & Toronto: Heinemann, 1961);

Travels With Charley (New York: Viking, 1962; London, Melbourne & Toronto: Heinemann, 1962);

America and Americans (New York: Viking, 1966; London: Heinemann, 1966);

Journal of a Novel (New York: Viking, 1969; London: Heinemann, 1970);

The Portable Steinbeck, enlarged edition, ed. Pascal Covici, Jr. (New York: Viking, 1971)—includes "Nobel Prize Acceptance Speech";

The Acts of King Arthur and His Noble Knights (New York: Farrar, Straus & Giroux, 1976).

John Ernst Steinbeck was in the course of his mixed career a common laborer, world traveler, novelist, short-story writer, essayist, and playwright. Although he will be most importantly remembered for his eighteen volumes of fiction and eight works of nonfiction, his three plays are an interesting sidelight in his long career. Of Irish and German ancestry, he was born in Salinas Valley, California, an area that served as the setting for many of his best novels and one of his plays, *Of Mice and Men* (1937).

Steinbeck was both a good student and athlete in high school, but his attendance at Stanford University was sporadic (1919-1920, 1922-1923, 1924-1925). In college he became interested in biological and ecological studies, but he never completed a degree. His first marriage in 1930 to Carol Henning ended in divorce in 1942; his second marriage in 1943 to Gwyndolyn Conger ended in divorce in 1948. He married his third wife, Elaine Scott, in late 1950 and they lived together until his death. Although his most notable award was the Nobel Prize for Literature in December 1962, his work was recognized in many other ways. Several of his novels reached a large popular audience when they were chosen by the Book-of-the-Month Club; his critical success peaked when *The Grapes of Wrath* won the Pulitzer Prize in 1940. His first two plays, *Of Mice and Men* and *The Moon is Down* (1942), were included in the Burns Mantle *Best Plays Yearbook*. The first play won the New York Drama Critics Circle Award for the 1937-1938 season and the second play won the King Haakon Liberty Cross, a Norwegian award, in 1946. Both plays appeared in film versions. During the 1940s Steinbeck also wrote several original screenplays. He died of a heart attack in New York City at the age of sixty-six; his ashes were buried in Salinas, California.

Some of Steinbeck's major themes and techniques are reflected in the three stories he dramatized for the stage. In discussing his attitude toward form, he remarked in *Saturday Review*, "If a writer likes to write, he will find satisfaction in endless experiment with his medium. He will improvise techniques, arrangements of scenes, rhythms of words, and rhythms of thought." This statement hints at his motivation for attempting the medium of theatre and also records some of the dramatic devices he employed, especially repetitions or "rhythms" of scenes and symbols. As far as the content of his works—including his three plays—is concerned, Steinbeck comprehensively summarized his major themes in his Nobel Prize acceptance speech: "The ancient commission of the writer has not changed. He is charged with exposing our many grievous faults and failures, with dredging up to the light our dark and dangerous dreams for the purpose of improvement. Furthermore, the writer is delegated to declare and to celebrate man's proven capacity for greatness of heart and spirit—for gallantry in defeat, for courage, compassion and love." Steinbeck's brief career as a dramatist, then, is of significance because his plays reveal his passion for experimenting with new forms and they dramatize some of the basic themes found in his best fiction.

By his own admission, Steinbeck had in mind, while he was writing the novel version of *Of Mice and Men*, the clear possibility of its performance on the stage. In an article which appeared in *Stage* (January 1938), he wrote: "Simply stated, *Of Mice and Men*

was an attempt to write a novel that could be played from the lines, or a play that could be read." Years later, he called this type of writing the "play-novelette" form. Several play agents were interested in the idea, but it was under the supervision of George S. Kaufman, the play's ultimate producer, that Steinbeck prepared his story for dramatic presentation. The opening and closing scenes of the play are set on a sandy bank of the Salinas River; the other four scenes take place in the several buildings on a ranch nearby. The two main characters are the itinerant ranch hands, George Milton and Lennie Small. George is described by the playwright as being "a small, sharp-faced ranch hand"; Lennie is his "huge, but not bright, companion." The two men have a close, but not always harmonious relationship, with George assuming responsibility for his simple-minded friend. There are five other ranch hands—Slim, Candy, Carlson, Whit, and Crooks—who appear on stage along with the boss of the ranch, his son Curley, and Curley's Wife, the only woman in the play and one who remains nameless throughout.

In the play Steinbeck develops two of his main themes—the exposition of our faults and failures as well as our dreams and schemes for improvement. These themes are suggested in the play's title which recalls Robert Burns' lines in the poem "To a Mouse" (1785) that "The best-laid schemes o' mice an' men/Gang aft a-gley." The play is a series of conflicts and confrontations as George and Lennie encounter troubles in their dealings with society. At a more fundamental level, the work is a study of the chilling loneliness that keeps men apart—an isolation that cannot even be remedied by such utopian dreams of a new community such as the repeatedly envisioned "little place" where George can "live off the fat of the land" and Lennie can tend his soft and lovable rabbits. In the opening scene George describes the harshness of the pair's present situation: "Guys like us that work on ranches is the loneliest guys in the world. They ain't got no family. They don't belong no place." In the scenes that follow, violence breeds violence in rhythmic patterns. Lennie loves to stroke soft animals, but his grip is suffocatingly possessive and means certain death for both mice and puppies. In the human sphere, Lennie unintentionally strikes out in childlike defense and confusion when he crushes every bone in Curley's hand in a bunkhouse fight; later he accidentally breaks the neck of Curley's Wife during the barn scene, which is the climax of the play. The emotional pitch is high in the play's final scene as the solitary George mercifully ends with a pistol shot

Caricature by Alfred Frueh of Broderick Crawford and Wallace Ford in Of Mice and Men

the life of his partner Lennie and pathetically spoils forever the dream the pair had of owning their own small plot of land, complete with chickens, rabbits, and a vegetable garden. Any audience would be moved to share in the feelings of sorrow, guilt, and love that are reflected on George's face as he contemplates the catastrophe and hears the voices of the approaching lynch mob, a group whose intentions have also been foiled.

There are positive and negative features to the way Steinbeck handles his themes in the play. Certainly he conveys a remarkably sincere and compelling compassion for the oppressed laborers and the half-witted, man-child Lennie. Also, the scene set in the separate room over a manure pile that is inhabited by Crooks, the negro stable hand, is one of the most powerful in the play and stands in the vanguard of American theatre for its naked and unsentimental revelation of what it is like to be a proud, intelligent, and sensitive black, but to be discriminated against and barred from as simple an entertainment as a bunkhouse card game. One of Crooks's intense statements conveys his hostile sadness: "A guy gets too lonely, he gets sick." The playwright is, however, less successful in delineating

several other characters and themes. While it is possible to accept the interpretation that Curley's Wife has no name because she has no real identity but instead mimics the movie-star image and the dream of being in Hollywood's "pichers," there is ample evidence that the delineation of the play's only female character is unclear and confusing. Claire Luce, who played the part in the original production, felt compelled to write Steinbeck for fuller directions concerning the nature of the character. Furthermore, why does Curley's Wife serve as not only the catalyst but the cause of the undoing of George and Lennie? She is a mysterious bringer of trouble and if the dramatist means to suggest that sex and female flirtatious behavior often lead men to murder and destruction, his presentation is unconvincing. Likewise, his social protest does not ring clear. Although Crooks delivers a bitterly pessimistic speech predicting the average man's inability to ever attain individual economic security, the deeper problems inherent in the labor-management system that exploits migrant workers are never adequately explored.

The critical reception of the play *Of Mice and Men* in 1937 was almost uniformly favorable. The greatest tribute to the work appeared on the citation that accompanied the Drama Critics Circle Award: "For its direct force and perception in handling a theme genuinely rooted in American life; for its bite into the strict quality of its material; for its refusal to make the study of tragical loneliness and frustration either cheap or sensational, and finally for its simple, intense and steadily rising effect on the stage." Other critics agreed with these sentiments. Brooks Atkinson called it "a masterpiece" that was "infinitely moving" and "somberly beautiful"; Stark Young called it "an absorbing work of theatre art"; Edith J. R. Isaacs claimed that the play deserved "extravagant praise"; and John Mason Brown called it "one of the finest, most pungent, and most poignant realistic productions." Only a handful of critics dissented. Several complained that the play relied for its emotional effects on melodramatic and sentimental elements. The strongest objections were raised against the play's dialogue, which several reviewers labeled as "starkly naked," "sacrilegious," "appalling," "offensive to good taste," "raw," "lusty," and "hair-raising." Before the play went on a road tour after its run in New York, some of the dialogue was prudishly modified by the producer, George S. Kaufman.

Although Steinbeck finished his dramatiza-

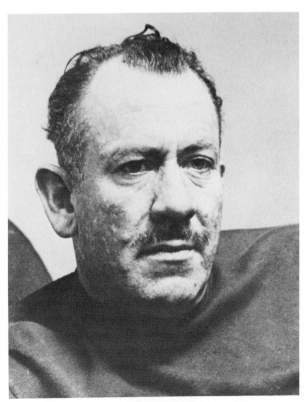

John Steinbeck

tion of the novel *The Moon Is Down* on the day of the Japanese attack on Pearl Harbor, 7 December 1941, it was 7 April 1942 before producer Oscar Serlin brought the play to the New York stage. The title is taken from Shakespeare's *Macbeth* (act 2, scene 1: "The moon is down; I have not heard the clock.") and implies a time of temporary but intense darkness. The drama, which has eight scenes and is divided into two parts, presents the thoughts and actions of both the invaders and the conquered people in a neutral country that is presumed to be Norway during World War II. In order to suggest the universality of the issues, the two nationalities involved are not explicitly stated. Yet by concentrating intently on one particular small mining town, the playwright presents a dramatic microcosm of the larger wartime struggle. Throughout the first half of the play the action per se is restrained and slow-paced as the dramatist concentrates instead on developing the opposing perspectives of the two contending forces. Various political concepts and positions are explored as the leaders negotiate, compromise, and sometimes collaborate. Outright resistance is exhibited at first by only two lowly and hot-tempered characters: the irate cook Annie throws boiling water on the soldiers who attempt to invade her kitchen and Alex Morden, a rebellious miner who refuses to work, strikes one of the invading officers fatally with a pickax. Otherwise, the plot moves forward through a series of long reflections that are a mixture of politics and philosophy, such as the interchange between the leaders of the opposing sides, Colonel Lanser and Mayor Orden:

MAYOR: Then we needn't talk any more.

LANSER: Yes, we must talk. We want you to help. . . . I suppose I knew it. Maybe Corell will have to be Mayor after all. You'll stay for the trial?

MAYOR: Yes, I'll stay. Then he won't be alone.

LANSER: We've taken on a job, haven't we?

MAYOR: Yes. The one impossible job in the world. The one thing that can't be done.

LANSER: Yes?

MAYOR: To break man's spirit . . . permanently.

Talk diminishes and violent action increases in the second half of the play as "the people" begin to fight for their freedom. In what is perhaps the most moving scene of the play, a young Lieutenant Tonder, who is lonely and tired of war, attempts to woo Molly Morden, the widow of the executed miner who rebelled against working in the mines. The scene conveys some vestiges of tenderness and humanity, but not for long as Molly, who symbolizes the resolve of the conquered to be free, transforms her sewing scissors into the steel dagger that ends the life of the lieutenant, a romantic who often "dreams of the perfect ideal love of elevated young men for poor girls." The time of collaboration ends as violent rebellion spreads. Using dynamite sticks dropped by British bombers, "the people" sabotage railroad lines, bridges, dynamos, transformers, and the mines. Although the town's mayor and doctor are executed in retaliation for the explosions set by the essentially unconquerable "free men," even the occupation commander, Colonel Lanser, admits that defeat is near for the invaders who are doomed to lose because they are "herd men, followers of a leader." The full implications of the play's central metaphor—"The flies have conquered the fly-paper"—are realized.

As a play dealing with a contemporary wartime situation, *The Moon Is Down* raises interesting questions concerning the function of theatre performed during wartime. Steinbeck eschewed dogmatic or simplistic thematic statements that would reduce his play to wartime propaganda. The invaders are presumed to be Nazis but they are never explicitly identified as such. There are degrees of civilized behavior and humane ideas on both sides throughout the play. If there is a compelling point that is impressed upon the audience in the drama it is that war reduces all men to a lowest common denominator; it is conducted at the expense of civilization itself. This point is effectively made in the stage directions: the settings become increasingly austere as the graceful art works and comfortable furnishings in the drawing room of the palace are replaced by the clutter and chaos of wartime gear, maps, and instruments.

Among both critics and the public, Steinbeck's wartime play sparked much controversy. Public support of the drama seemed to ebb and flow, but when the play closed after a nine-week run, over 56,000 theatregoers had seen it. Concerning the public's reaction Peter Lisca has observed that "the realities of the newsreel as well as the efforts of propaganda had led the public to expect more obvious heroics on the one hand and degenerate bestiality on the other." Critical reception was heated and mixed. The highest praise came from Rosamond Gilder, Brooks Atkinson, and Dorothy Thompson. Gilder wrote: "The power and the poignancy of Steinbeck's play lie in its immediacy, its ability to express world issues with the terrible nearness of little things, its affirmation of the dignity and nobility of man." Brooks Atkinson called it "a calm and reasonable story" and "a remarkably convincing play"; Dorothy Thompson affirmed her

basic faith in the German people by insisting that the "enormous power in Mr. Steinbeck's drama is that it is *not* an attack on *Nazis*. It is an attack on *Naziism*." Objections to the play were numerous and often intense. Critics complained that the playwright's overly confident thesis that the democratic forces must inevitably prevail was naive, misleading, and "even dangerous." Others objected to his "high-minded tolerance" in portraying Nazis who were not "sufficiently villainous." It was "unpatriotic" to present charming "gentle Huns" who showed qualities of humanity and civilization. John Mason Brown complained that "These Germans at the Martin Beck are too nice for comfort or belief"; Richard Lockridge argued that "By making his invaders more sinned against than sinning, Mr. Steinbeck has dissipated his drama." Several critics specifically objected to some of the play's dramatic devices. The dialogue was "rhetoric" and it was "wooden," "pedestrian," "stilted," or "stuffily unalive and somewhat pretentious." The *Time* reviewer's comment about the preponderance of offstage action that left at best a weak, secondary impression was trenchant: "The play lacks sustained action and commits the dramatic crime of having almost everything exciting take place offstage."

In his third and final attempt in what he now labels the "play-novelette" form, *Burning Bright* (the title is derived from William Blake's poem "The Tyger" 1794), Steinbeck intensified the tendency evident in *The Moon Is Down* to present a drama of ideas with a minimum of action on the stage. In fact, the third play leaves the realm of realistic drama in its use of expressionistic techniques. Concerning the heightened symbolism in the play Steinbeck remarked: "The attempt was to lift the story to the parable expression of the morality plays." It is the poetic language and the universal settings that elevate the play to an Everyman status above that of the play's particular action.

The plot outline is quite simple: over a telescoped period of about ten months, a woman bears a child and the four characters in the play adjust their attitudes to the new arrival. Joe Saul, who has been left sterile by a childhood attack of rheumatic fever, is forced—through the insistent pressurings of his Friend Ed—to face this fact and he comes to accept the child that has been conceived as a result of his devoted wife Mordeen's sacrificial relationship with a young, callous, and opportunistic lover named Victor. In the final scene Joe Saul proclaims gratefully that "There is a shining!" Somewhat melodramatically, Victor is pushed into the sea by

Friend Ed. It should be stressed that the story's primary focus is not upon the sensationalistic implications of a love triangle but upon the exploration of man's elemental fear of sterility.

What complicates the play's basic actions and ideas are the dramatic devices employed. Although the story and the characters continue through the three acts of the play, the settings and the characters' professions change in each act. Steinbeck said that "to indicate a universality of experience" he placed the characters in a series of "three professions which have long and continuing traditions, namely the Circus, the Farm, and the Sea." Furthermore, he poeticized the play's language: through "rhythm, sound, and image" Steinbeck sought, as he explained, to create "a kind of universal language not geared to the individual actors or their supposed crafts, but rather the best I was able to produce."

It was not the play's theme but its dramatic devices that the critics attacked with fury. A reviewer for *Theatre Arts*, for example, praised the play for being "an affirmation of faith in the human race, an avowal of belief in the dignity of man stated with unmistakable sincerity," but called the language "highly stylized" and "awkward" and the three background shifts "artificial" and "a theatrical trick." A host of other critics strongly condemned the dialogue and used such adjectives as "pretentiously archaic," "stilted," "improbable," "synthetic," "pseudo-poetic," "unwieldy," and "high-pitched and mawkish." Even though the play had the advantage of being produced by Rodgers and Hammerstein, it closed after only thirteen performances. In disappointed retaliation, Steinbeck wrote the essay "Critics, Critics Burning Bright." Warren French claims that during this period, Steinbeck's stature as a public literary figure "was at just about its lowest point."

In the defensive essay that Steinbeck addressed to the critics, he perhaps unwittingly provided the best epitaph to his career as a dramatist when he wrote: "But a book can wait until any frightening innovations have ceased to be objects of fear or derision. If my work had been exlusively for the theatre I believe that it would be unknown—and perhaps rightly so—for the theatre cannot wait." Although Steinbeck lived eighteen years after the failure of *Burning Bright*, he never again attempted what he once so enthusiastically called "this new form—the play-novelette." Neither the critics nor the public could accept the movement of his drama away from the earthy realism of *Of Mice and Men* to the expressionism of *Burning Bright*. Although the compassionate optimism for mankind and his future that informs Steinbeck's best works of fiction is evident in all three of his plays, his dramatic devices, especially the dialogue, ceased to impress theatre audiences. Ultimately, however, his experiments with drama will stand as a courageous and interesting sidelight in his remarkably diversified literary career.

–*William B. Thesing*

Screenplays:
The Forgotten Village, Arthur Mayer-Joseph Burstyn, 1941;
The Pearl, by Steinbeck, Emilio Fernandez, and Jack Wagner, RKO, 1948;
The Red Pony, Republic, 1949;
Viva Zapata!, Twentieth Century-Fox, 1952.

Periodical Publications:
". . . the novel might benefit by the discipline, the terseness. . . ," *Stage*, 15 (January 1938): 50-51;
"Critics, Critics Burning Bright," *Saturday Review of Literature*, 33 (11 November 1950): 20-21.

Letters:
Steinbeck: A Life in Letters, ed. Elaine Steinbeck and Robert Wallsten (New York: Viking, 1975).

Bibliography:
Tetsumaro Hayashi, *A New Steinbeck Bibliography (1929-1971)* (Metuchen, N.J.: Scarecrow Press, 1973).

Biography:
Thomas Kiernan, *The Intricate Music: A Biography of John Steinbeck* (Boston: Little, Brown, 1979).

References:
Warren French, *John Steinbeck* (Boston: Twayne, 1975);
Howard Levant, *The Novels of John Steinbeck: A Critical Study* (Columbia: University of Missouri Press, 1974), pp. 130-163;
Peter Lisca, *John Steinbeck: Nature and Myth* (New York: Crowell, 1978).

MEGAN TERRY
(22 July 1932-)

SELECTED PRODUCTIONS: *Ex-Miss Copper Queen on a Set of Pills*, 24 January 1963, Cherry Lane Theatre, New York;

Calm Down Mother and *Keep Tightly Closed in a Cool Dry Place*, 29 March 1965, Sheridan Square Playhouse, New York;

The Gloaming, Oh My Darling, Autumn 1965, Firehouse Theater, Minneapolis;

The Magic Realists, Winter 1966, La Mama Experimental Theatre Club, New York;

Comings and Goings, April 1966, La Mama Experimental Theatre Club, New York;

Viet Rock, 21 May 1966, La Mama Experimental Theatre Club, New York;

The People vs. Ranchman, 1 April 1967, Firehouse Theater, Minneapolis; 27 October 1968, Fortune Theatre, New York, 41 [performances];

Changes, by Terry and Tom O'Horgan, 4 January 1968, La Mama Experimental Theatre Club, New York;

Jack-Jack, 30 March 1968, Firehouse Theater, Minneapolis;

Massachusetts Trust, 21 August 1968, Spingold Theatre, Brandeis University, Waltham, Mass.;

The Tommy Allen Show, May 1969, College of the Immaculate Heart, Los Angeles; Spring 1971, Actors Studio, New York;

Approaching Simone, 26 February 1970, Boston University, Boston, 4; 4 March 1970, La Mama Experimental Theatre Club, New York, 5;

Nightwalk, by Terry, Sam Shepard, and Jean-Claude van Itallie, 8 September 1973, St. Clement's Church, New York, 15;

Hothouse, 13 February 1974, Circle Repertory Theatre, New York, 6;

The Pioneer, February 1974, Magic Theater, Omaha;

Babes in the Bighouse A Documentary Fantasy Musical about Life inside a Women's Prison, September 1974, Magic Theater, Omaha;

Pro Game, 24 October 1974, Theatre Genesis, New York;

100,001 Horror Stories of the Plains, by Terry, Judith Katz, James Larson, and others, 5 November 1976, Magic Theater, Omaha;

Brazil Fado, 21 January 1977, Magic Theater, Omaha;

American King's English for Queens, March 1978, Magic Theater, Omaha;

Attempted Rescue on Avenue B: A Beat Fifties Comic Opera, 3 March 1979, Chicago Theater Strategy, Chicago;

Goona Goona, 15 November 1979, Magic Theater, Omaha;

Winners, to be produced Spring 1981, Process Theatre, Santa Barbara.

SELECTED BOOKS: *Couplings and Groupings* (New York: Pantheon, 1963);

Calm Down Mother (New York: French, 1966);

Viet Rock and Other Plays (New York: Simon & Schuster, 1967)—also includes *Comings and Goings*, *The Gloaming, Oh My Darling*, and *Keep Tightly Closed in a Cool Dry Place*;

The People vs. Ranchman and Ex-Miss Cooper Queen on a Set of Pills (New York: French, 1968);

The Magic Realists, Sanibel and Captiva, One More Little Drinkie (New York: French, 1970);

Megan Terry's Home: or Future Soap (New York: French, 1972);

Approaching Simone (Old Westbury, N.Y.: Feminist Press, 1973);

Fifteen Million Fifteen Year Olds (Omaha: Magic Theater, 1974);

Henna for Endurance (Omaha: Magic Theater, 1974);

Hospital Play (Omaha: Magic Theater, 1974);

Hothouse (New York: French, 1974);

Two One-Act Plays: Pro Game and Pioneer (Holly Springs, Miss.: Ragnarok Press, 1975);

Sleazing Toward Athens (Omaha: Magic Theater, 1977);

Willa-Willie-Bill's Dope Garden, A Meditation in One-Act on Willa Cather (Birmingham: Ragnarok Press, 1977);

American King's English for Queens (Omaha: Magic Theater, 1978);

100,001 Horror Stories of the Plains (Omaha: Magic Theater, 1978);

Attempted Rescue on Avenue B (Omaha: Magic Theater, 1979);

Babes in the Bighouse (Omaha: Magic Theater, 1979);

Brazil Fado (Omaha: Magic Theater, 1979);

Advances (Omaha: Magic Theater, 1980);

The Trees Blew Down (Omaha: Magic Theater, 1980);

Flat in Afganistan (Omaha: Magic Theater, forthcoming 1981);

Goona Goona (Omaha: Magic Theater, forthcoming 1981);

Katmandu (Omaha: Magic Theater, forthcoming 1981);

Performance Piece (Omaha: Magic Theater, forthcoming 1981);

Winners: The Lives of a Traveling Family Circus and Mother Jones (Omaha: Magic Theater, forthcoming 1981).

Megan Terry came to international prominence in the 1960s as a playwright with the Open Theatre and as the author of *Viet Rock* (1966), America's first play about the Vietnam War. She is a prolific writer, having scripted over fifty musical plays, most of which have been published and produced. In Broadway's terms, her work is experimental and avant-garde—in content she confronts sexuality, politics, and sexual politics; in technique she pushes cultural cliches to extremes in order to expose the attitudes that breed them; in construction she formalizes the acting exercise known as "transformations" to create new dramatic structures. In American popular culture terms, however, her tone and sense of social responsibility are rooted in vaudeville, burlesque, evangelism, and stand-up comedy.

Born Marguerite Duffy in Seattle, Washington, to Harold Joseph Duffy, Jr., and Marguerite Cecelia Henry Duffy, Megan Terry had a "life long ambition . . . to be in the theatre. Of course, it was movies when I was four," she remembers; "it changed to theatre when I was seven." Seattle's Junior League sponsored a program which provided all children in the public schools with inexpensive tickets to see live children's theatre produced by the Seattle Repertory Playhouse, where at the age of seven, Terry had her first formal experience with the theatre: "I went and I looked at the stage and I fell madly in love. I knew I wanted to do that, whatever it was."

She participated in grade school dramatics when not creating theatre in her own backyard and, until the fifth grade (1942-1943), she felt very much a part of the "normal" world. When she was ten years old, however, her father "went to war. All the men went away, and there were only very old men left, and children. For the next four years I defended our home with my six-guns and wooden silver bullets." In the seventh grade she put down her weapons long enough to write, direct, and act in her first musical. "I remember being on stage and getting that terrific rush in the frontal lobes every time the audience laughed. I still get it, and that's one of the main reasons I'm still in it. Theatre is profoundly physically rewarding."

When she was fourteen, she and her sister moved to another town to live with their father. When her father returned to Seattle after World War II, her parents had divorced. The experience was a difficult one. Not sympathetic to the theatre as her mother had been ("He ridiculed my theatrical aspirations by calling me Tallulah Blackhead and Sarah Heartburn"), her father had taught her to survive in the wilderness. Terry remembers, "I caught my first fish at two, cleaned it, cooked it, and ate it. I still prefer to sleep outside whenever possible. I can build shelters and hunt and know how to use wild herbs and berries. My father also taught me to build houses, and I could lay bricks so accurately I didn't need a plumb line: he didn't know how I did it, and I didn't either. It was by feel." She returned to Seattle to live with her grandparents during her last year of high school. Having already read Chekhov and the Irish playwrights, she returned to the theatre she had fallen "madly in love" with at age seven.

The Seattle Repertory Playhouse was run by Florence and Burton James. Florence James, the director, had studied with Stanislavsky. Terry considered Burton James "the greatest actor I'd ever seen—and they believed in community theatre. The theatre was three blocks from my house, so I just hung out there until they took me in. I had a Greek education by the time I was seventeen. . . . It seemed to me that all of human wisdom was collected within the structure of the theatre."

Terry says she was "brought up" in the Seattle Repertory Playhouse; while being tutored by the Jameses she was also being instructed by their resident designer. She had written a junior class show (and played the drunken-clown master of ceremonies who held it all together) and designed, built, and painted the sets for all of the plays produced while she was in high school. She also discovered Gordon Craig and Adolph Appia, and "these two men had an enormous effect on the way I thought about theatre." To this early interest in design (plus the design skills she learned in her mother's florist shop and the building skills she learned from her father and grandfather), Terry attributes her later concern with plays as "structures." To the Jameses' political beliefs she attributes her early and ever-growing association of theatre with politics, remembering that "Mrs. James walked around with a copy of Jefferson under her arm at all times. Jefferson under this arm and an Oval cigarette. When she wasn't directing or lecturing, she ran for office in the Progressive Party." The closing of the Seattle Repertory Theatre under pressure from a state committee investigating un-American activities in 1951, "radicalized" Terry at a very early age. "It also," she says, "impressed me that theatre was pretty powerful if the politicians wanted to close it down."

In addition to their work in Seattle, the Jameses also taught at the Banff School of Fine Arts in Alberta, Canada, and, after graduating from high school in 1950, Terry went to Banff on a theatre scholarship to study acting and directing. That summer, under the stage name Maggie Duffy, she played Hermia in *A Midsummer-Night's Dream*, and in three later summers she played, among other roles, the title role in *Peter Pan* and Kate in *The Taming of the Shrew*. Peter and Kate were her "biggest successes."

She returned to Seattle in the fall of 1950, and enrolled at the University of Washington. (It was during this school year that the Seattle Repertory Playhouse was closed.) The following fall she returned to Canada to enroll as a sophomore at the University of Alberta in Edmonton, where she "met some great English comedians and a terrific comedienne named Myra Benson. Her humor influenced me terrifically; I learned timing from her."

While studying psychology and sociology in Edmonton, and while reading Antonin Artaud (the French director, actor, and aesthetician who evolved ideas about a "Theatre of Cruelty" and believed that theatre should make us alive to the fact that "we are not free. And the sky can still fall on our heads"), she was also designing sets for the university theatre and was technical director for the Edmonton Children's Theatre. It was this backstage experience which made her decide she would rather be a playwright, "responsible for the entire concept of not only what went on stage, but for the whole environment of the audience."

At the end of her second year in Edmonton, her grandfather became ill and she returned to Seattle to be near him. In fall 1953, she reentered the University of Washington to study creative dramatics for children. She also began teaching at the Cornish School of Allied Arts where she organized the Cornish Players. Terry calls the Cornish School, started by Nellie Cornish in the 1920s, "a school where all the arts would be under one roof and hopefully work together." Both Martha Graham and John Cage had taught there, and Nellie Cornish had brought the Jameses to Seattle from New York City. By teaching at the Cornish School, Terry was continuing in their tradition.

Remembering her own introduction to the Seattle Repertory Playhouse, she did not limit participation in the Cornish Players to students at the

Megan Terry

school; she remembers that she "went out in the street and got people," taking "anyone who was willing and began to train them to act, from teenagers to old people." As her experience at the Edmonton Children's Theatre had impressed her with the responsibility of the playwright to the theatre, so her experience with the Cornish Players impressed her with the responsibility of the playwright to children: "I got sick of the children's plays I was doing. They were what the people, the sponsors, wanted, but they had nothing to do with children as I knew them. . . . my first plays were. . . . improvisations I wrote up, dealing with sex as candidly as the children I knew did. I did a program of these plays, made adults buy them sight-unseen, and forbade any adult to view the plays with the kids. You never heard kids laugh so hard in your life. That clinched it for me about becoming a playwright."

Three of the improvisations she "wrote up" were produced in the spring of 1955: Seattle's KING-TV premiered *The Dirt Boat*, the Cornish Players premiered *Beach Grass* and *Seascape*; and the Cornish School's adult program premiered a fourth script, *Go Out and Move the Car*. Terry directed each production, but she did not claim authorship: "I made up outlandish names for the plays I wrote. One of them was 'Guinevere Boog.' I did it for two reasons. One because I thought it was presumptuous of me to be writing plays, and two because they were very sexy plays and I was afraid my colleagues would jump on me if they found out I wrote them." She calls *Go Out and Move the Car* "a comedy about a couple who tries to coerce each other with everything they've got to get the other one to go out and move the car." Acknowledging the influence of "Jackie Gleason and the early Honeymooner shows," she adds, "The head of the school said that the play was fit only for a burlesque house, which delighted me. That's where I'd have liked to have been anyway."

Terry resigned from the Cornish School, graduated from the University of Washington with a B.Ed. in June 1956, returned to Banff on a scholarship where she was awarded certificates in acting, directing, and design, and thus ended her affiliation with educational and theatrical institutions of the Northwest: "I decided New York would be more hospitable to the direction I felt I had to take my theatre work, and it was."

She had already changed her name for the last time ("Megan" from the Celtic root for "Marguerite," and "Terry" from the earth—*terra*—and from actress Ellen Terry), but it was not until 1958, when she had been in New York City for two years, and had written four more plays that, with some friendly encouragement, Megan Terry decided she *was* a playwright. "I wrote in secret and wouldn't tell anybody. It was involved with this whole thing of 'women shouldn't be able to do that.' Since I felt that playwrights were the pinnacle of civilization, for me to aspire to that seemed out of reach. But two of my friends found one of my plays [*Hothouse*, begun in Seattle and finished in New York] and took it to my agent [Elisabeth Marton]. She called me up and I went to her house and she kissed me on the forehead and said, 'You're talented.' I've cost her money ever since."

The first play she wrote after arriving in New York City was *Ex-Miss Copper Queen on a Set of Pills.* Based on a story Terry heard from a prostitute, a former Miss Cotton Queen, the basic situation involves two eccentric old lady garbage pickers who come upon a dying, drunken, pill-popping, good-hearted young whore in a back alley at dawn. The playwright explores the problems encountered by these women who have been uprooted from the West (as she had been) when their values clash with the vicissitudes of living in New York City. Terry was fascinated with the prostitutes she met, who

"took all kinds of drugs to do what they had to do to live." She was simultaneously fascinated with the garbage pickers who lived in her Lower East Side neighborhood; they worked very hard and kept to rigorous schedules, a life-style familiar to Terry because, she says, "the American Work Ethic was drilled into my head from the time I was little by my pioneer grandparents."

It was seven years before *Ex-Miss Copper Queen on a Set of Pills* was produced by the Playwrights' Unit (Edward Albee, Richard Barr, and Clinton Wilder) Off Broadway at the Cherry Lane Theatre on 24 January 1963; it was performed again in 1968 at the Players Workshop in New York. Reviewing the 1968 production, Robert Pasolli referred to Terry's play as "a good little one-act encounter play, in which Miss Terry's abilities at melodrama, comedy, character portrayal, and dramatic tension are eminently visible because they are conventionally conceived." He thought the play seemed to Terry's later work what "an early representational painting by an abstract expressionist" would be to the painter's more mature canvases: "you notice, perhaps with relief, that the artist really can draw after all, and then you forget it, for the throb and the life are all in the abstract work."

Between 1953 and 1960, Terry wrote four full-length realistic plays: the original version of *Hothouse*, written between 1953 and 1958, a full-length version of *Seascape* in 1957, *Avril and Helen* in 1958, and an early version of *Attempted Rescue on Avenue B* in 1959. Wanting to write a play about American business, however (inspired by her experience in a low-paying office job in Connecticut), she decided realism took too "bloody long to make a point if you use it as the only style in a play. I needed more ways of talking. I wanted to write a play using realism magically, but also ironically and politically, because these businessmen get to thinking they're magic after a while. . . ."

She called her play about the dangers of Big Business *The Magic Realists.* The subject is America's economic power structure, the mentalities it breeds and destroys, and the physical and emotional violence it perpetrates, but the tone is vaudevillean. The plot is a linear cartoon: T. P. Chester, sole executive of an interplanetary cartel, wants a "replica" to whom he can leave his business; none of his fourteen children (all named after banks) is suitable, so he advertises and finds his replacement in a young thief and murderer. Exploding the plot with dream sequences and songs, Terry knew she had found "a new style and a new way to deal with my experience."

This new style was not immediately realized in

production, however. When *The Magic Realists* premiered as an Open Theatre performance at La Mama Experimental Theatre Club in the winter of 1966, *Village Voice* reviewer Michael Smith thought that "as directed by Tom Bissinger, the play was incomprehensible and often irritating. Crucially lacking was a locus of reality or a clear link to the real world." Terry agreed that the production's confusion was based, ironically, in the director's and lead actor's insistence on realism: "I wanted T. P. to be a 'clown' businessman, a la Groucho Marx, Bert Lahr, or W. C. Fields, but it was produced before living American comic forms had come into double theatrical use."

The Magic Realists was composed in Connecticut (1960), where Terry had gone to rewrite *Hothouse* for production. Among other problems, her producers did not like the revisions, and *Hothouse* was not produced at that time, but it was this would-be production association which led to the premiere of *Ex-Miss Copper Queen on a Set of Pills* in 1963. Joseph Chaikin and Michael Smith attended the premiere; "they came back stage and said, 'We like your writing,'" Terry recalls. "Then they walked me home and said, 'You know, we can't stand the commercial theater. Do you want to come with us? We want to start some kind of a group that will make it possible to live. Because it's impossible to live in the commercial theater as it's set up in New York.' I said, 'Sure.' And then we began the Open Theater."

According to Pasolli, "The Open Theater limped into existence during the first half of 1963." At the first meeting on 1 February, "seventeen actors and four writers declared themselves to be a new theater group, did some warm-up exercises and two improvisations, and then went across the street for coffee." That fall, when Jean-Claude van Itallie was introduced to the Open Theatre, he found it an oasis in New York. The opportunity it created for actors, directors, playwrights, and critics to interact was unique, and the Open Theatre became, in van Itallie's words, "a workshop in which was eventually hammered out a new style of acting and directing to go with a new style of play."

A major element of the "new style" was the transformation technique, a familiar acting exercise to students of Viola Spolin, an innovative teacher of children and amateur adults who legitimized the use of theatre games and improvisations as tools of actor training. Transformations exploded the aesthetic and political conventions of realism or "naturalism," which Chaikin opposed because "the mode of behavior which a theater chooses to emphasize is a political choice, whatever the content.

Naturalism corresponds to the programmed responses of our daily life—to a life style which is in accord with the political gestalt of the time. To accept naturalism is to accept society's limits." Terry agreed.

One of the limits the Open Theatre wanted to transcend was the conceptual prison which defines a human being in terms of a single "personality" or "role"; their premise was that we are each (always) many-faceted aggregates of dramatic contradictions: change is always possible. To explore this premise theatrically, the rules of the transformation exercise require actors to be constantly and improvisationally alive to changes: each must respond, in kind, to spontaneous changes of action, or circumstance (time and/or place), or character. "It's the simple way children play," Terry explains. "You have a broomstick: this broomstick is a horse, is a magic carpet, is a rocket ship, is a gun, is a witch, is a broomstick. In the folk tales: I'm enchanted, I'm magic; I kiss you and you will turn into a frog, I kiss you again and you will turn into a Prince. It's all of *play*. It's just taking how children play and doing it on an adult level." As a writer, she had used transformations as early as 1955 in her TV play, *Dirt Boat*. Now, in community with other artists of similar interests, she returned to this technique and began to build plays as series of action blocs rather than as sequences of motivationally connected scenes.

Calm Down Mother and *Keep Tightly Closed in a Cool Dry Place* are two of Terry's most popular one-act transformation plays. In the former, three performers portray eight different character relationships in eight separate action blocs, each demonstrating a different aspect of relationships among women. The first bloc proclaims what is possible for a woman to achieve (active acceptance of the universe as a "living loving blinding mind"); the next six demonstrate the limitations women actually endure; the last suggests the source of those limitations. ("Our bodies Our bellies Our funnies Our eggies The eggies in our beggies are enough ARE THEY?")

When it was premiered by the Open Theatre on a double bill with *Keep Tightly Closed* at the Sheridan Square Playhouse on 29 March 1965, Pasolli reacted to *Calm Down Mother* as "a wildly funny and touching play," "imaginatively directed" and "impressively acted." After reading it, Ross Wetzsteon not only found it "a very funny and perceptive series of scenes united by the technique of 'transformations'"; he also thought "each scene taken individually, is remarkable."

Terry dedicated *Calm Down Mother*, subtitled *A Transformation Play for Three Women*, to the women in the Open Theatre who premiered it. She dedicated *Keep Tightly Closed*, a transformation play for three men (which some critics think is her most finely crafted play), to Joseph Chaikin. It was inspired by a story she read while in Minneapolis on an Office of Advance Drama Research grant in 1964 (she received another OADR grant in 1969): "There was a little paragraph in the newspaper about these men being in the same prison who'd been involved in the same murder, and they were going to have to break them up and transfer them to three different prisons because they were starting to hurt each other. So I just said, 'What if they were in the same cell?' "

In her production notes, Terry encourages directors and actors to bring their own realities to the script: "The play can be directed literally or as a fantasy or dream. . . . The director should decide if a murder *has* been committed, or if it is the desire *to* commit the murder, or if it is a dramatization of relief" and self-forgiveness. "Did he do it or not? The challenge of the play, aside from the doing of it, is to decide between the four involved, the director and the players, what matters to you." What matters to Terry, with any play, is the moment of engagement—for the actors with the script, for the audience with the production. Her scripts are catalysts for the moment of live theatre experience, not documents to be catalogued in the archives of literary history.

Because she is a theatrical writer rather than a purely literary one, successful productions of her plays demand the engagement of a director who feels a visceral connection to her theatrical vision. Sidney Schubert Walter, an early member of the Open Theatre, was such a director. In the 1965-1966 season of the Minneapolis Firehouse Theater, he directed a double bill of *Keep Tightly Closed* and the premiere production of *The Gloaming, Oh My Darling*. Written is 1965, *The Gloaming* is an expansion of one of the scenes in *Calm Down Mother*. Terry uses the transformation technique in this long one-act play to illuminate a single situation—two old women in a nursing home. Don Rubin has referred to this technique as Terry's "prismatic vision," van Itallie compares it to impressionism in painting, and Peter Feldman describes her method as "theatrical cubism."

The Gloaming is about the escapades and sentimental memory-fantasies of two old women, their engaging preoccupation with the sexual, and their attempts to cope with institutional routine and each other while they try to hide an old man they have kidnapped from the men's ward for one last fling.

Vickie Smith reported that "Miss Terry's completely open, unabashed wit brought consistent laughter from the audience" as they watched "the compassionate, subjective probing of the individual mind and spirit to expose some of the more hidden, often shamefully guarded, aspects of the personality."

Comings and Goings, yet another kind of transformation play, combines ever-changing situations, with ever-changing performers. The subject that unifies these transformations is male-female relationships. The unifying theme is the evanescence of such relationships but, as the play's subtitle *A Theater Game* implies, it "is meant for both actors and audience to be an enjoyment of technique—pure virtuosity on the part of the actors." Any production technique is permissible as long as the script is treated as play; Terry likes to think of a script "as a trampoline for actors and director." Premiered by the Open Theatre at the Cafe La Mama in April of 1966, *Comings and Goings* delighted New York reviewers, as well as Minneapolis and Los Angeles reviewers of later productions.

Essentially a virtuoso demonstration of techniques developed within the Open Theatre, *Comings and Goings* was nevertheless scripted outside the group. *Viet Rock* (1966) was the first play (since she "wrote up" children's improvisations in Seattle) which Terry wrote to express group as well as personal interests, the first "collaboration play" for her and for the Open Theatre, and her first play created *within* a workshop situation. The subject of this first collaboration, the Vietnam War, was an almost inevitable development of the Open Theatre's growing political interests.

"To understand about violence," Terry formed an all-day-Saturday workshop which met weekly for six months during 1965-1966. As a collaboration, *Viet Rock* grew out of this workshop "combined with the exploration of acting techniques discovered by Joseph Chaikin in his Monday workshops." The Saturday workshops, however, were devoted solely to exploring the actors' and the playwright's feelings as they related to the war in Vietnam. Her workshop techniques were improvisational methods she learned from Florence James, story-telling methods she learned from her mother and grandmother, and creative dramatics methods she learned at the University of Washington from Agnes Haaga and her cousin, Geraldine Sims. One of the actors in the workshops was Gerome Ragni who, inspired by the content and process of the experience, later collaborated with James Rado to create *Hair* (1967). "We used mate-

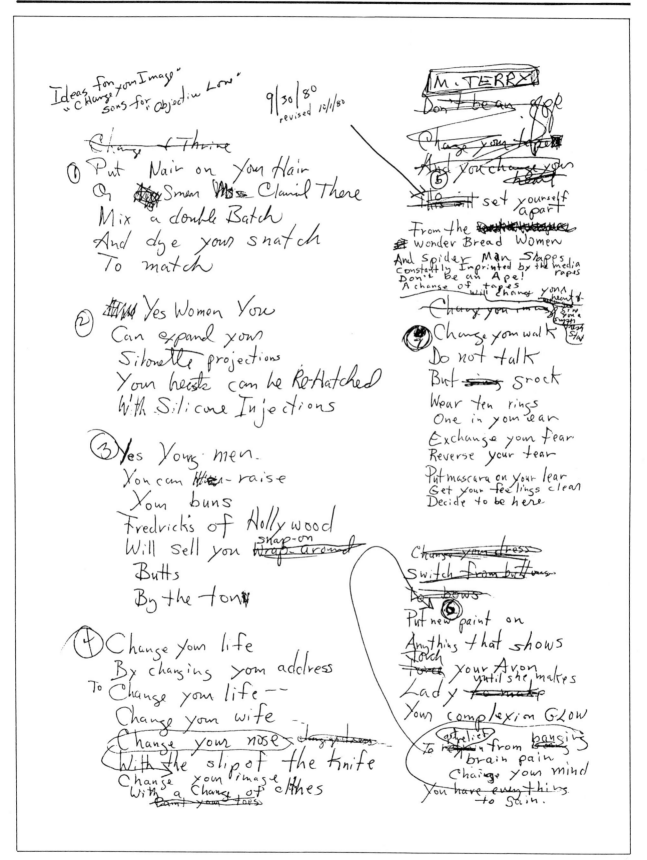

Lyrics for "Change Your Image," first draft

rial that bombarded us everyday from television and newspapers," Terry remembers. "We acted out personal stories and tried to get to the roots of our drives toward anger and aggression." "We pooled our fears, our violence, our knowledge, . . . to show our concern, our confusion, our anger, and our hope. . . . Through improvisation and acting exercises, guided by me, we evolved a script. The script was written and rewritten and rewritten and edited and shaped—not only by me, but by the exigencies of day-to-day events."

Viet Rock premiered at the Cafe La Mama on 21 May 1966 (Armed Forces Day), directed by Joseph Chaikin, Peter Feldman, and Terry. The production received favorable notices in the *East Village Other* and the *Village Voice*: "Theater magic!" wrote Jerry Benjamin: "The play isn't in the dialogue, it's ONTHESTAGE in the occurrence of the ensembles' vivid images." The purpose of including the audience in the action, Michael Smith evangelized, "is to reassert the real-life reality of the theater—not as a replica of or comment upon life but as a part of life—and thus restore its urgency and relevance."

The urgency and relevance also impressed Robert Brustein, newly appointed dean of the Yale School of Drama, and he invited cast and directors to come to New Haven that fall to present *Viet Rock* as the first production of Yale's professional season. Its two-week October run was received with mixed but predominantly favorable reviews and, on 10 November, *Viet Rock* opened Off Broadway at the Martinique Theater where it ran for sixty-two performances. Audiences were confronted with many "firsts" in this production. *Viet Rock* was America's first rock musical (the primitive and unamplified music, composed by Marianne du Pury, proved that popular folk-rock music could be adapted to the American musical form), the first realized theatre statement about the Vietnam War, the first play to expose transformations to a relatively wide commercial audience, and the first play in which actors left the stage to go into the house and touch the audience.

Because it was unprecedented in such a variety of ways, many critics found their expectations of an "anti-war" play unfulfilled and some deemed it a total failure. John Simon, for example, thought it was an "abject flop," Alfred Kazin thought it was "intense but harmless"; Catherine R. Hughes thought it failed through "lack of talent"; Harold Clurman called it inept, unoriginal, strained, and pretentious; and for Walter Kerr, "Not one cogent thing [was] said. . . ."

Subtitled *A Folk War Movie*, *Viet Rock* was meant to be a catalogue of cliches, conscientiously chosen to demonstrate the disparity between the reality of war and contemporary American attitudes toward it, attitudes expressed in habitual media-propagated language. Albert Bermel heard sound itself as a basic structural unit in *Viet Rock*: "Her vaudeville . . . consists of jagged, incomplete sentences, incantation, mountains of rhetorical slog, fierce ballads, footstamping, . . . and wisps of poetry that float out into silence and lightly collide. Miss Terry's is a theater of onomatopoeia, not sound as sense, though, rather sound as impressionism, an auditory *pointilliste* palette." A Minneapolis reviewer, Al McConagha, found Walter's 1968 Firehouse Theater production "a provocative, frequently wildly funny, series of theatrical metaphors," and Bradford F. Swan called the 1966 Yale production "completely fluid, one sequence . . . blending into another, with the biting, acidulous humor pervading everything and cementing its parts."

So earnest was Terry in creating *Viet Rock*, that she thought it would stop the war. Not only did the war continue—undeclared—until 1974, but some of her fellow writers berated her "for not writing something more timeless." The CIA and FBI taped the show and interviewed her, and even organizations who wanted to support the play tried to change it. In spite of all the pressure and in spite of the quantity of negative critical response, however, *Viet Rock* remains the best known of Megan Terry's plays; now listed in the Samuel French catalogue under "Popular Favorites," it has been widely translated.

Viet Rock was her first and last collaboration with the Open Theatre; Terry ended her close association with the group in 1967, and returned to Yale on an ABC "Writing for the Camera" Fellowship. Her next play to be produced was a script written before she joined the Open Theatre and completed the day John F. Kennedy was assassinated. Premiered at the Firehouse Theater in Minneapolis (where it played from 1 April to 6 May 1967) and directed by Walter, *The People vs. Ranchman* received three positive, thoughtfully critical reviews. A year and a half later a commercial production which opened Off Broadway at the Fortune Theatre on 27 October 1968 received five unreserved "pans." Using early transformation techniques and demonstrating her ever-keen wish to expose cliched language and attitudes, *The People vs. Ranchman* is, in Terry's summary, "a treatment of the criminal-as-star and how the Right and the Left will take up a personage like Charles Manson, Caryl Chessman, Angela Davis. It's a criticism of *everyone*. There's greed on both sides."

Still wondering if violence is ever justified and whether or not we can "control the fangs in our mouths," Terry began reading about population control and wondered, "What if the entire earth were honey-combed with billions of self-contained rooms and in such rooms lived nine people with all their needs met by dispensers, their communication via television with a central elite government that lived on the moon. They would be born in these rooms, and die in these rooms. They would not be allowed to have a child until one person died. Under these conditions, how would love show itself?"

In the spring of 1967, when channel 13's "New York Television Theater" commissioned her to write a full-length play, she channeled these questions into a futuristic soap opera called *Home: or Future Soap*. When officials for National Educational Television saw the script, they offered to coproduce it and, on 19 January 1968, *Home* received its nationwide television premiere, the first commissioned play ever presented on "NET Playhouse." George Gent's response was reluctantly positive: "typically feminine," he said, "she seems to prefer the emotional, even violent, expression of ideas, forcing her audience to question themselves. This is irritating, but it is also effective."

Making canny use of television's escapist genres—the soap opera and the science-fiction thriller—Terry seduced viewers into involvement before they realized the subject matter was of immediate relevance. Producer Glenn Jordan received a letter from a viewer grateful that "Someone is finally attempting a serious use of television medium to express something about the human condition of which television itself is a symptom and manifestation."

In contrast to *Home*, which received national exposure, *Changes*—developed with director Tom O'Horgan and the actors at Cafe La Mama—was seen by only one hundred people, one at a time. Each individual "was put into costume," Terry recalls, "and his name was changed. Then he was blindfolded and led by a guide to various spaces and events. Along the way he was talked to, lifted, touched, pushed, and caught. The work ends about a half hour later with the blindfolded person led to a bed where he lies between two nude persons making love. They make no references to him. . . . Then he's carried out and the actors gently call him by his real name, then they hold a mirror to his face and take off the blindfold." "It became an initiation rite

that blew not only the mind, but the body and soul." This unusual theatre piece, in which the audience member rather than the performer transforms, was presented for four evenings in the winter of 1968 at Cafe La Mama.

This interest in transforming audience members by disorienting them was incorporated into the structure and technique of *Jack-Jack*, a two-act rock musical which grew out of a two-and-a-half page script called "The Key Is on the Bottom." In addition to transformations and action blocs, which alternately contain realistic action, media parodies, metaphoric comment, and presentational statements, Terry uses a plethora of media devices— loud speakers, tape recordings, slides, films, psychedelic lights, a multi-leveled set surrounded by projection screens—to impress the audience with the omnipresence of Jack-Jack, a grotesquely affable giant who symbolizes all the repressive forces of society which destroy the individual.

Directed by Walter at the Firehouse Theater, with music by Paul Boesing, *Jack-Jack* (another early rock musical) was an unqualified hit with both audiences and reviewers. Opening on 30 March 1968, it played at the Firehouse until 14 April, was brought to the European Youth Drama Festival in Nancy, France, where it opened on 20 April, presented at Copenhagen and Aarhus, Denmark, and returned to Minneapolis on 11 May to play for four more weeks. Its run was later extended and it was still playing at the end of June, the longest run the Firehouse Theater had known since it opened in 1963. Peter Altman called *Jack-Jack* "a major theatrical event."

In *Jack-Jack*, Terry suggested American repressions might lead to fascism. In her next play, this darkening vision of American politics did not need to look to the future to despair; *Massachusetts Trust* presents a bleak American present underscored by a contemporary character called Prosperity, more insidious and spirit-killing than the giant Jack-Jack. He is so pervasively influential that, no matter how he is opposed "it is too late to make any difference." It is a contemporary morality play, an allegory presented, as one of the characters remarks, as an "orgasmic, volcanic cartoon." Although the play is raw and bitter in tone, its dream sequences contain some of Terry's most powerfully beautiful writing.

Her third collaborative work and her second with Tom O'Horgan, *Massachusetts Trust* was written and produced in the summer of 1968 for Brandeis Interact, the first international experimental theatre festival ever held in America. Terry worked with a company of La Mama actors and twenty students from Brandeis University; O'Horgan directed, wrote the music, and designed the sets. On 21 August 1968, one week after the script was completed, it was premiered as the principal work in the third and final week of the festival. Reviews tallied one unreserved condemnation (from Walter Kerr) and six appreciative critiques.

With "prosperity" still the *spiritus agens* of American culture, Terry moved out of the arena of practical politics and into the studios of establishment media to investigate prosperity's incarnations in the consumerism of both performers and audiences. *The Tommy Allen Show* deals with a live, late-night television talk show, hosted by Tommy Allen. Not only was Terry interested in the ritual in which live television audiences participate, she was also intrigued by the ritual form and content home viewers return to, night after night: "I spent a whole year looking at talk shows with the sound off. They're Comedies of Manners. They are ways of being and not being together, and it's so formal: how they behave and all the gestures and body language. They also have certain ways of talking: they start to get close and then they back off; and there are always triple and quadruple sexual entendres. They're really very sexy, but it's so hidden.

Megan Terry

What is really behind all of this very formalized and distant sexuality? What's really being sold to us through these talk shows?"

Terry examined these questions by pushing the talk-show format, complete with commercials that sell "good and evil," to a cartoonlike extreme; her handling of the cliched media rituals was so skilled that the audience, Dan Sullivan wrote, "as doesn't always happen in New Theater, could go and truly enjoy the author's bizarre fragmentation of [these rituals]." The themes that emerge from this fragmentation technique—such as sexuality, identity, marriage, commercialism, and the rituals of the media itself—confront American sexism and violence.

When it premiered in Los Angeles in May of 1969, *The Tommy Allen Show: LA* was billed as a work-in-progress. Terry had been invited to direct it at the College of the Immaculate Heart and, though the piece was basically completed before she arrived, she continued to build on it with her student actors even after it began its brief public run. In the summer of 1970, *The Tommy Allen Show: Omaha* was produced by the Magic Theater in Omaha, Nebraska, and in the spring of 1971, New York City's Actors Studio performed *The Tommy Allen Show: NY*.

Fragmented identity and repressed sexuality are subjects traceable in Terry's writings to *Ex-Miss Copper Queen on a Set of Pills*; fourteen years later she wrote *Approaching Simone* (1970). Simone Weil, born female, French, and Jewish, was a philosopher whose intense desire was to be an active and responsible citizen of Western civilization. Early in her life she wrote for socialist and Communist magazines, was active in the Spanish Civil War, and, after an epiphany, converted to Catholicism; much of her published work focused on metaphysical issues and the relationships between spirituality and politics.

Physically frail, she lived passionately, graced with an intuitive sense of social responsibility. She struggled much of her life to justify in her mind what she felt in her heart—that it is every person's right to have good done to her or him. Combined with her determination to grow beyond the limits imposed on her because she was a woman, her candid appraisal of herself and of the world pervades all her writing.

It is the struggle behind these writings that Terry dramatized in *Approaching Simone*, highlighting in events from Weil's life the development of her mind and spirit from the time she was five years old until 1943 when, at the age of thirty-four, she died of starvation refusing to eat as long as

World War II soldiers were starving at the front. In the play, Simone exemplifies the gradual liberation of a woman as she transforms herself into a creative person by the concentrated efforts of her own will. Terry makes this process theatrical by having all roles but Simone's played by ever-transforming members of the ensemble; Simone alone remains intransigently herself and thus, as supporting characters change with changing circumstances of her life, audience attention is focused on her struggle with herself.

Simone is not only the first self-aware protagonist to appear in Terry's plays, but the first heroic figure as well and, though Terry had known about Weil for almost as long as she had been writing plays, it took her "fifteen years to develop the form to contain the technique to express the breadth and humanity of this modern hero." The result is a play unique in Terry's oeuvre, rare in the history of dramatic literature, and critics unanimously applauded the achievement. Jack Kroll's enthusiasm is representative: "It is a rare theatrical event for these hysterical and clownish times, a truly serious play, filled with the light, shadow and weight of human life, and the exultant agonies of the ceaseless attempt to create one's humanity."

Terry finished *Approaching Simone* for presentation at the centennial of Boston University, where it premiered 26 February 1970. Directed by Maxine Klein, the play was performed by Boston University students; the production played only four nights, through 1 March. At Ellen Stewart's invitation, it moved to La Mama Experimental Theatre Club on 4 March. After a total of nine performances, only five of which were in New York City, *Approaching Simone* won the Obie Award for Best New Play of 1969-1970.

The role of Simone was played by JoAnn Schmidman who, in the summer of 1968, founded the Omaha Magic Theater in Nebraska. When cast as Simone, she was working for her B.F.A. at Boston University, and subsequently, having received the degree, she joined the Open Theatre to perform as a company member in their last three works: *Terminal*, *The Mutation Show*, and *Nightwalk*. Terry, although not a regular member of the company since 1967, had continued her interest in the theatre's work and was a contributing writer (with Sam Shepard and van Itallie) to their final production, *Nightwalk* (1973). This company piece, a theatrical exploration of waking and sleeping in America, attempted to bring dreams back into communal consciousness. Terry wrote the "Dinner with the Boss" scene in which Schmidman played the Hostess.

The Open Theatre completed its final tour and disbanded in December 1973; in January 1974, Terry moved to Omaha to join artistic director Schmidman as playwright-in-residence at the Magic Theater. They gathered around them—training those who were committed but unskilled—a company of people interested in acting, directing, writing, visual arts, music—and dedicated to developing new American musical plays. Located in a long, narrow store-front in downtown Omaha, the Magic Theater is a laboratory theatre seating from 25 to 100 people, operated by company members, and surviving on public grants, private contributions, the revenue from touring productions, and community support. With an on-going company at her disposal, Terry can pursue her interest in writing ensemble plays, an interest inspired by her outrage in New York at the "Typecasting Syndrome": "I consciously set to work to write plays so it wouldn't matter what type you were as long as you had the talent to play the part." Most of the scripts she has written since moving to Omaha have been produced by the Magic Theater and directed by Schmidman.

Two scripts she had written twenty years before, however, both realistic in form and both autobiographical in content, premiered elsewhere. *Hothouse*, originally scripted in 1953-1954 and rewritten in the early 1960s, won the Stanley Drama Award in 1964 and (after yet another rewrite) finally received its premiere production 13 February 1974 at the Circle Repertory Theatre in New York City. The play focuses on the relationships of three generations of women—Jody (based on Terry), her mother Roz, and Ma Sweetlove, her grandmother. This Irish-American family of women lives in a small fishing village near Seattle. It is a play of contrasts: the relationships suffocate and nourish, they provide warmth and humor as well as shock and pain. The characters, Richard Christiansen wrote, "make *Hothouse* boil with vitality. Lusty and free-wheeling, the script rushes along with the humor and lyricism of a rousing folk song." Emory Lewis thought it showed "a hint of O'Neill, laced with O'Casey's gift of mixing comedy and tragedy in a heady blend." "There aren't many American playwrights with such versatility," agreed Martin Gottfried, "with Terry's amazing combination of techniques, poetry, intelligence, stage sense and most of all, soul."

Subtitled *A Beat Fifties Comic Opera*, *Attempted Rescue on Avenue B* is set in New York City in the late 1950s, that period of Terry's life which was "like walking into a burning building." Twenty years after it was first scripted (and after several rewrites), *Attempted Rescue on Avenue B* was staged 3 March 1979 by the Chicago Theater Strategy. While it examines the relationship between an actress and an action painter (akin to Jackson Pollock), their relationships to their individual art, their friendships with other painters and actors and Beat poets, their struggle to love self and others, and the rise of political consciousness, it is also the portrait of a woman discovering herself as an artist. "People think that the fifties are 'Grease' and 'Happy Days,' " Terry complains. But "the whole Beat Generation arose, American Jazz came of age. . . . The sixties could not have been so brilliant or such a revolution without the work that went on in the fifties."

Likewise, Terry's work in the 1970s is rooted in her growth in the 1950s and 1960s. Michael Feingold writes about *The Pioneer*, for example, that "the preoccupations are the same as those in Megan Terry's large play *Hothouse*—the way parents pressure children into certain roles, by instruction and examples; the way society uses this pressure, making the home an horrific training ground for the horrific larger world." Other themes are re-sounded as well, says Feingold: "the disappearance of private space in an overpopulated world (*Home*); the obsessiveness of the consumer mentality (*Copper Queen*, and to some extent *Keep Tightly Closed*)." *The Pioneer* premiered in February 1974 at the Magic Theater as one of the several "family" plays Terry wrote in the 1970s. In this short two-character play set in an upper-middle-class dressing room, "a late-period Joan Crawford-style mother" tries to convince her daughter to get married.

Written in reaction to the football fervor Terry encountered when she arrived in Omaha, *Pro Game* is set in a working-class living room as a mother and three sons watch football on television. It premiered in New York City, 24 October 1974, at the Theatre Genesis. "Explosive theater," wrote New York reviewer Holly Beye, "wrought by a playwright of enormous theatrical control." Le Roy Perkins, a reviewer of a later Magic Theater production, called the play an "outrageous exposition of America's fascination with sports as a channeling of otherwise repressed sexuality."

The first full-length script Terry developed at the Magic Theater was *Babes in the Bighouse*. Written after more than a year of concentrated research, including visits to women's reformatories and interviews with inmates, *Babes in the Bighouse* premiered at the Magic Theater in September of 1974. The production was met with enthusiastic reviews. In addition to its B-movie title, the play is sub-titled *A Documentary Fantasy Musical about Life inside a Women's Prison*. Terry is again playing with contrasts: Gary Schweikhart saw the scaffold set as "a cross between Alcatraz and Hollywood Squares." Steve Jordan found the situations "so funny they're sad, so tragic they're hilarious," and he described the transformations, the basis of the play's structure, as "shifts from pathos to satire to parody to Broadway revue-style numbers."

When the production toured the East Coast, a Philadelphia reviewer, Victor Livingston, recognized Terry's purpose in using "razor-honed, sardonic gallows humor to coax sympathy and understanding from an audience without bludgeoning them with polemic vitriol," so that her theme, "the dehumanization of incarcerated people aided and abetted by sexist stereotyping and sadism. . . . comes across with even greater power and urgency"; thus "the play transcends the particular in its application to all persons stripped of their uniqueness and emotions by society's institutional attempts at behavior modification." Given the weight of the political issues in *Babes in the Bighouse*, he was thankful that "humor in the theater is the playwright's vehicle."

Meanwhile, Terry was conducting regular playwriting workshops for Magic Theater company members, most of whom were native midwesterners committed to their prairie community and its roots. They began to collect stories and songs of their ancestors' survival on the plains; *100,001 Horror Stories of the Plains* emerged from their research. As playwright-in-residence, Terry edited this patchwork quilt of true accounts, family histories, folklore, tall tales, poems, and songs which included contributions from over forty writers—not only writers from the Magic Theater (Judith Katz, James Larson, and Terry herself), but from "folks" in Nebraska, Iowa, Kansas, Colorado, and South Dakota as well. When the play premiered, 5 November 1976, the price of admission was a potluck dish for a supper shared by performers and audiences (which often included generations of families). The stories and songs of the play merged easily with this shared meal. The play was a popular success; Omaha reviewer Dan Taylor spoke for the audience when he said, "We share the Magic Theater's amazement that these pioneers—misled, mistreated, and misunderstood—survived at all only to spawn the television slaves of today."

Always alive to our television culture, Terry had been commissioned by WNET-NY to write another television script. *Brazil Fado* was written as a double-channel experiment: two different action lines were to be broadcast from two stations at the same time, necessitating watching at home on two television sets. Written when commissioned in 1972, it was never produced as a television project because "of political content," according to Schmidman. The play was transposed to the stage, as an hour-long one-act, which the Magic Theater premiered on 21 January 1977. "Operating on two physical levels, the play shows an American couple on a high platform engaged in sexual sado-masochism. On the floor a team of newspeople, movie stars, Brazilian peasants, and torture police enact recent violence in Brazil"—the physical and political rape of the Brazilian people. Reviewer LeRoy Perkins thought the production probed "brutality and sex with adroit commentary."

In 1978, Terry explored the brutality and sexism of language in *American King's English for Queens*, a musical, premiering at the Magic Theater in March. *American King's English for Queens* is another "family" play, the format being that of an all-American upper-middle-class family situation comedy. Mom and Dad send the children on a snipe hunt, which Dan Taylor found to be "the perfect metaphor for our futile pursuit of words that say exactly what we feel"; the children find a child raised by prairie dogs and try to teach her English. In that process, Terry exposes the interrelationship between language and sex roles and the effect of language on the status of women.

Pushing the cliche of the family sit-com even further, Terry combines this banal television staple with traditional Punch-and-Judy puppets, Buster-Keaton pratfalls, and burlesque slapstick to explore family abuse in *Goona Goona* (about the upper-middle-class Goon family). Billed in the premiere program (15 November 1979) as a "comic gymnastic extravaganza," *Goona Goona* contains bold images of traditional comic violence to analyze the sensitive issues of child and wife abuse and violence among children.

Some of Terry's scripts, especially those developed with companies, are published with a focus on performance rather than enduring literary merit. They remain rich theatrical resources for committed companies of performers and directors with clear visions and wills to edit. As she encouraged producers of *Keep Tightly Closed*, the challenge is in deciding "what matters to you."

Megan Terry says that nowhere does the moon shine so low and the sky seem so beautiful as in Omaha. She has always been happiest living in a community of artists and plans to continue her work

with the Magic Theater believing, as she wrote in 1968, that theatre artists must create plays "to bring people together for an entertainment, a celebration, a living theater to put down the fear and anguish that have got too many people in America by the throat."

–*Phyllis Jane Rose*

Television Scripts:
The Dirt Boat, Seattle, KING-TV, Spring 1955;
Home: or Future Soap, "NET Playhouse," PBS, 19 January 1968;
One More Little Drinkie, PBS, November 1969;
"Women and Law," (series of four half-hour shows), Nebraska Public TV, 1976.

Radio Scripts:
Sanibel and Captiva, Boston, WGBH, 1968;
American Wedding Ritual, "Earplay," National Public Radio, 1972;
Fireworks, "Earplay," National Public Radio, 1980.

Other:
Massachusetts Trust, in *The Off-Off Broadway Book*, ed. Albert Poland and Bruce Mailman (Indianapolis: Bobbs-Merrill, 1972), pp. 281-303;
Nightwalk, by Terry, Sam Shepard, and Jean-Claude van Itallie, in *Three Works by the Open Theater*, ed. Karen Malpede (New York: Drama Book Specialists, 1974), pp. 135-150;
"Janis Joplin," in *Notable American Women: The Modern Period*, ed. Barbara Sicherman and Carol Hurd Green (Cambridge: Harvard University Press, 1980).

Periodical Publications:
Introduction to *Viet Rock* and *Viet Rock*, *Tulane Drama Review*, II (Fall 1966): 196-227;
"Cool Is Out! Uptight Is Out!," *New York Times*, 14 January 1968, II:17;
"Who Says Only Words Make Great Drama?," *New York Times*, 10 November 1968, II: 1, 3;
"The Tommy Allen Show," *Scripts*, 1 (December 1971): 36-61;
"American Experimental Theater Then and Now," *Performing Arts Journal*, 2 (Fall 1977): 13-24;
"Two Pages a Day," *Drama Review*, 21 (December, 1977): 59-64;
"Playwriting in Omaha," *Southwest Review* (Fall 1980).

References:

Peter Altman, " 'Jack-Jack' Sets Excitement Mark," *Minneapolis Star*, 8 May 1968, p. 20;

Clive Barnes, "Stage: Terry's Simone," *New York Times*, 9 March 1970, p. 43;

Barnes, "Theater: *The People vs. Ranchman*," *New York Times*, 28 October 1968, p. 56;

Albert Bermel, "The Sound of Viet Nam," *New Leader*, 21 November 1966, p. 31;

Harold Clurman, "Theater," *Nation*, 203 (28 November 1966): 587;

Peter Feldman, "Notes for *Keep Tightly Closed*," in *Viet Rock and Other Plays*, p. 204;

George Gent, "TV: The Sterilized Nightmare of Megan Terry," *New York Times*, 20 January 1968, p. 59;

Henry Hewes, "Massachusetts Untrussed," *Saturday Review*, 50 (21 September 1968): 28;

Catherine R. Hughes, "The Theater Goes to War," *America*, 116 (20 May 1967): 759;

Alfred Kazin, "*Viet Rock*: 'I'm-Not-Afraid-to-Mention-Anything,' " *Vogue*, 149 (January 1967): 52;

Kevin Kelly, "Unforgettable Theater," *Boston Globe*, 22 August 1968, p. 49;

Walter Kerr, "The Theater: *Viet Rock*," *New York Times*, 11 November 1966, p. 38;

Kerr, "To Boo or Not to Boo—That Is Not the Question," *New York Times*, 1 September 1968, II: 1, 3;

Kerr, "Where Do You Draw the Line," *New York Times*, 10 November 1968, II: 5;

Jack Kroll, "New Baloney," *Newsweek*, 72 (11 November 1968): 121;

Kroll, "Waiting on God," *Newsweek*, 75 (16 March 1970): 64;

Elenore Lester, "At Yale: Joy, Baby, Joy," *New York Times*, 9 October 1966, II: 3;

Magic Dust, special Terry issues, 2 (Spring 1977); 2 (Fall 1977);

"New Plays: Gut Theater," *Time*, 92 (8 November 1968): 94;

Edith Oliver, "The Theater: Off Broadway," *New Yorker*, 44 (9 November 1968), 115-123;

Robert Pasolli, *A Book on the Open Theater* (New York: Bobbs-Merrill, 1970);

Stanley Richards, "Megan Terry," in his *The Best Short Plays of 1968* (New York: Chilton, 1968): 329;

Richard Schechner, "An Interview with Joseph Chaikin," *Drama Review*, 13 (Spring 1969): 141-144;

John Simon, "Theater Chronicle," *Hudson Review*, 20 (Spring 1967): 108;

Michael Smith, "Theater Journal: *The People vs. Ranchman*," *Village Voice*, 18 May 1967, p. 23;

Dan Sullivan, "Megan Terry's *Tommy Allen* a Player's Play," *Los Angeles Times Calendar*, 15 June 1969, p. 26;

Sullivan, "Theater: Even Minnesota; Avant-Garde 'Jack-Jack' a Hit," *New York Times*, 23 June 1968, p. 74;

Jean-Claude van Itallie, "The Open Theater," in *Theater 2: American Theater, 1968-1969* (New York: International Theater Institute, 1970), p. 83-86;

van Itallie, "Playwright at Work: Off-Off-Broadway," *Tulane Drama Review*, 10 (Summer 1966): 154-158;

Phyllis Jane Wagner, Introduction to *Approaching Simone* (Old Westburg, N.Y.: Feminist Press, 1973), pp. 9-34;

Bernard Weiner, "Love, Pain and Booze in Megan Terry's *Hothouse*," *San Francisco Chronicle*, 20 March 1979, p. 43;

Ross Wetzsteon, "Books: *Eight Plays from Off-Off Broadway*," *Village Voice*, 9 March 1967, p. 30.

JEAN-CLAUDE VAN ITALLIE
(25 May 1936-)

SELECTED PRODUCTIONS: *War*, 22 December 1963, Vandam Theatre, New York;

The Hunter and the Bird, Fall 1964, Sheridan Square Playhouse, New York;

Almost Like Being, February 1965, Sheridan Square Playhouse and Vandam Theatre, New York;

I'm Really Here, February 1965, Sheridan Square Playhouse and Vandam Theatre, New York;

Pavane, April 1965, Sheridan Square Playhouse and La Mama Experimental Theatre Club, New York, and Academy Theatre, Atlanta; produced again as *Interview*, in *America Hurrah* (*Interview, TV*, and *Motel*), 6 November 1966, Pocket Theatre, New York, 634 [performances];

America Hurrah, April 1965, La Mama Experimental Theatre Club, New York; produced again as *Motel*, in *America Hurrah* (*Interview, TV*, and *Motel*), 7 November 1966, Pocket Theatre, New York, 634;

Dream, December 1965, La Mama Experimental Theatre Club, New York; revised as *Where Is De Queen?*, March 1966, Firehouse Theatre, Minneapolis;

The Girl and the Soldier, 1965, La Mama Experimental Theatre Club; in *The Scene*, November 1967, Mark Taper Forum, Los Angeles;

TV, in *America Hurrah (Interview, TV, and Motel)*, 6 November 1966, Pocket Theatre, New York, 634;

Thoughts on the Instant of Greeting a Friend on the Street, by van Itallie and Sharon Thie, 1967, St. Mark's Playhouse, New York; in *The Scene*, November 1967, Mark Taper Forum, Los Angeles; in *Collision Course*, 8 May 1968, Cafe au Go-Go, New York, 79;

The Serpent: A Ceremony, 2 May 1968, Teatro degli Arte, Rome; 16 May 1969, Public Theatre, New York, 4;

Take a Deep Breath, in Eric Bentley's *The DMZ*, 10 October 1968, Village Vanguard, New York, 57;

Photographs: Mary and Howard, 7 October 1969, Mark Taper Forum, Los Angeles;

Eat Cake, 19 August 1971, Changing Scene, Denver;

Harold, 15 May 1972, Theatre for the New City, New York;

The King of the United States, music by Richard Peaslee, 15 May 1972, Theatre for the New City, New York; revised as *Mystery Play*, 3 January 1973, Cherry Lane Theatre, New York, 14;

Nightwalk, by van Itallie, Megan Terry, and Sam Shepard, 8 September 1973, St. Clement's Church, New York, 15;

The Sea Gull, adapted from Anton Chekhov's play, October 1973, McCarter Theatre, Princeton, N.J.; 21 January 1975, Manhattan Theatre Club, New York;

A Fable, music by Peaslee, 1975, Lenox Arts Festival, Lenox, Mass.; 18 October 1975, Exchange Theatre, New York;

The Cherry Orchard, adapted from Chekhov's play, 17 February 1977, Lincoln Center, New York;

The Three Sisters, adapted from Chekhov's play, August 1979, Bard College Center, Anandale-on-Hudson, N.Y.;

The Bag Lady, 21 November 1979, Theatre for the New City, New York.

BOOKS: *War and Four Other Plays* (New York: Dramatists Play Service, 1967)—includes *War, The Hunter and the Bird, Almost Like Being, I'm Really Here*, and *Where Is De Queen?*;

America Hurrah (New York: Coward-McCann, 1967);

America Hurrah and Other Plays (London: Penguin, 1967)—includes *Interview, TV, Motel, War*, and *Almost Like Being*;

The Serpent: A Ceremony (New York: Atheneum, 1969);

Seven Short and Very Short Plays (New York: Dramatists Play Service, 1973)—includes *Eat Cake, Take a Deep Breath, Photographs: Mary and Howard, Harold, Thoughts on the Instant of Greeting a Friend in the Street, The Naked Nun*, and *The Girl and the Soldier*;

Mystery Play (New York: Dramatists Play Service, 1973);

The King of the United States (New York: Dramatists Play Service, 1975);

A Fable (New York: Dramatists Play Service, 1976);

The Sea Gull, adapted from Anton Chekhov's play (New York: Harper & Row, 1977);

The Cherry Orchard (New York: Grove, 1977);

America Hurrah and Other Plays (New York: Grove, 1978)—includes *American Hurrah, The Serpent, A Fable, The Hunter and the Bird*, and *Almost Like Being*.

Jean-Claude van Itallie's theatre is naturalized American theatre. Like its author, its roots are anchored in the European tradition, but its metaphors and rhetoric are bound to the American experience. Emerging in the mid-1960s as a major young playwright associated with a significantly innovative theatre collaborative, the Open Theatre, under Joseph Chaikin's leadership, van Itallie created with his pieces a kaleidoscope of American images cast in European forms. The poetic vision belongs to a writer reared in the mid-twentieth-century world of pervasive displacement. Van Itallie straddles continents, languages, cultures; thus he is attuned to the patchwork nature of American culture while being suspicious of its panacea, the American dream, manifest in the notion of an American paradise preserved and everyone's inalienable right to pursue happiness. Van Itallie perceived that the theatre can provide potentially the sharpest depiction of the gap between the dream and immediate reality; the experience of the 1960s exacerbated the gap itself.

Van Itallie was born in Brussels, Belgium; his father was an investment banker. He came to the United States in 1940, although he was not naturalized until 1952. Van Itallie's encounter with theatre happened early in his life. According to his own testimony, he began acting in high school; he even directed there, which demonstrates an early critical streak in his theatrical endeavors. He continued his involvement with theatre while at Harvard. He took Robert Chapman's playwriting class; he acted in shows; he directed plays, among them the work of Michel de Ghelderode, a twentieth-century Belgian dramatist, and he read the twentieth-century obligatory avant-garde: Edward Gordon Craig, Antonin Artaud, the surrealists. The predilection for these artists indicates van Itallie's orientation: it is highly visual, dominated by space, color, and image sculpture, in which the word functions primarily as an evocative cue or as complementary force. Craig's and Artaud's theories supported van Itallie's "painterly" metaphorical approach by pointing out the metaphysical impact provided by a startling physical manipulation and subjugation of environment to one predominant metaphor. As a result, van Itallie's dramaturgy has persistently been characterized by compactness (most of his pieces are quite short); by the use of stereotypes, masks, and puppets as objective correlatives to features and themes of contemporary life; and by ceremonial and ritualized behavior sequences as reflective of archetypal or dreamlike processes. Admittedly more visual than aural, van Itallie treats sound, including that of words, in a painterly fashion as color and accent rather than for its musical potential. If van Itallie uses musical terms as structural metaphors, it is like Paul Klee's using musical symbols in his painting—for physical shape. Though van Itallie may use strains of popular music, it is not so much for the music itself but rather for the moral stereotypes projected, and therefore it too is subjected to the distillation of the controlling image. Other sources and inspirations which serve van Itallie are also the love of puppetry and masquerades characteristic of Belgian culture. The Belgian painter James Ensor created a great series of works depicting this national tradition, some of which find echoes in van Itallie's theatrical canvases.

Van Itallie received his bachelor's degree from Harvard in 1958. He studied acting at the Neighborhood Playhouse in New York during that summer, and the following year did graduate work at New York University. Between late 1963 and 1968 he worked as an editor for the influential monthly *Transatlantic Review*. The most formative period of van Itallie's work, however, begins with the Open Theatre and his collaboration with Joseph Chaikin. His connection with Chaikin and some of the actors associated with him, notably his sister Shami Chaikin, is still active, although the Open Theatre ceased to operate as a group in 1973. For five years, between 1964 and 1968, van Itallie functioned as a playwright-in-residence with the group, along with Megan Terry and Susan Yankowitz. Chaikin dedicated his book, *The Presence of the Actor* (1972), to Jean-Claude van Itallie and

Judith Malina (cofounder of the Living Theatre), an obvious acknowledgement of the writer's imprint on his work. The basic purpose of the Open Theatre was neither commercial nor to experiment in a communal art/life like the Living Theatre, but rather to be a study collaborative of a collaborative art. Actors, writers, and musicians (for example, the musician Richard Peaslee) came together in a loft on West Fourteenth Street to develop a theatrical vocabulary which bound together individual feelings, common social experiences, political orientations, into one cogent event. The inherent danger, for any collaborative, of course, lay in falling prey to the leveling power of the cliche. In such a situation, van Itallie served as observer and shaper who helped steer the group clear of cliches by infusing precise phrases and objectifying structures. When Gordon Rogoff introduced van Itallie to the Open Theatre, van Itallie had just had the first production of his first play, *War* (1963), by the Barr-Wilder-Albee Playwrights Unit at the Vandam Theatre. The new group's symbiotic relationship between performers and writers provided the playwright with an intimate working relation to theatre, quite unusual in American theatre. Since Chaikin had never presumed an actor to be a poet or even a structurer, he had from the beginning relied on writers to contribute that analytical and coordinating, perhaps even visionary, eye and voice, which would also push the actor beyond the immediate self. This is precisely how van Itallie functioned. He would observe, sometimes devise, but rarely participate in the exercises which were to help develop the vocabulary of the group and raise and define the particular territories investigated.

The Open Theatre and Jean-Claude van Itallie first drew major critical attention with the production of van Itallie's *America Hurrah*, which opened at the Pocket Theatre in New York on 7 November 1966. Robert Brustein remarked in his review in the *New Republic*: "if Mr. van Itallie provides the mind, spirit, and creative impulse of the evening, the Open Theatre actors provide the technique and invention, formed over three years of experimental work in histrionic transformation, and it would be criminal if the playwright's success led to any dissolution of this collaboration. With *America Hurrah*, the concept of theatrical unity finally becomes meaningful in this country and the American theatre takes three giant steps towards maturity. The triumph of this occasion is to have found provocative theatrical images for the national malaise we have been suffering in Johnsonland these last three years. . . ."

Van Itallie's first published play, *War*, had already introduced the technique of expanded metaphor which the trilogy *America Hurrah* was to take further. *War* is essentially a plotless series of increasingly aggressive encounters between an older and a younger actor who have met to rehearse a scene. An idealized lady in Edwardian apricot frills floats through their encounters without diffusing the hostility of the actors; at best she seems to provoke a regression to childishness in both while they continue to explore and exploit one another's weaknesses. The final image of the play: "The actors march in towards each other. They kneel at the center of the stage. They put their inner arms around each other but with their free arms they continue to hit each other. The Lady steps up from behind them, her face still covered by the parasol, which is twirling, and stands above them: this tableau forms a hieroglyph, an emblem, the two-headed eagle of war. There is silence. The curtain falls, slowly."

The next play, *The Hunter and the Bird*, which was prepared for the Open Theatre's Monday night series at the Sheridan Square Playhouse, opened under the direction of Joseph Chaikin in late 1964. The play lasts only a few minutes but in that time moments of ironic humor, of cruelty, of outrageousness, and of cold-blooded reason accumulate to form a powerful image of the delicate balance between victim and victor. The language has some of the madcap Alice-in-Wonderland quality which only serves to distill the final impact when the bird shoots the hunter: "Hoorah, hoorah. Oh frabjous day. He's dead. Kaloo Kalay and the bird she flew away." Two more short pieces, *Almost Like Being* and *I'm Really Here*, appeared under Chaikin's direction in February 1965 both at the Vandam and the Sheridan Monday night series. They are essentially spoofs on the Doris Day Hollywood fantasy. Van Itallie's stage direction for *I'm Really Here* (it is nearly the same for *Almost Like Being*) tells much about the style of the work: "The play is done by the actors as if it were a movie. When the actors are not, for a moment or two, 'on camera', their expressions are deadpan and bored. They are 'on' for their 'bits.' Often Doris will make a tried-and-true facial expression especially for the camera, turning her face into a 'cute' mask or a 'hurt' mask etc. She often addresses the camera instead of another actor . . . At the end of the play it is as if the cameras were locked into place. Doris cannot get out of this movie now if she wanted to." The grostesque ending resembles a Grand Guignol horror show, with the ideal lover, the toothsome Rossano Brassy, stabbing Doris after he had shown her around "Paree, whee, whee." She runs through her life in those last moments like a movie camera gone mad, expressing illusions of glory and final despair: "But the other man, the nice one, is coming to save me. I'm always saved. Someone will come. I'll be all right. Everything's coming up roses, Doris. Doris. Doris, take hold of yourself. I'm going to wash that man right out of my hair. I'm going to—I'm alone. Doris. Some enchanted evening you will see? meet? see? a stranger. But I'm Doris. I love Paris in the springtime when it drizzles. Doris. I'm alone. Help me. Forgive me. I'm alone. I can't die. Doris can't die. Die? Die? *I'm* dying. *I* am dying. Really dying. I'm *really*—(She screams very loudly in fear.) CURTAIN." This end is, of course, set in direct opposition to the fairy-tale ending of *Almost Like Being* where all join in singing a happy song and freeze into vacuous smiles. Though one critic, Elmer Borklund, considers these "cabaret sketches hardly worth the poetic skill or indignation of a writer as sophisticated as van Itallie," they can be considered successful preparation pieces for *America Hurrah* because of the theatricality of form, the use of masklike characters, the dialogue, which knits cliches and easily recognizable phrases together almost in Dada style.

Two of the plays in the *America Hurrah* trilogy, *Interview* and *Motel*, had previous single productions. In 1965 *Interview* opened under the title *Pavane* in Atlanta and simultaneously in New York at both the Sheridan Square Playhouse and La Mama Experimental Theatre Club under the direction of Peter Feldman of the Open Theatre. (Later Tom O'Horgan directed the La Mama tour of the play through Europe as well as its NETV production.) *Motel* was presented under the title *America Hurrah* at the La Mama Experimental

Theatre Club in April 1965 under the direction of Michael Kahn. But it was the 1966 production which combined *Interview*, *TV*, and *Motel* under the direction of Joseph Chaikin (*Interview*) and Jacques Levy (*TV*, *Motel*) into the epoch-making, though controversial, *America Hurrah* and which catapulted van Itallie into the forefront of American playwrights. Within the year there were productions in Europe; a German translation appeared in 1967. Especially the last play, *Motel*, projects a mythos of violence, hardly paralleled in its compactness—the printed text covers five pages. It is subtitled *A Masque for Three Dolls* and prefaced by the famous Yeats line, ". . . after all our subtle colour and nervous rhythm, after the faint mixed tints of Conder, what more is possible? After us the Savage God." And a savage vision indeed is invoked by the three larger than life-size dolls, two of whom mutely go about their business of destruction while the other intones a litany of junk. The destroyers are a Man doll and a Woman doll, mobile, grotesque George Segal-like figures who have come onto the set, a motel room with the discomfort of an Edward Kienholz environmental sculpture in its violent color combinations of "oranges, pinks and reds against a reflective plastic background." The Motel-Keeper's doll does not speak from her body but from a number of loudspeakers in the theatre. She moves little but her incessant litany grows harsher as it disintegrates into seemingly random thing-words. That the doll is an image of mythic dimension is established from the outset: "I am old. I am an old idea: the walls; that from which it springs forth. I enclose the nothing, making then a place in which it happens. I am the room: a Roman theatre where cheers break loose the lion; a railroad carriage in the forest of Compiègne, in 1918, and in 1941. I have been rooms of marble and rooms of cork, all letting forth an avalanche. Rooms of mud and rooms of silk. This room will be slashed too, as if by a scimitar, its contents spewed and yawned out. That is what happens. It is almost happening, in fact. I am this room." And then the ritual begins; the myth runs its course in a thoroughly modern American idiom. After the room has been demolished, the sentences decimated, leaving only disjointed words, the Motel-Keeper's doll itself is finally dismembered and the limbs thrown about. The Man and Woman dolls leave by way of the aisle, a fan blows from upstage through the "debacle," more excruciating noise is heard, then black-out, silence—and the audience is left with the reverberations of a pre-doomsday image, the last one of *America Hurrah*. In 1967, *America Hurrah* won the

Vernon Rice Award, Outer Critics Circle Award, and the Jersey Journal Award.

The final image of *Motel* is the strongest of the entire trilogy. The first play, *Interview*, subtitled *A Fugue for Eight Actors*, is Spartan by comparison, and perhaps too rooted in a highly technical acting exercise. Nevertheless, by opening the trilogy on a "white and impersonal set with eight grey blocks," with actors dressed in black and white street clothes and translucent plastic masks for the four interviewers, a progression from a cool order to violent chaos is created. The language in *Interview* consists mostly of common speech and phrases, such as "How do you do? Won't you sit down? Fill in the blank space, please. I am sorry." This speech is arranged in fugue-like patterns of theme, counterpoint, repetitions, and variations. At times musical accompaniment is provided by a harpsicord playing variations on a familiar American tune in dance rhythms, ranging from the minuet, to the Virginia reel, to the twist. The four applicant figures are given differentiating traits which, however, are no more than stereotypes. In the final variation on the theme "Can I help you?", the interviewers take on different prototypes; they become a priest, telephone operator, doctor, politician, psychiatrist, but none manages to help and some are actually robbed of their vocabulary; thus the final sense is one of impotence and social isolation.

The second piece, *TV*, also takes place on "a white and impersonal set," where pieces of furniture and a viewing screen indicate a televison viewing room. The play contains two concurrent actions. One group of actors plays a team of television researchers: Hal, Susan, and George. Another group of actors, made up with black lines across their faces to look like video images, plays multiple roles in various TV programs, anything from advertisement, to soap opera, to Western. Gradually the TV action takes over and engulfs the action of the three researchers until all is finally drowned in a sea of banality, wiping out any possible distinction between the improbable TV world and the "real" world of Hal, Susan, and George. A careful orchestration of the two sets of dialogue provides some amusing ironic spin-offs between the video characters and the "normal" characters. Van Itallie's epigraph quoting Marshall McLuhan's reference to the Narcissus myth leaves no doubt about the representation of "a closed system" of banality and illusion. Also between 1963 and 1967 van Itallie contributed as a free-lance writer on public affairs for NBC and CBS television. He has six television scripts to his credit; his first was *The Stepinac Case*

produced in 1963 by CBS, and the most recent, *Picasso, a Painter's Diary*, was shown on PBS in 1980.

A few very short pieces were also produced in the years 1965-1967. *The Girl and the Soldier*, which van Itallie called "a three-minute exercise in levels of reality" was produced at La Mama in 1965 and again in 1967 as part of *The Scene*, the original *Collision Course*, directed by Edward Parone at the Mark Taper Forum in Los Angeles. The soldier moves through his own life with the speed of lightning from being a young recruit to an old soldier while the girl remains the same, young and naive. He tells her about the cosmic dimensions of life and death, of screams of killing and of orgasm, of the possibility that another sun could cause "the infinitely slow disintegration of the earth, fragmented slowly into particles, boom, boom," and then for a long moment they embrace and the world seems to stand still while "their manner together is as full of love and quiet as his alone is full of war and movement." But the soldier returns to his race through life and his "boom, boom" destroys the idyll.

Thoughts on the Instant of Greeting a Friend on the Street, which van Itallie wrote together with Sharon Thie, had productions in 1967 by Joseph Chaikin at the St. Marks Playhouse in New York and by Edward Parone at the Mark Taper, also as part of the original *Collision Course*. The scene is indeed only an instant, the freezing of an encounter in order to reveal the reactions of the man and the woman. Alternately, one expresses the feelings and thoughts while the other continues to say the phrase, "Hi, how are you?" The woman's thoughts, written by Sharon Thie, deal with the impossibility of ever feeling safe, followed by the man's thoughts, by van Itallie, spinning off on visions of a nuclear holocaust.

The greatest endeavor for van Itallie and the Open Theatre was their creation of *The Serpent* which had its premiere in Rome at the Teatro degli Arte on 2 May 1968. It played subsequently in New York and later went on a European tour. The company stayed with the piece until 1970. The play, subtitled *A Ceremony*, became a testing ground of endurance for the Open Theatre but it must also have been a testing ground for van Itallie's conception of the playwright's function which to him is "not so much to write a play as to construct a ceremony which can be used by the actors to come together with their audience.... Words are a part of this ceremony but not necessarily the dominant part,... The important thing is what is happening between the audience and the action.... But the form must reflect contemporary thought processes.

8- ①

Clara ~~(checking which~~ (checking which objects to keep, which to throw out):
This whole city's like a hospital. I see 'em go by.
Breast cancer. Heart attack. Ass cancer. It's a joke. Everybody's
hustling, everybody's a patient, except me. I'm rich, you
see, ~~got everything I need.~~   ~~Not a little rich, very rich.~~
I have a subway map to get to Brooklyn, to the Welfare Center,
only I never take the subway so forget it. Anyone want a subway
map? Knitting needles---I don't use knitting needles. Out.
~~A yellow swatch to pick a fabric for the chairs in~~
~~the dining room in Hollywood. Okay. Lipsticks.~~ My Jackie
sweater. An electric toothbrush. Don't use the electric part
unless I'm in a hotel which I ~~XXXXXXXXXXXXXXXXXXXXXXXXX~~
never am. ~~Parasol.~~ Timetable of planes to Moscow.
Palm Beach telephone book. ~~letter paper.~~ Kleenex. Extra
purse. ~~Keys to the houses.~~ Telephone number of my yacht.
Want it? You can tell the captain I said it was okay, ~~for you~~
~~to visit.~~ ~~XXXXXXXXX~~   Robert Kennedy ~~Cushion-cover or bag,~~
~~depending. Okay. Dental floss, unused.~~ Potato chips.
Matches in a glass jar. Toilet paper purse. Plastic fork.
Tablecloth. Rubberbands. Sunglasses. ~~Vicks vap-orub.~~ ~~XXXXXX~~
Bravely, Cotton in this blue box. ~~Pins.~~ Letter to my brother,
the king of Moscow, unfinished. ~~XXXXXXXX~~   This city is going
to be a museum someday, soon, after it stops. All this is going
to be valuable. Piece of lace to make a collar.
~~My Irish coat. Silk underpants. Silk keeps you warm, you know.~~
Raincoat. Hat. ~~Embroidered slippers. XXXXXXXXXXXXXXXXXXXXXXX~~
~~Comb. Brush. Yellow blouse with sequins.~~ Chuckles for before
~~XXXXXXXXXXXXXXXXX~~.

The Bag Lady, revised typescript

And we don't think much in a linear fashion. Ideas overlap, themes recur, archetypal figures and events transform from shape to shape as they dominate our minds." Thus in *The Serpent* van Itallie functioned as the structurer of the archetypal figures and events and as the fixer of words. The subject was in Chaikin's words the remembered "first time," what the philosopher Mircea Eliade would call the *illud tempus* (that distant mythical time). The story of Genesis provided the narrative frame and much of the substance—the first man, the first woman, the first sexual encounter, the first murder. Chaikin describes in his book, *The Presence of the Actor* (1972): "Our aim . . . was that we should completely reunderstand the whole territory of shame, in the light of our retelling of the story. . . . What is deeply engaging in the biblical mythology is the discovery that its assumptions are even now the hidden bases of a lot of our own choice-making." And so by way of exercises, discussions, and improvisations, images were brought to the surface collaboratively which van Itallie refined, set down, and structured. The result is a scenario which recalls the structure of a shamanistic ritual whereby participants and audience proceed on a mythic journey downward to the *illud tempus*.

The play starts with a procession in which the actors indicate various sound and movement motifs which will be developed more fully. Then a doctor figure detaches himself from the group and begins his chant and "operation" to invoke memory. His chant is punctuated by gunshots. Then the chorus of four women, mythical figures who embody, among other things, the principle of memory, invoke the assassinations of John F. Kennedy and Martin Luther King. The company mimes the Kennedy assassination like an unreeling of the twelve frames of Zapruder's film depicting the scene in the car when Kennedy and John Connally were shot and Jackie Kennedy tried to climb out over the back of the car. The crowd and the assassins join in a brief chant of noninvolvement and the group then readies itself for the Garden of Eden. By sounds and movement the actors gradually make themselves into the creatures and become distinct. Above all, a Heron with his soft "brring," Eve, and a five-man Serpent stand out. The redemptive significance of the Heron and the number symbolism of the Serpent emphasize the mythic dimension. (The number 5, for example, represents not only the five senses with which one apprehends the world, but also the human microcosm; like the pentagram, it can represent radical intelligence and spiritual aspiration as well as witchcraft and fear.) Eve and the undulating, five-mouthed Serpent seduce one another, reaching the climax when Eve, seated in the middle of the Serpent/Tree, eats the apple—one of the many gorgeous apples dangling from the arms, legs, mouths, and crotches of the Serpent/Tree. What follows of the Genesis story is well known: Adam, after some doubt, eats; the curses follow: Cain's and Abel's offerings to God, the murder of Abel, and the begetting of the human race. Within this frame is created a network of transformations of time and sentiment: the curses spoken in rapid, alternating rhythm are made into specific stories of frustration; the murder is a *learning* to kill without the knowledge of death; actions are initiated by people blind to their results culminating in the Blind Men's Hell where death is difficult to ascertain for "even after the end, / Even when the body is on its own, / The human being can make such a variety of sounds that it's amazing. / A field of dead men is loud. / Teeth clack, bones crack, / Limbs twist and drop, / And the last sound of all / Is a loud trumpet / Of escaping wind." Out of this almost Hieronymus Bosch-like vision of hell, the group dissolves into the four women of the chorus wordlessly "davenning" while a man and a woman's slow approach to one another gives the cue for the mass "begetting." The women now start reciting from the Old Testament all the "begats" while the company joins together in an exploration of one another's bodies until the biblical connection is reached climactically as a rapid succession of birthing, rearing, and growing old brings the journey to an end. Now each actor is gradually "overtaken by a slow kind of dying . . . a kind of 'emptying out.' " They free themselves of the time and characters they have portrayed and return to a common time level with the audience. This is signified as they leave through the audience while singing "Moonlight Bay," an old sentimental, popular American song. The return, as it were, to the now of the audience, is also an important part of the shamanistic exercise. It marks the closure of the cyclic journey.

Walter Kerr, a critic hard to budge onto "the gymnasium floor," admired the Open Theatre's work on *The Serpent* as "plainly the best, because . . . it has humor . . . and the words, like the gestures are respected by the performers . . . not trampled on or turned into useless sounds." Kerr, who also expressed special admiration for van Itallie's script, was captivated by the fresh power and clarity of the images created. Clarity being van Itallie's aim, the author himself had warned against any improvisational tampering with the words. In a conversation with John Lahr, van Itallie expressed the desire to create in each moment a "vertical time," "to show an impression of all at once." In the same conversation van Itallie stated that "plays should be instruments to get into people's dreams. . . . If you can get into somebody's dream, that's exciting, perhaps the most profound change you can effect." And according to Lahr, he succeeded with *The Serpent*. It won the Obie Award in 1969.

In many ways *The Serpent* marked the high point and the end of a phase of a particular kind of theatre and collaboration. The next years saw the dissolution of the Open Theatre and van Itallie spent his time teaching, writing, and traveling with the support of Ford and Rockefeller Foundation grants. In 1971-1972 a journal on India, *Karma*, was prepared. A couple of small works were produced, one of which, *Eat Cake* (1971) directed by Michael Smith, resembled in grotesque violence the earlier *I'm Really Here*.

In 1972, however, van Itallie emerged not only with another full-length play but also as its director for a workshop production of a work-in-progress at the Theatre for the New City in New York. This musical mystery play, *The King of the United States* (1972), received very mixed reviews, ranging from Julius Novick's "evanescent and thin" in the *Village Voice* to a rave in *Showbusiness* by Deborah Wasserman, who was delighted by its "kaleidoscope whirl of narrative, scene, plot, non-plot, music, movement and satire." A version of the same play without Richard Peaslee's music was performed the following year under the title *Mystery Play* (1973). Though it too was received by some critics with polite reservation, two critics, Martin Gottfried and Michael Feingold, compared the play favorably with Tom Stoppard's mystery spoof, *The Real Inspector Hound* (1968). In fact, the play has a rather Pirandellian structure in which characters as well as the audience are manipulated into a gambit of role-playing and shifting complicity. The entire mystery seems arranged by a master *dompteur* (an expert manipulator)—in this case, a woman—the mystery writer who attends a party of her neighbor, "an important American statesman," in his elegant living room. But in the end she too seems to be the victim of another higher-up manipulator, most likely the author himself. For the basic conceit of this "playing at living," van Itallie is apparently indebted to Joseph Campbell. He includes in the published version a brief excerpt from Campbell's work *Myths to Live By* (1972) in which Campbell describes a peculiar speech pattern of the Japanese aristoc-

racy. For example, instead of saying "I see you've come to Tokyo," a person would say, "I see that you are playing at being in Tokyo." Campbell concludes that such control over one's life and powers makes one enter life as though it were a game. Van Itallie stresses in a note to the actors that they should fully explore "the familiar archetypal western-type mystery novel or movie" in order to find the appropriate style for their "as if" reality. As a farce the play takes advantage of the theatrical potential of the game playing and shifting perspective.

Van Itallie, like many other playwrights, has pursued his work by means of grants and associations with various universities. He taught playwriting at the New School for Social Research in 1967, 1968, and 1972; at the Yale drama school in 1969; at Amherst College in 1976; and at the Naropa Institute, Boulder, Colorado, from 1974 to 1976. Since 1973 he has been a lecturer at Princeton University. Moreover, he has received two Guggenheim fellowships for playwriting (1973 and 1980), a Creative Artists Public Service Grant in 1975, as well as grants from the Ford and Rockefeller Foundations. In 1977 he was awarded an honorary Ph.D. from Kent State University.

In 1975, another major collaboration with Joseph Chaikin and some of the actors of the former Open Theatre resulted in a wonderful work, *A Fable* (1975), with music by Richard Peaslee. Although it is another journey to and from *illud tempus*, in this case to the presumed Golden Time of the Kingdom of the People Who Fish in the Lake, it differs considerably from *The Serpent* in tone and structure. It is built on episodes of one person's journey, with encounters and feats proper to a heroic journey. Words play a more important role in controlling the images except at the beginning and the end of the journey, which are magnificently conceived dance mimes. The poetic fantastical, fairy-tale ambience and parable structure is more akin to folklore than to anthropology and thus informed though unencumbered by scientific knowledge.

Besides the above play and another collaboration, *Nightwalk* (1973), with Megan Terry and Sam Shepard, the major accomplishments of van Itallie in the 1970s have been his English versions of some of Chekhov's plays. The first one was *The Sea Gull*, originally produced by Princeton's McCarter Theatre in 1973. In 1974 Joseph Chaikin directed the same version for the Manhattan Theatre Club. Daniel Seltzer, who played Sorin in both productions, praised van Itallie's version for being an "act-able text in good American English for the first time," but more importantly he felt that its "specificity and . . . the potential for a sweeping overview . . . made it possible . . . to discover both the individual focus and the beautifully complex ironic sequences of the play." Andrei Serban has also directed van Itallie's version of *The Sea Gull* in the fall of 1980. Two more new English versions of Chekhov have followed, each praised for its clarity and concision. In 1977 *The Cherry Orchard* had a spectacular production at the Lincoln Center, directed by Andrei Serban. The humor, the economy and directness of Chekhov, the surprise of simple but rich imagery—all was supported by van Itallie's words. In the summer of 1979 *The Three Sisters* was performed in two mansions, one on the Hudson River. Though the overliteralness of the environment disturbed critic Erika Munk, she found van Itallie's language "a model of concision, idiomatic . . . perfect for the kind of flowing talk." Van Itallie has most recently made a new version of *Uncle Vanya* which has yet to be produced.

Before setting off for Ecuador in 1980 to look for the secret of long life, van Itallie produced another piece depicting another kind of perenniality, *The Bag Lady*, played by Shami Chaikin. Here is a solitary woman, a miniature representative of the most extraordinary garbage pile in the world, New York City. She tells us calmly that she is "the empress of New York," just as New York might be called the empress of cities. Reviewer Michael Feingold sees her as a metaphor for the city and considers her hour-long monologue "a melange of terror, good sense, and aliveness," which is shot through with prophecy. Van Itallie might well concur with this interpretation. After all, as a playwright he has been intimately connected with the theatrical scene in New York since the early 1960s and he will certainly retain his place there.

That van Itallie has been consistently interested in working with a community of artist/friends rather than the commercial sector is borne out by the very specific demand and quality of his work. It is not easily accessible to an actor or an audience; it needs slow piecing together. Though his theatre aspires to mythic dimensions, it is still chamber theatre, but then shamanistic rituals are performed in relatively small tents and Yeats wished to see his Cuchulain plays in living rooms.

Van Itallie has poetry stashed away in suitcases and is an avid letter writer. He lives in a most intrusive city, New York, and escapes to his Massachusetts farm. He delights in the ephemerality of

popular music and juxtaposes it with vertical journeys to First Times. Jean-Claude van Itallie is a poet of the theatre who sees words "as the top of the iceberg."

–*Beate Hein Bennett*

Screenplays:
Three Lives for Mississippi, adapted from William Bradford Huie's novel, Center Films, 1971;
The Box Is Empty, privately produced, 1975.

Television Scripts:
The Stepinac Case, "Look Up and Live," CBS, 1963;
New Church Architecture, I, "Look Up and Live," CBS, 1964;
New Church Architecture, II, "Look Up and Live," CBS, 1964;
The Sounds of Courage, "Look Up and Live," CBS, 1965;
Hobbies, or Things Are Alright with the Forbushers, "Look Up and Live," CBS, 1967;
Picasso, a Painter's Diary, PBS, 1980.

Other:
Nightwalk, by van Itallie, Megan Terry, and Sam Shepard, in *Three Works by the Open Theatre*, ed. Karen Malpede (New York: Drama Book Specialists, 1974), pp. 135-150.

Periodical Publications:
"Playwright at Work: Off-Off Broadway" *Tulane Drama Review*, 10 (Summer 1966): 154-158;
"Should the Artist be Political in his Art?," *New York Times*, 17 September 1967, II: 3.

References:
Robert Brustein, "Three Views of America," *New Republic* (3 December 1966); reprinted in his *The Third Theatre* (New York: Knopf, 1969), pp. 50-54;
Joseph Chaikin, *The Presence of the Actor* (New York: Atheneum, 1972);
Alex Gildzen, "The Open Theatre: A Beginning Bibliography" in *Three Works by the Open Theatre*, ed. Malpede (New York: Drama Book Specialists, 1974), pp. 188-191;
Walter Kerr, "God on the Gymnasium Floor," in his *God on the Gymnasium Floor* (New York: Simon & Schuster, 1971), pp. 21-27, 41-44;
John Lahr, "The Open Theatre's Serpent," in his *Up Against the Fourth Wall* (New York: Grove, 1970), pp. 158-174;

Robert Pasolli, *A Book on the Open Theatre* (Indianapolis: Bobbs-Merrill, 1970);
Serif, special van Itallie issue, 9 (Winter 1972).

Papers:
The largest collection of van Itallie's papers is at Kent State University, which also houses a collection on the Open Theatre.

DOUGLAS TURNER WARD
(5 May 1930-)

PRODUCTIONS: *Happy Ending* and *Day of Absence*, 15 November 1965, St. Mark's Playhouse, New York, 4 [performances];
The Reckoning, 4 September 1969, St. Mark's Playhouse, New York, 94;
Brotherhood, 10 March 1970, St. Mark's Playhouse, New York, 64;
The Redeemer, March 1979, Actors Theatre of Louisville, Louisville.

BOOKS: *Happy Ending and Day of Absence* (New York: Okpaku, 1966);
Brotherhood (New York: Dramatists Play Service, 1970);
The Reckoning (New York: Dramatists Play Service, 1970).

Douglas Turner Ward emerged from the Black Theatre Movement of the 1960s as a noted playwright, actor, and director. His plays, particularly *Day of Absence* and *Happy Ending*, brought a new, sharply satirical dimension to the dramatic presentation of black life. With the founding and development of the Negro Ensemble Company, a New York repertory theatre and workshop where Ward presently serves as artistic director, he solidified his position as a leading black artist.

Roosevelt and Dorothy Short Ward gave birth to their only child, Douglas Turner, 5 May 1930, on a rice and sugar plantation in Burnside, Louisiana, where they worked as field hands. Eight years later, the family relocated in New Orleans, where Roosevelt Ward worked on the loading docks and Dorothy Ward worked as seamstress. After World War II, they opened a tailoring business in their home. Despite his family's low-income status, Douglas Turner was noted to have a profound interest in reading and writing.

In New Orleans, Ward was enrolled at Xavier University Preparatory, a black Catholic high school. Wishing to become a writer, he decided to study journalism at Wilberforce University in Xenia, Ohio, and at the University of Michigan in Ann Arbor for one year in each place. He moved to New York City in 1948. The city at that time was going through tumultuous changes, and Ward engaged in the activities of several radical groups. "By the mid-sixties," Ward confessed in an interview with *New York Times* reporter Elenore Lester, "I had put behind me some of the attitudes the militants were just coming to. I had had my years of handing out leaflets on street corners, writing for *The Daily Worker*. . . . I had reached the point at which I felt this strong desire to deal with black experience in all its complexity."

Ward decided to prepare himself for dramatic writing by enrolling as a student in the Paul Mann Actors Workshop in New York. Not only did his two and a half years of studies there give him insight into writing from an actor's point of view, but they also raised his acting skills to a professional level. Ward did not use his last name in the early years of his acting career, appearing as Douglas Turner until 1972. He made his first stage appearance in 1956 as Joe Mott in Eugene O'Neill's *The Iceman Cometh* at the Circle in the Square Playhouse. In 1958 he appeared as Matthew Kumalo in Maxwell Anderson's *Lost in the Stars* at the New York City Center; in 1959 he appeared as a moving man in Lorraine Hansberry's *A Raisin in the Sun*. In addition to this role, he understudied actors Sidney Poitier as Walter Lee Younger and Lonne Elder III as Bobo. He then succeeded Poitier in the male lead and toured with the play in 1960-1961. In September 1961 he replaced Roscoe Lee Brown as Archibald Wellington in Jean Genet's *The Blacks* at the Saint Mark's Playhouse in New York. In December 1962 he took the role of a porter in Thornton Wilder's *Pullman Car Hiawatha* at the Circle in the Square; in November 1963 he was an understudy for the Broadway role of Fredricks in Dale Wasserman's adaptation of Ken Kesey's novel, *One Flew Over the Cuckoo's Nest*. In 1964 he played Fitzroy in Hugh Wheeler's *Rich Little Rich Girl* at the Walnut Street Theatre in New York, and also he followed James Earl Jones as Zachariah Pieterson in Athol Fugard's *The Blood Knot* at New York's Cricket Theatre.

Ward's ability as a playwright came into full view with the completion of his two satirical one-act plays, *Day of Absence* and *Happy Ending*, in 1964. His career as a dramatist was launched in November 1965 when these two one-acts were produced by

Robert Hooks at the Saint Mark's Playhouse. Set in a "spotless kitchen of a Harlem tenement," *Happy Ending* opens with two middle-aged black domestics, Ellie and Vi, weeping over the likelihood that their wealthy white employers, the Harrisons, will end their marriage in divorce. Ellie and Vi's nephew, Junie, a haughty twenty year old who has been to college but is unemployed, is angry to learn that his aunts feel sorry for their white employers and lectures them about black pride: "Here we are—Africa rising to its place in the sun wit prime ministers and other dignitaries taking seats around the international table—us here fighting for our rights like never before, changing the whole image, lumping stereotypes behind us and replacing 'em wit new images of dignity and dimension—and I come home and find my own aunts . . . drowning themselves in tears jist 'cause boss man is gonna kick boss lady out on her nose!" Junie, however, has misunderstood the cause of his aunts' tears. If the Harrisons divorce, his aunts will lose their jobs. Ellie runs the Harrison household, including balancing the budget, ordering the food, taking clothes to the cleaners. Mr. Harrison wears the same size clothes as Junie. All of the clothes in Junie's well-stocked closet were "gifts" from Mr. Harrison; Ellie and Vi's freezer is filled with expensive cuts of meat; the furniture in Junie's mother's house is courtesy of the Harrisons, who let Ellie and Vi make the arrangements when they moved from their old penthouse. All of Ellie and Vi's bills—phone, utilities, medicines, dry cleaning—have been secretly added to the Harrison accounts. Mr. Harrison is so wealthy he does not notice the difference. Ellie and Vi regard these benefits as salary supplements since their salaries are quite low. Junie begins to understand his position and also cries. When Arthur, Ellie's husband, learns the news, he needs no instructions to appreciate the severity of the situation. Finally the phone rings. It is Mr. Harrison, who asks Ellie to come over and babysit while he and his wife go out to celebrate: they have reconciled after all. In this "happy ending," Junie has learned quite a lot about survival and American Negro economics.

Day of Absence, subtitled *A Satirical Fantasy*, is even more farcical in its conception than *Happy Ending*. In an "unnamed Southern town of medium population on a somnolent cracker morning," the town's entire black population is, quite mysteriously, discovered to be absent. The whites, having had no warning, awake to find that nobody is there to cook the food, change the diapers, wash the

clothes, sweep the floors, shine the shoes, drive the cars, clean the toilets, or do the menial chores around the manufacturing and merchandising centers. Ward skillfully increases the traditional license of farce by having the white roles (such as the mayor, store owners, a Klansman, a minister) played by black actors presented in "a reverse minstrel show done in white face." Moreover, the stage instructions indicate that "this is a red-white-and-blue play—meaning that the entire production should be designed around the basic color scheme of our patriotic trinity." Lighting and costuming emphasize this ironic motif.

The central character of *Day of Absence* is the mayor, Henry R. L. Lee, who, after finally understanding the extent of the crisis caused by the blacks' departure, fears political death. He hears a succession of bad reports: an industrialist says that "seventy-five percent of all production is paralyzed"; a businessman reports an "almost negligible" volume of goods being sold; a clubwoman states that "food poisoning, severe indigestitis, chronic diarrhea, advanced diaper chafings and a plethora of unsanitary household disasters dangerous to life, limb and property" are threatening the community; even the sick blacks in the hospital have inexplicably fallen into comas.

The crisis atmosphere increases when a "Huntley-Brinkley-Murrow-Sevareid-Cronkite-Reasoner-type Announcer" appears to report the phenomenon. The Announcer interviews Mr. Clan (who blames the mayor for the problem); a social worker, Mrs. Aide (who deplores how the "Nigras" have sabotaged the white-sponsored "Nigra Git-A-Job movement"); a minister, the Reverend Reb Pious (who blames the departure of the blacks on Satan and voodoo). On television the Reverend Pious exhorts the departed blacks: "I say to you without rancor or vengeance, quoting a phrase of one of your greatest prophets, Booker T. Washington: 'Return your buckets to where they lay and all will be forgiven.'" As the Announcer interviews Mayor Lee, it appears that the absence of the blacks has caused a terrifying crisis in the marital, social, political, judicial, and economic life of the town. The mayor has even approached some of the bordering Southern states, which have expressed "their solidarity by lending us some of their Nigras temporarily on credit." But these states, apparently fearing that a similar crisis may affect them, renege on this promise. Finally, it appears that all means (including the mayor's promise, delivered on his knees before a national television audience, to kiss "the first shoe of the first one to show up" or "any other spot you request") to induce the blacks to return have failed. The Announcer reports that the town, unable to control itself, suffers rioting and looting and goes "berserk."

The finale shows two store owners talking the next day to a black named Rastus, who speaks in the manner of "Stepin Fetchit, Willie Best, Nicodemus, Butterfly McQueen and all the rest rolled into one." Rastus pretends that he cannot remember the day the store owners speak about: "I didn't know I had skipped a day," he says, and he shuffles on his way.

Both *Happy Ending* and *Day of Absence* are skillful modifications of the cunning servant character type found in much Greek and Roman comedy. The servant discovers his own personal freedom by manipulating his master's ignorance and stupidity. But *Day of Absence* is one of the most revolutionary plays written by an American black, for Ward depicts the enormity of the contribution of blacks to American life and in the same stroke the enormity of the exploitation that blacks have historically suffered. Although the play met with some unfavorable reviews, *Day of Absence* was broadcast by the Public Broadcasting Laboratory over educational television after its long theatrical run.

In a 1966 *New York Times* essay titled "American Theatre: For Whites Only?" Ward called for "a theatre concentrating primarily on themes of Negro life, but also resilient enough to incorporate and interpret the best of world drama, whatever the source . . . a theatre of permanence, continuity, and consistency, providing the necessary home base for the Negro artist." Contrary to some interpretations of this article, Ward was not advocating a theatre strictly for blacks. He argued for a theatre dedicated to the investigation and illumination of the Negro experience employing whites "if they found inspiration in the purpose." This article, despite controversy, led to an invitation from the Ford Foundation to apply for funds. A proposal, written with Robert Hooks and Gerald S. Krone, resulted in a grant of $1,200,000 covering the first three years to create the theatre which Ward had advocated. The Negro Ensemble Company, established in May 1967, was to be a combined professional theatre company and workshop to develop black actors, playwrights, directors, technicians, and managers, with Ward as its artistic director, Hooks as executive director, and Krone as administrative director.

The Negro Ensemble Company opened its

Douglas Turner Ward

first season in January 1968 with Peter Weiss's musical, *Song of the Lusitanian Bogey*, which was followed by a revival of Ray Lawler's drama *Summer of the Seventeenth Doll*, then by Nigerian playwright Wole Soyinka's *Kongi's Harvest*, in which Ward played Oba Daniola. The Negro Ensemble ended its first season with Richard Wright and Louis Sapin's *Daddy Goodness*. Again Ward participated in the production, acting the role of Thomas and also directing. In 1968, the Negro Ensemble received an Obie special citation.

In addition to his administrative duties, Ward continued acting and directing in the company. During the second NEC season, which opened in December 1968 with Ray McIver's *God Is a (Guess What?)*, the first professional performance of Lonne Elder III's *Ceremonies in Dark Old Men* (1969) was presented. The production was warmly received, and Ward won a Drama Desk Award for his portrayal of Russell B. Parker, the Harlem widower. In March 1969 he directed Alice Childress's *String* and Ted Shine's *Contribution*, two of a program of three one-acts. Ward's earlier plays, *The Reckoning* was performed independently of the Negro Ensemble Company at the Saint Mark's Playhouse in 1969. Not so humorous as Ward's earlier plays, *The Reckoning* tells the story of the blackmailing of a prejudiced white Southern governor by his "mistress," a beautiful and charming black prostitute, and her sly pimp. The play is actually a volleying of wits between the governor and the pimp, with the other characters on the sidelines adding to the "match game."

In 1970 Ward directed his one-act *Brotherhood*, as well as a revival of *Day of Absence*, on a double bill at Saint Mark's Playhouse. *Brotherhood* is also a farcical satire with a racial theme, although its tone is more brutal than that of Ward's earlier plays. The Jasons (a white middle-aged couple) have invited the Johnsons (their black counterparts, as the similar surnames imply) to their home for dinner. At the beginning of the play the Jasons are seen removing ashtrays and covering their furniture before their black guests arrive. When the Johnsons do appear they are very well dressed and pretend, in stilted language, to aspire to all the chic cultural advantages which their former environment had not provided. The Jasons make lame excuses for the absence of ashtrays, for the draped pictures on the wall, and for requesting that the Johnsons use a children's potty for a bathroom. (Mrs. Johnson decides to go outside.) Finally, when the Johnsons leave, the Jasons unveil their pictures which are scenes of blacks being tortured; they put back in

place their "bare-assed ashtray blacks," and other patronizing "Niggerphalia" artifacts. They release their children, who had been bound and gagged in a closet. In a brief epilogue Mrs. Johnson is seen stabbing a voodoo-doll likeness of Mrs. Jason, and Mr. Johnson is miming the action of slashing the throat of his white counterpart. The satire of *Brotherhood* is darker than in Ward's other plays. It underlines the falseness of facile "brotherhood" manners and implies strongly that pretense supplies no solution to radical differences between blacks and whites. Its deliberately stilted language and methods of caricature do not have the exuberant inventiveness of *Day of Absence*, but they certainly drive home Ward's point.

In January 1971 Ward directed Clarence Young III's *Perry's Mission* and produced Carlton and Barbara Molette's *Rosalee Pritchett* for the NEC; in May 1971 he directed John Scott's *Ride a Black Horse* and in March 1972 Lennox Brown's *A Ballet Behind the Bridge*. The Negro Ensemble Company continued its seasons of repertory productions until 1972-1973, when they were faced with financial problems; they then cut back to two full-scale productions per season, beginning in May 1972, with Arthur Burkhardt's *Frederick Douglass . . . Through His Own Words*, with Ward as Frederick Douglass. In December 1973, Ward directed Joseph Walker's *The River Niger* and played the role of Johnny Williams. This production ran for 120 performances at the Saint Mark's Playhouse and for 280 more on Broadway, after which it toured. The play received an Obie, and Ward was nominated for a Tony award for his portrayal of Johnny Williams. However, he refused the nomination because he felt that the category of "supporting actor" was not an accurate definition of the role.

Ward is aware of the irony that he, like Ossie Davis, gained wide recognition as an actor before his plays saw production. He enjoys acting but prefers writing: "I'll never think of acting as my first profession." Many of the Negro Ensemble Company's original productions in which Ward has acted are, however, finding wider audiences. In 1975, for example, Ward produced and performed in Lonne Elder's *Ceremonies for Dark Old Men* for the National Education Television Network.

During the last decade Ward has divided his time between writing plays and serving as artistic director of the Negro Ensemble Company. In an interview in 1973 Ward summarized the company's goals as it entered its fifth season: "to present on a permanent, consistent basis, quality theatre; to give a chance for mature black talent to continue to develop; to open the avenues for the development of new black talent; to train black artists in every phase of theatre—from artistic to administrative; to develop a workshop training program for young blacks with theatre aspirations; to do artistic works of relevance to black people; and to find and develop a black audience." Ward estimates that for any given show, the company's 150-seat house would be "60 to 65 percent filled by our black audience." Although financial straits have in recent years reduced the scope of some of the Negro Ensemble Company's ambitious goals, the company still profits from Ward's capable leadership. The contribution of the company to theatre in general and to an artistically sophisticated representation of black culture in particular is a major achievement. Ward was the recipient of the *Ebony* Black Achievement Award in November 1980. This honor was bestowed on him for his work with the Negro Ensemble Company and his overall excellence in dramatic arts. Ward's abilities as a playwright and artistic director have earned an enduring position in the history of American drama.

–*Gail Stewart*

Periodical Publications:
"American Theatre: For Whites Only?," *New York Times*, 14 August 1966, II:1;

"Needed: A Theatre for Black Themes," *Negro Digest* (December 1967): 34-39;
"Gut Response," *Newsweek* (December 1973): 82.

References:
Doris Abramson, *The Negro Playwright in the American Theatre, 1925-1959* (New York: Columbia University Press, 1969), pp. 279-281;
C. W. E. Bigsby, "Three Black Playwrights: Loften Mitchell, Ossie Davis, Douglas Turner Ward," in his *The Black American Writer*, vol. 2 (Deland, Fla.: Everett/Edwards, 1969), pp. 137-155;
Ellen Foreman, "The Negro Ensemble Company: A Transcendent Vision," in *The Theatre of Black Americans*, vol. 2, ed. Errol Hill (Englewood Cliffs, N.J.: Prentice-Hall, 1980), pp. 72-84;
Paul Carter Harrison, *The Drama of Nommo* (New York: Grove, 1972), pp. 174-176, 207, 228-229;
Elenore Lester, "We Exist to Create A Real Black Theatre," *New York Times*, 2 March 1975, II;
James A. Patterson, "The Negro Ensemble Company," *Players*, 47 (June-July 1972): 224-229;
Robert A. Raines, ed., *Modern Drama and Social Change* (Englewood Cliffs, N.J.: Prentice-Hall, 1972).

Thornton Wilder

Sally Johns
University of South Carolina

BIRTH: Madison, Wisconsin, 17 April 1897, to Amos Parker and Isabella Thornton Niven Wilder.

EDUCATION: Oberlin College, 1915-1917; A.B., Yale University, 1920; A.M., Princeton University, 1926.

AWARDS: Pulitzer Prize for *The Bridge of San Luis Rey*, 1928; Pulitzer Prize for *Our Town*, 1938; Pulitzer Prize for *The Skin of Our Teeth*, 1943; Litt. D., Yale University, 1947; American Academy of Arts and Letters Gold Medal for Fiction, 1952; U.S. Presidential Medal of Freedom, 1963; National Medal of Literature, 1965; National Book Award for *The Eighth Day*, 1968.

DEATH: New Haven, Connecticut, 7 December 1975.

PRODUCTIONS: *The Trumpet Shall Sound*, 10 December 1926, American Laboratory Theatre, New York, 30 [performances];
Lucrece, translated and adapted from André Obey's *Le Viol de Lucrèce*, 20 December 1932, Belasco Theatre, New York, 31;
A Doll's House, translated and adapted from Henrik Ibsen's play, 27 December 1937, Morosco Theatre, New York, 142;
Our Town, 4 February 1938, Henry Miller's Theatre, New York, 336;
The Merchant of Yonkers, 28 December 1938, Guild

Theatre, New York, 39; revised as *The Match-maker*, 5 December 1955, Royale Theatre, New York, 486;

The Skin of Our Teeth, 18 November 1942, Plymouth Theatre, New York, 355;

Our Century, 26 April 1947, Century Association, New York;

The Happy Journey to Trenton and Camden, 9 February 1948, Cort Theatre, New York, 318;

A Life in the Sun, 25 August 1955, Assembly Hall, Edinburgh, Scotland;

The Wreck of the 5:25 and *Bernice*, 20 September 1957, Congresshalle Theater, West Berlin, Germany;

Das Lange Weihnachtsmal (opera version of *The Long Christmas Dinner*), libretto by Wilder, music by Paul Hindemith, 17 December 1961, National Theatre, Manheim, Germany;

Plays for Bleecker Street (*Infancy*, *Childhood*, and *Someone from Assisi*), 11 January 1962, Circle in the Square, New York, 349;

Die Alkestiade (opera version of *A Life in the Sun*), libretto by Wilder, music by Louise Talma, 1 March 1962, Stadische Buhnen, Frankfurt, Germany;

Pullman Car Hiawatha, 3 December 1964, Circle in the Square, New York, 33;

Thornton Wilder's Triple Bill (*The Long Christmas Dinner*, *Queens of France*, and *The Happy Journey to Trenton and Camden*), 6 September 1966, Cherry Lane Theatre, New York, 55;

The Drunken Sisters, 28 June 1970, Spencer Memorial Church, Brooklyn Heights, New York.

SELECTED BOOKS: *The Cabala* (New York: A. & C. Boni, 1926; London: Longmans, Green, 1926);

The Bridge of San Luis Rey (London: Longmans, Green, 1927; New York: A. & C. Boni, 1927);

The Angel That Troubled the Waters and Other Plays (New York: Coward-McCann, 1928; London: Longmans, Green, 1928)—includes *Nascunter Poetae*, *Proserpina and the Devil*, *Fanny Otcott*, *Brother Fire*, *The Penny That Beauty Spent*, *The Angel on the Ship*, *The Message and Jehanne*, *Childe Roland to the Dark Tower Came*, *Centaurs*, *Leviathan*, *And the Sea Shall Give Up Its Dead*, *Now the Servant's Name Was Malchus*, *Mozart and the Gray Steward*, *Hast Thou Considered My Servant Job?*, *The Flight into Egypt*, and *The Angel That Troubled the Waters*;

The Woman of Andros (New York: A. & C. Boni, 1930; London: Longmans, Green, 1930);

The Long Christmas Dinner & Other Plays in One Act (New York: Coward-McCann / New Haven: Yale University Press, 1931; London: Longmans, Green, 1931)—includes *The Long Christmas Dinner*, *Queens of France*, *Pullman Car Hiawatha*, *Love and How to Cure It*, *Such Things Only Happen in Books*, and *The Happy Journey to Trenton and Camden*;

Lucrece, adapted from André Obey's *Le Viol de Lucrèce* (Boston & New York: Houghton Mifflin, 1933; London: Longmans, Green, 1933);

Heaven's My Destination (London, New York & Toronto: Longmans, Green, 1934; New York & London: Harper, 1935);

Our Town (New York: Coward McCann, 1938; London: Longmans, Green, 1956);

The Merchant of Yonkers (New York & London: Harper, 1939);

The Skin of Our Teeth (New York & London: Harper, 1942; London: Longmans, Green, 1958);

Our Century (New York: Century Association, 1947);

The Ides of March (New York & London: Harper, 1948; London: Longmans, Green 1948);

The Drunken Sisters (New York, Hollywood, London & Toronto: French, 1957);

The Matchmaker (New York, Hollywood, London & Toronto: French, 1957);

Three Plays: Our Town, The Skin of Our Teeth, The Matchmaker (New York: Harper, 1957; London: Longmans, Green, 1958);

Plays for Bleecker Street, 3 vols. (New York: French, 1960-1961)—includes *Infancy*, *Childhood*, and *Someone from Assisi*;

The Eighth Day (New York, Evanston & London: Harper & Row, 1967; London: Longmans, 1967);

Theophilus North (New York, Evanston, San Francisco & London: Harper & Row, 1973; London: Allen Lane, 1974);

The Alcestiad (New York, Hagerstown, San Francisco & London: Harper & Row, 1977);

American Characteristics and Other Essays, ed. Donald Gallup (New York, Hagerstown, San Francisco & London: Harper & Row, 1979).

On the strength of only three full-length plays and a bare handful of one-acts, Thornton Wilder ranks among the top half dozen playwrights in the history of American theatre. The modest volume of his dramatic work is the result not of a limitation of talent or interest; rather, it is due to the fact that his abilities and inclinations were multifocused, without becoming diffused. His career is marked with superior achievement in three fields: academics and fiction as well as drama. Beginning as a schoolmaster for young boys, he eventually held the Charles Eliot Norton Professorship of Poetry at Harvard. His fiction was rewarded with both the Pulitzer Prize and the National Book Award. In the field of drama, *Our Town* (1938) not only won the Pulitzer Prize, but has become this country's best-known and most-produced play. *The Skin of Our Teeth* (1942), another Pulitzer Prize winner, expanded Wilder's reputation to international status; the play's high esteem continues in the United States as well as Europe, and particularly in Germany. His light farce *The Matchmaker* (1955), designed as a spoof of conventional theatre, survives in transformation as America's most popular musical comedy, *Hello, Dolly!* A classicist and humanist with a profound interest in the past—both ancient and recent— Wilder has always appealed to the sentimental, yet his works skillfully avoid sentimentality. His literary career, punctuated by the crests of awards and renown, also survived momentarily devastating attacks: a lambasting for elitism amid proletarian suffering at the beginning of the Depression, and an accusation that *The Skin of Our Teeth* was plagiarized. His achievement in American drama lies in his employment of innovative, unconventional theatrical techniques to affirm conventional, humanistic values.

He was born Thornton Niven Wilder on 17 April 1897, in Madison, Wisconsin, the surviving member of a set of twin boys. His siblings included Amos, two years his senior, who later became a distinguished professor, theologian, and writer; Charlotte, born in 1898; Isabel, born in 1900, herself a writer who devoted most of her adult life to serving as Wilder's confidante, traveling companion, correspondence secretary, and general buffer against the world; and Janet, born in 1910. He was named for his mother, the former Isabella Thornton Niven, daughter of a Presbyterian minister. His father, Amos Parker Wilder, had earned a doctorate in political science and at the time of Wilder's birth was working as editor of the *Wisconsin State Journal*. Both this man's personality and his career were important influences on shaping his young son. Amos Wilder was a robust, stern, morally upright man who placed exacting demands on himself and his family, and Thornton Wilder's critics and biographers agree that the playwright sensed very strongly that his interests and achievements—both as a child and later as an adult—never won his father's approval. In addition,

Amos Wilder's decision in 1906 to enter the foreign service had a profound effect on the entire family. He accepted the post of consul general in Hong Kong; though Isabella and the children accompanied him, after six months they returned to the United States, and although they would again live in the same city, the entire family never again shared a household. Though Amos Wilder was a hemisphere away, however, his presence was continuously felt: through correspondence he kept abreast of his children's progress in school, constantly urging superior achievement and admonishing them when their marks fell below his expectations.

Because of his father's career, Wilder's early formal education came from a unique variety of institutions. After being uprooted from Wisconsin at the age of nine, he attended a German school in Hong Kong for six months before moving with his mother and siblings to Berkeley, California, where he was enrolled in public school. In 1909 his father was transferred to Shanghai, where the family rejoined him and the children were placed in boarding schools. After a brief period in a German school, fourteen-year-old Thornton was sent to the China Inland Mission School at Chefoo. He did not fare well at the Mission School (which was run like an English public school), and after a little more than a year his father sent him to join his older brother at the Thatcher School in Ojai, California. He withdrew after a year, joining his mother and sisters who were resituated in Berkeley, and in 1915 graduated from Berkeley High School. During his two years at Berkeley High he frequented the Liberty Theater in Oakland, participated in some of the school's dramatic productions, and dreamed of attending his father's alma mater, Yale.

Perhaps fearing the negative influence of Yale's worldliness, Amos Wilder instead enrolled his disappointed son at Oberlin College, far more isolated in location and religious in atmosphere. Despite his initial chagrin, young Wilder, who had up to this time been rather withdrawn, found at Oberlin an acceptance that he had never before enjoyed at an academic institution. He participated in student theatrics, studied the classics with Professor Charles H. A. Wager (according to Wilder, "the greatest lecturer I have ever heard"), and saw several of his writings published in the *Oberlin Literary Magazine* (some of which were later included in his volume of brief plays, *The Angel That Troubled the Waters and Other Plays*, 1928). After two years, however, he was again uprooted by his father, who had settled in New Haven, Connecticut, as executive director of Yale-in-China. Though Yale had previously been his supreme goal, Wilder was less than enthusiastic over the transfer, for he had thrived in the intimate and stimulating atmosphere of Oberlin. Though he never became part of the inner circle at Yale (he was lacking in athletic ability, masculine good looks, and social prominence), he did make a place for himself through his increasing gregariousness and his literary abilities. When World War I came, Wilder, like most of his classmates, was eager to participate, but nearsightedness prevented his acceptance by various branches of service. He finally entered the Coast Artillery Corps in September 1918, serving briefly at Fort Adams, Rhode Island, before being discharged in time to return to Yale in January 1919. Before his graduation in 1920, he was elected to the literary group Pundits and served on the editorial board of the *Yale Literary Magazine*, which published several of his short plays and essays and—in serialized form—his first long play, *The Trumpet Shall Sound* (1926).

Though Wilder knew upon his graduation that he wanted to be a writer, his father had other plans for the son he considered less than competent: a schoolmaster's wages, though meager, would provide a steady and stable income for the family, should they need to rely upon him as a source of support. Bowing to duty, Wilder acquiesced, agreeing to spend a preparatory year as a resident visitor studying archaeology at the American Academy in Rome. In addition to attending classes and participating in expeditions, he learned Italian and pursued the classics, with which he had become fascinated when studying with Professor Wager at Oberlin. He also began to collect material for "Memoirs of a Roman Student" (the working title of *The Cabala*, which would be published in 1926). After several months his idyll was interrupted by a cable from his father—still firmly holding the reins—announcing that he had secured for his son a position teaching French at the Lawrenceville School in Princeton, New Jersey. For four years Wilder remained at the select preparatory school for boys, teaching French and serving as assistant master of Davis House. In the time he could find to write, he continued work on "Memoirs of a Roman Student," an excerpt from which was published in the September 1922 issue of *Double Dealer*. Additionally, the February 1924 issue of *S4N* included "A Diary: First and Last Entry," Wilder's last short story published in a commercial periodical. His summers were spent escorting young students to Europe, their parents providing the passage he could not otherwise afford. On one such voyage he met drama critic Stark Young, who in 1924 intro-

duced him to Edith Isaacs, editor of *Theatre Arts Monthly*. Impressed with his readings from "Memoirs of a Roman Student," she recommended him for a scholarship at the MacDowell Colony in Peterborough, New Hampshire; the summer of 1924 was the first of several he spent at this mountain encampment for artists. She also commissioned him (in the temporary absence of John Mason Brown) to review for *Theatre Arts Monthly* the fifteen or so New York theatre openings in early 1925.

Encouraged by a former Yale classmate, Lewis Baer, who had become a partner in the new publishing firm Albert & Charles Boni, Wilder turned his attention to completing the novel begun in Rome. In order to have more time for writing, he resigned his position at Lawrenceville to enroll in the master's program in French at Princeton. After spending the summer at a tutoring camp for boys preparing for college boards (a source of income to which he would return several times), he began his studies at Princeton and, despite periodic writer's block, completed his first book. The fictitious memoirs of a young American among a wealthy and socially prominent coterie in Rome, the volume was retitled *The Cabala* and published in the spring of 1926 to a small but generally favorable reception.

In addition to the publication of his first novel, the year 1926 brought two other events of significance to Wilder's life: he was awarded the A.M. in French, and the first of his plays was professionally produced. On the recommendation of Edith Isaacs, Richard Boleslavsky produced *The Trumpet Shall Sound* (which Wilder had written while a student at Yale) at the American Laboratory Theatre. Trained by Stanislavsky at the Moscow Art Theatre, Boleslavsky was intrigued with the play's nonrealistic approach. A lengthy allegory, it presents a master who leaves his servants in charge of his house, returns to find that his maid has rented out the rooms of his mansion to a collection of undesirables, "sounds the trumpet" to place each of them in judgment, and ultimately forgives them for their wickedness. The link between the master of the mansion and God who in his mercy forgives even the worst of sinners is overly obvious. Except for bits of dialogue that ring true to conversational speech, the play is undistinguished, and the production was not a success.

Wilder himself was not involved with the premiere staging of his dramatic work. During the fall of 1926 he was touring Europe (again in the employ of the parents of a bored adolescent) where, in Paris, he began a seemingly unlikely friendship with Ernest Hemingway. Wilder's biographer Richard

H. Goldstone surmises that in addition to a common interest in writing, the two were attracted to each other as complementary opposites: "Wilder respected Hemingway's athleticism, his bravado, his openness, his professionalism; and Hemingway, in turn, admired Wilder's cultivation, his taste, his wit, his detachment."

During the European tour Wilder was at work on a second novel, which he completed in the summer of 1927 before returning to the Lawrenceville School, this time with a promotion to master of Davis House. Though he had published one novel and was certain of the publication of a second, he could not realistically expect a living income from royalties, so he unenthusiastically returned to teaching out of financial necessity. During the fall term his gloom increased, and his depression was compounded by appendicitis that necessitated serious surgery and a long convalescence. During his recovery, on vacation in Miami Beach, he introduced himself to Gene Tunney, whose title as world heavyweight boxing champion had made him an international celebrity. There began another of Wilder's celebrated incongruous relationships; the press would later have a heyday with the friendship between the diminutive, unathletic writer and the world-championship boxer with a taste for books.

The novel that Wilder had completed the previous summer was published in late 1927, and its reception came as a total surprise to its author. By early 1928, *The Bridge of San Luis Rey* had earned a monumental stack of favorable reviews, by spring its author had become a bona fide celebrity, and in May it was awarded the Pulitzer Prize. The novel is actually three separate stories, threaded together loosely through plot but tightly through theme, set within a rather obtrusive and unnecessary frame. The setting is early eighteenth-century Peru. A friar witnesses the collapse of a slat-and-vine bridge, sending its five travelers plunging to their deaths in the gorge far below. This friar's examination of the lives of the victims, in order to determine God's purpose in allowing them to die, provides the frame that opens and closes the novel; the three episodes within trace the lives of those who have perished. Their stories reveal a common theme: each had focused obsessively on an object of affection who either could not or did not reciprocate; the extensiveness of the obsession resulted in spiritual isolation from the rest of humanity. Shortly before traveling over the bridge, each had awakened to the folly of such an obsession and had set out in a new direction, attempting to make recompense. An expression of Wilder's Christian humanism, the novel

presents a concept that recurs in *Our Town*: there is wastefulness—sinfulness, even—in failure to examine and appreciate every experience. Though the book has been read by many for its "inspirational" value, it is unsentimental in its valuation of vigorous participation in life; it in no way encourages neglect of earthly experience in favor of promises of an afterlife. Wilder's prose style, influenced by his study of the classics, achieves a simple elegance that is neither ornate nor archaic. In addition to winning high critical acclaim, the novel has remained Wilder's most popularly successful work of fiction.

The book brought its author the financial security that allowed him to resign his position at Lawrenceville and sail to England in the summer of 1928. He was soon joined by Gene Tunney for a "walking tour" of Europe that brought him even wider press coverage than his Pulitzer Prize-winning novel. After the summer he extended his stay for several months, traveling with his sister Isabel and working on a third novel. While he was in Europe, in November 1928, *The Angel That Troubled the Waters and Other Plays* was published. The volume includes sixteen very brief works (its title was at one time to have been "Three-Minute Plays for Three Persons") composed over a twelve-year period beginning during Wilder's high school days. Though the short pieces exhibit the scope of Wilder's knowledge of literature, history, and philosophy, they fall short as dramatic works; their very brevity precludes any sort of development, and many of them contain actions or events totally impossible to stage ("Suddenly the thirty pieces of silver are cast upward from the revolted hand of Judas. They hurtle through the skies, flinging their enormous shadows across the stars and continue falling forever through the vast funnel of space"). However, what appears to be blatant disregard for the realities of theatrical production may in fact be the early (perhaps unconscious) rebellion against conventional staging by a playwright whose later innovations would supersede many of these limitations. Elements of some of the plays do prefigure later works: *Proserpina and the Devil*, for instance, combines past and present, as well as Christianity and Roman mythology, foreshadowing the omnidimensional world created so effectively in *The Skin of Our Teeth*. Also noteworthy is Wilder's foreword, in which he comments on the nature of the budding artist ("Authors of fifteen and sixteen years of age spend their time drawing up title-pages and adjusting the tables of contents of works they have neither the perseverance nor the ability to execute"), and straightforwardly voices the point of view he espouses ("Almost all the plays in this book are religious, but religious in that dilute fashion that is a believer's concession to a contemporary standard of good manners").

After returning to the United States in early 1929, Wilder set out on the first of several lecture tours. Though *The Bridge of San Luis Rey* had been a tremendous financial success, he felt that it would be imprudent to rely on his writing as a continuous source of income. By this time a failed venture in the newspaper business had broken his father both physically and financially, leaving the second son responsible for the support of his parents and his younger sisters. (The older son, Amos, had gone into the ministry, a choice of profession that had won his father's unqualified support, despite its lack of financial rewards.) Thus Wilder felt pressed to combine gainful employment with his writing efforts. In addition to the lecture tours, he accepted a post at the University of Chicago which allowed him to teach only part of the year, therefore freeing him to travel or concentrate on writing the remainder of the time.

Thornton Wilder

In early 1930 his third novel, *The Woman of Andros*, was published. Based on the Roman playwright Terence's comedy *Andria*, the book received reviews which, although mixed, were generally favorable, and so seemed destined for moderate success. Then in October 1930, to Wilder's complete surprise and dismay, a critical attack was launched that would temporarily demolish the reputation *The Bridge of San Luis Rey* had achieved for him. Michael Gold, a Communist journalist writing in the *New Republic*, lambasted Wilder as the "Prophet of the Genteel Christ" and his novel's religious stance as a "daydream of homosexual figures in graceful gowns moving archaically through the lilies." America had been plunged into the Depression, and Gold, a leader of the proletarian school of criticism, was enraged that in the midst of immediate social crisis Wilder, instead of using his art to champion reform, had chosen to display his New Humanist ideas in a setting as far removed as ancient Greece. He labeled Wilder's Jesus Christ "the First British Gentleman" and his religion "Anglo-Catholicism, that last refuge of the American literary snob." Though in retrospect the blatant vituperativeness of Gold's piece clearly nullifies it as criticism, in 1930 it created a literary controversy from which Wilder could not emerge totally unscathed, although he was ably defended in print by such notables as Edmund Wilson. Realizing that the fabric of American culture was indeed changing, he maintained his humanistic concepts but turned his talents in new directions, leaving behind temporarily both fiction and the past.

The publication of *The Long Christmas Dinner & Other Plays in One Act* in 1931 marks the beginning of Wilder's successful career as an American dramatist. If Gold's attack had forced his attentions to the subject matter of his own time and place, his European travels and experiences with that continent's experiments in nonrealistic theatre had also profoundly influenced his approach. While this volume may be considered the workshop in which he refined the techniques so highly lauded in the later *Our Town* and *The Skin of Our Teeth*, it is no mere testing ground; it contains some of his finest dramatic works.

The title work deals with one of Wilder's favorite subjects: time. Several conventional elements unify the play: its setting is the dining room of an American household, with the long table set for Christmas dinner, and its characters are the family members. However, the action of the one-act spans a period of ninety years, its characters changing as one generation passes on and another replaces it. As the play opens, a young couple celebrating their first Christmas in a newly built house share the festivities with the husband's mother, who remembers girlhood experiences "on this very ground." As the play progresses, characters exit through a portal representing death and enter through an opposite door representing birth, suggesting the ebb and flow of life. As babies are born and grow to adulthood, other family members quietly leave through death's portal—some dying of old age, one a victim of war, and one a baby who died at birth. The rhythm is gentle and smooth, sustained through the constant situation of the family Christmas dinner. Wilder's dialogue is simple and believable; as in *Our Town*, the focus is on the commonplace—the weather, the Christmas sermon, a parent's aspirations for a child—but here the time frame allows for a very effective use of repetition. As the generations pass, the same comments are echoed and reechoed as "Mother" is tempted with "just another sliver of white meat" and the head of the family toasts "the ladies" with a glass of wine. Thus Wilder masterfully fuses the recognizable, the ordinary of American life with an innovative nonrealistic theatrical technique.

Queens of France, though also consistent with Wilder's philosophy of celebrating the ordinary, is more conventionally realistic in technique. Set in New Orleans in 1869, it presents an unscrupulous lawyer who preys on the spiritual poverty of naive women. Convincing each that she is the long-lost successor to the French throne, he persuades her to "purchase" various of the royal artifacts, thereby providing funds necessary for locating documents that will prove the authenticity of her claim. Though Cahusac, the lawyer, is clearly a swindler, he inadvertently brings a new vigor to these women's lives. As one of the women, upon abandoning hope that proof will be discovered, observes dreamily, "It was so beautiful while it lasted. It made even school-teaching a pleasure." Though the external conditions of her life had remained unchanged, and the belief that she was in fact a monarch had been kept a secret between the lawyer and herself, by perceiving herself as uncommon, she had experienced greater appreciation of her very singular life.

Pullman Car Hiawatha is the most technically ambitious of the collection. Virtually plotless, it represents a slice of life (radiating from the narrow to the cosmic) on a train journeying from New York to Chicago on the evening of "December twenty-first, 1930." Here Wilder employs several of the devices used by the German expressionists and their

American followers, but to a significantly different end. The travelers are types rather than fully developed characters—a maiden lady, a young couple, a middle-aged doctor, an insane woman—and cities, fields, planets, and even units of time are personified by actors ("The minutes are gossips; the hours are philosophers; the years are theologians"). However, unlike the works of expressionists who seek to demonstrate the dehumanization and insignificance of man, Wilder's panorama displays a vast but ordered cosmos of which man is an integral part. Presiding over the presentation is the Stage Manager (employed most famously in the later *Our Town*), who introduces the audience to the characters and setting (represented by chairs placed within chalk-marked areas of an otherwise bare stage), takes various roles within the action, and provides commentary throughout.

Love and How to Cure It, in the vein of *Queens of France*, is conventional in presentation technique. Three performers—a young ballerina, a comedian, and a soubrette—await a rehearsal on the bare stage of a Soho music hall in 1895. Linda, the "beautiful, impersonal, remote, almost sullen" dancer, is plagued by an undesired suitor, a young student who she is convinced is about to shoot her because she refuses to return his affections. The older soubrette and the comedian invite the student to share their supper, secretly unloading the gun he has hidden in his cape. After putting the young man at ease with casual, friendly conversation, the comedian tells him gravely that he does not know what to make of newspaper accounts of "people who shoot the persons they love." He suspects that they want to be noticed, and for those who must shoot to get noticed, "it's themselves they love." Confessing that he had planned to shoot himself rather than his love, the young man apologizes to Linda, thanks the older pair for their kindness, concludes that "just loving isn't wasted," remarks on his own youth, and takes his leave. The young girl is still unmoved, but the older soubrette patiently notes, "Well, young lady, you're only sixteen. Wait 'til your turn comes. We'll have to take care of you."

Such Things Only Happen in Books is also a realistic drama; though it was removed by Wilder when the collection was reprinted, it is an effectively ironic piece. Set in a young couple's library / study / living room in a New Hampshire village, it comments on the major (rather than mere minor) details of life which may be missed by its unobservant participants. The husband, a writer, plays solitaire while his wife sews. He comments that the card game is "like fiction. You have to adjust the cards to make a plot. In life most people live along without plots." Through the course of the play the audience learns that the couple's house is filled with "plots": their maid, Katie, who is suffering from serious burns, actually received her injuries while harboring her brother, an escaped prisoner, in the kitchen; the wife is having an affair with the doctor who treats the maid; and two rather mysterious visitors are in fact the former inhabitants of the house who probably murdered their father. Holding fast to the notion that the excitement of fiction seldom touches real life, the unsuspecting husband maintains that "when you come down to it, the rank and file—rich and poor—live much as we do. Not much plot. Work and a nice wife and a nice house and a nice Katie."

The Happy Journey to Trenton and Camden is the most frequently anthologized and most frequently performed of the plays in the volume. In tone and technique it strongly prefigures *Our Town*. Its plot line is simple: Ma and Pa Kirby, along with their children Arthur and Caroline, take an automobile trip to visit their married daughter. Again a Stage Manager appears, but here he offers no comment on the action; instead, he plays various supplementary roles—a neighbor bidding the family goodbye, a gas station attendant—reading his lines from a typescript. Wilder again employs no scenery; four chairs suffice for the automobile, and all the props are imaginary. The focus is on the commonplace: as the lower-middle-class family ride through the countryside, they admire the scenery, read from billboards, eat hot dogs, bicker mildly, and eagerly anticipate their visit. Only in a moving scene after they arrive does the audience learn the full reason for the trip: the married daughter is recovering from a difficult childbirth in which her baby died. Emerging as the most strongly developed character is Ma Kirby, whose mundane aphorisms indicate a simple but clear and solid philosophy of life based on a positive outlook, appreciation of natural beauty, sincere devotion to family, and patient acceptance of a divine plan beyond human understanding. Of the six plays in this collection, this one best rebuts Michael Gold's charge that Wilder was incapable of writing an "American" work.

Although all of the plays in the volume were staged before the end of 1931 (on bills of various combinations at Yale, Vassar, the University of Chicago, and Antioch), and their stock productions soon began to provide Wilder with modest royalty checks, none was given a professional Broadway production until several years later. In 1948 *The Happy Journey to Trenton and Camden*, on a bill with

Jean Paul Sartre's *The Respectful Prostitute*, ran for 318 performances at the Cort Theatre. *Pullman Car Hiawatha* was produced in 1964 at Circle in the Square, and *Thornton Wilder's Triple Bill* (*The Long Christmas Dinner*, *Queens of France*, and *The Happy Journey to Trenton and Camden*) appeared at the Cherry Lane Theatre in 1966. An operatic version of *The Long Christmas Dinner (Das Lange Weihnachtsmal)*, with libretto by Wilder and music by Paul Hindemith, was presented in Germany in 1961.

Wilder's next writing for the theatre was a translation and adaptation of André Obey's *Le Viol de Lucrèce* (*The Rape of Lucrece*). A vehicle for Katharine Cornell, the production (entitled simply *Lucrece*) marked the first appearance on Broadway of a Wilder work. Despite a stellar list of collaborators (direction by Guthrie McClintic, music by Deems Taylor, choreography by Martha Graham), it was a failure. It opened in December 1932 at the Belasco Theatre, received unfavorable notices, and closed after only thirty-one performances.

During this period (the early and mid-1930s), Wilder's half-year position at the University of Chicago allowed him time to pursue interests beyond teaching and writing. His friendship with Alexander Woollcott provided him with an entree to the New York theatre circles that had long fascinated him. Although he was regarded by some as an academic unversed in the realities of professional theatre, he enjoyed an easy social relationship with many of New York's luminaries, and established more important friendships with a few. One was Jed Harris, a former Yale classmate who had become a successful producer; impressed with the volume of one-acts, he would a few years later produce Wilder's first Broadway success, *Our Town*. Another was actress Ruth Gordon, whose genuine friendship continued long after Wilder had parted ways with most of the other celebrities he reveled in socializing with during this period. The novel he was working on at this time was published in late 1934. *Heaven's My Destination*, a comic-spirited picaresque, presents the journey of a naive religious fanatic book salesman through the skeptical Midwest of the 1930s. Though the book's reputation has increased with time, on publication it met with generally unfavorable reviews. The stimulation provided by Wilder's theatrical friends, coupled with his dwindling success in the world of fiction, prompted him to once again turn his focus toward writing for the stage.

Among those few who lauded *Heaven's My Destination*—and her praise was high indeed; she called it *the* American novel—was Gertrude Stein.

Though he had been familiar with her writings, Wilder did not meet her until the mid-1930s when she visited Chicago as part of an American lecture tour. They began to correspond, and when she returned to conduct a lecture series at the University of Chicago, he gave up his apartment to her and Alice B. Toklas. The friendship that developed was one of the most enriching of Wilder's life. Something of an isolate as a child, he later developed a gregariousness and social self-confidence that made him entertaining company, and he took great pleasure in various types of socializing. However, despite his sincere conviviality, he remained essentially a very private person emotionally. Whenever questioned as to why he had never married, he responded that the emotional energy required by his writing precluded such a relationship. The consistent answer was only a half-truth, for he was a homosexual; however, his life included no long-term emotional relationship with a male. He never spoke publicly of his homosexuality, and his sexual preference was kept so private that even many people who were closely acquainted with him assumed that he was neither homosexual nor heterosexual, but asexual. He formed few strong emotional attachments. Throughout his life, however, he enjoyed several freindships with women (often older than he), among them Lady Sibyl Colefax, the celebrated London hostess whom he had met during the 1920s, and actress Ruth Gordon. The relationship with Gertrude Stein was the most important friendship with a woman (perhaps with anyone) of his entire life. Besides stimulating him intellectually, she nurtured him artistically and influenced him philosophically and aesthetically, and their visits and correspondence continued until her death in 1946.

By the spring of 1936 Wilder had become quite tired of his teaching duties, and he used the occasion of his father's serious illness and ultimate death to resign his post at the University of Chicago. Though his schedule still included lecture tours, he found himself free to travel, visit friends, and work on several long plays (some of which were never completed). He translated and adapted Ibsen's *A Doll's House* for a late 1937 production starring Ruth Gordon. Both the production (which ran for 142 performances) and the translation were reviewed favorably, encouraging the producer, Jed Harris, to maintain his interest in the playwright's talents; for several years he had insisted that Wilder would someday write a play of real significance, and he wanted to produce it. His opportunity came with the work that ultimately sent Wilder's reputation

back to the peak from which it had plummeted with Gold's 1930 attack in the *New Republic*.

Our Town, possibly America's most read and most produced play, opened in February 1938. Despite his confidence in both Wilder's script and the production he had mounted, producer and director Jed Harris experienced some uneasiness in anticipation of the critics' reaction to a play encompassing so many unusual elements. The out-of-town tryouts were met with a cool reception, but the New York critics—spearheaded by Brooks Atkinson—gradually built up a favorable response matched by public enthusiasm that resulted in a run of 336 performances. The play's success notwithstanding, the reviewers did not award it the New York Drama Critics Circle Award (which went instead to *Of Mice and Men*), but it won for Wilder his second Pulitzer Prize.

In *Our Town* Wilder combines in a full-length work several of the experimental elements employed in the collection of one-acts. As in *Pullman Car Hiawatha* and *The Happy Journey to Trenton and Camden*, an omniscient Stage Manager—with comfortable casualness and wry humor—provides exposition, narration, and commentary, occasionally playing a brief role as well. His verbal descriptions and the actors' pantomimed business create the imaginary props and scenery on an essentially bare-stage set. Like *Pullman Car Hiawatha*, this play begins with the specific details of specific lives and then expands to place those lives within a cosmic context. Wilder fuses his theatrical techniques with Gertrude Stein's notions of the relationship between the individual and eternity, as well as his own belief (echoed from, among other works, *The Bridge of San Luis Rey*) in the inestimable value of appreciating human experience.

In the first act, called "Daily Life," the Stage Manager introduces the audience to Grover's Corners, New Hampshire, on 7 May 1901. The action encompasses the events of a single ordinary, decidedly unspectacular day. The town's inhabitants meander in and out of the action, going about their daily routines of delivering newspapers, preparing breakfast, gossiping about the town drunk, walking home from choir practice. The focus is on two families, the Webbs and the Gibbeses, and particularly on the oldest child of each family. Emily Webb and George Gibbes, high-school students, are next-door neighbors whose collaboration on homework is obviously evidence of a budding romance. Although the townspeople's dialogue has the aura of verisimilitude, both the presence of the Stage Manager and the absence of scenery maintain the play's anti-illusionary effect. At the end of the act, as Emily's father whistles "Blessed Be the Tie That Binds," George's younger sister effectively links the day's events to a larger perspective by telling her brother of the remarkable address on a letter a sick friend had received from her minister: Jane Crofut; The Crofut Farm; Grover's Corners; Sutton County; New Hampshire; United States of America; Continent of North America; Western

over a lifetime have "eaten over fifty thousand meals" together. In the first act he demonstrated his omniscience; here he exhibits his control over conventional time. It is George and Emily's wedding day, and several minutes of dialogue present the early morning events of that day: meditativeness, nostalgia, and anxiousness characterize the parents of the bride and groom. Then the Stage Manager interrupts to turn back the scene to the events lead-

Our Town

Hemisphere; the Earth; the Solar System; the Universe; the Mind of God—"And the postman brought it just the same." The Stage Manager closes the act with a characteristically casual remark directly to the audience: "That's the end of the First Act, friends. You can go and smoke now, those that smoke."

Act 2 is called "Love and Marriage." Wilder points out in his preface to a 1957 volume including *Our Town* that "the recurrent words in this play (few have noticed it) are 'hundreds,' 'thousands,' and 'millions.' " He maintains that in the face of multiplicity of such magnitude, "each individual's assertion to an absolute reality can only be inner, very inner." The Stage Manager points up the vastness of the continuum of all human experience as he introduces the second act, set three years after the first: he speaks in terms of the sun having "come up over a thousand times" and elderly couples who

ing up to the marriage: "I'm awfully interested in how big things like that begin." George and Emily reenact a conversation in the drugstore (with the Stage Manager playing the druggist), just before their senior year of high school, during which they discuss the future and shyly but sincerely declare their affection for each other. Then time is returned to the present, and the act concludes with their wedding ceremony, officiated by the Stage Manager.

Act 3 takes place nine years later. Entitled "Death," it is set in the little town's cemetery, represented simply by rows of ordinary chairs on which the actors are seated. According to the stage directions, "The dead do not turn their heads or their eyes to right or left, but they sit in a quiet without stiffness. When they speak their tone is matter-of-fact, without sentimentality and, above all, without lugubriousness." The occasion is the funeral of

Emily Webb Gibbes, who has died in childbirth. As the mourners arrive, the dead note their presence and reminisce not unkindly, but with a detachment that indicates their transcendence of both earthly pains and earthly pleasures. As one comments, "I'm always uncomfortable when *they're* here." Despite strong warnings that she will regret her mistake, newcomer Emily insists on going back to relive a time in the past. She chooses her twelfth birthday, and as she and the Stage Manager verbally create the scenery on the bare stage, she returns to the home and family of her childhood. She quickly discovers that the warnings were well-founded, for the experience is impossibly painful. Knowing the future, she attempts to savor the moments, to express her love to her mother who is preparing breakfast. Breaking into sobs, realizing in frustration that "It goes so fast. We don't have time to look at one another," she requests permission to say goodbye to the world she has known before rejoining the dead. Recognizing too late the value of her everyday experiences, she bids farewell to her parents, Grover's Corners, clocks ticking, newly ironed dresses—a list whose commonplaceness brings her to the awareness that human beings never "realize life while they live it." As she calmly takes her seat and George mourns silently at her grave, the Stage Manager quietly closes the play with a conversational monologue that combines comments on sleepy Grover's Corners at eleven o'clock (most everyone is asleep, someone has heard a train go by, and "at the livery stable somebody's setting up late and talking") with remarks about the heavenly bodies, particularly "this one" which is "straining away all the time to make something of itself. The strain's so bad that every sixteen hours everybody lies down and gets a rest." Winding his watch, he bids the audience good night with, "You get a good rest, too."

The play established for Wilder a permanent place in American theatre. Since its opening in 1938, scarcely a day has passed that *Our Town* has not been performed somewhere in this country—in productions ranging from professional revivals to little theatres to colleges and high schools. The original production brought the playwright an opportunity shared by few others: temporarily replacing actor Frank Craven as the Stage Manager, for two weeks in September 1938 he starred on Broadway in his own highly successful show. (He subsequently appeared in stock productions of *Our Town* and, somewhat less successfully, as Mr. Antrobus in *The Skin of Our Teeth*.) Additionally, the acclaim awarded the New York production boosted sales of the play's published version, thus significantly increasing Wilder's financial rewards.

His next Broadway production was initially far less successful. *The Merchant of Yonkers*, based on Johann Nestroy's *Einen Jux will er sich Machen* (1842), opened 28 December 1938 and closed after only thirty-nine performances. Wilder had turned the direction over to Max Reinhardt, whose work he had admired for several years, but the critical consensus was that the production suffered from what Harold Clurman called the Viennese Reinhardt's "unfamiliarity with American theatre custom." The play's later success substantiates the notion that the director, rather than the script, may have been at fault: after highly acclaimed runs at the Edinburgh Festival and in London, it was brought back in a slightly revised form to the New York stage in 1955 in a production that ran for 486 performances. Director Tyrone Guthrie's light touch and rapid pace set off Wilder's farce (retitled *The Matchmaker*) to its best advantage. *Hello, Dolly!*, the adaptation by Michael Stewart, with words and music by Jerry Herman, opened in 1964; that production's run of almost 3,000 performances, a smash hit film version, and a later Broadway revival with an all-black cast have made it one of America's most successful and most popular musical comedies of all times.

Because *The Matchmaker* is essentially the same script as *The Merchant of Yonkers*, its discussion properly follows *Our Town* in a chronological examination of Wilder's career. The alterations of the earlier version involve only minor changes in dialogue and the addition of a closing monologue to point up the theme; the most significant difference is in the title change, which marks a shift in focus from one character to another. The appearance of something so close to a well-made play at this point in Wilder's career might appear peculiar, for all his efforts thus far had clearly countered the box-set, representational, realistic traditional conventions. However, as he states in his preface to the later *Three Plays* (1957), "One way to shake off the nonsense of the nineteenth-century staging is to make fun of it." As Wilder critics point out, he significantly chooses "to make fun of" rather than "to satirize." Thus the piece is a skillfully crafted bit of light entertainment, a farce which—true to the nature of its genre—delights and amuses, but challenges neither the emotions nor the intellect of its audience.

The Yonkers merchant is Horace Vandergelder, a sixty-year-old miser who is more grumpy than villainous. In amassing his wealth he has consciously turned his back on human feelings and emotions. He has absolutely no patience with his lovesick niece, Ermengarde, for the object of her affections, Ambrose Kemper, is an artist; he regards the choice of either love or art above money as total foolishness. Also suffering from his stinginess are his clerks, Cornelius and Barnaby, two provincials who long for adventure in the big city. Their love interests are provided by a young and pretty widowed milliner, Irene Molloy, and her giddy assistant, Minnie Fay. The focal character is Mrs. Dolly Levi, an older widow whose philosophy of life is the exact opposite of Vandergelder's: "Money is like manure; it's not worth a thing unless it's spread about encouraging young things to grow." Her goal is to marry the miser so she can live more comfortably and do good with his money. Barnaby and Cornelius, determined that life will not pass them by, rebelliously blow up their employer's canned tomatoes and head into New York City. Vandergelder is also in the city, so their adventure is increased by the necessity to avoid him. The plot relies on traditional farcical conventions: madcap chases, mistaken identities, females dressed in male clothing, collapsing screens. As both the day of adventure and the play come to a close, Mrs. Levi's matchmaking has paid off: the four couples— Ermengarde and Ambrose, Cornelius and Irene, Barnaby and Minnie Fay, Dolly Levi and Horace Vandergelder—are happily joined. Those who sought life's excitement have found it, the misanthropic merchant is on the road to reform, and Barnaby (as the "youngest person here") is summoned to the footlights by Mrs. Levi to "tell us what the moral of the play is": "Oh, I think it's about . . . I think it's about adventure. The test of an adventure is that when you're in the middle of it, you say to yourself, 'Oh, now I've got myself into an awful mess; I wish I were sitting quietly at home.' And the sign that something's wrong with you is when you sit quietly at home wishing you were out having lots of adventure. . . ." The work is both lighthearted and lightweight, but its continued popularity attests to the playwright's mastery of stage-worthy farce; and its celebration of experience and "adventure" echoes Wilder's humanistic philosophy.

When his next play, *The Skin of Our Teeth*, opened in November 1942, its author was a captain in the U. S. Army Air Force. After the failure of *The Merchant of Yonkers*, Wilder had traveled extensively, including an unsuccessful sojourn in Mexico where he had hoped to find the perfect climate for writing. A trip to Europe included a visit with Gertrude Stein and Alice B. Toklas in France, where he tried in vain to warn them of the impending war and to persuade them to return to America. Among his literary interests were the works of James Joyce,

upon whose death he wrote a memorial piece for the March 1941 issue of *Poetry*. He also devoted some of his time to writing film scripts, the most notable of which was *Shadow of a Doubt* (1943) for Alfred Hitchcock. At the request of the State Department, he made a goodwill tour of Latin America in the spring of 1941; his mission was to foster favorable feelings toward the United States among the cultural and intellectual circles of the countries he visited. A growing patriotism and sympathy for the Allied forces prompted him, at the age of forty-five, to enlist in the U. S. Army Air Force; his commission in Intelligence led to his service for three years, first in Africa and later Italy, and a promotion to lieutenant colonel before his separation from the military in 1945.

The Skin of Our Teeth made a much greater impact, both positive and negative, than *The Merchant of Yonkers*. Its topicality no doubt contributed to its success: it celebrates the human race's ability to survive disaster, an optimistic notion enthusiastically embraced by audiences in the midst of World War II. Despite the misgivings of several producers and actors who hesitated to align themselves with a play so unconventional in approach, neophyte producer Michael Myerberg, then-untried director Elia Kazan, and an experienced cast headed by Tallulah Bankhead (Sabina), Fredrich March (Mr. Antrobus), and Florence Eldridge (Mrs. Antrobus) combined forces to yield a production that won immediate critical and popular acclaim.

In previous works Wilder had tampered with conventional concepts of time. In *The Long Christmas Dinner*, events occur sequentially, but the chronology is selective and compressed. The Stage Manager in *Our Town* exhibits both omniscience and an ability to control time: he is able to allow Emily to relive part of her twelfth birthday, implying that the past continues to exist, but past and present are clearly separate entities. *The Skin of Our Teeth* represents an even further departure, for here major events of the entire history of the human race occur simultaneously. As the play opens, the setting is modern-day Excelsior, New Jersey, but its inhabitants are suffering the perils of the Ice Age. Act 2, spotlighting a convention on the Boardwalk of Atlantic City, ends with Mr. Antrobus loading a boat with his family and two of each kind of animal, preparing for the onslaught of the Great Flood. In the third act the characters are back in Excelsior, trying to put back together the pieces of civilization after surviving a seven-year war.

To further compound the violation of traditional perceptions of time, the illusion created by conventional realistic theatre is constantly broken. The play opens with a slide show that includes projections of the theatre in which the drama is being performed. Sabina, the maid, periodically drops her character, assuming the role of an actress playing the maid (Miss Somerset), to confide to the audience her misgivings about a script that she does not understand. The house area several times becomes part of the set, and at the end of the first act, in an effort to collect firewood for warmth against the impending glacier, Sabina entreats the audience to "Pass up your chairs, everybody. Save the human race." Act 3 opens with a rehearsal of production staff volunteers who will fill in for actors stricken with a digestive disorder, and later the actors playing Mr. Antrobus and his son abandon their characters to discuss events in their own lives and facets of their own personalities that make it difficult for them to play a father-son confrontation scene. The stage manager occasionally discusses interpretation of action with other characters, but his function here differs from his predecessors in the one-acts and *Our Town*; he is given a name (Mr. Fitzpatrick), and he clearly is in charge of overseeing the production. His more conventional stage manager's role includes rehearsing the stand-ins, settling differences between actors, and cajoling Miss Somerset back into her role of Sabina in her recalcitrant moments—albeit this typically "behind the scenes" action takes place as part of the play, in view of the audience. Although these devices are encompassed in the onstage action, they serve as constant reminders to the audience that they are in fact watching a play, rather than observing an enactment of real life, an anti-illusionary Brechtian technique that promotes intellectual rather than emotional involvement and response.

The characterizations also contribute to the effect of melding all of human history. George and Maggie Antrobus are at once Adam and Eve, the archetypical Everyman and Everywoman, and the average modern middle-class couple. Mr. Antrobus, the inventor of the alphabet, the lever, and the wheel, commutes across the Hudson River and serves as president of his fraternal order. Through glacier, flood, and war his primary concern is preserving for future generations the advances civilization has made: as the ice approaches and temperatures drop, he offers refuge to Moses, Homer, and the Muses; when he returns from the war, he is anxious to be assured that his books have not been lost. Mrs. Antrobus is a further development of *The Happy Journey to Trenton and Camden*'s Ma Kirby, elevated to the next social class. An inventor herself

(of, among other things, the apron), she keeps as her watchword "Save the Family." She faces disaster with energy, determination, and resourcefulness. Sabina describes her as a fine woman who lives only for her children: "If it would be any benefit to her children she'd see the rest of us stretched out dead at her feet without turning a hair,—and that's the truth. If you want to know anything more about Mrs. Antrobus, just go and look at a tigress, and look hard."

Like their parents, the Antrobus children are allegorical figures. In the first act Gladys is admonished to "Put down your dress!!" and scolded for painting her face with makeup. Despite her mother's constant exhortations that she be a lady and make her father proud of her, the daughter becomes more and more sluttish. She shocks her parents by appearing on the Boardwalk in a pair of probably ill-gotten red stockings, and by the end of the war she is the mother of an illegitimate baby. Her brother Henry has a penchant for throwing stones; his name has been changed from Cain (his hair is combed forward in an effort to hide the mark on his forehead), and his parents are still pained by the "accident" in which he killed his brother. In the third act, after he has been identified as the enemy against whom the war has been fought, the stage directions indicate that in the confrontation with his father "Henry is played, not as a misunderstood or misguided young man, but as a representation of strong unreconciled evil."

The adjunct to the Antrobus family who as often as possible places herself at the center of the action is Lily Sabina, a combination of Lilith and the Sabine women (supposedly Mr. Antrobus has "raped" her and brought her home to insult his wife). In the first act she appears as the family's good-natured but less than efficient maid. As she introduces the other characters, she prattles to the audience (both in and out of character) about the confusion in the world around her; her low-level panic in the face of adversity is in opposition to Mrs. Antrobus's firm resolve. On the Boardwalk in act 2, after she has won the bathing beauty contest (under the name Lily Fairweather—but Mrs. Antrobus recognizes her for who she really is), she makes a concerted but unsuccessful effort to lure Mr. Antrobus away from his wife. In the final act she has resumed her former position with the family; she goes about her duties "out of *habit*" but without conviction, for after so many disasters she holds little faith in new beginnings. Her character provides much of the play's comedy, and both the role and Tallulah Bankhead's performance in it were given large credit for the premiere production's success.

Taken as a whole, the play is a delightfully nontraditional comedy with substantial seriousness that provides ballast without overweighting it into pretentiousness. Wilder's vision is again affirmative, but because he encapsulates the whole of human history simultaneously rather than sequentially, and because the play cyclically ends where it begins (Sabina's curtain speech duplicates her entrance in act 1, with the whole world "at sixes and sevens"), he offers no traditional "happy ending" with all troubles vanquished and all problems resolved. Instead, he presents the human race—faced with disasters of the highest magnitude, some natural and some man-made—exhibiting the ability to survive, keeping intact the contributions of the past as well as a strong desire to make some slight advances for the future. The play's engaging theatrical, anti-illusionary technique—complete with slides and newsreels, walls that first totter and then disappear into the loft, actors who drop their roles to voice their apprehensions and opinions to the audience and each other, and ludicrously costumed animals who parade through the audience—provides an opportunity for entertainment, surprise, and intellectual challenge.

Scarcely three months after the play's opening, amid critical acclaim and popular success, Joseph Campbell and Henry M. Robinson launched an attack in the *Saturday Review of Literature* that was reminiscent of Michael Gold's 1930 onslaught in its effect on Wilder's literary reputation. In an article entitled "The Skin of Whose Teeth?" they noted the similarities in theme and technique between Wilder's play and James Joyce's *Finnegans Wake*; although they avoided a direct accusation, the implication was that Wilder had plagiarized. The effect of the charge was compounded by the fact that at that time, the number of Americans, even among the literati, with firsthand knowledge of Joyce's work (published in 1939) was very small. Wilder himself did little to abate the controversy; refusing to take a stand, he suggested that those in doubt should read both works and make up their own minds. (Not until years later did he publicly respond to the charge; and in the preface to *Three Plays* he acknowledges a debt to Joyce, commenting that he would be pleased if future authors should feel similarly indebted to him. "Literature has always more resembled a torch race than a furious dispute among heirs.") Several critics of the day adopted the view that has prevailed in retrospect: that Wilder, as most artists do, was making legitimate use of another's work for his own purposes, and that (as phrased by *Time*) the attackers were "trying to make headlines out of footnotes, were confusing influences with imitations."

The clamor did little damage to the play's popular success (it ran for 355 performances), but among literary critics the taint of possible plagiarism was slow to die. The work was voted down for the New York Drama Critics Circle Award (which went to Sidney Kingsley's *The Patriots*), reportedly on the basis of the unrefuted plagiarism charge. However, three weeks later it was awarded the Pulitzer Prize, Wilder's second in the field of drama. The play subsequently enjoyed a successful run in Britain, and a production in postwar Germany engendered an enthusiasm for Wilder's work that, though somewhat diminished, remains strong today; in fact, his work has generated more academic scholarship in Germany than it has in the United States.

For several years after World War II, Wilder's literary career leaned in the directions of fiction and academia. In June 1947 he was awarded an honorary doctorate by Yale University. Later that year he wrote a three-scene burlesque, *Our Century*, in celebration of the centenary of the Century Association of New York, of which he was a member. Because the production was not reviewed, and the distribution of the published version was limited, the short work did little to advance his career as a dramatist. *The Ides of March*, a fictionalized account of the last days of Julius Caesar, was published in 1948. The book displays the influence of—in addition to Wilder's previous concerns with history, ancient literature, and the notions of Gertrude Stein—the existentialism of Jean Paul Sartre. Eliminating the narrator, Wilder presents a randomly ordered collection of letters and journal entries almost entirely of his own creation. Although the novel was warmly received in England, American critics, balking at both the unconventional format and Wilder's alterations of historical facts, responded unfavorably. (A stage adaptation several years later, authored by Jerome Kilty with Wilder's unofficial but enthusiastic collaboration, was also a failure.) In 1950-1951 he held the Charles Eliot Norton Professorship of Poetry at Harvard, lecturing on nineteenth-century American writers in a series entitled "The American Characteristics in Classic American Literature." His scholarly publications included works on, among others, Emily Dickinson and Lope de Vega. In 1952 he was awarded the American Academy of Arts and Letters Gold Medal for Fiction.

Wilder's dramatic career in the 1950s was marked primarily by revivals, revisions, and foreign productions. *The Matchmaker*, the revision of *The Merchant of Yonkers*, was performed at the Edinburgh Festival in Scotland (August 1954) and in England before its successful run in New York. French productions of *The Skin of Our Teeth* and *The Matchmaker* increased his international reputation. His only original dramatic work of the period was *The Alcestiad*, a play based on Euripides' *Alcestis* on which he had worked for almost a decade. It was first performed in August 1955 at the Edinburgh Festival under the title *A Life in the Sun*; as *Die Alkestiade* it was produced in Germany in 1959, and a German operatic version, with libretto by Wilder and music by Louise Talma, opened in Frankfurt in March 1962. Though it saw German production, at the time only the fourth act, a satyr play entitled *The Drunken Sisters*, was published in English (both in the *Atlantic Monthly* and under its own cover in 1957); the complete work was not published in Wilder's language until 1977, two years after his death. The satyr play was performed in Brooklyn Heights in 1970, but as yet neither it nor the full-length work has been given a Broadway production.

Two other plays that received only German stagings were the one-acts *The Wreck of the 5:25* and *Bernice*. Performed in September 1957, as part of the dedication ceremonies for the new Congress Hall in West Berlin, both works exhibit a gloomy outlook uncharacteristic of Wilder's vision. The first focuses on a commuter who, even though he claims to have examined his life closely and determined to value it more highly, has in fact been averted from a suicide that would have eradicated a world he had cynically rejected. The second presents the alienation of an embezzler just released from prison; rather than being reunited with his daughter, who represents the society from which he has become estranged, he has her sent away, choosing to remain in permanent isolation. Unfavorably received in Berlin, the two plays remain unpublished.

Bernice was written as the "Pride" selection of a proposed cycle to be entitled "The Seven Deadly Sins"; "The Seven Ages of Man" was planned as a companion group. Neither cycle was completed, but works from each were performed together at Circle in the Square in 1962. Billed as *Plays for Bleecker Street*, the José Quintero production marks the final premiere of a Wilder drama. The first two *Plays for Bleecker Street* belong to "The Seven Ages of Man." *Infancy*, in which grown men appear in the roles of babies, extols the virtues of the young in a world marred by the errors of their elders. In *Childhood*, the most widely praised of the three, a father is allowed to become a participant in the enactment of his children's fantasies, and the ensuing mood of communication and harmony was likened by critics to that of *Our Town*. The "Lust" episode of the proposed "Seven Deadly Sins" cycle, *Someone from Assisi*, which focuses on a rejected lover of Saint Francis, was found unnatural and pretentious, in the mode of the early three-minute plays. Favorable response to the other two works, however, sustained the bill's run through 349 performances.

Although Wilder was to produce no further dramatic works, his literary career had not come to an end. Later in 1962 he was invited to Washington by President Kennedy's cabinet to present a reading from his works entitled "An Evening with Thornton Wilder," and in 1963 he was awarded the U. S. Presidential Medal of Freedom; having retired to the Arizona desert to write in seclusion, he did not appear in person to receive the award. In 1965 he was honored with the National Medal of Literature, and in 1967 the book he went into isolation to complete was published. *The Eighth Day*, lauded as a novel encompassing the best in theme and technique from his entire career, won the National Book Award in 1968. His final novel, *Theophilus North*, was published in 1973; a first-person account of a man who has just resigned a job at a prep school for boys, the work was found somewhat wanting for the author's insufficient detachment.

By this time Wilder, back in New Haven, was suffering the infirmities of age: failing eyesight, chronic back problems, a disposition that was becoming more waspish. However, rather than seeing his reputation fade as he grew older, he enjoyed the security of knowing that he had become an American institution. When he died in 1975, he was recognized as a novelist, dramatist, and man of letters.

Screenplays:
Our Town, by Wilder, Frank Craven, and others, United Artists, 1940;
Shadow of a Doubt, Universal, 1943.

Other:
Introduction to *Narration: Four Lectures*, by Gertrude Stein (Chicago: University of Chicago Press, 1935);
Introduction to *The Geographical History of America*, by Gertrude Stein (New York: Random House, 1936);

"Some Thoughts on Playwriting" in *The Intent of the Artist*, ed. Augusto Centeno (Princeton: Princeton University Press, 1941), pp. 83-98.

Periodical Publications:
The Trumpet Shall Sound, Yale Literary Magazine, 85 (October-December 1919, January 1920): 9-26, 78-92, 128-146, 192-207;
"A Diary: First and Last Entry," *S4N*, 32 (February 1924): 7-11;
"Three Sentences," *Double Dealer*, 4 (September 1924): 110;
"Playgoing Nights: From a Travel Diary," by Wilder and Isabel Wilder, *Theatre Arts Monthly*, 13 (June 1929): 411-419;
"James Joyce (1882-1941)," *Poetry: A Magazine of Verse*, 62 (March 1941): 370-374;
"Toward an American Language," *Atlantic Monthly*, 190 (July 1952): 29-37;
"The American Loneliness," *Atlantic Monthly*, 190 (August 1952): 65-69.

Bibliographies:
J. M. Edelstein, *A Bibliographical Checklist of the Writings of Thornton Wilder* (New Haven: Yale University Library, 1959);
Heinz Kosok, "Thornton Wilder: A Bibliography of Criticism," *Twentieth Century Literature*, 9 (1963): 93-100.

Biographies:
Richard H. Goldstone, *Thornton Wilder, An Intimate Portrait* (New York: Saturday Review Press / Dutton, 1975);
Linda Simon, *Thornton Wilder: His World* (Garden City: Doubleday, 1979).

References:
Carl Balliet, Jr., "The Skin of Whose Teeth: Part III," *Saturday Review of Literature*, 26 (2 January 1943): 11;
Rex Burbank, *Thornton Wilder* (New York: Twayne, 1961);
Joseph Campbell and Henry M. Robinson, "The Skin of Whose Teeth? The Strange Case of

Mr. Wilder's Play and *Finnegans Wake*," *Saturday Review of Literature*, 25 (19 December 1942): 3-4;
Campbell and Robinson, "The Skin of Whose Teeth: Part II, The Intention Behind the Deed," *Saturday Review of Literature*, 26 (13 February 1943): 16-18;
Robert W. Corrigan, "Thornton Wilder and the Tragic Sense of Life," *Educational Theater*, 13 (October 1961): 167-173;
Malcolm Cowley, "The Man Who Abolished Time," *Saturday Review of Literature*, 39 (6 October 1956): 13-14, 50-52;
Joseph J. Firebaugh, "The Humanism of Thornton Wilder," *Pacific Spectator*, 4 (Fall 1950): 426-428;
Four Quarters, Special Wilder issue, 16 (May 1967);
Michael Gold, "Wilder: Prophet of the Genteel Christ," *New Republic*, 24 (22 October 1930): 266-267;
Malcolm Goldstein, *The Art of Thornton Wilder* (Lincoln: University of Nebraska Press, 1965);
Richard Goldstone, "An Interview with Thornton Wilder," *Paris Review*, 15 (Winter 1957): 36-57;
Bernard Grebanier, *Thornton Wilder* (Minneapolis: University of Minnesota Press, 1965);
Tyrone Guthrie, "The World of Thornton Wilder," *New York Times Magazine* (27 November 1955): 26-27, 64, 66-68;
Donald Haberman, *The Plays of Thornton Wilder* (Middletown, Conn.: Wesleyan University Press, 1967);
Mildred Christophe Kuner, *Thornton Wilder: The Bright and the Dark* (New York: Crowell, 1972);
Helmut Papajewski, *Thornton Wilder* (New York: Ungar, 1968);
Harrison Smith, "The Skin of Whose Teeth: Part II," *Saturday Review of Literature*, 25 (26 December 1942): 12.

Papers:
Portions of Wilder's papers are held by the libraries of Yale University, Kent State University, and the University of Virginia.

Tennessee Williams

Sally Johns
University of South Carolina

BIRTH: Columbus, Mississippi, 26 March 1911, to Cornelius Coffin and Edwina Dakin Williams.

EDUCATION: University of Missouri, 1929-1931; Washington University, St. Louis, 1936; B.A., University of Iowa, 1938.

AWARDS: Group Theatre Award for *American Blues*, 1939; Rockefeller Foundation Grant, 1940; American Academy of Arts and Letters Award, 1944; New York Drama Critics Circle Award, Sidney Howard Memorial Award, Donaldson Award, and *Sign* Magazine Annual Award for *The Glass Menagerie*, 1945; New York Drama Critics Circle Award, Donaldson Award, and Pulitzer Prize for *A Streetcar Named Desire*, 1948; Elected to National Institute of Arts and Letters, 1952; New York Drama Critics Circle Award and Pulitzer Prize for *Cat on a Hot Tin Roof*, 1955; *London Evening Standard* Drama Award for *Cat on a Hot Tin Roof*, 1958; New York Drama Critics Circle Award for *The Night of the Iguana*, 1962; First place in London Critics' Poll for Best New Foreign Play for *The Night of the Iguana*, 1964-1965; Brandeis University Creative Arts Medal, 1964-1965; National Institute of Arts and Letters Gold Medal, 1969; First centennial medal of the Cathedral of St. John the Divine, 1973; Elected to Theatre Hall of Fame, 1979; Kennedy Honors Award, 1979.

SELECTED PRODUCTIONS: *Cairo, Shanghai, Bombay!*, by Williams and Doris Shapiro, 12 July 1935, Memphis Garden Players, Memphis;

Headlines, 11 November 1936, Wednesday Club Auditorium, St. Louis;

Candles to the Sun, 1936, Wednesday Club Auditorium, St. Louis;

Fugitive Kind, 1937, Wednesday Club Auditorium, St. Louis;

The Long Goodbye, 9 February 1940, New School for Social Research, New York, 2 [performances];

Battle of Angels, 30 December 1940, Wilbur Theatre, Boston; revised as *Orpheus Descending*, 21 March 1957, Martin Beck Theatre, New York, 68;

The Glass Menagerie, 26 December 1944, Civic Theatre, Chicago; 31 March 1945, Playhouse Theatre, New York, 561;

You Touched Me!, by Williams and Donald Windham, adapted from D. H. Lawrence's short story, 25 September 1945, Booth Theatre, New York, 109;

This Property Is Condemned, March 1946, Hudson Park Theatre, New York;

Moony's Kid Don't Cry, 1946, Actor's Laboratory Theatre, Los Angeles;

Portrait of a Madonna, 1946, Actor's Laboratory Theatre, Los Angeles;

The Last of My Solid Gold Watches, 1947, Actor's Laboratory Theatre, Los Angeles;

Summer and Smoke, 11 July 1947, Theatre '47, Dallas; 6 October 1948, Music Box Theatre, New York, 102; revised as *Eccentricities of a Nightingale*, 20 April 1966, Washington Theater Club, Washington, D.C.;

A Streetcar Named Desire, 3 December 1947, Ethel Barrymore Theatre, New York, 855;

The Rose Tattoo, 3 February 1951, Martin Beck Theatre, New York, 300;

Camino Real, 19 March 1953, National Theatre, New York, 60;

Cat on a Hot Tin Roof, 24 March 1955, Morosco Theatre, New York, 694;

27 Wagons Full of Cotton, in *All in One*, 19 April 1955, Playhouse Theatre, New York, 47;

Three Players of a Summer Game, 19 July 1955, White Barn Theatre, Westport, Conn.;

Garden District (*Something Unspoken* and *Suddenly Last Summer*), 7 January 1958, York Playhouse, New York, 216;

Talk to Me Like the Rain and Let Me Listen, 26 July 1958, White Barn Theatre, Westport, Conn,;

Sweet Bird of Youth, 10 March 1959, Martin Beck Theatre, New York, 375;

I Rise in Flame, Cried the Phoenix, 14 April 1959,

Theatre de Lys, New York, 1;

The Purification, 8 December 1959, Theatre de Lys, New York;

Period of Adjustment, 1959, Coconut Grove Playhouse, Miami, Fla.; 10 November 1960, Helen Hayes Theatre, New York, 132;

The Night of the Iguana, 28 December 1961, Royale Theatre, New York, 316;

The Milk Train Doesn't Stop Here Anymore, June 1962, Festival of Two Worlds, Spoleto, Italy; 16 January 1963, Morosco Theatre, New York, 69;

Slapstick Tragedy (*The Mutilated* and *The Gnädiges Fräulein*), 22 February 1966, Longacre Theatre, New York, 7; *The Gnädiges Fräulein* revised as *The Latter Days of a Celebrated Soubrette*, 16 May 1974, Central Arts Theatre, New York, 12;

The Two-Character Play, 27 November 1967, Hampstead Theatre Club, London; revised as *Out Cry*, 1 March 1973, Lyceum Theatre, New York, 12;

The Seven Descents of Myrtle, 27 March 1968, Ethel Barrymore Theatre, New York, 29; revised as *Kingdom of Earth*, 6 March 1975, McCarter Theatre, Princeton, N.J.;

In the Bar of a Tokyo Hotel, 11 May 1969, Eastside Playhouse, New York, 25;

The Frosted Glass Coffin and *A Perfect Analysis Given by a Parrot*, 1 May 1970, Waterfront Playhouse, Key West, Fla.;

I Can't Imagine Tomorrow and *Confessional*, 19 August 1971, Maine Theatre Arts Festival, Bar Harbor, Maine;

Small Craft Warnings, 2 April 1972, Truck and Warehouse Theatre, New York, 194;

The Red Devil Battery Sign, 18 June 1975, Boston; revised version, 17 January 1976, English Theatre, Vienna;

This Is (An Entertainment), 20 January 1976, American Conservatory Theatre, San Francisco;

Vieux Carré, 11 May 1977, St. James Theatre, New York, 5;

Crève Coeur, May 1978, Spoleto Festival, Charleston, S.C.; retitled *A Lovely Sunday for Crève Coeur*, 21 January 1979, Hudson Guild Theatre, New York, 36;

Clothes for a Summer Hotel, 26 March 1980, Cort Theatre, New York, 14.

SELECTED BOOKS: *The Summer Belvedere*, in *Five Young American Poets*, ed. James Laughlin, Third Series (New York: New Directions, 1944);

Battle of Angels (New York: New Directions, 1945);

The Glass Menagerie (New York: Random House, 1945; London: Lehmann, 1948);

27 Wagons Full of Cotton and Other One-Act Plays (Norfolk, Conn.: New Directions, 1946; London: Grey Walls Press, 1947)—includes *27 Wagons Full of Cotton*, *The Purification*, *The Lady of Larkspur Lotion*, *The Last of My Solid Gold Watches*, *Portrait of a Madonna*, *Auto-Da-Fé*, *Lord Byron's Love Letter*, *The Strangest Kind of Romance*, *The Long Goodbye*, *Hello from Bertha*, *This Property Is Condemned*, *Talk to Me Like the Rain and Let Me Listen*, and *Something Unspoken*;

You Touched Me! by Williams and Donald Windham (New York: French, 1947);

A Streetcar Named Desire (New York: New Directions, 1947; London: Lehmann, 1949);

Summer and Smoke (New York: New Directions, 1948; London: Lehmann, 1952);

American Blues: Five Short Plays (New York: Dramatists Play Service, 1948)—includes *Moony's Kid Don't Cry*; *The Dark Room*; *The Case of the Crushed Petunias*; *The Long Stay Cut Short, or, The Unsatisfactory Supper*; and *Ten Blocks on the Camino Real*;

One Arm and Other Stories (New York: New Directions, 1948);

The Roman Spring of Mrs. Stone (New York: New Directions, 1950; London: Lehmann, 1950);

The Rose Tattoo (New York: New Directions, 1951; London: Secker & Warburg, 1951);

I Rise in Flame, Cried the Phoenix (New York: New Directions, 1951);

Camino Real (Norfolk, Conn.: New Directions, 1953; London: Secker & Warburg, 1958);

Hard Candy: A Book of Stories (New York: New Directions, 1954);

Cat on a Hot Tin Roof (New York: New Directions, 1955; London: Secker & Warburg, 1956);

In the Winter of Cities (Norfolk, Conn.: New Directions, 1956);

Baby Doll (New York: New Directions, 1956; London: Secker & Warburg, 1957);

Orpheus Descending (London: Secker & Warburg, 1958); *Orpheus Descending with Battle of Angels* (New York: New Directions, 1958);

Suddenly Last Summer (New York: New Directions, 1958);

Garden District (London: Secker & Warburg, 1959);

Sweet Bird of Youth (New York: New Directions, 1959; London: Secker & Warburg, 1961);

Period of Adjustment (New York: New Directions, 1960; London: Secker & Warburg, 1961);

The Night of the Iguana (New York: New Directions,

1961; London: Secker & Warburg, 1963);

The Milk Train Doesn't Stop Here Anymore (Norfolk, Conn.: New Directions, 1963);

Eccentricities of a Nightingale and Summer and Smoke (New York: New Directions, 1964);

Grand (New York: House of Books, 1964);

The Knightly Quest: A Novella and Four Short Stories (New York: New Directions, 1966);

Kingdom of Earth (The Seven Descents of Myrtle) (New York: New Directions, 1967);

The Two-Character Play (New York: New Directions, 1969);

Dragon Country (New York: New Directions, 1970)—includes *In the Bar of a Tokyo Hotel*; *I Rise in Flame, Cried the Phoenix*; *The Mutilated*; *I Can't Imagine Tomorrow*; *Confessional*; *The Frosted Glass Coffin*; *The Gnädiges Fräulein*; and *A Perfect Analysis Given by a Parrot*;

The Theatre of Tennessee Williams, 6 vols. (New York: New Directions, 1971-);

Small Craft Warnings (New York: New Directions, 1972; London: Secker & Warburg, 1973);

Out Cry, (New York: New Directions, 1973);

Eight Mortal Ladies Possessed (New York: New Directions, 1974);

Moise and the World of Reason (New York: Simon & Schuster, 1975; London: Allen, 1976);

Memoirs (Garden City: Doubleday, 1975);

Androgyne, Mon Amour (New York: New Directions, 1977);

Where I Live: Selected Essays (New York: New Directions, 1978);

Vieux Carré (New York: New Directions, 1979);

A Lovely Sunday for Crève Coeur (New York: New Directions, 1980).

Tennessee Williams's playwriting career, already spanning more than four decades, has been marked by the highest acclaim, as well as the kind of critical controversy that is generated only by one whose achievements have been widely recognized and lauded. This recognition of achievement has taken many forms, most notably four New York Drama Critics Circle Awards and two Pulitzer Prizes. His choice to explore his basic themes through what have been labeled degenerate characters and sordid situations has created controversy. Because of his Southern roots, he is more closely tied in theme to twentieth-century Southern fiction writers than to other dramatists of the period. His concern with isolation, the difficulty of communication, and the solitary search for values in a chaotic world—as well as the frequent use of Southern settings and characters—links him to writers like William Faulkner and Carson McCullers. Though his work was preceded by the social protest of the 1930s, he has focused on the individual rather than on the fabric of society as a whole; this artistic direction, along with his use of lyrical language, differentiates his work from that of Arthur Miller, his only contemporary to achieve the same major status.

He was born Thomas Lanier Williams on 26 March 1911 in Columbus, Mississippi, the second child of a Puritan-Cavalier marriage. His mother, Edwina Dakin Williams, prim daughter of the Episcopal minister, had been "swept off her feet" by robust salesman Cornelius Coffin Williams, descended from a line of East Tennessee frontiersmen and political officeholders. During Williams's early years his father was on the road a great deal, so he, his mother, and his older sister, Rose, lived in the rectory with his maternal grandparents. The family moved to Clarksdale, Mississippi, when young Williams entered school.

An early childhood plagued by illness—a near-fatal bout with diphtheria left him to this day convinced that he suffered irreparable heart damage—kept him from the company of other children. A weak physical condition, combined with the influence of his delicate and protective mother, earned him the ridicule of both other children and his boisterous, highly masculine father, who according to Williams nicknamed his son "Miss Nancy."

When Williams was eight years old, his father's promotion to a managerial position uprooted the family from the safe and serene world of small-town Mississippi. Negative effects of the move to industrialized Saint Louis were felt by Williams, his mother, and his sister. His brother, Dakin, was born soon after the relocation. A few years later, the unhappy young Williams turned to writing as a means of both escape and recognition. Through poetry and short stories, he won prizes from advertising contests, school publications, and women's clubs.

His first published work came in 1927: an essay answering the question "Can a Good Wife Be a Good Sport?" was awarded third prize in a contest sponsored by *Smart Set* magazine. The next year his short story "The Vengeance of Nitocris" was published in *Weird Tales*; he received thirty-five dollars.

In 1929 Williams entered the University of Missouri, where he won small prizes for poetry and prose, pledged a fraternity, and discovered alcohol as a cure for the extreme shyness that had thus far kept him in virtual isolation. When he failed ROTC during his third year, his father withdrew him from school and set him to work in the International Shoe Company warehouse. His days were spent in the monotony and drudgery of dusting shoes and typing order forms; during the nights he turned to writing. The tedium and repression of his job led to a nervous breakdown in 1935, from which he recovered by spending a year in Memphis with his sympathetic grandparents.

During the year in Memphis, Williams was introduced to drama. A farce about two sailors on shore leave, *Cairo, Shanghai, Bombay!* was his first produced play. The Memphis Garden Players' production on 12 July 1935 introduced him to the thrill of watching an audience react to his work. Returning to Saint Louis to enroll at Washington University, he had decided that writing would be his career.

While studying at Washington University, Williams wrote *Me, Vashya* as an entry in the school's annual playwriting competition; he was disappointed to win only honorable mention. During this period he also became involved with The Mummers, a small Saint Louis theatrical group headed by Willard Holland. Willliams remembers the group as dynamic, nonconformist, and charged with electricity. He was invited to write a curtain raiser for their 1936 Armistice Day production of Irwin Shaw's *Bury the Dead*. The group subsequently produced two of Williams's longer early plays, *Candles to the Sun* (1936) and *Fugitive Kind* (1937) (a title later given to the film version of *Orpheus Descending*).

By 1937 his sister, Rose, who had since childhood become increasingly withdrawn and disturbed, was institutionalized as an incurable schizophrenic. She underwent one of the first prefrontal lobotomies performed in the United States. Williams had always felt an extreme closeness and fondness for his delicate sister, and the pain of watching her deterioration prompted his decision to leave Saint Louis. With his grandmother's financial assistance he entered the University of Iowa, where he studied with Professor E. C. Mabie, wrote two more long plays (*Spring Storm* and *Not About Nightingales*), and in 1938 earned a B.A. degree.

Following his graduation from Iowa, Williams spent a year as an itinerant writer, wandering from Chicago (where he tried unsuccessfully to work with the WPA Writers' Project—his writing lacked "social content" and his family was not destitute) to Saint Louis, New Orleans, and California. During this period he concentrated on writing poetry and short fiction, as well as one-act plays. He gathered valuable material which would appear later in the

characters, settings, and situations of his short fiction and dramatic works. His short story "The Field of Blue Children" was published in the summer 1939 issue of *Story* magazine. This was his first work to appear under the name Tennessee Williams, the permanently adopted nickname replacing his given name, Tom.

About this time he was awarded a special prize of $100 in a play contest sponsored by the Group Theatre. His entry was the four long plays written up to that time, in addition to a group of one-acts called *American Blues*. While his full-length plays did not win the contest, the judges thought his one-acts merited attention, and they created a special award for the collection including five short works.

In *Moony's Kid Don't Cry*, the first of the group (produced in 1946), a young couple have awakened and are bickering in the middle of the night. As Moony complains about having left his job as a woodsman to work in a factory, his wife Jane frets that he will awaken their one-month-old son. Moony misses the freedom of the outdoors and resents being restrained by a dull, repetitive job and the responsibilities of a wife and child. They quarrel, and Moony announces that he is walking out. Jane brings the sleeping infant to him, telling him that if he is going, he can take his kid with him. Jane returns to bed as her husband becomes completely absorbed in his baby and croons to the child that he has no intention of leaving. The theme of the restless, unfulfilled dreamer battling against the restraints of practicality is repeated frequently in later plays.

In *The Dark Room* a prim social worker interviews an Italian woman ("an avalanche of female flesh") about her fifteen-year-old daughter. The mother is reluctant to answer questions, but gradually the social worker learns that the father is in the city sanitarium, the older sons have deserted the family, and the daughter has spent the past six months lying naked in bed in a darkened room. She is visited regularly by her married lover, who brings her food. Just before the curtain, the mother reveals to her already shocked inquisitor that the girl is pregnant.

The Case of the Crushed Petunias (dedicated to Helen Hayes in February 1941) is included in the published collection with a publisher's note. The author on rereading found the piece immature and requested that it be omitted, but was persuaded to permit its inclusion. It is a didactic, unsubtle contest in which life wins over death (or death-in-life). Miss Simple of Primanproper, Massachusetts, is persuaded by a Young Man to forgive him for crushing the double row of petunias which serve to barricade her house and her heart from the world. She changes the name of her little shop from Simple Notions to Tremendous Inspirations and sets off to meet the Young Man on Highway No. 77 where she will exchange her spinsterish regimentation for thinking, feeling, experiencing, and living. The theme is handled much more effectively in later works.

The Long Stay Cut Short, or, The Unsatisfactory Supper is a three-character one-act which later served (with *27 Wagons Full of Cotton*) as the basis of the filmscript *Baby Doll* (1956). Archie Lee Bowman, a tooth-sucking rural Southerner, and his large, indolent wife Baby Doll commiserate over Aunt Rose's cooking. Aunt Rose is a senile eighty-five-year-old relative with no home of her own, who is passed from household to household; at present she is based with Archie Lee and Baby Doll, and they have grown weary of her forgetfulness and eccentricity. Despite his wife's protests, Archie Lee finally announces that it is time for Aunt Rose to move on. Sensing that despite all her efforts, she has become a burden, Aunt Rose wanders into the yard as a twister approaches. As the curtain falls, she struggles against the strong wind which is certain to blow her away. Though the conclusion smacks of deus ex machina, the play exhibits Williams's expertise at creating Southern dialogue and sharply defined characterizations.

The longest of the volume's one-acts, *Ten Blocks on the Camino Real*, was later expanded into the full-length *Camino Real* (1953). The dreamlike fantasy contains characters from history, literature, and contemporary folklore, placed in a Mexican setting. Kilroy, the all-American ex-boxer with a heart "as big as the head of a baby," has been dealt a losing hand—his naivete makes him an easy mark for swindlers—but he persists in seeking human goodness as he journeys down the hostile road known as Camino Real. When he dies, an autopsy reveals that his heart is solid gold. He comes back to life; attempts to win a gypsy's daughter with furs, jewels, and trinkets procured in exchange for his golden heart; and is rejected. At the end of the play he heads off with rusty-armored Don Quixote, who admonishes him to avoid self-pity.

Mollie Day Thatcher, one of the judges for the Group Theatre's award, was so impressed with this collection that she kindled the interest of Audrey Wood, a successful literary agent, who through a highly unusual procedure solicited Williams as a client, beginning a writer-agent relationship that would last for over two decades.

After exhausting the Group Theatre prize money, Williams returned to Saint Louis, where he worked on *Battle of Angels*. He soon received word that Audrey Wood had secured for him a $1000 Rockefeller Foundation grant, followed by a scholarship at the New School for Social Research in New York. There he worked with John Gassner and Theresa Helburn on revisions of *Battle of Angels* and saw produced his one-act *The Long Goodbye* (1940). In the one-act play, Joe is a young would-be writer overseeing the move from the apartment where his family has lived for twenty-five years. As he packs and supervises movers, his reminiscences of a quarter of a century of family joys and sorrows, people now dead or gone, are played out in periodic flashbacks.

In December 1940 the Theatre Guild opened *Battle of Angels* in Boston, with plans for a New York production to follow. What Williams anticipated as a glorious beginning of his career proved to be a glorious disaster. The opening night audience—those few who remained until the onstage conflagration at the end of the play—were driven from the theatre in a billow of smoke created by a stagehand overcompensating for his failure to produce more than a wisp during dress rehearsal. The critical response was negative, and the Boston City Council's reaction to the content of the play was even worse. Despite hasty revisions, the production was closed after its two-week Boston run.

The original story line follows the Lawrencian theme of repressed passion awakened by a wild and free poetic spirit. Disappointed in love and grieved over her father's death in a fire set by the town's leading citizens, Myra Torrance had years earlier consigned herself to a loveless marriage with a malicious, crotchety old storekeeper. At the beginning of the play, her husband's impending death from cancer has just been medically confirmed. Val Xavier, a vagabond poet dressed in a snakeskin jacket, is hired by Myra to do odd jobs in the dry goods store. Myra's repressed sexuality is awakened by the wild and mysterious Val, whose attractiveness creates quite a stir among the town's female population. Among those affected by his virility are Cassandra Whiteside, a fallen aristocrat who has given in to alcohol and promiscuity, and Vee Talbott, the sheriff's wife whose sexuality is sublimated through primitive painting and religious fanaticism. Through her affair with Val Myra blossoms, her former sharpness and tension replaced by a glowing softness. Both the townspeople and her dying husband are aware of the illicit relationship, and when on Good Friday Val is sought on a trumped-up rape

Tennessee Williams

charge, a lynch mob is ready. Jabe Torrance shoots his unfaithful wife, laying the blame on Val, who is carried off to the hanging tree by a hysterical posse armed with a blowtorch.

The production mounted by the Theatre Guild was the first version of Williams's perhaps most reworked play. Over the years it was to undergo numerous revisions and title changes. The original bears several of the Williams trademarks: it is set in a small Southern town, it presents the romantic theme of repressed passion and spiritual sterility, and it contains several sharply drawn minor characters. Though Boston's city fathers objected to the playwright's mix of sex and religion, other critics generally agreed that offense to a puritanical sense of propriety and decorum is not the play's only problem. Its chief flaws are also typically Williams: too much plot makes it overly complicated and confusing, as well as lacking in unity; the characters tend toward morality-play symbols rather than real people; and the playwright's lyricism gets out of hand.

Dejected over the failure, Williams returned to the Vieux Carré in New Orleans. From there he moved to New York, where he worked as a theatre usher, elevator operator, and waiter-entertainer. This bohemian period provided him with material for numerous short stories and one-acts. He also began collaboration with his friend Donald Windham on the comedy *You Touched Me!* (produced in 1945). In 1943, just when desperation over lack of funds was setting in, Audrey Wood secured for him a Metro-Goldwyn-Mayer scriptwriting contract in Hollywood at the incredible salary of $250 a week. He worked in Hollywood from May to November of that year. His first assignment was to write a Lana Turner vehicle (which he remembers as "The Celluloid Brassiere"); his script was rejected. With less than gracious comments about child actors, he refused his next assignment: a movie for Margaret O'Brien. He then presented an idea of his own for a film script, an outline of a work entitled "The Gentleman Caller." This idea was also rejected, and shortly thereafter he was advised to continue to draw his paycheck, but to stay away from the office. During the remainder of his contract he worked on his scenario, changing it to stage form and renaming it *The Glass Menagerie* (1944).

Agent Wood liked the play that had been rejected by Hollywood, and she found equal enthusiasm in Eddie Dowling, who agreed to direct as well as play the role of Tom. The production opened in Chicago in late December of 1944, bringing back to the stage the actress considered by many to be America's best, Laurette Taylor. Williams finally achieved the success that had eluded him four years earlier with *Battle of Angels*. Though audiences were sparse at first, a barrage of favorable newspaper criticism gradually generated interest, and after a few weeks people were flocking to see the play. By the time it opened in New York in March 1945, eager audiences were awaiting it. Scarcely two weeks later, it was chosen after only fifteen minutes' deliberation for the New York Drama Critics Circle Award. Its Broadway run lasted almost two years.

The Glass Menagerie is Williams's gentlest play. By virtue of frequency of productions and publication in anthologies, it is probably his most popular. Because its focus is away from the "sex, decay, and violence" motifs so prevalent in most of his later works, it has appealed to audiences who have found his other plays distasteful in subject matter. Nonetheless, in both its mood and its concerns, the play is characteristic of Williams's mature and best work.

In contrast to the overly complicated *Battle of Angels*, it presents a story simply told through only four characters. Williams looked to his own family and experience in creating the Wingfields—Amanda and her grown children Tom and Laura—who live in a dingy Saint Louis apartment building during the Depression. The autobiographical character Tom serves as narrator, setting the scene at the beginning and periodically addressing the audience in poetic monologues; he also participates in the action, thus giving the audience a representational view of the events as he remembers them, as well as his retrospective comments. A poet trapped in a mundane existence, he works days in a shoe factory and spends his evenings writing or going to the movies. His sister, Laura, whose crippled leg is symbolic of her psychic deformity, is so painfully shy that she avoids reality almost altogether, creating her world through playing old phonograph records and tending a collection of glass animals. Their mother, Amanda, combines obsesssion with her romanticized Southern debutante past and a fierce determination to survive a grim present. The husband/father of the family, referred to as "the telephone man who fell in love with long distances," deserted them years be-

fore. His prominent photograph is a constant reminder to Amanda of dreams gone sour; to Tom, the father with whom he is often bitterly compared represents escape.

The plot line is a simple one. Since high school, Laura has become more and more withdrawn. A business course proved a miserable failure; her shyness made her physically ill. Pinning all her hopes for the future on a marriage for her daughter, Amanda asks Tom to find a suitable young man among his friends at the warehouse. To pacify his mother—and missing the point of her grand design—he invites Jim O'Connor to dinner. Amanda is so excited over the prospect of a gentleman caller for her daughter that she practically redecorates the apartment in preparation. When Mr. O'Connor arrives, he proves to be everything Amanda could have desired: he is attractive, personable, and ambitious. He also turns out to be a former high school classmate of Laura's, someone she has quietly pined over for six years. After dinner, he and Laura talk, play music, and even dance. Their dancing is awkward, and they stumble into her animal collection, breaking the horn from a glass unicorn. The accident changes the mood from gaiety to tenderness, and what begins as Jim's attempt to build Laura's confidence becomes an expression of genuine admiration, ending in a kiss. Apologizing, Jim makes a clean breast by explaining

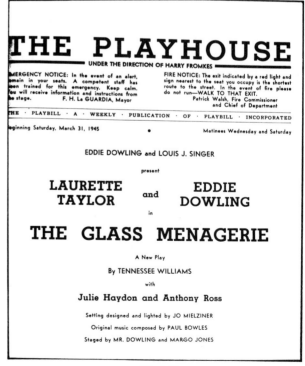

Playbill

that he cannot call Laura again because he is engaged to be married. His rather abrupt departure is followed by Amanda's railing at Tom for the cruel joke he has played on his family. Frustrated and angry, Tom leaves the house. As narrator, he reveals in the final lyrical monologue that soon after the fateful dinner he left his mother and sister for good, and has since then tried unsuccessfully to blot out his guilt.

The play's major theme is illusion versus reality. Laura, patterned after the playwright's sister, Rose, is the first of a long series of Williams characters who exhibit a fragility that renders them incapable of coping with the harshness, cruelty, and insensitivity of reality. Williams maintains his sympathy for these tortured people, no matter in what direction their escape takes them. Unlike later sufferers who turn to drugs, alcohol, or sex, Laura creates her own fantasy world of romantic music and tiny, delicate glass ornaments. Like the animals of her collection, she is beautifully fragile—but easily broken. Amanda, faced with economic hardship, a son who she fears is unambitious and irresponsible, a daughter both physically and emotionally crippled, and rejection by the man who swept her off her feet, seeks solace in the past. She is a survivor—she has great depths of energy, pride, and even practicality—but scraping and clawing for survival rub against her grain. She retreats into numerous anecdotes of her days as the belle of the Delta, entertaining gentleman callers by the droves, and even demonstrates her charming technique (complete with a girlish frock resurrected from a trunk) when Jim O'Connor comes to dinner. Tom as narrator is of course able to recognize and comment on the variance between truth and illusion, and he admits his own penchant for airbrushing his memories of the past. The Tom who appears in the play's action is facing the poet's conflict between the practical and the ideal. He feels love and responsibility for his mother and sister, but he yearns for romance, adventure, experience, and escape from his stifling "two by four situation." Though narrator Tom calls Laura's gentleman caller "an emissary from a world of reality that we were somehow set apart from," Jim O'Connor also has created his own world of illusion. The former high school hero relies on self-improvement courses and cliche-ridden bravado to soften the jar of unfulfilled dreams and unrealized potential.

Though the play is effectively simple in plot, it is rich in symbolism as well as a blending of production elements to create a mood of strong yet controlled grief. Both music and lighting are employed to produce the effect of memory—gentle and poetic. The language is highly evocative, particularly in Tom's monologues; some critics have found fault with what they see as strained, overdone lyricism. Another element of the original script has also been widely criticized. Williams conceived of the use of a screen device which would bear legends or images underscoring the particular point of each scene. Eddie Dowling omitted the screen device from the original show, and except for rare experimental productions, it has not been used since.

In September following the highly successful opening of *The Glass Menagerie* came the opening of a much less successful play. Actually written before *The Glass Menagerie*, *You Touched Me!* was a collaboration between Williams and his friend Donald Windham. An adaptation of the D. H. Lawrence short story of the same title, the play is a lyrical comedy with symbolic characters and action. A dying old captain lives with his unmarried daughter and sister. An adopted "charity boy," Hadrian, after an absence of several years returns in hopes of getting some of the old man's money. Hadrian is now a virile and attractive young man with romantic feelings toward the captain's hesitant daughter Matilda. Though she has been involved in a lengthy courtship with a clergyman, the captain's sister Emmie militantly disavows the flesh. Sex and freedom are pitted against reticence and frozen virginity, and a contrived ending leaves Matilda with Hadrian, Emmie with her clergyman, and the captain rejuvenated. The critics generally found the production disappointing; as a follow-up of *The Glass Menagerie*, Lewis Nicols termed it "a fall from grace."

The collection *27 Wagons Full of Cotton and Other One-Act Plays* was published in 1946. It includes *The Long Goodbye*, produced at the New School for Social Research in 1940, and a dozen other short works. Some in the collection later had New York productions; many contain characters and scenes that found their way into later longer works. The title work, for example, was later merged with *The Unsatisfactory Supper* to form the screenplay *Baby Doll*. *27 Wagons Full of Cotton*, written circa 1941 and produced in 1955, is set on the front porch of Jake Meighan's doll-like Gothic cottage near Blue Mountain, Mississippi. As the curtain rises, Jake, a fat man of sixty, leaves the yard carrying a gallon can of coal oil. A moment later his wife, Flora, a large, slow-witted, babyish woman, comes out looking for her lost purse. Jake has set fire to the cotton gin of the neighboring Syndicate Plantation; through sadistic arm-twisting combined with kisses, he forces Flora to provide his alibi. The next day the owner of the burnt gin, Silva Vicarro, brings twenty-seven wagons full of cotton for Jake to gin in his mill. Telling the small Italian that his wife was a huge baby doll when he married her, Jake leaves for the mill, instructing Flora to keep Vicarro comfortable in his absence. Vicarro has little difficulty in trapping the simple-minded Flora into revealing that her husband is the arsonist. Determined to get revenge, he begins a rape/seduction that includes flicking the large woman with his riding crop, while at the same time confusing her with sweet talk. The scene ends as he forces her into the house and her despairing cry is heard above the sound of the gin pumping across the road. Flora emerges from the house a ravaged mess: clothing torn, skin bruised, and blood trickling from the corner of her mouth. The scene takes place in moonlight, and when Jake arrives home from his day of work he is too tired and preoccupied with outsmarting Vicarro to notice his wife's condition. As Flora vapidly and laughingly explains that Vicarro was so impressed with Jake's "good neighbor policy" that he will probably bring twenty-seven more wagons of cotton to be ginned tomorrow, her husband is totally absorbed in gloating. As Jake wanders into the house, Flora idiotically croons "Rock-a-Bye Baby" to her large kid purse which she has stuffed with Kleenex "to make it big—like a baby!"

The Purification is a verse drama interesting for its experimental nature. Set in the breathtaking country around Taos, New Mexico (where Williams visited D. H. Lawrence's widow Frieda), it is a ritualistic trial involving incest, murder, retribution, and purification. Including guitar music, pageantry, pantomime, and dance, the play celebrates incestuous love between brother and sister as superior to the sister's barren, loveless marriage to a rancher who killed her. In style and structure it contrasts sharply with the other plays in the volume. Its first production was in December 1959.

The Lady of Larkspur Lotion depicts a dyed-blond woman of forty who lives in a rooming house in the French Quarter. Her crass landlady demands the rent and scorns her prostitute tenant's pretense of gentility. A derelict writer passionately defends the prostitute's right to live in a world of invention. As one who lives in his imagination, he pleads for compassion for the woman who awaits checks from the king of a mythical Brazilian rubber plantation. The prostitute who surrounds herself with dreams to compensate for life's brutality is a precursor of *A Streetcar Named Desire*'s Blanche DuBois.

The Last of My Solid Gold Watches (1947) presents a Willy Loman-type drummer at the end of the line. "Mistuh Charlie" Colton gets genuine respect from the old Negro porter who sets him up in his familiar hotel room, but the response from young salesman Bob Harper is only rudeness and impertinence. The contrast is sharp between "Mistuh Charlie," who takes pride in quality, craftsmanship, and strength of character, and the "young peckerwood" Harper, who represents the ignorance, bad manners, and cheap commercialism that have replaced the old values. "Mistuh Charlie" is an early version of *Cat on a Hot Tin Roof*'s Big Daddy. The sympathetic portrayal of the shoe salesman is indicative that Williams's feelings toward his own salesman father were by no means entirely negative.

The main character of *Portrait of a Madonna* (1946) is another preview of Blanche DuBois. Miss Collins is a middle-aged spinster who, without her knowledge, is being committed to the state asylum. While waiting for the authorities who will take her away, a sympathetic old porter and an impudent young elevator boy occupy her in conversation. Her illusionary role as hostess and coquette is reminiscent of Amanda and her gentlemen callers in *The Glass Menagerie*. Miss Collins is the epitome of repression. For the fifteen years since her mother's death, she has lived as a recluse in her apartment, surrounding herself with delusions and sexual fantasies. She imagines that she has been molested ("he indulged his senses with me") by the man who years before rejected her to marry a girl from Cincinnati, and that she is now pregnant with his child. She is led away by a dutiful doctor and his efficient nurse in a scene that anticipates the ending of *A Streetcar Named Desire*. The woman is obviously mad, but Williams draws her obsessive, over-refined character with a great deal of sympathy.

In *Auto-Da-Fé*, which the author calls "a tragedy in one act," a mama's boy in his late thirties bickers with his mother on the porch of their frame cottage in the Vieux Carré of New Orleans. Madame Duvenet, the frail mother, is a cleanliness fanatic; her son Eloi is a thinker of dirty thoughts. He reveals that by accident he has gained possession of a lewd photograph, and she orders him to burn it in her presence. Finding the corruption all around him inescapable, Eloi locks himself inside the house and sets it on fire in a lunatic mission of purification.

Lord Byron's Love Letter is set in the French Quarter during Mardi Gras. Two impoverished women attempt to cash in on the curiosity of the tourists by advertising that they possess a love letter written by Lord Byron to the grandmother of one of them. A matron from Milwaukee is intrigued with the story and persuades her husband to join her inside the women's parlor, but the sound of the parade draws them away without paying the dollar the two women request. The letter is a fake; it was written not by Lord Byron, but by the woman's grandfather—however, its lyrical romantic style is in ironically poignant contrast to the circumstances to which the pair have been reduced.

The Strangest Kind of Romance, a "lyric play in four scenes," is Williams's dramatization of his short story "The Malediction." In the first scene the Little Man moves into a furnished room in an industrialized midwestern city. The Landlady, an overbearing shrew, agrees to let him keep the cat that stayed in the room with the previous tenant. In the second scene she seduces the Little Man by arguing gently that "Nature says, 'Don't be lonesome.'" Three characters appear in the third scene: the Little Man, his cat to whom he lovingly feeds cream, and an Old Man who utters his malediction against corrupt industrialization. In the final scene the Little Man, who has been laid off at the plant because of his ineptitude with machinery, returns to find that his room has been rented to a Boxer and his beloved cat has been turned out. At the close, the Little Man has found his cat, the Boxer is slipping into the role of lover to the Landlady, and she gazes wonderingly out the window at "The funniest pair of lovers! The ghost of a man—and a cat named Nitchevo!" Though the social protest is a bit heavy-handed, the scenes between the Little Man and his cat are touchingly effective.

The main character of *Hello from Bertha* is another of Williams's prostitutes, but this one suffers no delusions of grandeur. She occasionally makes false claims of friends in high places, but she makes no attempt to deny her surroundings: she lies in a brass bed in a gaudy, disheveled bedroom in "'the valley'—a notorious red-light section along the river flats of East St. Louis." What Bertha does deny is that she is close to death. As the landlady, Goldie, argues that she must see a doctor, Bertha maintains that she is fully capable of returning to work—she only needs rest. As her physical and mental deterioration become more and more apparent, she dictates a letter to a beau of bygone days who stood her up to marry "a little choir singer." The play is a grimly realistic, sympathetic but unsentimental view of the demise of a pathetic isolate.

The lead character of *This Property Is Condemned* is also a prostitute, a thirteen-year-old combination of childish innocence and worldly experi-

ence. As the girl, Willie, balances on a railroad track, she explains her delinquent life to a slightly older boy, Tom. Her mother "run off with a brakeman on the C. &E.I," her father disappeared, and her sister Alva (who was "The Main Attraction" with the railroad men) died two years before of "lung affection." Since then Willie has worn her sister's clothes and makeup, inherited her beaux, and lived alone in a condemned house. She holds on to her doll, but speaks matter-of-factly about exchanging sexual favors for gifts from the railroad men, and dreams romantically of flowers, violin music, jewels, and going out with men who make good salaries. The play was produced in March 1946 at the Hudson Park Theatre in New York.

Talk to Me Like the Rain and Let Me Listen is a dramatic tone poem set in a furnished room in midtown Manhattan. As rain falls outside, the Man awakens from a drunken sleep and tells the Woman what he can remember of a days-long binge in various parts of the city. She then recites to him her fantasy of going away to a "little hotel on the coast" where she will live in quiet isolation for half a century, communing with no one except people in stories and dead poets. She imagines for herself a gentler version of Aunt Rose's demise in *The Unsatisfactory Supper*: she will grow thinner and thinner until she has no body at all, and the wind will "pick [her] up in its cool white arms forever, and [take her] away." Williams's stage directions at the beginning indicate that "the present scene between them is the repetition of one that has been repeated so often that its emotional contents, such as reproach and contrition, have been completely worn out and there is nothing left but acceptance of something hopelessly inalterable between them." The play was produced 26 July 1958 at the White Barn Theatre in Westport, Connecticut.

Something Unspoken reveals a love/hate relationship between two Southern women. Miss Cornelia Scott is a snobbish, elderly spinster of some social prominence; Grace Lancaster has been her live-in secretary since she was widowed fifteen years before. Cornelia wants to be elected Regent of the Daughters of the Confederacy, but, suspecting some opposition, has chosen to stay home from the meeting and periodically checks its progress through telephone conversations. A picture of the women's relationship emerges: there are hints of a lesbian relationship—perhaps unconsummated—between them. Cornelia dominates the weaker Grace, but the secretary is not totally overpowered. As Cornelia receives news that she has not been elected Regent, Grace responds with "a slight equivocal smile . . . not quite malicious but not really sympathetic." The play was presented with *Suddenly Last Summer* on the double bill *Garden District* in January 1958.

The success of *The Glass Menagerie* led Williams into a period of isolation and depression which he chronicled in "On a Streetcar Named Success," a *New York Times* essay reprinted as the introduction to *A Streetcar Named Desire* (1947). Having been accustomed to struggling fiercely for survival, he found financial security and artistic recognition difficult to handle. An eternal hypochondriac, he also suffered physically. After undergoing the fourth in a series of cataract operations, he left New York in search of less civilized, therefore less complicated, surroundings. He found them in Mexico, where he stayed for a few months, working on "The Poker Night," a play that would become *A Streetcar Named Desire*. He returned to the States and spent the summer of 1946 on Nantucket Island with Carson McCullers. As the two began a long-term friendship and mutual admiration society (he has persisted in calling her the best American novelist of the twentieth century), they spent their mornings writing at opposite ends of a long table.

On 3 December 1947, *A Streetcar Named Desire* opened for a New York run that would last well over two years. The opening marked a culmination of drafts and revisions that had spread over a number of years. The play is set in the picturesque French Quarter, a section of New Orleans that Williams had come to know well through several extended stays scattered over almost a decade. The locale is described as a poor section with "a raffish charm," situated between the tracks and the river. It is inhabited by hardworking young couples—both black and white—who enjoy an easy contentment that remains undisturbed by outbreaks of passion. The sounds of a "Blue Piano," characterizing the "spirit of the life which goes on here," are heard intermittently throughout the play. It is against this backdrop that Williams sets his dramatic conflict between dying aristocracy and a cruder, but more vital, working class.

Blanche DuBois, dressed in white and looking as if she were going to a garden party, arrives at the home of her younger sister, Stella. Stella is an aristocrat by birth, but as the family fortune dwindled, economic necessity forced her to seek a new life for herself. She has found happiness with her Polish husband, Stanley Kowalski, a sensual, attractive, high-tempered man who adores her. Her life with Stanley is a far cry from the plantation, Belle Reve, where the sisters grew up, but Stella accepts it with both honesty and pleasure. Stanley is unrefined— crude, even—but he has given her vitality and sexual passion. Sister Blanche's arrival on the scene disrupts Stanley and Stella's happy home; her presence threatens to destroy the contentment they have found.

The war that breaks out over the following months is one between gentility and commonness, illusion and truth, death and passion; and sex is the most frequently used weapon. Blanche is shocked by the coarseness of a life in which couples suddenly come to blows and equally as suddenly "kiss and make up," acting as though the violence had never occurred. She values the beauty that she associates with civilization: art, music, poetry, and refinement. Stanley is extremely threatened by this woman who does not hesitate to voice her dismay over the crudeness and coarseness she perceives. His love for Stella is genuine, and he fears that he is in danger of losing her, that Blanche's influence over her sister will take his wife away from him.

Blanche believes in illusion, while Stanley deals in hard reality. Recognizing that the world is not the beautiful ideal she would like, Blanche lives through creating illusions for herself and others. She claims to be on a leave of absence from her high-school teaching job; in reality, she has been fired because of an involvement with a seventeen-year-old boy. She tells Stanley and Stella's friends that she is the younger of the sisters, when she is actually the older by five years. A paper shade hung over the bedroom light symbolizes her need to soften the glare of harsh reality. Stanley, on the other hand, has no patience with the kind of feminine wiles he perceives as hypocrisy and deception. After having his home disrupted and his marriage threatened, he is only too happy to expose Blanche as a fraud. Desperately needing to find security and peace, she has almost reached the point of marriage with Mitch, a large, awkward, gentle man who is devoted to his ailing mother. In a gesture motivated as much by retaliation toward Blanche as by masculine loyalty to his friend, Stanley reveals to Mitch that Blanche is not the virtuous lily with old-fashioned sexual ideals that she has pretended to be. Rather, she has a past dotted with promiscuity: before coming to stay with Stanley and Stella, she had practically been thrown out of town for her numerous sexual escapades.

The conflict between Stanley and Blanche reaches physical culmination on the night that Stella is at the hospital giving birth to her first child. Dis-

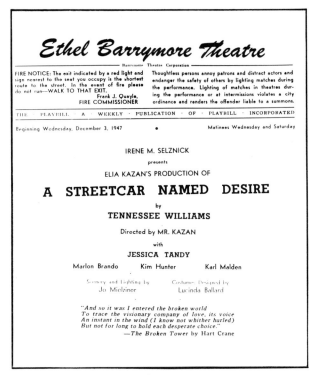

Playbill

traught over the loss of Mitch, Blanche has retreated into alcohol and illusions of being rescued by an oil baron (reminiscent of the delusions of Miss Collins in *Portrait of a Madonna*). Ecstatic over the impending birth of his child, Stanley returns home with a few celebratory drinks under his belt. His animalistic power has always frightened Blanche, but she also has been attracted by it. Her behavior toward him has often been flirtatious, even at times dangerously teasing. Her teasing has angered rather than aroused him, and, being a man who understands and respects power, he must retaliate for the threats to his manhood and self-esteem through an act of physical assertion. What begins as a conversation on a fairly even keel becomes a scene of violence. Feeling threatened physically, Blanche futilely attempts to use a broken bottle to fight off Stanley's advance. Announcing that, "We've had this date with each other from the beginning," he carries her inert figure to the bed for the rape that completely severs her tie with reality. In the final scene of the play, which takes place a few weeks later, a fragile, disoriented Blanche is led away to a state institution. As the curtain falls, Stanley "voluptuously, soothingly" comforts his sobbing wife, indicating that now that Blanche is gone, life for them will continue as before, that their relationship has weathered the enormous stress of her intrusion.

As attested by its tremendous popular and critical success, the play's strengths are many. Williams created a plot that is neither overly simplistic, nor burdened by the gratuitous complexities that marred the earlier *Battle of Angels*. With occasional expressionistic elements woven in to indicate Blanche's mental torment and deterioration, the action is for the most part straightforwardly representational, though heightened through the use of lighting, music, and details of set. The unique milieu of the French Quarter setting lends a vivid richness. The extensive use of symbols is less obtrusive and more intrinsic than in earlier plays. The excessive lyricism is confined for the most part to Blanche's speeches; given her character, they seem not inappropriate. Williams also deals quite successfully with the conflicts of sexuality. He does not allow his characters to become representative types, diametrically pitted against each other as embodiments of good and evil. Stanley and Blanche are at irreconcilable odds, but Williams gives them both complexity and sympathetic treatment. Stanley is coarse and at times brutal, but he also embodies a vitality and an energy that the dying aristocracy lacks. Additionally, he is a man under attack, and though his defensive counterattack is violent and destructive, it is mitigated somewhat by his devotion to Stella. Blanche, unequipped to deal with life's harshness and cruelty, hides in illusion and hypocrisy. Turning to promiscuity in search of warmth and comfort, she is unable to accept her own sexuality and creates a facade of virginal purity. However, her past is filled with traumas that justify psychological wounds—the suicide of her young husband, the prolonged illnesses and deaths of various relatives—and despite her hypocrisy, she exhibits genuine fragility, gentility, and compassion.

It is through the character of Stella that Williams best manages to avoid clear-cut dichotomy. Stanley is coarse and common, but he fully accepts, even revels in, his sexuality. Blanche, refined and aristocratic, denies hers. But Stella is proof that an overly simplified either/or choice is not necessary. Though she is by no means an easily derived combination of the two, she manages to maintain the gentility of her breeding while fully enjoying the sexual relationship that is central to her marriage.

The original production of *A Streetcar Named Desire* ran for 855 performances and won both the New York Drama Critics Circle Award and a Pulitzer Prize. It was followed by a highly successful film version, as well as London and Paris productions that drew unfavorable reviews but tremendous crowds. Thus, Williams's reputation as a playwright was established internationally as well as in America.

His next New York production, *Summer and Smoke*, is a less successful treatment of some of the same themes. Completed before *A Streetcar Named Desire*, it was produced in Dallas in July 1947, five months before *A Streetcar Named Desire*'s opening. Its 102-performance New York run began 6 October 1948. It grew out of Williams's short story "The Yellow Bird" and is dedicated to Carson McCullers. Set in Glorious Hill, Mississippi, it focuses on the relationship between a minister's daughter and a young doctor. Again resorting to allegorical figures rather than well-drawn characters, Williams juxtaposes Miss Alma Winemiller with Dr. John Buchanan.

In the brief prologue, Alma and John as children meet in the town square in front of a statuary angel named Eternity. She has given him a box of handkerchiefs in a prim effort to improve his careless appearance. Calling her "Miss Priss," he refuses the gift, but gives her a rough kiss before jerking her hair ribbon and running away. The rest of the play takes place several years later; John and Alma are now in their twenties. Because her mother has slipped into senility and infantilism, Alma has assumed the duties of hostess of the rectory. With her over-refined manners and frequent heart palpitations, she is a clear image of repression. Young Dr. Buchanan, who has returned to live with his father (also a doctor) next door to the rectory, has shown great medical promise but has a penchant for "indulging his senses" with booze and women.

John and Miss Alma again meet in the park, and he is intrigued by the attractive young woman whose laughter is somewhat hysterical. Alma, likewise, is attracted by the vibrancy and charm of the man who diagnoses her as having a doppelgänger, an inner self seeking release. Her invitation for him to attend a meeting of her literary club is a failure—he finds the members petty and dull—but a tenuous attraction-of-opposites rapport is established later that night when a hysterical attack sends her next door in search of the older doctor. Instead she finds John, who gives her sleeping pills, reveals that he is impressed with her sensitivity, and makes a date for the following Saturday.

On the date he takes her to Moon Lake Casino (Williams's ubiquitous romantic Mississippi night spot), a gambling, drinking, and gaming establishment "where anything goes." Alma explains her philosophy of life (man should reach beyond his grasp), chides him for his weak character and wasted talent, and confides that her unsatisfying relationships with men have been plagued by emotional distances, "wide stretches of uninhabitable ground." He kisses her, they discuss the various significances attached to sexual activity, he suggests going to a room above the casino, and Miss Alma, horribly offended, takes a taxi home.

A few weeks later John's house is the scene of a wild and noisy party in celebration of his engagement to Rosa Gonzales, a voluptuous Mexican girl seeking escape from poverty and deprivation. Goaded by a self-righteous neighbor, Alma calls John's father, who is working to eradicate a fever epidemic in a nearby town. Before his father's arrival, John is drawn from the party to the rectory, where he finds comfort in the touch of Miss Alma's cool hands on his face. The party ends with a sudden gunshot; Rosa's drunken father mortally wounds the older Dr. Buchanan, who is outraged upon arriving to find his house the scene of raucous revelry.

A few months later Miss Alma is beginning to emerge from a period of pyschologically induced illness and isolation. John has completed his father's work at the fever clinic and returned to town a hero. Miss Alma pays him a visit during which they discover that each has dramatically influenced the other. She has released her doppelgänger and, ready for life and experience, declares her love and offers herself to him. But, as Alma realizes, "The tables have turned with a vengeance." Taking to heart her pleadings that he strengthen his character and value spirituality, he has forsaken his wild ways and decided to settle down. He is now engaged to be married to Nellie Ewell, a young voice student of Miss Alma's who has flirted with him throughout the play. In the final scene, Miss Alma is again in the park near the stone angel. She strikes up a conversation with a young traveling salesman with whom she sets out for Moon Lake Casino, indicating that she is probably destined to become the town prostitute.

The culmination of the battle between the spirit and the senses seems to indicate that the flesh tempered by spirituality stands a better chance at survival than does its reverse. John has become respectable, but he has not sacrificed his vitality. Alma, however, too long locked in repressive physical denial, will know no limits once her bonds have been shaken. The battle between the mind and the flesh has excellent dramatic potential, but here Williams draws his symbols too sharply and distinctly for genuine flesh and blood characters to emerge.

Miss Alma is too singular an embodiment of the spiritual, the "soul" which her name symbolizes. John's representation of physicality and science is blatant and heavy-handed. (He even lectures Alma on the essential centers of the human being, the brain, the belly, and the sex organs, using an anatomy chart as visual aid.) Williams allows symbols to take the place of characters, and the reversal of roles between these two symbols is unmotivated, therefore too neat. The play's minor characters do not rise above the level of stereotypes. Alma's puritanical father and peevish mother, the pseudo-intellectual members of the literary club, the giggling Nellie, and the hot-blooded Gonzaleses are either gratuitous cardboard figures or underdeveloped plot advancers.

The poorly received New York production did face the disadvantage of following the far superior *A Streetcar Named Desire*, to which it was inevitably—and unfavorably—compared. However, the earlier Dallas production was extremely well received, and a revival in 1952 was the Off-Broadway hit of the season, even winning favorable reviews from some critics who had panned the Broadway debut. Both the Dallas and the Off-Broadway stagings were in small arena or thrust theatres. There is merit in the play's episodic structure which flows through lighting changes rather than scenery shifts, giving the piece an organic unity. Some critics believe that the less than subtle allegory and symbolism, which were so jarring in the larger-than-life emphasis of a large-scale production, dim somewhat in the more intimate setting of a small theatre.

Two other notable events occurred during 1948: the publication of *American Blues: Five Short Plays* (the collection for which Williams had won the special Group Theatre Award in 1939) and *One Arm and Other Stories*. The short-story collection includes "One Arm," "The Malediction" (dramatized as *The Strangest Kind of Romance*), "The Poet," "Chronicle of a Demise," "Desire and the Black Masseur," "Portrait of a Girl in Glass" (a germ of *The Glass Menagerie*), "The Important Thing," "The Angel in the Alcove," "The Field of Blue Children" (originally published in 1939; the first work published under the name Tennessee Williams), "The Night of the Iguana" (to be expanded into the later play of the same title), and "The Yellow Bird" (from which *Summer and Smoke* grew).

Williams's first attempt at longer fiction, the short novel *The Roman Spring of Mrs. Stone*, was published in 1950. His first visit to Rome, in 1948, provided him material for the physical setting and

social milieu. The title character is a recently widowed and recently retired actress who attempts to fill her life's emptiness by pursuing youth and sex. The protrayal is not sympathetic; her marriage to a rich "Easter bunny" businessman was a loveless one, and her acting career had depended on squashing others for her own self-advancement. As she seeks rebirth and rejuvenation in Italy, her predatory nature is no match for handsome gigolos who prey on rich, lonely women. The novel is much less successful than most of Williams's short fiction. The symbolism is too obvious and, as in some of his drama, the characterizations are weak as a result of his concern with making them representatives of ideas or types. Some critics saw a descent into the pornographic (Mrs. Stone is followed around by an exhibitionist tramp with a penchant for urinating on walls). Donald Windham has unkindly suggested that Mrs. Stone is Williams's "first fictionalized self-portrait after his success."

Also significant during this period was the beginning of Williams's major intimate relationship. Though his sexual preference would not be officially announced to the world for several years, he had for a decade practiced homosexuality. His *Memoirs* (1975) chronicle his young and sincere (though unconsummated) love for Hazel Kramer; his only sexual experience with a female; and his discovery that his physical attraction was for his own sex. In the early 1940s his social circle became more and more homosexual, and, according to his *Memoirs*, his own healthy-sized appetites were satisfied through almost constant sexual activity—often with pick-ups, sometimes with casual acquaintances, and occasionally with someone who would become a friend. The decade was dotted with a series of relationships, some of which Williams truly valued, but all of which were rather short-lived. In the fall of 1948, just before the opening of *Summer and Smoke*, he was reunited with a casual summer acquaintance, Frank Merlo, a young Sicilian from New Jersey. The two began living together, beginning a relationship that would continue until Merlo's death from lung cancer in 1963. They traveled together, and, though the relationship was not an exclusive one, their ties deepened so that *The Rose Tattoo*, which opened in 1951 after they had been together for two and a half years, was dedicated "To Frank in return for Sicily."

Williams had found in the Mediterranean region a world that perfectly suited the anti-Puritan side of his nature. He was drawn to the warmth, cheerfulness, lustiness, and excitement he found in the Italian people. He began work on *The Rose Tattoo* in Rome and, after several revisions, completed it two years later in Key West, Florida. It is set in a Sicilian community on the Gulf Coast, thus combining the South of his origins and the Latin country for which he was developing a deep affection. The play is a warm celebration of sexual love.

Serafina delle Rose is a voluptuous woman whose total devotion to her husband Rosario is both cheerful and passionate. Rosario is a truck driver who hauls contraband under loads of bananas. Serafina, a seamstress, is pregnant; she claims that on the night of conception she awoke to find that her husband's tattoo of a rose had appeared for a few moments on her left breast, indicating that another "rose" was growing within her body. Fearing for Rosario's safety, she anxiously awaits his return from his last haul in the employ of the Brothers Romano; tomorrow he will quit, pay for the ten-ton truck, and begin working for himself. As she waits, Estelle Hohengarten, a thin blond woman, promises to pay her an exorbitant price for the overnight construction of a rose silk shirt, an anniversary gift for a man she loves.

Serafina's worst fears are realized: Rosario is shot, his truck crashes, and he burns in the fire. A miscarriage results from her sudden grief. Three years pass; in the loss Serafina becomes slovenly and withdrawn. Having lost the husband with whom she made the marriage bed an altar, she now burns candles in front of the urn containing his ashes and worships the memories of her lost love. Her daughter, Rosa, grown into as passionate a female as her mother, has fallen in love with Jack, a young sailor, but Serafina, fearing impurity, shuts her daughter up in the house and locks away her clothes.

After a visit from Rosa's teacher, Serafina relents and allows her daughter to go to her high-school graduation and picnic, but not before extracting from Jack a sacred promise that he will respect Rosa's innocence. Alvaro Mangiacavallo (Alvaro Eat-a-Horse) enters Serafina's house in pursuit of a novelty salesman who has bullied him on the highway; a violent argument ensues between the two strangers. The cheap salesman calls Alvaro names and knees him in the groin, leaving with threats to have him fired from his truck-driving job. In despair over his woes, Alvaro begins to cry, and Serafina joins him in his tears and then offers a bottle of wine. She is amazed to discover that this young truck driver who has a clown's face also has the body of her dead husband Rosario. As they drink the wine, they share past experiences and present troubles and begin to be drawn to each other. As she mends his torn clothing, Serafina gives him the unclaimed rose silk shirt to wear. They plan to meet for supper that evening, provided that young Rosa is not at home; Serafina insists that she must set a good example for her daughter.

When Alvaro comes that evening, Serafina has corseted and dressed herself to receive her caller. As they continue to exchange confidences, Alvaro's bumbling is more and more apparent, but the warmth between them grows. Gossip that her husband had not been faithful continues to nag Serafina, and Alvaro's phone call to Estelle Hohengarten confirms her fears that the man she worshiped had deceived her. She smashes the urn containing his ashes, gathers her strength, and makes plans for Alvaro to make a noisy pretense of leaving, but to return through the back door.

At daybreak Rosa and Jack return from the picnic. The wildly passionate Rosa wants to make love, but Jack is bound by his promise to her mother. As they argue, Serafina's cries can be heard from the house; Rosa assumes that her mother is dreaming of making love with Rosario. Jack leaves and Rosa goes inside, falling asleep crying on the couch. The next morning, obviously suffering from the wine of the night before, Alvaro stumbles out of the bedroom and in his stupor exclaims in amazement over the beauty of the sleeping Rosa. She awakens with a scream, arousing her mother, who violently chases Alvaro from the house. Rosa is angered by her mother's hypocritical inventions to explain Alvaro's presence in her bedroom. She defiantly leaves to meet Jack before he sails away, and at the last minute her mother gives her blessing. Then Serafina, realizing that her dead husband's ashes have blown away during the night, calls Alvaro back as she feels the burning of the rose tattoo on her breast, indicating that once again she has conceived.

The play suffers from some of the same flaws as *Battle of Angels* (one critic even called it a comic version of the earlier work). The plot is overly contrived and the ending is a simplistically happy wrap-up of a situation that has up to that point been developed through character complexity. Much of the symbolism is overdone. Among the dressmaker's dummies that fill the interior set are a widow and a bride "who face each other in violent attitudes, as though having a shrill argument." And Williams's excessive use of roses—from character names to tattoos to actual flowers—ultimately renders their effect almost comic. However, despite its weaknesses, the play does achieve a rich, robust, and warm effect. Its high-spirited earthiness, comic sequences, and convincing dialogue in some measure compensate for plot contrivance and excessive symbolism. As in *Battle of Angels*, there is a mixture of sex and religion, but in this case it is not an unhappy one: for Serafina, there is no conflict, for to her the one is the other. Thus when she discovers that the husband she had worshiped was not what she thought him to be, her reaction is to reevaluate and to continue her life, rather than to become embittered or to crumble. And though a particular man may prove faithless, she does not break faith with her belief in physical passion as the raison d'etre of her universe. Pleased with his celebration of the warmth of the Italian people, Williams reportedly dared the critics to mention "neurotic" in connection with this play. Though the production was met with mixed reviews, it enjoyed a successful run of 300 performances from early February through late October 1951.

Another significant event of 1951 was the publication of *I Rise in Flame, Cried the Phoenix*, Williams's dramatized tribute to D. H. Lawrence. The play finds Lawrence in the final moments before his death, seated before a banner of "the Phoenix in a nest of flames." Having seen most of his fiction banned, he is informed of the equivalent chaos created by his London exhibition of paintings. As he battles "like a tiger" in the face of death, his two companions are his German wife Frieda ("rather like a Valkyrie") and the soulful Englishwoman Bertha who reports the reaction to his exhibition. Lawrence recognizes rather ruefully that in his own unsuccessful search for God, he has himself become a god for many of his female admirers; his wife observes that he is jealous of Jesus Christ for having "beaten him to it," for having suffered "the *original* crucifixion." As the sun sets, he speaks metaphysically of the harlot darkness seducing the light, but triumphantly proclaims that "he'll climb out of her belly" and in the end there will be "great blinding, universal light." The brief play is suffused with Lawrencian notions and symbols that permeate many of Williams's works: the idealistic search for truth through art, the attaching of cosmic significance to sex, and the artist as Christ figure. The play's first professional production (of one performance) was on 14 April 1959.

Camino Real, an extended version of the earlier *Ten Blocks on the Camino Real*, was produced in March 1953. Though the ten "blocks," or scenes, were expanded to sixteen, the later play is in essence quite similar to its predecessor. It opens with rusty-armored Don Quixote and Sancho Panza arriving in the plaza of an unnamed tropical seaport bearing resemblance to "such widely scattered ports as Tangiers, Havana, Vera Cruz, Casablanca, Shanghai, New Orleans." On the left is the luxurious Siete Mares Hotel; across the street are a pawnshop, the gypsy's stall, and the flophouse "Ritz Men Only." A crumbling arch in the background leads to "Terra Incognita." In the foreground is a fountain (the source of water for the town's poor) that has gone dry. Recognizing the place as the end of the line, Sancho leaves his knight to return to La Mancha. Don Quixote announces that he will sleep, and from the figures of his dreams in this place, he will choose a new squire to accompany him on his journey.

What follows is Don Quixote's dream, "a pageant, a masque," set in the mythical seaport and populated with characters from history, literature, contemporary folklore, and the "dregs of humanity." The surrealistic action flows from scene to scene, with no lapse of time between. The scenes are announced by Gutman, the fat proprietor of the Siete Mares who represents the corruption of money. The other characters can be divided into two general types, the low-lifers and the romantics. In the first category are the streetcleaners, the loan shark, and other minor figures who suggest the dismal way of life on the plaza. Among the romantics is Lord Byron, a poet in search of freedom whose speeches include a particularly graphic description of the burning of Shelley's corpse. Another is Jacques Casanova, a proud gentleman fallen upon hard times who is ejected from the Siete Mares because of lack of funds. He finds some comfort in a relationship with Marguerite Gautier (Camille), whose advancing years force her to pay instead of being paid for the "love" she seeks. The hero of the piece is Kilroy, the cartoon character ex-boxer whose gullibility makes him easy prey for the vultures of the Camino Real, but whose blind optimism is unflagging.

The action, within the frame of Don Quixote's dream, is a surrealistic blend of carnival-type scenes and characters, lyrical and idealistic outpourings of hope, and mad chases which spill from the stage into the balconies and aisles of the theatre. At the end Don Quixote awakens, water begins to flow from the fountain, and Kilroy accepts the old knight's invitation to travel with him into the Terra Incognita. The play closes with Don Quixote's optimistic and symbolic line, "The violets in the mountains have broken the rocks."

A few reviewers criticized the play for both obscurity and overwhelming negativism. Many critics, however, found instead of obscurity a damaging lack of subtlety. And while many who populate the Camino Real have sunken into filth, sordidness, and vice, Williams clearly celebrates the notion that though life continuously deals dirty blows, it is only through maintaining hope and belief in the human spirit that the romantic may triumph in a cynical world. Stung by the negative response to the play, Williams suggested that audiences had perhaps become "a little domesticated in their theatrical tastes." However, experimentation with nonrealistic style is not the source of the play's lack of success. Rather, the problems are the use of stock figures and types to replace characters, and the sentimentalizing of romantic idealism. The playwright attaches meaning and significance which do not legitimately grow out of the characters and situations. With his tendency to champion the underdog, Williams's fondness for the play (somewhat like his attachment for *Battle of Angels*) persists; in a 1970 interview with David Frost, he stated that because it deals with the necessity of a romantic ideal, *Camino Real* is his favorite play. (It must be noted, however, that one of his purposes in the interview was to promote a current production of the play.) The theme is a valid one, though one which Williams deals with far more successfully in other works. The critics generally found it to be the least successful work of the earlier and most pro-

ductive part of his career. The original production closed after only sixty performances.

In the following year, 1954, Williams's second collection of short stories was published. *Hard Candy: A Book of Stories* includes the title story; "Mysteries of the Joy Rio" (a variation on the same theme and setting as "Hard Candy," with different results); "Three Players of a Summer Game" (the germ of *Cat on a Hot Tin Roof*); "Two on a Party"; "The Resemblance Between a Violin Case and a Coffin"; "Rubio y Moreno"; "The Mattress by the Tomato Patch"; "The Coming of Something to the Widow Holly"; and "The Vine." A major source of material was his experiences in New Orleans, but some characters and situations grew out of both his early years and his stint in California with MGM.

The tremendously successful *Cat on a Hot Tin Roof*, which opened 24 March 1955, satisfied audiences and critics that the author of *Camino Real* had not lost his touch. In this play he returns to a Southern setting, a realistic presentation, and a focus on crisis in one specific family. The universality of the play's situations and themes is unstated, but rather allowed to grow naturally from its characters and events. Though various critics argue for one or another of the cast as *the* central figure, three emerge as major characters of the work. Brick Pollitt, a twenty-seven-year-old former athlete, has charm, good looks, and the possibility of inheriting a large Mississippi cotton plantation; but he has turned to alcohol and has formed a cool detachment from involvement of any sort. His wife Margaret, or Maggie, is a beautiful young woman intensely frustrated by her husband's rejection, but fiercely determined not to walk away from the struggle. The third major figure is Brick's father, Big Daddy, a wealthy plantation owner by virtue of his own hard work, a man coarse of manner, but compelling in his vitality and decency.

The play is set in Brick and Maggie's bed-sitting-room of Big Daddy's plantation house. The occasion is Big Daddy's sixty-fifth birthday, but the party is planned as a double celebration: they have just received news that Big Daddy's suspected cancer has been diagnosed as only a spastic colon. However, all the family members except Big Daddy and his wife, Big Mama, have been told the truth; Big Daddy does in fact have terminal cancer. In a drunken escapade the night before, Brick has broken his ankle attempting to jump hurdles on the high-school athletic field. To include him in the party, the family is bringing the celebration upstairs to Brick and Maggie's room.

As Brick and Maggie dress for the party, their

Playbill

conversation provides both character development and exposition. The other house guests are Brick's older brother, Gooper, his wife, Mae, and their five children (to whom Maggie refers as "no-neck monsters"). A long-term rivalry between brothers is apparent, though Brick has always maintained the favored position without exerting any effort at all. Gooper wants nothing more than he wants his father's approval, and he has doggedly followed all the rules in trying to win it. He has become an attorney, married a cotton carnival queen, and produced five grandchildren (with a sixth on the way) for his father. Brick, on the other hand, at present has little to recommend him. In his youth he was a football star, but an injury forced him out of his professional career, and he has given up a job as a sports announcer to do nothing but drink.

In addition to the obnoxiousness of the children, Mae's fertility is a sore point with Maggie, who is childless. Though Brick has no interest in taking over his father's plantation, Maggie urges her husband to fight for what is rightfully his. She knows, though, that their failure to produce children puts them at a disadvantage. However, she cannot admit to the rest of the family (though Mae's eavesdropping gathers the information) that her husband refuses to sleep with her.

Dialogue between Brick and Maggie reveals that the mysterious source of his discontent is somehow related to his relationship with Skipper, a college friend and football teammate who died of drugs and alcohol. The relationship between the two had been so strong that Maggie's jealousy had been aroused; after suggesting that their affection might be unnatural, she had forced Skipper into an unsuccessful attempt to prove her suspicions untrue. Taking Skipper's inability to perform in bed with her as proof, Maggie had concluded—and told Skipper—that the love he felt for her husband was indeed unacceptable in the world in which they were born and raised. Maggie assumes that it was her announcement of "truth" that led Skipper into a world of drugs, alcohol, and, ultimately, death.

The second act begins with Big Daddy's birthday party, punctuated by simperings from Mae and Gooper and their children, the preacher's unsubtle suggestions that Big Daddy make a provision in his will for air-conditioning the church, and Big Mama's feeble attempts to ease the tension by making herself the butt of crass jokes. Big Daddy and Brick are left alone for the play's major confrontation scene, which begins with Big Daddy's demand to know why Brick drinks. His father's persistence results in Brick's expressing disgust with mendacity,

to which Big Daddy replies that adjusting to lies and pretense is a necessity of life. After relentless probing, Brick reveals that Skipper's death came shortly after a phone call during which he made a drunken confession, and Brick hung up on him. Big Daddy announces his realization: Brick drinks because the disgust he feels is directed toward himself for his refusal to face the truth ("His truth, okay! But you wouldn't face it with him!"). As Big Daddy accuses Brick of being responsible for Skipper's death, of passing the buck, and of refusing to face truth, Brick completes the exchange by telling his father that he has been lied to about the clinic reports; Big Daddy is in fact dying of cancer: "Being friends is telling each other the truth. . . . You told *me*. I told *you*!" The act closes with Big Daddy's passionate curse against "ALL—LYING SONS OF—LYING BITCHES!"

The published play includes two versions of act 3. The author's note explains that he wrote an altered ending at the request of director Elia Kazan. Three concerns of the director prompted the revision, and mark the variation between the two versions. First, Kazan "felt that Big Daddy was too vivid and important a character to disappear from the play except as an offstage cry after the second act curtain." Second, he thought Brick's character should undergo some change as a result of the act 2 confrontation. Additionally, he felt that the character of Maggie should be made more sympathetic. Williams disagreed with the first two of the three, but deferred to Kazan and produced a third act incorporating all three suggestions. In his explanatory note he in no way acknowledges error in his original version, but indicates that the success of the playing script has more than justified the alterations made to satisfy Kazan. The Broadway version of act 3 is the one customarily used in production.

As Big Daddy exits cursing (there is no lapse of time between acts), Gooper and Mae gather the family members, the doctor, and the preacher to give Big Mama the truth about the cancer diagnosis. As the news is broken, Big Mama's evident partiality to Brick is agonizingly frustrating to Gooper and brings out all the nastiness in Mae. They have drawn up a dummy trusteeship which would give Gooper control over Big Daddy's holdings. In a sudden show of spunk Big Mama orders him to put away the papers, announcing that Big Daddy still lives, but even if he were to die, she might not be willing to let go of his rich land. When Big Daddy, disturbed by the stormy discussion, rejoins the family, Maggie announces that she is pregnant with Brick's child.

As she and her husband are left alone, she admits the lie, but plans to make it true by locking up Brick's liquor until he makes love to her. As Brick expresses his admiration for her cunning and perseverance, Maggie speaks gently and determinedly of taking hold of him and handing his life back to him.

The play was one of Williams's most successful. The continuous action is tightly woven, and the themes of family conflict, lies and truth, spiritual paralysis, and literal decay and death are allowed to emerge naturally through character, dialogue, and situation. Neither the posturing, excessive lyricism, nor superimposed mythic proportions which mar so many other works exist in this play. Some of the minor characters (the mercenary Reverend Tooker, for instance) are no more than stereotypes. Mae is largely one-dimensional, and even Big Mama and Gooper provide challenges to actors to keep them from being flat. But Big Daddy, Maggie, and Brick are all vivid, complex, believable, and complete creations. The play ran for 694 performances and won for Williams his third New York Drama Critics Circle Award and second Pulitzer Prize.

In December of 1956 the film Baby Doll, directed by Elia Kazan, was released in New York. The plot line of Williams's script, a merging of the short plays 27 Wagons Full of Cotton and The Unsatisfactory Supper, is essentially an interweaving of the two earlier plays; the major difference is that Baby Doll, instead of being middle-aged and fat, is a young and attractive blond. Archie Lee had married her two years previously, when her father died, agreeing that she would remain a virgin until her twentieth birthday (shortly approaching as the film opens). Long on physical appeal and short on intellect, she sleeps in a crib and sucks her thumb. The other characters from the two short plays—Archie Lee, Aunt Rose, and Silva Vacarro—remain virtually unchanged. As the story of arson in a Mississippi cotton town unfolds, Silva's seduction of Baby Doll varies from the original. He pursues the child/woman through her house, up into the rotting attic even, in a chase which frightens her at first, but gradually begins to excite her. When he finally gets what he wants—her signature on a statement that her husband burned Vacarro's gin—she is greatly disappointed. They spend the afternoon together (she sings a lullaby as he naps in her crib), but no consummation takes place. An attraction and rapport have been established, however, and he has awakened her sexually and given her a new awareness of her husband's meanness and brutality. Archie Lee returns, and in a drunken rage shoots Aunt Rose. As he is taken off by the police, Baby Doll and Silva (who have been hiding in a pecan tree) are free to celebrate her sexual awakening. Sensationally promoted, the film had tremendous popular appeal, but it elicited censorship battles and rousing critical condemnation. Thinking he had writtten only a funny story, Williams was mystified by critics who lambasted the film as "one of the most unhealthy and amoral pictures ever made in this country."

The volume of poetry In the Winter of Cities was published in 1956. It includes most of Williams's earlier poems (some revised) published in James Laughlin's Five Young American Poets (1944). Generally considered inferior to his drama, the poems express a range of ideas and themes which also appear in his plays: the artists as the "most destructible element in our society"; testimonials to D. H. Lawrence; sympathy for society's misfits; and the psychological merging of sex and religion.

In 1957 came the production of Orpheus Descending, a revision (according to Williams, seventy-five percent new writing) of the failed Battle of Angels. After the success of A Streetcar Named Desire, The Rose Tattoo, and Cat on a Hot Tin Roof, Williams thought audiences would be more ready than they had been in 1940 to accept the play's sexual and violent themes. He claims that despite its early failure, the work was never discarded, but remained "on the workbench" for the intervening seventeen years.

Orpheus Descending adheres closely to the story line of its predecessor. The revised play presents the downfall of a mysterious, charismatic wanderer, Val Xavier, as he kindles the affections of Lady Torrance, a middle-aged keeper of a dry goods store in a small Southern community. The title evokes comparison to the Greek myth of Orpheus, a skilled musician who goes into hell to retrieve his lost love Eurydice and is almost successful in shepherding her out. However, he is torn to pieces by the Furies when he gazes back at her before leaving the region of darkness. Val attempts to rescue Lady from the moribund psychological state she has entered as a result of being married to a tyrannical dying man, but he is eventually lynched by a vengeful and enraged mob.

A close reading of both Battle of Angels and Orpheus Descending reveals that Williams made significant alterations in characterization and events. For example, a frame device he had used in an earlier version of Battle of Angels—the play is opened and closed with brief scenes set a year following the horrible Easter weekend events—is eliminated.

Myra's name is changed to Lady, intensifying her connection to the Holy Vigin, and Cassandra Whiteside becomes Carol Cutrere, sister of Lady's lost young lover. Instead of a fallen aristocrat, Carol is a burned-out humanitarian whose failed projects for social reform have led her to disillusionment, alcohol, and promiscuity. Val as Orpheus descends into the hell of the small Southern town choked by malevolent provincialism. In this version, the culprit becomes a vicious and degenerate society that destroys the nonconformist. The characters are more believable and the plot line is more plausible and less complex than in the earlier version.

Despite the improvements in the script, the production was a failure. Though there was little negative reaction to the play's "shocking" subject and theme, critics found it clumsily written. Their quarrel was not with the playwright's grim vision—he had written successful plays whose views were dark—but rather with a lack of artistry, as evidenced by "snarled symbolism" and unintentional self-parody. The production closed after only sixty-eight performances. Hollywood bought the play and with minor script assistance from Williams made of it a modestly successful film entitled *The Fugitive Kind* (1960). Then, two and a half years after its Broadway failure, *Orpheus Descending* opened for an Off-Broadway run that received some critical acclaim and satisfied its author.

About the time of the failed Broadway production of *Orpheus Descending*, in 1957, Williams went into psychoanalysis. His friends had begun to comment that his plays were becoming more and more violent. The tensions of daily life that had always plagued him were becoming increasingly pronounced: he continued to suffer constant hypochondria, in addition to growing bouts with claustrophobia, fear of suffocation, and extreme dependency on alcohol. The death of his grandfather Dakin in 1955 and of his father in 1957 added to his depression. Seeking some relief from the growing anguish, he began a lengthy stint of expensive daily sessions with the Freudian analyst, Dr. Lawrence Kubie. He also did extensive reading in related areas. Out of this period of his own life, as well as continued concern for his schizophrenic sister, Rose, who had been institutionalized after undergoing a prefrontal lobotomy, grew *Suddenly Last Summer*, considered by critics to be Williams's most shocking play to date. Coupled with the earlier one-act *Something Unspoken* in a package billed as *Garden District*, the play opened in early January of 1958.

Suddenly Last Summer takes place in the garden adjoining Violet Venable's Gothic mansion in New Orleans. The fantastic tropical jungle-garden, filled with "massive tree-flowers that suggest organs of a body, torn out, still blistering with undried blood" and the cries and hisses of unidentified savage birds and beasts, had belonged to Mrs. Venable's late son Sebastian. As the play opens, she is reminiscing about her son with Dr. Cucrowicz (Polish for "sugar"), a handsome, white-clad young psychiatrist whom she has summoned to her home. According to Mrs. Venable, her son was an accomplished poet (though publicly unrecognized—he "abhorred" false values that come from fame) who produced a single poem per year for twenty-five years. The two of them traveled extensively, universally recognized as "Violet and Sebastian" rather than as mother and son, as she nurtured his talent and sensitivity. "I was actually the only one in his life that satisfied the demands he made of people." She believes that he died chaste at the age of forty.

Mrs. Venable has devoted her life to what she considers the pure nurture of her poet son. She even joined him in his obsessive journey in search of "a clear image of God." Together they traveled to the Encantadas, where they watched the sea turtles lay their eggs in the sand of the beach. They returned at hatching time to witness thousands of baby turtles struggling to reach the sea before they were ripped apart by swarms of predatory birds that fed on the flesh of their soft undersides. Sebastian guessed that only one in a thousand survived to reach the sea. In this horrible natural occurrence he believed he had found a clear view of God.

Sebastian has died a violent death a few months before the time the play opens, and Mrs. Venable is seeking the doctor's assistance in preserving her reverent memory of her son and their relationship. The threat is Catharine Holly, her niece, who traveled with Sebastian on his last vacation and witnessed his death. Mrs. Venable promises a large endowment to his hospital if the doctor will agree to perform the prefrontal lobotomy that will silence Catharine. The niece is being brought to the Venable house to tell her story, and her recitation will serve two purposes: first, it will afford the doctor an opportunity to observe the patient, and second, it will allow Catharine a final opportunity to retract the "obscene" tale that her aunt cannot accept. In addition to having witnessed the awful death, lost the cousin she loved, and been confined in a psychiatric hospital, Catharine suffers the additional pressure of a mercenary brother and mother. Mrs. Venable has their inheritance from Sebastian tied up in probate, and unless Catharine changes her story, they stand little chance of gaining the tax-free fifty thousand dollars each that he has left them.

Catharine, however, is compelled to tell the truth, no matter how hideous it is to her; an administration of truth serum assures that she cannot lie even if she were so inclined. Her lengthy monologue is punctuated with bird sounds from the jungle-garden and the doctor's calmly prodding questions. Catharine implies that Sebastian was a homosexual, using his attractive mother to lure young men. When a stroke prevented her from accompanying him on his last vacation, he took along his younger and more attractive cousin as procuress. Catharine was unable to provide the support that his mother had given him, and Sebastian went to pieces. He was unable to write, and he drifted from the elegant life into association with the hungry urchins who frequented the public beach. One day while eating a late lunch in an open-air restaurant, the pair was surrounded by a band of naked black children begging for bread. As the beggars refused to leave, and began a bizarre serenade using instruments made of tin cans, Sebastian fled from the restaurant up a steep hill, the children in pursuit. As she saw them overtake and surround her cousin, Catharine ran in terror down the hill, calling for help. When she and the waiters and the police returned, they found Sebastian's naked body. "They had *devoured* parts of him. Torn or cut parts of him away with their hands or knives or maybe those jagged cans they made music with, they had torn bits of him away and stuffed them into those gobbling fierce little empty black mouths of theirs." What was left of Sebastian looked like "a big white-paper-wrapped bunch of red roses." As Catharine ends her recital, Mrs. Venable attempts to strike her, is stopped, and is led away. As the play ends, the doctor muses reflectively, "I think we ought at least to consider the possibility that the girl's story could be true. . . ."

Williams had expected to be crucified by the critics, to be "critically tarred and feathered and ridden on a fence rail out of the New York theatre." To his surprise, the critical response was not unfavorable, and the play was a box office success, running 216 performances. No doubt the sensationalism of the subject matter is responsible for attracting numbers of curious thrill seekers. However, some critics found in the play evidence of artistic control that had sometimes been lacking in earlier works. Though the ending may be a bit far-fetched, Catharine's use of evocative rather than explicit language—as well as the fact that the story is

recounted rather than enacted—indicates the playwright's symbolic rather than literal intentions. All the jungle imagery, combined with the various direct and oblique references to cannibalism and predatoriness (Sebastian's jungle-garden even contains a Venus's flytrap), creates a dark view of man's survival chances as he struggles against nature and other men. Even the God that Sebastian discovers in the Encantadas only gives him an early vision of his own death. Dialogue and character development, which are Williams's strongest points, are virtually absent from this play. Still, the play is carefully structured for dramatic tension, and the setting, story, symbolism, and themes mesh to create an organically unified fable. The play is not easily staged, however. Williams provides almost an open invitation to both designers and performers to go overboard, to carry things too far. In performance the play can work only when handled with the utmost restraint.

Another play to grow out of the psychoanalysis period was *Sweet Bird of Youth*, which opened 10 March 1959 at the Martin Beck Theatre, the scene of the *Orpheus Descending* failure two years earlier. Dedicated to its producer, Cheryl Crawford, who had also produced *The Rose Tattoo* and *Camino Real*, the play deals with the theme of youth and innocence lost "to the enemy, time." It is set on Easter Sunday in St. Cloud, a small town along the Gulf Coast. Chance Wayne (symbolically named) at age twenty-nine has returned to the town of his boyhood with aging screen star Alexandra del Lago (the Princess Kosmonopolis). The first act, set in the bedroom they share in the Royal Palms Hotel, provides background for both characters while establishing the present situation. Chance was born in St. Cloud, a normal baby except for some kind of "quality 'X'" in his blood, "a wish or a need to be different." A would-be actor, he has never achieved the kind of success he desires, and though he says that stardom depends on luck and breaks, he is beginning to doubt his talent. He has found that he does have talent in the area of lovemaking, which he has turned to professionally. He has been able to give society matrons "a feeling of youth" and lonely young debutantes an illusion of being wanted and appreciated. But he never gets back the satisfaction he gives; all of his desire is directed toward Heavenly Finley, his high-school sweetheart whom he cannot forget. The relationship has been disapproved by Heavenly's father, Boss Finley, a corrupt, racist small-town politician who claims divine inspiration. Chance hopes that his arrival in St. Cloud with the wealthy and glamorous screen star will be impressive enough to win Heavenly permanently.

Alexandra, who tries to "put to sleep the tiger raging in her" with pills, vodka, and hashish, is running away from fear of advancing years and a finished career. She had fled in terror from the premiere of her comeback film, certain that the picture was a failure. After meeting in Palm Beach, she and Chance have traveled together, he serving as caretaker/male prostitute as she attempts to obliterate her past. As Chance provides her with oxygen and narcotics, he turns on a tape recorder and prompts her to talk about the hashish she has smuggled into the country. He has hopes of advancing his acting career through blackmail. When his plan is revealed, Alexandra at first fears that she has been robbed, but when all her valuables are accounted for, she admits that she is somehow touched by his ploy. A business agreement is reached between them: she will cover all expenses and he will provide lovemaking on demand, never mentioning her past, her possible ill health, or death.

Chance has been drawn to St. Cloud by his desire for Heavenly, but he is immediately met with warnings to keep away from her. Unknowingly, on a previous visit he had infected her with venereal disease, and she has undergone a hysterectomy ("a whore's operation," according to her father). Boss Finley has put out the word that if Chance reappears in town, he will have him castrated. Chance is threatened by the doctor who has been selected by Boss to marry Heavenly, and he is warned by Heavenly's Aunt Nonnie, a woman who likes Chance and fears for his safety. His compulsion is so strong that he ignores threats and friendly warnings alike.

Act 2 introduces the evil Boss Finley and his equally despicable son Tom. A political rally is planned for the evening, and Boss orders his daughter Heavenly to appear dressed in white to symbolize "the fair white virgin exposed to black lust in the South." Just prior to the rally, Chance appears in the hotel cocktail lounge, drinking and popping pills, again ignoring warnings that Boss has gathered support to carry out his castration threat. Through the loudspeaker Boss's supercharged political speech is heard; he garners support for the recent emasculation of a young black, chosen at random to serve as an example that the whites mean business when it comes to protecting the purity of their blood. A heckler who raises questions about Boss's use of Heavenly to symbolize white virginity is brutally beaten by the crowd.

In act 3 Chance telephones a Hollywood columnist, instructing Alexandra to announce that she is returning to Hollywood with a new discovery, a young male actor. When Alexandra learns that her comeback film was not a failure, but instead a triumph, she makes no mention of Chance, but talks only of herself. She excitedly plans to return, fully realizing that the success of the film is only a temporary reprieve, but willing to accept it. She recognizes the failure in Chance, but offers to take him with her to Hollywood. He refuses, knowing that he would only be "part of her luggage." He also knows that what awaits him in St. Cloud is castration, but "That can't be done to me twice. You did that to me this morning, here on this bed." As Alexandra leaves and the members of the mob quietly begin to surround him, he steps to the forestage to deliver his curtain line: "I don't ask for your pity, but just for your understanding—not even that—no. Just for your recognition of me in you, and the enemy, time, in us all."

Though there was some incredulity over Chance's curtain speech addressed directly to the audience, the critical response was favorable. The financial success of the production was instantaneous; the play that was termed "affluent Bird" ran for 375 performances and became an equally successful film. However, the appeal of both play and film very likely resulted in large part from the popularity of the stars (Paul Newman and Geraldine Page) and the sensationalistic portrayal of the racist South. Alexandra emerges as a powerful character; she is a unique Williams heroine who, even though she recognizes truth, gathers her dignity and her resources to continue the struggle, refusing to allow herself to be defeated. Chance has charm, and his predicament elicits a certain degree of sympathy, but he does not have the substance necessary to justify strong reaction to his downfall. The other characters are either blatant caricatures (like Boss Finley) or ineffectually flat figures (like Heavenly). The play is structured to create dramatic tension, with the intense horror of the political rally sandwiched between Chance and Alexandra's scenes together, but the dialogue (particularly some of Chance's speeches) is some of Williams's most lyrically overwrought.

Period of Adjustment, subtitled *High Point over a Cavern* and labeled "A Serious Comedy," opened in New York in November 1960. It is set in a " 'cute' little Spanish-type suburban bungalow" near Memphis, Tennessee, on Christmas Eve. It deals with two rocky marriages, one of five years and the other only twenty-four hours old. George and Isabel, on their honeymoon trip, drop in on George's old war buddy Ralph. George had met Isabel when he was a patient in a veteran's hospital—suffering from a case of inexplicable "shakes"—where she was a student nurse. Her sympathy turned to love and they married before getting to know each other. She has been dismissed from her first job for fainting at the sight of blood, and George has quit his job because he found it boring. A long drive in an unheated car with radio blaring and husband drinking led to a honeymoon night which Isabel spent locked in the bathroom or faking sleep in a chair.

As they arrive at Ralph's house, "built over a great underground cavern and sinking into it gradually, an inch or two inches a year," George roars off in his secondhand funeral limousine, leaving his slightly hysterical bride alone with his old friend. As they share confidences about their marriages, Ralph reveals that his is less than ideal also. He has also quit his job (he was employed by his father-in-law), and his wife, Dorothea, left him when given the news. He had been talked into the marriage by her father when he cured in one night the psychic frigidity that a psychiatrist could not overcome at fifty dollars an hour. Ralph's gesture was not all magnanimous; he had designs on the old man's fortune. But his father-in-law, suffering from multiple ailments, has continued to "cheat the undertaker" and has given him only one raise in five years, on the occasion of his son's birth.

Ralph and Isabel talk, a maid dispatched by Ralph's in-laws to fetch his son's things is sent away, and George returns. The two men engage in typical "male talk," reminiscences that exclude Isabel. As the hostility between the bride and groom becomes more and more pronounced, Ralph intermittently attempts to reassure them with his mundane comment that they are only "going through a little period of adjustment." Dorothea's parents arrive with a laundry basket to collect her belongings, and after an argument they leave, threatening a lawsuit. Dorothea herself returns, apologizing for her parents, and announcing that she intends to stay. The curtain falls with Ralph and Dorothea in their bedroom, George and Isabel on the sofa bed, implying that the "period of adjustment" has been weathered by both couples and everyone will live happily ever after—except that the house built over a cavern continues to tremble.

The critics found themselves at odds with Williams's apparent concept of comedy. Some of the dialogue rings true, and there are some entertaining stretches, but the extremely talky work is filled with the playwright's psychological posturings. There are endless discussions of virginity, inhibi-

tions, impotence, and sexual insecurity. Ralph fears that his wife is turning their son into a sissy ("They'll do it ev'ry time, man"), Isabel's ties with her father are suspiciously strong, and the intensity of the camaraderie between the old war buddies makes Isabel uncomfortable. Isabel's blithe assessment—"The world's a big hospital, a big neurological ward and I am a student nurse in it"—comes near the end of the play. The cliched metaphor is indicative of the level of both Williams's view and his presentation of it. The production closed after 132 performances.

The Night of the Iguana, Williams's last major prizewinner, opened in late December 1961. Three divergent characters create a triangular tension in this drama of man, like the iguana tied under the verandah, "at the end of his tether." The setting is the Costa Verde Hotel, a run-down tourist spot on Mexico's rather wild and primitive west coast, in the summer of 1940. The lustiest and most sensual of the trio is Maxine Faulk, the recently widowed over-forty padrona of the establishment. T. Lawrence Shannon, a defrocked minister suffering from consuming cosmic guilt aggravated by his penchant for young girls, has arrived at the Costa Verde with his disgruntled charges: a busload of school teachers and an oversexed teenager on a Blake Tour. The third point of the triangle is Hannah Jelkes, a "New England spinster pushing forty" who travels with her "ninety-seven years young" poet grandfather, painting portraits of tourists to make a meager living.

Maxine, who has taken her young employee Pedro as a casual lover, is thrilled to see Shannon; she immediately begins to talk him into settling with her in an arrangement that would provide the two of them with comfort and security. Though Shannon resists Maxine, he has been drawn to the Costa Verde in hopes of getting rid of his "spook," a familiar unwelcome guest who has precipitated periodic emotional breakdowns in the past. His life at present is complicated by Charlotte, the sexy teenager who has thrown herself at him and now insists on marriage. Knowing fully the ludicrousness of her proposal and totally regretting his involvement, Shannon is threatened with rape charges by Miss Fellowes, Charlotte's caretaker and the leader of the group of women. He is struggling not to drink, to extricate himself from Charlotte, to maintain control over his tour group who are beginning to mutiny because the ramshackle Costa Verde was not on their schedule, and to fight off the psychological demons that are beginning to engulf him.

As Shannon's torture increases, he draws some measure of comfort from the "fantastic" Hannah Jelkes. Though she in no way has designs on him as the jealous Maxine suspects, she does feel a kinship with the man whose psychic torment reminds her of similar past experiences of her own. An iron butterfly, the spiritual Hannah is by far the strongest of Williams's frail women. Her nature is totally gentle, yet she is shocked by nothing, and she has achieved a peace that allows her to accept gracefully that which she cannot improve. As Shannon

panicky fettered creature and the situations of the play's characters are apparent. As Shannon frees the lizard, Hannah's grandfather Nonno excitedly announces that his last poem, after twenty years of work, is finally completed. As he recites, Hannah writes down his words, tears streaming down her face because she knows that anticipation of this last creative act is the only thing that has kept him alive. Shannon joins Maxine for a moonlight swim, knowing that he will accept her invitation to stay, and as the curtain falls, Hannah, after fighting

Margaret Leighton, Williams, and Patrick O'Neal

rages—for a while Maxine even has him tied down in a hammock after he goes berserk when his tour bus leaves without him—Hannah offers him a sedative (poppyseed tea), observes that he finds some pleasure in his guilty suffering ("a *comfortable* crucifixion"), and offers the comfort of her philosophy: a full knowledge of grim reality, but a belief that demons can be withstood through endurance, and that occasional fleeting moments of human communication are possible.

As they talk, Shannon decides to "play God" and cut loose the iguana that the Mexican boys have tied under the verandah. The parallels between the

momentary panic over Nonno's death, presses her head to her grandfather's crown in a tender, dignified tableau.

The play has flaws, not the least of which is a family of German tourists who cheer over news of the bombing of London, participate in clumsy and confused chase scenes, and generally add a discordant element of slapsitck. The lusty, uncerebral Maxine is given less dialogue, therefore less development, than Shannon and Hannah, but her character rings true. Shannon is such a mess of confused rage and guilt that he elicits an audience's interest and sympathy, but not much respect. The complex Hannah is the best drawn of the three characters. Even so, her recounting of two experiences—one innocuous and the other called by Shannon "a dirty little episode"—proves unsettling. Her recital is dramatically effective, but the fact that she labels them the sum total of her "lovelife" suggests an incongruity. This woman of delicate appearance has proven that she has looked life hard in the face and is nothing if not realistic toward what she sees. It is clear that Williams's interest in her two rather pathetic stories is in conveying her acceptance of humanity: "Nothing human disgusts me unless it's unkind, violent." The acceptance is in keeping with Hannah's character, but her viewing these encounters as her "lovelife" is not. Still, through Hannah, Williams presents an altering view of the world. The cruelty and isolation are still there, but Hannah has learned to endure without impotently raging, escaping through sex, or sentimentally romanticizing. Both a critical and a popular success, the play ran 316 performances and won for its author his fourth Drama Critics Circle Award.

Though *The Night of the Iguana* was Williams's last major success, his productivity did not cease. In *The Milk Train Doesn't Stop Here Anymore* (1962) he extends the exploration of acceptance that was begun with Hannah in *The Night of the Iguana*. Here the comforter is Christopher Flanders, a thirty-five-year-old poet/Christ figure called the Angel of Death because of his frequent appearance with wealthy women about to die. In this case the woman is Flora Goforth, a rich widow who has survived four husbands, retreated to a guarded villa high on a peak of Italy's Divina Costiera, and begun to dictate her memoirs in a haze of drugs and alcohol as she fights against death. Chris appears to provide her with what she needs, rather than what she thinks she wants. As she rants and raves, alternately attempting to seduce him and accusing him of being a thief, he gives his message that is "vaguely Oriental with Occidental variations." He is gradually able to calm her, as her strength fades, into acceptance of death. The first version of the play was produced in 1962 at the Festival of Two Worlds in Spoleto, Italy. The first American production opened in mid-January 1963. Criticism was generally favorable; though Williams's formerly unrelenting dark vision was beginning to be altered, critics began to note the rehashing of old material that was to mark so much of his work thereafter. There was also negative response to the complicated symbolism, particularly embodied in and expressed through the poet/Christ figure, Chris. The New York premiere ran only

Tennessee Williams, 1979

sixty-nine performances, and a 1964 version closed after only four.

The play's lack of success was indicative of the remainder of the decade, which Williams refers to in his *Memoirs* as "my 'Stoned Age,' the sixties." His longtime lover and friend Frank Merlo died of lung cancer in 1963, precipitating a depression that ultimately led to even stronger drug and alcohol dependence than before. Williams continued to write, but with increased effort, and his plays continued to be produced. But (as he acknowledges) his "falling down state" made his pre-production involvement difficult, and the critics, as well as audiences, protested his exposing his private psychoses through his plays. The period is characterized by first version openings, summer stock try-outs, and revisions—none of which had long runs.

Eccentricities of a Nightingale was tried out in stock and published in 1964. A 1948 revision of *Summer and Smoke*, it is a definite improvement over the earlier work. The story line is essentially unchanged, but complexity and motivation are added to the characters of Alma and John, resulting in greater believability. The addition of the story of Alma's Aunt Albertine, who disgraced the family by running off with the proprietor of the Musée Mechanique, serves both to define Alma's expectations and to foreshadow her destiny. A Public

Broadcasting System presentation in 1976 gave the play its first major professional production and a national audience.

A double bill entitled *Slapstick Tragedy* opened in February 1966. Williams described the two one acts as kin to "vaudeville, burlesque, and slapstick, with a dash of pop art thrown in." *The Mutilated* presents the perverse Christmas celebration of two old New Orleans whores, Celeste, a well-endowed shoplifter, and Trinket, a wino who has suffered a breast mutilation. The play is framed by carolers whose song asks pity for the wild, the mutilated, the wanderers: "I think the strange, the crazed, the queer / Will have their holiday this year." *The Gnädiges Fräulein*, set in the Florida Keys, is a parable of the modern artist's struggle for success. The Fräulein, a one-time chanteuse (artist), must fight off the marauding Cocaloony birds (critics) for the fish which are her livelihood (success). Critic Harold Clurman, though he recognized the "effective mixture of gallows humor and Rabelaisian zest," could not bring himself to smile: "I was too conscious that the author was in pain." *Slapstick Tragedy* closed after only seven performances.

Also in 1966 came the publication of Williams's third volume of short fiction, *The Knightly Quest: A Novella and Four Short Stories*. Besides the title work, it includes "Mama's Old Stucco House"; "Man Bring This Up Road" (from which *The Milk Train Doesn't Stop Here Anymore* grew); "The Kingdom of Earth" (later dramatized, expanded, and retitled); and "Grand" (a moving reminiscence of his maternal grandmother Rose Dakin).

The short story "Kingdom of Earth" was dramatized as a one-act, then later expanded to full length and retitled. As *The Seven Descents of Myrtle*, it opened for a brief New York run on 27 March 1968. Lot Ravenstock, weak and tubercular, brings his new wife to his Mississippi Delta farmhouse. The third side of the triangle is Chicken, Lot's illegitimate half brother who is half Negro and who has a claim to Lot's property at his death. Scene locations alternate as Myrtle makes several descents from the upstairs bedroom of her dying husband to the crude kitchen below, which is the domain of the earthier, more virile Chicken. A flood approaches, Lot's adulation of his late mother culminates in his transvestite death scene, and Myrtle is won over by Chicken's crude philosophizing: "Ther's nothing in the world, in this whole kingdom of earth, that can compare with one thing, and that one thing is what's able to happen between a man and a woman." The critics generally found the play shabby; it closed after twenty-nine performances.

More than two years later, on 11 May 1969, *In the Bar of a Tokyo Hotel* opened for a short run Off Broadway. The intensely personal play chronicles the panic, uncertainty, and isolation of an artist facing either new insight and achievement or the disintegration of his talent; he cannot be sure which. The characters are the painter, Mark, who is obsessed with his discovery about color; his unsympathetic wife, Miriam, who becomes impatient with her husband's antics and attempts to seduce the barman; and Leonard, the homosexual gallery director who is in sympathy with the tortures suffered by the artist. Most critics found the play too painfully personal for the stage; some even sounded the death knell for one of America's major playwrights. Shortly thereafter Williams went into a state of nervous collapse that resulted in hospitalization; his three-month stay enabled him to break his alcohol and drug dependency.

In 1970 *Dragon Country*, his third collection of short plays, was published. The volume includes the already produced *In the Bar of a Tokyo Hotel*; *I Rise in Flame, Cried the Phoenix*; *The Mutilated*; *The Gnädiges Fräulein*, as well as four then-unproduced works. *I Can't Imagine Tomorrow* deals with problems of communication: the man named Two cannot complete a sentence without help from the woman One. *Confessional*, exhibiting the patrons of the beachfront bar, Monk's Place, would be expanded into *Small Craft Warnings*. *The Frosted Glass Coffin* presents the geriatric inhabitants of a Miami retirement hotel. In *A Perfect Analysis Given by a Parrot*, two women in "the late afternoon of their youth" attending a convention in Saint Louis are out to have a good time.

Small Craft Warnings, Williams's only commercial success since *The Night of the Iguana*, opened Off-Off-Broadway on 2 April 1972. Set in a sleazy bar on the California coast, the play, according to its author, is "about communication and how we see people and how they show themselves to be what they really are." The bar is populated by a group of derelicts, each of whom has his moment of confessional monologue while spotlighted on the forestage. Among them are Leona, who persistently gropes for companionship in a life she recognizes as sordid and solitary; Violet, who gropes for male genitals under tables; a pair of young homosexuals, one a boy from Iowa who is excited over the Pacific Ocean and the other a Hollywood scriptwriter who is excited by nothing; Doc, a physician with a philosophical bent who has lost his license to practice medicine; and the proprietor Monk, who insists that his place will not become "a pad for vagrants" or a gay bar, but for whom the tavern and its patrons are home and family. In an attempt to boost the production's box-office appeal, Williams himself performed for a period in the role of Doc. While critics found in the play little more than seamier versions of past Williams characters, it was fairly successful with audiences, running a total of 194 performances.

First produced as *The Two-Character Play* in London in 1967, then revised, retitled, and produced in Chicago in 1971, *Out Cry* opened for a brief Broadway run in March 1973. Structured as a play-within-a-play, the work is set on the stage of a theatre in an unspecified foreign country. Two actors, Felice and his sister Clare, have been declared insane and abandoned by the rest of their theatrical company. Nevertheless, they decide to perform *The Two-Character Play*, a vehicle which may be the story of their own lives. In the play the two have retreated into the house where their father killed their mother and then committed suicide. Dreadfully afraid of the world outside, they even find almost impossible the simple task of going to the grocer's for food. Uncertain over its ending, they come out of the play to discover the house empty, the audience gone. After a discussion of the various options available to them—none of them appealing—they decide to complete the play. Though the play-within-a-play is unobscured, Clare and Felice seem to wander from one world to the other, suggesting a thin line between art and life, reality and illusion, sanity and insanity. Though critics generally treated this most personal work with sympathy, their respect was for the past achievements of its author, and not for *Out Cry*. Its Broadway run closed after twelve performances.

Eight Mortal Ladies Possessed, published in 1974, is a collection of six short stories, five of which were written in the early 1970s. It includes "Happy August Tenth," "The Inventory of Fontana Bella," "Miss Coynte of Green," "Sabbatha and Solitude," "Completed," and "Oriflamme" (dated "January 1944, the month of my grandmother's death in St. Louis"). In 1975 came the publication of two more prose volumes. *Moise and the World of Reason* is supposedly the painter Moise's observations as told to the first-person narrator, but the narrator (who bears a striking resemblance to Williams himself) includes many of his own observations, experiences, and ideas.

Williams's *Memoirs* were also published in 1975. Written during the run of *Small Craft Warnings*, the volume is an unchronological, often stream-of-consciousness recollection of the play-wright's childhood, friendships, professional associations, periods of mental distress, successes and failures, heavily laced with detailed accounts of his sexual experiences. The book is illustrated with a wealth of photographs of Williams, his family, his friends, and productions of his plays. The Tennessee Williams who emerges is an engaging and likable human being—witty, articulate, self-aware, and candid. (In drawing a comparison between old crocodiles and old playwrights, he observes, "Scratching the hide of the latter, you will discover that it can only be noticeably indented by the cutting edge of a diamond or by a bit of dandelion fluff in the atmosphere of a late summer afternoon.") The *Memoirs* are an excellent source for understanding the overall tapestry that is Williams, but they are frustrating to anyone seeking an orderly account of the weaving of the cloth. More interested in "truth" than fact, he admittedly has difficulty placing events in exact time and place, and therefore abandons any attempt at chronology. Furthermore, his memories of many events have been colored by time and the artist's tendency to alter or embellish. As he wrote in a letter to Donald Windham, "Consistency, thy name is not Tennessee!"

Two plays produced in the mid-1970s are still considered "works in progress" and have yet to be performed in New York. Both combine complicated plots with contemporary social and political concerns (the stronghold of big business, international conspiracy, revolution). *The Red Devil Battery Sign* was produced in Boston in 1975 and, in revised form, in Vienna the next year. *This Is (An Entertainment)* was given an American Conservatory Theatre production in San Francisco in early 1976.

Vieux Carré, which ran briefly in 1977, bears strong resemblance to *The Glass Menagerie*. A young writer serves as both narrator and a participant in the action. Like Tom, this narrator faces the future with expectation, while others cling to the past, but *The Glass Menagerie*'s narrator does not abide in a house of ghosts. The boardinghouse in the French Quarter that provides the setting for *Vieux Carré* is inhabited by the dying—physically, spiritually, or both. The landlady who sleeps on a cot in the hall, armed with a flashlight against intruders, provides a home for a motley collection of down-and-outs: a homosexual painter, two penniless old women who scavenge for food, a would-be fashion designer from New York, and her junkie stud who works in a strip joint. Physical ailments abound in the boardinghouse: the painter is tubercular and the fashion designer is dying of leukemia. Critics were generally unreceptive; according to Clive Barnes,

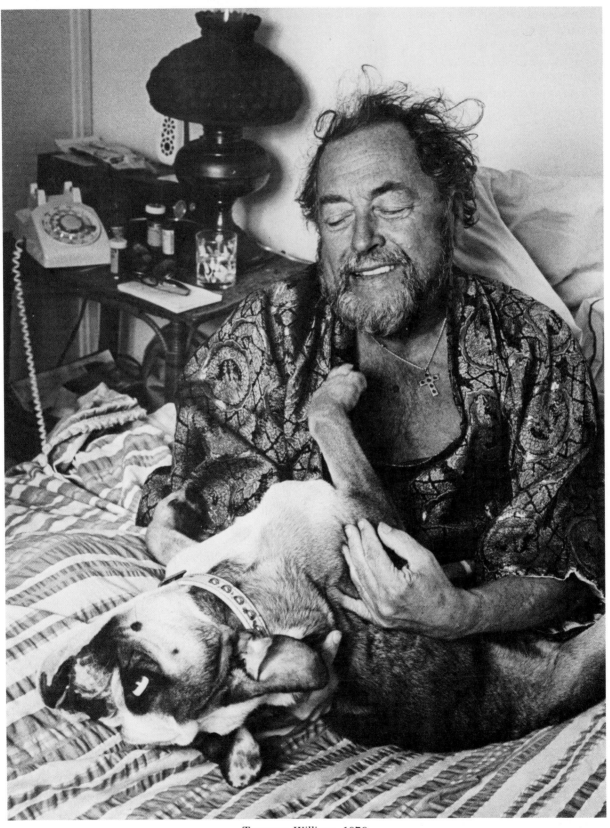

Tennessee Williams, 1979

"It is, unquestionably, the murmurings of genius, not a major statement." The production ran only five performances.

A Lovely Sunday for Crève Coeur was first performed as *Crève Coeur* at the Spoleto Festival in Charleston, South Carolina, in May 1978. Essentially the same production—a relatively unaltered script and most of the same cast—opened off-Broadway in January of the next year. Crève Coeur is a Saint Louis amusement park where Dorothea and Bodey have planned to go for a Sunday outing. Not wanting to spoil the picnic, Bodey spends much of the day hiding from Dorothea the newspaper announcement of the high-school principal's engagement. Dorothea, a civics teacher, has had a flirtation with the man; Bodey's plans are to be matchmaker for her roommate and her brother. They are visited by Helena, the chilly and refined art teacher who wants Dorothea to move with her into a very expensive apartment. The fourth character, a hysterical upstairs neighbor who speaks only German, occasionally adds confusion. Again critics noted the similarity to old material: the fading belle in the shabby Saint Louis apartment during the Depression. Some faulted the playwright for an unhappy mix of slapstick and pathos. The New York run lasted less than a month.

Clothes for a Summer Hotel, reuniting the playwright, director José Quintero, and Geraldine Page (who first worked together over a quarter of a century before on the Off-Broadway production of *Summer and Smoke*), opened 26 March 1980. Set outside the North Carolina asylum where she spent her last days and died in a fire, the play focuses on Zelda Fitzgerald, using flashbacks to include other stars of the Jazz Age: F. Scott Fitzgerald, Ernest Hemingway, and Gerald and Sara Murphy. Some critics wondered at Williams's choice of material, noting that he offered no new insight into characters already thoroughly familiar to the American public. Walter Kerr complained that Williams's personal voice is absent from the play, an observation that is rather ironic in light of the decades of criticism decrying a playwright for speaking too directly and too personally. Acutely missing the author's "inimitable flair for language," Kerr concluded that "*Clothes for a Summer Hotel* is Tennessee Williams holding his tongue." The critics were negative, and the play closed almost immediately.

Williams has not enjoyed a major success since *The Night of the Iguana* in 1961. Recently acknowledging that he seems to have been in "a period of eclipse" in recent years, and that perhaps he is "too old to write," he has insisted that he will nevertheless continue, because writing is his life. Over the past two decades much ink has been spilled—and a great deal of it with some glee—over the question of whether Williams is "written out." The question is a rather specious one; only time will tell. What he has put together over the past forty years is a richly checkered career, marked by tremendous successes and colossal failures. In many ways his greatest strengths also have been his greatest weaknesses. At times he was lambasted for parading across the American stage the products of his own psychosis; in recent years those of the "art grows from pain" school have wistfully concluded that in finding mental health Williams has lost his talent. His best work is lauded for its poetic language; his worst is marked by lush lyricism gone wild. His compassion for the tortured, the broken, the misfit, demonstrates his depth of feeling; but the line is thin between honest, compassionate portrayal of the unfortunate, and perverse fascination with sewer rats. Still, his best work is characterized by masterful use of poetic language, realistic human confrontation, and empathy with victims of loneliness and isolation. As Walter Kerr noted in his review of *Vieux Carré*, Williams "has already given us such a substantial body of successful work that there is really no need to continue demanding that he live up to himself, that he produce more, more, more and all masterpieces." Whether or not more great works are forthcoming, Williams's place is securely established as a major figure in mid-twentieth-century American drama.

Screenplays:

The Glass Menagerie, by Williams and Peter Berneis, Warner Brothers, 1950;

A Streetcar Named Desire, by Williams and Oscar Saul, Warner Brothers, 1951;

The Rose Tattoo, by Williams and Hal Kanter, Paramount, 1955;

Baby Doll, Warner Brothers, 1956;

Suddenly Last Summer, by Williams and Gore Vidal, Columbia, 1959;

The Fugitive Kind, by Williams and Meade Roberts, United Artists, 1960;

Boom, Universal, 1968.

Other:

Carson McCullers, *Reflections in a Golden Eye*, introduction by Williams (New York: New Directions, 1950).

Periodical Publications:

"Questions Without Answers," *New York Times*, 3 October 1948, II: 1;

"Tennessee Williams Presents His POV," *New York Times Magazine*, 12 June 1960, p. 19;

"Survival Notes: A Journal," *Esquire*, 78 (September 1972): 130-134, 166, 168;

"Let Me Hang It All Out," *New York Times*, 4 March 1973, II: 1.

Letters:

Tennessee Williams' Letters to Donald Windham, 1940-1965, ed. Windham (New York: Campbell, 1976; New York: Holt, Rinehart & Winston, 1977).

Interviews:

Robert Rice, "A Man Named Tennessee," *New York Post*, 21 April-4 May 1958;

Arthur Gelb, "Williams and Kazan and the Big Walkout," *New York Times*, 1 May 1960, II: 1;

Lewis Funke and John E. Booth, "Williams on Williams," *Theatre Arts*, 46 (January 1962): 16-19, 72-73;

Tom Buckley, "Tennessee Williams Survives," *Atlantic Monthly*, 226 (November 1970): 98ff;

"Playboy Interview: Tennessee Williams—A Candid Conversation," *Playboy*, 20 (April 1973): 69-84;

Mel Gussow, "Tennessee Williams on Art and Sex," *New York Times*, 3 November 1975, p. 49.

Bibliographies:

Delma E. Presley, "Tennessee Williams: Twenty-Five Years of Criticism," *Bulletin of Bibliography*, 30 (March 1973): 21-29;

S. Alan Chesler, "*A Streetcar Named Desire*: Twenty-Five Years of Criticism," *Notes on Mississippi Writers*, 7, no. 2 (Fall 1974): 44-53.

Biographies:

Edwina Dakin Williams (as told to Lucy Freeman), *Remember Me to Tom* (New York: Putnam's, 1963);

Catharine R. Hughes, *Tennessee Williams: A Biography* (Englewood Cliffs, N.J.: Prentice-Hall, 1978).

References:

Harold Clurman, "Tennessee Williams: Poet and Puritan," *New York Times*, 29 March 1970, II: 5;

Durante Da Ponte, "Tennessee Williams' Gallery of Feminine Characters," *Tennessee Studies in Literature*, 10 (1965): 7-26;

Francis Donahue, *The Dramatic World of Tennessee Williams* (New York: Ungar, 1964);

Frank Durham, "Tennessee Williams: Theatre Poet in Prose," *South Atlantic Bulletin*, 36 (March 1971): 3-16;

Signi Lenea Falk, *Tennessee Williams* (New York: Twayne, 1961; revised edition, 1978);

Norman J. Fedder, *The Influence of D. H. Lawrence on Tennessee Williams* (The Hague: Mouton, 1966);

John J. Fritsher, "Some Attitudes and a Posture: Religious Metaphor and Ritual in Tennessee Williams' Query of God," *Modern Drama*, 13 (September 1970): 201-215;

Paul J. Hurley, "Tennessee Williams: The Playwright as Social Critic," *The Theatre Annual*, 21 (1964): 40-56;

Esther Merle Jackson, *The Broken World of Tennessee Williams* (Madison: University of Wisconsin, 1965);

Jackson, "Tennessee Williams," In *The American Theater Today*, ed. Alan S. Downer (New York: Basic Books, 1967), pp. 73-84;

Robert Emmet Jones, "Tennessee Williams' Early Heroines," *Modern Drama*, 2 (December 1959): 211-219;

Sy M. Kahn, "Through a Glass Menagerie Darkly: The World of Tennessee Williams," in *Modern American Drama: Essays in Criticism*, ed. William E. Taylor (Deland, Florida: Everett/Edwards, 1968);

Albert E. Kalson, "Tennessee Williams Enters *Dragon Country*," *Modern Drama*, 16 (June 1973): 61-67;

Alvin B. Kernan, "Truth and Dramatic Mode in the Modern Theatre: Chekhov, Pirandello, and Williams," *Modern Drama*, 1 (September 1958): 101-114;

Francis L. Kunkel, "Tennessee Williams and the Death of God," *Commonweal*, 87 (23 February 1968): 614-617;

Marya Mannes, "Plea for Fair Ladies," *New York Times Magazine*, 29 May 1960, p. 16;

Gilbert Maxwell, *Tennessee Williams and His Friends* (Cleveland: World, 1965);

Jordan Y. Miller, ed., *Twentieth Century Interpretations of A Streetcar Named Desire* (Englewood Cliffs, N.J.: Prentice-Hall, 1971);

Benjamin Nelson, *Tennessee Williams: The Man and His Work* (New York: Obolensky, 1961);

William Peterson, "Williams, Kazan, and the Two

Cats," *New Theatre Magazine* (University of Bristol, England), 7 (Summer 1967), 14-19;

Henry Popkin, "The Plays of Tennessee Williams," *Tulane Drama Review*, 4 (March 1960):45-64;

Popkin, "Tennessee Williams Reexamined," *Arts in Virginia*, 11 (Spring 1971): 2-5;

Delma E. Presley, "The Search for Hope in the Plays of Tennessee Williams," *Mississippi Quarterly*, 25 (Winter 1971-72): 31-43;

Mike Steen, *A Look at Tennessee Williams* (New York: Hawthorne, 1969);

Jac L. Tharpe, ed., *Tennessee Williams: A Tribute* (Jackson: University Press of Mississippi, 1977);

Nancy M. Tischler, *Tennessee Williams: Rebellious Puritan* (New York: Citadel Press, 1961);

Kenneth Tynan, "Valentine to Tennessee Williams," *Mademoiselle*, 42 (February 1956): 130ff;

Gerald Weales, *Tennessee Williams* (Minneapolis: University of Minnesota Press, 1965).

Papers:

A substantial collection of Williams's manuscripts and letters is held by the Humanities Research Center, the University of Texas at Austin.

Lanford Wilson

Ann Crawford Dreher
University of South Carolina

BIRTH: Lebanon, Missouri, 13 April 1937, to Ralph Eugene and Violetta Careybelle Tate Wilson.

EDUCATION: Southwest Missouri State College, 1954; San Diego State College, 1955.

AWARDS: Rockefeller Foundation grants, 1967, 1973; Drama Desk Vernon Rice Award for *The Rimers of Eldritch*, 1967; ABC-Yale Fellowship, 1968; Guggenheim fellowships, 1970, 1972; New York Drama Critics Circle Award for Best American Play and Outer Circle Award for *The Hot l Baltimore*, 1973; Obie awards for *The Hot l Baltimore*, 1973, and *The Mound Builders*, 1975; American Institute of Arts and Letters Award, 1974; Pulitzer Prize for *Talley's Folly*, 1980.

PRODUCTIONS: *So Long At the Fair*, 25 August 1963, Caffe Cino, New York, 25 [performances];

No Trespassing and *Home Free!*, 16 January 1964, Caffe Cino, New York;

The Madness of Lady Bright, 19 May 1964, Caffe Cino, New York;

Balm in Gilead, 20 January 1965, La Mama Experimental Theatre Club, New York;

Ludlow Fair, 1 February 1965, Caffe Cino, New York;

This Is the Rill Speaking, 20 July 1965, Caffe Cino, New York;

The Sand Castle, 22 September 1965, La Mama Experimental Theatre Club, New York;

Days Ahead and *Sex Is Between Two People*, 28 December 1965, Caffe Cino, New York;

Wandering: A Turn, 10 April 1966, Caffe Cino, New York;

The Rimers of Eldritch, 13 July 1966, La Mama Experimental Theatre Club, New York;

Miss Williams: A Turn, 1967, La Mama Experimental Theatre Club, New York;

Untitled Play, 26 January 1968, Judson Poets' Theater, New York;

Lemon Sky, July 1968, Eugene O'Neill Memorial Theatre, Waterford, Conn.; 26 March 1970, Studio Arena Theatre, Buffalo, 37; 17 May 1970, Playhouse, New York, 17;

The Gingham Dog, 26 September 1968, Washington Theatre Club, Washington, D.C., 38; 23 April 1969, John Golden Theatre, New York, 5;

Serenading Louie, 1 April 1970, Washington Theatre Club, Washington, D.C., 35; 2 May 1976, Circle Repertory Theatre, New York, 33;

Sextet (Yes), 11 February 1971, Circle Repertory Theatre, New York;

The Great Nebula in Orion, 18 February 1971, Stables Theatre Club, Manchester, U.K.; 21 May

1972, Circle Repertory Theatre, New York;

Summer and Smoke, libretto by Wilson for Lee Hoiby's opera adapted from Tennessee Williams's play, Summer 1971, St. Paul; 20 March 1972, New York City Opera, State Theatre, New York;

Ikke, Ikke, Nye, Nye, Nye, 13 January 1972, Yale Cabaret, New Haven; 21 May 1972, Circle Repertory Theatre, New York;

The Family Continues, 21 May 1972, Circle Repertory Theatre, New York;

The Hot l Baltimore, 4 February 1973, Circle Repertory Theatre; 22 March 1973 transferred to Circle in the Square, New York, 1, 166;

The Mound Builders, 2 February 1975, Circle Repertory Theatre, New York;

Brontosaurus, 25 October 1977, Circle Repertory Theatre, New York;

5th of July, 27 April 1978, Circle Repertory Theatre, New York, 168; revised as *Fifth of July*, 5 November 1980, New Apollo Theatre, New York;

Talley's Folly, 3 May 1979, Circle Repertory Theatre, New York; 20 February 1980, Brooks Atkinson Theatre, New York.

BOOKS: *Balm in Gilead and Other Plays* (New York: Hill & Wang, 1965)—includes *Balm in Gilead*, *Home Free!*, and *Ludlow Fair*;

The Rimers of Eldritch and Other Plays (New York: Hill & Wang, 1967)—includes *The Rimers of Eldritch*, *The Madness of Lady Bright*, *This is the Rill Speaking*, *Days Ahead*, and *Wandering: A Turn*;

The Madness of Lady Bright and Home Free! (London: Methuen, 1968);

The Gingham Dog (New York: Hill & Wang, 1969);

The Sand Castle and Three Other Plays (New York: Dramatists Play Service, 1970)—includes *The Sand Castle*, *Wandering: A Turn*, *Stop: A Turn*, and *Sextet (Yes)*;

Lemon Sky (New York: Hill & Wang, 1970);

The Great Nebula in Orion and Three Other Plays (New York: Dramatists Play Service, 1973)—includes *The Great Nebula in Orion*, *The Family Continues*, *Victory on Mrs. Dandywine's Island*, and *Ikke, Ikke, Nye, Nye, Nye*;

The Hot l Baltimore (New York: Hill & Wang, 1973);

Serenading Louie (New York: Dramatists Play Service, 1976);

The Mound Builders (New York: Hill & Wang, 1976);

Brontosaurus (New York: Dramatists Play Service, 1978);

5th of July (New York: Hill & Wang, 1978);

Talley's Folly (New York: Hill & Wang, 1979).

Among American playwrights whose plays were first produced in the 1960s, Lanford Wilson deserves close study for several reasons. First, Wilson has been unusually prolific. In less than twenty years, from 1963 until 1980, over thirty of his plays were produced in New York City. Second, Wilson is a playwright with considerable artistic gifts. His plays have received numerous awards, including the Drama Desk Vernon Rice Award for *The Rimers of Eldritch* in 1967; the New York Drama Critics Circle Award, the Outer Circle Award, and an Obie for *The Hot l Baltimore* in 1973; another Obie for *The Mound Builders* in 1975; and, most recently, a Pulitzer Prize for *Talley's Folly* in 1980. And finally, Wilson's career as playwright parallels two important movements in the history of American theatre: the emergence of Off-Off-Broadway in the 1960s, and the important influence of regional theatre companies on theatre in the 1970s. Wilson's early plays were produced as part of an experiment which eventually gave rise to Off-Off-Broadway. His middle plays were first produced at regional theatres such as the Washington Theatre Club in Washington, D.C., and Buffalo's Studio Arena Theatre. Wilson's later plays have been launched exclusively by the Circle Theatre (or Circle Repertory Company, as it became known), a regional theatre group in Manhattan which Wilson helped found in 1969, and with which he has been long associated as playwright-in-residence.

Born in Lebanon, Missouri, Lanford Eugene Wilson ("Lance") was the only child of Ralph Eugene Wilson and Violetta Careybelle Tate Wilson. Five years after Wilson's birth, his parents divorced, and his father, who had been a shoe repairman in Missouri, went to San Diego to work in an aircraft factory. Wilson and his mother moved to Springfield, Missouri, where she worked as a seamstress in a garment factory. Six years later his mother married a dairy inspector named W. E. Lenhard, and Wilson moved with his stepfather and mother to a farm in Ozark, Missouri. Although Wilson described his family as "poor, very poor," he nevertheless had a happy childhood. He was popular in school, participating in track, painting and even acting in some high-school plays, notably as Tom in Tennessee Williams's *The Glass Menagerie*. Seeing a road-show production of *Brigadoon* won him over to theatre permanently. In a 1980 interview with Mel Gussow in *Horizon*, Wilson said, "After that town came back to life on stage, movies didn't stand a chance." Never earning a college degree, Wilson nevertheless attended Southwest Missouri State College in Springfield, Missouri, for one

term in 1954. In 1955, he went to San Diego State College and resided for one year with his father whom he had not seen for thirteen years. Wilson's father was then working at the Ryan Aircraft Plant in the experimental department. At San Diego State Wilson studied art, art history, and continued writing short stories, as he had since boyhood. He also worked as a riveter at the aircraft plant. But the father-son reunion was a fiasco, and in 1956, Wilson moved to Chicago, where he resided for six years. Although he had been writing for years, Wilson had actually focused more on drawing and painting. In Chicago, after working as a dishwasher and at other odd jobs, he landed a job as graphic artist with the advertising agency of Fuller, Smith & Ross. By 1959, Wilson had decided that he was not a painter and was about to write another story when he decided the idea would work better as a play. He says, "I wrote two pages and knew I was a playwright."

The embryonic first play was, according to Wilson, "rotten," so he enrolled in an adult educa-

tion class in playwriting at the downtown extension of the University of Chicago. In the course of the class he wrote numerous one-acts. One of these earliest plays was called "The Hour Glass," described by the playwright as "an O'Neill sea-story as if it were written by Tennessee Williams." Even though only one of these early plays, *Miss Williams*, proved stageworthy, Wilson has successfully pirated them for characters and bits of dialogue to use in later plays. In the summer of 1962, Wilson migrated to New York City, hoping to become involved in theatre. He lived in Greenwich Village, went to plays, and worked at numerous jobs, including waiting tables at a Cobbs Corner restaurant, where he was fired after serving one meal; taking complaints for a "fly-by-night furniture company"; taking reservations at the Americana Hotel; and working in the subscription office at the New York Shakespeare Festival. One night he happened to walk into Caffe Cino on Cornelia Street in the Village, and saw a production of Ionesco's *The Lesson*. It was a turning point in Wilson's life. He has since remarked, "I never knew that theater could be dangerous and funny in that way at the same time." That night Wilson was introduced to the proprietor, Joe Cino, who was intensely devoted to helping young artists. Cino asked Wilson to submit a play to be presented at Caffe Cino. Wilson, who had been writing plays for years, had a drawer full of scripts, and at last he had found a way to have them produced. Joseph Cino thus launched Wilson on a course which would eventually lead to his preeminence among American playwrights.

In the course of his theatrical career, Wilson, while foremost a playwright, has occasionally acted, built sets, directed, and served as producer. He has attended the Eugene O'Neill Memorial Theatre Center for Playwrights, and has received Rockefeller grants in 1967 and 1973, an ABC-Yale Fellowship in motion-picture writing in 1968, Guggenheim fellowships in 1970 and 1972, and the 1980 Creative Arts Achievement Award for theatre from Brandeis University. A bachelor, Wilson resides in Sag Harbor, Long Island, in a house built in 1845. He spends his spare time reading, restoring his house to its original appearance, and working in his garden. Wilson's plays typically contain a peculiar, theatrically vital tension which derives from his ability to represent universal truths through widely varying situations and characters. Humor, love, violence, jealousy, greed—all of the secret strivings of the human spirit appear in the fabric of his plays. Certain themes, however, surface repeatedly in his canon, connecting many of his plays. The playwright has an undying fascination with and respect for the past, and he is almost obsessed with how dangerous it is to forget the past or mindlessly destroy history. The family unit is another recurrent focal point. It is as though Wilson recognizes at once the necessity and impossibility of lasting family love. Playwright Robert Patrick has said that many of Wilson's characters are "trying to find the perfect family." And, perhaps most important of all, Wilson is imbued with an almost Shakespearean love of humankind. Wilson's characters are drawn with fine detail and understanding, regardless of sex, age, or social milieu. He is widely regarded as an actors' playwright. Most of his characters cling to their dreams. Although Wilson's plays squarely face the reality of life's pain, laughter and buoyancy ripple through them. Wilson's poignant comic tone arises from his characters stubbornly and almost idealistically maintaining their own private visions in the face of all opposition.

A 1980 Circle Repertory program referred to his style as "poetic realism," although this appellation may be misleading. While many of his plays are essentially written to be performed in the mode of twentieth-century realism, there are frequent nonrealistic, presentational departures: certain characters directly address the audience; some characters are clearly more symbolic than individualistic; treatment of time and place may be highly fluid or nonconventional. But the term *poetic* certainly applies to Wilson's work. Although his greatest strength as playwright may be his accurate ear for American speech, Wilson is at heart a poet because he is able to communicate his vision with language loaded with sensory appeal, yet natural to each particular character. Wilson has several other stylistic peculiarities. He is fond of deferred exposition. That is, he introduces his characters early on, but important facts about their pasts are revealed only gradually, as the action unfolds. He is also fond of simultaneous or overlapping dialogue, and characters onstage are often talking about several things at once. He prefers not to construct single lines of action but to render life in the style of an impressionistic painter: he shows snatches and glimpses of truth which can be apprehended clearly only at a distance, once the total pattern has emerged. While this mosaic style of writing makes for exciting theatre in performance, it can confuse the casual reader. Wilson's plays are rich with rhythm, innuendo, and delicate, interlocking pieces of action.

Like many new playwrights of the 1960s, Wilson was able to get his start as a professional play-wright because of the happy invention of a new producing arena: Off-Off-Broadway. In the 1950s, in an effort to break the large-house and mass-appeal cycle of Broadway, producers procured smaller, lower-rent spaces to mount productions, and the result was the innovative Off-Broadway movement. By the 1960s, however, even this new forum has succumbed to some of the same economic limitations as Broadway. Many Off-Broadway houses acquired small paid staffs, and to meet their payrolls, they were leaning toward productions that offered some chance of commercial success. Clearly, young, daring playwrights still needed theatres willing to take financial risks. Joseph Cino and Ellen Stewart, pioneering the Off-Off-Broadway theatre, provided an answer. They began producing plays in already existing cafes, the Caffe Cino and the Cafe La Mama specifically, creating a cabaret atmosphere suitable for theatrical experimentation.

In August 1963, Joseph Cino took Wilson's *So Long At The Fair* (written in one day) and put it on the boards at his Caffe Cino. Although the play was never published, the playwright describes *So Long At The Fair* as a "silly comedy" about a country boy who has "failed at every single art he has tried, including ice skating." The boy arrives in the big city only to be seduced by his boss's daughter into staying in the city and working at her father's cleaning plant.

Cino also produced, in January 1964, Wilson's next two plays on a double bill. The first was *No Trespassing*, which is also unpublished. Wilson wrote the play a few hours after reading Edward Albee's *The Zoo Story*, and, he admits, "it reads like it." In *No Trespassing*, a young man who has just killed his weak, henpecked father, runs into a vacant lot and encounters a bum. The young man confesses his crime to the bum in a cryptic manner (the bum does not understand the import of the confession), then allows his confidant to pick his pocket. The second half of this Cino double bill was *Home Free!*, which has received numerous subsequent productions in America and abroad. *Home Free!* concerns Lawrence and Joanna Brown, who are posing as husband and wife but are in reality brother and sister expecting a child from their incestuous union. The couple lives in a one-room apartment also inhabited by Edna and Claypone, who are imaginary young characters of the couple's creation. The play opens on a playful note as Joanna and Lawrence frolic in a world of their own. Lawrence is building an elaborate model Ferris wheel and never leaves the room. Joanna goes out on necessary errands. The brother and sister relate to each other tenderly and seem to be perfectly content. Their happiness is swiftly destroyed when Joanna falls ill, and while Lawrence battles with his fear of going outside for help, she dies. Following its Caffe Cino premiere, *Home Free!* moved to the Off-Broadway Cherry Lane Theatre on 10 February 1965. The play was produced there under the auspices of Theatre 1965, an association formed by Richard Barr, Clinton Wilder, and Edward Albee, which was sponsoring a New Playwrights' Series. The director of this Cherry Lane production of *Home Free!* was Marshall W. Mason, with whom Wilson has formed a highly productive and enduring professional relationship. Reviewers, on the whole, approved of *Home Free!*, which a *Time* magazine critic said was able to "achieve an astonishingly tender tension between sickness and sweetness." *Newsweek* said, however, that Wilson's "coy whimsy" threatened to make the play syrupy.

Wilson's next play was another one-act, *The Madness of Lady Bright*, which was first produced in May 1964, again at Caffe Cino. *The Madness of Lady Bright*, like *Home Free!*, was highly successful, moving from Caffe Cino to Theatre East 66, where it set an Off-Off-Broadway record with a run of 250 performances. Its star, Neil Flanagan, won an Obie for distinguished performance. Indeed, when *The Madness of Lady Bright* was published (1968), Wilson dedicated the play to Neil Flanagan, for Flanagan was a director at Caffe Cino when Wilson first had the idea for the play. While working at the Americana Hotel, Wilson had gotten to know a desk clerk there who was, in Wilson's words, "an outrageous queen." When Wilson took his play about this homosexual over to Caffe Cino for scrutiny, Flanagan and his wife went into a back room to read it. When they emerged, Flanagan said he did not want to direct it, he wanted to play it; and, as Wilson says, "He did—gorgeously."

The Madness of Lady Bright, which later enjoyed successful runs in London and Paris, is virtually a one-character play. The central character is Leslie Bright, a fortyish transvestite homosexual queen who is losing his beauty. Lady Bright rages in his one-room apartment, the walls covered with autographs of past one-night-stand lovers. There are also two characters designated Boy and Girl, who function more as stage managers to Bright's growing insanity than as separate characters. Boy and Girl occasionally assume the identities of characters from Bright's past, engage in dialogue with each other concerning Bright's mental state, play out their own subplot on the subject of loneliness, and often simply echo Bright's lines. The lonely Sunday

afternoon progresses, punctuated by Bright frantically trying to telephone friends who are not in, dancing to the music of neighbors' radios, and finally lapsing into complete fantasy, utterly mad. *The Madness of Lady Bright* represents the disintegration of a bizarre and memorable character in successive, highly poetic monologues. The horror of aging is described by Bright, who has survived for years on "her" beauty, in this way: "The veins in my arms and legs—my veins are old and brittle and the arteries break—your temples explode your veins break like glass tubes." Not all critics argued favorably for the worth of the play, however. Edith Oliver in the *New Yorker* said that were the central character an "old tart" instead of a man, the play would be hopelessly sentimental. She criticized Wilson for his "shameless old-fashioned mawkishness."

In January 1965, Wilson's first full-length play, the two-act *Balm in Gilead*, was produced by Ellen Stewart at the La Mama Experimental Theatre Club. *Balm in Gilead* takes place during the week or so before Halloween and spans a period of several days. The action is set in an all-night coffee shop and on the street corner outside, in the Upper Broadway area of New York City. The cast of thirty-two characters is composed of junkies, prostitutes, homosexuals of both sexes, and hustlers of all kinds. Wilson says in the stage directions that the cafe should look crowded and dialogue should overlap. Amid the general hubbub and jive talk, two characters gradually emerge as focal points. In fact, the stage directions suggest that the two be spotlighted against the dim general lighting soon after their first entrances. One of these characters is Joe, a young man from an obviously New York middle-class background, who is a dope pusher. The other is Darlene, a dumb prostitute from the Midwest who has just come to town. The central tension in *Balm in Gilead* comes from our interest in these two young people who have the embryonic promise of a real relationship. A few days before the action of the play begins, Joe had been given some heroin on consignment by Chuckles, a big-time operator who expects his dope or his money back within twenty-four hours. Days pass and Joe cannot make up his mind whether to deal or not. He meets Darlene, begins to spend time with her, and by the time he finally decides not to deal the dope, it is too late. In the climactic scene of the play, Chuckles sends one of his boys, the Stranger, to the cafe to kill Joe. While Darlene and the others look on, Stranger injects an overdose of heroin directly into Joe's heart. In *Balm in Gilead*, Wilson employs several staging devices to create the overall impression that life in the streets seems to move in a noisy circle. Rather than the dramatic action building in a typical linear fashion, there are frequent simultaneous conversations with no specific focus, single scenes rising out of the chaos. A cyclical effect is created as the play opens and closes with a rock 'n' roll song performed by "four Negro entertainers." Wilson also uses repeated action to emphasize that life recoils upon itself. For example, the Negro quartet can be frequently heard offstage rehearsing their song. Children dressed in Halloween costumes continue to run in and out shouting "Trick or treat." An original song entitled "Men on the Corner" is sung twice by characters who are commenting on their own conditions. A Colombian named Carlo is being given English lessons and at various times is heard repeating "One, two, three, four. . . ." Even Joe's chilling murder is performed once, then repeated twice, before the action continues. Other staging techniques in *Balm in Gilead* include two devices customarily thought of as nonrealistic in modern theatre: the monologue and direct address of the audience. At the end of act 1, a character turns to the audience and says, "We'll call an intermission here." The long monologue, used by Wilson extensively in his early short plays, becomes a polished tool in *Balm in Gilead*. One of the several monologues in act 1 is delivered by Dopey, whose name reflects the fact that he usually remains comatose on heroin. However, he suddenly comes to life and provides an elaborate explanation to the audience as to why prostitutes need pimps as status symbols, and how cockroaches will survive nuclear holocaust. In act 2, Darlene tells a long, strangely humorous story about how she almost got married. Even within the sordid souls of those lost in the gutter, Wilson manages to create sympathetic characters out of people named Rabe, Tig, Babe, and Fick. Wilson provides insight into this underworld microcosm by exploring the human needs behind the art of hustling. He examines the exotic boundaries of low-life morality, often with incongruous effects. Hoods habituated to crime are scrupulous in paying their diner tabs, prostitutes of both sexes form lasting love bonds, and big-time gangsters have primitive territorial instincts about the encroachment of small-time operators. Response to *Balm in Gilead*, although limited, was favorable. Michael Smith in the *Village Voice* praised the play as brilliant and "basically documentary." Perhaps it was sensation-seeking theatregoers who packed Cafe La Mama during the winter of 1965, but perhaps *Balm in Gilead*, out of a tradition as old as Gorki's *The Lower Depths* or as new as Gelber's *The*

Connection, is appealing to modern audiences because it portrays highest human aspirations springing from the lowest forms of humanity.

On 1 February 1965, three weeks after the opening of *Balm in Gilead* at Cafe La Mama, a new Wilson one-act, *Ludlow Fair*, opened at Caffe Cino. Along with the revival on 10 February of *Home Free!* at the Cherry Lane, Wilson had, for a period of three weeks, three plays running simultaneously in New York City. *Ludlow Fair*, directed and designed at Caffe Cino by Neil Flanagan, is a variation on the theme of loneliness so evident in *The Madness of Lady Bright* (in which Flanagan had starred). In *Ludlow Fair* two roommates, Rachel and Agnes, are each

Lanford Wilson

desperately looking for a man to marry. Rachel is the pretty one, who has been "in love" six times in nine months. Her last lover, Joe, turned out to be a thief, even stealing money from the girls. Rachel is near hysteria over her loss and her guilt for turning Joe in to the authorities. Agnes, on the other hand, has few beaux and is sick to death of Rachel's succession of men and endless lamenting. As each character is wrapped in her own misery, the two not only fail to communicate (Agnes is busy quoting Housman's poem "Ode to Terence"—hence the title of the play), but also they become overtly hostile during their interactions. The final picture is of two lost souls, searching for marriage as their salvation, unable even to provide friendship to reduce each other's misery. While Edith Oliver said in the *New Yorker* that *Ludlow Fair* was "almost worthless," Michael Smith in the *Village Voice* claimed the play "combines extreme precision in the writing with emotional discernment."

In summer 1965, Joe Cino, at the Caffe Cino, produced *This Is the Rill Speaking*, directed by Wilson himself. Subsequently the play toured Europe with the La Mama Repertory Company, under the direction of Tom O'Horgan, and was revived in April 1966 at the Martinique Theatre in New York as part of the *Six from La Mama* program. The play was also performed on educational television in New York in 1967. *This Is the Rill Speaking* takes its title from the words of Willy, one of the characters, who once wanted to be an artist (like Wilson himself) but now wants to be a writer of nature stories. Willy dreams of writing a story in which trees, brooks, rocks, and rills all speak, explaining life from their points of view. Willy's poetic vision is nestled within the kaleidoscopic patterns of seventeen other characters' lives. All seventeen roles are played by six actors, three men and three women, and all the characters live in a small town in the Ozarks, Wilson's homeland. Wilson employs simultaneous dialogue with many plots unraveling at once. There are rapid shifts of scene from pool hall to backyard to public park and so on. The settings are minimal, with each life study presented in a series of short scenes which are interlaced with others, creating from different threads a whole pattern. *This Is the Rill Speaking* opens and closes with Willy's family—Willy, his parents, and sister, Judy—engaged in harmless domestic chatter. In between are sandwiched a series of vignettes. Willy and his pal Tom conspire in secret masturbation. Willy's sister, Judy, and her friend Peggy dream of how Judy will decorate her house when she and her boyfriend, Keith, are married. Meanwhile Keith, a basketball star, is seducing Judy's friend Allison. Next door lives Maybelle Robinson, the town gossip, whose husband Walt's only occupation is walking to the post office daily. There are three other teenage boys, Manny, Ellis, and Ted, who are cooking up alibis to conceal a drunken escapade. In other scenes, Manny is shooting a pool game with Earl. Two farmers are seen discussing the best methods for harvesting hay. These continuous, overlapping dialogues are punctuated by Willy's mother calling him inside; by lullabies sung by a character named Martha, who occasionally loudly calls for someone named Carey; by at least half the male characters

whistling for their dogs; or by Willy whistling in code to Tom. *This Is the Rill Speaking* achieves its effect by using poetic, highly rhetorical dialogue. For example, Judy says to Peggy, "And I'll have a white Scotty dog or white yarn cat like Mrs. Carters makes on the bed and a few white throw pillows set up against the bed pillows there." *This Is the Rill Speaking* captures the essence of life in a small town, and one of the characters, never seen but the subject of much gossip, is Skelly, obviously the brunt of many town jokes. It is this character Skelly who later becomes the fulcrum of *The Rimers of Eldritch* (1966), also set in a small Ozark town. Elenore Lester, writing in the *Village Voice*, criticized Wilson's sentimentality, saying the characters in *This Is the Rill Speaking* were "stock types." However, she also called the play a "deft piece of dramatic poetry."

In September 1965 Wilson had his first volume of plays *Balm in Gilead and Other Plays*, including *Home Free!* and *Ludlow Fair*, published by Hill and Wang. In 1978 he would say, "I was lucky to get *Balm in Gilead* published by Hill and Wang when nobody had ever heard of me." He went on to praise Arthur Wang's courage, saying Wang "published everything I've done except for one or two pieces. Out of six he's published, he's only made money out of two."

The Sand Castle, Wilson's next one-act, opened in September 1965 at the Cafe La Mama, under the direction of Marshall Mason, who also served as set designer. The characters are Irene, a widowed poet and college professor about forty years old, and her three children: Owen, 22; Joan, 20; and Kenny, 12. Other characters are Clint, Irene's boyfriend, and Calvin and Sasha, friends of the family. *The Sand Castle* takes place during one evening at Irene's house in Ocean Beach, San Diego. Once again, Wilson employs overlapping dialogue, creating the impression that at Irene's house there are always lots of interruptions and at least two different conversations going on at all times. Every character in *The Sand Castle* is a loser in the game of love: Owen is blindly and unrealistically in love with his childhood sweetheart who is now pregnant and married to Calvin; Calvin tries unsuccessfully to seduce Sasha, who turns out to be a flirtatious iceberg; and Irene loses her truck-driving boyfriend, Clint, after he succumbs to a one-night stand with her daughter Joan. A musical motif punctuates the dialogue, a technique Wilson employed in *Balm in Gilead*. This time the song is an old favorite, "There is a Tavern in the Town," the first line of which is sung by Owen with all others in the cast creating an echo with "In the town!" At one point there are what the stage directions call "semi-choreographed dances" to the song, and the play ends with all the characters shouting "And may the world go well with thee!" Wilson also employs direct address of the audience by having the boy, Kenny, open the play: "I get to begin the play now. . . ." Other characters speak to the audience throughout the play, and finally Irene has to say, "This is the end of the play," because narrator Kenny has fallen asleep. The overall mood of *The Sand Castle* is gently somber, evoking the loneliness and the laughter of earlier Wilson pieces. It is as though Wilson reveals the heartbreak of the characters, at the same time demonstrating that their cheerful bravado and modes of coping with life can be very entertaining. A *Village Voice* review said that in *The Sand Castle* Wilson was "creating a flexible and promising technique." *The Sand Castle* was shown on educational television in 1970, and was selected by Stanley Richards for his *Best Short Plays* series in 1974. In December 1965 Caffe Cino presented a bill of two Wilson one-acts: *Days Ahead* and *Sex Is Between Two People*. The former is a monologue which, at Caffe Cino, was both directed and acted by Neil Flanagan. *Days Ahead* is a portrait of a middle-aged small businessman, who enters a room which has been divided in half by a wall. He raps on the wall and begins addressing someone the audience never sees. Gradually it becomes clear that on the other side of the wall is his wife whom he plastered inside twenty years before because he "began to feel restless." It appears that he has traveled the world, visiting the room once a year since then to tell his wife "the news." On this trip home he has brought with him a fork with which to tear down the wall, for at last he has had "a revelation." He has decided to come back to her and live in love and peace, reunited at last. The lights fade out as he scratches away at the wall with his fork and dreams about the long walks and talks they will have together in the days ahead. Michael Smith in the *Village Voice* praised Flanagan as both director and actor, but he faulted Wilson for illuminating "only a tiny area of experience." According to Smith, while Wilson's "considerable skill makes the play pleasing enough, he needs to find bigger uses for it."

The play which shared the Caffe Cino bill with *Days Ahead* was entitled *Sex Is Between Two People*. The brief play has never been published. It concerns two shy male homosexuals who meet at the Saint Mark's Baths. Again, Michael Smith of the *Village Voice* felt that *Sex Is Between Two People*, like its twin feature, was a minor example of Wilson's work. Smith called the play "anecdotal, unambitious, untheatrical."

In April 1966, Caffe Cino presented *Wandering: A Turn*, another Wilson one-act. In the Caffe Cino production Marshall Mason directed this three-character play in which he and Wilson played the two male roles. In May 1968, *Wandering* was included with ten other playwrights' one-acts in *Collision Course* at the Cafe au Go-Go, where it ran for eighty performances. *Wandering* also was produced on educational television in New York City. The language of *Wandering* is different from that of other Wilson plays, for it is built entirely of one liners, a mechanical kind of rapid-fire stichomythia broken only by deliberate pauses which are indicated in the script. The characters are He, She, and Him, and the stage directions say "The play runs through Him's life, recapping several times at the end." Him is badgered throughout by He and She who play various roles: Him's parents, his draft board, his wife, his friends, and the medical team attending his final illness. All Him really wanted out of life was to wander around, but He and She keep trying to make him toe the mark instead.

Wilson's second full-length play was *The Rimers of Eldritch*, written with the support of a Rockefeller Foundation grant. It was first produced at the La Mama Experimental Theatre Club in July 1966. Wilson himself directed the La Mama production. Like *This Is the Rill Speaking*, *The Rimers of Eldritch* is set in the Middle West, in Eldritch, a former coal-mining town with a current population of about seventy people. Whereas *This Is the Rill Speaking* has seventeen characters played by six actors, *The Rimers of Eldritch* is populated by eighteen small-town personae, played by seventeen actors. Eldritch itself unifies the action. The town is governed by the twisted morality of truly small and evil people who think themselves to be heroes and saints. The central plot revolves around the town hermit, Skelly, who was alluded to in *This Is the Rill Speaking*. Skelly has been the brunt of generations of Eldritch boys' jokes and is finally murdered. Skelly embodies evil to the rest of the Eldritch residents, so his death and the subsequent acquittal of his murderer, Nelly Windrod, serve to "free" the community of all blight—or so they think. As Skelly himself says of the townspeople, "What they want to think they think; what they don't they don't." What each character wants to think is that he or she is better than everybody else, and to that end they envy, gossip, and shift blame from themselves. Yet ironically, as the play unfolds, it becomes increasingly clear that the town heroes have grievous faults, and the town outcasts have noble spirits. As for the heroes, the same actor plays the Judge and the

Preacher, both authority figures busy "preaching" and "judging," calling Skelly names such as "the heathen in our fold" and "the evil in our lives." Nelly Windrod becomes the town hero for ridding Eldritch of Skelly, but the audience sees that she actually murdered in cold blood and, moreover, habitually mistreats her aged mother. Patsy Johnson, the toast of Eldritch, and the prettiest girl at Centerville High, is planning a June wedding. The action of *The Rimers of Eldritch* reveals Patsy as a conniving strumpet, pregnant by any of several boys, ready to lie to get herself a husband. As one by one the "good" people of Eldritch are discovered to have clay feet, Skelly reveals that the shining legend of Driver Conklin, town hero, is also tarnished. Driver was a champion stock-car racer who died in a racing crash. The wreckage of his car still stands in the town square as a memorial to the champ. Skelly has spent his lifetime lurking beneath windows and eavesdropping on his fellow citizens. He knows that rather than a hero, Driver Conklin was actually an impotent, viciously cruel malcontent. While the heroes are being debunked, the "outcasts" of Eldritch display many redeeming qualities. Cora Groves, whom one character calls a "daughter of Babylon," braves public opinion to testify to the true nature of Skelly's character. Mary Windrod, senile mother of Nelly, struggles with her fading mind to remember exactly what did happen on the night of Skelly's murder. And finally, in the most ironic touch of all, Skelly is killed because of his heroism. Nelly shot Skelly as a prowler while he was attempting to prevent Driver, Jr., from raping Eva, a crippled girl. *The Rimers of Eldritch* demonstrates how huge evil can grow from the maskings of small guilts; how appearances are more important to people than deeds; and how a town may identify and persecute a scapegoat.

In a 1980 *New York Times* interview, Wilson said of the people he grew up with in Missouri that "the people are so complicated and the texture is so rich . . . I go back and find that half the people in my high school class are divorced, and someone has murdered someone else, and soandso is cheating on suchandsuch, and Marylou just killed her baby, and one of my best friends is now an incredible alcoholic, and the guy least likely to succeed is now practically the mayor, and . . . yet all those idyllic values I remember, the warm human values, are still there, too, existing in parallel. That's what I mean when I say it's damned complicated." Stylistically in *The Rimers of Eldritch* Wilson disregards chronology and uses time in a fluid fashion, mixing together scenes from the spring, summer, and fall of the present year. The murder of Skelly is actually the inciting incident which propels the action of the play, but is not seen until the end. And once again, as in *This Is the Rill Speaking*, Wilson uses overlapping scenes, rapid shifts in locale, singing and whistling, with individual lines and bits of dialogue often repeated twice, sometimes three or more times. Such unrealistic treatment of time and place dictates a suggestive rather than a realistic setting, and the stage directions call for a set made up of "a series of areas, perhaps levels with porch and courtroom railings." Various indoor and outdoor locales suggested include a courtroom, a church, several houses, the forest, automobiles, store fronts, and a cafe. Most of the actors remain onstage throughout both acts, according to the stage directions, "grouping as needed to suggest time and place."

In February 1967, *The Rimers of Eldritch* moved to the Cherry Lane Theatre as part of Theatre 1967, a project of Albarwild (Albee, Richard Barr, and Clinton Wilder) Theatre Arts. The play was later produced on educational television in New York. Critics tended to compare the play to Dylan Thomas's *Under Milk Wood* and Thornton Wilder's *Our Town* with a few scattered accusations of oversentimentalization. *Time* magazine praised Wilson's "honesty of language" and said the title of the play was apt in that it showed "a people who blanket their lives with hoarfrost." Even Edith Oliver at the *New Yorker*, long a Wilson detractor, said that he "may not have invented people, but he has written parts." *The Rimers of Eldritch* won the Drama Desk Vernon Rice Award for Off-Off-Broadway achievement in 1967.

In 1967, the sky seemed to fall on the Off-Off-Broadway movement which had nurtured Wilson and so many of his theatrical contemporaries. Joseph Cino, the arch patron of struggling artists, committed suicide in that year. Wilson has remarked, "All he ever wanted for himself was enough money to keep the Caffe Cino going. . . . On nights when nobody came to see the play, we'd put it on just for Joe. . . . When your father and boss and preacher kills himself, you find yourself without much to believe in. Everyone—except Joe—knew that he was creating a new theatre in America. His excitement was responsible for half of the vitality of Off-Off-Broadway, and his death heralded the end of free activity. After Joe died, Off-Off-Broadway got less communal, more competitive."

Without the security of a steady producing organization, Wilson began to seek new theatres for his plays. At first he was content to put up already written pieces. When Robert Patrick asked some of his playwright friends to submit two-to-three-minute plays for a fire department benefit at La Mama Experimental Theatre Club, Wilson submitted *Miss Williams* (1967), which was actually written years before in Chicago. This unpublished play is extremely short, running about three minutes, with three characters: Miss Williams, a designer; a technician; and Miss Williams's secretary. Miss Williams is in charge of producing the sunrise over New York City every morning. On the particular morning in question, the designer awakens with a terrible hangover only to discover with dismay that everyone is expecting spectacle—the almanac has said there is to be an eclipse.

Wilson's next effort was a collaboration with some of his old Cino buddies. In January 1968, Wilson's *Untitled Play* was performed at Judson Poets' Theater (Judson Memorial Church) for several successive weekends. *Untitled Play* had been written the year before for a La Mama tour but was never performed. The Judson production was directed by Marshall Mason, house director at Judson at the time; and there were musical numbers written by Al Carmines, staged by Remy Charles and Aileen Passloff. Wilson describes *Untitled Play*, which is unpublished, as being "about the roots of patriotism. It is a free-form abstract play about the creating of a country, war, etc."

By September 1968, Wilson was ready to stage his third full-length play, the two-acter *The Gingham Dog*. What he needed to produce the play was a good regional theatre company of the type which was beginning to dominate serious American theatre by that time; fortunately he found the Washington Theatre Club in Washington, D.C., a highly respected regional theatre. The premiere of *The Gingham Dog* marked the first time a Wilson play had opened outside New York City. The Washington production was directed by Davey Marlin-Jones and ran for thirty-eight performances. Richard L. Coe, writing for the *Washington Post*, said *The Gingham Dog* was "a work of clear and substantial value." *The Gingham Dog* has four characters (two central ones) and is set in an apartment in the East Village. The play takes place on the last day of a marriage which is breaking up. Vincent, a twenty-eight-year-old white man, is leaving Gloria, his twenty-seven-year-old Negro wife. Wilson had actually known a couple in Greenwich Village on whom he patterned Vincent and Gloria. In his stage directions, Wilson makes it clear that the lengthy first act should be played as a tightly wound spring, with the negative energy generated by a bad marriage spewing forth in all directions. The couple is parting because of racial conflicts, from within the marriage and without. Robert, their neighbor, harbors secret curiosity, delighting in the details of the breakup. Barbara, Vincent's sister, has always been filled with jealous hatred for her black sister-in-law. However, the play focuses on the couple's towering hatred for each other and, by extension, for each other's values and the rest of the world. Tension builds throughout the act, as Gloria and Vincent direct their own unresolved feelings against each other and against those around them. Act 2 is shorter, written in only eight hours, and Wilson dictates that it should be played "very, very slowly." Vincent comes to see Gloria one last time in the wee hours of the morning, and although there are certain glimpses of their former tenderness toward each other, the overall impression from the last act of *The Gingham Dog* is the slow release out of anger into nothingness. The final curtain falls on Gloria gazing blankly out of the apartment window. Wilson suggests that after a marriage fails, once the violence dies down, what is left is a void. On 23 April 1969, *The Gingham Dog* opened at the John Golden Theatre in New York. It was Wilson's first production on Broadway. The regional-theatre-to-Broadway route was typical in the late 1960s. It was a road already taken successfully by Howard Sackler's *The Great White Hope* and Arthur Kopit's *Indians*. *The Gingham Dog*'s Broadway production was directed by Alan Schneider and was produced by Haila Stoddard, Mark Wright, Diane Wilder, and Harold Scott. George Grizzard played Vincent, and Diana Sands, making her last Broadway appearance, played Gloria. Critics praised the two stars, although Walter Kerr in his *New York Times* review said, "Mr. Grizzard was given the funnier lines, so Mr. Wilson must be white." Kerr went on to praise the play, saying "The loneliness on both sides was frightening." Clive Barnes said it was "beautifully directed and impeccably acted." Although a critical success, *The Gingham Dog* closed after only five performances. Indeed, Wilson would not have a commercial success on Broadway for another decade. For the most part during the 1970s he remained content to have his plays produced at regional, Off-Broadway, and Off-Off-Broadway theatres. At least one critic, Clive Barnes, mused that perhaps the state of the art on Broadway during the 1960s and 1970s was such that only the rare serious play could succeed at all. In a 1978 interview with Barnet Kellman, Wilson said, "We *want* our plays done Off-Off-Broadway. Very often I do, anyway. I guess a lot of us have had that Broadway thing, and know it's just impossible." Also Wilson candidly admitted in a 1980 *New York Times* interview, "Producers have not been beating down my door."

While 1969 was the year of Wilson's first Broadway failure, it was also the year in which an event transpired which would shape Wilson's playwriting career more than any other. Wilson, along with Marshall Mason, Rob Thirkield, and Tanya Berezin, founded the Circle Theatre. Their first theatre was in a loft at Broadway and Eighty-third Street, and during the early days Wilson designed and built scenery as well as acted, although his official title was playwright-in-residence. The Circle Repertory Company, as Circle Theatre soon became known, remains dedicated to the production of new scripts, as well as revivals of classical plays. The stated purpose of the group is "to make the action of the play become the experience of the audience." Throughout the 1970s Wilson's association with Circle Repertory would provide him with an opportunity unique for American playwrights: a close working relationship with a talented group of artists dedicated to taking his writing seriously. At Circle Repertory the playwright is present during the rehearsal process, and plays are rewritten and polished even after production opening. Wilson himself commented on his happy affiliation with Circle: "There is a group of six or seven of us who trust each other. We know we're after the same

thing, and we all know what that thing is, and we have open discussion amongst ourselves. . . . Marshall [Mason] actually says, 'What do you think?' . . . what he [Walter Kerr] regards as no more than an exercise—the working conditions in the workshop—we may feel produces the best poetry being written for the American stage."

In November 1969 Wilson's one-act, *Stoop*, was televised as part of "Foul" on the New York Television Theater. It is a play with three female characters, one of whom does not speak. The three women are seated on the steps of a run-down brownstone discussing life. It seems there is a plague, with dead bodies picked up and burned daily. There is talk of rats, canned water, and lack of radio communication. Through all this, these women are concerned with their petty physical ailments and complain only about offensive smells and tastes. The dialogue of this short play is broken up by someone practicing "Old Kentucky Home" on a nearby piano. The piano practicer makes repeated mistakes until the final moment of the play when, to the women's amazement, the whole first phrase of the song is correctly played.

By 1970 Wilson had two more full-length plays ready for production. Circle Theatre was still struggling for survival, so once again the playwright went to regional theatres outside New York. The

Marshall W. Mason and Lanford Wilson

first play, *Serenading Louie*, previewed during March and opened on 1 April 1970 at the Washington Theatre Club. Again, as for *The Gingham Dog*, Davey Marlin-Jones directed the premiere, and the play ran for thirty-five performances. The title is from a line in "The Whiffenpoof Song"—"We will serenade our Louie"—because the nostalgia of good old college days colors the lives of the four characters of the play. There are two couples here: Mary and Carl, who is an ex-football player, and Gabby and Alex. The couples, living in a suburb north of Chicago, are best friends, with all but Gabby having been together as undergraduates at Northwestern University. During the course of *Serenading Louie*, Alex is offered a gubernatorial appointment to an unexpired term in the U. S. Congress, while Carl becomes more and more depressed commenting that nothing "grabs" him anymore. Carl knows his wife Mary is having an affair with his CPA; Alex is in love with a teenager, leaving his wife Gabby sexually unfulfilled. Carl and Alex have long conversations about their unhappy sex lives and their disappointment with life. The set of *Serenading Louie* at the Washington Theatre Club premiere was a single interior, representing simultaneously the homes of both couples. Frequently entrances and exits overlapped and sometimes all four were in their two separate houses at once, "as though both homes were superimposed upon each other in the single proscenium frame." There is, in *Serenading Louie*, direct address of the audience, but time is treated in a realistic manner, with the action spanning two consecutive weekends in October and November of the present year. *Serenading Louie* is Wilson's hymn to suburbanites who expect more from marriage and their futures. The *Washington Post* reviewer pointed out that Wilson was "damned good at dialogue. The talk is not only listenable but, to the players' obvious pleasure, sayable."

The day after *Serenading Louie* began its preview in Washington, *Lemon Sky* opened at the Studio Arena Theatre in Buffalo on 26 March 1970. The Studio Arena production was directed by Warren Enters and starred Christopher Walken as Alan, the character who represents Wilson himself. *Lemon Sky* is highly autobiographical and had been written originally at the O'Neill Memorial Theater Center in 1968. It had taken Wilson twelve years to bring himself to write the painful story of his abortive attempt to become reconciled with his father. Finally, in a twenty-hour writing binge, the first act poured out. He says, "The entire play unfolded in front of my face." *Lemon Sky* is the touching story of

Alan, a sixteen-year-old college freshman, who travels (as Wilson did) by bus from the Midwest to San Diego to live with his father from whom he has been estranged since early childhood. Douglas, the father, has married Ronnie, a sympathetic woman, and they have two small sons. In addition, two teenage girls, Penny and Carol, live with Douglas and Ronnie as wards of the state. It is clear from the beginning of *Lemon Sky* that Alan and Douglas are not going to be able to forge a true father/son relationship. Time has made them strangers. Alan is suffering from a blinding migraine headache when he arrives, yet he valiantly tries to become part of his "new" family. Alan feels genuine affection for his two young half brothers, characters whom Wilson portrays as particularly appealing. Alan even tries to be friends with the two girls (his father's foster children) and comes to love and respect his stepmother. But Douglas and Alan do not see eye to eye on any issue, and ultimately, in an explosive scene, father accuses son of homosexuality, and son accuses father of whore-mongering and of contributing to the death of his baby sister (because the father was with another woman and could not be found when the baby was dying), leaving the son as only child. Alan returns to the Midwest, and the family ties he has worked to strengthen grow looser as the years pass. Time is fluid in *Lemon Sky*. A mature Alan greets the audience and narrates the play through flashbacks. Even in an almost soap-opera environment of domestic struggle, the characters' language is beautiful. Alan describes a California brush fire in this way: "The brush, some of it—the fire had gone through it so quickly, some of the brush stood—like ashes on a cigarette—stood three feet high—the white negative of the brush exactly intact, and you touched it and it disintegrated." Wilson has written some suggestions for the set and lighting for *Lemon Sky*. He prefers the play to be done before an "expanse of sky (which is never yellow)." Perhaps the playwright means that Alan's dream of happiness, a "lemon sky," is never realized. He further recommends that the actors pay no attention to room divisions in their movement, and that there be no green in either set or costumes, with "as many scenes as possible . . . bathed in a bright, cloudless sunlight."

Lemon Sky, which was included in the seventh series of John Gassner's *Best Plays 1967-1973*, is a highly visual, strikingly aural translation of a teenage Alan's vision of family. In May 1970, *Lemon Sky*, with its Buffalo director and cast, opened at the Playhouse, a new quasi-Broadway theatre on West Forty-eighth Street in New York. Three *Lemon Sky* producers, Stoddard, Wright, and Wilder, had produced *The Gingham Dog* as well. The fourth *Lemon Sky* producer was Neal DuBrock from the Buffalo Studio Arena Theatre. Critics raved about Charles Durning as the father, and especially about Christopher Walken in the role of Alan. John J. O'Connor, in the *Wall Street Journal*, commented on Wilson's "extraordinary use of language" and his "ability to compose not so much patches of interesting dialogue as sustained series of quiet lyricism, resembling vocal duets, solos or complex ensemble pieces." Clive Barnes praised Wilson's "impartiality" in depicting characters. However, *Lemon Sky* closed after seventeen performances, and the entire production moved to Chicago where it enjoyed a longer and more successful run.

After the New York failure of *Lemon Sky*, Wilson, who had been hard at work for the previous four years, seemed to run out of energy. For a year and a half, he was unable to write, even though he was officially the playwright-in-residence at Circle Repertory. As he puts it, "I had an incredible block after *Lemon Sky*. Maybe it was because I had grown up at the Cino, a theatre of participation, but I found that I just couldn't adapt to being a closet writer, to giving my play to a producer and waiting for the readings." Fortunately, Wilson had a few one-acts which had not seen production, so the Stables Theatre Club in Manchester, England, produced in February 1971 his *The Great Nebula in Orion*. Paul Hellyer served as director. The play has two characters, Louise and Carrie, old friends in their Bryn Mawr days, who have just run into each other in Bergdorf's. They have had a few drinks to celebrate their reunion and are now in Louise's posh New York apartment at Central Park West and Eighty-first Street. Carrie is married and lives outside Boston with her husband and two perfect children. Louise has never married and is a successful designer of women's clothing. The women are obviously from two different worlds now, and they cover their self-consciousness at being in each other's presence by talking to the audience. For instance Louise says, "It's a girdle, right? In this day and age, do you believe it?" And Carrie says, "I used to wait on her hand and foot." With the use of these comic asides, Wilson keeps the first part of the play light. The women are drunk and struggling to communicate. They discuss lost school chums like Phyllis Trahaunt, who Carrie hints was homosexual. They talk of a lost lover of Carrie's, Richard Roth, a poet who was briefly interested in astronomy, and taught Carrie about the Great Nebula in Orion. The nebula is not even a star; it is, ac-

cording to Carrie, "a lot of hydrogen gas that's lit up by a couple of stars behind it somewhere." As the play progresses Louise and Carrie both admit that they are less than happy with their lives. The mood becomes sober, and just as Carrie is about to leave, she looks into Louise's bedroom, sees a photograph of Phyllis Trahaunt, and realizes that Louise has loved Phyllis and lost. They both cry and, in their mutual misery, become again the friends they used to be.

Wilson had also previously written another one-act, *Sextet (Yes)*, commissioned by the Center Theatre Group at the Mark Taper Forum in Los Angeles. Circle Repertory staged this play in its 1971 fledgling season. *Sextet (Yes)*, subtitled *A Play for Voices*, has six characters, all of whose names begin with *B*—Bill, Betsy, Bob, Belle, Brenda, and Bert. All are middle-aged except Brenda, who is in her twenties. The play is built on the simultaneous stories of all six people. Each talks of the past, particularly past sexual experiences, without being aware that the others are speaking too. Occasionally one will softly agree with another's comment with a "Yes." The effect of the short play is of human isolation. People seem to use sexual encounters to reach out to each other, but they never quite succeed.

Wilson's *Ikke, Ikke, Nye, Nye, Nye* was first seen when directed by Michael Feingold at the Yale Cabaret in New Haven, Connecticut, in January 1972. Subtitled *A Farce*, the play concerns two characters, Edith, a telephone operator who is looking for a man, and Graham, the boss's son. The couple has been out on a date and is now back in Edith's apartment where she is attempting to seduce him with wine and sexual innuendo. The problem is that Graham has never been on a date before; he views the telephone as the ultimate object of forbidden sexual pleasure. Every time Edith leaves the room, Graham reaches for the telephone to make an obscene phone call. Edith and Graham continue at cross purposes, with Edith dreaming of being rich and/or getting raped by Graham, and Graham drunk and intent only on being able to make an obscene phone call. The hilarious climax occurs when Graham exits into the bathroom to pull himself together, and Edith receives an obscene phone call which arouses her to orgasm, though all the while she is yelling, "Smut!" Edith and Graham part civilly, without discovering how much they have in common.

During Wilson's dry period in which he could not write, he had continued to work at the Circle Theatre, answering the phone and selling tickets.

Finally, Circle announced a bill of one-acts by Wilson, including *The Great Nebula in Orion* and *Ikke, Ikke, Nye, Nye, Nye*. With the encouragement of the Circle Theatre group, Wilson wrote a new play, *The Family Continues*, to round out the bill. On 21 May 1972, Circle Theatre at 2307 Broadway presented a triple bill by Wilson. Marshall Mason directed all three plays, and as a result of this Circle production, *The Great Nebula in Orion* was included in Stanley Richards's *Best Short Plays, 1972*. *The Family Continues* was written with specific Circle actors in mind. In fact, the actors helped create some of the effects, since Wilson says the play "Should be considered a game, an exercise in swift characterization and ensemble co-operation." *The Family Continues* was revived at Circle Theatre in October 1972, and Wilson says that this second version, using only eight actors, was the more successful. The play is about Steve who, during the course of the play, is born, goes to school, enters the service, begins work in a service station, falls in love, gets married, becomes the service station manager, and fathers Steve, Jr. Then Steve, Jr., goes through all the same stages his father did. A narrator calls out, "Phase One—getting born. . . ," and so on all the way to "Phase Ten—passing away," and the play ends with Steve's demise. The other actors play all the characters in both Steves' lives, such as teachers, parents, customers, and friends. Frequent simultaneous dialogue is indicated in the margins with brackets around lines which are to overlap. Wilson suggests that no props be used and that the players dramatize the environment with their bodies. For instance, the Circle actors formed an automobile with which Steve recklessly kills a kid. Although the message of the play seems bleak, underlining the futile cycles of human life, Wilson suggests that the continual flow of the two Steves' lives be presented "with a sense of joy in creation." He writes in the script's notes, "I can't see it benefiting from a 'down' production."

Published in 1973 in a volume along with *The Great Nebula in Orion*, *Ikke, Ikke, Nye, Nye, Nye*, and *The Family Continues* is another one-act entitled *Victory on Mrs. Dandywine's Island*, subtitled *A Fable of Manners*. This strange, unproduced play is a blend of eighteenth-century drawing-room comedy, medieval morality play, and theatre of the absurd. In the stage directions Wilson says "The play should be treated in the exaggerated high style associated with an English comedy of manners." The character names include Miss Liveforever and Miss Companion; but rather than echoes of eighteenth-century characters like Congreve's Lady Wishfort, the characters in *Victory on Mrs. Dandywine's Island*

seem more didactically named. Miss Companion is a direct descendant of a character like Good Deeds in the medieval *Everyman*. And finally, with a character like the Gardener who says little more than "Mum mum mum," *Victory on Mrs. Dandywine's Island* is reminiscent of Beckett's or Ionesco's characters' failures to communicate. The plot concerns a mysterious bud which has poked up through the salty, arid land of the island. The remarkable survival of this tiny flower somehow constitutes Mrs. Dandywine's victory. Mrs. Dandywine maintains that she owns the island and therefore the flower. Miss Liveforever, a socialite neighbor, is infuriated. The Gardener resigns, and Mr. Orfington, an unwelcome guest in Mrs. Dandywine's home, leaves without his lunch. Of the few Wilson plays remaining unproduced, *Victory on Mrs. Dandywine's Island* is probably most deserving of that status.

In February 1973, Circle Theatre presented *The Hot l Baltimore*, directed by Marshall Mason. Written with the support of a Guggenheim grant, *The Hot l Baltimore* is without doubt Wilson's best-known play. The title represents the burned-out neon sign above a dilapidated hotel, once elegantly art deco. This image of urban decay is part of an idea Wilson had been considering for quite some time. In a 1980 interview the playwright said, "We change so quickly, we in America. I guess I might be saying something like, 'Look at what you're throwing away before you throw it away.'" Like *Balm in Gilead* and *The Rimers of Eldritch*, *The Hot l Baltimore* has a large cast (seventeen), and each character has a deathless dream to serve as counterpoint to the dying environment. As he had done with *The Family Continues*, Wilson found himself writing a play to fit most of the existing company of Circle Repertory actors. Wilson says, "I looked around and tried to use as many of the Circle actors as possible. As soon as I got a character in mind, I was able to say who should play it. Every character in that play was written for a particular actor." There are seven residents still living at the hotel. There is April, the large, sympathetic whore with heart of gold and a wisecracking sense of humor. There is Suzy, another prostitute who leaves the hotel deluding herself that she will find happiness at last with a new pimp. There is Mr. Morse, a craggy seventy-year-old who vocalizes, exercises, and plays checkers in the lobby, all the while exhibiting a marked degree of hostility toward the others. There is Millie, a retired waitress who sees ghosts and lives in a world altogether removed from reality. (The character of Millie was based on a waitress Wilson knew in Chicago and appeared in one of his early unpublished plays.) There is Jackie, a brusque-talking hustler who takes care of her slow-witted brother Jamie. And finally, there is the Girl, also a prostitute, whose youthful exuberance somehow is misplaced at the Baltimore. She can never decide what she wants her name to be and is romantically enthusiastic over train service and the geography of the United States. It is the Girl's flirtatious vulnerability that almost wins over Bill Lewis's heart. Bill is the night desk clerk who tries to avoid too much fraternization with the residents. Other nonresidents include Mr. Katz, the hotel manager, who has just given the residents one month's notice of the demolition of the hotel. Mrs. Oxenham is the day desk clerk whose iron rule is sometimes successful in keeping the whores' customers out of the hotel. There is Paul Granger III, who is searching for his lost grandfather, once a hotel resident. Granger is recently out of jail where he served a short sentence for a drug-related crime. Also, Mrs. Belotti comes in to pester Mr. Katz into keeping her thirty-six-year-old son, Horse, on the payroll. There are walk-on characters in the personae of a john, a cabdriver, and a delivery boy. As usual, Wilson employs simultaneous dialogue, and the action of the play is sprawling, with a constant stream of entrances into and exits out of the hotel lobby. The three-act play takes place on Memorial Day from half-past seven in the morning until after midnight. While there is no single line of action creating changes in the characters, there are bits and pieces of events that are interesting in and of themselves. Mr. Morse catches Jackie stealing jewelry from his room; Mr. Morse and Jamie come to feeble blows over a checker game; Jackie discovers that the Utah land she bought from a radio ad is utterly worthless; and Jackie clears out and abandons her brother. All the people at the Baltimore are either hurting each other or helping each other. The patchwork effect, when viewed at a distance, delineates a pattern of the human ability to go on feeling and striving in the midst of a crumbling world. In the end the Girl goes upstairs to take a bath, and April sends her a pizza. The curtain falls on April dancing with Jamie, who still does not know he has been abandoned. The play implies that the brave sing and dance in the teeth of destruction.

Critics and audiences alike loved *The Hot l Baltimore*. Clive Barnes in the *New York Times* said, "Mr. Wilson is both funny and sad about today, and the combination is an unbeatable winner." Michael Feingold in the *Village Voice* maintained, "Nobody has said enough about how good Lanford Wilson's *The Hot l Baltimore* is. . . ." and Harold Clurman,

writing in the *Nation*, said, "One can barely distinguish between the script and the acting. They become one with the entire fabric, which constitutes the real play in the theatre." The entire Circle Repertory cast was praised, particularly Conchata Ferrell, as April, and Mari Gorman, as Jackie. In March 1973, producers Kermit Bloomgarden and Roger Ailes moved the production downtown to the Circle in the Square Theatre where *The Hot l Baltimore* set a new Off-Broadway record with 1,166 performances. The play, which was sold to ABC for a television series, won the New York Drama Critics Circle Award for Best American Play of 1972-1973; an Obie Award for best Off-Broadway play; an Outer Critics Award; the John Gassner playwriting award; and it was included in the Burns Mantle/Guernsey *Ten Best American Plays* volume for that season. Wilson and the Circle Theatre had their first major commercial success, and the future seemed bright.

During the 1974-1975 season, the Circle Repertory Company moved to its new rented home at 99 Seventh Avenue South, formerly the Sheridan Square Playhouse. In its new 160-seat facility, Circle Repertory produced Wilson's *The Mound Builders*. The play was written with the support of a Rockefeller Foundation grant. Marshall Mason directed *The Mound Builders*, with John Lee Beaty serving as set designer. Opening night was 2 February 1975. In this two-act play Wilson explores the ravages of civilization on the past. Bulldozers are poised to create a recreational lake on top of a rich archaeological site, the burial place of an ancient Mississippian god-king. *The Mound Builders* takes place in Blue Shoals, Illinois, where five states come together at the confluence of the Wabash, Cumberland, Ohio, and Mississippi rivers. The specific setting is an old house which has been for three summers the residence of a team of university archaeologists racing to unearth the lost civilization before land development takes over completely. The script calls for a multimedia treatment, with the protagonist, August Howe, in the present time, dictating the story of last summer to send to his secretary. Howe illustrates scenes from the past with slides and a projector. The past, in this case, is the summer before, when the action of the play takes place. Howe is the chief archaeologist on the expedition and accompanying him are his wife, Cynthia; his eleven-year-old daughter, Kirsten; his assistant, Dan Loggins; and Dan's wife, Jean, a gynecologist who has recently become pregnant. All these characters, except Jean, are spending their third summer in the old farmhouse on the site.

University student apprentices and other assistants, who are only referred to, live below on a campsite, closer to the lake. Howe's sister, D. K. (Delia) Erikson, who has once again been bounced from an expensive psychiatric hospital, descends upon the group. Delia is a lapsed author with a penchant for drugs and men, but primarily for telling jokes when her psychic pain becomes acute. The only other character in the play is a local named Chad Jasker whose family owns the land on which the site is located. A new highway is planned near the new dam, making the Jaskers' surrounding acres ideal for new motels and chip 'n putt courses. Chad Jasker is already counting his money. The flashback format, also used in *Lemon Sky*, builds suspense in *The Mound Builders* by slowly revealing bits of information about the characters. Only gradually does the true nature of Chad Jasker emerge. He is the good-ole-boy fishing-and-drinking buddy of Dan's, but at the same time he covets Dan's wife. He is the landlord's son and as such plays host to August Howe and his archaeological team, but he is also Cynthia Howe's secret lover. As the deadline approaches when the site will be submerged by the new lake, tension mounts. Suddenly there is victory. Dan and August uncover the treasure-laden grave of an ancient god-king, and it is the most spectacular archaeological find ever in North America. They all "got it knocked," in Jasker's words, but Jean has been feeling all along that something is about to go wrong. Suddenly Jean's vision come true. Jasker is inadvertently informed of Jean's pregnancy. Then he learns that, thanks to August Howe's report to the state legislature on the importance of this Indian site, the highway is not going to be built on his side of the lake after all. In one fell swoop Chad Jasker loses the woman of his dreams and the wealth he had so hoped for. In revenge, Jasker destroys the treasure, the site, himself, and Dan Loggins. The play ends with Howe's family torn asunder after Cynthia and Jasker's affair is revealed; Jean is a pregnant widow; and the one brief glimpse of an ancient glorious civilization is wiped out completely. The expedition is over and as Howe plays back his taped version of the final moments before the inundation of the site, he says, "The lake had risen to half-cover the house. Much of the second level was above the water. The house looked more scuttled than inundated. The lake rises as a great long hand-shaped pond, slowly. . . ." *The Mound Builders* won praise from the critics as well as an Obie for Outstanding Playwright and the Circle Repertory production was part of the acclaimed "Theatre in America" series on WNET in 1976.

In 1976 Circle Repertory revived *Serenading Louie*, and the play ran there for thirty-three performances. Wilson had made some significant changes in the script since its Washington Theatre Club debut. Most notably, there was the addition of a chilling climax, reminiscent of the violent murders which end *Balm in Gilead* and *The Rimers of Eldritch*. In the new version Carl moves beyond depression into insanity. He shoots his unfaithful wife, Mary, as well as their daughter, Ellie, who never appears in the play. After a final, macabre telephone call to Alex in which he pretends that everything is fine, Carl shoots himself. This revised version of the script was included in the Burns Mantle/Guernsey *Ten Best American Plays* for the 1975-1976 season. In fact, Circle Repertory boasted two plays included in that volume edited by Guernsey, the other being Jules Feiffer's *Knock, Knock*.

In the fall of 1977, Circle Repertory did a one-act Wilson play, *Brontosaurus*, as a "late show." Since no Circle play is ever "frozen," the company continued to revise and rework the script. Directed by Daniel Irvine, a new version of *Brontosaurus* was part of the Circle's 1978 season. Although there are two characters, an outgoing antique dealer and her quiet young nephew, the woman dominates the play with long monologues. The nephew is a young theologian who, by his virtual silence, demonstrates little zest for questioning life. The antique dealer, played at Circle by Tanya Berezin, is, on the other hand, tantalized by life at every turn. *Brontosaurus* met with mixed initial reviews. Terry Curtis Fox, in the *Village Voice*, praised Wilson for his "musical speech," but dubbed *Brontosaurus* as "the artist's right to fail." Recently Wilson has toyed with the idea of turning *Brontosaurus* into a thriller. Admittedly a fan of mystery writer Rex Stout, Wilson says he may change the character of the young man, making him "active instead of passive—and dangerous."

The next two full-length plays Wilson wrote became the first two installments of a planned five-play cycle. The group deals with one Missouri family, the Talleys, and their history, particularly as affected by wars. The first, *5th of July*, was produced at Circle Repertory in April 1978 and was, as usual except in the case of *Brontosaurus*, directed by Marshall Mason. John Lee Beaty designed the set. The time of the action is the Fourth and Fifth of July 1977, and the location is the nineteen-room Talley place near Lebanon, Missouri, Wilson's birthplace. The house has been in the Talley family for generations, but now Ken Talley, Jr., is ready to sell. Ken is a paraplegic veteran of the Vietnam War. The year before, he thought he could move home and accept a teaching position at his old high school, in spite of his handicap. Now, after an awkward visit to the school, he is not so sure. Ken's male lover, Jed, is a botanist who has fallen in love with the Talley place and has spent months creating the beginnings of a formal garden out of an overgrown jungle. Another Talley in the play is Ken's sister, June, who was a ferocious antiwar activist during the early 1970s. June has a fourteen-year-old illegitimate daughter named Shirley, who has been raised, in large part, by Ken and June's aunt and uncle, Sally and Matt Friedman. Young Shirley has aspirations of becoming the greatest "artist" Missouri has produced since Betty Grable. Aunt Sally Talley Friedman is now a widow. She carries her dead husband Matt's ashes around in a candy box, looking for the right place to dispose of them. The Talleys are an eccentric, lovable, hearty lot whose wisecracking keeps them from cracking. Ken Talley plans to sell the country house to his old friends Gwen and John Landis, who have come to Lebanon for a twenty-one-hour visit. John grew up with Ken, and he and Ken and June were roommates back in their protest days. The three had been inseparable until John fell for Gwen, a wealthy hypochondriac who has fried her brains on drugs and now has plans of being a recording star. Gwen and John have brought along Wesley, a guitar-playing friend. Wesley entertains the assemblage with funny stories, including one about starving Eskimos trying to thaw frozen caribou meat with a fart. In fact, the mood of the whole play is comic, with fast-paced one-liners zipping between the madcap Talleys and their zany friends. Finally, it is the character John around whom the plot revolves and grows serious. John turns out to be a betrayer of friendship in the worst sense of the word. Fifteen years before, the audience learns, John and Gwen and Ken had planned to travel to Europe together to prevent the young men from having to register for the draft. At the last minute John abandoned Ken, took Gwen, and the two of them went to Europe alone. Moreover, it becomes clear that John is the father of June's daughter, Shirley. After ignoring his paternal responsibility for fourteen years, he now wants joint custody of the child. And finally, Ken realizes that John is not in love with his wife Gwen, but only manipulating her giant pocketbook. In the climactic scene Ken is about to sell John exactly what he has always wanted—the Talley place—when Aunt Sally comes to the rescue by outbidding the Landises' offer. It seems that Sally has sprinkled Matt's ashes on Jed's rose bushes and now refuses to leave him

behind. The curtain falls on the united family of Talleys who, along with Jed, plan to hold onto their past and face the future together. As Aunt Sally says, "You can't worry about the stopping, you have to worry about the going on." *5th of July* ran for 168 performances at Circle Repertory and received both negative and positive comments from the critics. Some critics failed to realize that Circle plays are always in a state of development and that *5th of July* would continue to be rewritten after both its Circle opening and closing. While Clive Barnes in the *New York Times* compared Wilson to Chekhov, Richard Eder called the play "appealing but unworkable," and Edith Oliver called it Wilson's "most ambitious play so far," and also "his most verbose." Audiences loved it, however, and Wilson remained enchanted by the Talley family.

During the rehearsals of *5th of July* Wilson had tried to help Helen Stenborg, who was playing Aunt Sally, get a feeling for Sally's dear, beloved dead husband Matt; so Wilson told her that Judd Hirsch, the actor, was the perfect image of Matt. As it turned out, Wilson was prophetic, for his next play was *Talley's Folly*, the story of Aunt Sally and Uncle Matt's courtship, in which Judd Hirsch played Matt Friedman. On 3 May 1979, *Talley's Folly* opened as the final play of Circle's tenth anniversary season. *Talley's Folly* was directed by Marshall Mason and designed by John Lee Beaty. Judd Hirsch was joined in the two-character play by Trish Hawkins. It was not the first time the two had played opposite each other, as Hirsch and Hawkins had played the desk clerk and the Girl in the original of *The Hot l Baltimore* cast. Just as *5th of July* concerns a celebration of Independence Day in the aftermath of the Vietnam War, so *Talley's Folly* is about people's lives during wartime, on 4 July 1944. The setting is a gazebolike boathouse, built with lots of Victorian flourishes by Sally's Uncle Whistler Talley. The title of the play refers to the townspeople's nickname for this architectural curio. The boathouse is more than a setting; it is a completely romantic environment, the site of Sally and Matt's first sexual encounter. Sally says of Talley's folly, "I used to think that he made the place for me. I was little when he died, but I thought he knew I'd come along, so he built it just the way it is—falling down—the way people used to build Roman ruins for their gardens. That way nobody else would come here and discover the magic of the place except me." *Talley's Folly* has been referred to by many as a valentine, a true love story. Matt Friedman is a forty-two-year-old Jewish accountant from Saint Louis. Matt had a seven-day love affair with Sally Talley the previous summer.

Sally is a thirty-one-year-old spinster who lives with her family in Lebanon, Missouri, in that same Talley farmhouse from *5th of July*. Throughout the winter Matt has continued to court Sally by letter, even driven to the hospital in Springfield where she works, all to no avail. Although most of Sally's family think of Matt as a "Communist, traitor infidel," there is one Talley aunt, Charlotte, who has taken pity on Matt, and has spoken with him, given him encouragement, on the telephone at frequent intervals all year. In spite of all odds, Matt realizes that he must have Sally and has come down to the boathouse to wage a no-holds-barred battle with her for her hand. The play opens with Matt telling the audience that the play will run for ninety-seven minutes with no intermission, and that the play is a waltz. This musical metaphor implies that the structure of the play is an elaborate mating dance—Sally and Matt butt heads, alternately contradicting each other and being playful or kind. Their confrontation exposes a tragic secret in each character's past, which each has thought would prohibit their marrying. Matt characteristically tells his story in third person. It turns out that Matt was nine years old during World War I, in 1911. He was the son of a "Prussian" engineer who happened accidentally to be privy to a new scientific process valuable in warfare. To discover what the invention was all about, French police tortured Matt's younger sister and she never regained consciousness. As his parents tried to flee Europe they were detained and murdered by the Germans, while Matt came to America with his uncle. As a consequence of this childhood tragedy, Matt decided long ago that "he would not bring into this world another child to be killed for a political purpose." Therefore he feels himself an unsuitable husband for Sally. He says, "I had fallen for a girl and could not give her the life she would surely expect, with a family, many children." Ironically, Sally's secret dovetails his. She was once engaged to Harley Campbell, a Lebanon man whose funeral she attends in *5th of July*. Everything between them was perfect, for Sally and Harley were heirs to the two largest fortunes in Lebanon. When Sally contracted tuberculosis and it rendered her sterile, however, Harley and the Campbells dropped her as a worthless commodity. The play ends with the couple convinced "some mischievous angel" has brought them together. *Talley's Folly* ran at the Circle for nine weeks, closing only because Hirsch had a previous television commitment. Critics were almost unanimous in their praise, with Walter Kerr, in the *New York Times*, calling the play "a treasure," and Clive Barnes, in the *New York Post*,

saying it was "perhaps the simplest, the most lyrical play Wilson has written. . . ."

During the last months of 1979, in Los Angeles, the Mark Taper Forum presented both *5th of July* and *Talley's Folly* in repertory. *Talley's Folly* turned out to be that rare Wilson play which underwent virtually no revision after its Circle debut. As Wilson said, "This is the best I'll ever be able to write it." In February 1980, with only six lines of original dialogue cut, *Talley's Folly* opened on Broadway at the Brooks Atkinson Theatre with its original cast. It was a serious, straight play, yet a tremendous Broadway success. Eleven years after the crushing failure of *Lemon Sky*, Wilson had scored a major Broadway triumph. In spring 1980 *Talley's Folly* was awarded a Pulitzer Prize for drama and was nominated for several Tony awards, with John Lee Beaty winning a Tony for his evocative design.

When *Talley's Folly* closed on Broadway in October 1980, Wilson and Marshall Mason were ready to present *Fifth of July* on Broadway at the Apollo Theatre. The script had undergone heavy rewrites twice: after its Circle debut and after its Mark Taper run. Wilson and Mason even recast the title by spelling out the date. Some of the original Circle cast were in the new New York production. *Fifth of July* enjoyed instant Broadway success, with critic Brendan Gill in the *New Yorker* applauding Wilson's ability "to depict so much life upon so comparatively small a canvas. . . ." Jack Kroll, writing in *Newsweek*, commented that "If Lanford Wilson's *Talley's Folly* won the Pulitzer Prize, as it did, then his *Fifth of July* deserves at least the Nobel."

The 1980-1981 Circle Repertory Company season featured Wilson's *War in Lebanon*, the third play in the Talley series. In it he explores what happens up at the main Talley house on that 4 July 1944, when Matt and Sally are courting down at the boathouse. He has plans for at least two other Talley plays. One will be about Sally's uncle, Whistler, and the other will take place in 1865, during the Civil War, when the Talley house was first built.

Lanford Wilson's association with the Circle Repertory Company dream has been mutually beneficial. *Talley's Folly* brought a sizable profit not only to its author, but also to Circle. Subscription sales for 1980-1981 at Circle topped four thousand, and the theatre enjoys the patronage of twenty-two corporations, including Exxon, Time, and the Ford Foundation.

Wilson, at forty-three, appears to have many productive years of playwriting ahead of him. And he is in a secure position, financially and artistically. Since most of Wilson's plays are relatively easy to stage technically, they are accessible and popular fare for community, regional, and academic theatres across the country. While Wilson is not the famous Missourian Tennessee Williams is, he has been frequently compared to Williams. He appears to have restored an element of nostalgic idealism to the American stage. Many exciting new American playwrights, such as David Mamet, cite Wilson as a principal influence on their writing. If his first twenty years in theatre are any indication, Wilson will continue to contribute his rich voice to American drama.

Television Scripts:

Stoop, in "Foul!," New York, WNET, November 1969;

One Arm, adapted from Tennessee Williams's short story, 1970;

The Migrants, by Wilson and Tennessee Williams, "Playhouse 90," 1973;

Taxi, "Hallmark Hall of Fame," 1978.

References:

Robert Berkvist, "Lanford Wilson—Can He Score on Broadway?," *New York Times*, 17 February 1980, D1, 33;

Guy Flatley, "Lanford is One 'L' of a Playwright," *New York Times*, 22 April 1973, D1, 21;

Mel Gussow, "*Talley's Folly* : A Valentine Hit / Lanford Wilson on Broadway," *Horizon* (May 1980): 30-37;

Barnet Kellman, "The American Playwright in the Seventies: Some Problems and Perspectives," *Theatre Quarterly*, 8, no. 29 (1978): 45-58;

Jim Laurie, "Theatre Club Author Seeks Relevance," *Washington Post*, 26 September 1968, D23;

"Young Genius on the Rise in U.S.," *U.S. News and World Report*, 78 (19 May 1975): 59.

PAUL ZINDEL
(15 May 1936-)

PRODUCTIONS: *Dimensions of Peacocks*, 1959, New York;

Euthanasia and the Endless Hearts, 1960, Take 3, New York;

A Dream of Swallows, 14 April 1964, Jan Hus House, New York, 1 [performance];

The Effect of Gamma Rays on Man-in-the-Moon Marigolds, 12 May 1965, Alley Theatre, Houston, Texas; 7 April 1970, Mercer-O'Casey Theatre(transferred 11 August 1970 to the New Theatre), New York, 819;

And Miss Reardon Drinks a Little, 1967, Mark Taper Forum, Los Angeles; 25 February 1971, Morosco Theatre, New York, 108;

The Secret Affairs of Mildred Wild, 14 November 1972, Ambassador Theatre, New York, 23;

Ladies at the Alamo, 29 May 1975, Actors Studio, New York.

BOOKS: *The Pigman* (New York: Harper & Row, 1968; London: Bodley Head, 1969);

My Darling, My Hamburger (New York: Harper & Row, 1969; London: Bodley Head, 1970);

I Never Loved Your Mind (New York: Harper & Row, 1970; London: Bodley Head, 1971);

The Effect of Gamma Rays on Man-in-the-Moon Marigolds (New York: Harper & Row, 1971);

And Miss Reardon Drinks a Little (New York: Dramatists Play Service, 1971; New York: Random House, 1972);

Let Me Hear You Whisper and The Ladies Should Be in Bed (New York: Dramatists Play Service, 1973);

The Secret Affairs of Mildred Wild (New York: Dramatists Play Service, 1973);

Let Me Hear You Whisper (New York: Harper & Row, 1974);

I Love My Mother (New York: Harper & Row, 1975);

Pardon Me, You're Stepping on My Eyeball! (New York: Harper & Row, 1976; London: Bodley Head, 1976);

Confessions of a Teenage Baboon (New York: Harper & Row, 1977);

The Undertaker's Gone Bananas (New York: Harper & Row, 1978).

A playwright who draws heavily on his personal experiences for the material of his plays, Paul Zindel is best known for his largely autobiographical award-winner, *The Effect of Gamma Rays on Man-in-the-Moon Marigolds* (1965). Using insights gleaned from his ten years as a high-school chemistry teacher, Zindel is also the author of several novels and three screenplays about young people. Zindel's art is one which realistically combines humor and pathos, poetry and terror.

Zindel was born on Staten Island, New York,

to Paul Zindel, a policeman, and Betty Frank Zindel, a practical nurse. His parents separated, and Zindel saw his father rarely. His mother had many schemes for supporting her family; she worked as a hatcheck girl, a shipyard laborer, a caterer, a real estate salesperson, and a collie breeder. In addition to these rather unsuccessful ventures, she boarded terminally ill patients, an occupation Zindel gives to characters in several of his works, including *The Effect of Gamma Rays on Man-in-the-Moon Marigolds*. Because of her eccentricity and restlessness, his mother moved her family from one apartment to another all over Staten Island. Zindel had difficulty forming friendships due to his mother's wanderlust and her isolation from and distrust of other people. As a result, he lived primarily in his imagination and developed early an interest in science. He recalls, "What a great love I had of microcosms, of peering at other worlds framed and separate from me."

In both elementary and high school, Zindel demonstrated an interest in the theatre. He acted in a few plays and wrote several skits for school performances. His high school years were interrupted by a bout with tuberculosis, which confined him at age fifteen to a sanatorium for a year and a half. His being the only adolescent in a hospital full of adults has had, he maintains, a complex and immeasurable influence on his life. While at the sanatorium, Zindel became fascinated with Chopin's *Warsaw Concerto*, and after he returned to Port Richmond High School, he wrote a play for a contest sponsored by the American Cancer Society about a seriously ill pianist who recovers to play the *Warsaw Concerto* at Carnegie Hall. For this effort, Zindel won a Parker pen.

Zindel attended Wagner College on Staten Island, majoring in chemistry. He obtained a B.S. in 1958 and a M.Sc. degree in 1959. While he was at Wagner, Zindel took a creative writing course taught by playwright Edward Albee. Though Zindel no longer reveres Albee as he once did, he credits Albee with being one of his major inspirations in writing plays. Under the direction of Albee, Zindel wrote *Dimensions of Peacocks* during his last year of college. It was performed in New York in 1959. The title, Zindel explains, is "a subtle way of expressing a fascination with . . . dementia praecox—which has nothing to do with the theme." The play deals with a troubled youth whose demented mother is a visiting nurse who steals monogrammed linen napkins from the homes of the patients she attends. As in most of Zindel's works, the eccentric, domineering mother and the

Paul Zindel

sensitive, confused young person create the major tension of the play.

Though he had written two plays already, Zindel says in a 1970 *New York Times* article that he saw his first professionally produced play in 1959—Lillian Hellman's *Toys in the Attic*, starring Maureen Stapleton. The impression made by the play and the actress was enormous. In fact, Zindel reports that he had Stapleton in mind when he wrote *The Effect of Gamma Rays on Man-in-the-Moon Marigolds*. He also greatly admired the work of Tennessee Williams: "I never missed an opening night of a Tennessee Williams play. . . ," Zindel recalls.

After college Zindel became a technical writer for a chemical company in Manhattan. He soon resigned, however, and became a teacher of chemistry and physics at Tottenville High School on Staten Island from 1960 through 1969. During these years he continued to write plays, though with little success. A New York City coffee house, Take 3, put on his second play, *Euthanasia and the Endless Hearts*, in 1960. His third play, *A Dream of Swallows*, was produced Off Broadway in 1964 and closed after one performance. The play's central character, Little Judith, is a nasty drunk who enjoys torturing the inmates of an asylum she visits. The critics were not impressed with Zindel's collection of eccentrics and misfits.

However, after a long delay, his next play confirmed his career as a dramatist. *The Effect of Gamma Rays on Man-in-the-Moon Marigolds* had its premiere at the Alley Theatre in Houston in 1965. Nina Vance, head of the Alley Theatre, liked the play so well that she took an option on Zindel's next play. As a result, he took a leave of absence from teaching and went to Houston in 1967 as playwright-in-residence at the Alley Theatre. Meanwhile, in October 1966, NET's "New York TV Theatre" presented the first of four television presentations of a condensed version of *The Effect of Gamma Rays on Man-in-the-Moon Marigolds*. Reviewers of the television drama found little to praise. But on 7 April 1970 the play opened Off Broadway at the Mercer-O'Casey Theatre and Zindel's talent as a playwright was widely acclaimed. In the summer of 1970, because of a fire, the Orin Lehman production, with a change of cast, moved to the New Theatre on Broadway. There the play remained until 14 May 1972 when it closed after 819 performances. In addition to its popular success, *The Effect of Gamma Rays on Man-in-the-Moon Marigolds* received an Obie Award (1970) as best play of the season; a New York Drama Critics Circle Award (1970) as best American play of the year; and the Pulitzer Prize in Drama (1971). In 1970 Zindel received a Vernon Rice Drama Desk Award as most promising playwright, and in 1971 was awarded an honorary doctorate of humane letters by Wagner University.

Many critics agreed with Clive Barnes, writing in the *New York Times*, when he described the title of *The Effect of Gamma Rays on Man-in-the-Moon Marigolds* as "one of the most discouraging titles yet devised by man." Most also agreed, however, that the title has its own thematic validity. It is essentially a domestic melodrama, with an occasional lapse into sentimentality, about a family composed of the mother, Beatrice Hunsdorfer, and her two teenage daughters, Ruth and Tillie, high-school students. Beatrice, known in her youth as "Betty the Loon," is the dominant character in the play. She is a bitter widow, cynical and half-mad, who dreams of opening a tea room but who lives in chaos and is paid to care for Nanny, an elderly woman who can neither speak nor hear. Beatrice fears the world's ridicule, so she makes her daughters dependent upon her and vents her rage and frustration upon them.

Everyone in the untidy house is psychically wounded. Nanny has been abandoned by a daughter who finds her existence a burden. Ruth, untidy

and wanton, has seizures brought on by memories of her mother's boarders' deaths and by her mother's threats of cruelty. Tillie, a shy, plain girl, bestows her affection on a rabbit given to her by her science teacher. Ruth longs to have the rabbit for herself, and Beatrice threatens daily to chloroform the pet. Tillie, however, has found an even more important release from her squalid environment— science. She is fascinated by the structure of atoms, and her science teacher has given her marigold seeds to grow which have been exposed to varying degrees of radiation. At the science fair, where she wins first prize, she describes the results of her experiment, showing how some of the seeds gave forth normal plants, while others bore mutations with double blooms or giant stems, and still others died. She ends her speech by expressing her belief that some of the "mutations will be good ones— wonderful things beyond our dreams—and . . . THE DAY WILL COME WHEN MANKIND WILL THANK GOD FOR THE STRANGE AND BEAUTIFUL ENERGY FROM THE ATOM."

The message is clear: Tillie is the mutant who has emerged from a horrifying environment with faith and potential intact—she is the double bloom. Life has bypassed Beatrice, and Ruth is a victim of her mother's despair. Tillie is Zindel's synthesis of the brutal and the beautiful. Zindel's own background was his source: in a *New York Times* interview, he remembers, "*Marigolds* is the kind of story that just sort of pops right out of you, because you've lived it." Beatrice, he has told a *Time* reporter, is his mother in "nightmarish exaggeration." In the introduction to the published version of *The Effect of Gamma Rays on Man-in-the-Moon Marigolds*, Zindel writes of his mother: "In her own way she told me of her secret dreams and fears—so many of which I had somehow sensed, and discovered written into that manuscript next to my typewriter, many years before." While Tillie is the heroine of the play, Beatrice, misfit par excellence, is the character who lives in the playgoers's memory.

Zindel's purpose in writing plays is, perhaps, best expressed in a *Life* interview: "I like trying to arrive at the sublime . . . through mundane common material." Theatre critics felt he had succeeded. *Time* called the play "splendid and tormented"; Edith Oliver in the *New Yorker* found it "touching and often funny"; and Harold Clurman in the *Nation* saw in it "intelligence, sensibility and humane feeling." Many critics found the play old-fashioned in the best sense of the word, praising its realism yet moved by its poetry. Several comparisons were made to Tennessee Williams's *The Glass*

Menagerie (1945), a play admired by Zindel.

The Effect of Gamma Rays on Man-in-the-Moon Marigolds was adapted and expanded for the screen by Alvin Sargent, and was released by Twentieth Century-Fox in 1972. The film, produced and directed by Paul Newman, starred Joanne Woodward as Beatrice. The play won additional awards when it was published by Harper & Row; it was selected as a 1971 Notable Book and as a Best Book for Young Adults by the American Library Association.

After the success of his eight-year-old play, Zindel resigned his teaching position and moved to Manhattan. His next play, *And Miss Reardon Drinks a Little*, was originally written in 1966. After many revisions it opened 25 February 1971 at the Morosco Theatre in New York City. Like his previous play, *And Miss Reardon Drinks a Little* is about women (Zindel has written few roles for men), three sisters, all schoolteachers, who have been psychologically maimed by a domineering, neurotic mother, now deceased. Ceil, the cool and capable supervisor of a school system, is the only sister who has married and who leads the semblance of a normal life. The play's action centers around Ceil's meeting with Catherine, the alcoholic Miss Reardon who drinks far more than a little. Ceil and Catherine must decide the fate of Anna, their half-insane sister.

All three sisters are sexually repressed. Ceil has married Catherine's former boyfriend; it is a loveless union. Catherine takes refuge in bourbon. Anna has made sexual advances to one of her male high-school students, and everyone involved feels that some action must be taken. Ceil favors committing Anna to a mental institution, and in the last act Catherine agrees to sign the papers. The play is a curious mix of high seriousness and low comedy, a combination of intense emotions, raw pain, sight gags, and coarse jokes.

Reviews of *And Miss Reardon Drinks a Little* were mixed. Martin Gottfried in *Women's Wear Daily* found it an "up and down play" but also "real theatre, strong and honest." T. E. Kalem in *Time* admired Zindel's "wacky humor" and "abrupt pathos," but was disturbed by the play's tendency to tell rather than show. Similarly, Clive Barnes of the *New York Times* faulted Zindel for describing his action rather than developing it. He, too, noted the lack of progress and movement. Henry Hewes in *Saturday Review* felt that "the sickness on which the play feeds is more exploited than explored." Brendan Gill in the *New Yorker* uses the occasion of *And Miss Reardon Drinks a Little* to suggest that Zindel has been "overpraised" for *The Effect of Gamma Rays on Man-in-the-Moon Marigolds* and runs the risk of being "underdamned" for his new play, which "has put [Zindel's] professional life in jeopardy."

Zindel's next play, *The Secret Affairs of Mildred Wild*, opened 14 November 1972 at the Ambassador Theatre in New York. Mildred Wild is another of Zindel's grotesque misfits—a sleazy and eccentric woman who excludes herself from society. Mildred and her diabetic husband live in the back of a shabby Greenwich Village candy store. Her husband overindulges in candy, causing him to go into sugar comas, and Mildred lives a vicarious life of the imagination through movies. She has lined her apartment with pages torn from fan magazines, and in her fantasies she becomes Scarlett O'Hara, Shirley Temple and Fay Wray, having encounters with Rhett Butler, Tarzan, and King Kong. In addition to this Walter Mitty theme, *The Secret Affairs of Mildred Wild* treats other types of phoniness. When Mildred wins a television game-show prize, a Hollywood screen test, it turns out to be as fake as all her fantasies. While the play is clearly a farce, the humor is muted by the sordidness and pathos of Mildred's life.

The critics were almost unanimous in their condemnation of *The Secret Affairs of Mildred Wild*. T. E. Kalem in *Time* accused Zindel of "huckstering kookdom for cheap laughs," and Martin Gottfried of *Women's Wear Daily* labelled it "untruthful to its own premise." Brendan Gill described the play as a "ramshackle comedy," and Harold Clurman found the "skimpy" script to be a "one-joke piece." In short, the critics began to question Zindel's predicted promise.

Zindel's *Ladies at the Alamo*, first produced at the Actors Studio in May 1975, evolved from a script called "Nymphs and Satyrs," which Zindel originally wrote in 1970. After he joined the Actors Studio, he used the Studio as a laboratory to rework the play, directing the other members in the roles as he rewrote. *Ladies at the Alamo* involves five very strong women in a power play for control of the most important theatre complex in Texas. The heroine of the play, Dede, has built this small playhouse into a multimillion-dollar complex and feels it slipping from her grasp. Zindel sees the powerful fighting ladies as "women in transition." When asked if Nina Vance of the Alley Theatre in Houston was the model for Dede, Zindel replied negatively, though the critics continued to speculate otherwise.

First performed in 1975 at the Actors Studio, *Ladies at the Alamo* opened on Broadway 7 April 1977 and closed after twenty performances. It was not generally well-received. Clive Barnes of the *New York Times* found the play "slick to the point of slippery," but with "some slap-bang moments of entertainment." Most of the critics found the play "stupid" and "weak in credibility." As with *The Secret Affairs of Mildred Wild* they were disappointed at what they viewed as unfulfilled promise.

In addition to writing plays, Zindel has been active in writing television plays, screenplays, and novels for young adults. In 1969 he wrote for NET's "New York TV Theatre" *Let Me Hear You Whisper*, a play about a lonely cleaning woman who saves a dolphin from vivisection by inducing it to talk. Zindel's standard theme of loneliness allied with science appears here as it does in most of his works. He also wrote the screenplays *Up the Sandbox* (1972), based on Anne Roiphe's novel about a housewife who lives in a fantasy world, and *Mame* (1974), based on Patrick Dennis's novel *Auntie Mame*, about a boy and his eccentric aunt.

In the mid-1960s after NET's production of *The Effect of Gamma Rays on Man-in-the-Moon Marigolds*, Zindel began to write novels for young adults. He was encouraged in this venture by an editor at Harper & Row. Themes from his plays often found their way into his fiction. His first novel, *The Pigman* (1968), depicts a lonely widower with a prized ceramic pig collection and two alienated teenagers, John and Lorraine, whom he befriends. This novel sold well over a million copies. Zindel's second novel, *My Darling, My Hamburger* (1969), deals explicitly with adolescent sex and contraception. The title refers to a teacher's suggestion that Liz, a troubled high-school senior, curb her boyfriend's lust by going out for a hamburger. Zindel's third novel, *I Never Loved Your Mind* (1970), describes a drop-out who falls in love with a flower-child; she deserts him, however, because of her inability to share his view of the world.

Zindel's next book also explores a recurring theme. *I Love My Mother* (1975) is a children's picture book narrated by a fatherless little boy who tells of his relationship with his mother. In *Pardon Me, You're Stepping on My Eyeball!* (1976) Zindel returns to young adult fiction with a story of a psychotic mother, an alcoholic father, a bizarre school psychologist, and two teenagers who are victims of the eccentric, misguided adults in charge of them. Typically, Zindel blends humor and pathos here in his treatment of death and guilt. His next novel, *Confessions of a Teenage Baboon* (1977), again focuses on outcasts, a fatherless teenager living with an eccentric mother who is a practical nurse. Zindel's

most recent novel, *The Undertaker's Gone Bananas* (1978), has the usual bizarre title, but it departs from his earlier works in that both of the central characters, misfit teenagers, have loving parents. Additionally, the novel is a mystery—another first for Zindel.

While Zindel has not fulfilled his early promise as a playwright after *The Effect of Gamma Rays on Man-in-the-Moon Marigolds*, he has continued to explore the recurrent themes of loneliness, eccentricity, isolation, and escapism. Much of his material is admittedly autobiographical, a working out and blending of his own past and his grotesque sense of humor. At his best he is sensitive, funny, warm, and perceptive, usually presenting an affirmation of life emerging even from the most desperate circumstances. His weaknesses, most apparent in his later plays, are lapses into melodrama, an overuse of cliches and slick material, a lack of direction in plot, and an overindulgence in a perverse, sometimes inappropriate, humor.

In a 1977 interview Zindel suggested that he has much in common with Dorothy Parker. He announced that he is collaborating with composer Paul Williams on a musical about Parker's life. He has promised, too, that he intends to write plays with substantial male roles in the future. Zindel sees himself as a born playwright, and he believes "that the seeds of theater are born inside of us." While he feels that few playwrights are writing honest plays, he also believes that "no one can kill Theater." He sees it as a "device for survival" that may experience a drought, but can never be starved out of existence; it will always reemerge. Though Zindel's screenplays and fiction have made him commercially successful, theatregoers are still awaiting a fitting successor to *The Effect of Gamma Rays on Man-in-the-Moon Marigolds*.

–*Ruth L. Strickland*

Screenplays:

Up the Sandbox, adapted from Anne Roiphe's novel, National, 1972;

Mame, adapted from Patrick Dennis's *Auntie Mame*, Warner Brothers, 1974.

Television Script:

Let Me Hear You Whisper, NET, 1966.

Periodical Publications:

"Interview with Edward Albee," by Zindel and Loree Yerby, *Wagner* [College] *Literary Magazine*, 3 (1962): 1-10;

"The Theater is Born Within Us," *New York Times*, 26 July 1970, II: 1, 3.

Interviews:

Guy Flatley, ". . .And Gamma Rays Did It!," *New York Times*, 19 April 1970, II: 1, 5;

Tom Prideaux, "Man with a Bag of Marigold Dust," *Life*, 69 (4 July 1970): 8-9;

"Prizewinning Marigolds," *Time*, 97 (17 May 1971): 66;

Patricia Bosworth, "The Effect of Five Actresses on a Play-in-Progress." *New York Times*, 3 April 1977, II: 1, 8, 9;

Jean F. Mercier, "Paul Zindel," *Publishers Weekly*, 212 (5 December 1977): 6-7.

References:

Clive Barnes, "The Stage: 'Ladies at the Alamo,' " *New York Times*, 8 April 1977, C: 3;

Barnes, "Theatre: 'Gamma Rays on Marigolds,' " *New York Times*, 8 April 1970, I: 32;

Barnes, "Theatre: Reardon Sisters Arrive," *New York Times*, 26 February 1971, I: 29;

Harold Clurman, "Theatre," *Nation*, 210 (20 April 1970): 476;

Clurman, "Theatre," *Nation*, 215 (4 December 1972): 572-573;

Brendan Gill, "The Theatre," *New Yorker*, 47 (6 March 1971): 67-68;

Gill, "The Theatre," *New Yorker*, 48 (25 November 1972): 111-112.

Appendix I:
Trends in Theatrical Production

Overleaf, from left to right: Scenes from David Belasco's Du Barry; *Clifford Odets's*
Golden Boy; *Eugene O'Neill's* The Emperor Jones; *David Belasco's* The Darling of the Gods.

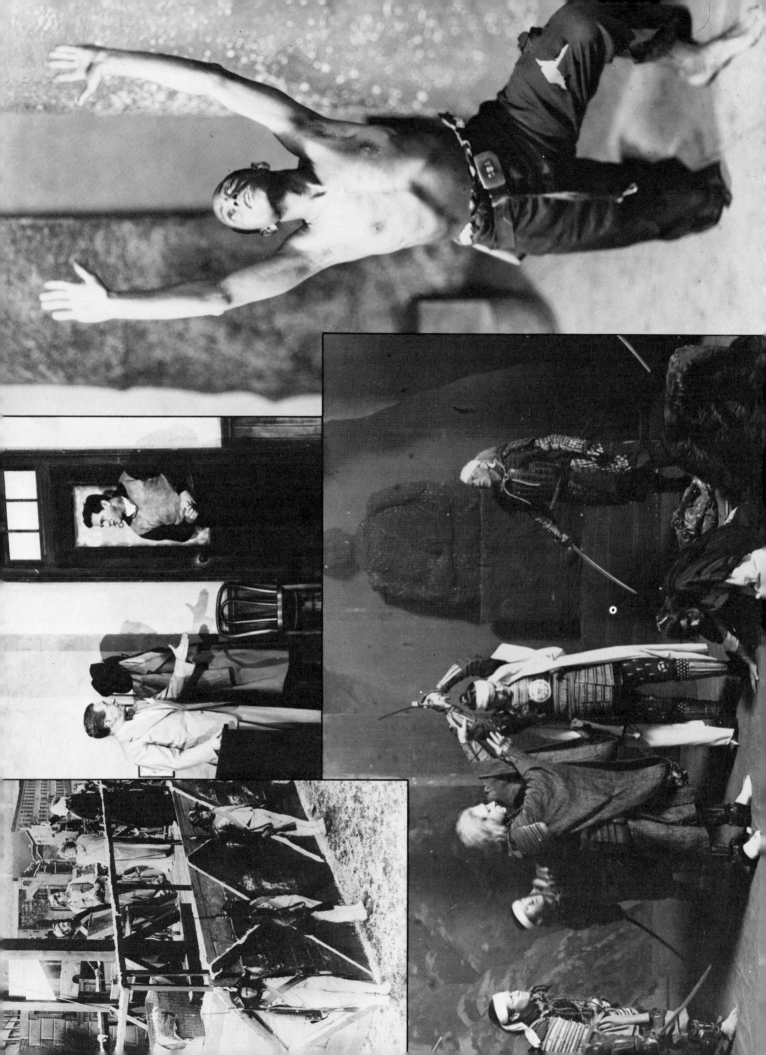

New Forces at Work in the
American Theatre: 1915-1925

The modern American theatre began in 1920, or so it is often said. Like all such historical declarations, it is only partially true. No single event occurred in 1920 to render 1919 old-fashioned and 1921 modern. The one occasion of the year was the Broadway opening of Eugene O'Neill's first significant full-length play, *Beyond the Horizon*. In light of O'Neill's primacy in urging the American theatre into the modern age, that opening gives 1920 a special importance. At any rate, 1920 stands midway in the most decisive decade in the history of theatre in this country, the ten years between 1915 and 1925. During that time, old patterns were broken, the theatre was freed of many arbitrary restrictions, and new forces went to work. As in Europe thirty years earlier, many of these new forces were part of the little theatre movement, a series of small theatres dedicated to the performance of plays that the established, commercial theatre could not or would not produce. These forces employed new, often experimental methods of production. Commercial theatre had become so dedicated to profits, so committed to its star system, its large box-pit-and-gallery theatres, and its repertory of proven "hits," that little chance existed to develop a drama more responsive to the modern world.

Space does not permit an investigation here of all the forces at work during the decade 1915 to 1925. A great many little theatres, as well as other enterprises and even individuals, contributed to the revolution. To gain a sense of the nature of the revolution, it should suffice to examine four particular developments that are highly indicative of the change that was wrought: the breaking of Theatrical Syndicate, the development of playwrights and other theatre artists in George Pierce Baker's Workshop 47, the emergence of the Provincetown Players, and the evolution of the Washington Square Players into the Theatre Guild. All of these began to exert influence around 1915 and all attained fruition by 1925. Together they provide an index to the modernization of American drama. Other events were taking place as well, of course, including the founding of various other little theatres, such as Winthrop Ames's Little Theatre in New York (1909), Maurice Browne's Chicago

Little Theatre (1912), the Toy Theatre in Boston (1912), the Arts and Crafts Theatre in Detroit under the direction of Sam Hume (1916), the Neighborhood Playhouse in New York (1915), and others. George Jean Nathan published attacks on American theatre culture and urged reforms in the pages of the *Smart Set* and elsewhere, and Sheldon Cheney began publishing the first serious theatre magazine, *Theatre Arts*, in 1916. Productions brought to the United States in this period by Max Reinhardt, Jacques Copeau, and Constantin Stanislavsky demonstrated potentials the American theatre had yet to tap. In short, serious thought was being given to the nature of theatre art, and it prompted a flurry of activity unequaled in the years previous and perhaps in all the years since.

The theatre is a curious form whose art depends upon the good health and vigor of the society of artists and audiences that make it work. It is at one and the same time an art form and a social institution. It depends upon the collaboration of all its artists, whose work comes to naught unless it encounters a vital, responsive audience. All this is difficult. That it happens at all is nearly miraculous. When it does, the theatre can engender an excitement beyond any aroused by any other art form. This is what began to happen in the United States about 1915. The appearance of a playwright of the stature of Eugene O'Neill requires a talent, to be sure, but also a theatre ready to receive the talent. The American theatre had made itself ready.

The major retardant to the development of theatre before this time was the commercialization of the institution, which became especially intense after 1870. Much of this derived from the "opening of the road," which transformed American theatrical organizations from permanent companies to touring companies. When the last spike was driven to join the East and the West by rail, on 10 May 1869, it occasioned a vast change in the theatrical system. Trains were an efficient means to new audiences, and hence larger profits. A touring company could be in another town playing to an entirely new paying audience the night after closing in the last one. Between 1870 and 1910, the number of permanent companies declined precipitously, rapidly replaced by touring companies. In 1870, there were

377

50 permanent companies in the United States, but by 1878 the number had dwindled to 20, by 1880 to 8, and in 1887 only 4 remained. In that same year, the number of touring companies had mushroomed to 282. This number reached its peak in December 1900, with 392 companies out on tour. Many of these were so-called combination companies, touring with only the principals and hiring local actors at each port of call.

Such a system can flourish only when theatre is treated as a commodity-producing industry, sending its products out to the marketplaces. In the early years of the road, the industry's distribution system was outrageously chaotic. Local theatre owners had to contact company producers individually to secure seasons of plays for their theatres. Producers tended to play their hunches on the road, and if it seemed more profitable to go to one city rather than another, they often felt no compunction about breaking the contract and doing so. Chaos ensued as producers regularly overbooked themselves, and, in retaliation, so did local theatre owners. New York booking agencies arose to ease the problem by serving as middlemen between producers and theatre owners; but even that did not eliminate the spiral of broken contracts.

The Theatrical Syndicate developed out of this mayhem. Six theatre owners banded together to bring some order to the booking system. Their prime motive, of course, remained profit. The six—Charles Frohman, Fred Zimmerman, Al Hayman, Sam Nixon, Marc Klaw, and Abraham Erlanger—met in 1896 to establish the new Syndicate to be dedicated to providing full seasons of guaranteed productions to local theatre owners. At the time, they themselves owned seventeen theatres and had control of thirty-three others in such diverse cities as New York, Philadelphia, Chicago, and San Francisco. The Syndicate met with success almost at once. Their seasons of guaranteed shows, many of them stellar attractions, not only solved the problem of chaotic scheduling but also assured theatre owners of success. This was the beginning of the period in which the Syndicate dominated American theatre.

The Syndicate adopted other measures, too, calculated to insure their own success. They adopted a policy of exclusive booking, which prohibited theatre owners who negotiated with them from negotiating with other agencies. Producers who refused to sign exclusively with the Syndicate were refused any bookings in Syndicate theatres. By the same token, actors who opposed them were blackballed and refused any appearance in Syndicate theatres. Such measures, to be effective, required that the Syndicate own many theatres, and they soon did. They began by buying up theatres that stood along key routes, so that rival companies would find it difficult to book themselves at points midway between major cities. They then began acquiring theatres in major cities, rapidly building an empire.

The Theatrical Syndicate reached its height of power in 1904. It is estimated that they controlled or owned as many as five hundred theatres in the United States, including all but two or three in New York and all but one in Chicago and one in Philadelphia. The Syndicate was in virtual control of the American theatre. Their bookings, true enough, were always star-studded shows capable of attracting mass audiences; but the art of theatre was entirely left out of consideration. Of the six men in the Syndicate, only one, Charles Frohman, had any direct involvement in theatrical production; the others were theatre owners for whom theatre was strictly an economic rather than artistic concern. For these men, change or experimentation was dangerous.

Naturally, the Syndicate inspired rebellion. The more they tried to hold it in check by blackballing and other means, the more intense became the rebellion. People such as Minnie Maddern Fiske, James A. Herne, and James O'Neill (Eugene's father) were adamant and courageous opponents of Syndicate power. They all refused to cooperate with the Syndicate, and as a result they were often forced to perform in makeshift theatres, such as tents or skating rinks. Sarah Bernhardt was so revolted by the high-handedness of the Syndicate that she conducted an American tour using a portable tent as her theatre.

The two most formidable foes of the Syndicate were the director, producer, and playwright David Belasco and the theatre owners the Shubert Brothers, Sam, Lee, and Jacob. These were strange bedfellows. Belasco rebelled to free theatre art from the restrictions of the Syndicate's narrow, self-serving practices; the Shuberts were simply interested in a piece of the pie. In 1907 Belasco and the Shuberts brought suit against the Syndicate, charging them with controlling a monopoly. The case was dismissed on three grounds: that the Syndicate had a right to control its properties; that neither Belasco nor the Shuberts were kept from controlling their own; and that the theatre is not a trade or commodity and so not subject to monopoly law.

The plaintiffs found other means to do battle.

By 1909, the Shuberts had enlarged the number of theatres they owned or controlled sufficiently to make inroads into the Syndicate's power. Belasco succeeded in creating such demand for his productions that the Syndicate finally had to accept his productions on his terms. Circumstance also militated against Syndicate power as the new film industry began to prove an efficient means of making money from dramatic art. Internal dissension, retirement, and death also reduced the Syndicate's power. When Charles Frohman died in 1915, only Marc Klaw and Abraham Erlanger were left, and their partnership was dissolved in 1918. In their place, the Shubert Brothers carried on the tradition, though never with quite the stranglehold the Syndicate had exerted. Ironically, they ultimately faced (and lost) a suit similar to the one they had brought against the Syndicate, and in 1956 they were forced to sell many of their theatres.

In 1904, when the Syndicate was in full power, one of the earliest and ultimately most powerful instruments for change in the American theatre had its quiet beginning in a classroom at Harvard University. Professor George Pierce Baker began to teach a course in playwriting. In itself, this was revolutionary, for universities at the time rarely offered courses in drama, and then only in its history. Baker, however, was tired of the old lecture system, and he insisted that learning would be deepened through doing creative work as well as studying it. Between 1906 and 1908, he spent much of his time in Europe, where he witnessed at first hand some of the extraordinary work accomplished by European playwrights, directors, and designers. These trips fired him with a zeal to convey to his students the challenge to be met in the theatre arts, armed with materials and slides to demonstrate the possibilities.

By 1913, Baker had added to his course a workshop designed to provide playwrights with exposure to the life of each of their plays on stage. This was the beginning of Workshop 47, named after the catalogue number of the course, English 47. It was supported by a subscription audience who also pledged themselves to provide brief written critiques of the plays they witnessed. Students were carefully screened before entering the workshop, and many who worked there became significant dramatists in the 1920s. Eugene O'Neill attended during the academic year of 1914-1915. The workshop also produced works by Philip Barry, Sidney Howard, S. N. Behrman, John Howard Lawson, and George Abbott. For a time, the workshop included Thomas Wolfe, whom Baker described as having "a genius for profusion rather than selec-

tion." If Baker did not succeed in transforming Wolfe into a playwright, he was obviously successful with others. The key to his success lay in his refusal to take a dogmatic approach. Rather, he insisted that each playwright, indeed each play, posed unique problems that needed to be resolved individually. These problems could only become apparent through the test of the stage. And so, with Baker's Workshop 47 came one of the first versions of an experimental theatre of the sort found among many of the little theatres of the mid-1910s and thereafter.

Workshop 47 derived much of its fame from its work with playwrights, but Baker also incorporated work with directors and designers. He spoke, cajoled, and prodded his students to seek new and more effective ways of staging and designing plays. As testimony to his success, many of his students went on to contribute significantly as designers (such as Robert Edmond Jones, Lee Simonson, and Donald Oenslager) and directors (such as Winthrop Ames, Samuel Hume, and Elia Kazan).

Baker's enterprise was to lead on to the creation of that uniquely American phenomenon: the university theatre. Some of his own disciples and others impressed by his example established theatre departments in universities across the country, beginning in 1914 when Thomas Wood Stevens established the first degree program in theatre at Carnegie Institute of Technology. Others included E. C. Mabie at the University of Iowa, Thomas H. Dickinson at the University of Wisconsin, Glenn Hughes at the University of Washington, and Frederick Koch at the University of North Dakota and later at the University of North Carolina. With time, university theatres were among the best equipped in the country, workshops for the further exploration of theatre art in the spirit Baker had established. Ironically, Harvard dropped out of the business of theatre education when Yale offered Baker a fully equipped theatre and the chance to develop a graduate program. Consequently, in 1925 Baker moved to New Haven and remained there until his death in 1935.

The breaking of the Syndicate and the development of new theatre artists out of Workshop 47 had both been realized by around 1915, the year in which two of the most significant of America's little theatres were founded, the Provincetown Players and the Washington Square Players. Both had humble beginnings, as small experimental amateur theatres. Both provided a challenge to the American theatre by the zeal, honesty, and dedication they brought to their art, perhaps the sort of enthusiasm only amateurs are capable of. Ultimately, their successes led them to become leading professional theatres in the 1920s.

The Provincetown Players began when a group of vacationing artists undertook to present plays on the front porches of their summer homes in Provincetown, Massachusetts, in the summer of 1915. By 1916, the group had remodeled a warehouse at the end of a wharf to make it into a small theatre seating some one hundred fifty to two hundred people. In that same year they encountered Eugene O'Neill, most of whose early one-act sea plays they presented, beginning with *Bound East for Cardiff*. After two summers in Provincetown, the Players began a winter program in New York City. They first took quarters in Greenwich Village at 139 MacDougal Street, and then in 1918 they moved down the street to a stable which they transformed into a theatre. Until 1920, the organization remained a small, experimental, coterie theatre, quietly practicing the art as devoted amateurs.

The prime mover behind the Provincetown Players was George Cram Cook, a novelist and indefatigable idealist. He was fully convinced that America was on the verge of creating a powerful culture for which the theatre could serve as a rallying point, as had the theatre of ancient Athens, itself an amateur theatre. He wanted the Players to create a model for this endeavor, one infused with unswerving love and devotion to Art. It was to be a combination workshop and temple. Susan Glaspell, novelist and playwright, and wife of George Cram Cook, was also a major force behind the Players. Together they conducted a revolt against the established theatre by providing an outlet for plays that would never be seen on the commercial stage, initially plays by members of the group itself. Indeed, one of their first productions was Susan Glaspell's Freudian one-act, *Suppressed Desires* (1915). They attracted a host of other artistic rebels to their cause, among them Theodore Dreiser, John Reed, Daniel Steele, Mary Heaton Vorse, Harry Kemp, Maxwell Bodenheim, Alfred Kreymborg, and Edna St. Vincent Millay. Among all those who joined the group, the three most important to its life were Eugene O'Neill, Robert Edmond Jones, and Kenneth Macgowan, the so-called triumvirate who directed it from 1923 to its end in 1929.

After the Provincetown Players' move to New York, which rapidly became their new home, their success had a perverse way of undermining the organization. Their work with Eugene O'Neill led to his emergence on Broadway, with *Beyond the Horizon* in 1920, followed by *Anna Christie* in 1921.

He continued to write for the Provincetown Players, and indeed throughout the 1920s he had the singular advantage of access to Broadway as well as to this experimental group. The Players presented his *Emperor Jones* in 1920 with such success that it moved uptown to Broadway where it was able to tap the profits it could so obviously produce. Cook vehemently opposed the move uptown, sensing that at best it would transform the group into something other than a small, close-knit society of devoted artists, and at worst break up the Provincetown Players. When the Players produced O'Neill's *The Hairy Ape* (1922), hiring Arthur Hopkins to direct and then moving uptown again, Cook called for a pause in the Players' activities to reassess their purpose for the season 1922-1923. He and Susan Glaspell left for Greece, whence he never returned.

Technically this was the end of the Provincetown Players, but the group reformed itself as the Experimental Theater in 1923, and continued its operation under the direction of O'Neill, Robert Edmond Jones, and Kenneth Macgowan who worked to give the theatre a more professional character. Between 1923 and 1925, they operated in two theatres, the old stable on MacDougal Street and the Greenwich Village Theatre near Washington Square. The repertory was expanded to include not only new plays, but also works of great Europeans such as Strindberg, Gozzi, Molière, and Hasenclever. Of course they continued to produce the bolder works of O'Neill as he wrote them: *All God's Chillun Got Wings* (1924), *Desire Under the Elms* (1924), and *The Great God Brown* (1926).

Another reorganization occurred at the end of 1925 when the group split, and James Light and M. Eleanor Fitzgerald attempted to reestablish the Provincetown Players at the MacDougal Street facility while the triumvirate of O'Neill, Jones, and Macgowan continued at the Greenwich Village Theatre. The former attempt failed, and rising costs and union problems began to nip at the heels of the triumvirate. Despite repeated help from philanthropist Otto H. Kahn, the Experimental Theater had to disperse in 1929 after one last valiant move, this time to Broadway. The Theatre Guild, having produced O'Neill's most recent experimental works, *Marco Millions* and *Strange Interlude* (both in 1928), had already become his new home.

The Provincetown Players made several significant contributions between their humble beginning in 1915 and the end in 1929. Their discovery of O'Neill and fostering of his career would themselves be sufficient to insure them a place in American theatre history. Their idea of an experimental theatre "to give American playwrights a chance to work out their ideas in freedom" was perhaps their greatest asset. They furnished a crucible for pounding out the New Stagecraft, and Robert Edmond Jones found himself wrestling with scenic challenges he might never have encountered otherwise.

In the autumn of 1914, another significant group began to form when various artists and theatre enthusiasts staged a production of Lord Dunsany's *The Glittering Gate* in the back room of a Greenwich Village bookstore. This experience fired the group with excitement, and they rented the Bandbox Theatre in 1915 and went to work organizing a theatre. They published a manifesto calling for subscribers, attacking the commercial theatre, and resolving to produce worthy plays that might otherwise never appear. First priority was placed on new American plays, and then on significant European scripts Broadway had ignored.

The founding group consisted of Lawrence Langner, Philip Moeller, Helen Westley, and Edward Goodman, among others. They soon attracted other artistic rebels, the most significant of whom were Rollo Peters and Lee Simonson. They formally opened as the Washington Square Players on 19 February 1915, with a bill of three one-act plays and a pantomime. The chief attraction was Maurice Maeterlinck's *Interior*, played with a rich and heavy atmosphere. The other two one-acts were new American plays: Edward Goodman's *Eugenically Speaking* and Lawrence Langner's *Licensed* (written under the pseudonym Basil Lawrence), pieces of avant-garde humor, as was the pantomime, *Another Interior*, which represented its protagonist, Gastric Juice, struggling inside a human stomach.

During the first season they presented bills of one-act plays on weekends, but by the second season they were playing seven nights a week. They augmented their ranks with professional actors such as Frank Conroy, Katharine Cornell, Roland Young, and Glenn Hunter. Productions included Philip Moeller's *Helena's Husband*, a spoof of the Trojan War, and Alice Gerstenberg's *Overtones*, a Freudian experiment using multiple actresses to play the various selves of two women, a device adopted later by Eugene O'Neill in *Strange Interlude*. Thereafter, the Washington Square Players began to move in a new direction, away from the experimental American one-acts and toward highly demanding European full-length plays. In 1916 they produced their first full-length play, Maurice Maeterlinck's *Ag-*

lavaine and Selysette, followed by Anton Chekhov's *The Sea Gull*.

This last play, which placed more demands on the company than they could satisfactorily meet, was indicative of the pattern that helped hasten the end of the Washington Square Players: the tendency to overreach themselves. They did so not only by being overly ambitious in their repertory, but also by expanding to a larger, more demanding theatre building. After *The Sea Gull*, they moved to the Comedy Theatre, closer to Broadway and much larger than the old Bandbox Theatre. There, in 1917, they produced Leonid Andreev's gloomy, symbolistic *The Life of Man*—the spectacle of Death shadowing a man from birth to death—and Henrik Ibsen's *Ghosts*. Although they continued to present a certain number of new American one-acts, such as Zona Gale's *Neighbors*, Susan Glaspell's *Trifles*, and Eugene O'Neill's *In the Zone*, they poured most of their energy into the large, ambitious European masterpieces. Among the last of these was George Bernard Shaw's *Mrs. Warren's Profession*, produced in 1918.

Several problems compounded to dispel the group. The move to the Comedy Theatre required larger houses, fuller sets, and more expense just as production costs were rising sharply. Finally, America's entry into World War I depleted its audiences and actors, and in May 1918, the Washington Square Players closed their doors. By that time, they had produced sixty-two short pieces and six full-length plays. They had been an eclectic, frenetic group of avid artists and experimenters. They had no fixed program aligned with one movement, but they made their discoveries one by one as the demands of new and varied plays were faced, if not always met. All styles of plays were performed, and they revered nothing more than what they saw as serious art.

This was not the end, however. In 1919, Lawrence Langner picked up that same banner and rallied his forces behind a new enterprise to succeed the Washington Square Players: the Theatre Guild. This theatre was to become the first truly successful art theatre in America. Langner was a remarkable man, a patent lawyer who managed to maintain his part in a successful law firm while he built up the Theatre Guild. He assembled a Board of Managers to help with the task. It consisted of himself, Helen Westley, Rollo Peters, Philip Moeller, Lee Simonson, Justus Sheffield, and Augustin Duncan, to whom were later added Theresa Helburn and Maurice Wertheim (both former students of George Pierce Baker as was Lee Simonson). They committed themselves at the outset "To produce plays of artistic merit not ordinarily produced by the commercial managers." To do so, they established a subscription system to insure sufficient money for a season of plays without having to have recourse to Broadway "angels" to underwrite each individual production. The initial 135 subscribers grew to six thousand by October 1922, and to twenty-three thousand by the fall of 1927. The Guild had as its home the Garrick Theatre, which had served Jacques Copeau as the home of the Théâtre du Vieux Colombier during their stay in America.

The Theatre Guild opened its doors 19 April 1919, with a production of Jacinto Benavente's *The Bonds of Interest*. The play uses a commedia dell' arte style for an engaging spectacle of pretense and truth, materialism and love. It is one of the masterpieces of modern Spanish drama, but it was not popular, gaining respect for the Guild but emptying their coffers. On this occasion, as well as several others, Otto Kahn helped them through the hard times. The Guild was rescued by their second production, St. John Ervine's *John Ferguson*. It cost the Guild under $1,000 to produce, but went on to turn a $40,000 profit. Thereafter the Guild was on solid ground, well established as a viable theatre.

In 1925, the Theatre Guild had become strong enough to support a permanent company of actors, whose close professional association, they felt, could only enhance the artistic effectiveness of Guild productions. They formed a nucleus of ten actors, to which they would add according to the demands of particular plays. The ten were Helen Westley, Alfred Lunt, Lynn Fontanne, Dudley Digges, Claire Eames, Margalo Gillmore, Edward G. Robinson, Earle Larimore, Henry Travers, and Philip Loeb. Shortly afterward they obtained their own specially designed theatre on Fifty-Second Street. It was not a remarkable theatre. It was a standard proscenium house, but spacious, comfortable, and still capable of sustaining the kind of intimacy the modern repertory calls for. At the time, it seemed a mark of triumph, although it became a financial burden during the Depression and ultimately had to be relinquished.

In addition to the strong sense of ensemble acting the Theatre Guild attained by virtue of the permanent company of actors, their long association with the brilliant director Philip Moeller, whose work went back to the first days of the Washington Square Players, had resulted in a succession of memorable productions. Moreover, they were able

to rely on the outstanding contributions of one of America's foremost designers, Lee Simonson, whose work also went back to the early days of the group.

Thus, the Theatre Guild accomplished an ideal long fought for: a permanent company of resident actors and staff artists performing plays in regular rotation—in short, a repertory theatre. It became a major force in establishing an especially American style of theatre, consisting of a selective realism reinforced by the ideas of the New Stagecraft championed by Lee Simonson and Robert Edmond Jones.

Still, for the first few years, the repertory of the Theatre Guild was composed almost exclusively of European plays, which occasioned considerable criticism of the group. Unlike the Provincetown Players, the Guild was not directly associated with any major American playwright, and if they were at the particular disposal of any playwright at all, it was George Bernard Shaw. They produced seventeen of his plays, several of them world premieres, including *Heartbreak House* (1920), *Saint Joan* (1923), and *Back to Methuselah* (1922). The last was an extraordinary tour de force, requiring two evenings and a matinee to perform, at considerable cost to the Guild's treasury.

If promotion of new American plays was slow in starting, it did happen. The first significant new American play produced by the Theatre Guild was Elmer Rice's highly experimental, expressionistic piece, *The Adding Machine*, in 1923. It was followed the next year by Sidney Howard's *They Knew What They Wanted*, which opened 24 November 1924 and won a Pulitzer Prize. Howard also contributed two other plays to the Guild's repertory, *Ned McCobb's Daughter* and *The Silver Cord*, both produced in 1926. They courageously produced a highly original and bold new play by John Howard Lawson called *Processional* (1925), described as a jazz symphony of American life and class tensions. In the spring of 1927, they introduced a new playwright of significance, S. N. Behrman, with his play *The Second Man*. Finally, the Guild inherited Eugene O'Neill from the Provincetown Players, and on 9 January 1928, opened his *Marco Millions* followed two weeks later by *Strange Interlude*, that demanding nine-act extravaganza of Freudian inner warfare, beautifully staged by Moeller and featuring Lynn Fontanne. Done with a dinner intermission, it was a daring feat which became "the thing to see" in New York, and ran for 426 successive performances (meanwhile undermining the repertory system of the Guild). All of these writers—Howard, Lawson, Behrman, and O'Neill—were products of George Pierce Baker's Workshop 47.

As a result of the Guild's growth in the 1920s, it succeeded in creating road companies with subscription seasons in six other cities: Baltimore, Boston, Cleveland, Pittsburgh, Philadelphia, and Chicago. At the height of this enterprise, the Guild employed two hundred actors and enrolled some seventy-five thousand subscribers. The crash of 1929 did not kill the Guild but did alter its adventurous spirit. It had to abandon seasons in cities outside New York and eventually (in 1935) lost the theatre in New York, although it continued to lease the facility. Most of the board members fell away, leaving behind only Lawrence Langner and Theresa Helburn. Eventually, by the 1940s, the Guild had lost much of its original character and conducted itself much as other commercial producers, using some of the very practices against which it had initially rebelled. Still, it did serve as the hatching ground of a new theatre which was to become one of the significant art theatres of the 1930s:

Harold Clurman, Cheryl Crawford, and Lee Strasberg began the Group Theatre in 1929 as a studio theatre of the Guild.

When the Guild and the Provincetown Players were at the height of their power, around 1925, they were contributing to a vastly different American theatre than had existed just ten years earlier. They themselves had worked to create it. It was now a theatre able to assimilate new ideas and to sustain the development of new talent, especially among playwrights. But all theatre artists profited by the change. Once the stranglehold of the Theatrical Syndicate had been broken, a new kind of theatrical organization had to emerge that could guarantee theatre artists that measure of freedom they needed to sharpen their craft, find their talent, and explore the possibilities of the theatrical medium. Workshop 47, the Provincetown Players, the Washington Square Players, and the Theatre Guild all contributed to building the new theatre. Without them the American theatre might well have withered in the old system of rigid commercial control.

–Stanley Vincent Longman

The Theatre Guild

New York

During the first third of the twentieth century, the Theatre Guild was the most innovative and important theatrical organization in the United States. From its fledgling days, when the company was known as the Washington Square Players, and was made up of a group of amateurs with a passion for the theatre, to the height of its development as a professional producing company—with audiences from coast to coast and an international reputation—the aim of the Guild was to present productions of the highest artistic merit. During its sixty-five-year career, it gave hundreds of gifted playwrights the opportunity of having their work done on stage, screen, radio, and television. Eventually the Theatre Guild achieved its goal of raising the taste of the playgoing public and the standards of the Broadway producers.

In the early years of the twentieth century, almost all the commercial theatres in the United States, including those in New York, were controlled by two companies, Klaw-Erlanger and the

Shuberts. To the men who ran these organizations, the theatre was simply "show business," and the play that turned a profit was a "great" play, though its quality was low and often coarse, and its production shoddy.

Disgusted with the theatrical fare being offered by the commercial producers, several literate and idealistic young men and women, who had studied drama at various colleges and academies, dreamed of founding a theatre—like the Abbey Theatre of Dublin or the Moscow Art Theatre—that would produce serious and artistic plays with style and beauty. These young people met frequently at the bookshop of Charles and Albert Boni, which was located on Washington Square in Greenwich Village, New York. In the group were Edward Goodman, Philip Moeller, Helen Westley, Lawrence Langner, and many other young hopefuls. It was Langner, an excellent organizer, who finally called a meeting in the winter of 1914 during which a company to be known as the Washington

Square Players was formed. A manifesto was drawn up stating some of the company's aims: to produce plays of artistic merit, with preference given to American plays as well as the works of European authors which have been ignored by commercial managers; to defray the expenses of production by the sale of tickets—the price of admission to be fifty cents a ticket or subscriptions for ten tickets at five dollars. In the beginning, the group planned to limit its efforts to one-acts, as no one was sufficiently experienced to write longer plays and the actors were equally unable to sustain them. Initially it was decided that the Washington Square Players would be run on a strictly democratic basis, with everyone in the group from director to office boy having a say in the selection and casting of plays. This soon proved to be highly impractical, so Moeller, Westley, and Langner were elected to make the final decisions. The Committee System of production was later adopted by the Theatre Guild under the title of the Board of Managers. Albert Boni and Langner, serving as business managers for the Washington Square Players, went looking for a playhouse and settled on the little Bandbox Theatre on East Fifty-seventh Street, just off Third Avenue. The house held 299 seats and rented for thirty-five dollars, since performances were to be given at first only on Friday and Saturday evenings. No one connected with the company received any money; and the capital available for the productions amounted to a few hundred dollars.

On 19 February 1915, the Washington Square Players gave their first performance, the inaugural bill consisting of three one-act plays and a pantomime. The plays were *Licensed* by Basil Lawrence (Lawrence Langner), *Eugenically Speaking* by Edward Goodman, who served as the company's stage director, and *Interior* by celebrated Belgian playwright Maurice Maeterlinck; the pantomime, called *Another Interior*, was a spoof that took place inside a man's stomach. Maeterlinck's play, staged with the help of Robert Edmond Jones, later to become one of America's most important scene and costume designers, created a hushed mood in the audience and caught everyone's fancy. Despite the fact that the acting for the most part in all the plays was amateur and at times fumbling (the critics complained of this), the theatre was sold out the next night, and soon a third weekly performance had to be added. The second bill of the first season was presented in March and consisted of five short plays. Among their authors were Leonid Andreev, a well-known Soviet dramatist; John Reed, who was soon to leave for the Soviet Union; and Philip

Moeller. The third bill, in April, featured plays by Edward Goodman and Maurice Maeterlinck; and the final bill of the first season reenacted three of the company's most popular productions and added *The Bear* by Anton Chekhov.

The Players reopened the Bandbox on 4 October 1915 for their second season, with an augmented staff of actors and other workers and now undertook to pay these workers $25 a week, to give seven instead of three performances weekly, to pay $250 instead of $35 weekly rental, and finally to ask the public to pay $1 instead of 50¢ for a seat. Already rising expenses had caused the increase in the price of a ticket. The general level of the acting remained amateur although the company had acquired a few trained actors like Frank Conroy and Roland Young. Two of the outstanding plays of this second season were Moeller's *Helena's Husband*, a historical burlesque, and Alice Gerstenberg's *Overtones*. This strange play shows two women who speak the commonplaces of polite society, while two other women, their "shadows," utter their real thoughts with outrageous honesty, a technique foreshadowing Eugene O'Neill's *Strange Interlude*. Slowly the acting of the company began to improve, and there was a noticeable increase in public attendance.

The most interesting play of the third bill was *The Clod* by Lewis Beach, a melodrama of the Civil War that was excellently acted and full of suspense. The fourth bill featured a play in verse about New York, *The Magical City* by Zoe Akins, who later made her mark as a playwright on Broadway; but it was Lee Simonson's beautiful and evocative setting that stole the show.

On 7 May 1916, the Players gave their first full-length play, Maeterlinck's *Aglavaine and Selysette*, in a single performance for their subscribers. Again the scenery was more notable than the acting or the script. The final bill of the season was Chekhov's *The Sea Gull*, acted from 22 May to 1 June. It was amateurish, overly "arty," and a financial failure.

The season over, the Players decided that the Bandbox Theatre was too small to yield sufficient revenue to meet their rising expenses and to satisfy their ambition to hire better actors. They could not increase their prices in a house so far from Broadway. After a search, and negotiations with the Shuberts, they were able to lease on reasonable terms the old Comedy Theatre on West Thirty-eighth Street; the house had a larger capacity than the Bandbox and was closer to the theatre district. By coming to Broadway, however, they entered into competition with it, lost much of the charm of their amateur standing, and still offered mainly one-act plays.

At the Comedy, the Players presented two summer bills, in June and August, 1916. These included *Pierre Patelin*, a famous medieval farce, author unknown; *The Bear* by Chekhov; and *Literature* by celebrated Viennese playwright Arthur Schnitzler. In their two remaining seasons at the Comedy, they presented several worthy plays, among them O'Neill's *In the Zone*, Susan Glaspell's *Trifles*, and Zona Gale's *Neighbors*. But they found the supply of one-acts running low; it was difficult to secure original work that would meet their literary standards as well as the test of Broadway popularity. They were driven back more and more to translations of foreign works and to full-length plays. Among the latter were *The Life of Man* by Andreev, *Ghosts* by Henrik Ibsen, *Youth* by Miles Malleson, and *Mrs. Warren's Profession* by Bernard Shaw. Shaw's play dealt with prostitution and created a furor, but the season was a financial failure. On the final bills of the fourth season, April and May 1918, there were *The Home of the Free* by Elmer Rice, *Salome* by Oscar Wilde, *The Rope* by O'Neill, and a play by Glaspell with a prophetic title, *Close the Book*. The experiment at the Comedy was no longer profitable. World War I was taking actors away from the company and the attention of the public away from "serious" theatre. The Washington Square Players had no choice but to disband.

In the four years of its existence, this organization had produced sixty-two one-act plays and pantomimes and six long dramas. Of these sixty-eight plays, thirty-eight were of American authorship, or slightly more than fifty percent. The Players had provided a showcase available in few other places for native playwrights, actors, directors, and designers. Those who came to public attention were dramatists O'Neill, Glaspell, Akins, and Rice; performers Katharine Cornell, Conroy, Westley, Young, Rollo Peters, and Glenn Hunter; directors Goodman and Moeller; and designers Simonson and Jones—almost all of whom were later to have a profound effect on the American theatre.

Although it ended its career with a record of artistic success and financial failure (Lee Shubert was left "holding the bag" because of nonpayment of rent for the Comedy), the Washington Square Players' most notable achievement, in the opinion of then drama critic Walter Prichard Eaton, was that "It accustomed a public, small perhaps, to look with interest on experimental work, and to relish the unusual, work done for the sheer joy of the doing.

Finally, it left among the workers themselves a sense of incompletion, of a vision striven for but not attained, a realization of mistakes, but a belief nonetheless that the vision was a sound one, that in a spirit of cooperation and united purpose some day it was not unattainable."

Six months after the Washington Square Players ceased to exist, World War I ended. On 18 December 1918, only a month after the armistice was signed, Lawrence Langner happened to meet Philip Moeller and Helen Westley and the discussion turned to the possible resumption in some form of the kind of art theatre they had originally been interested in. Several meetings were called which were attended by many of the former members of the Players; they were later joined by Theresa Helburn, a graduate of George Pierce Baker's Workshop 47 at Harvard, and who had been peripherally connected with the earlier group. The name chosen for the new organization was the Theatre Guild, suggestive of the excellence and skill of the famous medieval guilds. A new manifesto was drawn up which stated:

1. That we will form a group to carry out the idea of an expert theatre . . . made up only of artists of the theatre who are experts in their work;

2. That we will either lease or secure the building of a theatre seating a considerable number of people . . . (between 500 and 600 seating capacity), in some place where the rents were sufficiently low not to make rentals a burden;

3. To govern absolutely by a committee which will delegate its executive and administrative powers to the members thereof.

It was also decided that the Guild would finance its productions by selling subscriptions, would do no more one-act plays, and would not produce any play written by a member of the Board of Managers. Rollo Peters was named director of the board, and Theresa Helburn was designated play representative, but not yet a board member.

Langner and Peters, looking for a theatre, came upon the Garrick, on West Thirty-fifth Street, a house originally built for the famous comedians Harrigan and Hart. Otto H. Kahn, a banker and patron of the arts, owned the lease on the Garrick and generously offered it to the new company, saying they could pay the rent when they had it.

The choice of the first play was a matter of much debate. In keeping with their principles, it was to be a play of high quality, preferably one that had been ignored by the commercial theatre. They finally selected *Bonds of Interest* by Jacinto Benavente, a Spanish playwright who had won the Nobel Prize. The play was a comedy dealing with the mixture of good and evil in human nature, performed with the masks and characters of the commedia dell'arte. Moeller was chosen to direct, and Peters designed magnificent scenery and costumes. In the cast were several outstanding performers: Peters, Augustin Duncan (brother of Isadora Duncan), Westley, Mary Blair, Dudley Digges, and appearing briefly, Edna St. Vincent Millay. The actors performed for twenty-five dollars a week and the promise of sharing in the profits, if any. Opening night was 19 April 1919. In spite of the high praise of the critics, the play languished. It hung on for four weeks, the actors being paid first, and then the funds gave out. At this time, Maurice Wertheim, a banker and former student in the Workshop 47 of Professor Baker at Harvard, impressed by the work the Guild was doing, began to contribute generously to the company, and very soon became a member of the board.

The Guild had promised its subscribers two plays that season, and chose as its second offering *John Ferguson* by St. John Ervine, an Irish playwright living in London. Ervine wanted an advance payment of $1,000, but the Guild was able to talk him out of it, and rushed the play into rehearsal. It was the story of the tribulations of simple farm people and had a powerful emotional effect on audiences. It called for a small cast and one set that was designed by Rollo Peters, who was able to make it up out of odds and ends from the theatre's storeroom, at a total cost of $300. Augustin Duncan staged the play and appeared in the title role. When the curtain went up on 12 May 1919, the Theatre Guild had exactly $19.50 in the till. The critics' enthusiasm for the play decided the future of the organization; the public flocked to the theatre, and profits began to accumulate. That summer the members of Actors Equity Association started a long strike against the theatre managers and were able to force the closing of every legitimate theatre in New York. The Garrick was the single exception; that was permitted to operate because the Guild was run cooperatively and its management had been the first to recognize the actors' union. So for many weeks, the only play running in New York was *John Ferguson*, and business boomed. The Guild actors actually received their small percentages, Mr. Kahn got his rent, and the board began to lay aside a few dollars as a production fund for the next season.

The Garrick seated fewer than six hundred people, so it was impossible to make a great deal of money in it, even with a hit. *John Ferguson* would be capable of yielding a much larger return if it were moved to a bigger house, but inevitable risks would be involved in such a transfer. After a heated debate, the board agreed to move the play on 7 July to the Fulton Theatre, with cast and set intact. It had rung up sixty-six performances at the Garrick, then sixty-five at the Fulton, before closing on 30 August. In the heat of the summer, at a time when theatres were not air conditioned, this was considered an excellent run.

With the profits from *John Ferguson* and a membership of five hundred subscribers (a gain of three hundred fifty over the first season), the board felt it could splurge. On 19 October 1919, the second season opened and the first three plays—*The Faithful* by John Masefield, *The Rise of Silas Lapham*, adapted by Lillian Sabine from William Dean Howells's novel, and *The Power of Darkness* by Leo Tolstoy—were given elaborate and expensive productions, and all three proved to be dismal failures. With one hundred dollars in the bank and bills of two hundred dollars to meet, the Board of Managers could not decide on the next play. Emanuel Reicher, a great director who had come from Europe to work with the Guild, suggested that they do *Jane Clegg*, another play by St. John Ervine. Like *John Ferguson*, it was a moving story that featured a strong protagonist struggling nobly against adversity. It called for a small cast and a simple naturalistic setting. The play proved to be a good choice. It ran for 177 performances, until 24 July, and its success assured the continuation of the Guild. The season closed with a production of August Strindberg's *The Dance of Death* (the two parts condensed into one). It was given on two successive Sunday evenings, for the subscribers alone, whose numbers had increased by eight hundred, making a total of thirteen hundred.

At the end of the second season, important changes were made in the Guild's Board of Managers. Rollo Peters and Augustin Duncan, who had contributed greatly to the success of the company, preferred to work under one supreme director rather than under a cooperative, decision-making board. But as this was contrary to the principles and aims of the group, Peters and Duncan tendered their resignations. The board then assumed the composition it was to retain for the next twenty years. There were three artistic members—Helen Westley, Philip Moeller, and Lee Simonson—and three business or managerial members—Lawrence

Langner, Maurice Wertheim, and Theresa Helburn. Helburn became executive director and played an increasingly important part in production and administration.

The pattern that manifested itself during the first year of the Guild's operation—that is, two steps toward success and one back to failure—continued through the first ten years of its existence, with advances toward renown and financial independence taken in giant strides. In the beginning, the Guild leaned heavily on the work of foreign playwrights, among them, Bernard Shaw, A. A. Milne, Ferenc Molnar, Georg Kaiser, Karel Capek, Henrik Ibsen, and many others. Later on the Guild produced more American dramatists: Elmer Rice, Arthur Richman, Sidney Howard, S. N. Behrman, Rodgers and Hart, Maxwell Anderson, Philip Barry, and Eugene O'Neill. The Theatre Guild eventually became the exclusive producers of the works of Shaw and O'Neill.

In accordance with its aim to bring unusual plays to New York audiences, the Guild chose as the opening work of its third season, 1920-1921, David Pinski's *The Treasure*. This play, originally written in Yiddish, had been presented in German by Max Reinhardt. That great director's interest in it seemed to lend the play importance as a work of theatrical art. But *The Treasure*, set in a provincial Russian gravedigger's house adjoining a cemetery, was treated by the Guild as a farce. New Yorkers, not yet ready for gallows humor, rejected the play.

For its second offering of the season, the board wished to present *Heartbreak House* by Bernard Shaw. The playwright had begun this play in 1913 and had taken six years to complete it. Because the play dealt with the total madness of war and its effects on people, Shaw would not release it for production while World War I was in progress and the theatres were full of frivolous entertainments. In 1920, the war over, Shaw was confronted with a cable from the Guild seeking permission to present the play. Shaw asked in return if the Guild knew that the play would put a strain on the audience's attention for three hours and would "send them home exhausted but inspired." After much discussion, Shaw permitted the world premiere of the play to be given in New York under the auspices of the Theatre Guild (which was to present the premieres of four more Shaw plays). *Heartbreak House* was just about to open in the middle of October 1920 when Shaw cabled that the opening would have to be postponed until after 2 November, the day of the presidential election in the United States. From his experience, Shaw said, no one would pay any atten-

tion to the opening of a play while the electioneering fever raged. Despite the Guild's explanations and pleas, Shaw remained adamant; the play opened on 10 November and became a resounding success.

Encouraged by the response to their first Shavian production, the Guild approached the playwright for another work. They expressed a preference for *The Doctor's Dilemma*, which had been done years before in America by the English actor/manager Richard Mansfield. Shaw insisted, however, that the Guild do his latest work, *Back to Methuselah*, a play cycle in five acts dealing with the evolution of Man from 4,004 B.C. to 31,920 A.D. The play's ninety thousand words would take nine hours to perform. In spite of the financial and physical burdens such a work would place on the meager resources of the organization, the Guild decided to undertake the production for the prestige it would garner, presenting it as a festival. It would be done in three parts, with two evening shows and a matinee each week. Shaw would not allow any cuts in his plays and interested himself in every aspect of their production. He gave the Guild permission to split the play into three parts, but wrote: "You must sell . . . all . . . tickets on one sheet with perforated card divisions. If people buy them that way they will not throw them away. . . . The wording on your programmes and announcements must always rub in the fact that what the public is going to see is one play, with sections of various lengths. . . ." When Langner spoke to Shaw about a contract for this play, the playwright said, "Don't bother about a contract, it isn't likely that any other lunatic will want to produce *Back to Methuselah*." The play opened on 27 February 1922, lasted for nine weeks, and lost twenty thousand dollars. Shaw later remarked that the Guild had been prepared to lose thirty thousand dollars, but his name had "saved" them ten thousand dollars. The Guild considered this unconventional and financially unsuccessful production a worthwhile experiment, as Shaw now gave them an option on all his plays—those written previously and those to come.

The third season ended with money pouring in from three enormous hits—Bernard Shaw's *Heartbreak House*, A. A. Milne's *Mr. Pim Passes By*, and Ferenc Molnar's *Liliom*—and the members of the board were encouraged to move ahead with plans they had been considering for some time. These included a theatre building of their own, a permanent acting company, a school for actors, and a tryout theatre for playwrights.

During the Theatre Guild's third year at the

Garrick Theatre, the Board of Managers became aware of their need for a theatre of their own, one built to their specifications. They wished to establish a repertoire of plays, and this called for a backstage area large enough to accommodate at one time the sets for several productions. The Garrick, like most of the commercial theatres, was old-fashioned and cramped, and would not serve their purpose. In March 1922, just one month after the opening of *Back to Methuselah*, when the Guild was celebrating its fourth birthday, they announced their plans for erecting their own building. And to that end they held a banquet at the Waldorf Hotel to which they invited wealthy and influential citizens for the purpose of raising money by the sale of bonds; through an active campaign, bonds were also offered to the general public. These events netted six hundred thousand dollars; but before the new house, which was called the Guild Theatre and was erected on West Fifty-second Street, opened its doors on 13 April 1925, it was necessary for the Guild to arrange for a mortgage because the final cost was over one million dollars. Only the twelve thousand subscribers, who were now numerous enough to reduce greatly the losses on a failure, kept the Guild going.

The first aim achieved, the board turned its attention to forming a versatile and permanent acting company. By the 1926-1927 season, with twenty thousand subscribers, the Guild was able to engage a nucleus of ten players as a permanent company—as large a number as they felt their resources would permit. These ten performers were Helen Westley, Lynn Fontanne, Alfred Lunt, Dudley Digges, Claire Eames, Margalo Gillmore, Earle Larimore, Philip Loeb, Henry Travers, and Edward G. Robinson—most of whom were already familiar figures on the Guild stage. There were to be no "stars," but Lynn Fontanne and her husband, Alfred Lunt, a team known as the Lunts, became the most popular and idolized performers of their generation.

With the aid of its acting company, the Guild, in 1926-1927, had its most successful season up to that time, with five hits out of seven productions. The plays which drew packed audiences were Bernard Shaw's *Pygmalion*, Sidney Howard's two plays, *Ned McCobb's Daughter* and *The Silver Cord*, and Luigi Pirandello's *Right You Are If You Think You Are*. In order to keep these plays running, it was necessary for the Guild to rent two theatres—the Golden and the Garrick—in addition to occupying their own.

At the end of the season, the Philadelphia Art Alliance invited the Guild to send *Pygmalion*, with its original cast, to that city for one week's engagement.

This proved so successful that shortly afterward the Guild sent four of its plays to Chicago, again with enthusiastic response. This suggested the idea of touring the acting company each season with the Guild's most successful plays. A humble beginning was made in 1927-1928 when half a dozen plays, with the Lunts heading an excellent cast, were offered to audiences in Baltimore, Boston, Cleveland, Pittsburgh, and Philadelphia. Another first-rate company of actors, led by Frederic March, Florence Eldridge, and George Gaul, was engaged to take the hits of past seasons, such as Shaw's *Arms and the Man*, Howard's *The Silver Cord*, and Molnar's *The Guardsman*, with scenery that could be used in theatres, schoolhouses, or auditoriums, to 132 cities. Plans for the conquest of the "road" had thus begun. Now with over twenty-five thousand subscribers in New York alone, and an equal number on the road, the Guild decided to publish its own magazine, *The Theatre Guild Quarterly*, which later became a monthly called *The Theatre Guild Magazine*, and within two years achieved a circulation of fifty thousand.

On 9 January 1928, the Guild produced *Marco Millions* by O'Neill; no commercial producer would touch the script because it required an extremely lavish production. Although it satirized the American businessman, the play was set in Venice and Asia in the thirteenth century. The play received mixed reviews, and two weeks after it opened, the public was offered O'Neill's *Strange Interlude*, a play in nine acts; and again the Guild was prepared to defy theatrical custom, as it had done with Shaw's *Back to Methuselah*. *Strange Interlude*, which required four and one half hours for its performance, was presented in an unconventional manner. The play began at 5:30 in the afternoon, with a dinner intermission of an hour after act 5, and then continued till eleven o'clock. The play dealt with the life and loves of Nina Leeds in lengthy interior monologues, introspective asides, and Freudian overtones. It was one of the most profitable plays in the Guild's career, as well as in O'Neill's. The playwright now cast his lot permanently with the Guild, which presented eight of his works. In addition to *Strange Interlude*, the Guild had three other financially successful plays running at the end of 1928: Shaw's *Major Barbara*, Nichols and Browne's *Wings Over Europe*, and Sil-Vara's *Caprice*, a comedy with the Lunts that delighted their fans.

At the start of 1929, not quite ten years after it presented its first tentative production at the Garrick Theatre, the Theatre Guild had four plays running in New York and seven on the road, all of uniformly high standard. They had introduced many important dramatists to American audiences, built a powerful acting company of star quality, and had offered the public such experimental works as *R.U.R.* by Karel Capek, in which some of the characters were robots; *Porgy* by Dorothy and DuBose Heyward, a tragedy set in Charleston, South Carolina, with an all-black cast; and *The Garrick Gaieties*, a clever, satirical revue by Richard Rodgers and Lorenz Hart with a cast of youthful performers.

As early as 1919, Theresa Helburn had spoken about starting a school for young actors within the Guild. Applicants, who were accepted after auditioning, joined what was called the Studio and by 1924 were working on scenes from plays under Philip Loeb's direction. They prepared an act of Shaw's *You Never Can Tell*, and a play called *Fata Morgana* by Ernest Vajda, which the Guild later produced with a professional cast for its subscription audience. Members of the Studio, for practice, began to do songs and sketches for charity and social functions. When Rodgers and Hart's songs developed into *The Garrick Gaieties*, many of the young people from the Studio took part in that revue. Harold Clurman, a play reader for the Guild, served as stage manager for the revue, and Lee Strasberg, a Guild actor, appeared in it. This entertainment proved so successful it was done in two future editions.

Clurman, Strasberg, and Cheryl Crawford, the Guild's casting director, had the growing feeling, between 1927 and 1929, that the Theatre Guild was falling behind the times. This triumvirate was excited by the ferment in the Soviet Russian theatre that had taken place after the revolution. When a Soviet play called *Red Rust* by Kirchon and Ouspensky was sent to the Guild and optioned, Harold Clurman was asked to produce it for a special Sunday night performance for the subscribers. The play met with some success, but after its production the Theatre Guild gave up the Studio project. Clurman, Crawford, and Strasberg withdrew from the Guild and formed their own company, the Group Theatre, for the presentation mainly of plays of "social significance." Helburn helped the new organization to get on its feet, urging the Guild to provide half the funds for the Group's first two productions, and turn over to them two scripts— *The House of Connelly* by Paul Green, and *1931* by Paul and Claire Sifton. The Guild also released two actors it had under contract, Franchot Tone and Morris Carnovsky, who were engaged by the Group, and added the gift of a thousand dollars to

help defray the expense of rehearsals. Maxwell Anderson, a Guild playwright, contributed about two thousand dollars to the Group. During much of the time, in the thirties, when the Theatre Guild was in the doldrums, artistically speaking, the Group was actively functioning, with its playwrights Clifford Odets and Irwin Shaw, and doing brilliant work. The Group existed as an entity from 1931 to 1941, and its version of the Stanislavsky system of acting continued to influence the theatre long after the organization had vanished.

During the 1930s, the Theatre Guild, like the rest of the country, suffered from the effects of the Depression, but still managed to produce plays of exceptional quality—among them O'Neill's *Mourning Becomes Electra* and *Ah, Wilderness!*, Robert Sherwood's *Reunion in Vienna* and *Idiot's Delight*, Maxwell Anderson's *Elizabeth the Queen*, and Behrman's *Biography*. Two very interesting plays, neither of which then met with great response, were *Green Grow the Lilacs* by Lynn Riggs and *Porgy and Bess* by the Heywards and Gershwins. The latter was a folk opera based on the Guild's 1927 play, *Porgy*.

By the end of the decade, tensions within the Guild Board of Managers mounted, as difficulties in operating the organization became increasingly burdensome. The Guild Theatre was one of the severest drains on the company's resources; it had, in fact, become a white elephant. At the end of their road tour in *Reunion in Vienna*, the Lunts, now the most popular actors on the American stage, left the Guild to go into management with Noel Coward; and, in 1937, four of the Guild's most prominent dramatists, Anderson, Behrman, Sherwood, and Howard, for whom the Theatre Guild had produced sixteen plays, most of which were successful, joined forces with Elmer Rice to form the Playwrights' Company in order to mount their own works.

Perhaps it was the defection of these writers that reminded Theresa Helburn of the idea she had had years before of starting a tryout project for new dramatists. With the assistance of John Gassner, a play reader for the Guild, Helburn inaugurated the Bureau of New Plays, which would help authors to develop their scripts in seminars, and in productions conducted in conjunction with the Dramatic Workshop of the New School for Social Research, which was under the direction of Erwin Piscator. Between 1937 and 1940, many young playwrights were associated with the Bureau of New Plays, among them Arthur Miller and Tennessee Williams.

To increase the sale of tickets and to circumvent the so-called speculators, the Guild joined with the Postal Telegraph Company and had seventy-five clerks selling tickets by wire at a central ticket office off Times Square. Later, the Guild joined the Shuberts and Marcus Heiman in a merger of their subscription lists, which increased the audiences for the plays sent on tour. The Theatre Guild-American Theatre Society, as the new organization was called, offered its members the plays of other producers as well as those of the Guild.

The failure of Stefan Zweig's play, *Jeremiah*, in February 1939 left the Guild sixty thousand dollars in debt. Disagreement among the members of the board began to mount, and someone suggested that the Guild be dissolved. Plans for a new regime were being drawn up during the entire spring and summer of 1939. However, the very next production, *The Philadelphia Story* by Philip Barry, with Katharine Hepburn, Joseph Cotten, Van Heflin, and Shirley Booth in the cast, was a resounding hit and its long run gave the Guild a new lease on life for the next three years.

After *The Philadelphia Story* closed, a complete reorganization of the structure of the Board of Managers resulted in the resignation of Philip Moeller, Helen Westley, and Lee Simonson, each of whom received a pension and preferred stock in the company. Theresa Helburn and Lawrence Langner undertook to act jointly as administrative directors, with Armina Marshall (Mrs. Langner) serving as assistant director, and later on as associate director; and Warren Munsell as business manager. Maurice Wertheim continued as a member of the Board of Directors until his resignation in 1946, when Helburn assumed full artistic control.

America's entry into World War II had a negative effect on the theatre, and by January 1942 the Guild, with about thirty thousand dollars in the bank, was facing a financial crisis. Helburn, casting about for a play that would restore the Guild's fortunes, remembered Lynn Riggs's *Green Grow the Lilacs*, produced in 1931, which she had always liked because of the interpolated cowboy songs. Helburn felt that this piece of Americana, which dealt with life in the Oklahoma Territory, would make an interesting musical. Richard Rodgers and Oscar Hammerstein were asked to provide book, lyrics, and music. It took over a year to raise the money for the production of *Oklahoma!*, but at its opening on 11 March 1943 it was an immediate hit. It became one of the most successful and longest-running American musicals of the century, and its integration of story, songs, and ballet established a new standard for musical drama. *Oklahoma!* kept the

Guild from bankruptcy, and helped to support the organization for the next seven years. *Carousel*, a musical adaptation by Rodgers and Hammerstein of Molnar's *Liliom*, was another outstanding hit in 1945. But two years later, the musical *Allegro*, by the same creative team, using a book of their own invention, was not so well received.

Other plays which did well for the Guild during the forties, though they did not match the success of *Oklahoma!* or *Carousel*, were *Othello*, with Paul Robeson as the Moor; *Jacobowsky and the Colonel*, adapted by S. N. Behrman from a play by Franz Werfel; Philip Barry's *Foolish Notion*, with Tallulah Bankhead, which made money only on tour; and two plays with the Lunts, coproduced with John C. Wilson. These were Terence Rattigan's *O Mistress Mine* and S. N. Behrman's *I Know My Love*. Bankhead and the Lunts were able to charm their audiences by adding an aura of sophistication to the superficial plays they appeared in, thus assuring their success.

In 1944, the Guild moved its offices out of the Guild Theatre, which for a long time had proved unworkable so far as production was concerned. Its new quarters were in a magnificent mansion at 23 West Fifty-third Street, close by the Museum of Modern Art. This was a relatively inexpensive establishment for the Guild, as a large ballroom on the second floor was used for rehearsals, and there was ample space for a library, offices, and conference rooms.

Two plays by O'Neill, which fared better later under other managements than when done by the Guild in the forties, were *The Iceman Cometh*, presented on 9 October 1946, and *A Moon for the Misbegotten*, which opened on 20 February 1947 in Columbus, Ohio, toured several cities, but closed in Saint Louis and never reached New York.

During the fifties, several changes in policy and procedure were made by the Guild in the face of rising costs and falling profits, as well as competition from films and television. The Theatre Guild-American Theatre Society joined the Council of the Living Theatre and increased the subscription lists across the country to over one hundred thousand members; these were theatregoers who were willing to pay in advance for a series of from five to ten plays that were Broadway hits with star performers. The Guild also offered its subscribers notable films such as *Henry V* and *Hamlet*, both starring Laurence Olivier, Jean Renoir's *The River*, and *The Bridge over the River Kwai* with Alec Guiness.

In the opening years of the decade, the Guild did well with Christopher Fry's play in verse set in the fifteenth century, *The Lady's Not for Burning* (1950), and with two works by William Inge, *Come Back, Little Sheba* (1950), a melodrama of comedy and pathos, and *Picnic* (1953), a comedy of small town life, with Paul Newman in the cast.

In 1953 the Guild changed its legal designation from a corporation to a partnership, and three years later sold the building at 23 West Fifty-third Street to the Museum of Modern Art. The organization then moved to its present location, 226 West Forty-seventh Street, where it occupies the seventh and eighth floors of the ten-story office building it owns.

The Guild had always tried to meet its competition. In 1945, when Armina Marshall was made associate director of the organization, she turned her attention to radio, and with William Fitelson, the Guild's attorney, joined the United States Steel Corporation to sponsor radio drama. Thus began the radio program called "The Theatre Guild of the Air," on 9 September 1945, with an adaptation of the Robert Nichols and Maurice Browne play, *Wings over Europe*, starring Burgess Meredith. These radio programs were broadcast every Sunday evening to an audience that at times reached an estimated fifteen million people. For many listeners it was the first time they had heard the works of Shakespeare, Ibsen, O'Neill, and other major dramatists, with performances by stars of the stage, screen, and radio. After almost seven years, and the airing of about three hundred fifty plays, the series came to an end on 7 June 1953, with a production of Shakespeare's *Julius Caesar*, starring Maurice Evans and Basil Rathbone.

By 1953, television had captured the public's attention, and the Guild swiftly entered the newer medium. This program, called "The United States Steel Hour," was aired on television biweekly instead of weekly, but preserved the same format—adaptations of former Guild plays as well as those of other managements, and original scripts specially written for the series. This provided an opportunity for many new young playwrights to have their work done. The program premiered on 27 October 1953, with *P.O.W.*, a war drama by David Davidson, starring Gary Merrill; the series ended on 12 June 1963, with a production of *The Old Lady Shows Her Medals*, adapted by Robert Anderson from a play by James M. Barrie. In the cast were Alfred Lunt, Lynn Fontanne, Donald Madden, and Cathleen Nesbitt. More than 275 plays had been presented in the almost ten years of the program's existence.

By the mid-fifties, the Guild had become frankly commercial, seeking plays that looked like "show business" hits and tailored for popular stars. Because of increasing costs, many of these plays were staged in association with other producers. In December 1955, *The Matchmaker*, Thornton Wilder's adaptation of an old German play by Johann Nestroy, was a resounding success with Ruth Gordon and Eileen Herlie. This play was coproduced with David Merrick, and later served as the basis for Merrick's musical, *Hello, Dolly!* A year later, the Guild had another hit with *Bells Are Ringing*, a musical starring Judy Holliday and Sidney Chaplin (son of Charlie Chaplin); also connected with the production were Betty Comden, Adolph Green, and Jule Styne as writers, Jerome Robbins as director, and Bob Fosse as choreographer.

A revival of Shaw's *Back to Methuselah*, in a shortened form, was presented by the Guild in 1958, in the hope that it would succeed better than the original nine-hour version, but the public failed to respond. It was the last work of this dramatist offered by the Guild. Between 1920 and 1958, they had produced seventeen of Shaw's plays and two revivals. These were: *Heartbreak House* (1920), *Back to Methuselah* (1922), *The Devil's Disciple* (1923), *Saint Joan* (1923), *Caesar and Cleopatra* (1925), *Arms and the Man* (1925), *The Man of Destiny* (1925), *Androcles and the Lion* (1925), *Pygmalion* (1926), *The Doctor's Dilemma* (1927), *Major Barbara* (1928), *The Apple Cart* (1930), *Getting Married* (1931), *Too True to Be Good* (1932), *The Simpleton of the Unexpected Isles* (1935), *You Never Can Tell* (1948), *Saint Joan* (revival, 1951), *The Millionairess* (1952), and *Back to Methuselah* (revised and shortened by Arnold Moss, 1958).

In 1958, a play about President Franklin D. Roosevelt, *Sunrise at Campobello*, written by and co-produced with Dore Schary, featured motion picture star Ralph Bellamy and drew large audiences. The following year, *A Majority of One*, a sentimental comedy-drama by Leonard Spigelgass, starred Gertrude Berg, who was very popular with radio and television audiences. This play was cosponsored by Dore Schary, who did five productions in all with the Theatre Guild. In 1959, the Guild had four plays running simultaneously on Broadway, three of them coproduced with Dore Schary.

The 1960s saw the further disintegration of the Theatre Guild, with the cost of production—for sets and costumes, the salaries of actors, and the wages and demands of the backstage crews—on the rise. There was the occasional hit, or the play of serious intent, but for the most part the offerings were undistinguished; there was even a return to the production of one-act plays.

On 3 November 1960, *The Unsinkable Molly*

Brown, a colorful musical by Richard Morris and Meredith Willson, and starring Tammy Grimes, ran on Broadway for 533 performances, then continued on a long road tour. The road was still flourishing; there were almost 126,000 subscribers in about twenty cities, but the plays being offered them as time went on were more and more those of managements other than the Guild. The number of plays produced by the Guild was dwindling each season, from four plays to three to two, and occasionally just one. For the first time in its forty-five year history, the Theatre Guild had no production of its own in New York for the period from March to December 1963. By then, Helburn and Langner were no longer living, and the Guild was being run by Armina Marshall and her son, Philip Langner.

In 1959, there had been talk at the Guild of opening an Off-Broadway theatre, to be called Studio Three, where talent could be fostered and fine plays put on in the manner of the Washington Square Players, but the cost would be at least ten times more than it was in 1914. Nothing came of that plan. In 1964, *The Child Buyer*, a serious and literate play adapted by Paul Shyre from John Hersey's novel, was presented as an experiment in an Off-Broadway theatre. It did not succeed.

In association with Alexander Cohen, the Guild produced Harold Pinter's *The Homecoming* on 1 January 1967. The play was thought, by critics and public alike, to be ambiguous but significant; it created a great deal of discussion, and was a moderate success in New York, but failed on the road.

In 1968, Joel Schenker, a producer in his own right, who had been involved for about four years in several coproductions with the Guild, resigned from the company. And in 1968, Philip Langner decided to turn his attention to filmmaking and left for Hollywood; one of his productions, *Slaves*, was written and directed by Herbert Biberman, who had once directed for the Theatre Guild.

For six years, production at the Guild was in abeyance, but in 1974 Philip Langner returned to the theatre, and in association with the John F. Kennedy Center for the Performing Arts, and with British producer Michael Codron, presented *Absurd Person Singular* by Alan Ayckbourne. The play was seen first in Washington, D.C., and then in New York, and proved to be a success.

In 1975, a nostalgic entertainment called *American Musical*, with such former stars as Lillian Gish, Patrice Munsel, and John Raitt, had a brief run under Guild auspices at the St. James Theatre, New York.

Golda, a play adapted by William Gibson from the autobiography of Golda Meir, directed by Arthur Penn, and starring Anne Bancroft, opened on 14 November 1977 at the Morosco Theatre; it ran for ninety-three performances after sixteen previews and closed on 16 February 1978. Philip Langner, Armina Marshall, and Marilyn Langner—not the Theatre Guild—were named as the producers of this play.

During the 1970s, the Guild offered its members European theatre tours and Caribbean cruises on the S. S. Rotterdam, where plays were performed on shipboard. The latter venture was aptly named "Theatre at Sea."

On stationery headed "Theatre Guild Subscription Society, Inc. Philip Langner, Pres.," the plays for the 1980-1981 season were announced; all were to be Broadway hits and significant imports from London. There was no mention of a Theatre Guild production. The price of tickets in the orchestra for the series of five plays ranged from $97 at Wednesday matinees to $117 for Saturday evenings; as an inducement to prospective subscribers, this was said to be a $2 discount on the box-office price of each ticket. The high cost of theatregoing and the growth of excellent university and regional theatres in various parts of the country had cut deeply into the Guild membership.

"The Guild was a primary influence on bringing a childish theatre to maturity," said noted theatre critic Brooks Atkinson. "Without the broad views and the tenacity of the original board members, the Theatre Guild would have succumbed to the pleasant superficiality of the old theatre." In its old age, because of economic and social conditions beyond its control, the Theatre Guild did succumb, unfortunately, to the superficiality of the *new* theatre. The revolution conducted by the Guild that helped to liberate the American theatre from hackneyed formulas was essentially over by 1931, because by that time all reputable producers had adopted the standards that the Guild had set up. Those standards and ideals had attracted to the theatre intellectual, literate playwrights, brilliant performers, and creative designers for whose efforts the Theatre Guild won numerous prizes. For the splendid manner in which it presented some of Eugene O'Neill's most difficult plays, the Guild deserves a modicum of credit for the playwright's Nobel Prize of 1936. There were Pulitzer prizes for Howard's *They Knew What They Wanted* (1924); O'Neill's *Strange Interlude* (1928); Anderson's *Both Your Houses* (1933); Sherwood's *Idiot's Delight* (1936); Saroyan's *The Time of Your Life* (1939); Sherwood's *There Shall Be No Night* (1940); Inge's

Picnic (1953); and a special Pulitzer citation for Rodgers and Hammerstein's *Oklahoma!* (1943). In addition there were many Drama Critics Circle awards and dozens of Theatre Guild offerings listed among the ten best plays each year.

—Randolph Goodman

References:

Harold Clurman, *The Fervent Years* (New York: Knopf, 1945; revised edition, New York: Hill & Wang, 1957);

Walter Prichard Eaton, *The Theatre Guild: The First Ten Years* (New York: Brentano, 1929);

Theresa Helburn, *A Wayward Quest* (Boston: Little, Brown, 1960);

Lawrence Langner, *The Magic Curtain* (New York: Dutton, 1951);

Norman Nadel, *A Pictorial History of the Theatre Guild* (New York: Crown, 1969);

Roy S. Waldau, *Vintage Years of the Theatre Guild, 1928-1939* (Cleveland & London: Case Western Reserve University Press, 1972).

Papers:

The Theatre Collection of the New York Public Library at Lincoln Center has materials and clippings on the Washington Square Players and the Theatre Guild, 1914-1980.

Off Broadway and Off-Off-Broadway

Off Broadway and Off-Off-Broadway: these are terms originating in and applying specifically to New York City (more particularly to Manhattan), although the theatre production concepts they describe are known and practiced elsewhere. Off-Off-Broadway is the newer term, having been in general use only since 1960. Off Broadway, as a term, came into use at least a dozen years earlier, but the concept it embodies has been in existence over a much longer period of time. Any production that plays outside the thirty-five to forty comparatively large and privately owned theatres between Sixth and Eighth avenues and Forty-first to Fifty-sixth streets under the aegis of a limited partnership company specifically formed to produce a particular play is an Off Broadway or an Off-Off-Broadway production. Their auspices vary. Some are institutional theatres; some are repertory theatres; some are experimental theatres; some are simply rental spaces. The lines of distinction are not always clear: in the public and critical view any given performance or theatre group may at one time be designated Off Broadway, at another Off-Off-Broadway. And in recent years a few productions originating in Off Broadway or even Off-Off-Broadway have opened on Broadway. But it is possible to point out the basic concepts underlying Off Broadway and Off-Off-Broadway, and to trace the history of the movement, which is—as much as

anything else—both a protest to and an amplification of Broadway production.

If one were to trace the roots of the Off Broadway and Off-Off-Broadway movement back to its beginnings, one would arrive at the antiestablishment, "free" theatre movement in France, Germany, and England during the closing years of the nineteenth century and the early decades of the twentieth. The Théâtre Libre of Andre Antoine in Paris, formed to give voice to playwrights the establishment theatre of the 1880s would not produce, is the earliest and most famous of these. In 1889, Otto Brahm began the Freie Buhne in Berlin, and in 1892 Jacob T. Grein, in his Independent Theatre, produced *Widowers' Houses*, the first play of George Bernard Shaw to be staged in London. Later that decade (1898), Konstantin Stanislavsky began his Moscow Art Theatre, notably producing the plays of Chekhov, and in 1901 the Abbey Theatre in Dublin undertook the production of native plays, notably those of John Synge, William Butler Yeats, and Sean O'Casey. In 1907 Strindberg started the Intimate Theatre in Stockholm, chiefly to produce his own plays. It was in these antiestablishment or "free" theatres that a host of later significant playwrights had their first hearings.

However, such antiestablishment theatres were largely nonexistent in the United States until the second decade of the twentieth century. Then, in 1915, began the Washington Square Players, the Neighborhood Playhouse, and the Provincetown Playhouse. The first of these groups grew out of meetings of the Liberal Club, a group of writers and intellectuals living in the area around Sheridan, Washington, and Christopher squares in Lower Manhattan (called Greenwich Village). The group included such writers as Edna St. Vincent Millay, Vachel Lindsay, Susan Glaspell, Philip Moeller, and other intellectuals such as Lawrence Langner, a young lawyer. It was a one-act play of Langner's, called *Licensed*, which was first given in the Club space on 19 February 1915, that led to the formation of the Washington Square Players. In the first season they produced a series of short plays by John Reed, Philip Moeller, Holland Hudson, Leonid Andreev, Maurice Maeterlinck, and others in the Bandbox Theatre on Fifty-seventh Street near Third Avenue, which they leased. Their first printed program stated that their purpose was "to produce new works by American authors and important plays of foreign dramatists that would not otherwise be given a hearing." In their second year the group leased the somewhat larger Comedy Theatre on West Thirty-eighth Street, and by the end of the 1917 season they had produced sixty-two one-act plays by such American writers as Susan Glaspell, Theodore Dreiser, Zona Gale, and Percy MacKaye, and such foreign writers as Arthur Schnitzler, Chekhov, Andreev, and Maeterlinck, along with a host of others. After World War I, the group was reconstituted as the Theatre Guild, headed by Lawrence Langner and Theresa Helburn (and still in existence under succeeding leadership). The Guild gave first productions to many of the plays of Eugene O'Neill and George Bernard Shaw on Broadway; it also was the first sponsor of the organization that became the Group Theatre in the 1930s.

The Neighborhood Playhouse grew out of the activities of the Dramatic Club of the Henry Street Settlement House on the lower East Side, under the auspices of Alice and Irene Lewisohn, opening on 12 February 1915 in its own theatre on Grand Street. During the period in which it flourished (until 1927) it gave a widely heralded production of *The Little Clay Cart*, from ancient Hindu times, and introduced the Irish playwright, Lord Dunsany, to America. It also introduced actor-training under Richard Boleslavsky (a former member of the Moscow Art Theatre) and staged a staggering number of ethnic festivals, workshops, lectures, children's programs, and other such events for its neighborhood. Its memory and work are perpetuated to this day in the Neighborhood Playhouse School of the Theatre.

The Provincetown Players had their start in the summer of 1915, when a group of Greenwich Village residents summering in Provincetown produced a group of four one-act plays (including Susan Glaspell's *Suppressed Desires*) in John Reed's house there. The next year they renovated a building on the Provincetown wharf, calling it the Wharf Theatre, in which was produced for the first time the young Eugene O'Neill's *Bound East for Cardiff*. Now deciding to work through the winter, they leased a brownstone at 139 MacDougal Street in Greenwich Village and transformed its interior to a narrow 160-seat theatre, moving in 1918 to a slightly larger space at 133 MacDougal Street, which exists to this day as the Provincetown Playhouse. The Players themselves (originally George Cram Cook, Susan Glaspell, Floyd Dell, Max Eastman, Eugene O'Neill, Wilbur Daniel Steele, and Robert Edmond Jones) went through many changes of personnel until the group's final dissolution in 1929. But their fame is secure, primarily for the first performance of O'Neill's *The Emperor Jones* (1920) with Charles Gilpin in the MacDougal Street theatre and the play's subsequent move to Broadway and fame. Over the period of the group's troubled existence it not only fostered the genius of O'Neill, but also contributed to the careers of Sherwood Anderson, William Carlos Williams, Samson Raphaelson, E. E. Cummings, Paul Green, Hatcher Hughes, Cleon Throckmorton (designer), and Paul Robeson (actor).

By 1930, both the Neighborhood Playhouse and the Provincetown Players were no longer producing, and the Theatre Guild, which had grown out of the Washington Square Players, was a permanent organization producing for a subscription audience on Broadway. Meanwhile, the actor Walter Hampden had, for a five-year period (1925-1930), produced a series of plays in the leased Colonial Theatre which he renamed Hampden's, and the actress Eva Le Gallienne had given a noteworthy series of plays in true repertory fashion at the Civic Repertory Theatre. Both were victims of the Great Depression of the 1930s.

But it was the Depression, nonetheless, that fostered a growing social consciousness, and the appearance of several "socially conscious" theatres in New York City, all of which were—to some degree—antiestablishment though not always physically Off Broadway. Some of these were the Theatre of Action (which first performed Irwin Shaw's *Bury the Dead*, 1936), the Theatre Collective (which produced Paul Green's *Hymn to the Rising Sun*), the New Theatre League (Clifford Odets's *Waiting for Lefty*, 1935), the Theatre Union (Albert Maltz's *Peace on Earth*, 1933, and John Howard Lawson's *Marching Song*, 1937), as well as a series of black theatres: the New Lafayette Players (1919), the Harlem Experimental Theatre (1928), the Negro Art Theatre (1929), Rose McClendon's Negro People's Theatre (1935), and Langston Hughes's Harlem Suitcase Theatre (1938). It would be the Negro Playwrights' Company which would produce Philip Yordan's *Anna Lucasta* and would bring Paul Robeson to Broadway in *Othello*.

The most famous of these organizations in the 1930s was the Group Theatre, whose birth, life, and death are chronicled in Harold Clurman's *The Fervent Years*. It grew, in part, out of the interest in the acting methods of the Moscow Art Theatre on the part of Clurman, Lee Strasberg, Morris Carnovsky, Stella Adler, and Sanford Meisner. Since Clurman was then a play reader for the Theatre Guild and Cheryl Crawford a casting director, they persuaded the Guild to underwrite a production of Vladimir Kirshon's *Red Rust* as a Guild Studio production. Although favorably received, no other productions appeared as Guild Studio productions because Clurman, Crawford, Strasberg, and a serious group of young actors and actresses and directors began to plan for a new theatrical entity, and after an intensive summer of work in 1931, opened their first full production as the Group Theatre—Paul Green's *The House of Connelly*—at the Martin Beck Theatre on 23 September 1931. The Group Theatre received financial backing from the Theatre Guild, from Eugene O'Neill, Maxwell Anderson, and others. In its remarkable ten years of existence it developed a host of theatre workers who later became prominent not only in many areas of theatre but in the motion picture industry as well. Conceived primarily as an actors/directors theatre with a social conscience, it fostered the writing abilities not only of Paul Green, but also of Clifford Odets, Sidney Kingsley, John Howard Lawson, Irwin Shaw, and Robert Ardrey. Clurman, Strasberg, and Elia Kazan were to become outstanding directors; Mordecai Gorelik, Boris Aronson, and Donald Oenslager developed their skills as designers; and there were many performers who later became famous: Franchot Tone, John Garfield, Lee J. Cobb, Stella Adler, Morris Carnovsky, Luther Adler, Frances Farmer, and many others. Unquestionably, the Group Theatre had more influence in the twentieth century than any other single theatre organization.

The 1930s, of course, also witnessed the short and brilliant life of the Federal Theatre Project of the Works Progress Administration (1935-1939) under the direction of Hallie Flanagan, but its concept was different from that of most Off-Broadway theatres. During the war years, in 1941, Antoinette Perry began the Experimental Theatre of the Dramatists Guild to encourage playwrights, and Sam Jaffe and George Freedley set up the Equity Library Theatre (1944) to aid the careers of young actors and directors (a function it is still performing). Eva Le Gallienne had another try at repertory in partnership with Margaret Webster and Cheryl Crawford in the American Repertory Theatre (1946-1947), and Jean Dalrymple ran an enviable series of performances (1943-1966) at the New York City Center of Music and Drama, a huge Mecca Temple on West Fifty-fifth Street.

Though all of the above are a part of the lineage of Off Broadway, the movement did not coalesce until the establishment, in 1949, of the League of Off-Broadway Theatres and Producers. The League was formed by thirty Off-Broadway producers to deal with common problems such as the negotiating of favorable terms with various unions. For the most part, the Off-Broadway entities which formed the League were those interested in offering an alternative to Broadway production. Off-Broadway producers rented theatre space removed from the midtown theatrical district, which space typically would seat from one hundred to four hundred persons. The choice of material was most often revivals of plays hitherto presented on Broadway, revivals of classics or near-classics, interesting plays from foreign dramatists, and a modest number of new American plays. Ticket prices were low, scenic investiture modest, salaries miniscule. But there is no question that, by the early 1950s, Off Broadway was offering more productions from a more widely varied repertory than was Broadway. At the height of the theatre season, in the winter, as many as thirty or forty Off-Broadway productions might be available in a wide variety of locations as well as theatrical styles. In addition to the virtue of offering a theatregoing public some variety in theatrical fare, these houses also afforded performers more opportunity to work. Except for occasional approval in the pages of *Theatre Arts* magazine, however, the Off-Broadway houses were largely unnoticed by the critical press.

In 1952, however, The Circle in the Square (started as the Loft Players in 1950 by Theodore Mann, José Quintero, Emile Stevens, Jason Wingreen, Aileen Cramer, and Edward Mann, and changing to its present name in 1951 when it took over an abandoned night club in Sheridan Square and produced William Berney and Howard Richardson's *Dark of the Moon* to *no* critical notice) produced Tennessee Williams's *Summer and Smoke* with Geraldine Page in the leading role. Brooks Atkinson of the *New York Times* saw the production, wrote about it enthusiastically, and a year-long success was assured. Geraldine Page became a star; the Circle in the Square became a success, and the Off-Broadway movement became the focus of attention and concern. The seating capacity (maintained in pseudo-cabaret style) was 270, and the stage area was a three-sided arena. There followed a significant list of successes (interspersed with some failures, as Theodore Mann says) through the 1950s and 1960s, including Giraudoux's *The Enchanted* (1951), Steinbeck's *Burning Bright* (1953), Capote's *The Grass Harp* (1954), O'Neill's *The Iceman Cometh* (which made a star of Jason Robards in 1956) and Edwin Mayer's *Children of Darkness* (1958), among many others. In the 1960s the theatre relocated on Bleecker Street and then in 1972 opened a new theatre in the Uris Building (courtesy of revised building codes achieved under the leadership of then-Mayor John V. Lindsay) with Colleen Dewhurst in *Mourning Becomes Electra*. The 650-seat West Fiftieth Street theatre houses now each season four to five productions usually marketed on a subscription basis and produced by artistic director Theodore Mann and managing director Paul Libin. The theatre is, as the directors say, "dedicated to the revival of distinguished plays with eminent casts and the production of new plays with significant themes." It is, in essence, what elsewhere would be called an institutional theatre, and is considered by some a Broadway institution. It is certainly one of the three longest-lived and continuously producing of the noncommercial theatres in New York City. It has introduced new plays by Murray Schisgal (*An American Millionaire*, 1974), Michael Weller (*Loose Ends*, 1979), Jack Zeman (*Past Tense*, 1980), as well as works by Terrence McNally, Leonard Melfi, Jules Feiffer, and Israel Horovitz in previous seasons. After the move to the new house on Fiftieth Street, the management continued to maintain the older, smaller house on Bleecker Street, known as Circle in the Square Downtown, to present chiefly new plays on an ad hoc basis.

Another Off-Broadway entity still in existence began in the 1950s: the Phoenix Theatre. In 1953 T. Edward Hambleton and Norris Houghton renamed and assumed control of the old 1186-seat Yiddish Art Theatre (long a motion picture house) at Second Avenue and Twelfth Street. The first production was Sidney Howard's *Madam Will You Walk?* (1953) and the most brilliant of its early successes was the Jerome Moross/John Latouche musical, *The Golden Apple* (1954). By the end of the 1950s it had presented about sixty productions, half of them classics, with leading performers and directors from America and England. The enormous size and the downtown location of the theatre finally defeated the enterprising managers, but by 1961 the Phoenix rose again at the Eastside Playhouse on Seventy-fourth Street, having a major hit in the second season with Arthur Kopit's *Oh, Dad, Poor Dad, Mama's Hung You in the Closet and I'm Feelin' So Sad*. In 1964 the Phoenix entered into collaboration with the Association of Producing Artists (Ellis Rabb, Rosemary Harris, George Grizzard, Stephan Porter, and others) in a brilliant series of performances. In the fall of 1965 the associated companies took over the Lyceum Theatre on West Forty-fifth Street for several seasons, for some of which Helen Hayes was a member of the company. In the early 1970s the Phoenix and APA disengaged, but the Phoenix, now with T. Edward Hambleton alone at the helm, rose again in a new guise at the Marymount Manhattan Theatre on East Seventy-first Street. The recent emphasis is on new American plays. In a sense, the Phoenix is also an institutional theatre, since it has been, for twenty-seven years, a significant contributor to the New York theatrical scene, especially during the glorious years of the APA/Phoenix at the Lyceum.

The third institutionlike theatre in existence from the 1950s to the present centers around Joseph Papp. In 1954 he gave his first free Shakespeare performance in the East River Amphitheatre on a budget of $500. By 1957 the performances had moved to Central Park under the banner of the New York Shakespeare Festival, and by 1962 the Delacorte outdoor theatre had been built there for the summer performances after an epic battle fought out in the public press with City Parks Commissioner Robert Moses. Papp won the battle, standing firm in his conviction that the arts are indispensable to life and that a theatre "can and should be run for beauty and wisdom rather than for money." By 1967 Papp had added to the park performances the Mobile Theatre which toured the boroughs and the New York Shakespeare Festival Public Theatre in Astor Place. His budget was now about $3.5 million, and for this new headquarters he undertook a complete renovation of the old Astor Library, opening the first of several theatres in the building as the Florence Sutro Anspacher Theatre (named, of course, for the chief donor of funds), made from the main reading room of the beautiful old library. The opening production was *Hair*, the explosive rock-musical by James Rado and Galt McDermott which went on to Broadway and worldwide fame. Since that first opening on 29 October 1967, the Public has added six more theatre spaces to the interior of the building. The program in Astor Place is largely devoted to new works, and the roster of playwrights brought to public attention is impressive: Anne Burr, Adrienne Kennedy, Charles Gordone (*No Place to Be Somebody* won the Pulitzer Prize in 1969), Myrna Lamb, Robert Montgomery, David Rabe, Jason Miller (*That Championship Season* moved successfully to Broadway), John Ford Noonan, Edgar White, Robert Auletta, Susan Yankowitz, Murray Mednick, Ed Bullins, and innumerable others, including Michael Bennett, creator of *A Chorus Line*, which has been playing on Broadway for five years and has toured extensively. For three seasons (1973-1976) the Papp organization also produced at the Vivian Beaumont Theatre in Lincoln Center, opening with David Rabe's *Boom Boom Room*. But the politics and economics of being a Lincoln Center constituent, which had defeated the previous tenant of the Vivian Beaumont, caused Papp to withdraw after three seasons. He has concentrated his considerable energies since on Astor Place and Central Park, with an occasional foray to Broadway and the road. His accomplishments to date have been prodigious, and more may be expected. A whole generation of performers, writers, designers, have passed through his organization, and he continues to develop new talents, straddling the theatrical world like a colossus.

Other Off-Broadway theatres began in the 1950s and their fates have been various. One that began auspiciously in 1952 in a beautifully renovated theatre space was the Theatre de Lys on Christopher Street. After a few undistinguished presentations, Stanley Chase and Carmen Capalbo opened a highly successful production of *The Three Penny Opera* by Bertolt Brecht, Marc Blitzstein, and Kurt Weill in 1954. The production continued for almost seven years, long beyond the time when Lucille Lortel purchased the theatre in 1955. Under her proprietorship the Theatre de Lys has housed, over the years, a variety of productions, and the theatre itself is still one of the more comfortable of the Off-Broadway houses.

For a few years, beginning in 1956, David Ross ran what came to be called "the American home of Chekhov" at the tiny Fourth Street Theatre in the Village, while at the same time William and Elizabeth Landis devoted the Downtown Theatre, immediately next door, to productions of George Bernard Shaw's plays. The Greenwich Mews Theatre, in the basement of the Village Presbyterian Church on West Thirteenth Street, presented a lively series of plays during the 1950s, including Loften Mitchell's *A Land Beyond the River* (1957) and the widely heralded *Me, Candido!* by Walt Anderson (1956).

The Cherry Lane Theatre on Commerce Street, once a farm silo, then a box factory, was converted into a theatre in the 1920s by Edna St. Vincent Millay and a group of her friends and was saved from demolition in 1952 through purchase by Kenneth Carroad and other concerned Villagers. It has seen a variety of productions and producing units in its long history, and many new performers and directors have worked on its stage. Under the producing banner of Edward Albee, Richard Barr, and Clinton Wilder in the 1960s, it produced the early plays of Beckett, Genet, Ionesco, and Pinter, and gave a hearing to new American playwrights as well. In recent years it has housed David Mamet's *Sexual Perversity in Chicago* (1976), and since it has now been designated a historic landmark building it will no doubt continue to house Off-Broadway productions for the foreseeable future. Another Off-Broadway house still in use since the 1950s is the Orpheum Theatre at 126 Second Avenue, where *Little Mary Sunshine* ran for three years. It more recently housed the very successful run of *Your Own Thing* (1968) by Hal Hester and Danny Apolinar.

In the closing years of the 1960s, there were twenty-eight Off-Broadway theatres operating, some in the institutional style described above, but most as booking houses owned by a variety of landlords and rented by them to individual producers. The various successes scored in Off-Broadway houses since the inception of the movement called it to the attention of the various theatrical unions, who moved in to regularize treatment and payment of union members. By 1957, Actors' Equity had instituted a sliding scale for actors' salary minimums based on the potential gross of theatre revenue, increased required rehearsal pay, and mandated a package of benefits. Success and the improvements in theatre ambience and audience comfort such success seems to require, caused a rise in rents and maintenance. Through the 1960s, Off Broadway became more like a miniature Broadway than the experimental, antiestablishment movement of its early years. Production costs escalated from an average of $6,000 in the early days to $20,000 in the last years of the 1960s, and by the end of the 1970s they were twice that amount. Increasing costs almost invariably dictate increasing caution, particularly for houses of limited seating capacity—a caution manifested by the production, increasingly, of shows sure to be "hits" after the manner of Broadway. *The Fantasticks*, for instance, has been running at the Sullivan Street Playhouse for almost ten years, and *Scrambled Feet* is a long-running venture at the Village Gate. Or Off-Broadway producers have been led to seek foundation and/or government grant support for a particular "idea" theatre, as has Wynn Handman at his American Place Theatre. Handman's theatre began at St. Clement's Church in 1964 with the idea of having outstanding writers work in the dramatic form, and it had a signal success with Robert Lowell's *The Old Glory* (1964). It moved to a new theatre in an office building on West Forty-sixth Street in 1971. American Place Theatre has always been devoted to the production and development of new playwrights such as Frank Gagliano, Ed Bullins, Bruce Jay Friedman, William Alfred, Ronald Ribman, Anne Sexton, Joyce Carol Oates, Jack Gelber, Philip Hayes Dean. But Handman has always had to spend much of his time raising non-box-office money, as indeed have Papp and Theodore Mann, Robert Kalfin (Chelsea Theatre Center, founded in 1965), Lynne Meadow (at the Manhattan Theatre Club from 1971), and several others. Frequently enough to keep the hope ever before Off-Broadway eyes, productions have moved from that area to hit status on Broadway: *Hair*, *That Championship Season*, *Much Ado About Nothing*, *A Chorus Line* had been profitable Off-Broadway ventures for Joseph Papp; the Manhattan Theatre Club put the popular *Ain't Misbehavin'* on Broadway; Hugh Leonard's *DA* was originally a successful venture of the Hudson Guild Theatre; Samm Art Williams's *Home* arrived on Broadway from the Negro Ensemble Theatre; and there were others.

By and large, the adventure, the daring, the fervor has gone out of Off Broadway, except in a few rare instances like the Public Theatre, where the profitability of some ventures and the unexcelled ability of Papp to raise both public and private funds has made continuing experiment possible in a protected environment. It is inaccurate to say, of course, that Off Broadway has not produced good revivals of musicals, of ancient and modern classics, of new American and foreign plays, and has proved a fruitful field for the discovery and initial development of young actors, directors, designers,

and producers. And certainly most Off-Broadway productions are now accorded the same public, trade, and critical attention as are Broadway productions.

For the last ten or fifteen years, however, New York theatre audiences have looked for the new, the unconventional, the experimental in a group of theatres called by the rather awkward title of Off-Off-Broadway, a name said to have been coined by Jerry Tallmar, then critic for the *Village Voice*, in 1960. A recent count shows at least ninety active Off-Off-Broadway producing units as compared with less than a third that number which can be classified Off Broadway. Off-Off-Broadway is a very fluid world. New groups are always in formation; some disappear each season, never to be seen again. It is peopled by avant-garde actors and directors who moved into coffeehouses, lofts, churches, cellars, and storefronts to deal with theatrical elements no longer welcome in Off-Broadway houses. Many units have attempted a continuity of style, or of material, or of point of view from production to production. Several dedicated people have spent the greater portion of their professional lives working in Off-Off-Broadway; many others move freely from this to other forms of theatre and back again as their professional commitments permit. Since anyone can make an Off-Off-Broadway theatre by the simple act of declaring that one exists, quality varies from the rankest of amateur to trained and skilled professional. Geographically, the units are concentrated below Twenty-sixth Street in Chelsea, SoHo, NoHo, and the East and West Village, but an increasing number have been appearing in Clinton and the Upper East and West sides of Manhattan. Several groups have no permanent home, just a more or less permanent yearning to "make theatre" in a new way. Most have been influenced by camp and pop art, by American folk art, the movies, the theories of Artaud and Brecht, by Impressionism and Expressionism. Generally, what has evolved, according to some critics and observers, is a new aesthetic and a new means of experience.

The Caffe Cino at 31 Cornelia Street in the Village set the style and the ambience and is usually credited as the starting point for the Off-Off-Broadway movement. The date is December 1958. It is true that Julian Beck and Judith Malina had begun the Living Theatre at the Cherry Lane in 1951, opening with a production of Gertrude Stein's *Doctor Faustus Lights the Lights*, then moving to a basement on Wooster Street in 1954, and that

Julie Bovasso had founded her short-lived Tempo Theatre in the latter year, to present the works of Ghelderode, Genet, and Ionesco to American audiences. But it was Joe Cino's coffeehouse that became the real progenitor of Off-Off-Broadway. Part of the reason was the absolute freedom artists found there. Cino had not intended to create a theatre; he merely wanted a place where he could be surrounded by his friends "in the arts," as he put it. There was simply a central open space surrounded by tables and chairs where poets, musicians, actors—artists of all kinds—could present their works and be paid by passing the hat among the patrons. Cino personally chose the "acts"; the performances of plays grew almost inadvertently from actors reading scenes. But once begun, play production grew to take over the space. In the first four years, the repertoire was eclectic: Sartre, Inge, Chayefsky, Wilder, Aristophanes, Genet, Anouilh, Wilde, Molière, Shaw and a heavy infusion of Tennessee Williams. An occasional new young playwright's work was presented, but it was not until 1963, when Cino found Lanford Wilson—or Wilson found Cino—that the emphasis shifted to the production of new plays by new American playwrights that indelibly inscribed Caffe Cino in theatre history. Wilson's *So Long at the Fair* opened in August 1963; there was another new, untitled Wilson play in October, *Home Free!* in January, *The Madness of Lady Bright* in May, *Ludlow Fair* in February of 1965, *This Is the Rill Speaking* in July. Other new playwrights encouraged by Joe Cino include: David Starkweather, Barbara Guest, Michael Smith, Tom O'Horgan (who later became a director), Paul Foster, Lee Kalcheim, Ross Alexander, Robert Patrick, Jean-Claude van Itallie (before he went to the Open Theatre), Sally Ordway, Tom Eyen, Michael Benedikt, and John Guare. It is an impressive list. The pace was hectic, but the atmosphere was warm, personal, and friendly—like Joe Cino himself. When he committed suicide on 2 April 1967, his friends and fellow workers tried to carry on the work, but the heart had gone out of the place and it finally ground to a halt early in 1968. Having received much support through the columns of the *Village Voice*, Caffe Cino had achieved a kind of cult status in its ten years of vigorous life. Something of the Cino spirit lived on from 1967 to 1971 in the backroom of the Old Reliable Tavern on East Third Street, where Robert Patrick was a resident playwright and Neil Flanagan (who had played 205 performances of *The Madness of Lady Bright* at Caffe Cino) the resident chief actor. The works of many new playwrights were also presented at the Old Reliable Tavern: Sam Shepard's *Cowboys #2* and John Ford Noonan's *Rainbows for Sale* are only two of a long list.

Meanwhile, Julian Beck and Judith Malina had moved to a second floor loft space at Fourteenth Street and Sixth Avenue in 1959, and had mounted a production of Jack Gelber's *The Connection*. Its contemporaneity and production style made it popular with audiences, and when *Life* magazine did an article on the production and the 160-seat theatre space, the Living Theatre became the center of the American avant-garde. By 1963 they had done fifteen more works, but were in trouble with the Internal Revenue Service and with city authorities. The company then spent four years in Europe, returning in 1968. They did a season at the Brooklyn Academy, presenting four productions, two of which (*Antigone* and *Frankenstein*) had been remade to their avowedly revolutionary pattern, and two of which had been developed out of company work: *Mysteries and Smaller Pieces* and *Paradise Now*. By 1972 the company had disbanded. But over a long period of time they had declared themselves (and acted upon the declaration) opposed to the power structure of Western society and politics; they worked as a theatrical commune to create images which would surround and involve audiences and move them to action.

Stanislavsky once said that the spirited artistic life of a theatre organization is limited to twenty-five years. In America it often seems less. The Open Theatre is another example of a vigorous and innovative Off-Off-Broadway company which began in 1963 and had dispersed by the mid-1970s. Joseph Chaikin had been an actor with the Becks in the early days, but founded his own theatre group in 1963 to, as he has said, "redefine the limits of the stage experience, to unfix them . . . to encourage and inspire the playwrights who work with us . . . to develop the ensemble." Working with a fairly stable group of performers, and a few playwrights (primarily Megan Terry, Mariá Irene Fornés, and Jean-Claude van Itallie), performances were developed around an idea, an action, or a theme: war, death, creation, mechanization, etc. Actors, playwrights, and directors worked together to develop the performances. There was no emphasis upon character development or individual psychology; the scenes were not sequential or structured; the "play" was rather a succession of *action blocs* having associational relationships designed to confront the audience with its own aliveness in a world of change, as Chaikin says. The most effective of these "creations" proved to be Megan Terry's *Viet Rock*, van Itallie's *America Hurrah!* and *The Serpent*. When a performance was ready for an audience the Open Theatre performed in any proper and available space, like the Martinique Theatre. It was five years after the founding of the group before the actors were paid regularly, and then by virtue of grant money. But none had been interested in commercial success at any rate. The artistic vitality and exploration of the Open Theatre redefined many of the traditional limits of theatre.

There are other important groups founded in the 1960s which are still in existence. The most renowned is that centering around Ellen Stewart—La Mama—by now wreathed in legend, and deserving it. In 1962 she and Paul Foster rented a basement on East Ninth Street—she to have a boutique for the clothes she designed, he to "run a theatre" in the same space. There was room for twenty-five seats. Inevitably drawn into the play-producing side of the business (with little in her background to inform her), she fell in love with theatre and the idea of "doing plays." Leonard Melfi's *Lazy Baby Susan* was first presented in that cellar. The next year Stewart opened the Cafe La Mama in a second floor loft on Second Avenue, moving again in 1964 to another similar location just a bit further up the avenue, where there was room for seventy-four seats. Along with a variety of one-act plays of known playwrights, the Cafe La Mama also presented new works by Ross Alexander, Paul Foster, James Eliason, Rick Seay, Tad Mosel, Tom Eyen, David Starkweather, Tom O'Horgan and, in 1965, Murray Schisgal's *The Typist*. Lanford Wilson's *The Rimers of Eldritch* was performed in July 1966. Later that year Tom O'Horgan took a group of La Mama performers to Europe where they were hailed as the "New American Theatre." Early in 1967, Rochelle Owens's *Futz* was presented, and La Mama was on the map in New York. Megan Terry worked there, along with many others: Adrienne Kennedy, Israel Horovitz, Jerry Ragni, Julie Bovasso, Charles Ludlum, Wilford Leach, Ed Bullins, John Michael Tebelak—the list of playwrights whom La Mama discovered, encouraged, and supported is seemingly endless. Paul Foster's *Tom Paine* moved to a run Off Broadway in 1968; O'Horgan directed *Hair* on Broadway the same year. La Mama was established, and grant money began to flow. By 1970, Cafe La Mama had become La Mama Experimental Theatre Club and had moved into a renovated building on East Fourth Street with two theatres tucked inside.

Another building was later added. La Mama has become a worldwide organization, and Ellen Stewart has been listed by Esquire magazine as one of the 100 most important women in the world. Her Experimental Theatre Club remains to this day a mecca for theatre artists who wish to try innovative techniques in playwriting, acting, directing, designing. The purpose of La Mama has remained remarkably consistent through the years; it is one of the best examples of the Off-Off-Broadway spirit.

Another is the Judson Poets' Theater at whose center is the immensely talented Al Carmines. The theatre began in the fall of 1961 when the minister and congregation of the Judson Memorial Church invited Carmines to initiate a theatre program there. The first performance was that of Joel Oppenheimer's *The Great American Desert*, on a budget of $37.50. The next year Carmines, in collaboration with Lawrence Kornfeld, the director, began composing. With the integration of the new Judson Dance Theater was thus begun the kind of integrated arts performances for which the Judson has become justly famous. By the 1963-1964 season the new style was set, and Michael Smith in the *Village Voice*, writing about the Judson, said "Everything that happens has the casual inevitability of great art." Derek Walcott's *Women at the Tomb* first appeared at the Judson, as did Roslyn Drexler's *Home Movies*, Rochelle Owens's *The String Game*, Ronald Tavel's *Gorilla Queen*—to name only a few. The critical press is always interested in what goes on at the Judson Poets' Theater, to no little extent because of Carmines's talent as a composer. Jerry Tallmer in the *New York Post* once called him "the best living American composer."

Other Off-Off-Broadway groups founded in the 1960s and still in existence are Theatre Genesis (1964) at St. Mark Church-in-the-Bowery where, in addition to many new works by playwrights mentioned heretofore, Murray Mednick was introduced; the Chelsea Theatre Center (1965—Robert Kalfin, director) which produces in both Brooklyn and Manhattan; Douglas Turner Ward's Negro Ensemble Company (1966) from which Samm Art Williams's *Home* arrived on Broadway in 1980; Richard Schechner's The Performance Group (1968), whose most outstanding success remains *Dionysus in '69*; and Charles Ludlum's Ridiculous Theatrical Company (1967), which grew out of an earlier group begun by Ron Tavel and John Vaccaro. One should also mention Christopher Martin's Classic Stage Company, Gene Feist's Roundabout Theatre, Marshall Mason's Circle Repertory (from which Lanford Wilson's *Talley's Folly* arrived on Broadway and won the Pulitzer Prize in 1980), and Robert Moss's Playwrights Horizons (producing in Queens as well as Manhattan) because of their continuity and the excellence of their work.

By 1971 the Off-Off-Broadway scene had arrived at the point where Off Broadway had been in 1949. The Off-Off-Broadway Alliance (OOBA) was formed in 1972 by a group of more than fifty theatres with the common objective of focusing public attention on the movement and of effectively raising funds to support the work. Over the years since then, it has proved sporadically effective in both aims. In the last few years, the unions—especially Actors' Equity—have been trying to exercise the same control over Off-Off-Broadway as they had earlier imposed on Off Broadway. The outcome of this attempt is not yet certain.

To list here all the Off-Off-Broadway companies, or even to name those currently outstanding, would serve no useful purpose. On any given weekend during the season in New York (some theatres perform only on weekends), the Manhattan theatregoer is likely to have a choice among a hundred or more performances: thirty to thirty-five on Broadway, twenty to twenty-five Off Broadway, and fifty or more Off-Off-Broadway. It is the presence of this number and variety of plays, playhouses, and performances that makes New York City the theatre capital of the United States, if not—indeed—of the world.

–Vera Mowry Roberts

Appendix II:
Major Regional Theatres

Actors Theatre of Louisville

Located in the heart of downtown Louisville, Kentucky, near the banks of the Ohio River, Actors Theatre of Louisville (ATL) serves not only as the dominant arts organization in a community strongly committed to artistic endeavor but also as an institutional anchor in the revitalization of the central city. From its modest birth in a makeshift facility in 1964, Actors Theatre has drawn upon broadly based popular and corporate support to develop into an extremely active, flourishing institution boasting impressive facilities and one of the highest per capita subscription rates in the history of the regional theatre movement. In recent years ATL has gained national and international recognition for its extensive program for the production of new plays and the development of new playwrights, the scope of which has established the company as a leader in the fostering of original writing for the American theatre.

Actors Theatre of Louisville was established through the merger in 1964 of two struggling fledgling professional companies, Actors, Incorporated and Theatre Louisville. In their very brief existence, neither group had established a significant production record, nor had either reached a point of financial stability; in order merely to survive, they merged under the joint leadership of Richard Block and Ewel Cornett, and in the 1964-1965 season they presented a program of six plays in a small downtown loft seating only 100 persons. The program for that first season contained a very conventional selection of plays from the standard twentieth-century repertoire, such as Tennessee Williams's *The Glass Menagerie* and George Bernard Shaw's *Arms and the Man*, establishing a pattern of play selection that would continue until the development of the new play program in 1977. Catering to the expectations of a relatively unsophisticated audience, ATL attracted 419 season subscribers in its first year in operation, producing its season on a budget of $74,000.

Richard Block became the sole artistic director of the theatre after its first season, shifting operations in 1965 to a larger facility, a converted railway station. By 1967 the popularity of the theatre under Block's leadership attracted a list of season subscribers totaling 5,700 to an inconvenient, inadequate facility seating only 350. The most daring play selected for production during that season was Samuel Beckett's *Endgame*, but the balance of the season was made up of more typical, conventional choices such as Eugene O'Neill's *Long Day's Journey Into Night* and Robert Penn Warren's *All the King's Men*. Having built an audience through appeals to community pride and an undemanding selection of plays, however, Block was unable to maintain and to raise the artistic standards of the company; and after the 1967-1968 season, support for the theatre began to wane, with the most obvious symptom being a marked decline in attendance.

By 1969 the theatre's board of directors had concluded that new leadership was needed if Actors Theatre was to regain the support it needed for further development. They selected Jon Jory, co-founder in 1965 of the Long Wharf Theatre in New Haven, Connecticut, as Actors Theatre's producing director. Jory, son of film actor Victor Jory, entered the 1969-1970 season with these stated goals: to upgrade the quality of ATL productions, to expand the scope of the theatre's production and service programs, and to increase contributions to theatre on a national scale. Midway through that season, however, the very future of Actors Theatre was cast into doubt by the announcement that its facility was to be demolished to make way for a connector road. With the vocal support of the citizens and the business leaders of the community, Jory was able to obtain a two-year delay in the implementation of those plans, during which period he and the ATL board of directors planned and executed a move into the facilities the theatre occupies at present.

The site selected for the permanent facility contained two structures. Of principal interest was the old Bank of Louisville building, designed and built by Gideon Shryock, the father of Greek Revival architecture in Kentucky; completed in 1837, this building has been designated a Registered National Historic Landmark. Adjacent to the Bank of Louisville building stood an 1860-vintage red brick warehouse building, in which most of the theatre's production and administrative spaces could be located. That site was selected for four reasons: it was downtown, it was easily accessible, it could be converted for theatrical use at a reasonable cost, and its selection would guarantee the preservation of a significant architectural landmark. Thus, Actors Theatre became one of the first institutions in Louisville to make a commitment to the restoration of the decaying central city; the fact that it has continued to attract a substantial number of citizens back into the downtown area has been a significant factor in the ongoing revitalization of the riverfront area.

Having chosen its future home, Actors Theatre launched a capital fund drive to raise the $1.7 million needed to complete the planned conversion; within six months, $1.2 million had been raised from local sources, and an additional $360,000 was obtained through a Ford Foundation challenge grant. The conversion was begun; and today Actors Theatre boasts one of the most impressive lobbies in the country, with the old Bank of Louisville rotunda serving as the lobby for ATL's principal stage, the 637-seat Pamela Brown Auditorium, which features a modified thrust stage configuration. In the adjacent former warehouse building are housed production shops, administrative offices, a bar/restaurant in the basement, and—on the third floor—ATL's second stage, the

161-seat three-quarter arena Victor Jory Theatre.

By the time Actors Theatre vacated its old railroad station facility and moved to its permanent quarters, Jory had reversed the trend toward declining attendance and had increased the number of season subscriptions to 9,000; in addition, he had expanded the theatre's list of activities to include a children's theatre series and a rudimentary program of tours throughout the state of Kentucky. After a brief period of consolidation, ATL was designated the State Theatre of Kentucky in 1973, and another period of rapid growth began. By 1980, the theatre's operating budget had increased to $1.7 million (compared to Jory's initial $235,000 in 1969), a remarkable 70 percent of which was derived from earned income. The subscription audience had increased to 18,700 for the seven-play series in the Pamela Brown Auditorium; at that level, season subscriptions accounted for fully 96 percent of the available seats for ATL's main season. Total annual attendance at all Actors Theatre productions, including the "Off Broadway" series in the Victor Jory Theatre and the five-week regional tour, had reached 225,000; in addition, several cooperative nonperformance programs had

Actors Theatre of Louisville

been established with local elementary and secondary schools as well as with regional colleges and universities, through which ATL personnel conducted workshops, short courses, or discussions of the production program. Perhaps the most innovative program, though, was ATL's Senior Players, funded through the federal Comprehensive Employment and Training Act (CETA) program from 1977 to 1979; this performing group, composed entirely of senior citizens, presented a free forty-minute program based on their own life experiences, as well as a children's show. The former production proved to be one of the most popular of all ATL presentations.

Through all of these activities, Actors Theatre of Louisville was perceived as an integral part of the life of its community, and it drew upon widely based financial and political support. In addition to its substantial earned income, its principal funding source was the Greater Louisville Fund for the Arts, the oldest united arts fund in the country, having been formed in 1948 primarily for the purpose of supporting the Louisville Orchestra. Through the Fund for the Arts, ATL and ten other member agencies receive financial support from approximately three hundred businesses and corporations and from more than seven thousand individuals. In addition, several local corporations have sponsored specific projects and productions, and the number of such donations has increased steadily during recent years.

The generally high quality of its artistic work throughout its recent history has provided the foundation for the exceptionally rapid growth of Actors Theatre, but it is equally true that its present vitality and stability is due principally to the excellence of ATL's administration, which must be ranked among the best in the nation. As producing director Jon Jory serves as the chief executive officer of the theatre; but effective control of management policy and practice is shared, to an exceptional extent, by a tripartite team which also includes Alexander Speer, administrative director, and Trish Pugh, associate director. Speer joined the Actors Theatre staff in 1965 and Pugh in 1969, along with Jory; thus, the ATL management team has worked together for more than a decade, during which time they have developed a close rapport, a shared commitment to common goals, and an effective working method based upon both individual expertise and mutual consultation.

In his capacity as administrative director, Speer holds principal responsibility for all financial and physical plant operations of the organization.

Jon Jory

His specific duties include supervision of the budget, liaison responsibility between the board of directors and the administrative staff, and the management of all of the theatre's facilities, including the Starving Artist Bar/Restaurant located in the basement of the theatre. In addition to other outside service commitments Speer has served on the Executive Committee and the Equity Liaison Committee of the League of Resident Theatres.

As associate director, Trish Pugh is primarily responsible for what she refers to as "the people side of the business": she is in charge of all of Actors Theatre's public relations and audience development activities. With the subscription rate she has built, there is little room for growth, and so Pugh's primary concern is to maintain that rate in spite of the inevitable annual turnover among subscribers. In addition to her basic responsibilities Pugh also supervises all volunteer activities and coordinates the theatre's guest artist and speaker programs. She has served as a consultant in audience development for the Foundation for the Extension and Development of the American Professional Theatre (FEDAPT), sharing her expertise with such notable theatres as the Dallas Theater Center and the Eugene O'Neill Memorial Theater Center.

Jon Jory's principal responsibilities as producing director include the ultimate authority over all activities of the theatre, although he has chosen to delegate a considerable portion of effective authority to Speer and to Pugh. Jory's system of organization, however, reserves his final authority on all artistic matters, especially including the selection of plays and the hiring of the artistic staff and the acting company. Under Jory's direction, Actors Theatre hires a core acting company of twelve, for whom the average period of residence is three years; this company is regularly supplemented by actors hired to fill specific roles. Jory has also chosen to direct a large proportion of ATL's productions, particularly in the Pamela Brown series. He has also served on the Board of Directors of the Theatre

Lobby of the Pamela Brown Auditorium

Communications Group and on the Partnership Coordination Panel of the National Endowment for the Arts.

The exceptionally effective administration of Actors Theatre, though, is due less to the individual abilities of its team of managers than to a creative "blurring" of spheres of authority. Jory acknowledges that his system might not be appropriate for a more traditional business enterprise, and that it depends heavily upon close teamwork which requires many years to develop. It is, in short, a system which would be available to very few arts organizations in the nation because of the typical rapid turnover rate among administrative personnel. Because Actors

Theatre has been able to develop such a system, though, it has achieved an unusually effective level of integration between artistic and economic considerations and a closely coordinated program which simultaneously maintains strong popular support and a coherent, if somewhat commercial, artistic style.

As might be expected, the institutional artistic style of Actors Theatre is markedly similar to Jon Jory's personal style as a director. The early pattern of play selection at ATL, heavily weighted toward conventional modern plays, has continued under Jory's artistic direction. Thus, except for occasional ventures into the classical or the avant-garde, before the establishment in 1977 of its new play festival Actors Theatre chose to produce scripts drawn from the conventional commercial repertoire, with particular stress on comedies. Jory himself had consistent success in directing comedies, although the wide critical approval of his staging of the premiere and New York productions of Marsha Norman's *Getting Out* demonstrated his skill with serious material as well. That standard modern drama, and especially comic drama, was well suited to the artistic style of Jory and of his theatre was clear; that it was also to the taste of the local audience was regularly demonstrated at the box office and in the subscription list. It was notable, in fact, that a substantial number of season subscriptions were sold each year even before the final selection of plays was announced, an indication that the audience fully expected that each season would be very similar to those of the past. It was widely observed that ATL had produced only four premodern plays between 1975 and 1980, the last being staged in 1978; and the mixed critical and popular response those productions received clearly pointed to an artistic level well suited to contemporary material but not broad enough to accommodate the demands of the classical repertory. Still, the specific premodern plays selected were relatively consistent with regular Actors Theatre inclinations: *Oedipus Rex* (1975), *Much Ado About Nothing* (1976), *The Comedy of Errors* (1978), and especially an outer space rock musical adaptation of *Titus Andronicus* (1977).

The twin theatrical functions of teaching and of entertaining have been noted since the days of Horace; by this measure, Actors Theatre had made a conscious choice of artistic principle which informed both its selection of plays and its development of a characteristic artistic style. As Jon Jory put it: "We are in the business of entertaining. I've always hated the idea of educating an audience, I suppose because I loathed being educated all my life." That fundamentally commercial criterion did not automatically preclude literary merit or artistic integrity in the ATL production program, because Jory's definition of "entertaining" was broad enough to accommodate his desire "to show our audience things that they may not have seen before or have found any emotional or intellectual use for, in hopes that they'll relate to it." That desire partly accounts for Jory's extensive commitment of his theatre's resources, since 1975, to the support of new playwrights and the production of new plays: "We don't feel we are trying to educate our audi-

into the artistic and financial centerpiece of his organization.

As part of its 1975-1976 season, Actors Theatre had produced one new play (Paul Hunter's *Scott and Zelda*) and the American premiere of Charles Marowitz's version of *Hamlet* in its Victor Jory Theatre series. From that beginning, the enterprise now known as Actors Theatre's New Play Program quickly expanded to include four distinct elements: a national playwriting contest attracting nearly two thousand submissions each year; workshops and other developmental programs for

Pamela Brown Auditorium

ence or cure them of some unnamed disease with doses of contemporary drama. New plays aren't castor oil. They are exciting and that seems to be as much justification and relevance as we need." That the Actors Theatre audience found the production of original plays exciting was evident in the box-office figures for the annual Festival of New American Plays, and in the attendance at the other premieres which began to grace the production schedule. Jory had succeeded in converting a reputed financial gamble—an extensive investment in the production of untested, unproven material—

promising young playwrights; a commissioning program which developed over sixty works by American authors by 1980; and, at the center of the program, the Festival of New American Plays. To administer these activities, Actors Theatre formed a Literary Department which quickly grew to include a full-time literary manager, two full-time and several part-time salaried assistants, and a large number of volunteer readers and workers.

For the annual Great American Play contest a cash prize was established for the author of the winning manuscript; by 1980, the size of that prize had increased to $5,000. In keeping with general literary policy at Actors Theatre, the final selection each year was made by Jon Jory after a preliminary screening by the literary management staff. Although contest winners were not guaranteed production of their plays by the theatre, each winner between 1977 and 1979 was featured in the Festival of New American Plays: Frederick Bailey's *The Bridgehead* and Marsha Norman's *Getting Out* in 1977; Beth Henley's *Crimes of the Heart* and Olwen Wymark's *Find Me* in 1978; and John Pielmeier's *Agnes of God* and Adale Edling Shank's *Sunset/Sunrise* in 1979.

Marsha Norman's *Getting Out* serves as an example of the many potential benefits of this type of program for the playwright, the theatre organization, and the community. Marsha Norman is a native of Louisville, and while that fact was a source of great community pride the subsequent success of her play demonstrated that its inherent quality alone could justify its selection for the prize and for production. After its premiere in the Festival of New American Plays during the 1977-1978 season, *Getting Out* was produced at the Mark Taper Forum in Los Angeles and at the Theatre de Lys in New York, under the direction of Jon Jory. The play was selected as the Best Play in a Regional Theatre by the American Critics' Association, was published in *10 Best Plays of 1977-78*, and was the runner-up for the Susan Smith Blackburn Prize of 1978. National recognition was gained both by the quality of the play and by the phenomenon of a regional theatre producing an outstanding work by a local talent. As the crowning achievement, in 1980 the ATL production of *Getting Out* was selected by the U. S. State Department as the American representative in theatre festivals in Yugoslavia and in Ireland, and the production later traveled to Israel before returning to this country.

Simple numbers provide a clear indication of the extent of Actors Theatre's commitment to original works after 1975. Exclusive of productions in the Festival of New American Plays, in the five seasons beginning in 1975-1976 ATL staged fifty-one workshop productions, six American premieres of foreign plays, and twenty productions of original scripts. Notable examples of premiere productions include Brian Clark's *Whose Life Is It Anyway?* and D. L. Cogburn's *The Gin Game*, 1978 Tony Award nominee and winner of the 1978 Pulitzer Prize for drama after premiering in the 1977 festival.

It is in the intensely concentrated activity of the Festival of New American Plays that Actors Theatre's dedication to original work may be most clearly observed. The first true festival was staged in the 1977 season, when four works (including *The Gin Game*) were staged. That number increased to six in 1978, and to eight in 1979. During the five-week 1980 festival, when eight new works were premiered, ninety-four performances were given before a total audience of nearly 30,000.

One notable aspect of the 1979 and 1980 festivals was the production each year of an evening of commissioned, thematically related short plays averaging about ten minutes in length apiece. The first of those collections, *Holidays*, included ten playlets, each of which dealt with the meaning of, or events during, a specific holiday. While the quality of writing represented was markedly uneven, the list of contributing authors contained the names of many of America's most prestigious modern playwrights: Ray Aranha, Tom Eyen, John Guare, Oliver Hailey, Israel Horovitz, Preston Jones, Marsha Norman, Megan Terry, Douglas Turner Ward, and Lanford Wilson. It was reasonably clear that the restrictions under which the authors had been required to work (a severe limit on length, a predetermined subject, certain casting and production limits) had reduced the effectiveness of the work in several cases, but the production was sufficiently popular and challenging that the concept was repeated the following year. The second collection was titled *The America Project*, and for this production ten foreign playwrights submitted scripts interpreting various aspects of the American experience; the authors represented were Carol Bolt (Canada), Alexander Buzo (Australia), John Byrne (Scotland), Brian Clark (England), Keith Dewhurst (England), Gordon Dryland (New Zealand), Brian Friel (Ireland), Athol Fugard (South Africa), Stewart Parker (Ireland), and Wole Soyinka (Nigeria).

As a result of its Festival of New American Plays, Actors Theatre of Louisville gained national and international recognition it had previously lacked. Once it became clear that the national press would be interested in reporting on the festival, ATL accommodated the needs of out-of-town visitors in order to attract a larger number of reporters and critics: by scheduling a marathon series of performances during a selected weekend during the festival, the theatre was able to offer an opportunity to observe seven premiere productions during a three-day period. The result surpassed expectations, with observers arriving not only from this country but also from around the world, and the resulting series of articles and reviews served to consolidate and expand upon the gains the theatre had previously obtained in its own region. Largely as a result of the festival, ATL also won the 1978 Margo Jones Award, given annually for the production of new plays and the encouragement of new playwrights; the 1979 James N. Vaughan Memorial Award, given for exceptional achievement and contribution to the American theatre; and the 1980 Tony Award for regional theatres.

In choosing to devote its efforts to the fostering of new writers, Actors Theatre of Louisville came of age. In a single step, an excellent regional theatre had created a distinctive role for itself among its fellow companies, gained renown for the value and the quality of its work, and made a significant contribution to the future of the American theatre.

–Albert J. Harris Jr.

The American Conservatory Theatre
San Francisco

The American Conservatory Theatre in San Francisco is not only a resident professional company playing in true repertory but, as its name implies, also a conservatory, dedicated to a continuing program of theatre training for students from all over the United States. According to William Ball, its founder and general director, the "primary goal of the company is to bring each actor and student ever closer to the fulfillment of his own potential and, by extension, to help raise the standards of American acting as a whole." From its inception, the company has maintained its dual objectives as a producing organization and a full-time professional conservatory. One description of A.C.T. states: "Seeking to create an energetic atmosphere which would support and encourage theatre artists, William Ball has built a company in which actors teach, teachers act, directors act and actors direct, while students learn professional techniques and discipline through close association with experienced theatre artists." Several A.C.T. productions have been aired on Public Television: Dylan Thomas's *Under Milk Wood* in 1966, George Bernard Shaw's *Misalliance* in 1967, Anna Marie Barlow's Civil War play *Glory! Hallelujah!* and a sixty-minute documentary on the company, *A.C.T. Now*, in 1969, Edmond Rostand's *Cyrano de Bergerac* in 1973, and Shakespeare's *The Taming of the Shrew* in 1975—the last two on the "Theatre in America" series. Regional and international touring complements the company's San Francisco activities. In 1976, A.C.T. was sponsored by the State Department on a tour of the Soviet Union in celebration of the United States bicentennial. In 1978, the company was the first American resident theatre to tour Japan. In 1979, A.C.T. received the United States Institute for

Theatre Technology Award for Excellence and a Tony award for sustained theatrical excellence and commitment to the development of American theatre artists. During the presentation of the Tony, the League of New York Theatres and Producers American Wing cited the company's history of excellence "in presenting the finest classics of world drama with imagination, professionalism and boldly theatrical style."

The company's founder, William Ball (born 29 April 1931 in Chicago), graduated from Carnegie Institute of Technology (now Carnegie-Mellon University) in Pittsburgh with a B.A. in acting and design in 1953, and an M.A. in directing in 1955. While he was a student, he made his acting debut in 1948 in Anton Chekhov's *Uncle Vanya*. From 1948 to 1950 he was assistant designer as well as actor with Margaret Webster's Shakespeare touring company. He received a Fulbright scholarship in 1953 to study repertory theatre in England and Europe. He also won a Ford Foundation grant which enabled him to tour the leading regional theatres throughout the country as a visiting director. In the following year he directed Shakespeare's *As You Like It* in Yellow Springs, Ohio. From the Carnegie Institute of Technology he received an NBC/RCA Directors Fellowship in 1955. In the next year, he acted for the first time in New York as Acaste in Molière's *The Misanthrope* at the Theatre East. In 1958, twenty-seven-year-old Ball received a Ford Foundation grant for directing; the following year he was awarded an Obie for his direction of Chekhov's *Ivanov*. He continued to gain directing experience at such diverse theatres as the Alley Theatre in Houston, the Actor's Workshop in San Francisco, the Arena Stage in Washington, D.C., and the New York City Opera, where he directed Mozart's *Così fan tutte* in 1959. He has won two Lola D'Annunzio awards for his direction of Dylan Thomas's *Under Milk Wood* in 1961 and Luigi Pirandello's *Six Characters in Search of an Author* in 1963. In addition, he received the Outer Circle Critics Award for his direction of Molière's *Tartuffe* at the Lincoln Center Drama Repertory Theatre in 1965, where he, according to one critic, "redeemed the otherwise disastrous second season."

Ball was, therefore, well qualified to lead the American Conservatory Theatre, which he founded in 1965. He worked out a three-year joint program with Earle Gister, head of the drama department at the Carnegie Institute of Technology, and Richard Hoover, the managing director of the Pittsburgh Playhouse. According to Henry Hewes, Ball "pledged himself to the production of twelve plays at the Pittsburgh Playhouse's two theatres with a company of outstanding actors and promising newcomers who received fellowships to train and work with the company." A.C.T. received a Rockefeller Foundation grant of $115,000 as well as funds from the Pittsburgh-based Andrew Mellon Foundation. The advantage for Earle Gister to have a company such as A.C.T. in Pittsburgh was that he would have a number of professionals from A.C.T. to draw upon to teach supplementary drama courses. For Richard Hoover, having a repertory company in his theatres meant a secure season, in the sense of having an interesting selection of plays with established actors whose potentials could be expanded. Also, having a residential theatre company would ensure steady local support as the Pittsburgh audience became familiar with A.C.T.

The premiere season began on 15 July 1965 at the Craft Theatre and the Hamlet Street Theatre in Pittsburgh. The first six plays produced were Molière's *Tartuffe*, Edward Albee's *Tiny Alice*, Pirandello's *Six Characters in Search of an Author*, Jean Anouilh's *Antigone*, Tennessee Williams's *The Rose Tattoo*, and André Obey's *Noah*. In *Saturday Review* (4 September 1965) Hewes reported that "the attendance for all performances and previews has averaged 62 per cent of capacity, a figure which Mr. Hoover considers very good. The critical reception has been favorable with the Molière and the Pirandello receiving the highest praise." Hewes commended Ball's production of Albee's challenging *Tiny Alice*, a play which obviously fascinates Ball in view of the many and variously interpreted productions of it he has given since. According to Hewes's review of the first *Tiny Alice* production by A.C.T., "To capture the qualities he saw in the

William Ball

script, Mr. Ball did considerable transposing of lines, cutting, and—perhaps most important of all—included more of the long final speech as it appears in the published version than did the Broadway production." In the following description by Hewes, it is clear that Ball contributed to the shattering of the status quo of American theatre with its demand for realistic portrayals by emphasizing that actors and members of the audience have to be constantly made aware of the theatricality of the play: "Julian, played with constant distraughtness by young Paul Shenar, . . . faces Scooter Teague's rock-'n'-roll, pop-art Butler, and Ludi Claire's sophisticated, sensual Miss Alice. . . . Because the staging here is continually violent and dramatic, and crammed with directorial reinforcement such as the use of religious music, the play insists upon our attention throughout."

Because Ball deplores any approach to performing that inhibits the artist by making him constantly responsible for reproducing a naturalistic truth, he removes the actor's fear of extension (acting in a role that seems opposed to his own physical appearance or character) by concentrating his teaching in two areas: voice and body. Since 1965 the voice classes at A.C.T. have taught actors what their vocal ranges and stamina are, so that they can control and shape their speech. Ball points out that an actor "has all sorts of expressive devices at his command—jubilation, violence, roars, groans, giggles—that he never uses in the daily vocabulary of conventional behavior." Similar exercise periods are scheduled between rehearsal periods or at night after performances to extend body plasticity. Believing that extending an actor's range takes constant and sustained work, Ball often casts a handsome actor in a role famous for its ugliness, or a lively actor in a placid role. Ball says: "A ballet performer works out every day. An actor in a Broadway show can run for two years doing the same thing every night, performing like Pavlov's dog, and doing nothing all day to exercise his craft." In spite of the exhausting schedule, reviews point out the vitality and exuberance of the performances. Ball's practice counteracts the stultifying effects upon an actor caused by a single long-running show.

After one year A.C.T. left Pittsburgh under a cloud of controversy. According to Jack Kroll in *Newsweek* (20 November 1967), A.C.T. departed "in a blaze of bad feeling (the problem apparently was that Pittsburgh wanted local talent to get in the ACT)." But Fran Fanshel of the *San Francisco Sunday Examiner* (22 February 1976), asserted that the Pittsburgh Playhouse "was sufficiently impressed by Ball's work to invite ACT to become its resident company. When Ball refused to share artistic control with the theatre's board of directors—a nonnegotiable issue throughout his career—the Playhouse reconsidered its offer." With the help of federal funds, A.C.T. started a cross-country tour in 1966 which took them to New York, Connecticut, Michigan, and Arizona. In July, A.C.T. made its West Coast debut at Stanford University's Summer Festival in Palo Alto. Reviews reached San Francisco which caused an ad hoc civic committee to be formed to investigate the possibility of bringing A.C.T. permanently to San Francisco. Fanshel writes that committee members Mortimer Fleishhacker, Cyril Magnin, and Mel Swig drove to Palo Alto to see A.C.T.'s productions and were "highly impressed."

After four weeks in Palo Alto, A.C.T. moved to Chicago's Ravinia Park Festival, where its reception was equally enthusiastic. According to Hewes in *Saturday Review*, "it is expected that ACT will alternate between these two cities [Chicago and San Francisco]. Control of its destiny, however, remains with ACT, and should either San Francisco or Chicago find this cultural expenditure beyond their means, there seems little doubt other cities would be eager to have them." In Chicago, however, when the civic leadership was unable to raise funds to

support A.C.T. for the following year and interested groups in San Francisco made no firm offer of a permanent home for A.C.T., the company was forced to consider disbanding. During this period of uncertainty, Mortimer Fleishhacker, chairman of the newly formed California Theatre Foundation (since 1972 the California Association for A.C.T.), sent Ball a one-word telegram, "YES," promising to raise the necessary $200,000 to support A.C.T. for their first year.

The American Conservatory Theatre opened its first San Francisco season on 21 January 1967 with *Tartuffe*. Within twenty-two weeks it performed sixteen plays, in which forty-seven actors portrayed 187 characters. Jack Kroll commented in *Newsweek* (20 November 1967) that "San Francisco welcomed Ball with open arms and wallets. Last year, 222,685 paid to see 296 performances of sixteen plays at two theatres, with 62 percent capacity at the Geary and 86 percent capacity at the Marines' Memorial." Ball produced and directed new versions of *Tartuffe* and *Tiny Alice*, repeating the Pittsburgh season in part. Of *Tartuffe*, Hewes writes: "But just as important as this bravura performance is the way Ball directs his actors as he attempts the freest excursions within the very tight meter of Molière's rhyming couplets. So sure is this company's grasp that the entire cast can exit from the living room for a couple of beats and then come running back to pick up the next line." Of *Tiny Alice* Hewes notes: A.C.T.'s stylization, is "being made theatrically fascinating by the wildest possible exercise of performance antics. While one suspects that ACT has gone too far to make this difficult play effective, it should be pointed out that not only is it a smash hit here, but also that there is a certain nononsense sophistication that makes the play's strange events credible on a realistic level rather than metaphysically puzzling flights into abstraction." Other hits of the first San Francisco season were Jerome Kilty's *Dear Liar*, George Bernard Shaw's *Man and Superman*, and Samuel Beckett's *Endgame*.

The second season in San Francisco opened in October 1967 with a staggering total of twenty-seven new productions and revivals. Subscriptions rose from 12,000 to 17,000 during the forty-week-long season of double-theatre rotating repertory. A.C.T. leased two theatres and produced plays at both theatres simultaneously. Situated in the heart of San Francisco, at the corner of Geary Street and Mason Street, is the Geary Theatre, a historic building. (In 1980 A.C.T. started a three-year program to renovate and modernize this building, erected in 1910.) This theatre has a seating capacity of 1,049. Another arrangement with the Marines' Memorial Club gave A.C.T. the sole use of the 640-seat Marines' Memorial Theatre, which is located two blocks from the Geary Theatre. The proximity of the theatres enabled one actor, Jay Doyle, in 1966, to dash out of the Marines' Memorial Theatre, where he was performing in *Six Characters in Search of an Author*, and run down Geary Street to play in *Tartuffe*.

In November 1967, Kroll reported that "the once-peripatetic Ball is acting as if he is settling down. 'Until now we have concentrated on survival,' he says. 'At last we can direct our energy toward artistic excellence.'" Kroll also adds that "the local area has pledged $400,000, which, added to the $300,000 from the Ford Foundation and $350,000 from the National Endowment for the Arts, puts ACT within reach of its 2.3 million budget." Other foundations, such as Rockefeller and Mellon, contributed matching grants. Local support also came from the San Francisco Foundation, the California Arts Commission, and such corporations as the Crocker National Bank and Standard Oil of California.

During the second San Francisco season Ball produced three different versions of *Hamlet*: *Elsinore*, a stark "voice play" concentrating on poetry; *Hamlet*, a traditional Elizabethan version; and *The Bare Bodkyn*, a modern-dress version emphasizing alienation and madness. Other plays produced during the season included William Gibson's *Two for the Seesaw*, Arthur Miller's *The Crucible*, Jean Anouilh's *Thieves' Carnival*, Donald Hall's *An Evening's Frost*, Tennessee Williams's *A Streetcar Named Desire*, Martin Duberman's *In White America*, Edward Albee's *The American Dream, A Delicate Balance*, and *The Zoo Story*, Thornton Wilder's *Our Town*, and Eugene O'Neill's *Long Day's Journey into Night*. One critic charged that Ball's selection was "safe," to which Ball answered, "Well, we don't do them safely." Not only were new versions produced of plays already in A.C.T. repertoire, but Ball also had five world premieres: Jerome Kilty's *Don't Shoot Mable, It's Your Husband* and his *Long Live Life*; Nagle Jackson's *Caught in the Act*; a play written by A.C.T.'s press agent Brian McKinney called *Deedle, Deedle Dumpling, My Son God*; and a musical, *Your Own Thing*, by Hall Hester, Danny Apolinar, and Donald Driver.

Julius Novick reviewed seven A.C.T. productions in the *Nation* (19 August 1968). He explains that *Deedle, Deedle Dumpling, My Son God* "is a sort of modern *Candide*: the story of an ingenuous youth

and his attempts to make his way in a bewildering world." The leading character, Johnny, played by David Dukes, meets different men, all played by Peter Donat, and different women, all played by actress Michael Learned. Novick comments that the play "functions as a heap of fragments (some of them, however, quite interesting). . . . [and] is saved from pretentiousness by Mr. McKinney's comic gifts, and by the performance of David Dukes." Jerome Kilty's *Long Live Life* is an adaptation of Chekhov's letters "into a mosaic of monologues." In *A Streetcar Named Desire* Novick found that the important supporting roles were not well played. He also wrote that the entirely new production of *Long Day's Journey into Night* was a great improvement over A.C.T.'s previous production of the play. Novick also saw three plays directed by Ball: *Under Milk Wood*, ("Ball's gracefully fluid staging of what was meant as an essentially static 'play for voices' is always an embellishment, never a distraction"); *Tartuffe* ("Ball is more interested in making pleasing patterns and ingenious routines than in coming to grips with the hard core of the play"); and *Hamlet* ("a very oddly old-fashioned production, full of fine elocution and swirling capes; the actors keep striking attitudes that make them look like Garrick or Mrs. Siddon"). Novick also added an announcement that A.C.T. "would 'cease to exist' unless it could raise $104,000 within two weeks." This caused Novick to insert the following warning in his review: "That a theatre which has played to so many hundreds of thousands of people, and been the focus of so much attention and admiration, should find its existence in such immediate jeopardy, is an indication—one of many—of how dangerously shaky our noncommercial legitimate theatres are. In spite of what I consider to be its shortcomings, the closing of ACT would be a sad loss as well as a grim portent." The ambitious season as well as disappointments in funding plunged the company into a financial crisis, but a local fund-raising campaign temporarily averted disaster.

During its third season (1968-1969) in San Francisco, A.C.T. produced, among other plays, Georges Feydeau's *A Flea in Her Ear*, George Bernard Shaw's *The Devil's Disciple*, Jules Feiffer's *Little Murders*, Charles Dyer's *Staircase*, Anton Chekhov's *The Three Sisters*, Aleksei Arbuzov's *The Promise*, and Tom Stoppard's *Rosencrantz and Guildenstern Are Dead*. The company also presented the American premiere of *The Architect and the Emperor of Assyria* by the Spanish playwright Fernando Arrabal, and the world premiere of Anna Marie Barlow's *Glory! Hallelujah!*. (The latter play was directed by Edwin Sherin, who staged the 1969 Pulitzer Prize-winning *The Great White Hope* by Howard Sackler.) Jack Kroll, commenting on Barlow's play in *Newsweek* (9 June 1969), was disappointed that the lengthy Civil War "pageant-like chronicle in three acts and 27 scenes, with a cast of 23 principals and many subsidiary performers," did not even mention slavery and had no black characters. He concluded that its sentimental shallowness "won't wash in the age of Vietnam and of the tough and disturbing examinations of the morality of history by Hochhuth, Weiss and others." Henry Hewes in *Saturday Review* singled out Ball's direction of *The Three Sisters* and *Rosencrantz and Guildenstern Are Dead*, and also Edwin Sherin's direction of *Glory! Hallelujah!*, which he called "emotionally fulfilling." He also praised A.C.T.'s emphasis upon training repertory actors: "The company is a little like a versatile orchestra in which every musician can play several instruments. And the switching of instruments turns each performance into an adventure."

But financial and administrative problems continued to plague the company as the attendance dropped sharply. The dwindling box-office receipts forced an early closing of the third season. "The company was half a million dollars in debt," according to Fran Fanshel, "trying to perform twenty-four shows in forty-two weeks, and able to attract only thirty percent of its capacity audience." In addition, she wrote: "the company was split by a bitter schism between supporters of Bill Ball and those of ACT's young business manager, William Bushnell, who believed that Ball was too erratic to possess total control of the troupe and favored transferring authority from him to a board of directors." Bushnell was replaced by James McKenzie, a resourceful Broadway producer. McKenzie attacked A.C.T.'s financial difficulties with some bold measures which included closing the theatre for three months and coproducing a touring company production of *Hair* for seven months. *Hair* netted a profit of more than $100,000. The near-failure of his company as well as his battle for leadership had a profound effect on Ball. The result of this crisis was the postponed opening of the fourth season while extensive cutbacks and more compact scheduling were organized. To supplement their income, the company accepted special summer engagements sponsored by groups in Chicago and New York.

In 1969 the American National Theatre and Academy (ANTA) arranged for A.C.T. to start the New York season which presented a number of American resident companies. A.C.T. presented during its four-week engagement three plays: *Tiny Alice*, *A Flea in Her Ear*, and *The Three Sisters*. All three productions caused a great deal of controversy. Hewes explains one source of conflict: "While the *Tiny Alice* seen here at the ANTA Theater as the opening round in a campaign to bring to New York the best work of our resident theater companies is a splendid staging of the play, it is not quite as successful as the freely altered version the ACT presented in San Francisco. One cannot blame the playwright for refusing to allow that version to be done here, because even if he acknowledged it to be an improvement it would not be his. Yet, if he is willing to sell a play to the movies and allow it to be changed, why should he not permit an imaginative director such as Ball the same latitude with a new version of a play that has already had a previous Broadway hearing?" Jack Kroll and Stanley Kaufmann dismissed the production as ineffective. Harold Clurman praised the discipline of the A.C.T.'s acting and directing but concluded: "Finally it all becomes insufferably tiresome, for two reasons: because the numerous theatric devices employed are basically shallow, and because of the text to which they are applied. *Tiny Alice* is Albee's most pretentious and weakest play." The critical reaction to the other two plays was very much in the same vein. However, Robert Goldshy of the Univer-

Geary Theatre

415

sity of California at Berkeley, who worked with A.C.T. during its first four years in the Bay Area and established his own theatre with his wife Angela Patton in 1975, said of Ball: "His concerns are the things that move theatre toward circus or opera: form, color, line, and music. He's not interested in plummeting deep emotional or intellectual issues—he lets other people do that. Instead, he aims for maximum visual impact. He uses the actor as an artist uses paints. He is a virtuoso of stage movement, with meticulous care for costumes, sets, how the body moves. But his weakness is he doesn't get to the mind—that's not his intention." Ball himself added that the process of extending the limitations of a play, of daring to take chances and daring to fail, is what is important, not the results.

In March 1970, a streamlined twenty-two-week season opened which included nine new productions and two revivals. Among the productions were Oscar Wilde's *The Importance of Being Earnest*, Sophocles' *Oedipus Rex*, George Bernard Shaw's *Saint Joan*, Athol Fugard's *The Blood Knot*, David Halliwell's *Little Malcolm and His Struggle Against the Eunuchs*, Peter Luke's *Hadrian VII*, and George M. Cohan's *The Tavern*. Though the subscription sales remained low, overall attendance registered a slight increase. When the season ended, the company abandoned the double-theatre rotating repertory policy. Since 1970 Marines' Memorial Theatre has only been used for nonrepertory plays and musicals.

Both the 1970-1971 and the 1971-1972 seasons registered an increase in attendance. During the latter season, which had been expanded to twenty-eight weeks, A.C.T. produced nine plays. Also in 1972, the financial situation at A.C.T. improved through the spring fund drive which brought in a record amount of $120,000. Also, *Godspell*, which was coproduced by A.C.T., began its phenomenal sixty-one-week run. In addition, A.C.T. sponsored England's Royal Shakespeare Company in *A Midsummer-Night's Dream*, which broke all box-office records at the Geary Theatre. For the first time A.C.T. performed in Hawaii, an engagement which it has since repeated annually. In 1974, a Ford Foundation gift of $2 million enabled the company to purchase the Geary Theatre. The grant also provided funds for a four-year support plan and cash reserves, which ensured A.C.T. a permanent home in San Francisco. With each season subscriptions as well as attendance continued to rise. Nonetheless, the thirteenth season ended with a deficit of $430,000, and once again a local emergency fund drive rescued A.C.T. Currently

A.C.T. has 20,216 subscribers, a 73 percent paid capacity, an annual attendance of 600,000, and a budget of $7 million. The 1980 season, which extends for thirty-three weeks, offers nine plays, such as Shakespeare's *Much Ado About Nothing*, Henrik Ibsen's *Ghosts*, Noel Coward's *Hay Fever*, Jean Giraudoux's *The Trojan War Will Not Take Place*, Charles Dickens's *A Christmas Carol*, Tom Stoppard's *Night and Day*, Lillian Hellman's *The Little Foxes* and its sequel *Another Part of the Forest*, Richard Brinsley Sheridan's *The Rivals*, and Anton Chekhov's *The Three Sisters*. Between 1969 and 1972, A.C.T. presented five more world premieres: Nagle Jackson's *The Mystery Cycle*, Michael McClure's *General Gorgeous* (MacClure was a playwright-in-residence at A.C.T. in 1976), Tennessee Williams's *This Is (An Entertainment)*, Margaret Webster's *No Coward Soul*, and Stuart Hample's *The Selling of the President* (with lyrics by Jack O'Brien and music by Bob James). A.C.T. also presented the American premiere of Howard Sackler's *Monsieur Robert*.

Since the founding of the American Conservatory Theatre, Ball has emphasized the importance of continuous training for his students. The voice and body exercises initially held between rehearsals and after performances were organized into a small experimental eight-week program for the first time during fall 1967. The program included comic technique, Shakespearean diction, voice projection, nonverbal communication, suspense, rhetoric, scansion, dance, fencing, mime, improvisation, posture, hairdressing, and yoga. This was also the first time that A.C.T. offered to train students outside the company. According to Allen Fletcher, who has been associated with A.C.T. since its founding and has served as conservatory director since 1970: "In the first seasons, actors joined the company expecting to contribute something in the way of teaching their colleagues, but there was no thought of expanding that concept to include outsiders." In spite of low funds, A.C.T. started its first annual ten-week Summer Training Congress, which began in June of 1968 with 175 enrolled students. In 1969, the Advanced Training Program for young professionals outside the company was established as a full one-year course; and the Evening Extension Program offered beginning training for community members. In 1975, A.C.T. added the Young Conservatory to provide introductory theatre training for children, also enabling A.C.T. to fill children's roles satisfactorily. Moreover it instituted a full-scale student matinee program which has since offered special weekday performances to school groups. In 1972, the Advanced Training Program expanded to include a second year for young professionals. Also in that year, A.C.T. introduced the Plays-in-Progress series, a program of workshop productions of dramas by new playwrights (some of whom were playwrights-in-residence at A.C.T.). Another addition occurred in 1973, when the Asian-American Theatre Workshop was founded to increase communication between ethnic groups. In 1975, A.C.T. inaugurated the New Black Actor's Workshop. Both workshops became independent of A.C.T. in the late 1970s. Since 1977 the Advanced Training Program at A.C.T. has been offering the Master of Fine Arts degree in acting. Fletcher has observed an improvement over the years in the quality of training as well as in the caliber of students. He believes that "if the teacher isn't up to the student, he should get out. . . . The students look to the professionals as models, the professionals respond to that, and the interaction is valuable for both."

In addition to the Advanced Training Program, there is an Evening Extension Program which is open to everybody and meets for ten weeks, each meeting lasting between one and two hours. The Summer Training Congress is a ten-week intensive introduction to professional training. Graduates of the congress must wait a year before they can audition for the Advanced Training Program. Other programs and services which A.C.T. provides are classes for nonprofessionals and children; administrative and technical production internships; special performances for students, senior citizens and the disadvantaged; post-performance discussions; and productions of Plays-in-Progress.

One critic summarized the purpose as well as the necessity for the continuing existence of such an institution as the American Conservatory Theatre. While observing students' reaction to an A.C.T. matinee performance of *Hotel Paradiso* by Georges Feydeau and Maurice Desvallières, he noted that "they burst out into laughter and applause—not cruel laughter at the stutterer but pure, happy laughter at the preposterousness, the *theatricality* of the contrivance. Those kids did not 'learn' anything in the usual sense from *Hotel Paradiso*, but they learned that they themselves had the capacity to be delighted by something purely theatrical. Surely that is a lesson worth learning—the lesson that must precede all the others that the theatre can teach."

–Inge Kutt

Arena Stage
Washington, D.C.

Arena Stage in Washington, D.C., is one of the oldest and most prestigious of the theatres generally associated with the regional theatre movement. Since its inception in 1950, the theatre has occupied three different sites, while establishing an outstanding production record including premieres of *The Great White Hope* by Howard Sackler, *Indians* by Arthur Kopit, and Michael Weller's *Moonchildren* and *Loose Ends*. In 1973 it was chosen by the United States Department of State to be the first American drama company to perform in the Soviet Union. The company presented Jerome Lawrence and Robert E. Lee's *Inherit the Wind* and Thornton Wilder's *Our Town*. In 1976 it was the first company outside New York to receive a Tony Award for theatrical excellence, and in 1980 became the first American company to perform at the Hong Kong International Arts Festival.

Founded largely through the efforts of Zelda Fichandler, along with Edward Mangum and Thomas C. Fichandler, Arena Stage was conceived as a remedy to what was in 1950 an almost complete absence of dramatic art in the Washington area. Zelda Fichandler continues to serve as the theatre's artistic director, Thomas Fichandler as its executive director.

Zelda D. Fichandler, who is a native of Washington, D.C., studied Russian language and literature at Cornell University. After graduation in 1945, she returned to Washington, where she worked at the Pentagon in military intelligence. She married Thomas Fichandler, an economist. In 1950 she received an M.A. degree in dramatic arts from George Washington University. She then drew together enough volunteers to form a public stock company to raise funds for a theatre company. With approximately $15,000, Arena Stage opened on 16 August 1950 in the Hippodrome, a former movie house, with Oliver Goldsmith's *She Stoops to Conquer*.

The theatre slowly developed a subscription audience as its reputation spread and, at the same time, gradually evolved from the use of local and student talent to being a professional company. Building an artistic reputation and gaining the respect of a wide audience proved difficult, especially since the selection of plays intentionally steered away from those popular in the commercial market. But the theatre grew despite problems such as initially small audiences and limited facilities. In 1956 Arena Stage moved to a renovated brewery called the Old Vat, which accommodated more than twice the Hippodrome's seating capacity of 247 persons. Forty productions were presented there from 1956 to 1960. When the Old Vat was slated for demolition in 1960, Arena Stage commissioned a new building. This theatre and its additions are an integral part of Arena Stage's production capabilities and reputation.

The design of the current Arena theatre, which opened in 1961, was guided by the company's production experience. Its rectangular stage is surrounded by a seating area for 827 patrons with entrances for the players in the four corners. The building itself follows the octagonal outline of the seating area. At about the same time that these facilities were built, Arena Stage became a non-profit organization, enabling the theatre to seek major grants, such as those provided by the National Endowment for the Arts, to ease its financial problems.

In 1971 a second theatre, the Kreeger, was added to the Arena Stage complex. The fan-shaped building has a seating capacity of 514, with a modified thrust stage which can be altered to various sizes or can utilize a proscenium. Finally, in 1976 the Kreeger's basement was finished into a 180-seat cabaret called the Old Vat Room after Arena Stage's second home. An average of eight productions are presented per year by Arena Stage, each in the theatre most appropriate to the tone of the play.

From the first season through the present, Fichandler's artistic direction has carefully mixed critically established plays by writers such as Molière, Chekhov, and O'Neill, with new works by playwrights lacking established reputations or financial backing. Thus, the theatre serves both as a market for classical performances as well as an incubator for nonprofit artistic experimentation. For example, the first season in 1950-1951 balanced Shakespeare's *Twelfth Night* with Elmer Rice's *The Adding Machine*; the 1980-1981 schedule features plays by Bertolt Brecht, Jean-Paul Sartre, and Nikolai Erdman as well as four new works by American playwrights.

Arena Stage

Zelda Fichandler

Zelda Fichandler's philosophy has always been to produce plays that are enjoyable for both audience and actor, but do more than entertain—those dramas which are thought-provoking and contemporary in resonance. This outlook, plus Arena Stage's innovative productions and balanced scheduling, has often functioned as a model for regional theatres around the country. As a result, Arena Stage has been recognized as a forerunner in providing quality theatre beyond the boundaries of New York, and opportunities for the exposure of actor, audience, and playwright to each other in a noncommercial atmosphere.

Though not all of the theatre's productions have been met with critical acclaim, Arena Stage

maintains a subscription base of over 16,000 (a paid capacity of 91 percent)—one of the factors that allows the theatre to operate at a level of excellence and still take artistic risks. This willingness and ability to take risks has fostered premieres of plays such as *The Ruling Class* by Peter Barnes, *The Madness of God* by Elie Wiesel (filmed for PBS), and the Nemiroff/Zaltzberg musical *Raisin*. However, financial limitations persist and fund raising is still an important part of the theatre's administration.

As adjuncts to its main production program, Arena Stage at times offers post-performance discussions, readings, and workshops. But perhaps the most important outgrowth is Living Stage, now a nearly independent part of the program. Comprised of an entirely separate troupe of actors, Living Stage is a traveling improvisational group formed with the purpose of tapping the creative energies of its audience. Its basic repertoire of songs, poems, and improvisation encourages spontaneity of audience response. Started as a community outreach program for children from the inner-city part of Washington, D.C., Living Stage has expanded to include performances for the handicapped, the incarcerated, and others, as well as offering a summer training program open to the public. Living Stage is well respected in its field, having traveled as far as Hawaii to participate in special public programs utilizing its talents with the handicapped.

With a consistent philosophical and artistic background, a substantial following, and its present variety of facilities, Arena Stage has made a considerable contribution to regional theatre. Considerations and plans for the future are practical ones: economic survival, steady growth, and stability.

–Robert Klein and Susan Davis

Reference:

Boris Weintraub, "Close Up: In the Arena, Zelda Fichandler Does Not Stoop—She Conquers," *Washington Star*, 17 March 1980, D1-2.

The Dallas Theater Center

Founded in 1959, the Dallas Theater Center, located in Dallas, Texas, has been a prime force in the development of theatre in the Southwest. It is the only theatre designed by Frank Lloyd Wright, the only repertory theatre that from its outset was conceived as the location of a graduate program in drama, and the only repertory theatre, other than the Minneapolis Children's Theater, that is nonunion. Paul Baker, managing director of the center since its inception, has been mainly responsible for its philosophy and direction. With a salaried company of thirty-five permanent members, the Dallas Theater Center and Paul Baker have particularly promoted the writing and performance of new plays. Preston Jones, one of Baker's students of the early 1960s, achieved national recognition in the 1970s with his three plays, *A Texas Trilogy*, which were first performed at the center.

The founding of DTC dates to a "backporch meeting" in 1954 of a handful of people at the home of Mrs. Bea Handel, who had recently moved from Cleveland, Ohio, where she had been a supporter of the Cleveland Play House. She saw the need in Dallas for a nonprofit theatre supported by the community. Like the Cleveland Play House, it also would employ a permanent professional staff, train apprentices, encourage the participation of local amateurs, and offer classes for children. With the assistance of a few leading Dallas businessmen, particularly Robert Stecker, president of the Dallas Theater Center until his death in 1959, and Waldo Stewart, still active on the Board of Directors, the idea became a reality after five years of contending with many forceful personalities and numerous fund-raising problems and campaigns. In 1955 Stecker nominated Paul Baker, then the chairman of Baylor University's drama department, for the position of director of the new theatre. Baker had been a very successful director at Baylor during the 1940s and 1950s. In 1956 his production of *Hamlet*, starring Burgess Meredith and based on Baker's interpretation of Hamlet as three characters within one, attracted national attention. Baker is noted for his innovative approaches to theatre and for his respect for the integrity of the creative abilities of the individual. His philosophy of education, explained in his book *Integration of Abilities* (1972), is grounded in the idea that the creative individual is one who attempts to realize his or her potential in more than one area. His "Integration of Abilities" course, still required of DTC students, involves a progression of exercises that, ideally, lead to a better understanding of the elements that, according to Baker, shape and define space—rhythm, line, silhouette, color, and texture.

Paul Baker was born in Hereford, Texas, in 1911, the son and grandson of Presbyterian ministers. He received his B.A. degree from Trinity University in San Antonio in 1932 and his Master of Fine Arts degree in 1959 from Yale, where he studied drama under George Pierce Baker, whom he calls a major influence on his thinking. He also studied drama in London at the Central School of Speech and was one of the first ten theatrical specialists in the U.S. Army, serving in Iceland and France. In 1945 he received the Legion of Merit for his reorganization of the entertainment branch of the European theaters of operations.

His experiences at Baylor began in 1934, when he worked under almost impossible conditions on the third floor of an old building. As recounted by Joyce Burke Cory in her thesis, "The Dallas Theater Center, A History" (Trinity University, 1968), "By 1941 he had designed and built a new theatre and drama department that made Baylor a leader in Southwestern drama circles and received national and international recognition from professional as well as educational theater leagues." His theatre had six connecting stages surrounded by an audience in swivel chairs that could be moved; this innovation allowed for in-the-round staging as well as theatre-in-the-round. One critic, Al Dewlen, summarizes Baker's fresh approach to theatre: "Only a few of Baker's experiments have been labeled by critics as failures and, as one reflects, 'even those were worth seeing.' " Baker's experience and success at Baylor provided both the inspiration and the impetus needed for the building of a new theatre in Dallas.

The immediate problem facing the founders—finding a site—was solved in 1955 when Sylvan T. Baer, in memory of his parents, donated a wooded tract of land centrally located on scenic Turtle Creek Boulevard. Baer was to prove a dif-

The Kalita Humphreys Theater

ficult man to deal with, especially when after the ground-breaking ceremony on 15 September 1958, he attempted to regain the property by claiming the center had broken its contract by not beginning construction before 19 September 1958. Fortunately, in late September, the courts denied Baer's request and construction resumed. Baker and the founders agreed that Frank Lloyd Wright should be approached to design the building. With Mr. and Mrs. John Rosenfield, active supporters of the new theatre and acquaintances of Wright, Baker visited the architect at Taliesin East, his home and workshop in Spring Green, Wisconsin. Wright showed them the plans for a theatre which he had first presented in 1930 to a group in Hartford, Connecticut, and in 1951 to someone on the West Coast. According to Baker's account, Wright said he was very busy but could work with them if they accepted this basic plan. They wholeheartedly agreed, but the problems with technical details that were to develop nearly cost Wright's resignation.

Wright's concept of the theatre as a "temple" posed many of these difficulties. Among various other problems, his original plans did not allow for proper lighting and movement of sets on and off the stage. Wright did not appreciate Baker's requests for changes, in particular his request for an elevator to lift the props to the stage, and wrote several angry letters to Baker and the building committee about his concept of the "New Theater,"

as he termed it, threatening to resign over Baker's request for an elevator and insisting that the ramps in his design were "organically adequate" to the task of moving props. For Wright, "The original simplicity of '*the idea*' is being harmfully complicated to no good purpose related to the function of a *new* theater." Stage design should be accommodated to the demands of the building, he added: "Scene shifting becomes a simple matter of designed, sculptural, imaginative constructions. Directors come and go. The Building stays. Instead of painted back-drops and carpenter-work is the theater itself. A simplified sense of staging a show is made easy— but *organic simplicity* is needed there too for the best effects! I am no stickler for classification but I believe there is a definite line between the drama and the circus. Nothing can ever equal the *dramatic effects of organic simplicity*—in architecture or in Theater." The outcome of this confrontation was a compromise of sorts. The elevator was installed, unbeknown to Wright, but getting scenery on and off stage has still been one of the major technical problems of the building.

Although the building is stunning in appearance and has definite virtues to be found in no other theatre, there are certain difficulties as well. The lack of any ninety-degree angles can be very disorienting, and the very narrow stairs are dangerous for older theatregoers. The lack of sufficient working space and the cramped arrangement of what space does exist are major obstacles for the technicians. As one member put it, "When you're working, say on costumes, in some corner of the building you feel you're the only one struggling along, while on the other side of the wall is someone working away and most likely feeling the same way." But most observers admire the beauty and intimacy of the theatre itself which originally accommodated 416 people and now, with the addition of a balcony in 1979, contains 516 seats. The circular stage surrounded by an auditorium with hardly a bad seat in it superbly fulfills Wright's concept of a "New Theater" which eliminates the proscenium and blends

did visit the site before construction began, he died eight months before the theatre's opening on 27 December 1959, and thus never saw his last building, the only theatre building of the more than seven hundred structures he had designed.

Raising funds for the construction of the building was a never-ending struggle. The center first raised $315,000 in cash and pledges. This was augmented by a gift of $100,000 from Mrs. R. W. Humphreys of Liberty, Texas, in memory of her actress daughter, Kalita Humphreys, who had a successful acting career in New York before her untimely death in an airplane crash in 1954. She

World premiere of Preston Jones's The Last Meeting of the Knights of the White Magnolia (*Jones far left*)

the stage and auditorium into one entity. Baker says the auditorium-stage relationship "is probably the best of any theater anywhere. There is not any better audience-actor relationship. Wright called it a 'sympathetic audience,' no finer acoustics." Baker aptly summarizes Wright's attitude: "Mr. Wright didn't want us to have any scenery on the stage. It was to be a kind of a chapel where we would worship in his architectural shrine." Even after his disagreements with the architect, Baker regards Wright as one of the greatest geniuses of the twentieth century and stated that Wright taught him that "the power of one human will, focused and directed, has practically no limits." Although Wright

had acted in Baker's production of *The Barretts of Wimpole Street* at Baylor. In her honor, the center's main theatre bears her name. When funds were short, Dallas Theater Center president Robert Stecker suggested they cut the cost of seats from the budget, reasoning that the threat of no seats on opening night, more than anything else, would inspire people to donate money and it worked. As with all regional theatres, fund raising is a constant battle, but the Dallas Theater Center has survived due to strong local support, grants, and box-office sales.

In the summer of 1959 auditions for permanent members were conducted in New York, London, Dallas, and on the West Coast for the new theatre, as the building was taking shape. Charles Laughton and his wife, Elsa Lanchester, conducted the London auditions. Under the direction of Paul Baker and his associate director, Mary Sue Jones, a total of fifty-four company members, including nine staff members, were hired. One major problem was the misconception many of the company members had about the new theatre. Since many had no previous experience with Baker's work at Baylor, and the classes at the DTC were an extension of his drama program there, many had difficulties adjusting to his approach. As Baker put it some twenty-one years later, "Some were interested in Hollywood and New York, others in a quick result, or reputation, and they found out that the resident theater movement is an entirely different kind of movement. We are one of the few that have held on to developing a company. "

Adjusting to an entirely new space posed another problem, which the company discovered in its very first production, Baker and Eugene McKinney's adaptation of Thomas Wolfe's *Of Time and the River*, which had been produced earlier at Baylor. Those who had worked on the Baylor production found Wright's stage and auditorium to be quite different. Realizing that they could not simply recreate the Baylor production, they had to adjust to Wright's strong concept of space. In the earlier production, the Thomas Wolfe figure, Eugene Gant, was dramatically introduced to the audience on a ten-foot-high platform. The arrangement of space on Wright's stage did not permit this concept to work. Toward the end of the run, the character simply walked upon the empty stage toward the audience, followed by a single spotlight. This produced a wholly different yet desirable effect.

Other important discoveries of Wright's design were made during the first year. For *The Importance of Being Earnest*, stage designer Virgil Beavers found that "a successful set had to follow the basic 'units' of which the theater was constructed." Experimenting with the placement of chairs for the funeral scene of *Our Town*, Baker discovered that putting them in straight lines would not work. They had to be placed at angles that complemented the line of the stage.

For the first season, besides *Of Time and the River*, Baker remounted another of his most popular productions at Baylor, *Hamlet*, and he also produced *The Cross-Eyed Bear*, by his Baylor associate Eugene McKinney. Filling out the season were a double bill of *A Solid House* by Elena Garro and *The Bald Soprano* by Eugene Ionesco, Dylan Thomas's

Under Milk Wood, directed by Burgess Meredith, and Noel Coward's *Hay Fever*. The opening night audience of 27 December 1959 warmly received the highly emotional *Of Time and the River*. National critics, however, gave the production better reviews than did local critics who perhaps did not properly understand that a regional repertory company like the Dallas Theater Center is also intended to be an educational institution and needs time to mature before it can achieve the excellence of established commercial theatre. The so-called lack of polished acting has always been a criticism of the DTC, so much so that in 1980 Baker said that stress would be placed on acting above all else. Baker has always believed that the regional repertory theatre should not be "result-oriented," that the process of educating actors takes time, and that there needs to be room for experimentation.

Baker has long been a supporter of new playwrights and in 1964 helped to form the American Playwrights Theater, a national organization that promoted the production of new works. In the late 1970s, according to Mary Sue Jones, the organization ceased to exist for a fortuitous reason—the rising number of new plays being performed in theatres across the country. Down Center Stage, a small theatre in the lower level of the center building, was created in 1964 as a place for the production of original plays. As of 1980, approximately fifty plays have premiered there. The DTC has had many successful world premieres, including performances of Clifford M. Sage and Hal Lewis's *Joshua Beene and God*, starring Burl Ives (1961-1962 season); *Journey to Jefferson*, Robert Flynn's adaptation of William Faulkner's *As I Lay Dying* (1962-1963 season); Robert Anderson's *The Days Between* (1964-1965 season); Paddy Chayefsky's *The Latent Heterosexual*, directed by Burgess Meredith and starring Zero Mostel (1967-1968 season); *Jabberwock* by Jerome Lawrence and Robert E. Lee (1972-1973 season); DTC company member John Logan's *Jack Ruby, All-American Boy* (1973-1974 season); Mark Medoff's *Firekeeper* (1977-1978 season); and, perhaps most significant of all, Preston Jones's *A Texas Trilogy* (1973-1974 season).

Paul Baker sees his theatre as providing the ideal environment in which the writer as well as the performer, the director, and the designer may grow. Baker's philosophy proved a major influence on the career of his most popular student, Preston Jones. The enthusiastic audience response to the first productions of Jones's first two plays, *The Last Meeting of the Knights of the White Magnolia* and *Lu Ann Hampton Laverty Oberlander*, at Down Center

Stage in 1974 prompted Baker to move the plays, together with the newly written *The Oldest Living Graduate*, to performance in repertory in the main theatre. And the versatility of Jones's talents as actor and director as well as writer is testament to Baker's philosophy and training. Jones had acted in and directed several of the center's productions, and at the time of his sudden death in the fall of 1979, the playwright was preparing for a major role in the Dallas Theater Center's upcoming production of *A Man for All Seasons*.

Looking back over the first twenty-one years of the DTC's existence, Baker sees, besides Jones's success, the production of Flynn's Faulkner adaptation, *Journey to Jefferson*, as the major highlight. This production serves as an excellent example of Baker's overriding concern with proper integration of acting, designing, directing, and lighting. Representing the United States, the Dallas Theater Center company's production of this play at the summer 1964 Theater of Nations competition in Paris received the Special Jury Prize for the best production of the festival. Baker chose the play because, as he states in the booklet *Dallas Theater Center, Twenty Dynamic Years* (1979), it "represented the best we could do in theatrical art and technique. Also, we felt that we were authorities in some ways on the Faulkner country and characters, and that no other country could possibly have the insight into Faulkner that we had."

The DTC has programs for the promotion of new plays by established as well as new playwrights. One is the practice of having a playwright spend some weeks, usually in the spring, overseeing the production of his or her work. In the spring of 1978, Mark Medoff was in residency for the production of his play *Firekeeper*, directed by Baker. Also, late in the spring, occurs a showcase of new drama called the Playmarket, instituted in 1973. Jones attributed much of his success to the presentation of two plays of *A Texas Trilogy* at the first Playmarket. A major criticism of the programs in the late 1970s was that too many of the plays were written by Dallas Theater Center personnel and did not deserve being produced, but it is interesting to note that an audience survey conducted in 1978 placed four plays by Dallas Theater Center writers in the top five favorites: *A Midsummer-Nights Dream*, a musical adaptation of Shakespeare's comedy by Randolph Tallman and Steve Mackenroth (1973-1974 season), was at the top of the list; *The Last Meeting of the Knights of the White Magnolia* second; *Jack Ruby, All-American Boy*, fourth; and *The Oldest Living Graduate*, fifth. The third program that sup-

ports new plays is the Eugene McKinney New Plays Reading Series. Of particular note was a 1980 reading of John Gardner's *Death and the Maiden*, for which, as is customary, Gardner was present to answer questions about the play after the performance.

From 1959 to 1963 Baker remained chairman of the drama department at Baylor and commuted regularly between Dallas and Waco. Graduate students in drama lived in Dallas, though, and attended classes at the DTC. In 1963 a disagreement over Baker's production of *Long Day's Journey Into Night* resulted in the resignations of Baker and his entire staff from Baylor and their move to the faculty of Trinity University in San Antonio, where he was made chairman of the drama department. (The president of Baylor had insisted on the removal of certain words from the play, and Baker had refused to comply.) In 1977, Baker became chairman of Trinity's graduate program in drama. Graduate students at the Dallas Theater Center may never set foot on the San Antonio campus, although some are involved in summer workshops or productions that DTC performs in a modern theatre on Trinity's San Antonio campus. This theatre is built more to Baker's specifications than was the Wright building in Dallas.

The graduate program at the DTC is a rigorous three-year residency that requires the student become proficient in more than one area of theatre. The same requirement applies to company members, which has made for both virtues and vices. One reason the center has survived is the assistance the actors have given to the operation of the theatre and the Trinity graduate program, yet perhaps the quality of acting would be better if actors were allowed more time to study their roles and practice their art.

Community involvement is another major concern of the center. The children's theatre classes have involved the participation of thousands of children over the years. In 1969 the Magic Turtle program of Saturday morning shows began; it presents an average of four shows annually, many original adaptations of classics, such as *Rumpelstiltskin* by DTC member Sally Netzel and *A Christmas Carol* by DTC member John Figlmiller. Original productions have also been created by the center's mime troupe. In 1969 the Janus Players was formed to promote the participation of members of minority groups, particularly blacks and Hispanics, in theatre. The group played for five seasons and performed from two to five plays per season. Also, since 1961 the Dallas Theater Center has regularly taken plays on tour, mainly in Texas and surrounding states.

The Dallas Theater Center has enjoyed consistent support from the community; for the 1980-1981 season an unprecedented 10,606 subscriptions were sold. Associate Director Mary Sue Jones believes that the center has succeeded in providing a permanent place and program for so many theatre people—actors, designers, playwrights, directors. The Dallas Theater Center is likely to remain a leader in regional repertory theatre for many years.

–Donna Northouse

The Goodman Theatre
Chicago

In Chicago, the name Goodman means two things: the theatre which stands behind the Art Institute of Chicago close to the lakefront and the prestigious School of Drama to which the theatre was once connected. Both have had long and complicated histories, but both have had one aim since their beginnings: to create the best in theatre. The peculiar nature of these interrelated organizations was formed by changes in literary sensibilities in Chicago during the 1910s, a period that is frequently called the Chicago Renaissance. During the early part of the 1910s there were masses of little theatre groups forming in America, and Chicago was one of the leaders in the movement, with the most representative groups in the Windy City being Maurice Browne's Chicago Little Theatre, the Chicago Theatre Society, the Casino Players, and the Arts Students League. An active member in several of these groups was a wealthy socialite, Kenneth Sawyer Goodman, son of Thomas O. Goodman, an affluent lumberman. A graduate of Princeton (class of 1906), Kenneth Sawyer Goodman had majored in business, but he had written a good deal of poetry as well. After his graduation he worked for a year in one of his father's lumber franchises in Madison, Wisconsin. He also worked in his off hours with the Wisconsin Players where he learned much about the practical work in the theatre. After his return from Madison he continued to work for his father, but part of his days were spent in a new passion, writing plays. Fortunately his father, who was a board member of the Art Institute, approved of his son's artistic interests, as did young Goodman's wife, Marjorie. Three people Goodman met in these days before World War I would influence him greatly: Thomas Wood Stevens, B. Iden Payne, and Ben Hecht.

Stevens was best known at the time as the head of the drama department at Carnegie Institute of Technology, though in his long career in the arts he was a publisher, a lecturer at the Art Institute, a painter of murals, a stage designer, a stage director, and a writer of plays and pageants. B. Iden Payne, a friend of Stevens's, had already begun his distinguished career as an actor, a manager, and a stage director, both here in America and his native England. Hecht's friendship with Goodman has been chronicled by Hecht himself in his autobiography, *A Child of the Century* (1954). The abilities of Goodman and Hecht complemented each other: from Hecht Goodman learned about social conditions in Chicago and a great deal about working conditions among the poor; from Goodman, Hecht received invitations to groups that he probably would not have received otherwise. Despite Sherwood Anderson's advice to Hecht not to "collaborate with a millionaire . . . except in business," the two became collaborators, working together in the deserted board room of the Goodman lumber business, and wrote a couple of (admittedly minor) plays, most of which were performed by local theatre groups. Goodman's best plays are, however, those he wrote alone, the most frequently produced being *Dust of the Road* (1913) and *The Game of Chess* (1917).

Goodman's greatest wish was to found a theatre for the poor on Maxwell Street where plays could be produced free of charge for the largely immigrant population of the neighborhood. Unfortunately, he never lived to see this wish fulfilled. In 1917 Goodman joined the navy as an officer. While serving on active duty he died on 28 November 1918 of influenza (probably contracted at a football game) and was buried in Graceland Cemetery in Chicago, a place frequently called Chicago's Pantheon. In 1922 Goodman's parents along with his widow decided to honor Goodman's memory with a living memorial, a theatre and a school to be built not on Maxwell Street, but behind the Art Institute, according to a plan outlined by Goodman before he died. The trustees of the Art Institute accepted the gift of $350,000 from the Goodman family and shortly thereafter work was begun on the theatre. The architect for the new theatre was Howard Van Doren Shaw, not necessarily one of the great architects of the First Chicago School, but nevertheless the designer of several prestigious structures, such as the Fourth Presbyterian Church and the Quadrangle Club of the University of Chicago. The head of the new theatre was to be Thomas Wood Stevens, who made certain that the Goodman company's repertory in the first seasons reflected the kind of plays Goodman would have wanted to see.

In the spring of 1925, the acting company which Stevens selected did several evenings of plays at Fullerton Hall as a sort of calling-card season. The first use of the Kenneth Sawyer Goodman Theatre was on 20 October 1925 with a bill of three one-acts by the dead playwright—*Back of the Yards*, *The Green Scarf*, and *The Game of Chess*—staged by Stevens and Howard Southgate, the latter an actor and director with the newly formed company. This event was covered by both the drama critics and the society editors, since the audience was filled with the elite of Chicago's society. The official public opening on 25 October presented the American premiere of John Galsworthy's anti-imperialist play *The Forest*, staged by Stevens. The advent of the new theatre was applauded, the play less so.

Howard Van Doren Shaw's modified Doric temple of the arts was a difficult project to design because the zoning laws of Chicago prohibited building over a certain height near the lakefront. Therefore, except for the entrance foyer, the whole building was built underground, resting in the sandy soil on a sort of concrete disc. The front of the theatre was nondescript, its plainness earning for the theatre the nickname of "the pillbox" or "the mausoleum." The interior was warm, however, with a spacious lobby and dark wood paneling in the auditorium, and the busts of ten famous writers around the walls. The comfortable auditorium provided 725 seats arranged in continental fashion (no central aisle), wide spaces between the rows, a gradual rise in the floor, and convenient access to exits. The backstage was exceedingly well equipped, with a wide 37-foot proscenium opening and a distance of 165 feet from the front of the stage to the plaster dome which surrounded the stage. Since zoning restrictions prohibited a fly gallery, large side wagon stages were provided to shift scenery rapidly. Two quotations from Kenneth Sawyer

Goodman were prominently inscribed over two parts of the theatre. The first (not from a play) was over the front entrance of the theatre itself: "To restore the old vision, and to win the new." The second, still widely quoted, was from Goodman's allegorical play *The Edge of the Wood* and was enshrined over the proscenium arch: "You yourself must set flame to the fagots which you have brought." (The current management of the Goodman Theatre is considering an unveiling of this quotation, which is covered up at the present time.)

The acting company which Stevens had selected to present Galsworthy's play included several actors who were well known then (or who achieved fame later), including Mary Agnes Doyle, Eula Guy, Roman Bohnen, Whitford Kane, and Howard Southgate. (The last two served as stage directors for the company as well.) The critics were neither impressed with the play nor with the company, which had not meshed as yet. As J. Vandervoort Sloan put it in *Drama* magazine, "No other professional company could have made it a success and the Goodman Theatre Group is far from being professional." Only Eula Guy as Almina received consistently good reviews.

The second and third plays of the season proved more acceptable, and the fourth—the American premiere of Georg Kaiser's *Gas*, staged by Marion Gehring (who had been trained by Vsevold Meyerhold), with sets by Louis Lozowick—was a decided success though it confused many subscribers with its expressionistic techniques. Other plays followed with generally favorable reviews, the season closing with Shakespeare's *A Midsummer-Night's Dream*, staged by Whitford Kane who also played Bottom. This production did well at the box office and subsequently it was always Stevens's proud boast that he "made Shakespeare pay." Other playwrights who figured in the Goodman Theatre's opening season were Gregorio Martínez-Sierra, John Masefield, Molière, George Bernard Shaw, and the anonymous author of *Everyman*.

The fall of 1925 also saw the opening of the School of Drama that would work alongside the commercial company, something else young Goodman had wanted. Its job would be to train people for the professional theatre, with emphasis on acting and directing. In its first year 125 were enrolled from, the publicity said, "over 1,000 applicants." The theatre school curriculum was built around a three-year program with part of the professional company acting as teachers. Early in the life of the school Stevens planned a studio theatre (for student productions) and a children's theatre which would be a regular part of the student training (both became realities in 1929).

The most notable production of the professional company in its second season (1925-1926) was Sean O'Casey's *Juno and the Paycock*, with the directing honors going to Kane (who also played Boyle) and Mary Agnes Doyle as Juno. The season's opener Romain Rolland's *The Game of Love and Death* (directed by Stevens) was performed at the Goodman Theatre three years before the much-discussed Theatre Guild Production in New York. Other plays receiving critical acclaim that season were Luigi Chiarelli's *The Mask and the Face* (directed by Stevens) and Shakespeare's *As You Like it* (directed by Alexandra Carlisle and Kane). The season was adjudged more of a success than the first by the critics, but play selection was not exactly what Stevens, or more ominously the Board of Trustees at the Art Institute, had in mind.

The season of 1927-1928 was Stevens's best, boasting two of Ibsen's plays: *The Wild Duck* (directed by Kane) and the infrequently staged *The Vikings at Helgoland* (directed by Stevens). The latter play attracted huge crowds partly due to Chicago's large Scandinavian population, and partly due to the novel use in the setting of the Clavilus, a kind of electric-light organ. Another surprise hit of the season was a charming production of the Hindu drama usually attributed to King Shadraka, *The Little Clay Cart* (directed by Cloyd Head), which was revived the next season. Other writers represented this season were Shakespeare, Alexandre Dumas père, and L. W. Verdenne whose *Outbreak* received its world premiere (directed by Kane), much written about at the time, much forgotten today.

The 1928-1929 season in best remembered as the one in which David Itkin staged H. Levick's *The Golem* with Friendly Leon Ford as the Inquisitor. Itkin had been a member of the Habimah Theater (the national theatre of Israel, founded in Moscow) and a student of Stanislavsky's before immigrating to America. His English was broken, and tradition says he wandered in off the streets looking for a job at the Goodman. Stevens hired him and he was to remain a Goodman fixture until his retirement in the 1970s. Other plays offered in the season were Gogol's *The Inspector General* (directed by Kane); Pirandello's *Six Characters in Search of an Author*, with Roman Bohnen as the manager; plus Ibsen's *When We Dead Awaken*, with the production by B. Iden Payne (it was his only season with the company); and Richard Sheridan's *The Critic*, with Kane as Sir Walter Raleigh and Art Smith as Mr. Sneer.

The season of 1929-1930 continued Stevens's

The Goodman Theatre

policy of producing half classics and half modern works, but despite mostly good reviews, the stock market crash in the opening weeks of the season sent attendance down and the company lost a good deal of money—too much, said the trustees. Eventually Stevens quarreled with the trustees, and at the end of the season he resigned. His final play, *Escape*, was also by the author he had chosen to open the theatre four seasons earlier, John Galsworthy. Though the Chicago critics had occasionally argued with Stevens's choice of plays and productions, they lamented his departure. The kind of theatre which Stevens had envisioned was at least thirty years ahead of its time. He had successfully engaged a number of distinguished artists for his company. His choice of plays included several writers not seen on the commercial stage of the time. But the deficits killed him.

There was one final season for the professional theatre (1930-1931), managed by Hubert Osborne with Maurice Gneisen chosen to head the theatre school. Most of the actors associated with Stevens had left for New York. Mary Agnes Doyle, however, remained to teach at the school. Though Osborne cut the deficit to a manageable level with his choice of a more commercial repertory and despite the addition of new acting talent (Kent Smith, Judith Lowry, Margaret Wycherly) in the spring of 1931, the Board of Trustees at the Art Institute ended its support of the professional company. The final play staged was Somerset Maugham's *The Sacred Flame*; its premiere was on 31 March 1931.

In the fall of 1931 Gneisen was officially made head of the Goodman School of Drama, a position he was to hold until his death in 1956. It was his joke that he was the only Russian ever to work in the American theatre who had never studied with Stanislavsky; he received his theatre training from Syracuse University, Yale, and George Pierce Baker. Gneisen incorporated many of Stevens's ideas of running the drama school (admittedly Stevens's second love) with many of his own. As one of his former teachers put it, "Gneisen ran the school well, with a firm hand, and you always knew who was boss around him." He kept the studio, the main stage, and the children's theatre running with full seasons for eight months of the year. He brought in new teachers and kept the school alive during the dark days of the Depression. Among the more distinguished alumni of Gneisen's early years (to the end of World War II) are Karl Malden, Geraldine Page, Jose Quintero, Shelley Berman, Sam Wanamaker, and Ralph Alswang.

The productions on the studio and main

stages in the 1930s and 1940s, however, were both commercial and artistic. Gneisen reasoned that since most of his actors were going to work on Broadway, there ought to be a lot of commercial plays in the bill. But some noteworthy plays continued to be produced, including Percy Mackaye's *This Fine-Pretty World* (1931, directed by Itkin), Gneisen's own *Leonardo da Vinci* (1933, directed by Itkin), Ibsen's *The Master Builder* (1934, directed by Gneisen with Itkin as Solness), A. A. Milne's *Mr. Pim Passes By* (1935, directed by Sidney Breese), Shakespeare's *Romeo and Juliet* (1942, directed by Gneisen) and *King Lear* (1944, directed by Gneisen with Itkin as the King), and Chekhov's *The Sea Gull* (1944, directed by Itkin).

Earlier Stevens had opened a children's theatre on the main stage to present a season of four or five plays. The first director was Marion Brown, who was also Stevens's secretary. In the 1930s she was replaced by two of the early pioneers in the children's theatre movement, Charlotte Chorpenning and Louis Dale Spoor, both writers and directors of children's plays and close friends. Chorpenning wrote and directed a series of plays for the Goodman, most of which are still in print and still produced by children's theatres in the United States. She reasoned that a children's play should also please adults and that children should receive nothing but the best. Spoor and Chorpenning worked closely together and eventually founded the Coach House Press, which publishes children's plays.

After World War II both the Goodman student body and the faculty grew in size. The theatre was renovated and was one of the first to boast an Izenour board to control its lighting. Several graduates from the postwar era who later became famous were Lee Richardson, Harvey Korman, Lois Nettleton, and Theoni Aldredge. The acting training program remained the children's strong point of the Goodman, but the plays presented on the main stage (except the children's plays) were undistinguished. In the early 1950s Gneisen began to suffer from ill health, but he was reluctant to delegate power. Three people more than any others held the school together, all acting teachers: Joseph Slowik, David Itkin, and his daughter Bella (fondly known as Dr. Bella). Gneisen died in 1956. In the following year John Reich became head of the school, after Walter Martini's interim term as head of the school. Reich faced the difficult task of revamping the Goodman's entire program and image. For many years the theatre and the school were called "the best kept secret in Chicagoland."

Reich was born in Austria and his early academic training was in business, but he changed his mind and eventually studied theatre with Max Reinhardt. In Vienna he worked with both the Burgtheater and the Theater in der Josephstadt. In 1938 he immigrated to America before the Nazi takeover of Austria. He eventually earned a Ph.D. from Cornell (1944) and worked with various opera and theatre festivals and on Broadway before coming to the Goodman. With Reich came Charles McGaw who had considerable experience on the professional stage as a director and who had worked in Hollywood as well. McGaw eventually assumed control of the school as did Reich of the theatre.

Reich's whole attitude toward the theatre was decidedly professional. He hired Danny Newman to be publicity director and to increase the number of subscribers. He hired some new faculty members for the school, most with professional experience. His most notable accomplishment was to rejuvenate the Goodman's main-stage productions, to which he routinely invited the Chicago critics.

Under Gneisen's administration there had been occasional guest artists acting with the students, but this was not a permanent policy. Reich decided that the best way for students to learn acting was to observe professionals, so in his very first production at the Goodman, Eugene O'Neill's *Ah Wilderness!* (directed by McGaw), Sidney Breese, a well-known Chicago actor, played the father, Nat Miller. In 1959 Reich received a Ford Foundation grant of $10,000 which he used to hire a professional star to appear. The first actor hired was Murray Matheson, who appeared in Molière's *The Imaginary Invalid*, which Reich both translated and directed, to close the 1958-1959 season. This practice became a regular part of the Goodman season.

The guest star policy was good as long as the professional actor was receptive to working with student actors, and the best of the guest artists' plays were those in which the actor or actress gave completely of himself or herself. Some of the most critically acclaimed of the guest actor productions would include Shakespeare's *The Merchant of Venice* (1959, directed by McGaw) with Morris Carnovsky as Shylock; William Saroyan's *The Cave Dwellers* (1959, directed by Eugenie Leontovich and Joseph Slowik) with Leontovich as the Queen and Studs Terkel as the King; Pirandello's *Enrico IV* (1960, directed by Reich) with Ivor Harries in the title role; Hermann Gressieker's *Royal Gambit* (1961, directed by Melvin Bernhardt) with Sam Wanamaker as Henry VIII; Anouilh's *The Lark* (1961, directed by Bella Itkin) with Frances Hyland as Jean; Brecht's

The Caucasian Chalk Circle (1962, directed by Reich) with Carnovsky doubling as the Story Teller and Azdak; Shakespeare's *King Lear* (1964, directed by McGaw) with Carnovsky as the King; Shakespeare's *Macbeth* (1964, directed by Wanamaker with himself in the title role); the first American company production of Peter Weiss's *Marat/Sade* (1966, directed by McGaw) with Jerome Kilty as Sade; Brecht's *Galileo* (1966, directed by Howard da Silva) with Carnovsky as Galileo; Shakespeare's *Othello* (1968, directed by McGaw) with James Earl Jones as the Moor and Len Cariou as Iago; the world premiere of James Rosenberg's *The Death and Life of Sneaky Fitch* (1968, directed by Slowik); and Paul Foster's *Tom Paine* (1969, directed by Patrick Henry) with Michael Higgins and Ellen Travolta. Other guest artists to appear during the 1957-1969 years were Michael Hall, Fitzroy Davis, Donald Buka, Joseph Buloff, Walter Abel, Leo G. Carroll, Bramwell Fletcher, Signe Hasso, Tod Andrews, Lillian Gish, Brenda Forbes, Patricia Jessel, Peggy Wood, Zoe Caldwell, James Ray, Carrie Nye, Ronnie Graham, and Maurice Copeland. In most of the seasons from 1957 to 1969 Reich generally staged two plays as did McGaw.

By the 1967-1968 season the Goodman had more than twelve thousand subscribers with the theatre averaging 77 percent in attendance. In 1967 Mayor Richard J. Daley proclaimed a Goodman week; the same year Reich suggested that Chicago and the Goodman needed a professional resident company. In 1966 Mayor Daley commissioned a long and very expensive study to see if Chicago was ready for a professional theatre company. For a while there was talk of inviting several professional companies to make their home in Chicago but nothing came of this. In 1969 Reich moved into the breach and finally convinced a reluctant Board of Trustees at the Art Institute to support a resident theatre company that would present a full season of plays on the main stage. Reich then appointed two people to be his mainstays: Douglas Seale would be a coproducer and Douglas Campbell would be the company's lead actor with some responsibilities in staging. McGaw would assume the deanship of the theatre school. Seale had come from England where he had worked with both the Old Vic in London and the Shakespeare Memorial Theatre at Stratford-upon-Avon. In America he had worked with the Cleveland Play House, the Center Stage in Baltimore, the Front Street Theatre in Memphis, plus various other regional theatres. Campbell too had originally come from England (where he had worked at the Old Vic), but he had immigrated to

Canada where he had appeared as an actor at the Stratford Ontario Shakespeare Festival; he had also performed at the Guthrie Theatre in Minneapolis. Both men were talented and experienced, but sadly the triumvirate with Reich never seemed to function well.

The first season of the professional company (1969-1970) was undoubtedly Reich's best in terms of subscriptions (seventeen thousand) and audience support, though there was some grumbling by the critics. Reich's idea was the age-old one of splitting the season between classics and modern works (the opening publicity might have been written by Thomas Wood Stevens) with the permanent company (of about thirty actors) beefed up by guest artists. The opening production on 20 October 1969 presented Rolf Hochhuth's *Soldiers* (directed by Seale) with Campbell as Churchill. The play was not much admired, nor was the production, though Campbell received some good notices. Other works in the first season that Seale staged were Shakespeare's *The Tempest*, Robert Shaw's *The Man in the Glass Booth* with Leonardo Cimino as Arthur Goldman, and George Bernard Shaw's *Heartbreak House* with Campbell as Shotover. Other plays of the first season were Kaufman and Hart's *You Can't Take It With You* (directed by Edward Payson) and a double bill of Pinter's *The Basement* and *The Tea Party* (directed by Slowik). Critical reaction to the season was mixed, with *Heartbreak House* and *The Man in the Glass Booth* receiving the best reviews.

The next season (1970-1971) saw a dwindling in the number of subscriptions, despite the fact that the Goodman had the biggest hit it had ever had to this time: Patrick Henry's staging of Jerome Lawrence and Robert E. Lee's *The Night Thoreau Spent in Jail* with Christopher Walken as Thoreau and Campbell as Emerson. There were works by Brecht, Shakespeare, Anouilh, and John Whiting, but the only work besides *The Night Thoreau Spent in Jail* to gain wide public support was Seale's staging of an old Victorian clinker, *Lady Audley's Secret* (music by George Goehring, lyrics by John Kuntz) with Russell Nype. At the end of the season it was announced that the professional resident company would disband and that in the future each play would be treated as a separate entity. Campbell decided to leave and Seale returned for one season more to direct only. For the season of 1971-1972 Ken Myers became managing director for the Goodman Theatre Center (as it was then known). There were rumors that this would be Reich's last season and that Myers would continue alone after the season had closed. The first play was Stuart Vaughn's

much heralded *Assassination 1865*, staged by the author. The rest of the season was made up of Wilde's *The Importance of Being Earnest* (directed by Seale), Kaufman and Ferber's *The Royal Family* (Seale's last production), Peter Barnes's controversial satire *The Ruling Class* (directed by Patrick Henry), and the closing work of the season, Rogers and Hart's *The Boys from Syracuse* (directed by Christopher Hewett). In 1972 Reich left the Goodman.

The careers of Stevens and Reich have some parallels. Both were far more interested in the running of the professional company than in the daily chores of running a school. Both had their problems with the Board of Trustees of the Art Institute, though both had a large following with the general public. And the man hired to replace each in the running of the professional wing of the theatre lasted only one season. Ken Myers's season of 1972-1973 was neither a critical nor an audience success, and in the spring of 1973 he too handed in his resignation.

Myers had hired William Woodman to stage one work during his season as sole head of the theatre, and on the basis of this production and his past experience Woodman was offered the job as the head of the Goodman professional theatre in 1973. Woodman had considerable knowledge of regional theatres, having worked at the Barter Theatre, the Cleveland Play House, and the American Shakespeare Festival at Stratford, Connecticut, before coming to the Goodman. His goal was the same as Reich's had been (though he did not have to worry about the school): to restore faith in the crumbling Goodman, which is precisely what he accomplished. Woodman increased the number of subscriptions to what Reich had in his first season as head of the professional resident company; he also boosted a 90 percent attendance record. The Goodman currently has eighteen thousand subscribers.

Woodman's ideas were not the "balanced season" ideas of Stevens and Reich; he believed more in excitement in staging, whatever the play might be. In his next seasons with the Goodman he presented ten world and four American premieres. He also established in his second season a smaller theatre called Stage 2. Stage 2 had at least five locations and had been used exclusively for the presentation of modern or experimental works. Woodman also brought directors from abroad to the Goodman. His overall choice of repertory to be produced was decidedly modern, though Woodman's own classic productions were probably the best works he staged for the Goodman. Outstanding productions during Woodman's administration included plays by Brian Friel, Ibsen, Shakespeare, Chekhov, Brecht, Wilder, O'Neill, David Mamet, and David Rabe.

In the spring of 1978 Woodman voluntarily stepped down to be replaced by Gregory Mosher, who continues Woodman's emphasis on modern works and new plays. So far in the two seasons of Mosher's regime, he has produced five world and two American premieres. In the 1980-1981 season there will be five works which Chicago has never seen before; the season began with a specially commissioned translation of Erdman's *The Suicide*. Goodman Theatre Studio (located in the Goodman's old studio theatre) opened with a production of two plays by Beckett, staged by the author.

In view of Mosher's program, it is ironic that the greatest hit in the last two seasons has been Barbara Field's adaptation of Dickens's *A Christmas Carol*, first performed in the holiday season of 1978, but revived in the 1979-1980 season and again (with the same director, Tony Mockus) in November of 1980 to play through the holiday season. It is currently being underwritten by grants from the *Chicago Sun-Times*. Presumably *A Christmas Carol* will be revived for many holidays to come.

In his first season Mosher had two plays which were moved to Broadway, where they were critically attacked: Richard Howard's *Working* (1979, directed by Michael Feingold) and John Guare's *Bosoms and Neglect* (1979, directed by Mel Shapiro). Both these were rather well received by the Chicago critics. Other notable offerings in the last two seasons include Richard Wright's *Native Son* (1978, directed by Mosher); the world premiere of David Mamet's *Lone Canoe* (1979, directed by Mosher with music and lyrics by Alaric Jans); the American premiere of Slawomir Morozek's *Emigres* 1978, presented at Stage 2 directed by Mosher); Sam Shepard's *Curse of the Starving Class* (1979, directed by Robert Falls); Wole Soyinka's *Death and the King's Horseman* (1979, directed by the author); Arthur Miller's adaptation of Ibsen's *An Enemy of the People* (1980, directed by Mosher); the world premiere of Richard Nelson's *Bal* (1980, directed by Mosher); and Rostand's *Cyrano de Bergerac* (1980, directed by Michael Maggio), with Kenneth Welsh as the long-nosed poet.

Since 1977 the Goodman Theatre has separated itself from the Art Institute and is administered and funded by the Chicago Theatre Group, Incorporated. Stanley M. Freehling was the first chairman of the group, which supports the Goodman with a budget in excess of two million dollars, one-third of which is subsidized by grants from various organizations and private contributors. The Goodman Theatre has its own technical staff and administrative staff (one of whom is David Mamet) and is very much a self-sustaining organization. Over a typical season the theatre will mount six productions on the main stage plus a variable number at Goodman Theatre Studio for approximately eighteen thousand subscribers. The Goodman employs over one hundred actors a season and despite the fact it does not support a permanent resident company, there are clearly "Goodman favorites" who appear frequently. The Goodman Theatre seems assured of a long and distinguished future.

Since 1957 the Goodman School of Drama has fared poorly. As Joseph Slowik (a member of the Goodman staff since the 1940s) put it, "Reich . . . wanted a high profile for the theatre company which he regarded as more glamorous and exciting than the school." The losses from the school coupled with the losses from the professional theatre caused the Art Institute trustees to end their financial support of both. One member of the Goodman staff said bitterly that the trustees could instead "Buy a few more Cézannes." In 1975 the trustees announced that the incoming class of the school would be its last and in 1978 the school would close. Various institutions in the Chicago area were scouted with an eye for relocation, the best candidate being the Chicago Circle campus of the University of Illinois, but this possibility was squashed at the last minute by unknown sources. In 1978, and at the last minute, it was announced the Goodman would become the ninth school of De Paul University.

The current dean of the Goodman School of Drama is John Watts, formerly of Boston University and the University of California at Long Beach. The school presents five plays a year in its new theatre (created from an old building) on the De Paul campus, plus three children's plays on the main stage at the Goodman (this will cease in three years). The school has a four-year curriculum leading to a bachelor's degree, though students may attend the acting program only for three years and receive a certificate. Among its current faculty are Bella Itkin (head of the children's theatre since 1958, but a member of the Goodman faculty "since the year one," as she jokingly says), Joseph Slowik, Jack Jones, James Maronek, and others. Recent graduates of the school have included Carrie Snodgress, Charlaine Woodward, Ted Wass, Avery Schreiber, Concetta Tomei, Melinda Dillon, plus numerous actors, directors, and producers who are active in the various theatres which dot the north and south sides of Chicago.

Though the two Goodman organizations are now separated, both were created and continue to function according to Kenneth Sawyer Goodman's wish: "To restore old visions and to win the new." Given the quality of both organizations' work and the energetic and resourceful nature of their artists, both the Goodman School of Drama and the Goodman Theatre seem likely to provide Chicago with excellent talent and theatre for many years to come.

–Leon M. Aufdemberge

References:

Otto Maurice Forkert, *Children's Theatre . . . that Captures its Audience* (Chicago: Coach House Press, 1962);

Kenneth Sawyer Goodman, *More Quick Curtains* (Chicago: Stage Guild, 1923);

Ben Hecht, *A Child of the Century* (New York: Simon & Schuster, 1954);

Cora Jarrett, "The Goodman Theatre," *Theatre Arts*, 9, no. 9 (September 1925): 609-613;

Kenneth Macgowan, *Footlights Across America* (New York: Harcourt, Brace, 1929);

James S. Newel, "A Critical Analysis of the Development and Growth of the Kenneth Sawyer Goodman Memorial Theatre and School of Drama, Chicago, Illinois, 1925-1971," Ph.D. dissertation, Wayne State University, Detroit, 1973;

Martin Scott, "Drama School," *Theatre Arts*, 35, no. 7 (July 1951): 40-41, 90-91;

Thomas Wood Stevens, "What the Audience Wants," *Theatre Arts*, 15, no. 1 (January 1931): 59-67.

Papers:

The Kenneth Sawyer Goodman and Ben Hecht papers are on file at the Newberry Library in Chicago. The Cultural Center of the Chicago Public Library holds archives of the Goodman School of Drama and the Goodman Theatre. There are additional papers of the latter at the library of the Art Institute of Chicago.

The Guthrie Theater
Minneapolis

The Guthrie Theater is one of America's most distinguished and well-equipped regional theaters. It is located in downtown Minneapolis, in a specially built auditorium which is part of The Walker Art Museum cultural complex. It seats 1,441 spectators in an irregular semicircle around an equally irregular seven-sided stage. The Guthrie opened on 6 May 1963, with a production of *Hamlet* directed by Tyrone Guthrie and starring George Grizzard in the title role. In the years since, the Guthrie has maintained a steady reputation for responsible, if sometimes uninspired, repertory. Prior to the founding of the Guthrie, almost all professional theatre in the United States was concentrated in New York City. Most Americans came no closer than an occasional road company production of a Broadway hit to the experience of live professional theatre. Today, seventeen years after the Guthrie's opening, there are more than 175 nonprofit professional theatres in this country.

The expertise of the technical staff is world famous, especially in the areas of costuming and prop construction. The uncompromising use of the thrust stage has had an impact on recent theatre construction throughout the United States. Finally, the Guthrie Theater has transformed Minneapolis into one of America's most important theatrical cities, both for the number of theatres available and for the receptiveness of the audience.

In his book, *A New Theatre*, Tyrone Guthrie describes in some detail why the theatre was founded, and how and why it was built where it was. Guthrie, Oliver Rea, and Peter Zeisler conceived and developed the idea over a period of months. Rea offered his expertise as a theatrical businessman, and Zeisler brought a fund of theatrical technology to the project. Guthrie was the dominant creative spirit, and the name to be used for attracting public support.

After determining that they could not establish the sort of theatre they wanted in either New York or London, they cast about the United States in search of an appropriate site. A conversation with the New York critic Brooks Atkinson led to Atkinson's mentioning the project in a newspaper article. The result was an expression of interest from seven cities across the country: San Francisco, Milwaukee, Detroit, Boston, Cleveland, Chicago, and Minneapolis. One city was too close to other cultural centers which would detract from the special nature of the proposed theatre, another threatened artistic control, another seemed generally inhospitable; one by one the various possibilities were eliminated until only Minneapolis remained; besides, Guthrie freely admits that this was the location they preferred, relying purely on "hunch." Surely, part of Minneapolis's attraction was the easy readiness backers demonstrated to raise the necessary money.

The idea of the Guthrie Theater evolved slowly among Rea, Zeisler, and Guthrie; much of it occurred during a long retreat at Guthrie's home in Ireland in July of 1959. Many of their ideas were simply reactions against the coarse commercialism of Broadway and London's West End theatre district. The men were very much aware that American performers, directors, and technicians lacked the opportunity enjoyed by their British counterparts to try their skills, to hone their talents, in repertory companies.

In addition to providing a repertory experience for American theatre people, the three founders wanted the opportunity to do "Good Plays." They opted to define "Good" as applying to plays which had stood the test of time, which were still admired and enjoyed by artists and audiences alike after several generations. Guthrie's temporal litmus test would automatically exclude all American plays, a policy which immediately appeared shortsighted and not very complimentary to the host country. To avoid any appearance of cultural colonialism, they decided to include in each season one American play which seemed destined for classic standing. This policy was to be given a three-year test run, after which time it would be reexamined.

The play selection policy, like so much else about the Guthrie Theater, was the natural conclusion of the man who founded the troupe. Tyrone Guthrie was, at age sixty-three, an internationally acclaimed actor, director, and producer. Of Irish birth and breeding, he conquered the English stage, first with the Oxford Repertory Theatre, and later in various productions, both in the classical and the commercial theatre. He was an inspirational force behind the Scottish National Theatre, the Cambridge Festival, the Old Vic, and, most recently and most importantly for developments in Minneapolis,

the Stratford (Ontario) Shakespeare Festival. He had been knighted in 1961 for his contributions to the Canadian and British stage. He was to remain active in theatre after leaving Minneapolis until his death in 1971 at the age of seventy. His impact on the theatre which bears his name cannot be overestimated.

The Guthrie trio found quick and full support in the city's business world. John Cowles, Jr., vice-president of the leading newspaper chain in the Twin Cities, the "Minneapolis Star and Tribune," organized the financial community. When the theatre people were on the brink of decision, they were told that the Walker Foundation would contribute a handsome site, contiguous to its elegant museum, and that the Steering Committee, headed by Cowles, had further convinced the Walker Foundation to make an initial contribution of $400,000. Furthermore, the committee could assure Guthrie and company that an additional $900,000 could be raised quite readily.

The Steering Committee was made up of a group of local businessmen, mostly well under fifty years old, very comfortable financially, but not representing enormous wealth. They were socially well established, and seemed to Guthrie to be deeply committed to the project as a public service. Events appear to have born out Guthrie's conviction, and when the inevitable cost overruns occurred, the committee was able to raise a total of two million dollars to build the theatre. Strong support from the Twin Cities' business community has not faltered since. Contributions to the building fund came from large corporations and from individuals. The two-million-dollar fund represented a commitment from the entire community, and from surrounding areas as well. Clearly, Minnesota was ready for the sort of theatre Guthrie and his colleagues wanted to create.

Unlike many regional theatres, the Guthrie did not have to start out by renovating an existing building. In no way did the founders have to compromise their ideals to meet the exigencies of space designed for some other use. This is not to say that they got everything they wanted in their new building; considerable alterations had to be made during periods of design and construction in order to keep costs within the already generous budget. Throughout the building of the theatre, there was conflict between the theatre people and the architect, Ralph Rapson, professor of architecture at the University of Minnesota in Minneapolis. Guthrie was especially distressed by the need to cut off a large portion of the backstage and administrative areas, reducing not only their size, but also their attractiveness as places to work. This was particularly galling, since the lobbies and other public areas were never cut into, and remained spacious and lavish. In 1970, the backstage needs were alleviated by a sizable and comfortable addition.

It was in the architectural design of the theatre that Guthrie's association with the Stratford Shakespeare Festival became most obviously influential. Rapson felt that he could design a space which would convert readily from proscenium to thrust to arena; Guthrie and his fellow artists insisted that such a structure would inevitably be a compromise completely suitable to no one style. Guthrie had now been joined by Tanya Moiseiwitsch, a leading set and costume designer, and Douglas Campbell, an outstanding actor and director. Both were to remain with the Guthrie Theater for many years, and both had worked with Guthrie himself at Stratford. Indeed, Moiseiwitsch had designed the Stratford stage ten years before, and Campbell had been acting and directing on it ever since it had opened. This trio found itself frequently referring to their Stratford experience in dealing with the architect, and the group even made a trip to Stratford to view that playhouse. Rapson was not impressed; he found the Canadian house claustrophobic. Guthrie and his group, on the other hand, felt that the Stratford thrust stage and house held valuable lessons for them all. In the end, the Stratford frame of reference was valuable for providing a model of a thrust stage, and for leading the Minnesota group to aim for greater intimacy in the audience, and for greater set flexibility on stage than existed at Stratford.

The Guthrie auditorium is a large, irregular 200-degree arc. The seats are vari-colored, and rise in a steep "Alpine slope" on the audience right; no seat is more than fifty-two feet from the stage. The stage itself juts forth from the back wall as an asymmetrical seven-sided raised platform surrounded by steps leading down to the level of the audience. There are two entrance areas, or "vomitoria" sorts of tunnels rising from under the seating area and opening onto the stage, each placed about one third of the way into the audience. The back wall provides additional entrance areas. There is no place for a traditional stage set; productions are done with furniture pieces, hand and stage props, and costumes which are carefully selected and painstakingly constructed. Just as Guthrie intended, this has thrown the directorial emphasis on acting and human relationships, while the producer/designer concentrates on perfect evocation of period and mood with a few pieces, instead of a whole set. The asymmetrical quality of both the stage and the "house" or auditorium, combined with the lively color scheme, was "different" without being undignified, and favored movement over static solemnity. The Guthrie, very intentionally, does not look like a traditional opera house or movie theatre.

One of the factors which helped the Guthrie group decide on Minneapolis in the first place continued to be a source of help to them as they went about founding the theatre. The drama department of the University of Minnesota had been from the start cordial and open to Guthrie and his project. University theatre departments in other site cities were often hostile, fearing competition from a Guthrie repertory company. Frank Whiting, head of Minnesota's drama department, was determined that Guthrie should come to the Twin Cities, and he made the facilities and expertise of his department available to the new group.

Guthrie had long felt that there was an unnatural separation between academic and professional theatre, a gap which had to be bridged for their mutual benefit. Too frequently Guthrie had experienced the frustration of an educated man faced with talented but ignorant cast members or design technicians, people who could not seize the spirit of a classic piece of theatre because they knew nothing of the art, the politics, the religion of the period in which the play was written or set. On the other hand, he encountered too many young people, fresh from university drama departments, whose only previous practical experience with theatre had been in productions of *Brigadoon* in the college gymnasium; too often, they had had virtually no practical experience. Perhaps the flaw in academic training which irked Guthrie the most was the lack of adequate vocal training. Acoustics were at first a problem in the Guthrie Theater; spectators in the seats furthest from the stage had difficulty hearing the performers. Guthrie felt that the problem lay not in the acoustical design of the auditorium, but in the poor vocal training given to fledgling actors.

From the first year of the Guthrie operation, fellowships were established, first by the McKnight Foundation, later by the Bush Foundation, to fund a number of advanced graduate students for a year of work at the Guthrie. These young men and women were to work side by side with the professionals at the theatre, and acquire valuable experience for both their academic work and their future professional lives. In practice, it did not always work so well, and the original twelve McKnight fellow-

Sir Tyrone Guthrie

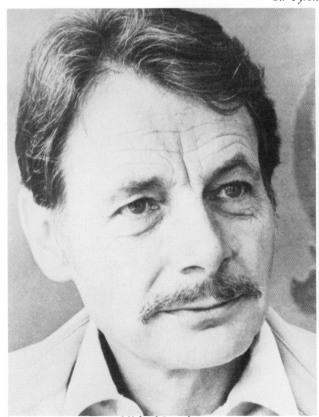

Michael Langham

Alvin Epstein

ships dwindled to three or four Bush fellowships. Not all the professionals at the theatre were as eager as Guthrie to welcome the students and to take valuable time to become their teachers, and not all of the students selected for the honor were as talented or dedicated as had been hoped. Nonetheless, the system has maintained a rapport between the university and the Guthrie which has fostered cooperation and prevented open hostility. A member of the university's Department of Theatre Arts sits on the governing board of the Guthrie, and the newly appointed (September 1980) dramaturge at the Guthrie is Arthur Ballet, a professor from that department. In addition, the mere existence of the fellowships has proved a strong point in attracting some highly talented youngsters to the university's department.

Once the building was under way and the design firmly set, once the money had been raised or at least pledged, once relations with the university and the Twin Cities in general had been established, it was time to choose the theatre's first season and first troupe. Guthrie opted to do both simultaneously, that is, to seek performers for certain roles he wanted to offer, and to choose plays that would suit the particular talents of the actors he could get. He began with two leading players, Hume Cronyn and Jessica Tandy. The breadth and depth of their experience, the versatility in which they both delight, made of them ideal fulcrums for a repertory troupe. In addition, their professional stature was such that it was bound to facilitate recruiting other outstanding actors. This decision was made in January of 1962, in preparation for an opening in May of 1963.

Guthrie decided to open the theatre with his own production of *Hamlet*, starring George Grizzard. Grizzard took on a great deal of voice training for the role, and he and the rest of the troupe worked steadily to form an ensemble spirit which would carry them through the first season. Once the opening play was chosen and cast, the rest of the season fell into place: Molière's *The Miser* would be the second night's offering, and a few weeks later would appear Chekhov's *The Three Sisters*, followed by Arthur Miller's *Death of a Salesman*.

While the troupe was being assembled, community involvement in the new theatre was rising. A group of public-spirited women, calling themselves the Stagehands, set about doing the office work on a volunteer basis and giving broad publicity to the ticket campaign for the first season. By the end of 1962 there were more than twelve hundred women in the society, and by March of 1963, when the campaign closed, almost twenty-two thousand people had bought season tickets, for a total seat sale of eighty-eight thousand.

While the Stagehands represent the most obvious form of community support, it was clear from the start that enthusiasm for the project was widespread. Theatrical activity throughout the upper Midwest, in high schools, colleges, summer stock, dinner theatres, and community theatres, had gradually and unwittingly prepared an audience for the Guthrie. Most especially, Don Stoltz, director of an equity company at the Old Log Theatre, had unflaggingly worked to develop a love for theatre in the general community. At the time the Guthrie opened, there were approximately ten theatres functioning in sporadic fashion in the Twin Cities. In 1976, thirteen years later, there were well over forty, some equity, some school-related, some community, some dinner. There had been a natural distrust among some of the local theatre groups that the incursion of a highly funded, handsomely equipped, professional theatre group into the Twin Cities area would hurt them more than help them; they feared that a theatregoing community which was already barely adequate to fill the few small theatres in the cities would be absorbed by the Guthrie to the detriment of their own work. However, it is now clear that, while some groups may have foundered, the general level of theatre in the Minneapolis area has risen greatly, in quantity, in quality, and in diversity.

While the tickets were being sold and the house reaching final readiness, the acting and technical staffs were assembled and working on the first two productions. To the trio of Cronyn, Tandy, and Grizzard were added Rita Gam, for the darker, more mature roles, and—after considerable dithering by equity who objected to the employment of a foreigner for the roles—Zoe Caldwell to do Frosine in *The Miser* and Natasha in *The Three Sisters*. Rehearsals began on 11 March 1963. One of Guthrie's first tasks was to convince his troupe of the validity of staging *Hamlet* in modern dress. He stressed that this style would help the audience to see through the murk of previous productions, to hear and feel the story as something fresh, something quite possible and real. Furthermore, American actors seem less at home than their British counterparts with period costumes, with the stances and gaits that must accompany an Elizabethan gown or a Renaissance doublet. Guthrie's setting in a royal court of contemporary Europe permitted the use of elegant fashions and flashing jewelry for the ladies, and striking military uniforms for the gentlemen.

Rehearsals ran every day for about six hours, and included class work in voice, fencing, and movement. Twenty minutes a day Guthrie led the troupe in the choral speaking of Psalm 118, both in preparation for the opening dedicatory services and to provide a common vocal experience for the actors. These exercises had that pragmatic value, but they also brought the entire group together on terms of equality, an essential ingredient, Guthrie thought, to a successful repertory company.

On Sunday, 5 May, the theatre was opened with an interdenominational service of dedication, and on Tuesday, 7 May 1963, took place the first public performance. The evening had become an event, something much more than a mere opening night. The audience was made up of all those "who counted" in the Twin Cities, and a large number of newspeople as well. Tension was high, and excitement at a fever pitch. It was probably not the best environment in which to present four hours of one of the most difficult plays. The audience's attention was lost in the first few minutes of the production, and even the most favorable reviews felt that the evening had been less than successful.

The second night's *The Miser*, with Hume Cronyn as Harpagon, fared somewhat better. It is a busy, antic piece, and was staged with considerable panache by Douglas Campbell. If the style became occasionally stylized, and the frothy turned into the arch, the production did succeed in attracting and holding its audience. By the time *The Three Sisters*, with Jessica Tandy, Rita Gam, and Ellen Geer, and *Death of a Salesman*, with Hume Cronyn, Jessica Tandy, and Lee Richardson, made their appearances later in the season, the entire repertory had taken shape. Even the earlier productions overcame their opening difficulties and settled into more mature, reflective, and polished pieces. On balance, it can reasonably be said that the first season of the Minnesota Theatre Company (as the Guthrie was called until 1970) was a success.

The next two seasons maintained the same pace, and remained under the artistic direction of Tyrone Guthrie. The 1964-1965 season repeated the formula of the first: one Shakespearean play, one modern classic (George Bernard Shaw's *Saint Joan*), and one classical comedy (Ben Jonson's *Volpone*), and one major American play (Tennessee Williams's *The Glass Menagerie*). George Grizzard returned (as Henry V), as did Ellen Geer (the first season's Ophelia). Tanya Moiseiwitsch remained as designer, and several other cast and production members returned for the second season.

The third season was to be Guthrie's last as artistic director. After *Richard III*, William Congreve's *The Way of the World*, *The Cherry Orchard*, Bertolt Brecht's *The Caucasian Chalk Circle*, and a reprise of *The Miser*, he returned to other theatrical ventures. He did come back to Minneapolis on occasion to direct one of the plays of a season, but his absence was felt keenly in the theatre. Douglas Campbell spent one year, 1966-1967, as artistic director, but the whole structure of the theatre's production and management shifted considerably; the lack of a clear hand at the helm made a difference in how the theatre was run, how plays were chosen and by what standards, and how the theatre was perceived by the public. By this time of course, the Guthrie was firmly rooted in the cultural life of the Twin Cities, and despite occasional setbacks, seemed assured of continuous support. "Going to the Guthrie" had become a staple of the lives of many Minneapolitans.

The basic problem that the Guthrie has had to face ever since its founder's departure has concerned the position of artistic director. The duties of the job are so vast, so time- and energy-consuming, that few people have come close to performing the task adequately. Tyrone Guthrie, endowed with talent, interest, and expertise in virtually every realm of theatre, and gifted with the ability to recruit first-rate assistance in areas he could not personally supervise, set an impossible standard for his successors. His protege Douglas Campbell found the task beyond him, and the theatre limped on with no artistic director at all, or with groups of "Producing Directors," until 1971, when Michael Langham assumed the position. A number of regulars provided a sense of continuity during this difficult transitional period; Tanya Moiseiwitsch was at the Guthrie every year until 1970, and a core of performers like Paul Ballantyne, Len Cariou, Ellen Geer, Ed Flanders, and Ken Ruta returned for almost every season. The plays chosen continued to reflect the theatre's original intent to present classical works and one major American play each season. Especially notable was Guthrie's stunning production of *Oresteia*, as adapted by John Lewin under the title *The House of Atreus*. That production, along with Guthrie's version of Brecht's *The Resistible Rise of Arturo Ui*, toured the United States, including New York City, with considerable success. *The House of Atreus* was typical of a sort of production the Guthrie does very well: it was highly theatrical, with a strong use of masks, large and striking prop pieces, emphatic use of ritual in movement and speech, and it drew the audience into its universe by underlining the dramatic qualities of the script and minimizing the realism.

Guthrie believed that theatre is the direct descendant of fertility rites, war dances, and all the ritual expressions used by human beings to relate themselves to God. He did not enjoy directing love scenes or quiet tea parties for two or three characters; he enjoyed moving masses of actors about the stage in large crowds and at spectacular moments.

Obviously, such productions must rely heavily on technical perfection, and this has also become a hallmark of plays at the Guthrie. The uniformly high quality of technical work has made the Guthrie a mecca for technical training throughout the

pushed by a stage crew of two or three people. For Tennessee Williams's *Cat on a Hot Tin Roof*, special wicker furniture had to be built out of steel; the appearance had to be light and airy, while the pieces had to stand up against heavy use and frequent set changes.

The lack of successful artistic direction after Tyrone Guthrie's departure led to the lowest point in the theatre's history. Audience attendance had sunk to 61 percent of capacity, and the Ford Foundation was no longer covering the growing operating deficits incurred by the company. There was even some sentiment for disbanding the company

The Guthrie Theatre auditorium

world. Trainees arrive from Europe and Asia to study with the Guthrie technical staff. The staff constructs almost everything used in a Guthrie production, whether furniture, costumes, wigs, jewelry, hand props, or large set pieces. In order to function economically and efficiently—a Guthrie set must be very mobile, since as many as three different productions may be presented within a twenty-four hour period—a broad range of new technical methods have been developed at the theatre. For example, to move sets on and off the thrust stage, the Guthrie technicians have pioneered an air pressure system that lifts the set one half inch off the ground, allowing it to be

altogether and renting out the building for other purposes. The public rallied, however, and the appointment of Donald Schoenbaum as managing director gave a sound and consistent financial policy to the theatre. Schoenbaum continues as managing director at this writing, and his steady hand and firm fiscal control have helped the Guthrie to weather some rather severe artistic storms over the past decade.

Michael Langham was appointed artistic director the year before Donald Schoenbaum joined the staff, and Langham gave some badly needed aesthetic stability to the acting company. He remained in this position from 1971 to 1977. During his tenure, he raised the level of artistic quality by staging plays which both entertained and stimulated Guthrie's audiences. He was particularly successful with the classics, especially *Oedipus the King* (1972-1973), which was the world premiere of Anthony Burgess's new version, *The Winter's Tale* (1976), and Nikolai Gogol's *The Government Inspector* (1973). Langham had had considerable success prior to joining the Guthrie as a director in his native England and at Canada's Stratford Festival Theatre, where he had succeeded Tyrone Guthrie in 1955. At the Guthrie Langham lengthened the seasons, building to eight mainstage productions in the 1977-1978 season, plus some other special events. During his tenure, a visually stunning adaptation of Charles Dickens's *A Christmas Carol* became a staple in the Guthrie repertoire.

Although the audience and finances of the theatre grew very solid during Michael Langham's career at the Guthrie, relations with the University of Minnesota grew more distant and strained. The McKnight fellows, who had been so important to Tryone Guthrie's concept of a symbiotic relationship between academic and professional theatre, became Bush fellows, fewer in number and less important in the life of the Guthrie. Finally, the entire fellowship program was abandoned, although a new grant, the Michael Langham Fellowship, enables promising actors, directors, and designers to spend a season at the Guthrie. The former McKnight/Bush fellowships have simply become internships, awarded through the university's theatre department.

Community outreach grew steadily in the Langham years, and now encompasses a broad range of activities. It includes classes in acting, directing, mime, movement, prop construction, costuming, and a host of other theatrical activities. The classes are taught by the members of the Guthrie staff, the actors, directors, and technicians. The theatre sponsors an "Artist in Residence" program for schools in Minnesota, and has a variety of traveling exhibits featuring Guthrie-built props and costumes. There are two tour groups providing productions of Shakespearean dramas and other Guthrie offerings to communities outside the Twin Cities area. The theatre has services for the handicapped, in particular special performances of each production which are signed for the hearing-impaired. The community's elderly are served not only with special performances which go to those citizens who cannot come to the theatre, but also with works written and performed by senior citizens themselves. In 1978, the Guthrie produced a forty-five-minute script, *Flashbacks*, a compendium of stories and recollections culled from several older Minneapolitans, and acted by the elderly. Another show, *Christmas Past/Christmas Present* was created on a similar format. Finally, the group of twelve hundred "Stagehands," the volunteers who did so much to get the theatre underway at its inception, has developed into a full-fledged community volunteer group who perform all sorts of tasks about the theatre, from ushering and staffing the gift shop to compiling the theatre's publicity records and helping with costume construction.

As early as 1968, people at the Guthrie saw that the Mainstage, with its enormous seating capacity and the need to fill it, could not serve all the needs of the theatregoing public, or of the Guthrie's artists. There needed to be a place where small-scale productions could be given the chance to succeed or fail, without entailing the tremendous costs of a mainstage production. Furthermore, the limited range of the Guthrie program, the classics and one contemporary American play, afforded no opportunity to experiment with avant-garde theatre. The Other Place, located just a few blocks from the Guthrie, became an exciting theatrical space, offering productions of plays by Sam Shepard, Jules Feiffer, Slawomir Mrozek, LeRoi Jones, Harold Pinter, Samuel Beckett, Lanford Wilson, and many others.

The Mellon Foundation awarded a grant to Langham which permitted him to move this second theatre to a more appropriate space near the university. The "Guthrie 2" continued the policies of the Other Place, and permitted many Guthrie actors and stage managers to have a hand at directing off-beat works. In addition, the Guthrie 2 gave encouragement to new playwrights by producing their works. Unfortunately, the Guthrie 2 fell victim to the bulldozers of urban renewal, and the Guthrie currently has no second space in which to offer opportunities for fledgling authors and directors.

When Langham left the Guthrie in 1977, he was replaced as artistic director by Alvin Epstein, most recently the associate artistic director of the Yale Repertory Theatre. His work at the Yale Rep included both acting and directing, in both classical and modern works. He had enormous enthusiasm for his new task, and a strong desire to rejuvenate what many felt was a stagnant, unadventurous company and season. His play selections placed greater emphasis on contemporary theatre, including *Teibele and Her Demon* by Isaac Bashevis Singer, *Boy Meets Girl* by Bella and Samuel Spewack, *Bonjour, La, Bonjour* by Michel Tremblay, as well as the classical *Pretenders* (Ibsen), *Marriage* (Gogol), *The Beggar's Opera* (John Gay), *Hamlet*, and the perennial *A Christmas Carol*; this represented his first (1978) season. Epstein's new approaches to play selection and production had limited success, and considerable turbulence ensued, both within the theatre and in the general public, about the personality and the policies of the new artistic director. He left rather precipitously in June of 1979, just three weeks into the mainstage season, and the theatre appeared once more to be directionless and foundering.

The flurry of the Epstein period moved those closest to the theatre to take stock of the institution's situation, and to reformulate and reaffirm the Guthrie's sense of mission. A new statement of purpose was adopted for the 1980s, and a new staff of artistic direction was engaged. The internationally acclaimed teacher and director, Liviu Ciulei, has been appointed artistic director, but his responsibilities will be shared by the young, progressive Garland Wright as associate director and Arthur Ballet, a professor from the university's theatre department, as dramaturge. The triumvirate approach is designed to alleviate the excessive burden placed on the artistic director, and to bring a fresh combination of attitudes—the Old-World, the avant-garde, and the academic—into creative collision. The theatre's governing board and its new staff have reaffirmed the original classical intent of the Guthrie, and comparative harmony seems to reign as America's foremost regional repertory theatre begins a new phase in its development.

With allowances made for the enthusiasm of its framers, the statement of purpose is probably an accurate reflection of the role the Guthrie can reasonably expect to play in the near future: "The mission of The Guthrie Theater is to entertain Upper Midwest audiences by achieving and sus-

taining a level of artistic accomplishments that exemplifies the highest standards of excellence of both past and present theatrical traditions.

"To this end the Theater looks to the great authors as its source of inspiration, and therefore its repertoire shall be drawn primarily from recognized classics and plays which reflect that level of theatrical genius.

"The Theater will strive also to attract and develop the artists and crafts people necessary to meet the challenge of bringing great works to life on the stage with vitality, vision, and skill.

"In support of the mission, the Theater also will produce works and create educational and outreach programs that extend the range of lively theatrical experiences for both its audiences and its artists.

"In performing this mission, the Theater will affirm its place as a major national resource and an important world theater." It seems likely that Tyrone Guthrie and the small band of people who gathered around him to found this adventure in theatre could gladly claim that statement as their own. It is no small tribute to their vision, and to the industry and talent of the people who have worked with the Guthrie, that such an optimistic and clearsighted statement could be made.

–*William A. Mould*

References:
Tyrone Guthrie, *A New Theatre* (New York: McGraw-Hill, 1964);
Guthrie, "Theatre in Minneapolis," in *Actor and Architect*, ed. Stephen Joseph (Manchester, U.K.: Manchester University Press, 1964), pp. 30-47;
Alfred Rossi, *Minneapolis Rehearsals: Tyrone Guthrie Directs Hamlet* (Berkeley: University of California Press, 1970).

The Mark Taper Forum

Los Angeles

The Mark Taper Forum, Los Angeles's regional theatre, is one of a complex of three theatres in the Music Center, located on Bunker Hill in the middle of downtown Los Angeles. The city was unusual in that a sizable audience was available from the approximately 12 million population of greater Los Angeles, yet it lacked a theatre district and cultural center. In 1955, the Southern California Symphony Association began a fund-raising effort to provide a permanent home for the Los Angeles Philharmonic Orchestra; and in that year the Los Angeles County Board of Supervisors appointed Mrs. Norman Chandler head of a committee to promote a performing arts facility for the county. As the project developed, the concept of a complete center to serve all the performing arts took shape, and by the time construction began in 1962, this had come to include the 3,217-seat Dorothy Chandler Pavilion, opened in 1964; the 2,083-seat Ahmanson Theatre, and the 742-seat Mark Taper Forum, both opened in 1967. The buildings, designed to be viewed from all sides, are now a prominent hilltop landmark in the center of the city.

The Music Center, A Living Memorial to Peace, as it is formally known, was funded by a blend of public and private financing. By 1960, the Southern California Symphony Association had raised $4 million, and in that year then-president Mrs. Chandler approached the Los Angeles County Board of Supervisors with a proposal to raise the rest of the money to construct the Music Center buildings on public land which had been considered for urban renewal. About $20 million was raised from private contributions, and the rest of the money needed to complete the theatres came from an issue of leasehold mortgage revenue bonds. The Music Center Operating Company was incorporated to operate the theatres on the county-owned property; and the rentals from the improved property will retire the bonds by February 1997, when the Music Center will be owned by the county. Los Angeles County, however, constructed the eight-floor parking facility under the Music Center and is also responsible for its maintenance; the parking revenues, about $1 million each year, go toward the county's costs in operating the center. The budget for each year is proposed by the Music Center Operating Company and approved by the Los Angeles County Board of Supervisors. In addition to use of the center for performances by the Los Angeles Philharmonic Orchestra and the Civic Light Opera, plays produced by the Center Theatre Group at the Ahmanson and Mark Taper Forum theatres, and performances by touring companies including opera and ballet, the two larger theatres are used occasionally as a federal courthouse for the swearing-in of new citizens, as a graduation stage for sheriff's deputies and nurses in county medical facilities, and for civic festival events. Nationwide audiences have seen the Dorothy Chandler Pavilion on television during the broadcasts of the annual Academy Award ceremonies.

Within this context, the Mark Taper Forum's role has been the production of new and experimental plays and above all the encouragement of new writers. "Its very name—Forum—suggests a 'sharing' of ideas, a spirited dialogue existing between audience and artist. Out of this comes provocative thought, perceptions, and—ultimately—the excitement of mutual expression," as Gordon Davidson, the Taper's artistic director, summed up the theatre's goals. The search for new writers gave rise to New Theatre for Now—new plays produced on otherwise dark nights in the theatre, or between the runs of the regular season—and the Forum Laboratory, located in the space under the John Anson Ford Cultural Center in Hollywood, formerly the Pilgrimage Theatre, for playwrights, actors, and directors "who need to work on concepts, problems, and ideas still in the exploratory stage." Other programs under the auspices of the Mark Taper Forum are the Improvisational Theatre Project, a group of young actors whose techniques grew out of Paul Sills's concept, *Story Theatre*, with its combination of mime, music, and narration, performed for young audiences in schools, community centers, and juvenile halls; the Deaf Audience Theater Encounter (DATE), with performances signed for the deaf, special program synopses, and post-play discussions; and provision of inexpensive tickets for halfway houses, prisons, churches, and community groups; student and senior citizen discounts; and regular reductions to the public on day

Mark Taper Forum

of performance. Staff members also meet with high-school and college drama and journalism classes; actors and directors perform programs at colleges. During the run of each play, there are several postplay colloquies with cast, crew, director, and sometimes the playwright. Audiences are further encouraged to express their opinions via questionnaires, and many each year respond by letter or telephone, by no means all with favorable reactions.

The Mark Taper Forum staff is headed by Gordon Davidson, the artistic director. Davidson, the son of Joseph Davidson, professor of speech and drama at Brooklyn College, was valedictorian at Brooklyn Technical High School and entered Cornell University as a scholarship student in electrical engineering, but soon changed his major to drama. After a year of graduate school at Western Reserve University and an M.A. degree, six months in the army reserve, a season of stage-managing at the American Shakespeare Festival in Stratford, Connecticut, three years with the Dallas Opera and some work with the Martha Graham Dance Company, Davidson was invited by John Houseman of the Theatre Group, a professional acting company on the UCLA campus, to assist in a production of *King Lear*. When offered the job of managing director for the company, he accepted and staged a number of successful productions between 1964 and 1966, including Lillian Hellman's *Candide*, scored by Leonard Bernstein, with lyrics by Richard Wilbur. From this background, he brought to the Mark Taper Forum in 1966 a philosophy of innovative and demanding theatre. In addition to overseeing all the Taper productions, he has directed a number of them, including the Pulitzer Prize-winning *The Shadow Box* and the Tony Award-winning *Children of a Lesser God*.

It is worth noting that Los Angeles now has over one hundred theatres, ranging from ninety-nine-seat Equity waiver houses to the Hollywood Bowl, which seats about twenty thousand. The Mark Taper Forum's contribution to the Los Angeles theatre scene is focus and continuity, especially for the development of writers. Though the presence of the film industry attracts a wide range of talent, the relationship between film and television and Los Angeles theatre is still not clear-cut, although a grant to the Taper from CBS for a Writer Development Program for new material for stage, film, and television indicates the possibilities of interchange. Also, the eight-week runs of the Mark Taper Forum's productions allow actors working mainly in film and television to return briefly to the stage. Over the years, for example,

Richard Basehart has appeared in *Uncle Vanya*, Faye Dunaway in *Old Times*, Jack Lemmon and Walter Matthau in *Juno and the Paycock*, Stacy Keach in *Hamlet*, Anthony Hopkins in *The Tempest*, and Tony Curtis in *I Ought to Be in Pictures*. Other performers appearing in early Mark Taper Forum productions later became more widely known for film and television work, such as Frank Langella (*The Devils*), Jill Clayburgh (*Othello*), William DeVane (*Henry IV, Part I*), Sam Waterston (*Volpone* and *A Meeting by the River*), and Richard Dreyfuss (*Major Barbara*). But usually, the Taper does not have a policy of star casting and often uses little-known players.

The Mark Taper Forum was dedicated in April 1967, with Lew Wasserman, then president of the Center Theatre Group; Governor Ronald Reagan; and County Supervisor Ernest E. Debs participating in the ceremonies. The theatre is named for S. Mark Taper, chairman of the board and president of the First Charter Financial Corporation, who has given substantially, through the Mark Taper Foundation, to education and civic affairs. For the first season, there were more than thirty thousand subscribers. As the opening production, Davidson chose the West Coast premiere of John Whiting's *The Devils*, followed by two world premieres, Romulus Linney's *The Sorrows of Frederick* and Oliver Hailey's *Who's Happy Now?*, and the West Coast premiere of Friedrich Dürrenmatt's *The Marriage of Mr. Mississippi*. It was an uncompromising commitment to the concept of producing new plays, encouraging new playwrights, and using the theatre as a forum for ideas. Reaction to *The Devils*, which is based on Aldous Huxley's history of witchcraft and demonic possession in a seventeenth-century French abbey, was one of outrage in a number of quarters, but the Taper's productions continued to reflect its basic philosophy and to outrage some of its audience. Ironically, by the eighth season, there was equally vocal criticism of the inclusion of a "trivial" comedy in the selection of plays, and in 1980 there were protests that a new play by Neil Simon did not belong at the Taper but at a more commercial theatre.

The design of the Mark Taper Forum reflects and reinforces the commitment to the new and experimental. The exterior is circular; Thomas Thompson, in the *New York Times*, called it "a round hatbox floating on an aquamarine pool—wedged between two majestic neighbors"—the Ahmanson behind it to the north, and across a long mall the Dorothy Chandler Pavilion to the south. Inside, the audience is seated around a forward thrust stage in about 180 degrees of a circle. This arrangement is not without its disadvantages; seats far down and very far around to the side are not optimum for viewing a performance and have poor sight lines that cut off much of the stage rear. However, seating only fourteen rows deep, combined with fluid staging, provides an intimacy and a give-and-take between actors and audience lacking in larger houses with more conventional staging. Davidson, by no means uncritical, said of the building, "The Taper has one of the best audience relationship houses I've ever been in, but there's no backstage. Notice this office [Davidson's] has no windows. We almost didn't have a box office. I prefer the vision to come first." (Since then, windows have been added.)

One aim of the Mark Taper has been to provide a forum for the city's large and diverse ethnic groups, especially the black, Chicano, and Oriental communities. Davidson is aware that so far this aim has not been fully realized: "If I could possibly pull it off, I'd like to do a festival . . . —I hate to call it ethnic theater—but with groups I can't book into the season, like the East/West Players, Chicano and black groups. I know we haven't succeeded in reaching out to the city multiracially." In some plays, notably *Hamlet* and *The Three Sisters*, black performers had major roles in mixed casts. (When asked what he thought about being a black actor cast as the Russian Colonel Vershinin in Chekhov's *The Three Sisters*, Lou Gossett quipped, "A little kahlua in the vodka.") Several outstanding productions dealt with black history or the black experience, notably Conor Cruise O'Brien's *Murderous Angels*, about Patrice Lumumba in the Congo; *Dream on Monkey Mountain* and the Calypso musical *The Charlatan* by Trinidad playwright Derek Walcott; *Sizwe Banzi Is Dead* and *The Island* by Athol Fugard; and Ntozake Shange's *for colored girls who have considered suicide / when the rainbow is enuf*. Perhaps the two most successful ethnic productions were a black musical, Vinnette Carroll and Micki Grant's *Don't Bother Me, I Can't Cope*, and Luis Valdez's *Zoot Suit*, both of which went on to long runs at other theatres. In 1978 the Center Theatre Group acquired the Aquarius Theatre in Hollywood in order to have space for extensive runs of shows that found wider audiences; the Mark Taper Forum plans eventually to branch out into a three-space complex in the Aquarius: a 1,000-seat main theatre, a 350-seat experimental theatre, and a cafe-cabaret theatre.

Zoot Suit is a good example of the Mark Taper Forum concepts in action. Davidson commissioned Luis Valdez, director of El Teatro Campesino (a San Juan Bautista-based troupe of Chicano players that had performed at the Mark Taper in the New Theatre for Now series) to write a play dramatizing the Chicano experience in Los Angeles. Davidson has long been an enthusiastic supporter of docudrama, or theatre of fact; and *Zoot Suit*'s predecessors in that area included Heinar Kippherdt's *In the Matter of Robert Oppenheimer*; Conor Cruise O'Brien's *Murderous Angels*; Daniel Berrigan's *The Trial of the Catonsville Nine*; and Christopher Hampton's *Savages*, a play about the program to exterminate the Indians in the Amazon jungle of Brazil. On *Zoot Suit*, Davidson worked closely with Valdez; the play was first put on for new Theatre for Now and, after further rewriting, was put on the main stage for the regular season in the fall of 1978. The play is based on the Sleepy Lagoon murder trial of 1942, in which seventeen Mexican-American youths were jailed for the murder of another Mexican-American youth after a party at Sleepy Lagoon, a swimming place in East Los Angeles. They were freed two years later by an appeals court, but in the meantime servicemen in the Los Angeles area began beating and stripping zoot-suited Chicano youths, and the ensuing riots spread across the country. The zoot suit became a symbol to the Mexican-American community, and Valdez created the character of El Pachuco, who remains onstage during the entire play, to symbolize and interpret the Chicano consciousness, plus another character who represents the press. Performed on an essentially bare stage, with setting provided by lighting and backdrops of giant-sized newspapers, *Zoot Suit* attempted to deal with the Sleepy Lagoon case and the riots both on a realistic and a symbolic level. *Zoot Suit* was so successful in Los Angeles that Davidson took it to the Winter Garden Theatre in New York. There it failed to attract audiences, who apparently were not interested in an episode of California Chicano history, no matter how dramatically presented. But *Zoot Suit* is an admirable example of regional theatre serving its own region.

The treatment of scripts submitted to the Mark Taper Forum underscores the theatre's commitment to finding and supporting new playwrights. Every script submitted is read, and scripts arrive at the rate of about twenty-five a week. The files of the Taper have some eight thousand scripts, representing a staggering number of person-hours of reading. Yet the effort is worth it; as it is, staff still recalls rejecting works that became hits elsewhere, such as Jason Miller's *That Championship Season* and Mark Medoff's *When You Comin Back, Red Ryder?* Scripts selected for some sort of production may be performed in the Forum Laboratory or the New Theatre for Now if they do not seem ready or suitable for the main stage.

Nearly one hundred scripts have been performed in New Theatre for Now productions, of which Edward Parone is staff producer and associate of the artistic director. The New Theatre for Now program was awarded a matching grant by the Rockefeller Foundation in 1968 and received a Margo Jones Award in 1969 for outstanding contribution to American playwriting. Some New Theatre for Now productions also reached the main stage and the regular season. In 1976, Davidson and the Mark Taper Forum were awarded a Margo Jones Award for "the most significant continuing effort to encourage playwrights by including new plays in [the] regular season production schedule." Over the years, a number of playwrights have brought new works to the Mark Taper Forum, including Oliver Hailey, Harvey Perr, Susan Miller, Derek Walcott, Israel Horovitz, Joel Schwartz, Richard Nelson, Michael Cristofer (who has acted in numerous Taper productions in addition to having four plays produced there), Ted Tally, Marsha Norman, and Mark Medoff, whose *Children of a Lesser God* won the 1980 Tony Award.

Children of a Lesser God is an instance of a play which, when announced, might have seemed a problem or social drama aimed at a very specialized audience. A last-minute replacement for another play scheduled for the season, it is also an instance of the Mark Taper Forum's adaptability. It is the story of a love affair and marriage between a hearing man and a deaf woman. True, the drama did bring out Deaf Audience Theater Encounter members in force and made Los Angeles and later New York audiences aware of problems facing the deaf, but the play goes beyond that to deal with the difficulty of communication of all kinds between human beings. Since the heroine, and Phyllis Frelich who played her, are both totally deaf and do not speak, Medoff incorporated sign language into the script; and John Rubinstein, who played the husband, mastered dialogue in sign language as well. Both Rubinstein and Frelich, an actress formerly with Theatre of the Deaf, gave remarkable performances that won them 1980 Tony Awards for best actor and actress.

One of the most impressive plays seemed in advance the most unlikely. *Terra Nova*, by the then twenty-six-year-old Ted Tally, dealt with the race between Scott and Amundsen to reach the South Pole. Subscribers who wondered how director Gordon Davidson could ever recreate Antarctica on stage did not fully take into account the imaginative powers of language and stagecraft. Tally's script presented, in poetically realistic language, a truly heroic play about our century; and Davidson, using projections of historic photographs salvaged from Scott's doomed expedition, a setting entirely in white, and powerful performances, evoked such a sense of the Antarctic that some audience members felt themselves freezing. Davidson was equally successful in evoking the Brazilian jungle and Indian culture for Christopher Hampton's *Savages*, another outstanding Taper production.

In 1972, the Mark Taper Forum inaugurated a program which it would be misleading to call "children's theater" as the term is usually understood. The Improvisational Theatre Project, working with techniques of music, mime, songs, narration, and dialogue devised by Paul Sills in *Story Theatre* has adapted fables and done original scripts in performances that tour the Los Angeles area. ITP also performs at the Mark Taper Forum during the Christmas season and takes an original production on the road to northern California. While the shows are aimed at audiences of young people, they are mature and lively theatre. One of the original productions, *Guns*, in which the main characters are various types of firearms telling their stories, became a mainstage production during the regular season. ITP has its own director, John Dennis, and a writer-in-residence, Doris Baizley, who wrote *Guns* among other scripts for ITP. For school audiences, ITP conducts workshops, with mime, games, story-building, and dance; completely improvised shows in which the plot evolves from audience suggestions; and the productions originating with the ITP staff. The program is funded through a combination of sources, including the National Endowment for the Arts, the California Arts Council, the Music Center Unified Fund, and the governments of the city and county of Los Angeles.

Productions of the classics have been the Mark Taper Forum's Achilles' heel. One major reason is the lack of a permanent acting company. As Davidson explained, "The reason we don't keep a corps of actors full time is partly financial, and also because I'm committed to the development of new plays." New plays often require special casting; the classics require a group of players skilled in certain techniques working in ensemble. Taper revivals of the classics, especially of Shakespeare, have often featured a star surrounded by an ad hoc company of mixed quality and mixed playing styles: Stacy

Keach as Hamlet, Victor Buono as Falstaff, James Earl Jones as Othello, Anthony Hopkins as Prospero. The results have been uneven. For John Webster's *The Duchess of Malfi*, the Taper imported Eileen Atkins, who had played the Duchess in a brilliant British television production; surrounded her with an inadequate and often inaudible supporting cast; and brought in as director Howard Sackler, author of *The Great White Hope*, who seemed out of his element with Jacobean tragedy. During the third season, the Taper imported Tyrone Guthrie's Minneapolis company to perform Aeschylus's *The House of Atreus*; the production by Guthrie's experienced repertory company was more successful than earlier Taper attempts.

Davidson acknowledges the tension and opposition between new and classical drama. "I've always felt that finally the mark of a theater is to create, not only new material, but new ways of looking at material, and finally something called 'style.' . . . We want to do something about the classical library now because it's in these plays that you get the great stretches for an actor and director, the language, the poetry, the imagery. I'm not saying there aren't great contemporary plays but. . . ." So far, however, the Mark Taper Forum style and strength has been the production of the new and the contemporary; revivals of the classics at the Taper have had their memorable moments, but few have been wholly satisfying.

As a step to the kind of ensemble experience that Davidson sees as necessary for the classics, a stretching of the actor's range and continuity of experience, the Mark Taper Forum began in 1975 to experiment with doing two or three plays in repertory. The first of these was Michael Cristofer's *The Shadow Box*, dealing with three very different families facing terminal illness, and *Too Much Johnson*, a classic American farce by William Gillette. So much critical energy went into denunciation of the juxtaposition of a deeply moving tragic drama with what one irate audience member referred to as "this—*titwillow!*" that the insights the pairing of the plays offered into the points where comedy and tragedy meet, and the total performances of players in widely divergent roles tended to be slighted. A more ambitious season was the spring of 1976, when three new plays—*Ashes* by David Rudkin, *Cross Country* by Susan Miller, and *And Where She Stops Nobody Knows* by Oliver Hailey—were done in repertory with Chekhov's *The Three Sisters*. The last, one of the most memorable classic productions at the Taper, suggests that the repertory experience is a valuable ingredient in productions of the classics.

The following season, Tom Stoppard's *Travesties*, which takes off on a mad tangent from Oscar Wilde's *The Importance of Being Earnest*, was offered in tandem with Wilde's play, provoking much discussion of two very different types of stylized acting and two plays that demand considerable verbal pyrotechnics from both actors and attentive audiences. Also during the 1976-1977 season, for the tenth anniversary of the Mark Taper Forum, four plays were offered in repertory. Christopher Durang's *A History of the American Film* played with Sam Shepard's *Angel City*, the former a hilarious look at images with which the movies have influenced several generations, the latter a turgid symbolic statement of the corruption oozing forth from the film capital. *Leander Stillwell*, David Rush's sensitive drama about a young man's experience in the Civil War, and *Bugs/Guns*, by Doris Baizley, a production from the Improvisational Theater Project, completed the repertory. In 1979-1980, two plays by Lanford Wilson, *Talley's Folly* and *5th of July*, each dealing with a different generation of the same family, were offered.

By the 1979-1980 season, the Mark Taper Forum had presented over two hundred productions, more than one hundred and fifteen of them world premieres. Of these, one play by a new playwright, Michael Cristofer's *The Shadow Box*, first performed at the Taper in the fall of 1975, won the 1977 Pulitzer Prize. *Talley's Folly*, by Lanford Wilson, also produced at the Taper, won the Pulitzer Prize for 1979. In 1977, the Mark Taper Forum was awarded an Antoinette Perry (Tony) Award for Theatrical Excellence. Eleven other Tony Awards and two nominations went to Taper-originated productions between 1970 and 1979. Taper productions have also received seven Obie awards, six New York Drama Desk awards, thirty-eight Los Angeles Drama Critics Circle awards, fifty-three Drama-Logue awards, and a number of special awards, including two Margo Jones awards for the encouragement of new playwrights. In recognition of its ethnic productions, the Taper won the Soul Award and NAACP Image Awards plus a special city council citation for *Don't Bother Me, I Can't Cope*, and two Nosotros Golden Eagle awards for *Zoot Suit*. Eighteen plays given first or major productions at the Mark Taper Forum have gone on to New York; *The Trial of the Catonsville Nine* was filmed under the direction of Gordon Davidson; and seven plays have appeared on television. The scope of the productions has included world premieres of contemporary American plays; a number of West Coast premieres; revivals of American plays; foreign plays, both contemporary and in revival; an occasional musical; and classics, including plays by Aeschylus, Shakespeare, Jonson, Webster, Wilde, Chekhov, and Shaw. Attendance continues to grow—the 33,458 subscribers for the 1980-1981 season broke all records—and audience members continue to walk out occasionally, expressing both involvement and dissent.

The Mark Taper Forum has provided a central focus and identity for theatre in Los Angeles and southern California, and it has gained impressive national recognition. Its major contributions have been to search for new plays, give major productions to works originating in smaller regional theatres, and encourage playwrights, especially in southern California. Another important contribution has been community involvement, though much remains to be done in this area, especially in relation to ethnic groups and to the film and television communities. It requires a delicate balance to keep a strong central focus while serving a community as diverse and geographically spread out as

Los Angeles. Recent acquisition of the Aquarius Theatre and association with the annual Los Angeles International Film Exposition (Filmex) may reinforce ties to the film community and the broader theatre community. In time, the repertory concept may develop more satisfying productions of the classics, thus providing a balance to docudrama and serious contemporary issues. The Mark Taper Forum has the problem of keeping in balance a philosophy of change and experiment with one of commitment to serious drama, which in itself, if too rigidly applied, can work against growth in all directions. A major asset is a large and loyal group of subscribers, growing larger each year, both willing to accept program changes in the middle of the season and capable of sending in the same envelope a blistering letter of complaint and a subscription renewal. Drawn from a one hundred mile radius from Santa Barbara to Riverside to San Diego, these people make the Mark Taper Forum truly a regional theatre.

–Katharine M. Morsberger

Off-Loop Theatres
Chicago

In the middle of the 1960s, Mayor Richard Daley formed a committee, on which Oliver Rea of the Guthrie Theatre served, to study the paucity of theatre in Chicago. The mayor felt that the amount of theatrical activity in Chicago was unworthy of the city. Productions were being imported into the Loop, the business district that is encircled by the city's subway and "L" trains, and there, at the Shubert, Studebaker, or Blackstone theatres, Chicagoans could see the most commercial— though not necessarily the best—of the previous New York season. There were, however, few local productions. The Goodman Theatre and the Second City were among the few groups contributing to the city's theatre; a city of Chicago's size, the mayor felt, deserved more.

Since the study commissioned by Daley, the Loop theatres have changed little. The Goodman Theatre, once a part of the Art Institute of Chicago, has grown and developed into one of the country's leading regional theatres, but the Shubert, Studebaker, and Blackstone theatres still import New York hits. In the 1970s, however, an Off-Loop

theatrical district, with little help from city hall, began to form. Chicago and its suburbs now claim almost seventy theatrical organizations; there are about as many actors working in the area as in New York; and local playwrights—David Mamet, Alan Gross, and Jeffery Sweet—are drawing national recognition. In a decade, Chicago has developed a sound theatrical community from a wasteland.

Though the Court Theatre, connected with the University of Chicago, and several black theatres, the most prominent of which is the Kuumba, are on the South Side, the Off-Loop theatre district proper is on the North Side. To the south of this district, in the Near North and Old Town areas, are scattered a few theatres. The Playwrights' Center, at 110 West Kinzie, a few blocks across the Chicago River, specializes in promoting new works of developing playwrights. The theatre attracts a sizable audience and has received a few Jefferson nominations, Chicago's equivalent of the Tony. Farther north, in the historic Old Town district, one of the few areas to survive the Chicago fire of 1871, is the Old Town

Players. The Players offers about four productions a year in a theatre of less than 100 seats at 1718 North North Park.

A few blocks from the Old Town Players is the Second City, one of the most influential comic and improvisational theatres in the country. In 1955, the group was formed as the Compass Players by a group of University of Chicago students. The Players, which eventually included Elaine May and Mike Nichols, performed a series of improvisations and comic skits in a Hyde Park bar. In 1959, the group evolved into the Second City. In its 300-seat club at 1616 North Wells, the Second City offers shows that consist of a comic revue followed by a series of improvisations. Some of the improvisations are reworked and included in the group's next revue. The Second City also produces a syndicated television program, manages a touring group, and offers programs for children. The major importance of the comic theatre, however, is its role in developing new talent. Among those who have worked and trained with the Compass Players or the Second City are: Alan Alda, Alan Arkin, Dan Aykroyd, John Belushi, Shelley Berman, Peter Boyle, Del Close, Valerie Harper, Ron Liebman, Gilda Radner, Joan Rivers, and David Steinberg. In the last few years, other comedy groups have developed in the Second City tradition. The Chicago Premiere Society, at 1548 North Wells, offers comic works like *Byrne, Baby, Byrne*, an irreverent look at the administration of Jane Byrne. The Chicago Comedy Showcase, at 1055 West Diversity, develops and produces comic plays like *The Life and Death of Sneaky Fitch*, presents improvisations, and lends its stage to traveling comedy groups.

North of the Second City, in the area surrounding De Paul University, are two important theatres, the Body Politic and the Apollo. The Body Politic was founded in 1969 when its mother organization, the Community Arts Foundation, purchased a building at 2261 North Lincoln Avenue. The purchase marked the start of the Off-Loop theatres, for the Body Politic instigated changes in the city's building code that hindered the development of small theatres. The building was converted into three small theatres of about one hundred seats each. The Body Politic produces about five plays a year in its subscription series and several more in its new works series. It has received numerous Jefferson nominations and has also con-

Founders of St. Nicholas Theatre:
David Mamet, Stephen Schachter, Patricia Cox, William H. Macy.

tributed to the development of other theatre groups. Several of Chicago's leading theatrical organizations, the Organic, Dinglefest (later the Performance Community), and Pary Productions, were once housed in Body Politic's building. Unfortunately, at the end of the 1979-1980 season, the group was forced to sell its theatre to remain solvent. It will, however, lease the building.

The Apollo Theater Center, at 2540 North Lincoln, was founded in 1978 by Stuart Oken and Jason Brett. The group produces plays and transports successful productions by other Off-Loop theatres to its theatre of 363 seats for extended runs. Steven Wade's *Banjo Dancing*, a one-man show, began at the Body Politic, moved to the Apollo for fifty-seven weeks, and then moved, under Apollo management, to the Century Theatre in New York. Before the Apollo group was founded, successful Off-Loop productions were offered for a set run and then closed to make room for a theatre group's next production. The Apollo organization has also begun to use Chicago talent in the production of feature films and television shows.

St. Nicholas Theater, located at 2851 North Halsted in the heart of the Off-Loop district, has a prestigious history, having earned more Jefferson awards than any other theatre. Founded in 1974 by William H. Macy, David Mamet, Patricia Cox, and Stephen Schachter, the St. Nicholas has grown steadily by offering a yearly assortment of classics and world premieres, including Mamet's *The Water Engine* and *The Woods*. It also presents five plays in its New Works Ensemble, produces children's theatre, and sponsors the St. Nicholas School of the Theatre Arts. In the 1979-1980 season, the St. Nicholas reached a crucial developmental stage. Its artistic director, Stephen Schachter, the last of the remaining founders, resigned. Cynthia Sherman, the acting artistic director, is faced with reorganizing and, perhaps, revitalizing the group. Critics have felt that the St. Nicholas seasons have been weak since 1978-1979, some citing overexpansion as the cause. In the 1979-1980 season, the St. Nicholas reached a budget of $1 million and a full-time staff of thirty-two. In that same season, after weighing the pros and cons of further expansion, it abandoned plans to move to a larger theatre.

Northwest of the St. Nicholas is the Theatre Building. The building is a warehouse that was converted into three theatres, of 100 to 150 seats, in 1977. It now houses three theatre groups, Performance Community, Travel Light, and Pary Productions. The Performance Community, which

David Mamet, 1975

leases and manages the Theatre Building, was founded in 1970 under the name of Dinglefest Theatre Company. It offers four or five productions each season. In 1970, they produced Alan Gross's *The Man in 605*, which has since been picked up by the Apollo and exported to New York. The Travel Light Theatre, founded in 1974 by Michael Cullen, originally staged its productions in pubs and coffeehouses on the North Side. In 1976, it won a Jefferson award for a pub production of Sam Shepard's *Cowboy Mouth*. The company now offers five productions a year, most of which are restagings of recent Off-Broadway hits. Pary Productions Company, founded in 1973, has many Midwest and world premieres to its credit but is best known for its avant-garde productions like Tom Eyen's *Women Behind Bars*.

The Steppenwolf Theatre lies east of the Theatre Building at 3212 North Broadway, just north of New Town. A small group of young actors formed the theatre in 1976 in the suburb of Highland Park. During the 1979-1980 season, it moved to a 135-seat theatre in the Jane Addams Hull House. The group offers six plays a year, casting most parts from its acting ensemble of sixteen. In its short history, the Steppenwolf has developed into one of the city's leading theatrical groups; a 1979 production of Tennessee Williams's *The Glass*

Menagerie received five Jefferson nominations. Though sets and direction are sometimes poor, the company consistently delivers brilliantly acted productions.

To the north of the Steppenwolf, in the Northside Auditorium Building at 3730 North Clark, is housed Victory Gardens Theater. Founded in 1974 by eight Chicago directors, actors, and playwrights, Victory Gardens has developed into one of the city's most ambitious and sound groups, receiving over thirty Jefferson nominations in seven years. Under the artistic direction of Dennis Zacek, it offers about ten productions a year, half in the 150-seat mainstage theatre and half in the 60-seat studio theatre. Of the group's fifty-six productions, thirty have been world premieres. In the 1980-1981 season, it will present world premieres of Jeffery Sweet's *The Unreasonable Man*, Steve Carter's *Dame Lorraine*, and Alan Gross's *The La Brea Tar Pits*. It sponsors theatre classes and a reader's theatre, which has showcased over fifty scripts. In 1979, Victory Gardens, using grant money from CBS, founded "Latino Chicago!," a company of six Hispanic performers. In 1980, the company presented its first program, a series of scenes of Hispanic Chicago and a one-act entitled *La Sorpresa*. Like the St. Nicholas, Victory Gardens has grown quickly. For the 1980-1981 season, it will have more than two thousand subscribers. It does not, unlike the St. Nicholas, seem to be suffering from its rapid growth.

One of the northernmost Off-Loop groups is the Organic Theater, housed in the Leo Lerner Theatre at 4520 North Beacon. The Organic, founded in 1969, is a theatre of the 1960s. Though the genres of its productions range from realism to fantasy, it always strives, through innovative staging, to astonish the audience and, like the Open Theatre of the 1960s, eliminate the separation between audience and performers. The group presented the first professional production of Mamet's *Sexual Perversity in Chicago* and has developed many original scripts: *Bleacher Bums*, set at Wrigley Field; *Fornicopia*, a Victorian pornographic musical; and *Warp*, a trilogy that blends comedy and science fiction. Organic productions have played on Broadway and Off Broadway, toured the United States four times, and toured Europe twice. In 1979, *Bleacher Bums* was adapted into a national PBS program. The group has won five Jefferson awards, one Obie award, one New York Drama Desk award, four Charles MacArthur awards, and a Chicago International Film Festival Golden Hugo Award.

The Wisdom Bridge Theatre, founded in 1974 by David Beaird, is located in a renovated second-story storefront at 1559 West Howard. Under the direction of Robert Falls, the group presents five plays a year. In 1978, it received a special Jefferson award for "quality and exciting theatre." Widsom Bridge productions do not bear a distinctive trademark; they are remarkable primarily for their consistent excellence.

Theatre in Chicago seems to be on firm ground. Though some theatre groups have recently disbanded, most notably the Halcyon Repertory Company, and some need better financing, such as the Body Politic, it seems certain that the St. Nicholas, Victory Gardens, Steppenwolf, Organic, and Wisdom Bridge theatres will form a stable nucleus of talent for many years, and the growth of the 1970s is continuing. Theatrical groups without their own theatres are beginning to make significant contributions. The San Quentin Drama Workshop, devoted to staging the works of Samuel Becket, has presented several excellent productions at the Goodman Theatre. Encouragingly, new theatre groups are still forming. In the last few years, the Chicago City Theatre, the Remains Theatre, the Commons Theatre, Chicago Theatre Strategy, Chicago Women's Theatre, and the Imagination Theatre have emerged. Of these groups, the Remains Theatre is especially promising. The suburbs, with the North Light Repertory Theatre of Evanston in the vanguard, are developing their own theatrical communities. The persistent growth of Chicago-area theatres has even initiated the formation of trade organizations, the Chicago Alliance for the Performing Arts and the League of Chicago Theatres.

The Windy City's theatre, however, is not without its weaknesses. It needs more groups—like the Apollo—that can extend and eventually export successful productions. It also needs a wider reputation and the profits of a large tourist audience. In 1979, Mayor Jane Byrne sponsored a theatre festival, which encouraged theatre excursions with advertising and half-price tickets, but the city needs to do more. The theatres must also contribute. There are far too few matinees, and little is done to entice tourists from the Loop to the Off-Loop theatres. If city hall and the League of Chicago Theatres can provide needed direction and unity, the Chicago Off-Loop district can rival and, perhaps, overshadow Off-Broadway.

–George H. Jensen

Eugene O'Neill Memorial Theater Center
Waterford, Connecticut

The Eugene O'Neill Memorial Theater Center was founded in 1964 by George C. White. That summer, White convened the first annual National Playwrights Conference, which, to date, has presented 214 new plays by 156 American dramatists. Numbering among its alumni such authors as John Guare, Arthur Kopit, Lanford Wilson, Israel Horovitz, and Albert Innaurato, the O'Neill, as it is commonly known, has emerged as one of the most notable sources of contemporary American drama.

Located in Waterford, Connecticut, on a hill overlooking Long Island Sound, the O'Neill is in session from mid-July to early August. Typically, a Conference consists of twelve to fourteen playwrights supported by "some of the most talented theater professionals we can assemble to work with these writers on the development of their material," according to artistic director, Lloyd Richards. The O'Neill's stated purpose is to give its authors a workshop production of their plays as performed and directed by proven theatre practitioners. Each play receives four days of rehearsal, then two staged readings before audiences which include both the general public and Conference personnel. There is no budget for props or costumes, and the settings are suggested by arrangements of steel and wood modules.

The day after the staged reading, the playwright himself takes the stage. Flanked by his director and dramaturge, and surrounded by Conference personnel, the playwright answers questions, considers suggestions, and absorbs criticism. "The purpose of criticism," Richards explains, "is to continue the process." Nor does "the process" end with the critique. The playwright is required to remain at Waterford until the Conference ends, during which time he works on his play.

In 1972, White and Richards inaugurated a Second Step Program, which fulfills the O'Neill's need to further its sphere of influence, while also affording regional and university theatre companies the opportunity to work with new plays and theatre professionals. The Second Step Program functions as follows: the participating regional or university theatre commits itself to a full production of a play that has been presented as a work-in-progress at the Conference. They also agree to have the playwright-in-residence for the entire rehearsal period and to accept a director from the O'Neill, or a suitable substitute, to direct the play. All rehearsals are open to the public; the participants are available for seminars, discussions, and critiques, and make community contacts that will benefit the project and its local sponsor. In its eight years of existence some eighty organizations have mounted more than one hundred sixty productions of Conference plays provided them through this Second Step Program.

The selection process for a Playwrights Conference begins in September with a nationwide call for submissions. Between December 1, the cutoff date, and the following April when the twelve to fourteen finalists are selected, Conference personnel consider nearly fifteen hundred plays. The finalists go to Waterford in May for a pre-Conference weekend, where each playwright reads his play aloud before an audience consisting of White and Richards, the directors who will stage their plays, and other members of the O'Neill community. Also during this weekend, the playwrights will confer with their directors on the matter of changes and revisions, after which they return home to work on their scripts.

Returning to Waterford in July, the playwrights are reunited with their directors and introduced to a dramaturge, or literary adviser, whose function is to assist the playwrights in the development of their material. This team of playwright, director, and dramaturge will remain intact throughout the four weeks of the Conference.

Waterford, being so close to New York City, attracts many agents and producers from the commercial theatre, and over the years, success itself has become a serious problem for the O'Neill. Many of the plays from the 1967 Conference were, in fact, finished works rather than works-in-progress and were quickly optioned for commercial production. This prompted the *New York Times* to describe the Conference as "Try-Out Town, U.S.A.," which put needless pressure on the playwrights, actors, and directors to create a perfect play, thus perverting

Preston M. Ransone, author of King Crab

Rehearsal of David Henry Hwang's FOB

Rehearsal of Judy Gebauer's Seconds

Ben Masters and Jeffrey De Munn in Judy Gebauer's Seconds

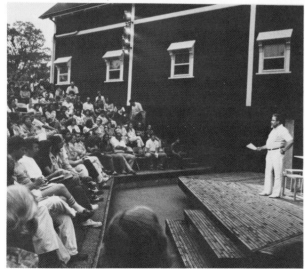

Lloyd Richards

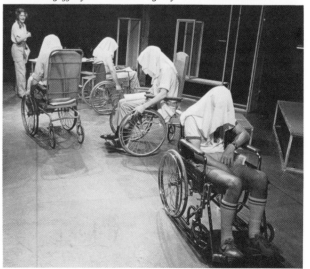

Stephen Davis Parks's Skidding into Slow Time

the purpose of the Conference by denying the participant's right to fail. This problem remains largely unresolved, and although Richards insists that he and White are "not concerned with selling a hit," their success factor, as evidenced by the Second Step Program and the O'Neill's growing list of awards, increases with every Conference.

In addition to its annual National Playwrights Conference, the Eugene O'Neill Memorial Theater Center also houses such diverse activities as the National Theatre of the Deaf, the National Critics Institute, the National Theater Institute, and the New Drama for Television Project. In addition, the O'Neill publishes a *National Playwrights Directory*, which contains biographical sketches of some five hundred living American playwrights and pertinent information about their work.

In 1967, designer David Hays formed the National Theatre of the Deaf, only the second professional theatre of the deaf in this century. (A company has existed in the Soviet Union since 1911.) Using elements of speech, sign language, dance, and pantomime, the National Theatre of the Deaf has developed a theatrical style which is readily understood by both hearing and deaf people. Since its inception, the National Theatre of the Deaf has made twenty-two national tours, totaling more than twenty-five hundred performances in the fifty states, and has performed in fifteen foreign countries throughout Europe, the Middle East, and the Orient. The National Theatre of the Deaf operates a school in Waterford for the purpose of developing new talent, including deaf playwrights, to help build deaf theatre companies in this country and abroad. In 1977, the National Theatre of the Deaf received a special Antoinette Perry Award for theatrical excellence.

The National Critics Institute is a workshop for journalists with a special interest in the performing arts. More than one hundred Critic Fellows from forty-seven states have participated in this annual program since it was first offered in 1968. The four-week workshop, which runs concurrent with the Playwrights Conference, focuses on the writing skills of its Critic Fellows and offers lectures and seminars in significant developments in the drama, opera and musical theatre, dance, and stage design. Critic Fellows review plays presented by the Playwrights Conference and by other summer theatres

in and around the Waterford area. Their reviews are then evaluated in daily tutorials led by critics of national renown. The purpose of this workshop is to improve the craft of reviewing of each Critic Fellow.

The National Theater Institute was established in 1970 as a school for college-aged students who have displayed a serious interest in the theatre as a career. It strives to give students a feel for life in the professional theatre through firsthand experience. Experimental in nature, the National Theater Institute presents its students with both classroom and workshop situations. Such basic courses as acting, directing, speech, and movement continue throughout the fourteen-week semester, with remaining time held open for workshops with guest artists. The semester culminates in a production prepared by the students and their instructors, and it tours colleges, high schools, and community and other theatres around New England.

The New Drama for Television Project, now in its fifth year, was created to give playwrights the opportunity to work on material especially suited for the medium of television and under the guidance of knowledgeable television practitioners, including a director and a story editor. As with the National Playwrights Conference, the emphasis of the Television Project is on the script. "This is an opportunity for the playwright to test his or her work while learning the craft of writing for television," Richards explains. From nearly four hundred applicants, he and White select four authors to participate in the Television Project. One television drama is produced for each week of the Playwrights Conference. For five days, the play is rehearsed, videotaped, and edited, and on Saturday, the results are screened and critiqued by Conference personnel.

During the 1970s, the story of the Eugene O'Neill Memorial Theater Center has been one of expansion, institutionalization, stabilization, and growing recognition in the theatre world. The decade ended with the Center receiving a Drama Desk Award "For Outstanding Contribution in Developing New Plays and Playwrights" and an Antoinette Perry Award "For Fifteen Years of Dedicated Service to the Theater."

–Howard Siegman

Appendix III:
Books for Further Reading

NEW THEATRE
A Magazine of Drama · Film · Dance
114 WEST 14TH STREET · NEW YORK
WAtkins 9-5473

May 15, 1935

Dear Miss Crist:

You and I are interested in the theatre. Not the dead part that's plenty. A small portion is alive. We have a burning problem to face: how to keep that alive.

Subscribe to the New Theatre Magazine -- that's one way. An important group of theatrical artists express their opinions, examine their own work and the work of others in the pages of the New Theatre Magazine every month. These artists, people of honest convictions like yourself, like myself, are determined to re-establish the theatre, the American theatre, as a vital force in leading mankind out of the barbarism of these chaotic and art-destroying times.

How much help do we need from you? $1.50.

What does it get you? The writings of men who make New Theatre sound like a "Who's Who" of the stage world. Sections of Archibald MacLeish's "Panic" were published months before its opening and New Theatre organized a special public performance of this fine poetic drama while other publications stood idly by or buried it. Eisenstein wrote on "Chapayev" and Pudovkin on "Youth of Maxim" months before these films reached the United States. Indispensable material like M. A. Chekhov's articles on the Stanislavsky Method have appeared in New Theatre. "Waiting for Lefty", in production and printed version, was sponsored by New Theatre long before the daily press became aware of its existence. In short, every issue manages in some way to scoop the theatre world.

Turn to the back page of this letter. Some of the most important critics of the daily papers tell you what they think. Atkinson of the "Times", Garland and Hansen of the "World-Telegram", Freeman of the "New Masses" - these men know their business.

You need this magazine. It needs you and your friends. $1.50 brings it to you every month. Please subscribe now!

Sincerely,

Clifford Odets

Author of:
"Waiting for Lefty"
"Till the Day I Die"
"Awake and Sing"

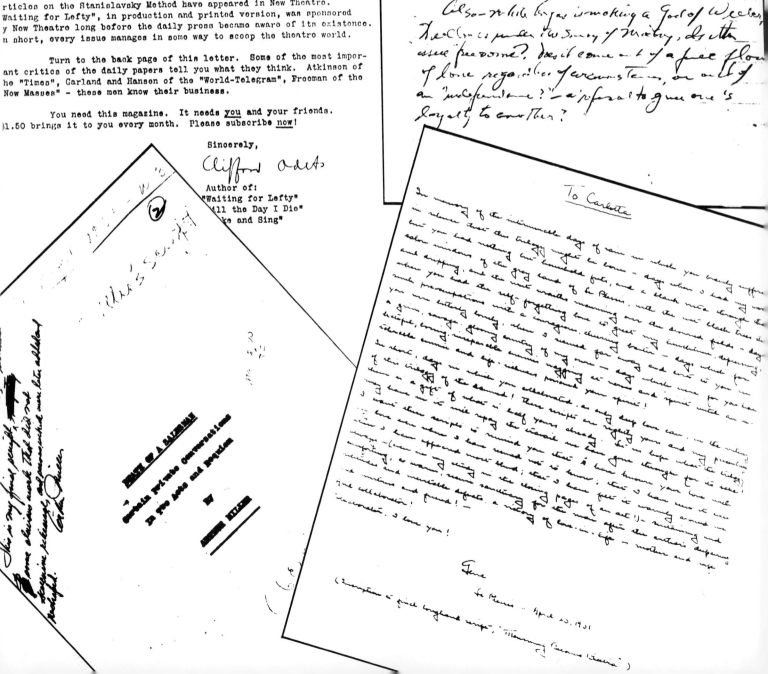

This is a selective list of general studies and guides to publications pertaining to American theatre in the twentieth century. Fuller bibliographies may be found in Eugene Hudson Long, *American Drama from Its Beginnings to the Present* (New York: Appleton-Century-Crofts, 1970); Lewis Leary, *Articles on American Literature, 1950-1967* (Durham: Duke University Press, 1970); Floyd Eugene Eddleman, *American Drama Criticism: Interpretations, 1890-1977*, second edition (Hamden, Conn.: Shoe String Press, 1979); Leary with John Auchard, *Articles on American Literature, 1968-1975* (Durham: Duke University Press, 1979); Charles A. Carpenter, "Modern Drama Studies: An Annual Bibliography," in *Modern Drama*, since 1974; and the annual MLA International Bibliographies. Useful reference works on the theatre are *Notable Names in the American Theatre* (Clifton, N.J.: J. T. White, 1976); Ian Herbert and others, eds., *Who's Who in the Theatre*, sixteenth edition (London: Pitman / Detroit: Gale Research, 1977); and Otis L. Guernsey, Jr., ed., *The Best Plays . . . : The Burns Mantle Yearbook* (New York: Dodd, Mead, 1964-   ).

Abramson, Doris E. *Negro Playwrights in the American Theatre, 1925-1959*. New York & London: Columbia University Press, 1969.

Adelman, Irving and Rita Dworkin. *Modern Drama: A Checklist of Critical Literature on 20th Century Plays*. Metuchen, N.J.: Scarecrow Press, 1967.

American Theatre, Stratford-upon-Avon Studies, 10. London: Arnold, 1967.

The American Theatre: A Sum of Its Parts (Collection of the Distinguished Addresses Prepared Expressly for the Symposium, "The American Theatre–A Cultural Process," at the First American College Theatre Festival, Washington, D.C., 1969). New York: French, 1971.

Arata, Esther Spring and Nicholas John Rotoli. *Black American Playwrights, 1800 to the Present: A Bibliography*. Metuchen, N.J.: Scarecrow Press, 1976.

Arata and others. *More Black American Playwrights: A Bibliography*. Metuchen, N.J.: Scarecrow Press, 1978.

Bentley, Eric. *The Dramatic Event, An American Chronicle*. New York: Horizon, 1954.

Bentley. *In Search of Theater*. New York: Knopf, 1963.

Bentley. *The Playwright as Thinker*. New York: Reynal & Hitchcock, 1946.

Bentley. *The Theatre of Commitment and Other Essays on Drama in Our Society*. New York: Atheneum, 1967.

Bentley. *Theatre of War*. New York: Viking, 1972.

Bigsby, C. W. E., ed. *The Black American Writer*, vol. 2. Deland, Fla.: Everett / Edwards, 1969.

Bigsby. *Confrontation and Commitment: A Study of Contemporary American Drama 1959-1966*. Columbia: University of Missouri Press, 1968.

Bonin, Jane F. *Prize-Winning American Drama: A Bibliographical and Descriptive Guide*. Metuchen, N.J.: Scarecrow Press, 1973.

Broussard, Louis. *American Drama: Contemporary Allegory from Eugene O'Neill to Tennessee Williams*. Norman: University of Oklahoma Press, 1962.

Brown, John Mason. *Two on the Aisle: Ten Years of the American Theatre in Performance*. New York: Norton, 1938.

Brustein, Robert. *Critical Moments: Reflections on Theatre and Society, 1973-1979*. New York: Random House, 1980.

Brustein. *The Culture Watch: Essays on Theatre and Society, 1969-1974*. New York: Knopf, 1975.

Brustein. *Revolution as Theatre: Notes on the New Radical Style*. New York: Liveright, 1971.

Brustein. *Seasons of Discontent: Dramatic Opinions 1959-1965*. New York: Simon & Schuster, 1965.

Clurman, Harold. *All People Are Famous*. New York: Harcourt Brace Jovanovich, 1974.

Clurman. *The Divine Pastime: Theatre Essays*. New York: Macmillan, 1974.

Clurman. *The Fervent Years: The Story of the Group Theatre and the Thirties*. New York: Knopf, 1945; revised edition, New York: Hill & Wang, 1957; revised again, New York: Harcourt Brace Jovanovich, 1975.

Clurman. *The Naked Image: Observations on the Modern Theatre*. New York: Macmillan, 1966.

Cohn, Ruby. *Dialogue in American Drama*. Bloomington: Indiana University Press, 1971.

Coleman, Arthur and Gary R. Tyler. *Drama Criticism*, 2 vols. Denver: Swallow Press, 1966, 1971.

Comtois, M. E. and Lynn F. Miller. *Contemporary American Theater Critics: A Directory and Anthology of Their Works*. Metuchen, N.J.: Scarecrow Press, 1977.

Crawford, Mary Caroline. *The Romance of the American Theatre*. Boston: Little, Brown, 1913.

Deutsch, Helen and Stella Hanau. *The Provincetown: A Story of the Theatre*. New York: Farrar & Rinehart, 1931.

Downer, Alan S. *Fifty Years of American Drama, 1900-1950*. Chicago: Regnery, 1951.

Esslin, Martin. *Reflections: Essays on Modern Theatre*. Garden City: Doubleday, 1969.

Esslin. *The Theatre of the Absurd*, third edition. London: Methuen, 1974.

Flanagan, Hallie. *Arena: The History of the Federal Theatre*. New York: Duell, Sloan & Pearce, 1940.

Flexner, Eleanor. *American Playwrights: 1918-1938*. New York: Simon & Schuster, 1938.

French, William P. and others. *Afro-American Poetry and Drama, 1760-1975*. Detroit: Gale Research, 1979.

Gassner, John. *Directions in Modern Theatre and Drama*. New York: Holt, Rinehart & Winston, 1965.

Gassner. *Dramatic Soundings*, ed. Glenn Loney. New York: Crown, 1968.

Gassner. *Form and Idea in Modern Theatre*. New York: Dryden Press, 1956.

Gassner. *Theatre at the Crossroads: Plays and Playwrights of the Mid-Century American Stage*. New York: Holt, Rinehart & Winston, 1960.

Gohdes, Clarence. *Literature and Theater of the States and Regions of the U.S.A., An Historical Bibliography*. Durham: Duke University Press, 1967.

Gould, Jean. *Modern American Playwrights*. New York: Dodd, Mead, 1966.

Guernsey, Otis L., Jr., ed. *Playwrights, Lyricists, Composers on Theater*. New York: Dodd, Mead, 1974.

Guthrie, Tyrone. *A New Theatre*. New York: McGraw-Hill, 1964.

Hart, Moss. *Act One: An Autobiography*. New York: Random House, 1959.

Hatch, James V. *Black Image on the American Stage: A Bibliography of Plays and Musicals, 1770-1970*. New York: Drama Book Specialists, 1970.

Hatch and Omanii Abdullah. *Black Playwrights, 1823-1977: An Annotated Bibliography of Plays*. New York: Bowker, 1977.

Hayman, Ronald. *Theatre and Anti-Theatre: New Movements since Beckett*. London: Secker & Warburg, 1979.

Helburn, Theresa. *A Wayward Quest: The Autobiography of Theresa Helburn*. Boston: Little, Brown, 1960.

Hill, Errol. *The Theater of Black Americans*, 2 vols. Englewood Cliffs, N.J.: Prentice-Hall, 1980.

Hornblow, Arthur. *A History of the Theatre in America from Its Beginnings to the Present Time*, 2 vols. Philadelphia & London: Lippincott, 1919; New York: Blom, 1965.

Houseman, John and Jack Landau. *The American Shakespeare Festival: The Birth of a Theatre*. New York: Simon & Schuster, 1959.

Houseman. *Front and Center*. New York: Simon & Schuster, 1979.

Hughes, Catharine R., ed. *New York Theatre Annual*. Detroit: Gale Research, 1978.

Hughes, Glenn. *A History of the American Theatre 1700-1950*. New York: French, 1951.

Hunter, Frederick J., ed. *Hoblitzelle Theatre Arts Library: A Guide to the Theatre and Drama Collections at the University of Texas*. Austin: Humanities Research Center, 1967.

Isaacs, Edith J. R. *The Negro in the American Theatre*. New York: Theatre Arts, 1947.

Jones, Robert Edmond. *The Dramatic Imagination: Reflections and Speculations on the Art of the Theatre*. New York: Arts Books, 1941.

Keller, Dean H. *Index to Plays in Periodicals*. Metuchen, N.J.: Scarecrow Press, 1971.

Keller. *Index to Plays in Periodicals: Supplement*. Metuchen, N.J.: Scarecrow Press, 1973.

Kernan, Alvin B., ed. *The Modern American Theater*. Englewood Cliffs, N.J.: Prentice-Hall, 1967.

Kerr, Walter. *Journey to the Center of the Theater*. New York: Knopf, 1979.

Kerr. *The Theater in Spite of Itself*. New York: Simon & Schuster, 1963.

Kerr. *Thirty Plays Hath November*. New York: Simon & Schuster, 1969.

Kinne, Wisner Payne. *George Pierce Baker and the American Theatre*. Cambridge: Harvard University Press, 1954.

Krutch, Joseph Wood. *The American Drama since 1918*, revised edition. New York: Braziller, 1957.

Langner, Lawrence. *The Magic Curtain*. New York: Dutton, 1951.

Langner. *The Play's the Thing*. New York: Putnam's, 1960.

Lewis, Allan. *American Plays and Playwrights of the Contemporary Theatre*, revised edition. New York: Crown, 1970.

Little, Stuart W. *Off-Broadway: The Prophetic Theater*. New York: Coward, McCann & Geoghegan, 1972.

Lowe, Claudia Jean. *A Guide to Reference and Bibliography for Theatre Research*. Columbus: Ohio State University Libraries, 1971.

Macgowan, Kenneth. *Footlights across America: Towards a National Theatre*. New York: Harcourt, Brace, 1929.

Mathews, Jane DeHart. *The Federal Theatre, 1935-1939*. Princeton: Princeton University Press, 1967.

Matlaw, Myron, ed. *American Popular Entertainment*. Westport, Conn.: Greenwood Press, 1977.

May, Robin. *A Companion to the Theatre: The Anglo-American Stage from 1920*. Guildford, U.K.: Lutterworth Press, 1970.

Mersand, Joseph E. *The American Drama since 1930*. New York: Modern Chapbooks, 1951.

Meserve, Walter J. *An Outline History of American Drama*. Totowa, N.J.: Littlefield, Adams, 1965.

Mielziner, Jo. *Designing for the Theatre: A Memoir and a Portfolio*. New York: Atheneum, 1965.

Miller, Arthur. *The Theatre Essays of Arthur Miller*, ed. Robert A. Martin. New York: Viking, 1978.

Mitchell, Loften. *Black Drama: The Story of the American Negro in the Theatre*. New York: Hawthorn, 1967.

Moderwell, Hiram Kelly. *The Theatre of To-day*. New York: Dodd, Mead, 1928.

Moses, Montrose J. and John Mason Brown, eds. *The American Theatre as Seen by its Critics, 1752-1934*. New York: Norton, 1934.

Nathan, George Jean. *Art of the Night*. New York: Knopf, 1928; Rutherford, N.J.: Fairleigh Dickinson University Press, 1972.

Nathan. *The Critic and the Drama*. New York: Knopf, 1922; Rutherford, N.J.: Fairleigh Dickinson University Press, 1972.

Nathan. *Encyclopaedia of the Theatre*. New York: Knopf, 1940; Rutherford, N.J.: Fairleigh Dickinson University Press, 1970.

Nathan. *The Magic Mirror*, ed. Thomas Quinn Curtiss. New York: Knopf, 1960.

Nathan. *The Morning after the First Night*. New York: Knopf, 1938; Rutherford, N.J.: Fairleigh Dickinson University Press, 1971.

New York Public Library. *Catalog of the Theatre and Drama Collections*. Boston: G. K. Hall, 1967.

Palmer, Helen H. and Anne Jane Dyson. *American Drama Criticism: Interpretations, 1890-1965 Inclusive, of American Drama since the First Play Produced in America*. Hamden, Conn.: Shoe String Press, 1967.

Pence, James Harry. *The Magazine and the Drama: An Index*. New York: Dunlap Society, 1896; New York: Burt Franklin, 1970.

Pendleton, Ralph, ed. *The Theatre of Robert Edmond Jones*. Middletown, Conn.: Wesleyan University Press, 1958.

Poggi, Jack. *Theater in America: The Impact of Economic Forces 1870-1967*. Ithaca, N.Y.: Cornell University Press, 1968.

Price, Julia S. *The Off-Broadway Theater*. New York: Scarecrow Press, 1962.

Quinn, Arthur Hobson. *A History of the American Drama from the Civil War to the Present Day*, revised edition. New York: Appleton-Century-Crofts, 1964.

Rice, Elmer. *Minority Report: An Autobiography*. New York: Simon & Schuster, 1963.

Rush, Theressa Gunnels, Carol Fairbanks Myers, and Esther Spring Arata. *Black American Writers Past and Present: A Biographical and Bibliographical Dictionary*, 2 vols. Metuchen, N.J.: Scarecrow Press, 1975.

Salem, James M. *A Guide to Critical Reviews*. New York: Scarecrow Press, 1966.

Salem. *American Drama, 1909-1969*, second edition. Metuchen, N.J.: Scarecrow Press, 1973.

Sheaffer, Louis. *O'Neill: Son and Artist*. Boston: Little, Brown, 1973.

Stagg, Jerry. *The Brothers Shubert*. New York: Random House, 1968.

Stratman, Carl J. *Bibliography of the American Theatre Excluding New York City*. Chicago: Loyola University Press, 1965.

Sumner, Mark Reese. *A Selected Bibliography on Outdoor Drama*. Chapel Hill: Institute of Outdoor Drama, University of North Carolina at Chapel Hill, 1965.

Taubman, Howard. *The Making of the American Theatre*. New York: Coward McCann, 1965; revised edition, 1967.

Tharpe, Jac, ed. *Tennessee Williams: A Tribute*. Jackson: University Press of Mississippi, 1977.

Timberlake, Craig. *The Bishop of Broadway: The Life and Work of David Belasco*. New York: Library Publishers, 1954.

The Vandamm Collection: New York Theatre 1919-1961. Teaneck, N.J.: Somerset House, 1980.

Wager, Walter, ed. *The Playwrights Speak*. New York: Delacorte, 1967.

Weales, Gerald C. *American Drama since World War II*. New York: Harcourt, Brace & World, 1962.

Wilmeth, Don B. *The American Stage from World War I to the 1970s*. Detroit: Gale Research, forthcoming.

Wilmeth. *The American Stage to World War I: A Guide to Information Sources*. Detroit: Gale Research, 1978.

Young, Stark. *Immortal Shadows, A Book of Dramatic Criticism*. New York: Scribners, 1948.

Zeigler, Joseph Wesley. *Regional Theatre: The Revolutionary Stage*. Minneapolis: University of Minnesota Press, 1973.

Contributors

Leon M. Aufdemberge ....*Kendall College*
Paul M. Bailey ....*University of Texas at Austin*
Fred Behringer ....*University of Tennessee at Chattanooga*
Beate Hein Bennett ....*Virginia Commonwealth University*
Terry Browne ....*State University of New York College at Geneseo*
George B. Bryan ....*University of Vermont*
John Bruce Cantrell ....*University of South Carolina*
Kathleen Conlin ....*University of Texas at Austin*
Susan Davis ....*Washington, D.C.*
Craig L. Downing ....*University of South Carolina*
Ann Crawford Dreher ....*University of South Calina*
David W. Engel ....*University of South Carolina*
Beth Fleischman ....*University of South Carolina*
Sheila Ennis Geitner ....*Asheville, North Carolina*
Randolph Goodman ....*Brooklyn College*
Ina Rae Hark ....*University of South Carolina*
Carol Harley ....*University of South Carolina*
Albert J. Harris Jr. ....*University of Louisville*
Jeffrey Helterman ....*University of South Carolina*
Jonathan Hershey ....*University of Alabama*
Lisa Hodgens ....*University of Alabama*
Robert W. Hungerford ....*University of South Carolina*
George H. Jensen ....*Chicago, Illinois*
Sally Johns ....*University of South Carolina*
Carol Johnston ....*Clemson University*
Richard W. Johnston ....*Barnwell, South Carolina*
Robert Klein ....*Washington, D.C.*
Inge Kutt ....*University of South Carolina*
Patricia Lewis ....*State University of New York College at Geneseo*
John Marion ....*Columbia, South Carolina*
H. W. Matalene ....*University of South Carolina*
James L. McWilliams III ....*University of Texas at Austin*
Katharine M. Morsberger ....*Los Angeles, California*
William A. Mould ....*University of South Carolina*
Sara Nalley ....*Columbia College*
Donna Northouse ....*Dallas, Texas*
James A. Patterson ....*University of South Carolina*
Jack Wright Rhodes ....*The Citadel*
Vera Mowry Roberts ....*Hunter College*
William Mattathias Robins ....*West Orange, New Jersey*
Phyllis Jane Rose ....*Minneapolis, Minnesota*
Paul Sagona ....*Columbia, South Carolina*
Bruce Serlen ....*New York, New York*

Howard Siegman..*Hofstra University*
Gail Stewart ....*University of Arkansas at Pine Bluff*
Ruth L. Strickland...*University of South Carolina*
Jane Isley Thesing ....*University of South Carolina*
William B. Thesing ....*University of South Carolina*
Laura M. Zaidman...*South Georgia College*
Richard Ziegfeld..*University of South Carolina*